DICTIONARY OF ALL
SCRIPTURES & MYTHS

DICTIONARY

OF ALL

SCRIPTURES

& MYTHS

G. A. GASKELL

GRAMERCY BOOKS
New York • Avenel, New Jersey

This 1981 edition is published by Gramercy Books,
distributed by Outlet Book Company, Inc., a Random House Company,
40 Engelhard Avenue, Avenel, New Jersey 07001.

Random House
New York • Toronto • London • Sydney • Auckland

Manufactured in the United States of America

Library of Congress Cataloging-in-Publication Data
Gaskell, George Arthur.
   Dictionary of all scriptures and myths.

   Reprint. Originally published: New York : Julian
Press, 1960.
   1. Symbolism—Dictionaries. 2. Mythology—Diction-
aries. 3. Religions—Dictionaries. I. Title.
BL603.G3   1981   291.1'3'0321   81-3499
ISBN: 0-517-34663-X   AACR2

8 7 6 5 4 3

"Unless we learn to understand this metaphorical or hiero-glyphic language of the ancient world, we shall look upon the Upanishads and on most of the Sacred Books of the East as mere childish twaddle."

MAX MÜELLER

PREFACE

THIS Dictionary of the Sacred Language claims to give the true solution of the age-long problem of the origin, nature and meaning of the Scriptures and Myths which are attached to the various religions of the world. It especially appeals to those thinkers who are dissatisfied with the many conflicting theories and expositions of both Christian and rationalist teachers and writers of modern times. To earnest souls who are distressed by doubts and difficulties concerning their scriptures and religion, this presentation of facts and their elucidation should bring peace, for it offers them all that is of eternal value in religion, and it entirely frees them from subservience to doubtful systems and conventional contradictory opinions.

The origin and nature of the various Scriptures have never been consistently explained either by religionists or rationalists, so as to account for their world-wide influence and the striking peculiarities of the writings. For more than a century clerical and lay thinkers have disputed about scriptures and doctrines, with no satisfactory result, for the theories of every disputant are open to fatal objections. It is usual to narrow the problem of Divine revelation to one particular religion, and to regard other religions as negligible, thereby making impossible a true understanding either of the accepted religion or of the general problem of religions. It will, I think, be found that the light thrown by this Dictionary upon the sacred writings, shows them to belong to a higher plane of thought than that hitherto conceded to them. On this high plane they are beyond the reach of all the controversies regarding them with which the world of thought is filled. There is indeed no room for scepticism on the general subject of religion and revelation when the full meaning of the Scriptures and their philosophy is apprehended. There is no conflict with science when the legends of old cease to be materialised in the notions of literalists. Doubt respecting Divine revelation only creeps in when history and verbalism are allowed to distort religious conceptions and obstruct the truth. When the fact is realised that the Scriptures belong to a category of writings which is unique in the world and can be recognised through the symbolism peculiar to it, the strength of the religious position is invincible in face of the attacks of materialists and other sceptics. The Scriptures can no longer be controverted because of any features in their appearance, while, in respect to their ascertained meanings, these are beyond the arguments of adverse rationalists.

This present exposition of Scripture exegesis, giving fuller knowledge of man's inner nature and the purpose of his life on earth, has taken the form of a dictionary because of the discovery, forecasted by the great orientalist Max Müller, of a metaphorical language underlying all sacred Scriptures of the world. The terms of this language will reveal themselves to students of the Scriptures who will follow the line of thought of this Dictionary. The Sacred Language will be seen to be the one and only instance where supernatural intrusion into mundane affairs is clearly cognisable ; for a universal language, such as this is, could not be invented and applied by man. It is possible for the Scriptures literally to be the work of man, but it is impossible for their world-wide under-meanings to be other than superhuman and transcendental. It matters nothing however grotesque the wording of Scriptures may be ; it is the symbolism alone which is precious, and worthy of our best efforts to elucidate.

The Five Planes in the World Systems

GREECE (Zeus)	ROME (Jupiter)	IRAN (Zerana Akerana)	SCANDINAVIA (Odin)	CHALDEA (Ea)
Apollo	Bacchus	Ormazd	Balder	Marduk
Hera	Juno	Armaiti	Frigg	Istar
Hermes	Mercury	Tistrya	Thor	Nebo
Hades	Pluto	Ahriman	Loke	Enlil
Hestia	Vesta	?	Sigyn	?

EGYPT (Rā)	JAPAN (Ameno)	NEW ZEALAND (Rangi)	CHINA (Heaven)
Osiris	Ninigi	Tangaroa	Water
Isis	Ama-terasu	Rongo-matane	Fire
Thoth	Shinatsu-hiko	Tuma-tauenga	Metal
Set	Susa-no-wo	Tane-mahuta	Wood
Nephthys	Haigi-no-kami	Haumea-tiki-tiki	Earth

In these tables the Five Planes of Existence are indicated by various symbols found in the Religious Systems of many nations. The correspondences run horizontally, and show that all religions are essentially the same and refer to the same facts of being on the higher and lower planes. The polytheism of the ancients is obviously the same in principle as the monotheism of the moderns. The only dissimilarities lie in the great variety of symbols for the same ideas, and in the many allegorical statements conveying the sacred language in which ideas are expressed.

IN THE WORLD SYSTEMS

CHRISTIAN (Father God)	KABBALAH (Ain Soph)	OTTOMAN SUFI (The Unity)	INDIAN (Paran-atma)
Son of God	The Crown	Absolutely Invisible	Atma
Holy Ghost	World of Emanation	Relatively Invisible	Buddhi
Mental faculties	World of Creation	World of Man	Manas
Lower emotions	World of Formation	World of Similitudes	Kama
Sensations	World of Action	Visible World	Sthula

GREEK (Father Æther)	MEDIÆVAL (Ineffable)	BOEHME (Verbum Fiat)	SWEDENBORG (The Infinite)
Good Mind	Light	Light-breath	Celestial
Fire	Fire	Fire-breath	Spiritual
Air	Mental	Air-breath	Rational
Water	Astral	Water	Proprium
Earth	Physical	Earth	Physical

The names between brackets are symbols of the Absolute or God-unmanifest, while the names on the highest of the five planes indicate God-manifest,—the Higher Self. In some systems the same symbols denote occasionally God-unmanifest or God-manifest. The fourth plane, counting from below, is the plane of the Holy Spirit, or Great Goddess, and feminine also is the lowest or physical plane. In most religions the highest plane is represented by numerous symbols or sun-gods, the sun being a universal symbol of the Higher Self traversing the Life-cycle or Zodiac.

FOREWORD

In this Dictionary the ancient doctrine of Verbal Inspiration is restored to its pristine position in the study of the Scriptures. It is obvious that no transcendental symbolism could be present in writings if the words on which symbolism depends were not chosen freely by the Wisdom within and set down unaltered by the inspired writer. Human interference with the wording of the Scriptures would prevent any symbolism being expressed. Verbal Inspiration was necessary in order to make possible the revelation of truths which are beyond the scope of human observation ; a symbolism of correspondences was also requisite in which to express the recondite knowledge offered to mankind. The vast amount of nonsense in the Scriptures is presumptive proof of verbal inspiration for no literate has been known to write in such terms as we find in the Avesta and many other Sacred Books.

Scriptures have very much the appearance of dreams in their grotesqueness and inconsequence, and to call them Cosmic Dreams would express much of their nature (see Appendix, p. 844). As personal dreams have their symbology, so also have cosmic dreams, and in both cases investigation and analysis lead to the interpretation of their terms. Ordinary dreams relate to the experience of a person : Cosmic Dreams relate to the experience of the soul. Psychoanalysis on a low level leads to the interpretation of dreams. Psycho-analysis on a high level opens the right way of interpretation of the Scriptures, and reveals truths of the greatest importance to humanity and the evolution of the Divine within the soul. Dr. Jung takes the low level course of thought with the Scriptures, and the result, empty of all value to man, is its own confutation.

In Scripture undermeanings the qualities of mind and emotion in man are regarded as of surpassing importance in the growth of the soul, and so these are found to be the principal subjects discussed in the interpretations, for the ever-changing and progressing human character and human faculty are of eternal moment in the development of the soul to a state of perfection.

There will be those who reject the idea of a cryptic language, and who cannot find the language in Scriptures. What then have these thinkers to fall back upon as explanatory of the origin and meaning of the mysterious literature which has been so powerful in the world ? The confused theories of theologians have all broken down : so also have the theories of the mythologists at their outset. There is no science in any of these theories, for they are only speculative in origin and they depend upon fancy, not fact. I venture to say there is no conceivable solution of the problems of Religions and Scriptures than the one set forth, however inadequately, in this Dictionary.

The present writer has done his best in difficult and arduous pioneer work. He has left very much to be done. Others who follow will do much better than he has been able to do, and will make far plainer the claims of the Sacred Language to elucidate the profound teachings of the Divine Wisdom which have been deposited in all inspired Scriptures and Myths. That these teachings are in many ways abstruse and hard to understand is reasonable to expect : what else, indeed, than intellectual depth could be expected of spiritual disclosures concerning the inner life of man and the universe ? There can be no pretence here of fully understanding all that is set forth in Scripture undermeanings, but much can be made out by those whose minds are receptive of inner truths.

For a right understanding of the thesis of the Dictionary it would be well for a reader to first peruse the articles on GOSPEL, GOSPELS, INSPIRATION, MYTHOLOGY, PROTOTYPES, RAMAYANA, RELIGION, RELIGIONS, REVELATION, SCRIPTURES, SELF, SIGN, UPANISHADS, and WORD :—these indicate the basis on which the whole philosophy of the Sacred Language rests,

INTRODUCTION

POPULAR religious systems and theories are notoriously unstable and changeful. They have altered greatly within the last fifty years. They are the sport of sentimentalists and the derision of rationalists, and they remain to this day destitute of logical coherence and unity. A majority of the most eminent philosophers and scientists disbelieve in religions which clash with that intelligence with which man is naturally endowed. They therefore repudiate them and endeavour to explain the origin and characteristic of religions by the methods solely of reason and research. Yet it must be admitted, the scientists have been no more successful than the religionists in solving the problem of the existence and influence of religions.

Religions arise from sacred Scriptures and Myths, and the requisite knowledge of these mysterious utterances has been sought with great assiduity by learned investigators for more than a century past, without any indisputable and satisfactory result having been arrived at. How is it, we may ask, there is so much disputation about the origin and value of concepts which, from the remotest times to the present, have influenced very greatly the minds and actions of men ? Surely we must conclude that nothing short of fundamental errors of investigation can account for the grave differences of opinion among thinkers on the subject of religions, scriptures and myths.

In regard to the origin of myths, I venture to say that the prevalent uncertainties and absurdities of the generally accepted Mythical theory are enough to arouse some suspicion that the theory is not well-grounded. Let us then examine its essentials. In the first place it is assumed, without any evidence, that there is in man a special faculty of the human mind for the invention of myths, and that this " innate faculty of myth is indigenous and common to all men " (T. VIGNOLI, *Myth and Science*, p. 3). This assertion, be it observed, is made in face of the fact that no person, living or dead, is known to have evidenced this faculty by producing a myth. Vignoli himself confesses, " it appears to me that the ultimate source whence myths really proceed has not been reached " (p. 13). The source of myth, then, being unknown, the Mythical theory is not founded on fact, but is purely speculative and unscientific.

I have been unable to find in the works of Sir J. G. Frazer, Herbert Spencer, E. B. Tylor, A. Lang, J. M. Robertson, Sir G. Cox, and other mythologists, any but speculative and imagined premises for a general theory of myth.

INTRODUCTION

The writers all tacitly assume that there existed a different human nature and motives for action in people of the past to what we observe in the human nature of to-day. Yet to prove this contention, these exponents of mythical lore are unable to indicate a single person, savage or civilised, who has invented and promulgated myths. This lack of evidential fact makes purely conjectural any surmise of a peculiar state of mind in a supposed myth-maker, and of his method of forming myths. Hence it is the simple truth that the whole mythical theory is devoid of foundation on the firm ground of ascertained and acknowledged fact. A theory that is not grounded on fact can have no pretensions to science.

Further than this,—a deliberative process of supposed myth-making must obviously be quite inconsistent with all known motives of intelligent action. What motive could there be for the very difficult production of a thoughtful myth ? People are not to be found who actually desire to express their thoughts in the tedious enigmas required by mythological theory. We know that men and women speak and write in order to be understood by others, and they never attempt to uselessly conceal their ideas in forms of expression which have a nonsensical appearance. The believers in myth-makers would have us imagine that to produce myths there were people in the past who were so eccentric and unnatural as to speak, write and act from motives unknown, and in ways quite contrary to human nature of the present day.

The mythologists suppose the myth-makers to have had a burning desire to say something weird and unintelligible about such commonplace subjects as the weather, the crops, the seasons, vegetation, sun, moon and stars, etc. They would not be so vulgar as to say straight out in plain language what they thought upon these subjects ; so it is supposed they took immense pains to cunningly clothe their remarks in mysterious and grotesque phraseology, so that people should not understand their trivial observations.

For example, Mr. J. M. Robertson writes of the passages in MATTHEW, ch. xxi, and ZECHARIAH, ch. ix, about a king riding to Jerusalem on two asses :—

" The just critical inference is that *both* passages had regard to the zodiacal figure of the Two Asses for the sign Cancer, from which we have the myth of Bacchus riding on two asses. Further, it is probable that the similar passage in the Song of Jacob has also a zodiacal basis."—*The Jesus Problem*, p. 45.

That is to say : in each of these two or three cases, the myth-maker or myth-adaptor, busy over his difficult work of concealing his thoughts in cryptic language, suddenly wanted, in his story, to mention the fact that the sun passes in summer through a certain part of the sky, so he chose to express this idea by relating the incident of a king (as the sun) riding in state to a city, seated grotesquely on two asses (as fixed stars) ; and he seemingly trusted that his readers would not detect his meaning for about two thousand years !

Mythologists have at the outset of their investigations taken for granted that myths must have originated through laborious rational processes in the working of ignorant minds observant of natural occurrences. They have supposed that the myth-makers have been searching for the causes of phenomena, imagining them to be personal. We are told by Vignoli that " man personifies all phenomena, first vaguely projecting himself into them." No evidence worth naming is given for this supposed primitive working of the human intellect. Mythologists are expected to hold with Mr. Robertson that—'

" All primitive beliefs and usages, however strange and absurd, are to be understood as primarily products of judgment, representing theories of causation, or guesses at the order of things."—*Pagan Christs*, p. 3.

The apparently absurd stories of Gods and Goddesses, and the strange usages in popular religions do not strike one as being primarily products of judgment, but rather as denoting ideas presented to unreasoning minds for acceptance, —credulous minds such as we observe among all religious and superstitious people. The mythologist assumes that myths arise from the exercise of reason in the minds of certain persons of a bygone age, which results in the invention of curious statements and stories : in short, that myths are intelligent productions of the self-conscious brain-mind of man. Now, as a matter of fact, there is no necessity whatever to assume that myths arise in this ordinary prosaic, thoughtful, imaginative way. Myths are extraordinary historical survivals, and it is surely reasonable to expect that they have originated in a manner also extraordinary.

In this relation our learned mythologists seem never to have given attention to the now well-known phenomena of trance-speaking and automatic writing, in which the speakers and writers present statements in the framing of which their conscious minds have had no part. Miss Evelyn Underhill writes :—

" St. Catherine of Siena, we are told, dictated her great Dialogue to her secretaries whilst in the state of ecstasy ; which probably means a condition of consciousness resembling the ' trance ' of mediums, in which the deeper mind governs the tongue." —*Mysticism*, p. 352.

" Madame Guyon states in her autobiography that she would experience a sudden and irresistible inclination to take up her pen ; though feeling wholly incapable of literary composition, and not even knowing the subject on which she would be impelled to write. If she resisted the impulse it was at the cost of the most intense discomfort. She would then begin to write with extraordinary swiftness ; words, elaborate arguments and appropriate quotations coming to her without reflection, and so quickly that one of her longest books was written in one and a half days. ' In writing I saw that I was writing of things which I had never seen : and during the time of this manifestation, I was given light to perceive that I had in me treasures of knowledge and understanding which I did not know that I possessed.' "—*Ibid*. p. 78.

Trance-speaking is a rare occurrence ; so is the formation of myth ; but while myth-making is totally unknown and incredible, trance-speaking has been carefully investigated in recent years, and found to show peculiarities which seem to make it a fitting external source of myth. What reason, then, is there for choosing the incredible myth-maker as the utterer of myth, rather than the credible trance-speaker ? No argument against this latter choice can be based on the fact that the subjective mind in trance has not for many centuries brought forth a myth ; for neither has the inventive mind produced a myth. The reason why myths are exclusively ancient must obviously reside in hidden causes about which we can only at present speculate.

The weakness and incompetence of the mythical theory to explain the subject it deals with is also very evident when we come to consider the question of the why and the wherefore of the popular acceptance and veneration of myths. The mythologists suppose that myths are calmly invented by students of nature and tradition through a process of cold reasoning and judgment, ill-calculated to appeal to their own feelings or the feelings of others. How, then, could the myths, when publicly announced, appeal to the emotions of the populace so as to command reverence, and be memorised ? Such a question as this does not apparently occur to any mythologist. In modern times the expounding of a seeming myth by its inventor would, I think, only arouse feelings of amusement and derision, and no one would have any impulse to believe in the absurd concoction. The newness of a legend would in these times also tell strongly against its acceptance. When missionaries of a religion try to gain proselytes, they never seek credence for new stories, but always for old and venerable narrations not supposed to be the inventions of human beings, and which they can expound in an impersonal and impressive manner.

Contrast any possible method of foisting invented myths upon a group of persons, with the very different occasion of an acknowledged trance-utterance, and the natural effect the strange speech would have upon ignorant or uncivilised auditors. The trance-speaker would be recognised as not speaking from himself, but from the inspiration of an invisible being who had taken temporary possession of him. This solemn and mysterious condition of things would certainly arouse in simple minds deep emotions of wonder, awe, and reverence, and ensure strong belief both in the powerful unseen intelligence and in the trance-spoken message, however absurdly it might be worded. In afterwards promulgating the utterance far and wide, its origin would be described or taken for granted, so that religious emotions would always be attached to it and give it persistency in believing minds.

Travellers have described scenes where persons entranced have declaimed to awe-stricken hearers who presumably would never forget what they had seen and heard. It seems to be certain that sacred myths in their inception must have had strong emotions behind them to give them the requisite power of impression and endurance in the minds of priests and devotees.

Sir George Grey, the principal collector of the myths of New Zealand, brings before us a remarkable figure :—

"For the first time, I believe, a European reader will find it in his power to place himself in the position of one who listens to a heathen and savage high priest, explaining to him, in his own words and in his own energetic manner, the traditions in which he earnestly believes, and unfolding the religious opinions upon which the faith and hopes of his race rest."—*Polynesian Mythology*, Preface.

Examining the contents of Sir G. Grey's book, I think it would be difficult for anyone to imagine that the grotesque myths this priest unfolded were the products of cold and cunning invention, rather than of impassioned entranced speech in some former age.

It is impossible to draw a line between sacred Myths and sacred Scriptures ; they flow into each other, and they obviously have the same kind of origin. Yet scant notice is taken of the mythical theory by most religionists, just as if it had nothing to do with their Scriptures. Nevertheless the theory they espouse is practically indistinguishable from the mythical theory, but with the added absurdity of a self-contradictory exposition of it. They affirm the Divine inspiration of their Scriptures, and at the same moment deny the necessary condition of inspiration, which is that the inspired writer is unaware of the theme on which he is writing, and therefore irresponsible for either the words or the meaning. They apparently assume that Scriptures are produced by an impossible co-ordination of two mental determinants, human and divine, with a nondescript result which could be attributed neither to man nor God.

This abortive theory has been invented to serve what is called the "higher criticism," which destroys entirely the old belief in verbal inspiration ; thus reducing the Scriptures to the level of all other writings, and treating them as rubbish, more or less, according to the fancies of the impious critics. Therefore, instead of discarding a theory which is obviously false, as it does not fit the facts, these thinkers cling to it, and so find themselves confronted with difficulties innumerable, created by their own theory out of the neglected facts, and which to their great distress they find it impossible to get rid of. This indicates the present position of Biblical exegesis among learned scholars who always refer to scripture writers as knowing what they wrote about.

On the question of symbolism, it is quite evident, from the structural resemblances we see in sacred Myths and Scriptures collected from all parts of the world, that the symbolism is one and universal, and therefore not of human origin. This unity, implying one Source for all sacred utterances, and the logical inference that the same symbols have the same meanings everywhere, has to be realised. When this highly important fact of symbolic unity is grasped, it completely sweeps away the possibility of the past existence of myth and scripture-making persons. No persons, however learned, could be credited with having knowledge of this obscure universal symbology so as to be able to compose true Myths or Scriptures.

Scriptures are merely extensions of myths; as the same symbology rules all sacred declarations. We are compelled by the facts before us to believe that all genuine Myths and Scriptures were produced in some way by persons in peculiar but not unnatural states of mind usually called inspired. In these states the will and brain-mind exercise no control over the means of speech or writing. The ancient Scriptures claim to be Divinely inspired, and it is highly reasonable to suppose that they were written down automatically. If they are examined freely and without prejudice, they show plainly, by the very large amount of absurdity and nonsense they contain, that they could not have been thoughtfully composed by either intelligent or unintelligent men. The allegation that the Sacred Books have proceeded from the intelligence of the writers of the books is a mere groundless assumption, for there is no evidence in history, or among living people, of any person composing and writing a sacred book.

Max Müller was probably, in his day, the greatest of all investigators of the world-scriptures. He died disappointed of his life-work, as the following statements indicate :—

"I confess it has been for many years a problem to me, how the Sacred Books of the East should, by the side of so much that is fresh, natural, simple, beautiful and true, contain so much that is not only unmeaning, artificial and silly, but even hideous and repellent. This is a fact and must be accounted for in some way or other."
"There will always remain in the Upanishads a vast amount of what we can only call meaningless jargon, and for the presence of which in these ancient mines of thought, I, for my part, feel quite unable to account."—*S.B.E.*, Vol. I. xii, Vol. XV. xx.

The nature of the Scriptures is not understood while they are regarded as of human origin and having no undermeanings. As a matter of fact, the Sacred writings bear no trace of human origin beyond the superficial presence of common ideas and language. Their varying contents, broadly considered, seldom relate to mundane experience, and usually purport to be revelation of unseen potencies. We find described an unnatural condition of things in the past, present, and for the future. Regarded as sincere expressions of thought, the sacred utterances are quite incongruous with all that is proved to be produced by the human mind.

In viewing our natural environment, we note the complete absence of beneficent and maleficent superhuman powers interfering with natural laws and human arrangements; but when we turn to the sacred writings we are confronted with such powers described as apparently active in the outer world. Gods, angels and devils move freely in a fantastic world unknown to our experience. Assuming that Scriptures are written truthfully, we can, from this peculiarity concerning them, judge with certainty that the sacred narrations are not historical but imaginative, and were not meant to be taken objectively in any sense. The world of Inspiration is not the physical world, or world of history, but is really the inner world of spirit, mind, emotion, and desire, in which the human ego always lives, moves, and has his being. In this inner world the Ideals of truth and goodness (the Gods) and their opposites (devils) are active, and it is here that the tragedy of each life is enacted. This conception of the nature of the Scriptures brings order out of the confusion of thought in which the modern mind involves them.

If now it be conceded that the Sacred Books are not of human origin, then it follows that they do not come under the ordinary methods of analysis, criticism and judgment applicable to human productions. Neither the historical nor the verbal criticism of scholars is of the least use in their exegesis.

INTRODUCTION

Not being literary compositions, they cannot properly be dealt with as such, but must be treated *differently* to all other books. They must be considered in view of what they *really are,* if rational use is to be made of them.

In popular religions, we find an inconsistent mixture of two different modes of scriptural interpretation, one spiritual and the other material (historical), with the inevitable result of interminable disputations over opinions, and the formulation of incoherent pronouncements which are the laughing-stock of sceptics. Popular religions partially teach truth ; and every religion is vindicated by the truths it has derived from the Spirit, while every religion is condemned by the superstitions it has imposed upon belief through having mistaken the dead letter of the Word for the living idea signified by it.

The Scriptures, as proceeding from the Omniscient Wisdom, are therefore in their undermeanings quite consistent treatises, never contradicting each other, and teaching universally the great truths of the nature of man, of the soul-process, and of the cosmos. The cryptic language of the sacred books is not at all of arbitrary formation, but accords with correspondences in nature, higher and lower, and being quite simple in its general features, can be readily made out by all open-minded, intelligent students who set themselves to learn it. When the clue to the language is found, it can be deciphered just in the same way as the hieroglyphs of Egypt were made out. Each hieroglyph when revealed aided the revelation of associated hieroglyphs. In the Scriptures, to make decipherment easier, there are certain spiritual ideas which are partly expressed on the surface and so can greatly help interpretation. These ideas have been embodied in the different religions of the world and constitute the active spirit of the religions, and are the source of their idealistic power over the mental and emotional nature of mankind.

In regard to the scheme of the symbolism, it will be found that in the sacred writings the activities which apparently are of the outer world of sense stand really for the activities of the inner world of thought. The apparent sense-world of consciousness symbolises the real soul-world of humanity, in which we become aware of all the emotions, faculties and activities of the soul's experience of life.

If in the country on a fine day, we stand fronting a pool of water, we may observe a prospect which beautifully pictures the higher and the lower things of the soul and the cosmos, as expressed in the Sacred Language of all Myths and Scriptures.

Sun-realm ;	Light ;	Celestial.
Sky-realm ;	Fire ;	Spiritual.
Air-realm ;	Air ;	Mental.
Water-realm ;	Water ;	Astral.
Earth-realm ;	Earth ;	Physical.

These ideograms are universal symbols of the Five Planes of Existence, all in their proper order, that is, from the highest (most inward) to the lowest (most outward) states of existence. They are recognised in all the Sacred Books of the world, and this Dictionary cannot be understood without regard to them. Knowledge of the Five Planes and their symbols makes it easy to at once make out the meanings of many other associated symbols. In the Sun-realm is the Sun, a symbol of God-manifest, or the Higher Self who passes through the whole Cycle of Divine Life (zodiac) in a series of twelve stages (year). In the Sky-realm are the higher emotions (bright clouds), and the transmuting Fire of Wisdom (the lightning) which purifies the human soul, life after life. In the Air-realm are the mental faculties (people) and lower emotions (animals), also instincts (plants), and aspirations (birds). In the Water-realm are reflected inversely the motives and things of the higher planes, and these bring delusion and error into the soul. In the Earth-realm are the outer conditions of mental activity (work) and progress (walking).

There is nothing mysterious in the original choice of particular symbols to express psychic ideas. The Divine choice was evidently restricted to just the various ordinary ideas which were to be found in the minds of the inspired writers ; and the ideas selected were those which corresponded in some way to the psychic and spiritual ideas which the Divine Wisdom sought to express for the information of the human race. It was obviously impossible for the Holy Spirit in any other way to impart to a but slightly civilised humanity some of the deep truths of being which minds are slow to receive and comprehend.

Symbols taken from the ideas of everyday life, such as Seeds, Fields, Ploughing, Sowing, Cultivation, Fruits, Garden, Corn, Bread, etc., correspond in their higher meanings quite reasonably with their lower significations, and are easily understood ; and they fit in perfectly with the ideograms of the Five Planes. Investigation will show that the Sacred Language is perfectly consistent in itself, and that it demonstrates the perfect consistency of each and all of the inspired Scriptures of the world. Uninspired interpolations can be readily detected by the absence of response to the sacred symbolism ; and, of course, all human compositions fail entirely to show the presence of the symbolism.

For the esoteric ideas there are many symbols in the Scriptures. This multiplicity is inevitable, in order to suit the discursive and figurative character of the narrations which contain the undermeanings. A few symbols have double meanings, i.e. higher and lower significations. The only cases I know are Fire, Water, Earth, Ocean, Serpent, Dragon, Darkness, Night, Riches, Garments ; also in some degree Clouds, Black, Children, Marriage, Māyā, Tongue, South, North, Demon, Stars and Sword. The right meanings in particular cases of these symbols are easily found by consideration of the contexts. The reason for these double meanings follows from the universal fact of the duality of manifestation.

The deific names for the manifest God, or Higher Self, on the highest plane are very numerous. The deific names for the Wisdom principle on the spiritual plane are rather less numerous. The deific names for the higher-mind principle appear to be no more than one in any religious system. The only ones I know are Thoth, Hermes, Mercury, Nebo, Thor, Hanuman, Shinatsu, and Tumatauenga. The Higher Self is sometimes symbolised by certain animal names ; as Ram, Bull, Lion, (white) Elephant, (white) Goat, and Fish. These represent centres of Divine activity in the stages of manifestation pictured in the zodiac. Time, Space, Justice, Evolution, Power have sometimes deific names ; while Desire, Relativity, Limitation, Illusion, Ignorance have demonic ones. Gender when present in symbols is often a great aid to the elucidation of undermeanings ; for the masculine gender relates to Spirit, Mind, Desire, or Time ; while the feminine relates to Matter, Intuition, Emotion, or Space. Also it must be borne in mind that the Spiritual and Earth planes are feminine, and the three other planes masculine.

The land of the country of origin of a Scripture becomes in that Scripture a symbol of the mental plane of the soul, the arena on which the various soul-qualities (people) develop and progress. The mental plane is the plane of conflict for the fighting and wars so much dealt with in the sacred books. The principal river of a country then symbolises the ray of the Divine Life which comes from above and brings life and truth to the mind and soul (e.g. Nile, Ganges, Jordan). The higher land stands for the higher mind, and the more remote and inaccessible districts for the higher planes of the soul. Foreigners or Gentiles represent little-developed qualities and adverse experiences invading the soul at times.

INTRODUCTION

National Scriptures vary from each other very much in character both outwardly and inwardly. In some the teaching is more advanced and intellectual, as in Greece and India; in others more emotional and elementary, as in Palestine and Scandinavia; in others more formal, as in Egypt and China; and so on, according to the needs of the souls in the nationalities. The use of particular symbols also varies naturally according to the customs, industrial conditions, foods, animals and climates in the different countries. For example, the Cow symbol, so common in the Scriptures of Egypt and India, is almost absent in the Bible of Palestine.

Some knowledge of the Divine Scheme of Existence, in combination with symbol meanings, is of great use in the elucidation of Scripture undermeanings. This knowledge has been in some degree known to the mystics of several religions, and is further revealed in the undermeanings.

I venture to say that only by accepting the Sacred Language as a well-ascertained fact, and by learning of truths by means of it, can the present controversies over religions and their Scriptures be ended, and a consistent and deep Philosophy of Religion be reached.

The Absolute or Unconditioned.

The Unmanifest God or God the Father.

| V
CELESTIAL | The Manifest God or God the Son.
The Self, Higher Self, or Christ. | *Atma* |

| IV
SPIRITUAL | The Wisdom Nature or Holy Spirit.
The Higher Emotion Nature or Madonna. | *Buddhi* |

| III
MENTAL | The Higher Mind or Individuality.
. . . .
The Lower Mind or Personality. | *Manas* |

| II
ASTRAL | The Lower Emotion Nature. Lower Self.
The Desire Nature. Teleplasm. | *Kama* |

| I
PHYSICAL | The Etheric Medium in all things.
The Solids, Liquids and Gases. | *Sthula* |

THE FIVE PLANES OF MANIFESTATION.

These range from the most outward below, to the most inward above. Behind or within, all physical things are the four other essential constituents, without which they could not exist, and from which they proceed.

Dictionary of all Scriptures and Myths

DICTIONARY OF THE SACRED LANGUAGE

AARON, THE HIGH PRIEST :—

A symbol of the spiritual mind, that is, the inner mind which is moved by the higher emotions. "Aaron" represents "Abel" on a higher mental sub-plane. The spiritual mind operates subjectively on the higher-mind plane, and ministers to the development of the causal-body.

See ADVARYA, AGNIDHRA, ATHORNE, CALF (molten), CHRYSE, HIGH PRIEST, PONTIFF, POPE, PRIEST, SCAPEGOAT, TEMPLE, URIM.

AARU :—See SEKHET.

AAT,—REGION :—

A symbol of a state of being in a period during the progression of a manvantara, or great cycle of existence.

See ÆONS.

AAT-SHATET :—

A symbol of a state of the soul during the seventh period of the celestial cycle of evolution. It is known as a haven of refuge.

AAT OF THE WATERS :—

A symbol of the astral condition during a state of disruption at the end of a cycle.

"Hail, thou Aat wherein the *Khus* gain no mastery. Thy waters are of fire, and the streams which are in thee burn with fire, and thy flame is a blazing fire. . . . The gods and *Khus* look upon the waters thereof and retreat without having quenched their thirst and their hearts are not set at rest, . . . the stream is filled with reeds, even as the stream which flowed from the issues which came forth from Osiris. I have gained the mastery over the waters thereof. . . . The gods are more afraid to drink the waters thereof than are the *Khus*."—BUDGE, *Book of the Dead*, Ch. CXLIX. p. 496.

In the state of being that occurs when a great cycle terminates, the physical plane is transmuted by spirit (fire), and is absorbed into the astral condition. The lives (*Khus*) in the forms are no longer manifest. They retreat, together with the Ideals (gods), without further experience of illusion (water). The astral plane is obstructed, but the soul that is perfected is master of it. The Ideals are not attracted to the life of desire and sensation as the form-lives, or souls, are.

"When the number of perfect souls shall be completed, I will then shut the Gates of the Light, and from that time none will be able to come in thereby, nor will any go forth thereafter, for the number of perfect souls shall be completed, and the mystery of the first Mystery be perfected,—whereby all hath come into existence, and I (Jesus) am that Mystery. From that hour no one shall any more enter into the Light, and none shall come forth, in that the time of the number of perfect souls shall be fulfilled, before I set fire to the world, that it may purify the æons, and veils, the firmaments and the whole world, and also all the matters that are still in it, the race of human kind being still upon it" (*Pistis Sophia*).—G. R. S. MEAD, *Fragments, etc.*, p. 503.

This refers to the end of a cycle when the Life-wave passes from one globe to another. The souls that are perfected are ready for union with the Higher Self (Jesus) on upper planes, and no longer will the causal-bodies (gates) send forth the ego to the life below. The Life process will cease for a time, and there will be a transmutation of the lower nature, a purification by buddhi (fire) of the physical and astral planes.

See BUDDHA, CHRIST'S SECOND COMING, COMETS, CONFLAGRATION, HORSE (white), JUDGMENT DAY, KALKI, KARSHVARES, PLANETARY,

17

REGIONS, REGNAROK, RENOVATION, SOSIOSH, SPRINGTIME, THIRST.

AB, THE HEART :—

A symbol of the causal-self, or the atma-buddhic principle in the causal-body,—the perfect archetype potential within. The spiritual ego.

"The heart is regarded as having been the centre of the spiritual and thinking life, and as the organ through which the manifestations of virtue and vice revealed themselves, and it typifies everything which the word 'conscience' signifies to us. . . . The heart amulet is made in the form of a scarab or beetle."—BUDGE, *Book of the Dead*, Vol. I. p. lx.

"The heart is a distinct personality within him : it is the god Khnum, the creator, strengthening and making sound his limbs. . . . This formula and its explanatory texts teach the curious doctrine that it is not the heart which sins, but only its fleshly envelope. The heart was and still remained pure, and in the Underworld accused its earthly covering of any impurities contracted."—WIEDEMANN, *Rel. of Anc. Egyptians*, p. 287.

The "heart," signifying the spiritual ego, or Divine spark, within the soul, cannot act wrongly. It becomes obscured in evil doing, and manifests in righteousness. It is the Divine Image, or Microcosm.

See CAUSAL, HEART, IMAGE, JOB, JUDGMENT-HALL, MICROCOSM, TEMPLE.

ABEL, A KEEPER OF SHEEP :—

A symbol of the dawning of. that moral element in the soul which works by love. This state is a faint correspondency of the Higher Self, and tends the virtues (sheep).

"Until the soul brought forth the God-loving doctrine (Abel), the self-loving (Cain) dwelt with her. But when she brought forth 'Abel,' or unanimity with God, she abandoned unanimity with that mind 'Cain' which was wise in its own conceit."—PHILO JUDÆUS, *Works*, YONGE, Vol. IV. p. 207.

"And Cain told Abel his brother. And it came to pass, when they were in the field, that Cain rose up against Abel his brother and slew him."—GEN. iv. 8.

And the lower self,—the personal "I,"—now gains the power necessary for its evolution, and contrives to obscure the love element in the soul. The "death of Abel" occurs when the higher general motive of love gives place to the dawn of individuality on the astral and mental planes.

"The Cain in man—the sense-nature symbolised by the 'fruits of the ground' —has killed the Abel in man, the intuitional faculty symbolised by the 'lamb' of a pure and guileless spirit."—ED. MAITLAND, *Bible's Own Account*, p. 10.

"The feeling of each one of us that we have a Cain and Abel within, and that our business here is to reverse the Scripture story and to make our Abel kill our Cain, is in itself a kind of revelation and an element of immense hope about the future."—J. BRIERLEY, *Studies of the Soul*, p. 214.

See ATOM, CAIN, LAMB, SETH.

ABERAMENTHO :—A MYSTERY NAME OF JESUS IN THE "PISTIS SOPHIA" :—

An appellation signifying the "Glory of the Sun," or the "Radiance of the Light." A "Mystery name" is a name used to obscure the meaning of a symbol from the lower personality, but one which serves to identify the individuality signified to the higher mind.

See MYSTERY NAME.

ABLUTION BY USE OF WATER :—

A symbol of purification through the acceptance and assimilation of truth.

See BAPTISM, WASHED, WATER.

ABODE, HOUSE, DWELLING :—

A symbol of a sheath of the soul, or body of mental, astral, or physical matter on the respective planes. The causal-body is usually signified as being the abode of the Self or Divine Spark. In the case of Loke's "house with four doors," all the four bodies are meant.

See CLASSES, DWELLINGS, HOUSE, PALACE, VESTURES.

ABODE OF CATTLE :—

A symbol of the field of manifested life in which the soul acquires experience. The "cattle" symbolise the emotions, desires and mental qualities on the lower planes, which constitute the field of the soul's activities.

See CATTLE, KARSHVARES.

ABORTION PRODUCED BY WISDOM :—

A symbol of the abnormal forcing of a certain side of the nature which,

unless evolved under favourable conditions of growth, does not yield the perfect fruition of maturity, and is as fruit unripe, without flavour, and lacking in full development.

See SOPHIA.

ABORTION OF ST. PAUL :—

A symbol of the forcing of the conditions of soul-growth whereby for a moment a vision of higher things is perceived by the lower consciousness.

"And last of all he (Jesus) was seen of me also, as of (an *abortive* or) one born out of due time."—1 COR. xv. 8.

This is the utterance of a soul when it has attained direct vision of the Supreme. It refers to that state wherein personality is transcended and its imperfections and limitations have been surmounted.

See BORN (due time), CONVERSION (Paul).

ABOVE THE EARTH :—

Symbolical of the planes of being superior to the lower nature (earth). Heaven in its widest sense comprises the higher mental, the buddhic, and the atmic planes, in the present stage of soul-growth.

See HIGHER AND LOWER.

ABRAHAM :—

A symbol of a phase of the Divine nature active in the soul. It stands for the Supreme Being in the parable of Dives and Lazarus. The symbol " Abram " signifies an earlier phase of the Divine.

"And if ye are Christ's, then are ye Abraham's seed, heirs according to promise."—GAL. iii. 29.

If these qualities are in harmony with the highest Ideal, then are they of spiritual descent, or begotten of the power of the Divine (Abraham),—inheritors of the " fruits of the Spirit," according to the Divine scheme.

"Abraham is in many respects a figure of Christ."—ST. CHRYSOSTOM, *Hom. III.*

"Abraham signifies to us the virtue of faith in Christ."—*Glossa Ord.*

See HADES, LOT, RAM.

ABRAHAM, ISAAC, AND JACOB :—

Symbolic of the Higher Triad active within the soul ; or a dim reflection of the Divine principle in the lower nature in its highest aspect.

" ' Just men made perfect,' that is, ' Abraham, Isaac, and Jacob,' brought to *their perfection*, and whose names consequently are now, ' Father,' ' Son,' and ' Holy Ghost.' "—JOHN WARD, *Zion's Works*, Vol. V. p. 271.

" Abraham, Isaac, and Jacob are types of the divine life in man, manifesting itself in the spirit, in the understanding, and in the body respectively ;—for this is only another way of saying that they are the spirit of faith, of sonship, and of service : for sonship is the bringing of the divine life into our understanding, and service is bringing it into our outward and bodily acts ;—and this cannot be done at once, but by degrees and successively. Sonship is come, when the things which are in the spirit are in the understanding also. Service is come, when the things which have been in the understanding are seen in the body and wrought outwardly. Each of these, then, is the same elect spirit, only seen at different stages of its development, and taking at each stage a different form, by which the same One Spirit may show itself in its sevenfold variety. . . . The same Spirit of God shows variously through the different mental atmospheres which are furnished by the successive stages of man's development."—AND. JUKES, *The Types of Genesis*, pp. 250-1.

" Mr. Worsley's notion respecting the Patriarchs briefly is, that Abraham, Isaac, and Jacob, ' present to us the eternal triune object ' of worship,—Father, Son, and Holy Ghost."—P. FAIRBAIRN, *The Typology of Scripture*, Vol. I. p. 25.

See APOSTLES, HADES, TEETH (gnashing), TRIAD, TRINITY.

ABRAXAS, THE SACRED NAME :—

A symbol of the Divine nature as expressed in the great Cycle of Life, and in the conflict through which the Self passes in its progress through the lower worlds.

" The figure may be taken as a speaking type of the *Pleroma*, the *one* embracing *all* within itself."—C. W. KING, *Gnostics*, p. 245.

" The name Abraxas, which consisted of seven elements or letters, was a mystery-designation of the God who combined in himself the whole power of the Seven Planets, and also of the Year of 365 days, the sum of the number-values of the letters of Abraxas working out to 365. This mysterious Being was the ' Year ' ; but the Year as the Eternity."—G. R. S. MEAD, *T. G. Hermes*, Vol. I. p. 402.

The " Year " has the same significance as the " Zodiac,"—the pathway of the Sun, i.e. the Self ;—it is a symbol of the Cycle of Life with all its divisions, content, and activities. "Pragāpati the year" is the same as "Abraxas the year." They both mean the One mysterious Being who is the life and source of all that has been, that is, and that shall be.

See MANVANTARA, PLEROMA, PRA-GĀPATI (relaxed), SAMSARA, TUAT, YEAR, YMER, ZODIAC.

AB-SHAW :—
See CROCODILE.

ABSOLUTE, THE : THE FATHER :—

The potential and unmanifest Source of existence, about which nothing can be predicated.

"Prior to truly existing beings and total principles there is one God, . . . immovable, and abiding in the solitude of his own Unity. . . . He is the fountain of all things, and the root of the first intelligible forms. But from this one Deity, the God who is sufficient to himself, unfolds himself into light. For this Divinity also is the principle of the God of Gods,—a monad from *The One*,—prior to essence, and the principle of essence. For from him entity and essence are derived ; and hence, also, he is denominated the principle of intelligibles."—IAMBLICHUS, *The Mysteries, etc.*, ed. Taylor, p. 301.

"In Geberol's philosophy, the Highest above all things is an Absolute Unknown Unity ; the Emanator of the created is a different Creator, getting all potentiality from the former."—I. MYER, *Qabbalah*, p. 152.

"The Absolute is called in Eckhart's terminology the Godhead, being distinguished from God. God is subject to generation and corruption ; not so the Godhead ; God works, the Godhead does not work. . . . The Godhead as such cannot be revealed. It becomes manifest first in its persons. The Absolute is at once absolute process. The Godhead is the beginning and final goal of the whole séries of essences which exist. . . . The Father uttered himself and all creatures, in the Word,—his Son,—and the return of the Father into himself includes the like return of all creatures into the same Eternal Source. The logical genesis of the Son furnishes a type of all evolution or creation ; the Son is the unity of all the works of God. . . . God is in all things, and God is in all things."—UEBERWEG, *Hist. of Philos.*, Vol. I. pp. 473, 475.

"The spiritual man knows already something of what life is, and whence it came ; it is the forth-putting of the

eternal divine substance under temporal conditions and limitations that it may declare its inmost quality. Things are ever in flux, the universe is ever in the making, but nothing is being produced— nothing great, or beautiful, or good— which is not already present in the being of God waiting to be lived."—R. J. CAMPBELL, Serm., *The Bundle of Life.*

See AIN SOPH, APARÂGITA, ARHAT, ATMAN, BRAHMA, DEITY, FATHER, GOD, GODHEAD, HIRANYAGARBHA, MONAD, TRINITY, VIVANHÂO, ZERANA.

ABSTINENCE :—

A symbol of the soul's refraining from the lower attractions :—ceasing from the pursuit of sensation and the satisfaction of desire ; in favour of impersonal aims, and attention to the higher nature evolving from within.

"But those who have sought the Self by penance, abstinence, faith, and knowledge, gain by the Northern path Aditya, the sun. This is the home of the spirits, the immortal, free from danger, the highest. From thence they do not return, for it is the end."—*Prasna Upanishad*, I. 10.

But those spiritual egos, or individualities, who have sought the inner Self through limitation of external activity, cessation from pursuit of desire and sensation, faith in the Divine within, and devotion to Truth, gain by the path of the Ideals (Deva-yana) union with the Higher Self (sun). This perfects the causal-body, the abode of the egos, the immortal soul which is above all conflict, and forms the highest state from whence the égos return no more to incarnation, for they have attained their end.

See ASCETICISM, AUSTERITIES, FASTING, PENANCE.

ABSYRTIAN ISLES :—

A symbol of a higher mental condition conducive to spiritual vision.
See ARGO, CIRCE.

ABSYRTUS, BROTHER OF MEDEA :—

A symbol of divine outgoing energy in the lower vehicles, allied to the buddhic principle.

"Medea seeing her father Æetes gaining on the Argo, cut her brother to pieces, and scattered his limbs on the waves : while Æetes was engaged in collecting them, the Argo escaped. He

went back and buried the remains of his son at a place which he called Tomi."
—*Argonautic Expedition*, KEIGHTLEY.

The Logos (Æetes) descends, as it were, from above to aid the Wisdom and Love principles to return to their Source. The intuition (Medea) realising the accession of power within, acquires strength such as shatters the astro-mental vehicle in which the lower mind is ensheathed, and thereby the consciousness rises, being free of the lower vehicle, the fragments of which the Logos uses in the formation of other vehicles : acting through the monad of form, he works the discarded matter into forms of the lower planes.

"No part of the universe has value in and for itself alone ; it has value only as it expresses God. To see one form break up and another take its place is no calamity, however terrible it may seem, for it only means that the life contained in that form has gone back to the universal life, and will express itself again in some higher and better form."—R. J. CAMPBELL, *The New Theology*, p. 24.

See ÆTES, ARGO, AUSONIA, JASON, MANEROS, MEDEA, NASU, SALVE, TOMI.

ABTU FISH, OR ANT FISH :—

A symbol of the indwelling Self, or Saviour, active on the higher planes (Abtu).

" 'May I see the Abtu fish at his season.'—*Hymn to Ra*. The name of a mythological fish which, on coffins, etc., is seen swimming at the bows of the boat of the Sun-god."—BUDGE, *Book of the Dead*, p. 6.

The soul when perfected anticipates union with the Higher Self at the end of the cycle.

The Higher Self symbolised as a Great Fish in the Ocean of Truth, leads the soul (boat) onwards in its course through the cycle of life on the lower planes.

See BENNU BIRD, DELUGE, FISH (great), JESUS (fish), OCEAN, RESTAU, SHIP (Manu).

ABYSS, THE :—

A symbol of a condition of being out of relation to the manvantara or cycle of life. It may also signify the state of formless matter of the lower planes, prior to the involution of Spirit.

See CHAOS, DEEP, GINNUNGA, PO, TANAOA.

ACACIA AND SYCAMORE (SHITTIM) TREES :—

Symbols of " trees of Life," indicative of Truth and Goodness.

"Acacia wood was held to be 'wood of life.' According to Kercher it was sacred to the Sun-god in Egypt."—A. JEREMIAS, *Old Test., etc.*, Vol. II. p. 123.

"Hero-behutet (Horus) was made the God of the region, and the acacia and the sycamore were sacred to him."—*Legend of the Winged Sun-disk*, WIEDEMANN.

The Christ (Horus) now became the Lord of the soul, inasmuch as he united mind to God, and thereby established Truth and Goodness which live and endure throughout all time.

See BOWS, SYCAMORE, ZACCHEUS.

ACHAIANS (GREEKS) :—

A symbol of the lower mental qualities.

" Of a truth (said Achilles) Agamemnon raveth with baleful mind, and hath not knowledge to look before and after, that so his Achaians might battle in safety beside their ships."—*Iliad*, Bk. I.

Assuredly the Desire-mind has strange fancies, and has little knowledge to perceive before and after, i.e. it has little steadiness of mental vision, which steadiness is needed in order that the mental qualities (Achaians) might successfully carry out their evolution.

See DANAANS, GREEKS.

ACHAIANS, THE GREAT-HEARTED :—

A symbol of the higher mental qualities.

See GREEKS (great-hearted).

ACHAIANS, SONS OF THE :—

A symbol of the " Sons of Mind." These are the spiritual egos brought forth by the evolutional activities of the lower mental qualities. Though they are of higher origin than mind, yet they are the atma-buddhic fruit, as it were, of the Self striving through the lower nature.

See AGNISHWATTAS, FRAVASHIS, MANASAPUTRAS, MONAD OF LIFE, SONS OF GOD.

ACHE, OR PAIN :—

A symbol of mental and spiritual disharmony and disorder.

ACHILLES, SON OF PELEUS AND THETIS :—

A symbol of the personality or lower self begotten of the Higher Self (Peleus) and brought forth by Nature (Thetis).

"But though thou (Achilles) be of superior strength, and a goddess mother has given thee birth, yet he (Agamemnon) is superior in power, inasmuch as he rules more people."—*Iliad*, Bk. I.

Though the Personality be superior in its extent or range, touching high and low, and is the child of Buddhi, still, judged from below, the Desire-mind possesses greater strength since it supplies the motive power to the lower activities, and it energises the qualities.

"Human personality, as we now know it, arises out of the conjunction and interrelation of two factors,—the eternal, imperishable Divine life and the material envelopes in which it is broken up and conditioned."—R. J. CAMPBELL, *Serm., God's Life in Man.*

See AGAMEMNON, ARJUNA, BRISEIS, GOLDEN HAIR, HEEL, HONOUR, MENIS, MYRMIDONS, NOD, PATROCLUS, PERSONALITY, SHIPS, SOUL (lowest), THETIS.

ACROPOLIS :

A symbol of the causal-body as a centre of the mind.

"O friends, ye who inhabit the great city of sacred Akragas up to the acropolis, whose care is good deeds, who harbour strangers deserving of respect, who know not how to do baseness, hail !"—*Verses of Empedocles*, 352, FAIRBANKS.

O higher qualities, which are evolved through the mental centre which is in the causal-body : these qualities are occasioned of good thoughts and deeds, which attract higher emotions, and are the means of aspiration, and of lifting up the lower self,—all praise to you !

See AKRAGAS, CITY.

ADAH AND ZILLAH, WIVES OF LAMECH :—

Symbols of theory and practice, or wisdom and experience utilised, in alliance with reflection.

"Lamech said, . . . Adah and Zillah hear my voice. For I have slain a man for wounding me, and a young man for bruising me : if Cain shall be avenged sevenfold, truly Lamech seventy and sevenfold."—GEN. iv. 23, 24.

Reflection calls upon theory and practice to attend to its cogitations. For reflection has killed out somewhat of the prejudice (young man) with which the mind started on its evolution. If the lower personality (Cain) be the means of causing sorrow, surely the reflective mind shall cause much more sorrow.

"By 'Adah' is signified the mother of the celestial and spiritual of that Church : by 'Zillah,' the mother of the natural things of the same Church."—SWEDENBORG, *Arc. Cel. to Gen.*, iv. 19.

See LAMECH.

ADAM (LOWER ASPECT) :—

A symbol of the lower mind energised from the desire plane, but receptive of impressions from the higher nature. This is the "fallen" mind (Adam).

"We must consider that the man who was formed of earth, means the *mind* which is to be infused into the body."—Vol. I. p. 60.

"God, when first of all he made the *intellect* called it Adam."—PHILO, *Yonge's Trans.*, Vol. IV. p. 312.

The "Adam of dust" is described by Zosimus as

"the Adam of fate, him of the four elements."

That is, the lower mind subject to Karma, and related with the lower quaternary.

"In reading the first and second chapters of Genesis, a distinction was made by the learned of the Israelites, between the higher Adam, i.e. the Adam Qadmon, or First Paradigmic Ideal Man, and the inferior (the terrestrial) Adam."—I. MYER, *Qabbalah*, p. 114.

The Kabbala describes four Adams, the two highest of which are celestial and spiritual.

"The Third Adam is the terrestrial Adam, made of 'dust,' and placed in the Garden of Eden. This Adam was also an androgene. . . . It had, when first created, a glorious *simulacrum* or light body, and answers to the Yetzeeratic World."—*Ibid.*, p. 418.

This indicates an early form of man in an astral body on the astral plane, directed at first from the buddhic plane (Eden).

"The Fourth Adam was the Third Adam as he was after the Fall, when he was clothed with skin, flesh, nerves, etc. This answers to the lower *Nephesh* and *Guff*, i.e. body, united. He has the animal power of reproduction and continuance of species, and also answers to the Aseeyatic World, but in him is some of the Light of all the preceding (Adams)."—*Ibid.*, p. 418.

This signifies man as he is now encased in astral (nephesh) and physical (guff) bodies united; and living in the physical world of action (aseeyatic), but enlightened from his inner nature of mind and spirit. These four Adamic humanities stand for four root-races, the last of which reached the physical plane; this is known as the Atlantean race, the race which preceded the Aryan.

"Together they form the Great Universal Man. . . . The Qabbalah names man as the purpose of creation, and the first step is the Upper Adam or Celestial Man" (*Zohar*, III. 48A).—*Ibid.*, p. 418.

(This account of the four Adams may be compared with the Chinese "dynasties.")

"And the Lord God formed man of the dust of the ground, and breathed into his nostrils the breath of life; and man became a living soul."—GEN. ii. 7.

And the Will-Wisdom established the lower mind, which is the direct offshoot of the higher element (dust) of the lower nature; and into this mentality the spiritual essence, or spark, was projected, to connect the lower nature with the higher: and thence the *man*,—manasic being,—became a creature capable of independent existence.

"And the Lord God took the man, and put him into the garden of Eden," etc.—GEN. ii. 15.

And the Wisdom-Love introduces the mind into the heavenly plane,—or starts the evolution through buddhic action.

See ASEEYATIC, COUNTERFEIT, DEAD, DUST, DYNASTY, EARTH (ground), EDEN, EPIMETHEUS, EVE, FALL, GOLDEN AGE, HEEL, HOUSE (frequented), IMMORTALITY FORFEITED, MAN, MATRO, NEPHESH, PERSONALITY, PYLUS, RACES, RAGHA, RUAH, SKINS, SWEAT, TYRUS.

ADAM (HIGHER ASPECT) :—

A symbol of the Divine nature of humanity,—the Archetypal Man on the three higher planes.

"The Great Androgene, the Adam Illa-ah or Adam Qadmon, which includes in itself all the ideas, and all the content of all the prototypes of the existences. . . . This (First) Adam is considered as the first distinctive beginning in the finite, and therefore is the sole occupant of the Atzeel-atic World."—I. MYER, *Qabbalah*, p. 401.

This signifies the Macrocosm, or Pleroma, which occupies the planes of atma and buddhi,—the world of emanation (Atzeel-atic).

"Man, who at first stretched from end to end of the world, was afterwards diminished by the hand of God (Ps. cxxxix. 5). See *Chagigah*, 12A, where it is also said, that the First Adam *extended from the earth to the firmament*, for it is said that he was created upon or *above the earth*."—CH. TAYLOR, *Sayings of the Jewish Fathers*, p. 71.

This indicates the Archetypal Man on the upper planes,—the Macrocosm from which comes the Microcosm, both existing above the lower nature (earth), the second being a diminution of the first.

"The Chaldæans and Parthians and Medes and Hebrews call the First Man Adam. . . . So the First Man is called by us Thōyth (Thoth) and by them Adam, not giving His true name in the Language of the Angels, but naming him symbolically according to His Body by the four elements" (*Zosimus*).—G. R. S. MEAD, *T. G. Hermes*, Vol. III. p. 277.

The suggestion here is, to give to the symbol "Thoth" its highest meaning, i.e. atma-buddhi-manas, the same as "Thrice Greatest Hermes," and therefore Thoth stands for the Archetypal Man which has its reflection in the lower quaternary (four elements).

"Philo's ingenious theory of the two original Adams : (1) the Heavenly, (2) the Earthly. The former is the Scriptural first man who was made in the image and likeness of God; he is imperishable, ' an idea or a genus perceptible only by the intellect.' The latter is man as we see him now in the races of the world, imperfect and corruptible."—J. ABELSON, *Immanence of God*, p. 75.

"The whole universe was incomplete and did not receive its finishing stroke till Man was formed, who is the acme of creation and the microcosm uniting in himself the totality of beings. The Heavenly Adam who emanated from the highest primordial obscurity created the Earthly Adam."—*Zohar*, II. 70b.

"Eckhart speaks of Christ as the representation of Collective Humanity—the ideal *Man*, in whom all *men* have their unity and reality, so that when a person rises to the ground and reality of his essential being he partakes of Christ and becomes one with Him and

so one with God : 'All creatures that
have flowed out from God must become
united into one Man, who comes again
into the unity Adam was in before he
fell. This is accomplished in Christ.
According to this truth all creatures are
One Man, and this Adam is God (Christ
the Son of God).' "—R. M. JONES,
Mystical Religion, p. 236.

" Christ Jesus is the 'Adam' that the
Bible talks of in *Genesis i.*—a Man of a
new order or kind."—JOHN WARD, *Zion's
Works*, Vol. III. p. 198.

In the Clementine writings Christ
is identified with the Heavenly Adam.

" The first man Adam became a living
soul. The last Adam is a life-giving
spirit. Howbeit that is not first which
is spiritual ; but that which is natural ;
then that which is spiritual. The first
man is of the earth, earthy : the second
man is of heaven."—1 COR. xv. 45–7.

The transposition of the two Adams
is explained in the text as referring
to *evolution* wherein the lower gives
birth to the higher. In *involution* the
reverse order obtains, for the heavenly
precedes the earthly, as in GEN. i.

" Ye have put off the old man with
his doings, and have put on the new man,
which is being renewed unto knowledge
after the image of him that created
him."—COL. iii. 9, 10.

Here, the Divine Image, the heavenly Prototype, the First Adam,
precedes the " Adam of dust," the
second Adam, as described in Genesis.
The evolution of the " new man "—
the Christ within,—is beautifully indicated as according to the primordial
Archetype which again is the Christ.
The " New Man " is weak and little
developed at first ; but by increments
of truth he is gradually renewed or
evolved after the perfect pattern of
Christ his Divine Progenitor, until the
two again become one.

" Whenever I attribute sinful properties and dispositions and inclinations to
our Lord's human nature, I am speaking
of it considered as apart from Him, in
itself. . . . As Adam was the perfect
man of creation, Jesus was the perfect
man of regeneration ; perfect in holiness,
by being perfect in faith."—E. IRVING,
Col. Writings, Vol. V. p. 564.

" It has been already established by
no contemptible arguments from Scripture, that the First Man may be properly
referred to Christ Himself, and is no
longer a type and representation and
image of the Only-begotten, but has
become actually Wisdom and the Word.
For man, having been composed, like
water, of wisdom and life, has become

identical with the very same untainted
light which poured into him. Whence
it was that the apostle directly referred
to Christ the words that had been spoken
of Adam " (1 COR. xv. 22).—METHODIUS,
The Banquet, etc., Ch. VIII.

" Humanity is Divinity Self-limited.
And if the divine and the eternal imply
each other, if that which is divine is that
which is uncreate, which never needed a
beginning and will never have an end,
then there must be something in every
human being which can only be thus
described."—R. J. CAMPBELL, Serm., *Our
Eternal Glory.*

" ' In the image of God created He
man.' God made man like Himself.
The creation had made man in the image
of God. Now if we can comprehend
that truth at all, it must be evident
that before man was made, the man-
type existed in God. In some part of
His perfect nature there was the image
of what the new creation was to be.
Already before man trod the garden in
the high glory of his new Godlikeness,
the pattern of the thing he was to be
existed in the nature of Him who was to
make him. Before the clay was fashioned
and the breath was given, this humanity
existed in the Divinity ; already there
was a union of the Divine and human ;
and thus already there was the eternal
Christ. See how this exalts the human
nature that we wear. In the midst of
the eternity of God there bursts forth
into being the new life of man. . . .
What if the type of this life I live were
part and parcel of the everlasting Godhead ? What if it be the peculiar glory
of one of the persons of that Godhead
that He has worn for ever, bound with
His perfect deity, the perfect archetype
and pattern of this humanity of mine ?
At once is not my insignificance redeemed ?
Every power in me grows dignified and
worthy, catching some of the importance
of the eternal type it represents."—
PHILLIPS BROOKS, *Mystery of Iniquity*,
p. 312.

See ADAPA, ARC. MAN, ATZEELATIC,
BOLTS, DISMEMBERMENT, EVOLUTION,
IMAGE, INDIVIDUALITY, INVOLUTION,
LIMBS, MACROCOSM, MALE-FEMALE
(divine), MICROCOSM, PRAGÂPATI,
THOTH.

ADAM, DUAL :—

A symbol of the union in the soul
of the mental and buddhic principles,
—Buddhi-manas,—the Divine Image.

" In the day that God created man,
in the likeness of God made he him ;
male and female created he them ; and
blessed them, and called their name
Adam in the day when they were created."
—GEN. v. 1, 2.

This passage refers first to the

progeny of the mind, which are thought-states which proceeded successively when the mind came forth in its perfection as the image of God. The mind was endowed with " sparks " of the eternal " Fire," namely the reason and intuitive principles. The " blessing " signifies the Divine Will operating through the human consciousness. The reference to the reason and intuition being " Adamic " implies that the intellect is supreme over the intuition first of all.

See LIVING THINGS, MALE-FEMALE, TYRUS.

ADAMANT :—

A symbol of the fabric of the universe,—the world-essence, forerunner of the physical condition.

" And they girded me with adamant which can crush iron."—" Hymn of the Soul," in the *Acts of Judas Thomas.*

And I, the soul, was invested with that world-essence which precedes the physical.

ADAMAS (HIGHER ASPECT) :—

A symbol of the Archetypal Man.

" ' But Cyllenian Hermes summoned forth the souls of men mindful ' (Od. 24, 1 ff.). . . . That is, from the Blessed Man Above, or Original Man, or Adamas, as they think they have been thus brought down into the plasm of clay, in order that they may be enslaved to the Demiurge of this creation, Esaldaios a fiery God, fourth in number, for thus they call the Demiurge." (Gnostic.)— HIPPOLYTUS, *Philosophumena*, Bk. V. Ch. 2.

The Divine Mind (Hermes) centralises the spiritual egos on the mental plane, endowing them with mind. That is, the egos take forms provided by the Archetypal Man, and are thus brought down to the lower vehicles, in order that they may be enslaved to the lower desire principle (Esaldaios), ruler of the lower quaternary.

" The ' rock ' means Adamas : this is the ' corner stone.' "—*Ibid.*

" The rock was Christ." " Adamas " signifies the Archetypal Man which is Christ incarnate,—the inner God.

See ARC. MAN, DEMIURGE, HERMES, I E O U.

ADAMAS (LOWER ASPECT) :—

A symbol of the lower self as ruler of the soul's lower qualities.

" The Six Æons under Adamas have refused the mysteries of Light, and persisted in sexual union and procreated rulers and archangels, angels, workmen and decans."—*Books of the Saviour.*

The qualities in the descending cycle of six signs are those attached to things of the lower nature,—those in whom the sense of separateness is not killed, and who are of the " old dispensation." They persist in the union of desire and mind which entails endless progeny of illusions. The procreation is the begetting and multiplying *means* of existence when the end should be all and in All.

See ÆONS (twelve), DISPENSATIONS, IABRAOTH, SEASONS (six), SIX, TYRANTS.

ADAM'S DEAD BODY :—

A symbol of the old self, devoid of spiritual life, and through discarding which the soul rises.

" Noah carries the body of Adam into the Ark, his three sons following with the sacred tokens."—*Book of the Conflicts of Adam.*

" Noah," the individuality or sublimated " Adam," conveys his old self with him, as it were, in the causal-body (ark), as it is only through it, and by surmounting it, that he rises. His " sons " stand here for the fruit of the affectionate nature, and these willingly follow with the tokens of the essence of his aspiration,—Faith, Love, Wisdom, Power.

See ARK (Noah), HAM, NOAH, NOAH'S SONS, ROCK, TOKENS.

ADAPA, THE SON OF EA, OR OF ERIDU :—

A symbol of the Archetypal Man, son of the First Logos, the Lord from Heaven.

" Ea had created Adapa without a helpmate ; he had endowed him with wisdom and knowledge, but had denied to him the gift of immortality."—SAYCE, *Rel. of Anc. Egypt. and Babyl.*, p. 383.

At this stage creation on the lower planes had not taken place, and it is upon the lower planes that duality is involved. Man's Prototype is endowed with " wisdom and knowledge," that is, with buddhi and manas, yet is devoid at this stage of those aspects of the Self which shall entitle him to life eternal, and which justify his *individual* existence in the manifested Cosmos.

"Man (Adapa) remained mortal, and it was never again in his power to eat of the tree of life."—*Ibid.*, p. 384.

Humanity in its lower nature so continued mortal; nor was it possible for man, i.e. man limited to the three lower planes, ever to become more than man and immortal.

"Adapa is called the 'seed of mankind.'"—DR. FRITZ HOMMEL.

See ADAM (higher), ARC. MAN, BOLTS, GATES, HEEL, IMMORTALITY, INDIVIDUALITY, PERSONALITY, SOUTH WIND, TAMMUZ.

ADEPT ; GURU :—

A symbol of the higher mind as an active agent in the instruction of the lower.

See GURU, HERMES, MASTER OF WISDOM.

ADITI :—

A symbol of primordial Space on the higher planes in relation to the manifestation of the Self (Aditya).

"Goddess Aditi, 'the Infinite Expanse,' conceived of subsequently as the Mother of all the gods."—MON. WILLIAMS, *Indian Wisdom*, p. 12.

"Aditi is mentioned by the side of heaven and earth."

"In X., 63, 2, the gods in general are represented as born from Aditi, the waters, and the earth."—MAX MÜLLER, *S. B. of E.*, Vol. XXXII. pp. 248, 251.

Space is the arena of the operations of spirit and matter.

The Ideals (gods) are produced from Space, the outpouring of Truth, and the aspiring lower nature.

"As Living Substance, God is One. As Life and Substance, God is Twain. HE is the Life, SHE is the Substance. . . . She is not Matter : but is the potential essence of Matter. She is not Space ; but is the *within* of space, its fourth and original dimension, that from which all proceed, the containing element of Deity, and of which space is the manifestation. As original Substance, the substance of all other substances, She underlies that whereof all things are made ; and like life and mind, is interior, mystical, spiritual, and discernible only when manifested in operation. In the Unmanifest, She is the Great Deep, or Ocean of Infinitude, the Principium or Archë, the heavenly Sophia, or Wisdom, who encircles and embraces all things."
—*The Perfect Way*, p. 55.

See ANTELOPE, BUDDHIC PLANE, DAWN, HORSE SACRIFICE, MĀYĀ

(higher), NUT, RHEA, SUBSTANCE, SUN-RISING.

ADITYA, THE SUN :—

A symbol of the primordial Self.

"Aditya (the sun) is Brahman, this is the doctrine."—*Khand. Upanishad*, III. 19, 1.

See SAVITRI, SUN, SURYA, VAISVĀNARA.

ADITYAS, THE TWELVE :—

These are symbolic of twelve aspects of the Self or Soul in the twelve signs of the Zodiac ; that is, they signify twelve states in the Soul's development through the Cycle of Life (the year).

"Varuna became relegated to a position among seven secondary deities of the heavenly sphere called Adityas (afterwards increased to twelve, and regarded as diversified forms of the sun in the several months of the year), and subsequently to a dominion over the waters when they had left the air and rested on the earth."—MON. WILLIAMS, *Indian Wisdom*, p. 13.

The last sentence signifies that Truth (Varuna) rules the aspirations arising from the lower nature (earth), responding to them by showering down truths (waters) into the mind (air) in order to fructify the lower nature (earth).

See ÆONS (twelve), DELUGE, FLOOD, NIDANUS, PRAGÂPATI, SUN, TUAT, TWELVE, VARUNA, YEAR, ZODIAC.

ADONAI OF THE HEAVENS :—

A symbol of the Archetypal Man, the ideal image of the soul.

ADONIS OR TAMMUZ :—

A symbol of the Higher Self,—the incarnate God born in the soul. Adonis was conceived of the Divine Father, and born of Myrrha—the purified lower nature. But before the birth, Myrrha was changed into a tree, the "Tree of Life" from which alone, as the Divine Ray from the Supreme, the Self may be born. The lower love nature (Aphrodite) concealed the Holy Babe in the soul (chest) and entrusted it to the emotion-nature (Persephone) which being allied with the desire-nature (Hades) is detained in the "underworld," or lower nature, subject to the developing process of transitory form lives. The incarnate God is therefore bound by the Divine (Zeus) law of the re-

incarnating cycle, and has to pass through short periods of earth life or physical existence, with intermediate periods of astral and mental existence of longer duration. The death of Adonis through being wounded by a boar, signifies the release of the soul from the underworld. The soul being perfected, the last thrust of evil (the boar) causes, as it were, the rise of the consciousness from the lower life to the higher.

"Now the Assyrians call this [mystery of soul-growth] Adonis (or Endymion). And whenever it is called Adonis, it is Aphrodite who is in love with and desires Soul so-called. And Aphrodite is Genesis according to them. But when Persephone (that is Korē), is in love with Adonis, Soul becomes subject to Death, separated from Aphrodite (that is from Genesis)."—HIPPOLYTUS, *Philosophumena*, Bk. V. Ch. 2.

The birth and evolution of the Higher Self in the human soul is this "mystery of soul-growth." When the lower love nature (Aphrodite) aspires towards the incoming Self, the Self responds to the lower attractiveness for growth and production (Genesis). But when the emotion-nature (Persephone) is allied with the Self, the Soul or Self is drawn down to the lower planes and is obscured and imprisoned in mortal bodies, unable to grow and produce its own nature until it is again allied with buddhi.

See APHRODITE, BOAR, HADES, PERSEPHONE, PERSEUS, TAMMUZ, VENUS, ZEUS.

ADOPTION :—

A symbol of the union of the personality with the individuality, that is, the absorption of the lower nature into the higher. The same as "redemption."

"For we know that every creature groaneth and travaileth in pain together until now. And not only they, but ourselves also, which have the firstfruits of the Spirit, even we ourselves groan within ourselves, waiting for the adoption, to wit, the redemption of our body."—ROM. viii. 22, 23.

The outgoing desires and passions have always been causes of pain and sorrow to the lower nature. So also, when the higher emotions are being evolved, the soul is still subject to suffering while progressing on its upward path, awaiting the time of liberation, when union with the Higher Self shall take place, and the lower nature be discarded by the "sons of God," the egos.

"Apparently this world is to go on, and material existence is to go on until everything human has been assimilated to Christ, and then the goal of redemption is reached, and God is all in all."—R. J. CAMPBELL, Serm., *The Ceaseless Quest.*

See ATONEMENT, REDEMPTION, REMISSION, UNION.

ADORNED WITH GEMS, ETC. :—

Symbolic of being endowed with virtues,—qualities of the buddhic nature.

See GEMS, JEWELS.

ADRASTIA, CRETAN NYMPH :—

A symbol of the law of cause and effect, or karma on the lower planes.

"The Demiurgus (Zeus), as Orpheus says, is nursed by Adrastia ; . . . but he marries Necessity and begets Fate."—PROCLUS, *Tim.* V. 323.

"Adrastia is said to guard the Demiurgus ; with brazen cymbals and sounding drums in her hands (at the mouth of the Cavern of Night), she sends forth sounds so that all the gods may turn to her."—PROCLUS, *Theol. Plat.* IV. 16, 206.

The Higher Self (Zeus) is brought up in the Soul (Cavern) by the laws of nature. Through the operations of karma, the ideals (gods) are aroused and evolved. The "sounds" signify the vibrations of emotion arising from the lower planes, which as the nature becomes raised and purified, arouse the higher qualities (gods) so that they may evolve in the soul.

See CAVE, DEMIURGE, KARMA, MUSIC, NECESSITY, ZEUS.

ADULTERY :—

A symbol of the ego's forsaking of the higher life for the lower, that is, the turning away from Wisdom's teaching, to effect union with desire and the sense activities.

"Whosoever shall put away his wife and marry another, committeth adultery."—MARK x. 11.

The soul which acts contrary to the spiritual law of the evolution of its own being, that is, who forsakes the Divine ordinance at the foundation of the cosmos,—commits adultery.

"To commit adultery and whoredom

27

signifies to adulterate and falsify the goods and truths of the Word."—SWEDENBORG, *T. C. R.*, n. 313, 314.

See COURTEZAN, DIVORCING, FOLLY, HARLOT, MARRIAGE, WIFE, WHORE-DOM, WOMAN (adultery).

ADUMBLA :—

See AUDUMBLA.

ADVARYA PRIEST :—

A symbol of the spiritual mind.

"The Advarya is the mind, and the Hotri is speech."—*Sata. Brâh.*, I. 5, 1, 21.

See AARON, AGNIDRA, ATHORNE, CHRYSE, HOTRI. PRIEST, POPE.

ADVERSARY, THE :—

The desire-mind which strives against the Divine nature within the soul.

"Your adversary the devil, as a roaring lion, walketh about, seeking whom he may devour : whom withstand steadfast in your faith."—1 PETER v. 8–9.

The desire-mind, motived by the strength of the desires and the senses, seeks to dominate the soul. But the soul is exhorted to resist by relying upon its higher nature.

See AESHM, AHRIMAN, ANTICHRIST, COUNTERFEIT, DEVIL, JOB, SATAN.

ADYTUM :—

A symbol of the causal-body on the higher mental plane, as the seat or vehicle of the Higher Self, Atma-buddhi.

See AKRAGUS, CABIN, HEART, HOUSE, KAABA, SHRINE, TEMPLE.

AEA :—

A symbol of the fifth sub-plane of the buddhic plane.

See CIRCE.

AEGAEON, ONE OF THE URANIDS :—

A symbol of the analytical function of the critical intellect, in the discernment of differences.

"Aegaeon is one of the giants who attacked Olympus."—*Smith's Class. Dict.*

The critical intellect casts doubt upon the existence of supreme Goodness, Love, and Wisdom, above a world of evil, suffering, and imperfection.

"Here we are, born into this world without any free choice of our own, so far as we know ; hedged about all along

with limitations through which we cannot break ; visited with sufferings and disabilities we cannot escape ; compelled to do things we do not want to do and to bear burdens of which we would fain be rid. There is not a single soul among us who is absolutely free to choose his or her own course in life ; we have not even control over our own dispositions—we cannot say what kind of temperament we shall possess, and only to a very limited degree what kind of character we shall exhibit or what thoughts and feelings shall dominate us from time to time. In fact, we are enslaved more or less, every one of us, both by our circumstances and our propensities. . . . We come whence we know not, and go whither we know not, driven along by forces against which we are helpless."

"We do not realise that we are being thrust along in this world by the dynamo of our own deeper self which is indissolubly one with all the divine power in the universe. At times we cry out against the conditions under which the eternal glory becomes manifest in us, and we think we would change or destroy them if we could. We are quite mistaken ; we should do nothing of the kind ; we should, if we could see the end from the beginning, demand exactly what is taking place."—R. J. CAMPBELL, Serm., *Who Compels ?*

See BRIAREUS, GUARDIAN SPIRITS, TALUS, WILL.

ÆGEUS, FATHER OF THESEUS :—

A symbol of spiritual knowledge which begets wonder-awe.

See CORD, TAURT.

AĒLOPUS, OR NICŌTHEA, THE HARPY :—

A symbol of desire through the sense of sight ; or the lust of the eyes.

See HARPIES, NICŌTHEA, OCYPETE, PHINEUS, ZETES.

ÆON :—

A symbol of the Divine primordial Unity, the manifesting Spirit emanating from the Absolute. The primal Monad of Life.

"Æon, moreover, is God's image ; Cosmos is Æon's ; the Sun (is the image) of Cosmos ; and Man the image of the Sun."—*Corpus Hermeticum*, XI.

Divine Unity,—the manifesting Spirit or Monad of Life,—is the projection of God ; the Archetypal Form-universe, or Monad of Form, is the projection of Divine Unity ; the Individuality is the projection of the Archetypal Form-life ; and the Personality is the projection of the Individuality.

"The Lord of the Eternity (the Æon) is the first God, the second is Cosmos ; man is the third" (*The Perfect Sermon*).—G. R. S. MEAD, *T. G. Hermes*, Vol. II. p. 325.

The Higher Self,—the Divine Life of the manvantara,—is the First Being produced by the Absolute ; the Second Being is the Archetypal universe ; the human Soul is the Third.

See COSMOS, MONAD, RULER OF ÆON, SUN, TRIAD, UNION.

ÆON, THE THIRTEENTH :—

This Æon signifies the period and state of completion, entered upon after the close of the cycle of twelve Æons.

"And so He (Jesus) passed inward to the veils of the thirteenth Æon."—*Pistis Sophia*.

So it is, the Christ-soul passed onward and inward to those states which lead to perfection and final liberation. This is the triumph of the Higher Self when the lower and the higher natures become one.

See ASCENSION, BORN (due time), COMPARTMENTS, MYSTERIES, THIRTEEN, UNION.

ÆONS :—

Periods and states within manvantaras ; or cycles and their states.

"Tumult arose in the pleroma lest the creations of the Æons should become formless and imperfect, and destruction in no long time seize on the Æons themselves."—HIPPOLYTUS, *Refutation*, Bk. VI. Ch. 26.

The "tumult" is the power to anticipate the result of the causes at work when the manvantaric law actualises, allied with a sense of apprehension of the upshot, as it were, of given conditions to produce effects. This involves the care with which nature ensheaths the life in its various aspects, and so carries forward the plan of evolution.

See AAT, PLEROMA, SOPHIA.

ÆONS, THE TWELVE :—

These are the same as the twelve signs of the Zodiac, the twelve Adityas, etc. The signs, or constellations, stand for every department of human experience. Æons are portions of great cycles, and

each Æon is distinguished by special features corresponding with the "twelve tribes," the "twelve apostles," "twelve loaves of shewbread," etc.

"Twelve Æons,—six being ruled by Adamas, and six by Iabraōth."—*Books of the Saviour*. See *Pistis Sophia*.

The Æons here referred to are the twelve divisions of the cycle of life,—six of which are ruled by the lower nature, and six by the Divine nature. The six under Adamas are those containing the souls attached to the things of the lower self,—those in whom the sense of separateness is not killed, and who are of the "old dispensation." The six under Iabraōth are the six signs above the "earth" or lower nature, and which correspond with the triumph and ascent of the Christ in the soul. These are of the "new dispensation."

"Jesus soared to the space of the Twelve Æons ; and all the Rulers and Orders were amazed."—*Pistis Sophia*.

The Christ-soul now completes its spiral ascent through the twelve departments of human experience, whose cyclic progression corresponds with the Twelve signs of the Zodiac, or fields of the Tuat. The "amazement" among the activities of nature, is simply the process of awakenment of the qualities and potencies (evolution) which takes place in the spiritual ascent.

See ADAMAS, ADITYAS, ANTHROPOS, APOSTLES, DISCIPLES, IABRAŌTH, SAVIOURS, SEXUAL, TRIBES, TUAT TWELVE, ZODIAC.

ÆSCULAPIUS :—

A symbol of the Higher Self as the healer and saviour.

"Æsculapius was said to have been smitten with lightning for raising the dead. It is evident that this could never have been the case in a physical sense. But view it in a spiritual sense, and then the statement is just this, that he was believed to raise men who were dead in trespasses and sins to newness of life."—A. HISLOP, *Two Babylons*, p. 236.

See SERPENT ÆSCULAPIUS.

AESHM ; WRATH, THE EVIL DOER :—

A symbol of the lower mind united with the instincts and desires.

"And many opponents have watched there (at the Kinvat bridge), with the desire of evil of Aeshm, the impetuous assailant, and Astovidad, who devours creatures of every kind and knows no satiety."—*The Minok-hired*, II. 100.

And many are the difficulties in the path of the soul, by reason of the opposition of the passions and desires. The lower mind (Aeshm) when rendered impetuous by desire for outward things, assails the higher nature at the "bridge" of mind. The "devouring of the creatures" signifies the assimilative action of the kama-manasic function (Astovidad), whether exercised in the pursuit of mere sensual indulgence, or in pursuit of knowledge for self-seeking ends. Its capacity for desires (creatures) is as a "bottomless pit" which cannot be filled.

See ADVERSARY, ASTOVIDAD, BOTTOMLESS PIT, BRIDGE, DEVIL, DEVOURER, EVIL, IRON AGE.

ÆSON, FATHER OF JASON :—

A symbol of the Second Logos from whom proceeds the incarnate Higher Self (Jason). "Æson" is the Son of God who reigns in the stead of his Father the First Logos (Cretheus).

See CRETHEUS, JASON.

ÆËTES, KING OF COLCHIS :—

A symbol of the Supreme Being, the First Logos, as ruler of the buddhic plane (Colchis).

See ABSYRTUS, CADMUS, COLCHIS, MEDEA.

ÆTHER OR FATHER ÆTHER :—

A symbol of the fifth plane of being ; the plane of Atma. The highest plane of manifestation.

"The fifth element some call Heaven, some Light, others Æther."—PLUTARCH, *On the E at Delphi*, § 11.

"Æther was considered one of the elementary substances out of which the universe was formed. It was regarded as pure upper air,' the residence of the Gods, and Zeus, Lord of the Æther, or Æther itself personified."—*Smith's Class. Dict.*

"Out of this same Self the ether rose, from ether air, from air fire, from fire water, from water earth, from earth plants, from plants food, from food the germ of life, from the germ of life man."—*Tait. Upanishad.*

See ATMA, DÆMONS, ELEMENTS (five), WORLDS (five).

ÆTHEREAL WORLD :—

A symbol of the Universe of Spirit (atma-buddhi) which precedes the lower universe which is patterned upon it.

See ARC. MAN, IMAGE.

AFU-RĀ, i.e. THE SUN-GOD RĀ IN-THE-FLESH, DEAD :—

A symbol of the Incarnate God,—the Higher Self involved in matter of the planes of manifestation during the Cycle of Life, and indiscernible (dead) to the lower consciousness.

"In the cabin of the boat stands the Sun-god, with a sceptre in one hand, and the sign of life in the other, his head is a ram's head surmounted by the solar disk. This god is Af Rā, 'Flesh of Rā,' not Rā himself, for the Sun is dead, but his flesh and blood. . . . In front of the cabin stands Apūat, 'Opener of the Ways,' a form of Anubis, whose office it was to introduce the soul of Rā as well as the souls of departed men into the underworld."—WIEDEMANN, *Rel. of the Egyptians*, pp. 86, 87.

The "boat" is a symbol of the World-soul or prototypal causal-body which passes through the Cycle of Life (the Tuat) and contains the cabined God, which ram-headed, represents the Higher Self sacrificed for humanity,—the "Lamb (Ram) slain from the foundation of the world." God limits and obscures himself in producing his creatures. He involves himself in matter, and thus is sacrificed that we may live in him. "Anubis" is a symbol of the human body of flesh which introduces the Divine and human souls to the physical existence which carries with it astral and mental activities of the lower planes (the underworld). In the early human races, the "opener of the ways" of life may be a buddhic, mental, or astral body, prior to the formation of a physical body. Hence the relation of "Apuat" to "Anubis."

"On looking into the Boat of the Sun-god we see that this deity has transformed himself, and that he no longer appears as a fiery disk, but as a ram-headed man, who stands within a shrine ; in other words Rā has taken the form of Osiris. The name given to this form is Af, or Afu, which means literally 'flesh,' and 'a dead body'; it was as a dead body that Osiris first entered the Tuat, and those who wished to become what he became subsequently had to enter the Tuat as dead bodies and with

the attributes wherewith he entered it."
—BUDGE, *Egypt. Heav. and Hell*, Vol. III.
p. 106.

It must be remembered that "corpse" or "dead body" is a symbol of the lower self or personality in its natural aspect of possessing no sign of Divine life. Osiris (Christ) enters the lower nature in evolution as a completely hidden Spirit, and every spiritual ego follows the same course. Osiris passes successfully through all states of the lower nature and carries his Osirified egos with him to rise finally to life immortal. "For if we have become united with him by the likeness of his death, we shall be also by the likeness of his resurrection" (ROM. vi. 5).

"From first to last Osiris was to the Egyptians the God-man who suffered and died and rose again and reigned eternally in heaven. They believed that they would inherit eternal life, just as he had done, provided that what was done for him by the gods, was done for them."—BUDGE, *Gods of the Egyptians*, Vol. II. p. 126.

"This Self is hidden in all living things, it shines not forth; but it is seen by the keen and penetrating mind of those that see into the supersensible."
—*Katha Upanishad*, III.

See AGNIHOTRA, AMEN, ANUBIS, APUAT, ARC. MAN, ARK (safety), ASCENSION (Osiris), BOAT, CABIN, CHILDREN OF HORUS, CORPSE, DEITY, EQUINOX, INCARNATION, JESUS (lamb), KHEPER, LAMB OF GOD, NET (under), PRAGÂPATI, RÂ, RAM, RESURRECTION, SEKER.

AGAMEMNON (ATREIDES), SON OF ATREUS :—

A symbol of the desire-mind, kama-manas, which is the offspring of illusion (Atreus).

"Nor do thou, O (Achilles) son of Peleus, feel inclined to contend against the king (Agamemnon); since never yet has any sceptre-bearing king to whom Jove has given glory, been allotted an equal share of dignity."—*Iliad*, Bk. I.

Nor must the personality (Achilles) begotten of the Higher Self (Peleus), seek to exterminate and crush out the desire-mind which has its own purpose in the soul's evolution; for never previous to its advent has any aspect of the Self, endowed with powers by the Supreme, attained to

so important a position in the Divine scheme (compare Haman).

"Agamemnon, although the chief commander of the Greeks, is not the hero of the *Iliad*, and in chivalrous spirit, bravery and character, altogether inferior to Achilles. But he nevertheless rises above all the Greeks by his dignity, power and majesty."—*Smith's Class. Dict.*

The "Greeks" signify the lower mental qualities.

See ACHILLES, ATREUS, BRISEIS, ESTHER, GREEKS, HECTOR, HONOUR, KLYTAIMNESTRA, MYRMIDONS, NOD, ODYSSEUS, PELEUS, PRIZE.

AGATE STONE :—

A symbol of acquired truth.
See RUBIES.

AGATHODÆMON :—

A symbol of the Divine Life and Energy arising within the soul.

"The 'Good Deity,' in honour of whom the Greeks drank a cup of unmixed wine at the end of every repast."—*Smith's Class. Dict.*

The "cup of wine" is the symbol of Divine Life and Truth which needs to be partaken of by all the qualities.

See CUP, DÆMON, MIND, SACRAMENT, SERPENT KING, SERPENT (solar), WINE.

AGENOR, SON OF POSEIDON :—

A symbol of the Divine Mind, begotten of the Eternal Truth.
See POSEIDON.

AGNI, THE FIRE-GOD :—

A symbol of the force-aspect of the indwelling Higher Self, directed to the higher channels of manifestation.

"Agni is the light, the burner of evil: he burns away the evil of this sacrificer; and the latter becomes a light of prosperity and glory in this, and a light of bliss in yonder world."—*Satapatha Bráhmana*, XI. 2, 3, 6.

The force-aspect of the Self is the light of Truth which causes the disappearance of the ignorance and shortcomings of the personality (sacrificer). And the personality becomes perfected in wisdom and righteousness on the lower planes, and has a blissful consciousness on the higher.

"The gods then established that fire (Agni) in their innermost soul; and having established that immortal element and become immortal and unconquerable, they overcame their mortal, conquerable enemies (the asuras). And so this sacrificer now establishes that immortal element in his innermost soul; and—though there is for him no hope of immortality—he obtains the full measure of life."—*Sata. Brâh.*, XI. 2, 2, 14.

The higher qualities, or ideals, involved and latent at first, establish through aspiration the Spirit or "fire" of evolutionary life in their innermost being. This confers immortality upon them and gives them the force necessary to overcome the desires (asuras). In the same way the personality takes to itself the Divine Spark, which though it does not confer immortality upon it, yet enables it to become perfect on the lower planes.

"I am the Fire-god, the divine brother of the Fire-god, and I am Osiris, the brother of Isis, . . . I am Osiris, the first-born of the divine womb, the first-born of the gods, and the heir of my father Osiris-Seb."—BUDGE, *Book of the Dead*, Ch. LXIX.

The Divine aspects on the higher planes cannot be differentiated the one from the other by the lower mind. The Higher Self (Osiris) is the first-born of Time (Seb) and Space (Mut) and emanates upon the plane of atma.

See ALTAR (fire), ASHES, GOLD PLATE, HORSE (red), HORSE SACRIFICE, LOTUS LEAF, PRANA, PRAGÂPATI, SOMA PLANT, TORTOISE.

AGNIDHRA PRIEST :—

A symbol of the spiritual mind working almost unknown to the personality on the higher mental plane.

"The Agnidhra goes round to the north, for he is virtually the same person as Agni himself."—*Sata. Brâh.*, I. 2, 4.

The spiritual mind standing, as it were, between the lower mind and the higher planes (the north) occupies the place of the Higher Self (Agni) to the lower personality.

"But one night, after I had been in great distress praying about this, I went to sleep, and at one o'clock in the morning suddenly I was waked up out of my sleep, and I found myself, with unspeakable joy and awe, in the very presence of the Almighty God. And for the space of four hours I was privileged to speak face to face with Him as a man speaks face to face with a friend," *Evan Roberts.*—W. T. STEAD, *Revival in the West*, p. 43.

See ADVARYA, ATHORNE, CHRYSE, POPE, PRIEST (altar), PRIEST OF APOLLO.

AGNIHOTRA HOUSE OR SHIP :—

A symbol of the causal-body, or vehicle of the individuality or spirit.

"The Agnihotra, truly, is the ship that sails heavenwards. The Ahavaniya and Garhapatya are the two sides of the same heavenward-bound ship; and that milk-offerer is the steersman. Now when he advances towards the east, then he steers that ship eastwards towards the heavenly world, and he gains the heavenly world by it. When he ascends from the north it makes him reach the heavenly world; but if one were to sit down in it after entering from the south, it would be as if he tried to enter it after he has put off and he were left behind and remained outside."—*Sata. Brâh.*, II. 3, 3, 15 and 16.

The causal-body, verily, is the vehicle of soul-development. The buddhic and causal aspects are the two means of development, and the personality offering the higher emotions (milk) promotes its growth towards perfection. Now when the personality aspires, then the soul progresses towards the buddhic plane and the ego gains by it the higher consciousness. When he seeks Truth through the intellect (north), then also the soul reaches the higher plane. But if the personality "sits down" to accept the rule of the desires (the south), the result is that the soul is deprived of the means of progression, and the personality is rendered useless.

See AFU-RÂ, AHAVANIYA, ARGO, EAST, GARHAPATYA, NORTH, SOUTH.

AGNISHTOMA, A PLACE OF WORSHIP BUILT TOWARDS THE CARDINAL POINTS :—

A symbol of the abode of the religious consciousness in the highest part of the lower nature. A reverent state of soul in close relation to the higher emotions of goodness, love, and truth.

"They (the sacrificers) choose a place of worship. Let them choose the place which lies highest; for it was from thence that the gods ascended to heaven, and he who is consecrated indeed ascends to the gods. He thus sacrifices on a place of worship frequented by the gods. . . . It should incline towards the east, since the east is the quarter of the gods; or else it should incline towards the north, since the north is the quarter of men. It should rise somewhat towards the south, that being the quarter of the Fathers (lunar pitris). . . . On this ground they erect either a hall or a shed, with the top beams running from west to east; for the east is the quarter of the gods, and from the east westwards the gods approach men."—*Sata. Brâh.*, III. 1, 1, 1–6.

The personalities accord a place in the mind for religion. Let them reserve in the highest part of the mind a spot sacred to the ideals (gods) which rise heavenward. The mental quality which aspires and is transmuted becomes an ideal on the buddhic plane. The personality therefore offers up the lower qualities in the highest part of his nature where he reverences the ideals. This sacred spot should be open to where Love and Truth rise in the soul, since the ideals are harbingers of the Self. It should also be open to the intellect (north), since the intellect co-ordinates the mental qualities through aspiration towards Truth. But it should be closed somewhat towards the desires (south), for these are of the form and not of the Life. On this high ground of the mind, the personalities erect the structure of their religion either complex or simple, with the highest intelligence (top-beams) directed towards the ideals which wait upon the Self, and approach the mind from above.

See CHURCH, HEART, PAPYRUS-BOAT, RELIGION (popular), TEMPLE, WORSHIP.

AGNISHVATTA PITRIS :—

A symbol of the monads of life; the spiritual egos central in every soul, and of atma-buddhic nature. These are the " Sparks from the Flame,"—the Divine egos which render human souls immortal.

" As from a blazing fire consubstantial sparks proceed in a thousand ways, so from the imperishable Spirit various living souls are produced, and they return to Him again."—*Mundaka Upanishad*, II. 1, 1.

" The spirit of man contains a spark from the power and light of God."—BEHMEN.

" Only the 'little spark' of the soul is to be at all times with God and united with God."—ECKHART.

" What is clear to my mind is that every individual human soul is a detached, or seemingly detached, portion of the Universal Substance, and that all the potencies of divinity are in it waiting to be revealed. . . . We have come from the One; unto the One shall we return, but not empty-handed."—R. J. CAMPBELL, Serm., *The Son of Man Ascending*.

See FIRE, FRAVASHIS, MANASAPUTRAS, MARUTS, MONAD (life), MUSPELL (sons), PITRIS (solar), SONS OF GOD, SPARKS.

AGRICULTURALIST, OR HUSBANDMAN :—

A symbol of the Higher Self as director of the qualities which bring about the cultivation of the lower nature.

See HUSBANDMAN, CULTIVATION, SEED, SOWER.

AGRICULTURE :—

A symbol of the cultivation of the qualities of the soul so that they shall bear fruit on the higher levels, that is, be productive of higher faculties and emotions through spiritual growth.

" The chief occupation (of the 'dead') was agriculture, which differed from that of earth only in that the harvest never failed, and the corn grew far more luxuriantly, its stems surpassing the height of a man. The Fields of Aalu (or Aaru) were tilled to provide the dead with food, in so far as their wants were not met by offerings, and by magic formulas made and spoken for them on earth."—A. WIEDEMANN, *Rel. of Anc. Egyptians*, p. 254.

The " dead " are the personalities in their lives on earth (not *post-mortem* states), who cultivate their natures and gain experience. The result of cultivation from the seed (corn) of the Spirit, " surpasses the height of man " (mind) because its fruit is above mind and on the buddhic plane. The " Fields of Aalu " symbolise the astral plane of the desires. The desire-nature is " tilled " by the personalities in order that through sacrifice and aspiration the best results should be transmuted by buddhic agency (magic formulas) and spiritual food be produced for the soul.

See ANIMALS, CORN, CULTIVATION, DEMETER, FIELD, HARVEST, OX AND ASS, PHALLIPHORIA, PLOUGHING, SEED, SEKHET (aaru), SHABTI.

AHANKARA :—

A symbol of the reflected or lower self-consciousness. The sense of a

separate self or personality. The
" I am I " feeling.

See CAIN, I AM, KERESANI, MAHAT,
SEPARATION.

AHAVANÎYA FIRE :—

A symbol of the centre of outpouring
spiritual activity on the buddhic
plane.

"Now Indra, in truth is the same as
the Ahavanîya ; and king Yama is the
same as the Garhapatya."—*Sata. Brâh.*,
II. 3, 2, 2.

"Indra" is a symbol of Divine
energy (atma-buddhic), and "King
Yama" is the causal self in the
causal-body.

"That Ahavanîya fire is the Sacrificer's divine body, and this body of his
is his human one."—*Sata. Brâh.*, VI. 6,
4, 5.

The buddhic outpouring is the
Divine vehicle of the Self, and the
causal-body is his mental one.

See AGNIHOTRA, GARHAPATYA,
YAMA.

AHRIMAN, OR AHARMAN :—

A symbol of the lower principle,
the opposite of the Higher. The
relative or illusive self during manifestation which implies duality.

"The destruction which Ahriman produced in the world was terrible. Nevertheless the more evil he tried to do, the
more he ignorantly fulfilled the counsels
of the Infinite, and hastened the development of good."—*Zoroastrian System.*

Upon the planes of form and illusion
the havoc produced among the lower
qualities was terrific, and the transformations which occurred were innumerable and various. Nevertheless,
the lower principle unwittingly acting
for good, although from low aims
and unworthy ideals, the counsels of
the Most High are established and
fulfilled ; and so all is done in the
interests of the great Law of the
development of the soul. The duality
of good and evil is a primal, necessary
means for the soul's experience, exercise and growth.

"God is not neutral between goodness
and badness, nor is His nature compounded of the two. For since evil is
inwardly self-discordant and self-destructive, and rebellious against the law of
the whole, its inclusion in the will of
God means its complete transmutation
and suppression in its character as evil.
. . . It is plain that morality is entirely
occupied in striving to abolish the con-

dition and object of its own existence.
For unless evil had at least a relative
existence as evil, there could be no
morality. Evil is thus in a sense a
cause, as being a necessary antecedent
condition, of good, and if so, it cannot
be radically bad. 'Things solely evil,'
says St. Augustine, 'could never exist,
for even those natures which are vitiated
by an evil will, so far as they are vitiated,
are evil, but so far as they are natures
they are good,' or, as Plotinus says, 'vice
is always human, being mixed with
something contrary to itself.' We believe
that all that is good is preserved in the
eternal world, but not the evils which
called it forth. For that which is not
only manifold but discordant cannot
exist, as such, in the life of God."—
W. R. INGE, *Paddock Lectures*, p. 132.

"If the Zoroastrians' good principle,
called God by us, is taken as a being ;
and their bad principle as only a condition privative ; one as a positive and
real cause, the other as a bad possibility
that environs God from eternity, waiting
to become a fact, and certain to become
a fact, whenever the opportunity is
given,—it is even so. And then it follows
that, the moment God creates a realm
of powers, the bad possibility as certainly
becomes a bad actuality, a Satan or devil
in esse ; not a bad omnipresence over
against God, and His equal,—that is a
monstrous and horrible conception,—but
an outbreaking evil, or empire of evil
in created spirits, according to their
order. For Satan or the devil, taken
in the singular, is not the name of any
particular person, neither is it a persona-
tion of temptation or impersonal evil,
as many insist ; for there is really no
such thing as impersonal evil in the
sense of moral evil ; but the name is a
name that generalises bad persons or
spirits, with their bad thoughts and
characters, many in one."—H. BUSHNELL,
Nature and the Supernatural, p. 88.

"Sin arises from our bondage,—from
the dualism in our nature,—from the
opposition between the lower and the
higher in our desires. There are tendencies in our nature pulling one way
while the moral sense is pointing another.
We have to fight for our promised land.
It is the only conceivable means whereby
nobleness as distinct from innocence
could become part of our conscious
experience."—R. J. CAMPBELL, Serm.,
The Meaning of Retribution.

See ADVERSARY, AIDONEUS, AKEM-
MANO, ANGRA-MAINYU, ANTICHRIST,
APEP, DEVIL, ENIGORIO, EVIL, LAW
OF ZOROASTER, OPHIONEUS, OPPO-
SITES, SATAN, SERPENT (mighty),
SPENTO, TYPHON, ZERANA.

AHURA-MAZDA, OR ORMAZD :—

A symbol of the Supreme Being,

or of the Divine Will in manifestation. The Logos. The Higher Self.

"Zoroaster's fitness for the prophetic mission which he is to undertake is divinely recognised, and Ahura Mazda selects him as his own messenger to the world."—*Dinkard. S. B. of E.*

The Incarnate Self discerns the destiny which awaits it under the manifold cycles of evolution and rebirth ; and the Logos appoints him as His only-begotten Son to be His special interpreter to the lower self, and be the Saviour of the souls of humanity.

See GATHA, HOMA, SPENTO, ZERANA, ZOROASTER.

AHURA RELIGION :—

A symbol of the love of ideals of truth and righteousness. It is through the awakenment of Love that the affinity of the soul with the Higher Self is seen and known.

See RELIGION, LAW OF ZOROASTER.

AIAS :—

A symbol of the understanding, or ready wit of the lower mind.

AIDONEUS OR HADES :—

A symbol of the lower principle,— the desire-mind (kama-manas), active upon the astral plane of the soul.

"But the notions of the Greeks are, I suppose, plain enough to everyone, for they make the good part that of the Olympian Jove; that of the hostile deity they give to Hades."—PLUTARCH, *Isis and Osiris*, § 48.

The antagonist of the higher nature is desire, and we find that Plato in *Cratylus* explains "Hades" to mean "desire." (*See* JOWETT, *Dialogues, etc.*, Vol. II. p. 225.)

"Hear first the four roots of all things ; bright Zeus, life-giving Hera, and Aidoneus, and Nestis."—*Empedocles*, FAIRBANKS, 33.

The fourfold nature is that of man apart from higher mind :—bright Atma, life-giving Buddhi, the Desiremind, and the Physical body.

"Hades was the son of Cronus and Rhea. His wife was Persephone, the daughter of Demeter, whom he carried off from the upper world. In the division of the world among the three brothers, Hades obtained the Nether World, over which he ruled. Hence he is called the infernal Zeus, or the king of the shades."—*Smith's Class. Dict.*

Desire is the product of a process in Time and Space (Rhea). It is allied with the emotion-nature arising from Buddhi, and which Desire captures. The lower planes with their illusions are ruled by Desire.

See AHRIMAN, CRONUS, DEMETER, DEVIL, HADES, HERA, NESTIS, PERSEPHONE, RHEA, SERPENT.

AIN SOPH :—

A symbol of the Absolute, the potential and unmanifest God, the Source of the Higher Self and its manifestation.

"The Supreme Unity is the *Ain Soph* of the Qabbalah and the Zoharic writings, termed also in them Ayin or No-thing."—MYER, *Qabbalah*, p. 199.

"It is so named because we do not know, and it is impossible to know, that which there is in this Principle, because it never descends as far as our ignorance, and because it is above Wisdom itself" (*Zohar*).—*Ibid.*, p. 127.

"Non-being is 'Absolute Being,' in Esoteric Philosophy. In the tenets of the latter even Adi-Buddha (the first or primeval Wisdom) is, while manifested, in one sense an illusion, Māyā, since all the gods, including Brahmā, have to die at the end of the Age of Brahmā ; the abstraction called Parabrahman—whether we call it Ain Suph, or with Herbert Spencer, the Unknowable—alone being the One Absolute Reality."—H. P. BLAVATSKY, *Secret Doctrine*, Vol. I. p. 84.

See ABSOLUTE, FATHER, GODHEAD, NOSE, TRINITY, WELL, ZERANA.

AIR ; THE ATMOSPHERE :—

A symbol of the mental plane ; the plane midway between " earth " the lower planes, and " heaven " the higher planes. Air (mind) is that element in which " animals " (desires and emotions) and " plants " (instincts, feelings, etc.) live and move.

The higher mental plane is the plane of creation in which ideas take form for embodiment beneath.

"The air, moreover, is the engine or machine, through which all things are made."—HERMES, *The Perfect Sermon*, § 3.

"By air as by a thread, O Gautama ! this world and all beings are strung together."—*Brihad. Upanishad*, III. 7, 2.

"The intermediate space of air, between heaven and earth. . . . These three, heaven, earth, and air, are the favourite group of three in the Rigveda, underlying all manner of applications of the number."—H. W. WALLIS, *Cosmology of the Rig-Veda*, pp. 113, 114.

" By the air is signified all things relating to perception and thought, . . . and respiration corresponds to the understanding, thus to perception and thought, and also to faith, because faith is of the thought according to the perception of the understanding."—SWEDENBORG, *Apoc. Rev.*, n. 708.

" The air is the guru, water our father, and the great earth our mother ;

" Day and night are our two nurses, male and female, who set the whole world a-playing " (*The Japji*).—M. A. MACAULIFFE, *The Sikh Religion*, Vol. I. p. 217.

The higher, or spiritual, mind is the teacher of the soul ; the Divine Reality, or Truth, is the source of all things ; and Buddhi gives birth to, and directs, the lower nature.

Involution and Evolution are the processes, masculine and feminine, by which the Self is tended and brought up, and through which the lower nature is filled with activity.

When a novel opinion begins to be widely accepted it is said to be " in the *air*," that is, in the mental atmosphere or general mind of humanity. Thus this very common sacred symbol *air* as signifying *mind* is generally recognised by people, though so seldom applied in the interpretation of the Scriptures.

See DÆMONS, ELEMENTS (five), PETER, PILLARS (light).

AIR AND ÆTHER :—

At their highest significance these conjoined symbols stand for Matter and Spirit.

" All things were together, infinite both in number and in smallness ; for the small also was infinite. And when they were all together, nothing was clear and distinct because of their smallness ; for air and æther comprehended all things, both being infinite ; for these are present in everything, and are greatest both as to number and as to greatness."—FAIRBANKS, *Anaxagoras*, 1.

At the beginning, that is, prior to involution, the parts of being were contained within the whole ; and the parts themselves were not what they were destined to appear, since within them also was that infinite possibility which was the reflection of That whose image they bore. And in homogeniety, no part was distinguishable from the whole. Spirit and Matter,—Mind and Form, were the

root of all existent things. All things comprise them, and these elements are the sum total of existence, and are eternal.

See INVOLUTION, HEAVEN AND EARTH, MONAD OF LIFE.

AKĀSA, ETHER-SPACE :—

A symbol of primordial matter which brought forth from within it the Second Logos, the Word, or Higher Self.

" First in order, Akāsa, ' ether,' with the distinguishing property of sound, or in other words, the substratum of sound (which sound is the *vishaya* or object for a corresponding organ of sense, the ear). Footnote,—The Rāmāyana, II. 110, 5, makes Brahmā spring from ether, but the Epic and Purānic accounts of akāsa are very inconsistent. Some say that it was created and is perishable, others that it was not created and is eternal."—MON. WILLIAMS, *Indian Wisdom*, p. 93.

" He (Brahman) who, dwelling in the âkâsa, is distinct from âkâsa, whom the âkâsa knows not, whose body the âkâsa is, who rules the âkâsa from within, he is thy soul, the inner guide, the immortal."—*Brihad. Upanishad*, III. 7, 12.

" It is the âkâsa, out of which all these creatures proceed, and into which they are again received, the âkâsa is older than they all, the âkâsa is the ultimate end."—*Khand. Upanishad*, I. 9, 1.

See BRAHMA, MĀYĀ (higher), MOTHER (divine), MULA-PRAKRITI, PRAKRITI.

AKEM-MANŌ, THE EVIL MIND :—

A symbol of the lower principle, the obverse of the Higher ; its seat is in the desire-mind.

" In the beginning there were twin spirits. The One who produced the ' reality ' is called Vohu-manō, the ' good mind,' the other, through whom the ' non-reality ' originated, bears the name Akem-manō, the ' evil mind.' "—HAUG, *Essays, etc.*, p. 303.

Manifestation implies duality of consciousness, and the two selves are aspects of That which appears to be continually striving together in itself. There is apparent conflict and recognition of contraries. It is, however, as the contraries are perceived to be not in reality opposites to, but mutually helpful of the other, that the Christ's reign may be said to begin.

" And we know that to them that love God all things work together for good, even to them that are called according to his purpose."—Rom. viii. 28.

See AHRIMAN, ENIGORIO, OPPOSITES, VOHUMANO.

AKERT, THE UNDERWORLD :—

A symbol of the lower quaternary, i.e. the four lower planes of nature.

"Homage to thee (Osiris), O Soul of everlastingness, thou Soul that dwellest in Tattu, Un-nefer, son of Nut; thou art lord of Akert (the underworld)" (*Litany to Osiris*).—BUDGE, *Book of the Dead*, Ch. XV.

The Higher Self is invoked as the "Good Being" brought forth of space (Nut), and supreme over the lower nature.

"The Egyptian sphinx plays the part of guardian of a temple or deity, and hence the god *Aker*, the watchman of the Underworld and the guardian of the god Rā during the hours of the night, is generally shown as a Sphinx with the body of a lion when represented as going forth to destroy the enemies of the Sun-god."—WIEDEMANN, *Rel. of Anc. Egyptians*, p. 194.

The higher nature within the lower overcomes the desires (enemies).

See HOLD OF SHIP, NUT, OSIRIS, QUATERNARY, SPHINX, TATTU.

AKERU GODS, OR GODS OF AKERT :—

The phases of the lower consciousness of the soul; i.e. the negations and limitations which are outgrown and left behind.

"I know the name of the snarers who lay snares therewith (net); Akeru gods, ancestors of Akhabin gods are their names. . . . I know the names of the fowlers and of the fishermen; Akeru gods, ancestors of Rā is their name."—BUDGE, *Book of the Dead*, Ch. CLIIIA. pp. 511, 513.

"Set hath delivered the interior of the body of Horus from the Akeru gods."—*Ibid.*, Ch. CX. p. 324.

The astral plane corresponds to the level from which evolution of form proceeds. The deliverance through the desire-nature comes when the individuality is at length born, and then all the experiences which have accrued through the evolution of the group-soul are welded into a unifying centre of consciousness.

In the lower states of consciousness ("fowlers and fishermen") the experiences are collected by means of the astral mechanism (net) of the senses, and transferred to the mental vehicle.

See FISH, HORUS, NET, SET.

AKESI CITY :—

A symbol of the centre or source of manifest existence, and of the outpouring and indrawing of the Divine Life.

"Hail, thou city Akesi, which art hidden from the gods, the *Khus* know the name of which the gods are afraid. None can enter therein, and none can come forth therefrom except that holy god who dwelleth in his egg. . . . He hath made the city so that he may dwell therein at will, and none can enter therein except on the day of great transformations."—BUDGE, *Book of the Dead*, Ch. CXLIX. p. 492.

The Divine source of existence is extolled. The higher qualities (gods) on the buddhic plane, being derived, know nothing of the underived into which they must disappear. The spiritual monads (khus) on the plane of atma know the Spirit by their spirit. Multiplicity cannot enter into the Absolute, only One alone—the Higher Self (holy god) who dwells centrally within his universe. When the cycle closes, all the results of the manifest will be indrawn.

See CITY, EGG, KHUS, JUDGMENT DAY, MONAD.

AKRAGAS, THE SACRED CITY :—

A symbol of the causal-body.

See ACROPOLIS, ADYTUM.

ALAGHOM NAOM (MOTHER OF MIND) :—

A symbol of the principle of buddhi.

"Otherwise called Iztat Ix, a goddess of the Izental Indians, a Mayan tribe dwelling in Mexico. She was the spouse of Patol, their chief deity, and was credited with the creation of mind and thought, in fact with the higher part of man."—*Non-classical Mythology*, p. 7.

The buddhic principle is allied with the Higher Self (Patol), and from it proceeds the mental plane which is the plane immediately below the buddhic. Through the functioning of buddhi the higher nature of the human being is manifested when mind is awakened in animal man.

ALBORDJ, OR ALBURZ, MOUNTAIN :—

A symbol of aspiration. A sense of possibility of reaching the summit of attainment—the ideal set before the lower self. It therefore also stands for the buddhic plane.

"On the earth Ormazd created the high mountain Alborj."—*Zoroastrian System.* J. F. CLARKE, *Ten Religions.*

On the lower planes the Divine Will created the religious instinct or sense of possibility of the attainment of the Ideal set before the lower consciousness.

"From Albordj the sun sets out on his course, he circles the earth in the highest spheres of heaven, and at evening returns."—*Ibid.*

The Incarnate Self (sun), from the first moment of manifestation, goes forth, traverses the higher planes and descends to the lower, and from thence rises to return to his source.

See AMARÂVATI, ANDUISAR, EARTH, HEROIC, HIMAVAN, KAILASA, KHORDAD, MOUNTAIN, OLYMPUS, PUITIKA.

ALCHEMY :—

This signifies the production, by unperceived processes, of the higher qualities from the lower ; that is, from the baser metals, or lower mental qualities, the precious metals, or higher mental (silver) and buddhic (gold) qualities, are by transmutation produced. Also, the process of purification by fire, whereby out of earth (lower nature) there is made gold (higher nature).

"According to Greek writers the Egyptians employed quicksilver in the processes whereby they separated the metals gold and silver from the native ore. From these processes there resulted a 'black' powder or substance which was supposed to possess the most marvellous powers, and to contain in it the individualities of the various metals ; and in it their actual substances were incorporated. In a mystical manner this 'black' powder was identified with the body which the god Osiris was known to possess in the underworld, and to both were attributed magical qualities, and both were thought to be sources of life and power. . . . The knowledge of the chemistry of the metals and of their magical powers were described by the name 'Khemeia.' . . . To this name the Arabs affixed the article *al*, and thus we obtain the word Al-Khemeia, or Alchemy."—DR. BUDGE, *Egyptian Magic,* p. 20.

Osiris with a black complexion signifies Deity unmanifest in the profound darkness of potentiality. In the black body of the dead Osiris, we may see a symbol of the Archetypal Man,—the Logos involved in Matter at the end of the cycle of Involution. Deity manifests again in Evolution,— Osiris comes to life in the new order of unfoldment. The lower nature (earth) gives birth to the higher nature (gold). This is the Divine Alchemy in which the black earth of ignorance appears to be transmuted into the gold of Wisdom.

"The transmutation of the normal physical consciousness of man into the divine consciousness was the *magnum opus* on which the true alchemists were engaged, and much that is grotesque imbecility in the directions and recipes they have left behind, if we read it simply as nineteenth-century chemists, becomes beautiful spiritual philosophy in strictest harmony with the laws governing human spiritual evolution, when we put a symbolical construction on the quaintly expressed formulæ relating to coctions and distillations and the mercury of the wise, and fiery waters and ferments."— A. P. SINNETT, *Growth of the Soul,* p. 371.

"The prime object of alchemy was held to be the production of the Philosopher's Stone ; that perfect and incorrupt substance, or 'noble Tincture,' never found upon our imperfect earth in its natural state, which could purge all baser metals of their dross, and turn them to pure gold. The quest of the Stone, in fact, was but one aspect of man's everlasting quest of perfection, his hunger for the Absolute. . . . Gold, the Crowned King, or Sol, as it is called in the planetary symbolism of the alchemists, was their standard of perfection, the 'Perfect Metal.' Towards it, as the Christian towards sanctity, their wills were set. It had for them a value not sordid but ideal. . . . Upon the spiritual plane also they held that the Divine Idea is always aiming at 'Spiritual Gold'—divine humanity, the New Man, citizen of the transcendental world,—and 'natural man' as we ordinarily know him, is a lower metal, silver at best, a departure from the 'plan'; who yet bears within himself, if we could find it, the spark or seed of absolute perfection, the 'tincture' which makes gold. . . . The art of the alchemist consists in completing the work of perfection, bringing forth and making dominant, as it were, the 'latent goldness' which 'lies obscure' in metal or man."—E. UNDERHILL, *Mysticism,* pp. 169, 170.

"Gold, the Crowned King" is a symbol of the Higher Self (sol), and the "noble Tincture" signifies the Divine Life or buddhic functioning in the human soul. The "natural man " is the lower mind (silver at best), and the " New Man " is the perfected personality transmuted to the higher mind.

" The Sulphur and the Salt, or ' metallic soul and body ' of the spiritual chemistry are the body and the ' rational ' soul or mind of man—Sulphur his earthly nature, seasoned with intellectual salt. The Mercury is Spirit in its most mystic sense, the Synteresis or holy Dweller in the Innermost, the immanent spark or Divine Principle of his life. Only the ' wise,' the mystically awakened, can know this Mercury, the agent of man's transmutation : and until it has been brought out of the hiddenness, nothing can be done."—*Ibid.*, p. 173.

" Sulphur " stands for the desire nature with its appetites and passions, and " Salt " for the reasoning faculty of the lower mind. " Mercury of the Wise " is the indwelling Spirit without which no transmutation of lower qualities into higher can be effected. The Higher Self must be born in the soul in order that its dross may be turned into pure gold.

" The Three Principles being enclosed in the vessel, or Athanor, which is man himself, and subjected to a gentle fire— the Incendium Amoris—the process of the Great Work, the mystic transmutation of natural into spiritual man, can begin. . . . The first matter, in the course of its transmutation, assumes three successive colours ; the Black, the White, and the Red. These three colours are strictly analogous to the three traditional stages of the Mystic Way : Purgation, Illumination, Union."—*Ibid.*

The desire, mental, and spiritual natures interactive within the human soul, or causal-body (Athanor), are subjected to the slow process of combination and evolution, whereby development proceeds in three stages.

" The alchemists call the first stage, or Blackness, Putrefaction. In it the three principles which compose the ' whole man ' of body, soul and spirit, are ' sublimated ' till they appear as a black powder full of corruption ; and the imperfect body is ' dissolved and purified by subtle Mercury,' as man is purified by the darkness, misery, and despair which follows the emergence of his spiritual consciousness. . . . The ' black beast,' the passional element of the lower nature, must emerge and be dealt with before anything further can be done."—*Ibid.*

The first stage represents the present state of human nature, full of imperfections, and undergoing ethical and spiritual discipline and purification in conditions of conflict and suffering. The lower nature is gradually dissolved away by the Spirit (Mercury).

" The second stage, Whiteness, the state of Luna, or Silver, the ' chaste and immaculate Queen,' is the equivalent of the Illuminative Way : the highest point which the mystic can attain short of union with the Absolute. This White Stone is pure and precious ; but in it the Great Work of man's spiritual evolution has not yet reached its term. That term (third stage) is the attainment of the Red, the colour of Perfection or alchemic gold ; a process sometimes called the ' Marriage of Luna and Sol '— the fusion of the human and divine spirit. Under this image is concealed the final secret of the mystic life, that ineffable union of finite and infinite—that loving reception of the inflowing vitality of God—from which comes forth the *Magnum Opus*, deified or spiritual man."—*Ibid.*, p. 174.

In the second stage the personality (Luna) is perfected in goodness and truth, and transmuted to the higher mental plane. The third stage culminates in the union of the Lower Self (Luna) with the Higher Self (Sol) on the buddhic plane, when the soul enters into the joy of its Lord at the cycle's end.

" ' This,' says the author of *A Suggestive Enquiry*, ' is the union supersentient, the nuptials sublime, *Mentis et Universi*. . . . Lo ! behold I will open to thee a mystery, cries the Adept, the Bridegroom crowneth the Bride of the north [i.e., she who comes out of the cold and darkness of the lower nature]. In the darkness of the north, out of the crucifixion of the cerebral life, when the sensual dominant is occultated in the Divine Fiat, and subdued, there arises a Light.' "—*Ibid.*, p. 174.

The Higher Self (Bridegroom) perfects (crowns) the Soul (Bride) which has come forth from the lower nature (north) wherein it was crucified mentally and emotionally. When the self-will of the desire nature is obliterated in the Divine Will, and overcome, then there arises in the Soul the light of Truth.

See Arc. man, Barsom, Beast, Black, Earth, Fire, Gold, Green lion, Higher, Imhotep, Isis, Light, Magic, Medicine, Metals, Moon, North, Osiris, Physician, Red (rose), Serpent Æsculapius, Silver, Spark, Stone, Sun, Transmutation, Transubstantiation, Valmiki, White.

ALCINOUS, KING OF THE PHAEACIANS :—

A symbol of the higher aspect of the soul, or of the higher mind and will ("strong mind") ruling the higher mental faculties (Phaeacians).

"Meanwhile Odysseus went to the famous palace of Alcinous, and his heart was full of many thoughts as he stood there or ever he had reached the threshold of bronze. For there was a gleam as it were of sun or moon through the high-roofed hall of great-hearted Alcinous."—*Odyssey*, Bk VII.

The "palace" of the higher nature of the soul (Alcinous) is the potential causal-body centralising the higher and lower consciousnesses—the individuality (sun) and the personality (moon). Enterprising courage (Odysseus) is said to penetrate deep within the soul and ally itself with the intuition (Nausicaa). The "fifty handmaids in the palace" are the higher emotions which form the robe of wisdom which clothes the liberated ego on the buddhic plane.

See ARETE, HOUSE, MARRIAGE, ODYSSEUS, OLYMPUS, PHAEACIANS.

ALMSGIVING OR CHARITY :—

A symbol of the element of universal love which must always be in the active truth-goodness (food) which nourishes and builds up the soul or causal-body.

"St. Thomas (Aquinas) tells us, with admirable clearness : 'An act can be derived from Charity in one of two ways. In the first way, the act is elicited by Charity itself, and such a virtuous act requires no other virtue beside Charity,—as in the case of loving the Good, rejoicing in it, and mourning over its opposite. In the second way, an act proceeds from Charity in the sense of being commanded by it : and in this manner,—since Charity' has the full range of and 'commands all the virtues, as ordering them (each and all) to their ultimate end,—an act can proceed from Charity whilst nevertheless belonging to any other special virtue.' "—F. VON HUGEL, *Mystical Element*, Vol. II. p. 164.

"The Lord of created beings (Pragâpati) has declared that alms freely offered and brought by the giver himself may be accepted even from a sinful man, provided the gift had not been asked for or promised beforehand."—*Laws of Manu*, IV. 248.

In the Divine scheme of things it is so arranged and established that when the lower self, out of love of truth and goodness, voluntarily offers the best within it to serve the higher aims, then the soul's qualities are transmuted, and these become the sustenance of its higher nature. The offering of his best efforts by the imperfect personality (sinful man) is acceptable by the Higher Self provided he has not acted from outward considerations or from expectation of reward to follow well doing.

"Love the love which loves you everlastingly—for the more you love the more you desire to love," and "when we spirits hold fast by love, He by His Spirit remakes us, then joy is ours. The Spirit of God breathes us out toward love and good works, and it breathes us into rest and joy ; and that is eternal life, just as in our mortal life we breathe out the air which is in us and breathe in fresh air."—RUYSBROCK, *Ladder of Love*. R. M. JONES, *Mystical Religion*, p. 311.

"Prayer is good with Fasting and Alms, more than to buy up treasures of gold. For Alms delivereth from death. . . . They that practise mercy and justice shall live long."—TOBIT xii. 8, 9.

"The *Theologia Germanica*,—'Be assured, he that helpeth a man to his own will, helpeth him to the worst that he can. Nothing burneth in hell but self-will. Therefore it hath been said, Put off thine own will, and there will be no more hell. As long as a man is seeking his own good, he doth not yet seek what is best for him, and he will never find it. For a man's highest good would be and is truly this, that he should not seek himself and his own things, *nor be his own end in any respect, either in things spiritual or in things natural*, but should seek only the praise and glory of God, and His holy will.' 'He that hateth his soul for my sake shall keep it unto life eternal' (JOHN xii. 25)."—W. R. INGE, *Paddock Lectures*, p. 89.

See CAUSAL-BODY, FOOD FOR SOUL, LAZARUS, LOVE OF GOD, MENDICANT, PRAGÂPATI, SANNYASIN, TRANSMUTATION, WILL.

ALPHA AND OMEGA :—

A symbol of the Higher Self as constituting the Soul-process in its entirety.

"I am the Alpha and the Omega, saith the Lord God, which is and which was and which is to come, the Almighty."—REV. i. 8.

The manifesting Spirit from the Supreme, is the outgoing and the incoming of the Divine Life, the present, the past, and the future in the Eternal Now.

"Signifies, who is the self-subsisting and only subsisting from first principles to ultimates; from whom proceed all things."—SWEDENBORG, *Apoc. Rev.*, n. 29.

"What is it that is the beginning and the end of existence? It is Christ. Christ is that in God which has produced man, and seeks full manifestation in man."—R. J. CAMPBELL, Serm., *Apoc. Vision.*

"To the author of Revelation it is not only God the Father, and not only our Lord Jesus Christ, but the *eternal in man himself* that says: 'I am Alpha and Omega, the beginning and the end, the first and the last.' "—R. J. CAMPBELL, Serm., *The Eternal Self.*

"The eternal relates to the past as much as to the future, and abolishes both. In the eternal, past and future are one. If your eternity lies in the future, it lies also in the past; you belong to the one as much as to the other. From the standpoint of eternity there is no question of 'I shall be' or 'I have been,' but 'I am.' "—R. J. CAMPBELL, Serm., *Reaping for Eternal Life.*

See COSMOS (higher), FIRST, I A O, PRAGÂPATI, TIME, YEAR.

ALTAR GROUND,—THE EARTH :—

A symbol of the lower nature which serves as a means whereby the egos are enabled to build up from it the structure (altar) of their higher nature.

"The sacrifice is a mystic union in which the sacrificer generates from out of the Vedi (fem.) or altar ground, his future divine self."—J. EGGELING, *S. B. of E.*, Vol. XLIII. Intro.

"By it (sacrifice) the gods obtained this entire earth, . . . therefore the sacrificial ground is called vedi (the altar). For this reason they say, 'As great as the altar is, so great is the earth'; for by the altar they obtained this entire earth."—*Sata. Brâh.*, I. 2, 5, 7.

Through the giving up of the lower qualities, the higher qualities (the gods) obtained rule over the entire lower nature: therefore the offered-up lower, forms the structure of the higher. The higher nature is then reflected fully in the lower; and into the divine Self the lower Self is merged.

See ALTAR (fire), EARTH, PRAGÂPATI, SACRIFICE, SACRIFICER.

ALTAR BUILDING TO THE LORD :

A symbol of the setting up in the mind of a structure of spiritual idealism on which the lower qualities may be sacrificed for the sake of the higher.

"And Noah builded an altar unto the Lord; and took of every clean beast, and of every clean fowl, and offered burnt offerings on the altar."—GEN. viii. 20.

And the individuality is said to "build an altar," that is, to raise a means of reciprocal action between it and the Self of which it is the manifest embodiment. And every desire and emotion become the means of this offering of the lower self to the Higher Self.

See BEASTS, BURNT OFFERING, GOD (smelling), NOAH, SACRIFICE, SAVIOUR.

ALTAR OF SACRIFICE :—

A symbol of a structure of the religious consciousness in the highest part of the lower nature, on which the lower desires and aims are offered up to the Supreme Goodness.

"The altar is 'the table of the Lord': whatever was put upon it was 'the food of God.' The fire from heaven, emblem of God's holiness, consumes the offering; and it all ascends as sweet incense before Him."—A. JUKES, *The Law of the Offerings*, p. 49.

"There is something sublime, something that is not wholly of this world, in the deed that costs the doer his personal happiness, the surrender of his own gratification in the interest of something higher. The world is always ready to reverence that when it sees it, perhaps without quite knowing why; but more often than not the essence of the deed consists in the fact that the world does not see it for what it is, but either ignores it or mistakes it for something else. It is this principle which lies at the heart of all the sacrificial systems of all the religions that have ever existed. Human nature is curiously constituted in this respect. It is damnably selfish, and yet never fails to respond in some degree to the call for self-immolation. There is something in us all which makes us want to lay ourselves on the altar when any great crisis demands it, any super-personal ideal has to be served. We may not yield to it, but the impulse is there; it is in everybody."—R. J. CAMPBELL, Serm., *Life's Great Antinomy.*

See ATONEMENT, BURNT OFFERING, CHURCH, FOOD, INCENSE, PROCESSION, TABLE, THUNDERBOLT.

ALTAR OF THE GODDESS :—

A symbol of the buddhic function in accepting and transmuting the offerings of the lower nature.

See BUDDHI, ISIS, WISDOM.

ALTAR, FIRE :—

A symbol of the Soul in its complete and perfect, but *latent*, condition at the commencement of the evolutionary cycle. It requires to be evolved by the Spirit (Fire) from within it.

"That Pragâpati who became relaxed is this very Fire-altar which here is built."—*Sata. Brâh.*, X. 1, 1, 3.

The Archetypal Man having become perfected through involution, ceases to manifest, and becomes the potential Soul of the next sub-cycle.

"Once granted that the real purport of all sacrificial performances is the restoration of the dismembered Lord of creatures, and the reconstruction of the All, it cannot be denied that of all ceremonial observances, the building of the great Fire-altar was the one most admirably adapted for this great symbolic purpose."—J. EGGELING, *S. B. of E.*, Vol. XLIII. Intro.

"Moreover, this process of transmutation, this rebuilding of the self on higher levels will involve the establishment within the field of consciousness, the making 'central for life,' of those subconscious spiritual perceptions which are the primary material of mystical experience. The end and object of this 'inward alchemy' will be the raising of the whole self to the condition in which conscious and permanent union with the Absolute takes place ; and man, ascending to the summit of his manhood, enters into that greater life for which he was made."—E. UNDERHILL, *Mysticism*, p. 108.

"But thou, O Lord, shalt abide for ever ; and thy memorial unto all generations. Thou shalt arise, and have mercy upon Zion : for it is time to have pity upon her, yea, the set time is come. For thy servants take pleasure in her stones, and have pity upon her dust. So the nations shall fear the name of the Lord, and all the kings of the earth thy glory : for the Lord hath built up Zion, he hath appeared in his glory."—Ps. cii. 12–16.

This refers to the building-up of the soul (Zion), or higher nature, when the higher qualities (servants) are stirring in the lower nature.

"Now that Pragâpati is no other than the Fire-altar which is here built up, and what five mortal parts there were of him (viz. the hair on the mouth, the skin, the flesh, the bone, and the marrow), they are these layers of earth ; and those which were immortal (viz. the mind, the voice, the vital air, the eye, and the ear) they are these layers of bricks."—*Sata. Brâh.*, X. 1, 3, 4–5.

The Archetypal Man becomes the latent Soul in which the five planes of manifestation are potential to the new cycle,—these are on the matter side,—the physical, the astral, the mental, the buddhic, and the atmic planes. On the side of Spirit there are five immortal modes of being, namely, Atma, buddhi, higher manas, the higher consciousness, and the lower consciousness ;—these build up the immortal Soul within the cycle.

"And the Fire that is laid down on the built altar, that is yonder Sun ;—that same Agni is indeed raised on the altar, and that just because Agni has restored him (Pragâpati)."—*Sata. Brâh.*, VI. 1, 2, 20.

And the Spirit dawns in the fully-formed Soul, and is the incarnate Self (sun) which is indeed raised up in the Soul, for it is a restoration of the Self involved within.

"In the fire the gods healed him (Pragâpati) by means of oblations ; and whatever oblation they offered that became a baked brick and passed into him. And because they were produced from what was offered (ishta), therefore they are bricks (ishtaka).—*Ibid.*, VI. 1, 2, 22.

Through the purifying and transmuting Spirit the higher qualities healed the Soul by means of the offering up of the desires ; and whatever the higher nature offered up, that was transmuted, and it became a spiritual quality which passed into the evolving Soul. And because the spiritual qualities are transmuted desires therefore they are desirable.

"On which side is the head of the brick ?—'Where he touches it and says a prayer,' so say some. . . . Those bricks, doubtless, are Agni's limbs, his joints. . . . But indeed, the fire which is deposited on the pile, that is the head of all those bricks."—*Ibid.*, VI. 1, 2, 31.

The aspiration (prayer) of the lower nature is at the head of the qualities that are transmuted. Those spiritual qualities are " the body of Christ and severally members thereof " (1 COR. xii. 27). But indeed, the Spirit within the Soul,—the indwelling God,—that is the head of all the higher qualities.

"For the perfecting of the saints, unto the work of ministering, unto the building up of the body of Christ."—EPH. iv. 12.

"Think of a spiritual altar on which Christ is being offered unceasingly for the life of the world, for the atonement, or making-one of man and God. That one spiritual altar has a possible manifestation in every human soul. It is there that Christ is being offered for the doing away of sin and the uplifting of our poor sunken race to its eternal home. No sharp line of division can be rightly drawn between the sacrifice of Christ for man, and the sacrifice of Christ in man. It is indeed Christ who saves, but that is how he does it; in all outpouring of human love, human self-devotion, human effort and struggle in the service of the true and the good, Christ is being offered on the spiritual altar, and the day of his final triumph is coming ever nearer."—R. J. CAMPBELL, Serm., *The Souls under the Altar.*

See AGNI, ARC. MAN, ASHADHA, ASHES, BRICKS, DHRUVA, DISMEMBERMENT, DURVA, DVIYAGUS, GARHAPATYA, GODDESS, GOLD MAN, LIMBS, LOTUS LEAF, MARROW, MEASURE, MEMBERS, PRAGÂPATI (relaxed), PRIEST (altar), RAVANA, SACRIFICE, SEASONS (five), STONE (building), TEMPLE (fire), THUNDERBOLT, TRANSMUTATION, ZION.

AMAKHIU :—

See APOSTLES (twelve).

AMALTHEA, THE GOAT WHO SUCKLED ZEUS :—

A symbol of the buddhic nature which brings up the nascent indwelling Self by means of the transmutation of the desires, symbolised by their being raised to become "stars of heaven,"—higher qualities. Desire (goat) is a means of growth.

See BUDDHI, GOAT, STARS, TRANSMUTATION, ZEUS.

AMARÂVATI :—

A symbol of the planes of atma-buddhi.

"The city of Indra is called Amarâvati or Home of the Immortals."—GRIFFITH, *The Ramayan,* Vol. I. p. 36.

Devotion to the Highest (Indra) establishes the spiritual qualities (Immortals) on the higher planes of manifestation.

"On the top of mount Meru lies the city of Amarâvati, wherein the gods dwell; and beneath Meru lies Irâvati, the city of the Asuras: between these two lies the earth."—SÂYANA, *S B. of E.,* Vol. XII. p. 110.

See ALBORDJ, ARCHED, ASURAS, CITY OF GOD, JERUSALEM, KAPILA, OLYMPUS.

AMA-TERASU, OR TENSHŌDAI-JIN, THE SUN-GODDESS :—

A symbol of Wisdom, the principle of buddhi. The same as the "Holy Spirit" of the West.

"The Sun-Goddess was born from the washing of Izanagi's left eye, and the Moon-god from that of his right, while a third deity, named Susa-no-wo, was generated from the washing of his nose. To the Sun-Goddess Izanagi gave charge of the 'Plain of High Heaven,' and to the Moon-god was allotted the realm of night. Susa-no-wo was at first appointed to rule the sea."—W. G. ASTON, *Shinto,* p. 95.

The Divine Will purifies the Individuality (left eye) and makes manifest the Buddhic nature. He purifies the Personality (right eye—Moon-god), and also the Desire-nature (Susa-no-wo). The Buddhic principle operates on the buddhic plane (High Heaven). The Personality organises the underworld (night). The Desire-nature rules on the astral plane (the sea).

"Ama-terasu being offended with Susa-no-wo went away and concealed herself in the Cave of Ameno Tuaya, closing the entrance with a large piece of rock. From this time the country was dark all over, and given up to the noise and disturbances of all sorts of inferior gods."—*Nihongi.*

Wisdom's influence on the lower nature being frustrated by Desire, she ceased from direct action in the soul, and retired into the inner being or Divine realm which is concealed from the lower nature by spiritual law. (That is,—the "Fall" having taken place, the Desire-nature rules the soul, and the direct vibrations from buddhi (Eden) cease.) After this event, the lower nature was bereft of the light of Truth, and immersed in the darkness of ignorance. The soul was given over to the turmoil and conflict of instincts, desires, opinions and feelings.

"Ama-terasu slightly opening the Cave door, asked, 'Why has Usumé danced, and why do the Gods laugh?' Usumé replied, 'I dance, and they laugh because there is an honourable deity here' (pointing to the mirror) 'who surpasses you in glory'; and as she said this, the mirror was pushed forward, reflecting her own radiant loveliness, and her surprise was greater even than before. As she peeped out of the door to look around, the Strong God pulled the rock-door open and drew the bright Goddess forth."—*Ibid.*

This refers to the end of the cycle when the consciousness rises to the buddhic plane. It was requisite that the emotions (Usumé) should be raised and the ideals be attained (Gods laugh). Perfection of the lower nature being at last realised, there was to be found in the causal-body (mirror) a reflection of the Wisdom-nature more glorious in so far as it signifies Victory,—the end of strenuous effort. The perfected lower nature disappears in the Higher, for they are alike, and joy ineffable fills the soul. As Wisdom (peeping out) becomes manifest in the evolved consciousness, the Divine Will (Strong God) makes the spiritual mind its fitting vehicle in the exalted soul.

"The above episode is the kernel of the mythical lore of Japan. Belonging to the class of light and darkness myths, it professes to give the origin of some of the principal ceremonies of the Shinto religion. . . . Modern Shinto explains the darkness produced by the Sun-Goddess's retirement as emblematic of the darkness of sin. The renewal of light typifies repentance. Of course this was far from the thoughts of the original myth-makers."—W. G. ASTON, *Shinto*, pp. 101, 102.

Nevertheless, modern Shinto is right in this. A shallow Mythology destroys religion and reduces the sacred writings to foolishness.

See BUDDHI, CAVE, DANCE, DARKNESS, EYES, HIDING PLACE, INSIGNIA, IZANAGI, LAUGHTER (gods), MAST, METZTLI, MIRROR, MITEGURA, MOON, NIGHT, NINIGI, RETURN, SEA, SUSANOWO, UKEMOCHI, UZUMÉ, WOODEN PALACE.

AMAZEMENT :—

A symbol of a process of awakenment.

AMAZONS :—

A symbol of the higher emotions,—the buddhic,—which oppose the desires.

"A mythical race of warlike females, are said to have come from the Caucasus, and to have settled in the country about the river Thermoden. Their country was inhabited only by the Amazons, who were governed by a queen : but in order to propagate their race, they met once a year the Gargarians in Mount Caucasus."—*Smith's Class. Dict.*

The higher emotions which contend against the desire-mental qualities, arise upon the buddhic plane as a result of aspiration from below, and are contiguous to the "river of life." They are above the mental qualities, and are co-ordinated by Wisdom. At one period of the cycle (year) they become allied with the higher mental faculties, and this alliance brings into activity many qualities, buddhic and mental.

See CAUCASUS.

AMBAS (SCRIPTURES) :—

A symbol of the teachings of the Spirit of Truth from the buddhic plane ; that is, the Divinely implanted inner meanings underlying the outer expressions of all the world-scriptures and sacred myths.

See DEVELOPMENT, INSPIRATION, KAYAN, REVELATION, SCRIPTURES.

AMBAYÂS RIVERS :—

A symbol of the channels of wisdom in the soul, leading from the Fountain of Truth or the Supreme Reality.

See CHANNELS, EDEN RIVER, RIVERS, TREES AND RIVERS.

AMBÂYAVÎS (UNDERSTAND-ING) :—

A symbol of the spiritual vision awakened in the soul, which recognises the inner meanings of the sacred scriptures ; for the meanings are already engraven on the secret tables of the heart.

"In the same Kingdom of Christ all things are inward and spiritual ; and the true religion of Christ is written in the soul and spirit of man by the Spirit of God ; and the believer is the only book in which God Himself writes His New Testament" (William Dell).—R. M. JONES, *Mystical Religion*, p. 493.

"In addition to reason man has a certain faculty by which he can understand hidden mysteries. It is called by Shams-i-Tabrizi the 'eye of the heart,' which is constant in its desire for God, and by Jelálu'd-din the 'inward sense.' This idea is not peculiar to Sufis. It was held by other mystics."—VAUGHAN, *Hours with the Mystics*, Vol. I. p. 158.

See GOSPEL, INSPIRATION, KORAN, PEN, REVELATION, SACRED TEXT, UPANISHAD, VEDA, WORD.

AMBROSIA, FOOD OF THE GODS :—

A symbol of Truth, Wisdom, and Love, which are the attributes of life immortal, and are the spiritual nourishment of the higher qualities (gods) in the soul of man.

See BUTTER, CHURNING, FOOD, HONEY, SACRAMENTAL CAKES, ZARAMAYA OIL.

AMEN, OR AMON (THE HIDDEN ONE) :—

A symbol of the Higher Self incarnate on the lower planes of the soul.

"As Amen-Rā he was worshipped as the supreme 'King of the Gods,' a creator and soul of the universe, inscrutable and eternal. He is usually figured in human form, with two long upright plumes rising above his head, holding a sceptre and the symbol of life. The ram was sacred to him, and in this animal he was believed to be incarnate."—*Non-classical Mythology*, p. 9.

The incarnate Self is symbolised by the ram of sacrifice,—the "Lamb of God."

See AFU-RĀ, CROWN (sekhet), DEITY (hidden), MUT, PLUMES, SCEPTRE.

AMENI, THE SON OF MAN :—

A symbol of the Higher Self born in the Soul.

"An Egyptian poet in the reign of Thothmes III had said :—A king shall come from the South, Ameni, the Truth-declaring, by name. He shall be the son of a Woman of Nubia, and will be born in [the south]. . . . He shall assume the crown of Upper Egypt, and lift up the red crown of the North. He shall unite the double crown. The people of the age of the Son-of-man shall rejoice and establish his name for all eternity. He shall be removed far from evil, and the wicked shall humble their mouths for fear of him."—*Papyrus* 1116, St. Petersburg.

"The words 'son of man' are a literal translation of the original *si-n-sa*."—SAYCE, *Gifford Lectures*, p. 248.

The Christ shall appear from within, and shall declare the Truth and the Right. He shall be born of Wisdom on the higher mental plane. He shall be ruler of the upper planes, and raise up through love the lower self. He shall triumphantly unite the higher and lower natures in the soul. The qualities (virtues) of the evolutionary period of the Divine Son-of-mind shall be transmuted, and his differentiation, or upward rise of consciousness, shall be established for ever. The Soul shall then be exalted above all

relation to the lower planes, and illusion and error shall no longer be expressed within it.

"The half-mythical country in the South was known to the Egyptians as the land of the Gods.' "—*Ibid.*, p. 134.

"Nubia," therefore, is a symbol of the Buddhic, or Wisdom plane ; Upper Egypt, of the higher mind plane ; Lower Egypt of the lower mind plane. The " great sea " is the astral plane. In *evolution* the " Son " is necessarily greater than the " father " ; so Son-of-mind is greater than mind.

The " wicked " are the bad qualities which cannot be expressed (mouths) in the higher nature.

"Look not abroad for the blessings of Christ. His reign and chief blessings are within you. The human soul is his kingdom. There he gains his victories, there rears his temples, there lavishes his treasures. His noblest monument is a mind redeemed from iniquity, brought back and devoted to God, forming itself after the perfection of the Saviour."—W. E. CHANNING, *Works*, Vol. II. p. 204.

"One like unto a Son of Man " (REV. i. 13). "I saw in the night visions, and, behold, one like unto a son of man came with the clouds of heaven, and came to the Ancient of days and they brought him near before him. And there was given him dominion, and glory, and a kingdom, that all people, nations and languages should serve him ; his dominion is an everlasting dominion, which shall not pass away, and his kingdom that which shall not be destroyed."—DAN. vii. 13, 14.

"There is very little doubt but that the imagery of the book of Daniel has inspired to a great extent that of the author of Revelation. The governing idea is the same in both, namely, that at the heart of the universe there is enthroned a being, a principle, a divine intelligence and power, so closely akin to ourselves that it (or rather he) might be said to wear the likeness of our humanity. It is remarkable how this conception rose and grew both in later Judaism and in Greek thought till it reached its culmination in Christianity. . . . This assertion of the cosmic significance of Christ is of the greatest value and importance to religion. It is nothing less than the revelation that that which has produced the world of worlds, that which has both created and redeemed us, that which is our source and our goal, has a nature like our own—nay more, is in a sense verily and undeniably Man. This idea did not come into the world with Christianity, it was here before it ; it has received its highest development in Christianity, but one is glad to know that spiritually minded people had felt it to be a necessity of religious belief."—R. J. CAMPBELL, Serm., *The Eternal Man.*

See ARC. MAN, BIRTH OF JESUS, BUDDHIC PLANE, CHRIST'S SECOND COMING, CLOUDS OF HEAVEN, CROWNS (Egyptian), EGYPT (higher and lower), EVOLUTION, FATHER (lower), HIGHER AND LOWER NATURES, JESUS (son of man), KING (great), MAN (bad), NAME, NUBIA, SEA, SON OF MAN, SOUL (middle), SOUTH, WICKEDNESS, WISDOM, WOMAN, WORLD.

AMENT, AMENTI, OR AMENTET, IN ITS HIGHER ASPECT :—

A symbol of a state of consciousness on the buddhic plane which is the plane of the first division of the Western Tuat, and of the corresponding division of the Eastern Tuat ; that is, the first and the last portions of the cycle of life.

" Beginning of the opening of *Amenti* (that is the West, and hence the Underworld) of the limit of the gathered darkness " (*Book, Am-Tuat*).—WIEDEMANN, *Rel. of Egyptians*, p. 85.

" The gods of this Court (first division of the Tuat) say unto Rā, ' O great God, . . . the portals of the secret Ament are thrown open before thee, the doors of Nut the great are thrown wide open, illumine thou the darkness of night.' "—BUDGE, *Egypt. Heaven and Hell*, Vol. I. p. 19.

" Life to thee, O governor of Amentet, Osiris, who art over the beings of Amentet."—*Ibid.*, p. 276.

" O Rā of the beautiful Ament."—*Ibid.*, p. 86.

" Isis of Amentet."—*Ibid.*, p. 85.

See APES (nine), ARIES, BUDDHIC PLANE, HEAVEN, MOUNTAIN, PISCES, SI-OSIRI, TAURUS, TUAT.

AMERDAD, KING OF VEGETATION :—

A symbol of the principle of growth of forms on the astral plane, and concerned with the development of the instincts, feelings and desires.

See ASTRAL PLANE, SHELTER, WOOD.

AMITAUGAS COUCH (ENDLESS SPLENDOUR) :—

A symbol of contemplation of the Supreme and repose upon the Infinite, when the consciousness is exalted to the buddhic plane.

" He (man) approaches the couch Amitaugas : that is prāna (breath, speech)."—*Kaush. Upanishad*, I. 2.

The soul comes to the state which signifies a sense of infinite rest and serenity,—which is comparable to the rhythm of the Great Breath which is perfectly harmonious and complete.

See ATOMS, BREATH, PRANA, PROSPERITY, SPEECH.

AMMIT MONSTER :—

A symbol of negation ;—that into which the lower illusion will finally descend, and by which it will be swallowed.

See JESUS (son of God), JUDGMENT HALL, NEHAKA, SCAPEGOAT.

AMRAPHEL, KING OF SHINAR :—

A symbol of greed, or acquisitiveness, as a ruler of the lower nature.

See KING, SHINAR.

AMSHASPANDS OR AMESHASPENTAS, THE IMMORTAL BENEFACTORS :—

A symbol of high Intelligences or Devas, which are modes of manifestation of the Divine nature. They are the ideals of Truth and Righteousness, which enlist the veneration of the soul. They are the bringers of " glad tidings," and so serve to evolve the inner capacities which are inherent within the soul. The six Amshaspands are faintly described as,—(1) Glorious Achievement, (2) Inspiration, (3) Wisdom, (4) Intellect, (5) Emotion, and (6) Love.

" God works from within outwards ; for God's kingdom is within, being interior, invisible, mystic, spiritual. And God's Spirits, the Spirits of the Invisible Light, are Seven :—the spirit of wisdom, the spirit of understanding, the spirit of counsel, the spirit of power, the spirit of knowledge, the spirit of righteousness, and the spirit of divine awfulness. These are the Powers, or Elohim, of God. They are co-equal and co-eternal. Each has in itself the nature of the whole. Each is a perfect entity. Of them all is the whole of God's substance pervaded. And in their individual manifestations they are the Gods."—*The Perfect Way*, p. 54.

" The seven Amshaspands, who are most assuredly our Archangels, designate also the personifications of the Divine Virtues."—BURNOUF, *Comm. on Yashna*, 174.

See ANGELS, APSARAS, ARCHANGELS, ARDEBEHESCHT, ASHA, BAHMAN, DEVAS, GODS, GUARDIANS, MESSENGERS, VOHUMANO.

AMULETS :—

A symbol of the germs of the Divine life evolving in the lower qualities and resisting evil influences. The higher nature of the soul.

See PARTICULAR AMULETS.

AMYCUS, KING OF BEBRYCIA :—

A symbol of the illusion of self-dependence and trust in the Higher as if separate from the ego.

"The Argo next touched at Bebrycia, where Amycus reigned. Every stranger who arrived in this country was forced by Amycus to engage him at the cestus. He therefore challenged the Argonauts, and Polydeukes engaged and killed him."
—Argonautic Expedition.

The soul arrived at a state of confidence, and here it is that trust in the Higher and self-dependence are both enthroned. Having arrived at this state, all the qualities were forced to test their power to rise higher. The encounter resulted in the Son of God overcoming the illusion of self in the forms mentioned. (Argonauts).

See ARGO, BEBRYCIA, DIOSCURI, POLLUX.

ANAGĀMIN :—

A symbol of the third initiation of the personality, implying attainment by the soul of a resolve to go through to the bitter end of experience and finish the course. In the Gospel Drama it is the equivalent of the three years' ministry of Jesus which ushers in the fourth initiation at the Crucifixion (the Arhat), when the lower nature is discarded and liberation is effected.

See INITIATIONS, WALKS.

ANAPHE, THE ILLUMINED ISLAND :—

A symbol of the soul suffused in Truth, implying its salvation.

"Apollo taking his stand on the rocks called Melantian Necks, shot an arrow into the sea : the arrow flashed a vivid light, and the Argonauts beheld an island which they named Anaphe."—Argonautic Expedition.

The Higher Self taking his stand on the sense of truth and duty, sends forth a ray of Itself which illumines the whole nature. And so the qualities behold a way of escaping danger. This experience being illuminating, it may be called salvation.

See APOLLO, ARGONAUTS, LIGHT, MELANTIAN NECKS.

ANAURUS RIVER :—

A symbol of the mentality which separates the lower nature from the higher. It stands for limitation and definition in mental forms of intellection.

See GJOLL RIVER, JASON, SANDAL.

ANCESTORS, OR PROGENITORS :—

A symbol of preceding states of the soul, from which the present state is derived.

See ARITS, FILIAL, PATRIARCHS.

ANCEUS, THE PILOT :—

A symbol of the buddhic consciousness which becomes the director of the evolution of the soul.

See ARGO, LYCUS.

ANCHORAGE OF THE SHIP :—

A symbol of the attachment of the lower self to the Higher Self, through the growth of the higher qualities.

"Your only freedom is in intercourse with Christ. Bind your soul to His, and it must rise with Him into His liberty."—PHILLIPS BROOKS, Mystery of Iniquity, p. 183.

"The promise (of salvation) is like a mighty cable, that is fastened by one end to a ship, and by the other to the anchor : the soul is the ship where faith is, and to which the hither end (nearest end) of this cable is fastened ; but hope is the anchor that is at the other end of this cable, and which entereth into that within the veil."—J. BUNYAN, Israel's Hope.

See DELUGE, HIGHER AND LOWER SELVES, MOORING-POST, SHIP.

ANCHORITE OR HERMIT :—

A symbol of the soul which undergoes many acts of self-discipline, and withdraws attention from the objects of sense.

See ARHATS, ASCETICS, ASRAMAS, BRAHMACARIN, HERMIT, MONK, ORDERS, SANNYASINS, SNATIKA, STUDENT.

ANDREW, THE DISCIPLE :—

A symbol of the subjective astral self which builds up and adapts the astral nature to ordinary requirements, and is the directive agency which has charge of the senses in their ordinary practical capacity, and is also controller of the sympathetic nervous system. As a symbol of one of the four elements or planes " Andrew " signifies Water (astral).

"One of the two that heard John speak, and followed him, was Andrew, Simon Peter's brother."—JOHN i. 40.

The subjective astral self is influenced by the moral nature (John) and also by the spiritual (Jesus). The astral self (Andrew) is allied with the lower mind (Peter).

See ASTRAL, JOHN BAPTIST, MESSIAH, PETER, SIMILITUDES, VAISYA, VESTURES, WATER (lower).

ANDROMEDA, DAUGHTER OF CEPHEUS AND CASSIOPEA :—

A symbol of the emotion-nature produced by the astral and buddhic principles.

"Andromeda, the Soul, the better part of Man, is on the point of being devoured outright by the baleful dragon of Negation, the agent of the lower nature, and the ravager of all the hopes of mankind. Her name—identical with the terms in which is described the first Woman of Hebrew story—indicates her as the helpmeet and ruler of man ; her parentage denotes the origin of the Soul from the astral Fire or Æther, signified by the land of Æthopis (the kingdom of Cepheus) ; the brazen fetters with which she is bound to the rock typify the present bondage of the Divine in man to his material part ; and her redemption, espousal, and exaltation by the hero Perseus, prefigure the final and crowning achievement of the Son of God, who is no other than the Spiritual Manhood, fortified and sustained by Wisdom (Athena) and Thought (Hermes)."—*The Perfect Way*, p. lxv.

See CUSH, EVE, GIHON, PANDORA, PERSEPHONE, PERSEUS, WOMAN.

ANDUISUR FOUNTAIN :—

A symbol of Truth flowing from the eternal Source of Life and Reality.

"Khordad was chief of the seasons, years, months, and days, and also protector of the Water which flowed from the fountain Anduisur, on Albordj."— *System of Zoroaster.* CLARKE, *Ten Rel.*

"Khordad" is a symbol of Time, and under the aspect of a ruling condition of manifestation, it becomes the elucidator of Truth in those terms which are reflected in cycles, succession, duration and evolution. The fount "Anduisur" signifies eternal Truth from the summit of attainment (Albordj).

See ALBORDJ, FOUNTAIN, KHORDAD, VOURUKASHA, WATER.

ANGELS :—

A symbol of spiritual influences able to minister to the aspirations of the soul. They are messengers of the inner light to arouse the higher faculties. There are many intelligences who point the way to Truth, and are a means of aiding the soul's evolution.

"And of the angels he saith, Who maketh his angels winds, and his ministers a flame of fire."—HEB. i. 8.

"Winds" and "fire" indicate that the "angels" are on the higher mental and buddhic planes.

"The *Kether Malkhuth* says of the angels : 'Some of them sheets of flames, and some of them breathing winds, some of them composed of fire and water, some Seraphim and some Cherubim.' "— I. MYER, *Qabbalah*, p. 192.

"And there were shepherds in the same country abiding in the field, and keeping watch by night over their flock. And an angel of the Lord stood by them, and the glory of the Lord shone round about them : and they were sore afraid."—LUKE ii. 8, 9.

And there were in this pure and peaceful condition of the soul, simple qualities attracted to virtue instinctively, and co-ordinating in a subjective state (night), the virtues and living truths possessed by them. And a messenger from the Spirit,—a sweet influence which put them in touch with the Highest,—vibrated within them, and, as it were, startled them in their quietude.

"As God is everywhere, so also the angels are everywhere ; but each one in its own principle, and in its own property, or (if you had rather) in its *own place.* The same Essence of God, which is as a Place to Spirits, is confessed to be everywhere ; but the appropriation or participation hereof is different to everyone, according as each hath attracted it magically in the earnestness of Will. The same Divine Essence which is with the Angels of God above is with us also below. And the same Divine Nature which is with us is likewise with them ; but after different manners and in different degrees communicated and participated."—J. BEHMEN, *The Supersensual Life*, pp. 94–5.

"By angel in the Word is everywhere understood the *angelic heaven*, and in a supreme sense the Lord himself. . . . Sending by his angel, signifies the things which are revealed from the Lord through heaven to those who are in the good of life."—SWEDENBORG, *Apoc. Rev.*, n. 4.

"Eichorn in regard to the many apparitions of angels, refers the supernatural to the figurative, in which, for example, a happy accident is called a protecting angel; a joyous thought, the salutation of an angel; and a peaceful state of mind, a comforting angel."—D. F. STRAUSS, *Life of Jesus*, p. 18.

"God's Ideas, like God, are real beings, Divine Personages, that is, Gods. Put forth by, and in a sense divided from, God, in order to accomplish God's purposes, these become *messengers* of God, that is, Angels."—ANNA KINGSFORD, *The Perfect Way*, p. 213.

"No angels come to us! No celestial voices speak to us! Oh! believe it not. Every deep impression of the rightness of an action, every keen conviction of a truth, every inward cry for light and impulse onwards, are messengers, voices of God."—STOPFORD A. BROOKE, Serm., *Angelic Life, etc.*

See AMSHASPANDS, APSARAS, ARCH-ANGELS, BIRD'S NEST, BIRTH OF JESUS, COLCHIANS, DÆMONS, DEVAS, GANDHARVAS, GUARDIANS, KHORDAD, KHUS, LADDER, MESSENGERS, SIRENS, WIND.

ANGER OF GOD :—

Symbolic of a relative and false conception which arises from the fear and hate of the lower nature directed against the Higher which it does not understand. It is the feeling engendered in the lower self that the Higher Self is an enemy. The Higher nature wears a forbidding aspect to the self-seeking personality. This is reflected in the semblance of Divine wrath.

"I (Moses) did neither eat bread nor drink water, because of all your sin which ye sinned, in doing that which was evil in the sight of the Lord, to provoke him to anger. For I was afraid of the anger and hot displeasure, wherewith the Lord was wroth against you to destroy you. But the Lord hearkened unto me that time also. And the Lord was very angry with Aaron to have destroyed him: and I prayed for Aaron also the same time."—DEUT. ix. 18–20.

The rational and ethical nature has been unable, in this backward state of soul, to partake of goodness and truth, because the lower mind has been so full of the activities of desire and sensation. The conscience, nevertheless, has been stirred and there is hope of progression. The spiritual mind (Aaron) was obscured, but the moral nature became a means for its revival.

See AARON, CLEANSING, JEALOUS GOD, MOSES, SELF (lower), SLAUGHTER, VULTURE, WRATH OF GOD.

ANGRA-MAINYU, OR ANGRO-MAINYUSH :—

A symbol of the evil power in the desire-mind, or the illusory principle of the lower mind, which creates opposites.

"Thereupon came Angra-mainyu, he created the serpent in the river, and winter the work of the daevas."—*Vendidad*, I. 2. *S.B. of E.*

This refers to the time when the mind distinguishes between good and evil. The "serpent" signifies the subtle nature of that which first ensnares, but which ultimately proves to be the means of enlightening the Self. The power of evil, or the illusory lower self, fashions "winter" or that which is the obverse of the fruitful principle above.

See AHRIMAN, BLACK MAGICIANS, DEVIL, OPPOSITES, SERPENT DAHAKA, SERPENT (mighty), SERPENT (water), UNBELIEF, WINTER.

ANHAT AND TEHAR OR TANIS :—

Symbolic of a condition of soul in possession of pure knowledge.

ANIMALS, TAMED AND WILD :—

A symbol of the desires, passions and appetites, both disciplined and undisciplined. They are of the astral plane, and pertain to animal-man of the lunar-pitri development.

"Thus in the living soul shall there be good beasts in gentleness of action, . . . and good cattle, . . . and good serpents, not destructive to do hurt, but *wise* to take heed."—AUGUSTINE, *Confessions*, p. 377.

"The animal nature, the fighting nature, even the ape and tiger qualities, have their use as the sheathing of the divine humanity that is to be; they have to be transcended, but never wholly destroyed."—R. J. CAMPBELL, Serm., *Coming to the True Self.*

"If the animal in us is not subject to the mind, it is because the mind or man is not subject to the Lord."—A. JUKES, *Types of Genesis*, p. 125.

"In the Levitical Law, the inferior *animals* were made by God to be symbols to man of his own *vicious propensities*, and so became instruments of moral and spiritual teaching to His people."—WORDSWORTH, *Bible, Job*, p. 96.

"A twice-born man who, knowing the true meaning of the Veda, slays an animal for (sacrifice), causes both himself and the animal to enter a most blessed state."—*Manu*, V. 42.

An individuality who realises the truth of the Divine scheme, offers up his desire-nature, and by so doing attains a state of bliss, while the desire-nature itself is transmuted to the buddhic plane.

See APE, BEASTS, CATTLE, CREATURES, GOAT, LION, SACRIFICE, SERPENT, VITAL AIRS, WOLF.

ANIMALS, REARED AND DOMESTICATED :—

Symbolic of the disciplining of the lower emotions and qualities, in such a way as to make them of use to the progress of the soul.

"Fuh-he recommended pastoral employments and the rearing of domesticated animals."—KIDD, *China*, p. 103.

The Logos (Fuh-he) arranged that the intelligence should be awakened through the activity of the desires, and the need that would arise for their restraint and regulation (animals domesticated). This refers to the dawn of mind when related with the desires (pastoral life), and the commencement of the cultivation and utilising of the lower faculties to aid development of the higher nature of the soul.

"Want, instinct, curiosity, with all the mental activity excited and quickened by them, the association of ideas, reflection, deliberate volition, have gathered, carved, polished, embellished the materials, adapting the occupant to the dwelling and the dwelling to the occupant."—A. LEFEVRE, *Philosophy*, p. 549.

See AGRICULTURE, CULTIVATING, FUH-HE, GEORGE, MITHRA (bull), PASTORAL.

ANNA, THE PROPHETESS :—

A symbol of a subjective mental condition, or type analogous to many souls patiently awaiting the coming of the Christ.

See SIMEON.

ANNAS, THE PRIEST :—

A symbol of a mental state dominated by conventional ideas which grow into sectarianism and professional systems of religious observances.

See CAIAPHAS, HIGH PRIEST (lower), PRIESTS AND ELDERS.

ANNU (HELIOPOLIS) :—

A symbol of the higher planes, atma, buddhi, and higher manas.

"The great house of the Aged One (Rā) who dwelleth in Annu."—BUDGE, *Book of the Dead*, p. 41.

The "Temple of the Soul" (great house) is the inner sanctuary of the Eternal Spirit whose abode is on the higher planes of the soul.

See CITY OF GOD, PLACE (Annu), TEMPLE.

ANOINTING WITH OIL :—

A symbol of the endowment of the soul with Divine Love, arousing sympathy with all beings.

"Thou preparest a table before me in the presence of mine enemies : Thou hast anointed my head with oil ; my cup runneth over."—Ps. xxiii. 5.

The Self hath prepared for the ego the "fruits of the Spirit" on the higher planes, to be the food of the soul ; and the desires (enemies) have been transmuted to this end. The Divine love has been bestowed upon the aspiring mind, and Wisdom has filled the understanding.

See CHRISTOS, CUP, HEAD, LAYING ON OF HANDS, OIL, OINTMENT, TABLE.

ANPU (ANUBIS), THE "OPENER OF THE PATH" :—

A symbol of the astro-physical body with its mechanism of sensation and action, which opens the pathway of the soul's development, life after life.

"The god Anpu, who dwelleth in the city of the embalmment, the governor of the divine house, placeth his two hands upon the lord of life of Nebseni, . . . and he furnisheth him with the things which belong to him. 'Homage to thee, O happy one, divine lord (Osiris Nebseni) . . . Ptah Seker hath bound thee up, Anpu hath exalted thee, and Shu hath caused thee to be lifted up, . . . Thy brow is in the protection of Anpu." —BUDGE, *Book of the Dead*, Ch. CLIB, p. 507.

The physical body equipped with its powers, is at the service of the personality whose need is purification in the interest of the causal-body (divine house). The physical activities, active and passive, are to subserve the Divine life within the soul, and be the means of bringing experience to the ego, which shall lead to the acquirement of spiritual capacities.

The Spirit has been involved in the lower nature by the will of the Supreme, and in the life of the physical human body, the evolution of the Spirit commences, for the Divine Will draws it forth. The truth-acquiring faculty is dependent upon the physical lives.

See ANUBIS, APUAT, CITY, EMBALM-MENT, HOUSE, JACKAL, PTAH, ROPE, SEKER, SHU.

AN-RUT-F DISTRICT :—

A symbol of the higher nature newly evolved in the soul.

" Thou great and mighty Prince (Osiris), dweller in An-rut-f, lord of eternity and creator of everlastingness (*Litany to Osiris*)."—BUDGE, *Book of the Dead*, Ch. XV.

The Higher Self (Osiris) abides in the soul's higher nature.

" A truce for six days and six nights then followed, and Horus had rest, while Isis made use of her words of power to keep away Set from the district called ' An-rut-f.' "—*Legend of the Winged Sun-disk.* WIEDEMAN, *Religion, etc.*

And now there intervenes a period of relative inaction proceeding up to an anti-climax, while no longer the centrifugal energy (Horus) is in the ascendancy : for the centripetal force (Isis) is substituted, so that, instead of being *driven*, the soul is *led* onwards, —the word of Wisdom being substituted for the act of Power. The " woman " corresponds to the ability of answering to the higher rates of vibration from within, which gives the feminine intuition. The " district " stands for the function of the so-symbolised feminine principle of in-tuition in keeping ignorance and evil (which are one and the same illusion) from the newly awakened higher nature.

See INTUITION, ISIS, MAGIC, OSIRIS, SET.

ANTELOPE, SKIN OF BLACK :—

A symbol of the soul in its aspect of a manifesting surface for the presentation of the higher and lower qualities.

" If there be only one (black antelope skin), then it is an image of these three worlds. Those hairs which are white are an image of the sky ; those which are black are an image of this earth ;— or conversely, black of sky, and white of earth. Those which are of a brownish-yellow colour are an image of the atmosphere."—*Sata. Brâh.*, III. 2, 1, 3.

The " black antelope " itself is the potential (black) soul after involution of all qualities : the skin is its surface of evolution whereon it displays its qualities (colours) of three orders,— higher (sky), lower (earth) and mental (air), or buddhic, astral, and mental qualities (three worlds).

" The sacrificer spreads it on the ground with the hairy side upwards, and with its neck-part turned to the west, with the text :—' The skin of Aditi art thou ! May Aditi acknowledge thee ! '— For Aditi is this earth, and whatever is on her, that serves as a skin to her. . . . Thereby he establishes a mutual under-standing between her and the black antelope skin."—*Sata. Brâh.*, I. 1, 4, 5.

The Self commences to manifest in the new cycle of evolution, and arranges that the purified emotions (neck) shall progress towards buddhi (west). The externalising of the quali-ties in space (Aditi), or the evolution of them from matter (earth), is the process whereby the soul is enabled to grow. For which purpose there is established in the mind a discrimina-ting faculty which adjudicates between nature and the soul.

See ADITI, AIR, COLOURS, EARTH, HAIR, NECK, PHINEUS, SKIN, SKY.

ANTHRŌPOS AND ECCLESIA :—

Symbols of the Divine Mind and the Soul or Buddhic function, in relation to human development.

" The Valentinians maintain that the twelve apostles were a type of that group of twelve Æons which Anthrōpos in conjunction with Ecclesia produced."—IRENÆUS, *Against Heresies*, Bk. II., Ch. 21.

The relationship of the twelve disciplined qualities with the twelve stages of the cycle of life, is to be seen when we recognise the close corre-spondence that obtains between the greater cosmic cycle and the lesser individual cycle—between the macro-cosmic and the microcosmic processes. Each is typical of the other, or rather, the lesser indicates the greater ; so that it will be seen that the individual epitomises, as it were, the entire manifested life-experience of the Logos. In each soul there are the twelve " apostles " more or less developed, and these disciplined qualities are to become more and more purified, and are to teach the lower qualities and lead them upward to the Light.

See ÆONS (twelve), APOSTLES (twelve), FATE-SPHERE, CHURCH, DISCIPLES (twelve), SAVIOURS (twelve), TRIBES (twelve).

ANTICHRIST :—

A symbol of the adversary of the Higher Self, which is the lower principle or the desire-mental nature.

"Hereby know ye the Spirit of God : every spirit which confesseth that Jesus Christ is come in the flesh is of God : and every spirit which confesseth not Jesus is not of God : and this is the spirit of the antichrist, whereof ye have heard that it cometh ; and now it is in the world already."—1 JOHN iv. 2, 3.

Hereby know ye the Spirit of Love and Truth : every impulse which is in harmony with Jesus Christ now born in our lower nature (flesh) is " of God " : and every impulse which annulleth Jesus in us, is " not of God," and this is the antichrist which is the impulse of the desire-mind in opposition to the indwelling Jesus. The antagonist of righteousness and truth is in our mental condition (world), but " greater is he (Jesus Christ) that is *in you* than he that is in the world " (verse 4), for he that is of the lower nature is Antichrist.

"St. John is not speculating on ultimate existences ; he is dealing with active powers ; and from this point of view the power of evil has its place in his system. As Christ is the principle of truth, so the devil is the principle of error. He remains as the anti-Christ, though all his attendant demons have vanished in this Gospel. The devil is *de facto* ruler of this world, which as his domain is contrary to God."—W. R. INGE, *Camb. Biblical Essays*, p. 272.

See ADVERSARY, AHRIMAN, COUNTERFEIT, DEVIL, HEROD, SATAN.

ANTS :—

A symbol of the monads of life and form.

" Ye divine ants—for it was they that produced this (ant-hill),—' the first-born of the world,'—the first-born of the world, doubtless, is this earth."—*Sata. Brâh.*, XIV. 1, 2, 10.

The spiritual monads (atma-buddhic) build up the forms and endow with life all the atoms and beings of the lower nature, which manifest first,—prior to spiritual qualities. The first to manifest in the cycle of evolution is the lower nature (earth).

See DEVAS, EARTH, MONAD OF FORM, MONAD OF LIFE.

ANU, GOD OF THE SKY :—

A symbol of the manifest God,—an aspect of the One Life extending through the universe, visible and invisible.

"A mighty king is Anu, the first born of the gods."—SAYCE, *Rel. of Anc. Babyl.*, p. 483.

The Logos or Higher Self appears first upon the highest plane, and thence upon the buddhic plane.

See NECK, PERSONALITY, SKY, SOUTH WIND.

ANUBIS, SON OF OSIRIS AND NEPTHYS :—

A symbol of the physical body as the most outward vehicle of the soul ; the product of Divine energy and matter on the physical plane (Nepthys).

"Isis found the child and bred it ; so that in process of time it became her constant guard and attendant, and from hence obtained the name of Anubis, being thought to watch and guard the Gods, as dogs do mankind."—PLUTARCH, *Isis and Osiris*, § 14.

Wisdom (buddhi) takes charge of the physical body and tends it, and assumes direction of its evolution while it guards the Divine nature within. In this way a perfect reciprocity is established between the higher and lower planes, through the actions and re-actions of the physical vehicle which thus becomes the constant attendant and nurturer of the Ideals (gods), or higher activities within the soul.

"According to Egyptian belief Anubis was a special patron of the dead, guarding them and superintending their embalmment, he or Thoth being their guide into the next world, and leading them by the hand into the Hall of Judgment."—WIEDEMANN, *Rel. of Anc. Egyptians*, p. 230.

"Anubis who is at the head of the divine hall and who dwelleth upon his mountain, the lord of Ta-tchesert, saith :— I have come to protect Osiris Mut-hetep, triumphant."—BUDGE, *Book of the Dead*, Ch. CLIA. p. 504.

"Anubis hath bestowed upon thee (Osiris Nebseni) thy winding-sheet, he hath wrought for thee according to his will, he hath provided thee with the ornaments of his bandages, for he is the overseer of the great god."—*Ibid.*, CLXXII. p. 586.

The physical body (Anubis) is a great factor in the mental expression of the personality (corpse), its activities, and its purification (embalmment). The physical mechanism and the higher mind (Thoth) lead the personality by its activities (hand) to the test of completeness of the perfecting process when the consciousness should rise to the higher planes. The physical body is in the forefront of the means of developing the causal-body (divine hall) which is exalted above it ; and it serves the spiritual ego (Osiris) within. It is also the external means provided for the education and enlargement of the ego.

See AFU-RĀ, ANPU, APUAT, BOAT, EMBALMMENT, ISIS, JACKAL, NEPHTHYS, ROPE, SUDRA.

APARÂGITA, PALACE (UNCONQUERABLE) :—

A symbol of the perfected Soul as a vehicle of the Eternal Spirit.

"He (man) approaches the palace Aparâgita, and the splendour of Brahman reaches him."—*Kaush. Upanishad*, I. 2.

The Soul approaches the condition of perfection,—the sense of the holy, or the entire and complete Unity of the All,—when the ineffable grandeur of the Living Whole appeals in its entirety to the exalted consciousness. This state of being is a sense of the all-embracing,—that which includes all manifestation yet is itself unmanifest,—which embraces each, yet is itself the opposite of each ;—that which is above, through, in, and without all.

See ABSOLUTE, BRAHMA, FACE (Lord), GODHEAD, PATH (twofold), TEMPLE, YESHTIKA.

APE, DOG-HEADED (LOWER ASPECT) :—

A symbol of the automatic mind, or subjective mind.

See JUDGMENT HALL.

APE AND TIGER NATURE :—

Symbolic of the automatic mind in ancestral traits and habits, and in unruled instincts and desires.

See ANIMALS, BEASTS (wild).

APEP, THE SERPENT :—

A symbol of the desire-mental nature.

"The undulating length of the serpent Apep, of whom it is said, 'his voice goeth round the Tuat.'"—BUDGE, *Egypt. Heaven and Hell*, Vol. II. p. 268.

In the relativity of the lower mind it may be said that the expression, or utterance, of the desire impulse allied with mind in the lower nature of the human soul, extends through the whole cycle of manifested life (the Tuat).

The desire-mind (Apep) is the adversary against which all the higher qualities (gods) contend. It is for ever being cut to pieces, but comes to life again all the same in other states and conditions of the soul's development.

See AHRIMAN, GREEN, NET, SATAN, SERPENT, TUAT.

APES (CYNOCEPHALI) NINE,— "WHICH SING TO RĀ AS HE ENTERETH THE TUAT " :—

These are symbolic of the myriad of egos who shall rise through Christ to divine manhood. "Nine" is their symbolic number, in that man becomes more than man when the "tenth"—signifying completion and accomplishment,—is reached.

"The Souls of the East (i.e. the Souls or Spirits who take the forms of apes immediately the Sun has risen) pay homage to thee, and when they meet thy Majesty they cry :—'Come, come in peace !' (*Hymn to the Setting Sun*)."—BUDGE, *Book of the Dead*, p. 80.

"Open to me (Osiris) the doors with your hands, O ye Apes, unfold to me the portals of the Courts, O ye Apes, and welcome the gods or goddesses who have come into being from my divine Souls ; come ye into being for Khepera, O ye who have your being at the head of the Tuat." *Ibid.*

This statement refers to the first division (Aries) of the cycle of life (the Tuat). It is on the upper levels of the buddhic plane that the Self (Sun) commences to manifest *in abscondito* (night). The spiritual egos (apes) are represented as opening the

"way of the Lord," because it is
through their *volition* in harmony
(singing) with the Supreme (RĀ), that
manifestation takes place ; and they
enter into being in order to undergo
the suffering and sorrow of the lives
on earth. They come into being for
Christ (Khepera) that they may triumph over ignorance and evil, and
rise with him to power and glory at
the end of the cycle.

"All protest against being coerced by
an almighty power outside ourselves
ceases to have any point when we realise
that the power outside ourselves is what
we ourselves essentially are. Indeed
there would be no power outside ourselves,—we should never feel it or know
anything about it,—if there were no
power within ourselves impelling us to
enter into relations with it."—R. J.
CAMPBELL, Serm., *Who Compels ?*

See AMENT, ARIES, EAST, GUARD-
IANS, NET-RĀ, RĀ, SERPENTS (emit-
ting sparks), SONS OF GOD, STRIDES
(soul), SUN, TUAT, WILL.

APHRODITĒ, FOAM-SPRUNG :—

**A symbol of the love aspect, or
attractive quality, of the desire-
nature, which promotes growth of
the lower qualities in the forms.**

"In the Asiatic religions Aphroditē
was the fructifying principle of nature."
—*Smith's Class. Dict.*, "Adonis."

See ADONIS, ATALANTA, ATTRAC-
TION, FOAM, MESCH, POURUSHASPA,
VENUS.

APIAN LAND :—

A symbol of the lower mental plane.

APIS, BULL OF THE WEST :—

**A symbol of the outgoing activity
of the Divine Will on the buddhic
plane.**

"In Memphis is kept the Apis, the
'Image of the soul of Osiris,' where his
body also is said to lie."—PLUTARCH,
Isis and Osiris, § 20.

On the buddhic plane (Memphis)
there appears the matrix of all forms
in prototype, directing the outgoing
energy of the Logos.

"The identification of Apis with Osiris
was easy enough, because one of the
commonest names of Osiris was 'Bull of
the West.' "—BUDGE.

"In course of time the bull, like other
animals, was regarded as a symbol, and
Apis is hence identified with Osiris or
the Sun."—*Smith's Class. Dict.*, "Apis."

See BULL, MEMPHIS, OSIRIS,
SERAPIS.

APOCATEQUIL, SON OF GUA-MANSURI :—

**A symbol of the Higher Self, pro-
ceeding from the Supreme.**

"He was the first mortal to descend
to earth. Associating with certain dwel-
lers of the dusk called Guachimines, he
seduced their sister, for which they slew
him. But his offspring by her, born
from two eggs, survived although their
mother was slain. These were the twin
brothers Apocatequil and Pigueras. The
former recalled his mother to life, slew
the treacherous Guachimines, and under
the guidance of the god Ataguchu, made
an aperture in the earth with a golden
spade, through which the race of Peru-
vians emerged and took possession of
the land." — *Non-classical Mythology*,
p. 12.

The Self in involution became
immersed in matter (earth) and
obscured by the desires (Guachimines).
When perfected as the Archetypal
Man he dies. But the Divine Life
through the emotion-nature (sister)
brings forth in the new cycle (evolution) the dual consciousnesses—the
Individuality and the Personality.
The Divine Individuality restores the
emotion-nature and eventually the
desires are overcome. The indwelling God operating through buddhi
(gold) penetrates the lower nature
(earth) and rises with his saints to
heaven.

See ASVINS, DIOSCURI, GEMINI.

APOLLO, SON OF ZEUS :—

**A symbol of the Second Logos
proceeding from the First. God
manifest, or the Higher Self.**

"Nine days through the army went
the arrows of the God (Phœbus Apollo) ;
but on the tenth, Achilles called the
people to an assembly ; for to his mind
the white-armed Goddess Juno had suggested it ; for she was anxious concerning
the Greeks, because she saw them perishing."—*Iliad*, Book I. *trans.* BUKKLEY.

For nine periods the life-giving
force of the Logos ensouled the egos,
or monads of form ; but at the tenth
period, the personality (Achilles) is
evolved sufficiently to enable the
lower mental qualities to assemble
to it as a centre. For at this period
of soul-growth there was some glimmer
of such higher perception as is essential
to the further development of the
individuality. And the Wisdom

aspect is directly concerned with the evolution of the mental qualities which had begun to languish.

"Dionysius proclaims : 'The Divine Goodness, this our great Sun, enlightens, nourishes, perfects, renews.' Even the pure can thus be made purer still. 'He, the Good, is called spiritual light ; he cleanses the mental vision of the very angels : they taste, as it were, the light.' All this imagery goes back, in the first instance, to Proclus. For Proclus puts in parallel 'sun' and 'God,' and 'to be enlightened' and 'to be deified'; makes all purifying forces to coalesce in the activity of the Sun-God, Apollo Katharsios, the Purifier, who 'everywhere unifies multiplicity . . . purifying the entire heaven and all living things throughout the world'; and describes how 'from above, from his super-heavenly post, Apollo scatters the arrows of Zeus,—his rays upon all the world'" (In Par. IV. 34).—F. VON HUGEL, *Mystical Element*, Vol. II. p. 93.

"Nothing can be more profound, more entire, than the reverence of Homer's mortals for Apollo and Athenè." —W. E. GLADSTONE, *Juventus Mundi*, p. 177.

See ACHILLES, ANAPHE, ARGIVES, AROUERIS, ARROWS, DELOS, EXILE, GALE, HECATOMB, HERA, HYMN, LATONA, NINE, NINE DAYS, PESTILENCE, PRIEST OF APOLLO, WRATH OF APOLLO.

APOSTATES WITH TWO LEGS :—

A symbol of relative conditions which are always short of the truth, as may be seen in the pairs of opposite qualities.

"And the vigour of Azi Dahak (raging elephant) increases, the fetters being removed from his trunk, and his impetuosity remains ; he swallows down the apostate on the spot, and rushing into the world to perpetuate sin, he commits innumerable grievous sins."— *Bahman Yast*, Ch. III. 57. *S. B. of E.*

The lower principle, with its illusions, strengthens as the Divine law gives it more liberty ; and relative conditions promote activities which produce innumerable evils in the external life.

"The apostate's mind is a furious elephant which wandereth distracted in the forest of worldly love. Impelled by Death it rusheth here and there, while the pious search and find God in their hearts" (*Guru Nanak*).—MACAULIFFE, *The Sikh Religion*, Vol. I. p. 315.

See ELEPHANTS RAGING, OPPOSITES, SERPENT (Dahaka).

APOSTLE OR DISCIPLE :—

A symbol of a developed and disciplined quality of the soul, in harmonious relation with the central Ideal, and which becomes a means for teaching and raising the lower mental qualities.

"The highest faculty in the soul is not, like each of the inferior faculties, one faculty among others ; it is the Soul itself in its totality ; as such it is called the 'spark,' also *Synteresis* (corresponding to the soul-centre of Plotinus). This highest faculty is served by all the faculties of the soul, which assist it to reach the Source of the soul, by raising the latter out of the sphere of inferior things. The Spark aspires to the Absolute, to that unity outside of which there remains nothing" (Eckhart).— UEBERWEG, *Hist. of Philos.*, Vol. I. p. 472.

The "apostle" is one of the superior faculties grouped about the highest faculty (Jesus)—the Divine Spirit within.

"We are assimilated to divinity by virtue."—PLOTINUS, *On the Virtues*, § 1.

See ANDREW, DISCIPLE, JAMES, JOHN, JUDAS, PETER, PHILIP.

APOSTLES, THE TWELVE :—

A symbol of the twelve highest qualities or virtues in the soul. They form a group nearest to the central indwelling Christ. The "apostles" are specialised conditions of the "disciples" and all are qualities which follow the leading of the Higher Self. The "apostles" are "disciples" raised to a state of close companionship with each other, whereby the Christ is brought into near relationship with the lower nature now gradually being drawn towards him.

"By the twelve apostles are signified all things of doctrine concerning the Lord, and concerning a life according to his commandments."—SWEDENBORG, *Apoc. Rev.*, n. 915.

"Jacob begot the twelve apostles in the Spirit, not in the flesh ; in word, not in blood."—*Pseudo-Chrysostom.*

"Abraham, Isaac, and Jacob are types of the divine life in man. . . . These children (of Jacob) by Leah and the bondmaids, are the different forms of life which are produced by the spirit of service in us out of different principles, Leah and Rachel representing the higher principles ; the bond-maids, other lower principles."—A. JUKES, *Types of Genesis*, p. 340.

In the book Am-Tuat, the twelve

amakhiu (apostles) of Rā, draw Afu-
Rā (the embodied Self, or Lamb of
God) through the body of the Serpent
(lower nature) and bring him out at
its mouth, transfigured.

The amakhiu "enter the tail of the
serpent as loyal servants, but like their
master, are transformed during their
passage through its body, and they
emerge from its mouth as 'rejuvenated
forms of Rā' each day."—Budge, *Egypt.
Heaven and Hell*, Vol. III. p. 193.

"Buddha, like Christ, had twelve
'great disciples.' 'Only in my religion,'
he said solemnly a little before he died,
'can be found the twelve great disciples
who practise the highest virtues and
excite the world to free itself from its
torments' (*Bigandet*, p. 301)."—A.
Lillie, *Budd. in Christendom*, p. 138.

The "apostles" are the qualities
which "practise the highest virtues,"
and stimulate the mind to free itself
from the causes of bondage in matter
(suffering). In the one religion of
the Higher Self (Buddha or Christ)
those qualities which are more advanced help those behind them to rise.

"The Marriage Supper can be celebrated in the kingdom of the Father
only, when all the 'Twelve Apostles,'
or elements corresponding to the twelve
degrees (of the Perfect Man), have been
brought into perfect harmony and at-
one-ment, and no defective element any
longer exists among them. In the central
place at this divine feast is the Thirteenth
Personage, the Master or Adonai of the
system, the founder and president of the
banquet. He it is who in later times
found a representative in the pure and
heaven-born Arthur, — Ar-Thor — the
'Bright Lord' of the Round Table."—
The Perfect Way, p. 247.

"In St. Clemente at Rome, in the
apsis, is a cross in mosaic, on which are
represented twelve doves, signifying the
twelve apostles united to, or having their
life in, Christ."—H. C. Barlow, *Essays
on Symbolism*, p. 74.

See Æons (twelve), Anthropos,
Argonauts, Dance (circle), Disci-
ples, Feeding (5,000), Heroes,
Peter, Saviours (twelve), Sparrows
(twelve), Tribes (twelve), Twelve,
Zodiac.

APPENDAGES :—

A symbol of modes of activity of
the lower qualities, which functionings are hung upon the personality
until it has risen above them.

"The Basilideans are accustomed to
give the name of appendages (or accre-
tions) to the passions. These essences,
they say, have a certain substantial
existence, and are attached to the
rational soul, owing to a certain turmoil
and primitive confusion."—Clement
Alex., *Ante Nic. Lib.*, p. 276.

The "appendages are merely modes
of activity of the qualities ; and the
passions have to obtrude themselves
so long as the functionings occur and
are attached to the lower self until its
limitations be outgrown.

"Isodorus, son of Basilides, advises
man to 'battle with the constraints of
the appendages ; (and says) our duty is
to show ourselves rulers over the inferior
creation within us, gaining the mastery
by means of our rational principle.' "—
Ibid.

The one alternative course to adopt
is the suppression of the lower qualities
by coercion from without : the other
is the conquering of the animal nature
from within.

See Dhruva, Personality, Qualities, Viscera.

APPLES OF THE HESPERIDES :—

A symbol of the buddhic emotions
and faculties, the "fruit of the
Spirit."

"The golden apples which Ge (Earth)
gave to Hera at her marriage with Zeus."
—*Smith's Class. Dict.*

The "marriage" is the union of
Wisdom (Hera) and Love (Zeus).
Love struggles upward from below to
meet Wisdom above ; and Matter
(Ge) yields up the results of experience
and effort, on to the Wisdom plane.

See Ge, Gold, Grail, Hesperides,
Hikoboshi, Marriage.

APSARAS :—

A symbol of high Devas,—intelligences who are co-operating with
evolution upon the highest planes of
the manifest universe.

See Angels, Archangels, Colchians, Devas, Gandharvas,
Guardians.

**APUAT, "OPENER OF THE
WAYS " :—**

A symbol of the external body or
vehicle of the soul, which opens the
way to manifestation in the lower
worlds.

See Afu-rā, Anpu, Anubis.

**AQUARIUS, THE ZODIACAL
SIGN :—**

A symbol of the eleventh period of
the cycle of life. It signifies the

buddhic vehicle of the Spirit, as the container of Truth (water) from the fountain of the Divine Reality. It refers to the rise of consciousness through the lower buddhic plane, far advanced in the present period of evolution.

See FOUNTAIN, WATER, ZODIAC.

AQUEDUCT :—

A symbol of a channel of truth established from the higher nature to the lower.

See CHANNELS, IRRIGATION, RIVER.

ARA LAKE :—

A symbol of a high state of Truth and Bliss upon the buddhic plane.

"He (the departed) approaches the lake Ara, and crosses it by the mind, while those who come to it without knowing the truth are drowned in it."— *Kaush. Upanishad*, I. 2.

He, the liberated ego, who has advanced beyond the conditioned, now hath known and realised his true nature to be Bliss. This he has discovered by means of the higher mind—buddhi. But those egos who, having acquired some powers of the mind, would pass beyond the conditioned without having the Truth and without purifying the lower nature, work destruction to themselves, as far as that state is concerned.

See BLACK MAGICIANS, BLISS, RAFT, VIGARA, YATUS.

ARABS ENTERING IRAN :—

A symbol of the emotion-nature (Arabs) and the mental-nature (Iran) becoming united on the mental plane. The emotions are, as it were, invaders (by vibrations) from another plane, of the mental realm which they in a measure conquer for themselves, though in doing so they come under the restraint and discipline of the mind (Iran).

See COUNTRIES, GREEKS, TAZ, TROJANS.

ARARAT MOUNTAINS :—

A symbol of the lofty aspirations which point the soul to Wisdom.

See CAUCASUS, FLOOD, MOUNTAINS.

ARBOURS, FESTIVE :—

Symbolic of virtues of the soul, which bring joy and satisfaction to the ego.

See ARCHED GATEWAYS.

ARCHANGELS :—

A symbol of primordial Divine Powers on the highest planes of manifestation. These have their part in the construction of the spiritual universe which underlies the perceptible and visible phenomenal universe. "Archangels" also signify messengers of the Logos on high planes; and exalted Intelligences who introduce the spiritual Life-element into the vehicles, or forms, fully prepared and awaiting its reception.

See AMSHASPANDS, ANGELS, APSARAS, BAHMAN, BUILDERS, DEVAS, GABRIEL, GUARDIANS, MESSENGERS, MICHAEL, VOHUMANO.

ARCHED GATEWAYS :—

A symbol of mental qualities which open the way to knowledge.

"The City of Kapila with its festive arbours, its arched gateways and pinnacles, it was radiant with jewels in every dwelling; and unable to find any other rival in the world, it could only feel emulation with its own houses."— *The Buddha-Karita*, Bk. I.

The abode of the Self on the higher planes of atma, buddhi, manas, is the perfection of all virtues, mental qualities, and aspirations. Within the soul (potential) is all beauty and excellence. At this stage of early involution, the Self is absolute unity, there is no Second Self to manifest. At this period no duality is apparent; there are no opposites, therefore no conflict takes place.

See AMARĀVATI, ARBOURS, GATEWAYS, GOLDEN AGE, JEWELS, KAPILA, PINNACLES, WORLD.

ARCHETYPAL MAN :—

This important symbol, the signification of which is a key to the knowledge of the soul's evolution to perfection, represents humanity perfected potentially on the higher planes in a past cycle of involution, and now subsisting as the directive efficient cause of imperfect actual humanity evolving on the lower planes in the present cycle. When the evolution is complete, the potential is actualised, and the souls are perfected.

"The Spiritual Man is both the import and the highest degree of creation, for which reason he was formed on the sixth day. As soon as the Man was created, everything was complete, including the Upper and Lower Worlds, for everything is comprised in the Man. He unites in Himself all the forms."—*Zohar*, III. 48A.

"Now the heavenly Man, as being born in the image of God, has no participation in any corruptible or earthlike essence."—PHILO, *Works*, Yonge, Vol. IV. p. 60.

"The first world, or the Archetypal Man in whose image everything is formed, is occupied by no one else."—C. D. GINSBURG, *The Kabbalah*, p. 111.

"The soul carries her knowledge with her to the earth, so that everything which she learns here below she knew already, before she entered into this world" (*Zohar*, III. 61, B).—*Ibid.*, p. 116.

"We have referred to the ancient Asiatic idea, that above the earth, in the heavens, existed a true and perfect ideation of everything created in the universe, visible or invisible. That this perfect ideal, true, and real, paradigm, was in opposition to, yet in harmony with, its imperfect shadow, the changeable,—by man considered real,—universe ; but the really untrue and unreal. . . . The Qabbalah holds fully to this idea. It also claims that the first account of the Creation in Genesis, referred exclusively to this ideal world and to an Ideal Man. In this first account there is not any Garden of Eden, nor any Eve, and the Ideal Man is created as an Androgene, but in the similitude of Elohim."—MYER, *Qabbalah*, pp. 121–2.

The process of involution of all qualities and forms into matter, eventuates in the creation of the Archetypal Man, the perfect prototype and source of all the souls of humanity, when the One becomes the many in the new cycle of evolution.

"These (Naassenes) honour as the Logos of all universals Man, and Son of Man. This Man is male-female, and is called by them Adamas."—HIPPOLYTUS, *Philosophumena*, Intro.

"Particular souls, by reason of what they have in common, can only be understood as derived from a General Soul which is their cause, but is not identical with all or any of them, . . . containing as identical with its own nature the eternal ideas of all the forms, general and particular, that become explicit in the things of time and space" (*Plotinus*).—T. WHITTAKER, *Neo-Platonists*, p. 55.

"All things are from eternity in God, not indeed in gross material form, but as the work of art exists in the master. When God regarded himself, he saw the eternal images of all things prefigured in himself, not, however, in multiplicity, but as one image. Eckhart follows Thomas in proclaiming the doctrine that there exists an eternal world of ideas.

Distinct from this is the world of creatures."—UEBERWEG, *Hist. of Philos.*, Vol. I. p. 475.

"These Ideas (*i.e.* the eternal archetypes of things), which are the first causes of individual existences, are contained in the Divine Wisdom or the divine Word, the only-begotten Son of the Father. Under the influence of the Holy Ghost (or the fostering divine love) they unfold their effects, which are the created objects, or the external world." (*J. Scotus Erigena.*)—*Ibid.*, Vol. I. p. 362.

"Speaking about the Son of God, Ruysbrock said—'I believe that the Son is the Image of the Father, that in the Son have dwelt from all eternity, foreknown and contemplated by the Father, the prototypes of all mankind. We existed in the Son before we were born. He is the creative ground of all creatures —the eternal cause and principle of their life. The highest essence of our being rests therefore in God,—exists in his Image in the Son.' "—VAUGHAN, *Hours, etc.*, Vol. I. p. 326.

"The Celestial Man is the 'seventh day'; all combat then ceaseth and it is sanctified. Every regenerate person is a 'sabbath,' when he becometh celestial ; because he is a likeness of the Lord."—SWEDENBORG, *Arc. Cel. to Gen.* ii. 2.

The Higher Self descends into matter during six stages of Involution (six days). The seventh stage is the completed Archetypal Man in whom activity ceases for a time and he is said to die. Every soul is destined to become perfect on the higher planes and be made the image of the Divine Archetype.

"It is taught (in the Upanishads) that the âtman created the universe and then entered into it as soul. Here for the first time we meet with the word *jîva âtman*, which later denotes 'the individual soul' as contrasted with the supreme. But no such contrast yet exists here. It is the âtman himself who alone exists and creates the universe, who as *jîva âtman* enters into the universe that he has created. Neither from the point of view of pure idealism, nor in its empirical varieties of pantheism and cosmogonism, does any opposition exist between the supreme and individual souls. The contrast between them is first seen at the moment in which the âtman who creates the universe and then enters into his creation becomes a duality, the parts of which are set over against one another. We have described this further accommodation to the empirical consciousness as Theism, since here the original unity of the âtman is divided into God and the Soul."—DEUSSEN, *Phil. of Upanishads*, p. 258.

From the Absolute (Father) proceeds the manifest God (Son), the Higher Self (Christ) who descends as Spirit into Matter, imparting by the process of involution all qualities and forms of growth which are subsequently to be evolved in nature. The Higher Self is the Agent of the Supreme, He is all and in all, and operates in countless ways in the Divine scheme. At a certain stage in the involutionary cycle the Self starts forth to become the Archetypal Man by being born on the mental plane in order to commence his evolution in the aspiring mind. As the germ-soul in the causal-sheath, he begins to evolve as the ideal life of the Soul. This spiritual evolution (or potential involution), then, having proceeded upward when evolution is begun, is capable of being reflected downwards to the lower planes. The Self makes, as it were, a trial trip, and thereby becomes organised as the Archetypal Man. The greater Self undergoes beforehand on the higher planes the ideal life experiences of the lesser Self which transpire subsequently. In human evolution these primal experiences of the Self are distorted beyond recognition, owing to the fact that they do not appear on the lower planes in a sequential or coherent form.

"The image and likeness of God . . . more probably points to the Divine pattern and archetype after which man's intelligent nature was fashioned; reason, understanding, imagination, volition, etc., being attributes of God; and man alone of the animals of the earth being possessed of a spiritual nature which resembled God's nature. Man in short was a spirit, created to reflect God's righteousness and truth and love, and capable of holding direct communion with Him."—STANLEY LEATHES, Smith's Dict. of Bible, art. Adam, p. 44.

"In reference to the world, Christ is the Agent in creation; 'through Him are all things' (1 COR. viii. 6), and we through Him. He pre-existed 'in the form of God' (PHIL. ii. 6) from the beginning. He is 'the first-born of all creation; in Him and through Him and unto Him are all things. He is before all things, and in Him all things hold together' (COL. i. 15, 16). All things are to be summed up in Him (EPH. i. 10). 'He is all and in all' (COL. iii. 11). His reign is co-extensive with the world's history. 'He must reign till He hath put all His enemies under His feet.

The last enemy that shall be abolished is death.' Only 'when all things have been subjected unto Him, shall the Son also Himself be subjected to Him that did subject all things unto Him, that God may be all in all' (1 COR. xv. 24–28). —W. R. INGE, Paddock Lectures, p. 40.

"Christ is the ideal, representative man, the archetype of the race, as Adam is the concrete, imperfect copy of the archetype. 'In Christ,' the pure archetype is imparted to man. As Christ is the image of the invisible God, so we are 'transformed into the same image from glory to glory.' By the resurrection the earthly flesh was overcome, and the spirit of the heavenly man was set free as the animating principle of a new humanity. This is the meaning of the 'new creation.' "— W. R. INGE, Constructive Quarterly, June, 1913.

"Underlying this ceaseless flux is something abiding, archetypal, spiritual, —something by which these ever-floating atoms are for the time compelled to take upon themselves the bodily form in which they are manifested to the senses,—something which holds the same relation to the ordinary body as that which is held by the Platonic Idea to the Platonic Eidolon, or by the body celestial to the body terrestrial. Without such something the ordinary body is simply nothing. Ordinary body, in short, must hold its very existence in fee from Spirit, and there is no escape from this conclusion. Moreover, the traces of archetypal unity which are everywhere perceptible in the organic world may be looked upon as supplying evidence to the same effect; for may not these show that the bodies of different living creatures are not things apart, as they would seem to be at first sight, but parts of a connected whole which has its real foundation in the unity of the Divine Being?"—C. B. RADCLIFFE, Man Trans-corporeal. Cont. Review, Dec., 1874, p. 128.

"Unless God had been first we—our whole human race in general and each of us in particular—never would have been at all. We are what we are because He is what He is. Everything which we do God has first made it possible for us to do. Every act of ours, as soon as it is done, is grasped into a great world of activity which comes from Him; and there the influence and effect of our action is determined. Everything that we know, is true already before our knowledge of it. Our knowing it is only the opening of our intelligence to receive what is and always has been a part of His being, who is the universal Truth. Every deed or temper or life is good or bad as it is in harmony or out of harmony with Him."—PHILLIPS BROOKS, Light of the World, p. 40.

"Christ is that perfect Humanity

ARCHETYPAL MAN

CELESTIAL PLANE		Realm of Love	*Atma*
		World of Potency	
SPIRITUAL PLANE		Realm of Wisdom	*Buddhi*
		World of Fixed Prototypes	
Higher **MENTAL PLANE** Lower		Realm of Causes . . . . World of Man	*Manas*
ASTRAL PLANE		Realm of Desires	*Kama*
		World of Similitudes	
PHYSICAL PLANE		Realm of Effects	*Sthula*
		World of the Senses	

ARCHETYPAL MAN (vertical, center upper) — *Natural Man* (vertical, center lower)

The potential Evolutionary Scheme of Divine manifestation in the universe and man is called the Archetypal Man for three reasons : (1) Because the human being is the only example of life on this planet which is individually conscious on the mental plane, and is mentally in touch with the emotions proceeding from the higher planes. (2) Because this unique constitution of man makes him a measure of the universe, for he subtends, latently and actively, the whole of the five planes of manifestation. (3) Because as man is thus the Microcosm of the Macrocosm, his totality on the higher planes is identical with the Archetypal Man, while on the lower planes he is active as the natural man.

The Archetypal Man, or World-soul, is to be regarded as the Divine Life of the solar universe, visible and invisible, and also of the human soul both as to formative idea and phenomenal action. The Divine Life became organized for phenomenal activity in time and space, by means of the process of spiritual Involution whereby mental, astral and physical matter became endowed with all the qualities needed for Evolution, qualities which we observe to-day in all natural conditions and growth of forms. The Sacred Books teach us that the Archetypal Man became complete in plenitude at the close of the cycle of Involution ; whereupon there was a period of rest, or pralaya, before renewal of activity in the present cycle of Evolution.

The supreme intelligence of the Archetypal Man proceeds from the higher mental plane and is manifest throughout all nature. On this plane are the *directive causes* of all phenomena, while on the physical plane are the *directed forces* producing the effects which we perceive by means of our five senses. The laws of physics and chemistry are expressed by science in mental terms, thus proving that the causation of the phenomena investigated is mental and not physical. The causative intelligence from within is very obvious in the building up of plant and animal organisms. In their growth these are constructed molecule by molecule ; each molecule being directed in purposeful accordance with a fixed scheme or plan of the growth and maturity of each particular species of organism.

within us, from which we have been
momentarily estranged by selfishness and
the want of self-sacrifice, but which is
ever at hand to weld us again into Itself
and restore us to God. . . . For Christ
is not ' a man ' but ' MAN.' "— J. G.
ADDERLEY, *Symbolism of the Mass.*

" It is impossible to think of God
except as the infinite and perfect of
ourselves. If it was a human conception,
then it was a true human conception or
intuition, of God, of ourselves, and of
our relation to God, that in the beginning
laid the foundation of religion in the
fact that we are created or constituted
in the image of God ; and that the
beginning and principle of all spiritual
instinct and impulse is the natural
movement and effort of the spirit in us,
to fulfil itself in that image, to realise
itself as Son of God, to become perfect
as our Father in Heaven is perfect."—
W. P. Du BOSE, *Constructive Quarterly,*
March 1913, p. 11.

" ' Man may change, but thou art
God, and Thy nature is perfection.'
When God begins the nobler creation in
any heart, it cannot be that anything
short of the full completion and entire
working out of His purpose and His
plan, shall be the goal and end of His
activity. If a Spirit, all-powerful and
infinite, is working in me, never can its
work be finished until its work is perfected."—A. MACLAREN, *Sermons, 1st
Series,* p. 49.

" For other foundation can no man
lay than that which is laid, which is
Jesus Christ."—1 COR. iii. 11.

" Christ recognised Himself as the Man
to whom all the past history of the race
had tended, the Man from whom all the
future history of the race was to flow.
He declared Himself not only to be a
Man, but the archetypal Man."—STOP-
FORD A. BROOKE, Serm., *The Baptism of
Christ.*

" We are justified in holding that,
whatever else He may be, God is essentially man, that is, He is the fount of
humanity. There must be one side, so
to speak, of the infinitely complex being
of God in which humanity is eternally
contained, and which finds expression
in the finite universe. Humanity is not
a vague term. We ought not to interpret it in terms of the primeval savage,
or even of average human nature to-day,
but in terms of what we have come to
feel is its highest expression, and that is
Jesus. If we think, therefore, of the
archetypal eternal Divine Man, the
source and sustenance of the universe,
and yet transcending the universe, we
cannot do better than think of Him in
terms of Jesus ; Jesus is the fullest
expression of that eternal Divine Man
on the field of human history."—R. J.
CAMPBELL, *The New Theology,* p. 89.

" Aristotle's dictum in the *Politics,*
that ' the nature of a thing is that which

it has become when its process of development is completed.' That is the other
side of the Platonic doctrine of ideas,
that behind and antecedent to things as
we see them are the ideas of them which
are perfect and eternal. Every man
carries in him the plan „of a Perfect
which his own nature at once suggests
and craves after."—J. BRIERLEY, *The
Eternal Religion,* p. 227.

See ADAM (higher), ADAMAS (higher),
ADAPA, AFU-RĀ, ALTAR (fire), AMENI,
ARHATS (three), ASO, ATONEMENT,
ATZEEL, BALDER, BOLTS, BUDDHA,
CARAPACE, COSMOS, CREATION, CRU-
CIFIXION (Christ, Purusha), DEATH
OF BALDER, OSIRIS, ETC., DEMIURGE,
DHRUVA, DIONYSUS, DISMEMBER-
MENT, EVOLUTION, FATE-SPHERE,
FRAVASHI, GATHA (days), GLORY,
GOSPEL STORY, HEALING, HIGHER
(natures), HUMAN BODY, IMAGE, IN-
CARNATION, INVOLUTION, ISVARA,
JESUS (son of God), KAGU-TSUCHI,
KAIOMARTS, LEMMINKAINEN, LIMBS,
MACROCOSM, MAHAVIRA-POT, MEASURE,
MEDIATOR, MEMBERS, NET (golden),
OANNES, OHONAMOCHI, OSIRIS, PRA-
GÂPATI, PROTOTYPES, PTAH, PURUSHA,
RAGHA, SABBATH, SEAL, SEASONS
(five), SELF, SEPHIROTH, SHEPHERD
(good), SIMILITUDES, SINA, SON OF
GOD, SON OF MAN, SOUL AND BODY,
SOUL (highest), TOMB, TORTOISE,
VIRGO, VISVAKARMAN, YAO, YMIR,
ZAGREUS, ZODIAC, ZOROASTER.

ARDEBEHESCHT, KING OF FIRE :—

A symbol of the Atma-buddhic
principle.

See AMSHASPANDS, ASHA, DEVAS,
FUDO.

ARENA OF LIFE :—

A symbol of the lower quaternary,
or the mental, astral and physical
planes on which the Soul expresses
itself under the aspects of Will,
Wisdom and Love.

See FIELD, KNOWER, QUATERNARY,
SETTLEMENTS, TUAT, VARA, WORLD,
ZODIAC.

ARES (MARS) :—

A symbol of the astral function
intensified through the action of
manas.

" Ares is the personification of bold
force and strength, and not so much
the god of war, as of its tumult, confusion, and horrors."—*Smith's Class. Dict.*

" Ares " signifies the desire-mind not so much an adversary of the Self, as the natural impulse towards maintaining life in the forms.

See BOAR, MARS.

ARETE, WIFE OF ALCINOUS :—

A symbol of the perfected emotion-nature allied with the Divine will in the soul.

See ALCINOUS.

ARGIVES :—

A symbol of the lower desires and emotions active on the desire-mental plane.

" Apollo aimed against the Argives his deadly darts. So the people began to perish in multitudes, and the God's shafts ranged everywhither throughout the wide host of the Achaians."—*Iliad*, Bk. I.

The Higher Self opposed with the Will (sword of the Spirit) the workings of the lower self. Hence the lower qualities gradually diminished in strength and numbers ; and the action of the Divine Will being directed to the suppression of the lower mental qualities, these are overcome.

See APOLLO, ARROW, ODYSSEUS, PEOPLE, PESTILENCE, PRIZE.

ARGO, THE SHIP OF JASON :—

A symbol of the causal-body as a vehicle of the Spirit and the higher qualities, in the evolutionary cycle.

" The ship which the Greeks call the Argo was the representation of the barque of Osiris."—PLUTARCH, *Isis and Osiris*, § 22.

" Argus with the aid of Athena, built for Jason a galley, called from himself Argo. In her prow Athena set a plank, cut from the speaking oak of Dodona."—*Argonautic Expedition.*

The Higher Self with the aid of Wisdom, built a buddhic vehicle,—the higher causal-body,—for his evolution. In the forefront, Wisdom placed a mast of Truth (speaking oak).

" And as they were passing by the Absyrtean Isles, the Argo spoke, and said that the anger of Zeus would not be appeased until they went to Ausonia, and were purified by Circe."—*Ibid.*

And as the consciousness is raised to the condition of spiritual vision, so it becomes aware of its own nature, and realises the Divine intention (anger of Zeus), which is that the soul shall attain to perfection (Circe) and possess the knowledge of all its possibilities.

See ABSYRTUS, AGNIHOTRA, AMYCUS, ANCEUS, ARGUS, ARK, BOAT, CIRCE, JASON, PHÆATIANS, SHIP OF MANU.

ARGONAUTS :—

A symbol of twelve, or fifty, higher qualities and Divine attributes, centred about the incarnate Self (Jason) in the causal-body (Argo).

When the heroes were all assembled, they took auguries, and offered sacrifices to Zeus, the Winds, and the Waves, the Night, and Paths of the Sea. The signs being favourable, they got on board and put to sea."—*Argonautic Expedition.* KEIGHTLEY, *Mythology.*

And when the higher qualities were assembled, they sanctified themselves, or consecrated their powers to the service of the Infinite which they beheld, as it were, by regarding the manifestations of God's wondrous might in the Universe. And all being now favourable, they embarked in the vessel of the soul which should carry them to the " promised land " whither they went. The " sea " signifies the reflection upon the astral plane, of what occurs from buddhi ; the higher plane being the plane of causation and prototypal perfection.

Nature is the realm of things, the supernatural is the realm of powers. There the spinning worlds return into their circles and keep returning. Here (within) the grand life-empire of mind, society, truth, liberty, and holy government, spreads itself in the view, unfolding always in changes, vast, various, and divinely beneficent. There we have a Georgic, or hymn of the seasons ; here an epic that sings a lost Paradise. There God made the wheels of His chariot and set them rolling. Here He rides forth in it, leading His host after Him ; vast in counsel, wonderful in working ; preparing and marshalling all for a victory in good and blessing ; fashioning in beauty, composing in spiritual order, and so gathering in the immense populations of the worlds to be one realm—angels, archangels, seraphim, thrones, dominions, principalities, powers and saints of mankind—all to find, in His works of guidance and new-creating grace, a volume of wisdom, which it will be the riches of their eternity to study."—H. BUSHNELL, *Nature and the Supernatural*, p. 189.

See APOSTLES, ATALANTA, BULLS (brass), CHARIOT, CRETE, DISCIPLES, HEROES, SACRIFICE, SHAVING.

ARGOS (PELASGIC) :—

A symbol of the domain of the potential on the higher planes, or the potential beginning of things.

See PELASGIANS.

ARGUS, SON OF PHRIXUS :—

A symbol of the Higher Self who proceeds from the Supreme (Phrixus).

See ARGO.

ARHAT,—"HE WHO SEES NIR-VANA" :—

A symbol of the ego who has attained consciousness on the buddhi-manasic levels, through the consummation of the physical life at the end of the present period, when the Self within the soul has arrived at every experience which it is necessary that he should undergo. This condition of consciousness implies the having passed an initiation equivalent to that symbolised in the "crucifixion of Jesus."

See ASCETIC, ASEKA, INITIATIONS, MASTER, WALKS.

ARHAT WITHOUT A COUNTER-PART :—

A symbol of the Absolute Being, the unmanifest Supreme Self.

"That Arhat is here saluted, who has no counterpart,—who as bestowing the supreme happiness, surpasses (Brahman) the Creator, — who as driving away darkness, vanquishes the sun,—and as dispelling all burning heat, surpasses the beautiful moon." — *Buddha-Karita*, Bk. I. 1.

The Supreme Self is hailed as One without a Second,—as the Unmanifest,—That in which all things consist and subsist,—That which is Bliss,—That which is above the Creator in that it is both Creator and created, and beyond them both ; the Ineffable Unity who is all Light, and comprehends all light,—who is all Truth, and surpasses the moon in that the One is not a reflection, but is True Being,—Divine Reality.

See ABSOLUTE, BRAHMA, FATHER, GODHEAD, KAPILA, TRINITY.

ARHATS OF THREE GRADES :—

Symbolic of three states of consciousness successively experienced on the higher mental and buddhic planes, after the attainment of perfection on the lower planes.

"First, the simple Arhat (who is perfect, freed from all pain, from all the ten fetters and from all attachment to existence). Second, far above the simple Arhat, the Pratyeka-Buddha or Solitary Saint, who has attained perfection for himself and by himself alone. . . . Third, the supreme Buddha or Buddha *par excellence*, who having by his own self-enlightening insight attained perfect knowledge, and having, by the practice of the transcendent virtues and through extinction of the passions and of all desire for life, become entitled to that complete extinction of bodily existence, in which the perfection of all Arhatship must end, has yet delayed this consummation that he may become the Saviour of a suffering world by teaching men how to save themselves." —MON. WILLIAMS, *Buddhism*, p. 134.

The first Arhat signifies the perfected individuality in the causal-body freed from attachment to the lower nature and without a personality. In this state the consciousness is buddhi-manasic. The second grade is represented by the individual monad or Divine Spark (Paccekabuddha) on the plane of atma, who is perfect of himself and has no lower nature. The third grade specifies the Higher Self (Buddha) who has descended into the matter of the lower planes in the cycle of involution, and, as the Archetypal Man, has attained all knowledge, power, and virtue, with complete control over the lower nature of humanity in its desires, passions, and appetites. He, the indwelling Self, being perfect and complete in the inner being of each striving human soul, remains in manifestation to be the Saviour of the suffering world of humankind. He saves all souls by teaching them how to discipline their lives and thoughts so that they may fit themselves for the redeeming grace which he is ever ready to bestow.

See ARC. MAN, ASRAMAS, BUDDHA, HOUSEHOLDER, MONAD OF LIFE, PACCEKA, SHORE (other), TRI-RATNA.

ARID :—

A symbol of a condition empty of active qualities.

ARIES, THE ZODIACAL SIGN :—

A symbol of the first period of the cycle of life. The Ram or Lamb (Varak) signifies the Divine Sacrifice at the outgoing of the Spirit on the upper buddhic plane, in which the Higher Self limits himself to conditions of manifestation. The "Lamb" is slain in involution, for the nourishment of the souls and qualities in evolution.

"Christ's special symbol is Aries, which in India is a Horse. In a figure from the catacombs we see the horse emerging from the waters."—A. LILLIE, *Budd. in Christendom*, p. 8.

"'Once when thou (Buddha) wert the White Horse, in pity for the suffering of man, thou didst fly across heaven to the region of the evil demons to secure the happiness of mankind.' (From Buddhist Gâthâs.) *Footnote.*—Yearly the sun-god as the zodiacal horse (Aries) was supposed by the Vedic Aryans to die to save all flesh. Hence the horse sacrifice."—A. LILLIE, *Pop. Life of Buddha*, p. 58.

The "region of the evil demons" is the present existence wherein are the desires (demons).

"In Persia, the sign Aries, the ram, was known as the lamb; and in the Mithraic mysteries at the Christian era, it was a lamb that was slain."—J. M. ROBERTSON, *Religious Systems*, p. 202.

In the second chapter of the *Bundahis*, Varak (the *Lamb*) is given as the first of the twelve signs or constellations. It is as a *Ram*-headed man that Afu-Rā, the incarnate God, enters the first compartment of the twelve divisions of the Tuat-night of twelve hours. The Zodiac with its twelve signs, the Year with its twelve months, and the Tuat with its twelve hours, all signify the great Cycle of Life in which the Self (sun) first becomes obscured in matter, and second, rises from matter to become fully manifest in the souls of humanity at the end of the cycle. The reason the sign is named "Lamb" rather than "Ram" is that the Self is *born* in the sign, and therefore is young.

"Cosmically Aries represents the initial stage in evolution where spirit descends into matter to bring into existence a universe. It is the supreme act of Divine sacrifice, which is again reflected when man is made 'a living soul.'"—J. H. VANSTONE, *Lecture on the Zodiac*.

See AFU-RĀ, AMENT, APES (nine), BUDDHA, DAWN, DEMONS, EQUINOX, EVOLUTION, HELL, HORSE SACRIFICE, HORSE (white), INVOLUTION, JESUS (lamb), LAMB, MARRIAGE (lamb), NET-RĀ, NIGHT, RAM, SACRIFICER, TAURUS, TUAT, YEAR, ZODIAC.

ARITS, SEVEN, — HALLS OR GATEWAYS OF OSIRIS :—

Symbolic of seven states of the Soul in the cycle of Life, through which the Divine ego of the individual passes.

"The Osiris Ani, triumphant, shall say when he cometh to this (seventh) Arit :—'I have come unto thee, O Osiris, who art cleansed of thine impurities. Thou goest round about heaven, thou seest Rā, thou seest the beings who have knowledge."—BUDGE, *Book of the Dead*, Ch. CXLVII. p. 478.

This signifies the triumph of the individual soul over the lower nature at the end of a cycle. The soul purified of the lower desires and emotions, identifies itself with its Higher Self, and becomes conscious of conditions on higher planes. It perceives intuitively the Divine love and wisdom.

"You draw the life of the soul immediately from the immanent God, the Christ who is the life of the world. The Holy Spirit, the light divine, coming straight from the Eternal Father, through the Christ, is revealing that Christ within your soul and fashioning you into his spiritual likeness."—R. J. CAMPBELL, *Serm., The Divine Trinity.*

See ANCESTORS, COME UNTO THEE, CONSUMMATION, HAST, PATRIARCHS, TUAT.

ARIZURA, NECK OF :—

A symbol of desire for the objects of sense, or the lust of the eyes.

"The first place (whereon is most sorrow) is the neck of Arizura wherein hosts of friends rush forth from the burrow of the Drug."—*Vendidad*, III.

The "first place" in the lower nature producing suffering and sorrow, is the lust of the eyes—desire. The "fiends" are the sense objects which allure. The "burrow of the Drug" signifies the same as the "bottomless pit of the Beast," that is, the sense nature, or desire nature, that is never satisfied.

See BOTTOMLESS PIT, DRUG, HARPIES, NICOTHEA, PIT, SERPENT.

ARJUNA, SON OF INDRA AND PRITHA :—

A symbol of the personality ensouled by the spiritual ego or divine spark. "Arjuna" is therefore the progeny of God (Indra) and nature (Pritha).

"Achilles has qualities in common with Arjuna."—MON. WILLIAMS, *Indian Wisdom*, p. 425.

The symbols "Achilles" and "Arjuna" have the same signification.

"At this time Krishna and Arjuna, standing in a splendid chariot drawn by white horses, also sounded their conches, which were of celestial form : the name of the one which Krishna blew was Pânchajanya, and that of Arjuna was called Deva-datta—'the gift of the gods.' "—*Bhagavad-Gita*, Ch. I.

At this period of soul-growth, the Higher Self and the lower Self (personality) were established from centres in the causal-body (chariot) in the higher mind (white horses), and commenced to function,—the one above and the other below. The "conches of celestial form" signify the spiritual means of development. "Krishna's conch sounded," is a symbol of the Spirit operating from within as proceeding from the incarnate archetypal Self. "Arjuna's conch sounded," symbolises the buddhic transmutations of the lower qualities ; or spiritual gifts. "Arjuna's crest was Hanuman," signifies the personality's possession of intellect (Hanuman).

"To get well into the mind Rothe's conception of the universe, as having for its one end the development of spiritual personality by the conflict in all worlds, of free-will with circumstance, a view in which difficulties, sorrows, pains are regarded as factors in the process, and heaven and the angelic hierarchy as some of its achieved results, is to sweep as with a keen north wind the fogs out of our brain, and to set us cheerfully to work."—J. BRIERLEY, *Studies of the Soul*, p. 191.

"We must make a distinction of the two great forms of being, and ask : What is that which is and has no becoming, and what is that which is always becoming and never is ? "—PLATO, *Timæus*.

"The being which is always becoming and never is, is our being in this world of sense ; that which is and has no becoming is the being of God, eternal, unchangeable, all-complete. The former is never wholly satisfied, nor can be until it is at one with the latter ; it is a state of lack and hindrance, a state of discord and trouble, a state of sin and woe."—R. J. CAMPBELL, Serm., *The Eternal Satisfaction*.

See ACHILLES, BHISMA, BIRTH OF KRISHNA, CHARIOT, GOPIS, HANUMAN, KARNA, KRISHNA, PANDAVAS, PERSONALITY.

ARK OF BULRUSHES OF THE BABE MOSES :—

A symbol of the mental condition of simplicity and aspiration in which the nascent moral nature is brought up.

"And when she (the mother) could no longer hide him, she took for him an ark of bulrushes, and daubed it with slime and with pitch ; and she put the child therein, and laid it in the flags by the river's brink."—EXOD. ii. 3.

And when the growing moral nature (Moses) became distinguishable from the emotion-nature (woman) that gave it birth, the emotions separated it off and by craft limited its scope, leaving it in simplicity and solitude to its aspirations (bulrushes, flags). The ethical beginnings (Moses) could not have endured the complexities of the external warring conditions, or multifarious lower plane activities : and must needs be nurtured in isolation and truth (water), and reared by an affection,—the daughter of a ruler of the lower nature.

See JOHN BAPTIST, MANGER, MOSES, PITCH, RULER.

ARK OF SAFETY :—

A symbol of the causal-body in which the Higher Self and its higher qualities traverse the changing lower nature during the manvantara or great cycle of life.

"Christ is the Ark, . . . we must bear the Christ upon us, and have the Temple of this Ark within us."—BOEHME, *Myst. Mag.*, p. 200.

"Christ is the Ark, taking the chosen family (of faithfulness and piety) from the world of judgment to the new heavens and the new earth (after destruction has passed on the old)."—A. JUKES, *The Law of the Offerings*, p. 21.

"The elect are delivered, first mystically by baptism, that passage through the waters, which figures death and resurrection ; and then actually, through that dying to the world and nature, which is both the judgment of the old, and the way for God's children to the new creation."—A. JUKES, *Types of Genesis*, p. 114.

"The ship of Ea is Destiny."—SAYCE, *Rel. of Anc. Babyl.*, p. 67.

See AFU-RĀ, ARGO, BOAT, BOAT (sektet), HOUSE IN HEAVEN, SHIP (Manu), TEMPLE.

ARK OF NOAH :—

A symbol of the causal-body as a means for the preservation of the individuality and the qualities of the soul, while lower conditions of growth are swept away.

"Make thee an ark of gopher wood; rooms shalt thou make in the ark, and shalt pitch it within and without with pitch."—GEN. vi. 14.

The Divine command is given the individuality (Noah) to form a causal-body, and in this higher mental vehicle several compartments for different functions are to be made. And it is to be limited in its nature within and without. "Pitch" is a symbol of limitation which provides for the distinguishment of truth.

"The ark, by which Noah (the spiritual mind) goes through the judgment,—formed by cutting down and judging the pride and strength of that soil in which the curse works,—figures the cross by which we are severed from the world, by which it is crucified to us, and we unto the world. As that ark was made up of many beams, so is the cross which delivers us from the world composed of many parts. . . . While in the old world, or amid the waves, the cross, like the ark, is our safety."—A. JUKES, *The Types of Genesis*, pp. 109, 110.

The "Ark" does in a measure correspond with the "Cross," in that they both indicate the junction between the higher and lower natures.

"The stories of the Ark are the three Principles. The seven persons point at the seven properties of the material life, that God will have children out of all the properties into his eternal Ark. The eighth person was Noah—the Righteous one."—J. BOEHME, *Myst. Mag.*, p. 196.

The "lower, second, and third stories" are the three higher sub-planes of the mental plane; as the causal-body is situate on the higher mind plane above the lower consciousness which perceives it not.

See ADAM'S BODY, BEASTS (clean), CAUSAL-BODY, CROSS, DELUGE, FLOOD, FOOD (man), LIVING THING, NOAH, WINDOW (ark).

ARK OF THE TESTIMONY :—

A symbol of the causal-body as the receptacle of evidence to bring conviction to the lower consciousness of the reality of the indwelling Divine nature as an Ideal for reverence and aspiration.

"And he (Moses) took and put the testimony into the ark, and set the staves on the ark, and put the mercy seat above upon the ark."—EXOD. xl. 20.

And the law of the moral nature was the means of preparing the mind for the reception within its most sacred shrine, i.e. the causal-body, of the Divine law of Love and Wisdom to be to the soul its Ideal for reverence and aspiration. The "mercy-seat" indicates forgiveness, that is, the Divine ignoring of past failures, and the concession of the soul's privilege of constant progression. And above this soul-state are the laws of the higher intelligence (cherubim), and the beautiful wings of aspiration.

"In the Ark of the Covenant there was but the Book of the Law, the Rod of Aaron, and the Pot of Manna. Even so that soul, which has no other aim than the perfect observance of the law of God, and the carrying of the Cross of Christ, will be a true Ark containing the true Manna, which is God" (*Catherine of Genoa*).—F. VON HUGEL, *Mystical Element*, Vol. II. p. 51.

See CAUSAL-BODY, CHERUBIM, FOOD (God), KARSHIPTA, MANNA, MOSES, SHEKINAH, SHEWBREAD.

ARMAITI, THE HOLY SPIRIT :—

A symbol of the principle of buddhi—Wisdom.

"Armaiti doubles righteousness by her actions."—*Gatha Ushtavaiti*.

The Wisdom principle transmutes the highest of the lower qualities on to its own plane, the buddhic.

See BUDDHI, GOLD, HOLY GHOST, ISIS, WISDOM.

ARMS, WEAPONS :—

Symbolic of outgoing energies of the soul on the mental plane,—the plane of conflict.

See BLACKSMITHS, WEAPONS.

ARMS OF THE BODY :—

Symbolic of action in relation to will on the mental plane. The use of the "left arm and the right" signifies the energy of the will incoming and outgoing. An "arm bent of Thoth" signifies inability of the mind to act with perfect unanimity, for unaided it cannot show perfect truth. Human figures shown without arms signify inaction, latency of powers and qualities.

"The prow and stern of the fourth boat terminate in heads of uraci, each of which is turned towards the deity who is kneeling in the middle of the boat. In the centre kneels a woman without arms, and before and behind her stands a man, who is likewise without arms."—BUDGE, Egypt. Heaven and Hell, p. 26.

The boat signifies the causal-body as the vehicle of the Divine Husbandman (Osiris Neper) who cultivates the lower nature (herbs and plants). But at this early stage the emotions (woman) and mental faculties (men) remain latent in regard to transmutation of qualities.

Arms "wandering bereft of shoulders," signify action destitute of directive capacity. "White arms" signify the pure and unsullied activities of the higher nature. This symbol is attached to the Wisdom Goddesses of the Greek scriptures (see Iliad).

See ASCENSION (Osiris), BOAT, CORN, HAND, RIGHT ARM, SHOULDER, THOTH, WHITE ARMED.

ARMY OF THE GODS, OR HOSTS OF THE LORD :—

A symbol of the disciplined mental qualities, ready to do battle with the desires and lower impulses, for the sake of ideals.

See HOSTS, SOLDIERS, WARRIORS.

ARMY BEING FORMED OF THE PEOPLE OF A COUNTRY :—

Symbolic of the organising and focalising of the mental qualities, so as to bring the powers of the soul to act from a common centre.

See CAMP, COUNTRIES, PEOPLE, QUALITIES.

ARMY OF THE DEMONS :—

A symbol of the desire-mental qualities.

"The army with a wide front shouting and flying in the air."—Homa Yasht.

This signifies the activity of the kama-manasic nature, wherein the desires and lower thought processes give rise to an unsettled state of the lower self.

See DAEVAS, DEMONS.

AROUERIS, THE ELDER HORUS :—

A symbol of the Second Logos, the indwelling God born upon the buddhic plane.

"Upon the second (of the five new days), Aroueris, whom some call Apollo, others, the elder Horus, was born."—PLUTARCH, Isis and Osiris, § 12.

The "five days" signify the five planes of manifestation, upon the second of which,—the buddhic,—the incarnate Self has his first birth.

See APOLLO, BIRTH OF HORUS, DAYS (five), GATHA DAYS, HORUS, WORLDS (five).

ARREST OF THE SUN, MOON, AND STARS IN THEIR COURSES BEFORE THE BIRTH OF THE HOLY CHILD :—

Symbolic of the individuality, personality, and several modes of their mental expression, being, as it were, formed through a special operation which corresponds to a change in the direction of their activities. Before the Soul is emanated, the various departments of being are said to be arrested inasmuch as the efforts of the Logos which produce them, require that the forces concerned with their emanation shall be conducted into new channels, prior to which an arrest in their previous course appears to be made. This, refers to the period of involution when the Soul is born into the lower nature.

See ARROWS (divine), BIRTH OF ZOROASTER, BOAT (sektet), MOON (waxing), SUN (catching), SUN (motionless).

ARROGANT, ONE OF THE THREE TRIPLE POWERS :—

A symbol of the sense of separateness,—the "prince of this world,"—which rules the three self-seeking passions, love of power, lust, and avarice, each triple, because they act on the three lower planes.

"Pistis Sophia grieving because of the sufferings brought upon her by Arrogant one of the three Triple Powers."—Pistis Sophia.

This signifies the solicitude of the Higher Self for the sake of the lower :—it is a portrayal of the process of suffering through which the consciousness is lifted complete and entire to the realisation of Bliss.

"The Asuras came to naught even through arrogance : wherefore let no one be arrogant, for verily arrogance is the opening (or beginning) of ruin."—Sata. Brâh., V. 1, 1, 1.

The desires (asuras) in being energised by the sense of separateness bring about their own destruction as the ego rises to a wider consciousness.

See ASURAS, BLISS, SEPARATION, SOPHIA.

ARROW OF THE SPIRIT :—

A symbol of the higher will, harmonious with truth and aspiration :— a ray of the indwelling Self.

"Having taken the Upanishad as the bow, as the great weapon, let him place on it the arrow, sharpened by devotion ! Then having drawn it with a thought directed to that which is, hit the mark, O Friend, namely, that which is Indestructible ! Om is the bow, the Self is the arrow, Brahman is called the aim. It is to be hit by a man who is not thoughtless, and then as the arrow becomes one with the target, he will become one with Brahman."—*Mundaka Upanishad*, II.

The soul is directed to rely upon the Word of God, i.e. the expression of the Truth within ; and determine the will in accordance with the same. Then, with the mind aspiring towards the Highest, the soul is required to rest upon the Divine Reality which underlies the illusions of thought and sense. The expression of the indwelling Spirit (Om) is the energy outpoured in the soul ; the spiritual Ego is the will, and union with the Higher Self is the aim. Union is to be achieved by the mind which is above the lower mind (thoughtless), and then as the will becomes one with the aim, so the lower Self merges into the Higher Self.

"For the arrows of God to go forth in light (HAB. iii. 11), is for His words to resound with manifest truth." "Job bears witness saying, 'Because He hath opened His quiver and afflicted me.' For as arrows lie hid in the quiver, so do sentences lie hid in the secret counsel of God : and an arrow is drawn, as it were, from the quiver, when God launches forth an open sentence from His secret counsel. The machination of the wicked is also designated by the word 'quiver,' as is said by the Prophet, 'They have made ready their arrows in the quiver, that they may shoot in darkness at the upright in heart.' "—GREGORY THE GREAT, *Morals on the Book of Job*, Vol. III. pp. 365, 472.

"Thine arrows are sharp in the heart of the king's enemies ; whereby the people fall under thee."—Ps. xlv. 5.

"But God shall shoot at them (the wicked) with an arrow ; suddenly shall they be wounded."—Ps. lxiv. 7.

The will united with truth and righteousness causes the lower qualities which are adverse to the Spirit, to fall below the consciousness. The shaft of the Spirit directed against the unruly desires and passions weakens and subdues them.

See APOLLO, ARGIVES, OM, PESTILENCE, PONIARD, SWORD, UDGITHA, UNION.

ARROW, THE SELF-MOVING :—

A symbol of the illusive will of the lower self, which is moved to action by desire.

"The man who fills himself with meat, is filled with the good spirit. It is this man that can strive against the onsets of Astovîdhôtu : that can strive against the self-moving arrow."—*Vendidad*, IV. *S. B. of E.*

The mind that assimilates knowledge is filled with that which is necessary for its growth. The mind thus stored is able to withstand the temptations which may assail the ego from the plane of the desires, and hold in check the lower personality, or lower will.

See ASHEMOGHA, ASTOVIDAD, MEAT, PERSONALITY.

ARROWS, DIVINE :—

Symbolic of spiritual force which rises from within and dissipates desire, and also causes transmutation of lower qualities into higher on the buddhic plane.

The Adhvarya priest "then hands him (the Kshatriya king) three arrows. That first one by which he pierces on shooting, that is this earth, that one is called 'dribâ.' And the one by which (the enemy Vritra) being pierced lies either living or dead, that is the second, that is this air, that is called 'ruga.' And this one with which he misses (his aim), that is the third, that is yonder sky, that is called 'kshuma.' "—*Sata. Brâh.*, V. 3, 5, 29.

Through the individuality (priest), the personality (king) receives the means for conquering the desires and rising victorious. The first means is the lower nature (earth) by which the soul rises stage by stage. The second is the mental nature (air) by which knowledge is gained and the desire nature (Vritra) is controlled or rendered ineffective. The third is the higher emotion nature (sky) which is above the personality, and so is uncontrolled by it.

" The sun and moon stood still in their habitation ; at the light of thine arrows they went, and at the shining of thy glittering spear."—HAB. iii. 11.

The individuality (sun) and the personality (moon) were sometime latent in the causal-body ; then at the outpouring of the Spirit within, they went forth to manifest, having in them the enlightenment of the Divine Ray which dispels illusion.

" I (Lakshmi) reside in an arrow."—*Inst. of Vishnu*, 99, 15.

The buddhic principle is spiritual force symbolised by an arrow.

" Let a man take the five arrows (the five virtues), put them on the bow of his brain and kill Death " (*Guru Nanak*).—MACAULIFFE, *The Sikh Religion*, Vol. I. p. 368.

Let the mind act in accord with the highest ideals of virtue, and immortality will be reached by the consciousness.

See ADVARYA, ARREST, BHISMA, FUNERAL, NINE DAYS, PESTILENCE, SLAUGHTER, SOUND, SPEAR, VRITRA.

ARSH, THE " THRONE OF GOD :—

A symbol of the plane of atma, the highest of the five planes of existence.

See ATMA, KURSI, PARADISE, THRONE.

ARTEMIS, THE GODDESS :—

A symbol of the principle of buddhi under various aspects. As a " huntress " it signifies the quelling of desires (beasts) through the " arrows " of the Spirit.

See ARROWS (divine), BEASTS (wild), DIANA.

ARTERY :—

A symbol of a channel in the soul of the Divine life (blood) which flows from the " heart " or centre of being.

See BLOOD, CHANNELS, HEART.

ARTIFICER, OR ARTISAN :—

A symbol of the ego active on the physical plane,—the plane of work, contrivance, and adaptation. The activity is manifested through the physical body (Artisanship).

See ANUBIS, CLASSES, SUDRA.

ARURU, GODDESS :—

A symbol of the feminine, or matter, aspect of Divine manifestation.

" Ea under the mask of Merodach, is the creator of mankind as of all things else. In this act of creation the goddess Aruru is coupled with him."—A. H. SAYCE, *Rel. of Egypt. and Babyl.*, p. 382.

The First Logos (Ea) under the aspect of the Second (Merodach) produces all things. " Aruru " signifies the feminine, receptive principle, for duality is necessary to manifestation, matter and spirit being essential thereunto. " Ea, Merodach, and Aruru " constitute the Higher Triad or Divine Trinity.

See BUDDHI, EA, MĀYĀ (higher), MERODACH, MOTHER, TRIAD, TRINITY.

ARYANA-VAÊJO, THE FIRST GOOD LAND, BY THE RIVER DAITYA :—

A symbol of the buddhic plane, the first to possess relative truth.

" Aryana-Vaêjo was created a region of delight by Ahura-Mazda."—*Vendidad*, I.

The buddhic plane exists in the innermost remembrance of the ego as it descends in the period of involution, to the lower planes.

See BUDDHIC PLANE, BULL (man), DRAGON (red), EDEN, GATHA (ahuna).

ARYAVARTA, THE LAND OF THE ARYAS :—

A symbol of the mental plane, the plane of the mental qualities (Aryans).

See COUNTRIES, NAVEL.

ASAR, ÆSIR, OR ASES :—

A symbol of the three Divine Principles, or the Logos under the aspects of Will, Wisdom, and Activity.

" Then the three Ases of this band, full of power and goodness, descended towards the sea ; they found in the country some wretched beings, Ask and Embla, needing destiny. They had no soul, they had no understanding, neither blood, nor language, nor good exterior ; Odin gave the soul, Hoenir gave understanding, Lodur gave the blood and the good exterior."—*Voluspa*, 33–40.

Then the Logoi in might and love, descended, as it were, to the astral plane (sea) to endow the forms, now developed thereon, with human attributes. There they found in pre-human forms, Desire and Instinct, needing further powers of growth. These creatures had no spiritual or mental natures, no true life, no intelligent expression, no proper human forms. To these lower personalities the Divine Will (Odin) gave the Divine Spark, Wisdom (Hoenir) imparted the mind, and Activity (Lodur) through slow evolution brought about the inner life connections with the higher nature, and the effective, erect human form.

"Thereupon (Balder's death) the Asar (at Asgard) sent messengers over the whole world, and besought that all would weep Balder out of the power of Hell."—*Prose Edda.*

The Divine Triad establishes in the lower nature the means by which the indwelling Self (Balder) shall be released through the suffering of the lives in the forms. Thereupon the urgent necessity for the triumph of the Self becomes apparent, and within the entire nature a desire for liberation is manifest. This craving must needs be first of all thoroughly established in the lower self ere the prayer may penetrate to the sanctuary of the Higher One.

See ASGARD, ASKR, BALDER, DEATH OF BALDER, EYE (third), HIRUKO, HODER, MAN (born), MAN (crawled), MIMER, NET OF ASAR, ODIN, THOCK, WEEPING, YGGDRASIL.

ASCENSION OF JESUS :—

A symbol of the union of the Christ-soul with the Christ: that is, the Soul or lower Self (Jesus) having been perfected on the lower planes and raised to the higher, becomes merged in the Higher Self seated in the causal-body on the higher mental plane.

"And Jesus led them out until they were over against Bethany: and he lifted up his hands, and blessed them. And it came to pass, while he blessed them, he parted from them, and was carried up into heaven. And they worshipped him, and returned to Jerusalem with great joy: and were continually in the temple, blessing God."—LUKE xxiv. 50–53.

The Christ soul as the highest ideal led, as it were, the disciplined qualities to the level of the "abode of the Lord," where their affection for the highest enabled him to bless and strengthen them. And as they aspired they became aware of their shortcomings, and so lost sight of the Christ-soul as he disappeared in the Christ. But the Divine Love was not parted from the qualities which were attached to him. The parting was only apparent. They had to continue their work on the lower planes, having been blessed by his presence. He would return to them as soon as they were able to receive him, for they were only shut off from him, insomuch as their limitations were necessary for the fulfilling of their special work. The "worshipping" signifies the devotion and aspiration of those qualities which were awaiting union with the Highest. The "temple" typifies the veiled mysteries of inner being, before whose presence they bowed in adoration, mindful of the glories which awaited them.

"The Ascension, with which the Drama terminates, is that of the whole Man, now regenerate, to his own celestial kingdom within himself, where—made one with the Spirit,—he takes his seat for ever 'at the right hand of the Father.'"—*The Perfect Way*, p. 215.

"'I come again,' said Jesus, 'and receive you unto myself that where I am there ye shall be also.' Interpret that promise as being for to-day; interpret it spiritually, and you have what it was meant to impart. Our dear Lord is always coming in like manner as we have seen him go. The cloud of new and harsher conditions has veiled him from your sight for a time, but he has not really gone; he has but called you upward, bidden you aspire through those very conditions to the place he has prepared for you in the everlasting kingdom. And he will come back to you with a greater fulness of life and power when you can receive him again with the heart of a little child."—R. J. CAMPBELL, Serm., *Christ Going and Returning.*

See ÆON, (thirteen) BETHANY, BLESSING, CHRIST, CHRIST'S SECOND COMING, GLORIFYING, JERUSALEM, JESUS (gospels), JESUS (son of man), LIBERATION, QUALITIES, REDEMPTION, REGENERATION, RESURRECTION, TEMPLE, UNION.

ASCENSION OF OSIRIS :—

A symbol of the rising of the lower Self to become one with the Higher Self.

"He who is in this picture in the invisible form of Horus in the thick darkness, is the hidden image (of Osiris) which Shu lifteth up beneath the sky, and Keb-ur cometh forth in the earth in this image."—BUDGE, *Egypt. Heav. and Hell*, Vol. I. p. 278.

The entity depicted as Horus is the Osirified-soul perfected and ascending from the lower planes (darkness) in the "night of the Tuat," as the cycle (Tuat) closes. The Osirified-soul becomes lost in the Osiris, that is, the perfected lower Self becomes one with the Higher Self in the causal-body. The Divine Will (Shu) raises the personality (Keb-ur) which has developed from the lower nature (earth).

(The picture)—"The end of the Tuat, which is represented by a semi-circular wall or border formed of earth. At the middle point of this border is the disk of the sun which is about to rise, and joined to it is the head of the 'image of Shu,' with his arms stretched out along the rounded border of the Tuat. Above his head is the beetle, symbol of Kheper, who has emerged from the boat of the Sun-god ; and below is the 'image of Af,' that is to say, the body of the night Sun-god, which has been cast away."—*Ibid.*

This symbolical picture exactly describes the ascension of "Horus into Osiris" or "Jesus into Christ." The future period indicated is the end of the cycle,—the termination of the "12th hour of the Tuat." The "black sun-disk" represents the unapparent Higher Self (Osiris). It rises from the cycle through "Shu" the Divine Will. The "beetle Kheper" signifies the indwelling Self (Horus) ready now to rise from the lower nature (earth) and to become united with the Self (Osiris) in the causal-body (*image* of Shu). Now the lower Self (Kheper-Horus) having become perfected and resurrected, discards the personality (*image* of Af) it has worked through for so long. The image therefore lies as a corpse at the end of the cycle ; but it is depicted as *embalmed*, and has a large X cross marked upon it. This means that the personality has been perfected at the crucifixion and therefore dies to be re-born spiritually (as Horus) in the new life. The "image of Shu" has neither body nor lower limbs, thus signifying that the individuality in the causal-body no longer puts forth personalities to occupy bodies on the lower planes. After the cruci-

fixion (arms outstretched) the soul has ceased to possess any lower nature.

"Verily, verily, I say unto thee (Peter), When thou wast young, thou girdest thyself, and walkest whither thou wouldest : but when thou shalt be old, thou shalt stretch forth thy hands, and another shall gird thee, and carry thee whither thou wouldest not. Now this he spake, signifying by what manner of death he should glorify God."—JOHN xxi. 18, 19.

As "Peter" means the lower mind or lower personality, the symbolism precisely corresponds with the swathing of the mummy of "Af-Rā." "Peter's" arms are girded to his body, signifying inactivity of the personality, through the withdrawal of Spirit ("another"). But being perfected he, by dying, "glorifies God."

Truly hereby is declared the fate of the lower personality. When the lower mind (Peter) is undeveloped (young) it is a law to itself, and it directs the outer activities of the soul according to its will. But when it is perfected at the end of the cycle, then (another) the indwelling Self,—the spiritual ego,—becomes supreme over it and reduces it to impotence. The personality is permitted no longer any directive action, and so it yields up its life, being, as it were, crucified in matter with head (mind) downwards. The death of the lower mind signifies the perfecting of the soul or the glorifying of God.

See AFU-RĀ, ARMS (body), BOAT CAUSAL-BODY, CORPSE, CROSS, CRUCIFIXION, EMBALMMENT, FEED, GLORIFYING, HORUS, KHEPER, MUMMY, OSIRIS, PERSONALITY, PETER, SCARABÆUS, SHU, SUN-RISING, TUAT.

ASCETIC ; SELF-RESTRAINED MAN :—

A symbol of an individuality who, after liberation from all below the higher mind, "departs from his house," that is, rises above the causal-body, and continues his progress upward through the buddhic plane.

"Having performed the Ishti, sacred to the Lord of creatures (Pragâpati), where he gives all his property as the sacrificial fee, having reposited the sacred fires in himself, a Brâhmana may depart from his house as an ascetic, . . . after giving a promise of safety to all created beings. . . . Making over the merit of his own good actions to his friends, and the guilt of his evil deeds to his enemies, he attains the eternal Brahman by the practice of meditation."—*Laws of Manu*, VI. 38, 39, 79.

Having renounced as lower all that he has attained and is now possessed of, and putting his trust in the supreme sacrificial Law, the liberated ego turns his attention to the atma-buddhic energies within, and aspires beyond the causal-self ; firm in his resolve not to use his powers in frustration of the Divine scheme. To higher and lower plane activities, in schemes of manifestation which in him are to go forth, he bequeaths his acquirements. Then, freed from all relativity, he passes into the Supreme.

See AGNIHOTRA, ANCHORITE, ASRA-MAS, ARHAT, HERMIT, HOUSEHOLDER, LIBERATION, MONK, ORDERS, PRAGÂ-PATI, SANNYASIN, SOUL.

ASCETICISM, OR AUSTERITY :—

A symbol of the voluntary abandonment of outgoing activities in preparation for a new form or course of manifestation. It is an inbreathing of the ego or Self prior to an outbreathing of renewed life.

"As early as the creation myths we saw how the Creator of the universe prepared himself for his work by the practice of *tapas* (asceticism) ; in which word the ancient idea of the 'heat' which serves to promote the incubation of the egg of the universe blends with the ideas of the exertion, fatigue, self-renunciation, by means of which the creator is transmuted (entirely or in part) into the universe which he proposes to create. According to this conception, everything that is great in the universe is dependent on *tapas*,"—DEUSSEN, *Phil. of Upanishads*, p. 66.

The perfection of the manifest Self is the absolutely necessary end of the Soul-process, and is the condition that must be attained ere a life-cycle can close in the complete indrawal of the Self. The toil and fervour of the Self to perfect its manifested Life, and its renunciation of all outgoing energy, become the preparation for the next life cycle. The actual then disappears into the potential, which then is, as it were, a germ or

egg out of which a new universe, outer and inner, proceeds into actuality. Everything great is dependent on asceticism, because perfection attained implies the subjugation and cessation of every activity of the lower nature in its widest sense.

"The souls on their entrance into heaven are apostrophised :—'Which invincible by *tapas*, have won their way by *tapas* to the light, that have accomplished the severest *tapas*,—to these now enter in' (*Rig-Veda*, X. 154, 2)."—*Ibid.*, p. 66.

The spiritual egos or individual souls on the higher mental plane having become perfected through their efforts in a stage of their progress upward to the truth, withdraw entirely from the lower life, and enter into the consciousness of the buddhic plane. (It is obvious that the asceticism practised in India by "Yogins," has its origin in a literal and mistaken interpretation of the sacred writings.)

See ABSTINENCE, AUSTERITIES, BREATH, EGG, FASTING, HIRANYA-GARBHA, LIGHT, MANVANTARA, PENANCE, PRALAYA, SANNYASIN.

ASEEYATIC WORLD—THE WORLD OF ACTION :—

A symbol of the physical plane, the lowest plane of the quaternary.

See ADAM (lower), COUNTENANCE (greater), WORLDS (five).

ASEKA ADEPTSHIP :—

A symbol of the state of consciousness of the ego when raised to the highest possible point it can attain in the present cycle of twelve stages through which growth is accomplished. This would mean an atma-buddhic level, whereas the Arhat consciousness is buddhi-manasic. The next globe period will be capable of carrying the advanced ego up to the Aseka stage of being ; so it may be imagined this stage will probably be achieved in the future.

See ARHATS, ASCETIC, INITIATIONS, MASTER OF WISDOM, WALKS.

ASGARD :—

A symbol of devachan,—a state of rest on the higher mental plane wherein the ego withdraws after manifesting in an incarnation.

"Hermode then rode home to Asgard and related everything which he had both heard and seen."—*Story of Balder*.

And now the Soul passes inwards to devachan, and continues for awhile in a blissful and comparatively passive state, wherein every experience is digested and so incorporated in the substance of its being.

See ASAR, BALDER, DEATH OF BALDER, DEVACHAN, MUSPELHEIM, VALHALLA.

ASHÂDHÂ BRICK FOR ALTAR :—

A symbol of the lower quaternary out of which the immortal Self arises.

"This earth then is one brick (called Ashâdhâ), for Agni is this earth, since it is thereof that the whole Agni is built up. Now this earth is four-cornered; for the quarters are her corners : hence the bricks are four-cornered; for all the bricks are after the manner of this earth."
—*Sata. Brâh.*, VI. 1, 2, 29.

The lower nature (earth) is the one means by which the Spirit (Agni) manifests in a multiplicity of forms, for the Spirit is within the lower nature in its operations, since it is through the operations of the lower nature that finally the whole Spirit is fully evolved. Now the lower nature is of fourfold composition, for the four planes compose it ; hence the means (bricks) of development are fourfold, for all the means are organised conditions of the lower nature.

See AGNI, ALTAR (fire), BRICKS, EARTH, QUARTERS, QUATERNARY, SPEECH.

ASHA-VAHIST, OR ARDI-BAHIST, THE ARCHANGEL :—

A symbol of a high intelligence on the buddhic plane ; a messenger of the Logos to do his will.

See AMSHASPANDS, ANGELS, ARDA-BEHESCHT, DEVAS, GEUSH-TASHA, ZOROASTER.

ASHA-VANUHI, OR ASHISH VANUHI, DAUGHTER OF AHURA-MAZDA :—

A symbol of Wisdom, the principle of buddhi, an emanation of the Supreme.

"Let the water drops fall here for the destruction of the daevas and devis. May the good Sraosha slay them ! May Asha-vanuhi take up her abode here ! May Asha-vanuhi grant happiness here, in this sacred abode of Homa, the transmitter of righteousness.—*Homa Yasht.*

Let the truth of the Supreme be the means of dispelling the misconceptions and illusions which have been formed by attachment to the opinions and desires of the lower mind or desire nature. May the Divine power (Sraosha) be the means of annihilating the unreal ! May Wisdom now come into her birthright ! May Wisdom be the means of securing the bliss which is to flourish in the kingdom of Love, the dispenser of Righteousness !

"Ashish vanuhi makes the wisdom of all the prophets continue, and inspires them in their turn with the original wisdom."—M. HAUG, *Essays on Rel. of Parsis*, p. 215.

See BUDHI, DAEVAS, HOMA, SROSH, WISDOM.

ASHEMOGHA, THE UNGODLY :—

A symbol of ignorance and prejudice which retard mental growth, and obstruct knowledge.

"A man filled with the good spirit, can strive against the wicked tyrant and smite him on the head ; it is this man that can strive against the ungodly Ashemogha who does not eat."—*Vendidad*, IV. *S. B. of E.*

The mind that assimilates knowledge and truth, is able to withstand the pretensions of illusion (tyrant), and overcome it in its most subtle forms, such as pride. The ego thus equipped, can strive against ignorance and prejudice which do not allow of intellectual development. "Not eating" signifies not incorporating knowledge (meat).

See ARROW (self-moving), EATING, ILLUSION, MEAT, TYRANT.

ASHES OF PLANTS SCATTERED ON THE WATER FOR THE BIRTH OF AGNI :—

A symbol of the preparation for the birth of the indwelling Self in the lower nature of the soul.

"While meditating, the gods saw this,—'Let us take the fire-pan down to the water ; for the water is the foundation of this universe : having settled it thereon, we shall reproduce from out of the water what there is of Agni's nature in this heap of ashes.'—They then took it down and threw the ashes into the water ; and in like manner does this Sacrificer now take it down to the water. 'O divine waters, receive ye these ashes, and put them in a soft and fragrant place !'—that being consumed, matter has run its course. . . . 'Bear it on the waters, even as a mother bears her son.' 'In the waters, O Agni, is thy womb, . . . being in the plants' womb thou art born again. Thou art the child of the herbs, the child of the trees, the child of all that is, O Agni, thou art the child of the waters,—the child of the universe.' "—*Sata. Brâh.*, VI. 8, 2, 2–4.

The quiescent higher nature (the gods) then perceived that the time had arrived for God to manifest directly in the lower nature. The latent soul (fire-pan) is therefore to be brought down, as it were, to the astral plane (water) ; for the Divine Reality operates through the astral nature as a foundation for evolution. The soul, or higher nature, being firmly connected with the lower, there will then be reproduced from the astral nature what there is of spiritual quality in the latent matter of the soul (the ashes). So the higher and the lower natures were united for the expression of the Spirit. In like manner the individuality now emanates the ego into the lower vehicles at every incarnation.

O probationary existence, receive ye these latent higher qualities and place them in a mental condition of gentleness and purity, that becoming raised from latency, there may be no further need for the life of matter on the lower planes ! Bear ye the germ of Spirit in the purified lower nature, even as the virgin mother bears her Divine Son. In the purified emotions (waters) is the matrix of the Christ. In the transfigured emotion-nature (plants' womb) the Christ is re-born. Thou O Christ-soul ! art the child of the affections and aspirations, and of all nature. For, O indwelling God ! thou art brought forth from out of the waters of life and the phenomenal realm.

See AGNI, ALTAR (fire), CHILD, HEIFER, PLANTS, TREES, WATER (lower), WATER (higher).

ASHES AS DUST :—

A symbol of the lower mind or transitory lower nature of the soul.

"He hath cast me into the mire, and I am become like dust and ashes. I cry unto thee, and thou dost not answer

me : I stand up, and thou lookest at me."—JOB xxx. 19, 20.

The incarnate Self (Job) is unable to express himself in the natural man.

See DUST, INCARNATION, JOB, MAN (natural).

ASHNYMPHS :—

A symbol of the higher emotions attached to the "Tree of Life."

ASITA, THE SAGE :—

A symbol of the mental and emotional natures united primordially in the Cycle of Involution. This condition constitutes the higher state of the lower self on the mental plane, at the period indicated.

"Then having learned by signs and through the power of his penances, this birth of him (Buddha) who was to destroy all birth, the great seer Asita in his thirst for the excellent Law came to the palace of the Sakya king (Suddhodana)." —*Buddha-Karita*, Bk. I. 54.

Then having apprehended the meaning and significance of the coming of the Ego which is by suffering and travail to attain perfect Bliss, and to pass beyond the planes of manifestation (birth), the mental-nature united to the emotion-nature, draws nigh to the causal-self.

"Asita is called Kaladevala in the Pali version, both words having for root the adjective 'black.' "—A. LILLIE, *Budd. in Christendom*, p. 20.

The symbol "black" so applied indicates the unmanifest or subjective condition of the mental-emotional lower self at the beginning of involution.

"A holy One, a Rishi, called Asita or Kâla, the 'Black One,' 'dwelling at peace above the thirty-three heavens, seeing celestial signs, and hearing the celestial song,' descended to the grove, 'where he usually dwelt on earth.' But according to other accounts, he was a Tapaso or ascetic, from the Himalaya, called Kâla devala, which name corresponds with that of Asita. He gets to Kapilavastu, where Mâya tries to make the child bow its head in reverence towards the feet of Asita. But the child, 'by its spiritual power, turned himself round in his mother's arms, and presented his feet towards the Rishi, who begged to worship his feet.' "— E. DE BUNSEN, *Angel Messiah*, p. 36.

The lower self (buddhi-manas) in the involutionary cycle, recognises its coming development, and joy is aroused within it. It is illusion (Mâya) that imagines the Self (Buddha) making obeisance to the lower nature. The Higher Self must always be supreme over the lower self : hence the presentation of the feet to Asita, who now aspires towards the higher nature.

See ASCETIC, ASCETICISM, BIRTH OF BUDDHA, BLACK, BUDDHA, BUDDHA (marks), HEAVENLY VOICE, KAPILA, MÂYÂ, NURSE, PENANCE, SIMEON.

ASKR (ASH TREE) AND EMBLA (ALDER TREE) UPON THE SEA-SHORE :—

Symbols of the desire-nature and the instinct nature, fully developed through the astral evolution.

"The most perfect objects of vegetation are two trees Askr and Embla, upon the sea-shore. The Gods change these trees into man and woman by giving them the human soul and body" (*Voluspa*, V. 33–40).—IDA PFEIFFER, *Iceland*, p. 314.

This refers to the perfecting of the desire and instinct natures in the forms on the astro-physical plane (sea-shore), and the conferring by the higher nature, of mind and spirit on the lower personalities. This development requires the union of mind (man) with emotion (woman) in a fitting human body.

See ASAR, MAN, MATRO, RIMTHURSAR, SHORE, TREE, WOMAN, YMER.

ASO, QUEEN OF ETHIOPIA :—

A symbol of the receptive or feminine aspect of the potential on the higher planes.

"It is said that it was Queen Aso who secretly measured the body of Osiris, and made the chest in which it was laid."—PLUTARCH, *Isis and Osiris*, § 13.

The actual becomes the interpreter of the potential (Aso) and a vehicle of the measure of the Archetypal Man (Osiris) is builded of astro-mental matter for the Ego, by the forces which are controlled and guided from the potential.

See ARC. MAN, CHEST, DEATH OF OSIRIS.

ASPAHI-ASTRA WHIP :—

A symbol of the Cosmic Will in the laws of nature for the disciplining of the soul.

"If a man shall bury in the earth the corpse of a man or of a dog, and

not disinter within half a year, he shall pay penalties of 500 stripes with the Aspahi-astra and 500 with the Sraoshokarana."—*Vendidad*, III. *S. B. of E.*

If the lower personality (corpse) is not outgrown within a certain period, the ego continues to undergo those trials and sufferings which must come to it so long as it identifies itself with its lower nature (earth), imprisoned in the meshes of the matter of the lower planes (earth). The "500 stripes" signify the operations of the Cosmic Will. "Sraoshokarana" means the Divine purpose The "corpse of dog" signifies the lower or desire will.

See BONDAGE, CAPTIVITY, CORPSE, DOG, MAN, SRAOSHA, SUFFERING.

ASPIRATION :—

A symbol of the expression or reflection of the Divine life on the lower planes of the soul. It is the yearning within the lower nature for communion and union with the higher. It implies dissatisfaction and discontent with present states and conditions, and means the setting up of ideals of what is better and worthier. Aspiration must of necessity by the Divine law meet with response from above and the bestowal of higher qualities and faculties on the mind which turns from the world to God.

"We are united to God, when, in the practice of the virtues, we deny and forsake ourselves, loving and following God above all creatures. We cannot compel God by our love to love us, but He cannot sanctify us unless we freely contribute our effort. There is a reciprocal desire on our part and that of God. The free inspiration of God is the spring of all our spiritual life. Thence flows into us knowledge—an inner revelation which preserves our spirit open, and lifting us above all images and all disturbance, brings us to an inward silence. God dwells in the heart pure and free from every image" (Ruysbroek).—R. A. VAUGHAN, *Hours with Mystics*, Vol. I. p. 328.

"Our experiences in this world now and then lay bare unexpected spiritual sublimities, sweet and awful wonders of heart and soul, which forbid us to believe that that from which we have come forth is less than the highest the mind can conceive. Doubtless it is infinitely higher. My faith in God rests on the fact that the spirit that indwells all things makes response to mine when it calls, and that that response is always forthcoming,

however. high we pitch the note of our
appeal. There is something at the heart
of things that is more than equal to
every venture of the soul."—R. J.
CAMPBELL, Serm., *Man's Case against
God*.

See BLESSING, GOD BLESSING, GRACE,
PRAYER.

ASRAMAS, FOUR LIFE-STAGES :—

**Symbolic of four successive states
of consciousness of the ego as he
progresses upward to final union
with the Supreme Self.**

"The four *âs'ramas*, or life-stages,
according to which every Indian Brâhman
was under obligation to devote himself,
first as a *brahmac'ârin* to the study of
the Veda, then as *grihastha* to the duties
of the sacrifice and other good works,
next as *vânaprastha* to the practice of
asceticism in the jungle, and finally
towards the end of life as *parivrâjaka*
(*bhikshu, sannyâsin*) to a wandering
existence without possessions or home,
awaiting only his soul's release and its
reception into the supreme âtman."—
DEUSSEN, *Phil. of Upanishads*, p. 60.

The Brâhman is the spiritual ego,
which expresses itself first in the
personality under the Divine law of
truth and right (veda); second, in the
individuality sacrificing the lower
for the higher and following the law
of the soul's growth; third, in the
super-individuality, a centralised consciousness without a vehicle and
therefore having no outward expression; fourth, in the highest individuality which is a centre of consciousness also without a vehicle, on
the buddhic plane.

The four orders or states of consciousness in the soul's evolution
must be conceived of as all existing
together at the same time in the
same human being. All the states
are incomplete and but partially
evolved. The two lower states have
bodies in which to acquire experience
and manifest on the mental plane;
but the two higher states are without
any vehicles or mechanism of manifestation. They are "houseless" on
their own planes, and entirely withdrawn from external existence. The
highest state is unattached to a
particular ego, but is common to all
egos in the present epoch.

"These four life-stages of the Brahman,—as student, householder, anchorite
and wandering beggar,—were at a later
time very significantly named *âsramas*,
i.e. 'places of mortification.' The whole
life should be passed in a series of
gradually intensifying ascetic stages,
through which a man, more and more
purified from all earthly attachment
should become fitted for his 'home'
(astam), as the other world is designated.
The entire history of mankind does not
produce much that approaches in grandeur
to this thought."—*Ibid.*, p. 367.

See ARHATS, ASCETICS, BRAHMA-
CARIN, FOREST, HERMIT, HOUSE-
HOLDER, INITIATIONS, MONK, ORDERS
(four), SANNYASINS, SNATIKA, STU-
DENT, VEDA, YELLOW DRESS.

ASS, OR MULE :—

**A symbol of the lower nature,
stubborn, but capable of direction
by a ruling power or quality of
mind.**

"The difference between that which
was within and without is well illustrated by a similitude (in the Zohar)
which says that those who interpret
Scripture according to the literal sense
set the Sacred King and his Bride upon
an ass, while those who understand it
according to a mystic sense mount them
nobly on a horse."—WAITE, *Secret Doctrine in Israel*, p. 15.

ASS AND COLT :—

**A symbol of the lower nature and
an affection thereof, which require to
be ridden or kept under. If the
"ass" is "tied," it signifies that
the lower nature is attached to some
dead form of thought.**

"Jesus sent two disciples, saying, Go
into the village that is over against you,
and straightway ye shall find an ass
tied, and a colt with her: loose them,
and bring them unto me."—MAT. xxi. 2.

The Christ sending two "disciples"
to the "village," indicates the raising
of two disciplined qualities to a higher
state. The "village" signifies the
assembling to a centre of a few
qualities on the plane upon which
they have hitherto been working,
from which they are to rise as soon
as the Christ and his attached qualities come to the state of loving
aspiration (Mount of Olives). The
"ass tied and a colt" signify respectively an old doctrine and a new
truth to which it has given birth.
Upon these the Christ-soul progresses
to the higher state (the heavenly
Jerusalem), as he comes not to
destroy but to fulfil, and presents

many an old fable as a new and
enlightening fact. The " colt " represents the new truth whereon no mind
as yet can sit as master.

See DISCIPLES, JERUSALEM, PARABLE,
VILLAGE.

ASSEMBLY OF PEOPLE :—

A symbol of the gathering together
and co-ordinating of qualities on the
mental plane.

See ATTRACTION, CITY, NINE DAYS,
PEOPLE, PILGRIMS (shrine), SHIPS
(Greeks).

ASSEMBLY OF ADJUDICATING
PRIESTS, ELDERS, AND
SCRIBES :—

A symbol of official theology,—
the habit of mind which clings to
authority and tradition, and is ready
to kill out any new truth that presents
itself.

" The chief priests mocking Jesus,
with the scribes and elders, said, He
saved others ; himself he cannot save.
He is the King of Israel ; let him now
come down from the cross, and we will
believe on him."—MAT. xxvii. 41, 42.

The " chief priests " signify a mental
condition full of prejudice and without
spiritual insight, therefore without
recognition in the least of the position
in which the Christ-soul is placed.
It is thought that by an appeal to
the lower life, proof of the existence
of the Higher may be obtained, a
proceeding which is contrary to the
truth and the divine life of the soul.

" It is only the adherents of the dead
letter which religion rejects, who have
filled the world with the clamour and
uproar of religious controversies."—
F. D. E. SCHLEIERMACHER.

See CAIAPHAS, GABBATHA, PILATE,
PRIESTS AND ELDERS, TRADITION,
TRIAL.

ASSUMPTION OF THE BLESSED
VIRGIN MARY :—

A symbol of the completely purified
human soul rising in its perfection,
through the power of the Spirit, to
the higher planes at the end of the
cycle.

" As the Immaculate Conception is the
foundation of the Mysteries, so the
Assumption is their crown. For the
entire object and end of kosmic evolution
is precisely this triumph and apotheosis
of the soul. In this Mystery is beheld
the consummation of the whole scheme

of creation,—the perfectionment, perpetuation, and glorification of the individual human ego. The *grave*—that is
the astral and material consciousness—
cannot retain the Mother of God. She
rises into heaven ; she assumes its
Queenship, and is—to cite the *Little
Office of the Blessed Virgin Mary*—
' taken up into the chamber where the
King of kings sits on his starry throne.' "
—*The Perfect Way*, p. 143.

See CONCEPTION (immaculate), DE-
VAKI, VIRGIN MARY.

ASSUMPTION OF THE
MADONNA :—

A symbol of the raising by the
indwelling Self, of the purified emotion nature.

" The Church speaks of the Ascension
of Christ, and of the Assumption of Mary.
Christ being deific in nature and of
heavenly origin, ascends by his own
power and will. But the soul is ' assumed ' or drawn up by the power and
will of her Son. Of herself she is nothing ;
he is to her all in all. Where he abides,
thither must she be uplifted, by force
of the divine union which makes her
one with him. Henceforth she abides in
the real, and has the illusions of sense
for evermore under foot. It is not of
herself that Mary becomes Mother of
God in man. The narrative of the
Incarnation implies a conjunction of
human, — though not physical, — and
Divine potencies. Mary receives her
infant by an act of celestial energy overshadowing and vitalising her with the
Divine life."—*The Perfect Way*, p. 243.

" In the Babylonion system it was
taught that Bacchus went down to hell,
rescued his mother from the infernal
powers, and carried her with him in
triumph to heaven (*Apollodorus*, lib. iii.).
. . . Now, when the mother of the
Pagan Messiah came to be celebrated
as having been thus ' *Assumed*,' then
it was that, under the name of the
' Dove,' she was worshipped as the
incarnation of the Spirit of God, with
whom she was identified. As such she
was regarded as the source of all holiness,
and the grand ' *Purifier*,' and, of course,
was known herself as the ' Virgin '
mother, ' *pure and undefiled*.' Under the
name of Proserpine (with whom, though
the Babylonian goddess was originally
distinct, she was identified), while celebrated, as the *mother* of the first Bacchus,
and known as ' Pluto's honoured wife,'
she is also addressed in the *Orphic
Hymns*, as ' All-ruling Virgin,' bearing
heavenly light.' To the fact that Proserpine was currently worshipped in
Pagan Greece, though well known to be
the wife of Pluto, the god of hell, under
the name of ' the Holy Virgin,' we find
Pausanias, while describing the grove
Carnasius, thus bearing testimony : ' This

grove contains a statue of Apollo Carneus, of Mercury carrying a ram, and of Proserpine, the daughter of Ceres, who is called "the Holy Virgin."' The purity of this Holy Virgin did not consist merely in freedom from actual sin, but she was specially distinguished for her 'immaculate conception'; for Proclus says, 'She is called Corè, through the purity of her essence, and her *undefiled* transcendency in her *generations.*'"—A. HISLOP, *The Two Babylons*, pp. 125, 126.

See BIRTH OF JESUS, OF MAN-CHILD, BACCHUS, CROWN OF TWELVE STARS, DEMETER, DRAGON (great), HADES, HELL, INCARNATION, PERSEPHONE, VIRGIN MARY.

ASSYRIA IN THE EAST :—

A symbol of the dawn of the personality on the astral plane (Hiddekel river).

"The rational faculty of the Church."—SWEDENBORG, *Apoc. Rev.*, n. 444.

See EAST, EDEN RIVER, HIDDEKEL, PERSONALITY, PITRIS (lunar).

ASTABET :—

A symbol of an abode of strength from above.

ASTARTE, GODDESS OR QUEEN :—

A symbol of wisdom on the buddhic plane.

"The king Melcarthus. The queen Astarte, or Saosis, or Nemanoun, the same as the Greek Athenais."—PLUTARCH, *Isis and Osiris*, § 15.

The "king" is a symbol of the ego as governor of the astral activities. The names of the queen signify aspects of wisdom, i.e. Wisdom-love, Wisdom-power, and Wisdom-activity.

"The goddess Astarte, or Asthertet, is in a chariot drawn by four horses which trample on the foes of Râ."—BUDGE, *Book of the Dead*, Vol. I. p. 478.

Wisdom is seated in the causal-body (chariot), directing the lower quaternary (horses), which through the mind overcomes the desires.

See FIRE OF HELL, ISTAR, MELCARTHUS.

ASTOVIDAD, OR ASTOVID-HOTU :—

A symbol of the desire-mind, or the function of kama-manas.

See AESHM, ARROW (self-moving).

ASTRAL PLANE :—

A mediæval term for the plane of nature between the physical plane and the mental plane. This plane is called in the Ottoman Sufi philosophy, the "world of similitudes"; in the Kabbalah the "world of formation." In Indian philosophy the plane bears the name of "kama," signifying desire. The astral plane is the field, or medium, of the desires, sensations, passions, and instincts of the lower nature.

"Included in the subconscious region of an average healthy man are all those automatic activities by which the life of the body is carried on : all those 'uncivilised' instincts and vices, those remains of the ancestral savage which education has forced out of the stream of consciousness; all those aspirations for which the busy life of the world leaves no place. Hence in normal men the best and the worst, the most savage and most spiritual parts of the character, are bottled up 'below the threshold.'"—E. UNDERHILL, *Mysticism*, p. 62.

The astral plane is also the plane of formation of the physical organisms which are built up, or grow up, in the similitude of the patterns on the astral and mental planes. These patterns are living patterns of growth of which a clumsy analogy may be found in the film pictures of the cinema show. Life on the physical plane is a mental directive agency from the astral plane which uses the forces of the physical plane to build up structure according to its pattern of growth. Death is the extrusion of this directive life of the physical forms, which thereupon disappears entirely, being non-physical. The origin of the astral patterns is not to be found on the astral plane any more than on the physical. The invention of the patterns is on the buddhic and mental planes, for high intelligence is needed for the complexities and efficiencies of phenomenal existence.

See AMERDAD, ELEMENTS, GREEN, KAMA, PROTOTYPES, SIMILITUDES, WOOD, WORLDS (five).

ASTRAL SHEATH, OR BODY, OF THE HUMAN BEING :—

This is the instrument of the incarnate ego on the astral plane. It contains the mechanism appropriate to the forces of the plane, and the means by which the desires, lower emotions, and sensations function in the soul and are perceived by the lower consciousness on the mental plane.

"Arranged in numerical order, the seven principles may be described in the following way :—
1. Physical Body.
2. Etheric Double.
3. Jiva.
4. The Astral Vehicle.
5. Manas.
6. Buddhi.
7. Atma.
"The Etheric Double is an Etheric rather than an Astral counterpart of the physical body, and at the same time, the intermediate organism through which the Jiva, or life force, influences the whole system. . . . Etheric matter is still physical according to the most accurate classification that can be adopted."—A. P. SINNETT, *Growth of the Soul*, pp. 156–7.

The astral body may be taken to be next in order to the physical body, including the etheric double, as the life (jiva) is not a sheath but a directive agency from a higher plane. On the mental plane (manas) there are two sheaths, viz. the causal-body and the mental body. This makes four bodies in which humanity at present manifests. The life force of the lower planes works strictly according to the patterns on the higher planes, the results being modified by obstructions on the lower. The patterns are brought forward, as it were, to the astral-plane where they guide the growth of all animal and vegetable organisms.

In the astral body are to be found the apparatus of sensory and motor conduction paths which convey vibrations from the brain and nerves to the mind, and from the mind to the brain and nerves. It must never be forgotten that consciousness is on the mental plane, and not below it.

See ANDREW, CASTES, CAUSAL-BODY, CHILDREN OF HORUS, CLASSES, INCARNATION OF SOULS, MARRIAGE (castes), NEPHESH, NET, PRANAS, PROTOTYPES, QUATERNARY, SENSE ORGANS, SHEATHS SKANDHAS, VESTURES, VITAL AIRS.

ASTRO-MENTAL AND ASTRO-PHYSICAL PLANES :—

These terms express the combined activities of the astral and mental planes, and of the astral and physical planes.

See ASTRAL PLANE, KAMA, MANAS, MENTAL PLANE.

ASURA, SURA, AHURA (HIGHER ASPECT) :—

A symbol of the Divine energy expressed through the higher, or atma-buddhic, qualities of the soul.

"The name for gods in the Veda is not only deva, but likewise asura. This name, if derived from asu, breath, meant originally the living, he who lives and moves in the great phenomena of nature, or, as we should say, *the living God*. Certain Vedic gods, particularly Varuna, are in the Veda also called Asura in the good sense of the word. But very soon the Sanskrit asura took a bad sense, for instance, in the last book of the Rig-veda and in the Atharva-veda, and particularly in the Brâhmanas. Here we constantly find the Asuras fighting against the Devas."—MAX MÜLLER, *Theosophy, etc.*, p. 181.

The "gods" signify the higher qualities or ideals in the soul, and these "asuras" proceed from the outbreathing of the Divine Life on the buddhic plane. The astral plane contains the desires (asuras) which are of the same Divine Life, but work outwardly in the opposite direction to the spiritual life which tends inwardly.

See BREATH (divine), COLCHIS, DEVAS, GODS, VARUNA, VEDA.

ASURA (LOWER ASPECT) :—

A symbol of the reflected Divine energy on the lower planes, expressed in desire which is the opponent of the higher energy.

"A new change appears in the later Sanskrit literature. Here the Asuras, instead of fighting with the Devas, are represented as fighting against the Suras; that is to say, by a mere mistake, the 'A' of Asura has been taken as a negative 'a,' whereas it is the radical 'a' of *asu*, breath, and a new name has been formed, *Sura*."—MAX MÜLLER, *Theosophy, etc.*, p. 187.

"By the breath of his mouth Pragâpati created the gods : the gods (deva) were created on entering the sky. . . . Having created them, there was, as it were, daylight for him. . . . And by the downward breathing he created the asuras : they were created on entering this earth. Having created them there was, as it were, darkness for him."—*Sata. Brâh.*, XI. 1, 6, 7–8.

The Divine out-breath of the Life produced the higher qualities (the gods) on the buddhic plane (the sky), and these served to express the nature of the Self (daylight). The Divine down-breath produced the lower qualities, the desires (asuras) which were reflected from the lower nature (earth) in opposition to the higher qualities, hence the Self was obscured by evil and ignorance (darkness), and rendered unapparent to the lower consciousness.

The double signification of " asura " is only an instance of the double meanings of symbols, whereby the higher and the lower conditions of the same origin are indicated. It is likely enough that a new symbol " sura " originated in the manner stated, and was used to better distinguish the higher from the lower in the inspired communications of a later date. Of course, no mistake has been made. The Spirit of Truth knows everything, and cannot possibly be in error about anything. The truth is set down in the scriptures if the lower mind does not interfere and insert its own opinions.

See BREATH (divine), DAEVAS, DAIMONS, DAWN, DEMONS, DEVAS, DEVILS, GODS, HORSE SACRIFICE, INSPIRATION, PRAGÂPATI.

ASVINS, THE TWO :—

Symbols of centres of consciousness on the mental plane for the Higher and Lower Selves,—the Individuality and the Personality, the immortal and the mortal lives.

" The gods called Asvins were a great enigma, . . . 'Heaven and Earth,' say some ; 'Day and Night,' say others ; 'Two kings, performers of holy acts,' say the Aitihasikas."—MON. WILLIAMS, *Indian Wisdom*, p. 169.

" The Asvins were fabled as connected with Ushas, as ever young and handsome, travelling in a golden car, and precursors of the dawn. They are sometimes called Dasras, as divine physicians, 'destroyers of diseases'; sometimes Nasatyas, as 'never untrue.' They appear to have been personifications of two luminous points or rays imagined to precede the break of day."—*Ibid.*, p. 14.

" These ever-youthful twin sons of the Sun, by his wife Sanjnâ, transformed into a mare (asvini), resemble the classical Dioscuri both by their exploits and the aid they render to their worshippers."—*Ibid*, p. 426.

" The Asvins are the (Brahman) physi-

cians of the gods, and it is by them that he heals this Sacrificer. . . . The two Asvins, indeed, are the eyesight, fiery spirit. . . . He-goats are sacred to the Asvins."—*Sata. Brâh.*, XII. 7, 2, 3–7.

The twin consciousnesses of the higher and lower minds, temporally separate, yet essentially connected, are known as the immortal Individuality and the mortal Personality. They precede in evolution the rise of the Sun of Righteousness, the Higher Self, in the soul. Through their functioning life after life, the soul is developed and healed of its diseases, and finally made whole and perfect. They are never untrue to themselves, that is, they work together in an indissoluble relationship under the laws of karma. They have been emanated by the Self (sun) and brought forth in the mind (Sanjnâ-mare), in order that the spiritual egos (gods) may be perfected in their manifestation in the lower worlds. By them the soul, or sacrificing lower Self, is restored and brought up to perfection. They are the means of perception (eyesight) and of purification (fiery spirit). Errors and desires (goats) are offered up by them.

See APOCATEQUIL, DIOSCURI, GEMINI, MARE, NAKULA, SACRIFICER, SPADE.

ATALANTA, THE FAIR MAID :—

A symbol of the love of beauty, harmony and perfection set before the lower nature.

" She required every suitor who wanted to win her to contend with her first in the foot-race. She conquered many suitors, but was at length overcome by Mīlanion with the assistance of Aphrodite. The goddess had given him three golden apples, and during the race he dropped them one after the other : their beauty charmed Atalanta so much, that she could not abstain from gathering them, and Mīlanion thus gained the goal before her."—*Smith's Class. Dict.*

The love of beauty and perfection, being at first unattached to the lower nature, requires, in order to be utilised, that means should be found to enlist it. Mental imagination (Mīlanion) having received from the astral love development (Aphrodite) love of form, sound and colour (the apples), is able to attract and draw down the higher love of beauty to itself. And thus an aspect of buddhic emotion becomes united with mind and originates the æsthetic feelings in sculpture, music and painting.

Evolution is an unfolding of qualities which are latent, and this unfolding is in response to stimuli from without. Æsthetic feeling (Atalanta), being of the higher planes, is too subtle to respond to ordinary mental processes. But when imagination (Milanion) is touched with love of form, sound and colour, this mental faculty arouses æsthetic feeling which, from being at first potential and inactive in the soul, is now made manifest.

"Some day, I doubt not, we shall arrive at an understanding of the evolution of the æsthetic faculty; but all the understanding in the world will neither increase nor diminish the force of the intuition that this is beautiful and that is ugly."—T. H. HUXLEY, *Evolution and Ethics*, p. 80.

"Beauty, Goodness, Splendour, Love, all those words of glamour which exhilarate the soul, are but the man-made names of aspects or qualities picked out by human intuition as characteristic of this intense and eternal Life in which is the life of men."—E. UNDERHILL, *Mysticism*, p. 35.

"All things that *are*, are the shadow and image of heavenly things. The highest lesson they can teach is, to remind us of and to symbolise for us the uncreated and everlasting Wisdom and Love and Beauty which lie beneath them, and ripple up through them."—A. MACLAREN, *Sermons, 1st Series*, p. 16.

See APHRODITE, ARGONAUTS, SCENT.

ATEA AND ATANUA, GOD OF LIGHT AND GODDESS OF DAWN :—

Symbols of Divine Will and Divine Wisdom, i.e. Atma-buddhi.

"Light (Atea) having been evolved from darkness (Tanaoa), the god Ono or 'Sound' was evolved from Atea, and he destroyed 'Mutuhei' (silence). But from the foregoing struggle between Tanaoa and Atea, Ono and Mutuhei, arose Atanua or the dawn. Atea then took Atanua for a wife, and from them sprang their first-born Tumea. After that Atea created the host of inferior deities, etc.,"—A. FORNANDER, *Polynesian Race*, Vol. I. p. 63.

The Divine Will having proceeded from the potential (darkness), the

"Word," or expression of God, became manifest in putting an end to the unmanifest (silence). Then from the interaction of matter (Tanaoa) and Spirit (Atea), and of activity (Ono) and inertness (Mutuhei), arose Wisdom (Atanua). Love (Atea) united with Wisdom and the Divine Son was born. Afterwards the Divine Will created the lower nature with its desires, etc.

See ADITI, DARKNESS, DAWN, LIGHT, TANAOA.

ATHENA, PALLAS; DAUGHTER OF ZEUS :—

A symbol of Wisdom, the principle of buddhi, in various aspects, proceeding from the Supreme.

"Unto men Athena gives good things —namely wisdom, understanding, and the creative arts; and she dwells in their citadels, I suppose, as being the founder of civil government through the communication of her own wisdom."— EMP. JULIAN, *The Sovereign Sun*, p. 243.

Unto the mental faculties buddhi brings intuition, dwelling in the mind-centre (citadel) and founding moral order.

"Pallas Athene came to Achilles from heaven, sent forth of the white-armed goddess Hera, whose heart loved both (Achilles and Agamemnon) alike and had care for them."—*Iliad*, Book I.

The Wisdom from the Highest descended forth from the potential Wisdom (Hera) in the realm of pure Love which included sympathy for both the personality (Achilles) or mental element, and the desire-mind (Agamemnon) with its appetites; and was to become the means of reconciling them.

See ACHILLES, APOLLO, BUDDHI, GODDESS, HERA, MUSE, PIETY, WHITE-ARMED, WISDOM.

ATHORNE; ATHRAVA; ATHARVAN; PRIEST OF THE ALTAR OR FIRE :—

A symbol of the spiritual mind or deeper intelligence which serves to direct the will.

"The very name for 'priest' in the Zend-Avesta, *âthrava*, is to be recognised in the *atharvan* of the Vedas, by which term a priest of Fire and Soma is meant." —HAUG, *Essays on Rel. of Parsis*, p. 212.

See AARON, ADVARYA, AGNIDHRA, BARSOM, CHRYSE, FIRE PRIESTS, PONTIFF, POPE, PRIEST.

ATHWYA, THE SECOND MAN :—

A symbol of the Second or manifest Logos.

"Athwya was the second man who prepared me (*Homa*) for the material world" (*Homa Yasht*).—HAUG, *Essays*.

This signifies the forth-pouring of the Second Logos upon the higher planes, which prepared the World-soul (Homa) for its expression upon the lower planes.

See ATMA, HOMA, SELF.

ATHYR (HATHOR) MONTH :—

A symbol of the period at the commencement of evolution, when there is liberation of the life from the form —a rising from the dead.

See HATHOR, SCORPIO.

ATLAS, THE HEAVEN-BEARER :—

A symbol of the higher mind which separates the lower (earth) from the higher nature (heaven).

"According to Homer, Atlas bears the long columns which keep asunder heaven and earth."—*Smith's Class. Dict.*

See PILLARS OF THE LIGHT.

ATMA PLANE :—

A designation for the highest plane of manifestation in the present cycle of life. It is the plane of the Second Logos, or Higher Self, and expresses the power-love aspect of Deity.

See ÆTHER, ARSH, ATHWYA, ELEMENTS, PROTOTYPES, WORLDS (five).

ATMAN :—

A symbol of the Supreme. The Logos or Self which enters upon manifestation and indwells in the universe and soul.

"Brahman = Atman, that is, Brahman, the power from which all worlds proceed, in which they subsist, and into which they finally return ; this eternal, omnipresent, omnipotent power is identical with our âtman, with that in each of us which we must consider as our true Self, the unchangeable essence of our being, our Soul. This idea alone secures to the Upanishads an importance reaching far beyond their land and time ; for whatever means of unveiling the secrets of Nature a future time may discover, this idea will be true for ever, from this mankind will never depart ;— if the mystery of Nature is to be solved, the key of it can be found only there where alone Nature allows us an *interior* view of the world, that is, in ourselves."
—P. DEUSSEN, *Outlines of Ind. Phil.*, pp. 22–3.

"This is my Self in my innermost heart."—*Sata. Brâh.*, X. 6, 3.

See ARC. MAN, BRAHMA, COSMOS, FIG-FRUIT, GOD, HIGHER, MACROCOSM, MICROCOSM, MONAD, SELF.

ATOM, PERMANENT ASTRAL :—

An atom on the astral plane attached to each causal-body, and forming a centre for personality in the whole series of incarnations.

"And the Lord said unto him, Therefore whosoever slayeth Cain, vengeance shall be taken on him sevenfold. And the Lord appointed a sign for Cain, lest any finding him should smite him."— GEN. iv. 15.

And the Divine Wisdom-love pronounced a benediction upon that Individuality within, which shall not be slain, and decreed that "sevenfold" shall be the suffering which shall come about when the lower self by the Higher Self is slain. And a "sign" or permanant astral atom, is provided, which answers to the personality throughout the cycle.

"Each man who is born into the world is provided with an imperishable bone in his present physical body, and it is from or on this that his organisation will be built up anew at the time of the resurrection" (*Zohar*).—A. E. WAITE, *Secret Doctrine*, p. 187.

See ABEL, CAIN, FUGITIVE, ONOGOROJIMA, PERSONALITY, SOUL (lowest).

ATOMS, PERMANENT, ON EACH PLANE :—

Buddhi, mental, astral, and physical, atoms attached to each Individuality as centres of life and form on the several planes.

"He approaches the couch Amitaugas : that is prâna (breath, speech). The past and the future are its eastern feet. Prosperity and earth its western feet." —*Kaush. Upanishad*, I. 2.

The soul comes to the state which signifies the sense of infinite rest and serenity,—which is comparable to the rhythm of the Great Breath. The "past and the future" symbolise the course which evolution has taken to enable this state of consciousness to be arrived at, and so the Eternal Now is verily realised. "Prosperity and earth" signify the sublimated lower or natural man, through which the Higher Ego has attained its final liberation. Although the lower is "unreality," it has been absorbed into the Self. The germ of this state exists and will persist through eternity; for nothing is ever lost. The state is transformed, but still visible to the Self, though now seen to be of It. There is a permanent atom or centre on each plane, which, when communicated with, will respond to vibrations which answer to the varied aspects of the Self.

See AMITAUGAS, GOLD-COLOURED SPOT, PLANES, PRANA, PROSPERITY.

ATONEMENT BY THE BLOOD :—

A symbol of the reparative effect of the Divine Life in the soul's growth. The forming and healing Life gradually making perfect the imperfect soul, in proportion as the soul aspires toward the ideal.

"For the life (or soul) of the flesh is in the blood : and I (the Lord) have given it to you upon the altar to make atonement for your souls : for it is the blood that maketh atonement by reason of the life (or soul)."—LEV. xvii. 11.

For the power of upward growth of the lower nature (flesh) of humanity, resides in the recuperative Divine Life (blood) which the Higher Self sheds upon the highest part of the lower nature (the altar) in order that the souls shall have the means of development : for it is the Divine Life that maketh perfect by reason of the perfect Archetype within.

"Among the ancient Hindus an atonement was asserted to be through the sacrifice of Purusha the Great Hindu Universal Ideal Man."—MON. WILLIAMS, *Indian Wisdom*, p. 24.

See ALTAR, ARC. MAN, BLOOD, FOOD, HOMA-JUICE, SCAPEGOAT, SOMA-JUICE.

ATONEMENT OF CHRIST :—

A symbol of the unfinished, continuous and progressive work of human perfectionment, by the substitution of the merits or perfection of the Redeemer for the imperfections of the redeemed. The indwelling Christ having laid down his life in Involution, takes it again in Evolution as he rises in the souls of humanity. In this process of spiritualisation he makes atonement for the sins of the world and unites man to God,—the made-perfect to the Perfect.

"For if, when we were enemies, we were reconciled to God by the death of his Son, much more, being reconciled, we shall be saved by his life. And not only so, but we also joy in God through our Lord Jesus Christ, by whom we have now received the atonement."—ROM. v. 10, 11.

For if, when we (the egos) were following only our natural desires, we were turned to God through the previous death of the Divine Life within the lower nature, and the consequent birth of the Christ in our souls ; much more, being turned thereby to God, shall we be saved by his Life within us. And not only so, but our souls in their innermost being now rejoice in the Ideal of Wisdom, Truth, and Love, through the growth of the indwelling Christ by whom we now receive a gradual perfectionment of being.

"William Law says,—'Christ given *for* us, is neither more nor less than Christ given *into* us. He is in no other sense our full, perfect, and sufficient Atonement, than as His nature and spirit are born and formed in us.' "—DR. INGE, *Christian Mysticism*, p. 281.

"The Atonement of Christ is the reconcilement of humanity in all the length and breadth of its complex duties and experiences. Hence he summons every man to a fellowship with His own life,—not only to follow Him, but to become one with Him."—T. T. MUNGER, *The Atonement, etc.*, p. 367.

"If Christ be the Eternal Son of God, that side of the Divine nature which has gone forth in creation ; if He contains humanity, and is present in every act and article of human experience, then, indeed, we have a light upon the fact of redemption. For Jesus is thus seen to be associated with the existence of the primordial evil which has its origin in God. . . . Evil is an experience for the sake of the far-off holiness it makes possible. The eternal Son, the going forth of God, must therefore be associated with responsibility for the bias without which neither guilt nor sainthood could have come into being. He, and He only, therefore, can sever the entail between man and his responsibility for personal sin."—R. J. CAMPBELL, *Ibid.*, p. 25.

"The Atonement that is a vital human need is no making up of a previous strife, but the fulfilment of the Divine idea of man. It is effected through self-development and self-realisation. Man comes to God as he comes to himself ; and to come to himself he must come to God. Atonement is, further, the reconciliation of the whole man,

and his whole life and world, to God."—
DR. J. HUNTER, *Ibid.*, p. 312.

See ADOPTION, ARC. MAN, BLOOD,
BLOOD OF THE LAMB, HOMA-JUICE,
LIBERATION, PASSOVER, RANSOM,
REDEMPTION, REGENERATION, REMIS-
SION, RESURRECTION, SALVATION,
SOMA-JUICE, TAUROBOLIUM, WASHED.

ATREUS, AND HIS TWO SONS,— LEADERS OF THE PEOPLE :—

Symbols of the illusion of separateness, and its products, love of power
and love of possession, rulers of the
lower qualities.

"And Chryses supplicated all the
Greeks, but chiefly the two sons of
Atreus, the leaders of the people."—
Iliad, Book I.

The spiritual mind, through illusion, captivates the lower minds and
principally through love of power and
possession.

See AGAMEMNON, CHRYSES, GREEKS,
MENELAUS, TROY, TYRANT.

ATRI AND HIS WISE SON :—

A symbol of the Soul centred in
the astro-mental nature, together
with its Divine deliverer and healer
born within it. For the Soul must
through its own evolution be its own
saviour, by reason of its inherent
Divine nature.

See REDEEMER, SELF, SOUL, VAL-
MIKI.

ATROPOS :—

See MOIRAE.

ATTACHMENT TO THE WORLD OR THE OBJECTS OF SENSE :—

A symbol of the captivity of the
ego to desire and sensation.

"The man stands in the middle between
the two worlds of light and darkness,
left to his own free-will" (*Zoroastrian
System*).—J. F. CLARKE, *Ten Religions.*

Seated in the causal-body upon the
higher mind plane, and midway between the physical and the atmic
planes, the Soul starts its career as a
responsible entity, and is thenceforth
accountable to itself for its conduct,
thoughts and experiences. These mental experiences are ultimately collected,
re-viewed, and co-ordinated in the
causal-sheath, and thus it is that
man is able eventually through identifying himself with the true Self of

his being, to attain final liberation,
and freedom from the thraldom of
desire and attachment to the things
of the lower nature.

"Existence is caused by attachment
(upādāna). Attachment is a kind of
falling off which makes a being come
under the fatal law of transmigration.
It is itself only an effect, which has for
cause desire (trishna, thirst). Desire is
caused by sensation (vedanā)."—J. B.
SAINT-HILAIRE, *The Buddha*, p. 135.

"Only that form of religion whose
inception of God is that of an Ideal
which satisfies the religious needs, and
which calls forth and fixes upon Itself
the choices of the human soul, can fully
develop the potentiality of freedom which
lies hidden in the soul's depths. There
is profound moral philosophy in the
promise of Jesus to those who are his
disciples indeed : ' Ye shall know the
truth, and the truth shall make you
free ' (JOHN viii. 31)."—G. T. LADD,
Phil. of Religion, Vol. I. p. 339.

"The various functions assigned by
Philo to the Logos may be thus summed
up. He is the agency by which God
reveals Himself. The theophanies of the
Old Testament are appearances of the
Logos, who also inspired the patriarchs
and prophets. Every man, in virtue of
the highest faculty residing in his soul,
is akin to the divine Logos, and may
become an image or fragment of the
divine nature. The majority of mankind
are entangled in illusions, and the divine
image in them is obscured by ignorance
and sensuality. But a man may raise
himself out of this sad condition, and
advance to the contemplation of the
Logos, which enables him to judge all
things in the light of divine truth. In
this way the Logos is the instrument
of deliverance and salvation. 'Those
who have real knowledge of the one
Creator and Father of all things are
rightly called sons of God. And even
if we are not yet worthy to be called
sons of God, we may deserve to be called
children of His eternal image, the most
holy Logos ' (*Conf. Ling.*, 28)."—W. R.
INGE, *Camb. Biblical Essays*, p. 276.

"The tumultuous senses and organs
hurry away by force the heart even of
the wise man who striveth after perfection. Let a man, restraining all these,
remain in devotion at rest in me, his
true Self ; for he who hath his senses
and organs in control possesses spiritual
knowledge. He who attendeth to the
inclinations of the senses, in them hath
a concern. . . . But he who, free from
attachment or repulsion for objects,
experienceth them through the senses
and organs, with his heart obedient to
his will, attains to tranquillity of
thought."—*Bhagavad-Gita*, Ch. II.

See ATMA, BONDAGE, CAPTIVITY,
CAUSAL-BODY, DARKNESS, EXPERI-

ENCES, FALL, HIGHER AND LOWER, IMAGE OF GOD, INCARNATION OF SOULS, LIBERATION, LIGHT, LOGOS, MAN, MEMBERS, METEMPSYCHOSIS, NIRVANA, PERSONALITY, SEPARATE-NESS, SERPENT (subtil), SPARK, THIRST, WALKS (six), WORLD.

ATTRACTION WHICH BUILDS UP THE STRUCTURE OF THE SOUL :—

This is the love-element on the different planes, which draws forces, atoms, or qualities, towards centres.

"For unto every one that hath shall be given, and he shall have abundance : but from him that hath not, even that which he hath shall be taken away."— MAT. xxv. 29.

This indicates that the strength of attraction is in proportion to the number of grouped forces or faculties attracting to a common centre. Where a force is unattached to a group, there is no balance about a centre, therefore it flies off to join a group, or it is dissipated. The teaching is, that higher qualities must not be isolated, but must be brought into harmonious relation with kindred qualities, so that all may work together for good. "Where *two* or *three* are gathered together, there am I in the midst of them."

See APHRODITE, ASSEMBLY, CITY, LOVE (uniter), PILGRIMS (shrine), STRIFE.

ATZEEL-ATIC WORLD OF EMANATION :—

A symbol of the higher planes (atma-buddhic) of manifestation.

See ADAM (higher), HIGHER, PROTO-TYPES.

ATZEEL-OOTHIC WORLD :—

A symbol of the three higher planes,—atma, buddhi, manas,—as containing the pattern of that which appears on the three lower planes.

"God has, in fact, erected (primor-dially) another and higher system, that of spiritual being and government for which nature exists ; a system not under the law of cause and effect, but ruled and marshalled under other kinds of laws, and able continually to act upon or vary the action of the processes of nature. If, accordingly, we speak of system, this spiritual realm or depart-ment is much more properly called a system than the natural, because it is closer to God, higher in its consequence, and *contains in itself the ends or final causes for which the other exists*, and to which the other is made to be subser-vient. There is, however, a constant action and reaction between the two, and, strictly speaking, they are both together, taken as one, the true system of God ; for a system, in the most proper and philosophic sense of the word, is a complete and absolute whole, which cannot be taken as a part or fraction of anything."—H. BUSHNELL, *Nature and the Supernatural*, p. 19.

"The spiritual is the world of causes, the material that of effects."—R. J. CAMPBELL, Serm., *Book of Destiny*.

See ADAM (higher), ARC. MAN, BREATIC, IMAGE, MACROCOSM, SEAL (great).

AUDUMBLA, THE COW :—

A symbol of the primordial buddhic nature which at first potential, be-comes actual.

"Then came the cow Audumbla, formed of the melting ice-drops. She nourished Ymer with four streams of her milk, and herself licked the sea salt-stones covered with the rime-frost, whence sprung Bur whose son was Borr, who married a giant's daughter, and was the father of Odin, Vili, and Ve, the ruling powers of heaven and earth."—*The Voluspa.*

This refers to the period of involu-tion of the qualities. Then there arose from latency (ice) the nascent buddhic life (cow) which vitalised on the four planes the Archetypal Man (Ymer). The buddhic activities were applied to the astro-physical nature (the sea salt-stones) and from the latent (frost) condition there sprung the desire-nature (Bur) whose issue was the mind (Borr) who became allied with the perfected emotions and then produced Divine Will, Wis-dom, and Action, the ruling principles of a new stage in the development of the higher and lower natures.

See ARC. MAN, BUR, COW, FROST, ICE, ODIN, TRIAD, YMIR.

AURVA'S BIRTH FROM THE THIGH :—

A symbol of the birth of the desire-nature which took place upon the astral plane.

See THIGH.

AURVAITO-DIH, THE TUR :—

A symbol of the soul on the buddhic plane.

"At the age of twenty, abandoning worldly desires and laying hold of righteousness, Zoroaster departs from the house of his father and mother and wanders forth, openly enquiring :—'Who is most desirous of righteousness, and most wishful to nourish the poor ? And they said,—'He who is the youngest son of Aurvaito-dih the Tur.' Zoroaster goes to 'that place,' and co-operates in serving the poor with food" (*Zatsparam*).—JACKSON, *Zoroaster*, p. 33.

When the cycle of the lower life is completed,—the lower self with its affections and lusts having been abandoned,—then the mind or manasic principle is said to be detached, because the mind no longer cleaves to the desires. Liberation, therefore, having been obtained, the Soul, instead of being anxious to seek its own well-being, identifies itself with the Will of the Supreme, and enquires to what purpose it may be used. It requests that it may be the means of furthering the interests of the other souls that are struggling to reach enlightenment. It learns that the soul most ready for aid from the higher, is the soul which is learning to discipline itself through the adoption of principles by means of which ultimate attainment of liberation is possible. The Soul now reaches the stage of freedom from all the lower limitations, and is said to go to the place of Bliss on the buddhic plane, from whence it may inspire souls which are ready.

See BIRDS (heaven), DUGHDHOVA, FOOD, POOR PEOPLE, POVERTY, POURUSHASPA, ZOROASTER.

AUSHEDAR, OR HUSHEDAR :—

A symbol of the Higher Self, Son of God.

"The marvellousness of Aushedar as to birth, glory of person, sayings and actions ; the standing of the sun ten days amid the sky ; the perishing of the fiend of the four-legged race, the production of a three-spring cloudless influence for vegetation ; the weakening of superfluity and destitution ; the extreme strengthening of alliance ; the gratification due to the good friendship of foreigners."—*Dinkard*, Bk. VII. Ch. 9, 2.

This declares the glory of the birth,

life, activities, and development of the Self,—the Son of the Logos,—commencing from the buddhic plane whereon the Self (sun) culminates above the lower evolution. The consequent ultimate perishing of the lower quaternary with its desire-mental nature (the fiend) : the production of the higher triad of truth, love, and wisdom, or the higher emotion nature nourishing the soul : the dispensing with the lower vehicles which are afterwards superfluous : the complete union of the lower Self with the Higher Self : the arrival of the Soul at Wisdom which relates all experiences, even adverse and evil experiences, with the evolution of the Self.

See ANIMALS, FOOD, PISCES, QUATERNARY, SUN MOTIONLESS, UNION, ZENITH.

AUSONIA :—

A symbol of the state of the soul on the buddhic plane which ushers in perfection (Circe).

See ABSYRTEAN-ISLES, CIRCE.

AUSTERITIES, PRACTISING :—

Limiting or restraining the outgoing activities in prescribed directions according to the Divine Law of the growth of the Soul.

"All the bliss of Gods and men is declared by the sages to whom the Veda was revealed, to have austerity for its root, austerity for its middle, and austerity for its end. The pursuit of sacred knowledge is the austerity of a Brahmana, protecting the people is the austerity of a Kshatriya, the pursuit of his daily business is the austerity of a Vaisya, and service the austerity of a Sûdra."—*Laws of Manu*, XI. 235–6.

The blissful, exalted life of Spirit and higher mind, is declared to have restraint or limitation for its source, its means, and its end. The Individuality, or spiritual mind, seeks truth from within by restraining the lower nature. The Personality, or lower mind, nurtures the qualities by restraining the desires. The Desire-nature co-ordinates the desires by restraining physical energies. The Physical-nature is subordinated to the requirements of the desires, the mind, and the higher nature.

See ABSTINENCE, ASCETICISM, CASTES, FASTING, PENANCE, RAJAS, SATTVA, VAIVASVATA, VEDA.

AVALOKITESVARA :—

A symbol of the Higher Self or Incarnate Self under the aspect of Love.

"The Buddha Amitabha, 'He of Infinite Light.' His chief minister is Avalokitesvara, a Bodhisatva who has taken a vow not to enter Nirvāna until he has led thither all living creatures, and who for this supreme grace is worshipped throughout the North with a corresponding fervour of devotion."— L. D. BARNETT, *The Path of Light*, p. 25.

"In the duty of watching over and protecting the whole Buddhist world, Avalokitesvara (=[Padma-pāni), that is, 'the Lord who looks down with pity on all men,' certainly takes the lead, and his name was in keeping with the reputation for answering prayer which he soon achieved. . . . People, therefore, pray to him more frequently than to any other Bodhi-sattva, and not only for release from the misery of future re-births, but in all cases of present bodily danger and domestic affliction. Hence he has numerous other names or epithets, such as 'God of mercy,' 'Ocean of pity,' 'Deliverer from fear,' 'Lord of the world,' 'World-protector,' 'Protector of the Aryas.' "—MON. WILLIAMS, *Buddhism*, p. 198.

The higher Love-nature within the soul always attracts, never repels. Hence the aspiring lower self is attracted to the Higher, and there is development of the buddhic emotions which purify and eventually save the soul.

See BODHISATVA, BUDDHA, CHRIST, ISVARA, PRAYER.

AVENGING THE DIVINE SACRIFICE :—

Symbolical of vindicating the Divine intentions by producing the result intended, namely perfection.

"Horus now gathered his followers around him, and prepared himself to avenge his father's death (that of Osiris)." —PLUTARCH, *Isis and Osiris*, § 19.

So soon as the Christ (Horus) had evolved above in the soul, he proceeded to choose those qualities (disciples) wherewith he should accomplish his work upon the lower planes ; and so he prepared himself to establish the kingdom of His Father in the souls of humanity, even as it exists above in the Heavens (buddhic plane).

"I (Rā) have come to avenge myself the blood of my members which have risen up against me, and I will bring to destruction that which hath been made for it. I will make perfect."—BUDGE, *Egypt. Heaven and Hell*, Vol. I. p. 19.

The Self within is ready to vindicate the Divine life (blood) which flows in the desires which act in opposition to the higher motives, and will bring to dissolution the lower nature which has been the means of its evolution. The indwelling Self will make perfect the soul.

"Avenge not yourselves, beloved, but give place unto wrath : for it is written, Vengeance belongeth unto me ; I will recompense, saith the Lord."—ROM. xii. 19.

Vindicate not yourselves in anger and passion, but in love make explanation. For the Divine Life of the soul will establish truth and righteousness, and bring all to perfection.

See BLOOD, DEATH OF OSIRIS, DISCIPLES, HORUS, MEMBERS, TATTU.

AVIDYA :—

See IGNORANCE.

AWALIM-I-KHAMSA—THE FIVE WORLDS ; OFTEN SPOKEN OF AS HAZRAT-I-KHAMSA,—THE FIVE PLANES :—

A symbol of the five planes of manifestation which proceed from the Absolute (World of Godhead) of which nothing can be predicated.

See WORLDS (five).

AXE :—

A symbol of Divine Truth uttered on the higher mental plane. Or the critical faculty.

"And now also the axe is laid unto the root of the trees : therefore every tree which bringeth not forth good fruit is hewn down, and cast into the fire."—MAT. iii. 10.

"Trees" here signify mental qualities. The "axe" is the Word of God which is to try men's "hearts" and to search to the roots and foundation of their being. If the qualities are unprogressed and rotten to the core then they will be cast forth as rubbish ; that is they will be dissolved and so be resolved into their primary constituents.

"MAT. iii. 10.—This is as much as to say to them : Since you have come to baptism without having done fruits meet for repentance, you are a tree that does not bring forth good fruit, and which has to be cut down by the most sharp and piercing axe of the Word which is living and powerful and sharper than every two-edged sword."—ORIGEN, *Comm. on John*, Bk. VI. § 13.

"There is much in the Bible which is neither true nor edifying."—CANON H. HENSON, *Christ and the Nation*, p. 266.

"We must always remember that a thing may be literally false and ideally true. A legend may be doubtful; the faith and devotion which it excites in religious but uncritical minds are very real."—W. S. LILLY, *Ancient Religion*, p. 285.

"What now is the condition of men's minds in respect to the *historical* element of the existing religion? None but those who through lack of education stand necessarily upon the old ways, have any reliance upon it. Critical analysis—that function of the mind which, in its nature destructive, is nevertheless, really harmful only to that which, in being untrue, has not in itself the element of perpetuity—has laid an unsparing axe to the forest of ancient tradition. The science of Biblical exegesis has made it obvious to every percipient mind that sacred books, so far from being infallible records of actual events, abound with inaccuracies, contradictions, and interpolations; that sacred persons, if they existed at all, had histories differing widely from those narrated of them; that sacred events could not have occurred in the manner stated; and that sacred doctrines are, for the most part, either intrinsically absurd, or common to systems yet more ancient, whose claims to sanctity are denied."—*The Perfect Way*, p. 26.

"For this sharp-edged axe hath led thee forward unto great bliss."—*Sata. Brâh.*, III. 6, 4, 14.

See INSPIRATION REVELATION, SCRIPTURES, TREE.

BA, THE SOUL :—

A symbol of the spiritual ego, or Divine spark, within each individual soul.

"In many texts the *Ba* is made to live with Râ or Osiris in heaven. . . . In the Papyrus of Nebquet it is seen in the form of a human-headed hawk flying down the funeral pit, bearing air and food to the mummified body to which it belongs."—BUDGE, *Book of the Dead*, Vol. I. p. lx.

As the spiritual ego is atma-buddhic it is the same with "Osiris (atma) in heaven (buddhi)." The "human-headed hawk" signifies the spiritual aspect of man. The "mummified body" signifies the purified personality which the spirit vitalises in its inner being, though its astro-mental form is left inactive and dead. The Ram-headed form of Osiris is sometimes called *Ba*.

See EMBALMENT, HAWK, MONAD OF LIFE, MUMMY, SON OF GOD, SPARK.

BABEL CITY :—

A symbol of a mental centre established in the soul, at an early period of human evolution, when the entire lower nature of the soul was in a homogeneous condition.

"From the very commencement of man's evolution, which was always meant to be spiritual only, he was a Temple (house of the Divine). At first his life was simple. It was onefold, so to speak, in order to express how simple it was. But even then the Divine Presence was within it potentially. It was not simple in its structure, but only in its powers of functioning. It was always a conscious being upon the spiritual planes, though its consciousness was what we might express by the term onefold: that word expresses its limitations, just like a child-consciousness. And then, as it performed its evolution upon the spiritual planes, it gradually unfolded more and more in its consciousness."—J. TODD FERRIER, *New Reformer*, Nov. 1911.

See CONFUSION, LANGUAGE, SPEECH.

BABEL TOWER :—

A symbol of the false conception that the highest truth may be reached through the exercise of the lower mental faculties.

See SHINAR, SPEECH.

BABYLON :—

A symbol of the lower nature of desire and sensation, which holds the soul in captivity.

"The old temple has been thrown down and despoiled, and the 'children of Israel' have been carried away captive to 'Babylon,'—the mystic name of the stronghold of Materialism. As it is written : 'The vessels of the House of the Lord'—that is, the doctrines of the Church—'great and small, and the treasures of the Temple and of the King and of the princes, were carried away to Babylon. And the enemies set fire to the House of God, and broke down the wall of Jerusalem,' that is, the Soul—'and burnt all her towers, and whatsoever was precious they destroyed.' (2 CHR. xxxvi. 19)."—*The Perfect Way*, Pref. to 1st ed., KINGSFORD & MAITLAND.

"All the vessels of gold and silver were five thousand four hundred. All these did Sheshbazzar bring up, when they of the captivity were brought up from Babylon unto Jerusalem."—Ezra i. 11.

The higher qualities (gold and silver) were preserved in the soul above its lower experiences.

See Bondage, Captivity, Exodus, Fetters, Suffering, Temple.

BACABS, FOUR :—

Symbols of the buddhic, mental, astral, and physical bodies of a human being.

See Children of horus, Pillars of shu.

BACCHUS :—

A symbol of the Higher Self incarnate in the lower nature.

"To the ordinary reader the name of Bacchus suggests nothing more than revelry and drunkenness, but it is now well known, that amid all the abominations that attended his orgies, their grand design was professedly ' the purification of souls,' and that from the guilt and defilement of sin."—A. Hislop, The Two Babylons, p. 22.

See Dionysus, Intoxication.

BACK PARTS OF THE DEITY :—

Symbolic of the passive aspect of the higher nature, which is negative to the lower.

(Exod. xxxiii 23).

BACKBONE :—

A symbol of aspiration, or of the Divine ray,—the Sushumna Solar Ray,—the " backbone of Osiris,"—or the " Tree " of the Divine Life in the soul.

See Brahmarandram, Sutratma, Tet, Tree of life.

BAHMAN (VOHU-MANO) :—

A symbol of a messenger of the Supreme, signifying victory over the lower nature.

"When the kinvat bridge has been crossed, the archangel Bahman rises from a golden throne : ' Now hast thou come hither to us, O righteous one ! from the perishable life to the imperishable life."—Minok-hired, Haug, Essays.

When the " bridge " of mind between higher and lower has been passed, and a high mental state has been arrived at by the perfected soul, —the condition of the consciousness now being centred in the causal-body, —the " archangel," or type of glorious

achievement manifests, and the wondrous power of the Self is declared, in that " this mortal shall have put on immortality ; then shall come to pass the saying that is written, death is swallowed up in victory."

See Amshaspands, Archangels, Bridge (kinvat), High-priestship, Man (righteous), Victory, Vohuman.

BAKHDHI THE BEAUTIFUL :—

A symbol of the higher mind, or devachanic plane.

"The fourth land was the beautiful Bakhdhi with high lifted banners."—Vendidad I. S. B. of E.

The fourth region is the devachanic plane, above which are the activities of atma-buddhi.

See Banners, Devachan, Manas, Nisaya.

BALANCE OF SPIRITS :—

A symbol of the comparative valuation of the forces (spirits) for good and evil in the soul, between incarnations.

"The weighing of Rashnû the just, with the balance of spirits which renders no favour on any side, neither for the righteous, nor yet for the wicked."— The Minok-hired, Haug, Essays.

The " weighing " is the point where the balance in favour of the Higher Self may be estimated. The righteous and the wicked are symbolic of the individuality and the personality.

See Bridge (kinvat), Gilgoolem, Horse (black), Mitro, Rashnu.

BALANCE IN THE " WEIGHING OF THE HEART " PICTURE :—

A symbol of the summing up of the soul's experience of relative existence, at the end of the life cycle.

"All that was required of the deceased was that his heart should balance exactly the symbol of the law."—Budge, Egyptian Ideas, etc., p. 136.

When the personality (feather symbol) exactly corresponded with the individuality in the causal-body (heart), then the lower consciousness could rise and become one with the higher.

"They whose balances shall be heavy with good works shall be happy, but they whose balances shall be light are those who shall lose their souls, and shall remain in hell for ever."—Koran, Surah, 23, 104.

" If the dead was found to be righteous he received back his heart, the rest of the immortal parts of his soul were re-united in him, and he was again built up into the man who had walked the earth, but who now entered upon new and eternal life."—WIEDEMANN, *Rel. of Anc. Egyptians*, p. 249.

If the personality (dead) was perfected, then he became one with the individuality in the causal-body.

See BRIDGE OF HEAVEN, CAUSAL-BODY, DEFUNCT, FEATHER, HEART, HELL, JUDGMENT HALL, PRAGÂPATI (relaxed), SAU.

BALARĀMA (RAMA THE STRONG) :—

A symbol of the Individuality, Ego, Divine Spark, or Monad, in the soul.

" Balarāma who is reputed to be an avatara of Sesha or Ananta, the serpent without end, which serves as a bed to Vishnu, appears to be an ancient agricultural deity, that presided over the tillage of the soil and the harvest. He is armed with a ploughshare, whence his surname *Halabhrit*, the plough-bearer."—BARTH, *Religions of India*, p. 173.

The Individuality, which is a resultant of the forces of the soul in the process of the cycle of manifestation (Ananta) of the Higher Self (Vishnu), presides over the cultivation, development, and transmutation of the lower nature. The Individuality fashions the lower bodies—mental, astral, and physical,—and produces the conditions (ploughing) necessary for the growth of the soul.

The two brothers Balarāma and Krishna were brought up together by the herdsman Nanda ; signifying that the Individuality and the incarnate Self are closely associated in the purified mind (Nanda).

See BIRTH OF KRISHNA, BROTHER OF JESUS, INDIVIDUALITY, INTOXICATION, KRISHNA, PLOUGHING, RAMA, SERPENT (ananta), SILENUS, VISHNU.

BALDER THE GOOD :—

A symbol of the Higher Self who sacrifices himself for the sake of humanity, and descends as Spirit into Matter to become the Archetypal Man—dying in involution, to rise again in the evolution of the myriad human souls.

" It may truly be said of Balder that he is the best, and that all mankind are loud in his praise. So fair and dazzling is he in form and features, that rays of light seem to issue from him ; and thou mayest have some idea of the beauty of his hair, when I tell thee that the whitest of all plants is called ' Balder's brow.' Balder is the mildest, the wisest, and the most eloquent of all the Æsir, yet such is his nature that the judgment he has pronounced can never be altered."— *Prose Edda*, MALLET, p. 418.

The Higher Self is the Ideal and centre of the mental qualities (mankind) which extol and venerate it. The light of Truth shines from it, and through faith there may be perceived something of its purity and perfection ("His head and his hair were white as white wool, white as snow." REV. i. 14). The "whitest of all plants " is the "tree of life" which is the spiritual ray of Truth and Life (Balder's brow) which vitalises every soul. The Higher Self who is love and wisdom (atma-buddhi) is the Word of God (eloquent). "For the word of God is living and active, and sharper than any two-edged sword, and piercing even to the dividing of soul and spirit " (HEB. iv. 12).

"After that, Hermod rode forward to the palace (in the underworld), alighted, went in, and there he saw Balder, his brother, sitting in the highest place : and there Hermod remained overnight. The next morning he entreated from Hel that Balder might ride home with him, representing to her the sorrow which prevailed among the Asar."—*Prose Edda*.

And following that, the Christ-soul, or progressing soul, reaches the stage where the Christ within is enthroned as a supreme Ideal. Then there ensues a devachanic condition wherein the soul passes an intervening period of relative inaction or subjectivity. That state concluded, and when the soul was to go forth again, the petition is made that the Divine Vision within may accompany it. The excuse given for this request is the need which exists for further co-operation upon the planes whereon the forces of nature are working.

"Hel replied, that it should now be tried whether Balder was so universally beloved as they said ; if, therefore, everything in the world, the living as well as the dead, wept for him, then should he return to the Asar ; but that he should remain in Hel if any single thing excused itself or would not weep."—*Ibid*.

Now the promise is made that the Christ from within shall come forth and manifest in the soul, and that the choice shall be given to the activities and intelligences operative on the lower soul levels, to be made one in Him,—the soul being composite and full of all potencies. If then, every emotion or quality earnestly yearns for the Christ,—that which is actively as well as passively engaged co-operatively,—then He would come to them and raise them. But where there should be no ardent desire for Him, no sense of incompleteness, no sense of spiritual need, then the Christ should remain in the realm of the potential and unmanifest.

" In most of the religions of the ancient world, the relation between the soul and God has been represented as a return of the soul to God. A yearning for God, a kind of divine home-sickness, finds expression in most religions."—MAX MÜLLER, *Theosophy*, etc., p. 92.

"The One is not far away from any one, and yet is liable to be far away from one and all, since, present though It be, It is efficaciously present only to such as are capable of receiving It."—PLOTINUS *Enneads*, VI, ix. 4.

"Perfect Love pertains to Charity which clings to God for His own sake." —AQUINAS.

See ASAR, ASGARD, DEATH, DEATH OF BALDER, FORMS, FROST, GANGLER, HERMOD, HUNGER, THOCK, URNA.

BANNERS, HIGH LIFTED :—

A symbol of the rays of the Self, or the Divine effluence of truth, streaming down on the higher mental plane.

See BAKHDHI.

BANQUET OR FEAST :—

A symbol of the assimilation of Wisdom and Love by the soul, and of the enjoyment of what it has earned through its efforts. A banquet may also stand for a completed period, or stage of soul-growth, when the results of experience are gathered.

"So the king and Haman came to the banquet that Esther had prepared. And the king said unto Esther at the banquet of wine, What is thy petition ? "— ESTHER v. 6.

This represents a stage when soul-growth is due to the natural order under the lower principle (Haman) the prime minister of the Supreme

(king), before the Self (Mordecai) is established in the soul to rule over it. The buddhic principle (Esther) directs the evolution and transmutes the results of experience (prepares the banquet). The " petition " on the plane of wisdom (wine) signifies the perception on the buddhic plane that a new order is to supplant the natural order, and the Self is to preside in the soul.

See BUDDHIC FUNCTION, COW OF PLENTY, ESTHER, FEAST, HEROD, HIGHER AND LOWER, MUSIC, TRANS-MUTATION.

BAPTISM OF WATER :—

A symbol of purification of the soul-qualities by Truth (water), effected through development of the moral nature.

"Go ye therefore and make disciples of all the nations, baptising them into the name of the Father, and of the Son, and of the Holy Ghost."—MAT. xxviii. 19.

A command which is full of the spirit of Christ. The disciplined qualities must extend their influence to the more backward qualities of all kinds, and bring about their purification through the attuning of the nature upon the three lower planes whereby the evolution of the soul is to be accomplished.

"The Lord washes or purifies man by the divine truth and the divine good ; and John represented this by his baptism : for the Holy Spirit is divine truth, fire is divine good, and water is the representative of both ; for water signifies the truth of the Word which becomes good by a life according to it." —SWEDENBORG, *Apoc. Rev.*, n. 378.

"He bathes. For impure indeed is man : he is foul within, in that he speaks untruth ;—and water is pure."— *Sata. Brâh.*, III. 1, 2, 10.

The mind acquires truth ; for the mind at first is ignorant and full of illusions and evil while desire rules the soul ; and it is truth (water) that purifies.

" 'We are all of us under the dominion of evil and sin because we are children of the water,' says the ancient Mexican formula of baptism, and Citatli and Atli, ' moon ' and ' water ' are constantly confounded in Aztec mythology."—*Non-classical Mythology*, p. 117.

In this statement the "water below " is meant, namely, the astra plane on which the desires are developed in the unar cycle. The "moon" is a common symbol of the astral plane, as also is "water." The personality is developed on the astral plane, hence we are "children of the water," at first under the rule of the desires.

"High principle, which is, in other words, the baptism of John, is the very basis on which is most naturally raised the superstructure of religious faith."— F. W. ROBERTSON, *Sermons, 1st Series,* p. 184.

"John's disciples come up out of Jordan, at the best but superficially cleansed, and needing that the process begun in them should be perfected by mightier powers than any which his message wields. They need more than that outward washing,—they need an inward cleansing ; they need more than the preaching of repentance and morality, —they need a gift of life ; they need a new power poured into their souls, the fiery stream of which, as it rolls along, shall seize and burn every growth of evil in their natures. They need not water, but Spirit ; not water, but Fire. They need what shall be life to their truest life, and death to all the death within, that separates them from the life of God."— A. MACLAREN, *Sermons, 2nd Series,* p. 236.

"Baptism is the declaration that this new-born life, which seems only a new-born animal, has in it, bound up with it, a divine nature. Baptism is the claiming of that nature. It is the assertion of the regeneration, the deeper and higher birth, the birth from heaven which is coincident with the birth from earth, and which is to use the physical basis for its servant, and its power of development."—PHILLIPS BROOKS, *Mystery of Iniquity,* p. 244.

See DISCIPLES, HOMA-TREE, I AM BULL, JOHANNA, JOHN BAPTIST, NATIONS, POOLS (goddess), RITES, SACRAMENT, SUDDHODANA, TCHESERT, WASHED, WATER, WOMAN (adultery),

BAPTISM OF FIRE :—

A symbol of purification by means of the buddhic function, of the souls of those egos who have attained Christhood.

"He shall baptise you with the Holy Ghost and with fire."—MAT. iii. 11.

This signifies the descent of the Spirit upon the faithful souls, which takes place when they are gathered together in one accord, looking within for the selfsame Light of Wisdom ; when they know that religion is progressive, and when they realise that the floodgates of Truth are never closed up, but that REVELATION is a reality of now and for ever. (*See* ACTS ii.)

"The Fire entereth into the soul secretly."—*Pistis Sophia.*

"The Fire" (buddhi) cometh not to the ego with observation, for it is not in the scope of the lower consciousness to perceive it.

"The fiery baptism will burn up the chaff of error with the fervent heat of Truth and Love, melting and purifying even the gold of human character."— Mrs. EDDY, *Science and Health,* p. 565.

"*The Holy Spirit is fire.* Now, whatever may be the meaning of the emblem in the preceding and subsequent clauses (of MAT. iii. 11), it can have but one meaning in our text itself—and that is, the purifying influence of the Spirit of God. Baptism with the Holy Ghost is not one thing and baptism with fire another, but the former is the reality of which the latter is the symbol. It may be worth while to dwell briefly on the force of the emblem. *Fire,* then, all over the world has been taken to represent the Divine energy. Scripture has from the beginning used it. . . . Thus, then, there is a continuous chain of symbolism, according to which some aspect of the Divine nature, and especially of the Spirit of God, is set forth for us by *fire.* The question, then, comes to be—What is that aspect ? In answer, I would remind you that the attributes and offices of the Spirit of God are never in Scripture represented as being destructive, and are only punitive, in so far as the convictions of sin, which He works in the heart, may be regarded as being punishments. The fire of God's *Spirit,* at all events, is not a wrathful energy, working pain and death, but a merciful omnipotence, bringing light and joy and peace."—A. MACLAREN, *Sermons, 2nd Series,* pp. 229–31.

See BORN AGAIN, FIRE, HOLY GHOST, 'PARACLETE, REGENERATION, REVELATION.

BARABBAS, MURDERER AND ROBBER :—

This symbol stands for a type of the lower instincts which kill out the Spirit, but it has no direct, or at best a very slight and obscure, meaning within the Gospel Drama.

BARHIS, SACRIFICIAL GRASS :—

A symbol of the life currents passing between the buddhic and astral planes, relating to the desires and their transmutations.

"At the beginning of the sacrifice the Advarya makes of a load of Darbha, or sacred grass, which has been brought to the sacrificial compound, seven bunches, each of which is tied together with a stalk of grass, just as the Baresma (Barsom) of the Parsis." (Footnote.)— J. EGGELING, *S. B. of E.*, Vol. XLIV. p. 84.

"As large as the altar is, so large is the earth; and the plants are represented by the barhis; so that he thereby furnishes the earth with plants; and those plants are firmly established in this earth; for this reason he spreads the barhis."—*Sata. Brâh.*, I. 3, 3, 9.

The soul (altar) that has to be evolved from latency is commensurate with the qualities of the lower nature (earth), for the desires (plants) are the outgrowths of the buddhic life forces (barhis) which furnish the lower nature with its qualities (plants), and these qualities when transmuted raise the lower nature. Hence the spiritual mind extends the scope of the buddhic energies.

See ADVARYA, BARSOM, BIRTH (SECOND), BUCKLE, GIRDLE, KUSTI, PLANTS, TAMA-GUSHI, WOOD (HOLY), YAGNA-PAVITA.

BARHISHAD PITRIS, OR LUNAR SPIRITS :—

Symbols of monads of form which become the centres of consciousness for the personalities. They are the "pitris of the demons," that is, the astral centres of the desires, passions, appetites, and instincts of the lower nature. They have been developed in animal-man on the moon in the lunar cycle.

See LUNAR CYCLE, MONAD OF FORM, MOON (waxing), PITRIS (lunar).

BARLEY AND WHEAT OR RICE :—

Symbols of high emotions on the buddhic plane, being the harvest of the ego's experience and efforts. Red barley is a symbol of love; and white wheat or rice, that of wisdom.

"The sacrificial essence entered into this earth. The gods searched for it by digging. They found it in the shape of those two substances,—the rice and barley."—*Sata. Brâh.*, I. 2, 3, 7.

The Divine Life entered into the lower nature of the soul. The spiritual egos sought for it by disciplining the lower qualities. They found it in the spiritual qualities of wisdom and love.

See CORN, EARTH, HARVEST, WHEAT AND BARLEY.

BARLEY MEAL EATEN :—

A symbol of experiences gathered and transmuted; or fruits of action as higher qualities laid up on the buddhic plane.

See TREASURE IN HEAVEN.

BARLEY-CORNS :—

Symbolic of Wisdom and Love,— the food of the soul.

"You are clarified butter and honey, O ye barley-corns; you are water and ambrosia. May you efface whatever sinful acts I have committed. Sins committed by words, by acts, and by evil thoughts."—*Institutes of Vishnu*, Ch. 48, 18.

Signifying; may Love and Wisdom and celestial Truth, purify my soul in expression, in deed, and in thought!

"He throws the barley-corns in with, 'Thou art barley (yava), keep thou (yavaya) from us the haters, keep from us the enemies!'"—*Sata. Brâh.*, III, 7, 1, 4.

The spiritual mind receives and transmits the vibrations of wisdom and love which are to rescue the soul from captivity to the desires (enemies).

See AMBROSIA, BUTTER, FOOD, HONEY, WATER.

BARSOM,—a ceremonial implement used in the Parsi ritual. It consists of a bundle of twigs or metal rods, which when not in use is placed across two crescent-shaped supports. The barsom is ceremonially sprinkled with milk :—

The bundle of twigs symbolises the currents or vibrations passing to and fro between the buddhic and astral planes. The currents represent the buddhic responses to the astral aspirations, and also the consequent growth of higher emotions as the indwelling Self is awakened through sensation and feeling. The two crescents at either end stand for the moon, which is a symbol of the astral nature, and through that of the buddhic. The Wisdom Goddesses are superlunar and often shown standing on the crescent moon. The "milk" signifies wisdom and love to nourish the soul.

"For our welfare the fire-priest, (athrava) Spitama Zarathushtra was born, he offered sacrifice for us and arranged the holy twigs (barsom). Thus comes forth from the waters (i.e. from its source) the good religion of the Mazdayasnians spreading over all the seven regions of the earth."—*Fravardin Yasht*, HAUG, *Essays on the Rel. of the Parsis*.

For the salvation of our souls, the great High Priest, the Higher Self, was born into the lower nature as the World-soul (Zoroaster) in the cycle of involution, becoming thereby a sacrifice for us, that through His limitation of himself we might attain to His perfection. For this end He provides the means, namely, the astro-buddhic process (barsom), for the growth of the higher nature in our souls. Thus comes forth from the eternal Truth (waters) the spiritual life of the Divine Monads, which outflows through all beings that exist in the seven globes of the planetary chain.

See ALCHEMY, ATHORNE, BARHIS, BIRTH (second) BLASPHEMY BUD-DHI, BUCKLE CRANIUM, DÆMONS, EPHOD, GIRDLE, KUSTI, MOON, REGIONS, RELIGION, SACRIFICE, SELF, TAMA-GUSHI, WOOD (holy), YAGNA-PAVITA, ZOROASTER.

BATTLE :—

A symbol of the conflict between mind and emotion, or the spiritually energised mental qualities and the desires, passions, and instincts of the lower nature.

"Every struggle of the people of God against evil in this world must be fired with eternal principles, must be instinct with thoroughness and with justice. . . . All the true battles of the earth really are God's battles, and are to be fought only in God's spirit and God's way. The old history of Israel and Edom sinks back into a parable. All that history was a crude and elementary utterance of the great truth that there must ever be, so long as the world remains imperfect and is struggling towards perfection, two parts of the world, one of which is God's and one which is not. What that chosen people represented is perpetual. There always is in the world some part of the world consecrated to the struggle to make the world divine. It is that part of the general humanity, that part of any race, nay, that part of any man— for even the individual life may be divided between God and the enemy of God— it is that part of human nature which is consecrated to God, and trying to do His will. That is the everlasting Israel. In more spiritual ways therefore, with less formality, more flexibly and freely, all that is said of God's relation to the Judaism of the Old Testament, must be the picture and the parable of the rela-

tion which God holds to all struggle after goodness, all effort of noble and devoted life everywhere and always."—PHILIPS BROOKS, Serm., *The Sword Bathed in Heaven*.

See BLACKSMITHS, CONFLICT, CONQUEROR, MAB, PER-AHA, PILLAR (temple), STRIFE, VICTORY, WAR, WARRIORS.

BDELLIUM AND THE ONYX STONE :—

Symbols of wisdom and power on the buddhic plane.

See HAVILAH.

BEANS :—

A symbol of a false philosophy.

"Miserable men, wholly miserable, restrain your hands from (plucking) beans."—*Empedocles*, verse 441, FAIRBANKS.

Those souls which are plunged in despair are to abstain from false conceptions of life, the product of emotion. "Beans" signify the fruit of the emotion-nature which is aptly symbolised by the quickly running and irregular growth of the bean plant.

BEARS :—

Symbolic of passions or illusions which hug the mind and stifle effort.

"And there came forth two she bears out of the wood, and tare forty and two children of them."—2 KINGS ii. 24.

The young undeveloped mind (children) is unable to appreciate a higher mental state, and is also lacking in faith and hope, hence it is condemned to be buffeted by the passions and illusions of the lower life of desire and sensation.

"Bears signify fallacies,—the literal sense of the Word, read indeed, but not understood."—SWEDENBORG, *Apoc. Rev.*, n. 573.

See ANIMALS, APE AND TIGER, BEASTS (wild).

BEAST OF THE BOTTOMLESS PIT :—

A symbol of the desire-mind which is the adversary of the Spirit. It is energised by the desire-nature never satisfied, i.e. "bottomless."

"Here is wisdom. He that hath understanding, let him count the number of the beast ; for it is the number of a man : and his number is Six hundred and sixty and six."—REV. xiii. 18.

He that hath knowledge of the

higher and lower planes in the structure of the soul, knows what constitutes man in his lower nature ; and this lower nature is the animal-man, or the " beast " in man. " Six " is a number of completion, and 666 indicates completion of nature on the three lower planes, i.e. the lower mental, astral, and physical planes, which three completely organised states make up the desire-mind embodied, or " beast." It must be remembered that the human consciousness is on the mental plane only.

See BOTTOMLESS PIT, DEVIL, PIT, SERPENT (hissing), WITNESSES (two).

BEASTS, ANIMALS :—

Symbolic of desires, passions and instincts of the lower nature.

" And as many pretend that the soul of Typhon himself is divided amongst these animals, the fable may be thought to express enigmatically that every irrational and bestial nature belongs to the share of the Evil Spirit."—PLUTARCH, *Isis and Osiris*, § 73.

See ANIMALS, BURNT OFFERING, HAND OF BEAST, SACRIFICE.

BEASTS, CLEAN :—

Symbolic of the superior emotions of the lower nature, that is, emotions in the astral course of production which are ready for transmutation.

" Thus in the living soul shall there be good beasts, in gentleness of action, . . . and good cattle, which neither if they eat, shall they over-abound, nor if they do not eat, have they any want ; and good serpents, not destructive to do hurt, but ' wise ' to take heed. (*Footnote*. In his *De Gen. con. Manich.* i. 20, Augustine interprets the dominion given to man over the beasts, of his keeping in subjection the passions of the soul, so as to attain true happiness.) "—AUGUSTINE, *Confessions*, p. 377.

" Of every clean beast thou shalt take to thee seven and seven, the male and his female ; and of the beasts that are not clean, two, the male and his female."—GEN. vii. 2.

The " seven and seven clean beasts " signify the higher emotions and aspirations which are to be established in the soul. These numbers 7 and 7 indicate perfection and completion, and correspond to the " fruit of the Spirit " (GAL. v. 22). The " unclean beasts " signify the pairs of opposites which are of the lower planes.

See ALTAR, ARK (Noah), CATTLE, FLOOD, FRUIT (spirit), GOSHURUN, OPPOSITES, SEVEN, TWO.

BEASTS, UNCLEAN :—

Symbolic of the inferior emotions which appertain to the " natural man."

" Of clean beasts, and of beasts that are not clean, and of fowls, and of everything that creepeth upon the ground, there went in two and two unto Noah into the ark, male and female, as God commanded Noah."—GEN. vii. 8, 9.

These injunctions refer to the way in which the higher and lower emotions, aspirations, and instincts, are said to go in by two and two, since each is to be perceived by its opposite. They " went in unto Noah into the ark," that is, the emotions entered a certain state of the soul (ark) and were attached to the individuality (Noah).

See ANIMALS, FLOOD, NOAH, GOSHURUN.

BEASTS OF THE EARTH :—

Symbolic of the desires of the lower nature, with the animal instincts and appetites (serpents).

" And the fear of you and the dread of you shall be upon every beast of the earth, and upon every fowl of the air ; with all wherewith the ground teemeth, and all the fishes of the sea, into your hand are they delivered."—GEN. ix. 2.

And the lower nature of the soul is first to be subdued and disciplined by the fear and dread of consequences, which are to bring it eventually into subjection. Into the power of the indwelling Self are all things of the lower nature to be delivered.

" ' The fear and dread of you, etc.' Animal faculties now are not only restrained by the ark or cross, but reduced to submission : the man or reason governs them. The ox strong to labour, the strength in us formed to serve, is not henceforth to spend its energies without direction. The lion and the bear, fierce thoughts, must be still. . . . I know indeed that even after this, after man has passed the flood and is regenerate, lions may be loosed in judgment by the Lord : the man in us may be slain, and the beast may be seen standing by the carcase ; or, as in another case, the man may be blind, and the beast, which should be guided by the man, may see more than that inward man which was formed to govern it. All this may be through sin. Yet our calling as regenerate is to rule the beasts, not to be ruled by them."—A. JUKES, *The Types of Genesis*, p. 125.

"And the Lord God said unto the serpent, Because thou hast done this, cursed art thou above all cattle, and above every beast of the field ; upon thy belly shalt thou go, and dust shalt thou eat all the days of thy life."—GEN iii. 14.

And the Divine nature decides that the desire-mind is indeed lower and grosser than the sub-human desires and instincts which preceded its evolution. It is doomed to remain on the lower planes, and it shall feed upon the sensations and forces which proceed from the lower nature as long as it exists.

"Here the craft and subtlety of the Serpent was manifest, and the precious Image (of God) was corrupted, and became a Beast of all beasts ; whereupon there are now so many and various properties in man ; as one a Fox, Wolf, Bear, Lion, Dog, Bull, Cat, Horse, Cock, Toad, Serpent, and in brief as many kinds of creatures as are upon the earth, so many and various properties likewise there are in the earthly man."—J. BEHMEN, *Mysterium Magnum*, p. 92.

See ANIMALS, CATTLE, DUST, FALL, FISH, MAN (natural), SACRIFICE, SERPENT (subtil).

BEASTS, WILD :—

Symbolic of the unruled baser passions of the lower nature.

"Fuh-he invented nets for fishes, and snares for wild beasts, in the use of which he instructed the people, for the twofold purpose of supplying their wants and procuring victims to offer in sacrifice."—KIDD, *China*, p. 103.

And now it is that in the scheme of the Logos an astral mechanism comes to be developed in the soul, which is to be used by the Ego in gathering the facts (fish) which it is necessary that he shall collect through sensation for his experience. The "wild beasts" symbolise the baser passions, which are to be checked and so transmuted through the gradual growth of the Self within. The "people" are the undeveloped instincts and activities which are to be disciplined and used ; as means to the end of Self-realisation. The "supplying" of the "wants" is realising that the powers within are to be utilised only for the highest purpose ; and this is the attitude that becomes the offering up of the Self,—or consecration of

the life,—to the One, in return for His own sacrifice.

"These (fierce wild beasts) are terrestrial dæmons, to whom the Chaldean oracle alludes, which says, 'the wild beasts of the earth shall inhabit thy vessel,' i.e. as Psellus explains it, the composite temperature of the soul."—IAMBLICHUS, *The Mysteries*, etc., trans. Th. Taylor, p. 98.

"Man begins his inward career, to use a sentence of Amiel, 'as a tamer of wild beasts, and these wild beasts are his passions. To cut their claws, to muzzle them, to tame them, to make of them domestic animals and servants, foaming at times, but submissive, that is personal education.'"—J. BRIERLEY, *Studies of the Soul*, p. 108.

See ANIMALS, APE AND TIGER, CREATURES, FISH, FUH-HE, NETS, PEOPLE, SACRIFICE, VESSEL.

BEASTS OF THE MOUNTAINS :—

Symbolic of ambitions, or elevated desires of a selfish nature.

"Separated by evil strife, the human members wander each in different directions along the breakers of the sea of life. Just so it is with plants and with fishes dwelling in watery halls, and beasts whose lair is in the mountains, and birds borne on wings."—*Empedocles*, FAIRBANKS, 247.

When evolution commenced, and the struggle for separate existence began, the functions of the Oversoul are said to be scattered, inasmuch as through desire and opinion a continual surging and unrest serve to stir the latent emotions by means of which growth is accomplished. So it is with the dawn of the emotions (plants), the astro-mental nature, the ambitions (beasts), the ideals and aspirations (birds).

See ARC. MAN, BIRDS, DISMEMBERMENT, EVOLUTION, FISH, MEMBERS, MOUNTAIN (lower), PLANTS, SEA, SEPARATION, STRIFE, WINGS.

BEASTS OF THREE SORTS ON EARTH :—

Symbolic of the first three root-races, being of an astral nature.

"Ahura Mazda and Yima called meetings of Gods and mortals, as bad times were coming, and the three sorts of beasts would perish."—*Vendidad*, II.

The Supreme through the Higher Self, calls a gathering together of the higher aspirations and practical forces, as a reckoning time was shortly to be arrived at : that is, the period when the carrying on of involution on another globe takes place. The period described is the period preceding evolution. The first three root races in evolution would in turn perish.

See ASTRAL PLANE, GODS, MAN (born), MOON, PLANETARY CHAIN, PYLUS, RACES OF MEN, RAGHA, ROOT-RACES, ROUND, SEEDS (men), YIMA.

BEASTS, BIRDS, AND FISHES :—

Symbolic of desires, aspirations, and facts or feelings.

"The affections and consequent perceptions and thoughts of spirits and angels in the spiritual world appear at a distance in the forms of animals or creatures upon the earth, which are called beasts, of creatures in the air which are called birds, and of creatures in the sea which are called fishes."—SWEDENBORG, *Apoc. Rev.*, n. 405.

BEASTS AND BIRDS SACRIFICED :—

Symbolic of the lower nature offered up for the sake of the higher.

See BURNT OFFERINGS, OBLATIONS, OFFERING, SACRAMENTAL CAKES, SACRIFICE.

BEATIFIC VISION :—

The soul realising its identity with the Infinite.

"The first stage of progression from the hiddenness (of the unrevealed Godhead) is made through the 'Great Intelligencies' which are nearest to God. These beings have first-hand illuminations, they 'participate in the One Himself, and have the feast of the beatific vision, which makes divine all who strain aloft to behold it '; and the Divine energy which 'bubbles forth' from the Godhead is passed on by them to the next rank, and so on down, until 'every existing thing participates in the Beautiful,' i.e. in the Godhead" (From *Dionysius*).—R. M. JONES, *Mystical Religion*, p. 106.

"To be completely filled with God, and perfected in the eternal movement of God ; in a word, to be conscious of God and dwell in the Divine impulse or inspiration—that is the perfect state." —H. BUSHNELL, *Nature, etc.*, p. 365.

See AMSHASPANDS, ARCHANGELS, BLISS, GODHEAD, SERMON, UNITY.

BEATRICE OF DANTE :—

A symbol of wisdom,—the buddhic principle, the fount of all virtue and intuition.

See HELEN, SERPENTS (sparks).

BEAUTY AND UGLINESS :—

Symbolic of attractiveness and repulsiveness.

BEBRYCIA :—

A symbol of a state of confidence in the Higher.
See AMYCUS.

BED :—

A symbol of a phase of thought or opinion, on which the ego reposes.

"That a bed signifies doctrine, is from correspondence, for as the body rests in its bed, so does the mind rest in its doctrine."—SWEDENBORG, *Apoc. Rev.*, n. 137.

BED, OR COUCH OF ZEUS :—

A symbol of the quiescent or unmanifest condition of the Self, at the beginning or end of a cycle.
See HEPHAISTOS, ZEUS.

BEE-INMATE OF LOTUS :—

Symbolic of intuitional perception, or understanding of wisdom (lotus).
See BEES, LOTUS.

BEELZEBUB :—

A symbol of evil, unreal and negative, which is to be overcome by truth and goodness the real and positive.
See EVIL, ILLUSION.

BEES :—

A symbol of the higher emotions, or of the spiritual egos.

"The Ancients, moreover, used to call the priestesses of Mother Earth (Dēmēter) Bees, in that they were initiates of the Terrene Goddess, and the Maid (Korē) herself Bee-like. They also called the Moon the Bee, as Lady of Generation ; and especially because [with the Magians] the Moon in exaltation is the Bull, and Bees are Ox-born—that is, souls coming into birth are Ox-born—and the 'God who steals the Bull' [Mithra] occultly signifies generation" (*Porphyry*). —G. R. S. MEAD, *Mysteries of Mithra*, p. 63.

"Bees appear to have been considered by the Greeks as emblems of purity, and as the symbols of nymphs, who are sometimes called Mellissæ, as were also priestesses in general."—ISAAC MYER, *Qabbalah*, p. 229.

"The gods Indra, Krishna, and Vishnu, on account of their name Madhavas (that is, born of Madhus, belonging to or in connection with it) were compared in India to bees ; the bee as making and carrying honey (madukaras) is especially the moon ; as sucking it, it is especially the sun."—GUBERNATIS, *Zool. Mythology*, Vol. II. p. 216.

The "priestesses of Demeter" signify the emotions of buddhi, that is, the higher emotions of the soul. The moon in its higher (exaltation) aspect is a symbol of buddhi which is allied with the Self (the Bull). The higher emotions (bees) are from buddhi (ox-born), as also are the spiritual egos (atma-buddhi) descending into incarnation. The Self "steals" the Archetypal Man (Bull-Mithra) when he becomes the myriad selves of humanity. The Higher Self in his active aspects (Indra, etc.) is comparable to the higher emotions (bees) which produce wisdom and love (honey) as food for the soul. The higher emotion nature (bee) producing the soul's nourishment, is of buddhi (moon), while the soul's assimilation of wisdom and love, raises the lower Self to the Higher Self (sun).

See ARC. MAN, BULL, CANDLES, DEMETER, HONEY, INDRA, KRISHNA, MITHRA, MOON, OX-BORN, SUN, VISHNU.

BEES, LIBATIONS FROM :—

A symbol of the voluntary relinquishing of the results of efforts, in favour of an ideal, by the lower self.

"Queen Kypris they worshipped with hallowed offerings, with painted figures, and perfumes of skilfully made odour, and sacrifices of unmixed myrrh and fragrant frankincense, casting on the ground libations from tawny bees."—*Empedocles, verse* 405, FAIRBANKS.

"Queen Kypris" signifies the buddhic ruler of the forthcoming evolution, for buddhi is the commencement of evolution ; the appeal being first of all made to the desire nature which is inverted buddhi. "Hallowed offerings with painted figures" are symbolic of those blissful conditions and transmuted desires which are appropriate to this early stage of soul-growth on the astral plane. "Perfumes" signify the inbreathing effects upon the higher planes, which become the causes, in turn, of mental evolution. "Sacrifices of myrrh and frankincense" symbolise the Truth and Wisdom which are transmuted from the lower experiences through

buddhi to the Higher Self. The "libations from bees" signify the free-will offerings or fruits of industry (bees), which are exacted of the lower self.

"We are working for a God just as a bee, without knowing it, is making honey for man."—RENAN, *Dial. Philos.*

See HONEY, KYPRIS, LIBATIONS.

BEGETTING SONS AND DAUGHTERS :—

Symbolic of mind and emotion creating, or giving rise to, states of reason and affection.

"And Seth lived a hundred and five years, and begat Enosh : and Seth lived after he begat Enosh eight hundred and seven years, and begat sons and daughters."—GEN. v. 6, 7.

And hope or mental desire (Seth) existed its appropriate time (105 = 6) and therefrom proceeded faith in the Divine (Enosh). And hope still existed and produced phases, or states, of joy and peace (807 = 15).

See CHILDREN, ENOSH, FIFTEEN, PATRIARCHS, SETH.

BEHEADING :—

A symbol of the cutting off of the lower mind, or a phase of opinion, at the end of a period or cycle.

See HEAD (living), HEAD OF SET.

BEHEMOTH, THE GREAT BULL :—

A symbol of the astro-physical matrix of all living things in the lower nature. It proceeds from its prototype upon the buddhic plane, and is fertilised by the mental seed-germs of all forms.

"The word *behemoth* literally means *beasts*, from the singular noun *behemah*, from the word *baham*, to be dumb." "By Behemoth and Leviathan are symbolised the two great hindrances of human salvation, viz. the Flesh and the Devil. . . . To speak more precisely, it seems probable that Behemoth represents the Evil One acting in the animal and carnal elements of man's own constitution, and that Leviathan symbolises the Evil One energising as his *external* enemy. Behemoth is the Enemy *within* us, Leviathan is the Enemy *without* us."—WORDSWORTH, *Bible, Job*, p. 95.

"Behold now behemoth, which I made with thee ; he eateth grass as an ox, etc."—JOB xl. 15–24.

The astro-physical nature is said to be made in alliance with the mental nature, and to have its life awakened by the faint aspirations or desires (grass) on the lower planes. Its manifestation (strength) is in the lower nature (loins, belly, etc.). It is the means whereby the Divine scheme of soul-probation is to be carried out (chief of the ways of God), the "sword of the spirit," or Divine will, being exercised upon it.

"Hail, holy Bull, beneficent, who makest increase. Who dost bestow thy gifts upon the faithful. Hail to thee whom Ahriman kills."—*Vendidad*, XXI. 1.

The prototype of the lower quaternary being on the buddhic plane, it is said to die on its descent to relativity (Ahriman) on the lower planes. As it contains the promise and potencies of perfection, it bestows the higher qualities upon the faithful in proportion to their efforts.

"In the names Behemut and Levitiya, sometimes given respectively to this Bull and Fish (of the Ottoman Sufi cosmogony) we seem to recognise the Behemoth and Leviathan of the book of Job."—GIBB, *Hist. of Ottoman Poetry*, Vol. I. p. 39.

See AHRIMAN, BULL, GRASS, JOB, LEVIATHAN, OX (sarsaok), VISCERA, VITAL AIRS, WOMB (cosmic).

BEHÛDET, GOD OF :—

A symbol of the Higher Self seated upon the buddhic plane.

"Thoth spake to Horbehûdti : 'Thou art a great protector.' From that day the sacred bark of Horus is called Great of Protection." (God of Behûdet is the same as Horus, or Horbehûdti.)—*Legend of Winged Sun-disk*.

The higher mind (Thoth) uttered itself to the Self : "Thou art indeed a great protector of myself." And from that period of development the causal-body (bark) is known to be a haven of protection for the qualities ; for through its functionings the soul is brought to a state of stability, centralised on the higher mind plane.

See BOAT, CAUSAL-BODY, DWELLING (palace), HORBEHÛDTI, HORUS, THOTH.

BEL OF NIPUR, OR MUL-LILLA, THE LORD OF THE LOWER WORLD :—

A symbol of the lower mind, - astro-mental.

"Now when Bel drew nigh, he saw the ship, and was very wroth ; he was filled with anger against the gods, the Igigi,

(saying) : Who then hath escaped with his life ? No man shall live after the destruction."—*Babylonian Flood Story*.

Now as the lower mind reached the zenith of its power, and was mightily increased in pride of the intellect so that the ideals (gods) were obscured, the quality of mental exclusiveness was developed, and it came to imagine that nothing it could not account for had any existence in the soul, or could survive death.

See NECKLACE, HERPEST, HIPPO-POTAMUS.

BELIEF :—

Union of the mind with a percept or concept presented to it. The mind unites with any idea if there is no opposing idea already accepted.

"Truth utters itself in outward symbols. Belief and resolution declare themselves in forms. It is the natural law of expression, and so long as the form remains soft and pliant, full of the spirit of the belief or resolution it expresses, all is right. Form and belief are like body and soul to one another. But when form hardens into formalism, when the real substance of belief, instead of remaining soft and pliant, grows stiff, and will not let belief grow and enlarge, will not let the food of belief which is new truth come pouring in, then you have got the most crusted and impenetrable armour that can be imagined. Forms ought to be the medium through which truth comes to the inner nature."—PHILLIPS BROOKS, *Mystery of Iniquity*, p. 157.

"Belief is of the very substance of the life. 'As he thinketh in his heart, so is he.' It is that through active service, through the will to do God's will, belief is ever struggling to become true, and feeling is ever struggling to grow healthy." —PHILLIPS BROOKS, *Light of the World*, p. 267.

"'Believe on the Lord Jesus Christ and thou shalt be saved.' It means that the one invincible force in your life is the Christ out of whom your soul has arisen ; not the evil that seems to bear it down. Believe that, and it will set you free, but believe it in the way that a man has to believe anything that lifts him to power. Your fetters are only made to be broken ; evil is only there to be transmuted to good."—R. J. CAMPBELL, Serm. *The Freedom of the Son of God*.

BENNU BIRD :—

A symbol of the spiritual ego which aspires and rises upward from the lower nature of the soul.

"I go in like the Hawk and I come

forth like the Bennu bird, the morning star of Rā."

"And grant that I may sail down to Tattu like a living soul, and up to Abtu (Abydos) like a Bennu bird."—BUDGE, *Book of the Dead*, pp. 20, 61.

The hawk descending on its prey, symbolises the spiritual ego falling into matter from which it afterwards ascends to the buddhic plane. The "living soul" descends to the lower planes (Tattu) to rise again to the higher planes (Abtu). The "morning star," or ascending soul, heralds the coming of its Lord the Sun of righteousness (Rā).

See ABTU, HAWK, KARSHIPTA, MORNING STAR, MORROW, PHANG, PHŒNIX, SONS OF GOD, STRIDES, TATTU.

BERSERKS, OR WARRIORS :—

Symbolic of active and combative qualities of the lower mind.

"The giantess Hyrrocken came riding on a Wolf, and had vipers for her reins. When she alighted from her steed, Odin ordered four berserks to mind him ; but they could not hold him in one place except by throwing him to the ground."—*Story of Balder, Edda.*

On the lowest sub-plane of the mind the activities take the form of Terror (Hyrrocken), fear (wolf), and cunning (vipers). And when the lower mind is given the rein, to guide the soul at this early stage, nothing good can be done with it through fear. By the will of the Supreme, the "berserks" courage, strength, avarice, and self-interest, partly neutralise its stultifying influence, but it must needs be kept in check altogether, by overthrowing fear completely.

See HYRROCKEN, MJOLNER, ODIN, ROMAN SOLDIERS, SOLDIERS, WOLF.

BERYLS AND GOLD :—

Symbols of love and wisdom.
See GEMS, JEWELS.

BES, GOD :—

See PILLOWS (mummies).

BETHANY :—

A symbol of the "abode of the Lord,"—a subjective state of consciousness on the higher mental plane in which the Higher Self dwells.
See ASCENSION OF JESUS, LAZARUS.

BETHESDA :—

A symbol of a state of bliss ; being a haven of rest for those who have outgrown the tribulations of the flesh and have cast off its fetters.
See CROSS, POOL, PORCHES.

BETHLEHEM :—

A symbol of the condition of purity and peace of mind, wherein the Christ-soul can be born as the Son of mind (man), and be protected at first from the strife of the lower emotions and desires.

"Wherefore every soul which receives that bread which comes down from heaven is the house of bread, that is, the Bread of Christ, being nourished and supported, and having its heart strengthened by that heavenly bread which dwells within it. Hence Paul also says, ' For we being many are one bread.' Every faithful soul is Bethlehem, as Jerusalem also is said to be, which has the peace and tranquillity of that Jerusalem which is above in heaven. That is the true Bread, which, when broken into pieces, fed all men."—ST. AMBROSE, *Letters*, p. 416.

See BIRTH OF JESUS, BREAD, VIRGIN MARY.

BETRAYAL OF JESUS :—

A symbol of the voluntary falling away from the Christ-soul of the lower element at the last, thus initiating the crossing over.

"And straightway Judas came to Jesus, and said, Hail, Rabbi ; and kissed him. And Jesus said unto him, Friend, do that for which thou art come."— MAT. xxvi. 49, 50.

"Judas" stands for the lowest, or least raised, quality in the not yet perfected Christ-soul, consequently that is the quality which requires the Soul to go through the anguish at the final crossing over from the lower to the higher state. The exercise of choice of action is the means whereby evolution is accomplished. Choice has previously been offered to the quality "Judas," when, having fallen away, he approaches to do that for which he has come. " Judas " by getting his selfish gratification (money) forfeits his claim to the Christ whom he betrays with a kiss ; that is, he retains the semblance of affection without the reality.

"The great problem of existence is our perfection ; the perfection, that is, of our liberty, the schooling of our choice or consent as powers, so that we may be fully established in harmony with God's will and character ; unified with Him in His will, glorified with Him in the glory of His character, and so perfected with Him in His eternal beatitude. Persons or powers are creatures who act, not by causality, but by consent; they must therefore be set in conditions that invite consent."—H. BUSHNELL, *Nature, etc.*, p. 62.

"In the lower stages of man's religious life we find this competition between different kinds of the good :—between the sensuous valuables to which the will is compelled by appetite, passion, and desire, and the spiritual values which religion, in its higher stages of the activity of intellect and imagination, presents as rivals to the sensuous And the man is called to choose between the two. This choice it is which seems to religion as a choice between the flesh and the spirit, or between the world and God, or between human favour and the Divine Approval; or, finally, between a widening moral separation from the Source of all spiritual Life and its voluntary acceptance as the indwelling and welcome Source of the soul's true and highest life."—G. T. LADD, *Phil. of Religion*, p. 338.

See DISCIPLES, JESUS OF THE GOSPELS, JUDAS, NIGHT (darkness).

BHARATA, THE VICE-KING :—

A symbol of the moral nature which rules the soul in the absence of the greater spiritual nature which is to follow.

"Bharata consents to take charge of the kingdom as a deposit. He bears away Rama's shoes on his head in token of this. . . . Until the return of the rightful king, never transacting any business without laying it before the shoes."—MON. WILLIAMS, *Indian Wisdom*, p. 354.

The moral nature rules for the soul's welfare until the spiritual nature is sufficiently evolved to take charge; when love of the ideal supersedes duty. The moral nature venerates the spiritual and puts it in the highest place in the mind (head). It recognises that in the spiritual is the power of progress (shoes), and it therefore, in all its operations, defers to the Higher Self—the Love nature which sooner or later will enter upon the kingdom which the moral nature is preparing for it.

See JOHN BAPTIST, MAHABHARATA, RAMA, SHOE-LATCHET, SHOES.

BHIKSHU :—

A symbol of a quality motived by love.

See ALMSGIVING, MENDICANT, MONK, SANNYASIN.

BHIMA, SON OF VAYU AND PRITHA :—

A symbol of the intellect, the product of the higher mind and nature.

"Bhima's great strength had to be maintained by plentiful supplies of food; as his name Vrikodara, 'wolf-stomached,' indicated a voracious appetite."—MON. WILLIAMS, *Indian Wisdom*, p. 382.

The intellect, which has such great power in the soul, requires to be supplied with knowledge (meat) of innumerable facts of nature and of life. The intellect is voracious for learning, and assimilates all it can for the support of its opinions, and for the formation of its theories. "Wolf-stomached" indicates the appetite of the intellect for the facts of the lower nature.

See FOOD, MEAT, PANDAVAS, PRITHA, STOMACH, VAYU, WOLF.

BHĪSMA, SĀNTANAVA, THE TERRIBLE :—

A symbol of the power for evolution active in the natural organism and environment during the early struggle for life and reproduction.

"The two brothers, Dhrita-rashtra and Pandu, were brought up by their uncle Bhīsma, who, until they were of age, conducted the government of Hastināpur."—MON. WILLIAMS, *Indian Wisdom*, p. 378.

The instinct-nature and the dawning mental nature were evolved in the undisturbed order of natural growth to which the soul was subject until the time arrived for the mind to assert itself through the personality.

"The first great single-combat was between Bhīsma and Arjuna. It ended in Arjuna transfixing Bhīsma with innumerable arrows, so that there was not a space of two fingers' breadth on his whole body unpierced. . . . Bhīsma had received from his father the power of fixing the time of his own death, and now declared that he intended retaining life till the sun entered the summer solstice."—*Ibid.*, p. 403.

The personality (Arjuna), as a centre of Divine life, commenced a new order by fighting nature (Bhīsma) through mind. It followed that the intelligent use of nature for personal ends took the place of subservience to nature. In the life of the soul, nature becomes transfixed by will-power (arrows) in every part and detail through the ingenuity of mind, and lives on. The natural order is said to receive from the Supreme the power of fixing its own term of life. It is a means to an end, and that end is the completion of the soul's growth : when nature has finished its work in the soul's evolution, " the sun enters the summer solstice," that is, the Self (sun) culminates in the soul, and the karmic natural order then exists for it no longer.

See ARJUNA, ARROWS, AUSHEDAR, DHRITA-RASHTRA, FALL, HASTINA-PUR, KARMA, PANDAVAS, PANDU, SUN-MOTIONLESS, ZENITH.

BIFROST, THE HEAVENLY BRIDGE :—

A symbol of the higher mind.

"Which is the path leading from earth to heaven ? 'That is a senseless question,' replied Har, with a smile of derision. 'Hast thou not been told that the gods made a bridge from earth to heaven, and called it Bifrost ? You must surely have seen it ; but perhaps thou callest it the rainbow. It is of three hues, and is constructed with more art than any other work. But strong though it be, it will be broken to pieces when the sons of Muspell, after having traversed great rivers, shall ride over it."—MALLET, *North. Antiq., Prose Edda,* pp. 408–9.

This refers to the period before the spiritual egos (sons of Muspell) had descended to incarnate in the lower nature. After traversing the buddhic states (rivers) they passed by means of the higher mind (bridge) to be attached to the personalities of the lower mind. Then, as it were, the bridge is broken down, for the lower consciousness is unable to rise to higher levels. The " three hues " are the three sub-planes of the higher mind.

See BOW, BRIDGE, CLOUDS, FALL, GANGLER, GODS, HEIMDALL, MUSPELL, RAINBOW.

BINAH, THE SEPHIRAH, OR IM-MAH THE MOTHER-UNDER-STANDING :—

A symbol of the principle of matter in which Spirit (Hokhmah-wisdom) becomes involved. The Understanding is receptive of Wisdom.

"For Divine Matter receiving that which defines and bounds it, possesses a definite and intellectual life."—PLOTINUS, *On Matter,* § 5.

"From the bosom of this Unity (Kether), two parallel principles proceed in apparent opposition, but which in reality are inseparable ; one is female, passive, negative, called Binah, Under-standing ; the other male, active, positive, called Hokhmah, i.e. Wisdom."—ISAAC MYER, *Qabbalah,* p. 193.

"The universal spiritual passive matter of Ibn Geberol is paralleled by Binah. In the Qabbalah matter always corresponds with the female passive principle, to be influenced by the active, or male, the forming."—*Ibid.,* p. 261.

At the manifestation of a solar universe, the Absolute outbreathes the Relative, which is dual as Spirit and Matter. The first is the active informing agent, and the second the passive, receptive condition.

See HEAVEN AND EARTH, HOKH-MAH, MALE-FEMALE, MALKHUTH, MATTER, MĀYĀ, OCEAN (feminine), PRAKRITI, SEPHIROTH, SHEKINAH.

BINDING AND LOOSING ON EARTH AND IN HEAVEN :—

Symbolic of the determinations of the law of karma. Cause and effect exemplified in higher and lower conditions.

"What things soever ye (the disciples) shall bind on earth shall be bound in heaven : and what things soever ye shall loose on earth shall be loosed in heaven."—MAT. xviii. 18.

The binding or loosing by the disciplined qualities (disciples) in the lower nature (earth), signifies the use made of the powers of the soul in their outgoing to bind or loose the desires. The binding or loosing in the higher nature (heaven) is the corre-sponding result arrived at by such activities within the soul in their incoming. That is, if the lower quali-ties are under control on earth, the higher qualities are under control in heaven ; or if the lower qualities are unrestrained on earth, the higher qualities remain unclaimed in heaven.

See DISCIPLES, FEEDING, KARMA, QUALITIES, TRANSMUTATION.

BIRD, GREAT,—" the God-like Bird which sits upon the Tree of Life,"—under the names, Hiran-yagarbha, Karshipta, Simorg, Sinamru :—

A symbol of the Higher Self or the Individuality, seated, as it were, upon the Divine Ray direct from the Absolute.

"There are times when we all get glimpses of that greater Self, that Self beneath the self, that Life within our life, that struggles for expression like a bird behind the bars of a cage ; that Soul within the soul which as a fourteenth-century mystic puts it, 'hath never consented to sin, nor ever shall.' That is the real you, the real me, the real Man in every man."—R. J. CAMPBELL, Serm., *Our Solidarity in God*.

"In the Rig-Veda (x. 149, 3) the sun is called the bird of Savitri."—A. BARTH, *Religions of India*, p. 20.

The "sun" is the symbol of the Higher Self.

See ATMAN, BIRDS (two), FIG-FRUIT, HIRANYAGARBHA, KALAHANSA, KARSHIPTA, PHANG, SEB, SIMORG, SWAN.

BIRDS ; FOWLS OF THE AIR :—

Symbolic of aspirations ; aspiring tendencies in the qualities of the soul ; thoughts which soar heavenward in the mind (air).

"Birds signify such things as relate to the understanding, and thence to thought and deliberation."—SWEDENBORG, *Apoc. Rev.*, n. 757.

"To every man there come noble thoughts that pass across his heart like great white birds."—MAETERLINCK.

"All the powers of God are winged, being always eager and striving for the higher path which leads to the Father."—PHILO, *Works*, Vol. IV. p. 252.

"And God said, Let the waters bring forth abundantly the moving creature that hath life, and let fowl fly above the earth in the open firmament of heaven."—GEN. i. 20.

And the Supreme now directs that the desire-nature (lower "water," astral) shall be the means of gradually giving rise to the lower emotions that have evolving life, and these are gradually to take wings and be the means of raising the lower impulses through aspiration, to the mental and higher planes.

See CREATURES, FIRMAMENT, PATH (birds), WATER (lower), WINGS.

BIRDS OF THE HEAVEN :—

A symbol of the Elder Brethren of humanity : those Egos who have "gone before," and who,—having aspired to the things which are above, and conquered the things below,—are now free and able agents of the Supreme working upon the buddhic plane. These Egos not having any lower nature, are unlikely ever to use vehicles of matter below the higher mental plane, though they could, of course, do so if they chose, because they necessarily have command of all lower conditions. But they act under the Divine law never to assist the lower until the lower is ready and prepared to receive help from them and profit by it.

See ARHATS, AURVAITO, BIRD'S NEST, TREE OF LIFE.

BIRDS, TWO, OF THE HOLY FIG-TREE :—

Symbols of the Higher Self seated above, and the indwelling Self evolving below in the human soul. Both are allied with the "tree of Life," the Divine Ray from the Absolute.

"Two birds (the Paramātman and Jivātman, or supreme and individual souls) always united, of the same name, occupy the same tree. One of them (the Jivātman) enjoys the sweet fruit of the fig (or fruit of acts), the other looks on as a witness. Dwelling on the same tree (with the supreme Soul), the deluded (individual) soul, immersed (in worldly relations), is grieved by the want of power ; but when it perceives the Ruler, (separate from worldly relations) and his glory, then its grief ceases. When the beholder sees the golden-coloured maker (of the world), the Lord, the Soul, the source of Brahmā, then having become wise, shaking off virtue and vice, without taint of any kind, he obtains the highest identity."—*Mundaka Upanishad*, III. 1, 1–3.

The Supreme Self (Paramātman) and the Incarnate Self (Jivātman) are one in essence and are both on the primal Ray from the Absolute (the Tree of Life). The Incarnate Self evolving in the souls of humanity, struggles upward to enjoy in the buddhic consciousness the fruit of experience and aspiration, while the Supreme Self is a witness and inactive. The Incarnate Self is immersed in illusion and ignorance, suffering and sorrow, but when having conquered the lower nature and risen above it, it perceives the Supreme Self, then its sorrow ceases ; ignorance and illusion are dispelled, and the Truth is made manifest. The pairs of opposites are discarded, and perfection having been attained, the two Selves become one Self in complete identity.

"All that is in the Godhead is *one.* Therefore we can say nothing. He is above all names, above all nature. *God works; so doth not the Godhead.* Therein they are distinguished—in working and not working. The end of all things is the hidden Darkness of the eternal Godhead, unknown and never to be known (Eckhart)."—R. M. JONES, *Mystical Religion,* p. 225.

"We discover in our inner self that we are not masters even in our own house. The inward economy of thinking and feeling which we call ourselves is, we find, to a large extent strange to us and independent of us. What power have we over our own sensations ? We cannot create sensation. We can only experience it. That a given set of circumstances should produce a given result of pleasure or pain is an arrangement entirely outside our own will. We accept it, we perhaps wonder at it. What we cannot do is either to explain it or alter it. It gives one an eerie, haunted feeling to realise that within us, yet not of us, there is this unseen agent who arranges for us all the phases of our consciousness, leaving the task of them simply for our part in the business. This strange registering apparatus, which we did not create and do not regulate, is ready for every conceivable event that may happen to us. If it were announced to us that to-morrow we were to be married or to be hanged, to be made a millionaire or a pauper, a certain pre-ordained sensation would be the result. But what precisely it would be, either in its flavour, its intensity, or its duration, is beyond both our will and our power of prediction. We are, indeed, the spectator of the greater part of our inner life rather than its agent or producer."—J. BRIERLEY, *Studies of the Soul,* p. 82.

The subjective mind of the involuntary vital system creates and maintains the body for the use of the voluntary cerebral system of the objective mind or personality.

See ATMAN, BRAHMA, DARKNESS, DOER, FIG-FRUIT, FIG-TREE, GOD-HEAD, GOLD, HIGHER AND LOWER SELVES, INCARNATION, INDIVIDUALITY, JESUS (son of God), JOB, PERSONALITY, SELF (supreme), SELF (lower), SOUL (spirit), TREE OF LIFE, YELLOW.

BIRDS (LOWER ASPECT) :—

Symbolic of emotions of ambition, pride, vanity, and exaltation of the personality. These affections multiply themselves and bind the soul to the lower life.

"In Holy Scripture 'birds' are sometimes given to be understood in a bad sense, and sometimes in a good sense. Since by the birds of the air occasionally the powers of the air are denoted, being hostile to the settled purposes of good men. Whence it is said by the mouth of Truth, 'And when he sowed, some seeds fell by the wayside, and the fowls of the air came and devoured it'; in this way, because evil spirits besetting the minds of men, whilst they bring in bad thoughts, pluck the word of life out of the memory. Hence, again, it is said to a certain rich man full of proud thoughts, 'The foxes have holes, etc.' (MAT. xiii. 4). For foxes are very cunning animals, that hide themselves in ditches and caves ; and when they face the light, they never run in straight courses, but always by crooked doublings. But the birds, as we know, with lofty flight lift themselves into the air. So then, by the name of 'foxes,' the crafty and cunning demons, and by the title of the 'birds of the air' these same proud demons are denoted. As if he said, 'the deceitful and uplifted demons find their habitation in your heart'; i.e. in the imagination of pride, 'but the Son of Man hath not where to lay His head,' i.e. 'My humility findeth not rest in your proud mind.' "—GREGORY THE GREAT, *Morals on the Book of Job,* Vol. II. pp. 394–5.

"Demons," "powers of the air," and "evil spirits" are symbols of the lower emotions and desires, which are hostile to the higher nature.

"By a foul spirit and an unclean bird are signified all the evils which pertain to the will and consequent actions, and all the falses which pertain to the thought and consequent deliberations."—SWEDENBORG, *Apoc. Rev.,* n. 757.

"For every kind of beasts and birds, of creeping things and things in the sea, is tamed, and hath been tamed by mankind."—JAMES iii. 7.

The desires, ambitions, lower propensities and passions are subjected to the mind.

See DEMONS, DEVILS, HOUSES FOR CORPSES, MONSTERS, WHALES.

BIRD'S NEST:—

A symbol of the buddhic plane (heaven) in which the aspirations (birds) lodge, and in which are reared their progeny—the higher emotions.

"Bird is a Hebrew term for angel; the Bird's Nest is heaven. . . . In the Zohar the Bosom of God is called 'the Bird's Nest.' 'When the Messiah shall be made perfect, through the instrumentality of the righteous, he will enter the Garden of Eden, into that place which is called the Bird's Nest' (*Zohar,* 2 8b)."—ISAAC MYER, *Qabbalah,* p. 217.

The "Messiah" signifies the Christ-soul, or indwelling Self, not yet perfect in expression but to be made so through the instrumentality of the evolving higher qualities (the righteous). When perfection on the lower planes is attained then the Christ consciousness rises to the buddhic plane (Eden), or the "bosom of God"—the "nest" of the great Sun-Bird, the eternal Self of all ; the "nest of Brahman" over which he broods.

"Birds of the heaven come and lodge in the branches thereof."—MAT. xiii. 32.

See ANGELS, BIRD (great), BIRDS (heaven), EDEN, TIME, TREE OF LIFE.

BIRTH AND DEATH OF FORMS :—

Human birth is the entrance of the ego with its qualities into a new body, or vehicle of consciousness, while death is the exit of the ego from a body of any age. The first implies the out-breathing of the spirit and personality into material forms on the mental, astral, and physical planes, while the latter implies the inbreathing of the same from out of the forms which then die and decay.

The life manifest in forms is not an element existing on the plane of the forms, but is an influence coming down from the plane next above the form-plane. Life apparent on the physical plane evidences a directive mental agency operating on the astral plane. The living human body derives its nourishment from the physical plane, but its life relates to the patterns and order of growth on the astral and higher planes ; these agencies direct the bioplasts in the building of the organisms.

Death implies cessation of direction from higher planes of the lower forces in forms.

See ASTRAL, CREATION, DEVAS (builders), FORMS, MAN BORN, MENTAL, MONAD OF FORM, PROTOTYPES, SIMILITUDES.

BIRTH OF BUDDHA :—

Symbolic of the entrance of the Self, or World-soul, into the lower nature of the Life cycle during the period of Involution, when the Soul is one, not many.

"From the side of the Queen Māyā, who was purified by her vow, her son

was born, without pain and without illness. Like the sun bursting from a cloud in the morning,—so he, too, when he was born from his mother's womb, made the world bright like gold, bursting forth with his rays which dispelled the darkness."—*Buddha-Karita* I. 25, 26.

The "side of the queen" is an allusion to the outgoing spiritual force which regulates the manifestation of the World-soul. The "purification by the vow" signifies the consecration or dedication of the matter of the lower planes to the expression of the Self within. The Son is born and comes forth on the astromental plane, since he is the centre of the solar universe, and becomes the means of uniting all principles, powers, and forces into one focus, and of co-ordinating all the fragments of the Divine nature in their harmonious expression in the cosmos. "Pain and illness" are absent from the birth of the Soul, inasmuch as the spiritual effort which is made is the deepest realisation of bliss in the nature of the Self.

Then as the sun shines forth from the dazzling rim of the morning cloud, so the inner Self, emerging from the prison-house of Matter wherein it had lain potential, brought out of chaos its vehicle the cosmos, and revealed the truth involved within himself. Forth from the inmost recesses of his being, proceeded the rays of his effulgence,—the Divine modes of functioning which turn apparent nothingness into the beginnings of the manifested all.

"The infant Buddha came forth, and the great kings of the four cardinal points received him in a cloth or net."—LILLIE, *Budd. in Christendom*, p. 18.

The Soul is received by the four principles of the quaternary in an astral mechanism of desire and sensation, that is, the four lower planes are organised for the manifestation of the incarnate Self.

"The resemblances between the Christian and Buddhist legends are so close that we can scarcely imagine it to be a mere coincidence. Jesus and Buddha are both said to have been born of a 'pure virgin,' honoured by heavenly spirits at their birth, prayed to by kings, and loaded with presents. 'Happy is the whole world,' sing the Gods under the form of young Brahmins, at the birth of the child,—as we are told in the *Lalita*

Vistara, the legendary biography of Buddha, dating from before Christ, ' for he is indeed born who brings salvation, and will establish the world in blessedness. He is born who will darken sun and moon by the splendour of his merits and will put all darkness to flight. The blind see, the deaf hear, the demented are restored to reason.' "—A. DREWS, *The Christ Myth*, p. 104.

" Professor Kellogg points out that in the Chinese books Buddha is said over and over again to have been incarnate of the ' Holy Spirit.' "—A. LILLIE, *Budd. in Christendom*, p. 16.

As Buddha, Christ, and Zoroaster are all symbols of the Higher Self incarnate in the lower nature, some similarities in the allegories concerning them are to be expected. The " pure virgin " signifies the purified part of the lower nature, in which the Holy Spirit can implant the Divine germ of Righteousness and Truth. The higher qualities, intellectual faculties, and ideals (gods) rejoice at the birth of the Self who will bring salvation to the soul. The advent of the Divine Ruler and Saviour imparts fresh energy to all the impulses towards the higher life. He is born whose light of knowledge will by comparison make the learning of the lower mind seem ignorance (darkness), and he will set Truth in the place of ignorance. The spiritually blind shall be made to see the truth. The qualities deaf to the Divine voice shall be enabled to hear the words of Love and peace. Those egos whose qualities are distorted and unbalanced shall be restored to spiritual equilibrium.

See ASITA, AVALOKITESVARA, BODHISATVA, BUDDHA, DARKNESS, DESTROYING EVILS, GARDEN (lumbini), HEAVENLY VOICE, INVOLUTION, KA, LION-GAIT, MATTER, MĀYA (higher), NET (golden), VIRGIN, WATER (heaven), WOMB.

BIRTH OF CHRIST :—

Symbolic of the entrance into manifestation of the Word which was God, and was in the beginning with God unmanifest, namely, the Higher Self.

" But when the fullness of the time was come, God sent forth his Son made of a woman, made under the law, to redeem them that were under the law, that we might receive the adoption of sons."— GAL. iv. 4, 5.

When the manvantara, or great cycle of existence, commenced, God the Father potential, the First Logos, sent forth his Only begotten Son, God actual, the Second Logos, as the Divine sacrifice to be involved in matter, the Word becoming flesh and dwelling among us. He, the Lord of all, and the life and the light of men, begotten of the Father—the Absolute, submitted to limitation under the Divine law, and descended into matter (woman) to become united with it and conditioned by it. (Matter is feminine—passive, adapted to receive and take impressions, and so is moulded and fashioned into forms for the life activities.)

The object of the Divine sacrifice being the redemption of the souls ; then afterwards in the period of evolution, there arise inner vibrations from the Spirit within the mind, which, once established, play upon the soul and so raise it. The soul therefore is gradually freed from the law of desire, and rising upward it unites itself with the Christ who gives salvation from the transitory life, and lordship over the lower planes. And so is fulfilled the liberty of the children of God.

" The Holy Spirit having entered into Matter, the world thus received its form and motion. The Holy Spirit is present also in those who fell to earth, as the power which shall raise them up again to Heaven " (*Synesius of Cyrene*).— UEBERWEG, *Hist. of Philos.*, Vol. I, p. 349.

" The work of Christ in the soul is one with the work of Christ in the world of worlds, a cosmic sacrifice, and a new spiritual creation. If he had failed in the greater he could not accomplish the less." —R. J. CAMPBELL, Serm., *Christ Arisen*.

" For Eckhart, the forthcoming of God is in this wise. The Godhead, ' the unnatured Nature,' in an ' Eternal Now,' beholds Himself, i.e. becomes an object of consciousness to Himself, and thus He becomes revealed to Himself. This is the beginning of the process of revelation. This is called ' the begetting of the Son,' the uttering of the Divine ' Word.' When God becomes conscious of Himself, there is differentiation into subject and object, or, as Eckhart says, into Father and Son. But we must not suppose that it *happened* at a temporal moment, before which the Son was unborn and God was not yet God. That view is too crude. Eckhart insists that the Son is eternally begotten ; ' He beholds himself in an Eternal Now ' : ' God is ever working in one Eternal Now, and his working is a giving birth to His Son. He bears Him at every instant.' "—R. M. Jones, *Mystical Religion*, p. 227.

See Absolute, Arc. man, Atman, Bodhisatva, Cosmos, Evolution, First-born son, God, Godhead, Hiranyagarbha, Huitzilopochtli, Image, Incarnation, Involution, Jesus (son of God), Lamb of God, Matter, Māyā (higher), Monad, Mother, Redemption, Sacrificer, Seed, Self, Son of God, Time, Trinity, Woman (goddess), Woman (matter), Womb of māyā, Word.

BIRTH OF CONFUCIUS :—

A symbol of the entrance of the Higher Self into the mentality of the lower nature during the cycle of Involution.

"The birth of Confucius is surrounded with many prodigious occurrences. . . . As her time drew near, the mother, Ching-tsae, asked her husband if there was any place near called ' The hollow mulberry tree.' He told her there was a dry cave in the south hill of that name. She said, ' I will go there.' On the night when the child was born, two dragons came and kept watch, etc."—J. Legge, *Life and Teachings of Confucius*, p. 58.

When the emotion-nature (Ching-tsae) was sufficiently advanced, and it aspired upward, there was a presentiment of spiritual influx, and in due time the Self was born in the purified soul (dry cave). The ' hollow mulberry tree ' refers to the Divine Ray to which all souls are attached, and which proceeds from the higher planes (south hill). The ' two dragons ' symbolise wisdom and love which protect the infant Self by keeping it close within.

See Cave, Confucius, Dragon, Filial piety, South, Tree of life.

BIRTH OF HORUS THE CHILD, OR HARPOCRATES :—

A symbol of the emergence of the incarnate Self in human souls during the present process and period of evolution.

"Meanwhile Horus the younger had been born to Isis, and brought up secretly at Buto, in the marshes of the Delta, out of reach of Set."—Plutarch, *Isis and Osiris*.

Meanwhile the Christ was now born on the buddhic plane (Isis), in relation to the lower nature, and was nourished and sustained unknown to the lower self, in the " marsh " which signifies the purified nidus, wherein water (truth) is abundant, and which is soft to higher impressions, and is out of reach of the desire-nature (Set).

"Therefore Isis perceiving that she is pregnant, ties an amulet round her neck on the 6th of the first quarter of the month Paophi, and that Harpocrates is born about the winter solstice, unfinished (or, whose lower limbs were dwarfed and stunted)."—Plutarch, *Isis and Osiris*, § 65.

This is the same symbolism as that of the Christ. The " tying of the amulet " signifies that perfect junction formed between the higher and lower principles, which is necessary in order that their union shall give birth to the Son of God. The " first quarter " is a symbol of the first root-race (astral). In the fourth root-race (physical) Christ is born on the buddhic plane in the soul. The " winter solstice " (Christmas) signifies the deep immersion of the soul in matter. The lack of finish in the lower limbs means that the higher or potential is always relatively unmanifest ; and that the lower or actual is never able to express the potential.

The earlier birth of Horus (Aroueris) is that corresponding to the form, the latter is that which refers to the life.

"Furthermore, Isis is said to have united with Osiris after his death, and in consequence to have brought forth Harpocrates (Horus)."—*Ibid.*

This signifies the process of gestation which takes place when the soul or personality is evolving upon the astral plane, and is therefore the point when the Son of mind enters. This is the birth of the Christ in the soul on the buddhic plane.

"And as the Egyptians believe the Nile the issue of Osiris, so do they regard the earth as the body of Isis : not, indeed, the whole earth, but just as much as the Nile inundates, fecundating and mingling with it ; for from the union they beget Horus. Horus is that which preserves and nourishes all things, namely the seasons and the circumambient air ; and they tell that he was nursed by Leto in the marshes round Buto, because the watery and thoroughly soaked earth *nurses* the exhalations that quench the dryness of the air."—*Ibid.*, § 38.

The Divine Life (Nile) fertilises the productive buddhic nature (Isis) expressed upon the astral and physical planes, and brings about the gestation of the Self (Horus) in the lower nature. The Self is the preserver and sustainer of the higher qualities in the periods of emanation on the mental plane (air). The nascent Self is developed by the buddhic emotion nature (Leto) in the purified lower nature susceptible of the truth (water) and productive of aspirations which spiritualise the mind (air).

See ARC. MAN, AROUERIS, BUTO, CHEMMIS, DELOS, DIONYSUS, EARTH (mother), EVOLUTION, GARDEN OF REEDS, HARPOCRATES, HORBEHUDTI, HORUS, ISIS, LATONA, MARSH, NILE, OSIRIS, PEACHES, REED-PLAIN, SEASONS, SEKHET-AARU, SIX, VULTURE.

BIRTH OF JESUS :—

Symbolic of the bringing forth of the Christ in the souls of humanity during the present cycle,—that of evolution.

"And she (Mary) brought forth her firstborn son and wrapped him in swaddling clothes, and laid him in a manger ; because there was no room for them in the inn."—LUKE ii. 7.

"Mary the virgin" signifies the purified lower nature of the soul, which has become fit to give birth to the incarnate Christ. The "enwrapping clothes" typify the virtues which surround and shield the new-born Christ-soul ; while the "manger" is a symbol of simplicity of heart in which the spirit of Christ is received. It is in the lowly "stable" of humility, and not in the "inn" of pride and luxury, that the higher emotions surrounding the Christ-soul are developed.

"The Spiritual Life is the gift of the Living Spirit. The spiritual man is no mere development of the natural man. He is a New Creation born from Above." —H. DRUMMOND, *Natural Law, etc.*, p. 65.

"For Jesus himself was (Basilides says) mentally preconceived at the time of the generation of the stars, and of the complete return to their starting-point of the seasons in the vast conglomeration of all germs. This is, according to these (Basilidians), he who has been conceived as the inner spiritual man in what is

natural—[now this is the Sonship which left there the soul, not that it might be mortal, but that it might abide here according to nature, just as the first Sonship left above in its proper locality the Holy Spirit, that is, the spirit which is conterminous]—this, I say, is he who has been conceived as the inner spiritual man, and has then been arrayed in his own peculiar soul."—HIPPOLYTUS, *Refutation, etc.*, Bk. VII. 15.

For the Christ-soul (Jesus) was potentially present in the higher mind, at the time of the forthgoing of the spiritual egos (stars), and of the completion of the process of involution (conglomeration of germs), when the cycles (seasons) having, as it were, returned to latency, were ready to start anew in the process of evolution. The Christ-soul has been conceived in the mind as the inner spiritual Self within the natural man, that is, as the Son of mind (man) to bring immortality to the soul while abiding in it according to its natural development. Similarly Christ (first Sonship) was born Son of Buddhi (Holy Spirit) on the buddhic plane which is common in the soul to all human beings, and not differentiated to the particular egos. This Christ-soul, then, is he who indwells mentally as the inner Spiritual Self,—the central Ideal arrayed in all the higher qualities and faculties of the evolving soul.

"It is well known that whereas in the Gospels Jesus is said to have been born in an inn stable, early Christian writers, as Justin Martyr and Origen, explicitly say he was born in a cave. Now, in the Mithra myth, Mithra is both rock-born and born in a cave, and the monuments show the new-born babe adored by shepherds who offer first-fruits."—J. M. ROBERTSON, *Pagan Christs*, p. 338.

"Mithra" is here a symbol of the Incarnate Self, the same as "Jesus."

"Christ cannot be conceived save of a soul immaculate and virgin as to matter, and meet to become the spouse of the Divine Spirit. Therefore, as the soul as Eve gives consent to the annunciation of the Serpent, so, as Mary, become virgin, she gives consent to the annunciation of the Angel, and understands the mystery of the Motherhood of the Man regenerate. She has no acts of her own, all the acts of her Son are hers also. She participates in his nativity, in his manifestation, in his passion, in his resurrection, in his ascension, in his penticostal gift. He himself is her gift to the world. But it is always he who operates ; she who asks, acquiesces, consents, responds.

Through her he outflows into the mind and external man, and so into life and conduct. As Augustine says, ' all graces pass to us through the hands of Mary.' For the purified soul is the mediatrix, as she is the genetrix, of the Divine presence." —*The Perfect Way*, p. 242.

" It—the Very Truth of Heaven— comes to be wrapped in swaddling-clothes and laid in a manger, and to thoughtful minds its seeming humiliation will be the very sign of its Divinity."— H. P. LIDDON, *University Sermons*, p. 207.

" Macarius, following Methodius, teaches that the very idea of the Incarnation includes the union of the Logos with pious souls, in whom He is well-pleased. In each of them a Christ is born. Thus besides the ideas of Ransom and Sacrifice of Christ *for* us, these theologians placed the ideas of sanctification and inner transformation of Christ *in* us, and they considered the latter as real and as integral a part of our redemption as the former. But the doctrine of Divine immanence in the human heart never became quite the central truth of theology till the time of the mediaeval mystics. It is Eckhart who says : ' The Father speaks the Word into the soul, and when the Son is born, every soul becomes Mary.' "—W. R. INGE, *Paddock Lectures*, p. 66.

See AMENI, ANGELS, ASSUMPTION, BETHLEHEM, BIRTH OF HORUS AND KRISHNA, CAVE, CONCEPTION, DEMIURGE, DIONYSUS, GOLD (frank.), JESUS (son of man), JOB, KING (great), MAGI, MANGER, MITHRAS ROCK, VEIL OF ISIS, VIRGIN, VIRGINITY, VIRGIN MARY.

BIRTH OF KRISHNA AN INCARNATION OF VISHNU :—

Symbolic of the bringing forth of the Self (Krishna), Son of God (Vishnu), in the human soul during the present period of evolution.

" Like Astyages and Herod, in order to ward off the danger arising from his sister's son, of which he had been warned by an oracle, King Kansa caused his sister and her husband Vasudewa to be cast into prison. Here, in the darkness of a dungeon, Krishna comes into the world as Jesus did in the stable at Bethlehem. The nearer the hour of birth approaches, the more beautiful the mother becomes. Soon the whole dungeon is filled with light. Rejoicing choirs sound in the air, the waters of the rivers and brooks make sweet music. The Gods come down from heaven, and blessed spirits dance and sing for joy. At midnight his mother Dewaki (i.e. the divine) brings the child into the world, at the commencement of a new epoch. The parents themselves fall down before him and pray, but a voice from heaven admonishes them to convey him from the machinations of the tyrant to Gokala, the land of the cow, and to exchange him for the daughter of the herdsman Nanda. Immediately the chains fall from the father's hands, the dungeon doors are opened, and he passes out. Another Christopher, he bears the child upon his shoulders through the river Yamuna, the waters of which recede in reverence before the son of God, and he exchanges Krishna for the new-born daughter of Nanda. He then returns to the dungeon, where the chains again immediately fasten of their own accord upon his limbs. Kansa now makes his way into the dungeon. In vain Dewaki entreats her brother to leave her the child. He is on the point of tearing it forcibly from her hands when it disappears before his eyes, and Kansa gives the order that all newly born children in his country under the age of two years shall be killed."—A. DREWS, *The Christ Myth*, pp. 105-6.

The meaning of this is similar to that of the birth story of Jesus. The lower principle (Kansa) perceives subjectively the coming of that power which will eventually exterminate it. It therefore in self-protection sets limits to the spiritual activities from within, and strives to control the purified lower nature (Dewaki) and the Holy Spirit (Vasudewa). Then from latency (darkness) there comes forth the incarnate Self, the Christ-soul, bringing with him the light of Truth which illumines the purified nature (Dewaki), while joy and energy suffuse the soul. The higher qualities (gods) arise from latency, and in harmony and gladness they surround the new-born Self. The period of the manifestation of the Self in the soul is a turning point (midnight) in evolution, and the beginning of a new process of moral and spiritual development. The purified emotion-nature allied with the Spirit (the parents) reverence the Love-nature which has appeared, but at the call of Wisdom from above they prepare to convey the Holy Babe to an exalted condition safe from the power of the lower principle. Then the liberated Spirit caught up the child unto God and unto his throne, passing inwards and upwards through the higher mind (river) to the buddhic plane (Gokala), leaving the reflection, as it were, of the Divine presence (Nanda's daughter) on the planes below. But the Spirit is still in touch with the purified lower nature (Dewaki), which is threatened by the lower principle, now powerless to expel the Divine reflection from within the soul. Thwarted by the higher nature, the lower principle is stirred to take action against all newly evolved higher qualities, for the "evil one" seeks to destroy all germs of the virtues which would eventually abolish his sovereignty.

See ARJUNA, BALARAMA, CAVE (Nanda), DEVAKI, DURASROBO, GLORY (divine), GOLOKA, GOPIS, HEBDOMAD, HEROD, KRISHNA, OX-LEADER, RIVERS.

BIRTH OF THE MAN-CHILD :—

A symbol of the emergence of the Higher Self or Soul on the buddhic plane at an early period during the cycle of involution of all qualities and forms.

"And she was delivered of a son, a man child, who is to rule all nations with a rod of iron : and her child was caught up unto God, and unto his throne. And the woman fled into the wilderness."—REV. xii. 5, 6.

The Wisdom principle at its highest level brought forth the Self into manifest existence in which the dual aspects spirit and matter, or good and evil, are evidenced. The incarnate Self is destined to rule all the various qualities of the soul through the mind (iron) ; and the Self being involved it is retained in a state of subjectivity in the causal-body (throne) above the conflicts of the opposites, while the Wisdom principle also becomes subjective and inoperative for a season. The Christ is here represented as born upon the buddhic plane in relation to the purified part of the lower nature below.

"By the 'woman clothed with the sun,' John meant most manifestly the Church, endued with the Father's word, whose brightness is above the sun. And by 'the moon under her feet' he referred to her being adorned, like the moon, with heavenly glory. And the words, 'upon her head a crown of twelve stars,' refer to the twelve apostles by whom the Church was founded. And those, 'she being with child, cries, travailing in birth, and pained to be delivered,' mean that the Church will not cease to bear from her heart the Word that is persecuted by the unbelieving in the world. 'And she brought forth a man-child, who is to rule all the nations'; by which is meant that the Church, always bringing forth Christ, the perfect man-child of God, who is declared to be God and man, becomes the instructor of all the nations. And the words, 'her child was caught up unto God, and to His throne,' signify that he who is always born of her is a heavenly king, and not an earthly."—HIPPOLYTUS, *Christ and Antichrist*, § 61.

"Church" is a symbol of the religious consciousness which, when purified sufficiently, must bring forth the Christ in the human soul, the expression (Word) of the Truth within.

"There is to be mentioned the mystic suggestiveness of the declaration that the Christ born in any human heart is immediately caught up to the throne of God. . . . Once let a human soul attain to Christ-consciousness—that is, once rise from the merely natural to the spiritual plane—once look out upon life from that standpoint, and I do not believe it is ever really possible to lose the glad possession and be as though it had never been. For what comes, then, in this new birth, as it is rightly called, is an inrush of the eternal, of the invincible reality which is enthroned far above all the vicissitudes of time and sense. . . . Caught up to the throne of God, far above the reach of evil, does not mean taken away from the human heart. Spatial dimensions have nothing to do with the matter. The throne of God is in the soul itself ; the eternal dwells in the midst of time ; there is no leap to take, no gulf to cross, to reach the Christ of glory ; here he is."—R. J. CAMPBELL, Serm., *The Assumption of the New-born Christ*.

See BIRTH OF HORUS, CHURCH, CROWN OF TWELVE STARS, DRAGON (red), HORNS (ten), NATIONS, ROD OF CORRECTION, THRONE (heart), YAO.

BIRTH OF OSIRIS, OR RĀ :—

Symbolic of the emanation of the First Logos, God manifest, the Higher Self, on the plane of atma.

"On the first of these (five) new-made days Osiris was born, and a Voice from heaven proclaimed, 'The Lord of all things hath appeared !'"—PLUTARCH, *Isis and Osiris*, § 12.

The "five days" signify the five planes of manifestation, and the first of these is atma, the highest plane, on which the First Logos forthpours. The "Voice" refers to the "Word," or expression, of the Divine Will in manifesting.

" O Osiris, son of Nut, I have given unto thee the sovereignty of thy father Seb, and the goddess Mut, thy mother, who gave birth to the gods, brought thee forth as the firstborn of five gods, and created thy beauties and fashioned thy members."—BUDGE, *Book of the Dead*, p. 627.

The Supreme grants to the Higher Self the primal conditions of time (Seb) and space (Nut or Mut) which have brought forth from the potential the actual. For the Manifesting Self is " the image of the invisible God, the firstborn of all creation ; for in him were all things created, in the heavens and upon the earth."

" Homage to thee (Rā), O thou who riseth in Nu, and who at thy manifestation dost make the world bright with light ; the whole company of gods sing hymns of praise unto thee after thou hast come forth."—*Ibid.*, p. 10.

The Higher Self comes forth in possession of the Divine powers of the universe (Nu), and illumines the higher planes with the light of truth. The whole assembly of higher attributes and ideals vibrate in harmony with the Love and Wisdom which have appeared, and are centralised in the Manifesting Self.

See ARC. MAN, CURSE, DAYS (five), DEATH OF OSIRIS, ELEMENTS (five), GATHA DAYS, HYMN, KING (great), MUT, NU, NUT, OSIRIS, PAMYLES, RHEA, SEB, WORLDS (five).

BIRTH OF ZOROASTER :—

Symbolic of the emergence of the Soul or Self from the womb of matter in the cycle of Involution. For this consummation stupendous preparations had been made on the lower planes.

" A divine light shone around the house, and a shout of joy arose when life triumphed, and loud laughter burst from the Child as he came into the world. All nature rejoiced at Zoroaster's birth, the very trees and rivers shared in the universal thrill of gladness that shoots through the world."—*Dinkard*, VII.

The Divine illumination of the Higher Triad of wisdom, love, and truth shone within the lower quaternary, while a glad thrill passed through the lower planes as the higher rates of vibration were transmitted to them and raised their responsiveness. A sense of joy and energy filled the awakening Self,—the only-begotten Son,—as it came forth. For bliss and power are of the true nature of the Self who is to redeem the world which lies in ignorance and evil, indicative of negation and inertia. All the forces and elemental conditions of the lower planes contribute towards the formation and development of the World-soul. As science shows, the physical body comprises all the materials and properties which are appropriate to serve through nature the end in view. So, correspondingly, the Soul of humanity comprises the sum total of all the conscious life in the Logos which contributes under every phase of its manifestation to the upbuilding of the Soul. The " trees and rivers " signify channels of truth and love which are the very warp and woof of the World-soul.

" Christ when he comes finds the soul or the world really existent, really having within itself its holiest capabilities, really moving, though dimly and darkly, in spite of all its hindrances in its true direction ; and what He does for it is to quicken it through and through, to sound the bugle of its true life in its ears, to make it feel the nobleness of movements which have seemed to it ignoble, the hopefulness of impulses which have seemed hopeless, to bid it be itself. . . . The worthless becomes full of worth, the insignificant becomes full of meaning at the touch (of noble characters). They faintly catch the feeble reflection of His life who is the true Light of the World, the real illumination and inspiration of humanity. . . . The truth is that every higher life to which man comes, and especially the highest life in Christ, is in the true line of man's humanity. There is the quickening and fulfilling of what man by the very essence of his nature is. The more man becomes irradiated with Divinity, the more, not the less, truly he is man."—PHILLIPS BROOKS, *Light of the World*, p. 5.

See ARC. MAN, ARREST, BIRTH OF BUDDHA, CHANNELS, DUGHDHOVA, DURASROBO FORMS, GLORY (divine), INVOLUTION, MACROCOSM, POURUSHASPA, RIVERS, SON OF GOD, SOUL, TRIAD, WOMB OF MĀYĀ, ZOROASTER.

BIRTH, SECOND, OF AN ARYAN :—

A symbol of the bringing forth into manifestation of the spiritual egos already on the mental plane (the Aryans). These are born into the lower nature when mind begins to function in the human soul.

" According to the injunction of the revealed texts the first birth of an Aryan is from his natural mother, the second happens on the tying of the girdle of munga grass, and the third on the initiation to the performance of a Srauta sacrifice. Among those three the birth which is symbolised by the investiture with the girdle of munga grass, is his birth for the sake of the Veda.'—*Laws of Manu*, II. 170.

The "first birth" is from the "natural mother," that is, from the natural order, or lower evolution ; this is the birth of the personality. The "second birth" occurs when the spiritual-mental ego descends into the human form as mind awakens ; this is the birth of the individuality. In this second birth, the ego is tied, as it were, to the upward current of the Divine Life (girdle), "for the sake of the Veda," that is, for the purpose of spiritual evolution according to the Divine law of true life on the higher planes. It is through the development of the three human bodies, causal, mental, and astral, now interrelated in connection with the Divine Life, that the ego progresses in its upward course. The three bodies (Brahmana, Kshatrya, and Vaisya) partake of the second birth, for they are directly united with the higher evolution ; but the physical body (Sudra) is a product of the natural order (first birth) only, and does not develop from incarnation to incarnation. It is for the temporary use of the soul, and has to serve the other bodies and their life principles. Hence the Sudra is called "once born."

The "third birth" occurs at the end of the cycle, when the soul attains liberation, and the lower Self and the higher Self become one on the higher mental plane. The "Srauta sacrifice" signifies the final abandonment of the lower nature : this is equivalent to the crucifixion and resurrection of Jesus.

See ARYAVARTA, BARHIS, BARSOM, BUCKLE, CASTES, DEVAYANA, GIRDLE ROPE, IMHOTEP, KUSTI, SUDRA, TAMAGUSHI, VEDA, YAGNAPAVITA.

BIRTH CEREMONIES OF THE BUDDHA :—

Symbolic of stages in the Soul's course towards liberation from the lower nature.

"The monarch also, being well-pleased at the birth of a son, having thrown off all those bonds called worldly objects, caused his son to go through the usual birth-ceremonies in a manner worthy of the family."—*Buddha-Karita*, Bk. I. 87.

The Self, whose nature is bliss, is said to rejoice in its forth-going (masculine). It is Itself unconditioned, yet requires its phenomenal Representative to pass through those stages which will enable it to arrive at true liberty.

See DEVAYANA, INVOLUTION, LIBERATION, SELF (lower), SON OF GOD, STRIDES (soul), SUDDHODANA.

BIRTH-CHAMBER OF THE DIVINE CITY :—

A symbol of the buddhic nature ensouling the causal-body in which the Self can be born.

"He is begotten in the birth-chamber of the Divine City, and his rest shall come in the consuming of the Divine City. He it is that fashions Her likeness and unites Her to all that belongs to the chamber of birth in the City of God."—M. W. BLACKDEN, *Book of the Dead*, Ch. CX.

The indwelling Self is begotten in buddhi, which ensouls the causal-body. The Self "rests" and is withdrawn from manifestation in the lower worlds, when the causal-vehicle is dissolved at the end of the manvantara. The Self, as Atma, fashions the buddhic soul (negative, receptive), and through her (buddhi) is united with all things, and apprehends the whole universal plan which lives, moves, and has its being in God.

See BIRTH OF HORUS, BUDDHI, BUDDHIC PLANE, CAUSAL BODY.

BISHOP :—

A symbol of a spiritual principle, or spiritualised mental quality, ruling over and directing the disciplined qualities of the soul (church). In its highest aspect, Bishop signifies the individuality (overseer), or the Higher Self " Shepherd and Bishop of souls."—I PETER ii. 25.

"The bishop therefore must be without reproach, the husband of one wife, temperate, soberminded, orderly, given to hospitality, apt to teach."—I TIM. iii. 2.

This means that the spiritualised

quality must be free from the contamination of the lower self-seeking desires. Must be " the husband of one wife," that is, must be allied indissolubly with the higher emotion nature, and not with the lower. Must be so far developed as to be practised in all the virtues ; ready to help and teach all lower qualities, seeking after truth and righteousness. The meaning of the whole statement is that the higher nature of the soul should co-ordinate and rule over the lower nature, in order that the soul should progress.

See CHURCH, FLAIL, HUSBAND AND WIFE, MITRE, PRIEST, SHEPHERD, WIFE.

BITTER :—

A symbol of suffering undergone in the process of the purification of the soul-qualities.

See COW'S URINE, GALL.

BLACK :—

Indicates either the unmanifest and potential, or ignorance and evil. This explains the black figures of the higher gods and goddesses and the Madonna, and of the lower gods and demons.

See DARKNESS, HEIGHT OF OSIRIS, HORSE (black).

BLACK MAGICIANS :—

These are partial and incomplete expressions of egos which have as yet only partly realised their possibilities. They are unbalanced egos which have set in motion powers and forces in their own natures which they cannot control. They have not first purified their lower nature ; and having acquired some powers of the mind, they work destruction to themselves.

" Thereupon came Angra Mainyus and created the evil witchcraft of the Yatus. And this is how the Yatus nature shows itself,—by the look, and then whenever the wizard howls forth his spells, most deadly works of witchcraft go forth."— *Vendidad*, I.

The path of holiness, or the White Magic, having been established, the Evil power or illusory self brought about the Black Magic, or art of the Black Magicians, which leads to death. And the nature of the Black Magician exhibits itself by the form,

and wherever the matter of the lower planes is acted upon. The results of such efforts as are made are disastrous and productive of evil.

See ANGRA-MAINYU, ARA, MAGIC PRACTICES, YATUS.

BLACKSMITHS, OR WORKERS IN METAL :—

Symbolic of mental qualities disciplined by the Spirit, and directed and energised from buddhi.

" Then came hither Horbehūdti ; his servants were in his following as workers with weapons of metal ; each had an iron lance and a chain in his hand ; then they smote the crocodiles and the hippopotami."—*Legend of the Winged Sun-disk.*

Then came forth the Son of God,— the Second Logos ; and the advanced qualities which attended upon His advent, and which are typical as workers of metal, in that metal is comparable to that mentality which will endure and consolidate. And each of these workers is said to have a " lance and a chain," which signify that which strikes and that which withstands,—positive and negative,— that which goes forth and that which withholds itself. And in this way they smote or suppressed the lower desire elementals.

See BATTLE, CONFLICT, HORBEHŪDTI, METAL, WAR, WEAPONS, WORKERS.

BLACK STONE OF THE KAABA :—
See KAABA.

BLANDISHMENT OF WOMEN TOWARDS THE BUDDHA :—

Symbolic of the higher emotions in their perfect attractiveness within the soul on the buddhic plane.

" There the women delighted the Buddha with their soft voices, their beautiful pearl garlands, their playful intoxication, their sweet laughter, and their stolen glances concealed by their brows."—*Buddha-Karita*, Bk. I. 31.

At this high level in involution the higher emotions are able to appeal to the soul successfully. The " soft voices," " pearl garlands," " playful intoxication," " sweet laughter," and " stolen glances," are symbolic of the attractive aspects of Wisdom,— responded to from above in the soul. The higher emotions which delight the incarnate Self are the buddhi-manasic impulses from within, such as love of righteousness and truth, of justice, mercy, wisdom, gentleness, peace, harmony, perfection, humanity, etc. These are symbolised by the attractive pleasantries of women (emotions).

See BUDDHA, GOPIS, HOURIES, INTOXICATION, MOON-LIKE, WOMAN.

BLASPHEMY AGAINST THE HOLY GHOST :—

A symbol of the turning away from the means of salvation.

"Whosoever shall speak against the Holy Spirit, it shall not be forgiven him, neither in this world nor in that which is to come."—MAT. xii. 32.

This is the attempt which must always be unsuccessful (hence there can be really no blasphemy) to substitute for the living Spirit the dead letter of convention and authority. This attempt is made, not only by theologian and ecclesiastical formalists, but by all men who do not live in accordance with the Divine guidance within them, who do not take up what is committed to them to spiritually profit by, and who fail to accept the Holy Spirit as it comes to them to become the sustaining power in their daily lives. There is much of this incipient blasphemy, for which there can be no forgiveness and no remitting, since there can be no substitute for the Holy Spirit which is the means of the soul's evolution. Until the atma-buddhic vibrations are allowed to permeate the lower nature, and so raise it, there can be no salvation for the soul.

See BARSOM, BUDDHI, COW'S URINE, ESCAPE, HOLY GHOST, PARACLETE, QUALITIES, SACRED TEXT, TRANSMUTATION, WISDOM.

BLESSING OF GOD :—

The Divine Will operating through the human consciousness. When the mind has once found its ideal, and determined to serve it, God's blessing is secured.

See GOD BLESSING, PRAYER, SALVATION, TITHES.

BLESSING OF THE LESS BY THE GREATER :—

The unfailing response of the Higher Self to the aspiring and struggling lower self, in exact proportion to its endeavours and to the sacrifices it makes.

"Spiritual blessings can only be given to those who are in a certain spiritual condition. Always and necessarily the capacity or organ of reception precedes and determines the bestowment of blessings."—A. MACLAREN, Sermons, 1st Series, p. 69.

"In an hour of heaviness not so very long ago there was whispered into my mind with a new force and meaning, and with an intensity which I cannot convey to you by speech, the verse : 'Faint not, nor fear, His arms are near ; He changeth not, and thou art dear ; Only believe, and thou shalt see, That Christ is in all to thee.' That word was given to me just when I needed it, and divinely given, I am fully convinced."—R. J. CAMPBELL, Serm., The Saviourhood of Christ.

See PROMISES, TITHES, TRANSMUTATION.

BLIND MAN :—

A symbol of mentality immersed in the concerns of the lower life, and devoid of spiritual perception.

"Bartimæus, a blind beggar, was sitting by the wayside. And when he heard that it was Jesus of Nazareth, he began to cry out and say, Jesus thou son of David have mercy on me."—MARK x. 46, 47.

This "blind man" is he who is not spiritually awakened, but who reveres the form of religion, and who addresses his God according to hearsay, not recognising the Divine,—the Son of God. He has to learn the truth and aspire, ere his eyes can be opened.

"New spiritual sight does not create, but reveals, the reality. And in all such openings, whether gradual or sudden, the Lord cometh, and his coming is more often than not connected with some pain of the new birth, fires and purgings that accompany the operations for cataract performed by the Great Physician on the spiritual eye. He to whose intuitions the Lord has thus come is positively a new man ; I mean, all limitations are removed from his Godward thought."—BASIL WILBERFORCE, Serm., The Message of Advent.

"The blind (spiritually blind) man hath forgotten the Name ; the perverse is stone-blind. His transmigration shall cease not ; he shall be ruined by death and birth."—"Hymn of Gura Nanak."—MACAULIFFE, The Sikh Religion, Vol. I. 263.

"Blind and naked signifies that they

are without the understanding of truth, and without the will of good."—SWEDEN-BORG, *Apoc. Rev.*, n. 153.

See DAVID, GARMENTS, HEALING, MAN (blind), MIRACLES (healing), SEEING, SIGHT.

BLISS :—

The abode of Perfection ; the state of true Being ; the condition of Love. The nature of the Higher Self is bliss.

" Fixing the senses with the inward sense, may Savitri produce in us senses by which there shall be bliss, and which shall reveal the divine being, the great light, by spiritual intuition."—GOUGH, *Svetas Upanishad*, p. 218.

Queting the desires and enticements of sense by reliance upon wisdom and love, may the Higher Self arouse the qualities which lead to perfection, truth, and love, that there may be union of the soul with God.

" The view that the gods, in contrast to the suffering world of men, enjoy an untroubled felicity, is probably common to all peoples. But in the Upanishads bliss appears not as an attribute or a state of Brahman, but as his peculiar essence. Brahman is not *ânandin*, possessing bliss, but *ânanda*, bliss itself." DENSSEN, *Phil. of Upanishads*, p. 141.

" This state (in which all contrasts have disappeared) is then further described as one of pure knowledge, of existence as subject without object, and it is then added, ' This is his supreme goal, this is his supreme happiness, this is his supreme world, this is his supreme bliss ; by a small portion only of this bliss all other creatures live " (*Brihad. Upanishad*, IV. 3, 33).—*Ibid.*, p. 143.

" I like to dwell upon this precious thought that the day will come for the redeemed of God when no man will have to struggle to do right or fear to do wrong, when there will be no question of such a thing, but we shall simply live as the flowers bloom and shed their fragrance in the summer air ; and by so living, spontaneously, gladly, inevitably, fill our appointed place in God's universal plan and contribute our full share to the blessedness of his whole creation."— R. J. CAMPBELL, Serm., *From Subjection to Sovereignty*.

See ARA, MUSIC, SORROW, SUFFER-ING, TASTE, UNEN, VIBHU.

BLOOD :—

A symbol of the Divine Life mani-fested on the lower planes, either in a higher or a lower sense.

" But flesh with the life thereof, which is the blood thereof, shall ye not eat." —GEN. ix. 3.

But of the lower desires (flesh-life) with their instinctive rebellion against the higher nature, nothing, to nourish the soul, is to be derived.

" Blood everywhere signifies in a spiritual sense the divine truth of the Lord, which also is the divine truth of the Word ; and in an opposite sense, the divine truth of the Word falsified or profaned."—SWEDENBORG, *Apoc. Rev.*, n. 379.

See ATONEMENT, HAND OF BEAST, INCARNATION, MAHAVIRA-POT, SACRA-MENT, SCARLET, SOMA-JUICE, WASHED (blood).

BLOOD AND WATER :—

Symbolic of the Divine Life and Truth.

" But one (soldier) pierced his side, and forthwith came out blood and water." —JOHN xix. 34.

But an aggressive quality stirred into activity the purified nature of the soul which thereupon yielded life and truth.

" Blood and water are divine truth, spiritual and natural ; and to pierce the Lord's side is to destroy both by falses." —SWEDENBORG, *Apoc. Rev.*, n. 26.

See CRUCIFIXION OF JESUS.

BLOOD OF THE LAMB :—

A symbol of the Divine Life pri-mordially involved in the World-soul.

" These are they which come out of the great tribulation, and they washed their robes, and made them white in the blood of the Lamb."—REV. vii. 14.

These are the souls or the qualities which arise purified out of the suffer-ing and discipline of the lower life. Their mental vestures of opinion, etc. are made consistent with truth and right, and they are now spotless and pure through the indwelling Divine Life which has restored and perfected them.

" The blood of the Lamb is the divine truth proceeding from the Lord."— SWEDENBORG, *Apoc. Rev.*, n. 555.

" ' The blood of Jesus Christ cleanseth us from all sin.' But what is the blood ? It is life outpoured—outpoured in love, outpoured in sacrifice. . . . There is a cleansing flood flowing from Im-manuel's veins that saves, heals, renews poor guilty souls. Immanuel—God with us—God with us all the time."—R. J. CAMPBELL, Serm., *The Sense of Sin*.

" Faith in Christ is that power by which the vitality of Christ, through our love and obedience to Him, becomes our vitality. The triumph of the believing soul is this, that he does not live by himself ; that into him is ever flowing, by a law which is both natural and supernatural, the vitality of the Christ whom he loves and obeys. His whole nature beats with the inflow of that divine life. He lives, but Christ lives in him. And then add one thing more. Christ is the perfect man, the divine man. Add this, and then we know that his vitality filling us is the perfection of human life filling humanity."—PHILLIPS BROOKS, Serm., *The Safety and Helpfulness of Faith.*

"By this mystical blood we are saved ; —this blood, . . . whereby man is transmuted from the material to the spiritual plane, the secret of inward purification by means of Love. For this "blood,' which throughout the sacred writings is spoken of as the essential principle of the 'Life,' is the spiritual Blood of the spiritual Life,—Life in its highest, intensest, and most excellent sense,— not the mere physical life understood by materialists,—but the very substantial Being, the inward Deity in man. And it is by means of this Blood of Christ only—that is by means of *Divine Love* only—that we can 'come to the Father,' and inherit the kingdom of heaven. For when it is said that 'the blood of Christ cleanseth from all sin,' it is signified that sin is impossible to him who is perfect in Love."—*The Perfect Way*, p. 109.

"The Blood of Christ 'cleanses our consciences from dead works to serve a living God' (HEB. ix. 14), because 'the Blood of Christ' is the symbol, *not of His death*, but of His Eternal Life. The Blood, we read, as far back as GEN. ix. 4, 'is the Life.' "—F. W. FARRER, *The Atonement, etc.*, p. 45.

"The Life of grace and truth ; that is the Life of Christ, and, therefore, the Life of God. The Life of grace—of graciousness, love, pity, generosity, usefulness, self-sacrifice ; the Life of truth —of faithfulness, fairness, justice, the desire to impart knowledge, and to guide men into all truth. The Life, in one word, of charity, which is both grace and truth, both love and justice in one Eternal Essence. That is the one Eternal Life, which must be also the Life of God. For, as there is but one Eternal, even God, so there is but one Eternal Life, which is the life of God and of His Christ."—CH. KINGSLEY, *Water of Life*, p. 8.

See ATONEMENT, CRUCIFIXION OF CHRIST, EVOLUTION, INCARNATION, LAMB OF GOD, LITANY, MAHAVIRA-POT, MEDIATOR, PASSOVER, PRAGÂ-PATI (relaxed), ROBE, SACRAMENT, SACRIFICER, SOMA-JUICE, TAUROBO-LIUM, TRANSUBSTANTIATION, WASHED (blood), WINE, WORD.

BLOOD OF BULLS :—

A symbol of the Life in the lower nature operating through desire only.

"And her (Queen Kypris) altar was not moistened with pure blood of bulls, but it was the greatest defilement among men to deprive animals of life and to eat their goodly bodies."—*Empedocles*, FAIRBANKS, 405.

In an early state of the soul, the static condition of the functioning of Wisdom, was not defiled by the struggle which was later on begotten of the divorce between desire (bulls) and reason, or between understanding and intuition. At this stage the sundering of the life and the form,— which was incidental to subsequent evolution, i.e. through the functioning of the lower mind,—was unknown.

See HECATOMBS, KYPRIS, TAUROBO-LIUM.

BLOODY SWEAT OF JESUS :—

A symbol of the effort of the Divine life to effect union of the higher nature and the lower.

"The spiritual life follows certain well-defined laws of development, and these laws do not admit of the experience of joy at every stage of the upward road ; on the contrary, they necessitate at various points an acquaintance with darkness and the shadow of death, with pain and loss and loneliness of heart, with the agony and bloody sweat and the crucifixion of the soul."—R. J. CAMPBELL, Serm., *The Glorified Life.*

See CRUCIFIXION OF JESUS, PASSION.

BLUE :—

The symbolic colour of the higher mental plane ; also a symbol of the philosophic mind and intellect, as the higher mind (air).

"By blue is signified intelligence."— SWEDENBORG, *Apoc. Rev.*, n. 450.

See COLOURS, SKY.

BLUE HEAVEN :—

A symbol of the celestial region of bliss on the buddhic plane.

"For 'I am' is that God, even the Bull, the Lord of gods, when he setteth forth in the Blue Heaven."—M. W. BLACKDEN, *Book of the Dead*, Ch. CX.

The true and one Self is symbolised by the "Bull,"—the Lord of the Divine attributes which are set forth in the Kingdom of heaven on the buddhic plane.

"And they saw the God of Israel ;

and there was under his feet as it were a paved work of sapphire stone ; and as it were the very heaven for clearness."
—Exod. xxiv. 10.

The Divine activities (feet) are directed from the buddhic and higher mental planes to the planes below.

See I AM, KINGDOM OF HEAVEN, TURQUOISE.

BOAR :—

A symbol of the lower quaternary, or of the astro-mental nature.

" Frey drove in a chariot drawn by a boar called Gyllenborste, or Slidrug-tanne "—*Prose Edda.*

And now the Self animates the causal-body, only after, however, the evolution has been furthered upon the planes below, i.e. the quaternary.

" In the poetical tales of the ancient Scandinavians, Frey, the deity of the Sun, was fabled to have been killed by a boar ; which was therefore annually offered to him at the great feast of Yule, celebrated during the winter solstice."

The Self (Frey) being completely involved in the matter of the lower planes is, as it were, killed by the lower quaternary.

" It is said that Adonis was slain by a boar. Now Adonis is supposed to be the same with Bacchus ; and many rites in the worship of each confirm this opinion."—PLUTARCH, *Symposiacs*, 4, 5.

" Adonis " being the Self, the same explanation applies.

The Buddha died through eating " boar's flesh " : that is, the Soul having attained perfection through the consumption of the lower quaternary (boar), it dies out of the lower nature to be born into the higher.

See ADONIS, ARES, JUDAS, PIG SOW, SWINE.

BOAR OF ARES (MARS) :—

A symbol of the lower quaternary as energised by kama-manas.

" Ares in the form of a boar sets all evils in commotion."—PLUTARCH, *Of Love*, § 13.

" Ares in the form of a boar with savage teeth, bringing death, came to weave the web of fate about Adonis."
—NONNUS, *Dionysiacs.*

It is through the activity of kama-manas, the desire-mind or " devil," that evolution at first takes place, and that all the evils in the world exist. The " web of fate " entangling the Higher Self is the desire-mentality

which imprisons the Self, but which is the means, through Self-conquest, of the attainment of bliss and the results of experience.

See ADONIS, ARES, MARS.

BOAR AVATAR OF VISHNU :—

A symbol of the quaternary comprising the four planes below atma. In this signification, the Self (Vishnu) manifests in order to destroy the Demon of desire and raise the lower nature (earth).

" This universe was formerly water. Prajāpate, as a boar, plunged beneath. He found the earth below."—*Tait. Upanishad*, I. 1, 3, 5.

" All was water only in which the earth was formed. Thence arose Brahmā. He becoming a boar, raised up the earth."—*Ramayāna*, II. 110.

" *Varaha*, the boar. In this incarnation Vishnu descended to deliver the world from the power of a demon called Hiranyaksha, who had seized the earth and carried it down into the lowest depths of the sea. Vishnu, as a boar, dived into the abyss, and after a contest of 1,000 years, slew the monster and raised the earth. In the earlier legends the universe is represented as a mass of water, and the earth being submerged, was upheaved by the tusks of the divine boar. According to some, the object of this incarnation was to recover the lost Vedas."—MON. WILLIAMS, *Indian Wisdom*, p. 330.

The Higher Self descends by involution into the four lower planes (boar, four-limbed), and at the end of the cycle succeeds in exterminating the desire nature (the demon). The work is accomplished by the Divine expression of Truth (tusks). The lower nature (earth) of the soul requires to be raised by upward thrust of the God within, from the lower water of error and illusion The object of all this effort is to restore to the egos the buddhic consciousness and Divine life (Vedas) which they had lost in their " fall " to the lower planes.

See BRAHMA, CHURNING, PRAGÂ-PATI, VEDA, VISHNU, WATER (higher).

BOAR, WILD :—

A symbol of the quaternary of planes below atma.

" Here (at the Mariandyni) died Idmon the seer, wounded by the tusks of a wild boar."—*Argonautic Expedition.*

The soul having arrived at the state of right discrimination in the domain

of the higher intellect (King Lycus)
the quality of faith (Idmon) is extinguished. The " wounding by the tusks
of a wild boar " is symbolic of Divine
Truth, through the attainment of the
buddhic (fourth plane) consciousness,
penetrating the corresponding vehicle
faith, thus rendering the latter needless.

See ADONIS, FAITH, IDMON, MARIAN-
DYNI, TEETH, TUSK.

BOAT :—

A symbol of the causal-body, the
seat of the Higher Self. The soul
floating on the river of life.

"The True Guru is a boat ; few there
are who consider this, and those who do
he mercifully saveth " (*Asa ki war*).—
MACAULIFFE, *The Sikh Religion*, Vol. I.
p. 236.

See AFU-RĀ, ARGO, ARK, CHARIOT
OF THE SUN, SHIP, TUAT.

BOAT OF THE EARTH :—

A symbol of the sub-cycle of the
re-incarnations of the Self in the
lower bodies below the causal-body,
in the cycle of involution.

"Immediately in the fair way of the
course of Afu-Rā (in the third division
of the Tuat) is a group of eight gods who
bear on their shoulders a long pole-like
object, each end of which terminates in
a bull's head. This object is intended to
represent the long tunnel in the earth,
each end of which was guarded by a
bull, through which, according to one
tradition, the night Sun passed on his
journey from the place of sunset to the
place of sunrise. . . . There is no doubt
that it originally represented a kind of
Tuat which was complete in itself, as
the bull's heads, one at each end of it,
prove."—BUDGE, *Egypt. Heaven and Hell*,
Vol. III. p. 126.

The third division of the cycle of
life is on the mental plane. The
bull's head is a symbol of the lower
quaternary, and the eight figures
supporting the pole indicate, probably,
duality on the four lower planes. The
passage through the "tunnel in the
earth " signifies the incarnation of the
Self (Afu-Rā) in the lower nature
(earth).

See AFU-RĀ, BULL, CIRCLE AND
SQUARE, EIGHT, GILGOOLEM, INCAR-
NATION, QUATERNARY, REINCARNA-
TION, SUN, TUAT, WHEELS (holy).

BOAT ON THE RIVER :—

A symbol of the causal-body, the

vehicle of the spiritual ego in the life
on the lower planes (river of life).

"During his journey in the underworld
the deceased came to a huge river
which he was obliged to cross, to enable
him to embark in the mystical boat,
every portion of which possessed a name
which he was bound to know and be
able to repeat, he provided himself with
Chapters 98 and 99. But this boat only
served to take him across the river,
and he longed to be able to embark in
the Boat of Rā, and be with the god for
ever."—BUDGE, *Book of the Dead*, Vol. I.
p. xcii.

In his progressive life on the lower
planes, the ego, or lower consciousness,
has before and above him the higher
mind, as it were a great river which
the consciousness must cross over ere
it can be united with the higher
consciousness in the causal-body
(mystical boat). This union of the
higher and lower Selves requires that
the lower Self in all its qualities shall
become perfect and identical with the
higher Self in the causal-body (Boat
of Rā).

See AFU-RĀ, ARGO, ARK, BRIDGE OF
HEAVEN, CHARON'S FERRY, HIKOBOSHI,
HOLD, KEEL, OARS, PADDLES, PLANKS,
ROCK-BOAT, ROPE, RUDDER, SAIL,
SAILOR, SHIP, SHIPS (beaked).

BOAT SEKTET, AND BOAT ATET ;
—THE EVENING AND MORN-
ING BOATS OF RA :—

Symbols of the buddhic causal-
body, or World-soul ; first, in the
cycle of involution (morning), and
second, in that of evolution (evening).
The first is said to mean " becoming
weak," and the second " becoming
strong," which signifies that the
Spirit becomes weak in descent into
matter, and strong in ascent therefrom.

"Thy right eye is like the Sektet
(evening) boat ; thy left eye is like the
Atet boat (or Matet, morning boat)."—
BUDGE, *Book of the Dead*, p. 503.

The individuality is formed and
perfected in the period of evolution ;
the personality in that of involution.

" May the soul of Ani come forth with
thee into heaven, may he go forth in the
Matet boat. May he come into port in
the Sektet boat, and may he cleave his
path among the never-resting stars in
the heavens."—BUDGE, *Egyptian Ideas*,
etc., p. 33.

May the perfected soul come forth
and unite with the Self on the buddhic

plane ; may he first go forth as the personality in the period of involution. May he when perfected come into the haven of attainment and peace, as the individuality ; and may he rise triumphant among the Divine monads, —the spiritual egos who scintillate knowledge on the atmic plane.

See ARK (safety), ARREST, CAKE, CROCODILE, DECANS, KEEL, KHEPER, MOON (wax), NET-RĀ, NUT, SUN-CATCHING, UPLIFTING, UTCHATS.

BOAT OF THE TWO-HEADED-SERPENT :—

A symbol of the causal-body during the involution of the desire-mental qualities.

In the fourth division (kama-manas) of the Tuat (Life-cycle) according to the Book Am-Tuat, Afu-Rā (Higher Self) has to leave his Boat in order to pass through waterless deserts (illusion and error). He and his company (ideals) therefore proceed on the back of a two-headed serpent (desire-mind). The " hidden gods " (experiences to develop the soul), who march in front of the boat to help it along, are all under the control of Anubis (physical body of sensation and action).—*See* BUDGE, *Egypt. Heav. and Hell*, Vol. III. p. 133.

See AFU-RĀ, ANUBIS, DESERTS, SEKER, SERPENT, TUAT.

BOAT OF WISDOM :—

A symbol of the causal-body on the higher mental plane. This is the vehicle of wisdom (buddhi) through which the qualities are delivered by Truth from the attachment to desire and sensation.

" Even if thou wert the greatest of all sinners, thou shalt be able to cross over all sins in the boat of wisdom."—*Bhagavad-Gita*, Ch. IV.

However strongly the soul may be bound down by desire, yet the time arrives when liberation is brought about by the soul's own efforts and the buddhic transmutations.

" There is no purifier in this world to be compared to wisdom ; and he who is perfected in devotion findeth wisdom springing up spontaneously in himself in the progress of time."—*Ibid.*

" Buddha will deliver by the boat of knowledge the distressed world, borne helplessly along, from the ocean of misery which throws up sickness as its foam, tossing with the waves of old age, and rushing with the dreadful onflow of death."—*Buddha-Karita*, Bk. I. 75.

The Self will be the means of delivering the qualities from the plane of the lower emotions by Wisdom, so that they may be transmuted to the buddhic plane and no more assailed by the conflicting feelings which trouble the lower self. The " sickness " signifies the nausea which afflicts the ego so long as it is unsatisfied by the true knowledge and perception of the nature of the Higher. The " tossing " is a symbol of unrest which engenders a sense of perpetual insecurity in the lower self. The " rushing, etc.," signifies a sense of dread of the unknown, and lack of faith in the real ; it is a symbol which corresponds to the " bottomless pit,"—" death " standing for the not-self, the unreal.

See BOTTOMLESS PIT, BUDDHI, CAUSAL-BODY, PAPYRUS BOAT, PIT, RAFT, TRANSMUTATION, WISDOM.

BODHISATVA, THE GREAT :—

A symbol of the germ of the One-Soul in the cycle of Involution. The incarnate Higher Self.

" Then falling from the host of beings in the Tushita heaven, and illumining the three worlds, the most excellent of Bodhisatvas suddenly entered as a thought into her womb (that of Queen Māyā), like the Naga-king entering the cave of Nanda."—*Buddha-Karita*, Bk. I. 19.

Then descending from the buddhic plane by way of the mental planes, —by means of the Devas,—and enlightening the mental, astral, and physical planes, the germ-Soul,—whose nature is pre-arranged harmony,— passed unperceived into the " womb of Māyā "—the embodiment of pure Truth,—the opposite of illusion ; the conception taking place on the fourth sub-plane of the astral plane. The " Serpent-king " is a symbol of wisdom and enlightenment, and the " cave of Nanda " a symbol of the personality.

See AVALOKITESVARA, BIRTH OF BUDDHA, BUDDHA, CAVE OF NANDA, CONCEPTION, CRANBERRY. ELEPHANT (sacred), FIRST-BORN SON, HIRANYA-GARBHA, INSIGNIA, MĀYĀ, MONAD, SEED, TUSHITA, WOMB OF MĀYĀ.

BODHISATVAS :—

A symbol of the monads of form in the natural order of things below the mental level. These originate as prototypes on the buddhic plane, and become reflected through the mental on to the astral plane where they mould the forms of all the varied structures in the phenomenal world.

" Hundreds of thousands of myriads of Bodhisatvas who equal in number the atoms contained in a thousand worlds, have risen from clefts in the earth created by a ray of light projected from the centre of (Urnā) Bhagavat's eyebrows. —*Lotus of the Good Law*, Ch. XX.

The countless numbers of monads of form, which are the prototypes of all things that appear and develop in the mineral, vegetal, and animal kingdoms of creation, become operative in the lower nature (earth) when physical conditions are prepared to receive them. They are the out-pourings of spiritual truth (urna) into matter in the course of Divine manifestation.

" A Bodhisatva is a being who through all his bodily existences is destined in some final existence to become a Buddha, or self-enlightened man. Until his final birth, however, a Bodhisattva is a being in whom true knowledge is rather latent and undeveloped than perfected."—Mon. Williams, *Buddhism*, p. 180.

The monad, or spiritual ego, is a being seeking expression through a series of living forms or bodily existences. He is destined gradually to express his nature and to become ultimately a self-enlightened soul (Buddha) in union with the Highest. Until his final advent on the higher mental plane, Truth is incomplete in him, and as a power it is latent. Not until perfection is reached can Truth be fully expressed, and the expression is then on the higher plane to which the consciousness attains.

See Agnishvatta, Atom (permanent), Buddha, Buddhic plane, Forms, Fravashis, Incarnation of souls, Maruts, Microcosm, Monad of form, Muspell, Nakedness, Paccekabuddhas, Prototypes, Re-incarnation, Sons of god, Sparks, Sutratma, Tri-ratna, Urnā.

BODY OF OSIRIS, OR OF JASON :—

A symbol of the astro-mental vehicle, or body of desire, in which the Self is encased.

See Death of osiris, Jason, Mummy of osiris, Osiris.

BOLTS OF THE GATES OF ERIDU :—

Symbolic of the second and third Logoi which proceed forth as manifestations of the Divine Life on the lower planes.

" At night Adapa drew the bolts of the gates of Eridu, and at dawn he sailed forth in his bark to fish in the sea " (*Babylonian Legend*).—Sayce, *Religions, etc.*

In the period when the lower nature appeared to be cut off from the higher, the Archetypal Man (Adapa) initiated a new Divine forthpouring of life : opening, as it were, the door between heaven (Eridu) and earth (the lower planes). And at this time of forthgoing, he goes in search of that which will provide him with sustenance. The " bark " is the manasic vehicle which sails on the astral sea. The " fish " are those appearances which come to him as sensations, feelings, and emotions, impinging upon the soul at the dawn of consciousness.

" Thou (Horus) hast opened the two doors of Heaven, thou hast drawn back the great bolts, thou hast removed the seal of the great door."—Budge, *Book of the Dead*, p. cxxiii.

" The celestial Adam Qadmon is called the Bolt or that which unites Heaven and Earth, the Invisible and Visible."—Myer, *Qabbalah*, p. 115.

" Adam Kadmon," the Adam of the first chapter of Genesis,—the perfect image of God,—signifies the Archetypal Man, the same as " Adapa." Here, the Archetypal Man is called the " Bolt," since it is through him,—as the incarnate God,—that the way or path of the souls is opened between the lower and higher planes.

See Adam (higher), Adapa, Arc. man, Eridu, Fish, Gate (tchesert), Gates, Heaven and earth, Higher and lower, Image, Incarnation, Logos, Meat, Night, Path, Sea.

BONDAGE UNDER THE RUDIMENTS OF THE WORLD :—

A symbol of captivity to desire and sensation.

" Even so we, when we were children, were in bondage under the elements of the world."—Gal. iv. 3.

This refers to the infancy of the spiritual egos, and the early stages of evolution, during which the laws of nature, or pressure from without, in the organism and its environment, alone stimulate the egos into activity.

"When a man becomes regenerate he then first enters upon a state of freedom ; before he was in a state of bondage. It is bondage when lusts and falsities have dominion ; it is freedom when affections of good and truth hold sway."—SWEDENBORG, *Arc. Cel.*, n. 892.

"Human infirmity in moderating and checking the emotions, I name bondage : for when a man is a prey to his emotions, he is not his own master, but lies at the mercy of fortune : so much so, that he is often compelled, while seeing that which is better for him, to follow that which is worse."—SPINOZA, *Ethics*, Vol. II. p. 187.

"'And if they shall be in chains, and bound with the cords of poverty, He will show them their works, and their wickednesses, because they have been violent' (JOB xxxvi. 8, 9). The 'chains of bondage' are the very detention of their present pilgrimage. Paul had seen that he was bound by these chains when he was saying, 'I have a desire to be dissolved, and to be with Christ' (PHIL. i. 23). He perceived that he was bound with the cords of poverty, when, beholding the true riches, he entreated them also for his disciples."—ST. GREGORY, *Morals on the Book of Job*, Vol. III. p. 176.

"'By grace ye are saved.' 'To save, to redeem, to deliver,' are in the general terms equivalent, and they do all of them suppose us to be in a state of thraldom and misery ; therefore this word 'saved,' in the sense that the apostle here doth use it, is a word of great worth, forasmuch as the miseries from which we are saved is the misery of all most dreadful."—JOHN BUNYAN, *Saved by Grace*.

See BABYLON, CAPTIVITY, DISPENSATIONS, EXODUS, FETTERS, GOLDEN AGE, GUARDIAN SPIRITS, HOUSE OF BONDAGE, IGNORANCE, JERUSALEM, LIBERATION, PASSOVER, PEOPLE, POVERTY, PRISONERS, RAHU, REDEMPTION, REGENERATION, REMISSION, RESURRECTION, SALVATION, SEPARATION, SERVANT OF GOD, SUFFERING, SUN-SETTING, TARTARUS.

BONES OR SKELETON :—

A symbol of the spiritual nature to which the higher and lower qualities of the soul are attached.

"By bones in holy Scripture we understand virtues ; as it is written, 'The Lord keepeth all his bones ; not one of them shall be broken' (Ps.

xxxiv. 20). 'His flesh shall waste away, and his bones which were covered shall be laid bare' (JOB xxxiii. 21). For when every outward pleasure is worn away by the pressure of the rod, the bones of inward firmness are laid bare. For what is meant in this place by the word flesh but fleshly pleasure itself ? Or what by bones but the virtues of the soul ? The flesh therefore wastes away, and the bones are laid bare, because while carnal pleasure is brought to nought by the reproof of scourges, those steady virtues are laid open, which had long been concealed, as it were, beneath the flesh."—GREGORY THE GREAT, *Morals on the Book of Job*, Vol. III. pp. 40, 46.

See CORPSE DEVOURED BY BIRDS.

BONES, WHITE :—

Symbolic of the spiritual foundation of the structure of the vehicles of consciousness of the ego.

"And the kindly earth in its broad hollows received two out of the eight parts of bright Nestis, and four of Hephaistos, and they became white bones, fitted together marvellously by the glues of harmony."—*Empedocles*, FAIRBANKS, 199.

And the lower self through the physical vehicle (Nestis) which was now being organised and adapted for the functioning of the ego, became the seat of two senses,—taste and touch, the other inner senses are at this period unmanifested. The "four of Hephaistos" are sight, hearing, smell, and the intuitive faculty. The "white bones" are comparable to the firm foundation to which the consciousness is now attached, and the being "fitted together, etc." signifies the perfect adjustment of each condition to each.

See EARTH, FLESH, HEPHAISTOS, NESTIS, NET, PROMETHEUS, RIB, STONE.

BOOK OF THE LORD GOD :—

A symbol of the Life Process of the cycle of manifestation on the lower planes, which is to lead to the soul's enlightenment.

"And I saw in the right hand of him that sat on the throne a book written within and on the back, close sealed with seven seals."—REV. v. 1.

In the keeping of the Absolute and ready to come forth into actuality (right hand), is the Divine scheme whereby the souls shall gain experience and learn the Truth. It comprises the inner and the outer manifestation in potentiality complete (seven).

"And he (the Lamb that had been slain) came, and he taketh it out of the right hand of him that sat on the throne."
—Rev. v. 7.

Only the Higher Self who had laid down his life in Self-limitation could carry out the Divine scheme, and ultimately rise in the souls of humanity to wisdom and riches, and glory, and the dominion over the lower nature.

See CHAPTERS, HAND (right), LAMB OF GOD, SACRIFICER, SEAL, THRONE.

BOOK STUDIES :—

Symbolic of following the letter of the sacred scriptures blindly, but reverentially.

"Homa grants fame and learning to all those who are engaged in the study of books."—*Homa Yasht.*

The Spirit allows in due time the interior perception of Truth to be opened in those who have earnestly studied the scriptures according to the letter. For the reverential carrying out of injunctions entrusted to the soul, even blindly and unintelligently, is the means of arriving at the state when the interior perception of truths shall at length be awakened, and the intuition of Wisdom within shall revive from latency.

See HOMA, PAPYRUS BOAT, READING, SCRIPTURES, UR-HEKAU, WITNESSES (two).

BOOTHS :—

Symbolic of mental forms, or thought forms.

"Ye shall dwell in booths seven days; all that are Israelites born shall dwell in booths."—*Lev. xxiii. 42.*

The mental qualities (Israelites) shall be contained in limited concepts or forms of thought, for a complete period of evolution.

See ISRAELITES, SEVEN, TABERNACLES, TENT, VESSELS.

BOREAS, THE NORTH WIND,— SON OF ASTRÆUS AND EOS :—

A symbol of the higher mind produced by reason and intuition.

See CLEOPATRA, PHINEUS, ZETES.

BORN AGAIN, OR FROM ABOVE :—

Symbolic of the consciousness raised from the lower mind to the higher, which is the second birth.

"Except a man be born of water and the Spirit, he cannot enter into the kingdom of God."—JOHN iii. 5.

Except an ego be raised morally and purified by truth (water) and the buddhic function (fire) he cannot enter into the buddhic consciousness.

The first birth is the entrance of the ego into the underworld or cycle of the lower life. When the ego dies to the lower life, he is reborn into the higher.

See BAPTISM (fire), KINGDOM OF HEAVEN, RE-BIRTH, REGENERATION, SPIRIT, WATER.

BORN OUT OF DUE TIME :—

Symbolic of the raising of the consciousness in the process of the soul's evolution. The state wherein personality is transcended, and all imperfections and limitations have been outgrown.

"And last of all, as unto one born out of due time, he appeared to me also."
—1 COR. xv. 8.

This is the utterance of the soul when it has attained direct vision of the Supreme seated in the causal-body. It refers to that state of consciousness which supervenes when the lower nature has fallen away, and the soul finds expression in due course on the higher mental plane.

"Then I am born as the twelfth or thirteenth additional month, through the twelve or thirteenfold father."—*Kaush. Upanishad, I. 2.*

Then the ego shall be as one born on the higher plane out of due time in the Divine order of things,—the "thirteenth additional month" signifying the period answering to the conclusion of a certain number of periods through the cycle which shall enable the soul to become perfect through intellect fully matured (father).

See ABORTION, ÆON (thirteenth), CAUSAL-BODY, CONVERSION OF PAUL, MONTH, SALVATION, THIRTEEN.

BOTTOMLESS PIT :—

A symbol of the desire and sensation nature which is never satisfied. The "beast" within it is the desire-mind, the adversary of the Spirit.

"What does he call 'the bottomless

pit' but the hearts of men, which are at once by the Fall all floating, and by the mistiness of double-dealing full of darkness?"—St. Gregory, *Morals on the Book of Job*, Vol. II. p. 368.

"Self-disease, the satiety which consumes, the dreadful loneliness which corrupts the soul, that passionate lust for more which is itself the unsatisfied worm which eats away the heart."—Stopford A. Brooke, Serm., *Individuality*.

See Aeshm, Arizura, Beast, Boat of wisdom, Pit, Serpent (hissing), Stench.

BOUGH TO LEAN UPON :—

A symbol of the support nature gives the soul, through the tree of life external.

See Garden lumbini.

BOW OF SILVER, AND ARROW, OF APOLLO :—

Symbolic of the higher-mental stimulus to evolution, destructive to the lower mental qualities.

See Apollo, Arrows, Clang, Metal, Pestilence, Silver.

BOW IN THE CLOUD :—

A symbol of the higher mind as the bridge between the higher nature and the lower.

"I do set my bow in the cloud, and it shall be for a token of a covenant between me and the earth."—Gen. ix. 13.

Between the Divine nature and the soul there is to be a channel, or bridge, for purposes of conscious intercommunication, which is to extend from the cloud (truth, wisdom) downwards; and this is to constitute the connection between the personality (earth) and Me,—the Individuality, or the lower nature and the Higher.

See Bifrost, Bridge, Cloud, Covenant, Earth, Rainbow.

BOWL OF PURE WATER :—

A symbol of the causal-body wherein the Eternal Truth manifests Itself.

See Cup, Hylas, Water.

BOWS OF BOAT :—

A symbol of the foremost qualities of Truth and Right.

"The Osiris Nu maketh right and truth to go round about the bows in the Great Boat."—Budge, *Book of the Dead*, p. 394.

"'Tell us our names,' say the Bows;

'He who is at the head of his nomes,' is your name."—*Ibid.*, p. 300.

The "Bows" signify the most advanced qualities in the departments of life.

See Acacia, Boat, Sycamore.

BOX-TREE WOOD, AND LOTE-PLUM WOOD, FOR BURNING :—

Symbols of will and energy active on the astral plane.

See Fire (lower), Wood.

BOY, OR YOUNG MAN :—

A symbol of a primitive mind, or young mind. Mind in an early stage of development.

See Dwarf, Young man.

BOYS, BAD :—

Symbolic of uninstructed qualities of the lower mind, which need to be transmuted and raised.

"A boy, a worker of iniquity, ran up and came against the shoulder of Jesus, wishing to make sport of Him, or to hurt Him, if he could."—*Gospel of Pseudo-Mathew*.

A fault of the lower nature pressed sore upon the Christ-soul, and brought grievous trouble with it, so that it became necessary for the Lord to forbid the liability of future temptation to arise.

See Joseph (Mary), Man (bad), Sparrows.

BRAHMA, OR BRAHMAN :—

A symbol of the Supreme Spirit,—the One Absolute Being; or, it may be, the manifest God,—the Higher Self of all.

"In the beginning Brahman was all *This*. He was one and infinite; . . . infinite above and below and everywhere infinite. . . . The Highest Self is not to be fixed, he is unlimited, unborn, not to be reasoned about, not to be conceived. He is like the ether (everywhere), and at the destruction of the universe, he alone is awake."—*Mait. Upanishad*, VI. 20.

Prior to the commencement of the cycle of life, the Infinite Self was unmanifest in time and space. Absolute being had not outbreathed the Divine Life. The Highest Self had not limited himself and taken birth in a universe—a solar system. He is inconceivable and at the root of all; and when the manifested Life is indrawn and the cycle ends, He alone persists.

"One of the greatest favours of God, bestowed transiently upon the soul in this life, is its ability to see so distinctly, and to feel so profoundly, that . . . it cannot comprehend Him at all. These souls are herein, in some degree, like to the souls in heaven, where they who know Him most perfectly perceive most clearly that He is infinitely incomprehensible ; for those that have the less clear vision, do not perceive so distinctly as the others how greatly He transcends their vision."—ST. JOHN OF THE CROSS, *A Spiritual Canticle.*

"The question whether, on mystical principles, we can know God, must be answered by drawing, with Eckhart, a distinction between the Godhead and God. Our knowledge must be of God, not of the Godhead, and the God of religion is not the Absolute, but the highest form under which the Absolute can manifest Himself to finite creatures in various stages of imperfection. The God of religion is not the Father of lights with whom is no variableness, for life without change is a state of which we have no experience, but the Father revealed by the Son. 'No man hath seen God at any time. The only-begotten Son, who is in the bosom of the Father, He hath declared Him.' "—W. R. INGE, *Paddock Lectures,* p. 11.

"I have had glimpses of an all-pervading Intelligence and Power, a curiously intense apprehension of a life, a mind, a will higher than anything that we ordinarily know under these terms, and the fulfilment of them all, absolutely all-inclusive, subject to no vicissitudes, far above all flux and change, and yet comprehending all change within its own majestic stillness and completeness."—R. J. CAMPBELL, Serm., *Being and Becoming.*

"It is said : 'within this body (*Brahme-pura*) *Brahme's* abode, is a little lotus, a dwelling within which is a (*dahara*) small vacuity occupied by ether (*ácasá*). What that is within (the heart's ventricle) is to be inquired, and should be known.' A question is here raised, whether that 'ether' within the ventricle of the heart be the etherial element, or the individual sensitive soul, or the Supreme One ; and it is pronounced from the context, that the Supreme Being is here meant."—H. T. COLEBROOKE, *Essays,* p. 221.

See ABSOLUTE, AKASA, APARÂGITA, ARHAT, ATMAN, FATHER, GODHEAD, HEART, LOTUS, OGDOAD, PATH (twofold), SARASVATI, SEASONS, SLEEPING, TASTE, TRINITY, UNION, VIBHU, VIRAJ.

BRAHMA-CÂRIN, STUDENT OF THE VEDA :—

A symbol of the personality in its ethical and spiritual aspect or relationship, for the soul's evolution.

"The young Brâhman is to reside with his preceptor (guru) until he has gained a thorough knowledge of the three Vedas." —WILLIAMS, *Indian Wisdom,* p. 245.

The young ego or personality is to revere his spiritual mind (guru) and learn the Divine law of the soul's evolution on the three lower planes, as expressed in the Word of God, or sacred scriptures.

See GURU, SANNYASIN, STUDENT, VEDA.

BRAHMA-WEAPON OF DRONA :—

A symbol of trust in outward authority in religion.

See DRONA.

BRÂHMANA :—

A symbol of the individuality seated in the causal-body on the higher mental plane.

"The regular means of subsistence for a *Brâhmana* are assisting to sacrifice, teaching the *Védas,* and receiving gifts." —COLEBROOKE, *Essays,* p. 276.

The individuality, or causal self, raises the soul by imparting truth and receiving love offerings.

See ALMSGIVING, CASTES, OFERINGS, SACRIFICE, VÂGAPEYA, VEDAS.

BRAHMAN PRIESTS :—

A symbol of the mental forms, or ideals, through which the spiritual nature is apprehended.

"And the king gave to the brahmans for his son's (Buddha's) welfare, cows full of milk, with no traces of infirmity, golden-horned, and with strong, healthy calves to the full number of one hundred thousand."—*Buddha-Karita,* Bk. I. 89.

The "gift of cows" signifies the provision of the intuitive perception of spiritual things which is to enable the soul to rise. The "brahmans" are the forms through which spirit is perceived. The "no traces of infirmity" is an allusion to the perfect conception of the truth, implanted by involution within the Soul. The "golden horns" are symbols of zeal and love of the true. The myriad "calves" are the progeny of Buddhi (cow), and are the inexhaustible treasures of the Spirit, i.e. the higher emotions and faculties.

See BUDDHA, CALVES, COW (milch), EPHOD, GOLDEN, HORNS.

BRAHMARANDHRAM :—

A symbol of the ray of the Divine Life which enters into the highest range of the mind (head).

"The brahmarandhram is an imaginary orifice of the skull on the top of the head, through which, according to Ait. I. 3, 12, Brahman entered into the body and by which the soul, or according to the more usual view only the souls of the emancipated, having ascended by the hundred and first vein (subsequently named *sushumnâ*) attains to union with Brahman."—DEUSSEN, *Phil. of Upanishads*, p. 283.

The "orifice of the skull" is the aperture of the mind towards the Divine influence from above ; indicative of a receptive attitude to Truth. The "sushumna vein from the heart" is a symbol of aspiration from the love nature of the soul. It is by means of aspiration and receptivity that the soul mounts upward to union with the Divine.

See BACKBONE, DOOR (vara), SUN (as door), SUTRATMA, TET, WINDOW.

BRAINS :—

A symbol of the buddhic nature,—wisdom and love.

See COCOA-NUT, YMIR.

BRANCHES OF TREES ; PALMS ; USED PROCESSIONALLY :—

Symbolic of attainment of glimpses of higher things.

See PROCESSION.

BRASS, BRONZE, METAL :—

Symbolic of mentality, the mental plane ; comparable to that which is firm and endures.

"Brass signifies natural good ; iron, natural truth."—SWEDENBORG, *Arc. Cel. to Gen.* iv. 22.

See IRON, METALS, TUBAL CAIN.

BRATROK-RISH, THE KARAP :—

A symbol of the lower mind which functions through the stimulus of the sense nature.

See BROTHERS.

BRAVERA LAND :—

A symbol of the astro-etheric plane,—a plane of illusions and dreams.

BREAD, OR BREAD OF HEAVEN :—

A symbol of the spiritual food of the soul, namely, truth—the substance of goodness, which is the staff of the higher life.

"For the bread of God is that which cometh down out of heaven, and giveth life unto the world."—JOHN vi. 33.

For the Truth is of the essence of the Self, and is that which cometh forth from the higher planes to nourish the soul and dispel the illusions of the lower nature.

"Teta (the Osirified) liveth upon the daily bread which cometh in its season. He liveth upon that which Shu liveth. . . . He eateth and drinketh what the gods eat and drink."—BUDGE, *Book of the Dead*, p. cxxii.

The perfected soul (Teta) subsists upon the Truth which comes to it in the course of its further development, and its activities are in accordance with the Divine will (Shu). It taketh part in the life of the higher qualities (gods).

"By bread is meant all that is spiritual and celestial, which is the food of angels, 'the bread which came down from heaven.'" — SWEDENBORG, *Arc. Cel. to Gen.* iii. 18.

"The spiritual meaning of anything is its real meaning. Physical things are but shadows or symbols of spiritual realities. When Jesus spoke of physical bread it was really spiritual bread he meant. It is impossible for a deeply spiritual being, such as He is represented to be, to speak of physical things without having in his mind their spiritual equivalents."—R. J. CAMPBELL, Serm., *The Spiritual Meaning of Childhood*.

"Hence there follows, 'And ye shall know the truth.' The truth is unchangeable. The truth is bread, which refreshes our minds and fails not ; changes the eater, and is not itself changed into the eater. The Truth itself is the Word of God."—AUGUSTINE, *Gospel of John*, Vol. II. p. 30.

See CAKE, CORN, DOUGH, EATING, FEEDING (five thousand), FLOUR, FOOD, HOST, KHABIT, MANNA, MEAL, PROCESSION, SACRAMENT, SACRAMENTAL CAKES, SEASONS, SHEWBREAD, STONES AND BREAD, TRANSUBSTANTIATION, UNLEAVENED.

BREAST-EARED RACE :—

A symbol of the emotions constituting the receptive function which enables evolution to be initiated in the soul.

BREAST-EYED RACE :—

A symbol of the higher emotions which give rise to ideas ; sight being comparable to the establishment of mental perception.

BREASTS :—

A symbol of the affection nature.

"The breast signifieth charity.' "—SWEDENBORG, *Arc. Cel. to Gen.* ii. 21.

See GIRDLE (gold), RIB, WOMAN.

BREASTPLATE OF JUDGMENT :—

This symbol signifies an assemblage of twelve disciplined qualities, or aspects of the Divine life in the evolution of mental qualities, in close affectional relation with the spiritual mind (Aaron), and connected with the buddhic and astral centres of activity (shoulderpieces). These qualities are illumined by the Divine Ray (the girdle). The breastplate was "foursquare," that is, the field of the qualities is in the quaternary,—the four planes below atma. The double thickness relates to active and passive conditions of qualities.—*See* EXOD. xxxix.

See AARON, COLOURS, DISCIPLES, EPHOD, GEMS, GIRDLE, JEWELS, KUSTI, PRECIOUS, QUATERNARY, SHEWBREAD, TRIBES, TWELVE, URIM AND THUMMIN.

BREATH :—

A symbol of the mental interpretation of Spirit, or the expression of the Divine on the mental plane.

See MARUTS, MORTAR, WIND.

BREATH, DIVINE, OUTBREATHING AND INBREATHING :—

Symbolic of spiritual action from the Supreme in the rhythmic forthpouring and withdrawing of the Divine Life of the Invisible and visible universe in successive spirations.

"Invoke thou the strong wind created by Mazda Sapandar, the pure daughter of Ormazd."—*Vendidad*, XIX.

Entreat the Divine Breath, the Holy Spirit of Wisdom, which is the functioning of the Absolute upon the Buddhic plane.

"The Sun is the outer Self, the inner Self is Breath. Hence the motion of the inner Self is inferred from the motion of the outer Self."—*Mait. Upanishad,* VI. 1.

"Breath is the life of all beings."—*Tait. Upanishad,* II. 3.

The manifest (outer) Self, and the unmanifest (inner) Self. The potentiality of the unmanifest is implied in the activity of the manifest. The unmanifest out-pours the manifest.

See AMITAUGAS, ASURA, EVENING AND MORNING, GALE, INSPIRATION, MANVANTARA, MORNING, PRALAYA, PRANA, RÂMA, REMISSION, SABBATH, SAPANDAR, TEZCATLIPOCA, WIND.

BREATH OF LIFE :—

A symbol of the spiritual essence,—the Divine Spark, atma-buddhi, which is immortal.

"And (God) breathed into his nostrils the breath of life ; and man became a living soul."—GEN. ii. 7.

And into this lower mind, or astromental body, was projected the Divine spark, and thence the *man* (manasic being) became a creature capable of responsible, independent existence.

See ADAM (lower), FLESH, MAN, NOSE, PERSONALITY, SPARK.

BREEATIC WORLD :—

A symbol of the mental plane.

"From the Atzeeloothic World, through the conjunction of the King and Queen, proceeds the World of Creation, called the Breeatic, or Olam Breeah, also Qursaiyah, i.e. the Throne. In this condition, creation, as we understand the word, begun."—I. MYER, *Qabbalah,* p. 328.

From the atma-buddhic plane, by means of the alliance of the Self (king) and Wisdom (queen), there proceeds the establishment of the mental plane as the plane of ideas to take forms on the astral and physical planes. Also on the higher mental plane there is the causal-body (throne).

See ATZEELOOTHIC, COUNTENANCE, CREATION, KURSAYAH, MAHAT, MALKHUTH, MANAS.

BRIAREUS, OR AEGAEON :—

A symbol of the critical intellect,—synthetic and analytic,—which destroys errors and illusions.

"Then didst thou, O goddess (Thetis), enter in and loose him (Agamemnon) from his bonds, having with speed summoned to high Olympus him of the hundred arms whom gods call Briareus, but all men call Aegaeon ; for he is mightier even than his father—so he sat him by Kronion's side rejoicing in his triumph, and the blessed gods feared him withal and bound not Zeus,"—*Iliad,* Bk. I.

At this period the Child of Time, Illusion, or the Desire-mind, is loosed from its limitations by the buddhic nature which raises to the higher mental level the Critical intellect with its wide-reaching scope. By the Higher Self this faculty is apprehended as the Synthetic function, but by the lower mind as the Analytic, which respectively discern similarities and differences. The Critical intellect is more effective than the Astro-mental faculty : hence the Critical intellect takes its place beside Time, since it is seen to be itself a creator of illusion. And the higher mental qualities now attended upon the Self who is no longer imprisoned in low conditions as heretofore.

See AEGAEON, COTTUS, FIRST, HEDGEHOG, INTELLECT, JOB, MEN (centimani), TALUS.

BRICK FOR STONE :—

Symbolic of superstition which is put in place of spiritual knowledge (stone).

"And they had brick for stone, and slime had they for mortar."—GEN. xi. 3.

Further experiences are to be gathered through superstition and craft (slime) before higher qualities are evolved.

See BABEL, MORTAR, STONE.

BRICKS FOR ALTAR, NATURALLY PERFORATED :—

Symbolic of the lower planes, which are the means of the soul's development by reason of the passage through them of spiritual vibrations, while the ego can rise through them to the higher.

"The naturally perforated bricks are these worlds. . . . How is it that that gold man is not held down by the naturally perforated brick ? Well, the naturally perforated brick is food and breath ; and man is not held down either by food or by his breath."—Sata. Brâh., VII. 4. 2, 8–9.

The lower planes are permeable to Spirit. The atma-buddhic monad is not made nugatory by the lower nature. The lower activities cause truth and virtue to nourish the soul, and so the ego is not restrained by these, but enabled to rise to the higher planes.

"The naturally perforated bricks are meant to represent the three worlds, the holes being intended to afford to the Sacrificer (represented by the gold man) a passage to the highest regions"

(Footnote).—JULIUS EGGELING, Ibid., VI. 1, 2, 31. S.B.E.

See ALTAR (fire), ASHADHA, BREATH, DURVA-BRICK, DVIYAGUS-BRICK, FOOD, GOLD MAN.

BRIDGE OF HEAVEN :—

A world-wide symbol of the higher mental plane which lies between the lower mental plane and the buddhic plane or heaven-world, and therefore is, as it were, a "bridge" from the lower nature to the higher nature.

"I (the Father) also wish thee to look at the Bridge of my only-begotten Son, and see the greatness thereof, for it reaches from Heaven to earth ; that is, that the earth of your humanity is joined to the greatness of the Deity thereby. I say, then, that this Bridge reaches from Heaven to earth, and constitutes the union which I have made with man. . . . And observe that it is not enough, in order that you should have life, that my Son should have made you this Bridge, unless you walk thereon."—ST. CATHERINE OF SIENA, Revelations, etc., LIX.

"In Him, the heaven, the earth, and the sky are woven, the mind also with all the senses. Know Him alone as the Self, and leave off other names. He is the bridge of the Immortal, i.e. the bridge by which we reach our own immortality."—Mundaka Upanishad, II. 2, 5.

The Higher Self as the Individuality is seated in the causal-body on the higher mental plane, and thus he can be spoken of as the "bridge to immortality," the "way, the truth, and the life." The indwelling Self is the soul's Saviour by whom our deficiencies are made good, our imperfect nature built upwards to perfection.

See BALANCE (heart), BIFROST, BOW, HIKOBOSHI, KINVAT, RAINBOW, RECOLLECTION, REINGA.

BRIDGE OF GJALL :—

A symbol of the higher mind leading to spiritual illumination of the consciousness.

"Hermöd rode nine nights and days through dark and deep valleys, and saw no light until he came to Gjall, and rode over the bridge of Gjall, which is overlaid with glittering gold" (Story of Balder, in Edda).—HOWITT, Literature, etc.

At this stage the Christ-soul is described as taking a lengthy ride,— that is, the Self acts through the intellect (horse) alone, which functioning corresponds with riding through dark and deep valleys of the lower mind,—the avenue of approach to "Gjall," that is, to those faculties which at length lead up to the illumination which proceeds from intuition (gold). The "bridge" is the point of junction with the Higher Self, from which inspiration,—the expression of the Holy Spirit, the source of all Truth to humanity,—emanates.

See CHARON'S FERRY, GJALL RIVER, GOLD, HERMOD, INTUITION, MODGUNN, NORTH, VALLEY.

BRIDGE, KINVAT, OR CHINVAT:—

A symbol of the higher mind, above the lower mind (kama-manas) and lower consciousness.

"Between Heaven and Hell is Chinvat Peretu, 'the bridge of the gatherer,' or 'the bridge of the judge' (Chinvat can have both meanings), which the soul of the pious alone can pass, while the wicked fall from it down into Hell."— HAUG, *Essays*, p. 311.

This "bridge" of the higher mind between the lower and higher natures is pre-eminently that of the *gatherer* and of the *judge*, for in the higher mind are gathered the results of the experiences of the ego in the lower life, and between each incarnation the soul is judged unerringly regarding its past progress, and the conditions needed to aid its future growth. The soul cannot pass over the "bridge" until it is perfected. As long as it is attached to desire and sensation and needs purification, so long it falls back into the underworld life after life.

See BALANCE, DOG-STAR, DUSAKH, ELIJAH (res.), GARODMAN, HEAVEN, HELL, HIGHER AND LOWER, KARMA, MAIDEN, RE-INCARNATION, SIRIUS.

BRIDGES, NINE, SIX, AND THREE, IN THE SETTLEMENT :—

These are eighteen centres of organisation in the soul, on various planes.

"In the uppermost part of the settlement make nine bridges, in the middle six, and in the lowermost three."— *Vendidad*, II. S. B. of E.

The nine "bridges" are the nine centres on the higher planes, whose correspondences find representation on the lower planes. The six middle

centres are astral centres, and the three lowermost centres are etheric.

See FRAVAK, GATES (nine), SETTLE-MENTS, STREETS (nine), VARA.

BRIGHT AND DARK :—

Symbols of knowledge and ignorance.

See DARKNESS, LIGHT.

BRIHAT AND RATHANTERA VERSES :—

Signifying the rule of the soul by Divine love.

"He approaches the throne Vikatshana. The Saman (conciliation) verses, Brihat and Rathantera, are its eastern feet."—*Kaush. Upanishad*, I. 2.

The soul attains complete mastery over self, through Truth and Goodness, he knows that government is possible through Love. The Sun of righteousness arises in the east.

See SAMAN, VIKATSHANA.

BRISEIS OF THE FAIR CHEEKS :—

A symbol of the intuition of love expressed in the lower nature, but proceeding from the higher.

"I (Agamemnon) will go to thy (Achilles) hut and take Briseis of the fair cheeks, even that thy meed of honour, that thou mayest well know how far greater I am than thou, and so shall another hereafter abhor to match his words with mine and rival me to my face."—*Iliad*, Book I.

The Desire-mind will, it supposes, approach the mental vehicle of the Personality, and by so doing take captive the Love nature (lower) on the plane of instinct, through which the experience of the Personality is acquired ; in order that the Personality may be impressed with the irresistible power of seductiveness of the Desire-mind, and so make it impossible for any other power to gain the ascendency over the influence of the Desire-nature (as it is imagined).

See ACHILLES, AGAMEMNON, CHRYSEIS, INTUITION, SERPENT (subtil).

BROTHER OF THE PERSONAL SELF :—

A symbol of the causal-self, or the Individuality.

"An elder full brother the image of oneself."—*Laws of Manu*, II. 226.

See BALARAMA, POLLUX.

BROTHER OF JESUS :—

A symbol of the Individuality, with which the perfected Personality unites.

"Thy brother embraced Thee (Jesus) and kissed Thee, and Thou didst also kiss Him, ye became one and the same Being."—Mary's story of the Infancy, in the *Pistis Sophia*.

The lower limitations are transcended, the soul-consciousness below rises to the consciousness above in the causal-body, the salute of Love is given, and the Higher Self and the Lower Self are made One and indistinguishable on the plane of the higher mind.

See CONSUMMATION, MARRIAGE, UNION WITH GOD.

BROTHERS, FIVE, OF DIVES :—

Symbolic of the five senses on the astro-mental plane.

See FIVE, LAZARUS.

BROTHERS, THE FIVE KARAP :—

Symbolic of the five senses which stir the mental faculties.

See BRATROK.

BUCKLE OF ISIS :—

A symbol of the life currents between the buddhic and astral planes, whereby the lower qualities are transmuted into the higher.

"The buckle (amulet) was placed on the neck of the mummy, which it was supposed to protect ; the red material of which it was made represented the blood of Isis."—BUDGE, *The Mummy*, p. 256.

The astro-buddhic vibrations are necessary for the evolution and establishment of the purified emotions (neck). They represent the Divine Life (blood) proceeding from the buddhic plane (Isis).

"This amulet represents the buckle of the girdle of Isis, and is usually made of carnelian, red jasper, red glass, and of other substances of a red colour ; it is sometimes made of gold, and of substances covered with gold. It is always associated with the CLVIth Chapter of the *Book of the Dead*, which is frequently inscribed upon it, and which reads :—

"'The blood of Isis, and the strength of Isis, and the words of power of Isis shall be mighty to act as powers to protect this great and divine being, and to guard him from him that would do unto him anything that he holdeth in abomination.'

"But before the buckle was attached to the neck of the deceased, where the rubric ordered it to be placed, it had to be dipped in water in which *ānkham* flowers had been steeped. . . . It enabled the deceased to have ' one hand towards heaven, and one hand towards earth.' "
—BUDGE, *Egyptian Magic*, pp. 43, 44.

The meaning of Ch. CLVI is, that the Divine Life from the buddhic plane manifests in the higher emotions which are mighty to protect the indwelling God as he evolves, at first weak and helpless, in the soul, and to guard this Great One from being overpowered by the lower emotions and desires. The baptismal ceremony signifies that through truth (water) and the virtues (flowers) the soul is enabled by means of the higher vibrations to aspire towards the higher nature, and do its duty in the activities (hands) of the lower nature (earth).

See BARKIS, BARSOM, BLOOD, DEFUNCT, FLOWERS, GEMS, GOLD, HAND, ISIS, KUSTI, MAGIC, MUMMY, NECK, TAMAGUSHI, YAGNOPAVITA.

BUDDHA AS GAUTAMA AND AS MAITREYA :—

A symbol of the Self or Soul (atma-buddhi) which descends to the lower planes, in order first (as Gautama) to become by involution the Archetypal Man, and second (as Maitreya) to rise by evolution in the souls of humanity to the higher planes again.

"Born, then, at last as the child Gautama, son of Suddhodana, and purified by a long observance of the six transcendent virtues, Buddha ultimately attained to perfect knowledge and Arhatship under the Bodhi-tree, and in so attaining passed from the condition of a Bodhi-sattva to that of the highest of all Arhats—a supreme Buddha."—MON. WILLIAMS, *Buddhism*, p. 181.

The Germ-Soul produced of the Supreme Self (king) emerged upon the lower planes and began its development through the gradual involution of the higher qualities (virtues). The Soul ultimately attained to perfection and supremacy (umbrella) under the completion of one part of the Divine scheme of the manifesting Life (Bodhi-tree). It thereby passed from the partly enlightened condition to the fully enlightened, and so it then rose in potentiality to the higher planes as the Archetypal Man—the

Ideal pattern of the forthcoming actuality.

"At the moment of his attaining Buddhahood he had transferred the Bodhi-sattvaship to Maitreya, 'the loving and compassionate one,' who became the Buddha-elect, dwelling and presiding as his predecessor had done in the heaven of contented beings (Tushita). There he watches over and promotes the interests of the Buddhist faith, while awaiting the time when he is to appear on earth as Maitreya, or the fifth Buddha of the present age. . . . No wonder, then, that this Maitreya, whose very name implies love and tenderness towards mankind, and who was destined to become, like Gautama, a Saviour of the world by teaching its inhabitants how to save themselves—became a favourite object of personal worship after Gautama Buddha's death."—*Ibid.*

With the completion of the involution of spirit into matter, there followed the transference of the Divine germ (Bodhisatva) to the new order of evolution. This implied a fresh outpouring of the Self, who presides potentially on the higher planes, while actually engaged in the evolution of himself (Maitreya) on the lower planes. The Self promotes the growth of the Divine germ of Wisdom, Truth and Love (the Buddhist faith), which requires to be developed in the souls of humanity until they are perfected, and the germ of the Self has become the complete Self rising glorified with his saints from the bondage of the lower nature (earth). The incarnate Self (Maitreya) is born in the evolving soul as the Spirit of Love and Truth destined to become the soul's Saviour by teaching it how to rise above the things of the world and free itself from the passions and desires of the lower nature. As the incarnate Self draws all minds upwards by his infinite love and tenderness, he is adored by all who perceive him in the innermost sanctuary of their souls.

See AAT, ARC. MAN, ARHATS, ASITA, AVALOKITESVARA, BIRTH OF BUDDHA, BODHISATVA, BRAHMAN PRIESTS, CHRIST, CHRIST'S SECOND COMING, DESTROYING EVILS, DWELLING, HORSE (white), INVOLUTION, KA, KALKI, LION-GAIT, NURSE, PRAYERS, RAHULA, RENOVATION, SOSIOSH, SOUL, (highest), SUDDHODANA, TONGUE, TRI-RATNA, TUSHITA, YASODHARA.

BUDDHA, MARKS OF THE :—

Symbolic of powers inherent in the Soul through involution.

"Thus the great seer Asita beheld the king's son (Buddha) with wonder, his feet marked with a wheel, his fingers and toes webbed, with a circle of hair between his eyebrows, and signs of vigour like an elephant."—*Buddha-Karita*, Bk. I. 65.

So it is the primordial lower self (Asita) beholds the offspring of the Highest with wonder, that is, with instinctive rather than rational appreciation of Truth. The "feet" are symbols of obedience, which tread the cycle of life as the path to peace. The "fingers and toes webbed" signify the, as yet, fettered organs of action. The "urna," or "circle of hair" is a symbol of spiritual truth. "Signs of vigour" symbolise the powers which are to yield the results of effort which accrue on the buddhic plane.

See ASITA, BODHISATVAS, CIRCLE (hair), FEET, FOOTPRINTS OF BUDDHA, MARKS OF JESUS, URNA.

BUDDHI, OR THE WISDOM PRINCIPLE :—

A symbol of the fount of spiritual life on the buddhic plane, which transcends the highest intellect. It is the source of all the higher emotions and ideal qualities appertaining to Truth, Love, and Wisdom. It is described as outpouring these qualities in response to the aspirations and sacrifices of the lower consciousness.

"Buddhi, commonly translated by perception, but really a kind of perception that involves something like what we should call intellect. . . . As a cosmic force, Buddhi is that which gives light as the essential condition of all knowledge. *Budh* means literally to awake, and as a sleeping person is dull and inert to the world, but begins to perceive as soon as he is awake."—MAX MÜLLER, *Six Systems of Indian Philosophy*, pp. 370, 371.

"The life there (of the celestial region) is wisdom, a wisdom not obtained by a reasoning process, because the whole of it always was, and is not, in any respect deficient, so as to be in want of investigation. But it is the first wisdom, and is not derived from another."—PLOTINUS, *On Intelligible Beauty.*

The feminine Holy Spirit—Sophia—and most of the great Goddesses of polytheism are symbols of Buddhi under various aspects. She is the Divine Mother who gives birth to the Son of God on the buddhic plane, that Love and Truth may rule the soul in righteousness and peace when evolution is complete.

"For Isis is the Female principle in Nature, and that which is capable of receiving all generation, in virtue of which she is styled by Plato 'Nurse' and 'All-receiving,' but by the generality, 'the one of numberless names,' because she is converted by the Logos (Reason) into, and receives, all appearances and forms. But she has, implanted in her nature, the love for the First and Supreme, which is identical with the Good, and this she longs after and continually pursues : whereas the part that belongs to the Bad One she flees from and repels, though she is the *field* and *material* for them both ; of herself always inclining towards the Better One, and permitting It to generate . . . and fill her with births,—for birth is an image of existence in Matter, and that which is *born* is a copy of that which is."—Plutarch, *Isis and Osiris*, § 53.

For Buddhi (Isis) is the receptive principle in Spiritual Nature. From the plane above, Atma, there is poured forth the primal Ideas and potencies of existence, and these generate on the next plane, the buddhic, where they are received and "nursed," as it were, or prepared for their reflection downward on to the lower planes. From Buddhi all diversity (numberless names) proceeds, through the action of the Logos who fills the Spiritual Wisdom with the ideal prototypes of all appearances and forms, subsequently to be expressed on the mental, astral, and physical planes.

Buddhi is in direct and harmonious relation with the Supreme, and wholly guided from above, whereas her reflection downward on the astral plane is full of the strife of the evolving monads she has brought forth, for she is the *field* and *mould* for both the perfect and the imperfect. She repels the lower desires (the Bad One), being united only with the Higher Self who produces in her the Divine Monads who take birth, or become embodied in the forms

wherein to evolve ; for the separated monad is a microcosm which is a copy of the Macrocosm.

"Spiritual things, as Plotinus says, are separated from each other not by local division, but only by discordance of nature. The organ by which we apprehend divine truth is no special faculty, but the *higher reason*, which we distinguish from the understanding because we mean it to include the will and feelings, disciplined under the guidance of the intellect. The higher reason is that unification of our personality which is the goal of our striving and the postulate of all our rational life. God is the last object to be clearly known, precisely because He is at once the pre-supposition and foundation and consummation of all our knowledge."—W. R. Inge, *Paddock Lectures*, p. 4.

See Alaghom, Amaterasu, Armaiti, Aruru, Asha-vanuhi, Athena, Barsom, Bees, Birth-chamber, Blasphemy, Boat of wisdom, Clouds, Cow, Dharma, Earth (great), Esther, Fire, Frigg Goddess, Gold, Golden fleece, Hathor, Heifer, Helen, Hera, Holy ghost, Intuition, Isis, Istar, Kypris, Lady, Lakshmi, Magic, Malkhuth, Metztli, Mother, Prototypes, Pylons, Sarasvati, Sita, Sky, Sophia, Transmutation, Veil of isis, Viraj, Wisdom.

BUDDHIC-BODY :—

This is the vehicle of the soul on the buddhic plane, potential and latent as yet, but destined to become manifest and active when the consciousness of the perfected ego rises to its level and claims its inheritance—the "treasure in the heavens that faileth not. . . . For where your treasure is, there will your heart be also."—Luke xxi. 33, 34.

"And I stretched forth and received my bright embroidered robe. With the beauty of its colours I adorned myself" ("Hymn of the Soul ").—*Acts of Judas-Thomas.*

And I made a great effort to receive my buddhic vesture, and did at length achieve my purpose. With its brilliant qualities, lovely to regard, did I adorn myself.

The buddhic-body is described as full of intelligence, wisdom, truth, and love, to a degree impossible for the lower mind to have any conception of. The putting on by the saint of this " robe of glory " will introduce the soul to a state of bliss in which higher faculties and activities will be exercised without a trace of selfishness entering in.

See CHILDREN OF HORUS, COLOURS, HEART, INCARNATION OF SOULS, NESHAMAH, QEBSENNUF, ROBE, SAMKHARA, SHEATHS, SKANDHAS, TREASURE, VEHICLES, VESTURES.

BUDDHIC FUNCTION :—

The spiritual carrying-out of the means of transmuting the lower emotions into higher emotions, so that the indwelling Self shall evolve Itself, and the lower nature of the soul fall away. It is Buddhi who directs the evolution of the true Self in the human being. When the lower nature aspires, she sends down strong vibrations which assist in uplifting the mind. At first the nature of the upward aspiration is the vague, almost unconscious, unrest and dissatisfaction at present conditions. The mind is allied with the desires and lower emotions, and what is required is that the mind should relinquish these inferior motives, and accept the ideals and higher emotions in place of the lower attachments. The highest part of the subjective lower mind is on the fourth sub-plane of the mental plane. The vibrations from Buddhi enter the mind at this level, and there is then an impulse awakened in the lower self from this sub-plane, which causes a speedy upward movement and so accelerates the mind's progress to a better condition of being. The lower nature has correspondences with the higher, and a perfect reciprocity is set up and established between the two natures. The transmutations are the apparent changes in the soul from lower qualities to higher which are brought about by a spiritual process under immutable law. The ideals and higher emotions (buddhi manas) are the most powerful rulers of the mind when the will is in accord with them. It is these which lead the martyrs of all faiths to brave the external forces which are arrayed against their activities. It must be remembered that while forces are always restricted to their particular planes under the law of conservation of energy, guidance of the forces connected with life comes from higher planes. The guidance is not a force,

but a ruling of forces, as when a man *calls* his horse to drag the cart. Forces on a lower plane respond to a " word " on a higher. This indicates the meaning of the Divine Word which rules all forces on all planes.

See ALCHEMY, BARHIS, BARSOM, BUCKLE, CLOUDS, EPHOD, EVOLUTION, GODS, HIGHER AND LOWER, KUSTI, LOGOS, QUALITIES, SELF, TAMA-GUSHI, TRANSMUTATION, WINDOW, WORD YAGNA.

BUDDHIC PLANE :—

A symbol of the plane of manifestation next above the higher mental plane. It is the highest of the four planes which constitute the arena of life in the present cycle of spiritual evolution. It is not outwardly manifest in the soul as are the three lower planes, and is only indirectly known through the higher emotions which are the " fruit of the Spirit." It is the plane on which are the prototypes or patterns of things below in the phenomenal realm, things, that is, that are the result of any kind of growth, mineral, vegetal, animal. The buddhic is the first plane to which the Higher Self descends in manifestation. It contains the higher causal-body which is the seat of the Self and of the higher qualities. On this plane is situated the heaven of the perfected human souls. It contains the state of consciousness from which the souls have descended, and the state to which they ascend in glory at the last.

See AMENT, ARYANA, BIRTH-CHAMBER, CAUSAL-BODY, EDEN, FRUIT, GARODMAN, HEAVEN, KINEDOM OF HEAVEN, MUSPELHEIM, NIRVANA, SEKHIT-HETEP, WORLDS (five).

BUILDERS OF THE UNIVERSE :—

Those Devas or Arch-angels who become the first-born children of the manifesting God, i.e. who come forth first upon the highest planes in order to commence the structure of the innermost invisible universe of the solar system.

" To whom then will ye liken me, that I should be equal to him ? saith the Holy One. Lift up your eyes on high, and see who hath created these, that bringeth out their host by number : he calleth them all by name ; by the greatness of his might, and for that he is

strong in power, not one is lacking."—
Is. xl. 25, 26.

In the emanation of spiritual intelligences, the monads of life (stars) are produced in their differentiations (names) and in the order of their greatness.

"Nature, according to the Zohar, is the garment of God ; it is that in which He appears and wherein He is veiled, so that we can look upon Him in His vestured aspect ; but it is not the body of God—which is more properly Shekinah, at least in one of her aspects—and it is still less God manifest. It is that which He took upon Himself for the purpose of appearing. (Footnote.) In the transcendence God and Elohim are inseparable, being male and female, and the first movement towards the production of a manifested universe was to send forth their living images below. That which was of the nature of God became of the nature of the Cosmos."—A. E. WAITE, *Secret Doctrine in Israel*, p. 59.

The " Holy One " and " Shekinah " are symbols of Buddhi ; " Elohim " of Atma-buddhi, Love-Wisdom, " male and female."

See AMSHASPANDS, ANGELS, ARCH-ANGELS, COMPANY OF GODS, CY-CLOPES, DEVAS, FIRE ALTAR, GUAR-DIANS, I AM, MESSENGERS, MONAD (life), PRAGÂPATI (relaxed), VALKYRIOR.

BULL, PRIMEVAL :—

A symbol of the Divine matrix of forms and qualities on the buddhic plane and reflected below on the astro-etheric plane.

" In the second age Ormazd had also produced the great primæval Bull, in which the seeds of all living creatures were deposited."—*Zoroastrian System.*

During the second period of cosmic activity, the Divine Will had created on the buddhic plane the womb of all living things upon the astral and etheric planes, and therein the mental seed-germ of the lower activities and forms is placed.

" May he who is the strong Bull of the Vedas, assuming all forms, . . . may that Indra strengthen me with wisdom."—*Tait. Upanishad*, 4.

May the Divine life which germinates within all forms, bring the soul, through its devotion to truth and right, the strength of wisdom which is its heritage in heaven above.

" The original of the universe contains in itself all intelligible beings, just as this world comprehends us and all other visible creatures. For the Deity intending

to make this world like the fairest and most perfect of intelligible beings, framed one visible Animal comprehending all other animals of a kindred nature. . . . There is one heaven, for that which includes all other intelligible creatures cannot have a second or companion. . . . There is and ever will be one only-begotten and created heaven."—PLATO, *Timæus*, JOWETT, Vol. III. p. 614.

" The Mnevis Bull is called the ' renewing of the life of Râ.' "—BUDGE, *The Mummy*, p. 283.

" Leather straps were made from the hide of the Mnevis Bull, which was burnt by Suti."—BUDGE, *Egyptian Magic*, p. 168.

" There is no other thing besides like unto him ; he is the Bull that beareth heaven and earth ; of his own power he maketh his skin a source of light, when the bay horses carry him as the Sun."—*Rig-Veda*, X. 31, 8.

In the Ottoman Sufi cosmogony a great Bull is one of the supporters of heaven and earth. The symbol " Bull " indicates the positive aspect of activity on the buddhic plane (Cow), and as this is the highest plane of the quaternary, it therefore bears, as it were, the higher and lower natures which are formed in it. The " renewing of the life of Râ " signifies the Divine Life out-poured on the buddhic plane (sign Taurus) at the opening of the manvantara. The " skin " or " hide " of the " Bull " is a symbol of the ordinances of the universe, which are external to the Self (sun) on the mental plane (horses) ; and the " leather straps " are the Divine laws binding on nature. The " burning of the Bull by Suti (Set) " has the same meaning as the " killing of the Bull by Ahriman," with also a reference to purification of the soul by fire (buddhi).

See APIS, BEES, BEHEMOTH, GEUSH-TASHA, GOSHURUN, I AM, MITHRA, MITHRAS, OX, PROTOTYPES, SEED, SERAPIS, TAUROBOLIUM, TAURUS, WOMB.

BULL, MAN-HEADED :—

A symbol of the archetypal union of the higher and lower natures in the Soul,—the Triad above the Quaternary.

" Gopaito-shah is in Airan-vaego, within the region of Khvaniras. From foot to mid-body he is an ox, and from mid-body to the top he is a man. And at all times he sits on the seashore, and always performs the ceremonial of the sacred beings, and pours holy water into the sea (for the destruction of noxious creatures)."—*The Mainog-i Khirad*, Ch. LXII. 31–34. *S. B. of E.*

The soul comprises all potencies from the buddhic plane to the physical plane on the present earth globe. The "four-limbed ox or bull" signifies the lower quaternary, and the superior human part, the higher triad,—atma-buddhi-manas. The Soul is seated on the astro-mental plane (sea-shore), and inaugurates the process of purification of the mental qualities which have in them the sacred germ of Divine life, and outpours truth upon the astral plane (sea) for the destruction of the desires.

See ARYANA-VAEJO, GRIFFIN, KAR-SHVARES, QUADRUPED.

BULLS, TWO BRASS-FOOTED :—

Symbolic of desire and reason on the lower mental plane.

"The King Æetes assented to give up the Golden Fleece, provided Jason could yoke the brass-footed bulls. These were the gifts of Hephæstus to Æetes, in number two, and breathing flame from their throats."—*Argonautic Expedition.*

The Supreme consents to endow the soul with Wisdom, providing that the soul is able to completely control the dual aspects of the lower self, which are the desire principle and the reason. These were the gifts to the Supreme of experience, by Him (Hephæstus) who had overcome the lower planes, and they breathed forth "flame" or burning desire,—having not yet been quelled or mastered.

See ARGONAUTS, BRASS, CADMUS, GOLDEN FLEECE, HEPHAISTOS, JASON.

BUR, WHOSE SON WAS BORR :—

A symbol of the Desire nature which gives rise to the Mind (Borr), which unites with the emotion nature, and afterwards awakens the spiritual nature within the soul. (*See Edda.*)

See AUDUMBLA, CHILDREN OF HORUS, YMIR.

BURNING OF DRY GRASS AS FUEL :—

A symbol of the production of the sexual instinct or lust.

BURNING FOCUS :—

A symbol of the Self as a centre wherein all the rays of the Divine Life

merge into one for indrawing and outpouring.

See SUN.

BURNING OF CORPSES :—

A symbol of the destroying principle which, through the destruction of effete forms of thought, may be the means of transmutation of qualities.

See CORPSE, CREMATION.

BURNT-OFFERING TO THE LORD :—

A symbol of the offering up of the best of the lower desires (beasts) to the higher ideal, in order that they shall be purified by buddhi (fire), and so be transmuted.

"And Noah took of every clean beast, and of every clean fowl, and offered burnt-offerings on the altar."—GEN. viii. 20.

And every lower emotion and desire given up for the sake of an ideal, becomes the means of this offering of the lower self to the will of the Higher Self in reciprocal action between the two.

"The name given in Scripture to this species of sacrifice is *olah*, an ascension, so called from the whole being consumed and going up in a flame to the Lord. It also received the name kalil, the whole, with reference also to the entire consumption."—P. FAIRBURN, *Typology of Scripture*, Vol. II. p. 344.

"So far as it contained the blood of atonement, ever in the course of being presented for the covenant people, it shadowed forth Christ as the one and all for His people, in regard to deliverance from the guilt of sin—the fountain to which they must daily and hourly repair, to be washed of their uncleanness."—*Ibid.*, p. 346.

"In the burnt-offering we have seen Jesus as *our representative*. His offering was offered 'for us'; therefore 'as He is, so are we in this world'; the measure of His acceptance is the measure of our acceptance."—A. JUKES, *The Law of the Offerings*, p. 66.

"And when the burnt-offering is placed upon it he shall burn the fat of the peace offering' (LEV. vi. 12). For whoever kindles within himself this fire of love, places himself upon it as a burnt offering, because he burns out every fault, which wickedly lived within him. For when he examines the secrets of his own thoughts, and sacrifices his wicked life, by the sword of conversion, he has placed himself on the altar of his own heart, and kindled himself with the fire of love. And the fat of the peace offerings smells sweetly from this victim; because the inward fatness of new love, making peace between ourselves and God, emits from us the sweetest odour. But since this selfsame love continues inextinguishable in the heart of the Elect, it is there fitly subjoined, ' This is that perpetual fire, which will never go out on the altar ' (LEV. vi. 13). This fire in truth will never go out on the altar, because the glow of love increases in their minds even after this life."— GREGORY THE GREAT, *Morals on the Book of Job*, Vol. III. pp. 105-6.

See ALTAR, BEASTS, FAT, FIRE, GOATS, HECATOMB, OFFERING, ROASTED, SACRIFICES (burnt), SAVOUR.

BURYING OF THE DEAD :—

A symbol of the ridding the soul of effete forms of thought and habits.
See OINTMENT.

BUTES, THE ARGONAUT :—

A symbol of attachment by association with what is lower in grade.
See LILYBŒUM, SIRENS.

BUTO IN LOWER EGYPT :—

A symbol of a purified state of the lower emotions on the astro-mental plane.
See BIRTH OF HORUS, CHEMMIS, EGYPT (lower), HORUS, LION-GOD, MARSH.

BUTTER :—

A symbol of Divine love and wisdom, the produce of buddhi (cow).

" The sacrificer takes butter with the dipping spoon (breath), with the text, ' Verily thou art the favourite resort (or dainty) of the gods ! . . . an unassailable means of worship.' "—*Sata. Brâh.*, I. 3, 2, 17.

The spiritual ego assimilates the nourishment of wisdom and love by means of the spiritual nature (atma) within him. For this divine food (ambrosia) is the support of the ideals (gods) through which the lower aspires towards the higher.

See AMBROSIA, COW, FAT, GHEE, GUHU, MILK, OIL, OLIVE.

BYBLOS IN LOWER EGYPT :—

A symbol of the astro-mental stage in which lower knowledge is arrived at.
See COLUMN, SCENT, WORSHIP.

CABIN OF AFU-RĀ :—

A symbol of the innermost shrine of the causal-body, or World-soul, on the buddhic plane. It signifies the confinement or involution of Spirit in Matter, and stands for the Incarnation of Rā (Afu meaning *flesh*), or the sacrifice of the "Lamb of God " symbolised by the ram-headed Rā, the Divine Ram sacrificed in matter, for the redemption of mankind.

See ADYTUM, AFU-RA, CANOPY, CAUSAL-BODY, CRUCIFIXION OF CHRIST, HEART, INCARNATION, LAMB, RAM, SHRINE.

CADMUS, SON OF AGENOR :—

A symbol of experience or wisdom, the offspring of the Divine Mind. When intuition (the cow that Cadmus followed) ceases to function and guide (the cow laid down), then experience establishes itself, and finally is transmuted to wisdom (Thebes).

" When Jason had yoked the two brass-footed bulls, he was to plough with them a piece of land, and sow the serpents' teeth which Æetes possessed, to whom Athena had given one half of those which Cadmus had sowed at Thebes."—*Argonautic Expedition*, KEIGHTLEY, *Mythology*.

And when the desire-force and the reason had been yoked together, it was necessary for the Self (Jason) to apply those powers which had been acquired, to the development of the lower nature, and to adapt to useful purpose those faculties which the Supreme bestowed upon him, and which amounted to one half, i.e. the lower aspect, of those which were yielded to the Supreme by Wisdom (Athena), through experience (Cadmus).

See ÆETES, ATHENA, BULLS, EIDOTHEA, GOLDEN FLEECE, JASON, THEBES.

CADUCEUS, OR HERMES' ROD :—

A symbol of aspiration (rod) through the higher mind (Hermes), resulting from the activities of Wisdom and Desire (the two opposing serpents).
See HERMES, ROD, SERPENT.

CAIAPHAS, THE HIGH PRIEST :—

A symbol of formal and sterile notions of religion, which have to be broken up before the Christ-spirit can burst forth in its fullness in the mind.

" The chief priests therefore and the Pharisees gathered a council, and said, What do we ? for this man doeth many signs. If we let him thus alone, all men will believe on him : and the Romans will come and take away both our place and our nation."—JOHN xi. 47, 48.

The priests and Pharisees represent a mental state in which the outer expression of the scriptures is regarded as authoritative in the unquestioning mind. This state of formalism and dogmatism is aghast at the incoming of a new spirit which threatens to upset the old traditional notions and substitute fresh ideas. Literalism is afraid also of the aggressive champions of rationalism (the Romans) who would destroy cherished practices and a fixed mental state (nation).

"But a certain one of them, Caiaphas, being high priest that year, said unto them, Ye know nothing at all, nor do ye take account that it is expedient for you that one man should die for the people, and that the whole nation perish not."—JOHN xi. 49, 50.

Caiaphas signifies a long-headed representative of the orthodox spirit, who foresees the natural result of the literalist tendency, and who seeks to control those he deems below him, in such a manner as is opposed to the Christ. He believes only in systems and creeds, and not in the triumph of those qualities which make the soul truly great. But his commanding intellect suffices to show him that there must be some change of mind to meet new conditions and that the old mental state (one man) must die out, in order that the whole traditional view should not perish.

"There is nothing to prevent a sincere Catholic from going to any length with modern criticism, *which the evidence really warrants*, in dealing with the letter of our Sacred Books. The divine element in those books no criticism can touch. The details over which it has power are as the small dust in the balance in comparison of the idea, over which it is powerless. . . . Surely Mr. Carlyle is right when he says : 'The Bible has, in all changes of theory about it this, as its highest distinction, that it is the truest of books.'"
—W. S. LILLY, *The Great Enigma*, p. 109.

See ANNAS, ASSEMBLY (PRIESTS), HIGH PRIEST (LOWER), INSPIRATION, PHARISEES, PILATE, PRIESTS AND ELDERS, REVELATION, RITES, ROMAN, SCRIPTURES, TRADITION.

CAIN :—

A symbol of the centre of the personality—the I am I feeling in the lower mind, which causes the illusion of separateness, and represents the lower self.

"Cain was a tiller of the ground."—GEN. iv. 2.

The sense of self and separateness supervises the growth of the lower desires which spring from the lower nature.

"That is not first which is spiritual, but that which is natural; and afterwards that which is spiritual (1 COR. xv. 46). What is first developed out of man is carnal,—that 'carnal mind which is enmity against God ; which is not subject to the law of God, neither indeed can be.' (ROM. viii. 7). This is Cain. But there is a second birth ; another life is born, which by grace springs out of the same old Adam ; and this second birth, this 'spiritual mind,' is Abel."—A. JUKES, *Types of Genesis*, p. 88.

"By 'Cain' is signified faith separate from love." "A 'tiller of the ground' is one who is without charity, whatever pretensions he may make to faith which when separated from love is no faith."—SWEDENBORG, *Arc. Cel. to Gen.* iv.

"Cain, who refers everything to himself, is the self-loving opinion. Abel, who refers everything to God, is the God-loving opinion."—PHILO JUDÆUS, Yonge's trans. *Works*, Vol. IV. p. 249.

"Cain, whereby is understood in the language of nature, a source out of the centre of the fiery desire, a self-ful will of the fiery might of the soul."—J. BEHMEN, *Mysterium Magnum*, p. 166.

See ABEL, AHANKARA, ATOM (perm.), CITY, COUNTENANCE, FACE (ground), FRUIT (ground), FUGITIVE, MONAD OF LIFE, NOD (land), SETH, WANDERERS.

CAKE, SACRIFICIAL :—

A symbol of the higher qualities on the buddhic plane, the result by transmutation of the experiences below.

"I (Nu Osirified) am the lord of cakes in Annu, and my bread is in heaven with Rā, and my cakes are on the earth with the god Seb, for the *Sektet* boat and the *Atet* boat have brought them to me from the house of the great god who is in Annu."—BUDGE, *Book of the Dead*, p. 196.

The perfected soul has become possessed of the higher qualities in buddhi, and the truth (bread) which is its sustenance, is from God (Rā). The higher qualities are transmutations of the lower nature through process of time (Seb) ; for the growth of the causal-body in its incoming and outgoing life, has brought wisdom and love to the soul from the Divine nature on the higher planes.

"To the gods belongs what sacrificial

food there is, to wit, King Soma and the sacrificial cake."—*Sata. Brâh.*

To the ideals (gods) belongs the celestial nourishment which is to strengthen them, namely, the Divine Life (Soma), and the higher qualities laid up in heaven.

See ANNU, BOAT SEKTET, BREAD, CORN, FOOD, FRUIT (spirit), MANNA, SACRAMENTAL CAKE, SHEWBREAD, TREASURE IN HEAVEN.

CALAÏS, SON OF BOREAS :—

A symbol of the will proceeding from the higher mind, and controlling the sense-nature and the desires.

See BOREAS, HARPIES, NICOTHEA, ZETES

CALAMITIES :—

Symbolic of the breaking up of forms and releasing the contained life for wider action in fresh forms.

"And ye shall hear of wars and rumours of wars : see that ye be not troubled : for these things must needs come to pass ; but the end is not yet. For nation shall rise against nation, and kingdom against kingdom : and there shall be famines and earthquakes in divers places. But all these things are the beginning of travail." —MAT. xxiv. 6, 7.

Christ emphasises the truth that such evils as wars and natural calamities, with the sufferings entailed, are means to an end, and are not to distress the faithful, for they do not affect the Self behind, and are passing phases in no way final for the soul. We are to recognise in these troubles certain processes whereby the evolution of good is ultimately accomplished.

"God brings forth from all pain a spiritual somewhat for the sake of which the pain is sent. There is no waste, no wanton sacrifice, in the experience of men ; all human sorrow is the substance from which God is fashioning holy joy. . . . All pain, whether deserved or undeserved, is God's accumulating blessing in His Divine purpose, and it has its spiritual equivalent in the deeper life that is one with His own. No man can suffer except God be with him. Pain is no mark of the displeasure of heaven, but just the contrary. It is the summons to come up higher."—R. J. CAMPBELL, *Song of Ages,* pp. 64, 70.

See EARTHQUAKES, ENDURING, FORMS, GOVERNORS, JESUS WEPT, MURDER, SUFFERING.

CALF :—

A symbol of the intuition which proceeds from buddhi (cow).

"By the beasts of the earth are signified the various natural affections, for such indeed they are ; and by a calf is signified the affection of knowing things true and good."—SWEDENBORG, *Apoc. Rev.,* n. 242.

See BUDDHI, COW, INTUITION.

CALF, THE FATTED, EATEN WITH JOY :—

Symbolising the Celestial feast, i.e. the consciousness raised to the buddhic plane, and the soul partaking of the " fruits of the Spirit "—Wisdom and Love Divine.

See DANCES, FAT, FATTED, FEAST, HUSKS, PRODIGAL.

CALF, THE MOLTEN :—

A symbol of the opposite of wisdom, namely, superstition, or the following of the dead letter of the scriptures, together with forms and ceremonies, apart from moral and spiritual motives.

"They made a calf in Horeb, and worshipped the molten image. Thus they changed their glory into the similitude of an ox that eateth grass."—Ps. cvi. 18, 19.

The spiritual mind (Aaron) at an early stage had to prepare the soul for higher guidance. At first there must be reliance upon external authority (earrings) and outside show and observances (the molten image). The glory of the moral and spiritual must be hidden under symbolism and ceremonies which satisfy primitive desires (grass) and emotions.

"The people sat down to eat and drink and rose up to play."—EXOD. xxxii. 6.

That is, the lower mental qualities (people) sought only to satisfy desire and sensation at this early stage.

See AARON, EAR, EATING, IDOL, MOSES, PRIESTS AND ELDERS.

CALL OF GOD :—

A symbol of the admonition of the conscience.

See CONSCIENCE, VOICE.

CALVES, THE MYRIAD :—

Symbolic of the higher emotions— the progeny of buddhi (the " celestial cow "), the inexhaustible treasures of the Spirit.

See COW (milch), SUN OF RIGHTEOUSNESS, TREASURES.

CAMEL'S HAIR RAIMENT :—

Symbolic of the mind's obedience to higher guidance, and willingness to endure for the sake of right and truth.

See JOHN BAPTIST, GIRDLE (leather), ENDURING, ZACHARIAS.

CAMP, WIDE, OF THE GREEKS :—

A symbol of freer means for expansion of the mental qualities in the upward growth of the soul.

See ARMY, GALE, GREEKS.

CANA MARRIAGE :—

A symbol of the union of Truth and Love. The " six waterpots " signify the six vehicles of consciousness, to be made full use of. The " turning of the water into wine " symbolises the substitution of the love element for the duty, or moral, element. It means a transmutation (miracle) in fact. This " beginning of miracles " records the dawning of the supremacy of Christ (Love) whose triumph (glory) is begun by the perfect adjustment of all the vehicles and functions upon the several planes of consciousness.

" The story of the marriage-feast and the miracle of turning water into wine has reference to the final initiation of Jesus. The water was the symbol for the soul, the wine for the spirit. ' The beginning of miracles ' for the man regenerate is the spiritualisation of his own soul, which is therefore mystically called the changing of water into wine."—ANNA KINGSFORD, *Life, by Maitland*, Vol. II. p. 3.

" Philo speaks of the ' wine of the divine love of God.' This fact (of the water becoming wine), the context, the structure of the Gospel, and the traditions of Philo, combine to indicate that the whole of the narrative is spiritual and emblematic.— E.A.A. *Gospels*, (54), *Enc. Biblica*.

See GRAPES, INITIATIONS, MARRIAGE, WATER (wine), WATERPOTS, WINE.

CANAAN, SON OF HAM :—

A symbol of works or service, proceeding from action (Ham).

See HAM, NOAH'S SONS.

CANCER, THE ZODIACAL SIGN :—

A symbol of the fourth period of the cycle of life. It signifies the lower mind energised from the astral plane. The " crab " or the " tortoise " (Indian sign of Cancer), is a symbol of the lower nature into which the soul descends in involution.

" Porphyrius says, . . . Theologians admitted therefore two gates, Cancer and Capricorn, and Plato also meant these by what he calls the two mouths. Of these they affirm that Cancer is the gate through which souls descend, but Capricorn that through which they ascend (and exchange a material for a divine condition of being)."—MAX MÜLLER, *Theosophy, etc.*, p. 145.

See CAPRICORN, CRATER, EQUINOX, ZODIAC.

CANDLES, LIGHTED :—

Symbolic of the light of Truth in the human mind or soul (church). Held in the hands of acolytes, lighted candles signify the truth illuminating the soul-qualities which are disciplined by the higher qualities (priests) above them. The beeswax of which the ceremonial candles are made is a product of bees which are a symbol of higher emotions, thus signifying, in burning, the purifying fire of the Holy Spirit on the buddhic plane.

" ' The spirit of man is the candle of the Lord.' (PROV. xxii. 27). God is the fire of this world, its vital principle, a warm pervading presence everywhere. . . . And now of this fire the spirit of man is the candle. What does that mean ? If, because man is of a nature which corresponds to the nature of God, and just so far as man is obedient to God, the life of God, which is spread throughout the universe, gathers itself into utterance ; and men, aye, and all other beings, if such beings there are, capable of watching our humanity, see what God is, in gazing at the man whom He has kindled,—then is not the figure plain ? . . . In certain lands, for certain holy ceremonies, they prepare the candles with most anxious care. The very bees which distil the wax are sacred. They range in gardens planted with sweet flowers for their use alone. The wax is gathered by consecrated hands; and then the shaping of the candles is a holy task, performed in holy places, to the sound of hymns, and in the atmosphere of prayers. All this is done because the candles are to burn in the most lofty ceremonies on most sacred days. With what care must the man be made, whose spirit is to be the candle of the Lord ! It is his spirit which God is to kindle with Himself. Therefore the spirit must be the precious part of him."—PHIL. BROOKS, Serm., *Candle of the Lord*.

See ALTAR, BEES, CANOPY, CEREMONIES, CHURCH, FIRE, FLOWERS, LAMP, LIGHT, PRIEST, PROCESSION.

CANDLESTICKS :—

A symbol of the wisdom- and love-nature as bearing the light of Truth in the soul.

" These (two witnesses) are the two olive trees and the two candlesticks, standing before the Lord of the earth." —REV. xi. 4.

The two principles which testify to the greatness of God within the soul, are Love and Wisdom, and these stand for the Lord who rules the lower nature (earth).

"By olive-tree is signified love and charity ; and by candlesticks is signified illustration in truths, and thence intelligence and faith."—SWEDENBORG, *Apoc. Rev.*, n. 493.

"A derived and transient light is all that any man can be. In ourselves we are darkness, and only as we hold fellowship with Him do we become capable of giving forth any rays of light. The condition of all our brightness is that Christ shall give us light. He is the source, we are but reservoirs. He the fountain, we only cisterns. He must walk amidst the candlesticks, or they will never shine. He must hold the stars in His hand, or they will drop from their places and dwindle into darkness. Therefore our power for service lies in reception ; and if we are to live *for* Christ, we must live *in* Christ. But there is still another requisite for the shining of the light. The prophet Zechariah once saw in vision the great Temple lamp, and by its side two olive-trees from which golden oil flowed through golden pipes to the central light. And when he expressed his ignorance of the meaning of the vision, this was the interpretation by the angel who talked with him : ' Not by might, nor by power, but by My Spirit, saith the Lord of Hosts.' The lamp that burns must be kept fed with oil. Throughout the Old Testament the soft, gracious influences of God's Spirit are symbolised by oil."—A. MACLAREN, *Sermons*, 2nd Series, p. 162.

"Oil" is a symbol for love ; "lamp" for the causal-body ; "stars" for the mental faculties ; "gold" for wisdom. Christ is the "sun" of the soul giving out the light of truth to the personality (moon) which shines only by derived light.

See CHURCHES (Asia), CRUCIFIXION (Rev. xi. 8), LAMP, OIL, OLIVE, PERSONALITY, PROCESSION, WITNESSES (two).

CANOPY OVER EUCHARIST :—

A symbol of the higher planes to indicate the under-world of the lower planes (four rods supporting the canopy) in which the Self (Christ) incarnates, as symbolised in the Roman mass.

See CABIN, CANDLES, CHILDREN OF HORUS, FIRMAMENT, IRON PLATE, PILLARS (four), PROCESSION, QUATERNARY, SACRAMENT, SKY, TEE, UMBRELLA.

CAPRICORN, THE ZODIACAL SIGN :—

A symbol of the tenth period of the cycle of life. It signifies the higher mind (white He-goat) which is attained by the ego climbing the mount of aspiration, through the transmutation of the lower mind, in the cycle of evolution.

"The Indian Capricorn is an elephant emerging from a makara, or leviathan. It is called in the ' Lalita Vistara,' *Airâvana* (born of the waters)."—A. LILLIE, *Budd. in Christendom*, p. 7.

The higher mental nature (elephant) arising from the lower nature (sea-monster). The higher mind born of the astro-mental nature (lower "waters"). When the lower nature is perfected, then the higher nature is born, as it were, into the consciousness.

See CANCER, ELEPHANT, GOAT (white), LEVIATHAN, WHALE, ZODIAC.

CAPTIVE WOMAN :—

A symbol of the higher emotion-nature held latent through the activity of the desires.

See ANDROMEDA, PERSEUS, WOMAN.

CAPTIVITY OF THE ISRAEL-ITES :—

A symbol of the enslavement of the mental qualities (Israelites) by the desires, sensations, and lower emotions,—the " Egyptians " or " Babylonians," as related in the Hebrew scriptures.

"For I delight in the law of God after the inward man : but I see a different law in my members, warring against the law of my mind, and bringing me into captivity under the law of sin which is in my members."—ROM. vii. 23.

"By leading into captivity is signified being seduced and so drawn away from truths and goods into falses and evils."—SWEDENBORG, *Apoc. Rev.*, n. 591.

"We must care for justice ; justice is one of the concerns of the soul. The soul that is indifferent to justice is not in possession of itself. . . Excessive poverty and excessive riches are fetters upon human souls, prisons to human spirits. That is why they should be abolished, and that is my main reason for being a social reformer."—T. RHONDDA WILLIAMS, Serm., *The Promise, &c.*

See BABYLON, BONDAGE, EXODUS, FETTERS, ISRAELITES, JUSTICE, PEOPLE, PRISONERS, REMISSION, SUFFERING.

CARAPACE, THE COSMIC :—

A symbol of Matter as the encasement of Spirit, resulting from the process of involution.

"The Lord and Maker of all things. . . . when He perceived that the Essential Man could not be lover of all things, unless He clothed him in a cosmic carapace, He shut him in within a house of body."—"The Perfect Sermon," G. R. S. MEAD, *T. G. Hermes*, Vol II. p. 321.

It is necessary that the Essential or Archetypal Man should be fully involved in the soul or cosmos through love—the Divine Sacrifice,—in order that afterwards it shall be evolved in the many souls of humanity.

See ARC. MAN, INCARNATION, MATTER, SACRIFICE

CARAPACE OF THE TORTOISE:—

A symbol of that which shuts off the lower nature from the higher nature. A symbol of limitation, or of the mental plane.

See TORTOISE.

CARDINAL POINTS :—

See QUARTERS.

CARNELIAN :—

A symbol of wisdom or intuition.

"Carnelian to strengthen his steps,"— *Book of the Dead.* BUDGE, *Egyptian Magic*, p. 187.

Carnelian, being red, was sacred to Isis (Wisdom).

See GEMS, ISIS, JEWELS.

CARPENTER :—

A symbol of the Divine Artificer. That aspect of the One Life which constructs and puts together.

"Tvashtar is the clever-handed carpenter-god, who, in particular, manufactured with his hatchet the thunderbolt of Indra, but also, in general, 'adorned heaven and earth—the parents, and all things with their forms,' whence heaven and earth are called 'the artificer's pair.' 'Tvashtar produced thee (Brihaspati) from all existing things, from hymn after hymn, the skilled artificer.'"—H. W. WALLIS, *Cosmology of the Rig-Veda*, p. 23.

Spirit (heaven) and matter (earth) are "the Artificer's pair," because from them all things are produced, and from all qualities aspiration for growth arises.

See CREATION, GATHA-AHUNA, HYMN SINGING.

CARRIAGE AND OXEN :—

A symbol of the vehicle of the astral nature, with the desires subordinated to the will of the driver—the ego on the mental plane.

See OX, OXEN.

CARRIAGES AND OXEN DECKED WITH RICH GARMENTS :—

A symbol of the desires and emotions subordinated to the requirements of the higher will, together with the high results arrived at through individual effort.

See GARMENTS.

CARRIAGES OF GOLD :—

Symbolic of high mental qualities allied with wisdom.

See GOLD.

CARTS GAY WITH SILVER AND GOLD :—

Symbolic of active and passive aspects of the higher emotions. Passive — "silver" (moon). Active— "gold" (sun).

CASTES, FOUR, OF MANKIND, IN THE SCRIPTURES OF INDIA :—

Symbolic of the four soul-vehicles and their activities on the four lower planes. The life principles of the four bodies of the incarnating ego.

"In order to protect this universe He, the most resplendent One, assigned separate duties and occupations to those who sprang from his mouth, arms, thighs and feet.

To Brâhmanas he assigned teaching and studying the Veda, sacrificing for their own benefit and for others, giving and accepting of alms.

The Kshatriya he commanded to protect the people, to bestow gifts, to offer sacrifices, to study the Veda, and to abstain from attaching himself to sensual pleasures.

The Vaisya to tend cattle, to bestow gifts, to offer sacrifices, to study the Veda, to trade, to lend money, and to cultivate land.

One occupation only the Lord prescribed to the Sudra, to serve meekly even these other three castes."—*Laws of Manu*, I. 87–91.

In order to utilise the scheme of things in behalf of the soul, the Higher Self established centres of consciousness and energy for the soul's functionings, on the four lower planes of nature. The "mouth" signifies expression of intelligence ; the "arms," activities in conflict ; the "thighs," means of progress ; the "feet," foundation of advancing movement.

To the higher mind centre, or causal body (Brâhmana), is assigned the reception of Truth (Veda) and the transmission of knowledge to the lower mind as it is able to receive it ; also the giving up of the lower for that which is higher, in order to promote the growth of the qualities ; and the bestowal and reception of spiritual love.

The lower mind centre, or mental-body (Kshatriya), was enjoined to organise the qualities (people), to make good use of the faculties ; to give up lower forms of thought for higher ; to purify itself by Truth ; and to maintain supremacy over the desires and sensations.

The desire centre, or astral-body (Vaisya), was to nurture the emotions (cattle) ; to raise the lower desires ; to give up the lower for the higher ; to purify its nature ; to exchange the worse for the better ; and to make fruitful for good the lower nature.

The physical centre, or physical-body (Sudra), is for the senses and activities only, in complete subordination to the desires, the emotions, and the mind.

"It is declared that a Sûdra woman alone can be the wife of a Sûdra, she and one of his own caste the wives of a Vaisya, those two and one of his own caste the wives of a Kshatriya, those three and one of his own caste the wives of a Brâhmana."—*Ibid.*, III. 13.

It is explained that the "wives" or permanent atoms of the four bodies on their respective planes are inter-related, and that the lower are sub-ordinate to the higher. Thus, the causal-self (Brâhmana) possesses all the four atomic centres (wives), and these are co-ordinated in the complete human being who aspires, thinks, desires, and acts in the world, thereby producing results (children).

"Castes are as ladders whereby to ascend from the lower to the higher. They are properly spiritual grades, and, have no relation to the outward condition of life. Like all other doctrines, that of Caste has been materialised. The Castes are four in number, and correspond to the fourfold nature of man."—ANNA KINGSFORD, *Life*, Vol. II. p. 5.

See ALMSGIVING, ARMS, AUSTERI-TIES, BIRTH (second), BRAHMANA, CHARIOT, CHILDREN OF HORUS, CATTLE, CLASSES, CULTIVATION, FEET, HOUSE (clan), JOB, KSHATRIYA, MAR-RIAGE (castes), MOUTH, PURUSHA, QUATERNARY, RAGANYA, RULERS (world), SACRIFICES, SKANDHAS, SU-DRA, THIGHS, VAISYA, VEDA, VES-TURES.

CATTLE, OR OXEN :—

A symbol of those emotions of the lower nature, which are under control of the higher nature ; or of the higher desires among the astral qualities, wherein buddhi is reflected through the desire-nature.

"And God said, Let the earth bring forth the living creature after its kind, cattle and the creeping thing, and beast of the earth after its kind : and it was so." —GEN. i. 24.

And again the Divine nature directs that the lower nature of the soul shall bring forth that which is first in order, namely, the natural qualities. The " cattle " symbolise obedience and docility to higher rule : the " creeping thing," cunning and subtlety : and the " beast of the earth," animal instinct : and so involution proceeds without struggle or strife in perfect order and entirety.

See ANIMALS, BEASTS, CREATURES, CREEPING THINGS, EARTH, GOLDEN AGE, OX.

CATTLE, COWS, OR KINE :—

A symbol of the buddhic emotions active in the mind.

"Agni (born from the womb of earth or sky) is favorable to cattle. . . . Agni is yonder sun."—*Sata. Brâh.*, VI. 4, 1, 8–10. "Cattle is food," *Ibid.*, V 2, 1, 16.

The Self (Agni) brought forth of the purified lower nature, or of buddhi (sky), is in harmony with the buddhic emotions. "Agni" is a symbol of the Higher Self. The love of goodness, truth, right, justice, etc. is the soul's nourishment.

See ABODE, BEASTS (clean), FOOD, KARSHVARES, SUN, YIMA.

CATTLE FREE FROM DEATH :—

A symbol of those high emotions that persist through time, having in them the Divine life of atma-buddhi.
See DEATH, YIMA.

CATTLE OF NOMADS :—

Symbolic of useful transient

emotions, within more permanent forms.

See JABAL.

CATTLE OF TRAILING GAIT :—

A symbol of high emotions produced through the slow progress of evolution.

CAUCASUS MOUNTAINS :—

A symbol of the heights of aspiration, or of successful endeavour.

See AMAZONS, ARARAT, MOUNTAIN, OLYMPUS.

CAUSAL-BODY, OR KARANA-SARIRA :—

This term denotes the vehicle of the spiritual ego in the higher mind of each individual. It is usually called the immortal soul, for it persists throughout the cycle. To it are attached the vehicles of the personality or personal ego, on the lower planes.

"The Vedanta affirms the existence of a third body, called *Karana-Sarira*, or causal body, described as a kind of inner rudiment or latent embryo of the body existing with the soul."—MON. WILLIAMS, *Indian Wisdom*, p. 64.

This is the "cognitional vesture" of the Upanishads which is at first rudimentary, but is gradually perfected through the efforts of the personalities.

"Tauler said : ' The ground or centre of the soul is so high and glorious a thing, that it cannot properly be named, even as no adequate name can be found for the Infinite and Almighty God. In this ground lies the image of the Holy Trinity. Its kindred and likeness with God is such as no tongue can utter. Could a man perceive and realise how God dwelleth in this ground, such knowledge would be straightway the blessedness of salvation.—Arnstein."—VAUGHAN, *Hours with the Mystics*, Vol. I. p. 246.

The causal-body is the seat of the higher Triad,—atma-buddhi-manas.

"The inner habitat which the soul provides for itself, and which goes everywhere with it. The grandest fruit of our earlier moral victories is that their results are woven into this structure and help to make it and us invulnerable. . . . In a free and growing soul this structure, woven out of our past and present, and open sheer to the heavens, becomes growingly real in our consciousness. It regulates for us the temperature of the outside world, and amid the disorders of the external, creates an inner calm when the spiritual can have full play. It is, as it were, the condensed exhalation of our personality, which, when death has loosed the bond between us and the physical, may take

shape in the spiritual world as the form of life we have been leading."—J. BRIERLY *The Eternal Religion*, pp. 93, 94.

" The soul in its highest sense is a vast capacity for God. It is like a curious chamber added on to being, and somehow involving being, a chamber with elastic and contractile walls, which can be expanded, with God as its guest, illimitably, but which without God shrinks and shrivels until every vestige of the Divine is gone, and God's image is left without God's Spirit."—H. DRUMMOND, *Natural Law, etc.*, p. 110.

" The spiritual faculties are organised in the spiritual protoplasm of the soul, just as other faculties are organised in the protoplasm of the body."—*Ibid.*, p. 233.

The causal-body is at first potential only. It becomes actual by a process of building up, life after life, so that when perfected at the close of the cycle, it forms the resurrection body of the glorified spirit.

"We are content then to fall back on Scripture words, and to believe in the resurrection of the dead simply because it is, as we believe, told us from God. For all who accept the message, this hope shines clear,—of a *building* of God imperishable and solid, when contrasted with the *tent* in which we dwell here—of a body ' raised in corruption,' ' clothed with immortality,' and so, as in many another phrase, declared to be exempt from decay, and therefore vigorous with unchanging youth. Whether because that body of glory has no proclivity to mutation and decay, or whether the perpetual volition and power of God counteract such tendency, matters not at all. The truth of the promise remains, though we have no means of knowing more than the fact, that we shall receive a body, fashioned like His who dieth no more. . . . And if all this be true, that glorious and undecaying body shall then be the equal and fit instrument of the perfected spirit, not, as it is now, the inadequate instrument only of the natural life."—A. MACLAREN, *Sermons, 2nd Series*, p. 204.

See AB, ADYTUM, BIRTH-CHAMBER, DEFUNCT, DWELLING, GLORY, HEART, HEBEN, HERMES, KA, KARANA, KHABIT, LAZARUS, LINGAM, MAHAVIRA-POT, MANASI, MIRROR, NESHAMAH, PRANA, PROVINCE-RULER, RESURRECTION, SAHU, SHINTAI, SAMKHARA, SOUL (middle), STHULA, TABERNACLE, TEMPLE, TENT, TZELEM, VESTURES.

CAUSAL-SELF :—

This is the higher mental Self which arises from the duality of mind and emotion when union of the two takes place. The causal-self, or causal consciousness, communicates itself as inner memory or reminiscence, through the personality to the lower planes, and by attracting and enlisting the receptive and inquiring mental qualities, implants ideals in the mind, which in the form of mental images at once serve as symbols to typify the eternities of Wisdom, Love, and Truth and show the correspondency between things above and things below.

"And Achilles, fleet of foot, made answer to Kalchas and spake to him : Yea, be of good courage, speak whatever soothsaying thou knowest ; for by Apollo dear to Zeus, him by whose worship thou, O Kalchas, declarest thy soothsaying to the Danaans, no man while I live and behold light on earth shall lay violent hands upon thee amid the hollow ships ; no man of all the Danaans, not even if thou mean Agamemnon, that now avoweth him to be the greatest far of the Achaians." —*Iliad*, Book I.

The Personality or lower self,— swift in its processes,—is the means whereby intercommunication between the inner memory consciousness (Kalchas), or causal-self, and the outer nature is eventually established. The mental attitude becomes receptive, and through wonder and curiosity, a questioning spirit becomes aroused and active. The soul is thus perceived to be not only existing as a state of consciousness, but persisting as the spark of the Eternal Fire of God. Through the establishment of memory is the lower mind awakened. The lower mind, so long as the Personality exists, shall not succeed in extinguishing the ray of the Eternal which passes through the reflection from Above. No mental quality,—not even the collective Desire-mind —but is aware of the transcendent power of the Causal-self on the higher mental plane. The " hollow ships " are the higher mental patterns of the lower bodies of the incarnating ego.

" ' The region above the heavens is the place of true knowledge. There colourless, formless, and intangible being is visible to the mind, which is the only lord of the soul. And as the Divine intelligence and that of every other soul which is rightly nourished is fed upon mind and pure knowledge, such an intelligent soul is glad at beholding *being* ; and feeding on the sight of truth is replenished.'—(PLATO, *Phœdrus*, 247.) But whenever a soul is unable to maintain its vision of truth and fails to nourish its wings with the

sight of pure being, that soul falls to this lower world and lives here among the shadows. But it never altogether forgets the realities it has seen in the eternal home. Deep in its memory it holds those realities it has known and, when it sees the shadow-image of the real thing, it remembers the ' Idea ' which it knew in the other sphere, so that all true knowledge is *reminiscence*. . . . This means that the soul has within itself, whether by reminiscence or otherwise, the power of rising above the transitory to that which is permanent, and that there is something in the soul kindred to the Reality which it contemplates."—R. M. JONES, *Mystical Religion*, pp. 61, 63.

The " shadow-image " may be taken to mean a *symbol* of the real thing above.

See ACHILLES, AGAMEMNON, APOLLO, CONSCIOUSNESS, DANAANS, GREECE, GREEKS, HOLLOW SHIPS, INCARNATION OF SOULS, KALCHAS, PERSONALITY, PRIAM, PROTOTYPES, SPARK, TAURT, YAMA, YUDHI, ZEUS.

CAVE, OR CAVERN :—

A symbol of the lower quaternary or lower nature of the soul—dark and gloomy, because devoid of the light of Truth.

" Far back in the inner chamber of the Cavern of Night sits Light (Phanes), and in the midst Night, who delivers prophetic judgment to the gods, and at the mouth is Adrastia."—HERMIAS, *Phœdr.*, p. 148.

The Divine illumination is only in the adytum, holy of holies, or higher nature of the soul. In the midst is buddhi, under the guise of folly and ignorance, who yields up the transmuted results of effort and aspiration, under the law of karma (Adrastia).

" The Persians, mystically signifying the descent of the soul into the sublunary regions, and its regression thence, initiate the candidate in a place which they call a cavern. . . . A cave, according to Zoroaster, being an image of the world which was made by Mithra.—PORPHYRY, *Cave of the Nymphs*, VI.

Mithra, like Zeus or Jesus, is said to have been born, or brought up, in a cave, which signifies the Redeemer entering the lower nature of the soul.

" In the Zuni cosmogony, men, as in so many other myths, originally lived in the dark places of the earth in four caverns. Like the children of Uranus and Gaea, they murmured at the darkness."— A. LANG, *Myth. Rit. and Rel.*, Vol. II. p. 62.

The " four caverns " signify the four lower planes on which the progeny of

Spirit (Uranus) and Matter (Gaea) are emanated. The same idea is to be seen in the Maori myth of Rangi (Spirit) and Papa (matter),—their children found themselves in darkness, ruled by great mother Night.

"Now was Loke taken without any chance of respite. The Asar conducted him into a cave."—*Prose Edda.*

Now the desire-nature (Loke) is captured by the mind (Thor), through the varied experiences which have been collected. And these are now organised in the young soul (cave).

See ADRASTIA, BIRTH OF JESUS, DIONYSUS, HIDING PLACE, LOKE, MITHRA, NIGHT, PHANES, RANGI, ROCK (spiritual), VIRGIN MARY.

CAVE, THE OVER-ROOFED :—

A symbol of the World-soul or Over-soul.

"We enter beneath this over-roofed cave."—*Empedocles,* FAIRBANKS, 392.

The emotions and the mind enter the World-soul, wherein are the Higher and lower selves,—buddhi-manas and kama-manas.

CAVE OF NANDA :—

A symbol of the receptive personality.

"The Naga-king entering the cave of Nanda."—*Buddha-Karita,* Bk. I. 19.

The "Serpent-King" is the symbol of wisdom and enlightenment, which enters the personality to illuminate it and raise it upward to perfection.

See BIRTH OF KRISHNA, BODHISATVA (great).

CEILING OF THE SKY :—

A symbol of the higher mental plane which is next above the lower nature. It has the same meaning as the firmament.

"Pepi hath been purified. He hath taken in his hand the *mah* staff, he hath provided himself with his throne, and he hath taken his seat in the boat of the great and little companies of the gods. Rā maketh Pepi to sail to the West, he stablisheth his seat above those of the lords of doubles, and he writeth down Pepi at the head of those who live. The doors of Pekh-Ka which are in the abyss open themselves to Pepi, the doors of the iron which is the ceiling of the sky open themselves to Pepi, and he passeth through them ; he hath his panther skin upon him, and the staff and whip are in his hand. Pepi goeth forward with his flesh, Pepi is happy with his name, and he liveth with his *ka* (double) " (Inscription in Pyramid of Pepi I).—BUDGE, *Egyptian Magic,* p. 158.

The Personality hath been purified and become one with the Individuality. He hath been victorious, and hath completed the development of his own causal body. He therefore hath his place in the World-soul or Causal-body of the Higher and lower natures. By the law of the Supreme, the Individuality enters upon the next cycle. He is now evolved above the souls having unfinished causal-bodies, and he is at the head of those who are incarnating. He can now traverse the lower planes at will, and entrance to the higher mind (iron ceiling) is his, and Wisdom's heights. He hath the sign (panther skin) upon him that the lower emotions have been overcome and displaced by the higher ; and aspiration (staff) and the will are active within him. The personality has transcended his lower self, he is blest in his differentiation, and he has become one with his higher nature in the causal-body (ka).

See ABYSS, BOAT, CHILDREN OF HORUS, DEFUNCT, DOORS, FIRMAMENT, IRON PLATE, KA, NAME, PANTHER SKIN, REN, THRONE.

CELESTIAL :—

Pertaining to the "sky," that is, to the buddhic and atmic planes.

CELESTIAL STEMS :—

A symbol of cyclic or zodiacal correspondences, which, as it were, connect the general scheme of things with the various centres on the mental and other planes of the soul.

See ATTRACTION, CITY, DECANS, VESTURES, ZODIAC.

CENSERS OF BURNING INCENSE :—

Symbolic of the purifying fire and aroma of the spiritual nature (buddhi) which permeates the mind (air) or disciplined and devout lower qualities (worshippers) in the human soul (church). The swinging of the censers signifies the functioning of buddhi in the lower nature, whereby the purifying and transmutation of the lower qualities are brought about.

"And Moses said unto Aaron, Take thy censer, and put fire therein from off the altar, and lay incense thereon, and carry it quickly unto the congregation, and make atonement for them : for there is wrath gone out from the Lord ; the plague is begun."—NUM. xvi. 46.

The moral nature (Moses) enjoins the spiritual mind (Aaron) to ally itself with buddhi (fire) and bring about the purification of the qualities (congregation) during a spiritual out-pouring which shall destroy the lowest qualities. The atonement signifies transmutation in response to aspiration, and the substitution of higher for lower.

See AARON, ALTAR, ATONEMENT, CHRYSEIS, FIRE, INCENSE, MOSES, PESTILENCE, PROCESSION.

CENTAURS :—

A symbol of the lower mental qualities—half mind and half animal instinct. They "led a wild and savage life."

See CHIRON, PANS, SATYRS.

CENTAURS OF MOUNTAIN CAVES :—

Symbolic of the more obscure and least intelligent opinions of the dawning mentality.

CENTURION :—

A symbol of a leading mental faculty which directs other mental faculties and qualities of the soul.

"Mystically, the centurion is every-one who rules over his members, senses and faculties, so that they, as it were soldiers, may fight for and serve God."— ST. GREGORY, *Morals on the Book of Job,* Vol. I. p. 332.

See RULERS, SOLDIERS.

CEREMONIES IN RELIGIONS :—

These are usually symbolical of the process of transmutation of lower qualities into higher.

See BAPTISM, BARSOM, CENSERS, HOST, INCENSE, PASSOVER, PROCESSION, RITES, RITUAL, SACRAMENT, SACRIFICE, TAUROBOLIUM.

CHAFF OF WHEAT :—

A symbol of the lower qualities which are gradually discarded— "blown away by the wind," i.e. cast out by mind (air) energised by the Spirit (wind). Chaff is the husk of that food, wheat, which has been evolved as the "fruit of the Spirit." When the lower qualities have effected their purpose in life, they dry up, as it were, like chaff and pass away.

"The wicked are like the chaff which the wind driveth away. Therefore the wicked shall not stand in the judgment, nor sinners in the congregation of the righteous."—Ps. i. 4, 5.

The evil qualities are transient and unreal. They have no place in the estimate of the state of the soul's progress, nor can they disturb the harmony of the higher qualities, for they are on a lower plane.

"Corn in the field is touched by the sun, in that in this life the soul of man is illumined by the regard of the light above. It receives the showers, in that it is enriched by the word of Truth ; it is shaken by the winds, in that it is tried with temptations ; and it bears the chaff 'growing' along with it, in that it bears the life of daily increasing wickedness in sinners, directed against itself ; and after it has been carried away to the barn, it is squeezed by the threshing weight, that it may be parted from the hold of the chaff, in that our mind, being subjected to heavenly discipline, whilst it receives the stripes of correction, is parted from the society of the carnal sort, in a cleaner state ; and it is carried to the granary with the chaff left behind, in that while the lost remain without, the Elect soul is transported to the eternal joys of the Mansion above."—ST. GREGORY, *Morals on the Book of Job,* Vol. I. p. 362.

See CORN, FAN, HUSKS, WAY OF DEATH, WHEAT.

CHANNELS, OR PASSAGES :—

A symbol of means of communication established in the vehicles of the soul, between the higher and the lower natures, so that reciprocal action and transmutations may occur.

See AMBAYÂS, AQUEDUCT, ARTERY, IRRIGATION, PASSAGES, RIVERS, TREES AND RIVERS.

CHAOS, OR THE DEEP :—

A symbol of primordial formless matter. Matter in its primal state, devoid of qualities, involution of Spirit not having yet taken place.

"Orpheus declares that Chaos first existed, eternal, vast, uncreate,—it was neither darkness nor light, nor moist nor dry, nor hot nor cold, but all things intermingled."—*Clementine Recognitions,* Ch. XXX.

"And the earth was waste and void ; and darkness was upon the face of the deep ; and the Spirit of God moved upon the face of the waters."—GEN. i 2.

And the first state of matter was formless,—the involution of form not having begun. All was inchoate, for spirit was not permeating or informing matter with qualities ; and the Spirit of the Logos,—the Atman,—brooded upon the " waters " of ultimate reality. This statement refers to the formation in space of the invisible beginnings of the Solar system, with a correspondence also to the preparative involution of the life of the soul.

See ABYSS, DARKNESS, DEEP, DESERTS, EARTH, EREBUS, EROS, GINUNGAGAP, NARYANA, PO, TANAOA, WATER.

CHAPTERS :—

Symbolic of the planes of manifestation, or of periods and stages of progress.

" What is the Book of Mysteries ? It consists, said R. Shimon ben Yo'hai, of Five Chapters, contained in a grand palace and filling the whole universe. If, replied Rabbi Yehuda, they contain the fundamental ideas, they would be the most excellent of all things ! And so they are, replied R. Shimon, for the initiated."—MYER, *Qabbalah*, p. 101.

In the manifestation of the Logos (book of Life) there are five planes, and these are comprised in the Macrocosm. If these five planes, namely, the atmic, buddhic, mental, astral, and physical planes, contain all that is necessary for the soul's perfection, then the soul as the microcosm will ultimately attain in actuality the perfection of the Macrocosm.

See BOOK, GOING IN, MANIFESTATION UNTO DAY.

CHAPTERS OF MAGIC :—

A symbol of the Holy Scriptures. *See* MAGICAL FORMULÆ.

CHARIOT, OR CAR :—

A symbol of a vehicle of the Soul, Self, or consciousness, on one of the four lower planes. It is usually a symbol of the causal-body on the higher mind plane.

" The youthful men (the Maruts) placed (Rodasî) the young maid in their chariot, as their companion for victory, mighty in assemblies."—*Rig-Veda*, Mand I. Hymn 167, 6. *S. B. of E.*

The spiritual or atmic egos (Maruts) with the principle of buddhi (Rodasî) occupied the causal-body, for it is by atma-buddhi that victory is gained over the lower nature through the transmutation and segregation of the qualities.

" Know the soul to be sitting in the chariot, the body to the chariot, the intellect (buddhi) the charioteer, and the mind the reins. The senses they call the horses, the objects of the senses their roads. . . . He who has no understanding, and whose mind (the reins) is never firmly held, his senses (horses) are unmanageable, like vicious horses of a charioteer. But he who has understanding and whose mind is always firmly held, his senses are under control, like good horses of a charioteer. He who has no understanding, who is unmindful and always impure, never reaches the goal, but enters into the round of births (samsâra). But he who has understanding, who is mindful and always pure, reaches indeed the goal, from whence he is not born again (from whence there is no return)."—MAX MÜLLER, *Katha. Upanishad*, iii. 3.

The " body," or " chariot," is the causal-body. The charioteer is the spiritual ego (buddhi-manas). The " senses " are the mental activities aroused by the desires, and mentally guided (the reins). The little-evolved ego is full of illusions, and fails to control his activities, which drag him hither and thither. But the fully evolved ego has wisdom and knowledge, and his activities are completely controlled. The ego filled with illusion and ignorance fails to reach the goal of perfection, and is re-incarnated life after life, in the lower nature. The wise ego who is perfected is liberated, and returns no more to birth upon the lower planes.

" In *Mait. Upanishad*, II. 6, where the organs of knowledge are the five reins, the organs of action are the horses, the manas is the driver, and the prakriti his whip. By means of this, manas drives the organs of action (speech, grasp, movement, evacuation, begetting) to their work, and they are then guided and controlled by manas by means of the organs of knowledge (sight, hearing, taste, smell, touch)."—DEUSSEN, *Phil. of Upanishads*, p. 274.

The intellect-will (manas) by means of nature (prakriti) drives the activities of mind (the horses), viz. mental action (speech), discipline (grasp), progress (movement), riddance of lower qualities (evacuation), production of higher qualities (begetting), to their work of the evolution of the soul. These activities are guided and controlled by the intelligent will in the causal-body (chariot) by means of the knowing faculties (senses), viz. consciousness (sight), intuition (hearing), desire (taste), sensation (smell), and lower mind (touch).

See Castes, Causal-body, Gilgoolem, Horses (bay), Maruts, Pragâpati, Prakriti, Pranas, Re-incarnation, Samsara, Sense organs, Vaimanika, Vestures, Vital airs.

CHARIOT OF THE SUN, WITH FOUR HORSES :—

A symbol of the celestial causal-body, or World-soul on the buddhic plane, inter-related with the activities of the quaternary.

"The four Elements are the steeds of the Great Chariot of all things. The course of the first Winged Horse is beyond the limits of heaven itself. This Steed transcends the rest in beauty, greatness, and speed, and shines with purest brilliance. Its resplendent coat is dappled over with sparks of flame, the stars, and planets and the moon. Such is the Steed of Fire. The second Horse is Air. Its colour is black ; the side turned towards its shining mate is bright with light, but that in shade is dark. In nature it is mild, and more obedient to the rein ; it is less strong than Fire, and slower in its course. The third is Water, slower still than Air ; while Earth, the fourth of this great Cosmic Team, turns on itself, champing its adamantine bit. Round it its fellow Steeds circle as round a post. And this continues for long ages, during which the Cosmic Team work steadily together in peace and friendship. But after many ages, at a certain time, the mighty Breath of the first Steed, as though in passion, pours from on high and makes the others hot, and most of all the last. And finally the fiery Breath sets the Earth Horse's mane ablaze. In the suffering of this cosmic passion the Earth causes such distress to its neighbour Steed and so disturbs its course, that exhausted by its struggles it inundates the Earth with floods of sweat. . . . But at the end of the world's age a still stranger mystery is wrought : a Divine Contest takes place among the Steeds ; their natures are transformed, and their substances pass over to the mightiest of the Four. It is as though a sculptor had modelled four figures in wax, and melted them down again, and remade them into one form. The One Element becomes omnipotent, and finally in its triumph is identified with the Charioteer Himself."
—Dion Chrysostom.

The "Great Chariot of all things" is said to be the "most perfect vehicle," which signifies its archetypal nature as containing the perfection of all qualities, and the pattern types of all forms. It is the buddhic causal-body, the same as the "Boat of Râ."

It is served by the quaternary, or "four great elements,"—buddhic (fire), mental (air), astral (water), and physical (earth), representing the four lower planes of manifestation. The fifth or atmic plane is the plane of the Higher Self, the "Charioteer." The "Winged Horse of Fire" is the same as the Holy Spirit (Buddhi), and contains the spiritual egos, or Divine sparks (stars of heaven), and centres of consciousness (planets, moon) for the mental plane. Its "speed" refers to its high rate of atomic vibration. The "Horse of Air" is *black*, to signify that the higher mind is unmanifest to the lower mind which is *dark* from ignorance and illusion. But the higher mind is "bright with light" from above. The mind is "mild," that is, it is stimulated into activity by either the lower or higher emotions, and is obedient to higher or lower rulers. The "Horse of Water" signifies the desire-nature of the soul, slower to spiritualise than the mind. The "Horse of Earth" signifies the physical brain and body at the foundation of the evolutionary soul-process, the pivot round which the higher activities turn. During the enormous period of *involution* there is no strife in nature, it is the "golden age" when all the qualities are brought to perfection, and pronounced "very good." But after a period of cessation from activity,—a pralaya of "rest,"—there is a fresh spiritual out-pouring from Buddhi, which rouses the life-forces of the planes below, and starts *evolution* from the physical nature, the protoplasmic body being the lowest vehicle. Then the bodily activities stimulate the more or less latent astral organisation of sensation, instinct, and desire, which re-acts to bring about physical adaptation. At the end of the cycle of life, the lower planes of the soul become purified and perfected : their natures therefore are spiritualised and transmuted, and are resolved again into the higher element buddhi. Finally, as the lower planes have merged into the higher, and victory is achieved, the omnipotent buddhi is withdrawn into the Atman and becomes one with the Self Triumphant.

See AIR, ARJUNA, BOAT, CAUSAL-
BODY, CONFLAGRATION, EARTH, ELE-
MENTS (four), FIRE, GOLDEN AGE,
HORSE (white), INVOLUTION, JUDG-
MENT DAY, OPPOSITES, PIETY, PRA-
LAYA, RENOVATION, SAVITRI, SHIP,
SPIRIT, WATER.

CHARON, SON OF EREBUS :—

A symbol of the desire-mental,
or kama-manasic, nature by means
of which the soul progresses through
the lower planes—the underworld
of ignorance (darkness). The " payment of a coin to Charon " signifies
the sacrifice that must be made of
desire, in order to progress.

See EREBUS, MONEY.

CHARON'S FERRY :

A symbol of the division between
the lower mind and the higher—the
same as the " bridge of manas." It
implies a " way " by which the
consciousness may pass from the
lower nature to the higher. Through
the establishment of this " ferry "
the recollection of past incarnations
becomes possible. The " ferry " acts,
as it were, like sight through a tele-
scope in relation to the lower consciouness, and through it a vision of the
Higher Self may be gained. And in
this way the reflection of the Higher
nature in the lower nature is in
process of time and evolution fully
accomplished, and then " Charon's
Ferry " is over-passed by the soul.
The " ferry," which at first is
potential, becomes actual when the
soul is ready to cross it.

" The mystic is one who knows divine
things otherwise than by hearsay, who
sees them by an inner light ; one to whom
the Infinite and Eternal is no mere article
of belief, but an experience. The mystical
doctrine, in its essence, is that the highest
in man can hold immediate intercourse
with the Highest in the universe, that the
human soul can enjoy direct communion
with the Supreme Object, to which neither
the senses nor the logical understanding
can attain."—W. S. LILLY, *The Great
Enigma*, p. 256.

See AGNIDHRA, BOAT (river), BRIDGE
OF HEAVEN, DOG CERBERUS, HIKO-
BOSHI, PRAGÂPATI, RECOLLECTION,
REMINISCENCE, STYX.

CHEEKS, FAIR, OF WOMEN :—

A symbol of the instinct aspect of
the intuition.

CHEEKS AND HAIR OF DEMONS :—

A symbol of the higher aspects of
the desires.
See DEMONS.

CHEMMIS ISLAND, PANOPOLIS :—

A symbol of a centre of activity
established in the astral vehicle.

" The Egyptians say that in this island
(called Chemmis), Latona, who was one
of the eight primary deities, dwelling in
Buto, . . . received Apollo as a deposit
from the hands of Isis, and saved him
by concealing him in this, which is now
called the floating island, when Typhon
arrived, searching everywhere, and hoping
to find the son of Osiris."—HERODOTUS,
Euterpe, II. 156.

The higher-emotion nature (Latona)
working within the lower emotions of
the astro-mental plane (Buto), received
the inborn Self (Apollo-Horus) as
proceeding from Wisdom (Isis) the
Divine Mother, and attached the Self
to an astral centre (Chemmis) which
now established a fixed connection
between the mortal personality and
the immortal individuality in a
permanent astral atom. Then the
lower principle (Typhon-Set) sought
for the young child, the Son of God,
to destroy him.

See BIRTH OF HORUS, BUTO, DELOS,
IZANAGI, MANCO, ONOGOROJIMA, RING-
HORNE.

CHERUBIM AND SERAPHIM :—

Symbols of transcendental keepers
of the buddhic plane : that is, Divine
laws applicable to the higher nature
but not to the lower, and which,
therefore, cut off the lower consciousness from the higher.

" So he drove out the man ; and he
placed at the east of the garden of Eden
the Cherubim, and the flame of a sword
which turned every way, to keep the way
of the tree of life."—GEN. iii. 24.

Because of the downward attraction
to desire, the mind is now driven
forth from its condition of primeval
innocence. At " the east," that is,
where the Higher Self (sun) will
appear, a sentinel or watcher (Cherubim) stands to bar the direct way to
heaven which is now only to be
attained by struggle ; " men of violence
take it by force." (MAT. xi. 12.) The
lower mind is cut off from the higher
mind. The flame of a " sword " is a
symbol of the spiritual strength which

is necessary to possess in order to gain the secret of Life eternal.

"By 'cherubim' is signified the providence of the Lord to prevent man in such a state (deprived altogether of all will towards good and understanding of truth) entering into the things of faith."—SWEDENBORG, *Arc. Cel. to Gen.* iii. 24.

"Hail, ye divine beings who guard the doors, make ye for me a way, for, behold, I am like unto you. I have come forth by day, I have journeyed on my legs. I have gained the mastery over my footsteps before the God of Light."—BUDGE, *Book of the Dead*, p. 276.

This symbolises not the going forth, but the return of the soul to the buddhic plane (Eden). The soul is now at one with the "cherubim" and entitled to proceed. It has forthpoured in evolution and attained perfection through its own efforts. It has gained the mastery over the lower nature by obedience to the higher guidance of the indwelling God of Truth and Right.

"The passage from the Natural World to the Spiritual World is hermetically sealed on the natural side. The door from the inorganic to the organic from the natural to the spiritual is shut, and no man can open it . . . . The Spiritual World is guarded from the world next in order beneath it by a law of Biogenesis—except a man be born again ; except a man be born of water and of the Spirit, he cannot enter the Kingdom of God."—H. DRUMMOND, *Natural Law, &c.*, p. 71.

See ARK (test.), BORN AGAIN, DOORKEEPERS, EAST, EDEN, FALL, FLAME, HEAVEN, SERAPHIM, SHEKINAH, STATUTE, SURTUR, SWORD, TREE OF LIFE.

CHEST, OR COFFER (ARCA), OF OSIRIS :—

A symbol of the astro-mental vehicle of the soul, in which the indwelling Self (Osiris) is confined. It may be regarded as a sheath of mental matter enveloped in astral matter, and containing the potential and latent Archetypal Man on the higher planes inward.

"After this they carried the chest away to the river side, and out to sea by the Tanaitic mouth of the Nile ; which for this reason is still held in the utmost detestation by the Egyptians."—PLUTARCH, *Isis and Osiris*, § 13.

The sending forth to sea signifies the descent of the World-soul upon the lower planes, and its submergence in the astral tide of desire. Its passage through the Tanaitic mouth is a symbol that the Soul has ceased to be relatively at the mercy of the desire-nature, which is regarded by the educated mind (Egyptians) as abhorrent.

See ARC. MAN, ASO, COLUMN, DEATH OF OSIRIS, EGYPTIANS, NILE, PANDORA, WEEPING OF ISIS.

CHILD ; SON OR DAUGHTER :—

A symbol of a resultant, or new, state of being, produced, emanated, or evolved, by the interaction of masculine and feminine principles, or conditions, on the several planes of manifestation. Spirit is masculine, Matter is feminine, and these first emanate the highest qualities, sometimes called Gods and Goddesses, on the planes of atma, buddhi, and higher manas. Time is masculine and space is feminine, and these are said to produce results through the slow processes of involution and evolution. Mind is masculine, lower or higher emotion is feminine ; the results of their interaction are opinions and feelings (children).

"Thou canst have a word in thy heart, as it were a design born in thy mind, so that thy mind brings forth the design ; and the design is, so to speak, the offspring of thy mind, the child of thy heart."—AUGUSTINE, *Gospel of John*, Vol. I. p. 7.

See ASHES, LITTLE ONES, PEACE (sword), PARENTS, SON OF MAN.

CHILDREN OF THE EAST :—

A symbol of the sun, moon, planets, and stars which have their birth, as it were, in the east where they first become apparent. These again are the symbols of the Higher Self (sun), lower Self (moon), etc. Thus, the "greatest of all the children of the east" is the Higher Self, the Sun of righteousness.

See EAST, JOB, SUN.

CHILDREN OF GOD :—

A symbol of the spiritual egos, sparks of the Divine Fire, or monads of Life.

"The Spirit himself beareth witness with our spirit, that we are children of God."—ROM. viii. 16.

"We are children of the Most High because we are expressions of his own nature, limited portions of his own being, so to speak, seemingly separated from him, but not really so, and placed within the ring-fence of material existence that we may work out and make glorious the

eternal fact that we essentially are."—
R. J. CAMPBELL, *Manifesting the Works of God*.

"The divinity is stirring within the human breast, and demanding a culture and a liberty worthy of the child of God." —W. E. CHANNING, *Likeness to God*.

See AGNISHVATTAS, LITTLE CHIL-DREN, SONS OF GOD, SPARKS.

CHILDREN OF MEN AND WOMEN :—

Symbolic of new mental forms be-gotten of mind and emotion. These are opinions, ideas, and impressions formed in the lower mind ; or they are aspects of mental qualities seeking expression in various ways.

"That children signify truths, and in an opposite sense falses, is because in the spiritual sense of the Word, by ' genera-tions ' are meant spiritual generations, . . . neither does spiritual generation give birth to any other sons and daughters, than truths and goods."—SWEDENBORG, *Apoc. Rev.*, n. 139.

"' In sorrow shalt thou bring forth children,' points to the efforts necessary for attaining knowledge."—JOHN SCOTUS.

See BEGETTING, DAUGHTERS, CON-CEPTION, GENERATIVE, MULTIPLY, PARENTS, SEEDS OF FOODS, SONS AND DAUGHTERS, UNRIGHTEOUS.

CHILDREN GIVING INFORMA-TION :—

Symbolic of the budding mental faculties which are responsive to high vibrations, thus imparting wisdom or knowledge.

CHILDREN OF HORUS, FOUR :—

Symbols of the four planes of manifestation below atma, i.e. the buddhic, mental, astral, and physical planes.

"The four children of Horus, or the gods of the four cardinal points, were called Mestha, Hāpi, Tuamutef, and Qebhsennuf, and with them were associ-ated the goddesses Isis, Nephthys, Neith, and Serquet respectively. Mestha was man-headed, and represented the south, and protected the stomach and large intestines ; Hāpi was dog-headed, and represented the north, and protected the small intestines ; Tuamutef was jackal-headed, and represented the east, and protected the lungs and heart ; and Qebhsennuf was hawk-headed, and repre-sented the west, and protected the liver and gall-bladder. . . . They origin-ally represented the four supports of heaven, but very soon each was regarded as the god of one of the four quarters of the earth, and also of that which was

above it."—BUDGE, *Egyptian Magic*, pp. 89, 91.

The four cardinal points are symbols in all scriptures of the four planes of the quaternary. The significations of the " children " are indicated by their heads. Qebhsennuf, Hawk = Buddhi. Mestha, Man = Mind. Hāpi, Ape = Astral. Tuamutef, Jackal = Physical. Associated with the buddhic are the lower emotions (Serquet) ; with the mental, the buddhic emotions (Isis) ; with the astral, the physical activities (Nephthys) ; and with the physical, the pattern forms on the buddhic plane (Neith). The planes are said to "pro-tect" the functionings of the soul upon them. Buddhi conserves the transmutations of the lower qualities (liver and gall-bladder) ; Mind, the appetites and desires (stomach and large intestines) ; Astral, the mechan-ism of the senses (small intestines) ; and Physical, the life of action and experience (lungs and heart). The last sentence of the text expresses that the buddhic plane (Qebhsennuf) may be taken as either below the plane of heaven or above it. In the present cycle buddhi is above the lower nature (earth).

"Says Qebhsennuf, I am thy son, O, Osiris ! I have come that I may be in thy protection. I gather together thy bones, I collect thy limbs, I bring thy heart for thee, I place it for thee upon its seat in thy body. I make thy house to flourish."—BUDGE, *The Mummy*, pp. 198–9.

This text identifies the symbol " Qebhsennuf " with " Isis," who col-lects the " limbs " of Osiris after his death and dismemberment ; signifying that the buddhic functioning (Isis) harmonises and disciplines the qualities (limbs) now evolving in the soul. The placing of the " heart " is the establishing of the causal-body, and so making the soul flourish.

In the published facsimile of the *Papyrus of Ani* (plate 8) is to be seen a most striking emblem of the resurrec-tion of the Self in the human soul. The head of Osiris (the incarnate Self) is seen rising from the chest (lower nature) in which he has been immured. On the chest are pictured the four children of Horus (the four planes) to designate the lower nature in which the Divine Life is involved as the Sacrifice for the redemption of humanity. Osiris is represented as putting forth two forearms, signifying the Divine activity (right arm) and receptivity (left) now manifest in the human being. Each hand holds an *ankh cross*, not held by the handle, as is usual, but by the haft, which signifies the Divine Life subduing the lower qualities (the haft) of man's nature. At each side of the chest stand large figures of the children of Horus, indicating that Osiris comes forth to draw all things to himself. His face is turned to Mestha (mind), signifying that it is through mind the Divine power works for the salvation of the soul.

The children of Horus are often depicted standing upon an open lotus flower whose stem grows from water (Truth-reality) at the base of the throne of Osiris. The lotus indicates the manifestation of nature through buddhi.

Regarded in relation to humanity, the "children of Horus" symbolise the four soul bodies, buddhic (potential), mental, astral, and physical. In the present cycle the causal-body is in place of the buddhic.

"The Maya Indians of Yucatan supposed the firmament to be upheld by four beings whom they designated Bacabs, each of whom stood at one corner of the earth. The names of these were Kan, Muluc, Ix, and Cauac, representing the east, north, west, and south. Their symbolic colours were yellow, white, black and red. They corresponded in some degree to the four variants of the Mexican rain-god Tlaloc, for the races of Central America supposed that rain, the fertiliser of the soil, emanated from the four points of the compass, and may find a parallel in the Egyptian canopic deities."—*Non-classical Mythology*, p. 23.

By the "firmament" is meant the highest plane — atma — above the quaternary. Of the "four beings,"

"Jars containing their effigies held the entrails of the dead in vessels similar to those of the funerary genii of Egypt."—*Ibid.*, p. 84.

"Tlaloc was supposed to inhabit the four cardinal points and every mountain-top."—*Ibid.*, p. 174.

"Tlaloc" is a symbol of the Higher Self, as is "Horus." The "Bacabs" signify the four soul-bodies on the four planes, which bring experience and truth (rain) to the soul.

"From Ymer's skull, the sons of Bor formed the heavens, which they placed over the earth, and set a dwarf at the corner of each of the four quarters. These dwarfs are called East, West, North and South."—*Prose Edda*, MALLET, *North Antiq.*, p. 404.

From the higher nature (skull) of the Archetypal Man (Ymir), the Divine Will and Wisdom (sons of Bor) by evolution made manifest the higher planes (heavens) above the lower planes (earth) in the human soul. The four soul-vehicles (dwarfs) are the means of expression and perception by the ego on the four planes (cardinal points).

See AFU-RĀ, ARC. MAN, BUR, CASTES, CEILING, CHEST, CLASSES, CROSS (aukh), DEATH OF OSIRIS, DISMEMBERMENT, FIRMAMENT, FOUR BEINGS, HEART, IRON PLATE, ISIS, JOB, LADDER, LIMBS, LOTUS, MEMBERS, NEPHTHYS, OSIRIS, PILLARS (four), QEBHSENNUF, QUARTERS, QUETZALCOATL, TCHATCHA, TLALOC, VESTURES, VISCERA

CHILDREN OF THE KINGDOM :—

Symbolic of those minds which have the Word of God and keep it, but do not get beyond the lower interpretations and are not deeply spiritual. The result of having the word, but abiding by the letter is ignorance (outer darkness).

See KINGDOM OF HEAVEN, LITTLE ONES.

CHILDREN OF MEN :—

A symbol of mental qualities through which the wisdom principle, or higher emotion, is realised.

"And the Lord came down to see the city and the tower, which the children of men builded."—GEN. xi. 5.

And the Divine nature responded to the cry from within the soul for knowledge. By devices (city and tower) of the lower mind, through sense of separateness, it is at first conceived that wisdom will be attained. The ideals arising in the mind conjoined to the processes of the lower planes give rise to the "children of men."

See BABEL, LANGUAGE, PARENTS, SPEECH

CHILDREN OF JERUSALEM :—

Similar to "children of the kingdom."

" O, Jerusalem, Jerusalem, which killeth the prophets, . . . how often would I have gathered thy children together, . . . and ye would not ! Behold, your house is left unto you desolate. For I say unto you, Ye shall not see me henceforth, till ye shall say, Blessed is he that cometh in the name of the Lord."—MAT. xxiii. 37.

The Christ's lamentation is directed towards the old dispensation which his new order supersedes ; that is, towards the following of the letter of the Word and killing out the spirit or intuition (prophet). When, therefore, the " city of the Great King" (the soul) is ruled over by the Christ,—i.e. when the intellect is illumined by the spiritual factor,—then, from Above will shine the Light within which brings peace to the soul. Whereas, when such is not the case, the opinions, ideas, and impressions (the children) of the brain-mind, are without guide or adviser. The " children " shall not see the Christ until they can discern good, righteousness, truth, and love, in all things, and so meet the Lord.

See CHRIST'S SECOND COMING, DISPENSATIONS, JERUSALEM, LIGHT, LITTLE ONES, PRIESTS AND ELDERS, PROPHET.

CHIP OF THE SACRIFICIAL STAKE :—

A symbol of the germ of Divine Life —the Higher Self—which is placed on the fourth sub-plane of the astral plane of the soul.

" He inserts a chip of the stake under the rope with, ' Thou art the son of the sky.' For it is doubtless the offspring of that sacrificial Stake."—Sata. Brâh. III. 7, 1, 22.

" Moreover, that chip of the stake is made an ascent to the heavenly world ; there is this girdle rope ; after the rope the chip of the stake ; after the chip of the stake the top-ring ; and from the top-ring one reaches the heavenly world. . . . With that part of the Stake which is dug in, he gains the world of the Fathers; and with what is above the dug-in part up to the girdle rope, he gains the world of men ; and with what is above the rope up to the top-ring, he gains the world of the Gods ; and what space of two or three finger's breadths there is above the top-ring,—the Gods called the ' Blessed,' —their world he therewith gains ; verily, whosoever thus knows this, he becomes one of the same world with the blessed Gods."—Ibid., III. 7, 1, 23–5.

The Supreme places the germ of the Higher Self in the planes below, that it may manifest its nature as the Son of the Highest. For this germ is the seed of the Tree of the Divine Life,— the product of the Self-limitation of God. Verily, the germ of the Divine Life implanted in the soul, raises it upward to the buddhic plane. At first, growth is brought about through the outward activities of the emotions (girdle) ; afterwards the spiritual germ evolves and the personality is perfected ; then the personality unites with the individuality and rises to the buddhic causal-body (top-ring), and so the consciousness rises to the buddhic plane.

By means of the Divine Life working in astro-physical forms, the personality is developed on the astral plane (world of the Fathers). Then the Spirit within adds the lower mind and emotion-nature, and the personality gains the mental plane (world of men). The Spirit becoming active in the mind, gradually perfects the personality, and so the higher planes (world of the Gods) are gained. Then above the causal-body (top-ring) the soul rises to the buddhic plane after passing two or three sub-planes of the higher mind. On the buddhic plane the ego inherits the results of the experiences below. Truly, the soul who through experience of the lower life has attained to the higher, becomes in harmony with the highest ideals on their own plane.

It is said that in cutting down the Tree for the Stake, the first chip is taken as " full of vigour," and this is afterwards thrown into the hole in which the Stake is set up. Signifying that the Tree of the Divine Life becomes the Stake of aspiration, or the Ray from the Supreme which provides the spiritual germ. It is through the energy of the Spirit that all evolution is accomplished.

See DEVAYANA, GIRDLE ROPE, MONAD, PITRIS (lunar), PITRIYANA, QUARTERS, SEED, SKY, STAKE, TOP-RING, TREE OF LIFE.

CHIRON, THE DIVINE CENTAUR, SON OF CRONUS :—

A symbol of the spiritual mind,

the product of time in the course of the evolution of mind and the desire nature, signified by the horse-animal, to which the spiritual nature is subjectively attached, as in the human animal.

See CENTAURS, CHRYSE, CRONUS, SILENUS.

CHRIST :—

Christ, or the Higher Self, is the fundamental principle underlying the idea of personal Godhood ; and is the Divine Life which proceeds forth from the Absolute, as the Son from the Father, to enter the world of manifestation and animate all things. He it is who is the Divine Sacrifice, in that he limits himself within all his creatures. Again, when involution and evolution are accomplished, he leaves the world and departs to the Father, taking with him the results of the soul-process.

Now through that Divine effort of manifestation, all that is expressed and comprised in mineral, vegetal, animal, and human, is lived through in due order in this underworld, whilst the essential Christ, the Lord in heaven, is " seated at the right hand of the Father " ; that is, he lives as the Power Actual proceeding from Power Potential. He comes forth in the World-cycle as Saviour and Judge in innumerable cloaks (forms) as the One Life operating diversely in many sheaths.

Christ is in everything. The forms or sheaths—the outward expressions of potential Spirit—are as the borders of his garment, which he shall cast forth when their purpose is effected, and afterwards he shall reveal his full form and stature to himself, for there ιs not another beside him. The All is no other than the One.

We are rooted and centred in Him. In his sight, or upon the highest level, we, as spiritual egos, are within the outer as he is ; but in our lower consciousness we see things not as they are in reality, but illusively, and so we only behold the diversity and separateness which give rise to our misconceptions of the inner and real significance of our Individuality and of its ultimate re-absorption into the Infinite. It is He, the Inner Self of all beings, who is infinite. Our little personality, being transitory and finite, is but a poor and partial mirroring of his infinity.

It is the immortal Individuality within us which is the immediate manifestation of his unmanifested Self.

He alone is the Way, the Truth, and the Life ; for he is above all, and in all, and more than all. He is the Supreme Ideal set before us to conform to, that we may become like him, and so manifest his nature that is in us.

" You may depend upon it that the laws of all life, vegetable, animal, mental, soulal, and spiritual, are one and the same, though different in degree ; and all derived from one and the same sacrifice of our blessed Lord and Saviour, offered from all eternity ; without which there would have been no life, but a universal death. And you may rest assured, also, that the lower is always typical of the higher ; and that the knowledge of the higher is best ascended into through the progression of the lower. We ought not to wonder, therefore, that the Holy Spirit continually useth the emblems or symbols derived from vegetable and human life— the sowing of the seed and the harvest, the birth of the child, and the full-grown man—to set forth spiritual things withal. And you ought not to say, they are finely chosen similitudes, but, they are rightly appropriated types. And, however much our men of taste and sentiment do laugh at the spiritualisings of our fathers, I dare to believe and to say, that to spiritualise nature is rightly to interpret nature, and that the greater part of our Lord's discourses are nothing but divine exercises of this kind ; and so of His parables also."—ED. IRVING, *Works*, Vol. I. p. 80.

" This Epistle to the Ephesians is penetrated throughout by that idea of living union with Christ, and indwelling in Him. It is expressed in many metaphors. We are rooted in Him as the tree in the soil, which makes it firm and fruitful. We are built into Him as the strong foundations of the temple are bedded in the living rock. We live in Him as the limbs in the body. . . . The indwelling, we say, is reciprocal. He is in us, and we are in Him. He is in us as the source of our Being ; we are in Him as filled with His fullness. He is in us all-communicative ; we are in Him all-receptive. He is in us as the sunlight in the else darkened chamber ; we are in Him as the cold green log cast into the flaming furnace glows through and through with ruddy and transforming heat. He is in us as the sap in the veins of the tree ; we are in Him as the branches. 'As a branch cannot bear fruit of itself, except it abide in the vine, no more can ye except ye abide in me.' "—A. MAC-LAREN, *Sermons, 3rd Series*, pp.. 70–2.

" The Christ is the Divine Man in men,

that through which the power and wealth of God flow into human life. The rise of idealism in the soul is just the emergence of the deeper Christ-nature. Whenever a refusal is made to the things that would gratify the superficial nature for the sake of those things which alone can satisfy the deeper nature, it is the triumph of the Christ in man."—T. RHONDDA WILLIAMS, Serm., *The Great Choice.*

"The law, or principle, of the obligation imposed upon man by a supernatural Ideal. . . . Indeed, *the entire evolution of the race may be considered, from the point of view of the philosophy of religion when surveying the history of this evolution, as arising out of obligations to the Ideal.* And this Ideal which religion in its highest form of thought, feeling, and service, strives to realise, includes the ideals of truth, beauty, and goodness. Thus, religion itself, when most profoundly comprehended, is seen to be of the nature of that command which Jesus uttered to his disciples : ' Be ye therefore perfect even as your Father in Heaven is perfect.' The voice in which all religious doctrine and prophecy is expressed, and to which the soul of man responds by entering upon the ' way of salvation,' is the exhortation : ' Thou shalt so think, act, and be, as to bring into the reality of human life a harmony with the Personal Ideal of perfect truth, beauty, and goodness."—G. T. LADD, *Phil. of Religion,* Vol. I. p. 257.

"The Object of religious belief and worship must ever be regarded as something about whose real Being man must increasingly strive to know."—*Ibid.,* p. 314.

See AVALOKITESVARA, BUDDHA, DAVID, HIGHER AND LOWER SELVES, HOUSE IN HEAVEN, JESUS (son of God), SELF, SON OF GOD.

CHRIST MUST INCREASE, BUT JOHN MUST DECREASE :—

Symbolic of the spiritual nature transcending the moral nature.

"Ye yourselves bear me witness, that I said, I am not the Christ, but that I am sent before him. . . . This my joy therefore is fulfilled. He must increase, but I must decrease."—JOHN iii. 28, 30.

The soul's moralised qualities know in themselves that the moral nature (John) is not the source of Truth, but is a preparation for the influx of spiritual energy from above. The moral nature which is devoted to Truth rejoices in the influx of Love and Wisdom. The Christ must increase or grow to maturity in the soul, while the moral nature must decrease, that is, become absorbed into the Christ nature so that it cannot be dis-

tinguished from it. Love of the Truth and Right transcends Duty and Obedience ; also, Love and Wisdom include Justice and Morals.

"Spiritual life consists mainly in the discovery and exercise of our highest faculties ; and this means joy, joy ever increasing in depth and intensity with every enlargement of our consciousness of power. And I want to tell you that considerations of right and wrong, of meritoriousness and wickedness, are only incidental to this after all, and will ultimately be transcended altogether. . . Morality appears to be an intermediate stage between the un-selfconscious automatism of the lower creation and the full self-knowledge and exuberant spontaneity of the saints in heaven. The lowest forms of life in God's universe know nothing of struggle between right and wrong ; neither do the highest."—R. J. CAMPBELL, Serm., *The Non-moral Aspects of Religion.*

"No one is ever released from law. Those who think the law is abolished have not the Love of Christ formed in them. The law is not abolished, it is fulfilled in Love. He that loveth doeth the will. No one ever transcends righteousness, for the entire work of God toward salvation has been making for the fruits of righteousness. (Henry Nicholas)."—R. M. JONES, *Mystical Religion,* p. 436.

See BAPTISM, HIGHER AND LOWER SELVES, JOHN BAPTIST, ZACHARIAS

CHRISTMAS-TREE :—

A symbol of the Divine Life of the soul, through the efficacy of which the " treasures of wisdom and knowledge " hidden in Christ shall be attained when the consciousness rises to higher levels.

"The Christmas-tree, now so common among us, was equally common in Pagan Rome and Pagan Egypt. In Egypt that tree was the palm-tree ; in Rome it was the fir ; the palm-tree denoting the Pagan Messiah, as Baal-Tamar, the fir referring to him as Baal-Bereth. The mother of Adonis, the Sun-God and great mediatorial divinity, was mystically said to have been changed into a tree, and when in that state to have brought forth her divine son."—A. HISLOP, *The Two Babylons,* p. 97.

The purified lower nature is in unison with the Divine Life (tree) and becomes the mother of the Higher Self (Adonis) born in the soul. It is Christ, the " Tree of life," who dispenses the gifts of the Spirit to all the qualities in harmony with him.

See ADONIS, BIRTH OF JESUS, JESUS (mortal), MITEGURA, SHINTAI, TAMA-

GUSHI, TREASURE, TREE OF LIFE, VINE, YGGDRASIL.

CHRISTOS AND CHRĒSTOS :—

Christos—the "anointed One" is the indwelling Spirit who is Divinely inspired by Love from on High. Chrestos the "perfect One" refers to the perfected lower nature at the end of the cycle.

See ANOINTING, OIL.

CHRIST-PRINCIPLE :—

The Christ-principle is Atma-buddhi energising on the higher mental plane. It can only become related to the activities of the lower planes, as these purify their nature and become free from the desire-principle. When the lower qualities aspire, this affords the opportunity for the Christ to reveal himself under his second aspect—buddhi—which, as wisdom, is then ready to forthpour itself in response to aspiration. In the Christ-principle, therefore, it is the feminine element buddhi that predominates. The heavenly Ma-donna in this sense comes to be the counterpart of the Christ, for the Christ operates through her—the Paraclete.

"The first Adam is of the earth, earthy, and liable to death. The second is 'from heaven,' and triumphant over death. For 'sin has no more dominion over him.' He, therefore, is the product of a soul purified from defilement by matter, and released from subjection to the body. Such a soul is called virgin. And she has for spouse, not matter—for that she has renounced,—but the Divine Spirit which is God. And the man born of this union is in the image of God, and is God made man ; that is, he is Christ, and it is the Christ thus born in every man, who redeems him and endows him with eternal life."—*The Perfect Way*, p. 190.

"For, as cannot be too clearly and forcibly stated, between the man who becomes a Christ, and other men, there is no difference whatever of kind. The difference is alone of condition and degree, and consists in difference of unfoldment of the spiritual nature possessed by all in virtue of their common derivation. 'All things,' as has repeatedly been said, 'are made of the divine Substance.' And Humanity represents a stream which, taking its rise in the outermost and lowest mode of differentiation of that Substance, flows inwards and upwards to the highest, which is God. And the point at which it reaches the celestial, and empties itself into Deity, is 'Christ.' Any doctrine other than this,—any doctrine which makes the Christ of a different and

non-human nature,—is anti-christian and sub-human. And, of such doctrine, the direct effect is to cut off man altogether from access to God, and God from access to man."—*Ibid.*, p. 248.

"In the evolution of God's life in man there are no short cuts, but a gradual unfolding of a principle of interior vitality. And the motto from this thought is, 'Rest in the Lord and wait patiently for Him,' while the child-Christ nature within you 'increases in wisdom and stature, and in favour with God and man.'"—BASIL WILBERFORCE, *Problems*, p. 9.

"God as the Absolute can, in the nature of things, only come into contact with man by a self limitation. . . . In Christ, to begin with, we have a revelation of the Absolute in the limited. In Him, as the Church all along has joyfully confessed, we see God."—J. BRIERLEY, *Studies of the Soul*, p. 258.

See ADAM (higher), BUDDHI, HOLY GHOST, PARACLETE, VIRGIN, WISDOM.

CHRIST'S SECOND COMING :—

A symbol of the completion of the process of purification and development of the souls of humanity, when the lower consciousness rises to union with the higher.

"And then shall they see the Son of man coming in a cloud with power and great glory. But when these things begin to come to pass, look up, and lift up your heads ; because your redemption draweth nigh."—LUKE xxi. 27, 28.

This refers to the consummation of the physical at the end of the cycle. Then as perfection of the soul-state approaches, the indwelling Christ appears in glory within the souls of the saints, or is raised above the condition wherefrom at first his descent was made. The "cloud" signifies a temporary veil which obscures the splendour of the Highest. The "lifting up of heads" refers to the aspiration of the minds, needful so that liberation from the lower nature may be effected.

"Verily I say unto you, This generation shall not pass away, till all things be accomplished."—LUKE xxi. 32.

Christ here points out that each grade of evolution of qualities now existent, shall not be extinguished until the complete process of soul-growth on the lower planes has been carried out.

"Friends, do not mistake the resurrection of Christ. You expect that He shall come in one single person as He did when He came to suffer and die, and thereby to answer the types of Moses' Law. Let me tell you that if you look for Him under the notion of one single man after the flesh, to be your Saviour, you shall never, never taste salvation by him. . . . If you expect or look for the resurrection of Jesus Christ, you must know that the spirit within the flesh is the Jesus Christ, and you must see, feel, and know from Himself His own resurrection within you, if you expect life and peace by Him. For he is the Life of the world, that is, of every particular son and daughter of the Father. For every one hath the Light of the Father within himself, which is the mighty man Christ Jesus. And He is now rising and spreading Himself in these His sons and daughters, and so rising from one to many persons. . . . And this is to be saved by Jesus Christ; for that mighty man of spirit hath taken up His habitation within your body; and your body is His body, and now His spirit is your spirit, and so you are become one with Him and with the Father. This is the faith of Christ, when your flesh is subject to 'the Spirit of Righteousness" (Gerrard Winstanley).— R. M. JONES, *Mystical Religion*, p. 496.

"Now I admit that it is possible to spiritualise the whole conception (of the nature of Christ's second coming), to regard the resurrection and ascension of our Lord as the dramatised representation of a spiritual experience through which every regenerate soul must pass, and the second coming as a spiritual process, a gradual increase of the Christ spirit in the world, culminating in the complete assmilation of every human institution to his ideal."—R. J. CAMPBELL, Serm., *Christ Going and Returning*.

See AAT (waters), AMENI, BUDDHA (Maitreya), CLOUDS OF HEAVEN, CONFLAGRATION, DOORKEEPERS, GENERATION, HAND (right), HEAD, HORSE (white), JUDGMENT DAY, KALKI (avatar), REGNAROK, RENOVATION, RESURRECTION, SON OF MAN, SOSHYANS, SOSIOSH, SOUL (spirit, body), SPRINGTIME, STUDIES OF THE SOUL.

CHRYSA AND DIVINE CILLA :—

Symbolic of Love and Wisdom in the causal-body, constituting the causal-Self.

CHRYSE, PRIEST OF APOLLO :—

A symbol of the spiritual mind, which is at first enslaved by the desire-nature, but afterwards is a prime means of bringing the mind in relation with buddhi, since through its aspirations it becomes attuned to every high emotion, and opposed to the workings of the lower self.

See AARON, ADVARYA, AGNIDHRA, ATHORNE, CHIRON, HIGH PRIEST, HOLLOW SHIPS, ODYSSEUS, PONTIFF, POPE, PRIEST OF APOLLO, TENEDOS.

CHRYSEIS, HIS DAUGHTER :—

A symbol of the intuition of Truth—the buddhic consciousness reflected on the higher mental plane, and bringing true knowledge to the soul.

"Apollo, enraged with the king (Agamemnon) stirred up an evil pestilence through the army, because the son of Atreus had dishonoured the priest Chryse; for he came in the swift ships of the Greeks to ransom his daughter (Chryseis), and bringing invaluable ransoms, having in his hands the fillets of far-darting Apollo on his golden sceptre."—*Iliad*, Bk. I.

The Higher Self working from beneath is the means of causing strife and unbalanced conditions upon the lower planes, whereby the lower qualities are destroyed. Illusion (son of Atreus) has cast a veil over the features of the spiritual mind (Chryse), for illusion overlays the astral impressions which lead to the mind and engage it. The enlightened mind is eventually to be the means of liberating the intuition of Truth; and illusion having thus quickened the lower evolution, the aroused spiritual mind becomes the means of offering up gifts to the Self, that is, through buddhi, "laying up treasures in heaven."

See AGAMEMNON, BRISEIS, CENSERS, INTUITION, KLYTAIMNESTRA, NEHEMĀUT, ODYSSEUS, PRIZE, RANSOM.

CHTHONIE (EARTH) :—

A symbol of the lower nature, or kama-manas—desire-mind. The under-world, or matter.

See EARTH, OPHIONEUS.

CHURCH OF GOD :—

A symbol of the form of thought occupied by the religious consciousness which is a mental emotional state of soul venerative of conceptions of Wisdom, Love and Truth. The Church of the Living God was, is, and ever will be to the end of time, seated in the inner sanctuary of the human soul, or causal-body.

"Christ also loved the church, and gave himself up for it; that he might sanctify it, having cleansed it by the washing of water with the word, that he might present the church to himself a glorious church, not having spot or wrinkle or any such thing; but that it

should be holy and without blemish."—
EPH. v. 25–7.

To bring about the completion of
the evolution of the inner nature
(church) of the soul, the Self, who is
Love, involved himself in the soul's
lower nature. He became incarnate in
order that, being born in the soul, he
might sanctify it, and having purified
it by truth (water), and by the expression of the Divine Life (word), he
might, as the Saviour of the causal-
body (church), complete it in every
respect, so that it should be a glorious
vehicle of the Spirit, pure and perfect,
holy and without blemish.

"The Church is formed out of Christ's
bones and flesh ; and it was for this cause
that the Word, leaving His Father in
heaven, came down to be 'joined to His
wife,' and slept in the trance of His
passion, and willingly suffered death for
her, that He might present the Church to
Himself glorious and blameless, having
cleansed her by the laver (of regeneration),
for the receiving of the spiritual and
blessed seed, which is sown by Him, who
with whispers implants it in the depths of
the mind ; and is conceived and formed
by the Church, as by a woman, so as to
give birth and nourishment to virtue."
—METHODIUS, The Banquet, etc., Ante-
Nic. Lib., p. 28.

"The Lord's church in heaven."—
SWEDENBORG, Apoc. Rev., n. 191.

"Inward sanctity, pure love, disinterested attachment to God and man,
obedience of heart and life, sincere
excellence of character, this is the one
thing needful, this the essential thing in
religion ; and all things else, ministers,
churches, ordinances, places of worship, all
are but means, helps, secondary influences,
and utterly worthless when separated from
this. To imagine that God regards anything but this, that he looks at anything
but the heart, is to dishonour him, to
express a mournful insensibility to his
pure character. Goodness, purity, virtue,
this is the only distinction in God's sight.
This is intrinsically, essentially, everlastingly, and by its own nature, lovely,
beautiful, glorious, divine. It owes nothing
to time, to circumstance, to outward
connections. It shines by its own light.
It is the Sun of the spiritual universe. It
is God himself dwelling in the human soul.
—W. E. CHANNING, The Church.

"See what the religious world really is
in its idea. A world everywhere aware of
and rejoicing in the priority of God,
feeling all power flow out from Him, and
sending all action back to report itself to
Him for judgment,—a world where
goodness means obedience to God, and sin
means disloyalty to God, and progress
means growth in the power to utter God,

and knowledge means the understanding
of God's thought, and happiness means
the peace of God's approval. That is the
only world which is religious."—PHILLIPS
BROOKS, Light of the World, p. 47.

See AGNISHTOMA, ALTAR OF SACRI-
FICE, BISHOP, CONVERSION, EARTH-
QUAKES, HOUSE IN HEAVEN, MANSIONS,
POPE, PYRAMID, RIB, TEMPLE, TABER-
NACLE, WOMAN.

CHURCH OF THE FOUR QUARTERS :—

A symbol of the religious consciousness at the highest level of the quaternary or four lower planes of the soul.

"Church of the four quarters of the
world, those (monks) present and those
absent."—H. OLDENBERG, Buddha, p. 340.

The inner sanctuary of the heart is
in the highest reaches of the lower
consciousness. In that are placed the
ideas which seem to claim the soul's
religious reverence ; and it is said that
the disciplined qualities (monks) and
the higher qualities (absent monks) not
yet attainable, are there to be found.

See HEART, MONK, QUALITIES,
QUARTERS.

CHURCHES IN ASIA, SEVEN :—

Symbolic of seven states of soul
in which the light of Truth is shining
from their higher qualities (candlesticks).

"All states of the reception of the Lord
and of his church are signified by those
seven names, in the spiritual sense."—
SWEDENBORG, Apoc. Rev., n. 41.

"They are, in their primary sense,
various states of the soul which the
Apocalypse describes under the guise of
the Seven Churches of Asia.—The Perfect
Way, p. 238.

See CANDLESTICKS, COLD AND HEAT.

CHURINGA OF AUSTRALIAN TRIBES :—

A symbol of the causal-body which
endures life after life, and to which
the fleeting personalities (alcheringa)
are attached. The symbol is regarded
with great reverence as a thing
affecting the inner being of men and
women.

See CAUSAL-BODY, REINCARNATION.

CHURNING OF THE OCEAN OF MILK, FOR THE RECOVERY OF GODDESS LAKSHMI AND THE LOST TREASURES :—

Symbolic of the process by which
the soul attains to its ideals.

"In the Tortoise incarnation, Vishnu descended to aid in recovering certain valuable articles lost in the deluge. For this purpose he stationed himself as a tortoise at the bottom of the ocean, that his back might serve as a pivot for the mountain Mandara, around which the gods and demons twisted the great serpent Vāsuki. They then stood opposite to each other, and using the snake as a rope, and the mountain as a churning stick, churned the ocean for the recovery of the Amrita or 'nectar,' the goddess Lakshmi, and twelve other sacred things which had been lost in the depths."— Mon. Williams, *Indian Wisdom*, p. 330.

Involution being accomplished, the treasures of wisdom, love, and truth are in *abscondito*, and can only be recovered through a process of evolution. The Higher Self (Vishnu), therefore, has to operate from below through matter, first in evolving simple desires and instincts (plants and herbs) and afterwards in arousing the stronger desires and the mind. The "sea of milk" is the buddhic nature reflected in the astral plane. This is stirred by the desire-mind (the serpent) by means of mental aspiration (mountain), in alliance with the forces of the ideals (gods) and of the desires (demons), which as "opposites" pull in contrary directions and so produce the strife between good and evil, error and truth, which is necessary to bring about development of the lower nature. The Higher Self is, as it were, the pivot of the whole process, the result of which is the recovery of the higher qualities of the soul which were lost at the "fall of man," or descent of mind into the lower nature. First to appear is the intuition (sacred cow) bestowing wisdom (milk) and love (butter) : next comes direct spiritual perception (wine) ; then the perceived universality of the Divine Life (tree of Paradise). To crown all, as the consciousness rises through the buddhic plane, Wisdom herself (Lakshmi), as a "robe of glory," is conferred, while Love the Divine physician (Dhanvantari) holds high the "nectar" of Truth and loving service to ideals, without which sustenance Ideals (the Gods) cannot live.—(See the account from the Puranas given in *Indian Wisdom*, p. 499.)

See Ambrosia, Boar (avatar), Lakshmi, Nectar, Tortoise, Treasure in heaven, Vishnu.

CIRCE, DAUGHTER OF HELIOS :—

A symbol of perfection begotten of the Supreme. When the soul is perfectly free from attachment to the things of desire and sense, then even those qualities that seek perfection (the lovers of Circe) have the appearance of self-seeking desires (swine). As the "purifier of the Argonauts," "Circe" was found on the highest sub-planes of the buddhic plane of the soul.

See Æa, Argo, Ausonia, Pig, Swine.

CIRCLE :—

A symbol of the all-embracing principle of Divine manifestation, perfect and entire, including everything and wanting nothing, without beginning or end, neither first nor last, time-less, sex-less, absolute. The circle denotes the higher planes, the square the lower.

"When he established the heavens I was there : when he set a circle upon the face of the deep."—Prov. viii. 27.

When the Higher nature came forth on the upper planes, and the cycle of manifestation was described in the mentality of the lower nature, the Self was existent.

"What is spoken of (in the text) is the drawing of a limit in that which has no limit, giving bounds to the boundless, marking out the cycle of a cosmic order. In Hindu thought, as perhaps, you know, it is held that Brahm, the nameless, eternal, impersonal reality, without parts or passions, attributes or qualities, gives birth to a universe when Brahma, idea and purpose, arises within it. The emergence of Brahma means the drawing of lines where there were no lines before, the bringing into existence of relations, sequences, phenomena, space and time ; it is as though a Being rose out of a shoreless sea, and taking a pair of compasses, swept a circle around himself ; that circle is the universe. The universe has to run its course, as innumerable universes have done before, till it is reabsorbed in Brahm."—R. J. Campbell, Serm., *The Timeless Affinity*.

See Aditi, Brahma, Cosmos, Creation, Pragâpati, Serpent ananta, Sphere, Year.

CIRCLE OF EXISTENCE :—

A symbol of the passage of the spiritual egos, or monads of life through the cycle of manifestation.

"As Humanity is the crown of the animal kingdom, so is the ' Perfect Man ' the crown of Humanity. It is to this stage of the Perfect Man, who by contemplation and by virtue can enter into the pure thought of the First Intelligence, that all things consciously or unconsciously strive ; for when the soul has reached this point it is ready to pass back into the bosom of that glorious Being whence it issued on its journey ages ago. This journey is called the ' Circle of Existence.' The spark of Divine Light or effluent Being, descends through the Intelligences, the Souls, the Spheres, and the Elements till it reaches Earth which is the lowest point on its downward course ; and this is the ' Outward Track ' or the 'Arc of Descent.'

The upward journey is then begun through the Mineral, the Vegetable, the Brute, and Humanity, till the stage of the Perfect Man is reached, when the Soul passes back into the embrace of the First Intelligence whence it set forth ; and this is the ' Homeward Track,' or the ' Arc of Ascent.' And when it is achieved the journey is accomplished " (Ottoman Sufi's " Doctrine of the Soul ").—GIBB, *History of Ottoman Poetry*, Vol. I. p. 52.

The " Perfect Man " is the Personality perfected at the end of the cycle, and ready to be merged into the Individuality, or in other terms, the lower Self about to become one with the Higher Self (First Intelligence). The spiritual ego (Divine spark) descends through the higher planes, to be embodied on the lower planes (the earth), and from thence begins its upward course from low forms of life to higher. This represents the evolution of the personality until the human stage is reached : then there is a fresh spiritual outpouring and junction with the Individuality is effected. From this point the human personality starts on its long course upwards to the stage of perfection, when the spiritual ego is liberated from the lower nature and is born into the higher. " Ye must be born anew (or from above)."—JOHN iii. 7.

See ABRAXAS, DECANS, EVOLUTION, INVOLUTION, MANVANTARA, REGENERATION, SAMSARA, STRIDES, TUAT, WHEEL, YI SYSTEM, ZODIAC.

CIRCLE AND SQUARE :—

Symbols of the higher nature and the lower nature—the Triad and the Quaternary.

" Sixty-four diagrams which are represented in a circle as emblematical of heaven, because heaven, according to Chinese notions, is round ; and the same number of diagrams, so disposed in a square as to make eight every way, is a similitude of the earth, which, on the principles of the same philosophy, is an immovable square in the centre of the universe, around which the heavens constantly revolve."—KIDD, *China*, p. 306.

The number of the emblematic divisions, $8 \times 8 = 64$, signifies completion of a process which ushers in a new state of manifestation. The lower nature, or physical nature (earth) is the foundation and centre of the evolutionary process which brings forth the higher nature into a new state of actual being. From the point of view of the lower consciousness, the infinite revolves round the finite.

See BOAT OF THE EARTH, CIRCLE, HEAVEN AND EARTH, I A O, QUATERNARY, SQUARE.

CIRCLE OF HAIR BETWEEN THE EYEBROWS OF BUDDHA :—

A symbol of spiritual truth within the higher mind.

See BUDDHA (marks), URNA.

CIRCULAR BOX OR DRUM :—

A symbol of the incarnating cycle of the personalities in the lower life.

"A circular box or drum was placed for Uzumé to dance upon."—*Japanese Legend.*

The cycle of incarnations was entered upon by the soul, in order that the higher emotion nature (Goddess Uzumé) might be evolved and exercised. Then the earth lives were full of the play and conflict of the emotions which sent up vibrations to the buddhic plane, and caused the transmutations of the lower qualities until perfection was reached.

See GILGOOLEM, LAUGHTER (gods), UZUMÉ.

CIRCUMCISION :—

A symbol, ignorantly materialised, of the cutting off of the lower desires.

" The circumcision of the skin is said to be a symbol, indicating that it is proper to cut away all superfluous and extravagant desires, by studying continence and religion."—PHILO JUD., *Works*, Vol. IV. p. 451, Bohn.

"Circumcision, as we are told in 1 PETER iii. 21, represented ' the putting away of the filth of the flesh.' "—A. JUKES, *The Law of the Offerings*, p. 15.

See STIFFNECKED.

CITY OR TOWN :—

A symbol of a centre of activity or functioning, upon the buddhic, mental, and astral planes, to which the qualities (people) are attached, and about which they may congregate.

"A city signifies doctrine, because land, and in particular the land of Canaan, signifies the church in the aggregate."— SWEDENBORG, *Apoc. Rev.*, n. 194.

"And Cain builded a city, and called the name of the city after the name of his son Enoch."—GEN. iv. 17.

The personality (Cain) having acquired the quality aspiration (Enoch), was enabled to form a mental centre (city), and to this fixed point in the mind, aspiration was attached.

See ACROPOLIS, ASSEMBLY, ATTRACTION, CAIN, HUMAN BODY, JESUS WEPT, PILGRIMS, STREETS.

CITY, HOLY :—

A symbol of the soul.

"Then the devil taketh him into the holy city ; and he set him on the pinnacle of the temple."—MAT. iv. 5.

Then within the soul's lower mental centre, puffed up with self-importance and identified with the not-Self (devil), there yet arises an aspiration (pinnacle) and yearning towards the Higher.

See DEVIL, JERUSALEM, JESUS, MOUNTAIN (lower), STONES AND BREAD, TEMPTATION.

CITY OF GOD :—

A symbol of the higher planes of the cosmos, and of the soul, wherein the higher qualities reside.

"There was a city, the dwelling-place of the great saint Kapila."—*Buddha-Karita*, Bk. I. 2.

This "city," "immersed in the sky and clouds," signifies the higher planes of being,—atma-buddhi-manas ; and the "great saint Kapila" is the Supreme Self.

"But ye are come unto Mount Zion, and unto the city of the living God, the heavenly Jerusalem," and to innumerable hosts of angels, to the general assembly and church of the firstborn who are enrolled in heaven, and to God, etc."— HEB. xii. 22–4.

But the qualities being perfected, have risen unto the causal-body (Zion) and unto the atma-buddhic region, the heavenly aim of endeavour, and to the innumerable spiritual influences on the buddhic plane, and to the communion of saints and inner soul-state of those souls (firstborn) who have for the first time commenced to function on the higher planes, and unto the Higher Self as judge of the conditions of all souls and qualities

"The City of God is a beautiful figure of speech wherewith to indicate the goal of our spiritual pilgrimage, the glorious end towards which the purposes of God have been tending since creation began. In a manner of speaking, we do not have to make it ; it exists eternally ; it is the only reality ; it is the source from which all human life has come. It is the full realisation of what humanity eternally is in God. It includes everything that can rightly be thought of as constituting the ideal good." R. J. CAMPBELL, Serm., *The Gates of the City of God*.

See AMARAVATI, ANNU, ERIDU, GOLDEN PALACES, JERUSALEM, KAPILA, MEASURE, SIDES, ZION.

CITY OF PEACE :—

A symbol of a centre of consciousness in Nirvana which is an intermediate state of heavenly rest between periods of objectivity.

See NIRVANA.

CITY SACRED :—

A symbol of the causal centre, or centre of spiritual action in the causal-body on the higher mental plane.

See ACROPOLIS, AKRAGAS, GLORY.

CIVILISING THE PEOPLE :—

A symbol of the establishing of prearranged harmony of the qualities on the buddhic plane, prior to evolution.

"Osiris, being now king of Egypt, applied himself towards civilising his countrymen, by turning them from their former indigent and barbarous course of life ; he moreover taught them how to cultivate and improve the fruits of the earth ; he gave them a body of laws to regulate their conduct by, and instructed them in that reverence which they should pay to the gods. He also travelled over the world inducing all to submit to his discipline ; not compelling them by force of arms, but persuading them to yield to the strength of his reasons, which were conveyed to them in the most agreeable manner in hymns and songs, accompanied by instruments of music."—PLUTARCH, *Isis and Osiris*, § 13.

This symbolism means that the Logos (Osiris) having established the mental plane (Egypt) and other planes and globes on which the evolution of the qualities and the monads or souls (countrymen) should take effect, goes forth from the higher manas—the kingdom of knowledge and experience. For every universe pre-supposes one which precedes, and it is upon the experience which has been gained that a future solar universe is fashioned. The Logos then founds the laws, and prepares the way, by which man and the rest of the cosmic entities shall be produced and be able to proceed with their evolution. The civilising and disciplining of the people through persuasion and reason, and with songs and music, signify the completely concordant means by which the realisation of power will be accomplished. The " music " is the symbol of perfect adaptation of each part to the whole. This forth-pouring of the Logos from the mental plane is a process of spiritual involution proceeding upwards for the creation of the perfect prototypal world which shall direct future evolution on the lower planes. It is to be understood that the period described is that of the preparation of the way of the souls, or the path to perfection, and long prior to the appearance of man in a physical body on the earth.

" During Osiris' absence from his kingdom, Set had no opportunity of making any innovations, Isis being extremely vigilant in her government."— *Ibid.*

Isis (Wisdom) governing in the absence of Osiris implies the potential rather than the actual ordering of things, and signifies the stage when perfect *inner* harmony is established. The strife of opposites, represented by " Set," has no part in this Edenic condition of things.

See GOLDEN AGE, GOVERNMENT, HYMNS, IMAGE, INVOLUTION, ISIS, KINGLY OFFICE, MINISTERS, MUSIC, OANNES, OHONAMOCHI, OSIRIS, PROTOTYPES, RESPECTFUL, YAO.

CLANG OF APOLLO'S SILVER BOW :—

A symbol of the vibrations arising within the soul, in response to the activities of desire and sensation.

" Then Apollo sat down apart from the ships, and sent among them an arrow, and terrible arose the clang of the silver bow." —*Iliad*, Bk. I.

Then the indwelling Self, seated in the lower vehicles of the soul, first of all receives, through the impacts from without, the means for the commencement of its evolution. The " clang " is the thrill of response from within.

See APOLLO, ARROWS, BOW (silver).

CLASSES, FOUR, OF MANKIND, IN THE SCRIPTURES OF EGYPT :—

Symbolic of the four soul-vehicles and their activities on the four lower planes.

" The four great classes into which the Egyptians divided mankind, namely, the Reth, the Nethesu, the Themehu, and the Aamu. Of these the Reth, i.e. the ' men,' *par excellence*, were Egyptians, who came into being from tears which fell from the Eye of Rā. The Themehu, or Libyans were also descended from the eye of Rā. The Aamu were the people of the deserts to the north and east of Egypt, and the Nehesu were the black tribes (negroes)."— BUDGE, *Egypt. Heaven and Hell*, Vol. III. p. 146.

The " Reth " signify the individualities in the causal-bodies, produced from the solar " utchat,"—higher consciousness. The " Themehu " are the personalities in the mental bodies, produced from the lunar utchat,— lower consciousness. The "Aamu" are the desire natures in the astral bodies. And the " Nehesu " are the physical lives in the physical bodies.

" In the abode of Osiris are sixteen gods in mummied forms. The first four are bearded, and wear the *menat* and the *white crown*, and each is described by the title,—' King of the South.' The second four are bearded, and are described as *Heteptiu* ; the third four are bearded, and wear the *menat* and the *red crown*, and each is described by the title *Bat* ; and the fourth four are bearded, and are called *Khu*."—*Ibid.*, Vol. I. p. 118.

The " abode of Osiris " is the hidden causal-body, and all the figures indicate the latent (armless) condition. Now in this sixth division of the cycle (Tuat), when the Archetypal Man (Osiris) is perfected, these four vehicles of the soul exist only potentially ; they are ready to put forth their activities (arms) in the new cycle that will open in the next division. The " Kings of the South " are the individualities on the higher-mind plane (Upper Egypt). The " Kings of the North " are the personalties (Bat) on the lower-mind plane (Lower Egypt). The "Heteptiu" are the astral vehicles, and the "Khus" are the physical forms.

See ARC. MAN, CASTES, CHILDREN OF HORUS, CROWN (Egypt), CROWN (white), EGYPT, KHUS (lower), MENAT, OSIRIS, UTCHAT.

CLASSES, FOUR, OF MANKIND, IN THE SCRIPTURES OF ZOROASTER :—

Symbolic of the four soul-vehicles and their activities on the four lower planes.

"Auharmazd created the religion of omniscience like an immense Tree, of which there are one stem, two branches, three boughs, four twigs, and five shoots. . . . The four twigs are the four classes of the religion, by whom the religion and world are prepared ; which are Priesthood, Warriorship, Husbandry, and Artisanship."—*Sikand-Gumanik Vigar, S. B. of E.*, Vol. XXIV. p. 118.

The Supreme emanated the Divine Life as a process of growth from unity to diversity. The "one stem" is a symbol for the Absolute Source of all. The "two branches" signify Spirit and Matter, and the "three boughs" are the three higher planes,—Atma, Buddhi, and Manas. The "four classes of the religion" signify the four vehicles or bodies, on the four lower planes, concerned with the growth of the spiritual life in the human soul.

"Priesthood" signifies the causal-body with higher mental activities. "Warriorship," the mental-body with lower mental activities. "Husbandry," the desire-body with astral activities. "Artisanship," the flesh-body with physical activities.

The first and highest vehicle is the causal-body (Priesthood) which is the seat of the spiritual emotions in the higher mind. The second is the mental-body (Warriorship) in the lower mind, the arena of conflict between the higher and the lower motives. The third is the desire body (Husbandry) on the astral plane, the plane of cultivation and growth. The fourth is the physical body (Artisanship), on the physical plane, the plane of work, contrivance and adaptation.

"I want to remind you that the body is not the self ; it is the instrument of the self. Our passional instincts are not the self ; they are the instrument of the self. Even the mind is not the self ; it is the instrument of the self. The self is something greater than the body, greater than the feelings, greater than the intellect. The self is the reality at the back of all these, partly hedged in by them, and partly making use of them to utter itself. Consciousness has to rise through them all before it can attain to its own highest, the level of perfect self-realisation, which is perfect love."—R. J. CAMPBELL, Serm., *Evolution of the Spiritual Man.*

See ARTIFICER, CASTES, GATHA DAYS, HOUSE (clan), KSHATRIYA, PRIEST, RULERS (world), SUDRA, TREE OF LIFE, VAISYA.

CLEANSING OF THE TEMPLE BY JESUS :—

A symbol of the purging of the astromental nature by the indwelling spirit of Christ.

"Jesus went up to Jerusalem. And he found in the temple those that sold oxen and sheep and doves, and the changers of money sitting : and he made a scourge of cords, and cast all out of the temple, both the sheep and the oxen ; and he poured out the changers' money, and overthrew their tables ; and to them that sold the doves he said, Take these things hence, &c. —JOHN ii. 13–16.

This allegory represents the assertive activity of the Christ-soul in substituting truth and right for the conflict of low and selfish desires and hypocritical emotions which characterise the worldly mind. The evil conditions are, as it were, cast out of the soul by an influx of better feelings and truer opinions. The "oxen, etc." stand for professed virtues devoid of love and truth. The "merchandise" signifies the appearance of religion and morality as a cloak to greed.

"However, to seek the mystery of the deed in the figure, who are they that sell oxen ? Who are they that sell sheep and doves ? They are they who seek their own in the Church, not the things which are Christ's. . . . Who then are they that sell doves, but they who say, 'We give the Holy Ghost ' ? But why do they say this ? and at what price do they sell ? At the price of honour to themselves. They receive as the price, temporal seats of honour, that they may be seen to be sellers of doves. Let them beware of the scourge of small cords. The 'dove' is not for sale : it is given freely. . . . Well, who sell oxen ? They who have dispensed to us the Holy Scriptures are understood to mean oxen. The apostles were oxen, the prophets were oxen. Whence the apostle says : ' Thou shalt not muzzle the mout of the ox that treadeth out the corn. Doth God take care for oxen ? Or saith He for our sakes ? Yea, for our sakes He saith it : that he who ploweth should plow in hope ; and he that thresheth, in hope of partaking.' (1 Cor. ix. 9, 10.) Those ' oxen,' then, have left us the narration of the Scriptures. For it was not of their own that they dispensed, because they sought the glory of the Lord. . . . These men, however, deceive the people by the very Scriptures, that they may receive honours and praises at their hand, and that men may not turn to the truth. But in that they deceive, by the very Scriptures, the people of whom they seek honours, they do in fact sell oxen : they sell sheep too ; that is the common people themselves. And to whom do they sell them, but to the devil ? . . . These, however, so far as they can, sell oxen and sheep, they sell doves too : let them guard against the scourge of their own sins. But when they suffer some such things for these their iniquities, let them acknowledge that the Lord has made a scourge of small cords, and is admonishing them to change themselves and be no longer traffickers. . . By this zeal of God's house, the Lord cast these men out of the temple. Brethren, let every Christian among the members of Christ be eaten up with zeal of God's house. He who exerts himself to have all that he may happen to see wrong there corrected, desires it to be mended, and does not rest idle." —Augustine, *Gospel of John*, Vol. I. pp. 144–7.

" Tauler points out that as man is meant to be a temple—' a clean, pure house of prayer'—he must first drive out all ' traders,' i.e. all human fancies and imaginations, all delight in the creature and all self-willing thoughts of pleasure, aims at self-gratification, ideas of temporal things. These are the ' traders ' that keep God out of His house."—R. M. Jones, *Mystical Religion*, p. 280.

"Jesus' discipline is applied to the natural temple of the soul in which are found tendencies which are earthly and senseless and dangerous, and things which have the name but not the reality of beauty, and which are driven away by Jesus with his Word plaited out of doctrines of demonstration and rebuke." —Origen, *Comm. on John*, Bk. X. 16.

" Heracleon says that the ascent to Jerusalem signifies the Lord's going up from material things to the spiritual place, which is a likeness of Jerusalem. He considers the temple to be the Holy of Holies, into which none but the High-priest enters, and there, I believe he says, that the spiritual go ; while the court of the temple, where the Levites also enter, is a symbol of those psychical ones who are saved, but outside the Pleroma. Then those who are found in the temple selling oxen and sheep and doves, and the money-changers sitting, he took to represent those who attribute nothing to grace, but regard the entrance of strangers to the temple as a matter of merchandise, and who minister the sacrifices for the worship of God with a view to their own gain and love of money. And the scourge he expounds as an image of the power and energy of the Holy Spirit, driving out by His Breath those who are bad."—*Ibid.*, Bk. X, 19.

See Dove-sellers, Jesus' severity, Mouth-opening, Scourge, Temple.

CLEOPATRA, DAUGHTER OF BOREAS, AND WIFE OF PHINEUS THE BLIND PRINCE :—

A symbol of the discriminative instinct which is the offspring of the higher mind (Boreas), and is allied to the spiritually blind discriminative faculty of the lower mind (Phineus).

See Boreas, Harpies, Phineus.

CLIMBING A MOUNTAIN, EMINENCE, LADDER, OR STEPS :—

A symbol of aspiration towards ideals of truth, wisdom, and love.

See Goat (he), Ladder, Mountain, Staircase, Steps.

CLOAK :—

See Coat.

CLOTHING :—

A symbol of limitations of thought which envelop the ego on the mental plane in forms of truth or error. They consist of ideas, opinions, prejudices, conventions, habits, theories, etc. In a higher sense the symbol stands for spiritual faculties on the buddhic plane, with which the ego may be endowed.

"A man is impious and damned who lets fall a scrap of clothing on a dead body."—*Vendidad*, V.

That is because the clothing corresponds to that which would preserve and perpetuate the personality (corpse) which has to be discarded and not cherished.

" My soul shall be joyful in my God, for he hath clothed me with the garments of salvation, he hath covered me with the robe of righteousness."—Is. lxi. 10.

This refers to the perfected soul united to Christ and endowed with the faculties of Love and Wisdom.

See Coat, Garments, Nakedness Robe, Toga, Wooden.

CLOUD, WHITE :—

A symbol of the buddhic vehicle, the sheath of the Atman.

CLOUDS, A LINE OF :—

A symbol of Truth potential, or of buddhi preparing to outpour truth.

"Homage to you, O ye gods who dwell in the divine clouds, and who are exalted (or holy) by reason of your sceptres."— BUDGE, *Book of the Dead*, p. 146.

Aspiration is directed to the ideals (gods) on the buddhic plane, whose rule exalts the soul.

See KAPILA, YAO.

CLOUDS WHICH DROP RAIN :—

A symbol of the buddhic function which out-pours truth (rain) within the soul.

"I (Lakshmi) reside in that cloud from which the waters of the rain pour down, in that cloud which is adorned with Indra's bow, and in that cloud from which the rays of lightning flash forth."— *Institutes of Vishnu*, XCIX.

The "Goddess Lakshmi" is a symbol of the buddhic principle, hence the symbology of "residence."

"The planet Tistrya was commissioned to raise the water in vapour, collect it in clouds, and let it fall in rain with the aid of the planet Sitavisa. The cloud compellers were highly reverenced" (*Zoroastrian System*.)—J. F. CLARKE, *Ten Rel.*

The Self or spiritual ego (Tistrya) directs and initiates. In this way, the facts or truths which are collected in the lower vehicles are transmuted and passed up through the higher mind, which corresponds to the individual stage of growth,—experience, subjected to limitation, definition (Sitavisa), on to the buddhic plane (clouds); from whence the results (rain) are transferred to the lower planes whereon evolution is being furthered. The "formation of clouds" corresponds with the awakenment of ideals in the mind.

"Bright clouds are the divine truth veiled in appearances of truth, such as the Word is in the letter with those who are in truths; and dark clouds are the divine truth covered with fallacies and confirmed appearances, such as the Word is in the letter with those who are in falses."—SWEDENBORG, *Apoc. Rev.*, n. 24.

See BIFROST, BOW, LAKSHMI, PARGANYA, RAIN, RAINBOW, SOUND, TISTRYA, TLALOC, WEALTH SHOWER.

CLOUDS, DARK AND COLD :—

A symbol of the Higher nature regarded by the lower as obscure and stern.

"Behold the sun, warm and bright on all sides, and whatever is immortal and is bathed in its bright ray; and behold the rain-cloud, dark and cold on all sides." —*Empedocles*, FAIRBANKS, 96.

Observe the Self, loving and wise both above and beneath, and do thou regard all the virtues, and all that endureth, as living within It. And see the manifestation of the One, which being incomprehensible, appears glowering, obscure, and repellent to the lower mind.

See ANGER, JEALOUS' WRATH.

CLOUDS OF HEAVEN, AS MIST :—

A symbol of obscurity to the lower mind, in respect to the higher nature.

"Thereafter shall ye see the Son of man sitting on the right hand of power, and coming in the clouds of heaven."— MAT. xxvi. 64.

At the end of the cycle, when the qualities approach perfection, the indwelling Christ will be perceived in His positive, outgoing, evolutionary energy, yet under temporary veils which must for a time obscure the splendours of the Highest, but which will disperse as soon as the glory and power of the Redeemer are revealed through the rise of consciousness.

"If a soul has many doubts and bewilderments about Christ, and yet knows that there is a Saviour, and that that Saviour's home is in the land of righteousness and truth, then to that land of righteousness and truth that soul will go by any road that it can find, eager to get there, seeking a road, pressing through difficulties, that it may be in the same country with, and somewhere near, its unfound Lord. It may be that the clouds that for us mortals haunt that land of righteousness and truth may long hang so thick and low that living close to Him the soul may still fail to see Him, but some day certainly the fog shall rise, the cloud shall scatter, and in the perfect enlightenment of the other life the soul shall see its Lord, and be thankful for every darkest step that it took towards Him here. . . . And so for you hereafter, Christ in the highest experiences, the purest raptures of this life and the other, Christ in forgiveness, in communion, in fellowship of work, in fellowship of glory; but now Christ in these first steps that lead you towards Him, in the truthfulness and purity and unselfishness and humility, in the struggle to do right, and the sorrow when you have done wrong."—PHILLIPS BROOKS, *Mystery of Iniquity*, p. 150.

See AMENI, CHRIST'S SECOND COMING, HAND (right), ILLUSION, SIGHT, VAPOUR.

CLUB AS A WEAPON :—

A symbol of higher emotion which overcomes and deadens lower emotion, desire, and selfishness.

See HAIR (sidelock), KERESASPA, MOUTH (food), NERYOSANG, SERPENT (svara).

COAT AND CLOAK :—

Symbols of mental coverings or forms of truth or error. Principles of action (changed in "turncoat"); opinions, prejudices, conventions, mental disguises (cloaks).

"And if any man would go to law with thee, and take away thy coat, let him have thy cloke also. And whosoever shall compel thee to go one mile, go with him twain."—MAT. v. 40, 41.

And if any reason or functioning of mind (man) should prove (law) to thee the truth of something and so take away thy error (coat), let the reasoning also take away the outer profession of error (the cloak). And if intelligence (man) compels to a course of action, then fully carry it out.

"This striking exhortation is not a detailed individual precept meant to meet a particular case, but a figurative way of saying that the spiritual man must be content with no half measures in the service of truth. . . . If your fidelity to the ideal costs you the loss of your outer garment of self-protection, do not grudge the sacrifice; let the inner go with it, the coat follow the cloak, if need be. If your labour for God compels you to go one mile because of human ignorance and wrong, go two, if two be required to gain your end. Life is such that no impersonal good is ever gained except at the sacrifice of the personal."—R. J. CAMPBELL, Serm., *The Utmost for the Highest.*

See CLOTHING, GARMENTS.

COCOA-NUTS, OR TREES :—

Symbols of wisdom and love.

"These (Pacific) islanders anciently believed that the two varieties of the unripe cocoa-nut, viz. the reddish and the deep-green, sprang from the two halves of the brain of the god Tuna (= fresh-water eel). They still speak of 'tasting the brains of Tuna.' Red nuts were sacred to Tangaroa, the God of heaven; deep-green nuts to Rongo, the god of nether world."—W. W. GILL, *Jottings from the Pacific,* p. 209.

"Tuna" is a symbol of the incarnate Self who died to save mankind.

"Tasting his brains" has the same meaning as "drinking the blood of Jesus," that is, partaking of the Divine Life which springs up from the Redeemer within. The Life manifests as wisdom and love (red). "Tangaroa" is a symbol of the Logos on the plane of atma; and "Rongo" is a symbol of the Holy Spirit on the buddhic plane; the first represents Love, and the second Wisdom.

"The cocoa-nut is considered (in India) one of the most sacred fruits, and is called Sriphala, or the fruit of Sri, the goddess of prosperity. . . . One of the main causes of the respect paid to it seems to be its resemblance to a human head, and hence it is often used as a type of an actual human sacrifice."—W. CROOKE, *Pop. Rel. of N. India,* p. 106.

"Sri" is a symbol of the buddhic principle, and the fruit is the "fruit of the spirit" (GAL. v. 22). It is through the Divine sacrifice that wisdom and love are available to the evolving souls of humanity.

See BRAINS, EEL-GOD, FISH (great), RONGO, SINA, TANGAROA.

COLCHIS AND THE COLCHIANS :—

Symbols of the buddhic plane and its denizens the buddhic devas. The devas are the high conditions of intelligence which have been the means of the soul's evolution and of the informing of the causal-body.

See ÆETES, ANGELS, DEVAS, GANDHARVAS, HEAVENLY NYMPHS, SIRENS.

COLD AND HEAT :—

Symbols of opposite qualities such as evil and good, hate and love, inertia and activity, matter and spirit.

"I know thy works, that thou art neither cold nor hot : I would thou wert cold or hot. So because thou art lukewarm, and neither hot nor cold, I will spew thee out of my mouth."—REV. iii. 15, 16.

The Holy Spirit examines a state of the inner soul (church) and finds it sluggish and self-opinionated, neither evil nor good. So it must be roused, and the negative condition expelled.

See CHURCHES OF ASIA, CONTRACTION, HEAT AND COLD, OPPOSITES, PROPHETS (false), TAMAS.

COLOUR, AND BLACK AND WHITE :—

Symbolic of the different qualities

within the soul, and their various aspects.

"Colour is intended for qualities, differences, etc."—Max Müller, *S. B. of E.*, Vol. XV. p. 249.

"And since these thing are so, it is necessary to think that in all the objects that are compound, there existed many things of all sorts and germs of all objects, having all sorts of forms and colours and tastes."—*Anaxagoras*, Fairbanks, 3.

And as the universe is so appointed (of Spirit and Matter), it is logical to accept the thesis that in all nature heterogeneity exists potentially. There was infinite diversity, in that, with the material was involved the spiritual, and within the spiritual lay the ideal forms (archetypal) of all objects that were to exist, and these were to be replete in "form, colour, and taste," that is, as regards their astral, mental and physical contributions to requirement.

"The tissues of the life to be we weave with colours all our own, and in the fields of destiny we reap as we have sown."—R. J. Campbell, *The New Theology*, p. 216.

"Some years ago in going through an exhibition of art and industry, I was taken to a place where a fabric of many colours was being woven by skilled workers. Each worker had a separate colour to insert in the piece, and I noted to my surprise that they were all seated on the wrong side of the frame in which the fabric was fixed, so that they could not see what they were producing, and they actually had a wrong-side pattern given them to work from ; the pattern, as each operator held it in his or her hand, was quite different from, and utterly inadequate as a representation of, what was appearing on the further side. Every movement on the hitherside was producing something much better and more beautiful on the other, the completed whole of which was a harmony of colour. We are all like those pattern-weavers. We are weaving on the wrong side of the fabric, and our best earthly efforts are other than they seem, and are producing a diviner result than this world shall ever see. God grant us all to weave faithfully according to such pattern as we have, that the glory of the fullest revelation may be ours."—R. J. Campbell, Serm., *Life's Delusions.*

See Creation, Kapila, Prototypes.

COLOURS :—

Specific meanings of some colours—
Rose-red—Love.
Red—Ambition and Power—correspond to Mars.

Scarlet—Energy, life (blood).
Yellow—Kingship.
Green—Astral growth.
Blue—Intellect.
Purple—Wisdom.
White—Purity, Perfection.
Black—Ignorance, or the Potential.

See respective colours, Ephod, Zeus.

COLUMN, OR PILLAR :—

A symbol of aspiration towards the higher.

"The king of the land at Byblos seeing the Erica tree, had it cut down, and set up as a pillar of his palace, not suspecting that within it was the chest (in which lay the body of Osiris)."—Plutarch, *Isis and Osiris*, § 15.

Now it is that the Ego becomes alive to some of its faults, and so directs that the evil shall be done away with, not beholding in the evil the means whereby its power is arrived at. The "Erica tree" is a symbol of doubt and difficulty which imply inverted confidence and faith,—or scepticism,—upon which reposes the palace of Truth. The "pillar" stands for both scepticism and aspiration : the one is the result of the other. Scepticism as a state of the mind is only the doubt which is begotten of a distrust of some form of thought, and this doubt answers to an unconscious awakenment within.

See Byblos, Chest, Death of osiris, Fire of hell, Obelisk, Pillar

COMB, MANY-TOOTHED :—

A symbol of knowledge with its many ideas, wherewith to aid evolution.

"Izanagi went after Izanami into the land of Yomi. Izanami said to him,—'Why is thy coming so late ? I have already eaten of the cooking-furnace of Yomi. But I am about to lie down to rest. Do not thou look at me.' Izanagi did not give ear to her, but secretly took his many-toothed comb, and breaking off its end-tooth made of it a torch and looked at her. Her body was. already putrid, maggots swarmed over it, and the eight thunder gods had been generated in her various members. Izanagi, greatly shocked, exclaimed,—'What a hideous and polluted land I have come to unawares !' So he speedily ran away."—*The Kojiki.*

To understand this, it is necessary to remember that the lower planes

(Yomi) are a distorted, because incomplete, reflection of the higher, also that the astral plane is produced by, and in intimate relation with, the principle of buddhi (Izanami). Hence the symbol of the decomposed body of the higher nature is to signify the state of evil and ignorance which is to be found in nature. The soul had partaken of the lower nourishment of desire and sensation, and therefore was bound by karmic law to go through with the world-process. It objects to the spiritual urgings from within. Then the Self (Izanagi) made use of knowledge and experience, and brought the light of reason (end-tooth) to show the deficiencies of the lower nature and the many passions generated in it. The Spirit then, as it were, retires within, and is no longer perceived directly by the consciousness.

See DANIEL, DWARFS, EATING, EYE, IZANAGI, MEADOW, MEDUSA, PERSEPHONE, YOMI.

" COME INTO THEE," OR " COME UP HITHER " :—

A symbol of the final abandonment of the lower nature, in the rise of consciousness and perception.

"Consummation ! I have come into Thee (O Goddess). My heart watches, and my head is crowned with its own white crown. I traverse the zenith."—BLACKDEN, *Book of the Dead*, Ch. CX.

Consummation of the lower life and final liberation are reached. The emotion principle articulates the whispers of the Spirit, and the higher mind attains the summit of its efficacy. The Self rises to the zenith of its powers and in its true nature it exhibits its divine functions.

"'Come up hither' (REV. iv. 1) signifies divine influx, and thence an elevation of the mind, followed by manifest perception."—SWEDENBORG, *Apoc. Rev.*, n. 226.

See CONSUMMATION, CROWN (white), GODDESS, HEART, SELF, ZENITH.

COMETS :—

These are symbols of elemental disruptive forces at the close of a manvantara. They are liberated primarily on the mental plane, and produce feelings of unrest and disquietude which are reflected upon the astral and physical planes, and precede physical dissolution. The

mind and will are able to control them until the decree of the Absolute is to be fulfilled.

See AAT (waters), CONFLAGRATION, KALKI, RENOVATION.

COMING FORTH BY DAY :—

A symbol of the forth-pouring of the Divine Life at the beginning of the process of evolution. This "coming forth " is preceded by the "going in," which is the process of involution of Spirit or Life into matter, during the first half of the great cycle, i.e. the first six divisions of the Tuat or Zodiac. The symbol may also apply to the soul's coming forth for reincarnation.

See EVOLUTION, GOING IN, I A O, INVOLUTION, MANIFESTATION, TOMB, TUAT, ZODIAC.

COMPANY OF THE GODS, OR THE GODS OF HEAVEN :—

A symbol of the activities on the higher planes ; or the Divine attributes, that is, the ideals and highest qualities within the soul, harmoniously co-ordinated on the buddhic plane, and expressing the will of the Supreme.

"We maintain that God's attributes are intelligible and that we can conceive as truly of his goodness and justice, as of these qualities in men. In fact, these qualities are essentially the same in God and man, though differing in degree, in purity, and in extent of operation. We know not, and we cannot conceive of any other justice and goodness, than we learn from our own nature ; and if God have not these, he is altogether unknown to us as a moral being ; he offers nothing for esteem and love to rest upon."—W. E. CHANNING, *Against Calvinism*.

See AMSHASPANDS, DEVAS, GODS, GUARDIANS, HAST, HEROIC, I AM, NUBIA, QUALITIES (higher), TEM, WHEAT AND BARLEY.

COMPARTMENTS OR DIVISIONS OF THE TUAT :—

Symbolic of twelve periods or stages of the manvantara or great Cycle of Life. They correspond with the twelve "tribes," "disciples," and "signs" of the Zodiac. They are, as it were, sections of a spiral through which Life progresses in the order of time.

See ÆON (thirteenth), DISCIPLES, MANVANTARA, TRIBES (twelve), TUAT, TWELVE, ZODIAC.

CONCENTRATION OF MENTAL EFFORT :—

This signifies fixity of aim and purpose brought about through the steadying of the mind when stilled from the surgings of sensation, desire, and passion.

See STORM OF WIND, WAVES.

CONCEPTION OF THE DIVINE GERM :—

Symbolic of the energising of the Self within, when the moral nature is perfectly established in the soul.

See BIRTH OF JESUS, BODHISATVA, GLORY (divine), SEED, VIRGIN MARY, ZACHARIAS

CONCEPTION, IMMACULATE, OF THE BLESSED VIRGIN MARY :—

A symbol of the spiritual (buddhic) origin of the purified lower nature which bears and brings forth the Christ in the human soul.

"The Immaculate Conception of Mary concerns the generation of the soul, presenting her as begotten in the womb of matter, and by means of matter brought into the world, and yet not of matter, but from the first moment of her being, pure and incorrupt. Otherwise she could not be 'Mother of God.' In her bosom, as Nucleus, is conceived the bright and holy Light, the Nucleolus, which—without participation of matter—germinates in her and manifests itself as the express image of the Eternal and Ineffable Selfhood."—The Perfect Way, p. 142.

See ASSUMPTION, BIRTH OF JESUS, DEVAKI, GLORY (divine), MĀYĀ (higher), VIRGIN MARY.

CONCEPTION OF CHILDREN :—

Symbolic of the formation in the mind of new ideas and generalisations, produced by thought and emotion.

"Unto the woman he said, I will greatly multiply thy sorrow and thy conception ; in sorrow thou shalt bring forth children ; and thy desire shall be to thy husband, and he shall rule over thee."—GEN. iii. 16.

To the emotion-nature it is imparted that difficulty and distress shall attend the formulation of fresh ideas, and the realisation of Divine wisdom. All the future evolution of the soul shall be through sorrow ; and the ideas begotten of experience (i.e. through the functioning of the mind) shall be realised with pain. The emotion-nature

shall be beholden to the mind, that is, shall be subservient to knowledge : and intellect shall dominate the love-principle, or emotion-nature.

"By 'conception' is signified all thought. By the 'sons whom she would bring forth in sorrow' are signified the truths which she would thus produce."—SWEDENBORG, Arc. Cel. to Gen. iii. 16.

See CHILDREN OF MEN, CONQUEROR, EVE, HUSBAND AND WIFE, MARRIAGE, MULTIPLY, WIFE, WOMAN.

CONCH, OR SHELL-TRUMPET :—

A symbol of spiritual and also natural means of development, rendered active (sounded) during the outpouring of the Divine Life.

"I (Lakshmi) reside in the sound of repeating the Veda, in the flourish of the shell (trumpet), in the sacrificial exclamations addressed to the gods and to the manes, and in the sound of musical instruments."—Inst. of Vishnu, XCIX. 15.

Buddhi (Lakshmi) is to be found in the manifestation of the laws of the Supreme, in the higher and lower means of progress, in the efforts and aspirations towards the ideals (gods) and the Spirit within, and in the harmony which wisdom brings about.

"That tumultuous uproar of conches rent the hearts of the sons of Dhritarashtra filling the earth and sky with sound."—Bhagavad-Gita. I. 19.

The strength of the progressive activities in the lower and higher natures is said to pierce the "heart" of the desires (Kurus).

See DHRITARASHTRA, KURUS, LAKSHMI, MUSIC, VEDA.

CONDITIONED FINITE :—

This state of being is the symbol and evidence of the unconditioned and infinite. Without the latter the former could not be. The conditioned finite in its highest state is God-manifest, or the Higher Self. The unconditioned infinite is God-Absolute, the Source of all.

"To all eternity God is what He is and never can be other ; but it will take Him to all eternity to live out all that He is. In order to manifest even to Himself the possibilities of His being God must limit that being. There is no other way in which the fullest self-realisation can be attained. Thus we get two modes of God—the infinite, perfect, unconditioned, primordial being ; and the finite, imperfect, conditioned, and limited being of which we are ourselves expressions. And yet these two are one, and the former is the guarantee that the latter shall not fail in the purpose for which it became limited. Thus to the question, Why a finite universe ? I should answer, Because God wants to express what He is."—R. J. CAMPBELL, *The New Theology*, p. 23.

See ABSOLUTE, GOD, GODHEAD.

CONE, CUPOLA, OR SPIRE :—

A symbol of aspiration, as of matter tending towards spirit.

"Stupas are buildings in the form of cones and cupolas, erected by the piety of believers to enshrine and cover relics. They are found throughout India."—J. B. ST. HILAIRE, *The Buddha*, p. 87.

Stupas and pyramids may be taken as symbols of the causal-body built up through aspiration, sacrifice, and transmutation. The "relics" seem to stand for the higher qualities which have survived from the practice of virtues below.

See PYRAMID, SHRINE, SPIRE, STUPA.

CONFLAGRATION, GENERAL :—

The physical element transmuted by "fire" (buddhic) which thereby signifies its dissolution at the close of a cycle. Astral dissolution follows physical dissolution.

"And death and Hades were cast into the lake of fire. This is the second death, even the lake of fire. And if any was not found written in the book of life, he was cast into the lake of fire."—REV. xx. 14,15.

The first death is the death of the physical vehicles ; the second death is the death of the astro-mental (Hades) vehicles, and the "lake of fire" stands for transmutation and dissolution. If any mental quality was not perfected it was transmuted and its lower nature dissolved.

"The reality of all things even in this visible world is God, and thus the final issue must be upward, until everything ends in Him as it began in Him. 'This is the end of all things visible and invisible, when all visible things pass into the intellectual, and the intellectual into God, by a marvellous and unspeakable union.' 'Everything that is shall return into God as air into light. For God shall be all things in all things, when there shall be nothing but God alone.' (Erigena). As evil is a negation, an unreality, it has no place or being in the final consummation." R. M. JONES, *Mystical Religion*, p. 126.

"The only real is the spiritual, the physical is the unsubstantial, and when the time comes for the seeming duality to end, it can only be by the spiritual transmuting the physical into itself,

swallowing it up, as it were, in that which can never know corruption and decay."—R. J. CAMPBELL, Serm., *The Fact of Death*.

See AAT (waters), CHARIOT (sun), CHRIST'S SECOND COMING, FIRE (destroying), HORSE (white), JUDGMENT DAY, KALKI AVATAR, REGNAROK, RENOVATION, RESURRECTION, SOSIOSH.

CONFLICT AND VICTORY :—

Symbolic of the dual aspect which underlies the triumph over evil. On the one side there is Conflict, on the other side there is Victory, which implies union with God.

"In order that a spiritual being may achieve anything worthy to be called great, and in so doing reveal the latent grandeurs of his own nature, it is requisite that he should not know while the work is proceeding the full truth about the beginning and the end thereof. To know would be to render effort negatory and attainment meaningless ; it is just because he does not know, save what is necessary for the purpose in view, that the result becomes glorious. . . . The soul-stuff belongs to that which is above both time and sense, beyond the conflict of good and evil. God, the infinite life in whom we live, and move, and have our being, has placed us here that we may know by not knowing, learn through limitation, declare the truth by seeking it."—R. J. CAMPBELL, Serm., *Not Knowing*.

See BATTLE, BLACKSMITHS, CONQUEROR, MAB, MENIS, STRIFE, VICTORY, WAR.

CONFUCIUS :—

A symbol of the Higher Self active on the mental plane of the soul.

"Chung-ne (Confucius) handed down the doctrines of Yaou and Shun, as if they had been his ancestors. Above, he harmonised with the times of heaven, and below, he was conformed to the water and land. He may be compared to heaven and earth, in their supporting and containing, their overshadowing and curtaining, all things. He may be compared to the four seasons in their alternating progress, and to the sun and moon in their successive shining" (Doctrine of the Mean).—J. LEGGE, *Teachings of Confucius*, p. 315.

The Self on the plane of mind inherited, as it were, the powers and qualities of the Self on the planes of atma and buddhi Above, he conformed to the laws of the higher planes ; and below he was reflected in the activities of the astral and physical planes. For in him were all things created upon the higher and lower planes. By him the soul progresses through the periods of the cycle. He is the Divine Life in the successive changes of the individuality and the personality.

See BIRTH OF CONFUCIUS, EARTH, FILIAL PIETY, HEAVEN, MOON, SEASONS, SUN.

CONFUSION OF SPEECH; BABEL :—

A symbol of the disharmony which arises through the expression of mind and desire, in the evolving soul.

"Go to, let us go down, and there confound their language, that they may not understand one another's speech."—GEN. xi. 7.

The Divine Life therefore descends, since it is a means of causing disagreement and disharmony in the qualities of the lower nature, a necessary condition and state of soul which precedes a craving for higher things. The confusion is evidenced in the irregular character of the alliance of mind with emotion or desire. Its expression (speech) is a natural unbalanced result which the mind produces when coming under the sway of the emotions. Neither *manas* alone, nor *kama* alone, can produce confusion. It is as each struggles with the other that confusion results.

See BABEL, KAMA, LANGUAGE, SPEECH.

CONGREGATION OF PEOPLE :—

A symbol of an assemblage of mental qualities.

See CENSERS.

CONJUNCTION, SECOND FORTUNATE :—

A symbol of the second initiation of the Individuality. It is initiation on the mental plane, and corresponds to complete mastery of the astral vehicle.

See FORTUNATE, INITIATIONS, WALKS.

CONQUEROR :—

A symbol of the Higher Self triumphant over the soul's lower nature. The Spirit of Truth gives the death-blow to illusion and ignorance.

"The 'celestial man' is engaged in no combat; and in case he is assaulted by evils and falses, he despiseth them, and is therefore called a conqueror : he hath no apparent restraints by which he is tied, but is free."—SWEDENBORG, *Arc. Cel. to Gen.* ii.

"New light can only be got by a fight against darkness. The soul cannot be revolutionised except through battle. The elements of a new life can only be assimilated through resistance. Otherwise they would not be your own. They are woven with the fibres of the soul by daily struggle. Without struggle they would be mere surface things, which a breath of temptation would blow away. The darkness does not vanish all at once, nor the light flash upon us. But when in our contest with the gloom and in our patient feeling after God, there comes first a faint glimmering of the truth which we shall possess, we rejoice and make it our own, and go on in its strength."—STOPFORD A. BROOKE, *Serm., Lord, Increase Our Faith.*

"The kingdom of Christ advances by warfare as well as by growth. Every step of the road, you have to cut your way through opposing foes. Every step of the road is won by a tussle and a strife. There is no spiritual life without dying, there is no spiritual growth without putting off 'the old man with his affections and lusts.' The hands cannot move freely until the bonds be broken. If we fancy that we are to get to heaven by a process of persistent growth, without painful self-sacrifice and martyrdom, we know nothing about it. For every progress in knowledge there must have been a sacrifice and martyrdom of our own indolence, of our own pride, of our own blindness of heart, of our own perverseness of will. . . . For every progress in strenuous work for God, there must have been a slaying of the selfishness which urges us to work in our own strength and for our own sake."—A. MACLAREN, *Sermons, 1st Series,* pp. 255–6.

"'I buffet my body and bring it into subjection.' He subdues himself, conquers the animal man through the grace of God in Christ in order to produce the spiritual man perfectly conformed to the likeness of his Lord."—R. J. CAMPBELL, *Serm., Warfare of Life.*

See BATTLE, CONFLICT, HORSE, (white), LIBERATION, MAB, PILLAR (temple), SALVATION, SPENDYAD, STRIFE, TANGAROA, VICTORY, WAR.

CONSCIENCE :—

The Divine judgment on problems of action formulated by the mind.

"And Agamemnon's dark heart was filled with great anger, and his eyes were like flashing fire. To Kalchas first spake he with look of ill : 'Thou seer of evil, never yet hast thou told me the thing that is pleasant. Evil is ever the joy of thy heart to prophesy, but never yet didst thou tell any good matter nor bring it to pass."—*Iliad*, Bk. I.

And forthwith the desire-mind is greatly perturbed by the reflections of the inner memory (Kalchas). And this reacts upon the lusts and desires of the lower self, which thereby become intensified, and cause the lower self to experience the sense of unsatisfied desire which proceeds from the dawn of the higher consciousness within the soul.   The conscience decides that certain things are evil, and this being distasteful to the desire-mind, the sense of rebellion is stirred.   The desire-mind realises that the higher mind always foresees evil, since indeed it is through the apprehension of folly that wisdom is awakened. And never was the higher nature stirred, save through the unwisdom and inexperience which the Self is called forth to combat. How, unless the desire-mind opposes the higher nature or inclination contends against conscience, shall the process of spiritual evolution be brought about ?

"The voice of conscience tells us we ought to choose and follow the higher whenever desire comes into conflict with what we have learned to call duty. We cannot escape the struggle ; indeed, we are here on earth that we may realise our divinity by means of that struggle ; it is the very reason why there is an earthly life at all."—R. J. CAMPBELL, Serm., *Our Eternal Glory*.

" The claiming for a man of a conscience is not only to make him a responsible moral agent ; it is, there and then, to endow him with the right of private judgment, to postulate the capacity on his part to agree with or dissent from certain received opinions ; in short, to confer upon him the express privilege of deciding for himself *in the light of some higher law or experience*. . . . In contending for a man's *conscience*, religion has done nothing less than sanctify the rational nature in man. To acknowledge such a thing as a conscience is not only to claim for a man inner freedom,—the substitution of constraint from within, for coercion from without : it is an implicit avowal of Humanism."—R. DIMSDALE STOCKER, *Social Idealism*, p. 119.

See AGAMEMNON, HECATOMB, HIDING, KALCHAS, NOD OF ZEUS, VOICE OF GOD.

CONSCIOUSNESS :—

The passive aspect of Spirit on the mental plane—it is immortal and eternal.

In manifestation, consciousness becomes dual—higher and lower. As consciousness descends into matter from the higher mental plane, on the one hand, so it rises on the other. Hence, as the physical matter becomes replete with qualities, and fully informed and operated upon from above ; contemporaneously with this activity in matter, there takes place the highest expression of the Divine consciousness from the highest plane —atma.

The dual consciousnesses are aspects of that which appears to be continually striving together in itself. All manifestation involves this apparent conflict and recognition of contraries. It is, however, as the contraries are perceived to be not in reality opposites to each other, but mutually helpful of the good and the true, that the reign of the Higher consciousness (Christ) may be said to begin. This is possible only as the Divine Life within ourselves overcomes the forms, and conquers the planes whereon the sheaths of consciousness are employed.

The Higher consciousness is all in all when the functioning upon all planes is completed, and this stage practically implies the union of the lower and higher on the upper mental plane, when the twain, male and female (manas and buddhi) are no longer severed, but are one. This is the " sacred marriage " in all scriptures.

The lower, or separated, consciousness is in a sense illusory, since it answers to the partial realisation only of the nature of the Self. The consciousness itself is one, but in the forms it appears as many. The apparent breaks are due to the illusory limits of the forms.

The divergence of consciousness is to be understood in this way :—that there is, through the constitution of the mechanism of the Self (Higher Self and Māyāvic Self), an alternation in the action of the Self upon the planes—higher and lower—of its being. The energised mechanism appropriate to each plane tends to follow the line of least resistance through its own inherent capability of responding to those stimuli which enable it to exercise its functions on the respective planes.

" I build my belief in immortality on the conviction that the fundamental reality of the universe is consciousness, and that no consciousness can ever be extinguished for it belongs to the whole, and must be fulfilled in the whole. The one unthinkable supposition from this point of view is that any kind of being which has ever become aware of itself, that is, has ever contained a ray of the eternal consciousness, can perish."—R. J. CAMPBELL, *The New Theology*, p. 230.

" Our self-consciousness at any time is but a poor, limited expression of what we really are, and if we could get down far enough into the sub-conscious depths of our being, we should find ourselves one with all the rest of existence, and with God who is the ground thereof."—R. J. CAMPBELL, Serm., *The Self and the Body*.

See GLORY, HIGHER AND LOWER, ICHOR, INITIATIONS, LIGHT, MARRIAGE, MÂYÂ, OPPOSITES, SELF, SEPARATION, SPIRIT, UNION.

CONSCIOUSNESS, VINNĀNA :—

A symbol of the individuality, or of the causal-body, the seat of the individuality.

" If consciouness, Ananda, did not enter into the womb, would name and corporeal form arise in the womb ?—No, sire."

If individuality did not manifest on the lower planes, would personality and its constructed higher (causal) body be produced and developed ?—No.

"And if consciousness, Ananda, after it has entered into the womb, were again to leave its place, would name and corporeal form be born into this life ?—No, sire."

And if individuality manifested only on its own plane, and withdrew, would personality and its higher body be produced in the cycle of the lower life ? No.

"And if consciousness, Ananda, were again lost to the boy or to the girl, while they were yet small, would name and corporeal form attain growth, increase, progress ?—No, sire " (*Mahânidâna sutta*). —H. OLDENBERG, *Buddha*, p. 228.

And if individuality withdrew while the mind (boy) and the emotions (girl) were yet immature, would personality and its higher body develop and attain perfection ?—No.

"Consciousness must be in order that there may be name and material form ; from consciousness come name and material form. Whence comes consciousness ?—Name and material form must be, in order that there may be consciousness ; from name and material form comes consciousness. . . . consciousness conversely depends on name and material form : the chain goes no farther."—*Ibid.*, p. 230.

This statement is to bring out the fact that the potential archetypal individuality emanates the personality which in its turn builds up the actual individuality which succeeds it, and unites with it. There must be individuality in order that personality and its higher form should exist : and there also must be personality in order that its higher form should be developed into the individuality.

"As two bundles of sticks leaning against each other stand, so also consciousness grows out of name and material form, and name and material form out of consciousness."—*Ibid.*

See FORM AND NAME, IGNORANCE, NAME, NIRVANA, SAMSKARA, SKANDHAS.

CONSECRATION OR DÎKSHÂ :—

A symbol of the perfecting of the soul, and so setting it apart for a rise in consciousness.

" They choose a place of worship. Let them choose the place which lies highest ; for it was from thence that the gods ascended to heaven, and he who is consecrated indeed ascends to the gods. . . . He who is consecrated, truly draws nigh to the gods, and becomes one of the deities. Now the gods are secreted from men."—*Sata. Brâh.*, III. 1, 1, 1–8.

The laws of the higher nature determine the course that the souls shall pursue. The highest place in the mind is the nearest to heaven, and when this highest is perfected, the soul rises to the state of the buddhic qualities (gods) and becomes one with them. In the lower nature, the higher qualities are hidden, or unmanifest to the lower mind.

" I (Lakshmi) reside in the consecration of a king."—*Inst. Vishnu*, XCIX. 16.

Wisdom (Lakshmi) "maketh the Son, who is consecrated (or perfected) for evermore."—HEB. vii. 28.

See GODS, HEAVEN, KING, LAKSHMI, LIBERATION, RE-BIRTH, REGENERATION.

CONSTELLATION PUSHYA :—

A symbol of the forces which are focussed upon the astral sub-planes in order to subserve the formation of the soul.

CONSTELLATION OF THE SEVEN RISHIS :—

A symbol referring to the seven

planes, or the seven root-races of humanity.

See RACES, RISHES, ROOT-RACES, ROUNDS.

CONSTELLATIONS, OR ASTERISMS :—

Groups of stars (mental faculties) which stand for the various mental states and experiences of the souls.

" In the present universe divine wisdom is, as it were, codified in the constellations. The stars are called in Babylonian, ' writing of the heavens.' The moving stars of the zodiac in their constellations are especially interpreters of the divine will. . . . In the Babylonian religion the symbols of the gods are the same as those of the constellations."— A. JEREMIAS, Old Test., etc., Vol. I. p. 49.

See DRAGON (red) STARS (fixed), ZODIAC.

CONSULTING AN ORACLE :—

A symbol of meditation, or communing with the inner nature.

See GOLDEN FLEECE, ORACLE.

CONSUMMATION :—

A symbol of attainment of the object of life, in the rise of consciousness above the lower nature.

See COME INTO THEE, HAST, MARRIAGE, UNION.

CONTENTION, BLOODY ; AND HARMONY OF SEDATE FACE :—

Symbols of conditions in the soul of strife and peace.

See BATTLE, CONFLICT, HARMONY, PEACE AND SWORD, STRIFE.

CONTRACTION AND EXPANSION :—

Contraction and holding is a symbol of matter. Expansion and allowing of escape is a symbol of spirit. Hence, heat and cold, or fire and frost, are symbols of spirit and matter.

See COLD, FIRE, FROST, HEAT, ICE, MATTER, SPIRIT.

CONVERSION :—

A symbol of a change in an upward direction of the ruling energies in the personality.

" Except ye be converted and become as little children, ye shall not enter the kingdom of heaven."—MAT. xviii. 3.

The conversion signifies a change of purpose towards ideals : a rising from lower to higher views of life. Distaste for the lower is effected through contrasting the lower with an object of a higher character, and turning attention to the latter.

See CONVICTION, KINGDOM OF HEAVEN, LITTLE ONES.

CONVERSION OF ST. PAUL :—

A symbol of the soul's turning away from tradition, formalism, and the letter of Scripture, to the recognition and acceptance of the teaching of the Holy Spirit, who cries to the ego from within.

" For ye have heard of my manner of life in time past in the Jews' religion, how that beyond measure I persecuted the church of God, and made havock of it."—GAL. i. 13.

In the inner sense only did " Paul " persecute. This account has a universal application, and refers to the extinguishing of the Spirit through cherishing the letter. The " church of God," which is the inner sanctuary of the " heart," is obscured by attention to externals in religion, and laid " waste." The story of the vision near Damascus refers to the interior change when Christ calls to the soul that is ready ; and then after a brief interval, a new " manner of life " begins.

See ABORTION (Paul), BORN OUT, CHURCH, DISPENSATIONS, PRIESTS AND ELDERS.

CONVICTION OF SIN :—

A sense of dissatisfaction with a course of life which comes to the emotion-nature, and is the precursor of an extension of the moral range and of a resolution to arise and seek a higher spiritual condition.

" The very problems of evil are really the marks of an eternal progress ; how man's very consciousness as a sinner is the evidence of a movement towards an infinitely glorious ideal yet to be realised in him."—J. BRIERLEY, The Eternal Religion, p. 45.

" Presently I found two things within me, at which I did sometimes marvel, especially considering what a blind, ignorant, sordid and ungodly wretch but just before I was ; the one was a very great softness and tenderness of heart, which caused me to fall under the conviction (of the blessed condition of a truly godly man) ; and the other was a great bending in my mind to a continual meditating on it, and on all other good things which at any time I heard or read of."—JOHN BUNYAN, Grace Abounding.

See CONVERSION, PRODIGAL.

COOL WITH CONTEMPLATION :—

A symbol of cessation from strife and stress in the soul.

CORCYRA, THE ISLAND OF THE PHÆACIANS :—

A symbol of a state of tranquillity and stability.

See PHÆACIANS.

CORD DESTROYED IN PLACE OF SERPENT :—

A symbol of mistaking the unreal *symbol* for the real thing, with result destructive of truth and right.

"Thueris (Taurt), as she was coming over to Horus, was pursued by a serpent which then was slain by her soldiers,— the memory of which action, say the Egyptians, is still preserved in that cord which is thrown into the midst of their assemblies, and then chopt to pieces."— PLUTARCH, *Isis and Osiris*, § 19.

The "serpent" is a symbol of seductiveness which nearly has the effect of dragging down the aspiring emotion of wonder (Thueris), but is put an end to by the raised qualities (soldiers). The "cord" incident signifies that there is danger of mistaking the symbol (cord) for the substance (truth), and that such a result would be destructive of truth and right in the doctrines and practice of mankind.

"By reason of A-vidya, then, the Jivatman, or 'personal soul of every individual,' mistakes the world, as well as its own body and mind, for realities, just as a rope in a dark night might be mistaken for a snake."—MON. WILLIAMS, *Indian Wisdom*, p. 119.

See ÆGEUS, HORUS, IGNORANCE, RITIS, TAUROBOLIUM, TAURT.

CORN, OR WHEAT :—

A symbol of the higher qualities, the spiritual germs of which have been sown in the lower nature, where through cultivation they have fructified, grown upwards, and borne the "fruit of the spirit" in the higher nature of the soul.

"He who cultivates most corn, grass, and fruits, with the left arm and the right, rejoiceth.—*Vendidad*, III.

The ego is most satisfied in himself, who assiduously cultivates those virtues, qualities, and powers, which accrue through the exercise of the active functions of the mind, incoming and outgoing, during periods of incarnation in which Karma is incurred,

and results are achieved through the functionings of buddhi. What is sown in sorrow is reaped in joy.

See AGRICULTURE, ARMS (body), BARLEY, BREAD, CAKE, CULTIVATION, FRUIT OF THE SPIRIT, HARVEST, LEFT, PLOUGHING, REAPING, RICE, RIGHT ARM, SEED (good), SHEWBREAD, SOWER, SOWING, WHEAT.

CORNER STONE :—

See SINGERS, STONE (corner).

CORPSE, OR DEAD BODY (HUMAN) :—

A symbol of the personality in its lower aspect, that is, without the Divine spark. Compared with the immortal Individuality, the mortal personality is apprehended as dead— illusive, transient.

"I have heard from the wise men that we are now dead, and that the body is our sepulchre."—PLATO, *Gorgias*, fol. 493.

"He that toucheth the dead body of any soul of man shall be unclean seven days."—NUM. xix. 11.

The "touching of a corpse" signifies the cherishing of the personality with its desires and selfishness which render the nature "unclean" for a full period.

"It is well known that, in the minds of Hindūs, ideas of impurity are inseparably connected with death, and contamination is supposed to result from contact with the corpses of even a man's dearest relatives."—MON. WILLIAMS, *Buddhism*, p. 496.

"It grieves the sun, O holy Zoroaster, to shine upon a man defiled by a corpse ; it grieves the moon ; it grieves the stars." —J. M. MITCHELL, *Zend Avesta, etc.*, p. 35.

When the soul is steeped in the selfishness of the lower personality (corpse), the Higher Self (sun), the emotions (moon), and the mental faculties (stars), are unable to develop it.

"'For whosoever would save his life shall lose it ; but whosoever shall lose his life for my sake, the same shall save it." —(LUKE ix. 24.)

"We must keep up our individuality, but we ought to take care that it is true and not false individuality. The key to distinguish them from each other is given to us in the text. It speaks of a double nature in man ; one which asserts self, the other which denies it. The first has a seeming life which is *actual death* ; the second has a seeming death which is actual life ; and therefore, as life is inseparably connected with individuality, the development of the selfish nature is false individuality ; the development of the unselfish nature is true individuality, . . . Love for self, sympathy for self, activity for self, do not produce life, or the sense of life ; they produce self, disease, the satiety which consumes, the dreadful loneliness which corrupts the soul, that passionate lust for more which is itself the unsatisfied worm which eats away the heart. No vivid or exalted sense of individual being can ever fill the heart of this man until he escape from the curse of self-involvement, and spread his being over all the world."—STOPFORD A. BROOKE, Serm., *Individuality*.

"A 'dead man' acknowledgeth nothing to be true and good, but what regardeth the body and the world."—SWEDENBORG, *Arc. Cel. to Gen.* ii.

"The attitude of the natural man with reference to the Spiritual is a subject on which the New Testament is equally pronounced. Not only in his relation to the spiritual man, but to the whole Spiritual World, the natural man is regarded as *dead*. He is as a crystal to an organism. The natural world is to the Spiritual as the inorganic to the organic. ' To be carnally minded in *Death*.' ' Thou hast a name to live, but art *Dead*. ' She that liveth in pleasure is *Dead* while she liveth.' ' To you hath He given Life which were *Dead* in trespasses and sins.' " —H. DRUMMOND, *Natural Law, etc.*, p. 75.

See AFU-RĀ, ASCENSION OF OSIRIS, ASPAHI, CREMATION, DEAD, DEFUNCT, EMBALMMENT, HEEL, HOUSES (corpses), INDIVIDUALITY, MAN (natural), MAN WITHOUT WOMAN, MUMMY, PERSONALITY, POOR PEOPLE, SEVEN, VULTURE.

CORPSE-CARRYING :—

See MAN WITHOUT WOMAN.

CORPSE DEVOURED BY BIRDS :—

A symbol of the personality or lower nature (flesh) being dissipated by nature forces (birds), in order that the now purified soul may be liberated and rise to bless on higher planes.

" In the disposal of the dead by Parsis, ceremonies are performed close to the *dakhma*, or ' tower of silence.' This is a circular pit, very deep, round which is a stone pavement about seven feet wide. On this the corpses are exposed naked. The face of the dead is uncovered ; the birds of prey come in multitudes, and very soon the flesh is all devoured. Every morning the bones are swept down into the great receptacle—the pit."—J. M. MITCHELL, *Zend Avesta, etc.*, p. 39.

The ceremonies signify the final purification of the soul, prior to the casting off of the dead body of corruption,—the astro-mental nature in which the spiritual ego has been held captive during the cycle of reincarnation. The

flesh-eating birds signify the rulers or elementals of the lower planes, and the bones symbolise the spiritual nature which endures.

See BONES, CORPSE, DEAD, FLESH, HOUSES OF DEAD, LIBERATION, PERSONALITY, VULTURE.

CORPSES OF DOGS AND MEN :—

Symbols of the lower will and the lower mind, both being illusory and impermanent, and without true life.

" He who digs out of the earth most corpses of dogs and men has greatest joy." —*Vendidad*, III.

The " corpse of man " signifies the personality which is the lower equivalent of the Individual in its latent state, and, as it were, dead. The "digging for corpses of dogs and men" is the effort which is successfully made to seek the Self, and the reference to "dog and man" is the insistence upon the aspects of *will* and *intellect*, which are essential to the finding of the Self. The "corpses" sought are of "dogs and men" because the Self is found, or the Individuality is developed, through will (dog) and mind (man). As the personality is apprehended as a corpse, and as the soul is, as it were, self-consciously realised, the raising of the self through the Self is rendered possible.

See DOG, EARTH, MAN, SELF, WILL.

CORRUPTION AND VIOLENCE ON THE EARTH :—

Symbolic of a state of estrangement from the Spirit, and of strife among the qualities of the lower nature.

"And the earth was corrupt before God, and the earth was filled with violence."— GEN. vi. 11.

And the lower nature was gross and predominant. " Corruption and violence " correspond to the alienation and changes which occur through the approach of the spiritual activities which are to proceed from above.

" It must have been divinely ordained that we should be subject to the dominion of darkness, in which God dwells in his fullness, though we do not know it. We are curiously imprisoned within our own physical organisations, and with all our advance in knowledge how little we know of our own universe ! . . . We sit in darkness and the shadow of death. Ignorance is the root cause both of suffering and sin. We suffer because we do not know. Sin would be just as impossible as pain if men knew the truth about life and were able to pierce the darkness that conceals the face of God." R. J. CAMPBELL, Serm., *Veil of Darkness*.

See CONFLICT, DARKNESS, DELUGE, DEPRAVITY, EARTH, FLOOD, STRIFE, SUFFERING, VAIVASVATA, WICKEDNESS.

COSMOS (HIGHER ASPECT) :—

A symbol of the Archetypal Form-universe, or the Monad of Form. It is the spiritual universe which is the formative pattern of the mental, astral and physical universes. Cosmos is the Macrocosm.

"Cosmos is second God, a life (living thing) that cannot die ; it cannot be that any part of this immortal life should die. All things in Cosmos are parts of Cosmos, and most of all is man the rational animal . . . after the image of the Cosmos made and having mind beyond all earthly lives " (*Corpus Hermeticum*, VIII).—MEAD, *T. G. Hermes*, Vol. II. p. 125.

The Archetypal Pattern, or Life and Form Scheme of the solar universe, represents the Second Logos, or second Divine outpouring of Life on the higher planes. This spiritual Pattern is fixed and permanent and not subject to successive changes of state ; consequently it is free of time. (Time only enters into manifestation when the Pattern is reproduced bit by bit on the lower planes. This is very plainly taught in the same treatise,—" God, maketh Æon ; Æon, Cosmos ; Cosmos, Time ; and Time, Becoming."—*Ibid.*, p. 175.)

All things manifest are in degrees of representation of the Divine Pattern above. In humanity there is the greatest number of degrees, for mind is present in man. The human soul is the microcosmic unit of the Macrocosm, and possesses the Divine Spark which is beyond all lower lives.

"The basic element of most of the ancient, and to this day of many of the modern, religions of the world is, the *idea* of a perfect invisible universe above, which is the real and true paradigm or ideal model, of the visible universe below, the latter being the reflection, simulacrum or shadow, of the invisible perfect ideal above. . . . The idea of the Upper ideal but *real* and *true*, and the Lower *apparently* real, but in truth *changeable* and untrue, goes through the entire Apocalypse of St. John, is in St. Paul, and in the Epistle to the Hebrews."—I. MYER, *Qabbalah*, pp. 108, 109.

"The lower world is made after the pattern of the upper world ; everything which exists in the upper world is to be found, as it were, in a copy upon earth, still the whole is one."—SOHAR, ii. 20a. GINSBURG, *The Kabbalah*, p. 104.

"In the Zohar it is said,—' the form of man is the image of everything that is above and below.' "—*Jewish Enc.* art. *Cabala*.

"The universe did not begin with atoms and electrons ; its basis is not material but spiritual ; and if we could break our way through the whole phantasmagoria— the tremendous drift and play and clash and scream of force and life against life— we should know that the real is also the eternally perfect, and that nothing can be added to or taken away from that perfection ; not even infinite wisdom and omnipotence could improve upon it, for it is itself the sum of these, and the home and reservoir of everything they could produce. It is the state beyond both good and evil, for evil cannot be felt or known in a state in which all fullness dwells. . . . If we could only get out and up to that state of being which is the antecedent cause of everything in the visible universe, we should find that by its very nature, it is a state of absolute felicity, bliss, and completeness ; it must be all that we dimly visualise when we strive towards what we call the good ; the ideal and the real are one. I insist that the real could not be anything else than the ideal, for it is at once the infinite source and the perfect satisfaction of everything that every soul can possibly aspire to."—R. J. CAMPBELL, Serm., *The Two Orders*.

Language is, of course, quite inadequate to describe noumenal actualities and their phenomenal correspondences. Statical phenomena are always imperfect in every respect, and can bear only a grotesque resemblance to their prototypes on the plane of causes. But suffice it to say that science and philosophy recognise archetypal causation. Professor Wm. James observed :—

"The widest postulate of rationality is that the world *is* rationally intelligible throughout, after the pattern of *some* ideal system. The whole war of the philosophies is over that point of faith." —*Principles of Psychology*, Vol. II. p. 677.

See ÆON, ALPHA, ARC. MAN, ATMAN, CREATION, EVOLUTION, GOOD (light), GODS, HEALING, HIGHER AND LOWER, IMAGE, INCARNATION, MACROCOSM, MICROCOSM, NET (golden), PLEROMA, PROTOTYPES, SEED, SIMILITUDES, SOUL (higher), SPARK, SPERMATIC WORDS, WORLDS (five).

COTTAGE, WELL-FASTENED :—

Symbolic of the enduring abode of the ego, which is the causal-body builded upon the upper mental plane.

See CAUSAL - BODY, DWELLING, HOUSE.

COTTUS, HUNDRED-HANDED :—

A symbol of the spiritual mind, active in numberless ideas. Or of the intellect.

"Blameless Cottus."—HESIOD, *Theogony*, 649.

See BRIAREUS.

COUNTENANCE, OR FACE :—

A symbol of a mental aspect of the feelings or emotions.

"But unto Cain and to his offering He had not respect. And Cain was very wroth, and his countenance fell. And the Lord said unto Cain, Why art thou wroth ? and why is thy countenance fallen ? "—GEN. iv. 5, 6.

But the lower nature, as such, could not be received by the Higher. And the earlier stages of evolution of the lower self (Cain) are attended by a great sense of restraint and hardship. And the Higher Self questions within the lower mind as to why it is suffering through its experiences.

"By 'countenance' are signified the interiors, which are said to 'fall' when they are changed. 'Countenance' with the ancients signified internal things, because internal things shine forth through the countenance."—SWEDENBORG, *Arc. Cel. to Gen.* iv. 5.

See CAIN, FACE, JOB.

COUNTENANCE, GREATER AND LESSER :—

Symbols of the Higher Self and the Lower Self—the Self unmanifest and the Self incarnate and partly manifest in the soul on the plane of mind.

"The White Head, the Ancient, or the Great Countenance is described as Ancient of Ancients, concealed of all concealed. He who is symbolised thereby is the Master with the white mantle and resplendent visage, and he is also called Holy of Holies. . . . Connected by means of a white thread or bond of union with the Great Countenance, there is that which is called the Lesser Countenance, Little Form or Figure, which presents, however, a complete aspect of humanity and is extended through three symbolical worlds. The distinction between the two heads is that in this case the hair and beard are black."—A. E. WAITE, *Secret Doctrine in Israel*, pp. 45, 46.

The Supreme Self, who is beyond time and space, is perfect in potentiality and hidden within all things. He is the Central Ruler and promulgator of the scheme of existence, and in him is the perfection of all Wisdom, Love, and Truth. Essentially united with the Supreme Self is the Conditioned Self, the complete prototype of perfect humanity, but as yet little evolved on the three lower planes. The black hair is significant of youthfulness.

"The Lesser Countenance has eyelids, because it has periods of sleep, a complete visage in manifestation because severity is one of its attributes, and a distinctive name, being Lord, whereas the Great Countenance is called Aïn, or Nothing. It is laid down (1) that the Lesser Countenance emanates from the Greater, (2) that the Greater metamorphoses into the Lesser, (3) that the latter is actually the former, as if seen through a curtain, and more specifically that they are one and the same."—*Ibid.*

The incarnate Self withdraws from outward perception, between periods of reincarnation. The mental aspect of the lower consciousness is that of a "man of sorrows and acquainted with grief," yet behind this visage is the Divine Ruler obscured by a curtain of imperfections, but destined to shine forth in his beauty when the soul has become pure and translucent, and the two Selves become One Self.

"According to the symbolism of the *Idras*, the Great Countenance is in *Atziluth*, abode of the three supreme *Sephiroth*, which are *Kether*, *Chokmah* and *Binah*. It is located especially in *Kether*. Below this there is the Lesser Countenance and Form, the head of which is in *Daath* (knowledge), while the body is extended through *Briah*, *Yetzirah* and *Assiah*, the male being not without the female.—*Ibid.*, p. 48.

The abode of the Higher Self is on the three higher planes (Atziluth), atma, buddhi, and higher manas, but essentially on atma (Kether). The incarnate Self is involved in the lower nature of the soul,—mental (Briah) astral (Yetzirah), and physical (Assiah). It is centred in the mind as the Individuality (Daath) which is in alliance with the higher emotion nature, buddhi (fem.).

"According to later Kabalism, the Great Countenance is *Macroprosopus*, the soul of the greater world, while the Lesser Countenance or Figure is *Microprosopus*, the soul of the lesser world and Adam

Protoplastes, his Bride being the archetypal Eve."—*Ibid.*, p. 49.

The first Adam (GEN. i.) is the Archetypal Man containing the duality of mind (man) and emotion-nature (woman).

See ADAM (higher), AIN SOPH, ARC. MAN, ASEEYATIC WORLD, ASTRAL PLANE, ATMA, ATZEELOOTH, BINAH, BREEATIC WORLD, BUDDHIC PLANE, FACE, HIGHER AND LOWER SELVES, HOKHMAH, HUMAN BODY, INCARNATION, JOB, KETHER, MACROCOSM, MICROCOSM, PLANES, SERVANT OF GOD, WARP, WHITE, YETZEERATIC WORLD.

COUNTERFEIT OF THE SPIRIT :—

A symbol of the Anti-Christ—he who cometh as from God, but who doeth not the works of God.

"And it is the Hebrews alone, and the Sacred Books of Hermes, which tell us these things about the man of Light and his guide the Son of God, and about the earthly Adam and *his* guide, the Counterfeit, who doth blasphemously call himself Son of God, for leading men astray."— *Fragments of Zosimus*, 27.

The " Man of Light " is the individuality in harmony with the Higher Self. The " earthly Adam " is the lower personality that first becomes subject to the desire-nature which claims falsely to be its true ruler, and to take the place of the spiritual nature in the human soul.

See ADAM (lower), ADVERSARY, ANTICHRIST, INDIVIDUALITY, PERSONALITY, SON OF GOD.

COUNTRIES OF SACRED SCRIPTURES :—

The country in which a sacred scripture originates is always a symbol of the mental plane, while certain countries adjacent may stand for astro-mental and buddhi-mental planes. The people of the scripture country are invariably the mental qualities in different stages of growth, and these play their part in the scripture dramas. For instance, in the Hebrew and Christian scriptures, Palestine is a symbol of the mental plane, while the inhabitants, the Jews, are the more or less developed mental qualities. In the ancient scriptures of Egypt, Higher Egypt and Lower Egypt, stand respectively for the higher mind and the lower mind. The marshes of the Delta

signify astro-mentality, while Nubia and Ethiopia stand for spiritual planes. The Mediterranean — the " great green sea "—signifies, of course, the astral plane. In the Zoroastrian scriptures, Iran (ancient Persia) is the mental plane, and the Iranians are the mental qualities. The Arab invaders of Iran are the emotions. In the Iliad the Greeks are the mental qualities, and the Trojans are the emotions. The " blameless Ethiopeans " are the higher or buddhic emotions.

" As the Temple is the reputed centre of the world, so every district is a microcosmos in which the myths of the Creation, of the combat with and final victory over the powers of darkness, and all other phenomena of the celestial world, are supposed to repeat themselves." —A. JEREMIAS, *Old Test., etc.*, Vol. I. p. 58.

" The most common and comprehensive word for deity in the Japanese language is *Kami*. It has the general meaning of ' above,' ' superior.' *Kami* is the part of Japan which lies near the capital, as opposed to *Shimo*, the lower country or provinces. *Kaha-kami* means the upper waters of a river."—W. G. ASTON, *Shinto*, p. 7.

" Kami " and " Shimo " are symbols of the higher and the lower natures of the soul.

See ARABS, EGYPT, FOLK, GREECE, GREEKS, IRAN, ISRAELITES, JEWS, JUDAH, LANKA, MAZENDARANS, MEAOU TRIBES, NORTH LAND, NUBIA, PEOPLE, PHÆACEANS, QUARTERS, QUETZALCOATL, SOUTH LAND.

COURSE, OR HORSE-RIDING GROUND :—

A symbol of the mental plane, as the arena of experience and of progress.

" The time of my departure is come. I have fought the good fight, I have finished the course, I have kept the faith : henceforth there is laid up for me the crown of righteousness, which the Lord, the righteous judge, shall give to me at that day."—2 TIM. iv. 6–8.

This represents the soul's victory over the lower nature, the attainment of liberation, and the acquirement of the results of experience, which are laid up on the buddhic plane to which the consciousness rises at the end of the cycle.

See CROWN, HORSE (white), LIBERATION, VARA, VICTORY.

COURTEZAN, OR STRANGE WOMAN :—

A symbol of the lust or attractiveness of the lower nature, and the instability which attends attention directed to the objects of sense.

"To deliver thee from the strange woman, even from the stranger which flattereth with her words; which forsaketh the friend of her youth, and forgetteth the covenant of her God."—PROV. ii. 16, 17.

The lower attractiveness was once the higher (buddhic), and the "friend of her youth" is Love on the buddhic plane.

See ADULTERY, HARLOT, WHOREDOM.

COVENANT OF GOD :—

A symbol of the realisation of the Divine nature within the soul as an ideal to be attained through evolution of the qualities life after life. In this way is established the connection between God and man—the Divine and the human.

"And God spake unto Noah, and to his sons with him, saying, And I, behold, I establish my covenant with you, and with your seed after you; and with every living creature that is with you, the fowl, the cattle, and every beast of the earth with you."—GEN. ix. 8–10.

And the Divine Power communicates itself to the Individuality (Noah) and its aspects (sons), so that the soul is made aware of its Divine origin and possibilities. The Divine Power also discloses the unity of the One Life, and gives the assurance that all the emotions and desires, high and low, are but aspects and phases of the One Life which is supreme and eternal.

"They (the children of Israel) shall inquire concerning Zion with their faces hitherward, saying, Come ye, and join yourselves to the Lord in an everlasting covenant that shall not be forgotten."—JER. 1. 5.

The lower mental qualities (Israelites) are enjoined to be reverent of the higher nature within the soul (Zion), and to set their efforts and aspirations towards it, in order that they may unite in realising the Divine nature as an ideal which brings with it the assurance of immortality for the ego.

"The Covenant with man is a type of the Three Principles of the Divine Being. For the Rainbow is the sign and token of this covenant that God doth here mind, that man was created out of the Three Principles into an Image."—J. BEHMEN, *Myst. Mag.*, p. 207.

The "Three Principles" signify the higher nature, atma-buddhi-manas, which constitute the ideal.

"When we are told that '*in* the blood of Jesus we have boldness to enter into the holy place' (HEB. x. 19), the meaning is that the Life of Christ, shared by us and imparted to us by the Spirit, has given us consecration and ratified an eternal covenant."—F. W. FARRER, *The Atonement, etc.*, p. 46.

"This natural body of ours has in itself the fitness for two sets of processes,—the processes of growth and the processes of repair. You keep your arm unbroken, and nature feeds it with continual health, makes it grow hearty, vigorous, and strong, rounds it out from the baby's feebleness into the full robust arm of manhood. You break that same arm, and the same nature sets her new efficiencies at work, she gathers up and re-shapes the vexed and lacerated flesh, she bridges over the chasm in the broken bone, she restores the lost powers of motion and sensation, and beautifully testifies her completeness, which includes the power of the Healer as well as the Supplier. So it is to me a noble thought, that in an everlasting Christhood in the Deity we have from all eternity a provision for the exigency which came at last (at the fall),—a provision, not temporary and spasmodic, but existing forever, and only called out into operation by the occurrence of the need. . . . And when an earnest soul accepts this everlasting Christ, is there not a new glory in his salvation when he thinks that it has been from everlasting? The covenant to which he clings had its sublime conditions written in the very constitution of the Godhead."—PHILLIPS BROOKS, *Mystery of Iniquity*, pp. 317–9.

See BOW, CREATURES, CUP (wine), DISPENSATIONS, IRIS, ISRAELITES, LAW OF MOSES, MEDIATOR, MOSAIC, NOAH, RAINBOW, SHEPHERD (good), TESTAMENT, ZION.

COW :—

A symbol of Wisdom, or the functioning of the buddhic plane activities, that inner nature of the soul which feeds, as it were, on "grass and the herb of the field," i.e. is nourished on the lower growths and affections, which it transmutes within itself into the higher emotions (milk and butter), the sustenance of the evolving soul.

"The beneficent cow fed upon plants."—*Vendidad*, V.

The buddhic nature in its receptive and transmutative functions.

" 'Harm not the inexhaustible, wide-ruling cow,' the cow is indeed wide-ruling, and the wide-ruling is food, and accordingly the cow is food."—*Sata. Brâh.*, VII. 5, 2, 19.

"Cow, the prolific image of the all-mother goddess Isis."—APULEIUS, *Metam.*, xi. 15.

"Like unto a mother, a father, a brother and other relatives, the cows are our best friends, in which medicines are produced. They give food, they give strength, they likewise give a good complexion and happiness; knowing the real state of this, they (the Brâhmanas) did not kill cows."—*Sutta-Nipāta*, 295, 296.

See AUDUMBLA, BUDDHI, BUTTER, FLAYING, FOOD, HATHOR, HEIFER, ISIS, MILK, MOTHER (divine), PLANTS, SOPHIA, VACH, WEALTH SHOWER, WISDOM.

COW—PASSIVE :—

A symbol of the negative, receptive aspect of Buddhi.

"Scratching the back of a cow destroys all guilt, and giving her to eat procures exaltation in heaven."—*Institutes of Vishnu*, XXIII, 60.

The meaning of this quaint statement is evident. Doing that which is well-pleasing to the unmanifest Holy Spirit (cow) by exercising the higher emotions, destroys the lower attractions. Offering up the desires and affections results in their being transmuted by Buddhi (cow) on the higher planes.

"Cows alone make sacrificial oblations possible (by producing sacrificial butter), cows take away every sin."—*Ibid.*, 58.

The higher emotions alone make the sacrifice of the lower qualities possible through the response from above of Wisdom (milk) and Love (butter) to strengthen the aspirations. The higher or buddhic emotions take away all wish for the objects of sensation and desire which are regarded as transitory and unsatisfying.

See SACRIFICE.

COW, GODDESS MEH-URT :—

A symbol of primordial matter, Truth-Reality, which brings forth the Self (Bull) on the highest plane.

"The homage of the scribe Nebseni to the goddess Meh-urt, lady of heaven, and mistress of earth."—BUDGE, *Book of the Dead*, Ch. LXXI.

"I behold Râ who was born yesterday from the buttocks of the goddess Meh-urt;

his strength is my strength, and my strength is his strength. What then is this? It is the watery abyss of heaven, or as others say,—It is the image of the Eye of Râ in the morning at his daily birth. Meh-urt is the Eye (Utchat) of Râ."—*Ibid.*, Ch. XVII.

The soul acclaims the Self, who, at the beginning of the cycle, was brought forth from primordial matter. The life and energy of the Self is within the soul, and the soul's life and energy is the Self's. What then is Meh-urt? It is Truth-Reality (water); or in other terms,—It is the counterpart of the Self at his forthgoing into manifestation ;—It is the mode by which the Self perceives Himself.

See AUDUMBLA, BIRTH OF BUDDHA, OF CHRIST, BULL, MATTER, MĀYĀ, MOTHER, PRAKRITI, UTCHAT, WATER.

COW, BLACK :—

A symbol of the unmanifest reality on the matter side of existence at the beginning of the cycle.

"With milk from a black cow which has a white calf he makes offering; the black cow with the white calf is the night, and her calf is yonder sun."—*Sata. Brâh.*, IX. 2, 3, 30.

The higher mind transmits the spiritual influences which come to it. From the unmanifest (the mulaprakriti) is born the manifest, the Higher Self (sun).

See MULAPRAKRITI, NIGHT, SUN.

COW, MILCH :—

A symbol of the buddhic nature in its aspect productive of the higher emotions which it confers upon the lower self.

"For this earth is, as it were, a milch cow : she yields to men all their desires ; and the milch cow is a mother, and this earth is, as it were, a mother : she bears (or sustains) men."—*Sata. Brâh.*, V. 3, 1, 4.

This is a comparison between the functionings of the two natures,—lower and higher. As the lower nature (earth) produces the desires and all exterior attractions for the benefit of the mind (men); so the higher nature (cow) produces the interior qualities of wisdom and love (milk and butter) for the benefit of the mind. The lower nature is the first to produce the means for the manifestation of mind in the evolutionary cycle.

"And king Suddhodana gave to the

brahmans for his son's (Buddha's) welfare, cows full of milk, with no traces of infirmity, golden-horned, and with strong, healthy calves to the full number of one hundred thousand."—*Buddha-Karita*, Bk. I. 89.

This refers to the involution of the soul (Buddha) at an early period. The gift of the " cows " signifies the conferring of the intuitive perception of spiritual things, which is to enable the soul to rise. The " brahmans " are the higher mental forms through which the spiritual nature is apprehended. The " no traces of infirmity " is an allusion to the perfect conception of the Truth inplanted within the soul through the process of involution. " Golden horns " are a symbol of zeal and love of the true. The myriad " calves " represent the inexhaustible treasures of the Spirit, produced by buddhi (cow).

" The religion of the Hindû detaches him from this earth ; therefore, even now, the cow-symbol is one of the grandest and most philosophical among all others in its inner meaning."

" In Esoteric Philosophy the Cow is the symbol of Creative Nature, and the Bull (her calf) the Spirit which vivifies her, or the ' Holy Spirit.' "—H. P. BLAVATSKY, *Secret Doctrine*, pp. 436, 493.

See BRAHMAN PRIESTS, BUDDHA, CALF, CALVES (Myriad), EARTH, GOLD, GOLDEN AGE, INVOLUTION, LINEN GARMENT, MILK, SUDDHODANA, UDDER, VACH.

COW OF PLENTY, "DAPPLE-SKIN" :—

A symbol of the buddhic-nature which operates within, as it were, the astral-nature of desire, sensation, appetite, and instinct. The pure within the impure (spotted).

" He (Vasishtha) called the cow of spotted skin, all spot without, all pure within. . . . With sumptuous meal and worthy fare ; be thine the banquet to prepare. . . . All these (viands and drinks), O cow of heavenly power, rain down for me in copious shower. . . . On her mine offerings which ascend to Gods and spirits all depend : my very life is due to her, my guardian, friend, and minister. The feeding of the sacred flame, the dole which living creatures claim, the mighty sacrifice by fire."—GRIFFITH, *The Ramayan*, Vol. I. pp. 226–8.

The forces of the lower planes (Vasishtha) operate outwardly in the manifest imperfections of life, which express the fact of the essential perfection of the archetypal spiritual pattern within. Through the buddhic activities nourishment for the soul is prepared. Goodness, love, and truth are the gifts of the Spirit bestowed on the aspiring mind. On Wisdom depends the transmutation of the offerings of the qualities at her shrine to the ideals. The life of the soul is to be found in its intimate relation with the spiritual forces which raise and develop it. The qualities which have in them the divine germ claim from Wisdom the purifying and perfecting of their natures.

" Hail (the seven kine and their Bull) ye who give cakes and ale, and splendour to the souls who are provided with food in the underworld, grant ye cakes and ale unto the Osiris Nu ; provide ye him with food, let him be in your following, and let him be born upon your thighs."— BUDGE, *Book of the Dead*, Ch. CXLVIII. p. 481.

Here, Wisdom is expressed through all the highest emotions and faculties, and it is the Higher Self (the Bull) which fructifies them. The " Osiris Nu " is the indwelling God,—the Christsoul —coupled with the name of an individuality " Nu." The Christ can only be born within the highest emotions, and must be nursed and nourished by them.

See ALMSGIVING, BANQUET, BULL, CAKE, CLOUD, CREATURES, FEAST, FIRE, FOOD, FRUIT, MILK, RAIN, SACRIFICE, SEED, SPOTTED, VASISHTHA, WEALTH-SHOWER.

COW, SPOTTED, IS THE EARTH :—

A symbol of the buddhic nature inverted on the astral plane, and operating as the desires, passions, appetites, instincts, and sensations, of the lower nature (earth).

" ' Having become a spotted cow, go to the sky, and thence bring us rain hither,' (the sacrificer says.) The spotted cow, doubtless, is this earth : whatever rooted and rootless food is here on this earth, by that this earth is a spotted cow. ' Having become this earth, go thou to the sky,'—this is what he thereby says, ' Thence bring us rain hither.' From rain certainly spring vigour, sap, well-being." —*Sata. Brâh.* I. 8, 3, 15.

The ego having acquired the lower emotion nature (spotted cow) it becomes requisite that the emotions should be transmuted by buddh-

(sky), and so bring truth (rain) to the soul. The lower emotions are of the lower nature (earth). While desires (rooted) and illusions (rootless) nourish the lower nature, the lower nature remains full of " spots and blemishes " (2 PETER ii. 13). It is therefore necessary that the lower nature be purified by the Spirit, so that Truth be attained, for from Truth spring strength, life, and immortality.

See CLOUD, EARTH (MOTHER), FOOD, RAIN, ROOTED, SAP, SKY, SPOTTED.

COWS OF APOLLO :—

A symbol of the higher emotions led by the Higher Self.
See APOLLO.

COW'S MILK :—

A symbol of the spiritual sustenance which is yielded by buddhi ; or the produce of the Wisdom function necessary for the growth of the soul, i.e. higher emotions.—*See* 1 PETER ii. 2.
See MILK (cow), UDDER.

COW'S MILK POURED OUT TO-WARDS THE NORTH :—

Symbolic of Wisdom which, descending upon the lower planes, immersed in ignorance, becomes inverted and actuates as craft and cunning in the lower nature.
See BUDDHI, NORTH, WISDOM.

COWS' URINE DRINKING :—

A symbol of the drinking of the cup of bitterness and sorrow, which yields experience and wisdom. The operation of buddhi on the lower planes produces pain and sorrow to the lower self, but joy and liberty to the higher : because thereby the Self is vivified and proportionately released from the bonds of matter.

Of Wisdom, it is said :—
" For at first she will walk with him by crooked ways, and bring fear and dread upon him, and torment him with her discipline, until she may trust his soul, and try him by her laws. Then will she return the straight way unto him, and comfort him, and show him her secrets. But if he go wrong, she will forsake him, and give him over to his own ruin."—ECCLESIASTICUS, iv. 17–19.

" Suffering is the ancient law of love ; there is no quest without pain, there is no lover who is not also a martyr. Hence it is inevitable that he who would love so high a thing as Wisdom should sometimes suffer hindrances and griefs."—B. H. SUSO, *Leben*, CH. IV.

See BITTER, BLASPHEMY, GALL, SORROW, VINEGAR.

CRANBERRY (MARJA) :—

A symbol of the Divine germ or seed which develops in the purified part of the lower nature, and becomes the Higher Self born in the Soul.

" Come, O virgin, come and pluck me, Come and take me to thy bosom. . . . Like a cranberry in feature. Like a strawberry in flavour, But the Virgin Mariatta, Could not pluck the woodland-stranger. Thereupon she cut a charm-stick, Downward pressed upon the berry, When it rose as if by magic. Darted upward to her bosom."—J. M. CRAWFORD, *Kalevala*.

When the soul is purified, it cries to the Self to come and take possession. The Divine Seed is the Son of the Highest : his nature is sweet, for it is Love. " O taste and see that the Lord is good." But the purified lower nature cannot be more than receptive, it could not of itself draw down the Spirit. Hence it adopts the means at hand, and so, through the buddhic functioning, the higher emotions press as it were downwards on the spiritual germ, with the result that the Divine Life suddenly starts from latency into actuality.

" Where did that compassionateness come from ? I think there is a plain answer to the question. It is that all along there has been wrapped up in the human soul a seed of Christhood—I think that is the word—waiting for its opportunity to germinate. The Christ-quickened soul reveals hitherto latent spiritual capacities whose emergence stamps it as a new creature, the same yet not the same, the lower mastered by the higher, every faculty ' brought into captivity to the obedience of Christ.' It is the same self, but regenerated, made truly manifest. As the Apostle Paul puts it, ' The earnest expectation of the creature waiteth for the manifestation of the sons of God.' "—R. J. CAMPBELL, Serm., *The Eternal Man*.

See BODHISATVA, BUDDHI, EGG, HUITZILOPOCHTLI, LEMMENKAINEN, MARJATTA, SEED, SEED (good), SERPENT (water), VIRGIN.

CRANIUM, OR MACROCOSM :—

A symbol of the spiritual universe. The higher planes of being above the lower.

" In the Concealed of the Concealed there is formed and prepared the representation of a Cranium full of crystalline dew, (and) a membrane of air. Transparent and hidden filaments of pure wool are hanging in the Balance. And they manifest the Good Will of good wills, through the prayers of the lower ones," (Footnote by Myer : " The immense Cranium is the Makrokosm, the arched firmament. . . . Hanging threads of pure wool are a symbol among some of the Orientals for the efflux of wisdom and vitality.")—ISAAC MYER, *Qabbalah*, pp. 117, 118.

The higher nature is always ready to respond (dew) through the mind (air) to the aspirations (prayers) of the lower qualities. The " hanging filaments of pure wool " have the same signification as the " Barsom " of the Parsis. They represent the hidden mechanism by means of which communication is established between the higher and lower planes of the soul, and the efflux of wisdom and love imparted to the striving qualities.

" The heaven was made of the giant Ymer's skull."—*Voluspa*.

See BARSOM, DEW, HAIR, MACROCOSM, YMIR.

CRATER, OR CUP :—

A symbol of the World-soul, or buddhic causal-body as the vehicle of the Atman or Higher Self.

" Proclus tells us that the Demiurge is said ' to constitute the psychical essences in conjunction with the Crater ' ; this ' Crater is the peculiar cause of souls, and is co-arranged with Demiurgus and filled from Him, but fills souls ' ; thus it is called the Fountain of Souls."—T. TAYLOR, *Theology of Plato*, V. 31.

The Higher Self constitutes the qualities and forms on the lower planes from their prototypes in the universal causal-body on the buddhic plane. Thus the World-soul is the cause of the individual souls,—the fountain from which they spring.

"A symbol of this mystic secret (of the Soul's descent into matter) is that Starry Cup (Crater) of Father Bacchus placed in the space between Cancer and Leo— meaning that intoxication is there first experienced by souls in their descent by the influx of matter into them. From which cause also forgetfulness, the companion of intoxication, then begins secretly to creep into souls. For if souls brought down to body memory of the divine things of which they were conscious in heaven, there would be no difference of opinion among men concerning the divine state."—*Macrobius*, Bk. I. Ch. 12.

The individual soul, as a microcosm

and reflection of the World-soul, descends through the lower mind (Cancer) to the astral plane (Leo) and is attached to a permanent atom on the fourth astral sub-plane, and thus the human or mental (starry) soul (crater) commences its career as a vehicle of the Higher Self (Bacchus). The lower nature is stupefied by the influx of the higher, and the egos, manifesting as the lower consciousness, retain no remembrance of their higher state of being. The " Starry Cup " is a symbol of the human causal-body on the higher mental plane, which is at first latent, and has to be developed from below.

See CANCER, CAPRICORN, CHARON'S FERRY, CUP, DEMIURGE, DIONYSUS, FALL, INTOXICATION, LEO, RECOLLECTION, REMINISCENCE, STARS (fixed) ZODIAC.

CREATION OR EMANATION OF THE SPIRITUAL AND MATERIAL UNIVERSES :—

The potential and unmanifest, becoming the actual and manifest in a scheme of being in which the spiritual and mental precede the astral and physical.

" What creation is to God, that is thought to man." " Creation is in fact the thinking out of a thought."—ALICE GARDNER, *John the Scot*, pp. 128, 38.

" The Deity began (the Creation) by forming an imperceptible point ; this was Its own Thought ; then It turned Itself to construct with its own Thought a mysterious and holy Form ; finally, It covered this (ideal) Form with a rich and shining (visible) garment ; that is, the entire universe, of which the name necessarily enters into the Name of Elohim."—*Zohar*, I. fol. 1 and 2.

" The Zohar also says : 'All that which is found (or exists) upon the Earth, has its spiritual counterpart also to be found on High, and there does not exist the smallest thing in this world, which is not itself attached to something on High, and is not found in dependence upon it.' The basic element . . . is the *idea* of a perfect invisible universe above, which is the real and true paradigm, or ideal model of the visible universe below. . . . The idea of the Upper ideal but *real* and *true*, and the lower *apparently* real, but in truth *changeable* and untrue, goes through the entire Apocalypse of St. John, is in St. Paul, and in the Epistle to the Hebrews."—ISAAC MYER, *Qabbalah*, pp. 108, 109.

" All things that are on earth, O Tat,

are not the Truth, they are copies only of the True. . . . For all that alters is untrue ; it does not stay in what it is. . . . All that is subject unto genesis and change is verily not true " (" Of Truth ").—G. R. S. MEAD, *T. G. Hermes*, Vol. III. pp. 18, 21.

" It is at the command of Him who always covers this world, the Knower, the Time of time, who assumes qualities and all knowledge, it is at His command that this work (creation) unfolds itself, which is called Earth, Water, Fire, Air, and Ether."—*Svetas Upanishad*, 6, 2.

" Thou (Rā) art the lord of heaven, thou art the lord of earth ; thou art the creator of those who dwell in the heights, and of those who dwell in the depths. Thou art the God One who came into being in the beginning of time. Thou didst create the earth, thou didst fashion man, thou didst make the watery abyss of the sky."—BUDGE, *Book of the Dead*, p. 13.

The " watery abyss " is the ocean of Truth-Reality becoming manifest upon the highest planes.

" We find the following in Suidas, as Tuscan teaching, gathered from the Tuscan history-book : ' The Demiurg ordained twelve thousand years of life for the world, and placed each thousand under the dominion of a sign of the Zodiac. Creation continued during six thousand, and the duration will be six thousand. In the first, heaven and earth, in the second the firmament, in the third sea and waters, then the two great lights, the souls of beasts, and lastly man was created.' "—A. JEREMIAS, *Old Test.*, etc., Vol. I. p. 168.

" Modern evolutionists would argue that creation has never had a beginning ; it is an eternal process. Our universe has had a beginning, no doubt ; but then there must have been other universes before it ; this mysterious something that now shows itself as life and mind must always have been at work in some form or other. It did not lie asleep for a million million ages, and then suddenly begin to evolve a universe. It has always been active ; it is its nature to be active, it could not help it. It never began, and it will never end. Solar systems are born, grow old, and die ; and then the process starts all over again. And we are obliged to admit this to be true, whether we believe in God or not. It is inconceivable that from all eternity God did nothing until one fine morning he suddenly decided to create a universe and to bring humanity into being. He must have been doing something ; to be eternally living is to be eternally active."—R. J. CAMPBELL, Serm., *God's Gift of Life*.

See ARC. MAN, BREATIC, CARPENTER, COLOURS, COSMOS, DAYLIGHT, DAYS (five), ELEMENTS, EVOLUTION, HEAL-ING, HIGHER, IMAGE, INCARNATION, INVOLUTION, KHIEN, LOOM, MACRO-COSM, NIGHT, PLEROMA, PROTOTYPES, PURUSHA, SEED, SIMILITUDES, SOUL (highest), SPERMATIC, TEM, TIME, TYPE VIVANHĀO, WATER, WORLDS (five), YI SYSTEM.

CREATURES :—

A symbol of the outgoing desires, passions and emotions of the lower nature, which, as it were, feed upon the instincts and sensations.

" The living creatures of the earth represent the emotions connected with the will. . . . The instinct of mankind has always read these forms aright. To this day, wherever the primitive language of symbol remains, the passions are still characterised by the names of different beasts."—A. JUKES, *Types of Genesis*, p. 37.

" Stand firm and shrink not ; for at length all thy creatures will grow faint, weak, and ready to die ; and then thy will shall wax stronger, and be able to subdue and keep down the evil inclinations. So shall thy will and mind ascend into heaven every day, and thy creatures gradually die away."—J. BOEHME, *The Supersensual Life*, D. 4.

" And God said, Let the earth bring forth the living creature after its kind."—GEN. i. 24.

The Divine Will directs that the lower nature of the Soul shall bring forth that which is first in order, viz. the natural qualities.

See ANIMALS, BEASTS, CATTLE, COW (plenty), DAEVAS, NAME, VITAL AIRS, WHALES.

CREATURES, SMALL LIVING :—

Symbolic of germs of goodness and truth generated in the lower nature by the higher.

" He who is persevering, gentle and patient shuns the company of men of cruel conduct, and does no injury to living creatures, gains, if he constantly lives in that manner by controlling his organs and by liberality, heavenly bliss."—*Laws of Manu*, IV. 246.

" In order to preserve living creatures, let him always by day and by night, even with pain to his body, walk carefully scanning the ground."—*Ibid.*, VI. 68.

The lower nature (ground) must be carefully scanned, or tried by suffering, so that all germs of truth and righteousness may be preserved and nourished.

" Insects, snakes, moths, bees, birds, and beings bereft of motion reach heaven by the power of austerities."—*Ibid.*, XI. 241.

The germs of goodness, wisdom, knowledge, aspiration, and latent virtues are evolved and transmuted through abstaining from lower emotional activities.

" He sees the Self who sees Aditi, one with all the gods, who emanated out of Hiranyagarbha, and has entered into the cavity of the heart, and there abides with living creatures. This is that."—*Katha. Upanishad*, IV. 1.

See CUTIVATING, GERMS, HIRANYA-GARBHA, LITTLE ONES, MULTIPLY, SEEDS (good).

CREEPING THINGS :—

A symbol of the lower instincts, desires, and emotions, such as cunning craft, greed, subtlety, mischief, cruelty, destructiveness.

" If we look to the inward sense of it, then the creeping things represent the foul vices, but the clean ones represent joy."—PHILO, *Works*, Yonge's trans., Vol. IV. p. 387.

"And let them (God's image) have dominion over the fish of the sea, and over the fowl of the air, and over the cattle, and over all the earth, and over every creeping thing that creepeth upon the earth."—GEN. i. 26.

The Wisdom and Love principles united in Mind are to have dominion over the feelings, ideas, actions, and the entire human nature, including the lower mental nature with the desires and instincts.

"Ye shall not make your souls abominable with any creeping thing that creepeth, neither shall ye make yourselves unclean with them, that ye should be defiled thereby."—LEV. xi. 43.

This is an injunction to the qualities to cast off the lower desires and degracing instincts, which render the soul impure.

See ANIMALS, BIRDS, CATTLE, DWARFS, HEDGEHOG, IMAGE, STAR-WORMS, TORTOISE.

CREMATION OF THE CORPSE :—

A symbol of the purification of the soul or the lower self by means of the functioning of buddhi (fire).

" There is, indeed, no doubt that the very ancient association of the ideas of Fire and of spiritual Purification goes back, in the first instance, to the conception of the soul being necessarily stained by the very fact of its connection with the body, and of those stains being finally removed by the body's death and cremation. We find this severely self-consistent

view scattered up and down Hellenic religion and literature. . . . The Fire is, at bottom, so spiritual and so directly busy with the soul alone, that it is ever identical with itself in Heaven, Hell, Purgatory, and on earth, and stands for God himself ; and that its effects are not the destruction of a foreign substance, but the bringing back, wherever and as far as possible, of the Fire-like soul's disposition and quality to full harmony with its Fire-source and Parent, God Himself."—F. VON HUGEL, *Mystical Element*, Vol. II. p. 125.

See BURNING, CORPSE, FIRE, FUNERAL PILES, KABANDHA, NANNA, PURGATORY.

CRETE :—

A symbol of a state of perfect peace on the higher buddhic levels.

"The Argonauts thence proceeded to Crete, where Talus the brazen man, prohibiting their landing, was slain by the art of Medea."—*Argonautic Expedition*

When the aspiring Soul with its advanced qualities reaches the condition of peace, the critical faculty (Talus) delays its arrival, but is eventually superseded by Wisdom (Medea).

" Minos had Zeus for his father. At nine years old he received revelations from Zeus, and reigned over all Crete." —W. E. GLADSTONE, *Juventus Mundi*, p. 119.

The Divine Will proceeded from the Supreme. At the appointed time when all preparations were made, the Divine Will established ideal conditions on the buddhic plane. This was in the golden age of involution, when there was no strife.

See ARGONAUTS, ICHOR, MEDEA, TALUS.

CRETHEUS, FATHER OF ÆSON, AND FOUNDER OF IOLCUS :—

A symbol of the First Logos, from whom proceeds the Second Logos, and who has established the beginning and the ending of the cycle of the soul's evolution.

See ÆSON, ALPHA, IOLCUS, JASON.

CRIMINALS WITH TWO LEGS :—

A symbol of paradoxes of relativity, or distorted views of life, which mislead those who cleave to the things of the lower mind.

See MAN (bad).

CRIPPLES ABSENT FROM THE VARA :—

Signifying that in the involutionary cycle all monads are perfect, and capable of carrying out the work which is set for them.

"And God saw everything that he had made, and behold, it was very good."—GEN. i. 31.

"There should be no cripples, or diseased ; no poverty, no meanness there."—*Vendidad*, II. *S. B. of E.*

The "cripples" are said to be rejected from the lower quaternary (vara) ; for there must be no imperfection in the Archetypal Man. The "diseased," "poverty," and "meanness" refer to states adverse to the carrying out of the work assigned to the monads.

See ARC. MAN, GOLDEN AGE, INVOLUTION, VARA.

CROCODILE :—

A symbol of the lower desires and passions which are of the lower nature on the astral plane (water).

In the seventh division of the Tuat,—
"In front of the goddesses of the Hours is an enormous crocodile called Ab-sha-am-Tuat, which is described as 'Osiris the Eye of Rā,' The crocodile stands upon a long funeral mound, out of the end of which . . . appears a bearded human head, i.e. 'the head of Osiris.' Of the crocodile the text says : 'He who is in this picture is Ab-shaw, and he is the warden of the symbols of this city. When he heareth the voice of the boat of Rā, which is addressed to the Eye in his cheek, the head which is in his dominion maketh its appearance, and then it eateth its own form after this great god hath passed it by. Whosoever knoweth this picture, Ab-shaw shall not devour his soul.' "—BUDGE, *Egypt. Heaven and Hell*, Vol. I. pp. 159-60.

The goddesses of the hours signify the emotions or virtues. The crocodile is a symbol of the desire-nature used as an instrument of the Logos (Osiris). The funeral mound indicates the Divine Sacrifice, for the symbol of the Logos appears from it. Spirit has been buried or involved in Matter. Osiris is dead and buried but comes to life as evolution proceeds. "Osiris the Eye of Rā" signifies the manifest or perceptive aspect of Deity. God looks out, as it were, upon Nature by means of his instrument of manifestation.

The lower instincts and desires (Ab-shaw) rule the activities attached to this personal centre (city) of consciousness. When the experiences are dealt with in the causal-body (boat of Rā), then the qualities are trans-muted as higher aspects (cheeks) of lower desires. The head appearing signifies Divine action or birth in the soul. As the higher nature becomes active, the lower nature (crocodile) becomes inert, and then disintegrates and disappears as illusion. Finally, whosoever has knowledge and shuns evil shall no longer be ruled by desire.

Dr. Budge states (*The Mummy*, p. 360) that on a cippus of Horus is a small scene in which is figured a crocodile with the divine emblem,—a circle and ram's horns,— on its head, and inscribed "Hidden is his name." This evidently signifies the incarnate "Lamb of God" (Osiris) hidden in the lower nature (crocodile). In this cippus Horus is shown standing upon two crocodiles. This may be taken as meaning,—the Higher Self triumphant over the lower desires and passions.

"The crocodile never touches any persons who sail in a papyrus boat, as either fearing the anger of the Goddess Isis, or else respecting it on account of its having once carried her."—PLUTARCH, *Isis and Osiris*, § 18.

The "papyrus boat" is a symbol of the Scriptures, which serve as a vehicle for Divine Wisdom (Isis). Doubt of the Scriptures by the lower nature (crocodile) never assails those whose religious emotions are ruled either by fear, or by love that is reverence.

See AFU-RĀ, BOAT (sektet), LAMB OF GOD, LEVIATHAN, NEKHEBIT, OSIRIS, PAPYRUS, UTCHAT.

CRONUS OR SATURN :—

A symbol of time and limitation arising from the inter-relations of Spirit (Uranus) and Matter (Ge).

See AIDONEUS, FOAM, KHORDAD, KRONOS, NUT, RHEA, SATURN, SEB, TIME, TITANS, URANUS, ZEUS.

CROPS OF GRAIN—

A symbol of the growing higher emotions in the soul.

"Thou shalt break the power of untiring gales which rising against the earth blow down the crops and destroy them ; and again, whenever thou wilt, thou shalt bring their blasts back."—*Empedocles*, FAIRBANKS, 24.

The Self shall overcome the winds of erroneous doctrine which arise, and striking the lower self (earth) destroy the sprouting emotions of truth, wisdom, and love. And moreover the Self shall recall such doctrines, and shall turn the falsity of the lower planes into relative truth for the enlightenment of the mind, and through dissipating ignorance shall enable it to know the truth.

See GALES, HAIL, SEED (good), STORM, TAWHIRI, WINDS (various).

CROOK :—

See FLAIL.

CROSS :—

A symbol of the manifested life of the Logos—the higher and lower natures, and the Divine Ray passing through the quaternary.

" The cross was composed of four pieces of wood ; the upright beam, the cross beam, the tablet above the Saviour's head, on which was the superscription and the socket in which the cross was fastened, or as some say, the fourth piece was the wooden shelf upon which the Saviour's feet rested. And these four pieces were of as many kinds of wood, that is, of palm, cypress, olive, and cedar. The Jews had formed the upright beam of a piece of timber which they found floating in the pool of Bethesda. Now this beam had grown from the branch of the Tree of Life which the angel Michael gave to Seth, son of Adam, in paradise." —*The Golden Legend.*

The number four expresses the quaternary—the four planes of nature on which the incarnate God is crucified. In the " Tet-pillar " the four planes are symbolised by the four cross beams of the pillar. In the Latin cross there is only one cross beam which therefore signifies the division between the higher and lower natures. The upright beam is a symbol of the Divine Ray or " Tree of Life," which, as atomic vibration, passes from the Supreme directly downwards across all the planes. This, from the lower aspect, is a symbol of aspiration. The " four kinds of wood " represent the four different planes. The water of the " pool of Bethesda " signifies the perception of Truth in which aspiration, as it were, floats. The Divine Life imparted immortality to the quality Hope (Seth), or sense of the Real within.

" I stretched out my hands and sanctified the Lord : for the extension of my hands is His sign, and my expansion is His upright tree."—J. R. HARRIS, *Psalm of Solomon,* 27.

The soul aspires to increase its higher activities (hands) ; for the extension of the higher activities is the expression of the indwelling Self, and the soul's growth is through the upward tending Divine Life (tree) which has been involved in archetypal humanity.

" Man himself is in the form of the cross. Origen, the great Church Father, taught that the true posture of prayer is to stand with outstretched arms, which is the form of a cross ; and the man standing in space with outstretched arms was with the ancients the symbol of the Beneficent Deity. . . . The cross meant the great world Passion, the Sacrifice of God in Creation, Deity laying down His life in the universe of matter and form."—K. C. ANDERSON, Serm., *Cradle of the Christ.*

" The great open secret of Christianity is the Cross of Christ. In the cross is summed up, for all who care to learn, the whole meaning of the world's travail and agony ; in the cross, too, is our hope of ultimate triumph in alliance with the will of God. All the theologies that have ever been framed have just been so many efforts to express, in terms of the mind, what the humblest servant of Christ already knows quite well with the heart—namely, that it is right and inevitable that by the cross should the Saviour enter into his glory. And we are still at it. On we go with our theologising, and we cannot help it ; we must keep on trying to express this august truth of the soul in terms of our ever-changing earthly experience. . . . And this, at least, there is no gainsaying, that those who have entered most deeply into the fellowship of the cross have just been those who have been most sure that it contains the clue to the mystery of earthly existence as a whole."—R. J. CAMPBELL, Serm., *The Divine Mystery.*

See ARC. MAN, ARK (Noah), CRUCIFIXION OF CHRIST, CRUCIFIXION OF PURUSHA, JESUS (mortal), POOL OF BETHESDA, PRAGÂPATI, QUATERNARY, SWASTIKA, T (cross), TET, TREE OF LIFE.

CROSS, ANKH (CRUX ANSATA), A SYMBOL OF LIFE :—

This Egyptian cross has the same meaning as the Latin cross. The circular handle is a symbol of the higher planes, but inasmuch as the handle is not a perfect circle, it indicates that activities pass from above to the quaternary below.

"According to Pythagoras, when the Soul descends from the boundary where the Zodiac and Galaxy meet, from a spherical form, which is the only divine one, it is elongated into a conical one by its downward tendency."—*Macrobius*, I. 12.

When the soul enters upon the limitations of the cycle of life (Zodiac) it is no longer wholly divine, but its lower part gravitates towards desire and sensation. The "Galaxy" is a symbol of the celestial regions (atma-buddhi) from which the Soul has come. The World-soul descends to be involved in the matter of the lower planes, that it may rise again in the myriad souls of humanity.

See CHILDREN OF HORUS, CIRCLE, QUATERNARY, SPHERE, SQUARE, ZODIAC.

CROWD OF PEOPLE :—

Symbolic of a discordant concourse of lower mental qualities in the soul.

"But when the crowd was put forth, he (Jesus) entered in, and took her by the hand ; and the damsel arose."— MAT. ix. 25.

When the jarring and self-seeking qualities of the lower mind were put forth or subdued, the Christ-soul was able to enter in and exercise his power in awakening a slumbering affection and putting it to active use in the soul.

"So the crowd is cast forth without, in order that the damsel may be raised up ; because if the importunate throng of worldly cares be not first expelled from the inner recesses of the heart, the soul, which lies dead in the interior, cannot rise up. For whilst it lets itself loose amongst the countless imaginings of earthly desires, it never in any degree gathers itself up to the consideration of self."—ST. GREGORY, *Morals on the Book of Job*, Vol. II. p. 370.

"When the scornful deriders have been rejected, Christ enters into the minds of the elect."—GLOSSARY.

See HAND, HEALING, (dead) JESUS, MIRACLES, STRIFE, ZACCHEUS.

CROWN :—

A symbol of supremacy over the lower nature. In its highest aspect it stands for the power of atma.

"Kether (the Crown) is the principle of all the principles, the Secret Wisdom, the most exalted Crown, with which all crowns and diadems are adorned."—*Zohar*, III. fol. 288 b.

The highest plane (Kether) is the most interior of all. It is atma, the hidden Truth and Life which confer immortality upon all victorious souls.

"In that day shall the Lord of hosts be for a crown of glory, and for a diadem of beauty, unto the residue of his people." —Is. xxviii. 5.

When the cycle ends, the Higher Self shall be supreme in beauty and harmony within the higher qualities which have been evolved from below.

See COURSE, KETHER, LION (man), TIARA.

CROWN, ATEF :—

A symbol of the realisation of supremacy in a state of the soul.

"Herubehutet and Horus had the bodies of men and the heads of hawks, and they wore the white and red crowns with plumes and uraei."—*Legend of the Winged Sun-disk*.

The human body and hawk-head to the two "gods," aspects of the Self, stand for a symbol of human perfection-ment, culminating in the soul which aspires to become Divine. The "white and red atef crowns" are symbolic of lordship over the planes of the intellect and the emotions. The "plumes" signify the conditions in which supremacy is realised. The "uraei serpents" signify the triumph of Wisdom reflected upon the lower planes of the soul.

See COME INTO THEE, HAWK, HORUS, PLUMES, SERPENTS, URAEI.

CROWN, DOUBLE SERPENT :—

An emblem of Kingship over the lower nature through the power of Wisdom and the higher emotions.

See NEKHEBIT, UR-UATCHTI.

CROWN OF LOWER EGYPT :—

An emblem of Divine rule over the lower mental, or kama-manasic, plane. Its form is that of an open mouth with a projecting tongue curled at the end, i.e. returning upon itself. This symbolises the uttered Word of Power, or the expression of the Divine Life on the lower planes, which must return unto its source.

See EGYPT (lower), MITRE, MOUTH, SERPENT (north), TONGUE.

CROWN OF UPPER EGYPT, OR TALL WHITE CROWN OF OSIRIS :—

An emblem of Divine rule over the higher mental and buddhic planes, exercised from the summit of Power and Truth.

" Thou (Osiris) art stablished as king, the white crown is upon thy head, and thou hast grasped in thy hands the crook and the whip."

The "crook" and the "flail" are symbols of shepherding and agriculture, over which, in their inner sense, the Divine Shepherd and Husbandman, the Higher Self (Osiris), presides. The tall white crown of Osiris symbolises the higher nature, and the mount of aspiration which has to be climbed in order to attain perfection.

See COME INTO THEE, FLAIL, HUS-BANDMAN, KING, MOUNTAIN, OSIRIS, SERPENT (south), SMAM, WHITE.

CROWN OF UPPER AND LOWER EGYPT—THE SEKHET OR PSCHENT CROWN :—

An emblem of the Divine supremacy over the higher and lower natures in the Soul.

"Amen-Rā, Lord of the uraeus crown, exalted by the two feathers, beautiful of diadem of the white crown of Upper Egypt. . . . He is adorned in his palace with the Sekhet crown. Loving its south and its north (i.e. the two divisions of Egypt which are symbolised by the Sekhet crown)."—WIEDEMANN, *Rel. of Anc. Egyptians*, p. 113.

The "uraeus crown" signifies the triumph of Wisdom over the lower nature, and the "feathers" (plumes) signify the aspiring condition in which supremacy is realised. The "south and north" are the higher and lower divisions of Egypt which symbolise the higher and lower mental planes.

See AMEN, AMENI, EGYPT, HIGHER AND LOWER, PALACE, PLUMES.

CROWNS, RED AND WHITE :—

Emblems of lordship over the emotion nature and the intellect.

See NEKHEBIT, RED, WHITE.

CROWN OF TWELVE STARS :—

A symbol of supremacy over the conditions of the lower planes during the cycle of twelve divisions (zodiac).

"A woman arrayed with the sun, and the moon under her feet, and upon her head a crown of twelve stars."—REV. xii. 1.

The Wisdom principle (buddhi) with the power of the Self (sun), and ruling the astral region (moon) ; with supremacy over the lower planes as director of the evolution of the soul.

" This is the Soul invested with the light of supreme knowledge attained through the experiences undergone in the long series of her past existences ; standing on the moon as victor over materiality and firm in the faith of a full intuition,—states denoted respectively by the dark and light portions of the moon ; and superior evermore to the changes of mortal destiny, the stars which represent this being the jewels of her crown, each of them denoting one of the ' twelve labours ' necessary to be endured by the Soul on her path to her final perfection-ment, and the spiritual gifts and graces acquired in the process."—*The Perfect Way*, p. 190.

" It signifies wisdom and intelligence from knowledges of divine good and divine truth derived from the Word."—SWEDENBORG, *Apoc. Rev.*, n. 534.

" There was a wonder in heaven ; a throne was seen far above all created powers, mediatorial, intercessory, a title archetypal, a crown bright as the morning star, a glory issuing from the eternal throne, robes pure as the heavens, and a sceptre over all. And who was the predes-tined heir of that majesty ? Who was that Wisdom, and what was her name, the mother of fair love, and fear, and holy hope, exalted like a palm-tree in Engaddi, and a rose-plant in Jericho, created from the beginning before the world, in God's counsels, and in Jerusalem was her power ? The vision is found in the Apocalypse, ' a Woman clothed with the sun, and the moon under her feet, and upon her head a crown of twelve stars.' The votaries of Mary do not exceed the true faith."—J. H. NEWMAN, *Development*, pp. 405, 406.

See AMATERASU, ASSUMPTION, BIRTH OF MAN-CHILD, DRAGON (red), FEET, LATONA, MOON, STARS (fixed), SUN, TUAT, TWELVE, VIRGIN MARY, WOMAN (goodness), ZODIAC.

CROWNING WITH THORNS, OF JESUS :—

A symbol of the lower qualities' falsely assumed veneration for an Ideal far beyond them.

"And they plaited a crown of thorns and put it upon his head, and a reed in his right hand, and they kneeled down before him and mocked him." MAT. xxvii. 29.

This signifies a disruptive process between the lower and higher natures. The "reed" which is put in his hand is a symbol of power and volition which the Christ-soul will not exercise actively as ruler of the lower qualities of the soul (the Jews).

" The crown of thorns proclaims a sovereignty founded on sufferings. The sceptre of feeble reed speaks of power

wielded in gentleness. The cross leads to
the crown. The brow that was pierced by
the sharp acanthus wreath, therefore,
wears the diadem of the universe. The
hand that passively held the mockery of
the worthless, pithless reed, therefore,
rules the princes of the earth with the
rod of iron. He who was lifted up to the
cross, was, by that very act, lifted up to
be a Ruler and commander to the peoples."
—A. MACLAREN, *Sermons, 1st Series*,
p. 159.

See HAND, HEAD, REED, ROMAN
SOLDIER, SCEPTRE, THORNS, TRIAL OF
JESUS.

CRUCIFIX :—

A symbol of the death of the Archetypal Man on the cross of Matter at
the end of the period of involution.
Through the death of Christ all
human souls have life in the period
of evolution.

See ARC. MAN, CROSS.

CRUCIFIXION OF CHRIST, ACCORDING TO THE MA-NICHÆANS :—

A symbol of the Divine sacrifice,
that is, the limitation and involution
of the Divine energies and qualities
within forms of matter.

"Christ, the Divine Virtue, Wisdom, or
Mind, came down from the Superior region
to be crucified in Matter from which he
again departs" (*Manichæan Tenets*).—
ALEXANDER, Bp. of Lycopolis.

Christ, being God-actual, proceeding
from God-potential, descends into
matter as the Divine Sacrifice from
the commencement of manifestation.
He contains in himself the ideas of all
forms and qualities which have to be
impressed in matter. He willingly
involves himself within nature, and
gives up his life as a glad outpouring
in order that the many souls may have
life and may progress. He then
becomes, at the completion of *involution*, the Divine Archetypal Man ready
to pour forth in *evolution* all qualities
and forms of life. In the inner being
of all things He lives in secret, and
eventually is born, or manifests, in the
human soul, where as his power
increases he becomes the conqueror of
the lower nature, and finally returns
in his saints to his Father and Source.

"The (Mani) crucifixion was, of course,
a mere semblance. This seeming transac-
tion symbolised the crucifixion of the Soul,
sunk in matter, which the Spirit of the
Sun would raise up to itself. The cruci-

fixion of that Soul which was dispersed
through all matter served but to accomplish the destruction of the kingdom of
darkness."—NEANDER, *Church History*,
Vol. II., p. 224.

The crucifixion story was regarded
as symbolical of the Soul involved in
matter, which the heavenly Christ
(sun) would raise up to unite with him
in glory. The involution of that Soul,
or indwelling Self, in the lower nature
is the means whereby the negative
condition of ignorance (darkness) will
disappear in the light of incoming
Truth.

"The pain of the lower creation is part
of the grand cosmic sacrifice whereby the
eternal God lays down his life that he
may take it again. On the altar of the
material universe that sacred life has been
offered since the beginning of time, and
though at present we can do no more
than glimpse that for which it is done,
we are justified in feeling that no life
which has ever risen to the dignity of
being able to suffer will be missing from
the grand consummation."—R. J. CAMP-
BELL, Serm., *Divine Justice*.

"God is in all things, whether personal
or impersonal, and in God they live and
move and have being. And that stage of
purification through which the Kosmos is
now passing is God's Crucifixion ; the
process of Transmutation, and Redemption of Spirit from Matter, of Being from
Existence, of Substance from Phenomenon
which is to culminate in the final At-one-
ment of the ultimate Sabbath of Rest
awaiting God's redeemed universe at the
end of the Kalpa."—*The Perfect Way*,
p. 116.

"So ' I am crucified with Christ, nevertheless I live ; ' death, therefore—that is,
the sacrifice of self—is equivalent to life.
Now this rests upon a profound truth.
The death of Christ was a representation
of the life of God. To me this is the
profoundest of all truths, that the whole
of the life of God is the sacrifice of self.
God is Love ; love is sacrifice—to give
rather than to receive—the blessedness of
self-giving. If the life of God were not
such, it would be a falsehood to say that
God is Love ; for even in our human
nature that which seeks to enjoy all
instead of giving all is known by a very
different name from that of love. All the
life of God is a flow of this divine self-
giving charity. Creation itself is sacrifice
—the self-impartation of the divine Being.
Redemption, too, is sacrifice, else it could
not be love ; for which reason we will not
surrender one iota of the truth that the
death of Christ was the sacrifice of God."
—F. W. ROBERTSON, *Sermons, 3rd Series*,
p. 100.

See ARC. MAN, CHRIST, DEATH OF
BALDER, OF LEMMINKAINEN, OF OSIRIS,

EEL-GOD, FUH-HE, IMAGE, LAMB OF
GOD, QUETZALCOATL, SACRIFICER

CRUCIFIXION OF CHRIST, ACCORDING TO THE GNOSTICS :—

A symbol of the Divine Sacrifice, as before.

"The Lord said unto John, ' Thou hearest that I suffered, yet I suffered not ; that I was pierced, yet was I not smitten ; that I was hanged, yet was I not hanged ; . . . See thou therefore in Me the slaying of a Word (Logos), . . . the passion of a Word. And by a Word I mean Man. First, then, understand the Word, then shalt thou understand the Lord, and thirdly the Man, and what is his passion."—*Acts of John* (2nd cent.).

First, the " Word," i.e. the expression of the Divine Life on the lower planes. Second, the " Lord," i.e. the Divine Life indwelling in the lower nature. Third, the " Man," i.e. the Archetypal Man who is potentially perfect man, and is the Divine Life Incarnate. Thus, all three are the one Christ crucified in humanity. Christ, whose nature is bliss, cannot suffer, but he becomes through Self-limitation (passion) the Perfect Man within, who is slain and dies in order to be born again in every soul. It is said in this scripture,—" Not yet hath every Limb of Him who came down been gathered together," which means that the qualities of the perfect Christ nature are scattered abroad, as it were, no higher quality being fully evolved in any striving soul. The gathering together of the " Limbs of the Ineffable " in the myriad souls is when the Lord cometh in the clouds of heaven (buddhi), and the saints (individualities possessing the " limbs ") meet Him in the " air " (higher mind).

" Thy Head stretcheth up into heaven, that thou mayest symbol forth the Heavenly Logos, the Head of all things. Thy middle parts are stretched forth, as it were, hands to right and left, to put to flight the envious and hostile power of the evil one ; that Thou mayest gather together into one them (the Limbs) that are scattered abroad. Thy foot is set in the earth, sunk in the deep, that Thou mayest draw up those that lie beneath the earth and are held fast, . . . and mayest join them to those in heaven."—*Acts of Andrew* (2nd cent.).

The Heavenly Logos is the celestial Christ, the " Head of all things." The terrestrial Christ is Christ Incarnate,— the Archetypal Man stretched forth in the lower nature of the soul. The " hands to right and left " signify the outgoing and incoming energies which disperse the hostile forces of ignorance and evil, and also by gathering together the higher qualities (the Limbs), prepare the souls for union with the One. The " foot in the earth " signifies the physical foundation of the lower activities which advance the evolution of the soul. These activities enable the Christ to gradually raise the qualities which are held captive, and by transmuting them, join them to those on the buddhic plane.

See ARC. MAN, CHRIST'S SECOND COMING, CROSS, DIONYSUS, DISMEMBERMENT, IMAGE, INCARNATION, KAIOMARTS, LIMBS, MEMBERS, PRAGÂPATI, PURUSHA, SACRIFICER, SINA, VISVAKARMAN, WORD, YMIR, ZAGREUS.

CRUCIFIXION OF CHRIST, ACCORDING TO THE REVELATION OF JOHN :—

A symbol of the Divine Sacrifice, as before.

"And the dead bodies (of the two witnesses) lie in the street of the great city, which spiritually is called Sodom and Egypt, where also their Lord was crucified."—REV. xi. 8.

The two Divine " witnesses " are Love (olive) and Wisdom (caedlestick), which emanate from the Supreme. Love and Wisdom " die," that is, become obscured when, at the fall of mind, desire (the beast) takes possession of the soul. They remain latent and untouched in the path of the lower evolution, until the mind by putting away desire is prepared to receive them and ascend with them. The " great city Sodom and Egypt " is a symbol of the lower planes whereon Christ the Saviour is crucified, dead and buried.

" This city, then, is the world, the materialising, the idolatrous, the blind, the sensual, the unreal, the house of bondage, out of which the sons of God are called. And the world being all these, is cruel as hell, and will always crucify the Christ and the Christ-idea."—*The Perfect Way*, p. 108.

" The God who is crucified in the Cosmos, and laid in the tomb of matter.

to rise again in glory, becomes in the individual soul the Christ who is crucified to the lower self-hood, and dies to the flesh, to rise again in the triumph of the spirit. The drama of Calvary is being re-enacted in every soul that comes to spiritual consciousness. . . . Until the Son of God rises in you victorious over the old Adam,—the self that says 'not Thou but me,'—the Christ of long ago has done but little for you. . . . The sweet story of old has to become your story, told over again in you. In you the Christ-child has to be born anew ; in you grow and labour ; in you suffer and die to the world ; in you rise in power and ascend to the eternal Father."—R. J. CAMPBELL, Serm., *Crucified with Christ.*

See BEAST, CANDLESTICKS, CITY, EVOLUTION, FALL, OLIVE, PATH, SACRI-FICER, SODOM, STREETS, WITNESSES (two).

CRUCIFIXION OF JESUS, AC-CORDING TO THE CANO-NICAL GOSPELS :—

A symbol of the final anguish of the incarnate Soul as it reaches per-fection, and the lower nature drops away from it.

"And about the ninth hour Jesus cried with a loud voice, saying,—My God, my God, why hast thou forsaken me ? "—MAT. xxvii. 46.

The "ninth hour" refers to the period of the attainment of perfection on the three lower planes. The cruci-fixion not being yet completed, the cry of mental distress and despondency signifies that the soul is temporarily agonised by this transition state, for it is not yet entirely alive to the nature of the highest conditions of Being, when, in fact, it is not yet *completely* able to identify itself with the Highest. When the identification is complete, the consciousness has risen to the causal-body, and the suffering lower nature has been ex-changed for bliss.

"In the Apocryphal Gospel of Peter, the dying Christ cries, 'My Power, my Power, thou hast forsaken me,' the 'Power' being the heavenly Christ, who for a time had been associated with the earthly person of the Redeemer."—W. R. INGE, *Paddock Lectures,* p. 57.

The "heavenly Christ," or Higher Self, is to be understood as *always* associated with the struggling Lower Self symbolised by Jesus. This cry of the lower to the Higher indicates the lower consciousness on the verge of

union with the Higher, but still per-ceiving its separateness from it. The expression "my Power" must be re-garded as meaning "my Divine Life and strength," which for a moment the personality realised as departing from it—the mortal personality. It must be remembered that it is the "earthly person" or lower personality signified by the "body of Jesus," which dies when the Divine spark has been withdrawn from it.

"And Jesus cried again with a loud voice, and yielded up his spirit."—MAT. xxvii. 50.

This signifies the consummation — the ultimate suffering, and then the triumph over the ultimate ills of the lower planes,—the Soul's liberation and final withdrawal from the lower manifestation.

"Although Redemption as a whole is one, the process is manifold, and consists in a series of acts, spiritual and mental. Of this series, the part wherein the individual finally surrenders his own exterior will, with all its exclusively material desires and affections, is desig-nated the *Passion*. And the particular act whereby this surrender is consummated and demonstrated, is called the *Crucifixion*, This crucifixion means a complete, un-reserving surrender—to the death, if need be,— without opposition, even in desire, on the part of the natural man. Without these steps is no atonement. The man cannot become one with the Spirit within him, until by his 'Passion' and 'Cruci-fixion,' he has utterly vanquished the 'old Adam' of his former self. Through the atonement made by means of this self-sacrifice he becomes as one without sin, being no more liable to sin ; and is qualified to enter, as his own high priest, into the holy of holies of his own inner-most."—*The Perfect Way,* p. 215.

"All the 'pains' we have to take,— they form the Cross upon which the Body is stretched out and the Blood is spilt. But it is all tending Godward, it is all in the approach to Love and Justice. This is the 'death of Christ.' "—J. G. ADDER-LEY, *The Symbolism of the Mass.*

See CAUSAL-BODY, CONSCIOUSNESS, ELIJAH, HEEL, HIGHER, INCARNATION, JESUS, KHEPER, LIBERATION, NIDANAS, NINE, OINTMENT, PASSION, PERSON-ALITY, REDEMPTION, RESURRECTION, ROMAN SOLDIER, SIXTH HOUR, SPARK, UNION, VICTORY.

CRUCIFIXION OF JESUS, ACCORD-ING TO CERINTHUS :—

" Jesus suffered ; and Christ remained incapable of suffering, being a Spirit of the Lord."—Hippolytus, *Works*, Bk. X. p. 385.

"Jesus" is a symbol of the almost perfected soul whose personality suffers at the last. The Christ,—the Atman,—could not suffer, for suffering is only of the lower planes, and is the result of imperfect functioning.

"Christ suffered and died. The Godhead indeed could not suffer. But God could take a nature which is capable of suffering."—H. P. Liddon, *University Sermons*, p. 231.

CRUCIFIXION OF PURUSHA, OR THE SACRIFICE OF THE MAN :—

A symbol of the Divine sacrifice, that is, the limitation and involution of the Divine energies and qualities within forms of matter.

"Now the sacrifice is the Man. The sacrifice is the Man for the reason that the Man spreads it ; and that in being spread it is made of exactly the same extent as the Man : this is the reason why the sacrifice is the Man."—*Sata. Brâh.*

The Divine sacrifice is consummated in the Archetypal Man. The sacrifice is of God's nature, for God, in manifesting himself, limits himself. The Divine energy—Spirit, enters into the receptive principle Matter, and spreads through it fully and perfectly. The sacrifice is the preparation of the way of the Souls.

"I stretched out my hands and approached the Lord : for the stretching out of my hands is a sign : my expansion is the outspread cross."—*Psalms and Odes of Solomon*, ps. 42.

See Arc. Cman, ross, Involution, Mahâvira-pot, Pragâpati, Purusha, Sacrificer, Sign.

CRYSTAL :—

A symbol of Truth received in the mind and operating through the personality.

"Crystal to lighten his face " (Bk. of the Dead).—Budge, *Egyptian Magic*, p. 187.

Truth imparting knowledge to the personality.

"Preaching assumes the fact in men of a religious nature, higher than a mere thinking nature, which, if it can be duly awakened, cleaves to Christ and His salvation with an almost irresistible affinity. This religious nature is a capacity for the supernatural, that is, for the divinely supernatural ; in other words, it is that quality by which we become

inspirable creatures, permeable by God's life, as a crystal by the light, permeable in a sense that no other creature is."—H. Bushnell, *Nature and the Supernatural*, p. 363.

See Church, Firmament, Flames (twin), Glass, Maaseh.

CULTIVATION OF THE GROUND:—

Symbolic of the ordering and disciplining of the desires and emotions by the Ego, and the developing of the faculties of the lower nature (the ground).

"I, too, plough and sow, and from my ploughing and sowing I reap immortal fruit. My field is religion. The weeds I pluck up are the passions of cleaving to existence. My plough is wisdom, my seed purity."—(Extract) Hardy, *Manual of Buddhism*, p. 215.

"He (Osiris) reaps and I plough ; yea, and I also reap."—Budge, *Book of the Dead*, Ch. CX.

The Higher Self, or Individuality, reaps celestial grain, i.e. acquires in actuality, higher emotions. The lower Self "ploughs," i.e. fashions the life conditions for the seed of the Spirit ; and finally also, the lower Self "reaps" as it realises its true nature.

"This, too, is the ruinous effect of an education of accomplishments. The education of the taste, and the cultivation of the feelings in undue proportion, destroys the masculine tone of mind. An education chiefly romantic or poetical, not balanced by hard, practical life, is simply the ruin of the soul."—F. W. Robertson, *Sermons*, 1st Series, p. 169.

"None of the inscriptions mentions Sekhet-Aaru, but it is distinctly said that the reaping of the grain is taking place in Sekhet-hetep, or Sekhet-hetepet." "If now we compare this picture (of Sekhet-hetep) with that from the Papyrus of Nebseni, we shall find that the actual operations of ploughing, reaping, and treading out of the corn are depicted in the Papyrus, and that several figures of gods and the deceased have been added."—Budge, *Egypt. Heaven and Hell*, Vol. III. pp. 44, 58.

The cultivation of the soul being a spiritual process appertains to the higher planes, and the reaping of the harvest is on the buddhic plane (Sekhet-hetep),—the "corn" signifying the higher qualities transmuted from the lower.

See Agriculture, Animals, Corn, Field, Garden, Harvest, Ploughing, Reaping, Seed, Sekhet, Self, Shabti, Sower.

CULTIVATING CORN, GRASS, AND FRUITS :—

A symbol of the fostering of those virtues and utilities which accrue to the soul through the exercise of the active functions of the mind.

"You go to Nature and say, 'Feed me or I shall starve ; ' and her question comes back to you, 'How (much seed) have you ? Give me something to begin with, however little it may be.' Drop the old remnants of a past life into the ever fruitful soil, and all the possibilities of new life open. The spring-time finds last summer's roots still remaining in the ground, and quickens them to life again, and multiplies them into a richer summer still. Ingenious Nature finds a germ wherever it is dropped ; but without the germ she will do nothing."—PHILLIPS BROOKS, Serm., *How many Loaves have ye ?*

" 'God comes to man, yea, He comes closer, till He enters into men. No disposition is good apart from God. Seeds of the divine are planted in human bodies ; if they are well tended, they germinate and grow up into the likeness of That from whence they sprang (Seneca, *Ep.* LXXIII. 14). The teaching that there is a germinative principle—a seed of God in the human soul—was a fundamental idea with the Stoics. This doctrine, interpreted at its best, offers a basis for mystical religion and was very suggestive to the primitive Christians."—R. M. JONES, *Mystical Religion*, p. 70.

See AGRICULTURE, CORN, CREATURES (small), GERMS, PLOUGHING, SEED, SOWING.

CUP OR CHALICE :—

A symbol of the causal-body which is the receptacle of the Spiritual life or Monad—Atma-buddhi.

"A higher power bringeth a Cup full of intuition and wisdom, and also prudence, and giveth it to the soul."—*Pistis Sophia, Books of the Saviour.*

"The Cup . . . is the Cup offered by the Deity to the souls, from which they drink the wine of wisdom. This may be compared with the Grail Legend."—G. R. S. MEAD, *Orpheus*, p. 43.

"He filled a mighty Cup with Mind, and sent it down . . . to the hearts of men : 'Baptise thyself with this Cup's baptism, . . . thou canst ascend to Him that hath sent down the Cup, thou that dost know for what thou didst come into being.' As many then as understood . . . became partakers in the Gnosis ; and when they had 'received the Mind,' they were made 'perfect men.' "—*The Cup or Monad, in the Corpus Hermeticum.*

"Mind" is a symbol of atma-buddhi, Love and Wisdom, the Divine Monad. When the souls partake of this "Cup" then perfection of the souls is reached.

"For this blood of Christ and of the Covenant—this wine within the holy Chalice, of which we all must drink who nevermore would thirst—*is the Divine Life*, the vital, immortal principle, having neither beginning nor end, the perfect, pure, and incorruptible Spirit, cleansing and making white the vesture of the soul as no earthly purge can whiten ; the gift of God through Christ, and the heritage of the elect. To live the Divine Life is to be partaker in the blood of Christ and to drink of Christ's cup. It is to know the love of Christ which 'passeth understanding,' the love which is life, or God."—*The Perfect Way*, p. 109.

"I will take the cup of salvation, and call upon the name of the Lord."—Ps. cxvi. 13.

The "cup of salvation" is the receptacle of the Spirit, from which the soul drinks the "wine" of love and wisdom.

See ANOINTING, BLOOD, CRATER, GRAIL, HOMA - JUICE, SACRAMENT, SOMA-JUICE, TABLE OF THE LORD, WATER, WINE.

CUP, DOUBLE :—

A symbol of the principles of Love and Wisdom which are united in Truth.

"So speaking he (Hephæstus) rose up and set in his dear Mother's (Hera's) hand the Double Cup, and spake to her."—*Iliad*, Bk. I, trans. BUCKLEY.

Thus having manifested Its powers, the Creative Mind rises to Buddhi, where it delivers to the Wisdom-principle (Hera) the dual aspects of the Higher Self,—intuition and love,— and then addresses Itself to the Wisdom within itself.

See HEPHAISTOS, HERA, MUSIC.

CUP WITH WINE :—

A symbol of the purified psychic body, or soul, with the indwelling Divine life of wisdom and love.

"This cup is the new covenant in my blood, even that which is poured out for you."—LUKE xxii. 20.

The cup and the wine signify respectively the Soul and the Life,— the receptacle or sheath for the Spirit, and the Spirit itself. The Divine Life was poured out for the qualities in their involution. This assurance of the Spirit is a sacrament, because it is a *binding*,—a covenant between the Soul and the qualities.

See BLOOD, COVENANT, SACRAMENT, SACRIFICER, TABLE OF THE LORD.

CUP, VIAL, VASE, ETC. :—

Symbols of lower bodies or vehicles, as containers of higher bodies or energies.

"By cups, chalices, vials, and platters, the same is signified as by the things contained in them. The literal sense of the Word is a containing vessel."—SWEDENBORG, *Apoc. Rev.*, n. 672.

See AGATHODÆMON, DISH, SOMA (moon), VESSEL.

CUPID AND PSYCHE :—

Symbols of the indwelling Self and the Emotion-nature. The two eldest daughters of the Archetypal Man (king) are appetite and instinct, born on the astral plane. The third daughter, Emotion (Psyche), is born subjectively on the buddhic plane. Love of form life (Venus) draws, as it were, the Self (Cupid) to effect in the forms union between Emotion and Desire, but the Self is in harmony with buddhic Emotion and nurtures that subjectively (night) during periods of incarnation. Then, when all is prepared, Emotion awakens in the mind, and the Self disappears from consciousness. This constitutes the "fall" of mind and emotion into the lower life of desire and sensation. Love of form life (Venus) enslaves Emotion amid the sufferings and sorrows of the lives on earth. But the indwelling Self (Cupid) "who still loved her in secret, invisibly comforted and assisted her in her toils." As evolution proceeds, the Emotion nature becomes more and more apparent and active in love of righteousness, truth, justice, wisdom, and all the virtues, until at the end of the cycle, love of life in the forms (Venus) is overcome, and the soul rises immortal to be joined with the Self for ever.

"This fable, it is said is a representation of the destiny of the human soul. The soul, which is of divine origin, is here below subjected to error in its prison the body. Hence trials and purifications are set before it, that it may become capable of a higher view of things, and of true desire. Two loves meet it,—the earthly, a deceiver who draws it down to earthly things ; the heavenly who directs its view to the original, fair and divine, and who, gaining the victory over

his rival, leads off the soul as his bride " (HIRT, APUD CREUTZER, *Symbolik* III. 573).—KEIGHTLEY, *Mythology*, p. 117.

See BUDDHI, EROS, LOVE, PANDORA, PERSEPHONE, PRITHA, SELENE, SEPHI-ROTH, VENUS.

CURETES AND CORYBANTES :—

Symbols of the higher mental faculties and the buddhic emotions.

"They are the Guardians of the Creative Power, while it is yet too weak to defend itself. Therefore they watch over Zeus when a child."—PROCLUS, *Polit.*, p. 387.

"Zeus," the incarnate Self born in the soul, is protected at first by the higher qualities that surround him and are in harmony with him.

See BIRTH OF KRISHNA, DURASROBO, GUARDIANS (world), HEROD, ZEUS.

CURSE :—

A symbol of limitation of activity through Divine laws and conditions imposed upon matter.

"Rhea (Nut) having companied with Kronos (Seb) by stealth, was discovered by Helios (Rā), who laid a curse upon her, that she should not be delivered in any month or year."—PLUTARCH, *Isis and Osiris*, § 12.

Space (Nut) and Time (Seb), imply-ing Form and Number, are rendered apparent through the forthpouring action of the Logos (Rā). The "curse" is a symbol of limitation of matter in time and space, for matter of herself cannot bring forth in any period.

See BIRTH OF OSIRIS, DAYS (five), NUT, RĀ, RHEA, SEB.

CURSE ON THE GROUND :—

A symbol of limitation of the activities of the lower nature by moral law, through suffering.

"Because thou (Adam) hast hearkened unto the voice of thy wife, and hast eaten of the tree, of which I commanded thee saying, Thou shalt not eat of it : cursed is the ground for thy sake ; in toil shalt thou eat of it all the days of thy life."—GEN. iii. 17.

And to the mind (Adam) the con-science directs that, since the emotion-nature (wife) has been apparently led astray, and the moral nature (tree) has been acquired, the lower nature shall become abhorrent, stage by stage, and it shall be a burden so long as evolution upon the lower planes proceeds.

" By the ' man hearkening to the voice of his wife ' is signified the consenting of the ' man ' or ' rational principle '; and whereas the rational consented, it also averted or cursed itself, and on that account the whole external man was averted (from celestial life), which is signified by the ' ground being cursed for thy sake '; to ' eat thereof in great sorrow,' signifies that the state of his life would become miserable ; and that this state would continue to the end of that Church."—SWEDENBORG, *Arc. Cel. to Gen.* iii. 17.

See ADAM (lower), EDEN, EVE, FALL, GROUND, HEEL, SERPENT (subtil), TREE OF KNOWLEDGE.

CURSE ON THE SERPENT :—

A symbol of limitation of the desire-mind to the lower planes in the soul.

"And the Lord God said unto the serpent, Because thou hast done this, cursed art thou above all cattle, and above every beast of the field ; upon thy belly shalt thou go, and dust shalt thou eat all the days of thy life."—GEN. iii. 14.

And the judgment of the Divine nature is that the lower mind is indeed lower in quality than the sub-human desires and instincts which preceded its evolution. It shall remain upon the lower planes, and shall be nourished upon the activities which proceed from the lower nature.

See BEAST, DUST, EDEN, FALL, FIELD, MAN (natural), SERPENT (subtil).

CURTAINS OF THE TABERNACLE OR OF THE KAABA :—

Symbolic of the higher emotions, veiling the causal-body.

See KAABA, PILLARS (light), TABERNACLE.

CUSH, OR ÆTHIOPES :—

A symbol of the astro-mental nature.

"The parentage of Andromeda, the Soul, denotes the origin of the Soul from the astral Fire or Æther signified by the land of Æthiopes."—*The Perfect Way,* p. lxv.

See ANDROMEDA, EDEN RIVERS, GIHON.

CUSHION TO RECLINE UPON :—

Emblem of security and trust in the Divine nature.

See PILLOW.

CUTTING INSTRUMENTS OF BRASS AND IRON :—

Symbolic of the incisive intellectual powers of analysis and discrimination.

See BRASS, IRON, METAL, TUBAL.

CYBELE, GODDESS RHEA :—

A symbol of primordial space on the higher planes.

See CURETES, NUT, RHEA.

CYCLOPES—THEY WHO SEE ALL ROUND :—

Symbolic of Divine powers upon the higher planes. They are the Monads of form—the highest builders of forms on the planes of buddhi and manas.

The Cyclopes are the first principles and causes of the figures which subsist everywhere. Hence theology says that they are ' manual artificers.' For this triad (Cyclopes) is perfective of figures, ' And in their forehead one round eye was fixed ' (Hesiod)."—HERMIAS, *Phædr.,* Taylor, pp. 12–14.

The "one round eye" is a symbol of perception on each of the higher planes. The forms (figures) of organic life are modelled from growth-patterns on higher planes.

See BUILDERS, MEN (one-eyed), MONAD OF FORM, POLYPHEMUS, PROTOTYPES.

CYNO-CEPHALI, NINE PORTERS OF THIS GREAT SOUL :—

Symbols of egos who shall rise to Divine manhood. Nine is their number, in that they have attained perfection on the three lower planes, and that man becomes more than man when the tenth stage is reached.

See AFU-RĀ, APES (nine), ARIES, NINE, TEN, TUAT.

CYZICUS, KING OF THE DOLIONES :—

A symbol of faith arrived at through interior meditation wherein the possibility of achieving freedom from the thraldom of physical illusion occurs.

See DOLIONES, SHAVING.

DÆMON, OR GOOD DAIMON :—

A symbol of the Higher Self, or of the Individuality in the causal-body.

Epictetus teaches—" The important thing is, not that he should search out all things above and beneath the earth, but that he should commune with the dæmon within him and serve him with sincerity ; the greater are the difficulties which oppose themselves to the investigation of the Real, the more should a man hold to that which in the changefulness of things and of opinions can alone give us calm,—to the conviction that nothing can happen to us which is not according to the nature of the universe, and that none can oblige us to act against our own conscience."—E. ZELLER, *Eclecticism*, p. 278.

" By each man standeth, from his natal hour, a dæmon, his kind mystagogue through life."—Menander, quoted by PLUTARCH. *De Tranqu-Animi*, 15, 474 B.

" He (Mind) is the Good Daimon. Blessed the soul that is most filled with Him, and wretched is the soul that is empty of the Mind."—*The Key, Corpus Hermeticum.*

"Archedamus thinks that the voice which influenced Socrates was . . . the influence of a superior intelligence and of a Diviner soul, operating upon the soul of Socrates, whose calm and holy temper fitted him 'to hear this spiritual speech which, though filling all the air around, is only heard by those whose souls are freed from passion and its perturbing influence.' "—PLUTARCH, *On the Dæmon of Socrates.*

" Did Socrates therefore call his own nature, which was very critical and productive, God ? Just as Menander says ' our mind is God.' And Heraclitus, ' a man's character is his dæmon.' "— PLUTARCH, *Qu. Platon.* I. 2. p. 999.

The " dæmon " is the Higher Self or Individuality, in relation to the Personality (Socrates) which was approaching perfection and gradually accomplishing its salvation. The " taking poison " is a symbol of the final quietus given to the lower nature, after which the consciousness rises to the higher state.

See AGATHODAIMON, ATMAN, BIRDS (two), FIG-FRUIT, HIGHER AND LOWER SELVES, INDIVIDUALITY, MIND, PERSONALITY, SELF.

DÆMONS :—

A symbol of intelligences on the buddhic and higher mental planes, which assist evolution and are related to the higher emotions and thoughts.

" There are certain mediary divine powers, between Æther above and earth beneath, situate in that mid-space of air, by whom our desires and deserts reach the Gods. These the Greeks call dæmons, carriers between human and heavenly, hence of prayers, thence of gifts ; back and forth they fare, hence with petition, thence with sufficiency, interpreters and

bringers of salvation."—APULEIUS, *De Deo Socratis*, 6, 132.

The " mid-space of air " signifies the higher mental plane which is in the middle between the higher and lower natures. By means of the higher mind, the " bridge of manas," communications pass from the higher nature to the lower, and from the lower to the higher. The aspirations of the soul always elicit a Divine response.

See ÆTHER, AIR, ANGELS, BARSOM, DEVAS, HERMES, IRIS, ISIS, SPENTO, THOTH.

DAEVAS :—

A symbol of the lower desires, errors, and illusions, which are the the opposites of the higher emotions, truths, and ideals.

" While Ormazd was thus completing his Light-creation, Ahriman was making a corresponding evil being for every good being created by Ormazd. These stood in their ranks and orders, with their seven presiding evil spirits, or Daevas, corresponding to the Amshaspands." *Zoroastrian System.*

And whilst upon the upper planes of buddhi-manas, the archetypal creation was proceeding in accordance with the Divine Will, simultaneously upon the lower astro-mental planes of manifestation the dual, or opposite, of each ideal thing was produced. It is through the inverted reflection below of the things which are above, that the illusion of evil and error is created in the soul. The dual or relative creation in the lower nature comes as an opposite thing to the relationship of the mind with the higher nature ; and what is ranked and ordered above is correspondently arranged below. The order in which the ranks are maintained refers to the several planes upon which the universe is manifest.

See AHRIMAN, ASURA, DAIMONS, DEMONS, DEVILS, DOG-STAR, HOMA-JUICE, OPPOSITES, RAKSHASAS, SPENTO, ZAIRIMYANGURA.

DAIMONS, OR DEMONS (LOWER ASPECT) :—

A symbol of the desires which coalesce with thought and contain energies directed to the external world. Also the appetites, passions and illusions of the lower nature.

"Those species of the daimons which continue in the quality of their own class,—these love men's rational nature, and are called daimons proper."—*The Perfect Sermon*, V., HERMES.

"One alone is Good, whose free utterance is His manifestation through His Son ; it is by Him alone that the heart can become pure, when every evil essence has been expelled from it. Now, its purity is prevented by the many essences which take up their abode in it, outraging it in divers fashions. . . . Thus it is with the heart so long as it has no care taken of it, ever unclean and the abode of many daimons" (Valentinus).—CLEM. ALEX., *Strom.* II. 20, 114.

See ANIMALS, ASURAS, BEASTS, DAEVAS, DEMONS, DEVILS, HARPIES, HEALING, RAKSHASAS, SERPENTS.

DAHAKA, THE SERPENT :—

A symbol of illusion and the sense of separateness.

See SERPENT (dahaka), THRAETONA.

DAITYA, THE GOOD RIVER :—

A symbol of relative truth which purifies the mind.

DAKSHINA FIRE OR BREATH : THE SOUTHERN FIRE :—

A symbol of the desire-nature which ultimately leads to the purification of the soul. The " southern fire " signifies the astral plane of the desires.

See AGNIHOTRA, FIRE, SOUTH.

DANAANS (GREEKS) :—

A symbol of the lower mental qualities and faculties.

See ACHAIANS, CAUSAL-SELF, GREEKS.

DANCE, DANCING :—

A symbol of mental and buddhic activities exercised harmoniously and in accordance with a governing principle.

"Make the dispelling of worldly love thy true and perfect tune, and set thy heart a-dancing to the Word " (Hymn of Guru Amar Das).—MACAULIFFE, *Sikh Religion*, Vol. II. p. 175.

"Thou hast turned for me my mourning into dancing : thou hast put off my sackcloth, and girded me with gladness."—Ps. xxx, 11.

Through suffering the soul is disciplined, and conflict is changed to harmony when the higher activities are brought into play.

"The conception of a sudden presence of God goes back, among the Neo-Platonists, to Plato and the Greek Mysteries, in which the God was held suddenly to arrive and to take part in the sacred dance. Such rings of sacred dancers, ' choirs,' are still characteristic of Dionysius, e.g. *Heavenly Hierarchy*, vii. 4."—F. VON HUGEL, *Mystical Element*, Vol. II. p. 97.

See HARMONY, MUSIC AND DANCING, SACKCLOTH, SATYRS.

DANCE, CIRCLE, ROUND A CENTRE :—

A symbol of the harmonious exercise of the higher qualities, in unison with a central ideal.

"We perpetually revolve about the Principle of all things, even when we are perfectly loosened from it, and have no longer a knowledge of it. But when we behold it, then we obtain the end of our wishes. Then also we are no longer discordant, but form a truly divine dance about it."—PLOTINUS, *On the Good, or the One*, § 8.

"In the ' Acts of John ' the disciples are described as holding one another's hands so as to make a ring round Jesus, who stands in the midst, and to each line He sings, they intone in chorus the sacred word ' Amen.' "

Jesus exhorts a disciple thus,—

"Now respond thou to my dancing. See thyself in Me who speak, and when thou hast seen what I do, keep silence on my mysteries."

Then dancing,—

"Observe what I do, for thine is this passion (suffering) of the Man, which I am to suffer."—G. R. S. MEAD, *Fragments, etc.*, pp. 431–4.

The " disciples " are symbols of twelve of the most disciplined qualities of the soul, and they therefore stand, as it were, round the central Ideal (Jesus), and look for teaching and guidance to that which is highest. Then, as the Divine nature in the midst expresses the harmony (singing) within, the disciplined qualities vibrate in unison. The exhortation is the teaching of the Spirit that the quality must merge and identify itself with the Divine, and conform unreservedly to that which is higher than it can understand. It is to observe the harmony (dancing) within the spiritual and ethical Ideal, and to bear patiently the suffering which it has to undergo in the personality (man) in order that the Divine ideal may be realised.

"Scaliger, who astonished Charles V by his dancing powers, says the bishops were called ' Praesules ' because they led the dance on feast days. According to some of the Fathers, the angels are always dancing, and the glorious company of the apostles is really a 'chorus' of dancers."—*Encyclopædia Britannica*.

See ANGELS, APOSTLES, DISCIPLES, GOPIS, HARMONY, HOURIES, MUSES, MUSIC, PHAEACIANS, SATYRS.

DANCES OF HEAVENLY NYMPHS :—

Symbolic of the harmonious exercise of the higher emotions within the inner nature of the soul.

"And with the dances of the heavenly nymphs, that Palace shone like mount Kailasa."—*Buddha-Karita*, Bk. II. 30.

The "dances of the heavenly nymphs" are the higher activities in the soul. The "Palace" is the causal-vehicle, which is said to shine, inasmuch as it shows forth the splendours within it, which are perceived through the intuition.

"Now his elder son was in the field ; and as he came and drew nigh to the house, he heard music and dancing."— LUKE xv. 25.

The intellect (elder son) is still engaged with the things of the lower life. But it is appealed to through harmony (music) and rhythm (dancing), that is, through knowledge derived by means of avenues of perception awakened upon higher planes. As it then draws nigh to a higher state of consciousness (the house), so it becomes aware of that which had previously escaped its notice.

See CALF (fatted), HEAVENLY NYMPHS, HUSKS, KAILASA, MUSIC, PRODIGAL.

DANIEL AND JOSEPH :—

Symbols of the Self incarnate in the lower nature of the soul, and gradually expressing outwardly the Truth that is within.

"As Joseph was carried captive to Egypt, so was Daniel to Babylon ; (Ch. I. 2) like Joseph he must change his name ; (7). God makes the prince of the eunuchs favourable to him, as the chief butler to Joseph ; (9). he abstains from polluting himself with partaking of the king's meats and drinks, which are pressed upon him ; (8). a self-denial held as meritorious in the time of Antiochus Epiphanes, as that of Joseph with regard to Potiphar's wife ; like Joseph he gains eminence by the interpretation of a dream of the king,

which his wise men were unable to explain to him."—D. F. STRAUSS, *Life of Jesus*, Vol. I. p. 83.

The change of name signifies difference in aspect or condition of limitation. The head officials are the highest qualities of the lower nature, which therefore favour the Self. The "self-denial" indicates that the Spirit cannot be nourished or satisfied with the things of sense and desire. The interpreting of the dreams signifies the bringing knowledge of the problems of life which the lower mind and its faculties (wise men) are unable to solve.

See JOSEPH.

DARDANUS, SON OF ZEUS :—

A symbol of experience of the ego, produced by the Higher Self (Zeus).

DARKNESS—HIGHER ASPECT :—

Symbolic of the inscrutable Source of the One and the All, under the terms, the Absolute, the Potential, the Unknowable, and the Unmanifest.

"With the Egyptians, Darkness was the mystery of all mysteries. As Damacius (*On First Principles*) says : 'Of the First Principle the Egyptians said nothing ; but characterised it as a darkness beyond all intellectual conception.—a thrice unknown Darkness.'" —G. R. S. MEAD, *T. G. Hermes*, Vol. I. p. 91.

"It is necessary to point out that darkness is not to be understood, every time it is mentioned, in a bad sense ; Scripture speaks of it sometimes in a good sense. . . . Darkness and clouds and tempest are said in Exodus (xix. 9, 16) to be round about God, and in the 18th Psalm, v. 11,—'He made darkness His secret place, His tent round about Him, dark water in clouds of the air.'"— ORIGEN, *Comm. on John*, Bk. II. § 23.

See JOB xxxviii. 9.

"In the beginning darkness existed, enveloped in darkness. All this was indistinguishable water." — *Rig-Veda*, MANDALA, X. 129.

"This universe first existed only in darkness, imperceptible, undefinable, as if immersed in sleep."—*Laws of Manu*, I. 5.

"Darkness that knew no bounds was in Abyss, and Water, and subtle Breath intelligent ; these were by power of God in Chaos."—*The Sacred Sermon*, Hermes.

"Sanchuniathon supposes the beginning of all things to consist of a Dark Mist of a spiritual nature, or as it were a Breath of dark mist, and of a turbid chaos black as Erebus."—PHILO BYBLIUS, *Fragment*.

"According to Berosus.—In the

beginning all was darkness and water."
Cory's Anc. Frag., p. 58.

"The Marquesas Islanders have a legend which relates that in the beginning there was no life, light, or sound in the world, that a boundless night, *Po*, enveloped everything, over which *Tanaoa*, which means 'darkness,' and Mutu-hei, which means 'silence,' ruled supreme."
—FORNANDER, *Polynesian Race*, Vol. I. p. 63.

"The doctrine (of Christian mysticism) is ever that which is so emphatically enforced by the great non-Christian schools of mysticism, that the Being of Beings is cognisable only by the purified mind. At first the Supreme Reality appears to the inner eye as darkness. This apparent darkness is, however, in itself light, dazzling and blinding in its splendour, and it gradually becomes visible as such, when the spiritual vision is purged and strengthened and renewed by the stripping off of all love for the relative, the dependent, the phenomenal, and by the assiduous practice of all moral virtues."—W. S. LILLY, *The Great Enigma*, p. 267.

See ABYSS, ATEA, BLACK, CHAOS, DEEP, EGG,' NIGHT (primordial), PO, TAABOA, TANAOA, WATER.

DARKNESS—LOWER ASPECT :—

Symbolic of ignorance which is absence of the light of Truth.

"The profundity of each body is matter. Hence all matter is dark, because reason is light, and intellect is reason."—PLOTINUS, *On Matter*, § 5.

"Darkness is falsity proceeding either from ignorance of the truth, or from a false principle of religion, or from a life of evil."—SWEDENBORG, *Apoc. Rev.*, n. 413.

"For thou art my lamp, O Lord : and the Lord will lighten my darkness."
—2 SAM. xxii. 29.

"The Man stands in the middle between the two worlds of light and darkness, left to his own free-will."
—*Zoroastrian System.*

Seated in the causal-body upon the higher mental plane, and midway between the physical state and the Atman, the human soul starts its career as a limited but responsible entity, which is thenceforth accountable to itself for its thoughts, conduct, and experiences. These are periodically and ultimately collected, reviewed, and co-ordinated in the causal-body, and thus it is that the ego is able, through identifying himself with the true Self of his being, to attain final liberation from ignorance and evil.

" 'There is no darkness, and there is

no shadow of death, where they who work iniquity may be hid' (JOB xxxiv 22). What did he intend to designate by 'darkness' but ignorance, and what by the 'shadow of death,' except oblivion ? For it is said of the ignorance of certain persons, 'Having their mind obscured with darkness' (EPH. iv. 18.). And it is written again of the oblivion which comes on us at death, 'In that day all their thoughts shall perish' (Ps. cxlvi. 4). Since then, whatever is thought of during life is utterly consigned to oblivion by death ; oblivion is a kind of shadow of death."—ST. GREGORY, *Morals on the Book of Job*, Vol. III. p. 99.

See BIRTH OF BUDDHA, DAYLIGHT, DAYS, EXPERIENCES, HIDING PLACE, IGNORANCE, LIGHT, MATTER, NICODEMUS, NIGHT (darkness) WOMEN'S LIFE, YOMI.

DATE-PALM LEAVES, AS A SCREEN :—

An emblem of self-sufficiency, a shielding of the lower self from the light of the Higher Self.

See SHELTER FROM SUN.

DAUGHTERS OF MEN :—

A symbol of the lower affections and emotions which proceed from minds united with desires.

"The sons of God saw the daughters of men that they were fair ; and they took them wives of all that they chose."—GEN. vi. 2.

The Egos or ideals in the mind identified themselves with the sense-objects, and so affection for the things of desire was set up, and hence illusion was produced. The "taking of wives" is the seeking by the Egos for the Self through the taking of forms, or bodies.

"*Men* are certain minds or thoughts; and a host of thoughts are now discerned to be alive within us ; their 'daughters' are the affections springing from them."
—A. JUKES, *Types of Genesis*, p. 108.

"In the days when the sons of God came down to the daughters of men. Under this descent some have supposed that there is an enigmatical reference to the descent of souls into bodies, taking the phrase 'daughters of men' as a tropical expression for this earthly tabernacle."—ORIGEN, *Comm. on John*, Bk. VI, § 25.

See CHILDREN OF MEN, MAN, NEPHILIM, SONS AND DAUGHTERS, SONS OF GOD.

DAVID, KING OF ISRAEL :—

A symbol of the natural man, that is, the lower mental and

emotional nature which rules over the little-developed qualities of the soul.

"God's Son, who was born of the seed of David according to the flesh, who was declared to be the Son of God with power, according to the spirit of holiness, by the resurrection from the dead."—Rom. i. 3, 4.

This represents the genealogy of the indwelling Christ after the lower nature (the flesh),—the natural heredity, as it were. "David" is ruler of the lower nature (earth), and it is through this condition of ruler-ship of matter in the soul that the Invisible is embodied. The Christ cannot actually be manifested among men excepting through a physical vehicle of sufficiently exquisite re-sponsiveness to enable It to incarnate and reveal its nature in some degree. It must be borne in mind that the Christ is not ultimated in the human race until the physical brain matter is adapted to interpret the functionings which play upon it from Above. In this explanation of "Jesus" is to be found the connection between the supposed external or historic, and the inward or essential, Christ.

"What are the conquests of David, or the greater conquests of David's everlasting Son, over the kingdoms of the earth, but a shadow of that inward conquest which Christ worketh over his enemies within our souls, which is more valuable than the earth, and to conquer which is a higher achievement than to subdue the kingdoms of the earth ? The soul is a thing for the Son of God to conquer, the world is for Cæsar, or the son of Philip. The soul, the boundless world of the soul to recover, to reconcile its warring powers, to breathe the life of God over its chaotic wastes—this is a work whereof all outward works are only fit to be the emblems ; a work, in the execution of which every spiritual man feels the going forth of his Saviour conquering and to conquer."—Ed. Irving, *Writings*, Vol. I. p. 403.

See Blind man, Christ, Earth, Flesh, Incarnation, Israelites, Jonathan, Man (natural), Resur-rection, Rock of salvation.

DAVID, SON OF :—

A symbol of the mind in its lower evolutional aspect, or a state of the lower mind.

"A Canaanitish woman came out from those borders, and cried saying,

Have mercy on me. O Lord, thou son of David ; my daughter is grievously vexed with a devil. But he answered her not a word. And his disciples came and besought him saying, Send her away."—Mat. xv. 22, 23.

So long as Christ is appealed to as mind (man),—as a "son of David,"—the lower emotion-nature (the woman) is addressing Him from the lowest state. It is therefore really no appeal, and no answer to the prayer can be given. The qualities (disciples) do not relish the use to which they were to be put in order to allow of the gracious act of the Christ afterwards taking place.

"Jesus requires faith of the blind men (Mat. ix. 27), that he may thereby raise their thoughts higher ; they had called Him the son of David, therefore He instructs them that they should think higher things of Him. Thus He does not say to them, Believe ye that I can ask the Father ? but, Believe ye that I am able to do this ? They say unto Him, Yea, Lord. They call Him no more son of David, but exalt Him higher, and confess His dominion. Then He lays His hand upon them."—St. Chrysostom.

See Disciples, Healing, Man, Woman.

DAWN, DAYBREAK, DAY-SPRING :—

A symbol of the commencement of manifestation—the period of the Self's forthgoing to establish the planes of nature. This is typified in the approach of sunrise when the sun (the Self) appears.

"Verily, the Dawn is the head of the Horse which is fit for sacrifice ; the Sun its eye, the Wind its breath, the Mouth the Vaisvânara fire, the Year the body of the sacrificial Horse, etc."—*Brihad. Upanishad*, V. 1.

The "Horse sacrifice" has the same meaning as the "Lamb sacrifice," and is a symbol of the sacrifice of the Logos in the involution of Himself in matter. Hence the "Horse" often stands for the "Ram" in the first sign of the Zodiac, which represents the sun's (the Self's) entrance upon his course.

The "head of the Horse" signifies the beginning of manifestation. The "Year the body" represents the whole Cycle of Life. The "Sun its eye" stands for the Higher Self, the per-ceiving consciousness. The "Wind its breath " signifies the Divine Life active upon the mental plane. The " Mouth the Vaisvânara fire " signifies the Divine Will expressed in the energies of the atma-buddhic plane.

See ADITI, ARIES, ASURA, CREATION, EAST, HORSE-SACRIFICE, MĀYĀ (higher), MORNING, NUT, SUN-RISING, VAISVÂNARA.

DAY :—

A symbol of a period of activity upon the upper planes.

DAY, GREAT, OF BRAHMA :—

A symbol of a manvantara or cycle of manifestation upon seven planes. The " Great Day " is preceded, and also followed, by a period of inactivity,—pralaya.

See ABRAXAS, MANVANTARA, PRALAYA, SAMSARA, TUAT, YEAR, ZODIAC.

DAY AND NIGHT :—

Symbolic of periods of spiritual and material activity, in major or in minor cycles.

" Day and Night are Pragâpati, its day is spirit, its night matter."—*Prasna Upanishad*, I. 13.

" Learning through this treatise, by trouble and day and night painstaking." —Preface to the *Bundahis*.

Learning from the Book of Life is possible only by effort and " day and night painstaking," that is, through experience in a successive series of physical incarnations.

See GILGOOLEM, JOB, NIGHT, PRAGÂPATI, RE-INCARNATION, SICKLE, SONG.

DAYLIGHT AND DARKNESS :—

Symbolic of the spiritual and the material aspects of existence. Perception and non-perception of the higher activities of being.

" Now what daylight, as it were, there was for Pragâpati, on creating the gods, of that he made the day; and what darkness, as it were, there was for him, on creating the Asuras, of that he made the night : there are these two, day and night."—*Sata. Brâh.*, XI. 1, 6, 11.

Divine Wisdom (Pragâpati) is said " by the breath of his mouth " to " create the gods on entering the sky," which means that the highest ideals (gods) of goodness and truth are first produced on the plane of buddhi

(sky). Then their opposites, evil and error (the asuras), are necessitated to appear on the astral and lower mental planes. Thus manifestation becomes divided into higher and lower planes : the first, a realm of light (day) and the second, a realm of darkness (night).

See CREATION, DARKNESS (lower), DAWN, LIGHT, MORNING, NIGHT.

DAYS :—

Symbolic of periods of manifestation. Cycles of involution and evolution. The " six days " of Gen. i. are all periods of involution, not of evolution. It is stated that the " evening and the morning were one day," that is, the twelve hours between the evening and the morning were the period meant, which corresponds with the twelve hours of the night of the Egyptian Tuat. The under-world or lower world of our present experience is always said to be in darkness, because the Higher Self (the sun) is obscured, and we are plunged in spiritual ignorance and error.

" And God called the light Day, and the darkness he called Night. And there was evening and there was morning, one day."—GEN. i. 5.

The " light " is the consciousness, the spirit-side of being, whilst the " darkness " is the material, the form-side of nature. " Evening " and " morning " are symbolic of the indrawing and the outgoing forces, constituting the first Life-wave.

See DARKNESS, EVENING, LIGHT, MORNING, NIGHT, SEASONS (six), SEPHIROTH, SIX, WEEK.

DAYS, FIVE, SUPERADDED TO 360 DAYS :—

The five days are taken as signifying the five manifest planes of nature. When these five planes are emanated, they are, as it were, *added* to the 360 degrees (days) of the Zodiac, or potential cycle of life, making it the *actual* cycle (365 days) of the course of the sun (Higher Self).

" These several 70th parts of the moon's illuminations, making five new days, Thoth afterwards joined together and added to the 360 of which the year formerly consisted : which days are called by the Egyptians the epact or superadded, and observed by them as the birthdays of the gods."—PLUTARCH, *Isis and Osiris*, § 12.

Prior to the Earth cycle the Lunar cycle was established, which gives rise to the evolution of the human race. The higher mind (Thoth) becomes related to 72 conditions on the physical, astral, and mental planes, which serve to correlate the five planes upon which manifestation now proceeds, and within which related planes are chronically comprised the 360 degrees of the Zodiac (year)—symbol of the life-cycle through which the development of the soul is accomplished. On the five planes of primordial nature, the Divine life (the gods) in five aspects takes birth.

See AROUERIS, BIRTH OF OSIRIS, CREATION, DECANS, ELEMENTS (five), FIVE, GATHA DAYS (five), HORUS, LUNAR CYCLE, OSIRIS, PITRIYANA, PLANES (five), RULERS (five), THIEVES (five), THOTH, WORLDS (five), YEAR, ZODIAC.

DEAD, BURYING OF THE :—

A symbol of the painful ridding of the old dead self by the ego. The moralised personality putting under the " old Adam."

" ' Lord, suffer me first to go and bury my father.' Jesus answered, ' Leave the dead to bury their own dead ; but go thou and publish abroad the kingdom of God.' "—LUKE ix. 59, 60.

" This signifies the hankering after some time-worn association which is, as it were, ' father ' of the personal state of mind, and which effectually prevents the 'kingdom of God,' or first hand, interior, religion, from being understood. The Christ enjoins the leaving of such impedimenta to natural dissolution, and the turning of the soul to truth and righteousness."

" ' Why seek ye the living among the dead ' (LUKE xxiv. 5). We go to look for Christ in the tomb of moribund creeds, and refuse to believe that He can be anywhere else. . . . We fail to see the Living Christ standing in the midst of the mighty movements of the day and directing them to diviner issues."—R. J. CAMPBELL, *Serm., The Resurrection Life.*

See ADAM (lower), CORPSE, FATHER (lower), OINTMENT, PERSONALITY, TOMB.

DEAD TO BE JUDGED :—

Symbolic of the lower personalities to be estimated according to their merits and demerits.

" For unto this end was the gospel preached even to the dead, that they might be judged according to men in the flesh, but live according to God in the spirit."—1 PETER iv. 6.

The lower personalities having had placed before them spiritual knowledge as a means of development, they are in a position to profit through their experiences of the lower life (flesh), so that the Divine nature within them may unfold to the light.

" By the dead who are to be judged, in a universal sense are meant they who have died out of the world, but in a proper sense are meant they who have not any spiritual life."—SWEDENBORG, *Apoc. Rev.,* n. 525.

See CORPSE, GOSPEL, JUDGMENT-DAY, MAN (natural), PERSONALITY.

DEAD, RISING FROM THE :—

A symbol of the consciousness rising from the lower nature to the higher, from the personality to the individuality.

" The Naassene exclaims, ' The dead shall start forth from their graves,' that is, from the earthly bodies, being born again spiritual, not carnal. For this, he says, is the Resurrection that takes place through the gate of heaven, through which, he says, all those that do not enter remain dead."—HIPPOLYTUS, *Bk.* V. p. 143.

The " earthly bodies " are the mental, astral, and physical bodies of the lower nature (earth). The " gate of heaven " is the higher mental plane, the central plane between the higher and lower natures. The personalities which do not rise to the higher planes are mortal and " remain dead": the individualities which emanate them are alone immortal and seated in causal-bodies.

" ' Blessed are the dead ' (REV. xiv. 13) does not, I think, mean, ' Blessed are they whose bodies are dead '; the death referred to is not physical. Now the phrase ' in the Lord,' even in the ordinary interpretation, means in a state of faith, a state of conscious union with God. That I believe is the true meaning of the phrase, a conscious union with God, with the Source of all life, and therefore union with all God's world. Now what is it that dies in that consciousness of union with God ? It is the lower self, the illusion that we are separate from God, that dies in the other consciousness, as the stream dies in the sea, as shadows die in the sun, as darkness dies in the dawn. In the coming forth of the Divine Essence into manifestation we found individual existence. At first we did not know that we were individuals, but we discovered ourselves. Then we made the mistake of supposing that we were not only individuals but entirely separate entities."—T. RHONDDA WILLIAMS, Serm., *Dying in the Lord.*

See BORN AGAIN, CORPSE, GATE (higher), INDIVIDUALITY, PERSONALITY, REGENERATION, RESURRECTION.

DEAFNESS AND DUMBNESS :—

Symbolic of the absence of perception of the truth and love from within, and inability to express the same.

See GIFT OF TONGUES, HEALING, SIGHT.

DEARTH IN THE LAND :—

A symbol of a state of latency, or a condition unfruitful of the virtues and higher qualities of the soul.

See DEVASTATION, DROUGHT, SABBATHS, WINTER.

DEATH UNTO LIFE :—

The passage, as it were, of the human monad from the lower nature to the higher. The lower nature of the soul, centred by the personality, perishes, while the victorious ego rises to the higher mental plane and becomes one with its Lord (the Individuality) in the causal-body.

" ' Blessed are the dead who die in the Lord.' Rightly, indeed, does He call them the blessed dead, for they remain continually dead to themselves, and immersed beyond their own nature in the gladdening unity of God."—RUYSBROECK, Stoddart's trans., p. 85.

"The death that we have to die has little to do with physical dissolution ; it is the letting go, the laying down, one by one, of all the desires that seek their gratification in separateness from our brethren. One by one these shackles have to be broken, these attractions disowned, these illusions swept away."—R. J. CAMPBELL, Serm., *The Lifting up of Christ.*

The lower life is the outflowing limited life of the manifest which ends in death, while the higher life is the inflowing, increasing life towards the Ideal and Eternal within.

See MONAD OF LIFE, PERSONALITY, RE-BIRTH, RESURRECTION, SEPARATION.

DEATH OF THE FORM :—

A symbol of the withdrawal of life from the form in which it has been manifesting its qualities. All vehicles of a monad of life die after a period, and are dissipated into their primary atoms, but life and consciousness endure for ever, as they are aspects of the eternal Spirit. The human body yields up its life only in relation to its organising human monad which has withdrawn itself ; but the lives of its molecules remain, and these set up the changes called decomposition.

"When we know what *form* really is, we know what is life and what is death."

"Thus nothing is ever annihilated but the accidental, the exterior, material form ; both matter and the substantial form, i.e. spirit, being eternal " (Bruno).—J. L. McINTYRE, *Giordano Bruno*, pp. 160, 165.

"There is in ever living organism a law of Death. We are wont to imagine that Nature is full of Life. In reality it is full of Death. One cannot say it is natural for a plant to live. Examine its nature fully, and you have to admit that its natural tendency is to die. It is kept from dying by a mere temporary endowment, which gives it an ephemeral dominion over the elements—gives it power to utilise for a brief span the rain, the sunshine, and the air. Withdraw this temporary endowment for a moment and its true nature is revealed. Instead of overcoming Nature it is overcome. The very things which appeared to minister to its growth and beauty now turn against it and make it decay. . . . Life is merely a temporary suspension of these destructive powers ; and this is truly one of the most accurate definitions of life we have yet received—'the sum total of the functions which resist death.' " —H. DRUMMOND, *Natural Law*, etc., pp. 103–4.

The above presents only a negative view of life. Life is a directive agency from higher planes, guiding growth according to specific patterns of animal, vegetal, and mineral forms. The withdrawal of the directive agency is death of the form.

See ASTRAL, BIRTH (forms), DEVAS (builders), MENTAL, MONAD OF FORM, SIMILITUDES, SIVA.

DEATH OF THE PERSONALITY :—

A symbol of the perfecting of the lower nature of the soul, which implies its dissolution and the rise of the human consciousness to the higher mind. The personality is always said to be mortal. It disappears as it unites with the immortal Individuality at the end of the cycle.

"For since by man came death, by man came also the resurrection of the dead. For as in Adam all die, so also in Christ shall all be made alive."— 1 Cor. xv. 21, 22.

"Blessed are the dead which die in the Lord from henceforth." Rev. xiv. 13.

For since by the fall of mind (man) came obscuration of the Spirit, by the rise of mind comes also the return to spiritual life. For as in the lower mind or personality (Adam) there is no spiritual life, so in the higher mind ruled by the Spirit shall the individualities have immortality. Blessed are the egos whose personalities are perfected and disappear in their individualities from henceforth.

The Personality is represented in the whole series of changing incarnations of one ego. When the Personality is perfected and dissolves, the causal body is also perfected and becomes the seat of the ego in the manifest order.

See ADAM (lower), CAUSAL-BODY, CORPSE, DEAD, FALL, INCARNATION OF SOULS, INDIVIDUALITY, JESUS (mortal), LAZARUS, MAN, PERSONALITY, RESURRECTION.

DEATH OF A STATE OR CONDITION :—

A symbol of the withdrawal of life from a stage of growth or development of the soul. This occurs when the stage has effected the purpose for which it existed. Each soul-state is a specific limitation of the life within, and as the life evolves, the states begin to cramp, so that old states have to pass away and new states take their place after many degrees of overlapping.

"A truth or principle is that all life tends to encrust itself, to imprison itself within itself, and that its crust needs to be constantly broken and returned into the general mass out of which it was formed, in order that the best influences may be received. Ever there must be a return to primitive simplicity, to a condition of first principles, in which the power to receive may be freshened and renewed."—PHILLIPS BROOKS, *Mystery of Iniquity*, p. 160.

See ABSYRTUS, MULTIPLY, PATRIARCHS, SETH.

DEATH OF THE SPIRIT, SOUL, OR HIGHER SELF :—

A symbol of the descent of Spirit into Matter, or involution of spirit in matter. Of the obscuration of Spirit in the lower consciousness— the apparent withdrawal of the Self through the fall of the lower mind to the plane of desire and sense. Of an apparent passage of the Soul from a lower to a higher state of consciousness, implying death out of one state and birth into another.

"It is Christ Jesus that died, yea rather, that was raised from the dead, who is at the right hand of God, who also maketh intercession for us."— Rom. viii. 34.

It is the Higher-Self as Archetypal Man that died in the involution of the Soul, yea rather, that was in us raised from the dead in the evolution of our souls, who now is seated in our hearts to actively assist us in all well-doing and to bring our souls to perfection.

The death of the Divine Being is said to occur in the manifestation of a universe, for Spirit is unapparent in the realm of phenomena. God is always within and never without.

See AFU-RĀ, ARC. MAN, CHRIST, CROSS, CRUCIFIXION, DEATH OF OSIRIS, DISMEMBERMENT, EVOLUTION, FALL, HAND (right), INCARNATION, INVOLUTION, PRAGÂPATI RELAXED, PURUSHA, RESURRECTION, SOUL, SPIRIT.

DEATH OF BALDER :—

A symbol of the descent of the Self or Soul to incarnate on the lower planes.

"Then said Frigg : 'Neither weapon nor wood will hurt Balder because I have taken an oath from them.' but 'eastward of Valhalla there grows a twig which is called Mistletoe, and it seemed to me too young to require an oath from.' Loke now took Mistletoe, laid his command upon it, and went to the Assembly. There he found Hoder, who stood in the outermost circle of the crowd, because he was blind. Loke inquired, 'Wherefore dost thou not shoot at Balder ?' He replied 'Partly because I cannot see him, and partly because I have no weapon.' Then said Loke : 'I will point out to thee where he stands and do thou shoot at him with this wand.' So Hoder took the Mistletoe and shot at Balder. The shot pierced him, and he fell dead to the earth" (*The Prose Edda*).—HOWITT, *Literature, etc.*

Wisdom (Frigg) rules the evolutionary cycle, and sets limits on all forms (weapon, etc.) of relative experience, so that no harm can happen

to the One (Balder) who is deep
within the soul. But it appears that
in " the east " of, or above the astral
plane (Valhalla) in the new cycle,
there is the germ of mind (Mistletoe).
At present mind is latent, but as soon
as it grows into activity, the soul will
have its eyes opened, and become a
responsible being, knowing good and
evil. The Desire-nature (Loke) now
acquires the impetus of the added
mind (took Mistletoe), and so is the
means of evolving a separate will
which enables the instinct-nature
(Hoder) to co-ordinate a will and
intelligence. The instinct-nature is
lowest, and therefore lies at the outer
extreme of the evolving soul, where
it is blind, unreasoning and unenlightened. Now it is that the Desire-
mind (Loke) becomes capable of
tempting the soul, and asks why the
Higher Self (Balder), regarded as an
enemy, is not killed out ? The reply
is given that the Lower-nature (Hoder)
is unaware of its existence, and also
that there are no means in its power
for effecting such an end. Then the
Desire-nature, being higher, reminds
the Lower-nature that it must needs
play its part as an agent of the evolving
Self,—that it cannot continue to exist
in ignorance of It (the conscience),
and that it must recognise its relationship with the Divine Life within.
The desire-mind, therefore, enlightens
the Lower-nature, and becomes the
means of opening its eyes, as it were ;
and so directs its aim that a commencement is made of its eventful struggle
with its great Adversary the Higher
Self. The mind (Mistletoe) then
becomes engrafted in the desires, and
the sense of conflict, or resistance to
discipline, is introduced into the
evolving soul. By this means the
unconditioned becomes the conditioned
and limited, and the " Fall " into
the underworld, or descent into the
lower realm of births and deaths
is accomplished.

See ASAR, ASGARD, BALDER, DOORS,
DROPNER, FALL, FRIGG, HEIMDALL,
HERMOD, HODER, HYRROCKEN, LOKE,
MISTLETOE, MJOLNER, NANNA, ODIN,
RINGHORNE, SERPENT (water), VAL-
HALLA, WEEPING.

DEATH OF LEMMINKAINEN :—

A symbol of the descent of the Self
to the lower planes.

" The Lady of Pohjola imposed a third
condition on Lemminkainen (to giving
her daughter to him) that he should
kill with an arrow the Swan that lives
on the black waters of the river of Tuoni,
lord of the dead. And Lemminkainen
went down into the abysses of Manala,
the abode of the dead. But there, near
the river, lay in wait for him the evil-
minded Shepherd whom he had despised
and spared. And when he came near,
this Shepherd pulled from the waters a
monstrous Serpent and hurled it against
him; the viper penetrated into the very
vitals of the hero, and he died, thinking
on his mother. Then the Shepherd
threw him into the waters of the black
river, and Tuoni cut him to pieces with
his sharp sword and strewed his limbs
on the stream.—Professor COMPARETTI,
Traditional Poetry of the Finns, p. 86.

The astro-physical nature (Lady of
Pohjola) offers, as it were, to the
Higher Self (Lemminkainen) the
Sense-nature (her daughter) on condition that the spiritual nature or
Divine germ (swan on the dark
waters) is destroyed. So the Higher
self descends into the lower nature
(abysses of Manala) and becomes
involved therein, as the Archetypal
man. But the lower instincts (the
evil Shepherd), whose origin is beneath, had now evolved and become
allied with the Desire-nature (the Serpent). This combination killed out
for a time the higher promptings, and
so the Self is said to die. But the
hope of the Self's resurrection lies
in the Wisdom-nature (the Divine
Mother) and the transmutations to be
effected through it (buddhi). The
soul is now ruled by the Desire-
mind (Tuoni, lord of the nether
world), and the struggle below produces limitation and diversity. But
in all qualities (limbs of the Ineffable)
there is to be found the germ of progress.

See ARC. MAN, DISMEMBERMENT,
HODER, LEMMINKAINEN, PRAGÂPATI,
SERPENT (water), SWAN.

DEATH OF OSIRIS :—

A symbol of the immersion of the
Higher Self in the matter of the lower
planes, as the Archetypal Man.

" Osiris laid himself down in the chest

that had been prepared for him, and forthwith Set and his companions put the cover on, and nailed it down. Afterwards, Isis searched for and found the chest, which had been cast into the sea. This she eventually put in an unfrequented place. Set, however, as he was out hunting, accidentally met with it, opened it, and tore the body into several pieces, fourteen (or more) in all, dispersing them up and down in different parts of the country. Isis, hearing of this, set out in search of the scattered fragments, and wherever she found one, she there buried it, and erected a sepulchre."—PLUTARCH, *Isis and Osiris*, § 13.

The Higher Self (Osiris) in completing the process of involution into matter, occupied the lower World-soul (chest) which the laws of nature had built ; and he willingly submitted himself to the limitations imposed upon him by the lower nature (Set and companions). The Wisdom from above (Isis) was able subsequently to impress and raise the soul, after it had first been acted upon by environment through passion and desire (waves of the sea). But as the lower emotions evolve, a state of inertia supervenes (unfrequented place). Then the form-nature, motived by Desire (Set) attempts to force, as it were, the higher Life out of the soul, and the resistance being great, there is caused the evolution of many qualities which operate on various sub-planes. This implies individuation,—the homogeneous becoming heterogeneous.

Then Wisdom descends and endeavours to harmonise and discipline the qualities. The erection of a sepulchre signifies the establishment of a mode of functioning from an astro-mental centre. These sepulchres are forms of faith ; sectarian presentations which are too often but empty forms under which truth is buried.

John Scotus (Erigena) understood much of the processes of Involution and Evolution, as the following account will show. The first sentence may be taken as referring to the Archetypal Man (Osiris).

" The uncreated but creating nature is the source of all created things. First of all, the created natures or beings, which are endowed at the same time with creative power, were produced.

These include the totality of *primordiales causæ, prototypa, primordialia exempla,* or Ideas, i.e. the eternal archetypes of things. These Ideas, which are the first causes of individual existences, are contained in the Divine Wisdom or the divine Word, the only-begotten Son of the Father. Under the influence of the Holy Ghost (or the fostering divine love) they unfold their effects, which are the created and not creating objects, or the external world. . . . Creation is an act of God by which he passes through (*processio*) the *primordiales causas,* or *principia* into the world of invisible and visible creatures. . . . Scotus says expressly that he affirms the doctrine of the descent of the Triune God into finite things, not only with reference to the single instance of the Incarnation, but with reference to all created things, or existences. Our life is God's life in us. The knowledge which angels and men have of God is God's revelation of himself in them, or theophany."—UEBERWEG'S *Hist. of Philos*, Eng. trans., Vol. I. p. 362.

Ideas,—the archetypes on the mental plane of things to appear on the lower planes,—are contained in the Archetypal Man or Incarnate God. Under the influence of Wisdom (Holy Ghost) these Ideas take effect on the astral and physical planes and become the qualities and objects on those planes. The Creative Spirit in Involution passes through the matter of the planes to endow it with that which shall afterwards appear in the " world of invisible and visible creatures."

" And the water under the earth, which is in nature indeed one, but which flows through all the paths of earth and is divided into many parts, they call Osiris, as being cut in pieces."—*Clementine Homilies*, VI. 9.

The lower water is a symbol of the astral, or astro-mental nature,—the " body of Osiris,"—which is differentiated into the qualities of the lower nature (earth).

See ARC. MAN, ASO, AVENGING, BIRTH OF OSIRIS, CHEST, COLUMN, DIONYSUS, DISMEMBERMENT, DWARF, EVOLUTION, FEAST, INVOLUTION, ISIS, MUMMY OF OSIRIS, OSIRIS, PRAGÂPATI, PURUSHA, QEBHSENNUF, SEA, SEKER, SEPULCHRES, SET, WATER, YMIR, ZAGREUS.

DEATH, KING ; YAMA THE SON OF VIVASVAT :—

A symbol of perfection ; that is, of the personality (Vivasvat) perfected

(Yama). It therefore stands for an aspect of the Higher Self, or Causal Self.

"The sage that hears and recites this primeval narrative that Death recited and Nachiketas heard is worshipped as in the sphere of Self."—*Katha. Upanishad*, III.

The spiritual ego or monad that has progressed through the sacred drama in its own experience is thereby exalted to the higher planes. As death only comes to the lower nature when it is perfected, so "Death" stands for the perfected personality which becomes one with the Self. "Nachiketas" is a symbol of the Soul which learns by experience, or is taught by the perfected personality (Yama) during its long series of incarnations in personalities. *Death* is *king* because it signifies supremacy over the lower nature.

See Gilgoolem, Manu vaivasvata, Nachiketas, Personality, Re-incarnation, Sage, Vaivasvata, Yama.

DEATHS OF THE HIGHER SELF :—

As the Higher Self is born so must He die. But these Births and Deaths on the planes are appearances only, and are consequent on the limitations with which the Logos, in manifesting, set forth. It is these limitations of Spirit which constitute the Divine Sacrifice taught in all Scriptures.

The great process of existence involves the law of birth and death, and the Supreme in coming forth as the Divine Monad, or greatest centre of consciousness, voluntarily places Himself under the law.

He is born into existence under a scheme of limitation in which He eventually dies, and is born again under another scheme. But in all this, He is the Wisdom, Life, and Consciousness of the universe ; and all the lesser monads, or sub-centres of consciousness live in, by, and through Him ; and eventually merge themselves in Him, when at the end of the cycle He returns to His source, the Absolute.

The deaths are always below in matter, and when He dies below, His power is at its highest above. He provides His vehicles for Himself, for He is Lord over all.

DECANS, THE 36,—(36 × 10 = 360 degrees) :—

These are indicative of the degrees of power in the functionings of the Logos upon the planes, during the cycle of life.

"The 36 Egyptian decans are the stars who watched for ten days each over the 360 days of the Egyptian year, and were divided into two classes, or hemispheres, those of the day and of the night."— Sayce, *Rel. of Anc. Egypt. and Babyl.*, p. 237.

The 36 stars serve to symbolise the path of the sun through the Zodiac, that is, the path of the Higher Self, or Divine Ego, through the cycle of life (year). The "decans" signify degrees of spiritual energy shown in the functionings on the planes. In the outgoing (day) the Spirit appears to become weaker and weaker ; in the incoming (night) stronger and stronger.

"Beneath the Circle of this all-embracing frame, are ranged the Six and Thirty Decans, between this Circle of the Universe and that one of the Animals, determining the boundaries of both these Circles, and, as it were, holding that of the Animals aloft up in the air, and so defining it."—"The Perfect Sermon."—G. R. S. Mead, *T. G. Hermes*, Vol. II. p. 46.

The "Circle encompassing all things," signifies the Absolute,—the Eternal Source. The "Circle of the Animals, or the Life-giving Circle," signifies the Cycle of Life, represented by the Zodiac and its animal signs. When manifestation commences, the latent Cycle of Life is, as it were, held aloft in the heavens and energised.

See Boat-sektet, Celestial stems, Circle of existence, Days (five), Planes, Self, Year, Zodiac.

DECEASED :—
See Defunct.

DECEIT (MĀYĀ) :—

Significant of illusion, the opposite of Truth.
See Illusion, Māyā (lower).

DEEP OR DEPTHS :—

A symbol of the lower nature as a region of darkness below the higher nature.

"Who shall descend into the deep ? (that is, to bring Christ up from the dead). Rom. x. 7.

This refers to the mistaken notion that the lower nature can command the higher. It is Christ of his own power who rises from the dead lower nature in the souls of men.

"When there were no depths, I was brought forth."—Prov. viii. 24.

Prior to the reflection of the Higher Self (atma-buddhi) in the "depths," —lower nature—the Higher Self was manifest on the higher planes.

See Abyss, Atea, Chaos, Delos, Fountains, Ginunga, Po, Tanaoa, Windows of heaven stopped.

DEEP, OF EA THE CREATOR :—

A symbol of the manasic plane on which the Logos creates the forms of the material universe. The firmament.

See Creation, Ea, Firmament.

DEEP, OF TIAMAT :—

A symbol of the astral plane of the lower emotions and passions, at first devoid of order.

See Astral plane, Chaos, Tiamat, Water (lower).

DEER, THAT SPRING :—

Symbolic of aspirations towards the truth.

"The spotted deer are the recognised animals of the Maruts, and were originally, as it would seem, intended for the rain-clouds."—Max Müller, *S. B. of E.*, Vol. XXXII. p. 70.

The spottedness signifies the impure appearance of the lower manifestation, which nevertheless is all pure within, and representative of the activities of the spiritual monads or divine Sparks (the Maruts). The aspirations are responded to from above, and buddhi (rain-cloud) showers truth.

See Clouds, Maruts, Rain, Spotted.

DEFUNCT, DECEASED OR DEPARTED PERSON :—

A symbol of the human individuality or causal-self on the higher mental plane. The immortal soul.

"Everywhere in the texts of the Book of the Dead the deceased is identified with Osiris. Another point to notice is the application of the words *maa kheru* to the deceased, a term which I have, for want of a better word, rendered 'triumphant.' These words actually mean 'true of voice' or 'right of word.'" —Budge, *Egyptian Ideas, etc.*, p. 144.

The identification with Osiris signifies the union of the soul with God. When the personality is perfected it becomes one with the individuality in the causal body. The individuality is then completely expressed (true of voice) on its own plane, and is in possession of all the faculties and qualities to which it is entitled through the strivings of its personalities life after life.

"Whatever he (the deceased) hath found upon his path he hath consumed, and his strength is greater than that of any spiritual body (sāhu) in the horizon ; he is the firstborn of all the firstborn . . . he hath carried off the hearts of the gods. He hath eaten the wisdom of every God, and his period of existence is everlasting, and his life shall be unto all eternity, . . . for the souls and spirits of the gods are in him" (Inscription in the pyramid of Unas).—*Ibid.*, p. 172.

The fully expressed individuality "liveth upon his fathers and maketh food of his mothers," that is, the perfected soul has been produced and sustained by the lower conditions or prior mental and emotional states which have given it birth. His powers are greater than those possessed by any causal-body (sāhu) in the lower cycle (horizon). He has priority over all previously produced states. He has acquired the ideals (gods) of wisdom, love, and truth, which make him immortal.

"The deceased himself says, 'My soul is God, my soul is eternity.'" (Papyrus of Ani).—*Ibid.*, p. 173.

The soul in its highest aspect is one with the World-soul or Higher Self the Eternal.

"Some may ask, what is it to be a partaker of the Divine nature, or a Godlike man ? Answer : he who is embued with, or illuminated by, the Eternal or Divine Light and inflamed or consumed with Eternal or Divine Love, he is a deified man and a partaker of the Divine Nature."—*Theologia Germanica*, Cap. XLI.

See Causal, Corpse, Embalmment, Father (lower), Individuality, Mummy, Osiris, Personality, Sāhu Shabti.

DEITY, HIDDEN OR CONCEALED :—

A symbol of the one Unmanifest Being, the Absolute, the Source of all.

"Manetho the Sebennyte is of opinion that the 'hidden' or 'hiding' is expressed by this word 'Ammon' . . . Hecatæus of Abdera says that the

Egyptians invoke the Supreme God as being *hidden* and *invisible*, and implore Him to make himself visible and apparent, and therefore call him ' Amun ' ; so great was the piety of the Egyptians in their teaching about the Gods."— PLUTARCH, *Isis and Osiris*, § 9.

So far as God is unmanifest in the soul and its qualities, he is, as it were, hidden, or in hiding, from the lower consciousness. The aspiration, therefore, of the soul is that God should manifest his nature in the higher qualities, and appear as a centralising Ideal to the consciousness. When God is born in the soul, he becomes, as it were, " visible and apparent " in the religious consciousness, and receives the adoration of the higher qualities of mind and emotion.

See ABSOLUTE, AFU-RĀ, AIN SOPH, AMEN, FATHER, GOD, GODHEAD, HIDING, TRINITY, ZERANA.

DELOS, THE ISLAND :—

A symbol of a centre of activity and organisation in the astral vehicle, or the lower nature of the soul.

" Delos was called out of the deep by the trident of Poseidon, but was a floating island until Zeus fastened it by adaman-tine chains to the bottom of the sea, that it might be a secure resting-place to Leto, for the birth of Apollo and Artemis. Apollo afterwards obtained possession of Delos, by giving Calauria to Poseidon in exchange for it ; and it became the most holy seat of the worship of Apollo." —*Smith's Class. Dict.*

An astral centre was established in the lower nature (the deep), through the wisdom, love, and power (the trident) of Eternal Truth (Poseidon). But this centre remained unattached and free until the Divine Will, by means of a structure of pre-physical world-essence, connected it with an astrophysical soul-body, from the func-tionings of which the higher emotion-nature (Leto) should eventually be developed, and Divine Love and Wisdom be born in the soul.

See APOLLO, ARTEMIS, CHEMMIS, DEEP, IZANAGI, LATONA, MANCO, ONOGOROJIMA, POSEIDON, TRIDENT.

DELPHI :—

See NAVEL.

DELUGE OF WATER :—

A symbol of the outpouring of ideas from the fountain of Truth (water).

The " deluge " implies the awaken-ment of the mind in ignorance and error ; for the downpouring truth (rain) is at first reflected as falsity on the astro-mental plane. The ideas of the lower mind are varieties of error, for the mind cannot know the perfect truth.

" And now when all the world was deluged, nought appeared above the waves but Manu and the seven Rishis, and the Fish that drew the ship."—*Maha-Bhārata*, III.

And now when the lower nature was, as it were, submerged in the lower ideas, and transformed by the awaken-ment of the mind in error and ignor-ance, then above the illusions of desire and sense rose the intellect in the seven races of humanity, and the Higher Self (the Fish) who guided and energised the evolution of the soul (ship).

" Unwearied thus for years on years the Fish propelled the ship across the heaped up waters, till at length it bore the vessel to the peak of Himavān ; then softly smiling, thus the Fish addressed the sage,—Haste thee to bind thy ship to this high crag."—*Ibid.*

For æons the Self guided and drew the soul onwards, until at length it raised it inwardly to a high pitch of aspiration (the peak). Then the Higher Self inclined in love to the lower which now aspired, and in-structed the soul how to seize the opportunity afforded it to attain rest or stability in firm attachment to the higher.—(*See* 2 SAM. xxii. 2–5).

All the Deluge, or Flood, stories in the sacred books expound the theme of the awakenment of the mind in ignorance which is the prelude to the attainment of Truth. The reality (water) above, is reflected in illusion (water) below, while the higher nature of the soul awaits undisturbed its evolution in due course.

See ABTU FISH, ADITYAS, ANCHOR-AGE, ARK, DEPRAVITY, FISH (great), FLOOD, HIMAVAN, HORN, JESUS (fish), LAKE, MANU, MOORING-POST, OCEAN, RAIN, ROCK, SHIP OF MANU, STONE, VAIVASVATA, WATER.

DEMETER, OR CERES :—

A symbol of the buddhic principle as functioning in the soul, and bringing forth the " fruits of the spirit " through the cultivation of the lower nature.

" Demeter was the daughter of Cronus and Rhea, and the sister of Zeus, by whom she became the mother of Persephone."—*Smith's Class. Dict.*

The buddhic principle in its manifestation proceeds from the course of time (Cronus) in space (Rhea). Buddhi is allied with Atma (Zeus); and from Atma-buddhi the emotion-nature (Persephone) is brought forth on the mental plane.

" Demeter was the goddess of the earth. She was the protectress of agriculture and of all the fruits of the earth.—*Ibid.*

Buddhi is the transmuter of the lower nature (earth), and directs the cultivation of the lower qualities that they may bear fruit upon the higher planes.

" Ceres was worshipped as the ' *Mother* of Corn.' The child she brought forth was He-Siri, ' the Seed.' or as he was most frequently called in Assyria, ' Bar,' which signifies at once ' the *Son* ' and ' the *Corn*.' The uninitiated might reverence Ceres for the gift of material corn to nourish their bodies, but the initiated adored her for a higher gift— for food to nourish their souls—for giving them that bread of God that cometh down from heaven—for the life of the world, of which, ' if a man eat, he shall never die.' Does any one imagine that it is a mere *New Testament* doctrine that Christ is the ' bread of life.' ? There never *was*, there never *could* be, spiritual life in any soul, since the world began, at least since the expulsion from Eden, that was not nourished and supported by a continual feeding by faith on the Son of God, ' in whom it hath pleased the Father that all fullness should dwell,' ' that out of His fullness we might receive, and grace for grace.' . . . That the initiated Pagans actually believed that the ' Corn ' which Ceres bestowed on the world was not the corn of this earth but the Divine ' Son,' through whom alone spiritual and eternal life could be enjoyed," we have clear and decisive proof."—A. HISLOP, *Two Babylons*, p. 161.

See AGRICULTURE, BEES, BUDDHI, CRONUS, CULTIVATION, FOOD, PERSEPHONE, RHEA, SEED, SI-OSIRI, TRANSMUTATION, ZEUS.

DEMIURGE, OR DEMIURGUS :—

A symbol of the Archetypal Man— the Self completely immersed in the matter of the lower planes—who is the World-soul and progenitor of the human race.

" The Self is the maker of all things, and he knows all things. He is the soul of all and the source of all, the perfect and omniscient author of time. He is the sustainer of Pradhāna, the *principium*, and of the migrating souls ; the disposer of the *primordia*, and the origin of metempsychosis and of liberation, of the preservation of the world and the implication of the soul. Such is the immortal Demiurgus (Isvara), residing in the soul, knowing all things, and present everywhere ; the sustainer of the world, who rules over the world for ever. There is no other principle that is able to rule over it."—GOUGH, *Svetas. Upanishad,* VI.

" The Demiurgus is the internal ruler or actuator, the first and highest manifestation of the Self. He informs and animates the elements and all living things."—A. E. GOUGH, *Phil. of the Upanishads*, p. 166.

" The universal soul is Isvara, the Self in manifestation as the creative spirit and soul of the world."—*Ibid.*, p. 62.

The Higher Self, or World-soul, descending into matter, becomes perfected as the Archetypal Man from whom matter drops away. He is then the potential pattern of humanity to become actual in the perfected souls of all.

" But the (spiritual) offspring of the Mother Achamoth, whereof she became pregnant in her contemplation of the Angels which waited on the Saviour, being of the same substance with the Mother-spiritual, was unknown even to the Demiurgus. It was secretly lodged in him without his consciousness, in order that by him having been sown in the soul which he made, and in this material body, and having therein, like an unborn babe, received growth, it might be made ready to admit the perfect Word. That Spiritual Man therefore was unknown to the Demiurgus, who was sown by Wisdom in the Natural man at the moment of his breathing into his nostrils " (Gnostic).— IRENÆUS, *Against Heresies*, Bk. I. p. 18.

The Demiurge—" the Framer of the world "—signifies here the matrix on the buddhi-manasic plane of all forms and qualities of the natural order of evolution. In this the seed of the Divine, foreign (unknown) to it, is placed. Thus it is that the germ of the higher nature (spiritual man) which proceeds from buddhi (Achamoth) on the reception by her of the higher spiritual influences (angels) from Atma (Saviour), constituting the germ atma-buddhic, is placed in the lower nature where it is un-perceived by the lower consciousness. It remains latent in the soul until development enables it to grow and come forth as the incarcate Self (Word) working for the perfection of humanity. The spiritual essence projected into the lower mind by Wisdom, unknown to the lower self (Demiurgus), constitutes man a responsible being knowing good and evil.

"The Gnostics say that they themselves are spiritual, because a certain particle of the Father's entire nature is lodged in their soul, they having their souls of the same substance as the Framer of the World (Demiurge); while he, having once for all received the entire Seed from his Mother, and retaining it in himself, continued merely animal in his nature, and had no understanding at all of the higher order of things."—*Ibid.*, Bk. II. p. 148.

The Divine spark, or spiritual ego, from the plane of Atma (Father) is lodged in the human soul, which has the same astro-mental nature as the lower World-soul (Demiurge). This lower soul containing within it the spiritual essence, can never of itself rise, nor can it understand spiritual things.

"We shall, however, be quite correct in saying that the Demiurge who made all this universe is also at the same time Father of what has been brought into existence; while its Mother is the Wisdom of Him who hath made it,—with whom God united, though not as man with woman, and implanted the power of genesis. And she, receiving the Seed of God, brought forth with perfect labour His only beloved Son, whom all may perceive—this Cosmos."—PHILO JUDÆUS, *De Ebriet.*, § 8.

The Higher Self (Demiurge) emanates the Cosmos through the buddhic (Wisdom) activities, the lower nature being, as it were, a reflection of the higher.

"When, therefore, the creation received completion, and when after this there ought to have been the revelation of the sons of God—that is of the Demiurge, which up to this had been concealed, and in which obscurity the natural man was hid, and had a veil upon the heart;—when it was time, then, that the veil should be taken away, and that these mysteries should be seen, Jesus was born of Mary the virgin, according to the declaration in Scripture, 'The Holy Ghost will come upon thee'—Sophia is the Spirit—' and the power of the Highest will overshadow thee,'

—the Highest is the Demiurge,—'wherefore that which shall be born of thee shall be called holy.' For he has been generated not from the highest alone, as those created in the likeness of Adam have been created from the highest alone—that is from Sophia and the Demiurge. Jesus, however, the new man, has been generated from the Holy Spirit—that is, Sophia and the Demiurge, —in order that the Demiurge may complete the conformation and constitution of his body, and that the Holy Spirit may supply his essence, and that a celestial Logos may proceed from the Ogdoad being born of Mary" (Valentinus).—HIPPOLYTUS, *Refutation, etc.*, Bk. VI. 30.

When involution of all things had received completion, and when subsequently in course of evolution the spiritual egos (sons of God) had incarnated, then the indwelling Self (Demiurge), who up to this period had been unmanifest, should be revealed in the soul. Humanity (natural man) up to this time had been obscured in primitive human forms, and a veil was over the higher affections (heart). It was time, then, that this veil should be removed, and that the higher nature should manifest ; therefore the Christ-soul (Jesus) was born of the purified lower nature (Mary). This birth was brought about through the brooding of Buddhi (Sophia) and Atma (Demiurge) in the purified and receptive portion of the emotion nature. The Christ-soul, the " new man," is generated in order that the " body of Christ " may be completed in human souls by means of the functioning of Buddhi (Holy Spirit); so that ultimately a celestial expression of the Divine may proceed from the reality of the Highest (Ogdoad) being born of the purified lower (Mary).

"For Christ is, in a manner, the demiurge, to whom the Father says, ' Let there be light,' and ' Let there be a firmament.' But Christ is demiurge as a beginning (arche) inasmuch as he is Wisdom. It is in virtue of His being Wisdom that He is called *arche*."—ORIGEN, *Comm. on John*, § 22. Bk. I.

"A new idea has got into the air, so to speak—new in emphasis, anyhow. It is that the universal and eternal substance, whatever it is, is itself in process of becoming, and never can be anything else. It is a sort of push or drive towards betterment. The eternal something—I cannot think of a better name at the moment—which has produced everything that is, in-

cluding ourselves, is unceasingly trying
to express itself in fuller and more
adequate forms, and will go on doing
so for ever and ever. It cannot help
it; it is its nature so to do, though
it does not know it is doing it. It
does not begin to know till it evolves
human consciousness; it knows in us,
and in no other way. . . . The average
human mind is coming more and more
to feel a difficulty in believing in the
existence of a divine being, or indeed,
a being of any sort, who is eternally
perfect without the trouble of becoming
so. Men to-day are so habituated to
the thought of growth, development,
the slow and toilsome acquirement of
fuller knowledge and power, that they
simply cannot imagine an ideal excellence
which does not involve such a process
of becoming. . . . All the same, there
is that within us which forbids us to
rest contented with this, either as an
explanation of things as they are, or
an incentive to action on the plane of
our own highest. It seems to me that
if we dig down deep enough into the
motives of our best efforts, if we penetrate
far enough into our noblest feelings, we
shall find that we know in a way that
all the good we strive after already is,
and we would not strive if we did not
know."—R. J. CAMPBELL, Serm., *Being
and Becoming.*

See ADAMAS (higher), ADRASTIA,
ARC. MAN, BIRTH OF JESUS, BREATH,
BULL (primeval), COSMOS, CREATION,
DISMEMBERMENT, EVOLUTION, IN-
CARNATION, INVOLUTION, ISVARA,
MAN (natural), MICROCOSM, MOTHER
(divine), OGDOAD, PRAGÂPATI, SEA-
SONS, SEED, SONS OF GOD, SOPHIA
ACHAMOTH, VIRGIN MARY, WOMB
(cosmic).

DEMONS AND FIENDS :—

These are nature-spirits, or non-
human intelligences concerned with
the direction of lower plane activities.
They are elemental forces, instinctive,
blind, and persistent, working automatically on the astral plane. They
build up habits, and are adverse to
spirit, striving against the Higher
attempts which are made from above
to raise the soul.

"Owing to the gracelessness which
they practised, the demons became more
oppressive, and they themselves carried
on unnatural malice between themselves; they advanced one against the
other, and smote and tore their hair
and cheeks."—*The Bundahis,* Ch. XV. 17.

The mental-body (kama-manasic
vehicle) being now built up, this
serves to render the mind of the ego

impervious to the higher rate of
vibrations from above, but at the
same time, increasingly responsive to
the vibrations from below. The
warring of the "members" (qualities)
within the lower self, the conflicts of
lusts and affections, become increasingly troublesome, and produce disorder in the lower mind. One desire
advances against another, thus de-
feating each other's ends. The
"smiting of cheeks and tearing of
hair" signify the forcible check which
is put upon one desire by another.
But the check is possible only when
forethought and the more intelligent
phases of the desire-nature come to
be evolved,—and these are typified by
the "cheeks and hair," which symbolise the higher aspects of the desires.

"Then the demons shouted out of
the darkness thus : 'You are man,
worship the demon ! so that your demon
of malice may repose."—*Ibid.,* 18.

This implies that the faint dawnings
of the lower Self, reflected in the desires through efforts at Self-realisation,
cause stress and sorrow. The first
impulse of the ego is to work for the
benefit of self, hence the lower qualities
alone are observed to be of assistance
at this stage of development.

See AHRIMAN, ASURA, DAEVAS,
DAIMONS, DEVILS, IRON AGE, MEM-
BERS, RAKSHASAS, SPENTO, VISTASP.

DENDERA :—

A symbol of a mental centre of
knowledge, by means of which a
widened experience is arrived at.

DEPRAVITY, UNIVERSAL :—

Symbolic of the vehemence of the
unruled lower desires in the soul,
which require to be disciplined.

"And the Lord saw that the wickedness of man was great in the earth,
and that every imagination of the thoughts
of his heart was only evil continually."
—GEN. vi. 5.

And the Higher Self beholds the
necessity for its further descent into
the soul. And it sees that there is
increased necessity and opportunity
for its operations amid the mental
conditions of alienation and strife
among the desires, which have been
set up upon the lower planes.

"Manu . . . conciliates the favour of
the Supreme Being in an age of universal

depravity."—MON. WILLIAMS, *Indian Wisdom*, p. 394.

The individuality (manu) operating through the lower mind seeks to discipline the turbulent lower desires and emotions.

See CORRUPTION, DELUGE, FLOOD, GOD (repenting), MANU, VAIVASVATA, WICKEDNESS.

DEPTH ; BYTHOS :—

A symbol of the primordial Divine Reality—Truth.

See CHAOS, DESERTS, OCEAN, WATER.

DESERT PLACE :—

A symbol of the domain beyond the scope of reason, which mind is unable to penetrate.

DESERTS, OR FORESTS :—

Symbolic of the solitude due to the absence of impressions from the external world of the senses.

"And the child (John) grew, and waxed strong in spirit, and was in the deserts till the day of his shewing unto Israel."—LUKE i. 80.

The moral nature (John) has to undergo the solitude necessary for growth until the mental condition shall be able to endure alone. This solitude corresponds only to the appearance in being devoid of strife, —not to the reality. It signifies the weaning of the highest part of the lower mind from the things of this world, and after that has been accomplished, then the moralised lower mind can be "shown to Israel," that is, brought into unison with those qualities which are united with the higher nature.

See FOREST, ISRAELITES, JOHN BAPTIST, WILDERNESS.

DESERTS, VAST AND UNKNOWN :—

Symbolic of primordial chaos— the infinite expanse of formless matter.

"Pwan-koo is described as appearing from the vast unknown deserts. He was four times taller than man, had horns on his head, and teeth protruding from his mouth."—KIDD, *China*, p. 100.

The Logos proceeds from the Chaos or Depth. The statement about height, refers to the fact that the measure of a man, or ego, comprehends the five planes of his being, upon

four of which he has not yet become fully conscious. The "horns" symbolise victory : they are the sign of the One who conquers the conditions of the planes. The "Lamb" or "Ram," "slain from the world's foundation," possesses the same symbol. The "teeth" symbolise power of expression,—the potential becoming the actual,—the force of that which is uttered in the Divine Fiat or Spoken Word.

"The hidden God is far above every outward thing and every thought, and is found only where thou hidest thyself in the secret place of thy heart, in the quiet solitude where no word is spoken, where is neither creature nor image nor fancy. This is the quiet Desert of the Godhead, the Divine Darkness. . . . this Abyss is our salvation" (Tauler.)—R. M. JONES, *Mystical Religion*, p. 278.

See ABYSS, CHAOS, DEEP, FANG, FOUR TIMES, HEAVEN AND EARTH, HEIGHT (Osiris), HORNS, LAMB OF GOD, MEASURE, PWANKOO, STEM, TEETH, TUSK.

DESTROYING EVILS :—

Symbolic of transcending the sense of separateness, and the illusions and attractions presented to the ego by the lower mind during the life cycle.

"Buddha was born to destroy the evils of the world."—*Buddha-Karita*, Bk. I. 20.

The Soul is born in the womb of matter (mental, astral, and physical), with the object of overcoming the things of the world,—that is, conquering the falsities which are mind-created, and which are to be destroyed through the knowledge of the Real.

See BIRTH OF BUDDHA, BUDDHA, LIBERATION, MĀYĀ (higher), SEPARATION, WOMB (Māyā).

DEVACHAN :—

A state of consciousness of the ego on the higher mental plane, wherein there is complete withdrawal of the energies from the outer world of effects. It is a self-contained state of contemplation.

See ASGARD, BAKHDHI, SEKHET-HETEP, SLEEPING (waking), UNEN.

DEVAKI, THE MOTHER OF KRISHNA :—

A symbol of Buddhi, the heavenly

mother of the Son of God in the soul of Man.

See BIRTH OF KRISHNA, KRISHNA.

DEVAS, SHINING ONES :—

Exalted Intelligences of Truth, Wisdom, and Love, on the higher planes. These operate from the buddhic and higher mental planes in furthering the process of evolution. They are concerned with the higher emotions, and are attracted by aspirations from below. They are the natural opponents of the " daevas," the " asuras," which are the lower desires and emotions.

" Verily, the Devas are not dear, that you may love the Devas ; but that you may love the Self, therefore the Devas are dear."—*Brihad. Upanishad,* Ad. 2.

The higher emotions and intelligences are all centralised in the Self as the supreme source of all love and devotion. Adoration is directed to the Highest, and is truly shown in exercising the higher qualities (Devas) of Love, Justice, Truth, Goodness, Sincerity, Benevolence, Righteousness, etc., which are dear to the aspiring soul for the sake of its central Ideal.

See AMSHASPANDS, ANGELS, APSARAS, ARCHANGELS, ARDEBEHESCHT, ASHA, BAHMAN, BUILDERS, COLCHIS, COMPANY (gods), DÆMONS, GANDHARVAS, GUARDIANS (world), MESSENGERS, POTSHERD, SIRENS, VALKYRIOR.

DEVAS, OR LOWER BUILDERS :—

A symbol of nature spirits on the astral plane which undertake the formation of the material sheaths of the spirit, in which the Self's evolution is accomplished. They are elemental builders of forms, not architects, but directed by intelligences on higher planes according to the Divine scheme. The auto-intelligent action of some of the lower elementals may be discerned under the microscope in the behaviour of protoplasts or bioplasts in forming vegetable structure.

" In the work of creation Ptah had been helped by the Khnumu, ' the modellers,' who were generally counted as his children, although later as those of Râ. They were represented as dwarfs with big heads, crooked legs, very long arms, and long moustaches."—A. WIEDEMANN, *Rel. of Anc. Egyptians,* p. 137.

See BUILDERS, FIENDS, LORDS (material), NAIADS, SALAMANDERS, PTAH.

DEVASTATION :—

Symbolic of a state of barrenness and unproductiveness in the lower nature.

See DEARTH, DROUGHT, WINTER.

DEVAYĀNA—THE PATH OF THE GODS :—

A symbol of the course of the soul's evolution after the mind has begun to function, and the monad of Life, or Divine spark, has been added to the monad of form.

" Having reached the Path of the Gods, the man comes to the world of Agni (fire), to the world of Vayu (air), to the world of Varuna, to the world of Indra, to the world of Pragâpati, to the world of Brahman."—*Kaush. Upanishad,* I. 2.

Having reached the state when the spiritual egos (Gods) have entered in, implying the knowledge of good and evil, the soul has greatly enlarged possibilities before it, and first comes to the sphere of the force-aspect of development (Agni) ; to the sphere of intellect (Vayu) ; to the sphere of Truth (Varuna) ; to the sphere of steadfast devotion to the Highest (Indra) ; to the sphere of direct spiritual Vision (Pragâpati) ; to the sphere of Pure Spirit (Brâhman).

" As early as the Rigveda and the Brâhmanas mention is frequently made of the *Devayâna,* which was originally in all probability the way by which Agni bore the sacrificial gifts to the gods, or the latter descended to them. . . . The meaning of the whole is that the soul on the way of the gods reaches regions of ever-increasing light, in which is concentrated all that is bright and radiant, as stations of the way to Brahman."—DEUSSEN, *Phil. of Upanishads,* p. 335.

When at the " fall of man," the Divine sparks descended into the human astro-mental forms prepared for them, the personalities (pitris) became moral beings and entered upon the path of the higher qualities or ideals (gods). Then the forceful Divine life (Agni) working below, bears the offerings of the lower to the higher, which latter thereupon descend to actuality in the aspiring souls. By the gradual unfolding of the Divine life, stage by stage, in human nature, the souls become more and more radiant with the higher qualities of truth, wisdom, and love, until at last the darkness of ignorance and selfishness is entirely overcome and the glorified spirits enter into union with God.

"It is true that Nature is largely governed by mechanism, but in the world we find stages of development, and each stage is further removed from the coercion of mechanical laws. At every higher stage something *essentially new* comes into existence; this *new*, as it unfolds, becomes more and more independent of the mechanical laws found below it. This *new* has the essence of its being not in the elements which it has left behind, but in the ideals which are in front of itself. The full truth of all this comes out in man alone. There is much in him which belongs to the world below him, but this is not the real nucleus of his being—all that is found in a Beyond; and this is a Beyond not in space but within the soul."—E. BOUTROUX, *Education and Ethics.*

See AGNI, BIRTH CEREMONIES, BRAHMA, EVOLUTION, FALL, GIFTS OF GOD, GODS, GRACE, HEAVEN, INDRA, INVOLUTION, LAW OF ZOROASTER, LIBERATION, MAHAYANA, MAN BORN, MOON WANING, PATH (birds), PITRIYANA, PRAGÂPATI, SACRIFICE, SONS OF GOD, SPARK, VARUNA, VAYU, WAY OF DELIVERANCE, YESHTIKA.

DEVELOPMENT OF HUMANITY THROUGH MILLIONS OF YEARS :—

Development cannot be measured from the point of view of the lower mind, and there is no evidence to show that it proceeds appreciably on this physical plane. It is God the Highest who looks down; not we who look up, who can judge upon the growth of the soul. Eternal verities cannot be put into terms of space and time, for these illusions must be eliminated from the mind ere it can discern the celestial significance of the sublime teaching of the sacred scriptures of the world.

See AMBAS, INSPIRATION, REVELATION, SCRIPTURES.

DEVIL, THE ADVERSARY :—

A symbol of the illusory principle of evil. The tempting Not-Self which is opposed to the True Self. The desire-mind which is the adversary of the Divine Spirit within—the one

tending downward to matter, the other tending upward to God. Kamamanas is the inverted reflection of buddhi-manas, on the astral plane. "Demon est Deus inversus."

"Sin and the devil are one and the same."—SWEDENBORG, *Apoc. Rev.*, n. 578.

"The true devil, against whom we have to be sober and vigilant, is within man; is carried about within the human heart. He is the animal part of human nature, the devilish within; the power in ourselves that makes for unrighteousness; the lower affections, thoughts and appetites, by resisting which we can alone become moral beings."—B. WILBERFORCE, *Problems*, p. 99.

"Evil is a negative, not a positive term. It denotes the absence rather than the presence of something. It is the perceived privation of good, the shadow where the light ought to be. 'The devil is a vacuum.' Evil is not an intruder in an otherwise perfect universe; finiteness presumes it. A thing is only seen to be evil when the capacity for good is present and unsatisfied. Evil is not a principle at war with good. Good is being, and evil is not-being. When consciousness of being seeks further expression, and finds itself hindered by its limitations, it becomes aware of evil."—R. J. CAMPBELL, *The New Theology* pp. 42, 44.

See ADVERSARY, AESHM, AHRIMAN, AIDONEUS, ANGRA-MAINYU, ANTICHRIST, BEAST, DURASROBO, DRAGON (red), EVIL, HEROD, LOKE, MARA, MICTLAN, MIDGARD'S SERPENT, RAVANA, SATAN, SERPENT, SET, SUSANOWO, TANE-MAHUTA, TEMPTATION, TYPHON.

DEVILS; UNCLEAN SPIRITS :—

Symbolic of the lower desires, passions, appetites, and instincts, which, so far as they oppose the upward evolution of the soul, constitute the evil impulses of human nature.

"Christ drives out our legion of indwelling vices by His inworking presence and power."—E. GOUGH, *Barrowford Treatise*, p. 61.

"Certain women which had been healed of evil spirits and infirmities, Mary that was called Magdalene, from whom seven devils had gone out."—LUKE viii. 2.

Certain emotional states had been purified of lower desires and errors. "Mary" stands for some slumbering affection towards the Christ, but which is entangled in the pursuit of the objects of sense, seeking for satisfaction from without (which is

" whoredom ") instead of from within
—whence cometh all good. But Love
casts out the seven " devils " of
Greed, Egoism, Hate, Sorrow, Avarice,
Lust, and Pride, which are delusions
fostered by the lower activities,—or
due to the, as yet, not fully purified
soul.

" Human sins all show that wonderful
activity, mobility, facility, malignity,
which we always conceive of as belonging
only to a personality. We have almost
been driven to a personal phraseology
in speaking of them. When we see
some force working its way with restless
energy against the sluggishness of higher
forces, choosing its persons and points
of attack with some marvellous discrimination, putting on, when need
demands it, the cloak and mask of a
diviner power, malignantly, dexterously,
with such strange choice and ingenuity
doing its work, what better conception
can we form of it than that which the
sublime language of the Scripture gives
us of a personal evil, a Satan, a bad
spirit set to the endless work of thwarting
God and ruining the hope of man !
Reason may find what difficulties she
will in the doctrine of a personal Satan,
but she has yet to harmonise and arrange,
under any other idea, the phenomena
of human sin."—PHILLIPS BROOKS,
Mystery of Iniquity, p. 14.

See ASURA, DAEVAS, DAIMONS,
DEMONS, HEALING, RAKSHASES,
SPENTO, WHOREDOM.

DEVOTION :—

Reliance on the Higher Self, in
pressing forward towards a high
ideal of Goodness, Truth, and Love.
This implies the relinquishment of
desire and self-seeking.

See INDRA.

DEVOURER OF CREATURES :—

A symbol of the desire-mind which
draws to itself all instincts, sensations,
appetites, and desires, without limit
or satiety.

See AESHM, ASTODVIDAD, BOTTOM-
LESS PIT, KABANDHA.

DEW OR MIST TO MOISTEN
VEGETATION :—

A symbol of a natural desire for a
progressive existence, responded to
by Truth (water) from above.

" But there went up a mist from the
earth, and watered the whole face of
the ground."—GEN. ii. 6.

But from the lower nature there
went forth an instinctive desire and

hope for future evolution, and so a
reflection of power from above was
obtained, and growth of the soul was
promoted.

" And of Joseph he said, Blessed of
the Lord be his land ; for the precious
things of heaven, for the dew."—DEUT.
xxxiii. 13.

See EARTH, GRASS, GROUND, ICE,
IRRIGATION.

DHARMA OR PRAJNA :—

A symbol of the buddhic principle,
Wisdom.

" I salute that Dharma who is Prajnâ
Paramita (Wisdom of the Other Bank),
pointing out the way of perfect tranquillity
to all mortals, leading them into the
paths of perfect wisdom."—*Scriptures of
Nepal.*

" Worthy of remark is the treatment
of ' Wisdom,' ' Dharma,' ' Heart of
Wisdom,' etc. in the Buddhist ritual.
Here is another address to her :—' Thou
who art possessed of great mercy, and
who in virtue of thine infinite power
and wisdom art manifested throughout the
universe for the defence and protection
of all creatures, etc.' "—A. LILLIE, *Pop.
Life of Buddha*, pp. 240, 246.

" By the aid of Prajna or Dharma
the Supreme Buddha made the world."—
Ibid., p. 246.

" I (Wisdom) was set up from everlasting, from the beginning, or ever the
earth was."—PROV. viii. 23.

The Self (atma-buddhi) was, is, and
shall be ; and necessarily existed before
the lower nature which is only an
illusive reflection of the higher.

See BUDDHA, BUDDHI, PLOUGHING,
PRAGNÂ, SHORE (other), TRANSMUTA-
TION, TRI-RATNA, WISDOM, YUDHI.

DHRISTA-DYUMNA :—

A symbol of the Higher Self manifesting in the lower nature, and becoming the conqueror thereof.

Drupada initiates—
" a sacrifice for the express purpose
of obtaining a son who should be invincible in war and capable of slaying
Drona. The result. . . was completely
successful, for out of the sacrificial flames
emerged a stately youth, encased in full
armour, with a crown on his head, and
bearing a bow and arrows in his hands.
This was Dhrista-dyumna. After him appeared a beautiful maiden,—Draupadi."—
J. C. OMAN, *The Great Indian Epics*,
p. 120.

The spiritual mind (Drupada)
through purification of the lower
nature obtains conditions in which
the son of God can manifest and

take the supreme (crown) place in the
soul. The conditions are also suitable for the acquirement of the intuition (Draupadi). Love comes to fulfil
and supersede custom (Drona).

"The revenge (for the death of Drona)
taken by Açwathaman (his son inspired
by Siva) and his associates was complete
and bloody. The first to perish in the
nocturnal attack was the generalissimo
of the Pandava army, Dhrista-dyumna
himself, whom Açwathaman found sleeping
in his tent and whom he trampled to
death."—*Ibid.*, p. 187.

As "Siva" is a symbol of Divine
energy at the end of periods of manifestation, this passage refers to the
death of the Son of God and all
qualities at the termination of a
cycle. The qualities are afterwards
revivified under fresh conditions, as
described further on in the Epic.

See DRAUPADI, DRONA, KURUS,
PANDAVAS, RENOVATION, SIVA.

DHRITA-RASHTRA, THE BLIND KING :—

A symbol of the instinct nature,
sub-conscious and devoid of
intelligence.

"Dhrita-rashtra (a firstborn son) was
blind, but, although thus incapacitated
for governing, he retained the throne,
while his son Duryodhana really directed
the affairs of the state."—J. C. THOM-
SON, *The Bhagavad Gita.*

The lower instinct nature of the
soul is the first to appear in the
evolution of the qualities of the
human being ; but as it is devoid of
mind, it is incapable of organising
and directing the qualities. It retains
the lead, being potent and fundamental ; but that which has arisen
from it, namely, the desire-nature
which allies itself with mind, becomes
the ruler and regulator of the whole
of the lower nature.

See CONCH, DUR-YODHANA, HODER,
KURUS, SANJAYA, SERPENT (water).

DHRUVA, AS THE TRUNK (BODY) OF THE SACRIFICIAL MAN :—

A symbol of the lower nature having
as appendages or limbs the soul-
qualities which are to be outspread
as evolution proceeds.

"That guhu (spoon) further is to
him no other than yonder sky, and
the upabhrit this atmosphere, and the
dhruva this same earth. Now it is
from this earth that all the worlds

originate ; and from the dhruva, therefore, the whole sacrifice proceeds."—*Sata.
Brâh.*

The causal-body (guhu) is the
vehicle of buddhi (sky), and the
mental-body (upabhrit) of the higher
mind (air). The lower nature (earth)
is the arena of the soul's activities, and
it is through these activities that the
ego becomes conscious upon all the
planes. From the lower nature, therefore, the whole sacrifice of the lower
for the higher proceeds. That is, the
Divine Spark or Ego, having through
its descent into matter, become
strongly attached to the lower nature,
it is only by the offering up of that
nature, quality by quality, through
suffering and effort, that the ego can
finally liberate itself from the fetters
which hold it captive to the lower
planes of illusion (the worlds).

See ALTAR (fire), APPENDAGES, ARC.
MAN, ARENA, BODY OF OSIRIS, EARTH,
FETTERS, GUHU, LIMBS, MEMBERS,
SACRIFICE, SACRIFICER, SRUVA,
UPABHRIT.

DIADEM :—

See CROWN.

DIANA, OR ARTEMIS, GODDESS OF LIGHT AND THE MOON :—

An aspect of Wisdom (Buddhi),
presiding over the astral plane.

See ARTEMIS, LIGHT, MOON.

DICE, OR COUNTERS :—

Significant of number—relations
in respect to conditions of matter
on the lower planes.

DIGGING A PIT IN EARTH :—

Signifies the attempt made by the
lower self to attain to self-consciousness through the desire-nature
(earth).

"For they (my people) have digged
a pit to take me, and hid snares for my
feet."—JER. xviii. 22.

The lower qualities (people) of the
soul are charged with having sought
for satisfaction by the way of the
desires, thereby oppressing the Spirit
within and preventing its advance (feet)
towards lordship over the lower nature.

See EARTH, FEET, IRON BEATEN.

DIONYSUS, OR BACCHUS :—

A symbol of the Higher Self evolving
in all the lower nature and born in

the soul. The "vine" with which the symbol is connected is the same as the "tree of Life," which signifies the spiritual life which ramifies through all things. "Wine," the "blood of the grape," symbolises the spiritual truth and life which intoxicates the lower nature and renders it powerless.

"Zeus, in order to save his child (Dionysus), changed him into a ram, and carried him to the nymphs of Mount Nysa, who brought him up in a cave, and were afterwards rewarded by Zeus, by being placed as Hyades among the stars."—*Smith's Class. Dict.*

The Supreme, in order to effect the purpose of manifestation, set his emanation (Dionysus) under laws of limitation (the "ram" or "lamb" sacrifice), so that it should be developed in the lower nature of the soul (cave) by the buddhic qualities (nymphs) which were afterwards united to the mental qualities (stars).

"Bacchus, or the mundane intellect, is 'the *monad*, or proximately exempt producing cause.' Bacchus is said to be the 'spiritual part of the mundane soul.' "—G. R. S. MEAD, *Orphœus*, p. 182.

"The Platonists called Dionysus 'Our Master,' for the mind in us is Dionysiacal and the image of Dionysus."—*Ibid.*, p. 183.

This may be taken as meaning that Christ, our Master, is our indwelling ruler, for our mind is spiritualised and possesses the Divine image—Wisdom and Love.

"Dionysus, while a youth, was particularly captivated with beholding his image in a mirror; during his admiration of which he was miserably torn to pieces by the Titans; who not content with this cruelty, first boiled his members in water, and after roasted them by fire."—TAYLOR, *Eleusinian Mysteries*, p. 126.

The Higher Self having attained perfection through involution as the Archetypal Man, he, as it were, perceived his lower self to be like himself, which perfection occasioned, through the great forces of existence (the Titans), his death out of the lower state, and the cutting up of his astro-mental body of qualities as material for the new state now arising. The desire-mental qualities were infused in the soul's new astral (water) nature, in order that they should afterwards be purified (roasted) and raised by buddhi (fire).

"The legend (of Dionysus and the Titans) can be interpreted from the macrocosmic and microcosmic stand-points. From the former we see the symbolical drama of the World-soul being differentiated into individual souls; from the latter the mystical spectacle of the individual soul divided into many personalities, in the long series of re-births or palingenesis through which it threads its path on earth. As Macrobius says: 'By Father Liber [Dionysus] the Orphics seem to understand the Hylic Mind, which is born from the Impartible [Mind] and is separated into individual minds [or personalities]. And so in their sacred rites [Dionysus] is represented to have been torn into seperate members, and the pieces buried [in matter], and then again he is resurrected intact.' (Somn. I. xii. 67)."—G. R. S. MEAD, *Orphœus*, p. 184.

See ARC. MAN, BACCHUS, BIRTH OF JESUS, CAVE, CRATER, DEATH OF OSIRIS, DISMEMBERMENT, DRUNKARD, IMAGE, INTOXICATION, LAMB OF GOD, LIMBS, MEMBERS, NYMPHS, OSIRIS, RAM, ROASTED, SATYRS, SILENUS, STARS, TITANS, VINE, WATER, WINE, YMIR, ZAGREUS, ZEUS.

DIOSCURI; CASTOR AND POLLUX :—

Symbols of the higher and lower centres of consciousness on the mental plane of the soul—the Individuality (Pollux) and the Personality (Castor), or the Higher and the lower Selves.

"They were sons of Leda. Pollux and Helen only were children of Zeus, and Castor was the son of Tyndareus. Hence Pollux was immortal, while Castor was subject to old age and death like every other mortal."—*Smith's Class. Dict.*

They are said to be the product of the matter side of manifestation. The individuality and the buddhic principle (Helen) were begotten of the Spirit (Zeus), and the personality was originated by desire (Tyndareus). Hence the individuality is immortal. and the personality mortal.

"Zeus rewarded the attachment of the two brothers by placing them among the stars as *Gemini*."—*Ibid.*

The Supreme utilised the higher and lower centres of consciousness, by giving them important functionings among the mental qualities (stars), in the cycle of life (the Zodiac).

See AMYCUS, APOCATEQUIL, ASVINS, GEMINI, HEEL, HELEN, INDIVIDUALITY, LATONA, PERSONALITY, POLLUX, ZEUS.

DIPPING A PITCHER INTO WATER :—

A symbol of the effort to acquire truth in a mental form.

See HYLAS, VESSEL.

DIRT :—

Symbolic of an accumulation of prejudices and errors.

DISCIPLE :—

A symbol of a quality which has been so far disciplined as to be capable of attachment to an Ideal with which it strives to be in harmony, and from which it receives inspiration and guidance.

See APOSTLES.

DISCIPLE, CALLING OF A :—

This is the call by the Spirit within to a quality, inviting it to enter upon a higher vocation whereby it shall be put to a higher use.

"It is not the discipline that fits. That which fits goes before the discipline, and the discipline only develops the fitness. 'God *hath made* us meet for the inheritance of the saints in light.' That is a past act. The preparedness for heaven comes at the moment when a man turns to Christ."—A. MACLAREN, *Sermons*, 1st *Series*, p. 91.

See CONVERSION.

DISCIPLES, THE TWELVE, OF JESUS :—

These signify twelve disciplined qualities and faculties of various kinds, which are able to receive higher teaching and profit by it. They have determined to adhere to the instruction and admonition of the Higher Self as the Master within the soul.

"Jesus chose the twelve before he came into the world. He chose twelve powers, receiving them from the twelve saviours of the Light-treasure. When He descended into the world, He cast them as sparks into the wombs of their mothers, that the whole world might be saved."—*Pistis Sophia*.

The Higher Self prior to his birth within the lower nature (EPH. i. 4) chooses the means by which he is to accomplish his purpose; and these are agencies from the "saviours," i.e., the ideal qualities above, which have to be actualised below. The "Light-treasure" is the perfect nature within, which shall attain to the "Light-realm." When the Self descends into the lower soul, the spiritual germs enter the qualities attached to the forms (mothers) and become the means by which the qualities are to attain liberation, through triumphing over the limitations of the lower planes.

"The Father sends then the Messenger who shall bring about the salvation of the world. The Divine Benefactor has his abode in the sun, together with twelve virtues, his daughters; 'tis he who launches into space the Lightships of Heaven."—F. CUMONT, *Manichean Researches*.

The "Divine Messenger and Benefactor" is the Christ whose abode is in the individuality (sun) centralising the buddhic qualities as "twelve virtues." It is the Christ who draws forth the higher nature of the striving souls.

"By the twelve disciples or apostles of the Lord are understood all who are of the church in truth from good; and in an abstract sense, all things of the church; and by Peter, all who are in faith; and abstractedly, faith itself; by James, they who are in charity, and abstractedly, charity itself; and by John, they who are in the good of life from charity and its faith, and abstractedly, good of life itself derived from thence."—SWEDENBORG, *Apoc. Rev.*, n. 7.

"Jesus spake unto them, saying, All authority hath been given unto me in heaven and on earth. Go ye therefore, and make disciples of all the nations, baptising them into the name of the Father and of the Son and of the Holy Ghost."—MAT. xxviii. 18, 19.

Christ, the Higher Self within, is intuitively regarded by the disciplined qualities as the supreme ruler within the soul,—higher and lower. The Ideal within them, therefore, impels them to take their part in the work of raising the less advanced qualities (the nations), for the command is full of the spirit of the Christ. They serve their Lord in bringing the lower nature into subjection to the higher. They act as a magnet to draw forth and transmute the germ of like properties within the qualities less evolved than themselves. The three-fold constitution of the baptismal ceremony refers to the attuning of the nature upon the three lower planes in relation to the higher and perfect nature on the upper planes, of which the lower is an incomplete and defective representation. This is expressed in the prayer of the disciples,—" Thy kingdom come. Thy will be done, as in heaven, so on earth." The ideal above is to be realised below.

" Jesus called unto him his twelve disciples, and gave them authority over unclean spirits, to cast them out, and to heal all manner of disease and all manner of sickness. Now the names of the twelve are these : etc."—Mat. x. 1–5.

The Christ within called through the love nature to his disciplined qualities and instructed them for their work in the soul. Through the Truth and Righteousness within them they were possessed of power to dispel the illusions of the lower mind, and rectify the unbalanced emotions and misdirected affections of the lower nature.

The following are the twelve disciplined qualities :—

The analytical lower mind
　　　　　　　　(Peter)
Faith and inquiry　(Andrew)
Hope and progressiveness
　　　　　　　　(James)
Love and philosophy (John)
Courage and forcefulness
　　　　　　　　(Philip)
Perserverance　　(Bartholomew)
Intellectual truth-seeking
　　　　　　　　(Thomas)
Modesty and receptiveness
　　　　　　　　(James Alpheus)
Gentleness and attentiveness
　　　　　　　　(Simon Zelotes)
Broadmindedness　(Judas bro.of Jas.)
Critical deliberation (Mathew)
Prudence　　　　(Judas)

These qualities are not to attempt to assist those states which are too backward to be affected, but rather to minister to those which are more developed and capable of assimilating truth.

See Adityas (twelve), Æons (twelve), Andrew, Anthropos, Apostles, Baptism, Binding, Breast-plate, Dance (circle), Feeding, Germs, Healing, Heaven, Heroes, James, Jesus of the gospels, John, Judas, Liberation, Light-realm, Nations, People, Peter, Philip, Saviours (twelve), Self, Sparrows (twelve), Sun, Tribes (twelve),

Trinity, Twelve, Urns (twelve), Zodiac.

DISCIPLES SENT FORTH :—

Symbolic of the disciplined qualities freed from reliance upon objects of the external life, and directed to purify the life within.

" Go not into any way of the Gentiles, and enter not into any city of the Samaritans : but go rather to the lost sheep of the house of Israel."—Mat. x. 5, 6.

The advanced qualities are instructed not to interfere with those natural qualities which have their due place temporarily in the external order, nor seek to influence qualities as yet unprepared for the inner light ; but to seek rather to bring Truth and Love to the qualities or virtues having in them the spiritual germ, the Divine Spark that has gone astray from the Eternal " Fire " in order to acquire knowledge through experience, and be found again of the Spirit. These " lost ones " require instruction which will enable them to find the path to heaven.

See Sheep (lost), Sparrows, Treading.

DISCIPLES SEATED UPON TWELVE THRONES :—

Symbolic of the disciplined qualities raised to a higher state, in the order of development.

" Ye which have followed me in the regeneration when the Son of Man shall sit on the throne of his glory, ye also shall sit upon twelve thrones, judging the twelve tribes of Israel."—Mat. xix. 28.

The Christ points out that those qualities which have followed his guidance in the progress from the natural to the spiritual state shall be transmuted, and be with him when he ascends to the higher plane to occupy his throne in the causal-body. There they also shall be enthroned around him, being brought to a higher state than mortals can have any conception of. Intellect, reason, judgment, feelings, emotions, etc.—all shall be transmuted and raised to a condition which transcends the terms of expression now used. In this future exalted state the " disciples " will be able to judge of the lower stages (twelve tribes) from which they have arisen.

"When I (Jesus) am king over the twelve saviours, and over all the number of perfect souls which have received the mystery of Light, then whosoever shall have received the mystery of the Ineffable One, they shall be joint kings with me and shall sit upon my right hand and upon my left in my kingdom. Verily I say unto you, those men are I, and I am those men. For this cause have I said to you formerly, ye shall sit upon your thrones, . . . and ye shall reign together with me. For this cause I said of old time, in the place where I shall be, my twelve ministers shall be also."—*Pistis Sophia.*

When the perfected Christ-soul (Jesus) has ascended to the higher planes, and is exalted over the ideal qualities (saviours) and the perfected individualities (souls), then shall the transmuted qualities from below be raised and united with the Christ, being enthroned with him in the higher causal-body. "God,—quickened us together with Christ, and raised us up with him, and made us to sit with him in the heavenly places, in Christ Jesus."—EPH. ii. 5, 6.

See ARGONAUTS, CHRIST'S SECOND COMING, JUDGES, KING OF GLORY, REGENERATION SAVIOURS, SON OF MAN, THRONE, TRIBES.

DISEASE, OR SICKNESS :—

Symbolic of a malady of the soul in which disability is caused by a one-sided development of the lower nature, with failure of the mind to control the deformity. The result is that an affection of the lower nature ties the soul down and prevents the increase of spiritual faculty. The malady can only be healed when the qualities concerned become discontented with their condition, and then aspire towards the ideal.

See HEALING, MIRACLES.

DISEASES, WASTING AND PUTRIFYING :—

Symbolic of the lowest states of the instinct and desire nature, which become obnoxious and gradually disappear.

"And I wept and shrieked on beholding the unwonted land where are murder and wrath, and other species of fates, and wasting diseases, and putrefactions and fluxes."—*Empedocles,* FAIRBANKS, 385.

The lower self, through the awakenment within, "wept and shrieked," that is, feared, trembled, and suffered,

all through the earlier troubles and difficulties which befell it. "Murder and wrath" signify the primitive and fearsome manifestations of the Divine indwelling principle. The "other species of fates" are the karmic liabilities which are incurred during the early state of strife. The "wasting diseases, etc." are the lowest aspects of the soul's lower desires.

See FATE-SPHERE, KARMA, MURDER, PESTILENCE, STRIFE.

DISH, OR BOWL :—

Symbol of a form which is a receptacle of the spirit ; or is an emblem of limitation.

See CRATER, CUP, VESSEL.

DISK, WINGED SUN- :—

This symbol signifies the higher Individuality which dwells on the buddhic plane and ensouls the causal-body. It is the buddhic vehicle or vesture of the Atman.

"Horbehudti (Horus) changed his form into that of a winged sun-disk, that which rests over the prow of the bark of Rā."—*Legend of the Winged Sun-disk.*

Now from the perfect form of man on the lower planes, the Son of God assumed the vesture of the higher Individuality,—the buddhic, which ensouls the causal-body (the bark of Rā).

"When perfect and fully winged, she (the soul) soars upward, and is the Ruler of the universe."—PLATO, *Phædrus,* JOWETT, Vol. II. p. 123.

"Almost every jot or tittle in the Egyptian worship had a symbolical meaning. The round disk so frequent in the sacred emblems of Egypt symbolised the *sun.* Now, when Osiris, the sun divinity, became incarnate, and was born, it was not merely that he should give his life as a *sacrifice* for men, but that he might also be the life and *nourishment* of the souls of men."—A. HISLOP, *Two Babylons,* p. 160.

See BOAT ON RIVER, BUDDHIC PLANE, CAUSAL-BODY, HORBEHUDTI, INDIVIDUALITY, SON OF GOD, SPHERE, SUN, SUN-DISK.

DISMEMBERMENT AFTER DEATH OF THE BODY OF THE GOD :—

A symbol of the potentially perfect homogeneous Soul becoming throughout evolution the actual imperfect heterogeneous aggregation of qualities. This refers to the Archetypal Man, who is perfected by the completion of the process of spiritual involution, and therefore dies out of that state in order to be reproduced piecemeal in another.

"The soul of Osiris is eternal and incorruptible, but his body Typhon did tear in pieces and put out of sight; and Isis wandered about, sought for it, and joined it together again."—PLUTARCH, *Isis and Osiris*, §§ 2 and 54.

The Archetypal Man in his higher nature in immortal, but his potential perfect lower nature is subject to death and change of state, and so the form or limitation tendency (Typhon), motived by desire, presses apparently against the life within, resulting in the evolution of a number of astro-mental qualities which operate upon many sub-planes. Then the buddhic function (Isis) begins to act in disciplining and harmonising the qualities, so that eventually they may all be perfected and united in one,— the Higher Self (Osiris).

"The god Tem, the Governor and only One of the gods, hath spoken, and his word passeth not away. Horus is both divine food and the sacrifice. Horus hath passed on to gather together the members of his divine father; Horus is his deliverer. Horus hath sprung from the water of his divine father and from his decay. He hath become the Governor of Egypt."—BUDGE, *Book of the Dead*, p. 258.

The Higher Self in the expression (word) of Itself endureth for ever. The Self below (Horus) in the sacrifice of Itself, is the sustainer of all that arises by means of it. The evolving Self restores in perfection the qualities proceeding from the involved Divine Archetype (father). The evolved Self is the deliverer of the involved Self, and the twain are One. The Self hath evolved from the emanation of the Spirit within, and from the cessation of its externalising activities. The Self hath become the ruler of the mental plane (Egypt).

"Manichæaus says that God, in his own nature, was cut in pieces by the race of darkness."—AUGUSTINE, *Manichæan Heresy*, p. 549.

"The "race of darkness" is a symbol of the forces of limitation and ignorance.

"Philosophers figuratively tell of 'tearings asunder' and 'dismemberings'; and in these aspects Apollo is variously

called Dionysus, Zagreus, Nyktelius, and Isodaites, and his 'destructions' and 'disappearances,' his 'death' and his 'resurrection' are fittingly expressing the true nature of the changes in God's essence in the formation of the world."—PLUTARCH, *On the E at Delphi*.

The symbolism of the "Gods" and their doings can be understood by philosophers who rightly approach the subject, free from the prejudices of scholars and mythologists. The Higher Self is symbolised under a thousand names connected with ideas of emanation, sacrifice, obscuration, death, and resurrection, which symbolically express the true nature of the changes in the manifestation of the Divine Life during the formation and development of the soul.

"The theologists say the mind (the 'heart') in this Dionysiacal dismemberment was preserved intact by the wisdom of Athena; it was the soul that was first divided, and it was divided sevenfold."—PROCLUS, *Parm.*, III. 33.

The causal-body (heart) on the higher mental plane was not subject to the lower nature, but being immortal it was carried over from involution to evolution, as the seat of the buddhic or Wisdom principle (Athena). The lower soul, or astro-mental nature, yielded its qualities in due order and sufficiency for the time being.

"There is no member of my body which is not the member of some god. And I am Rā day by day."—BUDGE, *Book of the Dead*, Ch. XLIII.

"So we, who are many, are one body in Christ, and severally members one of another."—ROM. xii. 5.

As the Archetypal Man, or Christ, is divided into many qualities after involution, so the many qualities become one Christ after evolution.

"Adam was one man, and is yet the whole human race. He was broken as it were, in pieces; and being scattered, is now being gathered together, and, as it were, conjoined into one by a spiritual fellowship and concord. And 'the poor that groan' as one man, is that same Adam; but in Christ he is being renewed; that Adam might renew to himself the image of God. Of Adam then is Christ's flesh: of Adam the temple which the Jews distroyed, and the Lord raised up in three days."—AUGUSTINE, *Gospel of St. John*, Vol. I. p. 149.

The Adam referred to is the Adam of the first chapter of Genesis, a symbol of the perfect Archetypal

Man (atma-buddhic), the crucified Christ, who gives his life for the salvation of humanity. His members, or qualities, are scattered in every human soul and are now being gathered together, that Christ may be renewed and manifested in us as we show forth his qualities of Wisdom, Love and Truth.

See ADAM (higher), ARC. MAN, CHRIST, CRUCIFIXION (gnostic), DEATH OF OSIRIS, OF LEMMINKAINEN, DIONYSUS, DWARF, EVOLUTION, FLAYING, FOOD (god), GLORY, HEART, HORUS, INCARNATION, INVOLUTION, ISIS, KAGU, KAIOMARTS, KAMA, LIMBS, LITTLE CHILDREN, MEMBERS, OSIRIS, PAPYRUS, PRAGÂPATI (relaxed) PURUSHA, QEBSENNUF, QUETZALCOATL, RESURRECTION, SACRIFICE, SETTLEMENTS, TEM, TYPHON, YMIR, ZAGREUS.

DISPENSATIONS ; COVENANT OF LAW, AND COVENANT OF GRACE :—

Symbolic of stages and methods of the soul's evolution.

"Wherefore the law was our schoolmaster to bring us unto Christ that we might be justified by faith."—GAL. iii. 24.

Wherefore the law of cause and effect, of reason and experience,—was as a teacher to lead us unto Wisdom and Love, that at length we should be perfected by intuition and perceive the Truth of things direct.

The first dispensation which is the moral law learned through experience and reason, and enforced by the conscience and the demands of social preservation and order, is supported and enhanced by the second dispensation which bestows the law of Love—a law free of coercion either from within or from without. It operates through attraction to all that is higher in the life of the soul.

"Unless the Church has more than a high morality to offer, it has ceased to be Christian. For as in Art, so in Christianity, its direct end is not to make men moral, but to awaken in them those deep emotions, and to present to them those high ideals, which, felt and followed after, will not only indirectly produce morality, but aspiration and effort to do far more than men are absolutely bound to do by the moral law."—STOPFORD A. BROOKE, Serm., *Changed Aspect, etc.*

"In the religious idea is the solution of the moral problem. This idea is none other than the idea of Perfection, which is in us at the bottom of our inner life, and realises itself—in idealising itself—in the notion of a God-loving synthesis of the real and the ideal. *Perfection exists.* It is the summit of creative evolution. It surpasses reality (the actual) without separating itself from it. Religion is a reality which surpasses reason without ceasing to conform to the laws of the understanding. The worship of Perfection is the beginning of wisdom ; it is also the end of knowledge, the highest development of the inner life in the communion of united and fraternal souls."—E. BOUTROUX, *Sorbonne Lecture,* 1913.

"The soul takes satisfaction in progeny only because it finds in offspring a visible image of some everlasting possession. It rises steadily to everhigher types of progeny—lofty thoughts, poems, statutes, institutions, laws—the fair creations of the mind. But the highest stage of Love comes when the soul sees Beauty itself which is everlasting, 'not growing and decaying, not waxing and waning.' He, who under the influence of Love rises to see that Beauty, is not far from the end. (PLATO, *Symposium*)."—R. M. JONES, *Mystical Religion,* p. 65.

See BONDAGE, CHILD, CHILDREN OF JERUSALEM, CONSCIENCE, COVENANT, EXILE, GRACE, INTUITION, JUDAH, JUSTIFICATION, KARMA, LAW OF MOSES, LOVE, MOSAIC, TESTAMENT, WOMAN (adultery).

DISTRESSED WORLD :—

A symbol of the astro-mental plane—the field of the warring desires and lower emotions and passions, with entailed suffering and sorrow.

See BOAT OF WISDOM, LION-GAIT.

DIVORCE .—

A symbol of an apparent or delusive separation of Love from Wisdom, Emotion from Reason, Goodness from Truth ; for these pairs are indissolubly united by Divine law.

"Have ye not read that he which made them from the beginning made them male and female, and said, For this cause shall a man leave his father and mother, and shall cleave to his wife ; and the twain shall become one flesh ? . . . What therefore God hath joined together, let not man put asunder."—MAT. xix. 4–6.

Christ here points out that ideally reason and emotion are not at variance they are not separate but a duality. For this reason the mind shall quit sense and desire,—the outer parents,—and go in search of the Ideal,—the higher emotions,—for they are *one*, when the intellect and the buddhic emotions are in harmony together. This ideal duality no lower attraction can avail to separate.

See HARLOT, HUSBAND (wife), MALE-FEMALE, MAN AND WIFE, MARRIAGE, WHOREDOM, WIFE, WOMAN.

DIVORCING A WIFE AND MARRYING ANOTHER WOMAN :—

The "wife" is a symbol of the emotions allied with the mind. The seeking to sunder the union of mind and emotion is an attempt to transgress the law of the soul's progression, and form an alliance with lower attractions—folly. *See* PROV. vii.

See ADULTERY, FOLLY, MARRIAGE (lower), WHOREDOM. WIFE.

DODONA SPEAKING OAK :—

Signifying lofty aspirations eliciting intuition of truth.

"In the prow of the Argo Athena set a plank, cut from the speaking oak of Dodona."—*Argonautic Expedition.*

In the forefront of the causal body, Wisdom planted, as it were, a mast of truth, that is, a means whereby aspiration should ascend and meet with the response from above

See ARGO, ATHENA, CAUSAL-BODY, MAST, SHIP.

DOER OF ACTIONS :—

The Self knows Itself alone to be the doer. Choice is left to the illusory separate self of the lower planes.

See BIRDS (two), OPPOSITES.

DOG :—

A symbol of the will in its various aspects.

See ASPAHI, CORPSES, WILL.

DOG (HIGHEST ASPECT) :—

A symbol of the going forth of the Self as will.

"A dog ate the first meat of the sacrifice of a sheep."—*The Bundahis,* Ch. XV. 14.

This sacrifice is that of the mind to the lower emotions, and the "fire" is the symbol of desire. It is a correspondency of the sacrifice of the Logos which takes place, in so far as the ego is concerned, from the mental plane. The "dog" is a symbol of the Self under the aspect of will, which is the first aspect under which the Self goes forth. The "meat" symbolises the beneficial results of experience, knowledge.

"The dog is connected with Siva in his character of a mountaineer, or rather, perhaps, with Rudra, who also presides over horses."—MON. WILLIAMS, *Religious Thought in India,* p. 328.

A "mountaineer" is one who climbs a mountain, a symbol of aspiration,—one who rises from the lower to the higher, as does the Self (Siva) through the will (dog). The Self (Rudra) through the will directs the mental faculties (horses).

See FIRE, HORSE, LAMB MEAT, SACRIFICE, SHEEP, SIVA.

DOG CERBERUS, THE THREE-HEADED GUARDIAN OF HADES :—

A symbol of the Higher Self in its threefold aspect of Will, Wisdom, and Activity made manifest on the lower planes (Hades).

See CHARON'S FERRY, HADES, STYX, TRIAD.

DOG, GOOD, PESOSCHOROUN :—

A symbol of the true will in the mentality, showing activity of the Divine nature within the soul.

See WILL.

DOG, WATER, HOLIEST OF ALL DOGS :—

A symbol of the will prosecuting the search after spiritual Truth (water).

See WATER.

DOG, HOUSE :—

A symbol of the will exercised in self-control.

See HOUSE.

DOG, SHEPHERD'S :—

A symbol of the will active in co-ordinating the virtues (sheep).

See SHEEP, SHEPHERD.

DOG, TRAINED :—

A symbol of the will powerful in the disciplined self.

DOG, VOHUNASGA :—

A symbol of the will tenacious in holding on to the ideals of goodness and truth.

DOG, BAD, VESCHEROUN :—

A symbol of the illusory lower will which evidences captivity to the desires. This false desire-will is the inverted reflection of the Love-will of the higher nature. It is nothing but the activity of the mind enslaved by sensations, desires, and passions. It is blind self-assertion of the lower nature : pain and sorrow result therefrom. Its power is proportional to its lack of intelligence.

"Lust and anger shall not seduce, and the dog covetousness shall be destroyed" (*Guru Arjan*).—MACAULIFFE, *The Sikh Religion*, Vol. III. p. 129.

See BONDAGE, CAPTIVITY, IGNORANCE.

DOG, ZAIRIMYANGURA (THE TORTOISE) :—

A symbol of the opposite or negative will which has no discrimination and allows the higher impulses to pass unrecognised.

See DAEVAS, TORTOISE, ZAIRIMYANGURA.

DOG, VANGHAPARA (THE HEDGEHOG) :—

A symbol of the will active in the intelligence.

"The dog with prickles and long and thin muzzle, the dog Vanghapara is a good creature which from midnight to dawn destroys thousands of creatures of the evil spirit."—*Vendidad*, XIII.

A symbol of the Will active in the critical intellect which destroys superstition, error, ignorance, and doubt ; and gets rid of the incumbrances or outgrown notions of the lower mind.

See BRIAREUS, CREEPING THINGS, TALUS.

DOG, WHITE, WITH FOUR EYES :—

A symbol of the will functioning in the quaternary.

"But the fiend (druj) Nasu can be expelled from the corpse by bringing in 'a dog with four eyes,'—a white dog, according to modern Parsi usage,—and the demon, as soon as the dog looks at the body, flies back to hell."—J. M. MITCHELL, *Zend-Avesta*, p. 36.

The "druj Nasu" is a symbol of the process of Time which captures the residual elements of the lower personality (corpse), and claims the astral matter for future use. The "dog with four eyes" is a symbol of the will controlling the activities on the four manifested planes : the "four eyes" signifying perception on the four planes,—buddhic, mental astral, and physical.

The will is perfect (white) because the activities of the ego on any plane are perfectly regulated. Time is vanquished when the ego is endowed with full attributes by means of the perfected personality.

"The four-eyed brindled dogs—that watch for the departed."—*Vedic Hymn*.

In this case the wills in the many souls are lacking in perfection, and they await the further experience of the personalities.

See ABSYRTUS, CORPSE, EYE, HOUSES (corpses), NASU, WHITE.

DOG-STAR SIRIUS, OR SURA, AT THE KINVAT BRIDGE :—

A symbol of the fixed will in the higher mind, which the soul must attain to ere it be liberated from the lower nature, and become conscious on higher planes.

"Those who have chosen the good in this world are received after death by good spirits, and guided, under the protection of the dog Sura, to the bridge Kinvat : the wicked are dragged thither by the daevas."—*Zoroastrian System*.

They who have done well in their incarnations,—who have sown worthily, shall reap the fruits, or reward, hereafter, i.e. upon those planes whereon their consciousness is gradually awakening. The "dog-star" is a symbol of power, will, and tenacity of purpose, which qualities stand for the will of the faithful servant of the Higher Self, who has succeeded in crossing the "bridge" of manas (mind) which unites the lower and higher consciousnesses. The "wicked" are the unperfected souls,— they who are relatively undeveloped and who are drawn away to incarnation by the lust of life, attachment, pride, and egotism.

See BRIDGE (kinvat), DAEVAS, HARVEST, KARMA, LIBERATION, MAN (bad), MAN (righteous), REAPING, REINCARNATION, SIRIUS, SOWING AND REAPING, WICKEDNESS, WILL.

DOLIONES PEOPLE :—

Symbolic of a state of deep meditation upon truth, and confidence in the reality it discloses.

"Leaving Lemnos, the Argonauts came to the Doliones, whose king was named Cyzicus."—*Argonautic Expedition.*

And now leaving the condition of scientific knowledge, the consciousness comes nearer to the state of interior meditation and faith in its higher suggestions, wherein the possibility of achieving freedom from the thraldom of physical illusion occurs.

See ARGONAUTS, CYZICUS, LEMNOS, SHAVING, TEARS.

DOLPHIN OF POSEIDON :—

A symbol of atma-buddhi, i.e. truth-wisdom, a denizen of the Ocean of Truth-reality. Or, in the plural, the myriad spiritual monads or egos of humanity.

See MONAD OF LIFE, OCEAN, POSEIDON, PUNGA, TANGAROA.

DOOR (HIGHER ASPECT) :—

A symbol of an entrance to the mind for the vibrations from above, that is, access through the higher mind for the spiritual life to flow in from the atma-buddhic planes.

"Jesus said, I am the door of the sheep. All that came before me are thieves and robbers : but the sheep did not hear them, I am the door ; by me if any man enter in, he shall be saved, and shall go in and go out, and shall find pasture."—JOHN x. 7–9.

The Christ-soul (Jesus) is the highest nature of the soul, and is therefore the entrance for the buddhic virtues (sheep) which do not contact (hear) the desires (thieves). The desires precede the advent of the Christ in the soul, and, as it were, rob it of good or the vibrations from above. If any mental quality (man) is of the higher nature, it is immortal and shall return from activity and go out to activity, and find experience conducive to growth.

"There is in every man's heart an open door towards the eternal, and through that open door the messages of God can come." R. J. CAMPBELL, *Song of Ages*, p. 280.

See FALL, GATE, MURDERER, PASTURE, SHEEP, SHEPHERD, SUN (door), THIEF, VOICE OF GOD, WINDOW.

DOOR (LOWER ASPECT) :—

A symbol of an entrance to the mind for vibrations from below, enabling the consciousness to perceive phenomena of the astral and physical planes.

"When St. John says that God is a Spirit, and that He must be worshipped in spirit, he means that the mind must be cleared of all images. When thou prayest, shut thy door—that is, the doors of thy senses. Keep them barred and bolted against all phantasms and images. Nothing pleases God more than a mind free from all occupations and distractions. Such a mind is in a manner transformed into God, for it can think of nothing, and love nothing, except God ; other creatures and itself it only sees in God. He who penetrates into himself, and so transcends himself, ascends truly to God. He whom I love and desire is above all that is sensible, and all that is intelligible; sense and imagination cannot bring us to Him, but only the desire of a pure heart" (ALBERTUS MAGNUS, *De Adh. Deo.*).—R. M. JONES, *Mystical Religion* p. 219.

See ASTRAL, CROWD, GATE (lower), HEART, MAN (blind), Man (rich).

DOOR, NARROW :—

A symbol of the higher mind as an entrance to the higher planes.

"And one said unto him, Lord, are there few that be saved ? And he said unto them, Strive to enter in by the narrow door : for many, I say unto you, shall seek to enter in, and shall not be able."—LUKE xiii. 23, 24.

This refers to the large amount of promise,—or potential power,—in comparison to the little fulfilment,—or actual power,—in the evolving qualities. The qualities when spiritualised, are all, as it were, Christs in the germ, for eventually they will become one with the Christ. But though there be many qualities called forth by the Word of God,—or the Will of the Logos,—yet few are chosen ; or rather, few *choose* to carry their destiny to its logical conclusion. Truly, the way is narrow and the journey perilous ; yet shall it be that those who steadfastly continue till the end, shall be *saved*, that is, shall retain their individuality and become in ultimates actually, that which they are in primes potentially.

See ENDURING, SALVATION, TEETH (gnashing).

DOOR SHUT BY THE LOGOS :—

A symbol of the termination of the cycle of life on the lower planes.

"When once the master of the house is risen up, and hath shut to the door, and ye begin to stand without, and to knock at the door, saying, Lord open to us ; and he shall answer and say to you, I know you not whence ye are." —LUKE xiii. 25.

This signifies the manvantaric evolution brought to a conclusion, and describes the inability of those who have not kept pace with the scheme, to secure a place in its fulfilment. Excuses are useless : for unless the lower avails itself of the advantages offered by the Influence from On High, no grace is obtained, and nothing is achieved. The " door shut " implies that the distinction between the material and spiritual is realised. The insufficiently progressed qualities or souls shut out have to await further opportunities of improvement.

See JUSTICE, KARMA, MANVANTARA, VIRGINS (parable).

DOOR OF THE ARK OF NOAH :—

A symbol of the entrance from below to the mind within the soul. The desires and sensations reach the consciousness from the astral and physical planes.

See ARK, WINDOW OF ARK.

DOOR OF THE VARA (ENCLOSURE) :—

A symbol of the point where the lower Self is united with the Higher Self ; or the aperture towards the Divine in the higher mind, contacting the lower mind above the quaternary (vara). (See Vendidad.)

" At the apex of your spirit there is a little door, so high up that only by hard climbing can you reach it. There the Object of your craving stands and knocks ; thence came those persistent messages—faint echoes from the Truth eternally hammering at your gates— which disturbed the comfortable life of sense. Come up then by this pathway to those higher levels of reality to which, in virtue of the eternal spark in you, you belong."—E. UNDERHILL, Mysticism, p. 50.

See BRAHMARANDHRAM, HAIR OF HEAD, QUATERNARY, VARA, WINDOW OF ARK.

DOORKEEPER (FEMININE) :—

A symbol of one of the senses which, as it were, opens the door of the soul to the external world.

In the Gospels a maid who kept the door, and another maid, both accused Peter of being a disciple of Jesus, which Peter denied.

" The Lord turned and looked upon Peter. And Peter remembered the word of the Lord."—LUKE xxii. 61.

The two " maids " signify two of the sense organs,—sight and hearing,— which when exercised with discernment, serve to make it evident to the lower mind (Peter) that the central Ideal (Christ) is a reality. But the lower mind, engrossed with the objects of sense, indignantly repudiates any connection with its Divine Author. Then comes the warning of the Christ in the dawning of the higher mind upon the lower consciousness,—a dawning which brings with it certitude of the reality of the higher nature, and a stirring of the buddhic emotions. " Peter went out, and wept bitterly."

See JESUS OF GOSPELS, MAN (natural), PETER, TRIAL.

DOORKEEPERS, INDRA AND PRAGĀPATI, OF THE HALL OF BRAHMAN :—

Symbolic of the Divine Will and Wisdom,—or devotion to the Highest and a direct vision of the Truth. These stand, as it were, at the entrance of the " palace of Perfection " and adjudge the condition required previous to the soul's final liberation from the lower nature.

" He (a man) approaches the door-keepers Indra and Pragāpati and they run away from him. He approaches the hall Vibhu, and the glory of Brahman reaches him."—Kaush. Upanishad, I. 2.

The ascending soul approaches the aspects of the Self,—Will and Wisdom, and these now quit their former positions as conditioning access to the higher planes ; they are no longer needed, that is, they are no longer required to be manifested. The soul then comes to the Hall of final liberation, and then it is that the Glory of the Supreme is made evident to him,— for it can never be beheld so long as the thraldom of manifestation is imposed upon the Self.

See CHERUBIM, CHRIST'S SECOND COMING, DEVAYANA, INDRA, PRAGÂPATI.

DOORS, HOUSE WITH FOUR :—

Symbolic of the quaternary giving the ego access to the four planes by means of four connected bodies.

"When the Gods, as was reasonable, became incensed against him to the utmost, he (Loke) fled away and hid himself in a hollow of the hills, where he built for himself a house with four doors, so that he might have views on all sides."—*Prose Edda.*

This statement is explanatory of the fall of the ego into matter to inhabit forms therein ; and it describes the limitations which are imposed upon the soul when it descends to gain experience on the lower planes. Hereon a "house with four doors" is builded, that is, a connected series of bodies is formed,—a physical, an astral, a mental, and a buddhic vehicle,—is organised for the use of the ego, so that intercommunication between itself and the universe,—the within and the without,—is established. The "anger of the Gods" refers to the obscuration of the Ideals which the descent into matter implies.

See ASAR, DEATH OF BALDER, FALL, HOUSE (four), LOKE, NET, QUATER-NARY, VALLEY.

DOORS OPENED BY THOTH :—

Symbolic of the four vehicles of consciousness rendering the four planes accessible to the ego by means of the activities of the higher mind.

"The north wind belonged to Osiris, the south wind to Rā, the west wind to Isis, and the east wind to Nephthys ; and for the deceased to obtain power over each and all of these it was necessary for him to be master of the doors through which they blew. This power could only be obtained by causing pictures of the four doors to be painted on the coffin with a figure of Thoth opening each. . . . the rubric says, 'Let none who is outside know this chapter for it is a great mystery, and those who dwell in the swamps (i.e. the ignorant) know it not. Thou shall not do this in the presence of any person except thy father, or thy son, or thyself alone ; for it is an exceeding great mystery which no man whatever knoweth.' "—BUDGE, *Egyptian Book of the Dead.*

The buddhic plane is the plane on which the incarnate Self (Osiris) is born ; the physical plane is a reflection of Atma (Rā) ; the mental plane is allied with buddhi (Isis) ; and the astral plane is the modeller of the physical (Nephthys). In order that the individuality (deceased) should obtain mastery over the conditions on each and all of the four planes, it was necessary for him to have complete knowledge and control of his four bodies or vehicles which are his instruments of consciousness and action on the four planes. This mastery could only be attained by perfecting the four bodies in the image of their prototypes, by means of the higher mind (Thoth) during the embodiment (coffin) of the ego on the lower planes (tomb). It is the higher mind which has the keys of heaven and of hell, that is, the means of access by the ego to the higher and lower planes. The mystery is in the perfecting of the bodies, which perfecting is impossible for the outside or lower mind ; as the desires on the astro-mental plane (swamp) are oblivious of it. The mystery cannot be solved by that which is lower but only by that which is higher—the spiritual father or the spiritual son allied with the individuality.

See ADEPT, ARHAT, ASEKA, BUDDHI, CHILDREN OF HORUS, DEFUNCT, FOUR BEINGS, INDIVIDUALITY, INITIATION, ISIS, KEYS, MARSH, NEPHTHYS, OSIRIS, PROTOTYPES, QUARTERS, QUATERNARY, RĀ, THOTH, TOMB, VESTURES, WALKS, WINDS (four), WOOD, WORLDS (five).

DOUBLE FOLD OF FLESH AND FAT :—

This signifies the outer and the inner aspects of love.

See FAT, FLESH, ROASTED.

DOUGH OF MEAL, WATER AND LEAVEN :—

Symbolic of experience and knowledge, transformed by the Divine Life (leaven), and made ready to be transmuted by fire (buddhi) into truth the substance of goodness, the "bread of heaven," the sustenance of the soul.

See BREAD, FLOUR, FOOD, LEAVEN (higher), MEAL, WHEAT, WATER.

DOVE, OR PIGEON :—

An emblem of purity, aspiration, and gentleness, or the active principle animating the higher nature which descends into the lower nature in order to rise therefrom.

"And Noah sent forth a dove from him, to see if the waters were abated from off the face of the ground ; but the dove found no rest for the sole of her foot, and she returned unto him to the ark."—GEN. viii. 8, 9.

And from the Individuality or Self in the soul, is sent forth an aspiration of a loving and pure nature, and a tender thought, to discover the secret of Truth behind the prevailing illusions of the lower mind ; but the aspiration at this stage found no lodgement in the lower consciousness, so by the law of its nature it returned to the Self again.

"The dove is that spirit of gentleness and peace which appears more boldly now as heaven opens to us."—A. JUKES, *Types of Genesis*, p. 120.

"The dove was the bird sacred to Istar."—A. H. SAYCE, *Rel. Babyl.*, p. 271.

"Istar" is a symbol of Wisdom,— the Holy Spirit (Esther).

"Upon whom thou shalt see the Spirit descending as a dove, and abiding on Him, this is He which baptiseth with the Holy Ghost."—JOHN i. 33.

"By means of the dove we are taught that this is He ; and dost thou think that thou art baptised by his authority by whose ministration thou art baptized ? If thou thinkest this, thou art not as yet in the body of the dove ; and if thou are not in the body of the dove, it is not to be wondered at that thou hast not simplicity ; for by means of the dove simplicity is chiefly designated."— AUGUSTINE, *Gospel of John*, Vol I. p. 63.

See MYSTERY (first), OLIVE LEAF, RAVEN.

DOVE-SELLERS :—

Symbolic of hybrid qualities seemingly gentle and beneficent, but really hard and grasping.

"Jesus overthrew the tables of the money-changers, and the seats of them that sold doves."—MAT. xxi. 12.

The "dove-sellers" are those who profess to be kind and amiable, but who are in reality selfish and indifferent, and who therefore prostitute the ideals which they profess to be living up to.

SEE CLEANSING, JESUS SEVERITY.

DRAGON :—

This symbol has similar meanings to the "Serpent." The male Dragon signifies astral aspects, and the female Dragon, buddhic, as a rule. But the "Dragon" may be raised in signification both on the masculine and on the feminine sides.

See GEORGE AND DRAGON, GREEN LION, SERPENT.

DRAGON OF WISDOM :—

A symbol of the Higher Self,— atma-buddhi.

"The great Dragon of Wisdom (Kwan-sui-yin) is born of Fire and Water, and into Fire and Water will all be re-absorbed with him."—*Fa-hwa-King*.

The Higher Self as atma-buddhi is generated from Spirit (fire), and Reality (water) on the side of Matter, and into Spirit and Reality at the end of the manvantara, all things will be re-absorbed together with him.

"In the first or lowest line, undivided, we see its subject as the Dragon lying hid in the deep. It is not time for active doing. In the second line, undivided, we see its subject as the Dragon appearing in the field. It will be advantageous to meet with the Great Man." —*Yi King*, I. 1, 2.

In the first age, the inner Potencies prepare to emanate. The Eternal Wisdom, or Higher Self, lies hidden in the unknown darkness of the Unmanifest ; for the time of creative activity is not yet. In the second age, the Self is emanated as atma-buddhi, and enters the field of manifestation. It is the Divine purpose to form the Archetypal Man, the progenitor of the human race.

See ARC. MAN, DEPTH, FIELD, FIRE, SERPENT, WATER.

DRAGON RISING FROM THE DEEP :—

A symbol of the astral plane, the activities of which are a means of arousing the lower mental faculties. "Deep" signifies the lower nature or the womb of matter.

See ABYSS, DEEP, TABLES.

DRAGON, GREAT RED :—

A symbol of the lower principle as an adverse energy to the Higher during an early period of involution on the buddhic plane, before the three lower planes were organised.

"And there was seen another sign in heaven ; and behold, a great red dragon, having seven heads and ten horns, and upon his heads seven diadems. And his tail draweth the third part of the stars of heaven, and did cast them to the earth : and the dragon stood before the woman which was about to be delivered, that when she was delivered, he might devour her child."—REV. xii. 3, 4.

The buddhic (heaven) is the first plane on which manifestation takes place on the lunar chain of globes (moon under feet). Manifestation implies duality and relativity, hence the opposite of the Self appears as an antagonistic energy (red dragon). The "heads, horns, and diadems" signify the full endowment of the not-Self with the lower mental, desire, and passional qualities which are of the natural man. The "third part of the stars" refers to the complete number of the spiritual egos who descend into the lower nature (earth) to undergo their pilgrimage through life. The buddhic principle (woman) is ready at this early period to bring forth the Self, who in involution becomes subjective and free of conflict.

See ARYANA, BIRTH OF MAN-CHILD, CONSTELLATIONS, CROWN (stars), DEVIL, GREEN, HORNS (ten), MAN (natural), STARS, YAO.

DRAUPADI, DAUGHTER OF KING DRUPADA :—

A symbol of Wisdom or Intuition generated by the spiritual mind.

"Draupadi was born out of the sacrificial fire, and was a form of Lakshmi. . . . Divine perfume exhaled from her person. As the Pandavas were all portions of one deity (Indra), there could be no harm in Draupadi becoming the wife of all five."—MON. WILLIAMS, *Indian Wisdom*, p. 388.

Wisdom, or the buddhic emotion-nature, was born in the soul from out of the self-limitation of Spirit, and aspiration of the lower nature. The "perfume" expresses the beauty and harmony which comes into the soul through the higher emotions. Wisdom is allied to all the five higher attributes of the soul on the higher mental plane. These attributes arise and develop through devotion to righteousness and Truth.

See CHRYSEIS, DHRISTA, DRUPADA, LAKSHMI, PANDAVAS, PANDORA, PERFUMES, SCENT (sweet).

DRAWER OF WATER :—

A symbol of the soul or mind acquiring truth.

See HYLAS.

DREAMS OF THE SUPREME :—

A symbol of pre-perception or fore-ordination of the Divine scheme of the universe and of the soul.

"The beginning of this story is that Balder the Good was disquieted by dreams of ill-omen which foretold peril to his life. He related his dreams to the Asar, and they took counsel among themselves, and determined that means should be taken for the security of Balder against all possible danger."—*Prose Edda*.

The Supreme Being fore-knows all things in the manifestation of Itself when It creates a universe, and so, in view of the Self-sacrifice or Self-limitation involved, is said to be in peril of its Life. As manifestation proceeds, the Divine aspects (Asar) confer, as it were, together and perfect their plans, devising means for the security of the indwelling Self in its involution and evolution through the illusory regions of the manifested lower worlds. And thus completely the order of nature is wisely arranged to subserve the Divine end in view.

"He (Brahman), the knowing, gave himself up to confused fancies, and when he fell into the slumber prepared for him by Mâyâ, he beheld in amazement multiform dreams : I am ; this is my father, this my mother, this my field, this is my kingdom."—H. OLDENBERG, *Buddha*, p. 238.

The Supreme Truth, in commencing to manifest, pre-determined the nature of the coming universe, and having become obscured within the illusion of existence, awakened therein to formulate the Divine scheme through Self-limitation. The true and One Self is the central principle of manifestation : the Absolute Spirit (father) through the essence of the highest Matter (mother) have produced it. Potential within the Self is the Life-cycle, the arena (field) of manifestation, and the kingdom of the soul.

"How could the all-knowing God arrange a scheme of providential order, just as if He did not know the coming fact of sin, eternally present to His knowledge ? Mind works under conditions of unity, and, above all, Perfect Mind. What God has eternally in view, therefore, is the certain fact of sin, that fact about which all highest counsel in His government must revolve, and upon the due management of which all most eventful and beneficent issues in His kingdom depend, must pervade His most ancient beginnings, and crop out in all the layers and eras of His process, from the first chapter of creative movement onward. As certainly as sin is to be encountered in His plan, its marks and consequences will be appearing anticipatively, and all the grand arrangements and cycles of time will be somehow preluding its approach, and the dire encounter to be maintained with it."—H. BUSHNELL, *Nature and the Supernatural*, p. 136.

See ABSOLUTE, ARC. MAN, ASAR, BALDER, COSMOS, CREATION, DEATH OF BALDER, EVOLUTION, FIELD, INVOLUTION, MATTER, MĀYĀ, PROPHECY, SACRIFICER, SELF.

DREAMS, CHAOTIC :—

A symbol of the false simulating the true, or of superstition.

DRINK OF WINE OR WATER :—

A symbol of the sustenance of the Spirit,—the soul partaking of Life and Truth.

See THIRST, WATER, WINE.

DRONA :—

A symbol of the law of outer observance :—the following of tradition, and the obedience to authority, and codes of external laws.

"Drona was the son of a Rishi, but was not born of woman."—J. C. OMAN, *The Great Indian Epics*, p. 113.

That is, the Law principle proceeds from a state of the soul, and not from the emotion-nature. "Drona" was the preceptor both of the young Pandavas and the young Kurus, i.e. the nascent soul-qualities were nurtured and taught under the Law.

"The tutor's fee which Drona required of his pupils for their instruction was that they should capture Drupada, king of Pancala, who was his old schoolfellow, but had insulted him by repudiating his friendship."—MON. WILLIAMS, *Indian Wisdom*, p. 385.

The Law requires that the qualities should capture the spiritual mind (Drupada), which repudiates authority. The desires (Kurus) are said to try, but fail, while the Pandavas (higher faculties) succeed.

"When Drona was carrying everything before him, the Pandavas informed him falsely that his son had been killed. He did not credit the report at first, but when assured of its truth by the virtuous Yudhisthira himself . . . the old hero threw away his arms and, devoting himself to *Yoga contemplation*, passed away immediately. Dhristadyumna then beheaded his lifeless corpse."—J. C. OMAN, *The Great Indian Epics*, p. 184.

To the higher faculties (Pandavas) law and authority come to have no result (son) in the mind, consequently they (Drona) are completely discredited and immediately disappear. The beheading is the ridding the mind (head) of its legalism.

See CAIAPHAS, DHRISTA, KURUS, PANDAVAS, PRIESTS AND ELDERS, YUDHISTHIRA.

DRÖPNER RING :—

A symbol of the quality of tamas, i.e. inertia, or lack of progressive energy, and of initiative.

"Odin cast upon the funeral pile (of Balder) the ring Dröpner, which possessed the property of producing every month eight similar rings of weight equal to itself. Balder's horse and all his ridinggear were also laid upon the pile."—HOWITT, *Literature, Prose Edda, etc.*

And now it is that the Higher Self under the aspect of Will (Odin) casts forth the tamasic quality, which is eightfold, inasmuch as, being a condition of the four lower planes, it has duality of aspect on each plane. The "month" is a symbol of time or space, and indicates phenomenal changes. Thereupon the rajasic quality of outgoing energy, and the functioning of the mind are substituted.

See BALDER, DEATH OF BALDER, EIGHT, GUNAS, HORSE, MONTH, NANNA, ODIN, RAJAS, RING-HORNE, TAMAS.

DROUGHT ; WATERLESS :—

Significant of an inert mental condition, with absence of truth or opinions, and consequent barrenness and latency.

See DEARTH, DEVASTATION, DRY, WINTER.

DROUGHT, FREEDOM FROM :—

A symbol of the activity of the mental faculties, and the nourishing of the mind through truth (water).

See IRRIGATION, RAIN, YIMA.

DRUG, OR DRUJ NASU, OR DROUK :—

A symbol of desire and ignorance, warring against right and truth.

See ARIZURA, DAEVA, DOG (white), NASU.

DRUGS OF MEDEA :—

Symbolic of buddhic functionings which render desire inoperative in the soul.

"Medea led Jason by night to the Golden Fleece, and with her drugs she cast to sleep the serpent which guarded it."—*Argonautic Expedition*.

The intuition leads the soul secretly to the source of Wisdom, so soon as the lower mind is stilled, for with the powers exercised upon the higher planes she lulls to rest the tempter,—kama-manas.

See GOLDEN FLEECE, JASON, MEDEA.

DRUNKARD ON WINE OR SOMA-JUICE :—

A symbol of the spiritual nature which "intoxicates" or paralyses the lower self through an influx of the Divine life.

"In the *Rig-Veda*, Indra is the highest and greatest of the Gods, and his Soma-drinking is allegorical of his highly spiritual nature. In the *Puranas*, Indra becomes a profligate, and a regular drunkard on the Soma-juice."—H. P. BLAVATSKY, *Secret Doctrine*, Vol. II. p. 295.

"I drank and was inebriated with the living water that does not die ; and my inebriation was not without knowledge."—*Ode of Solomon*.

See DIONYSUS, INDRA, INTOXICATION, NOAH, SILENUS, SOMA-JUICE, WINE.

DRUPADA, KING :—

A symbol of the spiritual mind.

See DRAUPADI, DRONA, PANCALA.

DRY AND MOIST :—

Symbols of Falsity and Truth.
See MOIST ESSENCE.

DRYAD OF THE FOREST :—

A nature-spirit or builder of forms on the astral plane.

See DEVAS (lower), SALAMANDERS.

DRYAS, SHEPHERD OF THE PEOPLE :—

A symbol of command, or the lower will ; a director of the qualities of the natural man.

DRY-BACKED THROUGH THE DAEVAS :—

Symbolic of aspects of the Self obscured and unapparent, owing to the activities upon the astral and lower mental planes.

See DAEVAS.

DUCK OF ILMATER :—

A symbol of primordial matter which brings forth the Cosmos as a germ or egg in time and space.

See EGG, MONAD, SEB, SEED.

DUGHDHOVA, MOTHER OF ZARATUST :—

A symbol of primeval matter of the lower planes,—manasic and astrophysical,—which gives birth to the Soul in the cycle of Involution.

See AURVAITO, BIRTH OF ZOROASTER, MĀYĀ, POURUSHASPA, PRAKRITI, WOMB, ZOROASTER.

DUNG OF FLOCKS AND HERDS FERTILISING THE GROUND :—

Symbolic of the experience which the emotions yield, and through which the soul-growths are nourished in the culture of the lower nature.

See FLOCKS, GROUND, MAN WITHOUT WOMAN.

DURĀSRŌBO, THE KARAP :—

A symbol of the kamic or astral principle of the lower nature, in its lower instinct quality.

"The plotting Durāsrōbo, as a punishment for his wickedness in endeavouring to thwart the righteous (Zoroaster), comes to a violent and strange end."—A. V. W. JACKSON, *Zoroaster*, p. 32.

The lower instinct-nature comes to an end inasmuch as when the rein of reason is put on it to restrain it then transmutation takes place, and the lower desires, as such, become to all intents and purposes non-existent. This restraint and repudiation of lower motives to action, is equivalent to the killing-out or suppression of desire.

See BIRTH OF KRISHNA, CURETES, HEROD, HODER, KILLING OUT, MAGIC PRACTICES.

DURGA, OR KALI, GODDESS :—

A symbol of Buddhi as the destroyer of the lower mental qualities (men or people).

This symbol furnishes an instance of erroneous attribution of ferocity to an object of worship, when the meaning is simply the destruction of evil propensities in the soul.

See BUDDHI, EGYPTIANS, EXODUS, SIVA, SLAUGHTER, TONGUES, WAR.

DURVA-BRICK, OF THE ALTAR :—

A symbol of the personality, or the lower self in the mental body.

"Inasmuch as he lays down the dviya-gus brick close to the durva-brick (cattle),—the durva-brick being the breath and the dviyagus the Sacrificer,—those two bodies of his (human and divine) thus become connected by breath."—*Sata. Bråh.*, VII. 4, 2, 20.

The two centres of consciousness,—the Individuality and the Personality,—are interconnected upon the mental plane. The human personality is the expression on the lower planes of the Divine individuality.

See ALTAR (fire), BREATH, BRICKS, DVIYAGUS, PERSONALITY, SACRIFICER.

DUR-YODHANA, "DIFFICULT TO BE SUBDUED" :—

A symbol of the desire-mind, the principle of kama-manas.

"Dur-yodhana (like Ravana) is a visible type of the evil principle in human nature for ever doing battle with the good and divine principle, symbolised by the five sons of Pandu."—MON. WILLIAMS, *Indian Wisdom*, p. 383.

The "hundred brothers" of Dur-yodhana are the desires.

See ADVERSARY, DEVIL, DHRITA, KURUS, PANDAVAS, RAVANA.

DUSAHK ABYSS :—

A symbol of the lower planes, the arena of the desire-mental activities ; the lower life of suffering and discipline in which the incarnating egos find themselves.

See BRIDGE (kinvat), GARODMAN, HADES, HELL, PURGATORY.

DUST OF THE GROUND OR WORLD :—

A symbol of the lower mind which is unstable and subject to every wind of doctrine and opinion that obscures the truth.

"So long as we are in the dust, we see not the face of the Beloved."—TABRIZI, *Ode XLIV*.

So long as the egos are obscured in the activities of the lower mind, they are unable to apprehend the higher qualities which are the expression of the Love and Wisdom nature within. Dust being free from water, signifies a state of ignorance, absence of truth (water), which is the original state of mind (man).

See ADAM (lower), BEASTS (earth), CURSE (serpent), DRY, MAN, SOPHIA, SWEAT, WATER.

DUTY, WEALTH AND PLEASURE :—

These ideas are symbols of Justice, Wisdom, and Love.

DVIYAGUS BRICK OF THE ALTAR :—

A symbol of the potential causal-body, the seat of the incarnate Self and Individuality.

"Now were he only to lay down that Golden Man (Pragâpati or Agni), and not let this dviyagus brick remain, the Sacrificer surely would quickly pass away from this world ; but now that he allows this brick to remain, he thereby leaves to him this human form of his ; and so he attains with this body the full measure of life."—*Sata. Bråh.*, VII. 4, 2, 18.

If the Logos only manifested as the primordial Higher Self (Gold man), and did not establish the buddhic causal-centre as the seat of the Individuality, the Logos would withdraw into Himself and leave the lower planes, so that the purpose of existence would be unaccomplished. But now that the causal-body is formed potentially as the perfect pattern of Divine humanity, it will evolve in actuality to the full measure of its indwelling life.

See ALTAR (fire), BRICKS, DURVA BRICK, GOLD MAN, PRAGÂPATI, SACRIFICER.

DWARF :—

A symbol of the lower Self as being small in comparison with the Higher Self. But the two are aspects of the One Self.

"I stood on a lofty mountain and saw a mighty Man, and another a dwarf, . . . and a voice spake unto me and said, 'I am thou and thou art I ; and wheresoever thou art, I am there, and I am sown (or scattered) in all. From whencesoever thou willest thou gatherest Me, and gathering Me thou gatherest thyself.'"—*The Gospel of Eve* (EPIPH. 26, 3).

The ego, in its loftiest aspirations, sees, as it were, the Higher and the lower Selves,—the one great in its completeness, the other little in its deficiencies. Yet the two Selves are essentially the same, for the Higher is the potential-perfect, while the lower is the actual, and only imperfect because not yet fully evolved. In the many souls the Perfect Self is

sown or scattered, and waiting to be
evolved. The high qualities that go
to make perfection " are many members, but one body," and that body is
Christ. When these qualities are
gathered together in the soul, the
Christ is evolved and the soul is then
Christ,—the higher and the lower
Selves have become One.

See DEATH OF OSIRIS, DISMEMBER-
MENT, EVOLUTION, HIGHER (selves),
LIMBS, LIT, MACROCOSM, MEMBERS,
MICROCOSM, OAK TREE, OHONAMOCHI,
PRAGÂPATI, PURUSHA, SEED (good),
SUKUNA, YOUNG MAN.

DWARF, MISSHAPEN :—

A symbol of error and small-
mindedness.

See LIT.

DWARFS :—

A symbol of the lower mental
qualities full of ignorance and illusion.

" The dwarfs had been bred in the
mould of the earth, just as worms are
in a dead body. It was, in fact, in
Ymir's flesh that the dwarfs were engendered, and began to move and live.
At first they were only maggots, but
by the will of the gods they at length
partook both of human shape and understanding, although they always dwell
in rocks and caverns " (*Prose Edda*).—
MALLET, *North. Antiq.*, p. 409.

The astro-mental qualities are the
offspring of the higher element of the
lower nature (mould or dust). Through
the death of the Archetypal Man
(Ymir), the kama-manasic (flesh)
principle is reflected below, and from
this the lower qualities arise. At
first they are instinctive and cunning,
but they gradually develop in character
though always remaining in the lower
nature of the soul.

See ARC. MAN, CREEPING THINGS,
COMB, EARTH, FLESH, QUALITIES,
YMIR.

DWELLER ON HIGH :—

A symbol of the Atman or Higher
Self.

See ATMAN, TAE-KEIH.

DWELLING IN THE RECESSES OF THE PALACE :—

A symbol of the causal-body on
the higher mental plane, the abode
of the indwelling Spirit.

" 'The prince might perchance see
some inauspicious sight which could

disturb his mind,'—thus reflecting, the
king had a dwelling prepared for his
son (Buddha) apart from the busy press,
in the recesses of the palace."—*Buddha-
Karita*, Bk. II. 28.

The Higher Self anticipates that the
Soul or lower Self (Buddha), during
the cycle of its lower experiences,
would require periods of withdrawal
and rest, which necessitate having a
permanent sheath wherein it may
take refuge. It is here in the process of involution that the true
permanent Ego is established in its
causal sheath.

" 'Lord, thou hast been our dwelling
place in all generations' (Ps. xc. 1).
The Psalmist's perception here is that
from everlasting to everlasting that
which constitutes man has been latent
in God, and has never really left him,
numberless as have been the successive
generations of human life on earth."—
R. J. CAMPBELL, Serm., *Our Solidarity
with God*.

See BEHÛDET BUDDHA, CAUSAL-
BODY, COTTAGE, HOUSE, HOUSE-
HOLDER, INDIVIDUALITY, INVOLU-
TION, PALACE, PLACE, RE-INCARNA-
TION, SHIP OF MANU, SUDDHODANA,
VESTURES.

DWELLINGS FOR THE SEEDS OF THE BEST CREATURES :—

Symbolic of vehicles or forms for
the reception of the perfect monads
of all the qualities of the soul which
have now to evolve.

" Dwellings should be established, and
the seeds of the best men, women, cattle
and all things should be brought."—
Vendidad, II., *S. B. of E.*

This refers to the process and
period of involution,—the Golden Age,
where all is perfect, and there is no
struggle. The " dwellings," or forms,
are now ideally prepared, that is, the
means for their formation on the
lower planes is secured. The type
forms for the various mental, emotional,
desire, and other qualities, brought
over from the previous cycle of manifestation,—the Lunar,—are now introduced in their perfection.

See CATTLE, FORMS, GOLDEN AGE,
HOUSE, INVOLUTION, LUNAR CYCLE,
MAN, MATS, SEEDS OF MEN, VARA.

DWELLINGS SUPPLIED WITH CATTLE :—

Symbolic of the forms and limitations of the lower life of desires and personal feelings.

See CATTLE, FORMS.

DYNASTY, HEAVEN'S (OF CHINA) :—

This signifies the development of potential man during the Lunar cycle, in a state of involution on the buddhic plane, whereby the higher qualities are involved in order that they shall afterwards be evolved.

DYNASTY, EARTH'S (OF CHINA) :—

This means the formation of potential man at the commencement of the Mundane cycle, during which the astral vehicle with its mechanism is prepared, and the desire-nature involved.

DYNASTY, MAN'S (OF CHINA) :—

This refers to the appearance of astral man on this earth, the formation of the physical body with its mechanism, and the establishment of the differentiated sensorium.

See ADAM (lower), ARC. MAN, PYLUS, RACES.

EA, GOD :—

A symbol of the First Logos, or the Creator manifesting upon the higher mental plane.

"Ea, under the mask of Merodach (Marduk), is the Creator of mankind as of all things else. In this act of creation the Goddess Aruru is coupled with him."
—A. H. SAYCE, *Rel. of Anc. Egypt. and Babyl.*, p. 382.

The "Creator Ea" is the First Logos acting through the Second Logos (Merodach). The "Goddess Aruru" is the feminine principle buddhi,—duality being necessary to manifestation,—spirit and matter being essential thereunto. "Ea," "Merodach," and "Aruru" are the Higher Triad,—Father, Son, and Holy Spirit.

"Ea was god of the deep, both of the atmospheric deep, and of that watery deep, the Okeanos of Homer, which surrounds the earth like a coiled serpent. . . . Ea was lord of wisdom."—*Ibid.*, p. 104.

The "atmospheric deep" signifies the higher mental plane, the "firmament." The "watery deep," the "celestial ocean" is the Divine Reality, the Source of all. Truth (water) is the origin of all things.

See AIR, ARURU, COSMOS, DEEP, FIRMAMENT, MERODACH, OCEAN, SPIRIT, TRIAD, TRINITY, WATER.

EAGLE :—

A symbol of the Holy Spirit, which flies, as it were, through the mind (air) from the higher nature (heaven) to the lower nature (earth) and soars aloft to the Self (sun).

"Alála, the eagle, is stated to be 'the symbol of the noon-tide sun'; and Alála, whose name is of Accadian origin, signifies 'the great Spirit.' "—A.H. SAYCE, *Rel. of Anc. Egypt. and Babyl.*, p. 248.

"The dove is the well-known figure of meek innocence. The eagle's lofty flight and keen vision represent but another form of the same Divine Spirit."
—A. JUKES, *Types of Genesis*, p. 34.

"Flying eagle signifies the divine truth of the Word as to knowledge and thence understanding."—SWEDENBORG, *Apoc. Rev.*, n. 244.

"(The letter from the king, my Father) flew in the likeness of an eagle, the king of all birds; it flew and alighted beside me, and became all speech" (*Hymn of the Soul*).—GNOSTIC, *Acts of Judas Thomas*.

The message to the soul appealed through the higher side of the consciousness. It sped forth with a directness and sureness of aim that might be compared to the flight of an eagle, which is a symbol of the Holy Spirit descending. It took possession of the soul mightily, so that it had to express outwardly that which was communicated to it from within.

"There is a great deal of meaning in the fact that the Bible in our English churches is put to rest on the outspread wings of an eagle. The meaning of it has to do with the fact that the letter killeth, but the spirit giveth life. You have very often got to put the literal Bible on the wings of the bird that can soar high, i.e. the spiritual imagination, the insight of the seer, before you reach its heavenly meaning. Yet many a clergyman, while his Bible is on eagle's wings, the very symbol that tells him to carry it to high spiritual realms of meaning, will give a wooden interpretation. In sacred symbolism the eagle stands for that power of rising above the earth, above the physical and the literal, into the high heavens of a rarefied faith, a mystic intuition, a penetrating spiritual imagination."—T. RHONDDA WILLIAMS, Serm., *Dying in the Lord*.

See FATHER, GRIFFIN, HOLY GHOST, LETTER, PHŒNIX, PROMETHEUS, SPEECH, SUN, VULTURE.

EAR, OR HEARING :—

A symbol of the mental faculty in its passive aspect, receptive of ideas. It stands for trust in authority ; reliance upon external guidance. Or, in a higher sense, the ear signifies receptivity to inward guidance and to the admonitions of the conscience as the voice of God.

" ' He will open also their ear, to correct them, and will speak to them that they return from iniquity ' (JOB xxxvi. 10). To ' open the ear from iniquity,' is to lay open the understanding of knowledge. But a man is reproved, and his ear opened, when he feels within him a desire after eternal goods, and acknowledges the sins which he has outwardly committed."

" To ' open the ear in tribulation ' (JOB xxxvi. 15) is to open the hearing of the heart by the affliction of blows. Tribulation then opens the ear of the heart, which this world's prosperity often closes."—ST. GREGORY, Morals on the Book of Job, Vol. III. pp. 176, 182.

" To the soul that is awakened, and that is made to see things as they are ; to him God is what he is in himself, the blessed, the highest, the only eternal good, and he without the enjoyment of whom all things would sound but emptily in the ears of the soul."—J. BUNYAN, Christ a Complete Saviour.

See CAIAPHAS, CALF (MOLTEN), CON-SCIENCE, HEARING, HIDING, NOISE, SOUND, TRADITION, VOICE.

EARTH,—PRIMORDIAL :—

A symbol of matter which, when acted upon by Spirit, takes forms and qualities for manifestation.

" In the beginning God created the heaven and the earth. And the earth was waste and void."—GEN. i. 1, 2.

At the commencement of the emanation of the Solar Universe, the primordial elements, Spirit and Matter, are differentiated from that condition which is itself neither, but which is potential for both. And the matter is formless and devoid of special qualities, for Spirit is not yet permeating and informing matter, and the process of involution has not begun.

" Creation for Erigena means only a local and temporal exhibition of eternal essences. The visible world is nothing but the appearance of invisible primordial causes. Take away from any object in this visible world all that can be thought about it, i.e. its Idea which constitutes its ' primordial cause,' and nothing is left. In the last analysis everything turns out to be immaterial. ' Matter,' so-called, is no real being ; it is only an aggregation of ' qualities.' Remove the ' qualities ' which thought can seize and nothing remains."—R. M. JONES, Mystical Religion, p. 125.

See CHAOS, COSMOS, CREATION, ELEMENTS, HEAVEN AND EARTH, KHIEN AND KHWAN, MATTER, MĀYĀ, PROTOTYPES, QUALITIES, SPIRIT.

EARTH, THE GREAT SUSTAINING MOTHER :—

A symbol of the productive buddhic nature as the Divine expression upon the astral and physical planes. Buddhi acting as the moulder of forms and guide of the separated Self to enable it to manifest its true nature in the soul.

" I praise the earth, the wide-stretched, the traversable, the vast, the unbounded, thy mother, O righteous Homa ! "—Homa Yasht.

The " earth " here signifies the buddhic principle in consciousness, which is the means of assisting the gestation of the Self in the lower nature. The buddhic consciousness is specially made mention of, as it is from this aspect that the growth of the lower Self is assisted.

" Aditi is this earth, for this earth gives everything here :—' the all-containing,' for on this earth everything is contained." Sata. Brâh., VII. 4, 2, 7,

" Earth—Mother of the Gods, the wife of the starry Heaven."—HOMER, Hymn, 30, 17.

" By earth is meant the Lord's church in the heavens and on the earths ; the church, wherever it may be, is the Lord's kingdom."—SWEDENBORG, Apoc. Rev., n. 285.

See ADITI, BUDDHI, CHURCH, COW (earth), LADY, MOTHER (divine), SAPANDOMAD, WISDOM.

EARTH ; GROUND ; WORLD :—

A symbol of the lower nature of the soul,—lower-mental, astral, and physical planes, which constitute the arena of life for the ego.

" And God called the dry land Earth : and the gathering together of the waters called he Seas : and God saw that it was good."—GEN. i. 10.

And matter being further differentiated, " dry land Earth " stands for the lower nature,—the natural man,—and the " gathering together of the waters " signifies the forming of the astral " Sea " of the desires. And all is made perfect in the course of involution.

" These knowledges are the ' waters gathered together into one place ' and are called ' seas '; but the external man is called ' dry land,' and presently ' earth.' "—SWEDENBORG, *Arc. Cel. to Gen.* i. 10.

" Thoth spake after he saw the enemies lying upon the earth : ' Joyful is your heart ye gods of heaven ! Joyful is your heart, ye gods of earth ! ! ' "—*Legend of the Winged Sun-disk.*

The Higher-mind, now awakened in the soul, sees the " enemies " or desires, prone upon the " earth " or lower planes. Thereat the ego sings, ' Glad is the Christ who hath triumphed over the desire nature and its illusions ! ' ' Glad are the higher qualities of the lower mind, which are now raised victoriously ! '

" I have moved against the earth ; I have caused my inherited fate to rest." —BLACKDEN, *Book of the Dead,* Ch. CX.

The Self has come forth in the lower nature to contend against it. The Self has offered itself as a sacrifice ; for it has voluntarily imposed limitation upon itself, for the sake of the many.

" Christ's redemption of the world was a true man ; all the truer man because it was God in man ; it was the Father in the Son who showed what earth, used in the fear of God, might be. In him there could be no doubt of what sort had been the giving of the earth to the children of men of which David had sung so long ago. It could not for one moment seem to have been a gift to man's self-indulgence and selfishness. It certainly had not been a giving of the earth away from God. It had been given to the divine in man, to that in man which had in it the nature of divinity, and which was capable, by obedience, of becoming infinitely near to God. That this is the real nature of God's gift of earth to man was the assertion of the incarnation and of all the life of Jesus."—PHILLIPS BROOKS, Serm., *The Earth of the Redemption.*

" He who dwelling in the earth is distinct from the earth, whom the earth knows not, whose body the earth is, who rules the earth from within, he is thy soul, the inner guide, the immortal." —*Brihad. Upanishad,* III. 7, 3.

The Self incarnate in the lower nature (earth) is distinct from the lower nature, whom the lower nature knows not, whose vehicle the lower nature is, who rules the lower nature from within ; he is thy individual soul or Self, the inner guide to perfection, the immortal ego.

" (JOB ix. 24.) For what is denoted by the designation of ' the earth,' saving the flesh ? who by the title of ' the wicked,' save the devil ?—ST. GREGORY, *Morals on the Book of Job,* Vol. I. p. 526.

See ADAM (lower), ALTAR GROUND, CHAOS, DEW, FLESH, GROUND, INCARNATION, JESUS (mortal), LAND, MAN, MAN (natural), REDEMPTION, SEA, THOTH, TRIBUTE.

EARTH (SPECIALISED) :—

A symbol of the physical nature, or the physical plane, as the lowest plane of manifestation.

" And God blessed them saying, Be fruitful and multiply, and fill the waters in the seas, and let fowl multiply in the earth."—GEN. i. 22.

And now the Divine nature energises the functions of the physical, astral, and astro-mental natures, and enjoins that the higher emotions are to increase in the soul, through the discipline of the physical nature (earth).

" The first of four human beings flew from the North, ' son of the essence of Water ' ; the second from the South, ' son of the essence of red Earth.' " —*Chinese Legend.*

The first world-soul vehicle is the buddhic, which is ensouled by the Atman. The second is the physical, which is a response to the atmic from below, and, through the law of attraction, becomes the epitome of the atmic or love (red) aspect. (The third and fourth vehicles are the astral and the mental.)

See CREATURES, ELEMENTS, MULTIPLY, WATER (lower), WHALES.

EARTHQUAKES :—

Emblem of upheaval in the lower nature, in which disruptive forces break up conditions that are outlived, and which are no longer of use in the old forms.

" For nation shall rise against nation, and kingdom against kingdom : and there shall be famines and earthquakes in divers places."—MATT. xxiv. 7.

This represents the conflicts between groups of the lower qualities, resulting in certain processes whereby the evolution of good is ultimately accomplished. The shaking of the lower planes (earthquakes) answers to an increase of spiritual energy above. Vibrations communicated to the higher planes set up counter quivers on high levels which react upon the matter beneath.

"Earthquakes signify changes of state in the church, because the earth signifies the church, and because in the spiritual world, when the state of the church is perverted anywhere, and there is a change, an earthquake takes place."—SWEDEN-BORG, *Apoc. Rev.*, n. 331.

See CALAMITIES, CHURCH, FAMINE, NATION.

EAST ; THE SUN-RISE :—

Emblem of the direction in which the Self appears in the soul. The source of Life, and the light of knowledge is the Self (sun) rising in the mind.

"Behold the Man whose name is East (or Rising)."—PHILO, *De Confus. Ling.*, § 14.

"The east, indeed, is the region of the gods, for this reason he (the sacrificer) looks towards the East." *Sata. Brâh.*, I. 9, 3, 13.

"The man who will feel the shining of the Eternal Sun, which is Christ Himself, will have clear vision, and will dwell on the mountains of the east, concentrating all his energies and raising his heart towards God."—RUYSBROECK, Stoddart's trans., p. 127.

"From the East our home, my parents, having equipped me, sent me forth."—"Hymn of the Soul" in the *Acts of Judas Thomas.*

From the East, or along the celestial path of the Self, to which the rising of the sun in the heavens is comparable, was the Divine Ego or Spark sent forth of the Spirit in the buddhic vestures which clothed it with the full powers of the soul.

See AGNIHOTRA, CHILDREN OF EAST, CHRIST, DAWN, EDEN, GATE (tchesert), HORISONS, JOB, MAGI, QUARTERS, QUETZALCOATL, SHINAR, STAR IN EAST, SUN-RISING.

EATING :—

A symbol of the acquisition of knowledge as sustenance for the mind, by means of sensation and experience. Also, in a higher sense, the reception of spiritual food which is Wisdom, Truth, and Love.

"As the living Father sent me, and I live because of the Father; so he that eateth me, he also shall live because of me."—JOHN vi. 57.

As the Absolute and Unmanifest Supreme emanated the Divine life, which is the life of the Manifest Self, so the quality that partakes of the nature of the Self, it also shall live everlastingly by and in the Self.

"'Of every tree that is in the Paradise thou mayest freely eat.' He exhorts the soul of man to derive advantage not from one 'tree' alone, nor from one single virtue, but from all the virtues; for eating is a symbol of the nourishment of the soul, and the soul is nourished by the reception of good things, and by the doing of praiseworthy actions."—PHILO, *Works*, Yonge, Vol. IV. p. 77.

"'For my sighing cometh before I eat' (JOB iii. 24). All they are starved of the food of truth that take joy in the emptiness of this scene of our pilgrimage, but he 'sighs' (with sorrow), that 'eats,' because all who are touched with the love of truth are at the same time fed with the refreshments of contemplation."—ST. GREGORY, *Morals on the Book of Job*, Vol. I. p. 251.

"To eat signifies appropriation of good or of evil things."—SWEDENBORG, *Apoc. Rev.*, n 832.

See ASHEMOGHA, BREAD, CALF (molten), FEED, FOOD, MANNA, MEAT, MOUTH (opened), SACRAMENT, SUPPER, TREE OF KNOWLEDGE, OF LIFE.

EATING THE LOWER FOOD :—

A symbol of becoming attached to the things of the lower evolution, and partaking of the desires and sensations. When the fruit or food of the underworld is eaten by man (mind) and woman (emotion) the ego identifies itself with the lower qualities and loses all possibility of detaching itself from them and rising again to the upper planes, except by recourse to the means provided in choosing the good and refusing the evil through a long series of lives.

"When Izanami died she went to the land of Yomi, whither she was followed by her husband. But as she had already eaten of the food of that region, he could not bring her back with him. She forbade him to look on her, but he persisted and saw that she was already a putrid corpse. Izanami then complained that he had put her to shame, and caused him to be pursued by the Ugly Females of Hades and other personifications of corruption and disease who dwelt there" (Nihongi).— W. G. ASTON, *Shinto (Religions)*, p. 23.

The principle of Buddhi (Izanami) became inverted, as it were, on the astral plane of the lower quaternary (Yomi) and so had partaken of the life of the plane, which prevented the Self (Izanagi) finding communion with her. The death of the higher qualities became the birth of the lower, which are the foes of the Self. The lower nature appears corrupt to the Higher, and the desires and lower emotions (Ugly females) obscure and repel the Divine spirit within. The " fall " having taken place, a process of salvation is rendered necessary.

See BUDDHI, COMB, CUPID, DANIEL, EYE, FALL, HIGHER AND LOWER, IZANAGI, MEADOW, MEDUSA, PEACHES, PERSEPHONE, QUATERNARY, UNDERWORLD, YOMI.

ECHINADES ISLANDS :—

Symbolic of various conditions upon the astral and physical planes, such as should conduce to the ultimate success and safety of the soul (Argo), as it progresses through the experiences of the lower state of existence.

See ARGO, OCYPETE.

EDDY, OR WHIRL :—

A symbol of vibratory vortices caused by spiritual energy in atomic matter of the higher and the lower planes.

" When Strife reached the lowest depth of the eddy, and Love comes to be in the midst of the whirl, then all these things come together at this point so as to be one alone, yet not immediately, but joining together at their pleasure, one from one place, another from another."—Empedocles, FAIRBANKS, 169.

When diversity reaches its maximum at its lowest point,—that is to say, a condition of evolution is arrived at, when by a system of vortices in matter, vibrations are set up which serve to produce lack of equilibrium of part with part, which answers to the dawn of separate existence. Then the Self (Love), seated in the centre of all beings, commences to evolve, and all the infinite diversity of phenomena begins to appear. And since all things are mutually interdependent, evolution is proceeded with en masse. Yet not equally or completely is this possible, as here and there, and step by step, some qualities slowly, others more quickly, so they all gradually accomplish their own growth.

" In the unageing Time, Chaos, impregnated by the whirling of (Father) Æther, formed itself into the Cosmic Egg."— G. R. S. MEAD, Orpheus, p. 155.

See COSMOS, CREATION, EGG, EVOLUTION, SELF, SEPARATION, STRIFE.

EDEN, GARDEN OF :—

Symbolic of a condition of soul upon the buddhic plane. The buddhic or Wisdom consciousness which is above the mental.

" And the Lord God planted a garden eastward in Eden, and there he put the man whom he had formed."—GEN. ii, 8.

And the Divine Will-Wisdom established the buddhic consciousness, or higher soul. And from this the individuality proceeds to manifest. It is the ensouling life of the causal-body on the mental plane.

" By ' garden ' is signified intelligence ; by ' Eden ' love ; by ' the east ' the Lord ; consequently by the ' garden in Eden eastward ' is signified the intelligence of the celestial man, which flows in by love from the Lord. There is here no strife between the internal and external man. The ' garden in Eden ' is the kingdom of the Lord, or heaven."—SWEDENBORG, Arc. Cel. to Gen. ii. 8.

" Eden is a symbolical expression for correct and divine reason."

" Paradise symbolically taken, means wisdom, intelligence both divine and human, and the proper comprehension of the causes of things."—PHILO, Yonge's trans., Vol. IV. pp. 286, 293.

" Eden, or Paradise, was considered by the learned of the ancient Israelites as the place of the Understanding and Wisdom, the Intellect. ' The higher Wisdom is called the higher Eden.' (Zohar)."—I. MYER, Qabbalah, p. 205.

" The Garden of Eden (in the Ottoman Sufi Cosmogony) is the scene of the Beatific Vision, the Divine Epiphanies, the sight of which will form the highest felicity of the blessed."—GIBB, Ottoman Poetry, Vol. I. p. 37.

" The source and motive of Progress is a sense of want, of short-coming. It is the very voice of truth, which confesses imperfections and yearns to rise. This true, this humble sense of actual imperfection is provoked and kept alive by a vision, an ideal of possible perfection, which haunts the secret soul of man, and which is a relic of Eden. . . . In man, something, be it a memory or an anticipation, is perpetually protesting against the actual attainments of human life, and stimulating him to seek a more perfect and higher condition."—H. P. LIDDON, University Sermons, p. 34.

" Gerald Winstanly had come to regard the whole Biblical narrative as an allegory of which he gives a most poetical interpretation. The Creation is mankind. The Garden of Eden is the mind of man, which he describes as originally filled with herbs and pleasant plants, ' as love, joy, peace, humility, delight, and purity of life.' The serpent he holds to be self-love ; the forbidden fruit to be ' selfishness,' following the promptings of which ' the whole garden becomes a stinking dung-hill of weeds, and brings forth nothing but pride, envy, discontent, disobedience, and the whole actings of the spirit and powers of darkness.' "—L. H. BERENS, *The Digger Movement*, p. 44.

See ADAM (lower), ARYANA, BIRD'S NEST, BUDDHIC PLANE, CAUSAL-BODY, CURSE (ground), EAST, FALL, GARDEN, GARDEN (flowers), GARODMAN, GIL-GOOLEM, GROVES, HEAVEN, KINGDOM OF HEAVEN, LOTE-TREE, MAN, MUS-PELLHEIM, NOD, PARADISE, TREASURES (cave), TYRUS, WISDOM.

EDEN RIVER WITH FOUR HEADS :—

Symbolically the " river of Eden " is a channel of communication from the buddhic plane to the lower quater-nary (four elements). The first " head," Pishon, is the higher mental plane ; the second, Gihon, the lower mental plane ; the third, Hiddekel, the astral plane ; and the fourth, Euphrates, the physical plane.

" Sol. ibn Gabirol says, ' Paradise is the world supernal. The river going forth out of Eden is universal matter. Its four separating streams are the four elements.' "—*Jewish Enc.*,- article "Cabala."

" The Zohar says,—' Fire , air, water, and earth are all united with each other, and there is not any void between them, etc.' ; as is taught in the Holy Writings,— ' And from thence it separates and becomes four heads.' "—MYER, *Qabbalah*, p. 216.

" The Shekinah is the Eden which is above, whence the river of life flows forth that waters the Garden below."—A. E. WAITE, *Secret Doctrine in Israel*, p. 192.

" A ' river out of Eden ' signifieth wisdom proceeding from love, which is ' Eden.' To ' water the garden ' is to give intelligence ; to be thence parted into four heads is a description of intelligence by four ' rivers.' The first river, or ' Pison,' signifieth the intelligence of faith originating-in-love. . . . The second river, ' Gihon,' signifieth the knowledge of all things relating to goodness and truth, or to love and faith. What relateth to ' Pison ' hath respect to the will, what to ' Gihon,' to understanding. The ' river Hiddekel ' is reason, or the clearness and perspicuity of reason. ' Phrath,' or ' Euphrates,' is science, which is the ultimate or term. As by ' Egypt,' so also by ' Euphrates,' are signified sciences, or scientifics, and also the sensual things whereof scientifics are formed. The nature and quality of

celestial order, or the manner of the process in things relating to life, may appear from these rivers, viz. that it is from the Lord, who is the East,—he is the fountain of wisdom, and by wisdom, of intelligence, and by intelligence, of reason."—SWEDEN-BORG, *Arc. Cel. to Gen.* ii.

" In Eden the stream is one, but ' from thence it is parted,' and becomes four distinct rivers. What is this but that stream of living waters, which one and undivided for those who enter Para-dise,—and without a name while it is there, for in its undivided flow the one stream is beyond all human description,— without the garden, it is parted into four streams, giving its waters to the world as Pison, Gihon, Euphrates, and Hiddekel. For divine truth which is the living water, to those who can see it as it is within the veil, is one full stream, in undivided flow ; but to us on earth it ever comes by four distinct channels. It may be said in general that there are four sources of truth, and but four, which are acces-sible to men : . . . first, *intuition*, by which we get an acquaintance with moral or spiritual things : second, *perception*, through the senses, by which we only get an acquaintance with material things and their properties : third, *testimony*, by which we learn what others have found out through perception or intui-tion : fourth, *reasoning* or reflection, process of the understanding."—A. JUKES, *Types of Genesis*, p. 50.

See AMBAYAS, ASSYRIA, ELEMENTS, ERIDANUS, EUPHRATES, GIHON, GIL-GOOLEM, GOLDEN AGE, HAVILAH, HIDDEKEL, HOUSE (frequented), PISHON, QUATERNARY, RETURN, RIVER OF LIFE, RIVERS, RUAH.

EDFU (APOLLINOPOLIS MAGNA) :—

A symbol of a centre of conscious-ness in which is the perception of Truth,—the fundamental fact which is to be arrived at through the self-conscious recognition of the Supreme Reality in the soul.

" The god Thoth spake : ' This was a stabbing of my foes.' The nome of Edfu is called Stabbing from that day."— *Legend of the Winged Sun-disk.*

The higher Mind recognized that this was a putting down of the illusions of the mind ; and the place of Truth in known as the condition of disillusion-ment to this day.

See EGINA, HORBEHUDTI, ILLUSION, THOTH.

EEL-GOD ; TUNA :—

A symbol of the Logos as the Divine

Sacrifice, the Saviour and Redeemer within the soul.

"The eel, according to Agartharchides quoted by Hippolitus Salvianus, the Bœotians crowned as a victim and sacrificed solemnly to the gods, which, according to Herodotus, the Egyptians venerated as a divine fish."—GUBERNATIS, *Zoological Mythology*, Vol. II. p. 341.

"As the Eel-god (Tuna) I shall come ; low on thy threshold shall I lay my head, and thine (Ina's) must be the hand to take my life. The great gods have willed that under thy axe my head shall fall, and sweet will it be so to end my mortal life for thee. Thus shall the waters be stayed, and thou shalt be saved."—KATE McCOSH CLARK, *Maori Tales*.

"Tuna" represents the Spirit involved in matter,—the Divine Incarnation or Archetypal Man. "Ina" (moon) stands for the soul in its lower nature or psychic (astral) aspect. The first is the Saviour of the second to which the death of the first is primordially due. The flood of "waters" signifies the great life-wave of involution which subsides at the death of the Incarnate God. The "head of Tuna is buried on the seashore" signifies that the Spirit is immersed in the desire-mental nature ; and from it spring two shoots,—wisdom and love.

See ARC. MAN, COCOA-NUT, CRUCIFIXION, FISH (great), INCARNATION, MOON, SINA.

EGG, PRIMAL :—

A symbol of the Cosmos in its original abstract conception in the ideal or innermost state of existence, prior to the periods and processes of Involution and of Evolution.

"Verily in the beginning this universe was water, nothing but a sea of water. The waters desired, ' How can we be reproduced ? ' They toiled and became heated with fervent devotion ; when they were becoming heated, a golden egg was produced. The year, indeed, was not then in existence : this golden egg floated about for as long as the space of a year."—*Sata. Brâh.*, XI. 1, 6, 1.

"Orpheus declares that Chaos first existed, eternal, vast, uncreate,—it was neither darkness nor light, nor moist, nor dry, nor hot, nor cold, but all things intermingled. . . . in course of the eternity, its outer parts became denser and so sides and ends were made, and it assumed the fashion and form of a gigantic egg."—*Clem. Recognitions.*

"Before the beginning of things, the great and invisible God alone subsisted. There was no motion, nor darkness, nor space, nor matter. There was no other than God, the One, the Uncreate, the Self-subsistent."—*The Perfect Way*, p. 53.

From the Absolute Being must first be emanated Life, Energy, Spirit, but the first manifestation is objective, and therefore is primordial substance, or Monadic essence, the container and mother of all that is to be. This Divine Reality is symbolised by "water" or "Chaos," and is described as becoming active within itself, through "devotion," which refers to the Spirit within taking on the limitations of matter in order to manifest itself. After a long period, the primordial matter becomes so far generally organised as to bear semblance or analogy to an egg ready to bring forth the higher qualities (gods) and the structure of the universe. Only when this point is arrived at does the Cycle of Life (the year) commence. It would be useless for the higher qualities to emerge until material conditions were prepared to receive their activities.

"I (Osiris) rise out of the egg in the hidden land. May my mouth be given unto me that I may speak therewith in the presence of the great god, the lord of the Tuat (underworld)."—BUDGE, *Book of the Dead*, Ch. XXII.

"The ' Egg of Life,' having been brought forth from boundless Mother Substance, and kept in motion by this subjective and ever-moving Mother Substance, manifests endless changes. For within its periphery a male-female living Power is ideated by the foreknowledge of the divine Spirit (Father Æther) which is in the egg ; which Power Orpheus calls Phanes, for on its shining forth, the whole universe shone forth by the light of Fire,—the most glorious of the elements,— brought to perfection in the Moist (principle-Chaos). And so the Egg, the first and last of all things, heated by the Living Creature within it, breaks ; and the enformed Power comes forth, as Orpheus says,—' when the swollen wide-capacious Egg brake in twain ',—and thus the outer membrane contains the diacosmic evolution ; ' but he (Phanes) presides over the Heaven, as it were seated on the heights of a mountain range, and in secret shines over the boundless Æon.' "—*Clem. Alex.*

Primordial matter, the "Mother-substance," or "Mula-prakriti," having been energised and informed by the Supreme Spirit "Father Æther," and undergone development through many changes, brings forth that state of existence which can be the field of action of the higher powers of the invisible universe. The first to appear is "Light" (Phanes), implying the union of spirit with matter in its atomic condition. "God said, Let there be light, and there was light." The "Egg breaking in twain" signifies the dualism of Spirit (heaven) and Matter (earth) which now characterises manifestation. Spirit emanating from above, or within, vitalises the entire Cycle of Life, and establishes the Divine order of development in the Solar universe. The "male-female living Power" is the spirit-matter union which is the condition productive of consciousness (Light) in the monads of life.

"Orpheus tells us that Phanes is the father of all the Gods, for their sake he created the heaven with forethought for his children, in order that they might have a habitation and a common seat—he founded for the immortals an imperishable mansion."—Lactantius, *Inst.* I., V. 28.

"Of the three aspects (of Phanes), Phanes is said to be the 'father,' Erecapæus the 'power,' and Metis the 'intellect' in Platonic terms."—Mead, *T. G. Hermes*, p. 165.

As in the Rig-Veda, "the Gods are subsequent to the development of this universe." The higher qualities (Gods) could not manifest until the way had been prepared, and an enduring provision made for them on the higher planes. The three aspects of the Higher Self (Phanes) are Will (Phanes), Action (Ericapæus), and Wisdom (Metis).

"Aditya (the sun) is Brahman, this is the doctrine, and this is the fuller account of it :—In the beginning *this* was non-existent. It became existent, it grew. It turned into an egg. The egg lay for the time of a year. The egg broke open. The two halves were one of silver, the other of gold. The silver one became this earth, the golden one the sky, the thick membrane (of the white) the mountains ; the thin membrane (of the yolk) the mist with the clouds, the small veins the rivers, the fluid the sea. And what was born from it that was Aditya, the sun."— *Khand. Upanishad*, III. 19.

In the beginning the spiritual Monad, or primordial substance, became existent and developed into a fit condition for the manifestation of the Divine Life. After a cyclic

period of preparation, the condition (egg) permitted of the interactive duality necessary to the emanation of a universe. An efflux of spirit burst forth from within, distinct and separate yet united to atomic matter on which to operate. Matter (earth), primordial, pure and perfect (silver), became the receptacle of Spirit on the buddhic plane (gold-sky). The conditions of aspiration (mountains) truth-bestowing (clouds), channels of Life (rivers), and the Divine Reality (sea), were established, and so it became possible for the Higher Self (the sun) to be born into the universe (solar).

It will be seen from the foregoing passages of Scriptures that the emana tion of a solar universe begins from the simplest state of substance on the highest plane, Spirit commencing to express its qualities through matter ; and that long ages pass ere the conditions of existence allow of the advent of the higher qualities needed for the commencement of the process of Involution which starts from the highest, and consummates in the lowest, and thereby prepares for Evolution which in its turn progresses from the lowest material condition to culminate in the highest spiritual state.

"That which 'descends' into generative states is the Monad, or divine substance vivified by the divine life. And its first appearance in the sphere of Matter and Time is not as individual, but as diffuse existence ; not as self-conscious but as simply conscious. But the potentiality of all higher existences is contained and slumbers within it ; it is the efficient cause of all subsequent developments."— Anna Kingsford, *Life*, Vol. II. p. 208.

See Absolute, Aditi, Aditya, Æon, Æther, Akesi, Asceticism, Austerities, Brahma, Chaos, Cosmos, Cranberry, Cupid, Duck, Eddy, Evolution, Gods, Heaven and earth, Hiranyagarbha, Imperial, Involution, Matter, Māyā, Metis, Monad, Mother, Mouth, Mula-prakriti, Phanes, Prakriti, Seb, Seed, Soul, Spirit, Tuat, Water, Year.

EGINA ISLAND :—

A symbol of perfect Truth-reality, which condition may be attained at the conclusion of the cycle of the soul's evolution.

"There are those whose country my mouth declares to have been Aegina, that most renowned island ; and it has long ago been built up as a tower for lofty virtues to ascend." (*Footnote*. It has long been regarded as the model of highest excellence, and an example for others to imitate.)—PINDAR, *Isthmian Ode*, IV. Paley, p. 245.

"At the back of all our endeavours towards fuller life, at the heart of all our idealism, under whatever guise it operates, is faith in God, the unimprovable perfection, the superintending purpose, the one within the many, the real beyond the seeming, the fullness of the life that filleth all in all, to which nothing shall ever be added, and from which nothing can be taken away."—R. J. CAMPBELL, Serm., *Being and Becoming*.

See ALBORDJ, EDFU, IOLCUS, OLYMPUS, WATER (higher).

EGYPT :—

From the point of view of the Greeks and Hebrews, Egypt is a symbol of the lower mental plane with its knowledge of the things of the world, and the objects of desire.

"Out of Egypt did I call my son."—MAT. ii. 15.

Out of mental experiences, or learning, is the Divine Child, the Son of mind (man), educated as a means to the end of the soul's salvation.

"This Egypt, that is our present life which oppressed us ; when flattering may aid when pressing us : and that which, when cherishing, crushed us with the yoke of bondage, may show the way of liberty, while it tortures."—ST. GREGORY, *Morals on the Book of Job*, Vol. III. p. 147.

"In the Word, by Egypt is signified the science of the natural man."—SWEDENBORG, *Apoc. Rev.*, n. 134.

"In denoting the world and the body, Egypt denotes the lessons to be derived from both of these, the learning of which is indispensable to the soul's development."—*The Perfect Way*, p. 234.

See BONDAGE, EXODUS, PARABLE, PEARL, SOUTH LAND, THOTH

EGYPT, HIGHER OR SOUTHERN :—

A symbol of the higher mental plane, or of the buddhi-manas level of the consciousness.

"The half-mythical country in the south was known to the Egyptians as ' the land of the Gods.' "—SAYCE, *Gifford Lectures*, p. 134.

"And Cronus (Ammon), going to the land of the South, gave the whole of Egypt to the God Taaut (Thoth) to be his kingdom."—SANCHUNIATHON, *Cory's Fragments*.

"But the elder of the two children Isis took with her and set sail with the chest to Egypt ; and it being now about morning, the river Phædrus sending forth a sharp air, she in her anger dried up its current."—PLUTARCH, *Isis and Osiris*, § 16.

But the mental faculty was raised by buddhi (Isis) so that the consciousness was elevated to the plane of the higher intellect, it being now the dawn of Truth, or perception of Reality. Then the lower mind, which was filled with cut-and-dried opinions and wind of doctrine, was superseded.

"But there were others who said that the struggle between Horus and Set went on with alternating success, until at last Thoth was appointed arbiter and divided Egypt between the two foes. Southern Egypt was given to Horus, Northern Egypt to Set." PLUTARCH, *Isis and Osiris*, § 19.

But those minds of narrow vision who saw not the Life entering into glory, and who perceived only the shattering of form after form, as they watched from below the struggle between good and evil, said that union of the soul with God was not fully accomplished until the mind (Thoth) was appointed arbiter and reserved for the Spirit and the emotion-nature each its appointed sphere, which arrangement at length on the higher planes appears inverted, as Spirit operates seemingly on the lower planes. Spirit (Horus) manifests on the astral plane under the aspect of love through which the soul's evolution is proceeded with. Egypt signifies kama-manas. Southern Egypt (for Horus) is the more manasic and solar : Northern Egypt (for Set) is the more kamic and lunar.

See AMENI, CHEST, ISIS, NORTH LAND, NUBIA, SOUTH, SOUTH LAND, THOTH.

EGYPT, LOWER OR NORTHERN :—

A symbol of the lower mental plane, or of the kama-manas level of consciousness.

"Many are the marvels which Si-Osiri shall do in the land of Egypt."—GRIFFITH, *Tales, etc.*

Illimitable shall be the possibilities

which the indwelling Self (the Son of
God) shall disclose in the regions of
the lower planes.

See BUTO, JOSEPH, NORTH LAND.
SEED (good), SI-OSIRI, SON OF GOD,

EGYPTIANS :—

A symbol of the lower mental
faculties and functions connected with
the desires and sensations.

"And they spoiled the Egyptians."—
EXOD. xii. 36.

This refers to the valuable results
of experience (jewels, etc.) accruing
in a past soul-state, being acquired
by the qualities now pressing onward
in their development.

"And Israel saw the Egyptians dead
upon the seashore."—EXOD. xiv. 30.

"Do we believe—you and I—in the
death of our Egyptians ? What is your
Egyptian ? Some passion of the flesh or
of the mind,—for the mind has its tyran-
nical passions as well as the flesh. . . .
Look around ! Where are the Egyptians
which used to hold the human body and
the human soul in slavery ? The divine
right of rulers, the dominion of the priesthood over the intellect and conscience,
the ownership of man by man, the accepted
inequality of human lots, the complacent
acquiescence in false social states, the
praise of ignorance as the safeguard of
order, the irresponsible possession of
power without corresponding duty, the
pure content in selfishness—do you realize
how these bad tyrants of the human race
have lost their power over large regions
of human life ? They are dead Egyptians.
. . . Is there anything more wonderful
than the way in which men to-day are
daring to think of the abolition and
disappearance of those things which they
used to think were as truly a part of human
life as the human body, or the ground on
which it walks ? Ah ! my friends, you
only show how you are living in the past,
not in the present, when you see nothing
but material for sport in the beliefs of
ardent men and brave societies which set
before themselves and human kind the
abolition of poverty, the abolition of
war, the abolition of ignorance, the abolition of disease, the sweeping away of
mere money competition as the motive
power of life, the dethronement of fear
from the high place which it has held
among, aye, almost above, all the ruling
and shaping powers of the destiny of
man. I recognize in many a frantic cry,
the great growing conviction of mankind
that nothing which ought not to be need
be. . . . 'The Egyptian must die.' That
is the assurance which is possessing the
heart of man."—PHILLIPS BROOKS,
Mystery of Iniquity, p. 60.

See DURGA, EXODUS, FORTY DAYS,

PARABLE, PEOPLE, SHORE (sea), SIVA,
SLAUGHTER, TONGUES, WAR.

EIDOTHEA, THE SISTER OF CADMUS :—

A symbol of the sense of the Ideal,
which is an outcome of the growth
of experience (Cadmus).

See CADMUS.

EIGHT, NUMBER :—

A symbol of entrance into a new state
or condition of the soul, the number
seven signifying completion of the
former state. Or the symbol may
refer to duality of aspects on the four
lower planes.

"The 'eighth day ' is always typical of
resurrection. The day, after the seventh,
or Sabbath, answers to ' the first day of
the week ' on which Christ rose. . . .
' Seven days ' include the periods proper
to the first creation The eighth day
brings us in type into a new order of
things."—A. JUKES, *The Law of the
Offerings*, p. 30.

"Eight is the number of regeneration,
hence by far the greater number of the
old fonts and baptistries are octagonal."
—F. E. HULME, *Symbolism, etc.*, p. 14.

See BOAT OF THE EARTH, DROPNER,
OGDOAD, SABBATH, SUNDAY, UDGITHA.

ELEMENTS, FIVE :—

A symbol of the five manifested
planes of nature in grades of spirit-
matter, from the innermost spiritual
to the outermost physical, or in other
terms, from the highest to the lowest.

"Chinese writers maintain there are
five original elements, whose names and
order are, water, fire, wood, metal, earth,
of which the last occupies the centre of a
circle described by the other four : the
first two take precedence of the rest, both
on account of superior importance and
priority of existence."—S. KIDD, *China*,
p. 160.

The first two are atma (water)
and buddhi (fire). The others are
mind (metal), astral (wood) and
physical (earth). The physical is the
temporary centre about which the
others turn in the soul-process.

"It is at God's command that this
work (creation) unfolds itself, which is
called earth, water, fire, air, and ether."—
Svetas Upanishad, VI. 2.

The physical (earth), the astral
(lower water), the mental (air), the
buddhic (fire), and the atmic (ether).

"The world may in a certain sense be
considered as composed and compacted
out of five other worlds ; for example,

the ono is of earth, the other of water, the third of fire ; the fourth of air ; the fifth element some call *heaven*, some *light*, others *æther*.' —PLUTARCH, *On the E at Delphi*, § XI.

Homer was the first to divide the world into five portions. The three intermediate he has assigned to the three gods : the two extremes, Olympus and Earth, whereof the one is the boundary of things below, the other of things above, he has left common to all and unallotted to any."—*Ibid.*, § XIII.

Olympus, Heaven, Light, and Æther stand as symbols of the highest plane, atma. Buddhi (fire), mind (air), astral (water), physical (earth). The " three Gods " are Hera (buddhi), Hermes (mind), and Hades (astral).

" Know that when in the beginning all was perfect void, and the five elements were not, then Adi-Buddha, the stainless, was revealed in the form of Flame and Light."—*Buddhist Sutta*.

" God pervadeth the five *elements*, the three *worlds*, the nine *regions*, and the four *quarters of the universe*. The Almighty supporteth the earth and the heavens."—MACAULIFFE, *The Sikh Religion*, Vol. I. p. 314.

" From the time Yin and Yang united and the five elements were intermingled in the centre of the universe, moisture and heat operated on each other, and produced an intelligent being."—KIDD, *China*, p. 167.

That is, from the beginning when Matter and Spirit, or form and life, were allied and operative upon all the five planes of the manifested Cosmos, Will and Wisdom together united, and so produced the Monad which is atma-buddhic.

" That, then, from which the whole Cosmos is formed, consisteth of Four Elements—Fire, Water, Earth, and Air ; Cosmos itself is one, its Soul is one, and God is one, . . . For from (the Elements), o'er which the same God rules, there floweth forth a flood of all things streaming through the Cosmos and the Soul, of every class and kind, throughout the nature of all things " (" The Perfect Sermon ").—G. R. S. MEAD, *T. G. Hermes*, Vol. II. p. 312.

" For from these four elements come all things that are, or have been, or shall be ; from these there grew up trees and men and women, wild beasts and birds, and water-nourished fishes, and the very Gods, long-lived, highest in honour."— *Empedocles*, FAIRBANKS, 104.

For from these four principles of nature, or departments of existence, namely, atma, buddhi-manas, kama-manas, and the physical, proceed all that was, is, or shall be in this

manvantara. From these principles are developed lower emotions (trees), mental faculties (men), and the higher emotions (women) ; undisciplined desires (wild beasts), and aspirations (birds) ; truth-receptive ideas (water-nourished fishes) ; and these all become the instructors of the higher qualities (Gods), that is, they furnish with knowledge the higher mind, or buddi-manas, in the causal-body which persists beyond the lower vehicles, and is the supreme seat of the Divine nature in the soul.

" Antiochus teaches,—There are two natures, the active and the passive, force and matter, but neither is ever without the other. That which is compounded of both is called a body or a quality. Among these qualities the simple and the compound are to be distinguished ; the former consisting of the *four*, or, according to Aristotle, *five*, primitive bodies ; the latter of all the rest : of the first category, fire and air are the active, earth and water the receptive and passive. Underlying them all, however, is the matter without quality, which is their substratum, the imperishable, but yet infinitely divisible elements, producing, in the constant change of its forms, definite bodies (qualia). All these together form the world. The eternal reason which animates and moves the world is called Deity or Providence, also Necessity ; and because of the unsearchableness of its workings sometimes even Chance." — ZELLER, *Eclecticism in Greek Philosophy*, p. 94.

" Fire lives in the death of earth, and air lives in the death of fire ; water lives in the death of air, and earth in the death of water."—*Herakleitos*, FAIRBANKS, 25.

Wisdom (fire) is active in the soul when the physical and lower nature (earth) is dissipated. The mind (air) is active when Wisdom (fire) is latent. Truth (water) is revealed when the lower mind (air) ceases to function. The physical lower nature (earth) is active where Truth (water) is unmanifest.

" According to the Taoist teaching, the element of Earth generates Metal and overcomes Water ; Metal generates Water and overcomes Wood ; Water generates Wood and overcomes Fire ; Wood generates Fire and overcomes Earth."—*S. B. of E.*, Vol. XXXIX., p. 258.

The physical nature (earth), through the activity of the senses, generates mind (metal) and obscures the intuition of Truth (water). The mind (metal) by its functioning acquires knowledge (water) and dominates the astral principle (wood). Truth (water) is outpoured and reflected as error and illusion in the astral principle (wood), and so overcomes Wisdom (fire). The astral principle (wood), through the transmutation of the desires, evolves Wisdom in the soul, and by this means controls and disciplines the physical sensation nature (earth).

See ÆTHER, AIR, ASTRAL PLANE ATMA, BUDDHIC PLANE, COSMOS, DAYS (five), EARTH (specialised), FIRE, FIVE, FOUR, GATHA DAYS (five), GODS, GOLDEN AGE, HEAVEN AND EARTH, MANAS, METAL, MINISTERS (four), NECESSITY, OLYMPUS, PILLARS (four), PLANES (five), QUATERNARY, RULERS (five), SEASONS (five), THIEVES (five) VESTURES (five), WATER, WOOD, WORLDS (five), YANG.

ELEMENTALS :—

See DEVAS (lower).

ELEPHANT :—

An emblem of strength, wisdom and sagacity, as characterising the under-standing or higher mental nature. The four legs signify the quaternary and the trunk the Divine Ray from above.

See CAPRICORN, GANESA, QUAD-RUPED.

ELEPHANT, SACRED WHITE :—

Symbolic of the Self as the potential personality of the Soul,—perfect in all qualities, mental, astral and physical, in the cycle of involution.

"Assuming the form of a huge elephant, white like Himālaya, armed with six tusks, with his face perfumed with flowing ichor, the most excellent of Bodhisattvas (Buddha) entered the womb of the queen of king Suddhodana, to destroy the evils of the world."—*The Buddha-Karita*, Bk. I. 20.

The Self manifesting as the germ of the personality in the nascent Soul whose nature is pre-arranged harmony in the cycle of involution, was received into the ideal lower nature, or the "womb of Māyā." The Soul is born out of the matrix of matter,—mental, astral, and physical,—with the object of over-coming the things of the world, that is, of dispelling the falsities which are mind-created, and which are to be destroyed through the attainment of knowledge of the Real.

The "huge elephant" is a symbol of the archetypal personality :—the four legs signify the quaternary, and the trunk, the sutratma. The "white-ness" indicates the state of perfect purity in which the Soul is conceived. The "six tusks" signify the modes of the Self in three dual aspects func-tioning upon the three lower planes. The "face perfumed with flowing ichor" symbolises the attractiveness of Love, which is the Divine aim and purpose underlying the birth and growth of the Son of the Eternal. The "king Suddhodana" is the supreme Spirit behind manifestation.

See BIRTH OF BUDDHA, BODHISATVA, INVOLUTION, MĀYĀ, PERSONALITY, QUATERNARY, SOUL, SUDDHODANA, SUTRATMA, TOOTH, TUSHITA, TUSK, WOMB.

ELEPHANTS OF GOLD :—

Emblems of high Wisdom, or buddhic faculties.

See GOLD.

ELEPHANTS OF THE KING'S ENEMIES :—

Symbolic of nature forces organised during the process of the soul's involution.

"Falling smitten by his arm in the arena of battle, the lordly elephants of his enemies bowed prostrate with their heads pouring forth quantities of pearls as if they were offering handfuls of flowers in homage."—*Buddha-Karita*, Bk. I. 11.

"Falling smitten" implies the descent of Spirit into matter. The "elephants" signify nature-forces, which though blind are yet submissive to the will of the Logos. The "pros-trate position," and "pearls, etc.," are emblematic of absolute obedience, and the results in virtues which are secured through the play of these forces in involution.

See FLOWERS, GOLDEN AGE, INVOLU-TION, MATTER, SPIRIT.

ELEPHANTS FROM HIMAVAT, RAGING :—

Symbolic of physical energies, strong and devastating, but subject to law.

See APOSTATES.

ELEPHANTS AS WEALTH :—

Symbolic of Wisdom acquired as development proceeds.

ELEVENTH HOUR :—

This signifies the eleventh stage of the evolution of qualities in the forms of matter in which they manifest : the twelfth stage being the final.—*See* MAT. xx. 6.

Compare, Eleventh hour of the Tuat (cycle of life).

See JUSTICE, LABOURERS, TUAT, VINEYARD.

ELIAS OR ELIJAH :—

A symbol of the psychic or emotion nature.

ELIJAH THE PROPHET :—

A symbol of the higher emotion-nature which brings the dawn of the higher consciousness and recognition of Truth-reality.

"Behold, I will send you Elijah the prophet before the great and terrible day of the Lord come."—MAL. iv. 5.

"Elijah" is the "messenger of the Lord," that is, the awakening of the consciousness which brings the recognition of a higher order, but which does not of itself do more than extend the spiritual boundary, as it were. This stage of a higher consciousness is the forerunner of the Christ consciousness, and therefore announces to the attentive lower self the turning of the heart towards the Lord from whom redemption is to be obtained. The "terrible day of the Lord" is the period or moment when the lower personality must be extinguished, and if it be all cast away,— then indeed it is the Lord's dreadful day,—the day of the "crucifixion" or the crossing over from the lower to the higher planes.

See CRUCIFIXION OF JESUS, HORIZONS, PROPHET, REDEMPTION, TABERNACLES, TRANSFIGURATION.

ELIJAH THE RESTORER :—

A symbol of the spiritualised emotion nature which on the form side of being gathers and collects the experiences necessary to development and restoration of the soul.

"Elijah indeed cometh, and shall restore all things : but I say unto you, that Elijah is come already, and they knew him not, but did unto him whatsoever they listed. Even so shall the Son of Man also suffer of them."— MAT. xvii. 11, 12.

The spiritualised emotion-nature is born in the soul as one of the successive steps in the evolution of the soul, whose nature is many sided, and parts of whose character appear under different conditions at various times in the development and restoration of the whole. At first the lower qualities do not recognise the superior status of the higher emotion-nature, and so they disregard and abuse it. The case is the same when the spiritual-nature is born in the soul as "Son of mind," for the lower qualities then condemn and seek to kill out that which appears as a stern opponent of the desire-nature.

See BRIDGE (kinvat), EXPERIENCES, HEROD, SON OF MAN.

EMBALMMENT OF A CORPSE :—

A symbol of the purification of the personality (corpse) through faith and trust in the ideal, producing blissful effects (perfumes) on higher planes, and mental evolution below.

"The perfume of Arabia has been brought to thee to make perfect thy smell through the scent of the god. Here are brought to thee liquids which have come forth from Rā to make perfect thy smell in the Hall of Judgment. O sweet-smelling soul of the great god, thou dost contain such a sweet odour that thy face shall neither change nor perish" (*Papyrus du Louvre*).—BUDGE, *Egyptian Magic*, p. 185.

Wisdom and philosophy are within the personality that it may be purified by truth from above. Love and Truth proceed from the Supreme that the personality may be perfected as it riseth to the higher mind. O noble ideals and Love Divine ! there is such blissful effect on the higher planes that the mental aspects below shall neither diminish nor perish.

The anointing with oil and the bandaging with linen typify the love and devotion that must arise in the personality as it proceeds on its way to union with the Divine.

"The tomb of the (Christian) saint is prepared for him ; he is brought thither, enclosed within it, and the interior and exterior of the sepulchre is anointed with a fragrant unguent. The idea of an embalmment is still more clearly expressed in the subsequent ceremonies, in which the anointing with fragrant oil is accompanied by fumigation with incense."— L. DUCHESNE, *Christian Worship*, p. 406.

See ANOINTING, ANPU, ANUBIS, ASCENSION (Osiris), BA, CORPSE, DEFUNCT, HEART, INCENSE, JUDGMENT HALL, MUMMY, MYRRH, OIL, PERFUMES, PERSONALITY, PHŒNIX, PILLOWS, SPICES, UNGUENTS.

EMBALMMENT OF THE BODY OF OSIRIS BY ANUBIS :—

Symbolic that fresh means were provided for the perpetuation of manifested existence, and so on the physical plane the physical body (Anubis) was gradually built up as an external encasement of the soul.

See ANPU, ANUBIS, ARC. MAN, MUMMY OF OSIRIS, OSIRIS.

EMPEDOCLES :—

Symbol of a teacher of Truth through Divine inspiration.

EMPEROR, FIRST :—

A symbol of the First Logos, or the Higher Self.

" The name of the first celestial Emperor of China was *Tae-haou,*—excessive splendour,—because his perfect holiness and virtue were resplendent as the luminaries of heaven."—KIDD, *China,* p. 103.

The First Logos is the Supreme Ruler, and being equal to go forth in his universe and to accomplish his work below, he is said to have been perfectly endowed with every quality, and holy as the Light of Truth which lighteth the Heaven above.

See KING (great), SACRIFICER, SELF (supreme), SUN, VINEYARD.

ENCASEMENTS OF THE SOUL :—

The bodies formed on the different planes to enable the ego to resist the incoming vibrations. These bodies are of elemental formative essence enclosed by the mental, astral and physical bodies.

See VEHICLES, VESTURES.

ENDURING TO THE END :—

This implies living in tune with the Infinite. For a quality, or individual soul, cannot endure to the end of the cycle unless it becomes in touch with the entire universe of which it is a fraction.

See CALAMITIES, DOOR (narrow), PROPHETS (false).

ENEMIES OF GOD :—

A symbol of the desires and lower qualities of the soul which are in opposition to the higher nature of Truth, Wisdom and Love.

" But God shall smite through the head of his enemies, the hairy scalp of such an one as goeth on still in his guiltiness."—Ps. lxviii. 21.

The Divine Love shall in the soul overcome the selfish desire-mental qualities,—the state of mind which is not contrite for the shortcomings of the lower nature, and which seeks its own aggrandisement.

" And Horbehûdti (Horus) spake : ' Advance, Râ, that thou mayest see thine enemies lying beneath thee in this land.' Now when the majesty of Râ had traversed the way, and with him the goddess Astarte, then saw he the foe lying upon the earth, each lay stretched out like a prisoner."—*Legend of the Winged Sun-disk.*

And the Son of God,—the evolving Self,—aspired and cried to the Supreme : " Advance, within the soul, O Father, that Thy perfection may find the enemies of righteousness prone upon the lower planes beneath the feet of Thy Servant ; for the illusions of ignorance and evil have now been slain through a realisation of Truth and Goodness." Then when the Logos had declared himself in his dual aspect of Love and Wisdom, he came forward and saw the foes of the Self which were lying dead beneath ; each having been vanquished and devitalised through the evolution of the higher nature.

See DURGA, HAIR SHAVEN, HEAD, HORBEHÛDTI, KILLING OUT, OPPOSITES, RÂ, SERVANT OF GOD, SLAUGHTER, SWORD, THUNDERBOLT, TONGUES.

ENIGORIO AND ENIGOHATGEA :—

Symbols of the Higher principle and the lower principle as conflicting opposites on the mental plane.

" Twin brothers, who in the mythology of the Iroquois Indians symbolised the good and evil principles, the names signifying ' Good Mind ' and ' Bad Mind ' respectively. The good creative offices in the building up of the cosmic scheme of Enigorio were neutralised by his evil brother, who wandered over the earth transforming the beneficent creations of Enigorio into the things that have proved harmful to mankind." — *Non-classical Mythology,* p. 62.

This legend does not show alteration under Christian influence, but is paralleled exactly in the Zoroastrian scriptures. In the first part of the Vendidad there is an account of the creation of many " lands " by Spenta-mainyu (Good Spirit) followed by the creation of deleterious objects by Angra-mainyu (Evil Spirit). This refers to the duality and relativity which are inseparable from manifestation. The relatively good always implies the relatively bad and each good quality has its opposite.

See AHRIMAN AKEM-MANO, OPPO-SITES.

ENDYMION :—

See SELENE.

ENOCH :—

A symbol of the individuality ; that part of the soul which survives physical and astral dissolution,— or the first and second deaths, and is immortal.

See INDIVIDUALITY, JARED, SOUL (middle), WALKING WITH GOD.

ENOCH, SON OF CAIN :—

A symbol of aspiration proceeding from the personality.

ENOSH, SON OF SETH :—

A symbol of increased faith in the Divine nature within the soul.

" The name of the son of Seth was Enos, and Enos means hope."—PHILO, *Works*, Yonge, Vol. IV. p. 276.

See BEGETTING, SETH.

ENTOMBMENT :—

A symbol of detention of the Spirit in the lower nature.

" The Dark Night (of the Soul) brings the Self to the threshold of that completed life which is to be lived in intimate union with Reality. It is the Entombment which precedes the Resurrection, say the Christian mystics ; ever ready to describe their life-process in the language of their faith."—E. UNDERHILL, *Mysticism*, p. 480.

See CROCODILE, RE-STAU, SÉPUL-CHRE, TOMB.

EPHOD, HOLY, OF AARON :—

A symbol of the buddhic functionings between the higher and lower natures in the human soul.

" And he made the ephod of gold, blue, and purple, and scarlet, and fine twined linen. And they did beat the gold into thin plates, and cut it into wires, to work it in the blue, and in the purple, and in the scarlet, and in the fine linen, the work of the cunning workman."—EXOD. xxxix. 2, 3. See also verses 4–7.

The vibratory currents established between the buddhic and astral natures were produced in the mental qualities (colours) of the soul. The buddhic responses to the mental aspirations are indicated by the wires of gold (buddhi) worked into the structure of the ephod. The qualities of the structure are of intellect (blue), wisdom (purple), life-energy (scarlet), and devotion (fine linen). The " thin plates " refer to an earlier and less-differentiated state of the qualities. The " shoulderpieces " represent the buddhic and astral centres of energy coupled together by the currents in the qualities. The " onyx stones engraved with the names of the twelve tribes " stand for a variety of virtues involved in the currents. The " blue robe of the ephod " is a symbol of the causal-body which clothes the spiritual mind (Aaron). The " binding " so that " it should not rend " indicates the permanence of the causal-body through the cycle.

See AARON, BARSOM, COLOURS, LINEN, ROBE, TRIBES.

EPHOD GIRDLE :—

A symbol of the Divine Ray of Life from the Supreme.

" And the curious girdle of (Aaron's) ephod, that was upon it, was of the same, according to the work thereof ; of gold. blue, purple and scarlet, and fine twined linen."—EXOD. xxxix. 5.

The Divine Ray of vibratory Life extends throughout the mechanism of the soul and its qualities, and its presence is felt in the spiritual mind " the Lord's High Priest."

See BRAHMAN PRIESTS, BREAST-PLATE, COLOURS, GIRDLE, GOLD, KUSTI, SUTRATMA.

EPIMETHEUS (AFTER-THOUGHT) :—

A symbol of the personality, or lower mental nature.

" For Prometheus and Epimetheus are one Man, according to the system of allegory,—that is, Soul and Body." " But the Greeks call the earthy Adam, Epimetheus, who is counselled by his own Mind, that is, his brother (Prometheus)."—ZOSIMUS, *Fragments*, 26, 27,

The "earthy Adam" is the lower mind or personality in its mental-body, and this is emanated by the higher mind or individuality (Prometheus) in its causal-body or immortal soul.

"Hermes took Pandora to Epimetheus, who made her his wife."—*Smith's Class. Dict.*

The mental principle (Hermes) conveyed the emotion-nature (Pandora or Eve) to the lower mind (Epimetheus or Adam), and these became allied in the human soul.

See ADAM (lower), DIOSCURI, EVE, GOSHURUN, HERMES, INDIVIDUALITY, MARRIAGE, PANDORA, PERSONALITY, PROMETHEUS, WIFE, WOMAN.

EQUINOX :—

A symbol of a point of balance and change reached in the soul's development (sun's course), when a line, as it were, is crossed and a new soul-process is entered upon. The process of Involution is commenced when the Logos (sun) manifests on the upper buddhic plane, at the point symbolised by the first point of Aries ; and after the completion of the process in Virgo, the first point of Libra signifies the commencement of the new process of Evolution in which humanity is now taking part. The Zodiac is a symbol of the great Cycle of Life. As the sun (Logos) passes through the six northern signs, the process of Involution of the qualities is accomplished ; and as it passes through the six southern signs, so Evolution will be completed, and the qualities and souls returned to God who emanated them.

See AFU-RĀ, ARIES, CANCER, CAPRICORN, CRATER, EVOLUTION, INVOLUTION, LAMB, LIBRA, SUN, TUAT, VIRGO, YEAR, ZODIAC.

EREBUS, SON OF CHAOS :—

A symbol of Divine potency arising in formless matter (Chaos) at the dawn of manifestation prior to the interactions of spirit and matter.

"From Chaos came dark Nox and Erebus ; from Nox was Æther sprung and Hemera, whom she that big with them had grown, brought forth, mixed in affinity with Erebus."—HESIOD, *Theogony*, 123–5.

From formless matter came forth the unconscious form side of nature (Nox), and the latent Divine potency (Erebus) for the production of forms. Then from the productive union of these states, consciousness (Æther) and discreteness (Hemera) became apparent in the first life-wave (day) of the cycle, as spirit began to inform matter and qualities and properties were gradually involved.

"The name 'Erebus' signifies darkness."—*Smith's Class. Dict.*

"Darkness" is a symbol of the potential or latent.

See ÆTHER, CHAOS, CHARON, DARKNESS, EROS, HEAVEN AND EARTH, MONAD OF FORM, NIGHT (matter), NOX.

ERECTHEUS, SON OF HEPHÆSTUS :—

A symbol of the philosophic intellect, the product of the Creative Mind.

" Great Erectheus swayed,
That owed his nurture to the blue-eyed maid (Athena),
But from the teeming furrow took his birth,
The mighty offspring of the foodful earth."—*Iliad*, Bk. II.

The philosophic intellect arises from the culture and disciplining of the lower nature, symbolised by the ploughed earth, and it is nurtured from above by the buddhic or Wisdom principle (Athena).

"Erectheus was the first who used a chariot with four horses, for which reason he was placed among the stars as auriga."—*Smith's Class. Dict.*

The philosophic intellect was the first faculty to make use of resources from each of the four planes, in its mental operations (horses) regulated from the seat of its mentality (the chariot). The "placing among the stars" refers to the raising of the intellect to a higher capacity.

See ATHENA, CHARIOT, EARTH, FURROWS, HEPHÆSTUS, HORSE, SITA.

ERICA, OR TAMARISK TREE :—

A symbol of the lower knowledge which, by its profuse growth, induces aspiration for the higher knowledge.

ERICAPÆUS, LIGHT-GIVER, LIFE, OR POWER,—ONE OF THE THREE ASPECTS OF PHANES :—

A symbol of Action : the other

two aspects of the Self (Phanes) being
Will and Wisdom.

See EGG, EROS, METIS, PHANES.

ERIDANUS, CELESTIAL RIVER :—

A symbol of the Divine Life of atma-
buddhi flowing downwards through
the quaternary. The river of life ;
the same as the river of Eden, and the
Nile, Po, Ganges, Jordan, etc.

See EDEN (river), JORDAN, NILE,
RIVER OF LIFE.

ERIDU AND ITS GATES :—

" Eridu " is a symbol of the higher
planes,—atma-buddhi-manas, and its
" gates " stand for the higher mental
plane through which there is access
from the higher planes to the lower,
and from the lower to the higher.

" Eridu. This ancient city, the older
name of which was Eri-dugga (' The
Holy City ', was the Jerusalem, the
Umritza, the Mecca of Chaldea."—
G. RAWLINSON, *Rel. Systems*, p. 16.

" Men-nofer (Memphis), ' the good place,'
is the equivalent of the name of the
ancient seaport of Babylonia, Eridu."—
A. H. SAYCE, *Gifford Lectures*, p. 138.

See BOLTS, GATES, JERUSALEM,
MEMPHIS, TAMMUZ.

EROS, OR PHANES :—

A symbol of the Higher Self in its
aspect of Love,— that which draws
all things towards unity with itself.

" By the philosophers, and in the
mysteries, Eros was regarded as one of
the fundamental causes in the formation
of the world, inasmuch as he was the
uniting power of love, which brought
order and harmony among the conflicting
elements of which Chaos consisted."—
Smith's Class. Dict.

" At first Chaos was, and Night, and
dark Erebus, and wide Tartarus ; nor
was there earth, or air, or heaven ; but
first of all black-winged Night lays a
wind-egg in the boundless bosom of
Erebus, from which in revolving time
sprang the much-desired Eros, his back
glittering with golden wings, like the
swift whirlwinds."—ARISTOPHANES, *Aves*,
V. 692.

At first matter is homogeneous and
formless, and from it arises the
capacity for taking forms (Night),
and also the power of producing forms
(Erebus) in the lower manifestation
(Tartarus). But as yet there were no
physical, kama-manasic or buddhi-
manasic planes. Then it is that
the aspiring form side (Night) brings

forth a spiritual germ (wind-egg) of
Love and Truth for embodiment in
the natural order, so that in the course
of time and in the process of involution, the Higher Self should manifest
his nature in the soul and rise triumphant to the higher planes at the end
of the cycle.

" Love is the essence of divinity. . . .
Love is that by virtue of which all things
are produced, which is in all things, and
is the vigour of all things, by its guidance
souls rise in contemplation by the power
of flight it inspires, the difficulties of
nature are overcome, and men become
united with God " (Bruno).—J. L.
McINTYRE, *Giordano Bruno*, p. 292.

" Love is the creative action of the
Universe, the force which emanates
from God to individuate itself into
innumerable centres of Godhead which
all beings are, or shall become."—E. C. U.,
A Message to Earth, p. 39.

See CHAOS, COSMOS, CUPID, EGG,
EREBUS, ERICAPAEUS, HIRANYAGAR-
BHA, LOVE, NIGHT, NOX, PHANES,
TARTARUS, WINGS.

ESCAPE FROM EVIL :—

A symbol of the higher nature in
the soul rising from captivity to the
lower, through the perfecting of the
personality.

" How shall we escape, if we neglect
so great salvation ? "—HEB. ii. 3.

If the expression of the Divine
Life (word) within the soul is not
heeded, and the choice of the ego
is to cling to its lower nature, there
can be no rising from the dead.

" These three words, Salvation, Escape,
and Neglect, then, are not casually, but
organically and necessarily connected.
Their doctrine is scientific, not arbitrary.
Escape means nothing more than the
gradual emergence of the higher being
from the lower, and nothing less. It
means the gradual putting off of all that
cannot enter the higher state, or heaven,
and simultaneously the putting on of
Christ. It involves the slow completing
of the soul and the development of the
capacity for God."—H. DRUMMOND,
Natural Law, etc., p. 117.

See BLASPHEMY, CAPTIVITY, LIBERA-
TION, RESURRECTION, SALVATION.

ESTHER, BOOK OF :—

A Divinely inspired story symbolical
of the spiritual evolution of the human
soul.

" (The goddess) Istar appears as Esther
in the book of Esther, where Mordechai,
it may be noted, is a derivative from

Merodach (the god)."—A. H. SAYCE, *Hibbert Lectures*, p. 275.

" Merodach was the Divine Man, freed from the limitations of our mortal existence. . . . When Nebuchadnezzar prays to Merodach, he calls him ' supreme in earth and heaven, omipotent and creator of all things.' "—A. H. SAYCE, *Religions, etc.*, pp. 334–6.

The sacred symbols in the Book of Esther are to be understood as follows :—The king Ahasuerus signifies the Supreme or Unmanifest Self and Mordecai is the Higher or Manifest Self gradually evolving in the soul. The first queen Vashti is a symbol of the buddhic principle retiring into obscuration at the time of the " feast " when the lower qualities (people) enter the mind or soul (Sushan). The second queen Esther represents the buddhic principle becoming manifest in human souls, and operating secretly on the lower nature. The " Jews " are the higher qualities scattered in germ throughout the lower nature (kingdom). They are in " exile," and need to be " restored " or evolved. The grand vizier Haman symbolises the desire-mind, the adversary of the higher qualities (Jews) ; he is the ruler of the lower qualities by the will of the Supreme. The desire mind hates the Higher Self (Mordecai), who will not bow to it. Haman, like Herod, seeks to destroy the " innocents " from among his " people," the lower qualities. But the massacre of the " Jews " which he contemplates is frustrated, and eventually the higher qualities (Jews) become strong and destroy a multitude of the lower qualities. The choice and purification of the " virgins " signify the subjective development of the buddhic emotions which are in touch with the Divine Love within. But the Wisdom nature (Esther) is pre-eminent, and the fitting bride of Love. It is through the activities of buddhi (Esther) that the machinations of the lower principle (Haman) are defeated and brought to naught. " Hegai, keeper of the women " is a symbol of the higher intellect, or spiritual mind, which discriminates the emotions and initiates order among them. Esther's banquets to the king and Haman

emphasise the necessity of the opposites, good and evil, for the growth of the soul. But evil exists to be overcome, so the time arrives for each phase of evil to be exterminated. The glorifying of Mordecai by Haman shows how unwittingly evil makes prominent and admirable the splendid virtues which clothe the manifestation of the Divine nature in the soul. Haman can get no consolation from reason (wise men) for even the lower mind foretells the destruction of evil when the higher qualities (Jews) arise in the lower nature. Haman falls upon Esther's couch, for the desire-nature is the inverted reflection of the buddhic and could have no existence but for it. At the death of the ruling lower principle, the supreme power in the lower nature of the soul passes to the Higher Self (Mordecai), who begins his government by fostering all good qualities and setting restrictions on the bad. The feast of Purim refers to the satisfaction and joy experienced in the triumph of good over evil. (By no possibility could any lower mind have invented the symbolism in this wonderful story of old.)

" There is a true sense in which it may be maintained that the New Testament is even more unreservedly religious than the Old. Certainly a book such as Esther, where the Divine Name is not once mentioned, could not have found a place in the Apostolic writings. If the Song of Songs has commended itself to the Christian Church, it has found acceptance by the help of the mystical interpretation which has seen in it an allegory of the Divine Love."—H. B. SWETE, *Cambridge Biblical Essays*, p. 549.

See AGAMEMNON, BUDDHI, EVIL, EXILE, FEAST, GARMENTS (higher), GOPIS, HEROD, HOURIES, INCENSE, ISTAR, JEWS, JOB, MAGI, MERODACH, PALACE, RETURN, SLAUGHTER, VIRGIN, WOMAN.

ETHIOPIANS, NOBLE OR BLAMELESS :—

Symbolic of activities upon the higher planes. Buddhic faculties of Truth, Wisdom, and Love.

EUCHARIST :—

See SACRAMENT.

EUNEUS AND NEBROPHONUS :—

Symbols of Love and Truth.

"Hypsipyle became by Jason the mother of two sons, Euneus and Nebrophonus."—*Argonautic Expedition*.

The philosophic intellect is then united with the intuition,—the expression of the Higher Self,—and the union gives birth to the qualities of love and truth.

See HYPSIPYLE, LEMNOS, THOAS.

EUNUCHS :—

A symbol of those egos who control the desire-nature, mentally, morally, and spiritually. This condition is consistent with the spiritualising of the affections.

"And there are eunuchs which made themselves eunuchs for the kingdom of heaven's sake. He that is able to receive it, let him receive it."—MAT. xix. 12.

See CIRCUMCISION.

EUPHRATES, RIVER OUT OF EDEN :—

A symbol of the physical plane including the etheric.

See EDEN RIVER.

EURYDICE, WIFE OF ORPHEUS :—

A symbol of the intuition of Truth, allied to the Self in its aspect of the union of Wisdom and Love in the soul.

See ORPHÆUS.

EVE, WIFE OF ADAM :—

A symbol of the emotion-nature united to the mental-nature of the lower mind.

"And the man called his wife's name Eve ; because she was the mother of all living."—GEN. iii. 20.

And the mind recognises the life-principle within the soul to be the emotion-nature, for it is the originator or former of all qualities that subsist, that is, of all qualities that have in them the germ of the higher life.

"Eve is the right magical child, for she is the matrix in which the Love-desire stood in Adam. She was Adam's Paradisical Rose-garden in peculiar love wherein he loved himself."—J. BOEHME, *Mysterium Magnum*, p. 83.

See ADAM (lower), ANDROMEDA, CONCEPTION (children), EPIMETHEUS, FALL, MAN, MAN AND WIFE, MARRIAGE, PANDORA, PERSONALITY, SEED (good), SERPENT (subtil), SETH, SKINS, WIFE, WOMAN.

EVENING :—

Symbolic of the drawing in of a cycle towards its close. A period of calm, rest and accomplishment ; a time when the stress and struggle of life are o'er, and when the noon-day heat is past. It is, at the same time, emblematic of a season of darkness, doubt, and despair, when the Self does not give his light, and when men's hearts,—unless they be firmly fixed upon their mission and realise their object,—fail them for fear and quake unutterably, "for looking for those things which are coming upon the earth," or lower nature at the end of a cycle.

"'In the evening' signifies the end of a former state and the beginning of a new one."

"'Between the evenings' signifies the last and the first state."—SWEDENBORG, *Arc. Cel. to Gen.* i.

"It shall come to pass that at evening time there shall be light."—ZECH. xiv. 7.

See CALAMITIES, EARTHQUAKES, HEROIC RUNNER, SUNSETTING.

EVENING AND THERE WAS MORNING, ONE DAY :—

"Evening" and "morning" are symbolic of the indrawing and out-going forces of manifestation. This "first day" signifies the period of the first Life-wave passing through the buddhic plane.

"Each Day would consist of an evening that witnessed the decline of force, and its disintegrating consequences, and of a morning that beamed on the progress of force."—FITZ SIMON, *The Gods of Old*, p. 16.

"'The outward man perishes,' as Paul says, 'but the inward man is renewed day by day.' The perishing of a form and method in which we have lived may naturally bring a pensive sadness like that which always comes to us as we watch a setting of the sun, but he who is in the true spirit of the sunset turns instantly from the westward to the eastern look. The things the day has given him,—its knowledge, and its inspirations, and its friendship, and its faith,—these the departing sun is powerless to carry with it. They claim the new day in which to show their power and to do their work. Live deeply and you must live hopefully. That is the law of life."—PHILLIPS BROOKS, *Mystery of Iniquity*, p. 329.

See BREATH (divine), EAST, KARSHVARES, MORNING AND EVENING, PLANETARY CHAIN, RENOVATION.

EVIL OR SINFUL STATE :—

A condition of soul due to the partial and unbalanced development of the qualities, and to the ignorance in which the ego is immersed. It is a state of emptiness in its degree, and not of fullness ; and as emptiness is no real thing, but the absence of the real, so an evil state of soul has no reality in itself, but needs the presence of the good and true, which are realities and endure for ever. The evil state is, therefore, relative, negative, and transitory, and implies the absence of completeness during a process of evolution of qualities and of knowledge.

"The nature of evil is negative. If evil, as evil, positively subsisted, it would be evil to itself and would therefore, destroy itself" (*Pseudo - Dionysius*).— UEBERWEG'S *Hist. of Philos.*, Vol. I. p. 351.

"Eckhart, like his predecessors, conceded to evil only the character of privation. As denoting a necessary stadium in the return of the soul to God, evil is sometimes represented by Eckhart as a part of the divine plan of the universe, as a calamity decreed by God. . . . Regarded from a higher standpoint, evil is not evil, but only a means for the realisation of the eternal end of the world. To the permanent essence of the spirit sin is external only. Even after the commission of mortal sins the spirit retains in its essence its likeness to God ; even the good works may arise from the eternal basis of the soul, the fruit of which remains in the spirit."—*Ibid.*, p. 481.

"On the one hand evil is necessary for good, for were the imperfections not felt, there would be no striving after perfection ; all defect and sin consist merely in privation, in the non-realisation of possible qualities. It would not be well were evil non-existent, for it makes for the necessity of good, since if evil were removed the desire of good would also cease. In its whole life, however, the soul will realise all good, and therefore is only *per accidens* imperfect" (Bruno).— J. L. MCINTYRE, *Giordano Bruno*, p. 314.

"That which is evil or rebellious must be the cause of the manifestation of the good, for it occasions the will to press back (upward) to its original condition, and so towards God. In this way evil has a special relation to construction and movement, as good has to love, and roughness or rebellion to joy. For a thing that is only good and has no suffering desires nothing, for it knows nothing better in itself, or for itself, after which it can long" (Boehme).—PFLEIDERER, *Phil. of Religion*, p. 20.

"Evil is not true being, but the negation or privation of it."—A. JUKES, *The Names of God*, p. 40.

"In the crucible of earthly life God has, from generation to generation, been working out a glorious fact, whose completion will be seen in the eternal world,— the evolution of a Divine Humanity,

the express image of himself, the unfoldment of his own potentialities of truth and beauty ; and the risk he has had to take in so doing is that at every stage of the age-long effort, poison and foulness have been liable to appear instead of health and purity ; but without the risk there could have been neither the one nor the other."—R. J. CAMPBELL, Serm., *A Christian World-view.*

"It is the good, and not the evil, that denotes largeness of nature in any living being. Infinity and moral perfection imply each other if only because the former is all-complete ; evil, no matter how colossal and grandiose, implies incompleteness. It is as essentially finite as good is infinite ; it is not a thing in itself, but the privation of good ; evil is only experienced when there is not good enough to go round, so to speak. When you are suffering from disease, for instance, it is because your body cannot get the fullness of life it craves."—R. J. CAMPBELL, Serm., *The Source of Good.*

"Evil is the negation of God or good :— Man's need of expansion and nutrition and consequent perception of this negation, of this evil within and around him, are the cause of his further vision of God or good. This further vision of God is born of effort which promotes all growth. Thus evil and the recognition of evil by man must be an inevitable step in his further consciousness of and progress towards God or good. Thus are sin and suffering embodied in the Divine Love which manifests itself through the *individuation* and *evolution*, from the chaos of formlessness, of the *Godhead of man*."—E. C. U., *A Message to Earth*, p. 30.

"Every sin has no foundation ; because it has no subsistence in its own proper nature. For evil has no substance. But that which anyhow exists unites with the nature of good. The 'narrow opening' is said, then, to have no foundation beneath it, because the pollution of sin has no power of subsisting by itself." —ST. GREGORY THE GREAT, *Morals on the Book of Job*, Vol. III. p. 184.

"In truth, our evil comes out of our want of resemblance to God, and our ignorance of Him ; and, on the other hand, our great good consists in our resemblance to Him."—METHODIUS, *Against Porphyry.*

"It is even a great part of God's wisdom, in casting the plan of our life, that He has set us in conditions to bring out the evil that is in us. For it is by this medley that we make of wrongs, fears, pains of the mind, and pains of the body, all the woes of all shapes and sizes that follow at the heels of our sin—by these it is that He dislodges our perversity, and draws us to Himself."—H. BUSHNELL, *Nature and the Supernatural*, p. 361.

See AESHM, AHRIMAN, BEELZEBUB, CONFLICT, DEVIL, ESTHER, GUILTY,

HEALING, HEROD, IGNORANCE, ILLU-
SION, LAW OF REVENGE, MURDER,
OPPOSITES, SATAN.

EVOLUTION AND INVOLUTION :—

**Evolution is the gradual emerging
into objective activity of qualities
and faculties which have been previously involved to perfection in the
matter of the lower planes.**

"If the Monad begins its cycle of
incarnations through the three objective
kingdoms on the descending curved line, it
has necessarily to enter on the re-ascending
curved line of the Sphere as a man also.
On the descending arc it is the spiritual
which gradually transforms into the
material. On the middle line of the base,
Spirit and Matter are equilibrised in
Man. On the ascending arc, Spirit is
slowly reasserting itself at the expense
of the physical, or Matter, so that, at
the close of the Seventh Race of the
Seventh Round, the Monad will find itself
as free from Matter and all its qualities
as it was in the beginning : having gained
in addition the experience and wisdom,
the fruitage of all its personal lives,
without their evil and temptations.
This order of evolution is found in the
first and second chapters of *Genesis*, if
one reads it in its true esoteric sense ;
for Chapter i. contains the history of
the first Three Rounds, as well as that of
the first Three Races of the Fourth
(Round), up to the moment when Man is
called to conscious life by the Elohim
of Wisdom."—H. P. BLAVATSKY, *Secret
Doctrine*, Vol. II. p. 190.

When the soul is fully involved,
"Spirit and Matter are equilibrised"
in the Archetypal Man, the Adam
(Kadmon) of Genesis i., or the Christ
who "descended into the lower parts
of the earth," and of whose "body"
and "members" the human race
now consists.

"I say that Christ is the last Word
of Evolution just because it was the first,
if it had not been the Alpha it could not
be the Omega. It is the unveiling of
Reality, the Reality that changeth not,
the Reality without a second, without
rival or superior."—R. J. CAMPBELL,
Serm., *The Source of Good*.

"The putting forth of finite beings from
the Deity was called by Scotus (Erigena)
the process of unfolding, and in addition
to this, he taught the doctrine of the
return of all things unto God, or their
deification."—UEBERWEG, *Hist. of Philos.*,
Vol. I. p. 359.

"Rightly interpreted, religion is life.
*For all human life, on this side of death
and on the other, is the resurrection of Christ
and his ascension to the Father.* Whatever
this world may have been like at its

birth, it was the in-folding of the life of
God in preparation for a vast spiritual
unfolding which is now going on and in
which we individually and collectively
are taking part. That infolding was,
as it were, the laying of a divine body
in the tomb of matter, the sacrifice,
of a divine life to death ; we are now
watching and co-operating in the issuing
forth and rising up of that divine life,
'the Christ that is to be.' We are
individually members of the body of this
Christ and of one another ; to see it is
to find life, to miss it is to abide in death.
Christ rises in every man who has caught
this vision and given himself to it."—
R. J. CAMPBELL, Serm., *The Resurrection
Life.*

"You cannot have evolution without
something to evolve ; evolution does
not create anything, it only reveals it.
What we are to-day, therefore, is the
partial unfolding of some immeasurably
greater Fact than can probably ever be
fully expressed under material conditions."
—R. J. CAMPBELL, Serm., *The Persistence
of Jesus.*

"The doctrine of creation by development or evolution is a true doctrine,
and is in no way inconsistent with the
idea of divine operation ; but the development is not of the original substance.
Being infinite and eternal, that is perfect
always. Development is the manifestation of the qualities of that substance
in the individual. Development is intelligible only by the recognition of the
inherent consciousness of the substance
of existence. Of the qualities of that
substance as manifested in the individual,
Form is the expression. And it is because
development is directed by conscious,
experienced, and continually experiencing
intelligence, which is ever seeking to
eliminate the rudimentary and imperfect,
that progression occurs in respect of
Form. The highest product, man, is
the result of the Spirit working intelligently within. But man attains his
highest, and becomes perfect, only through
his own voluntary co-operation with the
Spirit. There is no mode of Matter in
which the potentiality of personality, and
therein of man, does not subsist. For
every molecule is a mode of the universal
consciousness. Without consciousness is
no being. For consciousness *is* being."—
KINGSFORD AND MAITLAND, *The Perfect
Way*, pp. 18, 19.

"Evolution itself cannot even be
conceived of except in connection with
some unitary Being, immanent in the
evolutionary process, which reveals its
own Nature by the nature of the Idea,
which, in fact, is progressively set into
reality by the process. . . . Without
help from the tenet of evolution, the
doctrine of God as perfect Ethical Spirit
cannot be vindicated against the charges
offered by the prevalence of evil ; and
the most precious dogmas of Christianity

concerning the Divine work of redemption, the growth of the Divine Kingdom by revelation and inspiration, and the final triumph of that Kingdom as the realised Ideal of an all-inclusive good, cannot even be stated in intelligible terms. Thus the beliefs, hopes, and practical motives of a religion that is compatible with the advance of race-culture require the unquestioning acceptance of the truth, that wherever 'the earth bringeth forth fruit of herself,' there it is always, 'first the blade, then the ear, after that the full corn in the ear.' "—G. T. LADD, *Phil. of Religion*, Vol. II. pp. 303–4.

"The Divine Self is the sum-total of the finite selves which compose the race, and which are ever on the way to becoming more and more truly personal."—*Ibid.*, p. 309.

"Evolution is the growing towards God individuated of that which went forth from God un-individuated. It is the gradual taking on of Godhead by means of the passage through matter: a returning to God full, concrete and concentred, of that which went forth from God empty, discrete, and scattered. . . . For is not evolution the passage through matter *of* Spirit; is not Faith the clinging of matter *to* Spirit; is not Love the transfusion of matter *by* Spirit?" —E. C. U., *A Message to Earth*, p. 8.

Evolution being found in so many different sciences, the likelihood is that it is a universal principle. And there is no presumption whatever against this Law and many others being excluded from the domain of the spiritual life."— H. DRUMMOND, *Natural Law, etc.*, p. 37.

See ADAM (higher), ALTAR (fire), ARC. MAN. CANCER, CIRCLE OF EXISTENCE, COMING FORTH, COSMOS, CRATER, DEATH OF OSIRIS, DEVAYANA, EQUINOX, FALL, FORM AND NAME, GOING IN, IMAGE, INVOLUTION, LION-GOD, MACROCOSM, MAHAYANA, MITHRA, MUSUBI, NIGHT, PLEROMA, RESURRECTION, SABBATH, SACRIFICER, SEPHIROTH, SPIRIT, T (letter), TUAT, WHEEL OF LIFE, ZODIAC.

EXILE :—

A symbol to express the banishment, as it were, of the manifesting God, or Self, from the higher planes which are His real habitat, and His protracted sojourn encased in forms on the planes of nature below.

"The God (Apollo), though by nature incorruptible and eternal, yet through some decree of fate submitted to changes of condition, at one time set all Nature on fire, making all things like to all; at another time he was metamorphosed and turned into various shapes, states, and powers in the same way as the universe now exists. The wiser sort, cloaking their meaning from the vulgar, call the change into Fire 'Apollo,' on account of the reduction to one state, and also 'Phœbus' on account of its freedom from defilement, and its purity; but the condition and change of its turning and subdivision into airs, water, and earth, and the production of animals and plants, they enigmatically term 'Exile' and 'Dismemberment.' "—PLUTARCH, *On the E at Delphi*, § IX.

This mythical statement describes how the manifesting Self (Apollo), unconditional and eternal, submitted to inscrutable Law, and became conditioned and limited in self-expression. The "change of Nature into Fire and reduction to one state" refers to the process of Involution, whereby at one time potential diversity or plurality of qualities becomes merged in complete unity on the buddhic (Fire) plane in the Archetypal Man (Phœbus Apollo), who is pure and perfect in all his qualities. At another time following, the process of Evolution commences by "dismemberment" of the Archetypal Man, that is, by the separation and scattering of the qualities in the myriad forms. There is subdivision into mental qualities (airs), astral qualities (water) and physical qualities (earth), and the production of desires (animals) and feelings (plants). In all the qualities and forms the God within is in "exile" and unapparent.

"We are all making homeward, as it were, getting back to God, and carrying with us as we go the fruits of our brief sojourn in the foreign land of the material world. No two of us have ever had, or ever will have, precisely the same experience of this exile."—R. J. CAMPBELL, Serm., *Our Quest for God*.

"The presence of God in the conscience, and the sense of alienation from God, are to Cardinal Newman the main truths of natural religion—the notorious facts of the case in the medium of his primary mental experiences."—W. S. LILLY, *Ancient Religion*, p. 98.

" 'God is not external to any one.' He is 'the root of the Soul,' the 'centre' of the mind, and the way home to Him is within every person. This is the heart of the mysticism of Plotinus. There is in the universe, as he conceives it, a double movement—the way down and the way up. The way down is the eternal process of the Divine emanation, or outgoing of God towards the circumference. At the centre of all is God, the One, the Good. The One is a Unity above all difference, an Absolute who transcends all thought, who is, in fact, even *beyond being*. Thought implies a contrast of knower and known; Being implies a substance with qualities or characteristics, and each quality limits the substance. . . . From the Perfect One there flows or radiates out a succession of emanations of decreasing splendour and reality."—R. M. JONES, *Mystical Religion*, pp. 72, 73.

See ABSOLUTE, APOLLO, ARC. MAN, DEATH OF OSIRIS, DISMEMBERMENT, ELEMENTS, EVOLUTION, FALL, FIRE, HOME, INVOLUTION, JOB, LAMB OF GOD, PRAGÂPATI (relaxed), VOICE OF GOD.

EXODUS OF ISRAEL FROM EGYPT :—

Symbolical of the raising of the lower qualities by the aid of the higher, through the stress and struggle of life, until the buddhi-manasic consciousness (the promised land) is attained. The forty years' wanderings have reference to the transitory conditions attending the soul's pilgrimage in the arena of the natural life of desire and sensation, barren of itself (wilderness).

"The Exodus of Israel, their deliverance from their enemies, and their passage through the Red Sea, and the destruction of their enemies in its waters, were figures of the liberation of Mankind from the dominion and bondage of Satan, and of his overthrow by Christ in the Red Sea of His blood."— WORDSWORTH, *Bible, Job*, p. 97.

"We have been led out of Egypt, where we were slaves to the devil as to Pharaoh ; where we applied ourselves to works of clay, engaged in earthly desires, and where we toiled exceedingly. And to us while labouring, as it were, at the bricks, Christ cried aloud, ' Come unto me, all ye that labour and are heavy laden.' Thence we were led out by baptism as through the Red Sea,—red because consecrated by the blood of Christ. All our enemies that pursued us being dead, that is, all our sins being blotted out, we have been brought over to the other side. At the present time, then, before we come to the land of promise, namely, the eternal kingdom, we are in the wilderness in tabernacles. . . . In the desert waste : because in this world, where we thirst in a way in which is no water. But yet, let us thirst that we may be filled. For ' Blessed are they that hunger and thirst after righteousness, for they shall be filled ' (MAT. v. 6). And our thirst is quenched from the rock in the wilder-

ness : for ' the Rock was Christ,' and it was smitten with a rod that the water might flow."—AUGUSTINE, *Gospel of John*, Vol. I. pp. 398–9.

"The journey of the Children of Israel illustrates the struggles, temptations and victories of those who, discerning the great purpose of life, are led by their higher faculties—Moses and Aaron—rather than their senses, to press through a wilderness of difficulties in the way till they find its promise fulfilled."— MRS. U. N. GESTEFELD.

"It means spiritually that in the Soul's liberation from sin (or in the exodus of the Soul from sin) it is made holy and free in its powers."—DANTE ALIGHIERI, *The Banquet*, Bk. II. 1.

"The only thing we really do know about life in its supersensuous aspects is that it is an appeal to us to disregard personal and mundane security and well-being when these conflict with the ideal, whatever it may be, which is revealed within our hearts. We may not know why we are enslaved in the land of Egypt, why we should be compelled to long wandering in the wilderness of material hardship and privation, why our struggle for a footing in Canaan should be so strenuous and prolonged, but we know that never in any one of these experiences have we been left without the knowledge that it is somehow a bigger thing, and authoritatively greater thing, to give one's life away in the service of a super-personal good than to retain it for oneself alone."— R. J. CAMPBELL, Serm., *Things Hidden, etc.*

"I will open my mouth in a parable ; I will utter dark sayings of old : which we have heard and known, and our fathers have told us. We will not hide them from their children. . . . Marvellous things did He in the sight of their fathers, in the land of Egypt, in the field of Zoan. He clave the sea, and caused them to pass through ; and he made the waters to stand as an heap. In the day-time also he led them with a cloud, and all the night with a light of fire."—Ps. lxxviii. 2–14.

The moral nature (Moses the lawgiver) utters itself within the soul, and addresses the disciplined qualities (my people) through symbolism (parable and dark sayings). They are reminded of past experience, and the need to profit by it. The workings of the Spirit in the lower nature (Egypt) are shown in suffering, and trouble, and effort, which gradually cause the qualities to leave their lowest condition (cleave the sea) and follow the higher guidance. In the periods of acquisition of knowledge (day-time) they aspire to truth (pillar of cloud), and in the times of sorrow and pain (night-time) they are purified (pillar of fire) and raised.

See BABYLON, BONDAGE, CLOUD, EGYPT, EGYPTIANS, FIRE, FORTY YEARS, HERMES, HORSE, HOUSE OF BONDAGE, JORDAN, MOSES, PARABLE, PASSOVER, ROCK (spiritual), SEA.

EXPERIENCE OF THE EGO :—

All experience in the lower lives is the partial reflection upon the lower planes of that which is above, and interpreted by the mind according to its stage of development.

"Christ comes into the world from without, to bestow himself by a presentation. He is a new premise, that could not be reasoned, but must first be, and then can be received only by faith. When he is so received or appropriated, He is, of course, experienced or known by experiment ; in that manner verified,—he that believeth hath the witness in himself. The manner, therefore, of this divine experience, called faith, is strictly Baconian. And the result is an experimental knowledge of God, or an experimental acquaintance with God, in the reception of his supernatural communications. Which knowledge, again, or acquaintance, is, in fact, a revelation within."—H. BUSHNELL, Nature and the Supernatural, p. 367.

"I say that this continuous quest, this unceasing pursuit of an elusive satisfaction, is not a fruitless thing. God not only ordains it, but secures that it shall fulfil a spiritual object. That object is to educate the soul to understand the true nature of eternal reality by experiencing and rejecting everything that falls short of it. Divine perfection has many facets, if I may so express it, and we can only realise what that perfection is by becoming conformed to it ourselves under its every aspect. To do this means that we have to transcend, outgrow, leave behind everything less than the perfection of Christ on every side of his divinely human nature. That is what our earthly discipline is for, and there is no reason to believe that that discipline ends with the moment of our passing into another world at the change called death."—R. J. CAMPBELL, Serm., The Ceaseless Quest.

"The truth from which we start is this, that so far as the life of this world is concerned, every spiritual operation has its physical basis, in close connection with which it lives its life and does its work. The growth of the tree is a mysterious and spiritual power. . . . There must be black earth and the brown seed, or nothing comes. What growth-power ever made manifestation of

itself, creating out of nothing, in the air, a tree that had no history and no progenitor ? The material is first, and then the spiritual."—PHILLIPS BROOKS, Mystery of Iniquity, p. 245.

EXPERIENCES OF THE EGO :—

These are the facts or truths gathered on the lower planes by means of the astral mechanism of sensation. They are transmuted and collected together in the causal-body where they are co-ordinated and their value realised. The complexity and diversity of emotions and experiences can alone provide for growth and expansion of consciousness. The soul collects through mind and desire all the experiences which are woven into the nature of the Self.

"The truth is that there is no such thing as an abstract right or good. A thing is only right and good as it enters into the experience of conscious beings and is lived out by them. . . . There is no such thing, I say, as abstract truth or abstract righteousness apart from living minds and souls to think them and utter them ; and it is not enough,— even were it possible, which it is not,— that one privileged generation only, or half a dozen generations, should be the full and final fruitage of the untold æons of noble effort which have gone to make them possible. . . . Brethren, you and I have a greater destiny than that. It is to find our place in a gloriously perfect Divine Humanity."—R. J. CAMPBELL, Serm., Our Earthly Race.

See DARKNESS (lower), ELIJAH (rest.), FISH, FOOD, GATHAS (chanting), GOLD (spot), NET, PEARL (precious).

EYE, OR EYESIGHT :—

A symbol of mental perception. Discernment of ideas and feelings as externalities of consciousness.

"The eye of intellect."—HERMES, The Perfect Sermon, § 1.

"May the enemy be paralysed in the feet ! may he be palsied in the hands ! may he not see the earth with his eyes ! may he not see nature with his eyes ! who injures our mind, or injuries our body." —The Homa Yasht, HAUG, Essays.

The supplication here is that the Self may gradually eliminate all the lower motives in thought and action, and be the means of controlling the physical foundation (feet), the astral will to action (hands) and the mental perception (eyes), so that all should be done for the furtherance of universal good in the Supreme Nature.

"For God doth know that in the day ye eat thereof, then your eyes shall be opened, and ye shall be as God, knowing good and evil."—GEN. iii. 5.

For the Divine Nature knows that when the fruits of action on the lower planes are tasted, then experience shall be acquired, which will be the means by which mental perception will be enlarged and Godhood achieved.

"And the eyes of them both were opened, and they knew that they were naked; and they sewed fig leaves together, and made themselves aprons."—GEN. iii. 7.

And both the emotion-nature and the mental-nature perceive their utter ignorance, i.e. the ego recognises the necessity for further evolution. Then the emotions and the mind cover themselves with secrecy, and conceal the inward growth of the Spirit.

"By eyes in the Word is meant the understanding, and thence, by the eye-sight, intelligence. As the eye sees from natural light, so does the understanding from spiritual light."—SWEDENBORG, *Apoc. Rev.*, n. 48.

"Not-being is the mirror; the Universe is the reflection, and man is the Personality concealed in it, like the eye in the reflection. Thou art the eye of the reflection, while God is the Light of the eye; by means of that eye the Eye of God beholds Itself."—*Gulshan-i-Raz.*

"Self-consciousness is the eye of the soul."—R. J. CAMPBELL, Serm., *Man and Moral Freedom.*

"*Eyes*, metaphorically ascribed to men, signify their mind, understanding, or judgment, which are *opened*, when they are made to observe what they did not before (GEN. xxi. 9); when their conscience clearly discerns their sin and misery (GEN. iii. 7); or their mind is savingly instructed in the knowledge of Christ and spiritual things (ACTS xxvi. 18); and are sealed up, *blinded*, *closed* or *darkened*, when the mind is destitute of spiritual knowledge, and so ignorant, obstinate or biassed that it cannot discern between good and evil (IS. xliv. 18; ACTS xxviii. 27; ROM. xi. 10). *Eyes* and *eyelids*, ascribed to God, signify his wisdom and knowledge, which are displayed in every place (PROV. xv. 3; PS. xi. 4).—W. GURNEY, *Bible Dictionary*, p. 164.

See EATING (lower), FALL, MAN (blind), MEN (breast), NAKEDNESS (lower), SIGHT, TREE OF KNOWLEDGE, UTCHATS.

EYE, "THIRD," AND PHYSICAL :—

The "third eye" is a clairvoyant faculty on the astral plane, which precedes physical sight.

"When now the Asar had arrived at the house of Loke, the wisest of them, Quaser, first entered, and when he saw the ashes of the burned yarn (net) on the fire, he comprehended that this must be a device for catching fish, which he showed to the Asar. They therefore took linen thread and made a net, after the fashion of that which they could see in the ashes, which had been made by Loke."—*Prose Edda.*

And when the functioning upon the astral plane has been accomplished by the Logoi (Asar), the first thing that is done is the transference of the sense of sight to the physical plane. Clairvoyance (Quaser) is exchanged for the physical sense, for it is seen to be relatively illusory, and but a poor and ineffectual attempt to capture facts (fisb) or reality. The clairvoyance refers to the astral function of the "third eye," which ceases to act when physical sight is fully acquired. And now the substance of the astral matter is taken in structural form, and upon that is built the mechanism of the physical eye, which is to be used as the apparatus of sight.

See ASAR, LOKE, NET OF ASAR, PINEAL GLAND, QUASER.

EYE OF MACROPROSOPUS :—

Significant of the omniscience of the Higher Self on the mental plane.

"The eyes of the White Head are diverse from all other eyes. Above the eye is no eyelid, neither is there an eyebrow over it. . . . This eye is never closed; and there are two converted into one. All is right; there is no left. He slumbereth not, and he requireth not protection."—*Kabbalah*, "The Greater Holy Assembly," Ch. IX.

There is a reference here to the personality being merged into the Individuality, when the two become one, and there remains no lower self.

See COUNTENANCE, FACE, HEAD, WHITE, YMIR.

EYE OF VISHNU :—

A symbol of the Higher Self seated on the atmic plane as the Individuality.

"The wise ever behold that highest step of Vishnu fixed like an eye in the heaven."—*Rig-Veda*, I. 22, 20.

The perfected become conscious of the supreme Love and Truth on the highest plane.

See STRIDES OF THE SUPREME, UTCHATS, VISHNU.

EYES OF HORUS OR OSIRIS :—

Symbols of the Individuality and the Personality as centres of perception on the mental plane, or higher and lower consciousnesses.

" Thou didst stretch out the heaven wherein thy two eyes (sun and moon) might travel, thou didst make the earth to be a vast chamber for thy Khus (i.e. the beatified dead and the gods of heaven), so that every man might know his fellow " (" Hymn to the Setting Sun ").—BUDGE, *Book of the Dead,* p. 87.

The Logos establishes the cycle of life wherein the Higher and Lower Selves may go through their pilgrimage. The lower nature of the soul is to be the container of the Divine Monads, so that by means of experience every ego may progress from separateness to unity again.

" Mankind went forth from his (Rā's) two eyes " (" Hymn to Amen Rā ").— WIEDEMANN, *Rel. of Anc. Egyptians,* p. 115.

Humanity goes forth in its higher and lower centres of consciousness on the mental plane ; that is, the egos manifest in the individualities and the personalities.

See DEFUNCT, EARTH, GODS, HEAVEN, KHUS (higher), LIPS, MOON, SUN, UTCHAT.

EYES, TWO, SUPERIOR AND INFERIOR :—

Symbols of the Higher Self and the lower self ; or the upward- and downward-looking faculties of perception in the soul.

" Unless the bountiful, superior Eye were to look down upon and bathe the inferior eye, the universe could not exist even a single moment."—*Kabbalah,* " The Greater Holy Assembly," Ch. IX.

" The two eyes of the soul of man cannot both perform their work at once : but if the soul shall see with the right eye into eternity, then the left eye must close itself and refrain from working, and be as though it were dead. For if the left eye be fulfilling its office toward outward things ; that is, holding converse with time and the creatures ; then must the right eye be hindred in its working ; that is, in its contemplation. Therefore whosoever will have the one must let the other go ; for ' no man can serve two masters.' "—*Theologia Germanica,* Ch. VII.

See HIGHER and LOWER, MIMER.

EYES ROAMING :—

Symbolic of perception without discrimination ; or the senses active without intelligence.

EYES, TWIN :—

Symbolic of the Individuality and the Personality, as centres of consciousness.

EYES, TWO, OF HEAVEN :—

Symbolic of the Higher Self under the aspects of Intellect and Will, piercing to the inner nature of things.

FABLES AND GENEALOGIES :—

These are sacred stories and personal histories regarded as literally true instead of symbolically true in a deep sense.

" Neither to give heed to fables and endless genealogies, the which minister questionings."—1 TIM. i. 4.

The soul is exhorted to leave the " letter " for the " spirit." The following of the letter plunges the mind into a sea of difficulties which cannot be overcome, and of questionings which cannot be answered. The mind must seek for the true means of progress, which consists in the perception of the ideal within, and in steadfast devotion to the highest concepts of goodness and truth.

See EXODUS, INSPIRATION, MYTHOLOGY, PARABLE, SCRIPTURES.

FABRIC :—

A symbol of the structure, or mechanism, of the planes of the universe, with the vibratory forces which play through them.

See LINEN, LOOM, WARP.

FACE :—

A symbol of the mental aspect of being. Knowledge acquired either through the senses or the intuition. Expression of truth within.

See COUNTENANCE, SWEAT.

FACE OF THE GROUND :—

A symbol of the knowledge of appearances, or of the surfaces of things of the lower nature.

" Behold, thou hast driven me (Cain) out this day from the face of the ground ; and from thy face shall I be hid."— GEN. iv. 14.

The lower self, or personality, is brought to realise that it may no longer depend upon the lower knowledge for subsistence or satisfaction, and it cannot tell where to seek for food convenient to its evolving nature. It does not yet know the Higher Self or source of its inspiration.

See CAIN, FORTY DAYS, GROUND.

FACE OF THE LORD :—

A symbol of the higher knowledge of the real ; or the Truth nature revealed to the mind.

"Turn us again, O God ; and cause thy face to shine, and we shall be saved." —Ps. lxxx. 3.

The qualities aspire, turning from the lower nature to the Ideal within, confident that in knowledge of the real lies the hope of emancipation from error and illusion of the lower mind.

See APÂRAGITA, LIGHT.

FACES, DOUBLE :—

Symbolic of dual mental aspects of the Self. Pairs of opposites of a mental nature.

See OPPOSITES.

FACES OF THE GODS :—

Symbolic of the diverse mental aspects of the manifesting Self, or of the Ideals within the human soul.

See GODS.

FACES OF MEN :—

Symbolic of the mental aspects of the qualities.

"We all, with unveiled face reflecting as a mirror the glory of the Lord, are transformed into the same image from glory to glory."—2 COR. iii. 18.

When the qualities are freed in their mental aspects from the illusion of separateness, then they reflect the unity and harmony of the One Higher Self and become transmuted on to higher planes.

See MIRROR, TRANSMUTATION, UZUMÉ.

FAITH :—

Perception of the ideal and of that which is coming in evolution. A sense of that which is superior to knowledge, i.e. intuition of Truth. Acceptance of the system of nature with all its invariable sequence, its suffering and evil, as inevitable and perfect in process, in regard to its end which is God.—*See* HEB. xii.

"To choose the ideal without the support or sanction of the natural universe, and without hope of compensation ; this reveals what man really is, and this autonomous affirmation is *faith*. And whenever that faith finds utterance —for it is in all—then you may inquire into the meaning of the natural order. Here, we say, is an imperfect world, society, or character ; and yet we are found longing for perfection. How, then, can the intrusion of the ideal be explained ? There are only two answers ; one is that there is a scheme other than the natural, also pressing upon us, but only discerned by spiritual vision."— W. E. ORCHARD, D.D., *Ch. Com.*, Nov. 23, 1910.

"But before faith came, we were kept in ward under the law, shut off from the faith which should afterwards be revealed."—GAL. iii. 23.

Before the intuition of Truth came into the evolving soul, the qualities were under law, reason, Karma, cause and effect, and were kept in bondage to authority ; but afterwards through intuition wisdom was acquired.

"Yet beyond all knowledge, properly so called, is the realm of faith, and here, as in the case of more strictly cognisable things, the object of contemplation must actually come within the human mind, and be assimilated, before its being can be realised. 'God is also said to come into being in the souls of the faithful, since either by faith and virtue He is conceived in them, or in a certain fashion, by faith, begins to be understood. For, in my judgment, faith is nothing else than a certain principle from which the recognition of the Creator arises in a reasonable nature' (Scotus). We seem to have here the doctrine of the Incarnation presented from an entirely subjective and individual standpoint."—ALICE GARDNER, *John the Scot*, p. 129.

"According to Zwingli, faith is the highest power of our reasoning activity altogether, and can, therefore, never come into conflict with the remainder of the reasonableness of man."—O. PFLEI-DERER, *Development of Christianity*, p. 196.

"Faith is nothing less than a uniting of our will with God's will."—J. BOEHME, *Mysterium Magnum*, Vol. V. p. 299.

"I hold that it is in Transcendental Feeling manifested normally as Faith in the value of life, and ecstatically as sense of Timeless Being, and not in thought proceeding by way of speculative construction, that Consciousness comes nearest to the object of metaphysics, Ultimate Reality."—J. A. STEWART, *Myths of Plato*, p. 43.

"When the seed of the new birth, called the inward man, has faith awakened in it, its faith is not a notion, but a real, strong, essential hunger, an attracting or magnetic desire of Christ, which as it proceeds from a seed of the Divine nature in us, so it attracts and unites with its like : it lays hold on Christ, puts on the Divine nature, and in a living and real manner grows powerful over all our sins, and effectually works out our salvation (*see* EPH. iii. 17–19)." —WM. LAW, *Grounds, etc.*

" Faith is not anti-rational, but super-rational ; it is that whereby we lay hold of the spiritual and eternal. . . . Man's whole nature longs for fuller satisfaction than it can find in the dark valley of material existence ; faith contacts the regions in which those satisfactions lie and brings the tokens of them into our conscious experience. This side of our complex human experience is just as reliable as any other, and is not only the highest but the one for the sake of which the rest exist. Unless you can interpret life in terms of the spiritual, it is a mere chaos, not even rational ; you could not reason about a world which had no sort of *order* in it, and the moment you predicate *that* you are dealing with spiritual ends."—R. J. CAMPBELL, Serm., *The Function of Faith.*

" Faith discovereth the truth of things to the soul ; the truth of things as they are, whether they be things that are of this world, or of that which is to come ; the things and pleasures above, and also those beneath. Faith discovereth to the soul the blessedness and goodness, and durableness of the one ; the vanity, foolishness, and transitoriness of the other. . . . Faith wraps the soul up in the bundle of life with God."—JOHN BUNYAN, *Justification, etc.*

" The truth is that faith is only our own higher nature asserting itself and vindicating itself against the lower, and without such assertion and vindication there could not be,—even omnipotence could not bestow,—fullness of life and power upon the aspiring soul. . . . Faith is simply spiritual instinct making straight for its goal."—R. J. CAMPBELL, Serm., *Necessity of Faith.*

" This unfounded and arbitrary declaration of the ultimate rightness and significance of things I call the Act of Faith. It is my fundamental religious confession. It is a voluntary and deliberate determination to believe, a choice made."—H. G. WELLS, *First and Last Things*, p. 48.

See GOLDEN HAIR, HAIR, INTUITION, LOVE OF GOD, VAIRAUMATI.

FAITH TO DO MIRACLES :—

The spiritual knowledge born of experience in the bringing of the lower nature into harmonious relation with the higher. This brings about adjustments of qualities and the evolution of higher faculties.

" If ye have faith as a grain of mustard seed, ye shall say unto this mountain, Remove hence to yonder place ; and it shall remove ; and nothing shall be impossible unto you."—MAT. xvii. 21.

If the disciplined qualities have spiritual knowledge comparable to a small seed which is capable of developing into a great tree, then shall they be able to remove a spiritual difficulty (a mountain) ; but the knowledge must be sufficient to effect the adjustment required. To the indwelling Spirit nothing is impossible in the line of evolution.

" I can do all things through Christ which strengtheneth me."—PHIL. iv. 13.

" If I have the gift of prophecy, and know all mysteries and all knowledge ; and if I have all faith, so as to remove mountains, but have not love, I am nothing."—1 COR. xiii. 2.

If the soul have the buddhic faculty of intuition (prophecy) and all intellectual knowledge of the invisible universe and the soul-process, and also have spiritual perception so as to solve difficulties of the lower mind, and yet be deficient in selfless love of the ideal, it is stagnant and unprogressive.

See LOVE OF GOD, MIRACLES, PROPHECY.

FALL OF MAN :—

A symbol of the descent of the evolving soul, or consciousness, from higher to lower planes, due to the mind and emotions being attracted by the desires and sensations of phenomenal existence. Through the Fall, man exchanges a blissful state of passive receptivity for a condition of active responsibility, becoming thereby a moral being knowing higher and lower, and involved in a struggle between good and evil, during which the potential qualities within him are evolved into actuality.

" Why then does the soul descend and lose knowledge of its unity with the whole ? For the choice is better to remain above. The answer is that the error lies in self-will. The soul desires to be its own, and so ventures forth to birth, and takes upon itself the ordering of a body which it appropriates, or rather which appropriates it, so far as that is possible. Thus the soul, although it does not really belong to this body, yet energises in relation to it, and in a manner becomes a partial soul in separation from the whole. . . . All,—descent and reascent alike,—have the necessity of a natural law. . . . The universal law under which the individual falls is not outside but within each."—*Plotinus.* THOS. WHITTAKER, *The Neo-Platonists,* pp. 67, 68.

The fall, or descent of the soul to the underworld, or lower nature, is variously described in the scriptures.

From a Babylonian religious text we read :—

"The evil curse has slain that man like a lamb. His god has departed from his body ; his guardian goddess has left his side ; he is covered with sorrow and trouble as with a garment, and he is overwhelmed."—L. W. KING, *Babylonian Religion,* p. 207.

The mind has become a sacrifice to Desire. The Divine nature is un-apparent to the astro-mental body. Wisdom, its guide, is obscured in the mind, and the soul has entered into the lower life of suffering and sorrow.

Then the god Marduk (the Higher Self) is enjoined by the Supreme to become his Saviour :—

"Take him to the house of purifica-tion, and remove the spell from upon him."—*Ibid.*

In the development of the causal-body (house) is to be found the soul's purification, when thraldom to the desire-nature will be removed on the attainment of perfection.

"Though a man journey from the perfect to the perfect : yet that which is perfect still remains over and above all."—*Brihad. Upanishad,* V. 1.

The account of the fall of mind (man) and emotion (woman) is given in Genesis iii. :—

"Now the serpent was more subtil than any beast of the field which the Lord God had made. And he said unto the woman, Yea, hath God said, Ye shall not eat of any tree in the garden ? "

Now the desire-mind (the serpent) is more insidious than any of the simple lower desires or appetites (the beasts), and thus is able to lead the emotion-nature astray from the higher intuitions, and to divert the vibra-tions of energy downward to the plane of the desires. And so the emotion-nature is drawn to the sense objects.

"And the woman said unto the ser-pent, Of the fruit of the trees of the garden we may eat : but of the fruit of the tree which is in the midst of the garden, God hath said, Ye shall not eat

of it, neither shall ye touch it, lest ye die."

And the emotion-nature surmises that of the sense-pleasures the soul may partake naturally as do animals, but of the fruit of experience, which is the moral nature, the soul cannot partake without incurring the death penalty, by entering upon the cycle of evolution which necessitates the repeated births and deaths of the forms which transitorily embody the soul.

"And the serpent said unto the woman, Ye shall not surely die : for God doth know that in the day ye eat thereof, then your eyes shall be opened, and ye shall be as God, knowing good and evil."

Then the desire-mind represents to the emotion-nature that death or extinction shall not supervene for such behaviour ; for the Divine nature knows that when the fruits of action are tasted, experience shall be acquired which will be the means by which Godhood will eventually be achieved through cleaving to the good, and shunning evil.

"And when the woman saw that the tree was good for food, and that it was a delight to the eyes, and that the tree was to be desired to make one wise, she took of the fruit thereof, and did eat ; and she gave also unto her husband with her, and he did eat."

And so when the emotion-nature perceives the desirability of descend-ing to the lower planes, and sees the beauty of the prospect, and recognises that this course will be the means of enabling the soul to increase its knowledge, then attachment to the lower life is set up, and the results are communicated to the evolving mind, whereby the mind partakes of new experiences.

"And the eyes of them both were opened, and they knew that they were naked ; and they sewed fig leaves together, and made themselves aprons."

And then it is, both the emotions and the mind perceive their utter lack of " clothing " (concepts), their " nakedness " or ignorance, and they become aware of the necessity for further evolution. And their endeav-ours result in producing an external mental condition which conceals the inward growth of the soul. (Fig-leaves so applied are symbolic of secrecy.)

" The tree of the knowledge of good and evil, by which man fell, changed into the Tree of Life by which Satan perished ; the fruit of disobedience becoming the fruit of the Tree that is in the midst of paradise : the garden whence the first Adam was driven forth replaced by the garden where the second Adam arose from the dead."—J. M. NEALE, *Comm. Psalms*, Vol. I. p. 139.

" To come to man, the microcosm, the human trinity, made in the image of God, but fallen from its original glory ; Scotus attributes that fall to a self-willed turning away from man's proper nature and first principle of being. In following the story in Genesis, he gives an allegoric interpretation to its several parts ; . . . the Fall is not regarded as an event in time, nor Paradise as a definite locality. The story of the forbidden fruit is interpreted as the leading away of the mind (= the man) by sensibility (= the woman), so as to seek pleasure in the things of sense and not in pure wisdom. The punishments inflicted have a hidden meaning. 'In sorrow shalt thou bring forth children,' points to the efforts necessary for attaining knowledge ; ' thy desire shall be to thy husband, and he shall rule over thee,' promises the ultimate subjugation of sense by reason. . . . The means by which the general restitution is effected is, of course, the Incarnation. The Logos entering into human nature, and then returning to the Father or First Principle."—ALICE GARDNER, *John the Scot*, pp. 107–9.

" The failure of one thing, through grace, brings in a better thing. Where sin abounds, grace yet more abounds. Thus that short-sighted wisdom which would prevent falling, would by so doing prevent all progress to higher things ; for each advancing form of life which God takes up springs out of the failure of that which has preceded it."—A. JUKES, *Types of Genesis*, p. 107.

" Adam represents the person, Eve the soul, and the Divine Voice the Spirit, so the serpent typifies the astral element or lower reason. For this subtle element is the intermediary between soul and body, the ' fiery serpent' whose food is the ' dust,' that is, the perception of the senses which are concerned with the things of time and matter only."

" Coming next to the philosophical reading of our parable (the Fall), we find that on this plane the Man is the Mind or rational Intellect, out of which is evolved the Woman, the Affection or Heart ; that the Tree of Knowledge represents Māyā or Illusion ; the Serpent, the Will of the Body ; the Tree of Life, the Divine Gnosis—or interior knowledge ; and the sin which has brought and which brings ruin on mankind, Idolatry (which is the adoration of the shadow instead of the substance—God)."—*The Perfect Way*, pp. 159, 161.

" The One, which consists of these two (Life and Substance), is always putting forth alike the Macrocosm of the universe and the Microcosm of the individual, and is always making man in the image of God, and placing him in a garden of innocence and perfection, the garden of his own unsophisticated nature. And man is always falling away from that image and quitting that garden for the wilderness of sin, being tempted by the serpent of sense, his own lower element. And from this condition and its consequences he is always being redeemed by the blood of the sacrifice always being made for him by the Christ Jesus, who is Son at once of God and of man, and is always being born of a pure virgin ; dying, rising, and ascending into heaven."—*Ibid.*, p. 178.

" Before Adam sinned he went up into and remained in the illuminated Wisdom (Eden) Above, and was not separated from the Tree of Life. But when he acceded to the desire to know, and to descend Below, then . . . he separated himself from the Tree of Life, and knew only the bad, and left the good alone."—*Zohar*, I. 52 *a* and *b*, Brody.

" I admit that the Genesis story (of the fall) as it stands cannot reasonably be regarded as history ; it is not history, it is something better ; it is a symbolic statement of certain facts of experience. . . . The whole drama should be removed from the material to the super-material world, the paradise of Eden being a figure of man's condition immediately before his descent into matter. Our real fall, speaking of the race as a whole, consists in having to live under conditions wherein the struggle between good and evil is inevitable and unescapable. I say that to have come into a world like this at all is a fall from something higher. . . . It is true that we came up from below, but it is also true that we first came down from above. We are of the eternal ; our true being has never had a beginning and will never have an end. But when man as man entered this world he had to make acquaintance with something very different. His beginnings then were lowly enough, and as he has been slowly fighting his way upward, back in fact to where he came from, he has been learning tragically the difference between good and evil."—R. J. CAMPBELL, Serm., *The Tree of Knowledge*.

See ADAM (lower), ATTACHMENT, CAUSAL-BODY, DEVAYANA, EDEN, EVE, EVOLUTION, EYE, GARDEN, HEEL, HIDING-PLACE, IMMORTALITY, INCARNATION, INVOLUTION, JOHN-BAPTIST, KARMA, LAW OF ZOROASTER, MACRO-

COSM, MAHAYANA, MAN, MITHRA, NEPHILIM, PITRIYANA, RESURRECTION, RETURN, SACRIFICER, SEPARATION, SERPENT (subtil), SONS OF GOD, SOUTH WIND, STRIFE, SWEAT, TREE OF KNOWLEDGE, TYRUS, WOMAN.

FAMILY :—

A symbol of qualities in close relation to each other, and attached to a single centre.

"I bow my knees unto the Father, from whom every family in heaven and on earth is named."—EPH. iii. 14, 15.

The moral nature restrains the activities of the lower nature in due regard to the central Ideal and source of all, to which the differentiated groups of higher and lower kindred qualities of the soul are primordially attached.

See FATHER, KNEE, NAME, NATION, TRIBES.

FAMINE IN THE LAND :—

Symbolic of a period of mental and emotional inertia wherein there is a lack of sustenance and satisfaction for the soul.

"Behold, the days come, saith the Lord God, that I will send a famine in the land, not a famine of bread, nor a thirst for water, but of hearing the words of the Lord."—AMOS viii. 11.

This refers to a preparatory state of inactivity of the qualities.

"By famine is signified the deprivation of the understanding of all truth."— SWEDENBORG, Apoc. Rev., n. 765.

See CALAMITIES, EARTHQUAKES, FOOD, PRALAYA.

FAN, PRODUCING WIND :—

A symbol of the Spirit energising the mental vehicle, for the dissipation of error.

"Holy Ghost, . . . whose fan is in his hand, and he will thoroughly cleanse his threshing-floor; and he will gather his wheat into the garner, but the chaff he will burn up with unquenchable fire."—MAT. iii. 12.

The Holy Spirit (Atma-buddhi) energises the mind, in order that the lower nature of the soul may be purified through suffering and aspiration. The fruit of experience shall be transmuted on to the buddhic plane, but the lower qualities shall disappear utterly.

"Servius, in his comments upon Virgil's First Georgic, after quoting 'the mystic fan of Bacchus,' says that that 'mystic fan' symbolised the 'purifying of souls.' Now how could the fan be a symbol of the purification of souls ? The answer is, The fan is an instrument for producing 'wind'; and in Chaldee, as has been already observed, it is one and the same word which signifies 'wind' and the 'Holy Spirit.' . . . Hence, when Bacchus was represented with the 'mystic fan,' that was to declare him to be the mighty One with whom was 'the residue of the Spirit.' Hence came the idea of purifying the soul by means of the wind."—A. HISLOP, The Two Babylons, p. 139.

See BREATH, CHAFF, FIRE (destroying), FIRE OF HELL, FLABELLUM, HOLY GHOST, MARUTS, WHEAT, WIND.

FANG OF THY MOUTH :—

A symbol of the Divine Will and Power. Force of that which is uttered in the Divine fiat. The same as the "sword of the Spirit."—REV. xix. 15.

"I make no choice therein, yet I have power therein, for the fang of Thy mouth is a wand of power"—Book of the Dead, Ch. CX. (trans. Blackden).

All the experiences of the lesser lives are collected, and all are of service to the ego who relies upon the power of the Divine Will.

"And I steer in Her pools that I may fetch to her cities of peace; for behold my mouth is provided with my Fangs." —Ibid.

The Self guides its evolution through the Wisdom nature which is the means of contributing to the growth of the buddhic function from its centres (her cities). For the Divine Will and Word (Fangs) are their own support and are constantly exercised; and the means of disciplining the lower self is thereby provided.

See CITY, DESERTS, MOUTH, POOLS OF GODDESS, SWORD, TEETH, TUSK.

FAR-DARTING APOLLO :—

A symbol meaning that the Will and Power of the Logos extend everywhere, as the sun's rays through the solar system.

See APOLLO, SURYA, SUN.

FASTING :—

This signifies abstention from sense impressions and abstinence from all external aid, while relying upon the indwelling Spirit for help in evolution.

"Except ye fast to the world, ye shall in no wise find the kingdom of God."—*A saying of Jesus*, discov. 1897.

See ABSTINENCE, AUSTERITIES, PENANCE.

FAT ; OIL ; BUTTER :—

Symbols of the Love-nature. If offered in sacrifice they signify the offering of the heart's affection.

"By 'fat' is signified the celestial principle itself which is also from the Lord."—SWEDENBORG, *Arc. Cel. to Gen* iv. 4.

"Fat or dainty things signify celestia goods, the affections thereof and the delights of those affections."—SWEDENBORG, *Apoc. Rev.*, n. 782

"And I will satiate the soul of the priests with fatness, and my people shall be satisfied with my goodness, saith the Lord."—JER. xxxi. 14.

The inner sanctuary of the soul shall be filled with Divine love, and the disciplined qualities shall be steadfast in righteousness and truth.

See BURNT OFF, BUTTER, DOUBLE FOLD, GHEE, OIL, OINTMENT, PRIESTS, PROMETHEUS, SACRIFICE.

FAT DRIPPING DOWN :—

A symbol of the desire nature which is directed to the sensations and the objects of sense.

"When the sacrifice was completed, they collected the dripping fat from it ; it formed the beasts of the air, of the wild places and of the village."—*Rig-Veda*, X. 90, 8.

The "dripping fat" signifies the love-nature inverted in the downward attraction of the mind (air), and to be found in the desires (beasts) and passions (wild) connected with the astral centre (village). The "sacrifice was completed" means that the Self was fully involved in matter, that is, the One Self had limited Himself in order that the many selves should have life through Him.

See ANIMALS, ARC. MAN, BEASTS, INCARNATION, INVOLUTION, LAMB OF GOD, SACRIFICE, SACRIFICER, SELF, VILLAGE.

FATE, EVIL :—

The personal self's false opinion of the sufferings of the lower life, and of the natural order of existence.

"But when light is mingled with air in human form, or in form like the race of wild beasts, or of plants, or of birds,

then men say that these things have come into being ; and when they are separated, they call them evil fate ; this is the established practice, and I myself also call it so in accordance with the custom."—*Empedocles*, FAIRBANKS, 40.

But when the monadic life is embodied in the human mind, or when it is exhibited in the sub-human kingdoms, then it is assumed by the lower mind that the phenomena which answer to the soul's present stage of experience and growth have only now begun to exist, and that they exist in themselves. And so when the illusive discontinuity is apparent, and the oneness of things is unapparent, then evil is apprehended to be real, or cruel fate is supposed to be the soul's destiny : and the personal self, being ignorant, is led to make these false implications under illusion of the senses.

See BEASTS, BIRDS, CONSCIOUSNESS, EVIL, IGNORANCE, ILLUSION, MAN, MONAD OF LIFE, NECESSITY, PERSONALITY, PLANTS, SEPARATION.

FATE-SPHERE :—

A symbol of the lower planes as subject to the law of cause and effect, or karma, in relation to the spiritual Monad.

"But All-Father Mind, being Life and Light, did bring forth Man co-equal to Himself" (Pœmandres). "This Man or Anthrōpos is the Spiritual Prototype of humanity and of every individual man."—MEAD, *T. G. Hermes*, Vol. I. p. 139.

The Man, the Heavenly Man, the Son of God, who descends and becomes a slave of the Fate-Sphere ; the Man who, though originally endowed with all power, descends into weakness and bondage, and has to win his own freedom and regain his original state."—*Ibid.*, p. 138.

The "Heavenly Man" is the Self, or World-soul, who descends into matter, and becomes the Archetypal Man when all his qualities are involved. He subjects himself to karma, and in the process of evolution rises from the dead and ascends in humanity to his original state on the higher planes.

See ANTHRŌPOS, ARC. MAN, BONDAGE, COSMOS, CRUCIFIXION, DISEASES, I E O U, INVOLUTION, KARMA, MAAT, MAZENDARENS, MOIRÆ,

NECESSITY, NORNOR, SHENIT, SON OF
GOD, THEMIS.

FATES, SPECIES OF :—

Symbolic of the karmic liabilities
which are incurred by the ego during
an early state of strife, trouble and
suffering befalling the lower self.

See KARMA, STRIFE.

FATES :—

See MOIRAE.

FATHER, GOD THE ; OR THE GREAT INVISIBLE FORE-FATHER :—

A symbol to indicate Absolute
Being,—the First or unmanifest Logos,
—the Source of all that is. No conception is possible of Potential Deity,
—it is a " thrice unknown Darkness "
to the lower mind.

From the Father proceeds the Son,
—the Second Logos, God manifest
and limited in His creation.

"Jesus calls the Life-Force Our
Father. ' My Father worketh hitherto,
and I work.' Then all the working of
the Life-Force in the past—even in
what to our perception has been most
gross and dreadful—has been the working of a Mind and Will which means
well by us and could not do otherwise,
for it is our Father. . . . We must
work that God's work may be done and
our own destiny fulfilled. And we
know it ; we all know it. There is
that within us all which makes us know
that that alone is great and worthy of
reverence in human character and deed
which is the outcome of life spent in
the service of objects wider and higher
than the purely selfish and personal."—
R. J. CAMPBELL, Serm., *Jesus and the
Life-Force*.

"There was, he (a Gnostic) says, at
first nothing whatever that is begotten ;
the Father was in solitude, unbegotten,
not circumscribed either by space or
time, with none to counsel Him, with
no kind of substance that can be apprehended by any ordinary mode of apprehension. He was in solitude, as they
say quiescent, and reposing in Himself
alone. But inasmuch as He had the
faculty of generation, it seemed good to
Him at last to bring to birth and to
put forth what He had within Himself
that was fairest and most perfect ; for
He was no lover of solitude. For He
was, the writer says, all Love ; but love
is not love, unless there be an object of
love."—HIPPOLYTUS, *Refutation*, VI. 29.

See ABSOLUTE, AIN SOPH, ARHAT,
ATMAN, BRAHMA, GODHEAD, MACRO-
COSM, MONAD, OGDOAD, PRAGÂPATI,
TRINITY, VIVANHAO, ZERANA.

FATHER (LOWER ASPECT) :—

A symbol of a prior and inferior
condition of soul which begets a
superior.

"You must learn, you must let God
teach you, that the only way to get rid
of your past is to get a future out of
it."—PHILLIPS BROOKS, Serm., *How many
Loaves, etc. ?*

See DEAD (burying), DEFUNCT,
JESUS (severe), PARENTS, POURU-
SHASPA.

FATTED CALF EATEN :—

A symbol of the celestial feast of
wisdom and love on the buddhic plane,
whereby the sacrifice of the lower
nature has brought joy to the higher.
This implies the awakenment of the
consciousness on the higher planes.
—See LUKE xv. 23.

See CALF, DANCES, FAT, FEAST,
HUSKS, KID, PRODIGAL.

FEAR ; TERROR :—

Lack of intellectual will. It is a
negative state, that is, absence of the
positive state,—courage. Fear is
possible only to that which has no
real existence, namely, the lower
nature. It stifles effort and paralyses
initiative.

See ROCKS (floating), SYMPLEGADES.

FEAR OF GOD OR THE LORD :—

A symbol of the perception of the
higher nature within, and its
attractiveness upward.

"The fear of the Lord is the beginning
of wisdom."—Ps. cxi. 10.
"The fear of the Lord is a fountain
of life, to depart from the snares of
death."—PROV. xiv. 27.

See FAITH, INTUITION.

FEAST ; BANQUET :—

A symbol of the Realisation of
Truth, Wisdom and Love, in a state
of bliss on higher planes.

"So when they had rest from the
task, and had made ready the banquet,
they feasted, nor was their heart aught
stinted of the fair banquet. But when
they had put away from them the
desire of meat and drink, the young
men crowned the bowls with wine, and
gave each man his portion after the
drink-offering had been poured into the
cups."—*Iliad*, Bk. I, trans. Buckley.

And when this process of evolution
was completed, and the results of
the labours of the Self were accom-

plished, the period arrived when the Soul should enjoy that which it had earned. Nor was aught lacking, for when the desires and appetites of the lower self were restrained (i.e. when the Ego no longer identified itself with its baser nature) the mental qualities brought truth from above to the lower Self. And each department of the Soul received satisfaction so soon as it had been nourished by Truth from on High.

" And in this mountain shall the Lord of hosts make unto all peoples a feast of fat things, a feast of wines on the lees well refined."—Is. xxv. 6.

On the higher planes (mountain) the qualities shall partake of the " fruits of the Spirit " bringing joy and satisfaction to the soul.—*See* 1 Cor. v. 8.

See Banquet, Calf (fatted), Cow (plenty), Fat, Food, Mountain, Wine.

FEAST, ROYAL, OF TYPHON (SET) :—

A symbol of the junction of mind with desire, bringing about greater and wider activities in the lower nature. It is the fall of mind to the desire nature which stimulates the lower principle (Set).

See Death of osiris, Fall, Set.

FEATHER OF MAAT :—

A symbol of the lower personality in its relation to justice and law. The feather, which is significant of the ephemeral, transitory character of physical life, is a sign of the illusory personality of the lower planes. It indicates the insufficiency of the personality, which is a lower expression of the Divine life, to continue to persist. A feather after serving its purpose in life is discarded, and is wafted away and lost.

See Heel, Judgment hall, Justice, Maat, Personality, Sau.

FEED ; FEEDING :—

Symbolic of the dispensing of truth and goodness to the qualities, or imparting instruction to the mind and soul.

" Simon Peter saith unto Jesus, Yea, Lord ; thou knowest that I love thee. He saith unto him, Feed my lambs. . . . Tend my sheep. . . . Feed my sheep."— John xxi. 15-17.

Here the disciplined lower mind (Peter) is represented as growing in grace and in truth, and therefore becoming capable of instructing the qualities. At first the command of the indwelling Christ is to give instruction to the minor virtues (lambs), but afterwards as love of truth and righteousness increases, the lower mind is enjoined to instruct the major virtues (sheep). Then the allegory goes on to describe how the lower mind, at first a law to itself, shall when purified and perfected and ruled by the Spirit within, be " crucified," and transmuted, and so disappear as lower mind, being carried away and its elements dissolved by the Supreme Law.

" To feed means to teach."—Sweden-borg, *Apoc. Rev.*, n. 383.

" God is Love and Goodness. Fill the soul with goodness, and fill the soul with love, *that* is the filling it with God. If we love one another, God dwelleth in us. There is nothing else that can satisfy."—F. W. Robertson, *Sermons*, 3rd *Series*, p. 259.

See Ascension of osiris, Bread, Eating, Food, Lazarus, Meat, Peter, Sheep, Water.

FEEDING OF THE FIVE THOUSAND :—

A symbol of instruction and knowledge given to the numerous lower qualities of the soul, by means of the senses and subtle perceptions (fishes) of the astro-physical body.

" And Jesus took the five loaves, and the two fishes, and looking up to heaven, he blessed, and brake and gave the loaves to the disciples, and the disciples to the multitude."—Mat. xiv. 19.

This means the consecration of the five senses to the highest use, and this nobler use could only be brought about through the intervention of the superior qualities of the soul (the disciples). Christ, the indwelling Self, never gives aid or instruction *directly* to the lower qualities ; the blessing from above must always come through the intermediary of the most highly evolved qualities.

" The feeding of the multitude was not the feeding of the body, but the soul. The whole story is symbolical. It was the bread from heaven, the bread of life, which Jesus distributed to His disciples, and which they, in turn, were authorised to distribute to those who were hungering and thirsting after righteousness."—R. J. CAMPBELL, Serm., *Ministering the Bread of Life.*

"The great law under which man is placed is that he shall receive illumination and impulse from beings more improved than himself. Now revelation is only an extension of this universal method of carrying forward mankind. In this case, God takes on himself the office to which all rational beings are called. He becomes an immediate teacher to a few, communicating to them a higher order of truths than had before been attained, which they in turn are to teach to the race. Here is no new power or element introduced into the system, but simply an enlargement of that agency on which the progress of man chiefly depends. . . . Why are the more advanced commissioned to teach the less informed ? A great purpose, I believe the chief purpose, is to establish interesting relations among men, to bind them to one another by generous sentiments, to promote affectionate intercourse, to call forth a purer love than could spring from a communication of mere outward gifts."—W. E. CHANNING, *Evidences, etc.*

See APOSTLES, BLESSING, BREAD, DISCIPLES, EATING, FOOD, HUNGER, JESUS (gospels), LIVING THINGS, PARABLE, PEOPLE, QUALITIES, SITTING, THIRST.

FEEDING OF THE FOUR THOUSAND :—

A symbol of the imparting by higher qualities of knowledge and goodness to lower qualities.

"And Jesus commanded the multitude to sit down on the ground ; and he took the seven loaves and the fishes ; and he gave thanks and brake, and gave to the disciples, and the disciples to the multitudes. And they did all eat and were filled."—MAT. xv. 35–37.

The Christ within enforces obedience. " Sitting " corresponds to the position of acquiescence and receptivity of mind,—in which attitude instruction could be given. The taking and giving of the " loaves and fishes " signifies the dispensing of such truths and goodness as were at the disposal of the disciplined qualities, which were then able to minister to the less-developed qualities of the soul. The eating and being filled correspond to a condition in which satisfaction for a time was arrived at.

See BREAD, DISCIPLES, EATING, FISH, MULTITUDES, SITTING.

FEET :—

A symbol of the physical foundation of the lower activities which are necessary to advance the evolution of the soul. Activity or Will exercised on the lower planes.

"I thought on my ways, and turned my feet unto thy testimonies."—Ps. cxix. 59.

The soul meditates on its condition and regulates the lower activities, so that it may advance towards the ideals set before it.

"By standing upon their feet is signified the external of man. The external man is in itself natural."—SWEDENBORG, *Apoc. Rev.,* n. 510.

See FOOT, FOOTPRINTS, RIGHT FOOT, SANDALS, SKY, STRIDES OF SOUL, WALKING, WASHED FEET.

FEMININE PRINCIPLE :—

This designates the passive and receptive aspect of the manifest Duality. Space, Matter, and Wisdom (buddhi) have this feminine aspect and are symbolised by the great Goddesses in all the polytheistic religions. The present phase of evolution is directed from the buddhic plane which receives the transmuted results of experience, and yields up the higher emotions (feminine) to the aspiring lower Self incarnate in the soul.

See ADITI, BUDDHI, GODDESS, MALE-FEMALE, MASCULINE, MOTHER, PRAKRITI, SOPHIA, VACH, WISDOM.

FENSAL, AN ABODE OF FRIGG :—

A symbol of the astral plane as a reflection (inverted) of the buddhic.

See ASTRAL PLANE, FRIGG, MISTLE-TOE.

FESTIVAL, SACRED :—

A symbolic performance to celebrate an auspicious occasion in the life and progress of the soul.

See CEREMONIES, RITES.

FESTIVE ARBOURS :—

Symbolic of virtues which bring joy and satisfaction.

See ARCHED GATEWAYS.

FETTERS ON A MAN :—

An emblem of attachment of the mind to the lower affections and desires, causing sorrows, troubles, and tribulations, and binding the soul to matter.

"Let, therefore, no man love anything ; loss of the beloved is evil. Those who love nothing, and hate nothing, have no fetters."—*Dhammapada*, XVI. 211.

"The (living Self) not being a lord, is bound, because he has to enjoy (the fruits of works) ; but when he has known God, he is freed from all fetters."—*Svetas Upanishad*, I. 8.

See ATTACHMENT, VITAL AIRS.

FETTERS ON THE SELF, OR SOUL :—

A symbol of the captivity of the Self in the matter of the lower planes, due to the process of involution.

"The object of (the San-khya-karika) is to effect the liberation of the soul (purusha) from the fetters in which it is involved by union with prakriti (matter)."—MON. WILLIAMS, *Indian Wisdom*, p. 92.

" ' When all desires that dwell in the heart cease, then the mortal becomes immortal, and obtains Brahman. When all the fetters of the heart here on earth are broken, when all that binds us to this life is undone, then the mortal becomes immortal : here our teaching ends.' This is what is called Vedanta."—MAX MÜLLER, *India, etc.*, p. 249.

"Our Self is neither our body nor our mind, nor even our thoughts of which most philosophers are so proud, but that all these are conditions only to which the Self has to submit, fetters by which it is chained."—MAX MÜLLER, *Vedanta Philosophy*, p. 97.

"Whatever separates us from God is but the deceptive semblance of self which chains our volition. Hence man must release himself from the fetters of self and creature love, must have nothing, and desire nothing excepting God, and experience God in the solitude of his spirit " (Eckhart).—PFLEIDERER, *Devel. of Chris.*, p. 152.

"When a soul succeeds in breaking the fetters of sin and ascending the throne of spiritual power, it invariably does so by the emergence of something *divine from within*, something which must have been there from the first, and which lies deeper than all the corruptions of the fleshly nature."—R. J. CAMPBELL, Serm., *The Faith that Saves.*

"Thy chain, which is made up of guilt and filth, is heavy ; it is a wretched bond about thy neck, by which thy strength doth fail. But come, though thou comest in chains ; it is glory to Christ that a sinner comes after him in chains. The chinkings of thy chains, though troublesome to thee, are not, nor can be, obstruction to thy salvation ; it is Christ's work and glory to save thee from thy chains, to enlarge thy steps, and set thee at liberty."—J. BUNYAN, *Come and Welcome to Christ.*

See APPENDAGES, BABYLON, BONDAGE, CAPTIVITY, LIBERATION, PRISONERS.

FIELD :—

A symbol of the lower nature ; the arena within which the soul's evolution takes place.

"The great elements (earth, etc.), egoism (self-consciousness), the understanding, the unperceived also, the ten senses, and the one (mind) and the five objects of sense, desire, aversion, pleasure, pain, body, consciousness, courage, thus in brief has been declared the Kshetra with changes (development)."—*Bhagavad-gita*, Ch. XIII.

The Kshetra, or field, is the arena in its largest sense of organism and environment of the soul's evolution. It includes all the planes of manifestation below atma, though the present lower nature below the buddhic is more especially indicated. The mental faculties, the emotions, the desires, passions, and sensations in all their varieties are the means of soul-development.

"The field is the world."—MAT. xiii. 38.

The " world " signifies the lower nature of the soul, in which the germs of higher qualities (seed) are sown by the Spirit.

"This human frame, O Earth ! is called ' field.' He who knows (how to enter and how to leave) it is denominated by those conversant with the subject, ' the Knower of the field ' (i.e. Self or Soul). . . . Those striving after final emancipation must constantly seek to understand the ' field ' and to obtain a knowledge of the Knower of the field."—*Institutes of Vishnu*, Ch. XCVI. 97, 98.

The human organism on the lower planes is the field of experience. To know it all is to rise above it and become one with the Higher Self. The human organism comprises the four vehicles of the soul on the four planes of nature ; i.e. the causal, mental, astral, and physical human bodies. It is through these bodies that the indwelling spiritual ego must manifest his nature, and he can only do so by fully understanding and controlling them. When he has mastered the lower qualities, he has developed the higher, and the consciousness rises to the higher planes and to union with the Higher Self.

See AGRICULTURE, ARENA, CASTES,

IGNORANCE, IRRIGATION, KNOWER, LAND, LIBERATION, MARKET-PLACE, QUATERNARY, SETTLEMENTS, SKANDHAS, VARA, VESTURES, VINEYARD, VIRGINS, VITAL AIRS, WILDERNESS, WORLD.

FIEND OF THE FOUR-LEGGED RACE :—

A symbol of the desire-principle of the lower quaternary.

See AUSHEDAR, BEAST.

FIENDS, OR DEMONS :—

Symbols of auto-intelligent forces which operate upon the lower planes : these are chiefly elemental, and have to do with the nature and habits of the sub-human and instinctual intelligences.

See DEVAS (lower), LORDS (material), MITHRA, NAIADS, NASU, SALAMANDERS.

FIENDS RUSHING FORTH FROM BURROWS :—

Symbolical of the objects of sense which allure and captivate the ego. They appear and disappear in the consciousness, and come from the earth or physical plane as vibrations to the mind.

See BOTTOMLESS PIT, HARPIES, OVERSEER, SERPENT (hissing).

FIFTEEN, NUMBER :—

A number signifying completeness of condition or period. It is a multiple of three,—a perfect number,— and five, the number of the manifest planes.

See BEGETTING, GOLDEN AGE, MAIDEN.

FIG-FRUIT :—

A symbol of the sweet fruit of the Tree of Life, i.e. the blissful results of the experience of the Self in its course through the lower nature. The "fruit of the Spirit is love, joy, peace, etc." (GAL. v. 22), which are emotions transmuted through the Holy Spirit (Buddhi). This "sweet fruit" is garnered and enjoyed on the buddhic plane to which the consciousness rises after the lower nature is transcended.

"Two birds (the Paramātman and the Jīvatman, or Supreme and individual souls) always united, of the same name, occupy the same tree. One of them (the Jīvatman) enjoys the sweet fruit of the fig (or fruit of acts), the other looks on as a witness."—*Mundaka Upanishad,* III. 1, 1–3; MON. WILLIAMS, *Indian Wisdom,* p. 42.

The "two birds" are the Higher and the Lower Selves which are essentially one, but dual in aspect respecting manifestation, only the lower aspect being in active relation with the soul as the Divine Indweller. It is the Divine life (jiva), the Christ within, who strives and eventually conquers the lower nature of the soul, and afterwards rises in his saints to partake of the fruit of the life process.

"There are hints which lead to the truth that it is only the lower self which suffers ; the higher ego in us, 'the angel' which 'always beholds the face of the Father,' goes scathless, awaiting the uniting of the lower self with it."— K. C. ANDERSON, Serm., *The Buried Life.*

"There sits a silent watcher within each of us, an entity unaffected by the swift, tumultuous passing of the years, yet carefully gathering up and storing within itself the tribute that they bring. It forgets nothing, loses nothing, allows nothing to escape that has ever come within its ken. And all this treasure is being accumulated for eternity ; this inner self of every soul cares only for the things of time as they bear upon its return to that state in which time is not. Language is of necessity inadequate here to express a fact which transcends our powers of thought. But I repeat that that timeless, ageless principle, that point and centre of being, which alone deserves to be called you, deeper far than your present consciousness of yourself, and greater than you have or could have any conception of while you are enclosed and battened down in your physical body, derives immediately from the eternal Son of God."—R. J. CAMPBELL, Serm., *In Change Unchanged.*

See ATMAN, BIRDS (two), EXPERIENCE, FRUIT OF SPIRIT, HARVEST, HIGHER AND LOWER SELVES, INCARNATION, INDIVIDUALITY, JESUS (son of God), PERSONALITY, SAINTS, SELF (supreme), SELF (lower), SON OF GOD, TIME, TREE OF LIFE.

FIG-JUICE :—

Emblem of the Divine Life from the Tree of Life.

"As when fig-juice curdles and binds white milk."—*Empedocles,* FAIRBANKS, 279.

As when spiritual perception encompasses or endows the wisdom-nature.

Atma ensouling buddhi, which may be expressed as atma-buddhi.

See BLOOD, HOMA-JUICE, SAP, SOMA-JUICE.

FIG-LEAVES AS APRONS :—

A symbol of spiritual growth unobserved by the lower nature.—*See* GEN. iii. 7.

See EYE, FALL.

FIG-TREE :—

A symbol of the Divine life in the scheme of things. The Tree of Life, which grows up from a small seed and forms a stem, branches, twigs, leaves, and finally fruit and seeds, all typifying the spiritual life which permeates in every part the structure of the universe and the soul.

" This everlasting, holy fig-tree stands with roots above, with branches downwards. Its root is that pure Self, that immortal principle."—*Katha. Upanishad*, VI. 1.

See BIRDS (two), OAK TREE, SEED, SOMA PLANT, TREE OF LIFE, YGGDRASIL.

FIG-TREE WITHERED AWAY :—

This fig-tree stands for the lower nature which can never of itself bring forth the fruits of the Spirit. The lower nature withers away at the word of the perfected Christ-soul. The emblem here is taken as the lower part, or obverse, of the Tree of Life.—*See* MAT. xxi. 19–21.

See MAN (natural), WORD.

FILIAL PIETY (ANCESTOR WORSHIP) :—

A symbol of the soul's reverence for its Divine nature, and of its determination to follow the will of its Father in heaven.

" Asked what filial piety was, the Master (Confucius) said, ' It is not being disobedient. That parents, when alive, should be served according to propriety ; that when dead, they should be buried according to propriety ; and that they should be sacrificed to, according to propriety " (Confucian Analects).—J. LEGGE, *Life and Teachings*, etc., p. 123.

The Higher Self within teaches that the spiritual ego should be obedient to its Divine parentage : that the Parents (Atma-buddhi), when recognised (alive) should be intuitively served according to the divine ordinance of the higher life : that when

the Spirit within is obscured (dead) in the lower life, it yet should be held in reverence according to the divine ordinance ; and the lower qualities should be sacrificed to the higher according to the divine law of the evolution of the Spirit within.

" Now filial piety is seen in the skilful carrying out of the wishes of our forefathers, and the skilful carrying forward of their undertakings. In spring and autumn, they repaired and beautified the temple-halls of their fathers, set forth their ancestral vessels, displayed their various robes, and presented the offerings of the several seasons. By means of the ceremonies of the ancestral temple, they distinguished the imperial kindred according to their order of descent."—*Ibid.*, p. 296.

Now true religion is exemplified in the soul's methodical endeavour to accomplish the purpose of all prior manifestations of the Self, and to make use of all the means provided for the ego's spiritual evolution. During the times of manifestation (spring, etc.) the causal-bodies (temples) of the incarnating egos are developed and perfected, and the inherited mental-vehicles (vessels) are endowed with higher qualities (robes) as they relinquish the lower qualities (offerings) in the several stages of evolution. In the successive transmutations of the qualities for the enrichment of the causal-body, the corresponding phases of the evolving Self are represented.

See CONFUCIUS, DYNASTIES, PITRIS (solar), ROBE, SACRIFICE, TEMPLE.

FILLET OF APOLLO UPON A GOLDEN STAFF :—

Emblem of the causal sheath established upon the sutratma,— the Divine Ray,—through Wisdom and the Divine Will. Within the causal-body is the " ransom beyond telling," —the " treasure in heaven " laid up on the buddhic plane.

See GOLDEN STAFF, HOLLOW SHIPS, SCEPTRE (Apollo), SUTRATMA.

FILLETS AND GARLANDS, CROWNED WITH :—

Emblem of dependence upon the Self ; and indicates the ego gifted with spiritual graces of Wisdom and Love.

" I go about among you an immortal

god, no longer a mortal, honoured by all, as is fitting, crowned with fillets and luxuriant garlands."—*Empedocles*, FAIRBANKS, 352.

The Immortal Self moves amid the qualities which are transmuted and no longer perishable, and It is distinguished from its modes of action, as is essential to right perception, for it is crowned with Self-dependence and the "fruits of the Spirit."

See CHRIST'S SECOND COMING.

FINGER, FOREFINGER :—

A symbol indicative of what is shown, manifested, demonstrated or done. The forefinger of Horus, which he places upon his mouth, signifies the expression, or manifestation, of the indwelling Self in the soul ; the evolution of the Self from small to great.

"But if I by the finger of God cast out devils, then is the kingdom of God come upon you."—LUKE xi. 20.

If the Christ-soul by the evolution of the Self from within cast out evil qualities, then will the consciousness rise to the higher planes, and the lower nature of the soul be overcome and dissipated.

See DEVILS, HEALING, KINGDOM OF GOD.

FINGERS, FOUR :—

This symbol stands for that which is accomplished through the activities of the qualities on the fourfold path that has been traversed in the lower quaternary.

See WAR.

FINGERS, TWO, OF HORUS :—

A symbol of the love of goodness, and truth which effects much in the soul's evolution.

"This amulet is intended to represent the two fingers, index and medius, which the god Horus employed in helping his father Osiris up the ladder into heaven." —BUDGE, *Egyptian Magic*, p. 55.

"Horus" stands for the Christ active within the soul, while "Osiris" is the potential Christ which the actual assists to evolve and become manifest. But the two are one. When Christ,—the Higher Self,—is fully evolved, then the Soul having completed its upward path (ladder) attains the buddhic consciousness (heaven).

The Papal sign of blessing is the exhibition to the people (the mental qualities) of the "Two fingers of Horus," thus symbolically setting before them the ideal of goodness and truth to which they in reverence must aspire in order that they may attain to bliss.

The amulet of the "Two Fingers" has often been found in the *interior* of mummies (personalities) where it becomes an emblem of the purification of the personality, by means of the treasuring of ideals in the mind and heart.

See HEAVEN, HORUS, LADDER, MUMMY, PADDLES, PEOPLE.

FIRE :—

This important symbol has higher and lower aspects. In its higher aspect it signifies Divine love on the buddhic plane, i.e. the active, masculine principle Atma-buddhi ; the Love-energy from the Atman working through Buddhi, the Holy Spirit.

In its lower aspect, it signifies strong desire or passion energising the matter of the astral plane, and stirring the lower emotions.

"Fire was the symbol of the Spirit of God, and thus of Wisdom."—ERN. DE BUNSEN, *The Angel Messiah*, Transl., p. 99.

"It is no tale apart from our subject or witness. In the first place there sprang up out of the earth forms grown into one whole, having a share of both, of water and of fire. These in truth fire caused to grow up, desiring to reach its like ; but they showed as yet no lovely body formed out of the members, nor voice nor limb such as is natural to men."—*Empedocles*, FAIRBANKS, 262.

This is the whole secret of Divine philosophy :—at the first came forth from the lower nature forms of life which were homogeneous in their character, equally compounded of astral matter and spiritual energy (fire). These aspects of the Self became accentuated by the Love-energy (fire) within,—the lower Self struggling from below upward to meet the higher Self above. But as yet, no causal-body was builded to enable the union to be effected ; and no powers of expression (voice) of the life, or means of execution (limb) such as are inherent in the

the First Logos, the Unmanifest God. In other terms,—the Higher Self, the first emanation of Spirit from the Absolute.

"For the Father of things that are hath made him rise as His Eldest Son, whom elsewhere He hath called His First-born, and who, when he hath been begotten, imitating the ways of his Sire, and contemplating His archetypal patterns, fashions the species of things."
—PHILO, De Confus. Ling. § 14.

"The Son of (the Father's) love; in whom we have our redemption, the forgiveness of our sins; who is the image of the invisible God, the firstborn of all creation; for in him were all things created, in the heavens and upon the earth, things visible and things invisible."—COL. i. 13–16.

"Hiranyagarbha came forth as the first-born of creation from the primeval waters which were created by the first principle (Brahmân). Because it is the first principle itself which appears in its creation as first-born, therefore the latter also is denoted by Brahmân (masc.)."—DEUSSEN, Phil. of Upanishads, p. 199.

"This conception of the first-born of creation as the original source of all wisdom is carried further first in the Svetâsvatara Upanishad (which in general inclines towards a personification of the divine), and here it is described as the Brahmân, Hiranyagarbha the 'golden germ,' or even in one passage (V. 2) with a poetic and metaphorical use of the word as the 'red wizard,' kapila rishi, an expression that has led many into the mistaken belief that here in a Vedic Upanishad, Kapila, the founder of the Sankhya system, was named as the first-born of creation!"—Ibid., p. 200.

Nevertheless, the "great rishi Kapila," being the Higher Self and founder of the system of existence, is rightly said to be "the first-born of creation!" None of the names in the Indian sacred writings are names of persons. Persons, however learned, are too insignificant to have any part in Divine inspiration which proceeds from the Buddhic plane above the human mind. There are no "thinkers of the Upanishads" (ibid., p. 213) who have tampered with Divine revelation of truths of which they could know nothing.

See ARC. MAN, BODHISATVA, COSMOS, CREATION, HIRANYAGARBHA, IMAGE, INCARNATION, JESUS (son of God), KAPILA, MONAD, PROTOTYPES, RISHI, SEED, SELF, SON OF GOD.

FISH OF THE SEA AND LAKES :—

A symbol of facts of the lower experience, namely, concepts, percepts, ideas, feelings, emotions.

"But Simon Peter, when he saw it, fell down at Jesus' knees, saying, Depart from me; for I am a sinful man, O Lord. For he was amazed, and all that were with him, at the draught of the fishes which they had taken."—LUKE v. 8, 9.

But the disciplined lower mind (Peter) was full of perplexity through being in the midst of acquiring a multitude of facts (fishes), some of which could not be reconciled or assimilated; it became, therefore, oppressed with its own limitations and shortcomings, which feeling implied aspiration towards Truth and the Divine power within (Jesus' knees). When minds become heavily weighted with knowledges, they are often apt to sink, spiritually, from over-valuation of externalities which cannot feed the soul.

"By fishes or creatures of the sea are meant the affections and consequent thoughts of those men who are principled in general truths, and are therefore more attracted by what is natural than by what is spiritual."—SWEDENBORG, Apoc. Rev., n. 405.

"Thou hast put all things under his feet: All sheep and oxen, yea, and the beasts of the field; the fowl of the air, and the fish of the sea, and whatsoever passeth through the paths of the sea" (Ps. viii. 6–8). "The fowls of the air as representing the higher order of human intelligences: and the fishes of the sea, those who are immersed in the waves of worldly affairs (Hesychius)."—WORDSWORTH, Bible, Psalms, p. 12.

"The sea is a figure of the world; wherefore the creatures that are in it, of the men of the world (Is. lx. 5). This sea bringeth forth small and great beasts, even as the world doth yield both small and great persecutors, who like the fishes of prey, eat up and devour what they can of those fish that are of another condition. Now also out of the world that mystical sea, as fishers do out of the natural; both Christ and his servants catch mystical fish, even fish as of the great sea."—J. BUNYAN, Exp. of Genesis.

"Success or failure can never be measured in terms of the outward and visible, but only of the inward and spiritual."—R. J. CAMPBELL, Serm., The Inner Voice.

See ASPIRATION, EXPERIENCES, IKATERE, JESUS OF GOSPELS, KNEES.

MAN, NET, PETER, SEA, WATER (lower).

FISH CAUGHT IN A NET :—

Symbolic of facts collected through the apparatus of the senses.

"Fuh-he invented nets for fishes."—*Chinese Mythology.* KIDD, *China.*

The Logos is active within nature when at a certain stage an astral mechanism of sensation comes to be developed, which is to be used by the ego in gathering the facts (fish) which it is necessary that he shall collect for the widening of his experience.

FISH, GREAT :—

A symbol of the Higher Self as the supreme fact in the Ocean of Reality. The Divine Life of primordial Truth (water).

"He (God) had his dwelling in the Great Sea, and was a fish therein" (Zohar).—MYER, *Qabbalah*, p. 336.

"St. Augustine says of Jesus : 'He is a fish that lives in the midst of waters.' ' So many fishes bred in the waters, and saved by one great fish,'—says Tertullian of the Christians and Christ and the Church."—BLAVATSKY, *Secret Doctrine*, Vol. II. p. 327.

Brahma, Vishu, Ea, Horus, Dagon were said to appear in fish form. In Christian iconography a symbol of the Saviour Jesus is a fish.

See ABTU FISH, DELUGE, EEL-GOD, HORN OF SALVATION, JESUS (fish), LAKE, OCEAN, PISCES, SHIPS OF MANU, WATER.

FIVE, NUMBER :—

This number appears in the Scriptures most often in two relations, namely, the planes of manifestation and the senses. Five elements, five worlds, five intercalary days, and five gathas are symbols of the five planes. Five brethren of Dives, five Karap brothers, five foolish virgins, five companies of dead men, five barley loaves, five-pronged fork, are symbols of the five senses.

"The five elements, so disposed that earth occupies the centre, exhibit a model to which men and things in varied positions are made conformable. The five antediluvian emperors seem naturally referable to this number and its properties ; especially since one reigns by wood, another by fire, a third by earth, a fourth by metal, and a fifth by water. Then there are five human

relations, and five constant virtues ; five ranks of nobility ; five points—east, west, south, north, and centre ; five household gods, which occupy the four corners and middle of the house ; the five tastes ; five colours ; five viscera."—KIDD, *China*, p. 166.

"Five is symbolic of imperfection, or incompletion generally."—J. GARNIER, *Worship of the Dead*, p. 220.

See BRATROK, DAYS (five), ELEMENTS (five), FEEDING (5,000), FORK, GATHA DAYS (five), HADES, MODGUNN, PLACES, SEASONS (five), VIRGINS, WORLDS (five).

FLABELLUM, OR SACRED FAN :—

When used, this is a symbol of the Spirit, the Divine Breath, energising the vehicles of the soul.

See BREATH (divine), FAN.

FLAIL, FOR THRESHING OUT WHEAT :—

A symbol of the Divine Will which is active to beat out the lower qualities (the chaff), and reveal in the soul the higher qualities of wisdom and love (the wheat) with which the causal-body is nourished.

The figure of Osiris is often shown holding the emblems of the flail and the crook, the first signifying the coercive driving away of evil, as by a whip, and the second, the attractive drawing upwards of the qualities towards goodness and truth.

The flail is a symbol of the disciplining of the lower nature, and the cultivation of the higher. The crook is a symbol of the nurture and accumulating of virtues (sheep).

See BISHOP, CAUSAL-BODY, CHAFF, CORN, CROWN (upper), OSIRIS, SHEEP, SHEPHERD, WHEAT.

FLAME OF A SWORD :—

A symbol of spiritual strength which is necessary to conquer the lower nature and gain the secret of Life Eternal.

See CHERUBIM, FUDO, SWORD.

FLAMES, TWIN :—

Symbolic of Wisdom and Love Divine.

"And if one shall rest in life as a crystal, he shall do all things in the Garden of Rest, after the manner of that which is done in the pool of the Twin Flames."—*Book of the Dead*, Ch. CX., trans. M. W. BLACKDEN.

During the life of the lesser Self

below, the bright shining Truth of the greater Self from above is reflected within the evolving soul, so that the Wisdom and Love of the Self are transferred as a benediction to the lower planes.

See CRYSTAL, GARDEN, POOL.

FLAVOUR OF BRAHMAN :—

A symbol of the sense of supreme bliss.

"He approaches the city Salagya, and the flavour of Brahman reaches him."—*Kaush. Upanishad*, I. 2.

The Ego approaches the abode of the Higher Self, and a sense of supreme bliss comes to him.—*See* Ps. xxxiv. 8.

See ODOUR, SALAGYA, TASTE.

FLAYING OF MAN AND PUTTING HIS SKIN ON COW :—

A symbol of the transferrence of the perfected qualities of the Archetypal Man to the buddhic plane from whence they may be reflected to the lower planes in the evolving souls of men.

"The gods spake, 'Verily, the cow supports everything here on earth; come, let us put on the cow that skin which is now on man : therewith she will be able to endure rain and cold and heat.' Accordingly, having flayed man, they put that skin on the cow."—*Sata. Brâh.*, III. 1, 2, 14–15.

On the buddhic plane (cow) are the prototypes of all things on the lower planes (earth). The perfected qualities are, as it were, the outer envelope of the Archetypal Man, and these qualities are now gathered up to the buddhic plane to be used in providing the spiritual egos with manifest qualities during their evolution on the lower planes through various conditions of life.

"The word *skin*, which occurs frequently in this Book of Job, denotes here what is most precious. To be deprived of the skin is to lose what is most valuable, and to give the skin for a thing is to make the greatest sacrifice for it (JOB ii. 4).—WORDSWORTH, *Bible, Job*, p. 5.

See ARC. MAN, COW, DISMEMBERMENT, FLESH OF JESUS, LINEN GARMENT, MAN, PROTOTYPES, SKIN.

FLESH :—

A symbol of the lower nature, with its desires and passions.

"So then, brethren, we are debtors, not to the flesh, to live after the flesh; for if ye live after the flesh, ye must die; but if by the spirit ye mortify the deeds of the body ye shall live."—ROM. viii. 12, 13.

"By flesh is signified man's proprium or self-hood, which in itself is evil."

"In a good sense flesh signifies the good of the church."—SWEDENBORG, *Apoc. Rev.*, n. 748, 832.

See BURNT-OFFERING, ROASTED, CREMATION, SACRIFICE, THIGHS, VULTURE.

FLESH IN WHICH IS LIFE :—

Symbolic of the lower nature in which the Spirit is involved.

"And behold, I do bring the flood of waters upon the earth, to destroy all flesh, wherein is the breath of life, from under heaven; everything that is in the earth shall die."—GEN. vi. 17.

From the Logos there issues forth an outpouring of truth which is to confound the lower mental nature and overwhelm falsity. This "destroying of all flesh" permits the new interpretation of life which is to be given through the interior revelation of the Spirit. The Spirit is involved in the lower nature of the soul, in mind and desire, and it is not liberated until life is known no more after the "flesh" but after the Spirit. Everything of the lower nature must die, i.e. end, since it is a condition of limitation.

"The spirit of man is—not shall be—eternally one with God, eternally pure and beautiful and good; we are here to make that truth sublime by manifesting it in the teeth of the direst odds. For a brief hour we are shut away from the full knowledge of what we are; the limitations of the flesh press hard upon us; we have to know fear, and pain, and conflict, that the eternal splendour may be revealed."—R. J. CAMPBELL, *Serm., The Flesh Transfigured*.

See AFU-RĀ, BREATH OF LIFE, FLOOD, INCARNATION, INVOLUTION, LIBERATION, LIVING, MAN, QUALITIES, SPIRIT, WATER.

FLESH OF JESUS AS BREAD FROM HEAVEN :—

This symbol of the "flesh" or "body" of the indwelling Christ signifies the evolving Truth nature which implies conformity of the outer nature (flesh) to the inner nature (spirit). This outer truth-nature of Christ is then the same as the "bread of God" which signifies the truth-substance of goodness which must be assimilated by the qualities to give them eternal life.

"Except ye eat the flesh of the Son of man and drink his blood, ye have not life in yourselves. . . . As the living Father sent me, and I live because of the Father ; so he that eateth me, he also shall live because of me. This is the bread which came down out of heaven."—JOHN vi. 53, 57, 58.

Except the qualities assimilate the outer Truth-nature of the Son of God born of mind, and partake of his Divine life, they are of the lower nature, dead, transitory. As the incarnate Christ below proceeds from the heavenly Christ above, and the Divine life is one life, so if a quality becomes permeated with that Life of Reality—Truth—it is transmuted to higher planes and abides for ever. This truth-substance of goodness is indeed the food of the soul falling as manna from above.

"The symbol was as much a metaphor in the historical ages of Egyptian history as are the metaphors of our own language. When the Egyptian spoke of 'eating' his god, he meant no more than we do when we speak of 'absorbing' a subject."—SAYCE, Rel. of Anc. Egypt. and Babyl., p. 244.

"'Me he (mâm sah)' will devour in the next (world), whose flesh I eat in this life ; the wise declare this to be the real meaning of the word 'flesh' (mâmsah)."—Laws of Manu, V. 56.

This refers to the dissolution of the personality (me) when the lower Self and the higher Self become one, and as the consciousness rises to the causal-body in the "next world." The eating of the "flesh" of "Svayambhu (the Self-existent)" is the partaking of the Divine Life from within the soul.

"His true flesh and blood were his Life ; and they truly eat his flesh and drink his blood who partake of that divine Life."—MRS. EDDY, Science and Health, p. 25.

See ATONEMENT, BLOOD, BLOOD OF THE LAMB, BREAD, CORPSE, DOUBLE FOLD, FATHER, FOOD AS GOD, INCARNATION, INVOLUTION, MANNA, PERSONALITY, REDEMPTION, REGENERATION, SACRAMENT, SALVATION, SON OF GOD, SVAYAMBHU, WORLD.

FLOCKS OF SHEEP THE MOST GLORIOUS :—

Symbolic of celestial qualities, or

virtues on higher planes, which enable the ego to aspire.

See JOB, QUALITIES, SHEEP, YIMA.

FLOCKS OF SHEEP ON THE EARTH :—

Symbolic of virtues evolved from the lower nature.

See EARTH, SHEEP.

FLOCKS PASSING OVER GROUND :—

This signifies gleams of wisdom coming to the lower self.

See MAN WITHOUT WOMAN.

FLOCKS AND HERDS YIELDING DUNG :—

Symbolic of emotions which yield experience to fertilise the lower nature.

See DUNG.

FLOOD OF WATER :—

This symbol signifies a forth-pouring of the Logic Life-Wave,— the waters of Truth,—producing in the first instance erroneous opinions, as the lower mind is the great creator of falsity and illusion.

"By a flood of water is signified truths in abundance, and in an opposite sense falses in abundance."—SWEDENBORG, Apoc. Rev., n. 563.

See DELUGE, FLESH, KARSHVARES, MANU, PLANETARY CHAIN, REGIONS, ROUND, WATER.

FLOOD OF NOAH :—

A symbol of the downpouring of Truth (rain) into the lower mind at a certain stage of evolution. This is equivalent to an enlargement of the field of consciousness in the illusions of the lower life, for the truth is reflected as false conceptions on the astro-mental plane (lower water) ; and implies the awakening of the mind in ignorance, which is the condition out of which Truth eventually arises.

"And the Flood was forty days upon the earth ; and the waters increased, and bare up the ark, and it was lift up above the earth. And the waters prevailed, and increased greatly upon the earth ; and the ark went upon the face of the waters. And the waters prevailed exceedingly upon the earth ; and all the high mountains that were under the whole heaven were covered."—GEN. vii. 17–19.

And for its appointed period, which

corresponds to a term of the re-incarnating cycle, the "flood" or buddhic outpouring continued; and whilst it submerged the lower personal self, it but served to glorify the causal-body (ark) which was raised high above the lower self (earth). And the truth, reflected as falsity, prevailed and increased, but upon the waters of illusion the Soul floated And the truth prevailed upon the lower nature (earth), so that all those projects and aspirations of the lower self, which are ideals distorted with error, were frustrated. The "high mountains" or loftiest aspirations of the lower nature, are also for the time overwhelmed with the influx of perceptions and ideas.

"In the inward meaning, the flood is symbolically representative of spiritual dissolution."—PHILO, *Works*, Bohn, Vol. IV. p. 356.

"With respect to the inner sense of the passage (GEN. viii. 2) since the deluge of the mind arises from two things, for it arises partly from counsel, as if from heaven, and in another degree also from the body and from sense, as if from earth, the vices being reciprocally introduced by the passions, and the passions by the vices, it was inevitably necessary that the word of the Divine physician entering in as a salutory visitation for the purpose of healing the disease should prevent both kinds of overflow for the future."—*Ibid.*, p. 365.

The "fountains of the deep" are those sources of error which produce illusion in the lower self; and the "windows of heaven stopped" signify the spiritual perceptions diminished.

"By the flood is signified an inundation of evil and falsity."—SWEDENBORG, *Arc. Cel.*, n. 660.

"'And the waters were strengthened exceedingly upon the earth,' signifies that false persuasions so increased. This appears from what has been said and shown before respecting the waters; namely that the inundating waters signify falsities."—*Ibid.*, n. 794.

See ADITYAS, ARK OF NOAH, BEASTS (clean), CAUSAL-BODY, DELUGE, DEPRAVITY, EARTH, FLESH, FORTY, GOD REPENTING, HEROD, HOUSE (frequented), MOUNTAIN, NOAH, OLIVE LEAF, RAIN, TEN DAYS, WATER.

FLOUR, FINE :—

Symbolic of truth and goodness derived through the activities of the lower nature.

"Fine flour is truth derived from good."—SWEDENBORG, *Arc. Cel.*, n. 9995.

See BREAD, DOUGH, MEAL, SHEWBREAD, WHEAT.

FLOWERS :—

A symbol of the virtues with which the soul is potentially endowed, and which blossom to the light as the Higher Self draws them forth in evolution.

"The latent divine reality within has come to itself and is rising up into living union with that from which it came, as the flower rises towards the sun in high heaven; for, indeed, all the beauty the flower possesses is that same sun incarnate;—buried light bursting forth from its prison."—R. J. CAMPBELL Serm., *Coming to the True Self.*

See ELEPHANTS, GARLANDS, HONEY, LOTUS, MANASI, WATER (heaven).

FLOWERS, WHITE :—

Emblem of purity in the higher qualities of the soul.

"The white flower of a blameless life.'
See QUALITIES, WHITE.

FOAM OF THE SEA :—

A symbol of the astro-mental nature; being a combination of water (astral) and air (mental).

"But the genitals (of Uranus), as after first severing them with the steel, he (Cronus) had cast them into the heaving sea from the continent, so kept drifting long time up and down the deep, and all around kept rising a white foam from the immortal flesh; and in it a maiden was nourished; first she drew nigh divine Cythera, and thence came next to wave-washed Cyprus. Then forth-stepped an awful beauteous goddess; and beneath her delicate feet the verdure throve around: her, gods and men name Aphrodite, the foam-sprung goddess."—HESIOD, *Theogony.*

This refers to the first beginnings of manifested life after the process of involution is completed and that of evolution commenced. The generative, or creative, powers of Spirit (Uranus) are applied in a new direction from the higher mind (steel) plane and take effect on the astral plane (sea), in due relation to the whole scheme. These powers are at first uncentered on the plane, but gradually there is brought about the production of forms composed of pure astro-mental matter, patterned on types above (immortal flesh); and in these forms the evolving life (maiden) is embodied, life which is of a buddhic (Cythera) nature, but afterwards becomes astral and attached to an astral centre (Cyprus). Thus evolution is begun through the birth of simple, natural desires (Venus) which urge the life into the forms and bring about the growth of the instincts and affections. This love-nature (Aphrodite) is to be understood as of astro-mental origin through the working of the Spirit within nature.

See APHRODITE, CRONUS, EVOLUTION, GENERATIVE, INVOLUTION, IRON, PHALLIPHORIA, PLANTS, PROTOTYPES, SEA, URANUS, VENUS.

FOCUS, BURNING :—

An emblem of the Self as the centre from which emanate the rays of the Divine Life to every human soul.

"O Burning Focus! I have come into Thee ; I have cast about me the robe of the waters ; I have girt myself with the girdle of knowledge."—*Book of the Dead*, Ch. CX., trans. M. W. BLACKDEN.

The Self is seen to be as a Centre wherein all the rays of the Divine Life are focussed into one Supernal Light ; and the ego perceives that about the Divine nature into which he has come there are the " garment " and " girdle " of Truth and of Wisdom, i.e. the causal and buddhic vestures.

See GIRDLE OF KNOWLEDGE, ROBE OF WATERS, SUN.

FOHAT, OR WORLD OF AGNI :—

A symbol of the force-aspect of the Logos, operative only on the mental plane of the cosmos or in the causal-body.

"Evolution is commenced by the intellectual energy of the Logos, . . . not merely on account of the potentialities locked up in Mulaprakriti. This Light of the Logos is the link between objective matter and the subjective thought of Ishvara (or Logos). It is called in several Buddhist books Fohat. It is the one instrument with which the Logos works."—T. SUBBA ROW, quoted in *Secret Doctrine*, Vol. I. p. 161.

See LIGHTNING, POLYPHEMUS.

FOLK :—

A symbol of the lower mental qualities.

See COUNTRIES, PEOPLE.

FOLLY :—

A symbol of the desire-mental activity of the lower self. The folly of the lower self is Wisdom inversely reflected on the lower planes, and this is the means whereby the Self is evolved. Never is the Higher Self stirred save through the unwisdom and inexperience which it is called forth to combat. It is through the apprehension of folly that the wisdom above is awakened.

"Nevertheless man being in honour abideth not : he is like the beasts that perish. This their way is their folly : yet their posterity approve their sayings." —Ps. xlix. 12, 13.

The lower-mental quality that is valued and preserved by the lower self is mortal and passes away as do the desires. This lower-mental activity is the obverse of the abiding wisdom above, and though doomed to destruction, yet the illusions it creates constantly foster its expression.

"Though thou lovest the Earthly wisdom now, yet when thou shalt be clothed upon with the Heavenly Wisdom, then thou wilt see that all the wisdom of the world is folly."—BEHMEN, *The Supersensual Life*, p. 38.

See ADULTERY, BEASTS, DIVORCING, HARLOT, MARRIAGE (lower), RAIN, WHOREDOM.

FOOD :—

A symbol of Truth—the Real, which gradually takes the place of Illusion —the unreal. The lower soul-states change and vanish as Truth is assimilated.

"Water is food, the light eats the food. The light rests on water, water rests on light. This is the food resting on food."—*Tait. Upanishad*, III. 8.

Truth is the Real to be assimilated ; i.e. the light of knowledge incorporates truth. Knowledge reposes on truth, truth permeates knowledge. This is the truth (perfect) which rests upon knowledge (imperfect), and which the lower Self takes unto itself, as the unreal gives place to the Real.

"From food are produced all creatures which dwell on earth. Then they live by food, and in the end they return to food. For food is the oldest of all beings, and therefore it is called panacea (i.e. consisting of all herbs, or quieting the heat of the body of all beings). They who worship food as Brahman obtain all food."—*Ibid.*, II. 2.

From Truth,—the Real,—are produced by inversion, as it were, all desires, passions and emotions of the lower nature. Then, being transmuted, they live by truth, and finally return to the Real again. For Truth is from all eternity, and therefore is the support and healer of all qualities which are deficient of itself. That is, it is through growth of the emotions, and the regulation and mastery of the burning desires of the lower nature, that the healing truth is obtained. They who earnestly seek the Truth as the Highest Ideal, on them is the Truth bestowed.

"From the Sacrificer it (the shower of milk and butter) goes to the gods; from the gods to the cow, from the cow to the Sacrificer: thus circulates this perpetual, never-ending food of the gods."—*Sata. Brâh.*, IX. 3, 3, 17.

From the Soul or Ego (Sacrificer) aspiration arises which nourishes the ideals (gods). The ideals being nourished, the buddhic nature (cow) is also fed and strengthened; thence the buddhic functioning is rendered active, and there is bestowed upon the Soul the celestial food of wisdom (milk) and love (butter). Thus circulates perpetually the Divine Life and Truth.

See ALTAR OF SACRIFICE, AURVAITO, BARLEYCORNS, BHIMA, BREAD, CATTLE, COW (spotted), EATING, EXPERIENCES, FEAST, FEED, GODS, HUNGER, LIGHT, MEAL, MORTAR, MOUTH OPENING, ROOTED, SACRIFICER, TIME, UDDER, UKEMOCHI, UNEN, VAGEPEYA, WATER, WEALTH-SHOWER, YIMA.

FOOD, AS GOD, BRAHMAN, VISHNU, JESUS, HORUS, RĀ, CHRIST :—

A symbol of the Divine Reality the Source and sustainer of all things. In other words, the Higher Self, Atma-buddhi,—Love and Wisdom, —God and the "food of the Gods."

"They who worship food as Brahman obtain all food. For food is the oldest of all beings, and therefore it is called panacea. From food all creatures are produced; by food, when born, they grow."—*Tait. Upanishad*, II. 2.

They who aspire towards the Highest obtain spiritual sustenance, for the life-giving Spirit is the eternal source of all beings, and is the healer of all deficiencies. From the Spirit

come all qualities: and by spiritual sustenance, when they arise in the lower nature, they develop.

"I am the divine Soul of Rā proceeding from the god Nu; that divine Soul which is God. I am the creator of the divine food, and that which is an abomination unto me is sin whereon I look not. I proclaim right and truth, and I live therein. I am the divine food which is not corrupted in my name of Soul."—BUDGE, *Book of the Dead*, Ch. LXXXV.

The Higher Self, or Soul, proceeds from the Divine Power of the universe, the supreme Source which is the Absolute,—the "Father of the Gods." The Higher Self is the manifesting Spirit sustaining all things. The imperfections below are due to the fact of the Self not being fully manifest in the human soul, but the deficiencies, being negative, are illusive and unreal. The Higher Self stands for right and truth and lives in the soul as an Ideal. The spiritual sustenance is of the higher nature of the Soul and not of the corruptible lower.

"Food, from an early date, was taken as a symbol of God Almighty, rice and milk and barley, and the intoxicating soma."—A. LILLIE, *Budd. in Christendom*, p. 307.

"This food is the body of the blessed Vishnu, called Visvabhrit (all sustaining)."—*Mait. Upanishad*, VI. 13.

"Jesus took bread, and blessed, and brake it; and he gave to the disciples and said, Take, eat; this is my body."—MAT. xxvi. 26.

"Battista Vernazza's 'impression of eating God, and of inviting all others to the same Divine food' is substantially identical with Catherine's doctrine as to the 'One Bread God' and 'all creatures hungering for this One Bread.' Battista's sight of 'God being diffused throughout human nature' is analogous to Catherine's teaching as to no creature existing that does not, in some measure, participate in His goodness."—F. VON HUGEL, *Mystical Element of Religion*, Vol. I. p. 352.

"Food is Pragâpati."—*Prasna Upanishad*, I. 14.

"I heard Thy voice from on high crying unto me, 'I am the Food of the full-grown: grow, and then thou shalt feed on Me. Nor shalt thou change Me into thy substance as thou changest the food of thy flesh, but thou shalt be changed into Mine.'"—AUGUSTINE, *Confessions*, Bk. VII. 10.

"Christ will come into us, not merely stand without us. He will come in and be Himself the power which lays hold of His own invitations. We may feed on Him. Nay, let us take His own strong word and say, 'He that eateth Me, the same shall live by Me.' That is the inner life, Christ is the soul rising up and laying hold of the infinite possibilities which redemption has prepared. To feed on Christ, then, is to get His strength into us to be our strength. But what is this strength of Christ that comes to us ? There can be only one answer. It is His character. There is no strength that is communicable except in character. It is the moral qualities of His nature that are to enter into us and be ours because we are His. . . . 'He that eateth my flesh and drinketh my blood dwelleth in me and I in him.' 'This is the bread that came down from heaven.' 'He that eateth of this bread shall live for ever."—PHILLIPS BROOKS, Serm., *Christ the Food of Man.*

"Horus is both divine food and the sacrifice. Horus hath passed on to gather together the members of his divine father ; Horus is his deliverer."—BUDGE, *Book of the Dead*, p. 258.

"Now ye are the body of Christ, and severally members thereof."—1 COR. xii. 27.

"There is an ancient Babylonian name Lugal-kurum-zigum, 'the King is heavenly food.' "—A. JEREMIAS, *The Old Test., etc.*, Vol. I. p. 215.

See ATONEMENT, BREAD, DISMEMBERMENT, FLESH OF JESUS, HOMAJUICE, HOST, NU, PARGANYA, PRAGÂPATI, REDEMPTION, REGENERATION, SACRAMENT, SOMA-JUICE, UNEN.

FOOD OF THE GODS :—

A symbol of Wisdom and Love, or Truth and Goodness, as sustenance of the soul's Ideals which grow up from within.

"Come unto me, Lord Hermes, who dost collect the food of Gods and men."—*Magical Papyrus.*

Footnote by Mr. Mead :

"In its highest sense the heavenly food, or Wisdom, the 'super-substantial bread' or 'bread of Life.' "—G. R. S. MEAD, *T. G. Hermes*, Vol. I. p. 86.

"Hermes " signifies the higher mind which collects the spiritual sustenance from above, and the experiences from below.

"'Tis Fire alone, in that it is borne upwards, giveth life ; that which is carried downwards is subservient to Fire. Further, whatever doth descend from the above, begetteth ; what floweth upwards, nourisheth " (The Perfect Sermon).—*Ibid.*, Vol. II. p. 310.

The buddhic vibrations bear the qualities upwards and are the Divine life of the soul. The lower qualities subserve the higher. Truth flowing downwards increases knowledge. Aspiration for Love and Wisdom brings food to the soul.

See AMBROSIA, FIRE, GODS, HERMES, SACRIFICE, USERT.

FOOD FOR MAN :—

A symbol of sustenance for the mind in knowledge and experience gained through the senses and the activities of the lower nature, during lives on earth.

"And take thou unto thee of all food that is eaten, and gather it to thee ; and it shall be for food for thee and for them. Thus did Noah."—GEN. vi. 21.

The "food" which is to be taken is the experience which is to be gathered and appropriated. This is to be, first, for the Self or Individuality (Noah), and, second, for the maintenance of those functions and qualities which are to further the growth of the soul.

See ARK, EXPERIENCES, FEEDING, MAN, MEAT, NOAH.

FOOD FOR THE SOUL :—

A symbol of spiritual sustenance ; truth, wisdom, and love, which enter into the higher emotions, and nourish the soul.

"Of the nourishments brought to the righteous man, the Zaremaya oil ; that is the food, after decease, of a youth of good thoughts, words, deeds, and religion ; that is the food, after decease, for a woman of very good thoughts, words, deeds, well-instructed, ruled by a master and righteous."—*The Hadokht Nask*, HAUG, *Essays.*

The Self within the soul is sustained by Love, the "oil of gladness," the food which satisfies the mind that is growing in grace, i.e. learning to depend on higher things of the Spirit. This love of Truth and Right is the sustenance also of the Wisdom nature (the holy woman) which is instructed only by the Supreme,—the Absolute.

"And he that supplieth seed to the sower and bread for food, shall supply and multiply your seed for sowing, and increase the fruits of your righteousness."—2 COR. ix. 10.

The Supreme from whom cometh the spiritual germs of the higher emotions and faculties to the Soul, and the "bread of heaven,"—truth-goodness,—for the Soul's sustenance, shall bestow and develop the spiritual germs within the qualities, so that the "fruits of the Spirit" shall be increased through the perfecting of the qualities of the Soul.

See BREAD, CORN, LAZARUS, MEAT, OIL, SEED (good), SHEEP, WHEAT.

FOOLS :—

A symbol of the lower minds or personalities entangled in the errors and illusions of sense and desire.

"Fools ! for they have no far-reaching studious thoughts who think that what was not before comes into being or that anything dies and perishes utterly."— *Empedocles*, V. 45, FAIRBANKS.

The lower mind is foolish because it falsely imagines that the unreal can exist of itself, and the Real cease to be.

"Fools dwelling in darkness, wise in their own conceit and puffed up with vain knowledge, go round and round, staggering to and fro, like blind men led by the blind."—*Katha. Upanishad*, II. 5.

The lower mind, full of ignorance, self-esteem and illusion, passes from life to life in the world, buffeted by circumstances, and without true knowledge and wisdom.

See BLIND MAN, FOLLY, MAN (blind), PERSONALITY, PRIESTS AND ELDERS.

FOOT :—

A symbol of lower activities exercised in the course of the progress of the soul.

"Gavest thou the goodly wings unto the peacocks ? or wings and feathers unto the ostrich ? Which leaveth her eggs in the earth, and warmeth them in dust. And forgetteth that the foot may crush them, or that the wild beast may break them."—JOB xxxix. 13–15.

This refers to the state of ignorance and feebleness which the indwelling Self (Job) experiences when involved in matter. Nature is not designed to subserve the desires or the will of man. The external conditions necessitate effort and suffering from which there is no escape. The ambitions (wings) allure, but are not kindly ; they are generated in the lower mind (dust), and in the soul's progress (foot) they may be frustrated, or the unruly desires (beast) may destroy them.

"What is understood by 'foot,' but the passing over of active work ? What is signified by the 'field,' but this world ? Of which the Lord says in the Gospels, ' But the field is the world.' What is expressed by the 'beast,' but the ancient enemy, who lying in wait for the spoils of this world is daily satiated with the death of men ? "—ST. GREGORY, *Morals on the Book of Job*, Vol. III. p. 437.

See FEET, JOB, RIGHT FOOT, SANDAL, WALKING.

FOOT OF HERA (JUNO) :—

A symbol of the lowest part, as it were, of the Wisdom nature, that is, the kama-manasic nature or lower mind—understanding.

FOOTPRINTS :—

A symbol of a succession of the physical forms assumed by the ego during the course of the soul's pilgrimage through the lower life.

See FEET, INCARNATION, RE-INCARNATION.

FOOTPRINTS OF BUDDHA :—

A symbol of the marks of the Self's progress on the pathway to perfection and peace. These marks of spiritual development appear in the successive incarnations of the soul.

See BUDDHA (marks), MARKS OF JESUS.

FOOTSTEPS OF BUDDHA :—

A symbol of the three higher and four lower planes of the universe and soul ; the arena of the Self's activities.

"Unflurried, with the lotus-sign in high relief, far-striding, set down with a stamp,—seven such firm footsteps did Buddha take,—he was like the constellation of the seven rishis."—*Buddha, Karita*, Bk. I. 33.

Of Sattvic energy, with the ideal of spiritual perfection held high before the Self (the soul in involution), with gaze intently set upon the things of the Eternal,—seven firm efforts in succession were then made by Him. These represented the Self's progress through the seven planes of cosmic activity. The "constellation of the seven rishis" symbolically refers to the seven planes of manifestation.

See BUDDHA, GEOMETRY, GUNAS, LOTUS, STRIDES OF SOUL.

FOOTSTEPS IN FOLLOWING A LEADER :—

Significant of obedience to the higher

guidance, through the stages of spiritual progress.

See WASHED THE FEET.

FOREHEAD :—

A symbol of high intelligence. Intellect.

See HEAD.

FORENOON :—

Symbolic of an early stage of the Self's forthgoing.

"In the forenoon Homa came to Zarathustra while he was cleaning around the fire, and chanting the Gathas."— *Homa Yasht*, HAUG, *Essays*.

At an early period of manifestation Divine illumination (Homa) descended upon the Soul (Zarathustra). The "fire cleaning" signifies purification of the sense-nature ; and the "hymn chanting," the raising of the consciousness through meditation.

See FIRE, GATHAS, HOMA, ZORO-ASTER.

FOREST :—

A symbol of meditation in the solitude of the soul ; a subjective state of mind wherein the consciousness is withdrawn from all external attractions into the higher intellect.

"A twice-born Snâtaka, who has thus lived according to the law in the order of householders, may, taking a firm resolution, and keeping his organs in subjection, dwell in the forest."—*Laws of Manu*, VI. 1.

An ego endowed with mind and moral responsibility, who has further completed his incarnations and risen to individuality in the causal-body, may, with steadfast resolve to conform to the Divine will, and controlling completely his mental qualities, withdraw consciously inwards to meditate and progress, free from all external things.

"O Bhârata, what need has a self-controlled man of the forest, and what use is the forest to an uncontrolled man ? Wherever a self-controlled man dwells, that is a forest, that is an hermitage."—*Mahâbhârata, Santiparva*, 5961.

In the name of moral rule (Bhârata) ! what need has a self-controlled mind of limitation of freedom from external attractions, and, on the other hand, of what use is such limitation to an uncontrolled mind ? In whatever environment a self-con-trolled mind is placed, that is freedom for meditation, that is solitude of soul.

"The word 'forest' is used in this district (New Forest) in its primitive sense of a wilderness or uncultivated tract of country."—MABEL COLLINS, *In the New Forest*.

See ASCETIC, ASRAMAS, DESERTS, HOUSEHOLDER, SNÂTAKA, TREES (tall), VITAL AIRS, WILDERNESS OF JUDEA.

FOREST PATHS OF LIFE :—

A symbol of erroneous and inconsistent opinions which mislead the lower mind and obscure the truth.

See LOST (forest).

FORK, FIVE-PRONGED :—

Emblem of the five senses used by the mind in the investigation of phenomena.

See FIVE (number).

FORM AND NAME, WHICH ARE SAID IN THE SCRIPTURES TO BE THE SAME AS MIND AND SPEECH :—

These are symbols of the Ideal and the Actual, or the Archetypal Spirit and its Unfoldment through and from Matter.

"The Brahman then descended again into these worlds by means of these two —Form and Name. . . . As far as there are Form and Name, so far indeed extends this universe. These, indeed, are the two great forces of the Brahman. . . . One of these two is the greater, namely Form ; for whatever is Name, is indeed Form."—*Sata Brâh.*, XI. 2, 3, 3–6.

The Supreme manifests upon the five planes of the universe and the soul by means of these two states of the Divine Life, namely, the Ideal and the Actual. As far extended as there are the Archetypal causes above, so far are the unfolding effects below. These states are the two great manifesting conditions of the Absolute. One of these two is primal and essential, i.e. the Archetypal ; for whatever is in process of evolution is the archetypal unfolding itself.

See CONSCIOUSNESS (vinnana), EVO-LUTION, IGNORANCE, INVOLUTION, MIND, NAME, SPEECH.

FORMS, PHENOMENAL :—

The vehicles or receptacles of Spirit —i.e. the monads of life replete with qualities. The forms are compounded of the matter of the planes, as builded by the monads of form to receive the monads of life.

"And since these things are so, it is necessary to think that in all the objects that are compound there existed many things of all sorts, and germs of all objects, having all sorts of forms and colours and tastes."—*Anaxagoras*, FAIRBANKS, 3. *Anc. Phil. of Greece.*

And as the universe is so appointed of Spirit and Matter, it is reasonable to conclude that in all nature heterogeniety now exists. There is infinite diversity, so that with the material there has been the spiritual involved, and within the spiritual lay primordially the forms (archetypal) of all objects afterwards to actualise. These perfect forms (germs) are complete in "form, colour and taste," that is, in their mental, astral, and physical constituent elements.

"Zoroaster's birth, moreover, is in answer to pious prayers addressed by his father (Pourushaspa) to Homa."—*Zoroaster's Life*, A. V. W. JACKSON.

The Son of God comes forth in the lower nature only when the force (love) aspect of the life below (the father) is directed to the higher channels of manifestation, and as the aspiration of the lower forms of life-expression leads to some consciousness of possible union with a higher nature or Self. All the lower forms of life are thus dimly groping,—they know not how or why,—towards that Reality which is to merge them eventually into Itself, even as the ocean receives into its bosom the several drops which go to swell its boundless whole. The time does arrive, however, when there is this dim consciousness, or reflection of love from Above, in the lower forms of life, and which then takes definite expression of yearning for union with That Reality. This is the stage of preparation when it becomes possible for the Son of God to come forth as he is in his love-nature, when, indeed, all things are drawn upwards, and when no creature, form, or quality, however feeble and faint-hearted, however ignorant and unprogressed, but is made aware of its destiny to unite with the Self of all beings,—

the One Sum-total of all that is,— the outward Embodiment of the Eternal.

"In every object matter and form are to be distinguished, with which correspond, in the Godhead, essence and the divine persons. The form of an object is that which the object is for others; it is the revealing element, and hence the persons of the Trinity are the form of the essence. . . . Form is the individualising principle" (Eckhart).—UEBERWEG, *Hist. of Philos.*, Vol. I. p. 474.

"The Cosmos hath, moreover, been prepared by God, as the receptacle of forms of every kind" ("The Perfect Sermon").—MEAD, *T. G. Hermes*, Vol. II. p. 312.

"Thou who createst light where there was no light, and form, O men! where there was no form, hast been born together with the dawns."—*Rig-Veda*, I. 6, 3.

"The first Light is the creative Will, the efficient faculty, which passes into the Universal Form,—the potentiality to act. Matter is the principle of unity, Form of multiplicity. There is Universal Matter and Form; the former corresponds with unity, and the latter with two-foldness, hence not unity; but the Triad is at the root of all. . . . Creation with Geberol is only the impression of Form in Matter, an impression emanating from the Will. Creation keeps within bounds the Universal Matter and Universal Form. All the rest emanate from these. Creation does not happen in time, but precedes it and is in eternity. . . . Geberol sets forth the Will or Divine Word as the intermediary and bond of the Universal Matter and Form. Yet they also are bound together and exist in the Divine for they were born simultaneously. The Will is one, the Matter and Form two, together the Triad, but they have never been separated."—I. MYER, *Qabbalah*, pp. 153-4.

"Matter and form can only be separated in thought; in logical analysis, but not in fact."—H. M. GWATKIN, *The Knowledge of God*, Vol. I. p. 70.

"Any form the life of the universe takes here is for the sake of the acquisition of qualities which will inhere in the spiritual substance when it has reached its highest degree of manifestation, which will certainly not be on the earth plane. God throws it into a form and withdraws it, throws it into another and withdraws it again, and again, and again, until by its sojourn and experience in form after form, it at length becomes capable of expressing in fullness the highest it contains. The breaking of a form does not matter much; it only means withdrawing the life that indwells it, that it may function through new and higher instrumentalities."—R. J. CAMPBELL, Serm., *The Seeming Waste of Life.*

"The form perishes, but the divine essence that made it is only withdrawn to re-express itself in other and higher forms."—R. J. CAMPBELL, Serm., *God's Use of Time*.

See BALDER, BIRTH OF ZOROASTER, COLOURS, COSMOS, CREATION, EVOLUTION, FATHER (lower), GERMS, HOMA, INVOLUTION, MATTER, MITHRAS, MONAD (form, life), POURUSHASPA, PROTOTYPES, SEEDS, SON OF GOD, SPERMATIC WORDS, SPIRIT, TRIAD, TRINITY.

FORTRESS OR ROCK :—

A symbol of the Higher Self seated in the causal-body.

"And David said, the Lord is my rock and my fortress, and my deliverer."—2 SAM. xxii. 2.

See DAVID, ROCK, STONE.

FORTUNATE CONJUNCTION :—

A symbol of initiation, that is, a junction effected between higher and lower on any plane. It indicates attainment of power over that which is below.

See CONJUNCTION, INITIATIONS, WALKS.

FORTY, NUMBER :—

Symbolic of completion of a process on the four lower planes. *Ten* signifying accomplishment, and *four* the quaternary. $4 \times 10 = 40$.

"How, then, is work perfected in the number forty? The reason, it may be, is because the Law was given in ten precepts, and was to be preached throughout the whole world : which whole world, we are to mark, is made up of four quarters, east and west, south and north, whence the number ten, multiplied by four, comes to forty. . . . Certain it is, however, that in the number forty a certain perfection in good works is signified, which good works are most of all practised by a kind of abstinence from unlawful lusts of the world, that is, by fasting in a general sense."—AUGUSTINE, *Gospel of John*, Vol. I. p. 240.

"The number forty is expressive of a period of probation or trial. The Israelites wandered forty years in the wilderness, and forty years of bondage they also had to serve under the hard yoke of the Philistines. Moses was forty days on the mount of Sinai. Elijah was in hiding forty days. For forty days the deluge fell, and for yet another forty days Noah was shut within the ark. The men of Nineveh had a like period of probation under the preaching of Jonah. The fasting of our Lord in the wilderness again was for forty days."—F. E. HULME, *Symbolism*, etc., p. 15.

See EXODUS, GNOSIS, RAIN (deluge), TEMPTATION.

FORTY DAYS OR YEARS :—

Symbolic of transitory conditions on the lower planes attending the accomplishment of the pilgrimage of the soul through a process and period.

"After the number of the days in which ye spied out the land, even forty days, for every day a year, shall ye bear your iniquities, even forty years, and ye shall know my alienation."—NUM. xiv. 34.

The disciplined qualities (the spies) were unable to make the lower qualities (the Israelites) understand the higher nature. The lower qualities had to go through to the full with their experience of the lower life of suffering and trouble, in order to develop within them the capacity to appreciate higher things. Then they should know how it was that the Ideal was hidden from them.

See EGYPTIANS, EXODUS, PARABLE.

FORTY DAYS AND NIGHTS :—

A complete series of re-incarnations in a stage or period of the soul's evolution. These re-incarnations are transitory conditions on the lower planes.

"For yet seven days, and I will cause it to rain upon the earth forty days and forty nights ; and every living thing that I have made will I destroy from off the face of the ground."—GEN. vii. 4.

"Yet seven days,"—a numerical period which signifies completeness of a stage of activity. A flood of truth (rain) is to descend and envelop the lower nature. This outpouring from above is to last "forty days and nights," meaning a period which corresponds to a term of the re-incarnating cycle. The lower nature at this stage is to be transformed, that is, raised and purified ; hence it will no longer exist as heretofore, but pass away.

See FACE OF GROUND, RAIN (deluge), RE-INCARNATION, WILDERNESS.

FORTY-TWO AND FORTY-NINE :—

Forty-two is the number which implies perfection upon the *lower planes,*—6 × 7 = 42. **Increase this number by seven, and there results the number forty-nine,—7 × 7 = 49, —which is the Christ number signifying perfection on the higher planes.**

FOUNTAIN OF WATER :—

A symbol of the source of Life, as an outpouring of Truth from above.

"Truth is compared in Scripture to a streaming fountain : if her waters flow not in a *perpetual* progression, they sink into the muddy pool of conformity and tradition."—JOHN MILTON, *Areopagitica,* Scott's Lib. Ed., p. 31.

"For with thee (O God) is the fountain of life ; in thy light shall we see light."— Ps. xxxvi. 9.

"The law of the wise is a fountain of life, to depart from the snares of death." —PROV. xiii. 14.

The law of Truth brings eternal life to the aspiring qualities.

"The fountain is treated as a living thing, those properties of its waters which we call natural are regarded as manifestations of a divine life, and the source itself is honoured as a divine being."—W. R. SMITH, *Religion of the Semites,* p. 184.

"I was set up from everlasting, from the beginning, or ever the earth was. When there were no depths, I was brought forth ; when there were no fountains abounding with water."— PROV. viii. 23, 24.

The Higher Self was, is, and shall be,—and existed before the lower nature. Prior to the reflection of the Self in the lower nature,—astrophysical,—(the depths), the Self had emanated from the Supreme. The Self existed before the Truth was declared.

"The fountain that rises in my heart can only spring up heavenward, because the water of it flowed down into my heart from the higher level. All love must descend first, before it can ascend." —A. MACLAREN, *Sermons, 1st Series,* p. 190.

See ANDUISUR, AQUARIUS, WATER, WELL, WHITE.

FOUNTAINS OF THE DEEP :—

Symbolic of sources of error (" the water below ") which produce illusions in the lower self. These are astral and lower mental.

"The fountains also of the deep and the windows of heaven were stopped, and the rain from heaven was restrained." —GEN. viii. 2.

The Divine power having energised the mental vehicle, the sources of error are diminished, as also are the spiritual perceptions (windows). The Self as downpouring truth (rain) withdraws from itself below.

"When he made firm the skies above : when the fountains of the deep became strong."—PROV. viii. 28.

When the buddhic principle was established and centralised : when the desires of the astral plane became active.

See DEEP, FLOOD, RAIN, WINDOWS OF HEAVEN, WATER.

FOUR, NUMBER :—

This is a number significant of system and order ; and so there are to be found in the universe and soul many arrangements in sets of fours, which sets have relations in correspondence with each other and binding them together.

"They that venerate the number Four do not ill to teach that by reason of this number every body has its origin. . . . The number four, after having carried Nature forward up to completing a body and producing double bulk and resistance has yet left it deficient in the most important article (Olympus)." PLUTARCH, *On the E at Delphi,* § 13.

This statement is to indicate that the number four applies rather to the natural order of things, the quaternary, and does not include the spiritual (Olympus).

"Four is symbolic of the world, and nature, and of man by nature."—J. GARNIER, *The Worship of the Dead,* p. 220.

See BACABS, CASTES, CHILDREN OF HORUS, CLASSES, ELEMENTS, IRON PLATE, JOB, MINISTERS, OLYMPUS, PILLARS (four), QUARTERS, QUATERNARY, WINDS (four).

FOUR ANGLES OR CORNERS OF THE WORLD :—

A symbol of the quaternary. The four planes,—buddhic, mental, astral, and physical.—*See* REV. vii. 1.

See FIRMAMENT, IRON PLATE, SWASTIKA, WINDS (four).

FOUR BEINGS AT THE CARDINAL POINTS :—

A symbol of the four vehicles of the soul, namely, the buddhic, the higher mental, the astral, and the physical.

"Four other human beings were made at the four points of the compass, each of whom flew to the spot from a different quarter (when the golden-coloured personage disappeared)."—KIDD, *China*, p. 167.

These four other beings are the vehicles of the World-soul on the several planes of manifestation. The specification of the points of the compass has reference to the polarities of opposite conditions or activities, which are respectively signified. The disappearance of the radiant Light and Life signifies the unobserved descent of Spirit into Matter.

"The gods with long, flowing hair are the four children of Horus, Mestha, Hapi, Tuamutef and Qebhsennuf, each of whom wore a lock or tress of hair, which became a pillar-sceptre, and supported one of the four corners of heaven; these four gods became at a later period the gods of the cardinal points and the lords of the four quarters of heaven."— BUDGE, *Gods of the Egyptians*, Vol. I. p. 210.

"Foursquare; that whose length and breadth are equal. The foursquare form of the altar and new Jerusalem figures out the stability and self-consistence of Christ and his church, EXOD. xxvii. 1, REV. xxi. 16."—W. GURNEY, *Dict. of Bible*, p. 183.

See BACABS, CEILING, CHILDREN OF HORUS, CHURCH OF FOUR QUARTERS, ELEMENTS, FIRMAMENT, LADDER, QUARTERS.

FOUR DAYS :—

A period which corresponds with the condition arrived at on four planes or four sub-planes.

"So when Jesus came, he found that Lazarus had been in the tomb four days already."—JOHN xi. 17.

When the Higher Self began to manifest in the soul, he perceived the inert condition of the causal-body (Lazarus) on the fourth mental sub-plane.

See LAZARUS, TOMB.

FOUR ELEMENTS :—

See ELEMENTS.

FOUR GOSPELS :—

Significant of four points of view in beholding truths of the soul's evolution from the lower nature.

See GOSPELS.

FOUR SEASONS, OR WORLD PERIODS :—

These four periods signify correspondences between the microcosm and the macrocosm ; — spring, summer, autumn and winter, within which seasons, which relate to the buddhic, mental, astral, and physical planes, human evolution is accomplished.

See MACROCOSM, MICROCOSM, SEASONS.

FOUR TIMES TALLER THAN MAN, WAS PWAN-KOO :—

This statement refers to the fact that the potential measure of the human soul comprehends the five planes of its being, upon four of which it has not yet become conscious. The Logos (Pwan-koo) manifests on the five planes.

See DESERTS, HEIGHT OF OSIRIS, PWAN-KOO, WORLDS (five).

FOUR YEARS OF AGE :—

This period signifies four cycles, four rounds, four globe-periods, or four races, according to context.

See GOLDEN AGE, IRON AGE, RACES, ROOT RACES, ROUNDS.

FOWLS OF THE AIR :—

Symbol of aspirations which rise in the mind (air).

See BIRDS, FISH.

FOXES HAVE HOLES :—

A metaphor of the lower personality which has places of shelter, such as associations, creeds, cults, sects, coteries, etc., which protect and preserve it from change.

"And Jesus saith unto him, The foxes have holes, and the birds of the air have nests ; but the Son of man hath not where to lay his head."—MAT. viii. 20.

This symbolism shows that the "foxes and birds," which stand for types of the lower personality, have places for mental retreat, but that the spiritual ego (Son of man) must go forth, steadfastly purposed to keep his mind alert and his vehicles responsive to whatever demands may be made upon them.

"We may venture to apply Christ's words to this subject (of man's dissatisfaction and unrest), 'The foxes have holes, and the birds of the air have nests, but' man 'has not where to lay his head.' If he could rest, he could not grow. And so from generation to generation, for the individual and for the species, the condition of our progress is a distance beckoning us, and a feeling that we have not already attained, neither are already perfect."—A. MACLAREN, *Sermons, 2nd Series*, p. 43.

See HEAD, JESUS (son of man), PERSONALITY, PHARISEES, SON OF MAN.

FRANANGER WATERFALL :—

A symbol of the astral plane and its activities energised.

See NET OF ASAR, WATER (lower).

FRANKINCENSE :—

A symbol of wisdom, or metaphysical knowledge, which purifies the mind and renders it fragrant.

See GOLD, ETC., INCENSE, MAGI, TREASURES OF CAVE.

FRANKINCENSE AND MYRRH BROUGHT BY ANGELS :—

Symbolic of purity, grace and truth, and peace and bliss, conveyed to the soul by the inner messengers of the Spirit.

"Frankincense denotes internal truth, myrrh external or sensual truth."— SWEDENBORG, *Arc. Cel.*, n. 10, 252.

"After Adam and Eve leave the Garden of Eden, then at God's command, gold, frankincense and myrrh are brought to them by angels."—*The Book of Adam.*

See GOLD, FRANKINCENSE, ETC., TREASURES OF CAVE.

FRAVAK AND FRAVAKAIN :—

Symbols of two astral centres established in the early evolution of the soul.

"Of those seven pairs one was Siamak, the name of the man, and Nasak, of the woman ; and from them a pair was born, whose names were Fravak of the man, and Fravakain of the woman."— *The Bundahis*, Ch. XV. 25.—*S.B. of E.*

Of the seven pairs of opposites, which are active and passive aspects of the several emotional and mental qualities,—one pair was produced which was typical of the Life and Form side of manifest being ; and from these two were begotten two astral centres. These centres are given as masculine and feminine because one actively transmits physical outer vibrations astrally, and the other passively interprets mental vibrations astrally. So that one acts outwards, and the other receives inwards ; vibrations objective and subjective respectively.

See BRIDGES (nine), OPPOSITES, SIAMAK.

FRAVASHI OF ORMAZD :—

A designation signifying the Divine Monad or spiritual Prototype in its dual aspect.

"Even Ormazd has his Fravashi in relation to Zerāna-Akerana."— *Zoroastrian System*, J. F. CLARKE.

On the highest plane the Divine Being is said to bear under its dual aspects of Spirit and Matter a similar relationship to Itself (Absolute) as the lower manifestations bear to each other. The relationship of life and form.

See ABSOLUTE, HEAVEN AND EARTH, MONAD, SPARK, ZERANA.

FRAVASHI, OR IDEAL IMAGE, OF ZOROASTER :—

This "ideal image" is the Archetypal Man which is "Adonai of the Heavens." It is the prototype of the individual human souls.

See ARC. MAN, GLORY, IMAGE, MACROCOSM, ZOROASTER.

FRAVASHIS, FRAVAHAR, OR FEREUERS :—

These are the monads of life and form which become linked in the forms or bodies containing them ; the monads of life being born into the forms prepared to receive them.

"Ormazd began the creation by bringing forth the Fravashis. Everything which has been created, or which is to be created, has its Fravashi, which contains the reason and basis of its existence."—*Zoroastrian System.*

The Divine Will commences the task of creation by brooding over the Monad which is within all separate existences. For every single existent entity has its purpose and use, its intelligence or ideal mental character, and its form, or ideal astral character, to entitle it to its separate identity. The monads of life and form have many names in the different sacred scriptures of the world. They represent the inner intelligent forces of which the outer qualities and forms are the expression on the lower planes. They are the ideal prototypes on the higher planes.

See AGNISHWATTAS, BODHISATVAS, CREATION, GARODMAN, GLORY, GUARDIAN SPIRITS, HIGHER AND LOWER WORLDS, HOM, INCARNATION, MANASAPUTRAS, MARUTS, MITHRAS, MONAD (life, form), MUSPELL (sons),

PACCEKA-BUDDHAS, PITRIS (solar, lunar), PROTOTYPES, SONS OF GOD, SPARKS, SPERMATIC WORDS.

FRAZISHTO THE DEMON :—

A symbol of an allurement of sensation deadening spiritual activity.

FREDUN :—

See THRAETONA.

FREJA, FRIEJA, FREYA, OR FREYJA, WIFE OF HODER :—

Symbol of the receptive, organised astral principle.

"Freyja's dwelling is named Folkrangr, the plains on which the folk troop together."—GRIMM, *Teutonic Mythology*, Vol. I. p. 305.

The astral plane is the plane of the lower qualities (the folk),—the desires, instincts, and passions, which are allied together.

See HODER.

FREQUENTED HOUSE :—

See HOUSE.

FRIENDS, AND FOES :—

Symbols of the higher emotions and the lower desires.

See GEMS (strings), MAN, RELATIVES, STEWARD (unjust).

FRIENDS' HOUSES :—

These are the connections which are established on the mental subplanes between the centres of the mental mechanism, to allow of the organising of the functioning by the Devas (friends) and the transmission of higher emotions.

See HOUSES (friends).

FRIGG, OR FRIKKA, WIFE OF ODIN :—

A symbol of Wisdom, the principle of Buddhi, allied with the Self.

"Frigg, the daughter of Fiorgynn (he of the mountain top), as consort of the highest god takes rank above all other goddesses : she knows the fate of men, she presides over marriages."—GRIMM, *Teutonic Mythology*, Vol. I. p. 304.

The Wisdom-nature proceeds from the Supreme, and is allied with the Love-nature of the Self. Through Wisdom the mental qualities (men) are purified and transmuted, in order that in the risen and glorified souls the marriage of Wisdom and Love shall be celebrated.

See DEATH OF BALDER, FENSAL, HERMOD, MARRIAGE, MISTLETOE, OLYMPUS, WISDOM.

FROST ; ICE ; SNOW :—

Symbolic of matter which in itself is lifeless, solid, and inert. A state of latency.

"Everything wept for Balder, men, animals, the earth, stones, trees, and all metals, even as thou hast seen everything weep when it comes forth from the frost into the warm air."—*Story of Balder, Prose Edda.*—HOWITT, *Litera.*

Within the entire nature of the soul the craving for liberation is manifest as the triumph of the Christ (Balder) approaches. The statement indicates the suffering of the lower nature from the outer aspect, through the shattering of the forms wherein the life is encased. The change from dry frost to moisture is a symbol of the relatively inert condition of congelation changing to that which is mobile and volatile. The contraction and holding is symbolic of matter. The expansion and allowing of escape is symbolic of spirit.

See BALDER, ICE, RIMTHURSAR, SNOW, SUMMER (unfruitful), THOCK.

FRUCTIFYING PRINCIPLE :—

A symbol of the Divine life within the lower nature embodied through the process of involution.

"The Golden Personage cried out :— 'The wings have long embraced you ; on the breaking forth of the fructifying principle, I knew that you (an intelligent being) had entered into the world.' "—KIDD, *China*, p. 167.

The Spirit energises the monad within, and now from below the sense of aspiration (wings) is apprehended, so that it seeks to evolve its nature. Thus from the liberation of the life within, through response to the impacts from without, the consciousness of the ego is evoked.

See ELEMENTS, INCARNATION, INVOLUTION, WINGS.

FRUIT :—

A symbol of results of action,— good and bad. Effect of the operation of the law of karma,—moral causation,—in the soul's progress.

"I the Lord search the heart, I try the reins, even to give every man accord-

ing to his ways, according to the fruit
of his doings."—JER. xvii. 10.

"Say ye the righteous, that it shall
be well with him : for they shall eat the
fruit of their doings. Woe unto the
wicked ! it shall be ill with him : for
the reward of his hands shall be given
him."—Is. iii. 10, 11.

To every mental quality (man)
shall accrue the due result of its activity
in well or ill doing.

See KARMA.

FRUIT OF THE SPIRIT, OR OF THE TREE OF LIFE :—

**Symbolic of the higher emotions
and faculties of the buddhic nature;
the produce of Wisdom (buddhi)
laid up for the soul when perfected.**

"But the fruit of the Spirit is love,
joy, peace, longsuffering, kindness, goodness, faithfulness, meekness, temperance :
against such there is no law."—GAL. v.
22, 23.

The transmutations of the mental
qualities through the operation of
Buddhi, the Holy Spirit, produce the
higher emotions,—love of truth and
right, peace, patience, kindness, steadfastness, fortitude, faith, hope, compassion, moral courage, justice, gentleness, etc. The buddhic emotions in
perfection are the "treasure in
heaven," "the inheritance of the
saints," the fruit of experience and
aspiration below.

"And on this side of the river and on
that was the tree of life, bearing twelve
manner of fruits, yielding its fruit every
month : and the leaves of the tree
were for the healing of the nations."—
REV. xxii. 2.

The "river" of the water of truth
encompasseth the "tree" of the out-
growing Divine life. The "twelve
manner of fruits" signifies twelve
kinds of virtues or higher emotions.
The "month" refers to a period
within a cycle, or a stage of progress.
The outspringing Divine life (the
"leaves") is for the perfecting of
the organised qualities of the soul.

See CAKE (sacrificial), HEIR, LIGHT-
TREASURE, MENAT, MERCHANDISE,
PEACHES, SHEWBREAD, TREASURE,
TREE OF LIFE.

FRUIT OF THE GROUND :—

**Symbolic of the sensations or sense-
nature of the lower nature.**

"And in process of time it came to
pass, that Cain brought of the fruit of
the ground an offering unto the Lord."—
GEN. iv. 3.

And as evolution proceeds, the
sensation nature has to be subordinated by the personality to the ends
it has in view.

See ABEL, CAIN, GROUND.

FRUIT-TREE BEARING FRUIT AND SEED :—

**A symbol of the law of karma linking
life with form, and the potencies
within, which are ready to unfold.**

"And God said, Behold, I have given
you every herb yielding seed, which is
upon the face of all the earth, and every
tree, in which is the fruit of a tree
yielding seed; to you it shall be for
meat."—GEN. i. 29.

And the Supreme acquaints the
Soul with the fact that it has contained within it that which will
enable it to unfold, and thus expand
its own nature. This unfolding must
proceed through the lower nature
(earth). And every emotion which
(as seed) is capable of becoming
exalted, and which can be the means
of affording growth to the soul,—to
the soul it shall serve as sustenance.

See EARTH, FACE, KARMA, MEAT,
PLANT, SEED (good), SEEDS OF FOODS.

FRUIT OF THE TREE OF KNOW-LEDGE OF GOOD AND EVIL :—

**A symbol of experience acquired
through the activities of the lower
nature and the development of the
moral nature.**

See EXPERIENCE, LAW OF ZORO-
ASTER, TREE OF KNOWLEDGE.

FRUITFUL CROP :—

**Signifying that from the functioning
of the lower nature there is produced
a goodly array of the higher qualities
through spiritual cultivation.**—*See*
HEB. xii. 11.

See AGRICULTURE, CULTIVATION,
HARVEST, REAPING, SEED.

FUDO, GOD OF FIRE :—

**A symbol of the Higher Self (atma-
buddhi).**

"A Japanese Buddhist deity, worshipped as a god of fire. He sits, stern
and 'immovable,' surrounded with
flames, and holding a two-edged sword
and a rope; the latter he uses like
some of the Indian gods to restrain the
wicked. The flames are interpreted as
symbols of wisdom, of which he is also

said to be a god (Murray)."—*Non-classical Mythology*, p. 71.

The "fire" and "flames" signify the buddhic plane, the plane of Wisdom. The "sword" is a symbol of the Divine Will exercised as spiritual force to dispel ignorance and evil. The "rope" indicates the buddhic functioning for the transmutation of the lower qualities into the higher. The "wicked" are the lower desires which must be overcome and cast out of the soul. The lower qualities have to be purified by the spirit (fire) within them, so that the higher may evolve through them.

See AGNI, ARDEBEHESCHT, FIRE, FLAME, GIRDLE ROPE, SWORD.

FUGITIVE AND WANDERER :—

A symbol of the ego or soul, separated apparently from its spiritual source and undergoing a series of transient terrestrial incarnations.

"Behold thou hast driven me (Cain) out this day from the face of the ground ; and from thy face shall I be hid ; and I shall be a fugitive and wanderer in the earth ; and it shall come to pass, that whosoever findeth me shall slay me."—GEN. iv. 14.

The ego, as the lower self, is brought to realise that it may no longer depend upon the lower knowledge for soul-subsistence, and it cannot tell where it shall seek for food convenient for its needs. Evolving from the lower nature, it does not yet know the Higher Self or source of its spiritual inspiration. It nevertheless sees that it must necessarily become a "fugitive and wanderer," condemned to traverse a series of terrestrial incarnations, each of which is but temporary. And the ego fears that it shall lose its identity, knowing that it is at the mercy of higher stages of growth which (practically as with animals) admit of its extinction as individual continuity of consciousness, at successive periods.

"There is an utterance of Necessity, an ancient decree of the gods, eternal, sealed fast with broad oaths : whenever anyone defiles his body sinfully with bloody gore or perjures himself in regard to wrong-doing, one of those spirits who are heir to long life, thrice ten thousand seasons shall he wander apart from the blessed, being born meantime in all sorts of mortal forms, changing one

bitter path of life for another. For mighty Air pursues him Seaward, and Sea spews him forth on the threshold of Earth, and Earth casts him into the rays of the unwearying Sun, and Sun into the eddies of Air ; one receives him from the other, and all hate him. One of these now am I too, a fugitive from the gods and a wanderer, at the mercy of raging Strife."—*Empedocles*, FAIRBANKS, 369.

There is an indwelling inspiration of the Divine nature expressing itself in conscience, which is adapted to interpret to the inner soul, by way of experience under karmic law, the spiritual Truth underlying evolution. The Truth is then perceived through appearance or the falsity of the form-side of nature ; or is seen in the mayavic reflection below of things above ; or is recognised whenever an effort is made to transcend the limits of the form of thought.

One of those spirits,—a monad, or ego, which inherits the eternal impress through its cyclic evolution, is separated from primordial perfection (the blessed) during the process of manifestation, being successively embodied in terrestrial forms of different kinds, exchanging one more or less hard and bitter pathway of life for another. For the Divine Mind (mighty Air) emanates the soul on the mental plane, and precipitates it to the astral plane, and the astral principle (Sea), as it were, forces the soul on to the physical plane. [That is, the functioning of the desire-principle,— which is the inverted reflection of the love-nature of the soul,—is the means of directing the physical vehicle through which the ego works ; and thus the consciousness is drawn to the physical brain and nervous system]. Then the physical (earth) activity is the means of bringing the soul upward to the Higher Self (the Sun) ; and thus is the ego brought to self-consciousness on the mental plane. From plane to plane of nature, growth towards perfection is accomplished ; and upon no one level is the pilgrim soul at home or at peace.

Such an ego am I ; as it were, a fugitive,—a wanderer,—passing from life to life, cut off seemingly from the Divine source of my being,—the inner Self of all,—and in sorrow and suffering immersed in error and conflict.

See ÆTHER, ATOM (permanent), CAIN, EARTH, FACE, GROUND, INCARNATION, PERSONALITY, PILGRIM, REINCARNATION, SEA, SHEEP (lost), SOSHYANTS, STRIFE, WANDERERS, WAYFARING MEN.

FŪH-HE, OR TAE-HAOU :—

Symbol of the Logos.

"Tae-haou was also called Fūh-he or Paou-he 'the Sacrificer.' The tradition is that he had no father, was the first to reign, and that his name was *Fung*, meaning wind, spirit, breath."—KIDD, *China*, p. 103.

Under this aspect of the going forth to manifest, the Logos is said to have been the "sacrifice" and the "sacrificer,"—that which offers Self-limitation to Itself, or is limited and offered up to the Absolute, for the sake of Its universe. It is mentally received that the Supreme is Self-derived, not begotten nor created, but Self-existent. The terms Word, Wind, Spirit, and Breath are all symbols of emanation,—to which the forth-pouring from the Absolute is comparable.

"You and I are here, and the whole cosmos of which we are a part exists in order that God may be able to express that which he eternally is. There are some things impossible even to omnipotence, and one of them is that love's fullest resources should ever be able to declare themselves apart from sacrifice or that good, as good, could rightly be called such if it had never been thrown upon the dark background of evil. I do not mean to suggest that God, the eternal reality, does not eternally know himself to be essentially goodness and love ; I only say that if he is to live it, he cannot do so on any other terms than I have just stated ; it is a necessity written in the very nature of things. . . . Understand what you are. You are one means whereby the eternal declares itself, brings into manifestation its latent wealth of ideal good. In fact, you yourself *are* the eternal in one of its manifold aspects. That which is essential to your being has neither beginning nor end ; it eternally is—in God. It is foolish to speak of life as though it were eternal only in one direction—the future."—R. J. CAMPBELL, Serm., *Solidarity of Spiritual Experience*.

See ABSOLUTE, ANIMALS, BEASTS (wild), BREATH, CREATION, INCARNA-

TION, LAMB, NET, PASTORAL, SACRIFICER, SPIRIT, TEZCATLIPOCA, TABLES.

FULFILLING THE LAW WITH LOVE :—

This signifies the functioning of the higher intellect which supersedes the lower and intuitively perceives the Divine Truth, Love, and Wisdom.

"He that loveth his neighbour hath fulfilled the law."—ROM. xiii. 8.

The quality in harmony with its compeers hath risen from the lower levels to the higher.

See LAW OF ZOROASTER, WOOD (holy).

FUNERAL-PILES OF THE DEAD BURNING :—

Symbolic of the lower mental qualities dissolved and superseded.

"Apollo afterwards despatching a pointed arrow against the Greeks themselves he smote them, and frequent funeral-piles of the dead were continually burning."—*Iliad*, Bk. I.

But afterwards the lower mental qualities (Greeks) are stirred and rendered impotent, the Divine Will ("shaft of the Spirit") being called into play ; and the while, the lower aspects of the Self, being effete at this stage, were outgrown and dissipated.

See ARROWS (divine), BURNING, CREMATION, FIRE, GREEKS, KABANDHA, MAN (natural), PESTILENCE, WRATH OF APOLLO.

FURNACE :—

A symbol of the functioning of buddhi in the purifying of the qualities. This is reflected on the lower planes in the suffering and sorrow which accompany the process.

"The Lord hath taken you, and brought you forth out of the iron furnace, out of Egypt, to be unto him a people of inheritance, as at this day."—DEUT. iv. 20.

"The Lord, whose fire is in Zion, and his furnace in Jerusalem."—Is. xxxi. 9.

"And shall cast them (the wicked) into the furnace of fire : there shall be the weeping and gnashing of teeth."—MAT. xiii. 50.

The qualities on the astro-mental plane of conflict (Egypt) have undergone the discipline necessary to prepare them for an influx of spirit which shall raise them. The purifying buddhic functioning is in the higher nature (Zion and Jerusalem). The lower qualities (the wicked) shall be subjected to the purifying discipline of the Spirit, and their lower astral conditions shall be dissolved.

"St. Catherine of Genoa, 'as she plunged in the divine furnace of purifying love, was united to the Object of her love, and satisfied with all he wrought in her, so she understood it to be with the souls in Purgatory ? This 'divine furnace of purifying love' demands from the ardent soul not only a complete self-surrender and voluntary turning from all impurity, a humility of the most far-reaching kind, but also a deliberate active suffering, a self-discipline in dreadful tasks. As gold in the refiner's fire, so 'burning of love into a soul truly taken all vices purgeth.'"—EVELYN UNDERHILL, *Mysticism*, p. 266.

See BUDDHI, EGYPT, FIRE OF HELL, FIRE (destroying), HADES, HELL, JERUSALEM, MAN (bad), PURGATORY, TEETH (gnashing), ZION.

FURROWS IN PLOUGHED EARTH :—

This emblem signifies the lower nature (earth) prepared by the operation of the Spirit (the husbandman) to yield the higher emotions (fruit) from the germination and growth of the seed (centres of spirit) sown in it.

"The river of God is full of water : thou providest them corn, when thou hast so prepared the earth. Thou waterest her furrows abundantly ; thou settlest the ridges thereof : thou makest it soft with showers ; thou blessest the springing thereof."—Ps. lxv. 9, 10.

Life and Truth suffice for the growth of the soul. The qualities are endowed with the spiritual germ (corn) when the lower nature is ready to receive it. Truth is bestowed on the disciplined lower nature, and aspirations (ridges) are fostered from above. Truth (showers) makes the lower nature pervious to spirit, and the Divine grace ensures the springing up of the higher emotions.

"The wife of Rama was called Sīta because not born from a woman, but from a furrow (sīta) while Janaka (the king) was ploughing."

"Sīta is Lakshmi."—MON. WILLIAMS, *Indian Wisdom*, pp. 348, 360.

"I (Lakshmi) reside . . . in earth recently thrown up."—*Institutes of Vishnu*, XCIX. 13.

Lakshmi, like all other great god-

desses, is a symbol of buddhi—the wisdom nature. Buddhi is the fount of the higher emotions. Sīta stands for the higher emotion nature which is the manifestation of buddhi in the human soul. Hence Sīta (buddhi actual) is born in a "furrow," and Lakshmi (buddhi potential) resides in the *ridges* of earth thrown up.

See ERECTHEUS, GROUND RIDGES, LAKSHMI, RIDGES, SĪTA.

FUTSU-NUSHI :—

See TAKE-MIKA.

FYLLA RECEIVES A GOLD RING FROM NANNA :—

This symbolises that at an advanced soul-state Wisdom (Nanna) yields the sense of dominion over the lower planes to illusion (Fylla), which signifies the consciousness of escaping from desire.

See BALDER, DROPNER, NANNA, RING (gold).

GABBATHA, THE PAVEMENT :—

A symbol of a careless general state of mind towards spiritual things.

"When Pilate therefore heard these words, he brought Jesus out, and sat down on the judgment-seat at a place called The Pavement, but in Hebrew, Gabbatha." JOHN xix. 13.

"Pilate" represents a mental state wavering between allegiance to the higher or the lower, but falling in with prevalent opinion. His "sitting down to judgment" signifies his acquiescence in the general attitude taken by the mental qualities and constitution,—an easy-going spirit widely spread.

See ASSEMBLY, PILATE, TRIAL.

GABRIEL, THE ANGEL :—

An inner messenger from the higher planes ;—the bringer of good tidings—a sense of joy at conceiving a higher element in the soul.

See ANGELS, ARCHANGELS, DEVAS, LOTE-TREE.

GADERINE DEMONIACS :—

Symbolic of unbalanced mental conditions at a very early stage of evolution. These having had some glimpses of truth and higher emotion presented to them, had rejected the higher light, not being ready to receive it. These low conditions were doomed to extinction in the soul, as fuller mentality evolved.

See GIANTS, NEPHILIM.

GAGATI METRE :—

A symbol of the mental plane in relation to the rate of vibration in the atoms of mental matter.

GALAXY :—

See CROSS (ankh).

GALE FROM APOLLO :—

A symbol of the action of the higher mind on the lower.

"And Apollo the Fardarter sent the Achaians a favouring gale."—*Iliad*, Bk. I.

And the Higher Self wafted the mental qualities inward by the "breath," or life influence, of the mind.

See APOLLO, BREATH (divine), CAMP, WIND (strong).

GALES ; BLASTS OF WIND BLOWING DOWN CROPS :—

Symbolic of diverse erroneous doctrines and opinions of the lower mind, which proceed from prevalent illusions, and which stifle the growth of the higher emotions.

"Thou shalt break the power of untiring gales which, rising against the earth, blow down the crops and destroy them ; and again, whenever thou wilt, thou shall bring their blasts back ; and thou shalt bring seasonable drought out of dark storm for men, and out of summer drought thou shalt bring streams pouring down from heaven to nurture the trees ; and thou shalt lead out of Hades the spirit of a man that is dead."—*Empedocles*, Bk. I. 24 FAIRBANKS.

The Self shall overcome the winds of doctrine which arise and, striking the lower self (earth), destroy the sprouting emotions. And, moreover, the Self shall recall such doctrines. And the Self shall turn the falsity of the lower planes into relative truth for the mind's sustenance, and from the mind's ignorance enable it to know. And from the spiritual effects of the Higher Self upon the personality shall proceed the truth which shall serve to enable the qualities to be raised. And from the lower planes, the under-world, the relatively dead self,—the lower mind (man) or lower personality,—shall be led upward to the light.

See CORPSE, CROPS, HADES, RAIN, STORMS, TAWHIRI, TREES (tall).

GALILEE :—

A state of advance in the environment of the ego, or the conditions of the soul,—implying progress.

"But after I (Jesus) am raised up, I will go before you into Galilee."—MAT. xxvi. 32.

When the perfected lower nature (Jesus) awakes transfigured on a higher plane, it will enable the disciplined qualities to follow in His steps. It is the Risen Christ who would appear when they had advanced to "Galilee,"—a symbol signifying a state of looking forward, and a commencement of the diligent quest of Christhood.

"Galilee, that is, Contemplation ; Galilee is as much as to say, Whiteness. Whiteness is a colour full of material light, more so than any other ; and thus, Contemplation is more full of Spiritual light than any other thing which is below."—DANTE ALIGHIERI, *The Banquet*, IV. 22.

"The complete resurrection will begin in Galilee" (Zohar).—A. E. WAITE, *Secret Doctrine in Israel*, p. 187.

"We may regard 'Galilee' as a symbol of that moral realm in which we enjoy the liberty wherewith Christ makes us free, and are no longer in bondage to Law and Egyptian fleshliness."—E. GOUGH, *Barrowford Treatise*, p. 53.

See NAZARETH.

GALL :—

Symbolic of a sensuous gratification which would appear nauseous to the higher nature.

"They gave me also gall for my meat ; and in my thirst they gave me vinegar to drink."—Ps. lxix. 21.

The lower qualities, "enemies" of the higher, offer the soul the pleasures of the life of the senses to satisfy its cravings for goodness and peace ; and to its thirst for Truth, they offer ignorance which brings sorrow and strife. Not by indulgences from without can the soul be nourished and satisfied.

"I see that thou art in the gall of bitterness and in the bond of iniquity."—ACTS viii. 23.

"They gave him wine to drink mingled with gall : and when he had tasted it, he would not drink."—MAT. xxvii. 34.

See COW'S URINE, BITTER, VINEGAR.

GANDHARVAS, OR SIRENS :—

Symbols of Devas of the buddhic

plane, which assist in establishing harmony in the soul through the æsthetic emotions.

See ANGELS, COLCHIANS, DEVAS, HEAVENLY NYMPHS, SIRENS.

GANESA, GOD OF WISDOM :—

A symbol of atma-buddhi-manas, or the Higher Life.

"Praise to thee, O Ganesa. Thou art manifestly the truth; Thou art undoubtedly the Creator, Preserver, and Destroyer, the Supreme Brahma, the eternal Spirit. . . . By thee was this universe manifested; for thou art earth, water, fire, air, and ether. Thou art Brahma, Vishnu, and Rudra. We meditate on they countenance; enlighten therefore our understanding. He who continually meditates upon thy divine form, conceiving it to be with one tooth, four hands, bearing a rat on thy banner, of a red hue, with a large belly, anointed with red perfumes, arrayed in red garments, worshipped with offerings of red flowers, abounding in compassion, the cause of this universe, imperishable, unproduced, and unaffected by creation, becomes the most excellent of Yogis."— *Ganapati Upanishad,* WILKINS, p. 331.

The universe is manifested through the Higher Self in the five planes,— physical (earth), astral (water), mental (air), buddhic (fire) and atmic (ether). The "one tooth" signifies power potential; "four hands," activities on the four planes below atma. The "rat" is an emblem of the lower quaternary. The "redness" signifies Divine Love which draws all things to the Self. The "large belly" denotes ability to transmute (digest) the lower qualities into the higher.

See ELEMENTS, FLOWERS, HAND, HOKKMAH, PERFUME, RAT, RED (rose), TUSK.

GANGES RIVER :—

A symbol of the Divine life, atma-buddhic (the "river of life") which flows from its source, the Absolute, downwards through the higher planes, being reflected, as it were, in the lower planes.

See RIVER OF LIFE.

GANGLER OR GANGLERE :—

A symbol of the spiritual ego as life's pilgrim; or the conscience.

"'Evil are the deeds of Loki truly,' said Gangler; 'first of all in his having caused Baldur to be slain, and then preventing him from being delivered out of Hel.'"—*Prose Edda,* MALLET, p. 449.

Then the conscience speaks :—The desire-nature (Loki) has done amiss apparently, in that it has become the means of drawing the Soul (Baldur) to the karmic planes whereon it is obscured, and that it now serves to prevent it from rising to union with the Higher Self.

See BALDER, BIFROST, HILL, LOKE.

GARDEN OF FLOWERS AND FRUIT :—

This symbol signifies a state of the soul in which virtues (flowers) blossom, and the higher emotions (fruit) ripen on the buddhic plane.

"And their soul shall be as a watered garden; and they shall not sorrow any more at all.—JER. xxxi. 12.

The water of Truth fructifies the buddhic plane whereon is no ignorance or suffering.

"'Gardens' and 'groves' signify wisdom and intelligence, and every tree something thereof,—as the olive, the good of love; the vine, truth from that good; the cedar, rational good and truth."— SWEDENBORG, *T. C. R.* n. 204.

See EDEN, GETHSEMANE, GROVES, OLIVE FRUIT, PARADISE.

GARDEN LUMBINI :—

In the cycle of involution this signifies the condition of the lower nature which is required in order that the Soul may take birth in it.

"Then one day by the king's permission the queen, having a great longing in her mind, went with the inmates of the gynæceum into the garden Lumbini."— *Buddha-Karita,* Bk. I. 23.

The Divine Will now requires that the perfect desire-nature (Māyā), aspiring to be of use, shall be raised to the productive state of the "garden," which signifies the condition which is favourable to the birth of the Soul (Buddha).

See BIRTH OF BUDDHA, BOUGH, MĀYA.

GARDEN OF EDEN :—

A symbol of the buddhic or wisdom plane.

"Eden which is the Wisdom of God."— PHILO, *Works,* Vol. IV. p. 68.

"That the paradise of God means the truth of wisdom and faith is evident from the signification of garden in the Word; garden there signifies wisdom and intelligence, because trees signify men of the church, and their fruits goods of life; nothing else is signified by the garden of Eden, for by it is described the wisdom of Adam."—SWEDENBORG, *Apoc. Rev.*, n. 90.

" Thou (prince of Tyrus) hast been in Eden the garden of God ; every precious stone was thy covering."—EZEK. xxviii. 13.

The mental nature (prince of Tyrus) has been endowed from the buddhic plane (Eden) with every virtue (precious stone). The mental nature was perfect from the day it was evolved, till iniquity was found in it, and " Adam," the " prince of Tyrus," fell.

See EDEN, GOLDEN AGE, HIDING, HOURIES, JEWELS, PARADISE, TREASURES (cave), TYRUS.

GARDEN OF REEDS :—

A symbol of the astral plane, containing the astral heaven,—Svarga, or the Summerland,—on its upper sub-planes.

" Of union in the Garden of Reeds."— *Book of the Dead*, Ch. CX.

This refers to the acquirement of Individuality as the self rises above the manifestation of the astral life.

See BIRTH OF HORUS, MARSH, PEACHES, REED PLAIN, SEKHET-AARU, UNION (reeds).

GARDEN OF REST, OR OF PEACE :—

A symbol of Nirvana, i.e. an interval between globe periods, passed on the buddhic plane. Or Devachan on the higher mental plane.

" The Lord of the Peace of Horus,—the throne of His heart is in the pools and the cities of the Garden of Rest ; for He is begotten in the birth-chamber of the Divine City, and His rest shall come in the consuming of the Divine City. He it is that fashions Her likeness and unites Her to all that belongs to the chamber of birth in the City of God."—*Book of the Dead*, Ch. CX., trans. M. W. BLACKDEN.

The centre of the soul's being,— the True Self,—is above the lower nature, and enthroned in the causal-body (throne) where It is within atma-buddhic Truth (the Garden). The Self is begotten in Buddhi which ensouls the causal body (Divine City). The Self " rests," or is withdrawn from manifestation in the lower worlds, when the causal vehicle is dissolved at the end of the cycle. The Self as Atman fashions the buddhic vehicle to supersede the

causal, and through Her receptivity the Self is united with all things spiritually, and apprehends in full consciousness the universal scheme of Nature which lives, moves and has its being in the Godhead.—*See* Is. lviii. 11 ; JER. xxxi. 12.

See ATMAN, BUDDHI, CAUSAL-BODY, CITY, DEVACHAN, GOING IN, NIRVANA, PEACE, PLANETARY CHAIN, POOLS, SEKHET - HETEP, SOWING, THRONE (heart).

GÂRHAPATYA FIRE :—

A symbol of the buddhi-manasic centre of activity in the causal-body on the higher mental plane of the soul.

" The reason then why the sacrificer places water (the thunderbolt) near the Gârhapatya fire is that the Gârhapatya is a house, and a house is a safe resting place."—*Sata. Brâh.*, I. 1, 1, 19.

" The reason why he brings forward water is that all this universe is pervaded by water ; hence by this his first act he pervades (or gains) all this universe."— *Ibid.*, 14.

The higher " water " signifying Truth—the Divine Reality—the Life of the universe, it is necessary that the causal-body (house) should be shown to have a part in that Life, and be a permanent resting place for the Ego while it periodically forthpours itself into human forms.

See AGNIHOTRA, AHAVANÎYA, ALTAR (fire), CAUSAL-BODY, GEMINI, HOUSE IN HEAVEN. MENTAL PLANE, SOUL, THUNDERBOLT, WATER. YAMA.

GARLANDS OF FLOWERS :—

Symbolic of assemblage of higher emotions and virtues,—tokens of joy and gladness in the buddhic consciousness.

See FLOWERS, WREATHS.

GARMENTS (HIGHER ASPECT) :—

Symbolic of the buddhic and causal vestures, or sheaths, of the soul ; signifying wisdom and the higher intellect. The higher emotions.

" To give unto them (the captives) a garland for ashes, the oil of joy for mourning, the garment of praise for the spirit of heaviness ; that they may be called trees of righteousness, the planting of the Lord, that he might be glorified."— Is. lxi. 3.

The egos are liberated from captivity to the lower nature, and are given the higher emotions in exchange for the lower illusions ; love and bliss for sorrow and suffering ; the buddhic vesture of wisdom for the trammels of ignorance ; that so they may become unified aspects of the Divine Life, instituted by the Higher Self for the fulfilment of the purpose of the Supreme.

"And Mordecai went out from the presence of the king in royal apparel of blue and white, and with a great crown of gold, and with a garment of fine linen and purple : and the city of Sushan rejoiced and was glad,"—ESTHER viii. 15.

The indwelling Self, or Christ incarnate, went forth of the Supreme invested with celestial attributes of intellect and purity, and having supremacy over the lower nature ; also endowed with devotion to truth and with wisdom,—the buddhic robe. Then was the soul abounding with energy and bliss.

"By garments in the Word are signified truths which invest good, and in an opposite sense, falses which invest evil ; for man is either his own good or his own evil, the truths or falses thence proceeding are his garments."—SWEDENBORG, *Apoc , Rev.*, n. 166.

"Man is essentially a spirit. When that is realised, and the soul within him is allowed to seek its proper goal, it will develop into glorious beauty and proportion, and as it grows, weave for itself a garment worthy its God-like origin and nature."—J. BRIERLEY, *Studies of the Soul*, p. 112.

See ASHES, CLOTHING, COAT, CROWN, ESTHER, GATE OF SALUTATION, GUESTS, OIL, RAIMENT, ROBE, TREE.

GARMENTS (LOWER ASPECT) :—

Symbolic of opinions, prejudices, confining notions, narrowness of ideas, habits of low thought, literalism, and the " higher criticism " of scriptures.

These limitations of mind pertain to the lower mental plane, and enclose the ego in shells of mental matter, often very difficult and painful to get rid of. They have to be broken up by the advent of life and truth from the Spirit within.

"And he (blind Bartimæus), casting away his garment, sprang up, and came to Jesus."—MARK x. 50.

The aspiring mind rises and " casts off his garment " because he has, first, to make the effort to rise of his own accord, and stand (as it would

appear) ; and second, he must needs cast away his old prejudices and confining opinions, symbolised by the garment, before he can go to the Christ within.

"Proclus has it : The soul, on descending into the body, forsakes unity, ' and around her, from all sides, there grow multiform kinds of existence and manifold garments ; ' ' love of honour is the last garment of souls ' ; and when, in mounting up, ' we lay aside our passions and garments which, in coming down, we had put on, we must also strip off that last garment, in order that having become (entirely) naked, we may establish ourselves before God, having made ourselves like to the divine life.' "—From HUGEL, *Mystical Element*, Vol. II. p. 98.

See BLIND MAN, CLOTHING, INSPIRATION, NAKEDNESS, PRIESTS AND ELDERS.

GARMENT OF SHAME :—

A symbol of the vehicle of the desires and the senses.

" ' When ye trample on the garment of shame, and when the two shall be one, and the male with the female, neither male nor female.' then shall these things be."—*Saying of Jesus*, from CLEMENT ALEX.

When ye have cast off the lower (astral) vehicle of the senses, and when the emotions have been raised and united with the reason, so the two becoming one ; and when the relatives, the twain, active-passive, male-female, have transcended their former aspects and have become one energy ; then shall the Christ-consciousness be attained.

"Return unto thy home, O Soul ! Thy sin and shame Leave thou behind on earth ; assume a shining form—Thy ancient shape,—refined, and from all taint set' free " (*Rig-Veda*, X.).—MON. WILLIAMS, *Indian Wisdom*, p. 22.

See ASTRAL PLANE, MALE-FEMALE, MAN AND WIFE, MARRIAGE, RENDING, VIRGIN BRINGING FORTH.

GARODMAN, OR GAROTMANO :—

A symbol of the buddhic principle, or vehicle of atma. The buddhic plane of monadic activity.

"Garodman is the dwelling of the Fravashis and of the Blessed, and the bridge leading to it is precisely above the Abyss Dusahk,—the monstrous gulf, the home of Ahriman beneath the earth."—*The Zoroastrian System*, J. F. CLARKE.

The buddhic principle is seated in the causal-body, and is the vehicle of the monads of life (atmic), and of the souls evolved on the buddhic levels. The " bridge " is the higher manas, the connection between higher and lower planes ; it is above the lower manas and the astral plane, which is the " Abyss Dusahk " energised by the desire-mental principle (Ahriman) of the lower nature (earth).

See AHRIMAN, BRIDGE (kinvat), BUDDHIC PLANE, CAUSAL-BODY, DUSAHK, EDEN, FRAVASHIS, HEAVEN, HYMN SINGING, KINGDOM OF HEAVEN, MUSPELLHEIM, PARADISE.

GATE (HIGHER ASPECT) :—

A symbol of the higher mind or causal body in its receptive capacity for vibrations from below and from above. It becomes thereby the entrance through which the lower consciousness rises to the higher planes (heaven).

" For this gate of the great mysteries is the gate of heaven, and this is a house of God, where the good Deity dwells alone. And into this gate no unclean person shall enter."—Naasene doctrine, HIPPOLYTUS, Refutations, Bk. V. Ch. 3.

This is the entrance to a condition exalted and inexpressible,—a celestial abode, a " temple not made with hands," where dwelleth the Divine Unity, Father-Mother, Atma-Buddhi, in the causal-body. Into this higher mental state can pass no soul who has not cast off completely the " old Adam " with its affections and lusts.— See GEN. xxviii. 17; Ps. cxviii. 19, 20.

See DEAD (rising), DOOR (higher), ERIDU, GJOLL, VIRGIN BRINGING FORTH.

GATE (LOWER ASPECT) :—

A symbol of the lower mind or mental body as the entrance for the ego to the lower planes, or underworld, where the soul gains its experiences, and is disciplined through suffering and sorrow (hell). —See MAT. vii. 13, 14 ; Ps. ix. 13.

See DOOR (lower), PORCH OF HOUSE.

GATE OF SALUTATION AND HOMAGE TO GOD THE FATHER :—

Symbolic of a buddhic sub-plane to which the consciousness rises ere it becomes one with the Self.

" And my toga of brilliant colours I cast around me, in its whole breadth. I clothed myself therewith, and ascended to the gate of salutation and homage ; I bowed my head and did obeisance to the majesty of my Father who had sent it to me."—Hymn of the Soul, GNOSTIC.

And also my " toga," the causal-body of variegated qualities, did I now assume to its complete extent of development. I was able to clothe myself in my bright vestures, so that I was not found naked ; and then did I ascend to the portal of reverence, filled with a sense of the majesty of God—the Creator and Sustainer of the Cosmic Scheme. I bowed my mind and did homage to his greatness ; and I reverenced my Father from whom had emanated such splendid endowments for the soul.

See BUDDHIC PLANE, DOOR (higher), GARMENT, NAKEDNESS, RAIMENT, ROBE, TOGA.

GATE OF TCHESERT :—

A symbol of the planes of buddhi-manas, as affording an opening for the manifestation of the Divine nature.

" Now the gate of Tchesert is the gate of the pillars of Shu, the northern gate of the Tuat (underworld) ; or, as others say, —it is the two leaves of the door through which the god Tem passeth when he goeth forth to the eastern horizon of heaven."—BUDGE, Book of the Dead, Ch. XVII.

The " pillars of Shu " are the four planes below atma, which constitute the Tuat, or underworld. The " northern gate " represents the entrance into the cycle of the lower life. The " two leaves of the door " signify the Buddhi-manasic outpouring of the Logos (Tem) at the dawn (east) of manifestation.

See BOLTS, BUDDHIC PLANE, EAST, HORIZONS, MANAS, PILLARS OF SHU, SHU, TEM, TUAT.

GATES OF ERIDU :—

A symbol of the higher manas which communicates between the higher and lower regions of existence.

" At night Adapa drew the bolts of the gates of Eridu, and at dawn he sailed forth in his bark to fish in the waters of the Persian Gulf."—Legend of Adapa. SAYCE, Rel. of Anc. Egypt, etc.

" Adapa " is a symbol of the Archetypal Man in the aspect of the lower self at an early stage. " At night,"— the period when the lower self appears to be cut off from the Higher,—he is said to "draw the bolts" of the gate between heaven and earth; that is, the condition of the soul requires the forthpouring of the Spirit to open a way to the lower planes. Then at the period of forthgoing (the dawn), he goes in search of that which will provide him with sustenance. The "bark" is the manas, or mental vehicle, which sails on the astral sea. The "fish" are those facts or appearances which come to him as sensations, feelings, and emotions, and which present themselves at the dawn of consciousness.

See ADAPA, ARC. MAN, BOLTS, BRIDGE, DAWN, ERIDU, FISH, MANAS, NIGHT, PYLONS, SEA, TAMMUZ.

GATES OF THE BODY, NINE :—

Physiologically, these are the nine openings of the body, six above (eyes, ears, and nostrils) and three below (mouth and two vents). They are intimately related with etheric, astral, and mental centres and activities, with which they correspond on the several planes of the soul.

These centres and their connections are mentioned under the symbols of "nine brothers," "nine streets," etc.—*See Bhag. Gita.*, V. 13.

See BRIDGES (nine), HUMAN BODY, NINE, STREETS OF EARTH.

GATEWAYS, ARCHED :—

A symbol of higher mental qualities which may gain access to the higher planes of the soul.

See ARCHED.

GĀTHA AHUNA-VAIRYA, FOUR TIMES CHANTED :—

Symbolic of the formation of the lower quaternary, through buddhic vibrations passing downward, or outward.

"Famous in Airyana-vaêjo, thou (Zarathustra) first recitest the Ahuna-vairya four times, with pauses between the verses, each successive time with a louder recitation."—*Homa Yasht*, HAUG, *Essays*, p. 179.

This refers to the inter-relation between the astral and buddhic (Airyana-varêjo) planes. And the repetition of the hymn four times is the establishment of the lower quaternary. The pauses are the distinctive operations of the elemental forces of

nature. The recitation of the verses and the louder utterance of them refers to the increasing density of the matter of the four lower planes, viz. lower mental, astral, etheric, and gross physical.

See ARYANA, ASTRAL PLANE, BUDDHIC PLANE, CARPENTER, HOUSE RULER, HYMN SINGING, MUSIC, PLANES, QUATERNARY, TRISHTUBH.

GĀTHA KAM-NEMOI-ZAM CHANTED :—

Symbolic of the giving attention to lower desires, affections, and attractions, when such habits of thought bring only dissatisfaction and regret.

"Zarathustra asked Ahuramazda, . . . 'When the wicked man dies where dwells his soul that night ? Then said Ahuramazda, . .. In the vicinity of the head it runs about, chanting the Gātha Kam-nemoi-zam, saying,—'To what land shall I turn ?' That night the soul experiences as much of discomfort as all that which it had as a living existence."— *Hadokht Nask*, HAUG, *Essays*, p. 222.

The "wicked man" is the lower mind attached to its desires, instincts and appetites; it is the expression of the soul upon the astral plane. When the soul vacates the physical body, into what state does it pass in the first instance ? The answer is, that on the astral plane the soul lingers for a period with no fixed place of abode, yet tending to the higher mental plane (the head). But being attached to desire, it is totally without aim or purpose before it; it has no anchorage, and in despair reaps the results of its shortsighted behaviour in the past life. The consciousness is detained for a protracted period in the lowest mental sub-plane (the first night), and experiences the sorrow which is ir.-evitable during the purgatorial process which must ensue from not realising the value of the opportunities for progress which it has had here below.

See AHURA-MAZDA, ASTRAL PLANE, HAND OF BEAST, HARLOT, MAN (bad), NIGHTS (three), PURGATORY, RE-INCARNATION, SVARGA, UNRIGHTEOUS, WICKEDNESS.

GĀTHA USHTAVAITI CHANTED :—

Symbolic of the giving attention to the higher emotions and aspirations,

for such habits of thought bring satisfaction and peace.

"Zarathustra asked Ahuramazda: O most munificent Spirit, creator of the settlements supplied with creatures! 'When a righteous man passes away, where dwells his soul that night?' Then said Ahuramazda: 'It sits down in the vicinity of the head, chanting the Gātha Ushtavaiti, imploring blessedness. . . . That night the soul experiences as much of pleasure as all that which it had as a living existence.' "—HAUG, *Hadokht Nask, Essays*, p. 220.

The Soul questions the Supreme, who is the Emanator of the manifested worlds,—' When the perfected soul is projected, at the death of the body, beyond the physical plane, into what condition does it then enter?' The reply is made that it returns inward towards the higher mental plane, and recapitulates the nature of the higher emotions and aspirations to which it had habituated itself when incarnate. And its enjoyment is proportionate to its capacity for realisation of bliss when in its physical life. The second and third "nights" of the perfected soul signify the arrival of the consciousness at the various sub-planes of the mental plane which contribute to the devachanic state. These three "nights" represent the intervening period between incarnations; also there is a connection between them and the cyclic periods. It must be remembered that only a very small part of a soul manifests in any particular incarnation, and that part is the lowest and least advanced part of the totality. Consequently a very advanced soul may be perfected all but that part.

See AHURA-MAZDA, CREATURES, DEVACHAN, GILGOOLEM, HEAD, HYMN SINGING. INCARNATION OF SOULS, MAN (righteous), MANAS, MUSIC, NIGHTS (three), RE-INCARNATION, SETTLEMENTS, SOUL, ZOROASTER.

GĀTHAS, CHANTING THE :—

A symbol of meditation in tune with the Infinite, so raising the consciousness as to be able to recover the memory of all past lives of the ego.

"Then thou wouldest sit down, chanting the Gāthas, and consecrating the good waters and the fire of Ahura-mazda, and extolling the righteous man coming from near and far."—*Hadokht Nask*, HAUG, *Essays*, p. 221.

Then by raising the consciousness through meditation, thou will be able to recover the past experiences collected in the causal sheath, and wilt be able to dedicate thyself to the pursuit of truth and to the love of God. "Extolling the righteous man, etc." signifies the exaltation of the purified mind, and of the lower self, which when united make for righteousness.

See CAUSAL-BODY, CONSCIOUSNESS, EXPERIENCES, FIRE, FORENOON, HYMN SINGING, KALCHAS, LITANY, MAN (righteous), RE-INCARNATION, REMINISCENCE, SPENTO.

GĀTHA DAYS, FIVE :—

These five intercalary days of the year are added to the 360 days (degrees) of the Zodiac, to complete the actual year of 365 days. They are then taken as symbolising, as in Egypt, the five manifest planes of being; because they imply the potential cycle (360) becoming the actual cycle (365) in which the Self (sun) manifests in time and space.

"These five Gāthas (hymns) are made up from the body of a Righteous Man." —*Shayast La-Shayast*, Ch. XIII., *S.B.E.*

The "Righteous Man" signifies the Archetypal Man from whom humanity proceeds; and his measure is the Macrocosm of the five planes in which he manifests completely, *potentially*, and will manifest completely, *actually*, in all souls at the end of the cycle. For every soul is a Microcosm of the five planes, the same as the Macrocosm in every particular.

See ARC. MAN, AROUERIS, BIRTH OF OSIRIS, CASTES, CLASSES, DAYS (five), ELEMENTS, MACROCOSM, MICROCOSM, MUSIC, RULERS, THIEVES (five), TREE OF LIFE, WORLDS (five).

GÂYATRI VERSE OR METRE :—

A symbol of the astral plane in relation to the rate of vibration in the atoms of astral matter.

GAYOMARD :—
See KAIOMARTS.

GĒ, GÆA, OR TELLUS :—

A symbol of matter in its essential

nature of mother substance bringing forth qualities and forms.

See APPLES, HESPERIDES, OCEANUS, RHEA, URANUS.

GEBAL, OR BYBLOS, SWAMP :—

A symbol of the fourth sub-plane of the astral plane.

See BYBLOS, MARSH.

GEMINI, THE ZODIACAL SIGN :—

A symbol of the third period of the cycle of life. The " Twins " signify the higher and lower Selves, or the Individuality and the Personality on the mental plane. These are the two centres of consciousness in the soul for the higher and lower activities. In the constellation *Gemini* are the two stars Castor and Pollux, which are symbols of the personality and the individuality in accordance with the story of the Dioscuri.

See APOCATEQUIL, ASVINS, DIOSCURI, INDIVIDUALITY, PERSONALITY, PISCES, POLLUX, ZODIAC.

GEMS, OR PRECIOUS STONES :—

Symbols of virtues and high qualities of mind and emotion.

" In that city (of Kapila), shining with the splendour of gems, darkness like poverty could find no place."—*Buddha-Karita*, Bk. I. *S.B. of E.*

In the centred Self on the higher planes is perfect bliss, emanating the highest qualities of Love and Wisdom. Ignorance (darkness) or privation (poverty), could not possibly enter into manifestation at this stage of forth-going towards involution.

See BREASTPLATE, CARNELIAN, JEWELS, KAPILA, NECK, PRECIOUS, RUBIES, SAPPHIRE, SARDONYXES.

GEMS, STRINGS OF :—

Emblematic of buddhic functionings productive of virtues in harmony with each other.

" Friends brought Buddha strings of gems exactly like wreaths of plants."— *Buddha-Karita*, Bk. II.

In the Soul are established the functionings upon the buddhic or emotional plane. The allusion to " wreaths of plants " is made because the idea suggests the budding of the feeling within the lower nature which will afterwards yield " fruit," that is, higher emotions.

See BUDDHA, FRIENDS, JEWELS, NECK, STRINGS, UNGUENTS, WREATHS.

GENERATIONS OF PEOPLE :—

A symbol of grades of qualities in stages of development.

See CHRIST'S SECOND COMING.

GENERATIVE FUNCTION :—

This symbol expresses the inter-active spirit-matter creative, or multi-plying function in nature, by means of which the consciousness evolves in the transitory forms.

" In memory of this event (of the birth of Osiris) the Pamylia were afterwards instituted, a festival much resembling the Phalliphoria, or Priapeia, of the Greeks."

In regard to the genetic power of the indwelling Self in the soul, the generative function (Pamylia) is made the symbol of the spiritual-material creative function producing forms, by means of which forms the growth of consciousness is rendered possible.

See CHILDREN, MITHRAS, MULTIPLY, PHALLIPHORIA, SEXUAL.

GENERATIVE FUNCTION TRANS-MUTED :—

The astro-mental generative function of mind and desire, by which ideas and lower emotions are pro-duced, is exchanged for the buddhi-mental function giving rise to higher emotions and concepts of truth.

" Isis was never able to recover the phallus of Osiris, which having been thrown into the Nile immediately upon its separation from the body had been devoured by the Lepidotus, the Phagrus, and the Oxyrynchus fish, which of all others, for this reason, the Egyptians have in more especial avoidance."—PLUTARCH, *Isis and Osiris*, § 18.

This signifies arrival at the point when the astro-mental generative function is no longer used in the blind, natural way, but when it is raised and consecrated to the highest uses. Then it is that the last trace of the lower personality, love of self (astro-mental " phallus "), is absorbed, as it were, by the " fishes," which are a symbol of that which is false in the eyes,—now opened,—of the lower self. The three " fishes " are illusions of kama-manas, and they seem to be superstition, prejudice, and false knowledge, which are condemned by the enlightened mind.

See CHILD, CHILDREN, DEATH OF OSIRIS, EGYPTIANS, ISIS, NILE.

GENTILES :—

Symbolic of mental qualities less developed than the " Jews," and standing, as it were, outside the " chosen people," or more or less disciplined qualities of the mind.

"The Gentiles are fellow-heirs, and fellow-members of the body, and fellow-partakers of the promise in Christ Jesus through the gospel."—EPH. iii. 6.

This is a recognition that all qualities, however backward in development, have their part in the perfect pattern behind the phenomenal deficiency, and that all are capable of being evolved by the Spirit of Truth through the means provided in the forms.

See ARC. MAN, GOSPEL, IMAGE, ISRAELITES, JEWS, MEMBERS.

GEOMETRY :—

Geometry and symbolism are the means whereby all spiritual facts are expressed, and by a knowledge of which they are to be interpreted.

"Thus the King took away the one and protected the seven ; he abandoned the seven and kept the five ; he obtained the set of three and learned the set of three ; he understood the two and abandoned the two."—*Buddha-Karita*, Bk. II. 41.

Thus the *One* manifested as *seven* planes and their activities. The two highest, or innermost, remain in obscuration ; the *five* are manifest. The *set of three* is the triad which is expressed in the triple nature of the manifested soul, that is, atma, buddhi, and higher-manas, which triad is reflected below as physical, astral, and lower-manas. The *two* stand for the desire-nature and the reason-nature, both of which must be experienced and eventually abandoned.

See FOOTSTEPS OF BUDDHA, INVOLUTION, OGDOAD, RĀ.

GEORGE AND THE DRAGON :—

Emblematical of Reason overcoming the lower Emotion nature ; or of Mind controlling Desire. The horse and rider signify intelligence under the direction of the will ; and the dragon is the lower nature which wars against the soul,—the selfish nature which devours the innocent and obstructs liberty and justice.

"The true end of man is moral perfection, not pleasure. And it is in bringing the animal nature into obedience to the rational, the particular will into subjection to the universal, that he advances towards that end. The moral quality, subjectively considered,—of course the act has also, or rather primarily, a moral quality,—resides, not in the result achieved, nor in the end pursued by him, but in the motive which prompts him in the inner spring of action, in volition. The only real and absolute good for man is a good will : that is a will determined by the moral law. The desire to do right, as right, is morality. No act is really ethical which is not motived by Duty, by obedience to the moral law. And that law, as Kant admirably teaches, is not a higher self, but an independent reality, which evokes the higher self within us."— W. S. LILLY, *The Great Enigma*, p. 21.

"We want a diffusion of knowledge and a prevailing habit of intellectual activity. The reason why the morally best men are so often in our experience the least intelligent and the most bigoted is the fact that they are intellectually undeveloped. The ancient and obstinate error of asceticism is rearing its head again among us, and wherever asceticism appears, fanaticism is not far distant. I mark already the familiar burden of ascetic preaching, the exaltation of the non-natural, the contempt of the intellectual, the parade of self-suppression, the depreciation of liberty. By authoritative lips and in persuasive terms you are often enough encouraged to absolve yourselves from the arduous yet uplifting labours of the intellect, and to drown thought in the hustle and bustle of social work. Against all such counsels I raise the short and pregnant sentence of St. Paul : 'Brethren, be not children in mind, howbeit in malice be ye babes, but in mind be men' (1 COR. xiv. 20)."— H. HENSLEY HENSON *Christ and the Nation*, p. 261.

See DRAGON, HORSE, MITHRA AND BULL, PERSONS, WILL.

GERMS, OR SEEDS :—

A symbol of the monads of Life and of Form, which proceed forth primordially into manifestation.

"Germs infinite in number, in no way like each other ; for none of the other things at all resembles the one the other."—*Anaxagoras*, FAIRBANKS, 4.

Prior to manifestation, the differentiated possibilities of life (monadic) were not apparent. Within the spiritual essence lay the monads,— the centres of the archetypal qualities and forms of all things in infinite diversity, for no one form of the One Life may resemble another, since that Life is infinite.

"Germs of all objects, having all sorts of forms and colours and tastes."— *Ibid.*, 3.

The "forms, colours, and tastes" refer to the astral, mental, and physical contributions from the monadic centres of manifestation.

See COLOURS, COSMOS, CREATION, CULTIVATING, INVOLUTION, MONAD OF LIFE, OPPOSITES, PROTOTYPES, SEED (good), SPERMATIC WORDS, WHEAT.

GETHSEMANE :—

A symbol of an interior and subjective mental state in which the soul truly lives in its evolving experiences.

"Then cometh Jesus with them unto a place called Gethsemane, and saith unto his disciples, Sit ye here, while I go yonder and pray. And he took with him Peter and the two sons of Zebedee, and began to be sorrowful."—MAT. xxvi. 36, 37.

Gethsemane stands for the Garden of the soul, the place of purity and fruition, wherein all the inner experiences are *lived*, as contrasted with expressed merely. The Christ-soul directs that the lower manifestations of the qualities (disciples) shall here have to abide quietly, and to suffer in silence, in order to await the call of the Highest. But the Higher Self —with whom Jesus is identified— always goes beyond the ken of the actual, and so raises the qualities. The lower mind (Peter), reason (James), and love (John) have to be raised. The suffering is the effect of the depression of the personality.

See DISCIPLES, EXPERIENCES, GARDEN, JAMES, JOHN (apostle), MOUNT OF OLIVES, PASSION, PETER, TRANSFIGURATION, VINEGAR.

GEUSH-TASHA, CUTTER OF THE OX ; AND GEUSH - URVA (GOSHURUN) :—

Symbols of the lower self which cuts off the intuition, and the personality which differentiates the qualities.

"The Geush-tasha frightened by this cry (of the Geush-urva for help), asked the archangel Asha as to who had been appointed to protect the Geush-urva. Asha referred him to Mazda, who is the most wise and the giver of oracles. Mazda answered that ' Geush-urva was being cut into pieces for the benefit of the agriculturalist.' "—*Yasna*, 29 ; HAUG'S *Essays*, p. 148.

The "Geush-tasha" is that principle of the lower self which defines and limits, causes contrasts and perception of differences ; and leads also to perception of affinities on the life side. The "Geush-urva" is the personality which had been imperilled of its homogeneity by onslaughts from without upon it, which cause it to exert such kama-manasic energy as suffices to enable the lower self (Geush-tasha) to function completely on the astromental plane. The conditions which give rise to this functioning are for the time powerless to withstand the strenuous attempts to triumph over them (or prematurely supersede them) made by the Self through its outgoing energy. In self-protection the impulse then comes to the lower self to turn within from the outer conditions, to that Divine Life which ordains them as a means whereby development is rendered possible. Then it is that the inner conviction is borne in upon the soul that the personality is being hewn in pieces (because homogeneity limits the Life) for the sake of the operations for growth which are being carried forward in the astral nature,— to wit, the resulting expansion of the higher emotions which necessitate that the lower and now outgrown and imperfect astro-mental receptacle of the reflection of the Self shall be superseded by the higher vehicle.

"The literal meaning of the word *Gĕush urva*, 'soul of the cow,' implies a simile ; for the earth is compared to a cow. By its cutting and dividing, ploughing is to be understood."—HAUG, *Ibid.*, p. 148.

See AGRICULTURE, ASHA-VAHIST, BULL, COW, CULTIVATION, GOLDEN FLEECE, GOSHURUN, ORACLE, PERSONALITY, PLOUGHING, VESSEL.

GHEE, OR BUTTER :—

A symbol of the intuition of Divine love and wisdom, or the buddhic emotion nature which proceeds from buddhi (cow).

"May the purifiers of ghee purify us with ghee !—For they, the divine, take away all taint ; now ' all ' means every, and ' taint ' means what is impure ; for they do take away from him every impurity."—*Sata. Brâh.*, III. 1, 2, 11.

The spiritual forces are called upon to purify the mental qualities by uniting them with the buddhic emotion nature (ghee) which takes away the taint of selfishness, pride, greed, attachment to desire and sense, and every impurity. The lower mind commences its activities under the stimulus of desire and lower emotion. This stimulus from below has to be superseded by the stimulus from above to be found in the higher emotions of wisdom, truth, and love.

See BUDDHI, BUTTER, COW, FAT, GUHU, MILK, OIL, OINTMENT, OLIVE.

GIANTS, NEPHILIM, MIGHTY MEN :—

Symbols of early mankind in great ape-like forms resident on continents now mostly submerged.

" There were giants in the earth in those days. . . . And mighty men which were of old."—GEN. vi. 4.

The pre-human forms in which mind began to dawn were rude and gigantic. In these early vehicles of human life the individuality is as yet only nascent.

See GADERINE DEMONIACS, NEPHILIM.

GIANTS OF THE MOUNTAIN :—

Symbolic of elevated mental qualities such as aspiration and hope.

See MOUNTAIN, RIMTHURSAR.

GIFT OF TONGUES :—

A symbol of the unfoldment of a spiritual faculty, or the power of presenting from within to the understanding the truth and love of the Spirit, which enables the lower mind to realise in some degree the beauty of the powers of high intellect and emotion which are above it and beyond its purview.—See 1 COR. xiv ; MARK vii. 35.

See DEAFNESS.

GIFTS OF GOD :—

These are higher powers and faculties bestowed on the soul when the soul is prepared to receive them. Causation is of the higher nature only. Phenomena are effects.

" For by grace have ye been saved through faith ; and that not of yourselves : it is the gift of God : not of works, that no man should glory."—EPH. ii. 8, 9.

It is through the action of the higher nature that the qualities progress towards perfection in response to the aspiration and faith of the lower. The lower nature of itself cannot progress. The activities of the lower mind are ineffectual without the aid of the Spirit of Truth.

" Consciousness of spiritual powerlessness, with its sequent dissatisfaction and struggle, when it results in renewed inspiration, insight, and moral correspondence to the Divine Ideal, which the psychology of religious experience observes is its own witness to the belief that the religious progress of the individual, and of the race, takes place by the gift and power of God. Thus experience creates the impression that the real cause of man's religious progress is to be found in the truth of the belief that God is making man more and more into the likeness of the Divine."—G. T. LADD, Phil. of Religion, Vol. I. p. 357.

See ATONEMENT, DEVAYANA, GRACE, IMAGE, MEDICINE, MICROCOSM.

GIHON RIVER :—

A symbol of the lower mental nature as a current of life on the lower planes.

" And the name of the second river is Gihon : the same is it that compasseth the whole land of Cush (Ethiopis)."—GEN. ii. 13.

And the second differentiation from the higher mental plane (Pishon) is the lower mental plane ; this includes all the activities of the astro-mental nature (Cush).

See ANDROMEDA, CUSH, EDEN RIVER.

GILGAMES AND EA-BANI :—

Symbols of the Incarnate Self or Individuality and the lower mind or Personality.

" The Epic begins with a description of his (Gilgames) rule at Erech, ' the seat ' of his power. Between him and the inhabitants of the city there seems to have been little goodwill. He had not left, they complained, the son to his father or the wife to her husband."—SAYCE, Rel. of Anc. Egypt. and Babyl., p 432.

The Self seated on the lower planes (Erech) brings dissension among the the lower qualities (people) by his operations. The activities of the indwelling Self are opposed to the lower emotions and desires. The Self sets the more progressed quality (son) at variance with the less progressed (father), and the mind (husband) in conflict with the lower emotion (wife).

" The gods, we are told, heard the cry of the people, and Aruru was instructed to create a rival to Gilgames, who might overcome him in the contest of strength. The goddess accordingly kneaded clay with her hands, and made it in the form of Ea-bani, half man and half beast. His body was covered with hair ; ' he knew neither kin nor country ' ; ' with the gazelles he ate the grass ' of the field and ' satisfied his thirst with the cattle.' " —*Ibid.*, p. 433.

Through buddhi (Aruru) as for the natural order, the personality is developed and the lower mind (Ea-bani) is embodied in matter (clay), that is, mind is endowed with a body on the astral plane of desire (beast). Thus the lower mind becomes kama-manasic, half mind and half desire-nature. The lower mind at first obeyed the intuitions (hair), but recognised neither higher nor lower qualities. He just accepted the higher qualities (gazelles) as means of growth (grass, milk). Afterwards, being attracted by love of form-life, he fell from his pristine purity to the lower planes (Erech).

"When once more he turned back to his gazelles and cattle, they fled from him in terror ; he had become a man, knowing good and evil."—*Ibid.*

When the lower mind had identified itself with the desires and sensations, the divine intuitions became obscured, and the higher qualities (gazelles, etc.) were no longer perceived by the consciousness. The Personality having within him the nascent mind and the germ of Spirit, began his career as a responsible being, but immersed in ignorance and the illusion of separateness. But deep within him was the Incarnate Self (Gilgames), who was "his fast friend and ally." It is through the alliance of the Individuality with the Personality, and their concerted operations, that the soul progresses on its upward path.

The Epic of Gilgames, like the Iliad, cannot be taken as sequential in its arrangement ; it gives instruction about the Divine scheme from various points of view, without order as to time and space. It is scrappy, no doubt by reason of many inspirations put together, as was the Kalevala in the 19th century.

See ADAM (lower), BUDDHI, CATTLE, COW (milch,) DEER, EA, EDEN, FALL, FATHER (lower), GOAT (milch), GRASS, HAIR, INCARNATION, INDIVIDUALITY, MAN, MILK, PARENTS, PEACE AND SWORD, PEOPLE, PERSONALITY, SATYRS, SELF, WIFE.

GILGOOLEM, OR REVOLUTION OF SOULS :—

A symbol of the cycle of periodical re-incarnations of the spiritual monads in human bodies.

"All the souls go up into the *gil'good-ah*, i.e. revolutions or turnings, and the children of man do not know the ways of the Holy, and how He judges the children of man every day and in all time, and how the *Neshamoth* souls go up to be judged before they come down into this world, and how they go up to judgment after they go out from this world. How many Gil'gool-em and how many hidden doings the Holy does with them ? How many naked souls and how many naked spirits go in that world (the other) which do not enter through the king's *pargoda* (curtain) ? . . . All the *Neshamoth* souls go out from that great Tree, and from that mighty River which flows out from Eden, and all the *Ru'hin* spirits come out from that other small tree. The *Neshamah* soul comes from Above, the Rua'h spirit from Below, and unite in one " (Zohar, II.).— MYER, *Qabbalah*, p. 413.

The " Neshamah " is the Divine Soul, atma-buddhi, in humanity. The " Neshamoth " are the Divine monads or egos, atma-buddhic, on the Ray from the Supreme (the Tree of Life). These spiritual egos in human beings outpour from the Divine life of the buddhic plane (the river of Eden). The " rua'h spirit from below " is the *rua'h nephesh*—the lower mind or personality which unites with the Divine soul. The " ru'hin spirits " are the personalities from the astral evolution below (the small tree), which provide forms for the egos and unite with them. The judging of the souls,—the children of mind (man),— takes place midway between the incarnations and karmically determines the nature of the next descent into the material world. The lower mind does not cognise the cycle of re-births (gil'-gool-em), for it is beyond its purview. The soul enters the heaven-world through the higher emotions (the king's curtain). The spiritual egos go forth from the Divine life. The personalities arise from the astral evolution below and unite with the former in the human mind.

" The doctrine of the pre-existence of the soul is shared by the Gallic Druids and the Druses of the Middle Ages ; it is maintained to-day by the Zulus and the Greenlanders, by the Indians of North America and the Dayaks of Borneo, by the Karens of Burma and the inhabitants of Guinea ; it counts among its adherents the worshippers of Brahma and Buddha, and it attracted the sympathetic assent of a Spinoza and a Lessing. The wide extension of this theory in space and time is sufficient evidence of its deep roots in human thought and sentiment."—T. GOMPERZ, *Greek Thinkers*, Vol. I. p. 124.

" The reincarnating Ego, or individuality, retains during the Devachanic period merely the essence of the experience of its past earth-life or personality, the whole physical experience involving into a state of *in potentia*, or being translated into spiritual formulæ. The term between two re-births is said to extend from ten to fifteen centuries, during which time the physical consciousness is totally inactive, having no organs to act through, and therefore no *existence.*"—H. P. BLAVATSKY, *The Key to Theosophy*, p. 132.

" Man is the thinking animal, the animal that plans and creates, and in whom the primordial life which inhabits all living things is pressing on and up to greater heights of aspiration and performance. But apparently the same thing holds good as before. The life which expresses itself as mind is still the universal life, and when the brain perishes in which it finds its temporary home, it goes back to where it came from, like the rest of the life of creation, and then from the standpoint it has won incarnates itself anew for some further and nobler effort towards self-realisation—if that be the right word."—R. J. CAMPBELL, Serm., *God's Gift of Life.*

See BALANCE, BOAT (earth), CHILDREN OF MEN, CIRCULAR, DAY AND NIGHT, DEVAYANA, EDEN, EDEN RIVER, GIRDLE (star), INCARNATION OF SOULS, JUDGMENT HALL, MARRIAGE, MONAD OF LIFE, NAKEDNESS (higher), NEPHESH, NESHAMAH, PITRIYANA, REINCARNATION, RIVER OF LIFE, RUAH, SOUL, TREE OF LIFE, UNION, WHEELS OF BIRTH.

GIMLI OR VINGOLF :—

A symbol of the buddhi-manasic plane.

See KINGDOM, RIMTHURSAR.

GINUNGA-GAP, THE YAWNING GULF :—

A symbol of primordial formless matter in space, prior to the involution of spirit.

" It was time's morning when Ymer lived. There was no sand, no sea, no cooling billows ; earth there was none, no lofty heaven ; only the Gulf of Ginunga, but no grass."—*The Voluspa.*

At the dawn of manifestation, the potential lay dormant. There was nothing firm, no outflow of life. There was no lower nature, nor higher nature ; only chaos, and no growth from below.

See ABYSS, CHAOS, DEEP, EARTH, GRASS, HIGHER, SANDS, SEA, WAVES, YMIR.

GIRDLE OF THE BODY :—

A symbol of spiritual purity and power invigorating the soul.

" And righteousness shall be the girdle of his loins, and faithfulness the girdle of his reins."—Is. xi. 5.

See MAN (righteous), REINS.

GIRDLE OF KNOWLEDGE :—

A symbol of the causal-body which implies the investment of the soul with intuition of truth.

See CAUSAL-BODY, FOCUS.

GIRDLE OF LEATHER :—

An emblem of spiritual support and confidence.

" And John was clothed with camel's hair, and had a leathern girdle about his loins, and did eat locusts and wild honey."—MARK i. 6.

The moral nature (John) was endued with capability of obedience and willingness to endure, and had the support which is derived from the things of the Spirit. " Locusts and wild honey " are the food which signifies the *natural* means of nourishment ; subsistence upon plain ascertainable *facts* of life, as upon uncooked simple fare, which can be procured direct from the natural environment by means of the senses.

See CAMEL'S HAIR, JOHN BAPTIST.

GIRDLE OF GOLD :—

Emblem of the endowment of wisdom ;—the consciousness upon the buddhic plane.

" And girt about at the breasts with a golden girdle "—REV. i. 13.

This signifies the Higher Self having the aspects of Love (breasts, and Wisdom (gold).

" To ' have a golden girdle about the paps ' is to restrain all the movements of our changeful thoughts by the bands of love alone."—St. Gregory, *Morals on the Book of Job*, Vol III. p. 639.

See Barhis, Barsom, Breasts, Buckle, Consciousness, Gold.

GIRDLE-ROPE OF THE SACRIFICIAL STAKE :—

A symbol of the higher emotions which encompass, as it were, the ray of the Divine Life (stake).

"He (the Sacrificer) girds the stake with a triple rope for three-fold is food, and food means cattle ; and there is the father and mother, and what is born is the third, therefore he girds it with a triple rope."—*Sata. Brâh.*, III. 7, 1, 20.

The Higher Self emanates the higher emotions as sustenance for the soul, for the buddhic emotions (cattle) nourish the soul. The triad of father, mother, and son, represents mind and emotion producing the indwelling Self born on the mental plane (son of mind).

See Birth (second), Cattle, Chip, Food, Sacrificer, Stake, Top-ring.

GIRDLE, STAR-STUDDED, SPIRIT-FASHIONED (BELT OF ORION) :—

A symbol of the wheel of re-births, or the sub-cycle of the soul's re-incarnations.

"Mazda brought to thee the star-studded, spirit-fashioned girdle, leading the Paurvas, or the good Mazdayasnian religion ; then thou art begirt with it, (when growing) on the summit of the mountains, to make lasting the words and long accents of the sacred text."—*Homa Yasht*, Haug, *Essays*.

The Divine Nature ordains that each soul shall go through the " wheels " of re-birth and gain experience through many lives, which process is to instruct the soul, and show it that by this means the love and truth latent within it (the good religion) shall be brought forth. As growth is arrived at, karma envelops the soul until it reaches the " mountain " stage, and aspires towards that which is to free it. The reference to " words and accents " made " lasting " signifies the means whereby the true message from within of the Divine is effectually translated into terms of the soul's experience. The " sacred text " is the message of love and truth indelibly written within the human soul.

See Ahura-Mazda, Gilgoolem, Mountain, Re-incarnation, Religion, Sacred text, Wheels.

GIVING A CUP OF WATER :—

Significant of presenting truth in a mental form as expressed by the giver.

"And whosoever shall give to drink unto one of these little ones a cup of cold water only, in the name of a disciple, verily I say unto you, he shall in no wise lose his reward."—Mat. x. 42.

The mental quality that shall convey truth to an incarnating ego (little one), while identifying itself with a disciplined emotion, shall be transmuted to a higher plane.

See Cup, Disciple, Hylas, Pitcher, Water.

GJOLL, OR GJALL, RIVER :—

A symbol of the higher faculties of the mind which lead to truth through the intuition.

"The Gjoll river being the nearest to the gate of the abode of death " (*Prose Edda*).—Mallet, *North. Antiq.*, p. 401.

The higher mental faculties are at the entrance of the higher planes which the consciousness attains to through the death of the lower nature.

See Anaurus river, Bridge of Gjall, Gate, North, Styx.

GLASS, OR CRYSTAL :—

A symbol of Truth on the higher mental plane.

"And I saw as it were a glassy sea mingled with fire."—Rev. xv. 2.

This represents the Truth and Love of the Spirit, which are the foundation on which the higher qualities of the soul rest. (Osiris is often depicted seated upon a throne which rests upon a " glassy sea " of water,—Truth.)

"What other thing, then do we understand by 'gold and glass,' but that heavenly Country, that society of blessed citizens whose hearts mutually one with another at once shine with brightness, and are transparent by pureness ; which John in Revelations had beheld, when he said, ' And the building of the wall of it was of jasper, and the city was of pure gold like unto clear glass.' "—St. Gregory, *Morals on the Book of Job*, Vol II. p. 377.

"You cannot fail to observe that the writer speaks of God as possessing the same attributes as the glassy sea which surrounds His throne. He speaks of the nature of God as crystal-clear and yet as filled with fire. I think I see what he means. 'God is light, and in Him is no darkness at all.' But He is also love, the burning flame that is never quenched and in whose embrace all foulness and corruption are destroyed. The sea before the throne is the truth about God, and about all being, made manifest to those who are worthy to behold it with unclouded vision. . . . It is crystal-clear with the light of truth, and mingled with the flame of eternal love that streams from the throne itself. The glassy sea is thus a beautiful figure for the perfect revelation of the glory and the grace of God."—R. J. CAMPBELL, Serm., *The Crystal Sea.*

See CITY OF GOD, CRYSTAL, FIRE, FOUR BEINGS, GOLD, JERUSALEM, OCEAN, WATER.

GLORIFYING OF GOD :—

This signifies the perfecting of the soul, which then returns into the Absolute, who gave it to the planes of the relative existence for the express purpose of Self-expression, which being completed, corresponds to the glorifying of God.—*See* MATT. v. 16 ; ROM. xv. 6).

See ASCENSION OF OSIRIS, JESUS (son of man), KING OF GLORY, SPENDYAD, SUN (moon).

GLORY, DIVINE SACERDOTAL AND KINGLY :—

Symbolic of the Divine Ray of Consciousness and Life which proceeds from the Absolute and passes through the upper planes to the lower.

"The Divine sacerdotal and Kingly Glory is handed onward from saint to saint, ever with a view to its illuminating the soul of the Inspired one. It is ordained of Heaven, moreover, that this Glory shall be combined with the Fravasi and the material body, so as to produce from this threefold union the wonderful child (Zoroaster)."—*The Dinkart,* VII. 2, 68–70. *S.B. of E.*

The Divine Monad of Consciousness and Life passes on, during the process of involution, from seed-ego to seed-ego, and ultimately in the epoch of evolution, incarnates as human soul monads in the lower vehicles which are prepared for it as a dwelling-place ; thus bringing Wisdom eventually to the Soul. It is so ordained by the Divine Law that the Spiritual Consciousness shall dawn in the soul, through the union on the higher mental plane of the Monad of Life (Fravasi) with the Monad of Form,—

the one representing Force, and the other Matter, and the junction of the two leading up to the third,—Spirit or Consciousness ; thus producing the threefold elements of the coming Soul.

(To explain further,—Life and Consciousness are aspects of the Self which illuminate every developing Son of God. These aspects are to be conceived of as passing through, or animating, each successive manifestation of the involved Self which is differentiated in them. Fundamentally there is, of course, but one Self,—the direct expression of the Logos,—and from this One proceed the several manifestations which function and produce the many phenomenal results which contribute to the growth and expansion of the soul. Ultimately, the way having been prepared during the process and period of involution, the incarnation of the Divine Monad,—the One becoming the many,—is possible. But this "dismemberment" can only occur when the Self comes forth, or evolves, into the realm of Māyā. Incarnation completes involution, and is the point when evolution commences.)

See ABSOLUTE, ARC. MAN, ASSUMPTION, BIRTH OF KRISHNA, OF ZOROASTER, BODHISATVA, CONCEPTION, CONSCIOUSNESS, DISMEMBERMENT, EVOLUTION, FRAVASHI, HEBDOMAD, INCARNATION, INVOLUTION, MĀYĀ, MONAD OF LIFE, SEED, SELF, SON OF GOD, VIRGIN MARY, ZOROASTER.

GLORY IN THE GREAT CITY :—

Symbolic of the consciousness and life of the Spirit in the Causal-body, the ego having actualised the potential with which the soul was endowed. The ego becoming in ultimates that which the Self is in primes.

See CAUSAL-BODY, CITY (sacred).

GNOSIS OF LIFE :—

A symbol of the Illuminator of the qualities, i.e. the Higher Self—he that brings Truth to the soul, from within.

"The Master, Manda d'Hajje, is the Gnosis of Life by whose power Johanna (the baptiser) has been teaching and initiating all the long forty and two years of his ministry."—*Codex Nazareus,* R. h. Genza, 11.

The "Master" is the Higher Self, who, unknown of the lower consciousness, has sufficed to illumine those qualities which have sought the way to Peace. "John" the moral nature, the aspirer towards Truth (water) has been purifying the qualities "forty and two years,"—the number 6×7 which implies perfection upon the lower planes of the soul. But during this period of probation, the Love-nature (the Master) is unknown to the moral nature (Johanna), which labours from conscientious, rather than from highly spiritual, motives. Nevertheless, grace has descended upon it from on High, for the moral nature is really sustained by the Highest, who, when its period expires, reveals to it that which supersedes its phase of evolution,—Love taking the place of Law and Duty

"The virtue of the soul is Gnosis. For he who knows, he good and pious is, and still while on the earth divine" (C. H., *The Key*).—MEAD, *T. G. Hermes*, Vol. II. p. 146.

"What is it that makes the Soul alive in sooth ? Life unto the soul is knowledge of the Truth.—ASHIQ, *Gharib-Name*; GIBB, *Hist. of Ottoman Poetry*, Vol. I p. 197.

"Reason is the head, and knowledge is the ground of blessedness. To know an object is to become really one with it. God's knowing and my knowing are one ; true union with God takes place in cognition. Hence knowledge is the foundation of all essence, the ground of love, the determining power of the will. Only reason is accessible to the divine light. But the knowledge here referred to is something supra-sensible, inexpressible in words, unaided by the understanding ; it is a supernatural vision above space and time, and is not man's own deed but God's action in him" (Eckhart).— UEBERWEG, *Hist. of Philos.*, Vol. I. p. 473.

See FORTY, JOHANNA, JOHN BAPTIST, LETTER, MYSTERY (first), PEARL, SERPENT (loud breathing), SOUL.

GOAT,—WHITE HE-GOAT, UNBORN, HORNLESS, BEARDED :—

A symbol of the Higher Self incarnate in the lower nature, from which it climbs upward to Itself above.

"The He-Goat sprung from Pragâpati's head." "The He-Goat is no other than Pragâpati." "The He-Goat doubtless is speech, and from speech the gods doubtless went to the God-head, to the summit ;—

'thereby they went to the height' ; the height, doubtless, is the heavenly world." —*Sata. Brâh.*, V., VI., VII. 5, 2, 36.

The Higher Self emanates from the supreme, and is the Supreme (actual). The Higher Self incarnate, expresses (speech) itself in its evolution of the ideals (gods) which aspire to the Highest (the summit). The Self in the qualities climbs the heights to atma-buddhi. White signifies perfection.

See CAPRICORN, GODHEAD, HEIGHT, INCARNATION, MOUNTAIN, PRAGÂPATI, SPEECH, WHITE.

GOAT, MILCH :—

A symbol of error and desire, the lower food of the soul.

"And Mashya and Mashyoi had gone thirty days without food, covered with clothing of herbage ; and after the thirty days they went forth into the wilderness, came to a white-haired goat, and milked the milk from the udder with their mouths."—*The Bundahis*, Ch. XV. 10.

And for the lunar cycle (30 days), the Soul, comprising the sub-mental and love natures, proceeded on the astral plane with the growth of the earlier desires and instincts ; afterwards it struggled up to the mental plane, and encountered the "goat" —a symbol of false knowledge and desire, "white-haired" because attractive and alluring. The "drinking of the goat's milk" signifies the partaking of sensuous enjoyment in external activities, resulting in the evolution of the kama-manasic or desire-mental nature. This constitutes the fall of mind and emotion into matter.

See ASTRAL PLANE, CLOTHING, FALL, HERB, LUNAR CYCLE, MATRO, MILK (goat), PITRIYANA, PLANTS, SERPENT (subtil), WILDERNESS.

GOATS :—

A symbol of lower qualities,—the desires, instincts, and passions.

"And he shall separate the nations one from another, as the shepherd separateth the sheep from the goats ; and he shall set the sheep on his right hand, but the goats on the left."—MAT. xxv. 32, 33.

At the end of the cycle judgment will be passed upon the qualities of the soul. The groups of qualities (nations) which belong to the higher nature will "inherit the kingdom," that is, enter upon activity on the buddhic plane of consciousness, while the groups of lower qualities will be deprived of activity and cast out for dissolution (see ZECH. x. 3). The higher qualities minister to the Christ within the soul in their work of raising those qualities below them, though they may seem in so doing to turn away from the Christ. But the lower qualities are incapable of understanding the higher, or giving sustenance to the germs of goodness and truth which the Christ implants in the lower nature. The lower qualities are left to be reabsorbed in the purifying "fire" of the buddhic plane (see verses 34–46).

"But suppose we leave souls out of account for the moment, and think only of spiritual qualities. I admit that these can only exist in the experience of souls, but it is these which constitute the sheep and the goats, and not the souls. Souls can be freed from them or acquire them as the case may be, can accept them or reject them as time goes on, but there is no necessary eternal association of a soul with any quality. Once we see this the parable becomes luminous. You can draw the dividing line then between the sheep and the goats with absolute clearness. The sheep are the good things in our nature, the Christlike qualities in our character and experience ; the goats are the opposite. And Jesus can say, and does say, to every soul in whom his own love and purity are all in all, 'Come, ye blessed of my Father, inherit the kingdom prepared for you from the foundation of the world.' And correspondingly he can say, and does say, to the evils of life, to the selfishness inherent in the natural man, to everything opposed to his own spirit of compassion and desire to help, 'Depart from me, ye cursed, into the eternal fire.' For the devil and his angels, read 'evil and its agents,' and you have the truth about that phrase too. . . . The eternal fire is the truth, the righteousness, the love of God. Nothing can live in that devouring flame that is of the nature of a lie or wars against the essential life of any being. That consuming fire is eternal as God himself ; it is because he is ; it is that which was from the beginning, is now, and ever shall be, world without end. . . . Note carefully that I do not say that it is these good and evil qualities and not the souls in which they are expressed, that will enter into blessedness or suffering at the word of our divine Redeemer. They (the souls) do. The qualities are attached to the souls and have no independent existence. . . . But note also, that in this

parable it is nowhere stated that the souls remain in the endurance of the eternal fire into which they are sent, or into which they are dragged by their own evil against which the curse has been pronounced. That is not what is stated. The eternal fire is the eternal fire, whatever goes into it or comes out of it or dies within it. The dross is burned up, but the pure gold remains. Hell ceases to be hell the moment a soul is free from sin,—it becomes heaven."—R. J. CAMPBELL, Serm., *The Eternal Fire.*

This sermon was published in the *Christian Commonwealth* for June 18, 1913. As it contains probably the first published reference to the very important idea of *soul-qualities* being meant in scripture instead of souls, in many cases,—it is memorable.

See APPENDAGES, BUDDHI, DEVIL, FIRE (destroying), FIRE OF HELL, FURNACE, GOLD, HAND (left), HAND (right), HELL, MAN (natural), NATIONS, PURGATORY, QUALITIES, SCAPEGOAT, SHEEP, SHEPHERD, WAR.

GOATS, UNBLEMISHED :—

A symbol of sincere faith tending upwards (desire exalted).

"Whether haply Phœbus Apollo may be willing, having partaken of the savour of lambs and unblemished goats, to avert from us the pestilence."—*Iliad*, Bk. I.

Whether it will be that the Higher Self, having accepted the contribution of the lower self in the thought of loving service (savour of lambs) and sincere faith (unblemished goats), will afford the lower self the means for overcoming the adverse conditions which surround it.

See APOLLO, BURNT OFFERING, GOD (smelling), LAMB, PESTILENCE, SAVOUR (sweet).

GOD, POTENTIAL AND ACTUAL :—

A symbol of the central principle of being, the only reality, and the source of the transitory manifestation of the external universe, and of the human soul.

"The only Life which exists entirely in itself, from itself, and by itself, is the Life of God, or of the Absolute ;—which two words mean one and the same thing ; so that when we say the Life of the Absolute, we only use a form of expression, since the Absolute is Life, and Life is the Absolute.

This Divine Life lies entirely hidden in itself ;—it has its residence within itself, and abides there completely realised in, and accessible only to itself. It is all being, and beside it there is no being. It is therefore wholly without change or variation. Now this Divine Life discloses itself, appears, becomes visible, manifests itself as such—as the Divine Life : and this its manifestation, presence, or outward existence, is the world."—J. G. FICHTE, *Nature of the Scholar*, p. 134.

"How little do we know of ourselves ! How unjust we are to ourselves ! We study everything else but the Divine Principle within our own persons. The truth may be on our lips ; but in how few hearts does it live ! We need a new revelation—not of heaven or of hell,— but of the SPIRIT within ourselves."— W. E. CHANNING, D.D., *The Perfect Life*, p. 57.

"Man can name and can think of God because in his inmost substance he is of God. 'All divine things,' says Dionysius, ' in so far as they are manifested to us, are known only by participation therein.' . . . The chief names of God allowed by Dionysius are Goodness, Love, Being, Life, Wisdom, Reason, Faith, Power, Justice, Salvation, Redemption."—ALICE GARDNER, *John the Scot*, pp. 33, 35.

"Symbolically or metaphorically speaking, God can be called truth, goodness, essence, light, justice, sun, star, breath, water, lion, etc. But in reality he is exalted above all those predicates, since each of them has an opposite, while in him there is no opposition " (*John Scotus* (Erigena)).—UEBERWEG, *Hist. of Philos.*, Vol. I. p. 361.

"As to the true God of the human conscience, He cannot be attacked. He has his *raison d'être* in an invincible faith, and not in more or less ingenious arguments. Within the conscience a sacred voice is to be heard, which speaks to man of quite another world, the world of the ideal, the world of truth, of kindness, of justice. If there were nothing but Nature we might wonder whether God were necessary, but since an honest man existed, God has been proved. . . . I have no need of miracles for believing in Him, I have only to listen in silence to the revelations of my heart."—ERNEST RENAN, *Letter to M. Géroult*, 1862.

"If you will be blind to sense and see with the mind ; if you will turn from the flesh and waken the eyes of the soul, thus and thus only shall you see God."— CELSUS, *Origen cont. Cels.*, 7, 36.

God is Love—internal. There is no external God—a supposed dispenser of rain or fine weather, of miraculous escapes and shocking fatalities, of mining rescues and dire effects of explosions, of healings and diseases, of beautiful landscapes and deadly earthquakes, etc. In God there are no opposites.

"We get no proofs out of nature that go farther than to prove a God of nature, least of all do we get any that show Him to be acting supernaturally to restore the disorders of nature. . . . Our God derived from nature, is a monosyllable only, or at best a mechanical first cause, and no such being as the soul wants. Resting here, therefore, or allowing ourselves to be retained by what we call our natural theology, Christianity dies out on our hands for the want of a Christian God. And accordingly it is a remarkable fact that we have lost faith in God just in proportion to the industry we have spent in proving His existence by the natural evidences. First, because the God we prove does not meet our living wants, being only a name for causes, or a God of causes ; secondly, because in turning to Christianity for help, we have rather to turn away from the God we have proved, than toward Him. There is no relief to this mischief, but to conceive at the beginning that nature is but a fraction of the complete system of God ; that the true living God is a vastly superior being still, who holds the worlds of nature in His hands, and acts upon them as the Rectifier, Redeemer, Regenerator,—this is the God that speaks to our true wants."—H. BUSHNELL, *Nature and the Supernatural*, pp. 357–8.

"Love strives after the good ; it is nothing other than God himself."— ECKHART.

"It is the divine in man that impels him to love God as He is in reality, and the aim of that love is to take God into himself,—to become one with God."— GIORDANO BRUNO.

"The very fact that you can love proves that God is love ; he must be capable of it or you could not have had it. He must be wisdom or you would never have been able to think a thought ; he must be goodness or the very idea of goodness would never have been yours. God is the limitless reservoir out of which all our idealism arises, and without which truth, beauty and righteousness could not be ; to see these is to see God."—R. J. CAMPBELL, Serm., *Our Solidarity with God*.

"The idea of God as a man is a just idea, for God is divine love and divine wisdom, with every quality belonging thereto, and the subject of these is man." —SWEDENBORG, *Apoc. Rev.*, n. 224.

"Ere yet time was, God dwelt alone in unrevealed loveliness and glory. . . . The desire of self-expression is an esential attribute of the Absolute Beauty whereof these phenomenal forms are so many partial manifestations. The phenomenal universe then results from this desire of self-manifestation on the part of Absolute Beauty " (Sufi doctrine).—GIBB, *Hist. of Ottoman Poetry*, Vol. I. p. 16.

See ABSOLUTE, ATMAN, BRAHMA, CONDITIONED, DEITY, FATHER, FOOD, GODHEAD, IMAGE, JESUS (son of God),

MACROCOSM, MIND (good), MONAD, OGDOAD, PRAGÂPATI, SEED, SELF, SON OF GOD, TRINITY.

GOD BLESSING HIS CREATURES :—

A symbol of the Divine nature energising the functions of the lower nature so that the processes of involution and evolution may be established.

See BLESSING, CREATURES.

GOD REPENTING OF PREVIOUS ACTION :—

A symbol of Divine realisation of the possibility of superseding the initial attempts at Self-expression in low forms by fuller and completer life processes within improved astro-physical forms.

See DEPRAVITY, FLOOD.

GOD SMELLING A SWEET SAVOUR :—

A symbol of the apprehension by the Higher Self of the strivings of the lower Self to secure its blessing. It implies the loving response of the Higher to the lower.

See ALTAR BUILDING, BURNT OFFERING, GOATS (unblemished), NOAH, SAVOUR (sweet).

GODDESS, LADY, OR WOMAN (CELESTIAL) :—

A symbol of the buddhic principle, or of the matter aspect of manifestation, in its highest condition.

"I have remembered in Her (Lady) what I had forgotten ; and I, even I, live and am not hurt to my destruction. Therefore give unto me, give Thou unto me bliss and Thy peace : that the grasping of the four winds may knit together my parts."—Book of the Dead, Ch. CX.

In the buddhic (Lady) nature of the soul is seen to be all that is contained and evolved in and by the lower vehicles through the building of which the recovery of the true inner Self-knowledge has alone been rendered possible. And the true Self lives and alone survives the temporary associations in the lower life, which have led to the Higher Self's apprehension of Itself. For this reason bliss shall be committed to the soul, inasmuch as bliss is of the true nature of the Self which in essence is pure bliss. The full control of the lower nature in the

quaternary, as the means of evolution, serves to knit together the nature which is to be expressed under manifold aspects on higher planes.

"Varro derives the male divinities from heaven or Jupiter as the active principle, and the female divinites from the earth or Juno as the passive principle, while Minerva denotes the ideas as prototypes."—ZELLER, Hist. of Eclecticism, p. 177.

"Heaven" and "earth" are symbols of Spirit and Matter. "Minerva" signifies the buddhic plane, which contains the prototypes of the manifest.

See ALTAR (fire), ATHENA, BUDDHI, COME, ESTHER, FEMININE, HERA, ISIS, ISTAR, LADY, MĀYĀ, (higher) PROTOTYPES, RETURN, WINDS (four), WISDOM, ZEUS.

GODDESSES IN THE FORM OF DOUBLE SERPENTS CROWNED :—

Symbolic of the buddhic ideals of Wisdom and Love.

See SERPENTS (Nekhebit), SERPENTS (sparks).

GODHEAD :—

A symbol of the Absolute,—the Divine Reality, potential and unmanifest,—the One Source of all.

"Above and beyond the universe, yet compassing all things, and the source of all things, is the ' World of Godhead,' of this nothing can be predicated, and It is not reckoned among the Five Planes " (Sufi doctrine of the Soul).—GIBB, Hist. of Ottoman Poetry, Vol. I. p. 55.

"The Absolute is at once absolute process. The Godhead is the beginning and final goal of the whole series of essences which exist. . . . The eternal Godhead, as the beginning and end of all things, is concealed in absolute obscurity, being not only unknown and unknowable to man, but also unknown to itself" (Eckhart).—UEBERWEG, Hist. of Philos., Vol. I. p. 474.

"The Platonic, and still more the Stoic, speculation had led to the recognition of something divine in the spirit of man. In the more pantheistic Stoical form the doctrine might be expressed as follows : ' The Godhead can unfold His essence in a variety of existences, which, while they are His creatures as to their origin, are parts of His essence as to their contents.' This is not expressed in religious language ; but the belief that the Spirit of God is actually the guest and guide of the human soul was the source of all that was best and most ennobling in the system of the

Stoics."—W. R. INGE, *Paddock Lectures*, p. 62.

"The idea of God that man has in his being is the wonder of all wonders. He has felt in the depth of his life that what appears as imperfect is the manifestation of the Perfect."—RABINDRANATH TAGORE, *Hibbert Journal*, July, 1913.

See ABSOLUTE, AIN-SUPH, APARÂGITA, ARHAT, ATMAN, BRAHMA, CONDITIONED, DEITY, FATHER, GOD, MACROCOSM, MIND (good), MONAD, OGDOAD, PATH (two-fold), PRAGÂPATI, SEASONS, SEED, SELF (supreme), TRINITY, VIVANHAO, ZERANA.

GODS, DEITIES :—

Symbols of the highest Ideals in the soul. Love and Wisdom, Truth, Goodness, and Justice.

"Not different gods amongst different people,—Barbarian or Grecian, of the South or of the North,—but like as the Sun, Moon, Sky, Earth, Sea are the common property of all men, but yet are called by different names by different nations ; in the same manner as one Reason regulates all things, and one Providence directs, and subordinate Powers are appointed over all things, yet different honours and titles are by custom assigned to them amongst different peoples ; and these have established and do employ, *symbols*, some obscure, some more intelligible, in order to lead the understanding into things divine."—PLUTARCH, *Isis and Osiris*, § 67.

"All the Gods are good, and invariably the causes of good ; and all of them are uniformly convolved to one good, according to the beautiful and good alone."—IAMBLICHUS, *The Mysteries, etc.*, Th. Taylor trans., p. 68.

"They are called gods who are in divine truths from the Lord, and abstractedly, the truths themselves."—SWEDENBORG, *Apoc. Rev.*, n. 44.

"The names of the Gods of whom Orpheus sings are not the titles of deceiving demons, but the designations of divine virtues."—PICUS MIRANDULANUS, *Opp.*, p. 106, ed. Basil.

"Justice, goodness, disinterestedness, truth, purity, love ; do you not transport these ideas to heaven ? Are they not in fact the essential elements of your conception of heaven ? Is it not through them that you imagine beings in higher stages of existence ? Is not the very idea of a higher being this,—that the elements of moral perfection dwell in him in fullness and unity, as they are not unfolded upon earth ? Here then we learn the greatness of human nature."—W. E. CHANNING, *The Perfect Life*, p. 51.

"'So that the gods might dwell upon the earth in joy of heart, Marduk created mankind ? Man therefore is created for the sake of the gods ; it is precisely so in the *Enuma elish*."—A. JEREMIAS, *Old Test., etc.* Vol. I. p. 143.

"Savitri is the mind, and the gods are the vital airs ;—' Savitri, having harnessed the gods going by thought to the light, to heaven,'—for as such are as going to the heavenly world by thought (devotion) he has harnessed them for this holy work."—*Sata. Brâh.*, VI. 3, 1, 15.

"Savitri" is the Self working through the higher mind, and the "gods" are the energies of the Divine Life, the buddhi-manasic qualities. The Self has attached to the soul the higher qualities (gods) which aspire to the truth (light), for it is by means of the higher qualities that the egos are raised to a higher state of consciousness.

"Everything earthly in the Light-world of Ormazd had its protecting deity. These guardian spirits were divided into series and groups. They had their captains and their associated assistants."—*Zoroastrian System*, J. F. CLARKE.

This means, that as it was below, so also it was in prototype above. The "deities" are the ideals which enlist the veneration of the soul. The divisions are the groups of ideals centralised, which have been responsible for the religious and other systems of thought in human development.

"What is God for humanity but the transcendental summary of its supra-sensible wants, *the category of the ideal*."—E. RENAN, *L'Avenir de la Science*.

See AMSHASPANDS, COMPANY OF GODS, COSMOS, FOOD OF GODS, GOLDEN SOLES, KALLIOPEIA, LIGHT-WORLD, NIGHT, PROTOTYPES, QUALITIES, SACRIFICE, SAVITRI, VITAL AIRS.

GOING IN AND COMING FORTH IN MANIFESTATION :—

Symbolic of Involution and Evolution of the Divine Life.

"Beginning of the chapters of the Garden of Rest,—one of the chapters of Manifestation into Day, of Going in and Coming forth in the possession of Divinity ;—of union in the Garden of Reeds, of ' being ' in the Garden of Rest, even in the Great City, the Lady of the Four Winds."—*Book of the Dead* (Heading of Chapter CX.), trans. BLACKDEN.

A description of the Soul's pilgrimage towards Nirvana (Garden of Rest) during a manvantara ; beginning with the cycles, first, of Involution (Going in), and second, of Evolution (Coming forth) of the Life of the Logos. The acquirement of Individuality, or union with the Higher, as the separated Self rises above the functionings of the Astral life (Garden of Reeds). The periodic retirement of the Ego between incarnations into the Causal-body or higher Mind-centre (Great City) through which Buddhi (Lady) rules evolution in the Lower Quaternary (Four Winds), namely on the Lower Mental, the Astral, the Etheric, and the Physical planes of the Soul.

See BUDDHI, CHAPTERS, CITY (sacred), COMING FORTH, EVOLUTION, GARDEN OF REST, I A O, INCARNATION, INVOLUTION, LADY, MANVANTARA, RE-INCARNATION, SELF, WINDS (four).

GOLD :—

A symbol of spiritual qualities of the buddhic plane. Divine Wisdom ; celestial Truth. The endowments of the soul which are above the mental plane. The " treasures in heaven."

" And the city was pure gold, like unto pure glass "—REV. xxi. 18.

And the higher state of consciousness was on the buddhic plane whereon Wisdom and Truth were clearly perceived.

" And what does he (the Psalmist) call *gold*, saving wisdom ; of which Solomon saith, ' A treasure to be desired lieth at rest in the mouth of the wise ' (PROV. xxi. 20.) ? That is, he saw wisdom as gold, and therefore called it a " treasure ' : and she is well designated by the name of ' gold,' for that, as temporal goods are purchased with gold, so are eternal blessings with wisdom."—GREGORY THE GREAT, *Morals on the Book of Job*, Vol. I. p. 228.

"Gold signifies the good of love."—SWEDENBORG, *Apoc. Rev.*, n. 913.

See APPLES, ARMAITI, BUDDHIC PLANE, CRYSTAL, GLASS, HAVILAH, METALS, NET (golden), SAVITRI, SILVER, TREASURE, WISDOM.

GOLD-COLOURED SPOT :—

A symbol of a permanent atom of the causal-body, as a centre of organisation on the higher mental plane, and to which are attached the buddhic qualities.

" There collect the water into a channel the size of a Hathra ; there fix landmarks on a gold-coloured spot, (provided) with imperishable food ; there erect houses (composed of) mats and poles and roofs and walls."—*Vendidad*, II.

The using of a water channel

signifies the transferring of the experiences from below to the causal-body. This " channel " is said to be the size of a soul, the extent of which is comparable to the degree of the capacity of experience. The " landmarks " denote the successive incarnations by means of which the soul garners its harvest ; and the " gold-coloured spot " is the permanent atom of the causal-body. The " imperishable food " is the Wisdom and Love which suffice eternity. The " houses " are the temporary habitations of the ego on the lower planes, and the " mats, poles, roofs and walls " stand for the physical, astral, kama-manasic, and mental sheaths, on the respective planes.

See ATOM, ATOMS, BUDDHI, CAUSAL-BODY, CHANNELS, EXPERIENCES, FOOD, HOUSE, INCARNATION, LANDMARKS, PROSPERITY, RE-INCARNATION.

GOLD, FRANKINCENSE AND MYRRH, AS OFFERING TO THE DIVINE :—

Symbolic of philosophy, metaphysics, and logic, the productions of intellectual concentration.

" And (the wise men) came into the house and saw the young child with Mary his mother ; and they fell down and worshipped him ; and opening their treasures they offered unto him gifts, gold and frankincense and myrrh."—MAT. ii. 11.

And the faculties enlightened intellectually and seeking for Truth came into the soul's innermost sanctuary, where the Divine Truth and Love ensouled in the purified nature that bore It was revealed to their opening intellectual vision. In deep veneration they bowed down before their highest Ideal, and then they were able to offer up to It their best, —their much valued treasures of philosophy, metaphysics, and logic, through which they sought for Truth.

" The Magi, opening the stores of Scripture, offer its threefold sense, historical, moral, and allegorical, or Logic, Physic, and Ethics."—*Gloss, Anselm.*

" The reason why the Magi offered these three was because gold signified celestial good, frankincense spiritual good, and myrrh natural good, and from these three goods all worship is derived."—SWEDENBORG, *Apoc. Rev.*, n. 277.

" After Adam and Eve leave the Garden

of Eden, then at God's command, gold, frankincense and myrrh are brought by angels."—*Book of the Conflicts of Adam.*

The Supreme, through His messengers or subjective agencies, imparts to the mind and emotion, nature in their innermost capacity,—spiritual wisdom (gold) purity or grace (frankincense) and peace or bliss (myrrh). These await their development within the soul.

See BIRTH OF JESUS, FRANKINCENSE, HOUSE OF GOD, JESUS (gospels), MAGI, MYRRH. STAR IN THE EAST, TREAURES (cave), VIRGIN MARY.

GOLD MAN :—

A symbol of the atma-buddhic monad or Divine spark ensouled in the buddhic causal-body of the human race. The higher individuality.

"If the dviyagus brick is that same Sacrificer who is that Gold man (Pragâpati or Agni), which then is that real form of his ? Well, that Gold man is his divine body, and this brick is his human one. As to that Gold man, that is his immortal form,—his divine form ; gold being immortal. And as to this brick being made of clay, it is because this is his human form."—*Sata. Brâh.*, VII. 4, 2, 17.

If the causal-body represents the Archetypal Self, who is the Divine Monad ?—which is the original Divine Self ? Well, the Divine Monad is the spiritual expression direct from above, and the causal-body, is the expression of the Self working from below upwards in the matter of the planes. As to the Divine Monad, that is the Self's primordial eternal condition,—his state of being in atma. And as the causal-body is formed of higher mental matter, so it is the expression of the Self through human involution and constitutes the Individuality.

See ALTAR (fire), BRICKS, CAUSAL-BODY, DVIYAGUS, MONAD, PRAGÂPATI, SELF.

GOLD PLATE (CIRCULAR) :—

A symbol of the sun which is a symbol of the Supreme Self the centre and source of all things.

"He (the Sacrificer) hangs a gold plate round his neck, and wears it ; for that gold plate is the truth. . . . Now that truth is the same as yonder sun. For gold is light, and the sun is the light ; gold is immortality, and he is immortality."—*Sata. Brâh.*, VI. 7, 1, 1–2.

The incarnate Self is related to the Supreme Self through the purified emotions (neck). The Supreme Self is the Divine Reality, the centre of all. The Divine Wisdom (gold) imparts Truth (light), and the Supreme Self is the eternal Truth.

"Indra and Agni are the same as these two, to wit, the gold plate and the gold man : Indra is the gold plate, and Agni the man."—*Ibid.*, X. 4, 1, 6.

See AGNI, CIRCLE, GOLD MAN, INCARNATION, INDRA, LIGHT, NECK, SACRIFICER, SELF (supreme), SUN.

GOLDEN AGE :—

A symbol of the cycle of Involution which preceded the present cycle of Evolution. It is the age of archetypal perfection.

"During the happy reign of Yima, there was neither cold nor heat, neither decay nor death, nor malice produced by the demons ; Father and Son walked forth, each fifteen years old in appearance."—*The Homa Yasht*, HAUG, *Essays.*

"Yima" represents the primordial Self,—the Spirit in its descent into matter of the higher planes. The "happy reign" refers to the Golden Age during which all contrasts, good and evil, and the like, were non-existent. Decay and death are consequent upon evolution, not involution. Malice implies the opposite of love, and the "demons" are those powers which are concerned with its administration : the evil powers had not yet functioned. The "Father and Son" signify the First and Second Logoi, or Divine outpourings. The "fifteen years" refers to the early part of the cycle of involution, which is on both the atmic and buddhic planes. Involution does not yet occur lower than these planes,—not until the Third Logos functions.

"During the Third Dynasty (man's), human beings among whom respectful manners and pure customs prevailed occupied one territory. The kingly office was not mere pageantry ; nor were the functions of state ministers empty show. Good government was established by rulers, and correct instruction diffused among the people."—*Chinese Mythology.* KIDD, *China*, p. 101.

And now it is that the nascent humanity of the Golden Age,—the early type in which the absence of all relative experience appears as Edenic perfection,—is developed. The "territory" is a symbol of limitation imposed upon the race by the Absolute through whom humanity is formed and organised. At this stage no self-consciousness has been arrived at, that is, things could not be other than they are. *Necessity* is at this stage of being imperative. The "kingly office" signifies the Divine Will, and the "state ministers" are those agents through whom the Divine Will is executed. At this period of involution all the principles or laws of the universe are, as it were, laid down and worked out ideally, and these serve for the guiding of the process of evolution which is to follow.

"In the age of perfect virtue they (the spirit-like men) attached no value to wisdom, nor employed men of ability. Superiors were but as the higher branches of a tree ; and the people were like the deer of the wild. They were upright and correct, without knowing that to be so was Righteousness ; they loved one another, without knowing that to do so was Benevolence ; they were honest and leal-hearted, without knowing that it was Loyalty ; they fulfilled their engagements, without knowing that to do so was Good Faith ; in their simple movements they employed the services of one another, without thinking that they were conferring or receiving any gift. Therefore their actions left no trace, and there was no record of their affairs."—KWANGTZE, *Writings*, Bk. XII. 2, 5, 13, *S. B. of E.*

The Age is that of Involution and of prototypal perfection. The "spirit-like men" represent the inner nature of humanity being formed on the planes of atma-buddhi. Mentality (men of ability) was not yet operative. The buddhic virtues were practised without thought of any contrary action. Perfect inner harmony was established through the perfect adjustment of all conditions. There was no sense of moral evil and therefore no appreciation of goodness. There was no karma, and therefore no fruits of action, nor individual responsibility.

"In times past, the divine nature flourished in men ; but, at length, being mixed with mortal custom, it fell into ruin ; hence an inundation of evils in the race."—PLATO, *Critias*, p. 400.

"In the beginning, All-father appointed rulers, and bade them judge with him the fate of men, and regulate the government of the celestial city. They met for this purpose in a place called Idavoll, which is in the centre of the divine abode. Their first work was to erect a court or hall wherein are twelve seats for themselves, besides the throne which is occupied by All-father. This hall is the largest and most magnificent in the universe, being resplendent on all sides, both within and without, with the finest gold. Its name is Gladsheim. They also erected another hall for the sanctuary of the goddesses. It is a very fair structure, and called by men Vingolf. Lastly they built a smithy, and furnished it with hammers, tongs, and anvils, and with these made all the other requisite instruments, with which they worked in metal, stone, and wood, and composed so large a quantity of the metal called gold that they made all their moveables of it. Hence that age was named the Golden Age. This was the age that lasted until the arrival of the women out of Jotunheim, who corrupted it " (*Prose Edda*).—MALLET *North. Antiq.*, p. 409.

At the commencement of the cycle of involution, the Supreme co-ordinates the primal forces and conditions of manifestation that they might work together with him in the development of human souls and their perfectionment on the higher planes. They began their operations upon the higher buddhic plane (Idavoll), and from a centre thereon the Soul or higher causal-body (Gladsheim) was constructed. This had twelve divisions corresponding to twelve stages of the cycle (Zodiac), and twelve powers. The potential Soul was made perfect on the buddhic plane, or in Wisdom (gold). There was also formed the buddhic vehicle (Vingolf) as centralising the higher emotions (goddesses). The "smithy etc." refers to the activities of the higher mind, which being allied with buddhi produced in perfection the buddhic qualities (moveables of gold), perfect on the higher plane in this " Golden Age " of involution. This age of harmony lasted until the mind was attracted downwards, and the lower emotions (women) from the astromental evolution entered into it and filled it with turmoil and suffering.

"If now we associate the four elements in their regular order with the corresponding Ages of man in their regular order, the dominating element during the Golden Age will be fire, during the Silver Age, air, during the Brazen Age, water, and during the Iron Age, earth.

The conclusion of this is that the descent of man himself is due to his ever-increasing distance, so to speak, from the Divine fire."—K. F. SMITH, "Ages," *Ency. of Religion and Ethics.*

This is very true ; and if the esoteric meaning of each element is also borne in mind, the entire correspondence is very striking indeed. *Fire* stands for the buddhic plane—the real arena of the Golden Age : *Air* for the mental plane, the next below : *Water* for the astral plane : and *Earth* for the physical plane, the lowest of all, and furthest from the Divine. The physical plane is the most in evidence in the present Iron Age. The spiritual ego (man) descends to incarnate and expressed itself on the lowest plane, in an age of suffering and sorrow.

"You would know nothing either of good or evil if you were absolutely free from all restraint or coercion ; it is just because you are not free that you have such a battle to fight between the lower and the higher. The ideal life, the unconditioned life of God, the life eternal, knows nothing of the conflict between right and wrong, for there is nothing to give rise to it."—R. J. CAMPBELL, Serm., *God's Life in Man.*

"Not merely revelation to those who received it, but even human reason to those who have made it their teacher, has always signified that the wrong was an importation, an intrusion, an invasion in the world. That there was a time when it was not, there was a moment when it began to be. This has been always one of the dearest and most precious thoughts of men, one that they laid hold of the most eagerly, one that they let go of last. And men have always seemed to carry a certain sort of proof of their idea about with them in the very pictures and ideals of perfect goodness,— which all ages have treasured and kept alive. I suppose there is no other way of explaining the strange fact that amid all the personal badness, and social corruption that is in the world, the human mind has been able to preserve the ideal of a pure society and a perfect life, to dream of it, sometimes to strive after it, except by acknowledging the reality of an entrance of iniquity into the world, and looking back to a time before that invasion when the world was sinless." —PHILLIPS BROOKS, *Mystery of Iniquity*, p. 4.

See ADAM (lower), BONDAGE, BUDDHIC PLANE, CIVILISING PEOPLE, CRIPPLES, DEMONS, DWELLINGS, DYNASTY, EDEN, ELEMENTS, EVOLUTION, GARDEN, GIMLE, GOOD (light), GOVERNMENT, INVOLUTION, IRON AGE, JOTUNHEIM, KALI-YUGA, MANCO CAPAC, METALS, MINISTERS, OANNES, OHONAMOCHI, PEOPLE, PYLUS, RACES, RAGHA, RESPECTFUL MANNERS, SETTLEMENTS, VARA, VISTASP (king), WORLDS (five), YAO, YIMA, ZODIAC.

GOLDEN AND SILVERN APPEARANCE :—

Symbolic of active and passive states. Gold, or sun, signifies activity : silver, or moon, passivity. *See* CARTS.

GOLDEN CARRIAGES :—

A symbol of high mental qualities allied with buddhic faculties.

GOLDEN CHILD :—

See HIRANYAGARBHA.

GOLDEN FLEECE, FROM THE GOLDEN OR PURPLE RAM OF GOD :—

A symbol of the buddhic vesture of the indwelling Spirit (atma)—the Incarnate Self, the "Lamb of God."

"On the arrival of Jason at Iolcus, Peleas, the king, remembered the oracle about being on his guard against the man with the one shoe, and so asked Jason what *he* would do if he were told by an oracle that he should be killed by one of his subjects ? Jason, at the suggestion of Hera, who hated Peleas, answered that he would send that subject to fetch the Golden Fleece. Peleas accordingly ordered Jason to fetch the Fleece."—*The Story of Jason*, KEIGHTLEY, *Mythology.*

On the Higher-Self (Jason, or Jasius) being born in the soul on the mental plane (Iolcus), and received of the lower-self (Peleas) ; the lower being in touch with the Higher, recollects that the Higher is never revealed in his fullness or perfect duality, and that the Unmanifest can never be apprehended in its true nature. So the lower, as it were, puts the Higher nature to the test, and inquires what would be done if he,— Jasius the Saviour,—were to be delivered up by one of his chosen qualities (a "Judas") for execution ? Then the Higher-Self prompted by the Wisdom (Hera) within, which disdains the opinionative knowledge esteemed by the lower-self, answers that if this execution or consummation of sacrifice,—the slain Son of Man rising as Son of God,—be accomplished, then indeed the endowment of the buddhic faculties (the Golden Fleece or the Purple Robe) shall be attained and the Higher Self be glorified in the risen lower Self. And so it follows that the prompting from Above impels the Higher nature in the soul to seek Self-realisation through Self-development.

"With her drugs Medea cast to sleep the serpent which guarded the Golden Fleece."—*Ibid.*

With the potent "drugs," or powers, exercised upon the higher planes, intuition (Medea) lulled to rest the desire-mind (the tempting serpent), and so revealed the buddhic nature to the consciousness.

The "Golden Fleece" has the same meaning as the "treasure in heaven," the "fruit of the Spirit," the "pearl," the "best robe," the "holy grail," "wealth."

See BULLS, BUDDHI, CADMUS, CONSULTING, DRUGS, EVOLUTION, GEUSH TASHA, HERA, INCARNATION, JASON, LAMB, MEDEA, ORACLE, PEARL (precious), PELEAS, ROBE, WISDOM.

GOLDEN HAIR :—

A symbol of the highest aspirations of the mind in contact with buddhi.

"Athene stood behind Peleus' son (Achilles) and caught him by his golden hair, to him only visible, and of the rest no man beheld her."—*Iliad*, Bk. I.

The Wisdom principle (Athene) appeals to the personality (Achilles) by inspiring it with loftier motives and higher aspirations, for by these only is Wisdom apprehended. To the lower mental qualities the buddhic nature remains unapparent.

See ACHILLES, ATHENA, BUDDHI, HAIR OF HEAD, PELEUS, WISDOM.

GOLDEN HORNS :—

A symbol of zeal and love of the true.

See BRAHMAN PRIESTS

GOLDEN HORSES :—

Symbolic of insight into the truth through the intellect; i.e. philosophy.

See HORSE.

GOLDEN HORSE TRAPPINGS :—

Symbolic of high mental perception revealing the intuition of truth or wisdom.

GOLDEN LIGHT :—

A symbol of the Divine radiance of Truth which flashes forth from above and illumines the soul.

See LIGHT.

GOLDEN PALACES OF THE CELESTIAL CITY :—

Symbolic of the ideal types of the lower vehicles of consciousness, which are on the buddhic plane.

See CITY OF GOD.

GOLDEN PILLAR :—

A symbol of the Divine Ray from the Supreme, linking the higher and lower natures.

See PILLAR, SUTRATMA.

GOLDEN SOLES MADE BY HEPHAESTUS, WHICH ENABLE THE GODS TO TREAD EARTH AND SEA AND AIR :—

Symbolic of the functionings of the causal-body, which the Divine Mind contrived to enable the Ideals (Gods) to operate upon the lower planes through the vehicles connected with the causal-body. These vehicles of the ego are upon the physical plane (earth), the astral plane (sea), and the mental plane (air). The "soles" or "shoes" signify power to advance in progression. By means of the Ideals which arouse aspiration, the soul grows towards perfection.

See AIR, CAUSAL-BODY, EARTH, GODS, HEPHAISTOS, SEA, SHOES.

GOLDEN STAFF :—

A symbol of the Divine Ray from the Supreme which vibrates downwards through the planes.

See FILLET OF APOLLO.

GOLGOTHA, THE PLACE OF A SKULL :—

A symbol of the emptiness of the lower affections if they are taken as an end in themselves, rather than as a means to an end. The empty skull is significant of the vanity of all earthly attachments. The procession of Jesus and the people to Golgotha is typical of the soul which has not yet entirely parted from those lower affections which are attached to the outer form and not to the spirit within.

See PILATE, SKULL, TRIAL,

GOLOKA OR GOKALA, WORLD OF COWS :—

A symbol of the buddhic plane.

"Goloka 'the world of the cows,' or the supreme heaven of Krishna."—A. BARTH, *Religions of India*, p. 228.

The plane of buddhi (cow) is the height of attainment for the Soul (Krishna) in the present cycle.

See BIRTH OF KRISHNA, COW, GOPIS, KRISHNA.

GOOD FRIENDSHIP OF FOREIGNERS :—

This symbol signifies the benefit derived from the experiences of the undisciplined and adverse qualities in furthering the soul's development.

"The extreme strengthening of alliance; the gratification due to the good friendship of foreigners."—*Dinkard*, Bk. VII. 9, 2, *S. B. of E.*

The complete union with the Self; the arrival of the consciousness in buddhi, where all experiences, even adverse experiences, are related with the evolution of the Self.

See AHRIMAN, BUDDHIC PLANE, EXPERIENCES, UNION.

GOOD, OR LIGHT CREATION :—

A symbol of the perfect archetypal production of qualities and forms upon the upper planes of being.

"And God saw that it was good."—GEN. i. 10.

All that was produced through involution was pronounced "good," that is, perfect for purposes of forthcoming manifestation upon the lower planes in the cycle of evolution.

See COSMOS, CREATION, GOLDEN AGE, IMAGE, INVOLUTION, PROTOTYPES.

GOOSE :—

See SEB.

GOPIS, COWHERDESSES :—

A symbol of the buddhic emotions which accompany the manifesting Higher Self or Divine Soul.

"In those same amours (with the Gopis) to which Krishna surrenders himself, we have a picture of the wanderings of the soul (for Krishna is also the universal soul) and the ineffable blessedness which it experiences when, restored to itself and yielding to the invitations of grace, it throws itself into the arms of God."—BARTH, *Religions of India*, p. 231.

"The Gopis were madly in love with Krishna. As he played the flute they came to dance with him; but as all could not hold Krishna's hand as they danced, he multiplied himself into as many forms as there were women, each woman believing she held the hand of the true Krishna."—*Story of Krishna*.

The higher emotions (Gopis),—those essentially of goodness, justice, truth, wisdom, kindness, patience, gentleness, serenity, peace, etc.,—were in close affection with the Divine Ideal born in the soul, and their activities were brought into harmony with the Divine activities. Each emotion became separately harmonised and in tune with the Divine soul, and so partook of the Divine nature, while they all worked together to promote truth and righteousness.

"Krishna is named Gopal, 'the Cowherd.'"—BARTH, *Religions of India*, p. 220.

"Gosvāmen—lord of cows—is an epithet of Krishna."—MON. WILLIAMS, *Indian Wisdom*.

"Cow" being a symbol of buddhi, these terms are accounted for as indicating that "Krishna" stands for the Higher Self,—atma-buddhi.

See ARJUNA, BIRTH OF KRISHNA, BLANDISHMENTS OF WOMEN, BUDDHI, DANCE (circle), ESTHER, GOLOKA, HOURIES, KRISHNA, MUSES, MUSIC, QUALITIES, SATYRS, WOMAN.

GOSHURUN :—

A symbol of the personality which proceeds from the astral principle.

"But when the Bull died Kaiomarts (Gayomard), the first man, came out of his right shoulder, and from the left Goshurun, the soul of the Bull, who now became the guardian spirit of the animal race."—*Zoroastrian System*, CLARKE.

This signifies the period at the commencement of evolution, when man is evolved from the involved Monad. "Kaiomarts" is the Archetypal Man who comes forth into activity upon the buddhic and higher manasic planes. The "right shoulder" signifies the outgoing, positive force; the "left" is the astral principle from which arises the personality (Goshurun) which becomes the regulator of the desires and lower activities. The "primal Bull" signifies the matrix of all living things upon the lower planes, and its "death" is the ensouling of the monad of form on the mental plane by the monad of life.

"Also the whole realm of the clean

animals and plants came from the Bull's body. Full of rage, Ahriman now created the unclean animals,—for every clean beast, an unclean."—*Ibid.*

From the same matrix proceeded also the " clean beasts," that is, those natural activities which were in the astral course of production. And in process of time the opposites of these were brought forth ; the positive implying negative,—the good, the bad ; the strong, the weak, and so forth.

" Thus Ormazd created the dog, Ahriman the wolf ; Ormazd all useful animals, Ahriman all noxious ones ; and so of plants."—*Ibid.*

The " dog " and the " wolf " symbolise the higher and lower minds or wills. The " useful " and " noxious creatures " represent those apparently beneficial, and those deleterious functions, both of which are, however, necessary to the evolution of the soul. The " plants " signify the minor activities in the earliest functionings of soul growth.

See AHRIMAN, ASTRAL, ARC. MAN, BEASTS, BULL, DOG, EPIMETHEUS, GEUSH-TASHA, HERB, KAIOMARTS, OPPOSITES, PERSONALITY, PLANTS, PROMETHEUS, WOLF, YEHEEDAH.

GOSPEL :—

The message of Wisdom from within to acquaint the soul of its Divine nature, its purpose, and its destiny.

" How that our gospel came not unto you in word only but also in power, and in the Holy Ghost, and in much assurance."—1 THESS. i. 5.

The message of Wisdom (Holy Ghost) may be suggested from outside, but its power, and the conviction of its truth, can only be found within.

" And this too we must bear in mind, that as the law contains a shadow of good things to come, which are indicated by that law which is announced according to truth, so the Gospel also teaches a shadow of the mysteries of Christ, the Gospel which is thought to be capable of being understood by anyone. What John calls the eternal Gospel, and which may properly be called the spiritual Gospel, presents clearly to those who have the will to understand, all matters concerning the very Son of God, both the mysteries presented by His discourses and those matters of which His acts were the enigmas."—ORIGEN, *Comm. on John,* Bk. I. p. 9.

" By the Gospel and the preaching of the Gospel is signified the annunciation of the coming of the Lord and of his kingdom."—SWEDENBORG, *Apoc. Rev.,* n. 626.

" The gospel is that of the revelation of God in Christ, who is the Alpha and Omega, the beginning and the end, the first and the last. The gospel of Christ would be powerless to help in readjusting life's beginnings and endings unless he were himself in very deed a revelation of the cosmic secret, the heart divine that beats at the centre of all existence and seeks its own by way of the cross. . . . He was and is the focus and embodiment of that which was from the beginning, and is the true and only end of all our strivings."—R. J. CAMPBELL, Serm., *Beginnings and Endings.*

" When the new light has come on a heart prepared to receive it ; when the new ideas, which are a gospel to us, are recognised at once as the masters of life, what is the main result ? They transfigure life, they make all things new, they exalt the common into the divine, they cleanse and ennoble all the world. It is the work that the ideas of the Gospel of Christ do upon the spirit that receives and loves them. . . . In the realm of the pure intellect all things are glorified as parts of a great whole."—STOPFORD A. BROOKE, Serm., *Peter and Cornelius.*

" Our confidence remains unshaken, that Christ and His all-quickening life are in the world, as fixed elements, and will be to the end of time ; for Christianity is not so much the advent of a better doctrine as of a perfect character ; and how can a perfect character, once entered into life and history, be separated and finally expelled ? It were easier to untwist all the beams of light in the sky, separating and expunging one of the colours, than to get the character of Jesus, which is the real gospel, out of the world."—H. BUSHNELL, *Nature and the Supernatural,* p. 231.

See AMBAYAVIS, INSPIRATION, KORAN, LAW OF ZOROASTER, PEN, RAMAYANA, REVELATION, SASTRA, SCRIPTURES, UPANISHAD, VEDA, WORD OF GOD.

GOSPEL STORY OF JESUS CHRIST :—

A Divine Drama of the Soul's descent in Involution, ascent in Evolution, and final return in glory to its Source.

" To sum up all things in Christ, the things in the heavens, and the things upon the earth ; in him, I say, in whom also we were made a heritage, having been foreordained according to the purpose of him who worketh all things after the counsel of his will ; to the end that we should be unto the praise of his glory, we who had before hoped in Christ : in whom ye also, having heard the word of the truth, the gospel of your salvation,— in whom having also believed, ye were sealed with the Holy Spirit of promise." —Eph. i. 10-13.

The container of all qualities and forms of the higher and lower natures is the involved Spirit, the Archetypal Man (Christ). In him the disciplined qualities are made the means of accomplishing his purpose according to the foreordained scheme of spiritual development, to the end that the qualities should be perfected and return with him into the Absolute. The less disciplined qualities having received the " word of truth " from within, now possess the means whereby they also may be perfected, for they have been allied indissolubly with the Wisdom nature which is to transmute them.

" The Gospel narrative is to be studied ' in order that we may know ' : it does not convey knowledge immediately. ' Getting to know ' is a gradual process, a progressive inner experience. God reveals Himself within us as we are able to receive Him."—W. R. Inge, Paddock Lectures, p. 51.

The deep meanings which underlie the teaching of the Gospel drama were crystallised, so to speak ; and to get at them, the crude external form of expression has to be broken up into fragments, and then,—and then only, —can be perceived the infinite wisdom concealed in the whole scriptural narration.

The deep meanings have always been recognised partially by a few, as will be found by consulting the writings of the seers of all past ages. But these interpretations of the seers are a question of interior illumination, and so are seldom seen or heard of in the world. But we may be assured that these inner meanings will in time become universally recognised, as indeed they are at present on higher planes of the soul,—which subjective fact makes people cling with such tenacity and unreasoning stubbornness to the Bible and the other scriptures, all of which contain similar ideas of the soul and God under their surface expression. All scriptures have been written down and preserved to suit certain stages of human evolution.

" The life and death and rising again of Christ are to St. Paul a kind of dramatisation of the normal psychological experience. We too must die to sin and rise again to righteousness ; nay, we must die daily, crucifying the old man and putting on the new man—the true likeness of Him who created us. And this is why the identification of Christ with the world-principle was so essential for him. The ' whole process of Christ ' (as some of our English divines called it) was thus proved to be the great spiritual law under which we all live."—W. R. Inge, Ibid., p. 45.

" In the sixth chapter of the Fourth Gospel, when both ' Jews ' and ' disciples ' show such a strange inability to grasp the symbolic meaning of the ' bread which came down from heaven,' our Lord closes the discussion by saying, ' It is the spirit that quickeneth, the flesh profiteth nothing. The words that I have spoken they are spirit and they are life.' . . . A purely historical faith appeals only to the understanding, to the faculty which judges of scientific or historical truth in other fields ; that the conclusions it arrives at are as liable to be upset as the conclusions of secular historians ; and that it is subject to the limitations which Bacon asserts of intellectual investigations generally—' Studies teach not their own use.' The words of Christ appeal not to the senses and understanding but to the heart and higher reason."—Ibid., p. 49.

" These Christian mystics see in the historic life of Christ an epitome—or if you will, an exhibition—of the essentials of all spiritual life. There they see dramatised not only the Cosmic process of the Divine Wisdom, but also the inward experience of every soul on her way to union with that Absolute ' to which the whole creation moves.' This is why the expressions which they use to describe the evolution of the mystical consciousness from the birth of the divine in the spark of the soul, to its final unification with the Absolute Life, are so constantly chosen from the Drama of Faith. In this drama they see described under veils the supreme and necessary adventures of the spirit. Its obscure and humble birth, its education in poverty, its temptation, mortification, and solitude, its ' illuminated life ' of service and contemplation, the desolation of that ' dark night of the soul ' in which it seems abandoned by the Divine : the painful death of the self, its resurrection to the glorified existence of the Unitive Way, its final reabsorption in its Source."—E. Underhill, Mysticism, p. 144.

See Arc. man, Ascension, Christ, Disciples, Evolution, Holy Ghost, Incarnation, Inspiration, Jesus, Multitudes, Qualities, Resurrection, Revelation, Scriptures, Soul.

GOSPEL OF THE KINGDOM :—

A symbol of the Divine message to the soul to make things below perfect, as their prototypes above are perfect.

" And this gospel of the kingdom shall be preached in the whole world for a testimony unto all the nations ; and then shall the end come."—MAT. xxiv. 14.

The " gospel of the kingdom " is the spiritual " book of life " which sets forth the course of the evolution of the soul ; it contains the history of " just men made perfect " in all their qualities (nations). The end must arrive for all that is less than perfection.

" Basilides added, that the life of Christ was the beginning of a progressive shaping and forming of the individual souls of believers, as thoughts of God, out of the shapeless form of unconscious material or psychical existence. . . The history of mankind is the type of the evolution of creation."—BUNSEN, *Hippolytus, etc.*, Vol. I. p. 120.

See BOOK, CREATION, DAY AND NIGHT, IMAGE, JUDGMENT DAY, KINGDOM OF HEAVEN, NATIONS, PROTOTYPES, QUALITIES.

GOSPELS :—

Writings symbolic of the evolution of the soul.

" In assigning to the Gospels their proper meaning, it is necessary to remember that as mystical Scriptures they deal primarily, not with material things or persons, but with spiritual significations. Like the ' books of Moses,' therefore, and others, which, in being mystical, are, in the strictest sense, prophetical, the Gospels are addressed, not to the outer sense and reason, but to the soul. And being thus, their object is not to give an historical account of the physical life of any man whatever, but to exhibit the spiritual possibilities of humanity at large, as illustrated in a particular and typical example. The design is, thus, that which is dictated by the nature itself of Religion. For Religion is not in its nature historical and dependent upon actual, sensible events, but consists in processes, such as Faith and Redemption, which being interior to all men, subsist irrespectively of what any particular man has at any time suffered or done. That alone which is of importance is what God has revealed. And therefore it is that the narratives concerning Jesus are rather parables founded on a collection of histories than any one actual history, and have a spiritual import capable of universal application. And it is with this spiritual import, and not with physical facts, that the Gospels are concerned."—KINGSFORD AND MAITLAND, *The Perfect Way*, p. 225.

" The Gospel narrative, while related, —in Scripture fashion,—as of an actual particular person, and in terms derived from the physical plane,—is a mystical history only, of any person, and implies the spiritual possibilities of all persons. And hence, while using terms implying or derived from actual times, places, persons and events, it does not *really* refer to these or make pretence to historical precision."—*Ibid.*, p. 230.

" Horst presented the symbolical view of the history of Jesus with singular clearness. . . . The history of the Gospel is in fact the history of human nature conceived ideally, and exhibits to us in the life of an individual what man ought to be, and, united with him by following his doctrine and example, can actually become."—D. F. STRAUSS, *Life of Jesus*, Vol. III. p. 430.

See FOUR GOSPELS, INSPIRATION, REVELATION, SCRIPTURES.

GOVERNMENT, GOOD :—

A symbol of the Divine order of the principles and laws of the universe, or of the soul.

" God is the Governor of all the world. The purpose of His government, the one design on which it all proceeds, is that the whole world, through obedience to Him, should be wrought into His likeness, and made the utterance of His character. Let that thought dwell before your mind, and feel, as you must feel, what a sublime and glorious picture it involves. Then remember that God does not treat the world in one great, vague generality. He sees the world made up of free souls of men and women. The world can become like Him by obedience, only as the souls of men and women become like Him by obedience. Each soul must enter into that consummation by its own free submission ; helped, no doubt, by the movement of souls all about it, and by the great promise of the world's salvation, but yet acting for itself, by its own personal resolve. To each soul God brings all the material of this terrestrial struggle,— all the temptations, all the disappointments, all the successes, all the doubts and perplexities, all the jarring of interests, all the chances of hinderance and chances of help which come flocking about every new-born life. . . . The real victory in the struggle can be nothing less than the accomplishment in us of that which it is the object of all His government to accomplish in the world."—PHILLIPS BROOKS, Serm., *The Pillar, etc.*

See CIVILISING, GOLDEN AGE, KINGLY OFFICE, MINISTERS, OANNES, OHONAMOCHI.

GOVERNORS OF THE EARTH :—

A symbol of ruling desires and passions of the lower nature (earth).

"Before governors and kings shall ye stand for my sake, for a testimony unto them."—MARK xiii. 9.

This signifies the bringing of the disciplined qualities (disciples) before the tribunal of the rulers of the lower soul,—such ruling forces as brute-power, greed, passion, lust, anger, self-interest, craft, cunning, all of which are "of this world." The qualities testify before these rulers for the sake of the Ideal.

See CALAMITIES, DISCIPLES, EARTH, KING, MURDER, RULER.

GRACE OF GOD :—

A symbol of the response of the Higher nature to the aspirations of the lower. It is through the action of the Higher nature alone that the soul is raised ; the unassisted lower nature being incapable of raising itself.

"We must learn to discern the true from the false, the higher from the lower, in all the relations of life, and trust to the redeeming grace of God to enable us to fulfil all righteousness."—R. J. CAMPBELL, Serm., *God's Life in Man.*

"If there is any sufficient infallible, and always applicable distinction that separates a Christian from one who is not, it is the faith, practically held, of a supernatural grace or religion. (Faith is the sister of reason ; grace is the medicine of nature.) There is no vestige of Christian life in the working-plan of nature. Christianity exists only to have a remedial action upon the contents and conditions of nature. That is development ; this is regeneration. No one fatally departs from Christianity who rests the struggles of holy character on help supernatural from God. No one really is in it, however plausible the semblance of his approach to it, who rests in the terms of morality, or self-culture."—H. BUSHNELL. *Nature and the Supernatural*, p. 356.

"A righteous man's reward is not the result of merit. It is in the order of grace, the (super) natural consequence of well-doing. It is life becoming more life. It is the soul developing itself. It is the Holy Spirit of God in man making itself more felt, and mingling more and more with his soul, felt more consciously with an ever-increasing heaven. You reap what you sow—not something else—but that. An act of love makes the soul more loving. The thing reaped is the very thing sown, multiplied a hundredfold. You have sown a seed of *life*—you reap Life everlasting."—F. W. ROBERTSON, *Sermons, 1st Series*, p. 219.

"To be saved by grace supposeth that God hath taken the salvation of our souls into his own hands. . . . God is not willing that men should be saved by their own natural abilities ; but all the works of the law which men do to be saved by, they are the works of men's natural abilities, and therefore called the work of the flesh, but God is not willing that men should be saved by these, therefore no way but by his grace."—JOHN BUNYAN, *Saved by Grace.*

"God is always the same—equally near, equally strong, equally gracious. But our possession of His grace, and the imparta-tion of His grace through us to others, vary, because our faith our earnestness, our desires vary. True, these no doubt are also His gifts and His working, and nothing that we say now touches in the least on the great truth that God is the sole originator of all good in man ; but while believing that, as no less sure in itself than blessed in its message of confi-dence and consolation to us, we also have to remember, ' If any man open the door, I will come in to him.' An awful re-sponsibility lies on us. We can resist and refuse, or we can open our hearts and draw into ourselves His strength."—A. MACLAREN, *Sermons, 2nd Series*, p 35.

"It is not that God is a great way off, but that we in spirit may be a great way off from the apprehension of his eternal holiness and truth. But the grace of God takes advantage of every smallest opportunity to find entrance to the soul. The faintest motion of our spirits Godward brings him to our assistance. There may be very little in us for his goodness to take hold of, but such as it is he makes use of it."—R. J. CAMPBELL, Serm., *God's Loving-kindness.*

See BLESSING, DEVAYANA, GIFTS OF GOD, INFIRMITIES, LADDER, PRAYER, SEED (good).

GRAIL, HOLY OR RICH :—

A symbol of the Divine Life, Wisdom and Love (atma-buddhi), vehicled in the causal-body (the chalice). The quest of the Grail is the search by the indwelling Self below in the Personality, of the Wisdom and Love-nature above in the Individuality. This search is the Divine drama of the Soul, in which the Self as a hero goes through the experiences of the lower life, contending against ignor-ance and evil and releasing the higher qualities held captive by the lower.

"Seen from different standpoints, the Grail became the emblem of moral purity, or of triumphant faith, or of soldierly heroism, or of gracious charity ; the radiance of it became the radiance of that ultimate perfection which allures those who struggle, and rewards those who attain."—ROSE, *Ency. of Religion and Ethics*.

See APPLES, CAPTIVITY, CAUSAL-BODY, CUP OR CHALICE, EXPERIENCES, GOLDEN FLEECE, GOSPEL, HESPERIDES, HIKOBOSHI, INCARNATION, INDIVIDU-ALITY, LOVER (maiden), MAIDEN, PEARL (precious), PERSONALITY, SELF, SOUL, TREASURE, WISDOM, WITNESSES (two).

GRAPES, OR WINE :—

A symbol of the spiritual nature of love and wisdom. The "fruit" of the "vine," or "tree of life."

"The common people like to mix water with the wine of their belief. They usually mix a great deal : sometimes so much as to drown the precious drop from the 'calix inebrians,' 'the chalice of the grapes of God.' But it is still there, potent in its divine virtue to slake the thirst of human nature for a good transcending sense ; to lift eyes, dim with tears and dull with pain, towards the Beatific Vision ; to heal and strengthen feet sore and weary from the rough ways of earth, for the steep ascent of Heaven."—W. S. LILLY, *The Great Enigma*, p. 288.

See CANA, CUP, FRUIT OF THE SPIRIT, HANGING, INTOXICATION, VINE, WINE.

GRASS :—

A symbol of the condition of awaken-ment of the Divine life in the lower nature of the soul.

"And God said, Let the earth put forth grass."—GEN. i. 11.

And the Supreme now directs that the earliest beginnings of the Divine life shall proceed to manifest. The "grass" symbolises the faint aspira-tion arising from the lower nature in the dawn of light and life. Grass upsprings from the soil which is sluggish and inert,—the mineral form of life.

"By green grass is signified that good and truth of the church or of faith, which first springs up in the natural man ; the same also is signified by the herb of the field."—SWEDENBORG, *Apoc. Rev.*, n. 401.

See DEW, GINUNGA, HERB.

GREAT INVISIBLE FORE-FATHER :—

A symbol of the First Logos, or of the Absolute, the Source of all.

See ABSOLUTE, FATHER, GODHEAD, SELF (supreme), TRINITY.

GREATNESS, MANY-CROWNED, CONTRASTED WITH LOW-NESS :—

Symbolic of honour in high en-deavours educing power over the lower nature, in contrast with dis-honour which attends the yielding to the lower allurements.

See CROWN, HIGHER AND LOWER.

GREECE ; GRECIAN LAND :—

A symbol of the mental plane in the sacred scriptures of Greece.

"O Gods ! surely a great sorrow comes upon the Grecian land. Verily, Priam would exult, and the sons of Priam, and the other Trojans would greatly rejoice in their souls, were they to hear these things of you twain (Agamemnon and Achilles) contending : you who in council and in fighting surpass the Greeks."—*Iliad*, Bk. I, trans. Buckley.

O Ideals ! certainly a great trial shall forthwith assail the mind. Assuredly the Causal Self (Priam) and its assemblage of high faculties shall thereby be developed ; and the lower emotions (Trojans) will be greatly stimulated if the Desire-mind and the Personality be stirred into more activity. For in the unwisdom of the emotional lower self there consists greater wisdom in latency than in the mental faculties.

See ACHILLES, AGAMEMNON, COUN-TRIES, GODS, NESTOR, PRIAM, PYLUS, TROJANS.

GREEKS ; ACHAIANS :—

A symbol of the mental faculties which contend against the emotions (Trojans).

See ACHAIANS, AGAMEMNON, ARABS, ATREUS, FUNERAL PILES, SHIPS (Greeks), WARRIORS.

GREEKS, GREAT-HEARTED :—

A symbol of the higher mental faculties which raise the lower nature and purify it, when allied with the buddhic emotions.

See HONOUR, PRINCES (Greeks).

GREEN COLOUR :—

The symbolic colour of the astral plane, being the plane of growth through desire. Hence the "green sea"; "grass," "herbs," "vegeta-tion," etc., also "wood."

"If thou wouldst destroy Apep, thou shalt say this chapter over a figure of Apep

which hath been drawn in green colour upon a sheet of new papyrus, and over a wax figure of Apep upon which his name hath been cut and inlaid with green colour; and thou shalt lay them upon the fire so that it may consume the enemy of Ra."
—From "The Book of Overthrowing Apep," DR. BUDGE, *Egyptian Magic*, p. 80.

The serpent Apep is a symbol of desire which inhabits, and energises upon, the astral plane. The "saying of the chapter" signifies the passing through the period of experience which shall develop the desire nature and make it of service in the soul's progress. The "drawing and figure of Apep" signify the illusoriness and transitoriness of the things of the lower planes, which truth the soul gradually realises; and the burning is the symbol of final purification, and the ridding the soul of the desire-nature the opponent of the Divine.

See APEP, ASTRAL PLANE, COLOURS, DRAGON (red), HERB, PLANT, SEA, WOOD.

GREEN LION HUNTING :—

A symbol of the pursuit and capture by the spiritual and ethical qualities of the lower personality with its passions and appetites.

"The Green Lion is the First Matter of the Great Work: hence, in spiritual alchemy, natural man in his wholeness—Salt, Sulphur, and Mercury in their crude state. ' Our lyon wanting maturitic is called greene for his unripeness ' (*Alchemic Tract*). Here the common opinion that a pious effeminancy, a diluted and amiable spirituality is the proper raw material of the mystic life, is emphatically contradicted. It is not by the education of the lamb, but by the hunting and taming of the wild, intractable lion, instinct with vitality, full of ardour and courage, exhibiting heroic qualities on the sensual plane, that the Great Work is achieved. The Green Lion, then, in his strength and wholeness is the only creature potentially able to attain Perfection. . . . The Kingdom of heaven is taken by violence, not by amiable aspiration. ' The Green Lion,' says one alchemist, ' is the priest by whom Sol and Luna are wed.' . . . The transmuting process is described as the hunting of the Green Lion through the forest of the sensual world. When the Lion is caught, when Destiny overtakes it, as the preliminary to the necessary taming process, its head must be cut off: . . . and its removal is that 'death of the lower nature ' which is the object of all asceticism—i.e. Purgation. The lion, the

whole man, is, as it were, 'slain to the world,' and then resuscitated; but in a very different shape. By its passage through this mystic death, the 'colour of unripeness' is taken away. Its taming completed, it receives wings, wherewith it may fly up to Sol, the Perfect or Divine; and is transmuted, say the alchemists, into the Red Dragon. . . For the Spiritual Chemistry, then, th Red Dragon represents Deified Man. Man has transcended his lower nature, has received wings wherewith to live on higher levels of reality."—E. UNDERHILL, *Mysticism*, pp. 174–6.

The personality full of the desires of the astral plane (green lion), and a union of mind (salt), desire (sulphur), and hidden Spirit (mercury), requires to be disciplined in suffering and sorrow (hunted), and finally spiritualised and made perfect (captured), which causes its death on the lower planes, and transmutation to the higher (Great Work).

See ALCHEMY, COLOURS, DRAGON, KINGDOM, LION, MAGIC, MAN (natural), PERSONALITY, QUATERNARY, SUN, WINGS.

GRIFFIN :—

A symbol of the higher and lower planes on which the Higher Self manifests.

"Apollo, whose car we may sometimes see drawn by griffins, was properly the symbol of Christ, and in this sense is introduced by Dante in the procession of the church. The eagle's head and wings represent the divine nature; the lion's body the human nature."—H. C. BARLOW, *Essays on Symbolism*, p. 76.

See APOLLO, BULL (man-headed), EAGLE, LION, QUADRUPED, SPHINX, WINGS.

GROUND : EARTH :—

A symbol of the lower nature of the soul, which requires "tilling" and "sowing" to produce good "fruit."

"Therefore the Lord God sent him (Adam) forth from the garden of Eden, to till the ground from whence he was taken."—GEN. iii. 23.

So the mind having ceased to be influenced from the buddhic plane (Eden) is directed by the Supreme law towards the lower plane activities whereof its own nature has been builded up.

See ADAM (lower), CURSE (ground), EARTH (ground), EDEN, FRUIT (ground), LAND.

GROUND RIDGES :—

A symbol of the lower planes.

" And Horus brought back 142 of the enemy, whom he slew ; and he tore out their tongues, and their blood gushed out upon the ridges of the ground."—*Legend of the Winged Sun-disk.*

And the Son of God went forth in his strength, and completely (142) mastered and dissipated the lower desires, and " tore out their tongues," that is, cast out falsity and perversity ; and the vitality which had before animated them was dispersed and flowed to the lower planes wherein it was resolved into its primary constituents. (1 + 4 + 2 = 7.)

See EARTH, FURROWS, SEVEN, TONGUE.

GROUND, HOLY :—

A symbol of the spiritual nature of the soul, which is the foundation of manifest existence.

GROVE, SACRED :—

A symbol of the buddhic plane, or the buddhic reflected in the astral. It represents the inner nature of the soul with its aspirations and higher emotions, and in which the ideals are exalted and worshipped.

" With the ancients worship was also in gardens and in groves, and also on mountains and hills ; for the gardens and groves signified wisdom and intelligence, and every tree something thereof,—as the olive, the good of love ; the vine, truth from that good ; the cedar, rational good and truth ; a mountain, the highest heaven ; a hill, the heaven below it."—SWEDENBORG, *T. C. R.* n. 204.

" And Asa did that which was good and right in the eyes of the Lord his God. For he took away the altars of the strange gods, and the high places, and brake down the images, and cut down the groves."—2 CHRON. xiv. 2-3.

This refers to the change from a lower condition of the soul to a higher.

See EDEN, GARDEN (flowers), GODS, IDOLS.

GROWTH TO BE ONE OUT OF MANY :—

This signifies the process of Involution whereby the many potencies emanated from the Supreme eventuate in the formation and completion of the Archetypal Man.

See ARC. MAN, EVOLUTION, INVOLUTION.

GROWTH TO BE MANY OUT OF ONE :—

This signifies the process of Evolution whereby the Archetypal Man (Christ incarnate) becomes " dismembered," or " scattered," for the sake of the incarnating egos (human monads), and so the One brings forth the many qualities for the use of each human soul according to its stage of development.—*See* Empedocles, verse 60 ; *also see* 1 COR. xii. 12-31 ; EPH. i. 10.

See ARC. MAN, DISMEMBERMENT, EVOLUTION, GEOMETRY, INCARNATION.

GROWTH OF MAN FROM THE EARTH :—

A symbol of the upward increasing stature of the manhood or mentality from the lower nature to the higher. First the natural man (kama-manas), and afterwards the spiritual (buddhi-manas).

See DISMEMBERMENT, EARTH, MAN CRAWLED, MAN (natural), PRAGĀPATI RELAXED.

GUARDIAN SPIRITS OF MEN :—

A symbol of the Divine monads or spiritual egos within all human beings, manifesting upon the mental plane.

" Auharmazd deliberated with the consciousness and guardian spirits (fravahar) of men ; and the omniscient wisdom brought forward among men, spoke thus : ' Which seems to you the more advantageous, when I shall present you to the world ?—that you shall contend in a bodily form with the fiend, and the fiend shall perish, and in the end I shall have you prepared again perfect and immortal . . . ; or that it be always necessary to provide you protection from the destroyer ? ' "—*Bundahis,* Ch. II. 10.

This statement refers to the primordial free decision of the monads to descend into bodies and go through the struggle of life with all its suffering and sorrow, in order to win self-consciousness and victory over the lower limitations.

The Divine Will is said to put before the separated wills and con-sciousnesses two alternatives for their free choice,—either to descend to incarnation on the lower planes in order to contend against evil and overcome it, and so ascend to perfection and immortality ; or to remain merely conscious and automatic on the higher planes.

"Thereupon, the guardian spirits of men became of the same opinion with the omniscient wisdom about going to the world, on account of the evil that comes upon them in the world from the fiend Aharman, and their becoming, at last again unpersecuted by the adversary, perfect and immortal in the future existence, for ever and everlasting."—*Ibid.*, V. 11.

The monads being of the same nature as the Supreme, and suffused with the same wisdom, energy, and courage, elected to go forth into the world of strife, and enter into conflict with the relative self (Aharman), confident of the coming time when the adversary shall be overcome and the perfected souls rise to life everlasting.

"Beings that are absolutely free have no reason to think of it. Now can we get this freedom ? Yes, says St. Paul, it is our heritage ; we came forth from it. It is the mother of us all. Our spiritual nature is, as M. Bergson would say, essentially free or derived from that which is absolutely free till it comes into contact with this material world. As far as we know, it is not our doing that we have been put here ; it is not of our own will that we have been subjected to this earthly bondage. Will not he who has made us so subject see to it that we are not left to perish in this prison-house of matter ? Whatever he has put us here for, he will take care that we are not allowed to fail of acquiring it, for it is on his account, as well as our own, that we are having to pass through it. Our guarantee of escape is the freedom of God, the immunity of the divine nature from the conditions under which we are having to struggle now. Perfect freedom is perfect self-determination. God cannot be necessitated by anything outside himself, for there is nothing outside himself. He can will nothing but what is good, and it is just because of this that we have hope in him. Our salvation stands in God's inability to fail or fall. This is the gospel. God in Christ has come to set us free from our grievous bondage and to usher us into the glorious liberty of the sons of God."—R. J. CAMPBELL, Serm., *Sources of Spiritual Freedom.*

See AEGAEON, AHRIMAN, AHURA-MAZDA, BONDAGE, FRAVASHIS, INCARNATION, JERUSALEM, LIBERATION, MANASAPUTRAS, MONAD OF LIFE, PITRIS (solar), SERVANT OF GOD, SHEEP (lost), SONS OF GOD, SPARK, STRIFE, TREE OF KNOWLEDGE, WILL, WORLD.

GUARDIANS OF THE WORLD :—

These are High Intelligences or Souls, agents of the Supreme to guide and guard the expression of the Divine Wisdom in the Sacred Scriptures, and to aid in human evolution.

"The guardians of the world hastened from heaven to mount watch over the world's one true ruler ; thus the moon-beams, though they shine everywhere, are especially bright on Mount Kailāsa."—*Buddha-Karita*, Bk. I. *S. B. of E.*

The Higher Intelligences come forth to quicken the growth of the Soul upon the mental plane, as it is upon this plane that the Selfhood is established, and rulership maintained. The "moon-beams" here signify the reflections of the light of Truth, which, though they are everywhere discernible, are especially brilliant through the intuition proceeding from the buddhic plane.

See AMSHASPANDS, ANGELS, APES, ARCHANGELS, COLCHIS, CURETES, DEVAS, KAILASA, MESSENGERS, VALKYRIOR.

GUESTS, WEDDING :—

Symbolic of higher emotions and higher faculties accompanying the lower Self when it becomes one with the Higher Self.

"But when the king came in to behold the guests, he saw there a man which had not on a wedding garment : and he saith unto him, Friend how camest thou in hither not having a wedding garment ? And he was speechless."—MAT. xxii. 11 12.

When the Supreme had regard to those attributes of the soul which were bidden at the summons of the higher nature, to attend the union of the Higher Self with the purified lower, then was perceived a mental quality in which the without and the within had not become one so as to be invested as one. The attribute which failed to wear the garb of truth was one that ignored the process of uniting the external and internal, and which therefore was unable to retain its place at the "feast." It was "speechless" because the conditions precluded any expression of an unperfected quality.

See GARMENTS, MARRIAGE (higher) RAIMENT.

GUHU (SPOON) :—

A symbol of the causal-body on the higher mental plane.

"The guhu (spoon) and upabhrit (spoon) are looked upon as yoke-fellows, they being the two horses that are supposed to convey the sacrifice (and consequently the sacrificer himself) to the world of the Gods."—J. EGGELING, *S. B. of E.*, Vol. XII. p. 68.

The causal-body, the seat of the individuality, and the mental-body the seat of the personality, are closely allied, and it is through the mental activities (horses) of both, working together for evolution, that the lower nature is sacrificed and the consciousness raised to the higher world wherein the ideals (Gods) are realised. The spiritual ego is conveyed heavenwards by means of the individuality and the personality operating upon the mental plane of the soul.

See BUTTER, CAUSAL-BODY, DHRUVA, EVOLUTION, GHEE, GODS, HEAVEN, INCARNATION, INDIVIDUALITY, PERSONALITY, SACRIFICER, UPABHRIT.

GUILTY PERSONS :—

Symbolic of anti-social qualities, such as hate, revenge, envy, malice, cruelty, etc., which become active in astro-mental forms in the lower nature of the soul.

"Guilty persons, even though he (the king) had sentenced them to death, he did not cause to be killed, nor even looked on them with anger ; he bound them with gentle words and with reform produced in their character,—even their release was accompanied by no inflicted injury." —*Buddha-Karita*, Bk. II. 42.

This refers to the involution of the lower passionate qualities,—hate, revenge, malice, etc., which though apparently abhorrent and condemned by the Higher nature to extinction, are not really doomed. Neither are they regarded as inferior nor useless, for they have their part in the Divine scheme. Through love and wisdom they can be transformed. They become gradually regulated and guided by the higher impulses from above within the soul, and in process of time transmuted into higher qualities. Their purification, or release from the thraldom of the lower personality, involves in reality no harshness, severity, or sudden transition. It

may be said of the method of purification, that "it is all triumphant art,—art in obedience to law" ; without coercion and in accordance with love and wisdom.

See ESTHER, EVIL, LAW OF REVENGE, MURDER, OPPOSITES, QUALITIES.

GULDTOPP HORSE RIDDEN BY HEIMDALL :—

Symbol of the Divine Will manifesting under the aspect of intelligence on the higher mental plane.

See HEIMDALL, HORSE.

GUNAS, THREE ; SATTVA, RAJAS, AND TAMAS :—

These are three states, or conditions, of the soul, made evident on the mental plane in the self-conscious mind.

In the Sattvic state, the mind is intent upon goodness and truth, wisdom and love. This condition leads to the evolution of the higher (the buddhic) emotions, and to the Ideals (state of gods).

In the Rajasic state, the mind is full of outgoing energy towards the acquisition of objects of sense, knowledge, fame, power, ambition, social benefit, etc. This condition leads to the evolution of the mental faculties in their widest range (state of men) and to the intuition of truth.

In the Tamasic state the mind is sluggish, unaroused, stupid, ignorant and without zest in the pursuit of any worthy objects. This condition leads to the evolution of the desires, passions, and appetites (state of beasts).

According to *Manu*,—Sattva (goodness) has the form of knowledge, and induces a deep calm full of bliss, and a pure light. Rajas (activity) has the form of love and hatred, and induces pain and dissatisfaction, and an activity difficult to conquer, which draws embodied souls to the objects of sense. Tamas (darkness) has the form of ignorance, and is coupled with delusion unfathomed by reasoning.—*See Bhag. Gita.*, Chs. 14, 17, 18.

See QUALITIES, RAJAS, SATTVA, SHINAR, TAMAS.

GURU, OR TEACHER :—

A symbol of the spiritual mind ; that faculty in the higher mind which brings knowledge from above to the

causal-self in accordance with the endeavours of the lower self to attain goodness and truth.

"That Brāhmana, who performs in accordance with the rules of the Veda the rites, the Garbhādāna (conception rite), and so forth, and gives food to the child, is called the Guru (the venerable one)."—*Laws of Manu*, II. 142.

That higher mental faculty which carries out the Divine laws of the higher nature in regard to the nurture and sustenance of the spiritual germ and infant "Son of mind" in the soul, may be called the spiritual mind, (buddhi-manas).

"Without the true Guru they find not the Real Thing. They who are purified by the True One walk in the true way." "There is no emancipation without the perfect Guru" (*Guru Nanak*.). —MACAULIFFE, *The Sikh Religion*, Vol. I. p. 365.

The true or perfect Guru signifies the Higher Self.

See AARON, ADEPT, BRAHMACARIN, BRAHMANA, CHRYSE, MASTER, PRIEST, VEDA.

HABIT :—

The functioning in old-established directions of the sub-conscious automatic mind. This section of astromentality is amenable to suggestion when constantly made ; hence change of habits.

See SPARROWS.

HADES ; THE UNDERWORLD :—

A symbol of the lower planes of existence. The lower quaternary, which is below the Upper world of the higher planes. More particularly it refers to the desire-mental conditions which involve suffering and sorrow. Souls are always in Hades until the consciousness has risen above the lower mental plane and entered the higher, where union with the Higher Self is effected.

"And in Hades he (Dives) lifted up his eyes, being in torments, and seeth Abraham afar off, and Lazarus in his bosom. And he cried and said, Father Abraham, have mercy on me, and send Lazarus, that he may dip the tip of his finger in water, and cool my tongue ; for I am in anguish in this flame."—LUKE xvi. 23, 24.

The "rich man" is the lower self (kama-manas) which is satisfied with the things of the world and the pleasures of sense. But by a change of state he is now cut off from those things in which he delighted. And in the midst of his suffering, when he has no means of satisfying those cravings to which his life has been given,—he is led at length to cast his eye upward and to aspire to something towards which he had not yet been able to look. And then he asks that mercy may be extended to him, and that the buddhic function of the causal-body (Lazarus) may be aroused in him, so that he may perceive Truth (water),—to receive which, however, his condition is not yet ripe, and he must undergo further purification.

See ABRAHAM, ADONIS, AIDONEUS, CAUSAL-BODY, FIRE OF HELL, FIVE, FURNACE, HELL, HERMOD, HINE, LAZARUS, MEADOW, MICTLAN, NIFLHEIM, PO, PURGATORY, QUATERNARY, RE-STAU, RICH MAN, TARTARUS, TUAT UNDERWORLD.

HAETUMANT, THE BRIGHT, GLORIOUS LAND :—

A symbol of the path of holiness, or of the white magic, which is the bringing into play of forces upon the higher planes which act upon the lower nature so as to purify and raise it.

See BUDDHI, MAGIC, TRANSMUTATION.

HAIGI-NO-KAMI, EARTH DEITY :—

A symbol of the physical plane.

"Haigi-no-kami is said to be the God of the space between the door of the house and the outer gate."—W. G. ASTON, *Shinto*, p. 146.

The extremity ; the outermost plane of manifestation is the physical. "House" means causal-body.

See HESTIA, NEPHTHYS.

HAIL DESTROYING CROPS, ETC. :—

Symbolic of erroneous opinions and doctrines destroying the germs of truth and goodness.

"By hail is signified falsity destroying good and truth."—SWEDENBORG, *Apoc. Rev.*, n. 399.

See CROPS, GALES.

HAIR OF THE HEAD :—

A symbol of faith, intuition of truth, or the highest qualities of the lower mind.

"My Mother the Holy Spirit even now took me by one of the hairs of my head, and carried me to the great mountain Tabor."—Cited by Jerome from the *Gospel according to the Hebrews.*

The Holy Spirit is the Mother of the Christ upon the buddhic plane : and it is through Her (Wisdom), and through the uplifting of the soul through the intuition, that the highest state of consciousness is attained ; which answers to the ascent of the " lofty mountain." The raising by " a hair of the head " is the lifting of the Christ-soul (Jesus) by a point of contact which is attached to its most receptive functioning towards higher things.

" Eckhart teaches,—at the ' apex of the mind ' there is a Divine ' spark ' which is so closely akin to God that it is one with Him, and not merely united to Him."—W. R. INGE, *Christian Mysticism*, p. 155.

" The most common and comprehensive word for deity in the Japanese language is *Kami.* . . . *Kami no ke*, or simply *Kami*, is the hair of the head. *Kami* is applied not only to Gods, but to Mikados and nobles."—W. G. ASTON, *Shinto*, p. 7.

See FAITH, GOLDEN HAIR, HOLY GHOST, MAUI, MEN (forest), MOUNTAIN, SPARK.

HAIR,—SIDE-LOCK :—

A symbol of intuition, or the buddhi-manasic functioning.

" Keresaspa, a youthful hero who wore a side-lock, and carried a club, who slew the serpent Svara."—*Homa Yasht.*

The Love-nature (Keresaspa) signifies the path of the soul in Devotion to the Ideal. The " side-lock " signifies the attainment of intuition. The " club " is a symbol of emotion. The nature is to be disciplined through the Love-element which conquers selfishness (Svara).

" The second sign (of a ' great man ' or Buddha) is to have hair curling towards the right side, of a deep black, changing colour with the light."—*The Lotus of the Good Law.*

When the consciousness rises to the higher mind (great man) the intuition becomes active (right) and no longer latent (black), for the light of Truth shines in it, and its quality (colour) becomes apparent.

" As to Isis (when she heard of the death of her husband Osiris), she immediately cut off one of the locks of her hair, and put on mourning apparel."—PLUTARCH, *Isis and Osiris*, § 14.

Wisdom (Isis) now appears obscured, so that the lower mind cannot perceive her, for she is to the personality " black." The cutting off of the " lock of hair " signifies that the ego was deprived of intuition, or psychic faculty, which had hitherto been vouchsafed to the lower self. The deprivation occurs as the lower emotion-nature becomes active in the soul.

" And his (Rā's) hand stayed not, and he made his form into that of a woman with a lock of hair which became the divine lock in Annu."—BUDGE, *Book of the Dead*, p. 342.

This refers to the activities of atma-buddhi energising the intuition from the buddhic plane.

" For what is a lock of the head but the thoughts of the mind gathered together, so as not to be scattered and dispersed, but to remain bound by discipline. A hand is therefore put forth from above, and the Prophet is lifted up by the lock of his head (EZEK. viii. 3) ; because when our mind collects itself by watchfulness, a heavenly power raises us upward from things below."—ST. GREGORY, *Morals on the Book of Job*, Vol. III. p. 440.

See ANNU, BLACK, BUDDHA, CLUB, COLOURS, FALL, INTUITION, ISIS, KERESASPA, MOURNER, RĀ, RIGHT HAND, SERPENT (svara), WOMAN.

HAIR OF MACROPROSOPUS :—

A symbol of the Divine Life emanated from the Source of all life and truth, in forms of infinite diversity.

" From the skull of His head hang down a thousand thousand myriads (of hairs). . . . All are in order. Each hair is said to be the breaking of the hidden fountains issuing from the concealed brain."—*Greater Holy Assembly*, Ch. VII.

The " hairs " from the " skull " are the atmic aspects of all things,—the spiritual truth (water) from the hidden source in the Godhead.

See CRANIUM, FOUNTAIN, MONAD OF FORM, OF LIFE.

HAIR TUFT BETWEEN THE EYEBROWS OF BUDDHA :—

An emblem of spiritual truth within the soul.

See URNA.

HAIR OF THE DIVINE BODY,— ITS SMOOTHNESS :—

Symbolic of the freedom of the perfected soul from the things of the lower planes.

HAIR SHAVEN FROM CROWN OF THE HEAD :—

A symbol of contrition for the shortcomings of the lower nature, and a sign of fervent desire to contact the Source of Truth and Power.

" For it is not the wearing of beards and the dressing in long gowns that makes people philosophers ; neither does the *linen surplice* and the *shaven crown* make votaries of Isis, but the real Isiacist is he that is competent to investigate by the aid of the Word, the symbolism, and the ceremonies connected with these duties (after he has been lawfully empowered so to do) ; and who meditates upon the Truth which is involved in them."— PLUTARCH, *Isis and Osiris*, § 3.

In the Catholic and the Buddhist Churches the tonsure—

"marks the passage from the worldly to the religious life."—H. OLDENBERG, *Buddha*, p. 321.

See ENEMIES OF GOD, SHAVING.

HAIR TOP-KNOT :—

See MAUI.

HALLOWED OFFERINGS TO KYPRIS :—

Symbolic of blissful conditions appropriate to an early stage of growth of the soul.

See KYPRIS.

HAM, SON OF NOAH :—

A symbol of courage, action, and works, generated by the individuality.

See ADAM'S DEAD BODY, CANAAN, NOAH, NOAH'S SONS, TOKENS.

HAMMER OF THOR :—

A symbol of will determined by the higher mind (Thor).

See MJOLNIR, THOR, WILL.

HAND :—

A symbol of the directive principle of activity either outgoing (right) or incoming (left). The positive and negative aspects of Divine action in the soul.

See ARMS OF BODY, HEALING (hand), STRIKING.

HAND, LEFT :—

A symbol of the externally passive incoming energy of the soul.

HAND, RIGHT :—

A symbol of the externally positive outgoing energy,—that which does. The evolutionary force from within outwards.

" Ye shall see the Son of man sitting at the right hand of power, and coming with the clouds of heaven."— MARK xiv. 62.

When the consciousness is raised above the lower planes, then shall the adoring soul behold the higher aspects of existence and the central Ideal of Love and Truth established in the evolutionary out-going power of the Supreme. The " clouds of heaven " signify the veils which for a time obscure the love and truth of the Supreme, but which disperse so soon as the Divine glory and power are revealed to the consciousness.

" Whilst on the one side Christ rests as from a perfected work which needs no addition nor repetition, on the other He rests not day nor night. And this aspect of His presence is as distinctly set forth in Scripture as that is. For is not ' the right hand of God ' the operative energy of the Divine nature ? And is not ' sitting at the right hand of God ' equivalent to possessing and wielding that unwearied, measureless power ? Is there not blended together in this pregnant phrase the idea of profoundest calm and of intensest action, *that* being expressed by the attitude, and *this* by the situation ? Therefore does the Evangelist who uses the expression expand it into words which wonderfully close his Gospel."—A. MAC- LAREN, *Sermons*, 2nd Series, p. 22.

See BOOK OF THE LORD, CHRIST'S SECOND COMING, CLOUDS OF HEAVEN, RIGHT HAND, SON OF MAN.

HAND OF EVERY BEAST AND MAN :—

Symbolic of self-directed activities of the desires and of the mental qualities.

" And surely your blood, the blood of your lives, will I require ; at the hand of every beast will I require it : and at the hand of man, even at the hand of every man's brother, will I require the life of man."—GEN. ix. 5.

And the life (blood) being now ensouled in forms, operates through the law of cause and effect, so that every form that it energises is the means of reproducing certain effects upon the various planes of its mani- festation. " At the hand of every beast " signifies that the lower desires are not exempt from the law of progress of the Causative Power at work within. " At the hand of man, etc." is meant, that the mind upon its own plane is held accountable ethically, not only for its individual conduct, but for that of the human race which is inseparably connected with its individual expression.

" You know what you know and do what you do, in order that the whole race may reap the benefit hereafter. You are just one point through which God is pouring himself. This accounts for all our differences of whatever kind they be. We live for one another, suffer for one another, achieve for one another, and all of us for God."—R. J. CAMPBELL, Serm., *Solidarity of Spiritual Experience.*

See BEASTS, BLOOD, EVOLUTION, GATHA (kam,), MAN (natural), MAN (bad), PURGATORY.

HANDS RAISED UPWARDS :—

A symbol of aspiration towards the higher life.

" Then Chryses, the priest of Apollo, lifted up his hands and prayed aloud for the Greeks suffering from pestilence."— *Iliad*, Bk. I.

Then the spiritual mind (Chryses) aspires towards the Divine within the soul, and seeks to raise the lower desire-mental qualities immersed in suffering and strife.

See APOLLO, CHRYSES, GREEKS, PESTILENCE.

HANGING   TENDRILS   OF HOMA :—

A comparison of the Divine Nature to the fruit of the vine,—grapes signifying Love of the Ideal.

See GRAPES, VINE.

HANUMAN, SON OF VAYU :—

A symbol of the intellect which proceeds from the higher mind (Vayu).

" From the south came the welcome tidings of the discovery of Sita by Hanuman, one of the chief captains of the Vanar host, a son of the wind-god by a nymph of paradise."—J. C. OMAN, *The Great Indian Epics*, p. 55.

The lower, or astral (south) emotions, when transmuted, bring about the evolution of the intuition (Sita) which the intellect recognises and saves from extermination. The " Vanar host " are the mental qualities. A " nymph of paradise " is a lower aspect of buddhi.

See INTELLECT, LANKA, RAMA, RAVANA, SITA, SOUTH, TRANSMUTATION, VIBHISHANA.

HĀPI GOD, OR NILE :—

A symbol of the Divine Life which, like a river, flows from the higher planes downwards to fertilise the lower planes.

" The living and beautiful Nile (god Hāpi), who loveth Nū, the father of the gods and of the divine cycle, he who dwelleth in the river. . . . Thou art lord of many fish and gifts ; thou givest food unto Egypt. The divine cycle knoweth not where thou art. Thou art its life."—*Hymn to Hāpi*, WIEDEMANN, *Rel. of the Egyptians*, p. 147.

The energising and bountiful Divine Life is united with the Divine powers (Nū) operating in the universe and the soul, according to the scheme of manifestation. Through the Divine Life truths (fish) are bestowed upon the soul, and the mind (Egypt) is nourished thereby. The forms embodying the life in the cycle of manifestation perceive not the indwelling Spirit by which they exist. God is hidden in his universe.

See EGYPT, FISH, FOOD, GODS, MOIST, NILE, NŪ, RIVER OF LIFE.

HAPTO-IRINGA, (MARS PLANET) :—

A symbol of force, resistance and will.

See ARES, MARS, PLANETS.

HARAVAITI,   THE   BEAUTIFUL LAND :—

A symbol of kama-manasic enlightenment during involution. It signifies the emotion-nature expressing itself so as to produce pleasure to the soul at this stage of the soul's growth.

See GOLDEN AGE, INVOLUTION, KAMA, PARADISE (lower).

HARLOT,   OR   STRANGE WOMAN :—

A symbol of the allurements of sensation and desire which capture the soul until it has learned that it is wisdom that must be sought after above all else.

" Of the nourishments brought to the soul of the wicked man are some from poison and poisonous stench ; . . . that is the food after death, for a harlot of very evil thoughts, words, deeds, and ill-instructed, not ruled by a master, and wicked."—*Hadokht Nask*, HAUG, *Essays* p. 233.

Of the food supplied to the soul at this stage are stimuli which inflame and excite the lower nature. These are the desires which must continue unsatisfied, and the longings which cannot end, since they are to be the means of drawing the soul again and again into incarnation ; for so alone will it work out its salvation. The folly (harlot) of the lower self is, indeed, Wisdom reflected inversely on the lower planes, and this is the means whereby at first the Self is evolved in the soul. " Not ruled by a master " signifies that the desire nature is not as yet regulated through the will and reason.—*See* PROV. vii. 6–27, and 1 COR. vi. 13–20.

See ADULTERY, COURTEZAN, DIVORCE, FOLLY, GATHA (kam.), MAN (bad), POISON UNRIGHTEOUS MAN, WHOREDOM.

HARMAKHIS, RĀ, THE EVER-LIVING :—

A symbol of the First Logos, the Divine Life of the universe.

See RĀ, STRIDES.

HARMONY AND MUSIC :—

Symbolic of perfect adjustment of all conditions during involution, implying complete adaptation of each part to the whole.

See DANCE, GOLDEN AGE, GOOD, HYMN, MELODY, MUSIC, NYMPHS.

HAROYN LAND AND LAKE :—

Symbolic of the condition of Bliss reflected in the astro-physical organism, thereby producing the basis of sensation.

See BLISS, GOLDEN AGE, INVOLUTION.

HARPIES :—

A symbol of the unregulated appetites of sensation and desire, which seize upon knowledge in order to promote their own aims.

" The Gods to punish Phineus struck him blind, and sent the Harpies to torment him : these fell monsters came flying the instant food was set before him, carried off the greater portion of it, and so defiled what they left, that no mortal could endure to eat it."—*Argonautic Expedition.*

Life becomes difficult at this stage,

and a condition of spiritual blindness overtakes the discriminating mind (Phineus), all of which implies torment and trouble. And so it came about that immediately knowledge (food) was placed for the mind to partake of, it was appropriated by the irregularities of the sense and desire natures, and in this way it was that the knowledge, instead of being assimilated by the understanding, was turned to base uses.

See NICOTHEA, OCYPETE, PHINEUS, ZETES.

HARPOCRATES (YOUNG HORUS), SON OF OSIRIS AND ISIS :—

A symbol of the Higher Self born in the soul upon the buddhic plane, prior to the birth upon the mental plane. This is when the soul is evolving upon the astral plane, and is, therefore, the point when the Son of mind enters as a germ.

" Harpocrates came into the world before his time, and lame in his lower limbs."—PLUTARCH, *Isis and Osiris*, § 65.

This signifies that the Higher or potential Self is always relatively unmanifested, and that the lower or actual condition is never able to express or support in fullness the Higher.

See BIRTH OF HORUS, HEPHAISTOS, HORUS (child), LAMENESS, LIMBS, PLEROMA, SEED, WORLD.

HARVEST AT THE END OF THE WORLD :—

A symbol of the gathering in of the " fruits of the Spirit " at the close of the cycle ; that is, the attainment of the spiritual results of experience and aspiration when the consciousness rises to the buddhic plane. It is the acquisition of perfected qualities of wisdom, love, and truth.

" The hour to reap is come ; for the harvest of the earth is over-ripe. And he that sat on the cloud cast his sickle upon the earth ; and the earth was reaped."—REV. xiv. 15, 16.

The period has arrived in the soul's evolution when the consciousness is ready to rise to higher planes. The Higher Self, therefore, having conquered the lower nature, sends forth from the plane of buddhi (cloud) his outgoing spiritual energy (sickle) to cut down all attachments to the desires and objects of sense, and so liberate the ego from the lower nature (earth) and enable it to rise to peace and bliss, and inherit the treasures above which are the fruit of its aspirations and efforts during the protracted period of conflict and suffering on the planes below.

" By harvest is signified the state of the church as to divine truth ; the reason is, because from a harvest corn is procured, from which comes bread, and by corn and bread is signified the good of the church, this being procured by truths."—SWEDEN-BORG, *Apoc. Rev.*, n. 645.

See AGRICULTURE, CLOUDS, CULTI-VATION, FRUITFUL, PLOUGHING, REAP-ING, SEED, SEED (good), SICKLE, SOWER.

HARVISPTOKHM, THE TREE OF ALL SEEDS :—

A symbol of the " tree " of the Divine Life growing from the atmic plane (Vouru-kasha) and containing the spiritual germs of all qualities and forms.

See SEEDS, SPERMATIC WORDS, TREE OF LIFE, VOURUKASHA.

HAST, OR COMPLETION :—

A symbol of the Self below having become one with Itself above.

" O Hast, I have entered into thee, I have driven back those who would come to the turquoise (sky), and I have followed the winds of the company of the gods."—BUDGE, *Book of the Dead*, Ch. CX. p. 334.

The Self is seen to be perfect and entire, and in its entirety the lesser Self abandons itself. The lesser Self has struggled with the opponents, as they have appeared to be, of the higher life, and has proved itself triumphant through the power of the Divine attributes.

See COMPANY (gods), CONSUMMA-TION, HIGHER AND LOWER SELVES.

HASTINA-PUR, THE CITY :—

A symbol of the mental centre of the lower nature.

See BHÎSMA.

HATHOR, COW AND MOON GODDESS :—

A symbol of Buddhi, reflected upon the astral plane, or as the vehicle of atma.

" Hathor means ' Abode of Horus.' She was the goddess of love and joy. The cow was sacred to her." " The

golden Hathor was goddess of the western sky which received the dying sun in the glow of sunset."—WIEDEMANN, *Rel. of Egyptians*, pp. 30, 142.

Buddhi (cow-Hathor) receives the incarnate God (dying sun) in the first division of the Tuat, and parts with Him in the last, when rising victorious to his own plane (atma).

See ATHYR, BUDDHI, COW, HORUS, PLACE (Annu), SEB, SHU, SUN, TUAT.

HAUMIA-TIKITIKI, THE GOD AND FATHER OF THE FOOD OF MAN WHICH SPRINGS UP WITHOUT CULTIVA-TION :—

A symbol of the instinctive sensa-tion-nature which receives impres-sions through the senses of the facts of the physical life, producing ex-perience and knowledge as nourish-ment for the mind and soul.

" Tumatauenga determined also to be revenged upon his brothers Rongo-matane and Haumia-tikitiki ; he soon found them by their peculiar leaves, and he scraped into shape a wooden hoe, and plaited a basket, and dug in the earth and pulled up all kinds of plants with edible roots, and the plants which had been dug up, withered in the sun."—GREY, *Polynesian Mythology*, p. 11.

Wisdom and sensation were known through the relation of mind to the emotions and sense perceptions. The " hoe and basket " operations signify the astro-mental methods of dealing with experience, whereby the fruits of experience pass upwards.

See EARTH, FOOD FOR MAN, PLANTS, RONGO, ROOTED, SUN, TUMATAUENGA, WOOD.

HAVILAH LAND :—

A symbol of the lower buddhic region.

" The name of the first river is Pishon : and that is it which compasseth the whole land of Havilah where there is gold ; and the gold of that land is good : there is bdellium and the onyx stone."—GEN. ii. 11, 12.

The " name " or symbol of the first answers to the higher mental plane : this comprises the circuit, as it were, below and around the buddhic state. The " good gold " stands for celestial Truth. Upon these levels exist wisdom and power.

See EDEN RIVERS, GOLD, PISHON.

HAWK ; SPARROW-HAWK ; AN EMBLEM OF RĀ, THE SUN-GOD :—

A symbol of the manifested Higher Self.

"The hawk stands for the Supreme Mind, and for the intelligent soul. The hawk is called in the Egyptian language *baieth*, from *bai* soul, and *eth* heart, which organ they consider the seat or enclosure of the soul."—HORAPOLLO.

"Races having no connection with the Egyptian have associated sun and sparrow-hawk. Homer, for instance,—*Od*, 15, 525,—calls the hawk the 'swift messenger of Phœbus.' "—WIEDEMANN, *Rel. of the Egyptians*, p. 27.

"A hawk was the symbol of God." —CLEM. ALEX., *Miscel.*, Bk. V. 7.

"The soul of man was often represented by a hawk, the symbol of the sun-god. Why the hawk should have thus symbolised the sun is a question that has often been asked. The Egyptians did not know themselves ; and Porphyry, in the dying days of the old Egyptian faith, gravely declares that it was because the hawk was a compound of blood and breath ! . . . Originally it was only the sun god of Upper Egypt who was represented even by the Egyptians under the form of a hawk. This was Horus, often called in the later texts 'Horus the elder' (Aroêris)."—SAYCE, *Rel. of Anc. Egyptians*, p. 71.

The sun, blood, and breath are all symbols of the Divine Life.

See BA, BIRD (great), BIRDS, BLOOD, BREATH, EAGLE, EGYPT (higher), HIPPOPOTAMUS, HORUS, RĀ, SUN, WORD.

HAWK-HEADED HUMAN BODIES :—

Symbolic of the perfected human souls arisen to the higher planes : or of the buddhic plane of the quaternary.

See CROWN (atef), QEBHSENNUF.

HAWK, MAN-HEADED :—

A symbol of the spiritual aspect of man, or of the Divine element in the human soul. The incarnate Self on the mental plane.

See JUDGMENT HALL, MAN (righteous).

HAWK-HEADED POLE :—

A symbol of aspiration towards the Highest, or that attribute which soars and attains perfection.

See COLUMN, POLE.

HEAD :—

A symbol of the mind, the intellect, the intelligence ; that which distinguishes man.

"Thou preparest a table before me in the presence of mine enemies : Thou hast anointed my head with oil ; my cup runneth over."—Ps. xxiii. 5.

The Self hath prepared for the ego the fruits of experience to be the food of the soul, while the desires have become inoperative. The Divine love is bestowed upon the aspiring mind, and Wisdom filleth the understanding.

"Let they garments be always white ; and let not thy head lack ointment."—ECCLES. ix. 8.

"There is the understanding, which may be termed the head ; because in that is placed the eye of the soul ; and this is that which, or by which the soul, discerneth things that are presented to it, and that either by God or Satan."—J. BUNYAN, *Greatness of the Soul*.

"The head being the uppermost, and a chief part of the body, is often put for the whole man ; so blessings come on the head, the whole person of the just (PROV. x. 6) ; and men have their way recompensed on their head (EZEK. ix. 10)."—W. GURNEY, *Bible Dict.*, p. 220.

"*Head* . . . the understanding ; a chief or leader. . . . *Head-work*, intellectual work. . . . *Off one's head*, demented, crazy."—*Chambers's Dictionary*.

See ANOINTING, CUP, ENEMIES, FOREHEAD, FOXES, GARMENTS, OIL, OINTMENT. WHITE.

HEAD OF HORUS ON A POLE :—

A symbol of aspiration and Divinely directed intelligence dominant over the lower nature.

See HORUS, POLE, SERPENT (hissing), SET.

HEAD OF SET CUT OFF :—

Symbolic of the mental element in the desire-mind being removed.

"Horus next cut off Set's head, and the heads of his followers, in the presence of Rā and the gods, and then dragged his body through all the land."—*Legend of the Winged Sun-disk*.

This means the depriving evil of its intelligent quality. And now the Self is enabled to unite the consciousness of the lower planes with his own ; so that no longer was there evil or separateness between himself above and the manifestation of himself on the lower planes.

See BEHEADING, GODS, HORUS, RĀ, SET.

HEAD, LIVING WITHOUT A :—

Symbolic of a spiritual condition in which mind is superseded by intuition of Truth.

"The sixteenth good land was the land by the floods of the Rangha where people live without a head."—*Vendidad*, I, *S. B. of E.*

This state of the soul signifies a condition receptive of a flood of Truth from above, whereby the processes of intellect may be dispensed with and pure thought,—the spiritual, impress of reality, that which is self-evident,—be substituted for the mind (head).

See BEHEADING, FLOOD, INTELLECT, INTUITION, RANGHA, WISDOM.

HEALING :—

A symbol of a spiritual process by means of which qualities are energised, harmonised, and purified. Evolution is often irregular and unbalanced through the vacillations of the egos ; and spiritual adjustments are made according to an ideal pattern, as the souls become prepared for them. The higher nature gradually conforms the lower nature to itself.

"Heal me, O Lord, and I shall be healed ; save me, and I shall be saved : for thou art my praise."—JER. xvii. 14.

"For I will restore health unto thee, and I will heal thee of thy wounds, saith the Lord ; because they have called thee an outcast, saying, It is Zion, whom no man seeketh after."—JER. xxx. 17.

The qualities after being disciplined by tribulations are prepared for the Divine upraising, wherein the lower conditions shall be surmounted. By the lower desires, the higher qualities are unregarded ; for the soul's divine nature (Zion) is uncared for by the lower mind (man) deluded by the things of sense.

" ' Who healeth all thy diseases ' : this is effected by the believer in the present life, while the flesh so lusts against the spirit, and the spirit against the flesh, that we cannot do the things we would (GAL. v. 17) ; whilst also another law in our members wars against the law of our mind (ROM. vii. 23) ; whilst to will is present indeed to us, but not how to perform that which is good (ROM. vii. 18). These are the diseases of a man's old nature which, however, if we only advance with persevering purpose, are healed by the growth of the new nature day by day, owing to the faith which operates through love

(GAL. v. 6) "—AUGUSTINE, *Anti-Pelagius*, Vol. I. p. 221.

"If you want to be happy and prosperous you must call upon your indwelling divine strength. You must realise that all you can possibly want or desire is already within you, and that it rests with you to bring it into manifestation. Thus, if you are poor, you must believe that all the wealth of the universe is within you, waiting to be drawn upon ; if you are sick, you must believe the same in respect to health ; if circumstances seem to be against you, you must understand and act upon the conviction that the spiritual nature of man is subject to no limitations, and can neither be hampered nor imprisoned by material things."— R. J. CAMPBELL, *Thursday Mornings*, p. 214.

"As transcending all mere development, I refer to that wondrous, inexplicable function of healing, discovered in the restoration or repair of animals and vegetables that are wounded or sick. When a tree, for example, is hacked or bruised, a strange nursing process forthwith begins, by which the wound is healed. A new bark is formed on the edges of the wound, by what method no art of man can trace, the dead matter is thrown off, and a growth inward narrows the breach, till finally the two margins meet and the tissues interweave, and not even a scar is left. So in all the flesh wounds of animals, and the fractures even of bones. So too in regard to all diseases not terminating mortally ; they pass a crisis, where the healing function, whatever it be, triumphs over the poison of the disease, and a recovery follows, in which the whole flesh and fibre appear even to be produced anew. . . . Regarding the body as a machine,—and taken as a merely material organisation,—it is plainly impossible for it to heal, in this manner, and repair itself. The disordered watch can never run itself into good repair. In machines, disorder can only propagate and aggravate disorder till they become a wreck. . . . Whatever view we take of this healing power in physiology, these two points are clear. First, that the healing accomplished is no fact of development. There is no difficulty in seeing how existing tissues and organs may create extensions within their own vascular sphere ; and this is development. But where a new skin or bark is to be created, or a new interlocking made of parts that are sundered, the ducts and vesicles that might act in development, being parted and open at their ends *want mending themselves*. . . . A fevered body does not cure itself by development. No shade of countenance, therefore, is given to the hope that human development, under the retributive woes of sin, will be any sufficient cure of its disorders, or will set the fallen subjects of it forward in a course of social progress.

This also, secondly, is equally clear, that, as the mysterious healing of bodies yields the development theory no token of favour, it is only a more impressive type, on that account, of some grand restorative economy, by which the condition of unnature in souls and the world is to be supernaturally regenerated—just such a type as regarding the relations of matter to mind, and of things natural to things spiritual, we might expect to find incorporated in some large and systematic way, in the visible objects and processes of the world. And how much does the healing of bodies signify, when associated thus with the grand elemental disorder and breakage of sin ! What is it, in fact, but a kind of glorious, everywhere visible sacrament, that tokens life and hope, and healing invisible, for all the retributive woes and bleeding lacerations of our guilty fallen state as a race apostate from God."—HORACE BUSHNELL, *Nature and the Supernatural*, pp. 156–8.

The physical body may be torn and disordered, but the astro-mental structure on which it was built by the life-forces of growth remains, of course, unaffected, and the subjective mind gives the necessary guidance to the life-forces which heal. As the body has grown, so it heals within the possibilities of environment. With regard to the soul, the atma-buddhic archetypal structure (Christ) within is the perfect guide to ultimate perfection. The below must become as the above.

"Wrong and wretchedness can find no place in reality, for the simple reason that wrong and wretchedness are experiences which imply inability to get at and draw upon ample reserves of life and power ; wrong and wretchedness would instantly vanish if we could all manage to do that. If we could only get out and up to reality, this is what we should find ;—and it is exactly what we are in process of doing. Step by step and bit by bit we are working our way upwards towards a state of spiritual consciousness which will put us at one with reality, which is only another way of saying at one with God."—R. J. CAMPBELL, Serm., *The Two Orders*.

See ARC. MAN, COSMOS, CREATION, DISEASE, IMAGE, LEPER, MEDICINE, MIRACLES, MULTITUDE, PHYSICIAN, POOL (Bethesda), RITES, SUN (of righteousness), TEN.

HEALING OF THE WITHERED HAND OF A MASON :—

A symbol of the energising of the will by the Spirit.

"Then saith he to the man, Stretch forth thy hand. And he stretched it

forth ; and it was restored whole as the other."—MAT. xii. 13.

The hand is the active and constructive instrument under the control of the will ; and Christ's cure refers to the energising of the will by the indwelling Self.

See HAND, MAN (natural), WILL.

HEALING OF AN EPILEPTIC :—

Symbolic of the steadying by the Spirit of the mental faculty which wavers between passion and error.

" There came to him a man, kneeling to him, and saying, Lord, have mercy on my son : for he is epileptic, and suffereth grievously ; for oft-times he falleth into the fire, and oft-times into the water."—MAT. xvii. 15.

The mind (man) referred to is one attracted towards the indwelling Christ, whom he supplicates to control the product of the mind, which is a mental state oscillating between passion (fire) and falsity (water). *Water* signifies Truth, but incomplete truth is dangerous,—is error. *Fire* signifies Love ; but on the astral plane it becomes passion. And so the Christ is brought to effect the cure of a vacillating and insecure mind or biassed opinion.

" This use of things natural, to represent things spiritual, is not the culling out the best and noblest, but likewise and equally the use of the worst and basest, or rather, I should say, the indiscriminate use of all. Sickness and vileness, wounds, bruises, and putrifying sores, leprosy, palsy, and death, are all used to shadow forth the evil conditions of our natural estate ; medicines, balms, and amputations, Christ's medical care of us ; and health or salvation, which is restoring to health, represents the efficacy of the Physician's care."—ED. IRVING, *Works*, Vol. I. p. 71.

See DISEASE, FIRE, MEDICINE, PHYSICIAN, WATER (lower).

HEALING A MAN SICK OF THE PALSY :—

A symbol of the restoration by the Spirit of a mental faculty which had been obstructed in its evolution.

" Jesus seeing their faith said unto the sick of the palsy, Son, be of good cheer ; thy sins are forgiven."—MAT. ix. 2.

This relates to a spiritual fact. It is the liberation of a disused power, which is effected in the soul by the faith or receptiveness, which brings forth the life when the Christ commands. The sins are forgiven in the fact of the spiritual adjustment and evolution of the Divine life.

"Paralysis is any disease of the soul whatsoever, but especially of fleshly lust, and the carelessness and indifference to spiritual things which it generates. For it so entirely prostrates the soul, that it is without power to lift itself up to virtue, to heaven, to God. Wherefore the man that labours under this disease must be carried by bearers, that is, by pastors, preachers, confessors, up upon the housetop, that is, to the desire of salvation and heavenly things ; and then must be let down through the roof to the feet of Christ ; and they must ask of Him by earnest prayer to heal them by His grace, and restore to him the power of motion and the sense of spiritual things."—C. À LAPIDE, *Great Comm.*, Vol. I. p. 358.

"They went up to the housetop, and let him down through the tiles with his couch into the midst before Jesus."—LUKE v. 19.

This signifies that the mental faculties (men) were exercised and the mind acquired knowledge, which prepared the mind for the spiritual adjustment which followed.

See FAITH, GRACE OF GOD.

HEALING BY CASTING OUT DEVILS :—

A symbol of the dispelling of illusions, and the driving forth of delusions.

"And he was casting out a devil which was dumb. And it came to pass, when the devil was gone out, the dumb man spake."—LUKE xi. 14.

This signifies a restoration to spiritual vision, perception of truth and ability to express the same in thought and action.

"The Pharisees said, This man doth not cast out devils, but by Beelzebub the prince of the devils."—MAT. xii. 24.

The literalist state of mind is illogical, as the spiritual teaching shows it to be. Literalists are nothing if not thorough-going, and so they accuse the Christ-soul of using means the very reverse of that which is really employed.

"If I by Beelzebub cast out devils, by whom do your sons cast them out ? "—MAT. xii. 27.

This is the retort of One who could see further than the literalists and formalists. The "sons of the Pharisees" cast forth illusions,—as they imagine and suppose,—by con-

demnation of the "evil," which of course shows that they *believe* in the "evil" as real, and therefore indirectly they are instrumental in encouraging error and delusion. Christ casts evil forth by *doing right* in thought and action.

"That was the Christ who went from haunt to haunt of the devils and bade them flee ; and they, the devils of hatred, cruelty, lust, selfishness, brutishness, superstition,—they all fled at His presence."—PHILLIPS BROOKS.

See DEVILS, EVIL, ILLUSION, PHARISEES.

HEALING BY RAISING THE DEAD :—

Symbolic of a spiritual awakening in the soul. The energising of a dormant, or latent, affection or mental faculty.

"And when the Lord saw the widow, he had compassion on her, and said unto her, Weep not. And he came nigh and touched the bier : and the bearers stood still. And he said, Young man, I say unto thee, Arise, And he that was dead sat up, and began to speak. And he gave him to his mother."—LUKE vii. 13-5.

The "widow" signifies that part of the nature which has lost a product and mental object of its affections. It grieves at the loss and imagines the quality to be dead. The Christ, however, re-animates the condition of interest, and revives the relationship, which thereby restores harmonious conditions.

"Jesus said, Give place ; for the damsel is not dead but sleepeth. And they laughed him to scorn. But when the crowd was put forth, he entered in, and took her by the hand ; and the damsel arose."—MAT. ix. 24, 25.

This story may have referred to the resuscitation of an affection in a quality which was developed as a ruler of qualities. This spiritual life-giving was effected through the interposition of the Christ in the manner symbolically described. It must be remembered that many of these minor incidents in the gospel drama, though mostly spiritual in their meaning, cannot be interpreted bit by bit (as Swedenborg imagined). They must be sensed, as it were, and they may all be classed as showing a general tendency of soul towards Christhood,—or an accession of Power through the Spirit. The saying of Jesus that "the damsel is not dead but sleepeth" signifies that an affection cannot die. It could only slumber until applied to its true purpose through the Christ. The "putting forth of the crowd" is the subdual of discordant elements so that the Christ may enter in and bring renewed life to the soul.

See CROWD, JAIRUS, INFIRMITY, LAZARUS, RULER, TRANSMUTATION.

HEARING (HIGHER ASPECT) :—

A symbol of the intuitive perception of truth from within the soul. An attitude of reception of wisdom from above.

"God speaks with a man, not by means of some audible creature dinning in his ears, so that atmospheric vibrations connect Him that makes with him that hears the sound ; nor even by means of of a spiritual being with the semblance of a body, such as we see in dreams or similar states ; for even in this case he speaks as if to the ears of the body, and with the appearance of a real interval of space. Not by these, then, does God speak, but by the truth itself, if any one is prepared to hear with the mind rather than with the body. He speaks to that part of man which is better than all else in him, and than which God himself alone is better."—AUGUSTINE, *City of God*, Bk. XI. Ch. 2.

See CONSCIENCE, HIDING, SOUND, VOICE OF GOD.

HEARING (LOWER ASPECT) :—

A symbol of the reception of knowledge without wisdom. "Hearing" proceeds from "the flesh," i.e. it is the outcome of the desire nature.

"To hear signifies to perceive."— SWEDENBORG, *Apoc. Rev.*, n. 448.

"I had heard of thee (the Lord) by the hearing of the ear : but now mine eye seeth thee."—JOB xlii. 5.

The condition and stage of the soul signified by "Job" became first cognisant of its higher nature through ordinary channels of information, but afterwards the mind perceived the truth within.

See EAR, EYE, JOB.

HEART :—

A symbol of the causal-body as a centre of being on the higher mental plane, and the receptacle of atma-buddhi, the spirit within. The heart also signifies the love principle and the higher affections.

"The heart—the heavenly city of Brahman."—*Mundaka. Upanishad*, 2, 7.

"God who is concealed within the heart. . . . O man meditate on the Name under the Guru's instruction, and thou shalt be happy in the temple of thy heart " (Nanak).—MACAULIFFE, *The Sikh Religion*, Vol. I. pp. 317–8.

"Sakalya said ; 'And in what does the True abide ?' Yagnavalkya said : 'In the heart, for with the heart do we know what is true, and in the heart indeed the True abides.' "—*Brihad. Upanishad*, III. 9, 23.

(*Footnote.* "Heart stands here for buddhi and manas together."—*S. B. of E.*, Vol. XV. p. 146.)

"My heart, my mother ! My heart whereby I came into being. May naught stand up to oppose me at my judgment ; . . . may there be no parting of thee from me in the presence of him that keepeth the Balance ! Thou art my double (ka), the dweller in my body. . . . Verily how great shalt thou be when thou risest in triumph."—BUDGE, *Book of the Dead*, Ch. XXXB.

The causal-body is the "mother" whereby the ego comes into being on the lower planes. It is the cause of the series of incarnations. In the "weighing of the heart before Osiris " the development of the causal-body is judged by its balance against the personality. The causal-body is the "double" on a higher plane of the personality, and when perfection is reached, the two Selves, lower and higher, become one and rise in triumph to the buddhic plane.

"The heart lies in seas of blood which dart in opposite directions ; and there most of all intelligence centres for men for blood about the heart is intelligence in the case of men."—*Empedocles*, FAIRBANKS, 327.

The "heart" or love principle, is in closest contact with the life essence (blood) which flows, or energises, in opposite ways, or to "pairs of opposites," in other words, the life essence is directed toward objects which involve opposite relationships. And through this conflict intelligence develops in the mind from the awakenment of the emotion principle. The life essence concentrated in the causal-body and higher affections, gives intuition when it is united with the mental principle.

"The heart was considered to be the source of all life and thought, and it was the part of the body that was specially taken care of in mummifying. . . . Sometimes the heart (amulet) is human-headed, with the hands crossed over it, and sometimes a figure of the soul, in the shape of a hawk with outstretched wings is inlaid on one side of it."—BUDGE, *The Mummy*, pp. 262–3.

The causal-body is perfected by the purification of the personality (mummifying). It is the immortal soul—the seat of the Higher Self (hawk).

"As the Æolian harp vibrates to the wind, so does the heart of man everywhere to the true message of God."—J. BRIERLEY, *Studies of the Soul*, p. 168.

"The soul is often called the heart of man, or that, in and by which things to either good or evil, have their rise; thus desires are of the heart or soul; yea, before desires, the first conception of good or evil is in the soul, the heart. The heart understands, wills, affects, reasons, judges, but these are the faculties of the soul; wherefore, heart and soul are often taken for one and the same. 'My son, give me thine heart.'—(PROV. xxiii. 26). 'Out of the heart proceed evil thoughts,' etc. (MAT. xv. 19; 1 PET. iii. 15; Ps. xxvi. 2)."—J. BUNYAN, *Greatness of the Soul*.

Both the symbols "soul" and "heart" have higher and lower meanings in accordance with the duality of manifestation.

"By the word *heart*, of course, we here mean not merely 'the seat of the affections,' 'the organ of tender emotion,' and the like: but rather the inmost sanctuary of personal being, the synthesis of its love and will, the very source of its energy and life."—E. UNDERHILL, *Mysticism*, p. 85.

"God's Spirit is throned in the heart, He walks with us as a friend, He breathes into our spirit the inspiration of power, and love, and a sound mind. In the secret places of our trial and our doubt, in the hour when our nature trembles on the verge of fall, in the hour when our being asserts its immortal righteousness against a base temptation, He is with us, inspiring us with the memory of Christ, calling on us to be worthy of our calling, pouring life and energy into the affections which raise us above our selfishness, into the aspirations which make us despise our sin; kindling hope in the midst of our despair, and faith to try again when life has failed."—STOPFORD A. BROOKE, Serm., *Pentecost*.

"The fact is that the 'Heart' is a symbol of the central life of the soul and the manifestations thence proceeding, for the Scriptural writers as well as for the Classical writers generally."—A. CALDECOTT, *Phil. of Religion*, p. 89.

See AB, BALANCE, BLOOD, CABIN, CAUSAL-BODY, EMBALMMENT, HAWK, INCENSE, JUDGMENT-HALL, KA, LOTUS, PROCESSION, PYLONS, QEBHSENNUF, QUETZALCOATL, SHENIT, SHRINE, SOUL, TEMPLE, VISCERA, ZAGREUS.

HEAT AND COLD :—

Symbols of the opposite conditions of relativity,—good and evil.

"Divine Truth proceeding from the Lord as a sun in heaven, is light in heaven, and Divine goodness is heat there."—SWEDENBORG, *White Horse*, p. 49.

See COLD AND HEAT, OPPOSITES.

HEAVEN :—

A symbol of the state of consciousness on the buddhic plane which is above the mental plane.

"The first man is of the earth, earthy: the second man is of heaven. As is the earthy, such are they also that are earthy: and as is the heavenly, such are they also that are heavenly. And as we have borne the image of the earthy, we shall also bear the image of the heavenly."—1 COR. xv. 47–9.

The "first man" is the personality (Adam of dust), which is developed from below through the astral evolution,—the matter (earthy) side of being. The "second man" is the individuality or Divine monad from above,—the spiritual (heavenly) side of being. To the personality are attached the lower qualities, and to the individuality the higher qualities. In the course of development, the ego more and more asserts its Divine nature, and finally rises from the lower nature to become united with the higher in consciousness on the buddhic plane.

"More and more distinctly over our human life, with all its best affections, hangs the serene heaven of the divine life, the heaven of the love of God, into which our human affections must enter before they become religious; into which they cannot enter till they have been *born again*. . . . These (affections) which the Spirit finds in you are not religion. Never let yourself think that they are, and so depreciate and disregard the work which the Spirit has to do in you. They are not religion; but they are the material of the religious life. They are the part of your nature in which you may become religious. They are the stone in your nature out of which the temple may be built."—PHILLIPS BROOKS, Serm., *How many Loaves, etc.?*

"The *quality* of the Eternal Life alone makes the heaven; mere everlastingness might be no boon."—H. DRUMMOND, *Natural Law, etc.*, p. 220.

See ADAM (higher), ADAM (lower), AMENT, ARC. MAN, BORN AGAIN, BUDDHIC PLANE, DEVAYANA, EARTH, EDEN, GARODMAN, IMAGE, INDIVIDUALITY, KINGDOM OF HEAVEN, MONAD OF LIFE, MUSPELLHEIM, PITRIS (lunar, solar), PITRIYANA, RE-BIRTH, REGENERATION, SEKHET-HETEP.

HEAVEN AND EARTH :—

Symbols of Spirit and Matter,— the life and the form sides of manifestation.

"There are, strictly speaking, only two *substances*, matter and spirit : all particular things result from the composition in varying degrees of these two,— are therefore mere 'accidents,' and have no abiding reality" (Bruno).—J. L. MCINTYRE, *Giordano Bruno*, p. 159.

"Heaven represents the male (Yang) principle and earth the corresponding (Yin) female principle, on which two principles the whole of existence depends." —C. T. R. ALLEN, *Chinese Poetry*, Preface.

"Varro derives the male divinities from heaven or Jupiter as the active principle, and the female divinities from the earth or Juno as the passive principle."— ZELLER, *Eclecticism*, p. 177.

"In the beginning God created the heaven and the earth. And the earth was without form and void ; and darkness was upon the face of the deep : and the Spirit of God moved upon the face of the waters."—GEN. i. 1, 2.

At the commencement of the emanation of the Solar Universe, the primordial elements, Spirit and Matter, are differentiated from that which is itself neither, but which is potential for both. And the primordial matter is inchoate and formless,—the involution of form not having yet begun, —for Spirit is not yet permeating and enlightening matter. And the Supreme Logos (the Atman) broods upon, or contemplates, the "waters" of Absolute Truth, the Ultimate Reality.

"In the beginning God, the Unity, created, or put forth from Himself, the Duality, the Heavens, or Spirit and Deep, Force and Substance, and their ultimate phenomenal resultant, generated of them, the Earth or Matter. And the Spirit, or Force, of God, moved on the 'face of the waters' or Substance of God, and God said, or found expression, and there was Light, or manifestation of God."—E. MAITLAND, *Life of A. Kingsford*, Vol. I. p. 199.

"Pwan-koo was the first Being after the separation of the heavens and the earth, between which he existed, and

whose heights and depths he comprehended. He knew the principles of creation, and was the original Ruler of the world. He is described as appearing from vast unknown deserts."—KIDD, *China*, p. 100.

"Pwan-koo" signifies the Second Logos, the Divine Artificer, from whom all emanates. The "separation of heaven and earth" refers to the duality of primordial manifestation, namely, the polarities of Spirit and Matter between which manifestation proceeds, and through which the heights and depths of the planes of creation are to be supplied. The Divine Ruler proceeds from the chaos (unknown deserts).

"Of old, Heaven and Earth were not yet separated, and the In (Yin) and Yo (Yang) not yet divided. They formed a chaotic mass like an egg, which was of obscurely defined limits, and contained germs. The purer and clearer part was thinly diffused and formed Heaven, while the heaven and grosser element settled down and became Earth. The finer element easily became a united body, but the consolidation of the heavy and gross element was accomplished with difficulty. Heaven was therefore formed first, and Earth established subsequently. Therefore divine beings were produced between them" (Commencement of the *Nihongi* and the *Kiujiki*).—W. G. ASTON, *Shinto*, p. 84.

This statement refers, first, to the period prior to Involution when Spirit and Matter were not yet differentiated from the Monadic essence in which they lay potentia . This essence on the atma-buddhic heights contained the prototypes (germs) of all things that were afterwards to exist. Second, the primal elements, Spirit and Matter, having come into being and become separated, the one from the other, by reason of their different natures of activity and passivity, there was established the interactive duality from which the highest qualities (gods) should first arise in preparation for the process of Involution.

"(In China there is) a belief in two higher Powers, which in the language of philosophy may mean *Form* and *Matter*, in the language of Ethics, *Good* and *Evil*, but which in the original language of religion and mythology are represented as Heaven and Earth."—MAX MÜLLER, *Science of Religion*, p. 92.

See AIR-ÆTHER, CIRCLE AND SQUARE,

COSMOS, CREATION, DESERTS, EARTH (primo.), EGG, HELIOPE, HIGHER AND LOWER NATURES, HORSE-SACRIFICE, KHIEN AND KHWAN, MATTER, MULA-PRAKRITI, OCEANUS, PILLARS OF SHU, PWANKOO, RĀ, RANGI, RHEA, RONGO RU, SALT, SEPARATION OF HEAVEN AND EARTH, SKY, SPIRIT, STEM, TANEMAHUTA, URANUS.

HEAVENLY NYMPHS, SIRENS, GANDHARVAS, COLCHIANS:—

These are symbols of buddhic faculties on the higher sub-planes of the buddhic plane in the soul.

See COLCHIS, DANCES, GANDHARVAS, SIRENS.

HEAVENLY REGIONS :—

A symbol of the higher mental or buddhic states of rest and bliss.

"Every evening Oro descended on the rainbow to the valley, and returned by the same pathway on the following morning to the heavenly regions."—W. ELLIS, *Polynesian Researches*, Vol. I. p. 231.

And at recurring intervals, descents,—evening, night, morning,—marking periods of embodiment on the lower planes, would be made by the Self or ego ; after which the Self would again quit the temporary abode of its incarnation, and return through the higher mind (rainbow bridge) to the devachanic state.

See DEVACHAN, ORO, RAINBOW, RE-INCARNATION, VAIRAUMATI.

HEAVENLY SPRINGTIME :—

A symbol signifying the Individuality rising joyously from the causal-body to progress on the celestial journey to heights of glory inconceivable. The Ego has in this case passed through the present cycle and attained Liberation and Union on the higher mental plane, for from that point is the true beginning of the Real Life.

"O 'Heavenly Springtime!' I have come into Thee ; I have eaten my sacramental cakes ; I have power over the sacrificial portions of my beasts and birds ; the feathered fowl of the light are given unto me, for I have followed the Gods when the Divine forms come."—*Book of the Dead*, Ch. CX., trans. M. W. Blackden.

The Divine Life is entered into, and the growth of the true Self is now apprehended and perceived to be the supreme fact of universal life. The "food of the Gods" has been eaten in the attainment of the Ideals in Wisdom and Love, and so spiritual power is acquired which renders sacrifice, asceticism, self-denial, or any form of self-abnegation or irksomeness, not only unnecessary but impossible. The aspirations, which formerly led to these necessary but contractive limitations, now yield their fruit ; for the rising Self within has fulfilled his ideals and been true to them.

"It seems to me that the very essence of the life eternal consists in the fact that it involves perfect self-expression, without the sense of lack, hindrance, or defeat. The life eternal, the life that God lives and is, is the life in which fullness of power, fullness of joy, and fullness of self-knowledge preclude any possibility of subjection to the limitations which in this world are the cause of our trouble and compel us to choose between one form of gratification and another. . . . We want not to have to think about giving up this and resisting that ; we want to be able to live as the trees and birds live, fulfilling our appointed tasks with perfect ease and harmony, and without the danger of going wrong anywhere. Now that, I say, is the life eternal, the goal of all our strivings, the life that in Christ we shall come to share with God. And you can see for yourselves at once that it must be a life in which considerations of right and wrong no longer hold good ; they are gone, transcended, swallowed up in the joy of being and doing exactly what we want and God wants, without the intrusion of any discordant factor."—R. J. CAMPBELL, Serm., *The Non-moral Aspects of Religion.*

See BEASTS (clean), BIRDS, BREAD, COME INTO THEE, FOOD, GODS, SACRAMENTAL CAKES, SPRINGTIME.

HEAVENLY VOICE IN THE PATH :—

A symbol of aspiration which is the expression of the Divine life within the soul.

"But hear now the motive for my coming and rejoice thereat ; a heavenly voice has been heard by me (Asita) in the heavenly path, that thy son (Buddha) has been born for the sake of supreme knowledge."—*Buddha-Karita*, Bk. I. 62.

The lower self (buddhi-manas) in involution, now realises the nature of the higher law whereby its development is to be quickened ; and within it joy is aroused. The Divine nature,—aspiration,—has awakened within it, and now it recognises that the Son of Righteousness (moral law and conscience) has been born upon the higher planes.

See ASITA, BIRTH OF BUDDHA, BUDDHA, SIMEON.

HEBDOMAD WHICH PROCEEDS FROM THE OGDOAD :—

A symbol of the Highest Being which emanates from the Absolute. The manifest Self from the unmanifest.

See GLORY, OGDOAD.

HEBDOMAD, SON OF THE :—

A symbol of the Son of God, or God manifest on the higher planes.

" The light, therefore, which came down from the Ogdoad above to the Son of the Hebdomad, descended from the Hebdomad upon Jesus the son of Mary, and he had radiance imparted to him by being illuminated with the light that shone upon him. This, he says, is that which has been declared : ' The Holy Spirit will come upon thee,' meaning that which proceeded from the Sonship through the conterminous spirit upon the Ogdoad and Hebdomad, as far as Mary." (*System of Basilides*).—HIPPOLYTUS, *Refutation, etc.*, Bk. VII. 14.

So from the Highest, the Divine Ray, which had already been latent within the Supreme (the Ogdoad), went forth unto Him who was the only begotten of the Highest, and descended through the upper planes to illumine the personal aspect of the Self,—the Christ-soul,—born of the purified portion of the lower nature (Virgin Mary). And the purified nature was made radiant with love and truth, through the Divine Light which was caught by Him to whom the purified nature had given birth.

See BIRTH OF JESUS, OF KRISHNA, OF ZOROASTER, GLORY (divine), JESUS, KINGLY GLORY, VIRGIN MARY.

HEBEN TEMPLE GROUND :—

A symbol of the causal-body and its relations with the lower planes.

" All these things took place on the temple ground of Heben, which measured 342 *khat* on the south, north, west and east."—*Legend of the Winged Sun-disk*.

All these activities of the indwelling Self (Horus) took place in the soul, which is the " temple " of the Holy Spirit, and is comparable to the measurement 342,—that number being

a symbol of wholeness and completeness (3), and significant of top and bottom, height and depth (4). Or, the 3 dimensions,—the number of the physical plane, and the 4 planes of the lower quaternary (cardinal points), together with duality (2) on each plane. It signifies the summing up of the soul's possibilities, when the soul is weighed and not found wanting.

See CAUSAL-BODY, JUDGMENT HALL, QUARTERS, QUATERNARY, TEMPLE.

HECATOMB,—THE SACRIFICE OF MANY UNBLEMISHED BULLS AND GOATS AND LAMBS :—

A symbol of the tribute offered by the lower self to the Higher Self : the tribute being the karmic results of the ethical activity of the mind in the sacrifice of the lower qualities which implies exercise of the higher (unblemished).

" Let us (said Achilles) consult some prophet or priest, or even one who is informed by dreams,—for dream also is from Jove,—who would tell us on what account Phœbus Apollo is so much enraged with us : whether he blames us on account of a vow unperformed, or a hecatomb unoffered ; and whether haply he may be willing, having partaken of the savour of lambs and unblemished goats, to avert from us the pestilence."— *Iliad*, Bk. I., trans. Buckley.

An effort is made by the personality (Achilles) through the mind to find authority and sanction for its self-preservative course of action, in the opinion or tradition current at that period of its activity. The " dream, etc." stands for the first theory of religion and life that is at hand. And thus a dim conception is gradually arrived at as to the nature of the activities of the Higher Self (Apollo). But a sense of doubt and uncertainty gains possession of the mind, on the question as to whether the mind is held accountable because it possesses the germ of conscience, or whether it is so from the karmic law of action and reaction exemplified in the moral nature ? The mind further inquires, whether it will be that the Higher Self, having accepted the tribute and contribution of the lower self in the thought of loving service (lambs) and sincere faith (unblemished goats), will afford the lower self the means for overcoming the adverse conditions which surround it, and profiting from the destruction of the lower qualities.

"Then was the noble seer (Kalchas) of good courage, and spake : ' Neither by reason of a vow is Apollo displeased, nor for any hecatomb, but for his priest's sake to whom Agamemnon did despite, and set not his daughter free and accepted not the ransom ; therefore hath the Far-darter brought woes upon us, yea, and will bring. Nor will he ever remove the loathly pestilence from the Greeks till we have given the bright-eyed damsel (Chryseis) to her father (Chryse, Apollo's priest), unbought, unransomed, and carried a holy hecatomb to Chryse ;— then might we propitiate Apollo to our prayer.' "—*Ibid.*

Then the inner memory (Kalchas) of the soul's true nature comes into play. Not on account of the surrender of the lower self to a partial conception of higher activities and cosmic law, nor because of the limiting and binding nature of the karmic order on the lower planes, will the indwelling Self (Apollo) fail to express its latent,— or as yet unmanifest,—potencies for good, but for the sake of restoring to action the spiritual mind (priest),— to which the desire-mind (Agamemnon) was opposed which took the intuition of Truth (Chryseis) captive, and would not seek to recover that which was to ransom the intuition, namely, by treasure or higher qualities above. Hence the Self is the means of disquieting the lower self. Nor will the erroneous theories of the lower mind be got rid of until the intuition of Truth is recovered by the inner memory, and voluntary effort is made on the part of the lower self to raise the consciousness to the spiritual understanding, in which case the reconciliation between the Higher Will (Apollo) and the lower mind will have been effected.

See ACHILLES, AGAMEMNON, APOLLO, BLOOD OF BULLS, BURNT OFFERING, CHRYSE, CHRYSEIS, CONSCIENCE, GREEKS, HIDING, INTUITION, KALCHAS, KARMA, PAPYRUS, PERSONALITY, PESTILENCE, RANSOM, RELIGION, ROASTED, SACRIFICE, SAVOUR, TREASURE, VOICE, VOW.

HECTOR, SON OF PRIAM :—

A symbol of the spiritual perceptive-

ness of the truth, begotten of the causal self (Priam).

"And then wilt thou (Agamemnon) in no wise avail to save the Greeks, for all thy grief, when multitudes fall dying before manslaying Hector."—*Iliad*, Bk. I.

And the Desire-mind shall in no wise avail to arrest the evolution of the soul, by the continuance of the lower mental faculties or "mortal mind." And all the sorrow of the Desire-mind shall prove unavailing to preserve the effete, before the unfoldment of the Spiritual law transcending the mind.

See AGAMEMNON, EVOLUTION, GREEKS, MORTAL MIND, PRIAM, TROJANS, TROY.

HEDGEHOG :—

A symbol of the critical intellect destructive of errors.

"The dog with prickles and a long and thin muzzle, the dog Vanghapara is a good creature which from midnight to dawn destroys thousands of creatures of the evil spirit."—*Vendidad*, XIII.

This "dog," with defensive points and insinuating methods of destructive inquiry, signifies the critical intellect which destroys superstition, error, delusion, and doubt, and gets rid of the prejudices and out-grown notions of the lower mind.

See AHRIMAN, BRIAREUS, CREEPING THINGS, DAEVAS, DOG, TALUS.

HEEL :—

A symbol of the lower nature of the human soul.

"And I will put enmity between thee and the woman, and between thy seed and her seed : it shall bruise thy head, and thou (serpent) shalt bruise his heel."—GEN. iii. 15.

And ethical distinction shall be drawn between the sense nature with its appetites and delights, and the higher emotion-nature ; and through this distinction shall the struggle within the soul proceed. From this conflict between higher and lower, the result shall be that the lower mental (head) directivity of desire, or lower will, shall be crushed out by the Divine nature (Christ within) grown up in the soul, and this will lead to the dissipation of the lower part of the soul (heel).

"To this serpent, this spirit of evil

in the world, God is speaking. What does God say ? There shall be a long, terrible fight between man and the power of evil. The power of evil shall haunt and persecute man, cripple him and vex him, hinder him and make him suffer. It shall bruise his heel. But man shall ultimately be stronger than the power of evil, and shall overcome it and go forth victorious, though bruised and hurt, and needing recovery and rest. He shall bruise its head. . . . Is it not true that everywhere the good is hampered and beset and wounded by the evil which it is ultimately to slay ; true also that the good will ultimately slay the evil by which it was wounded and beset ? These two facts, in their combination, make a philosophy of life which, when one has accepted it, colours each thought he thinks, each act he does. The two facts subtly blend their influence in every experience."
—PHILLIP BROOKS, Serm., *The Giant, etc.*

"As heels are the lowest part of the body, Christ's *heel* bruised by Satan is his humbled manhood, and his people who are subject to him. To have *heels bare*, denotes shame, contempt, captivity or distress (JER. xiii. 22). To lift up the *heels* or kick is to render evil for good to a superior, as a beast when it strikes its master ; so Judas acted in betraying our Lord."—GURNEY, *Bible Dict.*, p. 256.

"A day arrives when man becomes aware of a dual nature within him, a divine and an earthly, one in which he shares with the gods, and one which is his in common with the brutes. But he pays a heavy price for his self-knowledge. Henceforth he is at war with himself, the God and the serpent within him fighting for mastery. On the whole, victory rests with the former, and in the end will do so completely, but it will not be a scathless triumph ; the God will crush the serpent's head, but the latter will wound the heel that tramples it. . . . The whole upward progress of humanity towards the stature of the superman has been a continuous bruising of the serpent's head : but in the process we have had to suffer ; the heel that tramples down the evil has to feel the serpent's fangs."—R. J. CAMPBELL, Serm., *Trampling the Serpent.*

"Achilles is not quite invulnerable ; the sacred waters did not wash the heel by which Thetis held him. Siegfried, in the Nibelungen, is not quite immortal, for a leaf fell on his back whilst he was bathing in the dragon's blood, and that spot which it covered is mortal."—EMERSON, *Compensation.*

"Thetis endeavoured to make Achilles immortal by dipping him in the river Styx, and succeeded with the exception of the ankles (or heel) by which she held him."—*Smith's Class. Dict.*

"Achilles" is a symbol of the personality brought forth by nature (Thetis). The "river Styx" signifies the life of the soul on earth, through which the personality is developed and purified. But though the personality is purified ultimately, it misses immortality by reason of its lower nature (heel) which is mortal. When the lower nature vanishes, the personality vanishes with it. Nevertheless, within the personality there evolves the lower Self, which, when the lower nature is cast off, rises immortal to the higher planes and becomes one with the Higher Self. It is this which is signified by "Achilles" being said to be immortal all but his lowest part (heel).

"By ' heel ' is signified the lowest natural principle, as the corporeal, which the ' serpent ' should bruise."—SWEDENBORG, *Arc. Cel. to Gen.* iii. 15.

"Krishna finally died of an arrow wound which he sustained accidentally and in an unforeseen manner on his heel,— the only vulnerable part of his body (cf. Achilles, Balder, Adonis, and Osiris)."—A. DREWS, *The Christ Myth*, p. 107.

See ADAM (lower), ACHILLES, CURSE (ground), EVE, FALL, HEAD, HORSE (winged), IMMORTALITY FORFEITED, KEEL, MORTAL MIND, NIDHOGG, PERSONALITY, SERPENT (subtil), SHABTI, SOUL (lowest), STYX, WOMAN.

HEIFER, RED, PERFECT :—

A symbol of the buddhic nature,— Wisdom (cow), Love (red), prior to the soul's descent.

"A red heifer without spot, wherein is no blemish, and upon which never came yoke."—NUM. xix. 2.

This indicates that wisdom-love at an early stage of the soul's evolution is entire and latent in respect to the lower nature. The "killing" is the obscuration of wisdom-love which occurs on the descent of the ego (one) to the lower planes. The "burning" and the "ashes" signify the purifying function of buddhi operating through the lower nature. "Touching the dead" refers to the "dead selves" which must be got rid of. The ego allied with the lower personality (corpse) is "unclean until the even," that is, he is imperfect until the indrawing at the end of the cycle (day) of incarnation.

"In accordance with the general nature of the symbolical institutions, the body (of the red heifer) stands as the representative and image of the soul, and its defilement and cleansing, for actual guilt and spiritual purification."—P. Fairbairn, *Typology of Scripture*, Vol II. p. 404.

"The offering of Christ, as in 'the red heifer,' is without doubt the great end of the representation."—A. Jukes, *The Law of the Offerings*, p. 27.

"The ruddy cow with reddish-white eyes is the Father's own whom they slay here for the Fathers."—*Sata. Brâh.*, III. 3, 1, 14.

This signifies that wisdom-love operates through the higher mind for the benefit of the astral development of the forms and the personality, by which it becomes obscured in the soul. (The "Fathers" are the lunar pitris.)

In Ovid's *Epistles of the Heroines*, Helen is called "the Grecian Heifer," which can only mean the "cow," symbol of the buddhic principle.

See Ashes, Buddhi, Burnt offering, Corpse, Cow, Dead, Helen, Pitris (lunar) Red, Spotted.

HEIGHT, OR HEIGHTS :—

A symbol of the higher planes of manifestation. The buddhic plane, heaven. It has the same meaning as mountain top, or mountain upon which the Gods dwell.

See Albordj, Caucasus Goat, (white), Himavan, Kailāsa, Mountain, Olympus.

HEIGHT OF OSIRIS :—

A symbol of the planes of manifestation of the Logos.

"Osiris was beautiful of face, but with a dull and black complexion; his height exceeded five and a half yards."—Plutarch, *Isis and Osiris*.

The Higher Self (Osiris) was beautiful and perfect *potentially*, but was *actually* non-existent, and, as it were, "black," which stands for negation of existence. His "height" refers to the five planes whereon his complete evolution would be accomplished. The excess above five refers to two unmanifest planes above atma, which will become manifest in other cycles.

See Black, Deserts, Face, Four times, Heaven and earth, Osiris, Planes, Stem.

HEIMDALL :—

A symbol of the Logos, or the Divine Will in manifestation.

"Heimdallr was a god of light, of the early sun, 'the dawn and the beginning of all things' (Uhland), akin to the Greek Helios. He kept watch on the frontiers of highest heaven (Himinbjorg), guarding the rainbow bridge (Bifrost) against the assaults of the giants. Descriptions of Heimdallr speak of his golden teeth, of his horse with golden mane (Guldtoppr), on which he rode to Balder's funeral, of his wonderful sword, Hofud (head), of his horn (Gjallarhorn) with which the gods were summoned to the last great battle. He had deadly feud with Loki, with whom he fought daily."—*Nonclassical Mythology*, p. 80.

The Divine Will manifests on the plane of the higher mind (Bifrost) midway between the higher and lower natures, and judging the soul-qualities. The "golden teeth" symbolise wisdom and power. The "horse" signifies the highest intelligence; the "sword," spiritual force to dispel error; the "horn," the outpouring of the Divine Life for the development of the qualities. The Divine Will contends against the lower principle (Loki) in every stage of the soul's progress.

See Balder, Bifrost, Dawn, Death of balder, Gold, Guldtopp, Horse, Loke, Regnarok, Teeth, Tusk.

HEIR ACCORDING TO PROMISE :—

A symbol of the perfected Individuality seated in the causal-body, which succeeds the Personality and inherits the "treasures laid up in heaven," becoming "heir of the righteousness which is according to faith," that is, of the transmuted qualities of the lower nature, awaiting recognition upon the buddhic plane, when the consciousness rises to the heaven plane.

"Everything that your heart has ever longed for or possessed of things holy and blessed is yours now in Christ, part of his unsearchable riches, your eternal inheritance, marked with your name. There is something better for you than (the past), something vaster and grander. Make towards it at once. Delay not a moment. Christ is your way there, the companion of your pilgrimage and the goal of your hopes."—R. J. Campbell; Serm., *Sacred Memories*.

"This eternal God is of necessity to be the object of our hope. The church in heaven, called the body and temple of God, is to be a habitation for himself when it is finished, to dwell in for ever."—J. Bunyan, *Israel's Hope*.

See FRUIT OF SPIRIT, NALA-KUVERA, TRANSMUTATION, TREASURE, WEALTH.

HELEN OF TROY :—

A symbol of Wisdom on the buddhic plane. It is for the possession of the buddhic consciousness that the soul contends in the strife between the mental qualities (the Greeks) and the emotions (the Trojans). In the sack of Troy (the kingdom of heaven), "men of violence take it by force" (MAT. xi. 12); that is, it is through the striving of the mental qualities for Wisdom that the higher emotions are acquired and heaven gained.

"Simon Magus says that he has brought down this Helena from the highest heavens to the world; being queen, as the all-bearing being, and Wisdom, for whose sake, says he, the Greeks and barbarians fought, having before their eyes but an image of Truth; for she who really is the Truth was then with the chiefest God."—*Clementine Homilies*, Ch. 25. of *Hom.* II.

"Simon Magus, as the 'Great Power of God' . . . declared that she (Helena) was the 'Intelligence' that of old was imprisoned in the body of the Grecian Helen, then of the Lost Sheep, but now was restored to him for the salvation of the world" (from Hippolytus).—C. W. KING, *Gnostics and their Remains*, p. 21.

See GREEKS, HEIFER, ILIUM, POLLUX, SHEEP (lost), TROJANS, TROY, WISDOM.

HELIOS, THE SUN-GOD, RĀ :—

A symbol of the First Logos.

See ADITYA, AMEN-RĀ, RĀ, SAVITRI, SUN, SURYA.

HELIOPE AND CHTHONIE, OR SUN AND EARTH :—

Symbols of the higher and lower Selves, or of buddhi-manas and kama-manas,—the higher mind and the lower.

See EARTH, HEAVEN AND EARTH, SELF, SUN.

HELL, HEL, HADES, SHEOL :—

These are symbols of the underworld or four lower planes of nature, namely, the lower mental, the astral, the etheric, and the physical planes. The underworld is the arena of life for the spiritual egos who incarnate therein to gain experience and the development of their potential natures.

"Now Scripture language is symbolical. There is no salt, no worm, no fire to torture. I say not that a diseased soul may not form for itself a tenement hereafter, as here, peculiarly fitted to be the avenue of suffering; but unquestionably we cannot build upon these expressions a material hell."—F. W. ROBERTSON, *Sermons*, 1st Series, p. 117.

"If that soul of ours, that sheath of the spirit, belongs to earth rather than heaven, the Spirit will have to remake it, and that means hell until every earthborn desire has been renounced and overcome as such, and transmuted into its spiritual counterpart."—R. J. CAMPBELL, Serm., *Hell*.

The supposed scriptural authority for places of post-mortem everlasting torment for human beings is simply misinterpretation of texts. The symbol *man* or *men* signifies mind or mental qualities, and these qualities, as long as they are "wicked," have to be purified in the eternal "fire" of the Holy Spirit. The purification takes place in "Hell," i.e. the lower quaternary, in connection with the egos, and through the struggle and suffering which we observe around us.

Dr. Budge, after describing "the destruction of the dead in the Tuat," observes :

"Thus there is no doubt that there was a hell of fire in the kingdom of Seker, and that the tortures of mutilation and destruction by fire were believed to be reserved for the wicked."—*Egypt. Heaven and Hell*, Vol III. p. 137.

The "kingdom of Seker" was in the Fifth Division of the Tuat (underworld), that is, it centred in the astral plane of desire and sensation, in which the mental qualities were "purified as by fire," and had their lowest condition cut away. Dr. Budge continues,—

"Of the rewards of the righteous in this kingdom we have no knowledge whatever."

The "righteous" are the purified qualities, and there are no purified qualities on the lower planes. The "rewards of the righteous" are not on the lower planes. They are "the treasures in heaven," that is, the transmuted qualities on the buddhic plane. They are the "grain and fruits" of the garden of Sekhethetepet.

"For thou wilt not leave my soul in hell; neither wilt thou suffer thine Holy One to see corruption."—Ps. xvi. 10.

The "Holy One" is the spiritual ego,—immaculate and eternal in every human soul. This will not always be a captive to the lower nature, but will rise in glory at the cycle's end.

"Nobody who has lived — lived honestly, truly, deeply—who has thought for himself, or felt for others—but believes in hell. Earth and hell interpenetrate—there is no doubt about it. Earth is full of hell—full of mental and moral and social disorders, and wretchedness and suffering. Earth is full of hell—and countless souls are there ; and unless the fires of hell could purge and purify and refine mankind, we might well doubt whether life were worth while. But they can. Earth is full of hell. But it is not all hell. Indeed I would say that we realise hell only by that which we oppose to hell. I mean the thought of heaven—and this too exists on earth."—R. DIMSDALE STOCKER, *Social Idealism*, p. 78.

See ARENA, DUSAHK, FIRE OF HELL, FIRE (destroying), FURNACE, GARDEN, GATHA (kam.), GOATS, HADES, MAN (bad), NIFLHEIM, NORTH, PURGATORY, SEKER, SEKHET-HETEP, SIAMAK.

HELMET :—

A symbol of protection of the mind or soul from the assaults of the desires and passions.

"And take the helmet of salvation, and the sword of the Spirit, which is the word of God."—EPH. vi. 17.

The soul is exhorted to rely upon the Divine protection from evil, and to call forth the spiritual energy from within.

See SALVATION, SHIELD, SWORD.

HEPHAISTOS, OR VULCAN :—

A symbol of the Creative Mind which has conquered the lower activities :—the Higher Self which has been born in the soul on the mental plane, and grown upward to knowledge and power.

"Now when the bright light of the sun was set, there went each of the gods to his own house to sleep, where each one had his palace made with cunning device by famed Hephaistos the lame god ; and Zeus the Olympian, the lord of lightning, departed to his couch where he was wont of old to take his rest whenever sweet sleep visited him. There went he up and slept, and beside him was Hera of the golden throne."—*Iliad*, Bk. I. end.

Now when the cycle terminated, and pralaya supervened, each aspect of the Supreme Self returned to a quiescent condition,—for which, how-ever, a form or mode was provided by the Creative Mind. This means that nothing, no differentiation, was extinguished. In every case the Creative Mind had called into being that which was to endure eternally. The Creative Mind is said to be "lame" because he originates from that which is partial and incomplete. This means that all *forms* limit potencies ; and so that which is formed becomes but the expression of an *aspect* of Truth-reality.

And the Higher Self as Will (Zeus), the originator of the life activities of the universe, returned into Unmanifest Being, wherein He dwells from eternity in so far as no manifestation is called forth. So here *in abscondito* the Self abode, and here also was Wisdom who remained supreme with Him.

See CREATION, CUP (double), GODS, GOLDEN SOLES, HARPOCRATES, HERA, HOUSE (sleep), LAMENESS, LAUGHTER, MAHAT, MIND, PANDORA, PRALAYA, SUN-SETTING, WHITE-ARMED, ZEUS.

HERA OR JUNO :—

A symbol of Wisdom, the principle of buddhi, seated on the buddhic plane.

Zeus addresses Hera,—"Abide thou in silence and hearken to my bidding, lest all the gods that are in Olympus keep not off from thee my visitation, when I put forth my hands unapproachable against thee. He said ; and Hera the ox-eyed queen was afraid, and sat in silence, curbing her heart ; but throughout Zeus' palace the gods of heaven were troubled."—*Iliad*, Bk. I. (trans. Buckley).

The Higher Self interprets Wisdom, —'Within thyself be that which thou art in the Divine scheme, and fulfil thy function unless the higher ideal qualities (the gods) be the means of preventing me from accomplishing my destiny until the conditions make it necessary that I act from the Higher Will.' The Self having expressed itself,—Wisdom remains apart from Love, for at this stage the higher feelings (heart) are not fully aroused. But in the abode of the Higher Self on the higher planes, the aspiring qualities, or high ideals, begin to be stirred into activity. "Ox-eyed" is a symbol of spontaneous cognition, and refers to the intuition of truth.

"The Greek Hera was a daughter of Cronos and Rhea, and sister and wife of Zeus. . . . Her marriage, called the *Sacred Marriage*, was represented in many places where she was worshipped."—*Smith's Class. Dict.*

Wisdom is said to proceed from Time and Space, as it relates to the establishment of the planes of nature, of which the buddhic is the fourth, reckoned from below upward. The "sacred marriage" is the marriage of Wisdom and Love : the Love below (Zeus below) becomes united with the Wisdom above, at the end of a cycle.

"For Matter is Hera, and deity is Zeus."—Cf. *Clementine Homilies*, V. 18, 667, and ORIGEN, *Cont. Cels.* 4, 48.

The feminine symbol is always on the matter side of manifestation, and the masculine symbol on the side of spirit.

See ATHENA, BUDDHI, CRONUS, GODS, MARRIAGE (higher), MUSE, OLYMPUS, PALACE, PIETY, RHEA, WHITE-ARMED, ZEUS.

HERB OF THE FIELD, OR GREEN HERB :—

A symbol of the primitive desires and affections which are aroused by the activities of the senses.

"And no plant of the field was yet in the earth, and no herb of the field had yet sprung up : for the Lord God had not caused it to rain upon the earth, and there was not a man to till the ground."—GEN. ii. 5.

And at this early period of the soul's evolution, no desire had as yet appeared upon the lower plane (earth) ; and no sign of awakening life had yet thrilled the matter from which unfoldment was to take place. For the Divine Truth-Love had not yet caused the forthcoming of stimulative ideas to proceed from buddhi. And no mental faculty was up to the present actively functioning in the lower nature.

See AGRICULTURE, EARTH, FIELD, GRASS, GREEN, MAN, PLANTS, RAIN, THORNS.

HERB YIELDING SEED AFTER ITS KIND :—

Symbolic of the natural laws of growth and increase in the development of the desires, affections, and faculties of the soul.

"And the earth brought forth grass, herb yielding seed after its kind, and tree bearing fruit, wherein is the seed thereof, after its kind : and God saw that it was good."—GEN. i. 12.

And the physical or natural law of growth was set in operation, and the laws which worked upon the lower planes of being were established and commenced to act. And all was perfect in the period of involution. In other words, there was an awakenment of the divine life in the lower nature (earth) which then brought forth the desires and affections which give rise to higher states. Also there appeared the aspirations which are to bear fruit on higher planes. And all was made perfect in preparation for forthcoming evolution.

See EARTH, FRUIT, GOLDEN AGE, GOOD, GRASS, GREEN, INVOLUTION, PLANTS, SEEDS OF FOODS.

HERCULES, SON OF ZEUS :—

A symbol of the Divine Will active in the laws of terror and fear. The Divine Will acting through terror breaks down obstacles in the forms which impede the evolving life, and also subdues unruly desires (beasts and monsters) which while unconquered ravish the soul.

"And the fear of you and the dread of you shall be upon every beast of the earth, and upon every fowl of the air."—GEN. ix. 2.

And the lower nature with all its passions and desires, is to be subdued and disciplined by the "fear and dread" which are to bring it into subjection to the higher nature and Divine Will.

The meaning of the symbol Hercules may vary somewhat in the different legends. It signifies generally the coercive action of the environment through pain and trouble in stimulating the growth of the soul.

See ANIMALS, BEASTS, HYLAS, MONSTERS, VULTURE.

HERDS OF CATTLE :—

Symbolic of co-ordinated desires and emotions, as activities in the evolution of the soul.

See CATTLE, OX.

HERMES ; MERCURY ; THOTH ; THOR :—

These are symbols of the principle

of the higher mind, or the centralised activities of the higher mental plane, which is the medium of communication between the higher and lower natures in the soul. Hence Hermes is called the herald or messenger of the Gods.

" For the Egyptians relate that Hermes (Thoth) had one arm so bent that it could not be straightened."—PLUTARCH, *Isis and Osiris*, § 22.

This " bent arm of Hermes " signifies the inability of the mind to act with perfect unanimity. It is the function of the intellect to disclose differences and perceive similarities, and therefore, unaided by a higher faculty, it can never show perfect trueness.

" In the Iliad and Odyssey Hermes is characterised as a cunning thief."— *Smith's Class. Dict.*

" The ascription, in the mythologies, of a thievish disposition to this divinity, and the legends which represent him as the patron of thieves and adventurers, and stealing in turn from all the Gods, are modes of indicating the facility with which the understanding annexes everything and makes it its own. For Hermes denotes that faculty of the divine part in man which seeks and obtains meanings out of every department of existence, intruding into the province of every ' God,' and appropriating some portion of the goods of each. Thus the understanding has a finger upon all things, and converts them to its own use, whether it be the ' arrows ' of Apollo, the ' girdle ' of Aphrodite, the ' oxen ' of Admetus, the ' trident ' of Poseidon, or the ' tongs ' of Hephaistos. . . . His are the rod of knowledge wherewith all things are measured, the wings of courage, the sword of the unconquerable will, and the cap of concealment or discretion. He is in turn the Star of the East, conducting the Magi ; the Cloud from whose midst the holy Voice speaks ; by day the pillar of Vapour, by night the shining Flame, leading the elect soul on her perilous path through the noisome wilderness of the world, as she flies from the Egypt of the Flesh, and guiding her in safety to the promised heaven."—KINGSFORD AND MAITLAND, *The Perfect Way*, p. 269.

" Hermes, as the messenger of God, reveals to us his paternal will, and,—developing in us the intuition,—imparts to us knowledge. The knowledge which descends into the soul from above excels any that can be attained by the mere exercise of the intellect. Intuition is the operation of the soul. The knowledge received through it from above, descending into the soul, fills it with the perception of the interior causes of things. The Gods announce it by their presence, and by

illumination, and enable us to discern the universal order " (Proclus).—*Ibid.*, p. 270.

" Hermes has from time immemorial been, in the sacred science of the West, the symbol for the Understanding, especially in relation to divine things. In that science the sea—*Maria*—has always been the symbol for the Soul. And the tall, far-off hills, with their peaks glistening with snow, are the pure shining heights of spiritual attainment the Soul's goal."—E. MAITLAND, *Life of A. K.*, Vol I. p. 151.

The *sea* is a symbol for the lower or astral soul which when purified in its highest part is the *virgin* which bears the Christ.

See ADAMAS, ARROWS, CADUCEUS, CAUSAL-BODY, DAIMONS, EXODUS, GIRDLE, HORSE, HOUSE, IBIS, INTELLECT, INTUITION, IRIS, MAGI, MOUNTAIN, NARADA, NEBO, SEA, SHINATSU, STAR IN EAST, THIEVES, THOR, THOTH, TRIDENT, VIRGIN MARY, WILDERNESS.

HERMES TRISMEGISTUS :—

A symbol of the three-fold aspect of the Self,—Alma-buddhi-manas,—manifesting on the higher mental plane as Will, Wisdom, and Action.

" The ' thrice-greatest,' because he spoke of the ' three greatest ' powers that ' veiled the one Divinity ' "—(*Chron. Alexand.*, p. 47).—G. R. S. MEAD, *Orpheus*, p. 17.

" On the famous Rosetta stone, Hermes is called the ' Great-and-Great.' "—MEAD, *T. G. Hermes*, Vol. I. p. 117.

" Thoth is called ' Twice Great ' and ' Thrice Great.' "—BUDGE, *Gods of the Egyptians*, Vol. I. p. 401.

" Hermes Trismegistus " is the reputed author of many writings ; that is, the Divine Intelligence is the inspirer of many scriptures which have been written down by the receivers of these symbolical communications from the higher mind. The truth from the atma-buddhic planes is imparted to the higher mind and then expressed in symbols to the lower mind.

See HOLD, INSPIRATION, PAPYRUS BOAT, SCRIPTURES, TRIAD, TRIDENT.

HERMIT OR ANCHORITE :—

A symbol of an ego manifesting in a centre of consciousness on the sixth mental sub-plane.

" When a householder (a Snâtaka) sees his skin wrinkled, and his hair white,

and the sons of his sons, then . . . abandoning all food raised by cultivation, and
all his belongings, he may depart into the
forest, either committing his wife to his
sons, or accompanied by her."—*Laws
of Manu*, VI. 2, 3.

When an ego, through the individuality (householder), perceives that
his lower nature (skin) has fallen away,
and that he is gifted with pure intuition (white hair) and higher mental
qualities (sons of sons); then he turns
away from seeking knowledge (food)
through experience and discipline,
and gives up his lower mental faculties.
He is thus prepared to withdraw
from all externals into the solitude
(forest) of his soul, leaving the emotion-
nature with the mental qualities, and
uniting with the buddhic principle
(wife).

"Buddha laid aside weapons and pon-
dered the Sâstra, he practised perfect
calm, and underwent various observances,
like a hermit he refused all objects of
sense, he viewed all his kingdoms like a
father."—*Buddha-Karita*, Bk. II. 52.

The soul now casts aside its weapons
of offence and defence, that is, it
relinquishes its outgoing energies, and
relies upon the Word of the Lord,
which is the expression of the Supreme
within it,—that which unifies and co-
ordinates its experiences. The soul
realises itself as centrally situated,
and meditates within itself. And then
it undergoes many acts of self-
discipline as an anchorite. It withdraws from the many, and regards
all perceptions equally and dispassion-
ately, as a father his children.

See ANCHORITE, ASCETIC, ASRAMAS,
CULTIVATION, FOOD, FOREST, HAIR,
HOUSEHOLDER, MONK, ORDERS,
SANNYASIN, SKIN, SNÂTAKA, WHITE,
WIFE.

HERMOD, SON OF ODIN :—

A symbol of the Higher Self, son
of the Logos, born in the soul to become its ruler and redeemer.

"Hermod the Lively, Odin's son
took upon himself this mission from
Frigg, to find Balder in the underworld.
Odin's horse, Sleipner, was prepared for
the journey; Hermod mounted him,
and rode hastily away."—*The Story of
Balder, Prose Edda*. Howitt, *Litera*.

And now it is that the Christ-soul
is born upon the higher planes of
experience, and it is this indwelling
spirit which becomes the Saviour
of the soul. On the lower planes
(underworld) the Christ-soul is
deputed by Wisdom (Frigg) to seek
the Higher Self (Balder), the Christ
within. Then the higher mind (Odin's
horse) is equipped for the expedition :
and so the Self within, under the aspect
of mind goes forth in the soul conquering and to conquer. The "liveli-
ness of Hermod" is expressive of the
outgoing energy of the Self.

See BALDER, BRIDGE OF GJALL,
DEATH OF BALDER, FRIGG, HADES,
HORSE (Odin's), MODGUNN, NORTH,
ODIN.

HEROD THE KING :—

A symbol of the lower principle
as the ruler of the lower nature of
the soul. It represents the worldly,
sordid side of the lower nature in
which Spirit is at its lowest ebb.

"Then Herod when he saw that he was
mocked of the wise man was exceeding
wroth, and sent forth, and slew all the
male children that were in Bethlehem."
MAT. ii. 16.

The anger of the lower principle
when disappointed by the upward
trend of the intellectual faculties
(wise men) was the expression of the
malevolence and ignorance of the
animal nature. The seeking to kill
out the Christ from the soul is the
lower nature's rebellion, and the
instinctive fear and hate of what is
above itself. The lower principle
"slew the innocents," that is, took
measures to destroy growth from the
germs of virtues and truths,—the
spiritual children now born in the soul.

"Herod (i.e. sin, human pride) is
reigning, he is not yet dead, and he rises
up and seeks the life of the young child,
and slays all the children that were in
Bethlehem, 'from two years old and
upwards,'—that is to say, the Spirit of
God had visited by his power the human
mind, to bring forth the Good (the
children) and at the end of two years'
particular visitation the Son was born.
But sin (which lay concealed) broke forth
as a flood and deluged the soul, so that
all life died. All the work that the Spirit
had done was now swept away with
the flood of error and thoughts; and this
is in reality what is meant by 'Noah's
Flood'; 'all that had life died.'"—
JOHN WARD, *Zion's Works*, Vol. III. p. 5.

"Herod,—the grossest element of
mortal mind."—MRS. EDDY, *Science and
Health*, p. 565.

" We have seen that there is a natural principle in man lowering him, deadening him, pulling him down by inches to the mere animal plane, blinding reason, searing conscience, paralysing will. This is the active destroying principle, or Sin."—H. DRUMMOND, *Natural Law, etc.*, p. 108.

" Herod is the devil, the world, and the flesh, and the way to him is pleasure and greed. They therefore, who pass from him to Christ, walk by the other way of the cross and mortification ; and thus it behoves them to return to their own country,—that is, the heavenly paradise."

" Herod is the devil, who strives to cut off ' infants '—that is, those who are weak in faith and virtue, also the first inspirations from God, and good thoughts before they have become strong and increased."—C. À LAPIDE, *The Great Commentary*, Vol. I. pp. 71, 77.

The following portion of a leading article has evidently been written without a thought that its philosophy interprets the story of the birth and infancy of Jesus—the Divine Idea or Ideal.

" The story of the progress of the human race is the story of the birth of moral ideas, which attain their incarnation and manifestation in human society by one of two means, Evolution or Revolution. Evolution is the natural process. Some fundamental principle of truth, hitherto undiscovered by the human mind, becomes impregnated with the life-force and pushes its way through prejudices and misconceptions, meeting but the normal obstruction which the materialism of the present always offers to the spirit of the future. With gradual quiet growth it emerges into human consciousness, having secured its place ; material conditions gradually adapt themselves to its presence, and it becomes part of the social inheritance of humanity. But sometimes the process of birth is different. The *divine idea* is opposed by perverted human will. Those who hold the sceptre of rule in the world summon all the forces of materialism and all the forces of physical repression to their aid, with the intent to crush the new manifestation. They may seem to succeed for a time. But because there is the germ of indestructible life latent in the idea, it grows under the repression, and one day there comes a world-shaking upheaval. That upheaval is revolution."—*Votes for Women*, May 16, 1913.

See BETHLEHEM, BIRTH OF KRISHNA, CURETES, DEVIL, DURASROBO, ELIJAH (restorer), FLOOD, LITTLE CHILDREN, LITTLE ONES, MAGI, PHARISEES, RITES, STAR IN EAST.

HERODIAS' DAUGHTER DANCING :—

A symbol of the emotion-nature captivated by the desires and sensations.

" And when the daughter of Herodias herself came in and danced, she pleased Herod and them that sat at meat with him."—MARK vi. 22.

The lower nature led away by the allurements and distractions of the world is well-pleasing to the lower principle and all its affinities. It is on " Herod's birthday," signifying the glorying of the lower principle, that this sensuousness happens,—not on the birthday of the Christ and his exaltation in the soul.

" There is a higher good than enjoyment ; and this requires suffering in order to be gained. As long as we narrow our view of benevolence, and see in it only a disposition to bestow pleasure, so long life will be a mystery ; for pleasure is plainly not its great end. But this does not detract from God's love ; because he has something better for us than gushing streams of joy."—W. E. CHANNING, *Discourse on Dr. Follen*.

See EVE, FALL, MEDUSA, PANDORA.

HEROES, THE GREATEST OF THE DAY :—

A symbol of the twelve or more disciplined qualities and spiritual energies which are highest in the soul and have been evolved through the lower activities.

" When the ship Argo was completed, Jason consulted the oracle, and was directed to invite the greatest heroes of the day to share in the dangers and glories of the voyage."—*The Argonautic Expedition*, KEIGHTLEY, *Mythology*.

" When the causal-body of humanity was potentially completed, the Christ-soul (Jason or Jasius) communed with his inner nature whether the conditions were such that it would now be possible to gather together, or co-ordinate, the higher qualities which had now been evolved upon the lower planes of his being, and which would serve to assist in subjugating the lower qualities and perfecting the soul. The soul's salvation depends upon the development of the disinterested and heroic side of its nature, so that all selfishness and evil be overcome.

See APOSTLES, ARGO, ARGONAUTS, BOAT, DISCIPLES, JASON, ORACLE, SHIP, TWELVE.

HEROIC RUNNER,—THE SUN :—

The Higher Self ; the Divine Spirit as the energy within all things.

"First, Ormazd created 'the Heroic Runner,' who never dies, the Sun, and made him king and ruler of the material world. From Mount Albordj he sets out on his course, he circles the earth in the highest spheres of heaven, and at evening returns."—*The Zoroastrian System.*

First of all, the Higher Self,—the Divine indwelling Monad,—is said to be emanated, and this is indestructible through all changes of state. From the first moment of manifestation, he goes forth from the heights of aspiration, passes through the higher planes, involves himself in the lower planes, and from thence rises again to the higher as the cycle terminates.

"O Rā, O Runner, O Lord, O only One, thou maker of things which are , thou hast fashioned the tongue of the company of the gods, thou hast produced whatsoever cometh forth from the waters."—BUDGE, *Book of the Dead,* Ch. XV.

See ALBORDJ, CIRCLE, COMPANY (gods), EARTH, EVENING, KING, MONAD, SELF, SUN, TONGUE (higher) WATER.

HERPEST, " ON THE BACK " :—

This signifies the conquest of intellectual pride.

"As proof of victory Horus stood upon the back of a male hippopotamus, and so was called Herpest, i.e. He who is on the back."—*Legend of the Winged Sun-disk.*

As evidence of victory, the Christ-soul overcomes the pride of the mind, and thereby gives God the praise of spiritual upraising, recognising that the mind is not the real actor, but is an agent of the Supreme.

"If there is one lesson which more than any other ought by this time to be burnt in upon the human soul by much tribulation, it is that of the vanity of earthly pride and ambition ; it leads nowhere ; it yields nothing but pain in the end unless that which gives rise to it can be linked to something higher than one's own personality. It is no use living for oneself on the one hand or a blind universal on the other. And with this realisation is apt to come a sense of the futility of existence ; the heart goes out of our hopes and aims, and we flee into the wilderness of pessimism and despair."—R. J. CAMPBELL, Serm., *Being and Becoming.*

See BEL (Nipur), HIPPOPOTAMUS, HORUS.

HESED (CHESED), THE SUN :—

A symbol of the Individuality on the mental plane of the soul.

"*Chesed* (merit) is the right and *Geburah* (demerit) the left arm. The right side is life and the left is death. . . . The serpent constitutes the left arm and thence emanates the impure spirit. It is the side of water and the side of sadness. These engender darkness, and the way of escape is by the harmony which can be instituted between the Mercy or Grace of *Chesed* and the Severity of *Geburah*. A day will come when the evil, that is on the left side, shall disappear and good will ᴏbtain only. It is said further that the Mercy and Severity of *Chesed* and *Geburah* are united in *Tiphereth*."—A. E. WAITE, *Secret Doctrine in Israel,* pp. 35-7.

The immortal Individuality (Chesed) and the transient Personality (Geburah) work together for good. The desire nature (serpent) enthrals the Personality, but a time of liberation will come when the perfected Personality will disappear in the Individuality, which will then become one with the Self in the causal-body (Tiphereth).

See BONDAGE, FALL, INDIVIDUALITY, PAHAD, PERSONALITY, RIGHT ARM, SERPENT, SUFFERING, SUN, MOON, TIPHERETH.

HESPERIDES :—

A symbol of the buddhic emotions which guard, as it were, the " treasure in heaven," " the golden apples which Ge (Earth) gave to Hera at her marriage with Zeus," signifying that when Wisdom and Love are united after the struggle of the Self rising from below, the treasure, which matter, or the lower nature (earth), has been the means of securing, is presented to Wisdom as the consciousness rises to the buddhic plane.

See APPLES, GE, GOLD, HERA, TREASURE, ZEUS,

HESTIA ; VESTA :—

These symbols are the expression, through the feminine or negative principle, of the physical plane.

"According to a view that afterwards became current, under the influence of philosophers and mystics Hestia was regarded as personifying the earth as

the fixed centre of the world."—NETTLE-
SHIP, *Dict. of Class. Antiq.*

See EARTH (spec.), ELEMENTS, HAIGI,
NEPHTHYS, NESTIS.

HETEP, THE GOD :—

A symbol of the Divine Will ; the
Word, or the Logos.

"The god Hetep is hidden of mouth,
his mouth is silent, that which he uttereth
is secret, he fulfilleth eternity and taketh
possession of everlastingness of existence
as Hetep, the lord Hetep."—BUDGE,
Book of the Dead, Ch. CX.

The Logos is the unspoken Word,—
the inherent energy of the Divine
Will,—which is to be perceived only
by those egos who have transcended
the form levels. The secret utterance
is the emanation of the Divine Life
which is manifested through the
manvantara. The fulfilling of eternity
signifies the power which makes for
righteousness interpreted in the
natural, moral, and intellectual orders
of action, and which is realised when
the ego perceives that all things
work together for good,—since such
an intuition is a direct perception
of the Love of God. "Hetep, the
lord Hetep" signifies the attainment
of equilibrium in the soul.

"He (the god Hetep) is established
upon the watery supports (?) of the god
Shu, and is linked unto the pleasant
things of Rā."—BUDGE, *Book of the
Dead*, Ch. CX.

The Divine Life has its source above
the higher mind, and is held above
the devachanic state during the
periodic interval between two outpourings.

See LOVE OF GOD, MANVANTARA,
MOUTH, PILLARS OF SHU, WORD.

HETEP, LAKE OF THE GOD :—

A symbol of the Greater Self
wherein all the lesser selves unite
and are made One in Truth (water) ;
that is, become one on the higher
planes of atma-buddhi.

See LAKE, OCEAN.

HETHRA, THE MOTHER OF ALL LIVING :—

This is a symbol of the womb of
matter wherein the Divine conception
takes place, which is to give life and
immortality to every soul.

See MATTER, MOTHER, PRAKRITI,
VIRGIN, WOMAN (matter), WOMB OF
MĀYA.

HIDDEKEL RIVER :—

A symbol of the astral plane which
proceeds from buddhi.

"And the name of the third river is
Hiddekel ; that is it which goeth in front
of Assyria."—GEN. ii. 14.

The symbol "Hiddekel" stands for
the astral plane on which the personality develops, becoming as it were,
a dawn of consciousness—light in the
east —precursor of the rising of the
Higher Self (sun) in the soul.

See ASSYRIA ASTRAL PLANE, EAST,
EDEN (rivers), PERSONALITY, TIGRIS.

HIDING FROM GOD :—

Symbolic of the mental emotion-
nature paying no heed to conscience
and aspiration.

"And they heard the voice of the Lord
God walking in the garden in the cool
of the day : and the man and his wife
hid themselves from the presence of the
Lord God amongst the trees of the
garden."—GEN. iii. 8.

And by the mind and emotion-nature
the voice of the Divine within them is
partially interpreted, when they were
wandering at the close of a period,
among the objects of delight which
were in the soul : and the mental
emotion-nature is not developed
enough to reflect and interpret aright
the decrees of the Divine nature, so
it is said to "hide" from the presence
of Love-Wisdom, that is, it is unable
to respond to the vibrations from
within of the Spirit.

See ADAM, CONSCIENCE, DAY, EVE,
EVENING, FALL, GARDEN OF EDEN,
HECATOMB, MAN AND WIFE, VOICE,
WALKING.

HIDING PLACE OF THE GOD- DESS :—

Symbolic of the buddhic nature
which is unperceived by the lower
nature, and is deep within the soul.

"O Goddess of Power ! I have come
into thee, even into thy hiding place, and
power is born unto me."—*Book of the
Dead*, Ch. CX. (trans. Blackden).

The lesser Self has come into the
buddhic sanctuary of the greater
Self as Wisdom, and all its needs are
satisfied in the accession of higher
faculties.

"Amaterasu, the Sun-Goddess, being
offended with Susanoo, the god of the
Moon and Sea, went away and concealed
herself in the cave of Ameno Tuaya,

closing the entrance with a larger piece of rock. From this time the country was dark all over, and given up to the noise and disturbances of all sorts of inferior gods."—*Japanese Legend.*

Wisdom on the buddhic plane being frustrated by Desire (Susanoo) withdrew from direct action in the soul, and retired into the inner being or Divine realm, concealed from the lower nature by the higher mind. [That is,—the "Fall" of mind (man) having taken place, the Desire-mind rules the soul, and the direct vibrations from the buddhic plane (Eden) cease.]

This left the lower nature bereft of the light of Truth, and immersed in the darkness of ignorance. The soul was given over to the desires and sensations (inferior gods) in constant turmoil and conflict.

See AMATERASU, CAVE, DARKNESS, EDEN, FALL, MOON, RETURN, SUSA-NOWO, UZUMÉ.

HIGHER AND LOWER NATURES :—

Symbolic of the ideal and phenomenal phases of existence, of which the first is the enduring and real, and the second the changing and unreal. The first is archetypal and perfect ; the second proceeds from it but is always deficient as a copy of the first, and is changeable, being in process of becoming perfect in essentials. The higher nature comprehends the lower, but the lower cannot understand the higher. The greater can contain the less, but not the less the greater.

"Of course, it was recognised, even in antiquity, by thoughtful persons that such expressions as above and beneath, heaven and earth, were metaphors ; just as Plato in the seventh book of the *Republic* says : 'It makes no difference whether a person stares stupidly at the sky, or down upon the ground. So long as his attention is directed to objects of sense, his soul is looking downwards. not upwards.' For a long time the local and spatial symbols were regarded as literally true, concurrently with the spiritual doctrine that God is everywhere, and heaven wherever He is. St. Augustine did much to legitimise the spiritual doctrine, which is no after-thought, no explaining away of dogmatic truth. 'God' he says, 'is present everywhere in His entirety, and yet is nowhere. He dwells in the depths of my being, more inward than my innermost self, and higher than my highest. He is above my soul,

but not in the same way in which the heaven is above the earth.' So the scholastic mystics say that God has His centre everywhere, His circumference nowhere."—W. R. INGE, *Paddock Lectures,* p. 123.

"The fundamental thought of the Christian religion is that there are two orders, commonly called nature and grace ; the one discernible by sense and understanding, the other by a spiritual sight. From the first until now the mystic light of Tabor, before which the phenomenal world fades away into nothingness, has ever burned at the inner shrine of Christianity. Thence has come the illumination of those who, age after age, have entered most fully into the secret of Jesus ; thence are the bright beams which stream from the pages of *St. John's Gospel, St. Augustine's Confessions, The Imitation of Christ, The Divine Comedy, The Pilgrim's Progress.* The supreme blessedness of man, as all Christian teaching insists, is the vision, in the great hereafter, of Him who is the substance of substances, the life of life, who alone, in the highest sense, is—'I am,' His incommunicable name,—and who, even in this world, is seen by the pure in heart." —W. S. LILLY, *The Great Enigma,* p. 266.

See ARC. MAN, ATMAN, COSMOS, CREATION, EVOLUTION, HEAVEN AND EARTH, IMAGE, IMPERIAL, MACROCOSM, MAHAYANA, MICROCOSM, OCEAN, PLE-ROMA, PRANAS, PROTOTYPES, SIMILITUDES, SPERMATIC WORDS, WORLDS (five).

HIGHER AND LOWER WORLDS :—

Symbols of the inner ideal prototypal nature on the higher planes, and its outer emanation, the phenomenal nature, on the lower planes The lower proceeds from the higher.

"All that which is contained in the Lower World is also found in the Upper (in prototype). The Lower and the Upper reciprocally act upon each other."— *Zohar.*

"All that which exists upon the Earth has its spiritual counterpart also to be found on High, and there does not exist the smallest thing in this world which is not itself attached to something on High. . . . When the inferior part is influenced, that which is set over it in the Superior World is equally influenced, because all are perfectly united together." —*Zohar.*

"All that which is on the earth, is also found above in perfect prototype, and there is not anything so insignificant in the world, that does not depend upon another above : in such a manner, that if the lower moves itself the higher corresponding to it moves towards it."— I. MYER, *Qabbalah,* p. 109.

" A spiritual and invisible world preceded, therefore, this visible material world, as its prototype. In creating the material world, which was in reality only an incorporation of the spiritual world of Fravashis, Ormuzd first created the firm vault of heaven, and the earth on which it rests."—*Zoroastrian System.*

This refers to the fact that the Ethereal or Buddhic world, or Universe of Spirit, preceded the physical world which was patterned upon it. In devising the creation of the physical universe, the Divine Will first created that which corresponds to the prototypal evolution of the soul (potential), and afterwards the lower planes whereon its expression might proceed. This signifies the production of the mechanism of life and form through which the Divine power is realised. It is analogous to a process of involution, prior to an objective evolution.

" The whole natural world corresponds to the spiritual world, not only as a whole, but in every part ; and therefore whatever exists in the natural world is said to be the *correspondent* of that from which it derives its existence in the spiritual world ; for the natural world exists and subsists from the spiritual world, just as an effect exists from its cause."—SWEDEN-BORG, *The Future Life*, p. 29.

" All things accordingly, that are on earth, O Tat, are not the Truth ; they're copies only of the True. . . . Wherever the appearance doth receive the influx from above, it turns into a copy of the Truth ; without its energising from above, it is left false " (Of Truth).—G. R. S. MEAD, *T. G. Hermes*, Vol. III. p. 18.

" All (Sufi seers) agree in maintaining the pre-natal existence of the soul, and in declaring the physical world to be but a transient and distorted reflection of a far more glorious world, and in itself essentially unreal."—GIBB, *Hist. of Ottoman Poetry*, Vol. I. p. 58.

" What is heredity but the permanence of that invisible and yet most real type which Plato called the idea ? . . . We must postulate invisible but real types, because without them their visible effects would remain inexplicable."—F. MAX MÜLLER, *Theosophy, etc.*, p. 389.

See ARC. MAN, BUDDHIC PLANE, COSMOS, CREATION, EARTH, FRAVASHIS, HEAVEN AND EARTH, IMAGE, INVOLUTION, MACROCOSM, MICROCOSM, PROTO-TYPES, SUBSTANCE, WORLDS.

HIGHER AND LOWER SELVES :—

Symbols of the Spirit potential above, and the Spirit actual below. The two are aspects of the one Divine Life, but the second is in the process of manifesting itself, while the first is unmanifest. The first is to be thought of as seated regnant upon the higher planes, and the second as struggling upward through the lower planes. The first is never revealed to the consciousness in its fullness, for the unmanifest cannot be apprehended in its true nature. The second, in manifesting, is always *short* of itself, but as it develops its qualities, it gradually approaches completion, and when complete and perfect it unites with its counterpart on the upper planes.

" And what is all human life but this ; man having in his freedom, to *choose*, to choose under all kinds of circumstances, all kinds of feelings, under the stress and force of all kinds of motives—having to choose and *choosing*,—the right thing or the wrong—going straight onward or turning aside : giving proof of what is in him, of the inmost bias and inclination of his character, of the use he would make of his freedom, of the strength and mastery over himself, by which he can make his higher self govern his lower self, by which he can make his weaker and poorer and baser wishes yield to his nobler will."—R. W. CHURCH, *Cathedral Sermons*, p. 100.

" ' Howbeit that was not first which is Spiritual, but that which is Natural : and afterward that which is Spiritual.' (1 COR. xv. 46). St. Paul surveys the universe and finds the same truth everywhere. Everywhere the higher comes to make the lower perfect. Everywhere the lower is provided first, to be the basis and opportunity of the higher coming by and by. Everywhere the lips must be before the speech ; the canvas must be before the picture ; the candle must be before the flame ; the brain must be before the thought. It is the teaching which natural science is giving us profusely. . . . But our deeper observation teaches us a deeper truth. The material has within itself the power of spiritual life. Its total story has not been told until a waiting impulse has been felt within it dimly conscious of incompleteness, until it has answered to the spiritual call and roused itself to Life."—PHILLIPS BROOKS, *Mystery of Iniquity*, p. 242.

" The conception of the solidarity of man's spiritual part with the eternal substance is the root principle of all our Christian faith in immortality to-day . . . The mysterious entity which we are obliged to call the self is a vastly greater thing than its physical expression. . . . You, the mortal earthly you, began a few short years ago, and a few years hence at the most this frail, unstable, constantly changing you will have come to an end ; but the you behind all these shifting shadows, the you that derives immediately from God, the you whose angel doth ever behold the face of the Father, lives not by days and years; it simply is. . . . I am only insisting on the eternity of the spiritual substance out of which your soul arises, and which is truly you, a greater you than as yet you have knowledge of, or your present consciousness can more than feebly and fitfully express."—R. J. CAMPBELL, Serm., *Our Eternal Substance.*

See ARJUNA, BIRDS (two), CHRIST, CONSCIOUSNESS, FIG-TREE, IMMORTALITY FORFEITED, INDIVIDUALITY, LITTLE CHILDREN, MONAD, PERSONALITY, PRAGÂPATI, SELF, SOUL (highest), UNION.

HIGH-PRIEST OF THE GOOD RELIGION :—

A symbol of the spiritual mind (buddhi-manas), the upholder of the science of the Higher Self in building up the individualised causal-body.

"For every high priest, being taken from among men, is appointed for men in things pertaining to God, that he may offer both gifts and sacrifices for sins."— HEB. v. 1.

The subjective spiritual mind is set apart from other mental qualities; and its function is to minister to righteousness, and receive the higher powers and faculties,—the reward of giving up the lower desires,—in order to offer to the causal-body that which will promote its growth

See AARON, ATHORNE, CHRYSE, HECATOMB, POPE, PRIEST, RELIGION, SACRIFICE.

HIGH-PRIEST OF A DEAD FAITH :—

A symbol of conventional ideas of religion, and the rule of a formal creed which supports sectarianism and intolerance.

See ANNAS, CAIAPHAS, PRIESTS AND ELDERS.

HIGH-PRIESTSHIP OF THE GLORIFIED ONE :—

A symbol of authority and power over the lower nature, attained by the Self who has undertaken to go forth and accomplish his evolution.

See BAHMAN, MELCHIZEDEK, MICHAEL, VICTORY, VOHUMAN.

HIKOBOSHI, A STAR-GOD :—

A symbol of the spiritual ego on the mental plane, or the incarnate Self.

"By the ferry of Yasu, on the River of Heaven, the boat is floating : I pray you tell my younger sister (wife) that I stand here and wait. Though I (being a Star-god) can pass freely to and fro, through the great sky,—yet to cross over the River of Heaven, for your sake, was weary work indeed ! . . . From the time when heaven and earth were parted she has been my own wife ;—yet to be with her, I must always wait till autumn " (Legend from the Manyōshu). — L. HEARN, *Milky Way,* pp. 36, 37.

The "ferry of Yasu" has the same meaning as the "bridge of heaven," and signifies the higher mind which the consciousness most traverse in order to rise to the buddhic level. The "boat floating on the River of Heaven " signifies the causal-body on the higher mental plane. The "wife (Tanabata) " is Wisdom,—the buddhic principle,—the "younger sister " of the Higher Self. The Self can pass freely through the higher planes, but when it is incarnate it is "weary work indeed " to struggle upward, so that Love from below may be united to Wisdom above. From the time of the commencement of evolution when Spirit and Matter were dissevered,— matter alone being left apparent,—the Self-incarnate claimed his true mate ; but to be again united with her, he must wait until the cycle's close.

"(Footnote). By the ancient calendar, the seventh day of the seventh month would fall in the autumn season."— L. HEARN, *Ibid.*

The number seven signifies perfection and completion, and the "seventh period " therefore signifies the completion of the cycle, when the lower being perfected it unites with the Higher.

"In mysticism the will is united with the emotions in an impassioned desire to transcend the sense-world in order that the self may be joined by love to the one eternal and ultimate Object of love ; whose existence is intuitively perceived by that which we used to call the soul. . . . We at once see that these two activities correspond to the two eternal passions of the self, the desire of love and the desire of knowledge : severally representing the hunger of heart and intellect for ultimate truth."— E. UNDERHILL, *Mysticism,* pp. 84, 85.

"Thou hast ravished my heart, my sister, my bride ; thou hast ravished my heart with one of thine eyes with one chain of thy neck. How fair is thy love, my sister, my bride ! How much better is thy love than wine ! "—*Song of Songs*, iv. 9, 10.

See APPLES, BRIDGE, BUDDHI, CHARON'S FERRY, CUPID, GOLDEN FLEECE, LOVER, MAIDEN, RECOLLECTION, ROBE, SELF, SEVEN, SHORE (other), SONS OF GOD, STARS OF SOULS, WATER.

HILL COUNTRY :—

A symbol of aspiration.

"And Mary arose in these days and went into the hill country with haste, into a city of Judah ; and entered into the house of Zacharias and saluted Elisabeth."—LUKE i. 39, 40.

And the purified part of the lower nature bestirred itself at this period and centred itself in a state of aspiration and love of the Divine : and became in touch with the spiritual mind, aspiring towards the truth side which is to give birth to the moral nature (John).

"And most rightly was it in the hill country that these transactions took place, since no great thing can be entertained by those who are low and may be thence called valleys."—ORIGEN, *Comm. on John*, Bk. VI. § 30.

"I will lift up mine eyes unto the hills from whence cometh my help."—Ps. cxxi. 1.

"Any man who undertakes that struggle with temptation may look either to the valleys or to the hills for help, may call the lower or the higher powers to his aid."—PHILLIPS BROOKS, Serm., *Help from the Hills*.

See JOHN BAPTIST, JUDAH (land), MOUNTAIN, VALLEY, VIRGIN MARY, ZACHARIAS.

HIMAVAN PEAK, OR HIGH MOUNTAIN :—

A symbol of a high pitch of aspiration to which the soul may attain.

See ALBORDJ, DELUGE, KAILASA, MOUNTAIN, OLYMPUS.

HINE-NUI-TE-PO :—

A symbol of the matter and space side of manifestation which eventuates in the lower nature.

"There were two grand orders of gods : the first and most ancient were the gods of the night, as night preceded light ; and then followed the gods of the light. Of the former, the chief was Hine-nui-te-po, the great mother Night, the grandparent of the rest"—R. TAYLOR, *New Zealand*, p. 16.

The potential (darkness) precedes the manifest (light). Space-matter gives birth to both higher and lower qualities.

"Po, or night, was the great name for Hades."—*Ibid.*, p. 41.

The manifested lower nature in ignorance (darkness) is the underworld, —the lower planes.

See HADES, LEVIATHAN, MATTER, MĀYĀ (lower), MOTHER, NIGHT, PO, WOMB.

HIPPOPOTAMI :—

A symbol of the elementals of pride, craft, hate, etc., which disport themselves on the astro-mental plane (marsh).

See MARSH, NEKHEBIT, WATER (lower).

HIPPOPOTAMUS, MALE :—

A symbol of intellectual pride.

"In Hermopolis, the symbol of Typhon was a river-horse,—upon which a hawk was placed fighting with a serpent ;—representing by the horse, Typhon, and by the hawk, power and the origin of things. . . . They (the Egyptians) also picture Osiris as a hawk."—PLUTARCH, *Isis and Osiris*, § 50

The "hawk fighting the serpent" symbolises the Higher Self (Osiris) overcoming the desire-nature (serpent) in its subtlest form of intellectual pride (on the back of the river-horse).

See BEL, HAWK, HERPEST, SERPENT, TYPHON.

HIRANYAGARBHA, GOLDEN GERM :—

A symbol of the Divine Monad,— the primordial centre of manifestation arising from the Absolute.

"In the beginning there arose the germ of golden light, Hiranyagarbha ; he was the one born lord of all that is. He established the earth and the heaven."— *Rig-Veda*, X. 121.

"Hiranyagarbha came first into existence, for that golden child did come first into existence —born he was the one lord of being ; he upholdeth this earth and the sky."—*Sata. Brâh.*, 4, VII. 4, 1, 19.

"When God determined to manifest Himself, He summoned into being a glorious Radiance derived from His own light. . . . God looked upon it and loved it, and uttered this sentence,—'But for thee, verily I had not created the heavens !' And it was through this Light and for its sake, that all things were made" (Sufi Cosmogony).—GIBB, *Hist. of Ottoman Poetry*, pp. 34, 35.

As the Absolute is symbolised by

Darkness, so the first germ of manifestation is symbolised by *Light.*

"All the gods are based upon that divine being Hiranyagarbha, out of whom the sun rises, into whom the sun sets. No one is beyond identity with that divine being. This is That."—*Katha. Upanishad,* IV.

"Hiranyagarbha means literally the golden embryo, the golden germ or child, or born of a golden womb, and was no doubt an attempt at naming the sun. . . . The golden child was supposed to have been so called because it was Pragâpati, the lord of creation, when dwelling as yet in the golden egg, and Hiranyagarbha became in the end a recognised name of Pragâpati."—MAX MÜLLER, *Vedic Hymns,* p. 6.

The symbols of the manifested Self are many. From that Self all proceeds, and of that Self all consists. As the egg evolves the life-form, so the germ-Self evolves the inner and the outer universes.

See ABSOLUTE, ASCETICISM, CREATURES (small), EGG, EROS, FIRSTBORN SON, GOLD MAN, HEAVEN AND EARTH, IMPERIAL, MAN CRAWLED, MANES, MONAD, PHANES, PRAGÂPATI, SEED, SELF, SPHERE, SUN, SUTRATMA, SWAN, VAISVANARA.

HIRUKO (LEECH-CHILD) :—

A symbol of the astral human nature devoid of mind. The incipient personality.

"The child which was the first offspring of the union of Izanagi and Izanami was the Hiruko (leech-child), which at the age of three was still unable to stand upright, and was therefore placed in a reed-boat and sent adrift."—*The Kojiki.*

The union of Will and Wisdom as Life and Form, produced first in order the astral nature of man, which before it was endowed with mind and spirit, could not, "stand upright," but "crawled," as it were. It was therefore kept on the astral plane (sea) in an astral body (boat). The development of the astral nature of desire and instinct comes first, and when the animal-man is complete it is individualised by the evolution within it of the mental factor which gives it power to stand alone as a personality (astro-mental).

See ASAR, BOAT, IZANAGI, MAN BORN, MAN CRAWLED, MOON-WAXING, PITRIS (lunar), PITRIYANA, REED PLAIN.

HOA-TABU-ITERAI :—

A symbol of the lower mind or intellect, the personality.

"Oro's wife bore a son, whom he called Hoa-tabu-iterai, i.e. 'friend sacred to the heavens.' This son became a powerful ruler among men."—WM. ELLIS, *Polynesian Researches,* Vol. I. p. 231.

From the Self and the not-Self,— Spirit and Matter,—there is produced the astro-mental nature which is to triumph over the lower instincts and desires, and become a means for the ascent of the soul. This "son," therefore, is the personality which grows from small to great as it manifests more and more the Divine ego which is within it.

"(Aristotle teaches). By pure contemplation the mind may rise above the transitory and contingent, may get beyond space and time and contemplate the Absolute. This attainment is possible because man possesses at the 'top of his mind' an *active reason,* that is to say, 'a pure self-consciousness.' Aristotle distinguishes two *levels* of reason, which he calls the active and the passive reason. The active reason has no finite origin, is not bound up with, or dependent on, the body. It is 'pure,' i.e. not mixed with desire or passion, and does not receive its content through sense. The lower or passive reason is wholly dependent for its content on the body."—R. M. JONES, *Mystical Religion,* p. 67.

See INTELLECT, ORO, PERSONALITY, SPARK, TAATA, VAIRAUMATI, VAPOUR,

HODER :—

A symbol of the lower instinct nature, ignorant and undeveloped.

"Hoder stood in the outermost circle of the crowd round Balder because he was blind."—*Story of Balder, Prose Edda.*

The lower nature, instinct, or subconscious factor,—the astral dregs,— lies at the circumferential extremity of the evolving soul; whereas the germ-God (Balder), corresponding to the Spirit or Seer within, is the innermost super-conscious factor. The former is "blind," that is, unenlightened and unreasoning.

"Hodr, pictured as a blind god of tremendous strength, who without malice discharges the fatal arrow at Balder, is called Hotherus in Saxo (Grammaticus). He was imagined blind, because he dealt out at random good hap and ill."—GRIMM, *Teutonic Mythology,* Vol. I. p. 223.

"Instinct is blind, but has a wonderful power of going unerringly to the spot he 'sees' and finding what he wants;

without him there would be neither life nor light in the cave of the soul. Reason can see, but is clumsier in his movements than instinct, and is apt to follow wrong roads in his quests and sometimes to make grievous mistakes ; he often gazes upward to the mountain peaks."—R. J. CAMPBELL, Serm., *The Function of Faith.*

See ASAR, BALDER, BLIND MAN, CAVE, DEATH OF BALDER, OF LEMMINKAINEN, DHRITA-RASHTRA, EYE, FREJA, LOKE, MISTLETOE, PHINEUS, SERPENT (water).

HOKHMAH, THE WORD, OR WISDOM (MASCULINE) :—

A symbol of the Second Logos,—the manifesting Higher Self on the upper planes.

" The Word or Wisdom, represents the Creator of the Universe, and the Mediator between the Holy One (Ain Soph) and Its creation. In the Qabbalah it is called the Upper Wisdom to distinguish it from the Sephirah Malkhuth, kingdom, the Lower Wisdom, the manifested She'keen-ah or Glory of the Deity."—I. MYER, *Qabbalah,* p. 206.

The " Lower Wisdom " is the buddhic principle (feminine) the Queen, Malkhuth," the " kingdom of heaven," the Holy Spirit.

" The second emanation from *Kether,* is the Sephirah Hokhmah, Wisdom, the Word, also called the Son. . . . It is the male principle, and that which gives existence to everything, by giving Form to Matter."—*Ibid.,* p. 199.

" The Zohar says : ' For it (Hokhmah) generates all things.' "—*Ibid.,* p. 283.

Hokhmah, therefore, is the same as the Word, the Christ,—" All things were made by him " (JOHN i. 3).

See AIN SOPH, ATMAN, BINAH, CHRIST, GANESA, HOLY GHOST, KETHER, MALKHUTH, PAHAD, SEPHIROTH, SHEKINAH, SON OF GOD, TRINITY, WISDOM (masc.), WORD.

HOLD OF THE SHIP :—

A symbol of the lower consciousness and experience of life on the lower planes. The conditions of life and progress through self-love and attraction towards the lower nature.

" ' Tell me my name,' saith the Hold ; ' Aker is thy name.' "—BUDGE, *Book of the Dead,* Ch. XCIX.

" I am supplied with the books of Thoth, and I have brought them to enable me to pass through the god Aker who dwelleth in Set."—*Ibid.,* Ch. XCIV.

The " books of Thoth " are the sacred scriptures, veneration for which,

and obedience to the guidance of the indwelling Spirit, enable the soul to progress through the lower experiences of life and the conditions of limitation and separateness (Set).

See AKERT, HERMES (tris.), NAMES, SET, SHIP, THOTH.

HOLLOW OF THE HILLS :—

A symbol of the lower planes, below the higher ; or of the lower mind.

See DOORS (house), HILL COUNTRY, MOUNTAIN, VALLEY.

HOLLOW SHIPS :—

A symbol of the prototypes of the soul-vehicles (ships) ; hence they are the ideal patterns on the higher mental plane, and are therefore beyond the form levels.

" Let me not find thee, old man, (Chryse, priest of Apollo), at the hollow ships, either now loitering, or hereafter returning, lest the staff and fillet of the god (Apollo) avail thee not."—*Iliad,* Bk. I.

The lower self or desire-mind (Agamemnon) soliloquises thus :—' I look not to thee—spiritual mind (Chryse),—nor would I see thee at the ideal prototypes on the higher mental subplanes, either now or hereafter ' : that is, ' I apprehend thee not in the operation of those laws which make for the karmic compensation of deeds committed ; in case the will and wisdom of the Spirit (Apollo) satisfy not at the same time the lower needs of the personality.' The desire-mind does not recognise the place of the spiritual mind in the moral order, and it relies on the course of the natural order.

See APOLLO, CHRYSE, FILLET, KARMA, PROTOTYPES.

HOLY GHOST, OR SPIRIT :—

This symbol signifies properly the feminine aspect of the Divine Trinity, and has the same meaning as the great Goddesses of other religions than the Christian. It represents the activities and functioning of the plane of being above the higher mental planes, i.e. the buddhic plane. The Holy Spirit proceeds from the Godhead—the infinite source of all. It is the Breath of the Atman,—the infinite power of God. It is not separate from, but operative through the Christ—the Higher Self. Without

Christ there would be no Holy Spirit. With Christ there must be a Holy Spirit, which, however, is possible to be seen and known only as the personal is lost sight of, or transcended, and the Truth and the Life are realised. But the lower mind cannot distinguish between the Christ and the Spirit.

"Now in Hebrew the word 'spirit' (mach) is of feminine gender. As a consequence of this the Holy Ghost was looked upon by the Naassenes and the earliest Christians as the 'mother' of Jesus."—A. DREWS, *The Christ Myth*, p. 118.

See ATMAN, BAPTISM OF FIRE, BLASPHEMY, BREATH, BUDDHIC PLANE, CHRIST (pri.), GODHEAD, HAIR, INSPIRATION, JERUSALEM, MALKHUTH, OCEAN (fem.), PARACLETE, SAPANDAR, SELF, STIFFNECKED, TRINITY, WIND.

HOLY PLACES AND FEELINGS :—

Symbolic of exalted states of consciousness, and aspirations towards attaining them.

"King Suddhodana bathed to purify his body and mind with the waters of holy places and of holy feelings."—*Buddha-Karita*, Bk. II.

The Higher Self now withdrawing within itself, bathes, as it were, in the pure Truth which is to cleanse the intellect and the vehicle of the mind, and raise the soul to high states of consciousness in response to desires to attain such.

See BAPTISM, RIVER OF LIFE, SUDDHODANA, WATER, WELL.

HOM-PLANT STEM :—

A symbol of the inter-connected vehicles of the soul.

"The archangels convey to earth another of the three elements, the Fravashi, bearing it in a stem of the Hom-plant, the height of a man."—*The Dinkard, S. B. of E.*

The messengers of the Logos are the means of introducing the Life-element into the germ-vehicles of the human soul, which are awaiting its reception.

See AMSHASPANDS, FRAVASHIS, HEIGHT OF OSIRIS, PROMETHEUS, STEM, VESTURES.

HOMA-JUICE :—

A symbol of the Divine Life to be acquired through aspiration, and sacrifice of the lower desires offered to the Ideal before the soul.

"Homa grows when being praised. So the man who praises him becomes more triumphant. The least extraction of Hom-juice, the least praise ; the least tasting of it, O Homa ! is sufficient for destroying a thousand of the daevas."—*Homa Yasht*, HAUG, *Essays.*

The Self within develops as his laws of growth are reverently observed. So the mind which diligently attends to the higher laws of its being rises in power. The least degree in which the Divine Life functions is so far the means of furthering the evolution of the Self and of overcoming the manifold negations and illusions of the lower planes.

"There is in all who are born into this world as part of mankind, a universal Life, and that life is God's life, latent in some, more formed in others, vivid and full in the best of the race, but absent from none. None are divorced from the Life of Truth and Love and Righteousness, none able finally to be divorced from it, and though that Life in the man, like Truth in the world, may run wild and run to evil, it will be sovereign in him in the end and perfect him, as Truth will be sovereign in the race. . . . There is, indeed, a God with us—in our hearts. Believe in that, live in the truth that God is incarnating Himself in you, that His spirit is at one with yours. So that if you will, your thought and work and will may be God's thought and work and will. Worship God not only in yourselves in this truth, but live in it, and in its spirit among men, and your outward life will then be in it worship of God in spirit and truth."—STOPFORD A. BROOKE, Serm., *God is Spirit.*

"The Eternal indwells you now, though you cannot realise it ; it *is* you, though your surface consciousness that you mistake for yourself keeps you ignorant of it. Man, what you know about yourself now is but a tiny fraction of the glorious reality that is visible to the eyes of God. He sees, he cares, he saves."—R. J. CAMPBELL, Serm., *The Eyes Divine.*

See ASHA-VANUHI, ATONEMENT, BLOOD, CUP, DAEVAS, FORENOON, HYMNS, PRAGÂPATI, PRAISE, SAP, SOMA-JUICE, THRITA, VITAL AIRS.

HOMA TREE OR PLANT :—

A symbol of the Divine Ray or "tree of Life," which proceeds from the Absolute and conveys spiritual nourishment to the soul.

"Then spake Zarathustra : Reverence to Homa ! good is Homa ! well-created is

Homa ! rightly created, of a good nature, healing, well-shaped, well performing, successful, golden-coloured, with hanging tendrils, as the best for eating and the most tasting provision for the soul."—*Homa Yasht*, verse 16, HAUG, *Essays.*

The soul (Zarathustra) acclaims the Divine Life (Homa), or the spiritual consciousness. In doing so, it prepares itself to receive, to reverence, and to acknowledge the Truth and Life which proceed from the Divine illumination. This preparedness implies realisation of Right, Holiness, Harmony, Justice, Equilibrium, Victorship and Wisdom. The symbol of the " hanging tendrils," is the comparison of the Divine Nature to the fruit of the vine of Love, which is the best nourishment for the growth of the soul during its pilgrimage.

" The *Hom* of the Persians is spoken of in the *Zend-avesta* as the Word of Life, and has its echo on the earth ; also as the author of salvation, and at the same time the announcer of it ; as the Tree of Life, and source of the living Water of Life. The plant *Hom*, when consecrated, is regarded as the mystical body of God ; and when partaken of as a sacrament, is received as the veritable food of eternal life."—H. C. BARLOW, *Essays on Symbolism*, p. 116.

" The purification of the Homa twigs is accomplished by water and formulas. The priest takes the Homa twig (one is sufficient) in his right hand, holding a copper goblet of water, in his left, from which he pours water, at intervals, over the twig as he thrice recites, etc."—HAUG, *Essays on Parsi Religion*, p. 339.

See ATHWYA, BAPTISM, BREAD, CONSECRATION, CUP, FOOD, GRAPES, HEALING, PLANTS, SACRAMENT, SOMA-PLANT, SOUL, SUTRATMA, TABLE OF THE LORD, TREE OF LIFE, VINE, WATER, WINE, ZOROASTER.

HOME ; PLACE OF BIRTH :—

A symbol of the source of the soul's being. Abode of the spiritual consciousness prior to the descent of the Monad into the arena of the lower life. The descent of the Divine Sparks, or Monads of Life, is followed by their triumphant ascent on the upward path to their true abode in Divine bliss.

" Thou hast made us for Thyself, and our heart is restless till it find its home in Thee."—AUGUSTINE, *Confessions*, Opening words.

" The place where I was born is God. God is my fatherland, . . . before I lived in myself, I lived already in God."—TAULER.

" When I was a little child, and dwelling in my kingdom, in my Father's house, and in the wealth and glories of my nurturers had my pleasure, from the East our home, my Parents having equipped me, sent me forth."—" Hymn of the Soul," *Acts of Judas Thomas.*

When I, the Soul's prototype, was in the germ state,—a manifestation proceeding from the Divine Monad or radiation from God,—I dwelt as an undifferentiated unit in the bosom of the Eternal fullness ; and in the greatness and opulence of my nature had my delight. From the " East,"— or along the path of the manifesting life to which the rising of the sun is comparable,—was I sent forth of my parents Love and Wisdom, or the Spirit and the vestures which clothed me. And with the potential wealth of the spiritual treasury, as latent powers of the soul, was I endowed.

" Now there is not upon earth any creature but wisheth and willeth to come to that home, the high source of his being, where heart's ease is and endless rest, *that* plainly is Almighty God. Now there is not upon earth any creature but revolves like a wheel on itself ; why so it revolves is that it may return where it erst was, where its earliest impulse began."—KING ALFRED, *Works.*

" There is a raying out of all orders of existence, an external emanation from the Ineffable One. There is again a returning impulse, drawing all upwards and inwards towards the centre from whence all came."—*Plotinus to Flaccus.*

" Return unto thy home O Soul ! thy sin and shame leave thou behind on earth ; assume a shining form—thy ancient shape,—refined and from all taint set free."—*Rig-Veda.*

" Our spirits are eternally at home in God, even when in our particular generation retaining only the dimmest consciousness of our divine origin, we wander in the semi-darkness through the labyrinth of this strange, puzzling earth-world."—R. J. CAMPBELL, Serm., *Our Solidarity with God.*

See ATMA PLANE, BUDDHIC PLANE, CHILD, EAST, EXILE, FATHER, GERMS, INVOLUTION, JUDGMENT HALL, KINGDOM, LITTLE ONES, LOTOS TREE, MONAD OF LIFE, SHEEP (lost), SPARK, VESTURES, WEALTH OF TREASURY, WHEEL OF LIFE.

HONEY :—

A symbol of spiritual food and

nourishment, that is, of wisdom and love on the buddhic plane, which are the produce laid up above, of the higher emotions (bees).

"The theologers have used 'honey' in many different symbolic ways because it has both a purifying and preservative virtue. . . . Moreover it is sweet to taste, and collected from 'flowers' by 'bees' who happen to be 'ox-born.' When, therefore, they pour into the hands of those who are receiving the Leontic initiation, honey for washing instead of water, they bid them keep their hands pure from everything that causes pain or harm, or brings defilement ; just as when the purifying medium is fire, they bring the candidate appropriate means of washing, declining water as inimical to fire. Moreover it is with honey too they purify their tongues from every sin. . . . Porphyry then goes on to say that some think that honey further typifies the celestial nectar and ambrosia, and also the pleasure which draws souls down into generation. Then is the soul moistened and becomes watery " (*Cave of the Nymphs*).—G. R. S. MEAD, *The Mysteries of Mithra*, pp. 61, 62.

The celestial food,—wisdom and love,—is, as it were, collected and transmuted from the virtues (flowers) by the higher emotions (bees) which arise from buddhi (ox-born). Wisdom and love cast out from the mind all falsity and perversity (tongues) ; and the soul becomes suffused with Truth (watery).

"Honey the winds pour forth for the righteous, honey the rivers ; full of honey may the plants be for us !—Honey by night and morn, rich in honey may the region of the earth be for us, honey the father Heaven !—rich in honey may the tree be for us, rich in honey the sun, full of honey the kine."—*Sata. Brâh.*, VII. 5, 1, 4.

This statement enumerates the sources from which wisdom and love may be derived, according to the meanings of the various symbols.

"When the grace of the Holy Spirit bathes us, it fills us with 'honey and butter' equally. For 'honey' falls from above, but 'butter' is drawn from the milk of animals, and so 'honey' (sweetness) is from the air, 'butter' from the flesh."—ST. GREGORY, *Morals on the Book of Job*, Vol. II. p. 185.

"When Solomon gives the exhortation. Eat honey, my son, that it may be sweet to thy palate, he uses *honey* figuratively, meaning divine doctrine, which restores the spiritual knowledge of the soul."—HIPPOLYTUS, *On Proverbs*, Ante-N. Vol. VI. p. 431.

See AMBROSIA, BEES, BUDDHI, FLOWERS, FOOD, NECTAR, NORNOR, OX-BORN, PLANTS, TONGUE, TREE OF LIFE, WATER.

HONOUR, MEED OR PRIZE OF :—

This signifies the treasure of the things of the Spirit laid up in heaven as reward for merit, as it were, for those egos who have done valiantly and have conquered the lower nature.

"To him then made answer fleet-footed god-like Achilles : 'Most noble son of Atreus, of all men most covetous, how shall the great-hearted Greeks assign thee a meed of honour ? We know naught of any wealth of common store, but what spoil we took from captured cities hath been apportioned, and it is not fitting to collect all this back from the folk."—*Iliad*, Bk. I.

To the Desire-mind (Agamemnon) comes by way of the Intellect, the questioning spirit, and it perceives that the Personality (Achilles) is illusory and rooted in egoism ; and is led to ask how the higher mental qualities shall uplift and transform the lower self, assigning honour to it. The Personality is unaware of the existence of any inexhaustible mine of wisdom, and cannot conceive of that which is self-derived from within ; and falsely imagines that knowledge is only borrowed, or acquired through study, or captured from without. It perceives that the knowledge it has already acquired has been applied to life (i.e. turned to personal advantage), and the ends which were sought have been attained. These low ends which have been realised are not to be forfeited, but are to be expanded to the real objects of evolution.

See ACHILLES, AGAMEMNON, GREEKS (great), PERSONALITY, TREASURE.

HORBEHUDTI, OR HORO-BEHUTET :—

A symbol of the Second Logos.

"Then spake Thoth to Râ : 'Lord of the Gods ! there came the God of Behudet (Edfu) in the form of a great winged disk. From this day forth he shall be called Horbehudti' (Horus of Edfu)."—*Legend of the Winged Sun-disk.*

Then spake the mind or awakening intelligence to the Supreme ;—' Lord of the Ideals ! there came forth from the lower nature the Son of man arrayed in the buddhic vesture, and being raised up, he shall now be known as Son of God, born of the eternal Spirit of Wisdom.[1]

See BIRTH OF HORUS, DISK, EDFU, HORUS, ISIS, SON OF GOD, SON OF MAN, SUN-DISK, THOTH, WISDOM.

HORIZONS, THE TWO :—

Symbolic of the commencement and termination of the cycle of life through which the Self passes, as comparable to the sun in its diurnal course from east to west.

"Heru-khuti, i.e. Horus of the two horizons, is a form of the Sun-god ; the words ' two horizons ' refer to the mountains of Bakhatet and Manu, the most easterly and westerly points of the sun's course, and the places where he rose and set."—BUDGE, Book of the Dead, p. 4.

"I know the two sycamore trees of turquoise, from between which the god Rā doth emerge when he setteth out upon his journey over the pillars of Shu towards the door of the lord of the East wherefrom Rā cometh forth."—Ibid., Ch. CXLIX.

The "trees" or "mountains" signify the two highest planes, atma-buddhi, and the "pillars" denote the quaternary of planes below the plane of atma. The journey over the quaternary typifies the lower existence in which the Self (sun) is unapparent until he rises in the "East" in the great day of the Lord.

See EAST, ELIJAH, GATE (tchesert), HORUS, LION-GOD, MANVANTARA, PILLARS OF SHU, RĀ, SAND, SUN, SUN-RISING, SYCAMORE, WEST, ZODIAC.

HORN ON THE HEAD :—

A symbol in its higher aspect, of aspiration and lofty thought, and in its lower aspect of ambition, pride, vanity, conceit, egotism.

"Horns denote powers of truth from good."—SWEDENBORG, Arc. Cel., n. 10,186.

"I (the Soul) make a way among the horns of all those who make themselves strong against me."—BUDGE, Book of the Dead, Ch. LXIV.

"All the horns of the wicked also will I cut off ; but the horns of the righteous shall be lifted up."—Ps. lxxv. 10. (See Ps. xviii. 2, and Ps. xcii. 10.)

See SHIP OF MANU, TUSK.

HORN OF SALVATION :—

A symbol of aspiration toward the ideal of Love and Wisdom.

"Manu fastened the ship as directed to a horn in the Fish's head."—Deluge story in the Maha-bharata.

The higher Self, as the individuality (Manu), is established in the causal-body (ship), and the mind through which it manifests is attached to an aspiration from the striving Self within the soul.

"The God of my rock, in him will I trust ; my shield, and the horn of my salvation, my high tower, and my refuge ; my saviour, thou savest me from violence."—2 SAM. xxii. 3.

See ABTU FISH, CAUSAL-BODY, DELUGE, FISH (great), JESUS AS FISH, MANU, SHIP OF MANU.

HORNS OF GOLD :—

Symbolic of zeal and love for the true and good.

See JUPITER (planet).

HORNS OF THE GOD :—

These symbolise exaltation, and victory over the lower qualities. They also refer to the penetrative faculty of intuition which transcends the mind.

See DESERTS.

HORNS, TEN, OF THE DRAGON :—

These symbolise the self-centred qualities of the astral or desire principle of the lower nature, they are forms of greed, pride, love of power, etc.

"By ten horns is signified much power ; from the signification of the number ten as denoting what is full."—SWEDENBORG, Apoc. Rev., n. 101. (See REV. xii. 3.)

See BIRTH OF MAN-CHILD, DRAGON (red), TEN.

HORSE :—

A symbol in its higher aspect, of the intellect or intelligence, and in its lower aspect, of the lower mind subject to the desires and passions.

"Yea, as a horse that bears to the gods ; that which conveys to the gods is indeed the mind, for it is the mind which chiefly conveys the wise man to the gods."—Sata. Brāh., I. 4, 3, 6, S. B. of E.

"Man does not rightly know the way to the heavenly world, but the horse does rightly know it."—Ibid., XIII. 2, 3, 1.

"The horse is the nobility." The horse is related to the northern quarter," which is "the quarter of man."—Ibid.

"Horses denote the intellect."—SWEDENBORG, Arc. Cel., n. 10, 227.

"Wherever the horse is mentioned in the Holy Word, it signifies either true or false understanding. This is now, since Swedenborg, a universal induction valid in all particular instances."—J. J. GARTH WILKINSON.

" An endeavour is made by the sorcerers to have the babe (Zoroaster) trampled to death by horses, but the leading horse stands over the child and prevents it from perishing."—*Life of Zoroaster.*

The astral nature of desire and sensation, operating through the lower mind, is opposed to the Spirit and seeks to kill it out. On the mental plane are the ideas (horses) which are the means of furthering or retarding the progress of the soul. They require to be reined in and guided by the enlightened will. The " leading horse " signifies the disciplined mind which retains the impressions that are required for the evolution of the intellect, and it therefore protects the spiritual germ within.

" Now the Egyptians are men, and not God ; and their horses flesh, and not spirit : and when the Lord shall stretch out his hand, both he that helpeth shall stumble, and he that is holpen shall fall, and they shall all fail together."—ISA. xxxi. 3.

The " Egyptians " (in the Bible) signify the lower mind, which is illusory and unreal, i.e. not self-derived (God) ; and its ideas (horses) are energised by desire (flesh) and not by spirit. And so when the Higher Self shall energise the mind, the lower unreality of error (the helper) and delusion (the helped) shall fall away.

See CHARIOT, EGYPTIANS, EXODUS, GODS, GULDTOPP, HEIMDALL, HERMES, HOUSE, MAN, ZOROASTER.

HORSE, BLACK :—

A symbol of error or false knowledge.

" There (in the sea) the daeva Apaosho in the shape of a black horse with black ears and tail encounters Tishtrya (as a red horse). Both fight for three days and nights ; at length he is defeated by the daeva."—*Tir Yasht,* HAUG, *Essays.*

At this time the illusion of the lower mental plane assails the ego. This illusion is false knowledge which rises before him. The struggle continues for three successive periods during which the mind is preparing. The defeat of the higher intelligence of the ego is at the moment when the evolution is to be carried on upon the lower planes, so that reason and will appear to be dethroned.

" And when he (the Lamb) opened the third seal, I heard the third living creature saying, Come. And I saw, and behold, a black horse ; and he that sat thereon had a balance in his hand."— REV. vi. 5.

And when the Second Logos, involved in matter as the Divine Sacrifice (Lamb), entered upon the third period of evolution, the lower mental (third creature) plane was established, and energised from the astral plane. This produced false knowledge (black horse) and illusion (rider). The reference to the " balance," and, in the sixth verse, to the measures of wheat and barley, signify the soul becoming subject to the law of karma, whereby it shall reap according as it has sown. And " the oil and the wine hurt thou not," is an exhortation to protect the growth of love (oil) and wisdom (wine) from the adverse forces of the lower planes.

See BALANCE, BLACK, DAEVAS, DAYS, LAMB OF GOD, NIGHTS, TISTRYA, WHEAT AND BARLEY.

HORSE, RED :—

A symbol of the mind energised by the Spirit.

" Unless the prayers of men were addressed to him (Tishtrya), he was powerless to defeat the evil spirits, who kept back the waters in the sea. . . . He steps into the sea in the shape of a red horse with yellow ears."—*Tir Yasht.*

The Higher Self through the mind (Tishtrya) cannot operate immediately upon the lower planes, unless aspirations or petitions from below are first raised for spiritual realities : since, of course, the lower planes do not exist excepting in so far as they become channels for the activities of the functionings of the indwelling Self. The Self energises the mind by animating the higher emotions. The " red horse " symbolises the mind energised ; and the " yellow ears " signify the aspiring intelligence which is now coming into play as the astral plane (the sea) is reached.

" Tishtrya cannot bring the rain from the sea Voura-kasha over the earth, if not assisted by the prayers of men. In the same way Indra cannot release the celestial cows (the clouds) from the rocky cave, whither they have been carried by demons, without the assistance of *Brihaspati,* who is the representative of the prayers sent up by men to the gods, and the personification of their devotion and meditation."—M. HAUG, *Essays, etc.,* p. 279.

"And when he opened the second seal, I heard the second living creature saying, Come. And another horse came forth, a red horse : and to him that sat thereon it was given to take peace from the earth, and that they should slay one another : and there was given unto him a great sword."—REV. vi. 3, 4.

The astral plane (second) being established, the mind was energised by the Spirit, and thereupon began the conflict between the higher and lower qualities of the soul ; for in the first instance Christ "came not to send peace but a sword." The great "sword of the Spirit" signifies the spiritual energy from within, which by dissipating evil would in the end bring peace.

"O red-steeded, come hither ! for red indeed is Agni's horse ; . . . O Agni. overcome all evil doers ! "—*Sata. Brāh.,* VI. 6, 3, 4.

"Those who stand around Indra while he moves on, harness the bright red (steed) ; the lights in heaven shine forth." —*Rig-Veda,* Mand. I. 6, 1.

The agents of the Higher Self (Indra or Agni) as he progresses, bring about the evolution of the mind which the Spirit energises ; and so knowledge increases in the soul and love and truth shine forth from within.

See AGNI, CLOUDS, COWS, INDRA, IRIS, IRRIGATION, OCEAN, PEACE AND SWORD, PRAYER, RED, SLAUGHTER, SWORD, TISTRYA, VOURUKASHA, WATER.

HORSE, WHITE :—

A symbol of the pure and perfect higher mind (buddhi-manas) with its ideals and aspirations.

"Once when thou (Buddha) wert a white horse ; in pity for the suffering of man, thou didst fly across heaven to the region of the evil demons, to secure the happiness of mankind" (*Buddhist Gatha*).—A. LILLIE, *Life of Buddha,* p. 58.

"Pragâpati said, ' Whoever shall seek thee (Agni) in the form of a white horse, shall find thee.' . . . It should be a white horse, for that is a form of him (the sun) who burns yonder."—*Sata. Brâh.,* VII. 3, 2, 15–6.

The Higher Self (sun) must be sought for through the highest mental qualities in aspirations towards Truth and Love.

"And I saw, and behold, a white horse, and he that sat thereon had a bow ; and

there was given unto him a crown : and he came forth conquering and to conquer. —REV. vi 2.

The Higher Self (Christ) emanated in the higher mind, equipped with the mental stimulus to evolution (the bow), which is destructive of the lower qualities, and endowed with supremacy (crown) over the lower manifestation : and he went forth in the soul to "subject all things to himself."

"Every spiritual man feels the going forth of his Saviour conquering and to conquer. And he hath every outward action of holy writ realised inwardly— every groan of the conquered, every struggle of the Conqueror, His toil, His sweat, His wounds, His death, His resurrection, His second going forth in the plenitude of the Spirit, His unconquered resolution, His long-abiding labour, the turning of the tide of battle, His sword upon the neck of His enemies, the shout of victory, the treading of the nations in the winepress of His fury, His shivering them with His iron sceptre like a potsherd, His driving them with death, and the grave, and him that had the power of death, into the bottomless pit. His reign of peace, its joy, full contentment, and perfect assurance ; what are they all, but letters, words, and similitudes, whereby the believer may better understand, and better express the spiritual work which is going on within his own soul, by the casting down of imaginations, and every high thing that exalteth itself against the knowledge of God, and bringing into captivity every thought to the obedience of Christ."— E. IRVING, *Writings,* Vol. I. p. 402.

See AAT, AGNI, ARIES, BOW, BUDDHA (Maitreya), CHRIST'S SECOND COMING, CONFLAGRATION, CROWN, JUDGMENT DAY, KALKI, PRAGÂPATI, RACE-COURSE, REGNAROK, RENOVATION, SLAUGHTER, SOSIOSH, SPRINGTIME, STRIFE, SUN, VICTORY, WHITE.

HORSE, ODIN'S, SLEIPNER :—

A symbol of the higher mind. *See* HERMOD.

HORSE, WINGED :—

A symbol of the aspiring higher mind.

"By the Winged Horse, Pegasus, the Ancients understood the intellect of the truth by which wisdom is attained. By the hoofs of his feet, the experiences through which the natural intelligence comes."—SWEDENBORG, *True Christian. Religion,* p. 693.

See HEEL, WINGS.

HORSE, SACRIFICIAL :—

A symbol of Divine manifestation on the buddhic plane at the commencement of the great cycle of life. It signifies the sacrifice of the Logos in the limitation of himself in forms of matter.

"Yearly the sun-god as the zodiacal horse (Aries) was supposed by the Vedic Aryans to die to save all flesh. Hence the horse sacrifice."—A. LILLIE, *Popular Life of Buddha*, p. 58.

"The Asva-medha (horse-sacrifice) is Pragāpati."

"Pragāpati poured forth the life-sap of the horse (asva-medha). When poured forth, it went straight away from him and spread itself over the regions. The gods went in quest of it. By means of offerings they followed it up, by offerings they searched for it, and by offerings they found it."—*Sata. Brâh.*, XIII. 1, 4, 1.

The Supreme emanated the Divine Life in the sacrifice of himself. When emanated, it passed into the matter of all the planes (regions) to the outermost physical. The monads of life (the gods) became embodied in the forms and sought to be evolved in its qualities. By means of relinquishing lower conditions, the monads became attached to higher. By giving up the inferior qualities they secured the superior.

"He addresses the horse with,— 'Thus born, art thou the child of the two worlds,'—the two worlds, doubtless, are these two, heaven and earth; and he (Agni) thus born, is the child of these two."—*Ibid.*, VI. 4, 4, 2.

The descent of the Divine life into manifestation is both a sacrifice and a birth. The Higher Self (Agni) is born in matter both on the higher planes (heaven) and the lower planes (earth); and thus the indwelling Spirit becomes a "child," as it were, of duality,—the higher nature and the lower.

See ADITI, AGNI, ARIES, ASURA (lower), BLOOD, BLOOD OF THE LAMB, BURNT-OFFERING, CHILD, CREATION, DAWN, EVOLUTION, HEAVEN AND EARTH, INCARNATION, INVOLUTION, OFFERING, PRAGÂPATI, REGIONS, SACRIFICE, SACRIFICER, SOMA-JUICE, SUN, SUN-RISING, ZODIAC.

HORSES, TWO BAY :—

Symbols of mind and emotion, functioning on the mental plane.

"They harness to the chariot on each side his (Indra's) two favourite bays, the brown, the bold, who can carry the hero."—*Rig-Veda*, Mand. I. 6, *S. B. of E.*

To the causal-body (chariot) and the causal-self are attached the functionings of mind and emotion energised by the Self (Indra); and these are to develop the soul.

See CHARIOT, INDRA, MARUTS, PIETY, PRAISE OF GOD.

HORSES WITH LONG FLOWING MANES :—

These symbolise the faculties of the lower mind which would search for truth laboriously. The lower mind is in itself of the utmost use, as its exercise promotes patience, gentleness, and the grace of unremitting enquiry in the pursuit of truth and right.

See HAIR, INTELLECT, MANAS, PETER.

HORUS, THE ELDER, OR AROUERIS :—

The Second Logos, or the Self manifest primordially upon the higher buddhic plane.

"Isis and Osiris conceived the elder Horus while they were in their mother's womb."—PLUTARCH, *Isis and Osiris*, § 12.

Wisdom (Isis) and Will (Osiris) primordially produce Action (Horus) which is to go forth on the buddhic plane at the emanation of the universe or solar system.

"The Book of the Dead, Ch. XVIII, states that of Horus, the Avenger of his Father Osiris :—' His two eyes (i.e. Sun and Moon) are the two feathers on his head.'"—A. WIEDEMANN, *Rel. of Anc. Egyptians*, p. 259.

The two feathers therefore signify the Individuality and Personality by which the Self manifests.

See AKERU, AROUERIS, ASCENSION OF OSIRIS, AVENGING, BIRTH OF HORUS, DAYS (five), HORIZONS, PYLONS, TATTU, URNI, UR-UATCHI.

HORUS, THE YOUNGER :—

See HARPOCRATES.

HORUS, THE CHILD :—

The same as Harpocrates.

It signifies the birth of the Christ in the soul upon the buddhic plane, or the Self commencing to incarnate in the human being.

See BIRTH OF HORUS, BUTO, HARPOCRATES, HORBEHUDTI, INCARNATION.

HOSHANG AND GUZAK :—

Symbols of the outgoing and incoming, or inductive and intuitional, aspects of the mental faculty.

HOST, OR CONSECRATED WAFER :—

A symbol of the Divine Victim—the Incarnate Self,—abiding within Truth-goodness (bread of heaven, or body of Christ) : it signifies the Real Presence of God in the human soul, and object of the soul's adoration. Christ can only express Himself in the highest qualities of the mind so these highest qualities are, as it were, his body in which he lives in us.

See Bread, Food as god, Procession, Sacrament, Shrine, Transubstantiation.

HOSTS, LORD OF :—

A symbol of the Higher Self,—the ruler and director of the qualities (hosts), higher and lower.

See Army of the gods, Jewels, Qualities, Self, Soldiers.

HOTRI PRIEST (SPEECH) :—

A symbol of the religious expression of the emotional mind.

See Advarya, Priest of altar.

HOUR :—

A symbol of the twelfth part of a manvantara or great cycle of manifested life of the universe, or soul. The " hour " has the same signification as a sign of the Zodiac. It represents the twelfth part of the course of the Higher Self (sun) through the cycle of life in the lower nature or underworld. Sometimes the cycle is symbolised as a day of twelve hours, and sometimes as a night. When symbolised as a night of twelve hours, as in the case of the Tuat, the implication is that the Higher Self is concealed and unmanifest, as we find is the case in our present state of existence.

See Labourers, Manvantara, Tuat, Twelve, Zodiac.

HOUR OF MID-DAY :—

A symbol of the middle period of the cycle of involution, or of evolution. If the cycle is divided into seven periods, then the middle period is the fourth. Whether there are six or seven periods depends upon the manner of reckoning. The seventh counting downward is the turning point, or " day of rest," leaving six on each side : these are the twelve, as in the Zodiac.

See Æons (twelve), Iabraoth, Sabbath, Seven, Twelve.

HOURIES, NYMPHS OF PARADISE :—

A symbol of the higher emotions active on the buddhic plane.

" The Garden of Eden is the scene of the Beatific Vision, the Divine Epiphanies, the sight of which will form the highest felicity of the blessed. The native inhabitants of Paradise are the houries, maidens of celestial beauty and possessed of every virtue, who will be the heavenly brides and companions of the blessed, and the ' eternal youths ' who will be the attendants on the just."—Gibb, *Hist. of Ottoman Poetry*, Vol. I. p. 37.

When the consciousness rises to the buddhic plane (Eden) the soul will become possessed of the high faculties of that state of being. The higher emotions (houries) in harmony with Truth, Wisdom, and Love, will fill the consciousness with peace and bliss (*See* Koran, *Sura*, LVI.).

" In *The Pilgrim's Progress*, in the house called Beautiful, all the inmates, except the porter, are females."—Geo. Offor.

See Blandishments, Dance, (circle), Esther, Garden of eden, Gopis, Muses, Paradise.

HOUSE :—

A symbol of one of the vehicles, bodies, or habitations of the soul on the planes of the quaternary.

See Cottage, Dwellings, Gold-coloured spot, Palace, Wooden palace.

HOUSE OF BONDAGE :—

A symbol of an early state of the soul in which the indwelling Spirit is in bondage to the lower instincts, desires, and sensations.

" The Lord thy God which brought thee forth out of the land of Egypt, out of the house of bondage ; who led thee through the great and terrible wilderness, wherein were fiery serpents and scorpions, and thirsty ground where was no water."—Deut. viii. 14, 15.

The Divine Will leads the chosen qualities of the soul from a state of subservience to the desire-nature, into another condition full of trouble and

suffering, in which desires and passions
are rampant, and the lower nature is
steeped in ignorance.

See BONDAGE, CAPTIVITY, DRY,
EGYPT, EXODUS, HERMES, HORSE,
ISRAELITES, MOSES, PASSOVER, ROCK
(spir.), SCORPION, SERPENT, THIRST,
WATER, WILDERNESS.

HOUSE, FREQUENTED :—

A symbol of the causal-body as
an archetype of perfection set before
the soul.

"In the first or lowest heaven is the
so-called 'Frequented House.' This,
which is a great dome of red ruby, was
originally in the highest Paradise, the
Garden of Eden, from which, on Adam's
expulsion and subsequent repentance, it
was brought to earth as a solace to him.
It was placed where the Ka'ba of Mekka
now stands, and Adam was bidden
compass it ; and the angels who dwelt
in the Seven Heavens were commanded
to descend and perform the rite along
with him. It remained on earth till
Noah's time, but before the flood it was
caught up to the spot in the lowest
Heaven immediately above where it
used to stand, and there it will rest till
the Last Day, when it will be taken back
to its original place in Paradise."—GIBB,
Hist. of Ottoman Poetry, Vol. I. p. 37.

The lowest heaven is Devachan
on the higher mental plane, on which
level is the causal-body in process of
building up from the potential condition to the actual. The "dome of
red ruby" signifies the archetypal
Love and Wisdom of the upper
buddhic plane (Eden) whereon the
highest causal-body exists. The
"bringing to earth" refers to the
descent of the spiritual monad (atma-
buddhi) into the mind or personality
(Adam). The personality has thus set
before it the ideal of Wisdom and
Love which the higher qualities
(angels) are to assist it in attaining.
The "remaining on earth" indicates
an intuitional apprehension of higher
things which faded away in the human
race when the Individuality (Noah)
became firmly established. The
causal-body rests now in the higher
mind where it will remain until the
end of the present cycle ; after which
further evolution will require its
transmutation to the upper buddhic
levels.

See ADAM (lower), BUDDHIC PLANE,
CAUSAL-BODY, EDEN, FLOOD, GARDEN
OF EDEN, INDIVIDUALITY, JERUSALEM,
JUDGMENT DAY, KAABA, NOAH, PARA-
DISE, RED (rose), RUBIES, STONE
(black), STUPA.

HOUSE IN HEAVEN, OR HOUSE
    OF GOD :—

A symbol of the causal-body or
immortal soul, the seat of the Divine
nature of humanity.

"But Christ as a son, over his (God's)
house ; whose house are we, if we hold
fast our boldness and the glorying of
our hope firm unto the end."—HEB. iii.
6, 7.

The indwelling Self is the manifest
Divine,—the son of the Unmanifest,—
who is seated in the potential causal-
body. To evolve the actual from
the potential, the egos build up in the
spirit of Christ, the causal-body, and
become one with it in actuality as
they are victorious over the lower
nature and persevere unto the end of
the cycle.

"The piece of money—the groat, as he
(Walter Hylton) calls it—is lost in thy
house. That is to say, the Divine treasure
lies holden in thy *soul.* Jesus sleeps
in thy *ship,* as he once slept in the little
ship on the lake of Gennesaret."—
DR. INGE, *English Mystics*, p. 89.

"The body is the prâna's habitation,
of which the head forms the roof, in which
it is bound to the breath as posts, by
food as the rope. . . . Usually following
Brih. II. 5, 18, and especially *Chând*
VIII. 1, 1, the body is described as the
city of Brahman, heavenly, desirable,
the highest dwelling of Brahman, in
which as a house the lotus flower of the
heart abides, in which during sleep the
fires of the prâna keep watch."—DEUSSEN,
Phil. of Upanishads, p. 283.

The causal-body is the vehicle of
the Self (prâna) in the underworld,
who is attached to it by the processes
of soul-nourishment and growth. The
causal-body is the soul's centre (city),
perfect potentially if not actually ;
it is the seat of the Higher Self (Brahman) ; it is also the soul's innermost
shrine in which wisdom and love
abide. When the causal Self indraws
the life (sleep) after an incarnation,
the soul's energies await further outpouring.

"Catherine of Siena gave her testimony
to the fact that the soul 'bears ever
within it the place where God lives by grace
—the house of our soul wherein holy
desire prays constantly.' "—R. M. JONES,
Mystical Religion, p. 305.

"The second place of earth's joy is whereon the faithful one erects a house wherein every blessing of life is thriving."—*Vendidad.* III.

"Earth's joy" is so expressed, since the awakenment of the Self must proceed first from the physical plane. The "second place" signifies the plane of the higher mind whereon the indwelling Self, through the egos, builds up the causal-body within which the transmuted experiences are collected together.

"The earth brings forth for them many things of all sorts, of which they carry the most serviceable into the house and use them."—*Anaxagoras,* FAIRBANKS, 10.

The lower nature yields experiences for the mind, of which those which are capable of transmutation are conveyed to the causal-body wherewith to build it up.

See ARK, BOAT, CAUSAL-BODY, CHRIST, CHURCH, COTTAGE, DWELLING, GARHAPATYA, LOST SILVER, LOTUS, MANSIONS, PYLONS, PYRAMID, SHIP, SHRINE, STONE (building), TABERNACLE, TEMPLE, TREASURE, VICTORY.

HOUSE PROVIDED WITH FIRE, CATTLE, WIFE, SON, AND PLENTY :—

Symbolic of the causal-body within which the transmuted emotional, intellectual, and moral experiences are brought together, so that there is Truth and Love in abundance.

See CATTLE, CAUSAL-BODY, FIRE, TRANSMUTATION, WIFE.

HOUSE WITH FOUR DOORS :—

A symbol of the soul, with buddhic, mental, astral, and physical bodies which give openings of perception on the respective planes.

See DOORS, QUATERNARY, TET, VESTURES, WOODEN.

HOUSE OF A MAN :—

Symbolic of the state into which the mind or soul is brought through its own efforts. It is the mental environment to some extent. It is also the whole external aspect of the spiritual ego. Each room may signify a plane.

See ROOM IN A HOUSE.

HOUSE, CLAN, TRIBE, AND COUNTRY :—

Symbols of the four bodies, or

sheaths of the soul, on the four planes of the quaternary.

"O Homa! thou lord of the house, lord of the clan, lord of the tribe, lord of the country, thou successful physician ! I further invoke thee for strength and prosperity for my body, and for the attainment of much pleasure."—*Homa Yasht,* verse 27, HAUG, *Essays.*

The Supreme Self is Lord of the physical-body, Lord of the astral-body, Lord of the mental-body, and Lord of the causal-body. The "successful physician" is the Self under the aspect of Love. The Supreme Self is invoked for the purpose of granting the fulfilment of all right aims and good wishes upon the lower planes of the soul's activities, that so the true and lasting joy of the Spirit be attained.

See CASTES, CLASSES, HEALING, RULERS (world), SERPENT, ÆSCULAPIUS, TRIBE-RULERS, VESTURES.

HOUSE-RULER :—

A symbol of the sense-nature operating from a physical centre or centres in the human brain.

"The progress which is in the Ahunavaiti Gatha the house-rulers should carry on."—*Shayast La-Shayast,* Ch. XIII. 15.

The development of soul occasioned through the instrumentality of the physical body is due to the rule of the senses which arouse and inform the mind.

See GATHA (ahun.), RULERS (world), TRIBE-RULER.

HOUSE TO SLEEP IN :—

A symbol of ideal form or mode in which the Spirit withdraws from manifesting itself.

"Now when the bright light of the sun was set, there went each god to his house to sleep, where each one had his palace made with cunning device by famed Hephaistos the lame god."—*Iliad,* Bk. I.

Now when the cycle terminated, and pralaya supervened, each aspect of the Self returned to a quiescent condition—for which, however, the form, or mode, was provided, that is, nothing was extinguished. In every case the Creative Mind (Hephaistos) had called into being that which was to endure eternally.

See HEPHAISTOS, MANSIONS, PALACE, PRALAYA, SLEEP, SUN-SETTING.

HOUSEHOLDER (HIGHEST ASPECT) :—

A symbol of the First Logos or Supreme Self.

"The kingdom of Heaven is like unto a man that is a householder, which went out early in the morning to hire labourers into his vineyard."—MAT. xx. 1.

The First Logos, ruling on the higher planes, is as one who goes forth under many aspects, and calls all the forms of His own life within his universe, to discharge their appointed tasks in the arena of existence.

See JUSTICE, KINGDOM OF HEAVEN, LABOURERS, MONEY, PARABLE, STEWARD, VINEYARD, WAGES.

HOUSEHOLDER :—

A symbol of the Individuality, or causal Self, who occupies the " house " or causal-body on the higher mental plane.

"As all rivers, both great and small, find a resting place in the ocean, even so men of all orders find protection with householders."—*Laws of Manu*, VI. 90.

The "men of all orders" are the egos in four stages of consciousness on the mental plane, centred on various sub-planes. These are periodically withdrawn into the causal-body from which they are again emanated by the Individuality when manifestation is due.

See ARHATS, ASCETIC, ASRAMAS, CAUSAL, DWELLING (palace), FOREST, HERMIT, ORDERS, OVERSEER, SELF, SNATAKA.

HOUSES FOR CORPSES :—

The three houses for the dead bodies of Parsis are symbolical of the physical, astral, and mental bodies which have contained the personality (corpse) and which afterwards gradually disintegrate on their respective planes. The flesh-eating birds of the Dakhma stand as symbols of the rulers of the planes.—*See* EZEK. xxxix. 4.

See BIRDS (lower), CORPSE, DOG (white), TEMPLE (fire), VULTURE.

HOUSES OF BUDDHA'S FRIENDS :—

Symbolic of centres of energy spiritually organised on the mental plane.

"Then they brought Buddha as presents from the houses of his friends costly unguents of sandal wood, etc."—*Buddha-Karita*, Bk. II. 21.

The giving of gifts is comparable to the joy which is brought to the Self from the preliminary experiences which precede its evolution. The "houses of his friends" are the connections which are established on the mental sub-planes between the centres of the mental mechanism. The statement signifies the organising of the mental functioning by the Devas (friends) of the buddhic plane. The "unguents" are the rewards accruing for righteous acts. Love (oil) is its own reward, i.e. increased power and opportunity for well doing.

See BUDDHA, DEVAS, FRIENDS, OIL, OINTMENT, UNGUENTS.

HUITZILOPOCHTLI, WAR-GOD :—

A symbol of the indwelling Higher Self as the opponent and conqueror of the desires.

"His mother, Coatlicue, a devout widow, on entering the Temple of the Sun one day for the purpose of adoring the deity, beheld a ball of brightly coloured feathers fall at her feet. Charmed with the brilliancy of the plumes, she picked it up and placed it in her bosom with the intention of making an offering of it to the sun-god. Soon afterwards she was aware of pregnancy, and her children, enraged at the disgrace, were about to put her to death when her son Huitzilopochtli was born, grasping a spear in his right hand and a shield in his left, and wearing on his head a plume of hummingbird's feathers."—L. SPENCE, *Mythologies of Mexico, etc.*, p. 14.

The purified lower nature (mother of God) aspiring to the Highest, receives to her heart the Divine germ as that which is supreme (plumes) over the lower nature. Then the desire-mental activities, progeny of the unpurified lower nature, seek (like Herod) to kill out the higher nature ; but this they are unable to do, so the Divine Child is born in the soul, fully endowed with spiritual power (spear) and will (shield), and taking supremacy (crown) over all.

See BIRTH OF CHRIST, CRANBERRY, CROWN, HEROD, MARJATTA, PLUMES, SEED, VIRGIN MARY.

HUMAN BODY :—

Symbolically considered, the different parts of the human body are correspondentially related with the

higher centres, and it is through these centres on the higher planes the soul-nature is developed.

See ARC. MAN, BRIDGES (nine), CITY, COUNTENANCE, GATES OF BODY, HEAD, HEART, KHEPER, NAVEL, PINEAL GLAND, PRAGÂPATI, PURUSHA.

HUNGER :—

A symbol in the higher aspect, of a longing for truth and goodness as the "bread of heaven,"—the soul's sustenance ; and in the lower aspect, of a desire for externalities which cannot satisfy.

"Hunger signifies deprivation and rejection of the knowledges of truth and good arising from evils of life ; it also signifies ignorance of the knowledges of truth and good arising from a deficiency thereof in the church ; and it signifies likewise a desire to know and understand them."—SWEDENBORG, *Apoc. Rev.*, n. 323.

"Hunger is a cloud which rains down naught but wisdom." "None can worship rightly so he be not hungry" (Aphorisms of Sufi Saints).—BROWNE.

"It is this hunger for God, this unsatisfied yearning of the soul for union with its true centre, which is the dynamic of all the restless strivings of our complex modern civilisation. The world may not know it, but it is so ; we may be feeding upon husks instead of the bread of life, but it is the bread of life we want all the time."—R. J. CAMPBELL, Serm., *Our Quest for God.*

"These things that seem to be you are not you. The real you is that which feels hungry for something better than you have ever found yet, or than the things of the outer world can supply."—R. J. CAMPBELL, Serm., *Coming to the True Self.*

"For he (the Lord) satisfieth the longing soul, and the hungry soul he filleth with good."—Ps. cvii. 9.

"Blessed are they that hunger and thirst after righteousness for they shall be filled."—MAT. v. 6.

See BALDER, BREAD, CLOUD, FOOD, SACRAMENT, TEMPTATION, THIRST.

HUSBAND AND WIFE :—

Symbols of mind and emotion, or the mental-nature and the emotion-nature indissolubly united within the soul.

"Wives be in subjection unto your own husbands, as unto the Lord. For the husband is the head of the wife, as Christ also is the head of the church, being himself the saviour of the body."—EPH. v. 22.

The emotions must be ruled and regulated by the mind in its higher ranges of thought. For the mind is the intelligence wedded to emotion, as the Self is wedded to the soul, and become the transmuter of the body of desire.

See BISHOP, CHRIST, CHURCH, CONCEPTION OF CHILDREN, DIVORCE, MAN AND WIFE, MARRIAGE, WIFE, WILDERNESS, WOMAN.

HUSBAND, GOOD AND RICH :—

A symbol of the Spirit of goodness and truth to which the soul aspires.

"Homa grants a good and rich husband to those who have long been maidens, as soon as he (Homa), the wise, is entreated."—*Homa Yasht.*

The Supreme grants the fulfilment of those dearest wishes for "the fullness of him that filleth all in all," which are to be satisfied only through the abstinence and self-denial which are the means of rendering the soul responsive to higher joys.

See HOMA, NALI-KUVERA, RICHES (higher), WEALTH.

HUSBANDMAN :—

A symbol of the Higher Self as the tiller and sower of the lower nature (earth), so that it should bring forth a harvest of the "fruits of the Spirit" on the buddhic plane.

"The Lord is wise and forgetteth not : He is true and a great husbandman. He first prepareth the ground, then soweth the seed of the true Name. From the name of the one God the nine treasures are produced, and man obtaineth the marks of His favour" (Hymn of Guru Nanak).—MACAULIFFE, *The Sikh Religion*, Vol. I. p. 263.

"Behold a very fair and most resemblant image,—a husbandman casting the seed into the ground ; here wheat, there barley, and there again some other of the seeds. Behold one and the same man planting the vine, the apple, and other trees. In just the self-same way doth God sow Immortality in Heaven, and Change on Earth, and Life and Motion in the Universe."—MEAD, *Hermes to Asclepius*, § 10.

See AGRICULTURALIST, FIELD, INTOXICATION, JASON, KNOWER, PLOUGHING, REAPING. SEED (good), SOMA (moon), SOWER, VINE, WHEAT.

HUSKS :—

Symbolic of low objects of desire and sensation, devoid of the kernel of truth and goodness.

"And he went and joined himself to

one of the citizens of that country ; and
he sent him into his fields to feed swine.
And he would fain have been filled with
the husks that the swine did eat : and
no man gave unto him."—LUKE xv. 15, 16.

The emotion-nature finding no
longer delight in those things which
at first gave him pleasure, he hungered
for that towards which his evolution
was now directed. And he then
allied himself with the worldly wisdom
which corresponds to all that is
depraved, unclean, and unfit for the
kingdom of heaven. And he would
willingly have fed upon the food
which these lower instincts and desires
partook of ; but no mental quality
gave unto him, nor could this food
satisfy.

"So sure as you allow the lower to
master the higher, so sure will you have
to find out your mistake. Your spirit
cannot satisfy itself with the husks that
the swine eat, for it craves the bread of
God."—R. J. CAMPBELL, Serm., *Coming
to the True Self.*

See CALF, DANCES, FIELD, HUNGER,
PRODIGAL, SWINE.

HUT, OR TENT :—

A symbol of the mental body, or
vehicle of the lower mind.

See BOOTHS, TABERNACLE, TENT.

HVANIRATHA OR KHVANIRAS :—

A symbol of the Earth,—the physical globe in the planetary chain of
seven globes.

"I (Zaratusht) call upon the region
of Qaniratha the splendid ; this they
(the Gâthas) assert as they are stationed
in this one (of the seven regions)."—
Vendidad, XIX. 39 (129) ; HAUG, *Essays*,
p. 389.

The incarnate Self acclaims the
Earth planet as presenting conditions
of life and experience very conducive
to the growth of the soul. The inner
spiritual vibrations (Gâthas) from the
buddhic plane to raise the soul are
operative in the minds of those who
are living the physical life on earth.

See KARSHVARES, PLANETARY CHAIN,
REGIONS, RENOVATION, SOSHYANS.

HVERGELMIR FOUNTAIN :—

A symbol of life on the lower planes,
of illusion and separateness.

"Many ages before the earth was made
Niflheim was formed, in the middle of
which lies the spring called Hvergelmir,
from which flow twelve rivers."—*Prose
Edda.*

These are the twelve divisions of
the cycle (Zodiac).

See FOUNTAIN (deep), NIDHOGG,
NIFLHEM, YGGDRASIL.

HYLAS, AN ARGONAUT :—

A symbol of unbiassed search into
the truth of things.

"Hylas, a youth beloved by Hercules,
having gone for water in Mysia, was
laid hold of and kept by the nymphs of
the spring into which he dipped his
urn."—*Argonautic Expedition.*

Impartial investigation (Hylas), in
concord with the terror aspect of Divine
Will (Hercules), having undertaken to
search for truth (water) in the realm
of pure intellect (Mysia), was forced
to quail before the allurements of
metaphysical speculation (the nymphs),
as the effort was made to acquire
truth.

See HERCULES, NAIADS, PITCHER,
VESSEL, WATER.

HYMN-SINGING :—

A symbol for aspiration through
harmony and the uplifting of the
nature towards Truth, Wisdom, and
Love.

"So all day long worshipped they the
gods with music, singing the beautiful
pæan, the sons of the Achaians making
music to the Far-darter, and his heart
was glad to hear."—*Iliad*, Bk. I.

So "all day," i.e. during the outpouring of Life on the upper planes,
the Higher Self was adored with
"music," the expression of the spirit
of harmony. The Sons of Mind,—
the spiritual egos,—were then attuned
to the inspiration of the Self, and
response was made.

"The world of the word is to the
Indian another microcosm. In the
rhythm of the sacred song he hears the
echoes of the universe resound."—OLDEN-
BERG, *Buddha, etc.,* p. 27.

"The name for heaven is *Garôdemana*
(Garotman in Persian), 'house of hymns,'
because the angels are believed to sing
hymns there, which description agrees
entirely with the Christian idea as founded
on Isaiah vi. and the Revelation of
St. John."—HAUG, *Essays on Rel. of
Parsis*, p. 311.

See APOLLO, BIRTH OF OSIRIS,
CARPENTER, GARODMAN, GATHAS
(chanting), GODS, HARMONY, HEAVEN,
MELODY, MOUNT OF OLIVES, MUSIC,
SINGERS, SONG

HYMNS, TWO PRAISE :—

Symbolic of the paths of ideal attraction and of moral coercion, or of action and of meditation upon truth.

"Thereupon answered me Homa the righteous, who expels death. Address prayers to me, O Spitama ! (Zoroaster) and prepare me the Homa juice for tasting. Repeat about me the two praise hymns, as all other Soshyants repeated them."—*Homa Yasht.*

The Divine Life (Homa) which now appears as eternal, and is distinguished from the vitality of the form, makes answer, that in the functioning of the soul's Divine life (Homa-juice), aspiration is to be made, and the sacrifice of the lower is to be offered to the ideal now before the soul. The invocation of the Divine nature is to take a two-fold form, the " hymns " being the paths of Love and Duty, or Works and Wisdom. The " Soshyants " signify the pilgrim egos who must traverse the self-same paths to bliss.

See HOMA-JUICE, PILGRIM, SOSHYANTS, WAY OF THE LORD, WORKS AND WISDOM, ZOROASTER.

HYPERION, SON OF URANUS AND GE :—

A symbol of the Higher Self, or Consciousness, proceeding from Spirit and Matter.—Divine Love.

See GE, TITANS, URANUS.

HYPSIPYLE, DAUGHTER OF THOAS :—

A symbol of philosophic pride, produced by the germ of truth contained in forms of thought.

See EUNEUS, LEMNOS, THOAS.

HYRCANIA HEIGHTS :—

A symbol of the formless levels of the upper planes.

See HEIGHT.

HYRROCKEN, THE GIANTESS :—

A symbol of terror, fear, and cunning, which are activities on the lower plane of the mind.

"Hyrrocken went to the prow of the ship of Balder, and with one shove pushed it off, so that fire sprung from the underlaid rollers, and the whole earth shook."—*Story of Balder, Prose Edda.*

And now the emotion of terror takes possession of the mind, and in this way its evolution in the soul commenced ; corresponding with which the desire-nature is augmented, while to the physical body are communicated thrills which answer to increased responsiveness in the newly awakened astral centres.

See BALDER, BERSERKS, DEATH OF BALDER, EARTHQUAKE, FIRE, MJOLNIR, SHIP.

IABRAŌTH AND ADAMAS :—

Symbols of the Divine principle and the lower principle, each ruling six out of the twelve divisions of the cycle of life. The six æons ruled by the Divine principle are represented by the six signs of the Zodiac above the lowest point, or first point of Libra. This path corresponds with the ascent of the Christ (sun) who triumphs in the sign Pisces,—emblem of the Saviour,—wherein the two (fish), the higher and the lower Selves, become One.

"The six Æons under Iabraōth have repented and practised the mysteries ef Light, and have therefore been carried by Ieou to a pure atmosphere near the light of the Sun."—"*Books of the Saviour*," *Pistis Sophia.*

In the ascending cycle the qualities become purified. "Ieou" stands for the higher Triad which carries the risen or transmuted activities into the Higher Self (sun).

See ADAMAS (lower), ÆONS (twelve), EVOLUTION, FISH, HOUR (mid-day), I E O U, INVOLUTION, LIBRA, LIGHT, MYSTERIES, PISCES, SUN, TRIAD, ZODIAC.

"I AM" :—

A symbol of the self-conscious "I" of the Self, reflected on the plane of the mind as the individuality enthroned in the causal vehicle.

"For ' I am ' is my rest in His seasons ; even he who when He manifests His plan, the Company of the Gods become His firstborn children."—*Book of the Dead*, Ch. CX. (trans. Blackden).

The "I am" is the true Individuality which is arrived at only as the cycles (seasons) are seen to be illusory and impermanent. The Individuality persists ; for even the Logos, when he first determines the emanating of a universe, requires the help of the Builders, or Devas and Archangels, who become " his first-born children," that is, come forth first in order to do his will.

(The " I am I " feeling is produced through the forthpouring of the Divine life-consciousness into the forms which are temporary conditions and set limits for a time to the consciousness. The consciousness itself is one, but in the forms it appears as many. The apparent breaks are due to the illusory limits of the forms.)

See AHANKARA, APES, ARCHANGELS, BUILDERS, CAUSAL-BODY, COMPANY (gods), CONSCIOUSNESS, COSMOS, CREATION, DEVAS, FORMS, INDIVIDUALITY, PERSONALITY, SEASONS, SEPARATION.

" I AM,"—THE BULL :—

The " I am " is the sign of the " Bull " which is the positive, active, principle of Buddhi, the " Cow " being its negative, receptive aspect.

"For ' I am ' is that God, even the Bull, the Lord of Gods, when he setteth forth in the Blue Heaven."—*Book of the Dead*, Ch. CX.

The true and One Self is symbolised by the " Bull " (Atma-buddhi), the Lord of the Divine attributes which are set forth in the celestial regions, or "kingdom of heaven," when the Self attains the zenith of his powers at the end of the cycle.

"The Bull is a symbol of the Sephirah Hesed, i.e. Grace or Mercy—the spiritual Water or humidity : hence Baptism."— I. MYER, *Qabbalah*, p. 229.

The Sephirah Hesed signifies the Individuality or Higher Self, the Spirit of Truth (water). It is truth that purifies, and frees the soul from ignorance and evil,—in the meaning of " baptism."

See BAPTISM, BLUE HEAVEN, BULL, COW, GODS, HESED, KINGDOM OF HEAVEN, SEPHIROTH, SUN (motionless), WATER, ZENITH.

I A O,—THE NAME :—

A symbol of the Higher Self in manifestation.

I, the Pleroma hath gone forth ;
A, they shall return within ;
O, there shall be an end of ends.
—" *Books of the Saviour*," *Pistis Sophia.*

I stands for the going forth of the Divine Life into manifestation. It is a symbol of individuation, identity, and separation from the parent source.

A signifies the duality in the manifest, denoted in the sex principle, force-matter, active-passive, and expressed by the two sloping lines converging to a point and united by a line, thus introducing the idea of higher and lower, through experience of which, union of the *perfect* with the *perfected* is attained.

O stands for the circle which comes after and includes the other signs, and so typifies the all-embracing principle, sexless, perfect and entire, wanting nothing, Absolute, without beginning or end, first or last.

See ALPHA, CIRCLE, COMING FORTH, GOING IN, HIGHER AND LOWER, PLEROMA.

IBIS, A MARSH AND WATER BIRD :—

A symbol of the higher mind above the lower mind and astral nature.

" Horapollo tells us that the ibis was the symbol of Thoth as the ' master of the heart and reason in all men.' "— MEAD, *T. G. Hermes*, Vol. I. p. 48.

" Thoth " is a symbol of the principle of the higher mind, and therefore ruler of the causal-body and intelligence in the soul.

See BIRD, CAUSAL-BODY, HEART, HERMES, JUDGMENT HALL, MARSH, THOTH, WATER (lower).

ICE, FROST, OR SNOW :—

A symbol of latent truth (water), or truth unmanifest. A state of inertness of matter from which the life is not arising. It may indicate a period of pralaya.

" He casteth forth his ice like morsels : who can stand before his cold ? He sendeth out his word and melteth them : he causeth his wind to blow, and the waters flow."—Ps. cxlvii. 17, 18.

After pralaya comes an outpouring of the Divine Life (word).

" Not until the frozen Crust is broken, and the ice melts once more into the stream, and the hardened ground is crumbled into the general system of the soil again : not until then can power and influence easily find their way in and permeate the whole. Is not the parable plain ? Can we not recognise how that which takes place in the lake or on the roadside takes place also in the ordinary intellectual and moral life of man. Out of the very substance of a man's life, out of the very stuff of what he is and does, comes the hindrance which binds itself about his being, and will not let the better influences out. His occupations, his acquirements, his habits, his standards of action and of thoughts, make Crusts out of their own material, so that, beside whatever foreign barrier may stand between them and the higher food they need, there is this barrier which they have made out of themselves. That self-made barrier must be broken up, must be restored to its first condition and become again part of the substance out of which it was evolved, before the life can be fed with the dews of first principles and the rain of the immediate descent of God."—PHILLIPS BROOKS, *Mystery of Iniquity*, p. 156.

See BREATH (divine), DEW, FROST, PRALAYA, RAIN, SNOW, WATER, WIND, WORD.

ICHOR IN THE VEIN OF TALUS :—

A symbol of the lower consciousness which has its seat on the mental plane and is, as it were, a reflection of the spiritual ego—the real being within.

"But Medea, it is said, promising to make Talus immortal, persuaded him to let her pull out the pin (in the vein), which when she had done, the ichor all ran out, and he died."—*Argonautic Expedition*, KEIGHTLEY, *Mythology*.

Wisdom (Medea), however, by raising the lower mind (Talus) to its utmost, so that it is united with the higher mind, causes the lower consciousness (ichor) to be extinguished, it being illusion and separateness. The separate consciousness, then, is merged into the whole, and the lower self or personality is annihilated.

"From the clear vein the immortal ichor flowed. Such stream as issues from a wounded god."—*Iliad*, Bk. V.

See CONSCIOUSNESS, INDIVIDUALITY, MEDEA, PERSONALITY, TALUS.

IDÆA, DAUGHTER OF DARDANUS, AND WIFE OF PHINEUS :—

A symbol of the sense of the ideal, to aspire towards which is the spiritual outcome of the growth of experience ; and is allied to the reasoning faculty (Phineus).

See EXPERIENCE, PHINEUS.

IDMON, THE SEER :—

A symbol of the quality of faith, as intuition of Truth, and as perception of that which is imminent in evolution.

See BOAR (wild), FAITH, PROPHET.

IDOL-PRIEST :—

A symbol of the creed-bound, literalist mind, and the mental quality of subservience to ritual and ecclesiastical systems.

See CALF (molten), PRIESTS AND ELDERS, RITES, RITUAL.

IDOLATRY :—

A symbol of the worship of conventional and false ideas put in the place of the true, the beautiful, and the good.

"The superstitions of all religions—Catholic or Protestant, Christian or Pagan, Jew or Gentile—differ more in name than in reality. For there are idols of the mind which take the place of visible images : idols of tradition, of language, which come between us and God ; idols of the temple too, in which good and evil seem to be inseparably blended, and the good is near and present, and the evil is only recognised in some fatal but distant consequences."—B. JOWETT, Serm., *Image of the Invisible God*.

See PRIESTS AND ELDERS, TRADITION.

IDOLS :—

A symbol of conventional mental conceptions ; mistaken notions of the object of life ; fixed ideas which bar the way to Truth ; outward observances regarded as ethical or spiritual exercises ; unworthy objects of life.

See CALF (molten), GROVES, JEALOUS GOD.

IDOLS, GRAVEN :—

Symbolic of the objects of sense regarded as an end in themselves. "Idols graven in stone" signify the ideals inverted,—the mistaking of the shadow for the substance, due to the sense of separateness, and supposing the part to be the whole.

"Ashamed be all they that serve graven images, that boast themselves of idols."—Ps. xcvii. 7.

See SEPARATION.

IDOMENEUS :—

A symbol of the lower will as the principle of the desire nature.

I E O U :—

A symbol of the Higher Triad,—atma-buddhi-manas,—which apparently limits the lower quaternary which proceeds from it.

"The Six Æons under Adamas have refused the mysteries of Light. . . . They have accordingly been bound by Ieou in the Fate-Sphere."—"*Books of the Saviour*," *Pistis Sophia*.

The six divisions of the cycle of life ruled by the lower nature (six signs under Adamas) are those states of soul attached to things of the lower self,—those in whom the sense of separateness is not killed, and who are of the old dispensation under coercive law. These states have refused, as it were, to be led by Love upwards to the Truth. They have therefore had an apparent limitation imposed upon them by the Prince of Light, to remain under the law of karma. *Apparent* limitation, as obviously the lower cannot be the means of limiting the higher impulses. The allegory refers only to appearance and not reality.

See ADAMAS, FATE-SPHERE, IA-BRAÖTH, TETRAGRAMMATON, TRIAD.

IGNORANCE, *AVIDYA* :—

A symbol of matter as being of itself devoid of qualities, but which is the medium of Spirit, giving birth to the qualities. Ignorance is the negation of Truth or enlightenment, and it is by the influx of Spirit that enlightenment is brought about and matter (ignorance) dissipated.

"From Ignorance comes the combination of formations or tendencies (instincts derived from former births) ; from such formations comes consciousness (vijnāna) ; from consciousness, individual being (nāma-rupa, name and form) ; from individual being, the six organs of sense (including mind) ; from the six organs, contact (with objects of sense) ; from contact, sensation (vedanā) ; from sensation, desire (lust, thirst, tanhā = trishnā) ; from desire, clinging to life (upādāna) ; from clinging to life, continuity of becoming (bhava) ; from continuity of becoming, birth ; from birth, decay and death ; from decay and death, suffering" (*Mahā-vagga* I. 1, 2).—MON. WILLIAMS, *Buddhism*, p. 102.

From primordial matter arises on the buddhic plane the prototypal universe of ideal forms and qualities carried over from previous universes. From these ideal prototypes the potential causal-body is formed on the higher mental plane as the seat of the individuality (consciousness). From the causal-body, the mental body is projected in the lower mind

as the seat of the personality,—the actual (nāma) which builds up its potential higher body (rūpa). From the mental body come the means of perception on the lower planes. From the means of perception come the relations set up with the external world. From these relations comes the astral body (vedanā) in activity. From the astral body come desire, passion, appetite. From desire comes attraction to the lower life. From attraction comes detention of the ego upon the lower planes in a continuous life of evolution of qualities. From this continuous life come the periods of re-incarnation. From these come the struggles for life ending in death, which are attended with suffering and sorrow.

"But there is a taint worse than all taints, ignorance is the greatest taint. O mendicants ! throw off that taint, and become taintless."—*Dhammapada*, XVIII. 243.

"But if ignorance be removed by the complete extinction of desire, this brings about the removal of conformations ; by the removal of conformations, consciousness is removed ; by the removal of consciousness, name and corporeal form are removed ; by the removal of name and corporeal form, the six fields are removed ; by the removal of the six fields, contact (between the senses and their objects) is removed ; by the removal of contact, sensation is removed ; by the removal of sensation, thirst is removed ; by the removal of thirst, the clinging (to existence) is removed ; by the removal of the clinging (to existence), being is removed ; by the removal of being, birth is removed ; by the removal of birth, old age and death, pain and lamentation, suffering, anxiety, and despair are removed. This is the removal of the whole realm of suffering" (*Mahā-vagga*, I). — H. OLDENBERG, *Buddha*, p. 226.

But if matter (ignorance) be dissipated by the entire cessation of the outpouring of the Divine Life, this brings about the withdrawal of the ideal prototypes on the buddhic plane of the soul. By the removal of these prototypes, the causal-body ceases to exist. By the removal of the causal-body, the personality and its constructed ideal vanish. By the removal of the personality and its ideal, on the mental plane, the arena of perception on the lower planes is nullified. By the removal of perception of the lower nature, the relations with the external world are ended. By the removal of external relations, the astral-body is discarded. By the removal of the astral-body, longing for objects of desire is impossible. By the removal of this longing, attachment to the lower planes is severed. By the removal of attachment, the outer being of the soul exists not. By the removal of outer being, birth of the ego in the cycle of life cannot occur. By the removal of birth, its sequencies,—the wearing out of lives, the casting away of bodies, the passing through painful states of consciousness,—are extinguished. The inbreathing of the Spirit is the abrogation of the whole condition and extent of the bondage of Spirit in Matter.

"Sitting under the tree of knowledge Buddha says to himself : ' Difficult will it be for men to grasp the law of causality, the chain of causes and effects. And this also will be very hard for them to grasp, the coming of all conformations to an end, the loosening from everything earthly, the extinction of desire, the cessation of longing, the end, the Nirvâna.' "—*Ibid.*, p. 263.

"What keeps the soul bound in the cycle of birth, death, and re-birth ? Buddhism answers : desire and ignorance. Of the two, the greater evil is ignorance, the first link in the long chain of causes and effects, in which the sorrow-working destiny of the world is fulfilled."—*Ibid.*, p. 52.

The Higher Self (Buddha) realises the long and difficult course of the soul's evolution, and the slowness of the mind (men) to attain liberation from external attractions (desire) and the bondage of matter (ignorance).

"Matter has no intelligence of its own, and to believe intelligence is in matter is the error which produces pain and inharmony of all sorts ; to hold ourselves that we are a principle outside of matter, we would not then be influenced by the opinions of man, but held to the workings only of a principle Truth, in which there are no inharmonies of sickness, pain, or sin" (*P. P. Quimby MS.*).—G. MILMINE, *Hist. of Christian Science*, p. 129.

See BONDAGE, CAUSAL-BODY, CONSCIOUSNESS, DARKNESS (lower), EVOLUTION, FORM AND NAME, INVOLUTION, JERUSALEM, MONKS, NIDĀNAS, NIRVANA, ORIGINAL SIN, PROTOTYPES, RAHU, RE-INCARNATION, SAMSARA, SAMSKARA, SCAPEGOAT, SKANDHAS, SUFFERING.

IKA-TERE, THE FATHER OF FISH :—

A symbol of aspiration towards truth, which begets knowledge.

See FISH, PUNGA, RANGI, TANGAROA, TUTE.

ILIUM (TROY) :—

A symbol of the causal-body, the abode of the causal-Self, as a centre for the higher mental qualities and emotions. The personality (Achilles) is represented as seeking to capture the heavenly city by violence ; that is,—through the striving of the personality for perfection, the consciousness is raised to the higher mind, which involves the death of the personality.

"In the centre of the world was Turkland with its capital Troy. In this Turkland there were twelve kingdoms, and a chief king, who was Priam."—Preface to *Prose Edda*.

In the centre of the soul, or midway between the higher and lower planes, is the higher mental plane, with the causal-body, the seat of the causal-Self (Priam). On the higher mental plane are represented the twelve stages of the Life Cycle (Zodiac).

See ACHILLES, CAUSAL-BODY, CITY OF GOD, HELEN, MENIS, PERSONALITY, PRIAM, SHIPS OF GREEKS, TROJANS, TROY.

ILLUSION :—

An appearance devoid of reality in itself. The orderly succession of phenomena may be taken as proving the unreality of phenomena in themselves. They do not persist, and are interpreted in the mind as fleeting states of consciousness related to ideas and feelings of an impermanent nature.

"For all that alters is untrue ; it does not stay in what it is, but shows itself to us by changing into one another its appearances. . . . All that is subject unto genesis and change is verily not true "—(HERMES, *Of Truth*). MEAD, T. G. *Hermes*, Vol. III. pp. 20, 21.

" ' Brahma is true, the world is false, the soul is Brahma and is nothing else.' (N. N. GORE, 1862.) This is really a very perfect summary (of Vedanta)."—MAX MÜLLER, *Theosophy, etc.*, p. 317.

"Matter is darkness, as the Logos is light : it has no real being " (Plotinus),

—UEBERWEG's *Hist. of Philos.*, Vol. II. p. 246.

"The One who produced the 'Reality' is called Vohu-mano,—the Good Mind,—the other, through whom the 'Non-reality' originated, bears the name Akem-mano,—the Evil Mind."—HAUG, *Essays (Zoroastrianism)*, p. 303.

"The outward world, with the four Elements and stars, is a figure of the internal powers of the Spiritual World, and was expressed, or breathed forth, by the Motion of God. . . . It is as a smoking or vaporous steam of the Fire-Spirit and Water-Spirit; breathed forth, both out of the Holy and then also out of the *Dark* world; and therefore it is evil and good; and consists in Love and Anger; and is only as a smoke or misty exhalation, in reference and respect to the Spiritual World."—JACOB BOEHME, *Mysterium Magnum*, p. 20.

"Four astrums, elements, or properties of nature."—*Ibid.*, p. 58.

"The stars are nothing else but properties of the powers of nature."—*Ibid.*, p. 57.

Here, the lower quaternary is described as a reflection, or figure, of a pattern in the higher planes, becoming dual on the lower planes. The buddhic (Fire-Spirit) and the astral (Water-Spirit) commingle in opposition, causing strife, and educing the higher emotions (Love) and the lower (Anger). The lower world is unreal and illusory in respect to the higher world.

"This very capacity of ours for imagining a better world than this points to the fact that the Ideal World we desire already exists; our desire for it signifies, in a manner of speaking, that we already belong to it and that our souls can never find complete satisfaction in anything less. Indeed, it is the real world. This present world which seems to us so real, is both fragmentary and unsubstantial, and destined to pass away when it has served its purpose; behind and beneath it is the eternal world—changeless, perfect, all complete."—R. J. CAMPBELL, Serm., *What is Life Eternal?*

"The realm of the real is spiritual. The opposite of Spirit is matter, and the opposite of the real is the unreal, or material. Matter is an error of statement. This error in the premise leads to errors in the conclusion, in every statement into which it enters. Nothing we can say or believe regarding matter is immortal, for matter is temporal, and is therefore a mortal phenomenon, sometimes beautiful, always transitory."—MRS. EDDY, *Science and Health*, p. 277.

See BEELZEBUB, BRAHMA, CREATION, DARKNESS, ELEMENTS, FATE, FIRE, HIGHER, MATTER, MĀYĀ, MIXTURE, MOTHER, OGDOAD, PHENOMENA, PRAKRITI, PROTOTYPES, STARS, TYRANTS, UNBELIEF, VOURU-KASHA, WORLD.

ILYA TREE :—

A symbol of the Divine Life or Ray from the Absolute.

"He (the soul) approaches the tree Ilya, and the odour of Brahman reaches him."—*Kaush. Upanishad*, I. 2.

Free from all relativity, the soul approaches the Truth of the Divine Life which yields the fruit of Wisdom; and the "breath" of the Supreme invigorates his being.

"O taste and see that the Lord is good."—Ps. xxxiv. 8.

"How sweet are thy words unto my taste! Yea sweeter than honey to my mouth!"—Ps. cxix. 103.

"Plato 'keeps the faith' that the soul has in itself an eye for divine Reality, and that the mind has a native capacity for beatific vision. This doctrine has had mighty influence and is of vast import. The view which Plato's successors and the later mystics found in his teaching was rather an ultimate Reality 'beyond' the universe, and 'above' mind; 'beyond being' and 'above knowledge.' It is to be reached only by a sublime process which *negates* all finiteness; all multiplicity, all particularity. On this basis the Absolute Reality is nothing knowable or thinkable."—R. M. JONES, *Mystical Religion*, p. 66.

See ABSOLUTE, BRAHMA, BREATH (divine), FRUIT, ODOUR (sweet), SALAGYA, SUTRATMA, TASTE, TREASURE, TREE OF LIFE, VIBHU, YESHTIKA.

IMAGE OF GOD :—

This expression signifies a projection of the Divine nature on the two highest planes of the soul, and constitutes, when united with mind, the Archetypal Man energising as Love and Wisdom (atma-buddhi).

"And God said, Let us make man in our image, after our likeness: and let them have dominion over, etc. And God created man in his own image, in the image of God created he him; male and female created he them."—GEN. i. 26, 27.

At this stage of involution, the Divine nature projects a likeness of itself upon the highest planes. This is the Divine Ray or Spark, which is a direct emanation of the Logos,—Atma-buddhi,—dual, male-female, and consequently spoken of as *Us*. The two Divine aspects united, are essential to the making of Man as a spiritual being. The Love and Wisdom principles (Atma-buddhi) united in mind (manas), are to have dominion over the feelings, ideas, actions, and the entire nature, including the lower mental nature. And so the Divine Will caused to be created the Archetypal Man in the image (microcosm) of the Divine fullness (Macrocosm), as the dual expression of Truth-Wisdom.

"Man made after the image of God. This is the Word of God, the first beginning of all things, the original species or the archetypal idea, the first measure of the universe."—PHILO, *Works*, Yonge's trans., Vol. IV. p. 285.

"What is this image of God ? It is the mind of God ; for Christ is that Mind or Word to rule in us. The Man is Christ, the perfect mind of God. . . . This Man was created 'male and female,' that so he might be a perfect image of God. God is infinite Wisdom and Love : no image of Him would be complete which did not express both."—A. JUKES, *Types of Genesis*, p. 40.

"But All-Father Mind, being Life and Light, did bring forth Man co-equal to Himself, with whom He fell in love, as being his own child ; for he was beautiful beyond compare, the Image of his Sire."—*Pœmandres* (Hermetic), 12.

"This image of God, which is found in all men, may be considered under three aspects : first, as a natural aptitude for loving and understanding God, which belongs to the nature of the mind and is common to all men ; secondly, as actual and habitual knowledge and imperfect love, which is the conformity of grace ; and thirdly, as that perfect love and knowledge which constitute the image of God in a State of Glory. The first is in all men, the second in the just, the third in the Blessed. . . . The image of God in man is according to the Divine Nature and the Trinity of Persons, inasmuch as in God Three Persons exist in One Nature."—T. AQUINAS, *Comp. Summa Theol.*, p. 237.

"In every department of being, where the imperfect is found, the perfect pre-exists."—*Ibid.*, p. 129.

"As the soul is said to be of the breath of God, so it is said to be made after God's own image, even after the similitude of God. . . . This character the Holy Ghost, in the Scriptures of truth, giveth only of man, of the soul of man ; for it must not be thought that the body is here intended in whole or in part."—J. BUNYAN, *Greatness of the Soul*.

"The Platonists called Dionysus ' Our Master,' for the mind in us is Dionysiacal

and the Image of Dionysus."—PROCLUS, *Crat.*, LIX. 114, 82.

This may be explained in the words of Tauler, where he speaks of,— "the unseen depths of man's spirit wherein lies the Image of God."

"A conception which pervades the Midrash literature is that there is an ' upper ' and a ' lower ' Adam : a celestial man made strictly in the image of God, and a terrestrial man corresponding in detail to his archetype."—C. TAYLOR, *Sayings of the Jewish Fathers*, p. 70.

"Irenæus says, ' What we had lost in Adam, namely our possession of the image and likeness of God, we recover in Christ.' Adam, however, is humanity ; in other words, as all humanity is united and renewed through Christ, so also it was already summarised in Adam."—HARNACK, *Hist. of Dogma*, Vol. II. p. 273.

"Wisdom, Love, and Truth are the principle or image of God" (P. P. Quimby).—G. MILMINE, *Life of Mrs. Eddy*, p. 129.

"The soul who perceives himself to associate with God, will have himself the similitude of Him. And if he passes from himself as an image to the Archetype, he will then have the end of his progression."—PLOTINUS, *On the Good, or the One*, § XI.

"Because of the constitution of Man in Elohim's likeness, the Man, i.e. the Perfect, Primordial, Ideation Man or Adam, comprises (in itself as the similitude of Elohim) all things, and admits all things to settle (be contained or arranged) in it."—I. MYER, *Qabbalah*, p. 138.

"The Life-Force which speaks in the soul in the language of duty, truth, and love, must have been these things to begin with, or it could never have made us know them ; and the wiser and older grows the race the more plainly does the Life-Force speak of these. God and the Life-Force are one. To be in line with the Life-Force of the universe, to do the will of God, is to live in the spirit of the love that seeketh not its own. And he knows this best who gives himself for it most with unfaltering faith."—R. J. CAMPBELL, *Serm., Jesus and the Life Force*.

"As the Bird-life builds up a bird, the image of itself, so the Christ-life builds up a Christ, the image of Himself, in the inward nature of man."

"Observe the passive voice in these sentences : ' Begotten of God ' ; ' The new man which *is* renewed in knowledge after the Image of Him that created him ' ; or this, ' We *are changed* into the same Image ' ; or this, ' Predestinate *to be conformed* to the Image of His Son.' "—H. DRUMMOND, *Natural Law, etc.*, pp. 293, 310.

"That God is the true and supreme end of man we know by the simple fact that the end of man can lie only on true lines of himself, and all these lines lead directly and only to God. The end of his mind is Truth, the end of his feelings and affections is Love, the end of his will and activities is Goodness and Good : and the completeness and perfection of all these is God. No finite spirit, seeking and striving to be all itself, can will or conceive for itself anything short of the infinitely True, Beautiful and Good—infinite Wisdom, Virtue, Happiness—infinite Holiness, Righteousness, Life. *God, so far as we can know Him, is the Infinite, Eternal, Perfect of ourselves, as we are the finite, incomplete, and imperfect of Him.* If this is conceiving or creating God in our own image, I admit it and justify it. It is the only way and form in which we can know God at all."—W. P. Du Bose, *Constructive Quarterly*, March 1913.

"Manhood itself may be regarded as the product of countless æons of an evolutionary process ; but if the evolution is to be considered from this point of view, and subjected to the theory of reality, which the religious consciousness insists upon assuming, then the process is a divine procedure, and its product a divine creation. Man's evolution, for religion, is but God's way of making man in the divine image. The psychological truth involved in the assumption of an essential likeness between the two—a certain Oneness which accounts for the duality ; this is an assumption upon which is based the very existence of religion at all." . . . "Man makes God in man's image ; because God has made man in the divine image. Man as he becomes more fully man, more of a rational and free personality, more worthily and truly conceives of God ; but this is because God is himself making man more and more like God."—G. T. Ladd, *Phil. of Religion*, Vol. I. pp 347, 361.

"The great work of religion is to conform ourselves to God, or to unfold the divine likeness within us."—W. E. Channing, *Likeness to God*.

See Ab, Adam, Arc. man, Atzeel, Breath (divine), Buddhic plane, Cosmos, Creation, Creeping, Evolution, Fravashi, God, Good (light), Healing, Higher and lower, Imperial, Incarnation, Involution, Jesus (son of God), Macrocosm, Male-female (divine), Man and wife, Microcosm, Pleroma, Prototypes, Purusha, Salvation, Seal, Seed, Similitudes, Son of god, Soul (highest), South wind, Spark, Spermatic words, Sutratma, Tree of life, Trinity, Type, Tzelem, Worlds (five).

IMHETEP OR IMHOTEP :—

A symbol of the Higher Self manifesting upon the higher mental plane.

"The name of Imhetep signifies ' he who comes in peace ' ; the Greeks transcribed it Imûthes, and likened him to Asklepios. . . . He cured men of their diseases by means of medicine and of magic. He was generally regarded as a learned deity."—Wiedemann, *Rel. of Egyptians*, p. 139.

"Imhotep was reputed the first hierophant ; he it was who recited the liturgy of the dead, and the magic formulæ which restored health to the sick and raised the dead to life. (*Footnote.*) The office of Imhotep was to conduct the dead safely back to a second life."—Sayce, *Gifford Lectures*, p. 140.

The Higher Self from the beginning reveals His nature in the sacrifice of Himself. He is the way and means of salvation, that the lower qualities may be transmuted, and that the souls may be raised to the life immortal.

See Alchemy, Birth (second), Magic, Medicine, Physician, Serpent Æsculapius, Valmiki.

IMMORTALITY FORFEITED :—

The personality in identifying itself with its lower nature and the trials and sufferings which thereby come to it, is said to forfeit its immortality; for it is this lower personality which is mortal. The ego within, which does not so identify itself, remains unaffected, and is immortal.

"Isis nursed the child of King Melcarthus and fed it by giving it her finger to suck instead of the breast ; she likewise put him every night into the fire in order to consume his mortal part, whilst transforming herself into a swallow, she hovered round the pillar and bemoaned her sad fate. This she continued to do for some time, till the queen, who stood watching her, observing the child to be all in a flame, cried out, and thereby deprived him of that immortality which would otherwise have been conferred upon him."—Plutarch, *Isis and Osiris*, § 16.

The king is a symbol of the ego as governor of the astral or desire nature, and so his child signifies the personality nursed by buddhi (Isis). The wisdom (Isis) element now sustains the nascent soul and affords it the means of evolution through the stimulation of latent capacity by indication (finger), or suggestively, rather than by direct means. And whilst it was night, that is, unknown of it, all that in each stage was perishable in the soul was burned away through the buddhic functioning; whilst Wisdom herself, as the spiritual daylight broke, ascends as a bird upward. At length, however, the progress of Wisdom is arrested, inasmuch as the purification of the personality (child) is being accomplished with such pain and difficulty, that attention is directed through the reasoning mind (queen) to the sufferings, with the result that the ego identifies itself with the sufferings, which entails the forfeiture of immortality for the lower personality with its suffering, ignorance, and evil which are mortal.

"And the Lord God said, Behold, the man is become as one of us, to know good and evil; and now, lest he put forth his hand, and take also of the tree of life, and eat and live for ever : therefore the Lord God sent him forth from the garden of Eden, to till the ground from whence he was taken."—GEN. iii. 22, 23.

And now the Love-forceful aspect of the Logos, realising that the mind (man) is able to recognise the distinction between each of the many states of relativity; and that of the relative condition there will be begotten the pairs of opposites; directs that the descent into physical matter be accomplished, lest without the mind undergoing the experiential life beneath, absolute existence should again be claimed. So the mind is directed towards the lower plane activities whereof its own nature has been builded, and is required to develop and discipline its faculties and emotions.

"The true and fundamental selfhood of every human soul, best and worst, is the very life of God himself, though differentiated from the whole, and made over, as it were, in part at least, into the soul's own keeping. Therefore, you, the real you, deep down beneath the ignorant, suffering, sinful you, are eternal. You, the outer you, the mortal man, are of yesterday, and will be gone to-morrow; you, the spiritual you, the deathless you, are of that in which time is not, and will enter by and by upon the fullness of your glorious heritage in the living God."—R. J. CAMPBELL, Serm., *God's Life in Man.*

See ADAM (lower), BIRD, BUDDHI, EDEN, FALL, FINGER, FIRE, GROUND, HEEL, INCARNATION, INDIVIDUALITY, ISIS, JESUS MORTAL, JOB, MORTAL, PERSONALITY, SCENT, SHAI, SHORT-LIVED ACHILLES, SOUTH WIND, TREE OF LIFE.

"IMPERIAL REVERENCE" :—

A title signifying the acquirement by the individual monad or ego, of the attributes of the higher planes. It has the same meaning as "being made in the image of God."

"Having bestowed upon the Golden Personage the appellation,—'Imperial Reverence,' it informed him of the manner of creation ; of the divisions of the heavens and the earth ; of the Yang and the Yin ; of the separation of darkness from light ; and that all things were produced from an egg first formed in the water."—*Chinese Mythology.*

And now the truth of atma-buddhi-manas having entered through involution into the consciousness of the ego, the knowledge of the process of creation, of the higher and lower planes, of spirit and matter, of science, philosophy, religion, truth and negation, Self and not Self, etc., is made clear. And it is made evident that all things are first of all produced from a germ or egg,—the symbol of infinite expansion from the fount of Truth (water).

See EGG, HIGHER AND LOWER, HIRANYAGARBHA, IMAGE, MAN CRAWLED, MONAD, WATER, YANG.

INCARNATION OF SPIRIT :—

A symbol of the embodiment of Spirit in Matter, or of the Soul or Self in the lower nature (flesh). Involution of the qualities (spirit) is the process which precedes the express functioning of the Divine Life (the Self) upon the several planes of existence. Incarnation completes involution, and is the point where evolution commences. Incarnation is the completion of the Archetypal Man (Christ),—the perfect "image of God,"—or spiritual-human pattern within the soul. In the involution of the Self, Christ "sheds his blood," i.e. involves his life (blood). In the Self's evolution, "the blood of Christ taketh away all sin," i.e. the Divine Life welling up as an inner fountain, constantly brings Wisdom, Love, and Truth to the struggling souls

as they realise their deficiences and yearn for perfection.

"Schelling laid down the proposition, —the incarnation of God is an incarnation from eternity :—he understood under 'the incarnate Son of God' the finite itself in the form of the human consciousness, which in its contradistinction to the Infinite wherewith it is nevertheless one, appears as a suffering God subjected to the conditions of time." —D. F. STRAUSS, *Life of Jesus*, p. 432.

"May not the love which conquers the demon of selfishness, which raises the individual soul above the narrow world of self-interest, and in society transforms the natural struggle for existence into the endeavour to realise the moral solidarity of all men,—may not this love be rightly conceived as a supernatural power revealing itself as a divine all-attracting force in the souls of men, like the force of gravitation in the material world ? . . . Love is the fulfilling of the law, since it transforms the external compelling command into the free impulse and active force of the heart ; why then may we not perceive in love 'the incarnation of the divine Logos,' which was consummated not once only, but ever comes to pass where love unites the hearts of men and consecrates society so that it becomes the kingdom of God ? "—O. PFLEIDERER, *Early Christian Conception of Christ*, pp. 164, 165.

"Human nature did not begin to be with Adam, but existed forever in the eternal Christ. I hold, then, that the Incarnation was God's commentary on that verse in Genesis, 'In the image of God created He man.' Yes, 'from the beginning' there had been a second person in the Trinity,—a Christ, whose nature included the man-type. In due time this man-type was copied and incorporated in the special exhibition of a race. There it degenerated and went off into sin. And then the Christ, who had been what he was forever, came and brought the pattern and set it down beside the degenerate copy, and wrought men's hearts to shame and penitence when they saw the everlasting type of what they had been meant to be, walking among the miserable shows of what they were. . . . Suppose I find in Revelation this sublime truth, that the man-type for which I am so anxious has had an eternal existence as a part and parcel of the Deity ; that, however, this manifestation of it has been reached, there is manifest in every man the image of a pattern-life that is in God. Let me carry away from Revelation the supreme truth of the eternal humanity of Christ, and then my moral life, my reverence for the nature which I share, my high ambition after its perfection, all this is unimpaired. Let science show me my affinities with the lower life : a mightier hand points

me to my connections with the higher." —PHILLIPS BROOKS, *Mystery of Iniquity*, pp. 314, 316.

"God becomes incarnate through the eternal principles that underlie the *conscience* and the *affections* of man : in his reason and his faith, organised into character as intellectual light and noble love."—S. JOHNSTON, *Oriental Religions*, Vol. II. p. 77.

"Incarnation, then, is the ethical process by which the Divine Logos becomes one with a morally pure human person."—O. PFLEIDERER, *Develop. of Christianity*, p. 63.

"Man, conscious of inherent weakness, longs for union with God. In the incarnation, God and man become one. Man feels himself exposed to a strange fascination which attracts him towards evil and draws him away from God. In Christ he meets, baffles, and overcomes the personal agent of all temptation. Man feels that he is a slave to nature, over which a sure instinct tells him that he was destined to rule. In Christ he exercises that dominion, making all physical forces subservient to his will. Man fears disease, affliction, and bereavement. In Christ all sorrows become medicinal, and conduce to the perfection of our renewed nature. Man has two great foes—sin, and death, the penalty of sin. Christ crushes sin, and expels it from His dominions ; death He converts into the last best friend, the opener of the portals of eternal life."— F. C. COOK, *Aids to Faith*, p. 143.

"There can only be one reason why eternal spirit should ever consent to become imprisoned within material forms, and that is that its latent powers may declare themselves. Undifferentiated unity must become endless variety ; the unmanifest must split up to utter itself. There could be no such thing as a human soul if boundless spirit did not deliberately put some portion of itself in a ring fence, so to speak, that it may be cultivated and made to body forth its hidden riches. Every soul is thus a point through which the infinite expresses itself, declares a divine idea, absolutely separate and distinct from every other, though closely related thereto and destined to rich fulfilment in a wondrous whole which shall include all the good of all the race."—R. J. CAMPBELL, Serm., *God's Life in Man*.

"Birds and beasts, equally with ourselves, are the incarnation of an indestructible life whose greatest manifestations have yet to come, and the whole creation is a solidarity with man in the expression of the Divine Idea."—R. J. CAMPBELL, Serm., *Evolution of the Spiritual Man*.

"Christ is that perfect Humanity within us, from which man feels himself getting loose by sin, but to which he also feels that if he can only return and cling, he will once more be re-united to

God. The Incarnation is the supreme manifestation of this."—J. G. ADDERLEY, Serm., *The Symbolism of the Mass.*

" The Incarnation, which is for popular Christianity synonymous with the historical birth and earthly life of Christ, is for the mystic not only this, but also a perpetual Cosmic and personal process. It is an everlasting bringing forth, in the universe and also in the individual ascending soul, of the divine and perfect Life, the pure character of God, of which the one historical life dramatised the essential constituents. Hence the soul, like the physical embryo, resumes in its upward progress the spiritual life-history of the race."—E. UNDERHILL, *Mysticism*, p. 141.

" The suggestion of an Incarnation is the supreme potential excellence of human nature. The Gospel prohibits any doubt as to the moral competence of men to rise to the perfection exhibited in the Incarnate."—H. HENSLEY HENSON, *The Value, etc.,* p. 270.

See ARC. MAN, ATONEMENT, BIRTH OF CHRIST, BLOOD, CHRIST, COSMOS, CRUCIFIXION, EVOLUTION, FIRSTBORN SON, FLESH, GOD, HORUS, IMAGE OF GOD, INVOLUTION, JESUS (son), KRISHNA, LEMMINKAINEN, LOGOS, MATTER, OSIRIS, PRAGÂPATI, PURUSHA, QUALITIES, REDEMPTION, SELF, SON OF GOD, SPIRIT, UNION.

INCARNATION OF SOULS :—

The descent of the spiritual egos into human forms on the lower planes.

The Divine Monad (atma-buddhi), at a certain stage, splits up in a limited measure, as it were, into many monads, an enormous but limited number. Each of these spirits, sparks, or souls, is ready to incarnate in humanity when mind is attained. They become the deepest selves in every human being,—the immortal spirits in each. At first they are almost totally obscured by the activities of the desire and sense natures, but gradually the stimulation from without arouses the qualities and potencies latent within them, and man becomes not only a mental but a spiritual being.

" My God is my deeper Self, and yours too ; He is the Self of the universe, and knows all about it. He is never baffled, and cannot be baffled ; the whole cosmic process is one long incarnation and uprising of the being of God from itself to itself."—R. J. CAMPBELL, *The New Theology*, p. 35.

See ARC. MAN, ATMA, BUDDHI, COSMOS, CREATION, EVOLUTION, FALL,

FRAVASHIS, MANASAPUTRAS, MARUTS, MONADS, NAKEDNESS, REINCARNATION, SHEEP (lost), SONS OF GOD, SOUL, SPARK, VESTURES, WHEELS OF BIRTH.

INCENSE-BURNING :—

A symbol of the purification of the soul by the functioning of buddhi (fire), which transmutes the lower emotions into the higher. The perfume signifies the Love and Wisdom called forth on the higher planes, through the aspirations from below.

" The Egyptians burn for incense *Resin*, thereby rectifying and purifying the air by its virtue, and blowing away the corrupted exhalation naturally given forth by the body, because this perfume possesses a strong and penetrating quality."—PLUTARCH, *Isis and Osiris*, § 80.

" The burning of this sweet-smelling substance (incense) assisted in opening the mouth of the deceased and in strengthening his heart. . . . ' Incense hath been offered unto thee of the incense of Horus, and incense hath been offered unto Horus of thy incense.' (From papyrus.)"—BUDGE, *Egyptian Magic*, pp. 194, 202.

The Love and Wisdom (the incense) of the Higher Self (Horus) hath been bestowed in response to the soul's aspirations.

" Incense signifies worship from spiritual good which is the good of love towards our neighbour. What is signified by incense is also signified by the vials in which the incense is contained."—SWEDENBORG, *Apoc. Rev.*, n. 277.

" When the maidens were gathered together for the great king Ahasuerus, before they were brought to him into his royal presence, they were to be had to the house of the women, there to be purified with things for purification, and that for twelve months together—to wit six months with oil of myrrh, and six months with sweet odours, and other things, and so came every maiden to the king " (Es. ii. 9, 12, 13).—J. BUNYAN, *Greatness of the Soul.*

The oiling and spicing of the maidens signifies the raising and transmuting of the emotions to prepare them for union with the Higher Self (great king).

" In the tabernacle of Israel, day by day, there ascended from the altar of incense the sweet odour, which symbolised the fragrance of prayer as it wreathes itself upwards to the heavens."—A. MACLAREN, *Sermons, 2nd Series*, p. 33.

See CENSERS, EMBALMMENT, ESTHER, FIRE, FRANKINCENSE, HEART, KA,

MAGI, MUMMY, MYRRH, OIL, PROCESSION, SAVOUR, SPICES, VIRGIN.

INDIVIDUALITY :—

This term is taken in its highest sense as signifying the direct embodiment of the Self in the manifest, in which the Self for the time is limited to the mode of Its manifestation. The individuality, therefore, is the immediate manifestation of the Self's otherwise unmanifested Self. Regarded in relation to the myriad human souls, the individuality is the point at which we pass forth from the Higher Self wherein we are rooted and centred in unity within.

"He, the monarch of the Sākyas, of native pre-eminence, but whose actual pre-eminence was brought about by his numberless councillors of exalted wisdom, shone forth all the more gloriously, like the moon."—*Buddha Karita*, Bk. I. 14.

The Self as the individuality,—the essential One,—but whose actual power is ensured by the numerous modes of its activity upon the lower planes, shines forth all the more gloriously as it undertakes to manifest upon the planes of illusion as the personality (moon).

"There is one unborn being (feminine) red, white and black, but producing manifold offspring. There is one unborn being (masculine) who loves her and lies by her; there is another who leaves her, while she is eating what has to be eaten."—*Svetas. Upanishad*, IV. 5.

"The text must be interpreted in accordance with the context, and in harmony with a similar passage in the Chāndogya Upanishad : 'the red colour of fire is the colour of heat, white is the colour of water, and black the colour of earth.'"—A. E. GOUGH, *Phil. of Upanishads*, p. 204.

The feminine being signifies Buddhi functioning as goodness (heat) and truth (water) in the lower nature (earth). Buddhi produces the innumerable qualities of the soul, both higher (white) and lower (black). The masculine being is the Causal Self or Individuality who is united to Buddhi. The other being is the Personality who evolves under the influence of Buddhi, and when perfected dies and disappears while Buddhi transmutes the lower qualities to the higher planes.

"Christianity accepts the Platonic distinction between the higher and the lower self, and agrees with Plato that the higher self is born of influences which belong to the Eternal world, the supernatural source of truth and goodness. This law of growth through the clash and union of opposites runs all through the Christian experience. There is no self-expenditure (self-sacrifice) without self-enrichment, no self-enrichment without self-expenditure. . . . Anyone who tries to attain complete self-expression—to build his pyramid of existence, as Goethe put it, as an isolated individual, is certain to fail ignominiously. The self that he is trying to bring to perfection is a mere abstraction, a figment of his imagination. And conversely, any one who lived a purely external life, with no inner soul-centre to which all experiences must be related, would be nothing either. Our unifying consciousness is the type and the copy of all-unifying consciousness of God. Our individuality is a shadow of His."—W. R. INGE, *Paddock Lectures*, p. 87.

"The Rational Soul which rules over that which is under it, and comes to know the higher by means of the enlightenment given by the World-Spirit, is then the real Man—brought into existence, but as unmixed essence, as individual substance indestructible, immortal."—DE BOER, *Hist. of Phil. in Islam*, p. 142.

"Note clearly the unity of the Self. You individualised are but one being, though you do not yet know very much about the nature and potentialities of that being ; I individualised am another self of whom the same thing is true. And your Selfhood is in essence good, eternal, divine, because it is an expression of the very life of God ; so is mine ; so is that of all mankind. It is in the task of manifesting it that we have to a great extent gone wrong, and are conscious of discord and failure."—R. J. CAMPBELL, Serm., *The Self and the Body*.

See ADAM, ADAPA, ASVINS, BALARAMA, CONSCIOUSNESS, BIRDS (two), DEFUNCT, DIOSCURI, ENOCH, FIG-FRUIT, HIGHER AND LOWER, I AM, IMMORTALITY, INCARNATION OF SOULS, MANU, NOAH, PERSONALITY, PROMETHEUS, RUAH, SELF, SHRINE, SOUL (middle), SUDDHODANA, WALKING WITH GOD.

INDRA, THE THOUSAND-EYED :—

A symbol of the Divine Will, or steadfast devotion to the Highest through the higher spiritual qualities, all perceiving.

"By earnestness did Maghavan (Indra) rise to the lordship of the gods. People praise earnestness ; thoughtlessness is always blamed."—*Dhammapada*, Ch. II. 30.

"'Yonder Indra has been utterly

annihilated by the people when they saw the glories acquired by the Sakyas,' uttering this scoff, the city strove by its banners with gay fluttering streamers to wipe away every mark of his existence."
—*Buddha-Karita*, Bk. I. 7.

"Indra" is here a symbol of the higher spiritual qualities which are said to be annihilated by the lower qualities (people), inasmuch as power is transferred through the higher mental qualities (the Sakyas) to the lower planes of being. The Self in establishing itself upon the plane of the desire-nature appears to obliterate in nature all trace of the Divinity which is inherent within it.

See DEVAYANA, DEVOTION, DOOR-KEEPERS, PEOPLE, SINGERS, WATER (heaven), YAMA.

INFIRMITY, SPIRIT OF :—

An aspect of a spiritual quality exercised through the astral nature, and which has been misdirected.

"And behold a woman which had a spirit of infirmity eighteen years; and she was bowed together, and could in no wise lift herself up. And when Jesus saw her, he called her, and said to her, Woman, thou art loosed from thine infirmity."—LUKE xiii. 11, 12.

The indwelling Christ is teaching the qualities, when his wisdom attracts a contracted and well-nigh dead affection of the lower nature, i.e. a starved emotion. The Christ responds to the aspiration, and calls the emotion to a higher use, thus releasing it from its bonds and making its path straight.

See ASTRAL PLANE, HEALING (dead), JAIRUS, WOMAN.

INFIRMITIES OR WEAKNESSES PERCEIVED :—

A symbol of recognition of lack of completion or perfection in the manifestation of the qualities of the soul : the recognition being an aspiration for the grace of God to heal the soul.

See EVIL, GRACE, QUALITIES.

INITIATION OF AN EGO :—

A symbol of the introduction of an ego into a superior state with enhanced powers and wider activities. This introduction is operated from above, and can only be conferred when the soul is ready for it. The soul's evolution is accomplished through a series of successive stages of development. Each stage, each step, each advance, each growth in grace corresponds to an initiation, which is a spiritual leading forth to a fuller life. The mastery of each plane requires its initiation ; for the controlling of each soul-vehicle implies an initiation which confers powers and faculties sufficient to achieve success. The ego is to be conceived as obscured in the evolving soul and gradually expressing itself more and more. Each walk or stride forward implies the perfecting of the previous stage and then being endowed with fresh faculties and opportunities for their exercise, so that another stride forward may be possible.

INITIATIONS :—

There are two lines of initiations, a lower and a higher. The lower line refers to the perfectionment of the lower self,—the Personality, as it appears, or is expressed, regarded from below. The higher line is the expression of the Individuality in the causal-body,—the evolution of the "Lord from heaven," into which at length the lower Personality is absorbed, when the twain become One, and the final initiation is accomplished for this cycle.

Four higher initiations may be taken from the Christian and Buddhist scriptures, and compared together.

The Birth of Jesus from the Virgin is equivalent to the stage Srotapatti or Sohan (He who has entered the stream). This initiation is the entrance of the Christ-soul into the physical life—intent upon living it spiritually by consecrating it to noble and worthy Ideals.

The Knowledge disclosed by the child Jesus when he is said to discourse with the doctors is the equivalent to Sakridagamin (He who will receive birth, but once more). It consists in the arousing of the intellect to a perception of the Truth and the Life.

The Ministry of Jesus terminating in the Trial and Sentence is equivalent to Anagamin (He who will be re-incarnated no more). It is the high resolve to go through to the bitter end,—to drink the cup to the dregs in the three years (the number three signifying completeness).

The Crucifixion is equivalent to Arhat (He who sees Nirvana). It is the consummation of the physical life. The Christ-soul at this initiation has arrived at every experience which it is necessary he shall undergo.

"The lowest class is made up of the Srotâpanna, i.e. those who have attained the path (of sanctification). Of them it is said : ' By the annihilation of the three ties, they have attained the path ; they are not liable to re-birth in the lower worlds (hells, spirit worlds, and world of lower animals) ; they are sure (of deliverance) ; they shall attain the highest knowledge.' The next higher class is that of the Sakadâgâmi (' those who return once.') : ' By the annihilation of the three ties, by the suppression of desire, hatred and frivolity, they have become " once returning : " when they have returned once only to this world, they shall attain the end of sorrow.' Then follow the Anâgâmi (' the not-returning ') : ' By the annihilation of the five first ties they have come to be beings, who originate of themselves (i.e. who enter upon the state of being without being begotten or born ; this is the case of the higher worlds of the gods) ; they attain the Nirvâna up there (in the world of gods) ; they are not liable to return from that world.' . . . The highest of the four stages and last is that of the Arhat, i.e. the Saint."—H. OLDEN-BERG, *Buddha*, pp. 319, 320.

"Conduct corrects vice, meditation corrects lust, insight corrects error, Conduct is the virtue of the beginner (sotâgâmi), meditation of the advanced (anâgâmi), insight of the perfect (arhat)." —R. S. COPLESTON, *Buddhism*, p. 365.

See ADEPT, ANAGAMIN, ARHAT, ASEKA, ASRAMAS, BIRTH OF JESUS, CAUSAL-BODY, CONJUNCTION, CRUCI-FIXION OF JESUS, DEATH, EVOLUTION, FIELD, FOOTSTEPS, FORTUNATE, GOSPEL STORY, INCARNATION OF SOULS, INDIVIDUALITY, INTELLECT, JESUS OF GOSPELS, JESUS (severe), MAN (right-eous), NIRVANA, PATRIARCHS, PERSON-ALITY, REINCARNATION, SAKRIDAGA-MIN, SROTÂPANNA, STRIDES OF SOUL, UNION, VESTURES, WALKS.

INSANITY :—

The external expression of disordered conditions in one or more of the lower vehicles of the soul. Insanity is a general mental condition which proceeds from psychic instability, irregularity, or want of equilibrium. It is the result of inequable astral and mental activity, and may generally be traced to the ineffectiveness of the mechanism of the vehicles through which the consciousness, or ego, acts. Often, what amounts to insanity follows from a distorted or very partial reflection of the higher activities in the lower mind, and when these activities are very pronounced, there is found the want of balance which characterises the insane. In some cases mental disorder may be due to the intense automatic action of the mechanism of conduction of conflicting ideas. In cases of worry and trouble, the nervous mechanism is subjected to such strain as results in its being temporarily or permanently, dis-sociated, as it were, from the regulating factor which co-ordinates the mental activities in the normal person. In melancholia the related physical and astral mechanism is unable to function completely. Insane ideas arise from sub-conscious impulses,—many of them karmic,—and the reason why the reflective and comparing faculties are not operative on the delusions is that the true mind (higher manas) is temporarily detached from the opinionative lower mind (kama-manas). Direct mental action from above applied to the disused or infirm portions of the astro-physical, or astro-mental mechanisms, designed to remove the causes which obstruct the perfect performance of the mental functions, may sometimes be effective in opening up communication from above to below and restoring balance of mind.

See ASTRAL BODY, CAUSAL-BODY, MAN, MENTAL-BODY, VESTURES, VITAL AIRS, WORLDS (five).

INSIGNIA OF THE IMPERIAL POWER OF JAPAN :—

Symbolic of the spiritual endowments of the soul upon the mental plane (Japan).

"The Goddess Amaterasu proclaimed her grandson Ninigi sovereign of Japan for ever, and appointed his descendants to rule it as long as the heavens and the earth endure. Before starting for his kingdom he received from his grandmother the Three Divine Insignia, viz.—the Sacred Mirror, the Sacred Sword, and the Sacred Stone or Magatama."—*The Nihongi*.

The Wisdom Principle (buddhi) being the director of the evolutionary process, assigns to the Germ-Self on the mental plane the future sovereignty of the Soul in a series of stages, as long as the Cycle lasts. She is able at the outset to endow the Incarnate Self with the Causal-body (mirror), the Intuition of Truth (sword), and the Spiritual Ego (stone).

See AMATERASU, BODHISATVA, BUDDHI, CAUSAL-BODY, INCARNATION, MIRROR, MITEGURA, NINIGI, SHINTAI, STONE, SWORD, TAKE-MIKA.

INSPIRATION, DIVINE :—

This means the " breathing of the Spirit," or the " speaking of the Word," into the mind of man. The " Word " is the Divine expression of Truth from above, made possible of reception by the mind, when union between the mental and buddhic natures has been attained. Inspiration is given whenever there is a receptiveness towards the eternal theme of Truth, Love, and Wisdom, and, however the truths may be presented,—into whosesoever mind they may have been put,—the recognition of the Truths themselves in the sacred scriptures will furnish *the proof* that the scriptures are what they profess to be, namely, the utterance of the Holy Spirit from the buddhic plane. The scriptures are to be judged by their fruits, and by what they imply as suggesting conceptions of the inner life of the soul, embodied in symbols which provided a sheath for their perfect preservation through the ages of the past. The persons who received these buddhic communications, evidently understood but little of their meaning, but being profoundly impressed by the spiritual influx, earnestly gave them out to others, and in many cases set them down in writing.

Knowledge of the inner nature of humanity and of the soul's evolution, flowing down from above into the mind, can only find expression through the ideas that happen to be in the mind. Now these ideas are incompetent to express hidden mysteries ; but there are ideas of concrete facts of experience which offer analogies and resemblances to facts of the super-physical planes. These correspondences are utilised by the Spirit of Wisdom to serve as symbols of inward truths, and are woven into mysterious, absurd, and dramatic statements, to rivet the attention of mankind, promote enquiry into the meanings of the sacred symbols, and so raise the souls by means of the various religions established upon them.

The evidence in modern times relating to the phenomena of inspiration and automatic writing overwhelmingly shows that the objective and deliberative mind has no part whatever in the production of inspired statements. Yet the whole of modern Biblical criticism is founded upon the assumption that the sacred writings are " composed," " worked over," " altered," and " amended " by many minds ;—a process obviously destructive of Divine inspiration.

" Madame Guyon states in her autobiography, that when she was composing her works she would experience a sudden and irresistible inclination to take up her pen ; though feeling wholly incapable of literary composition, and not even knowing the subject on which she would be impelled to write. If she resisted this impulse it was at the cost of the most intense discomfort. She would then begin to write with extraordinary swiftness ; words, elaborate arguments, and appropriate quotations coming to her without reflection, and so quickly that one of her longest books was written in one and a half days. ' In writing I saw that I was writing of things which I had never seen : and during the time of this manifestation, I was given light to perceive that I had in me treasures of knowledge and understanding which I did not know that I possessed ' (VIE). Similar statements are made of St. Teresa, who declared that in writing her books she was powerless to set down anything but that which her Master put into her mind."—EVELYN UNDERHILL, *Mysticism*, pp. 78, 79.

" If God sends a message, he will choose the messenger. . . . We can all agree to the first step—that if man is not purely passive in receiving the message, it cannot escape the touch of human infirmity. The believer in verbal inspiration says that revelation is real, and therefore man's part is passive. . . . Some things the prophet could not understand if they were told him, and some that he does understand he will only understand in part ; for he can only understand them in terms of his own knowledge. He might no doubt be kept from error by a supernatural dictation overriding his human weakness as often as might be necessary ; and the believers in verbal inspiration had to suppose that this dictation was given."—H. M. GWATKIN, *The Knowledge of God*, Vol. I p. 179.

" We now know (from a study of telepathy) that, not merely are we bombarded unconsciously by stray thoughts from other minds, but that it is possible so to discipline the conscious mind that it may become a resonator to thought, even to a long series of precise impressions of words from beyond the threshold of consciousness. I could place my hand on a quantity of inspired writing which sounded without premeditation through the mind of one who belongs to the order of Illuminati."—J. H. COUSINS, *Address on Psychical Research.*

Inspiration is of many grades. Madame Guyon obviously did not receive *Divine* inspiration whose only known expression is in sacred symbols. Nevertheless her inspiration was submental and passively received by the objective mind in words chosen subconsciously, not consciously. The lower inspirations may have all the outward features of Divine inspiration ; therefore the one and only test of the Divine Word is the presence, in writings, of the specific symbolism which is the same in all inspired scriptures of the world.

" In accordance with what is said in 1 COR. ii. 14, the truth of the Scriptures must be ' spiritually discerned.' But what does this mean except that the inspired element is underneath the phraseology rather than in it." " If no conditions in the spiritual world can ever be communicated to men except through the use of material symbols or forms, and if these can never represent the conditions fully or adequately, nor to minds, differently constituted or cultured, in an exactly similar way, then different symbols or forms may be used, in different nations, for the purpose of expressing exactly the same truth or principle, and not only in Christianity, but in all these nations, they may be inspired."—G. L. RAYMOND, *Psychology of Inspiration,* pp. 154, 131.

" In his *Who is the Heir to Divine Things* (II. 52) Philo says : ' For a prophet says nothing of his own, but everything which he says is strange and prompted by someone else. . . . He alone is a sounding instrument of God's voice, being struck and moved to sound in an invisible manner by him.' Again, in par. 53, speaking of inspiration, he says : ' For the mind that is in us is removed from its place at the arrival of the Divine Spirit, but is again restored to its previous habitation when that Spirit departs ; for it is contrary to holy law for what is mortal to dwell with what is immortal.' Volz quotes several other passages, in which Philo speaks in the same strain. Interesting in this connection is the passage in Josephus, which runs : ' Thus did Balaam speak by inspiration, as not being in his own power, but moved to say what he did by the Divine Spirit ' (*Antiquities,* Bk. IV. Ch. vi. 5). In the same paragraph Josephus makes Balaam reply to Balak as follows : ' O Balak, if thou rightly considerest this whole matter, canst thou suppose that it is in our power to be silent, or to say anything

when the spirit of God seizes upon us ? For He puts such words as He pleases in our mouths and such discourses as we are not ourselves conscious of.' "—J. ABELSON, *The Immanence of God,* p. 256.

" The Scriptures were written by the Spirit of God, and have a meaning, not such only as is apparent at first sight, but also another, which escapes the notice of most. For those words which are written are the forms of certain mysteries, and the images of divine things. Respecting which there is one opinion throughout the whole Church ; that the whole law is indeed spiritual ; but that the spiritual meaning which the law conveys is not known to all, but to those only on whom the grace of the Holy Spirit is bestowed in the word of wisdom and knowledge."—ORIGEN, *De Principiis,* Preface.

" Let us notice, then, whether the apparent and superficial and obvious meaning of Scripture does not resemble a field filled with plants of every kind, while the things lying in it, and not visible at all, but buried, as it were, under the plants that are seen, are the hidden treasures of wisdom and knowledge."—*Ibid.,* Bk. IV. 23.

" ' All Scripture was held (by Origen) to be written " ab intus," *from the inward mystery,* and not " ab extra," with a mystical sense *put into it. In every case* the historical account is the rind or coating, the mystical meaning the essence of Holy Scripture, not the former *the* essential truth containing a mystical sense ' (Writer unknown)."—ST. GREGORY, *Morals on the Book of Job,* Vol. I. p. 13.

" Inspiration is the deepest question of our day ; the one which lies beneath all others. . . . It is this grand question of Inspiration which is given to this age to solve. Our subject will break itself up into questions such as these,—What the Bible is, and what it is not ? What is meant by inspiration ? Whether inspiration is the same thing as infallibility ? When God inspired the minds, did He dictate the words ? Does the inspiration of men mean the infallibility of their words ? Is inspiration the same as dictation ? Whether, granting that we have the Word of God, we have also the words of God ? Are the operations of the Holy Spirit inspiring men, compatible with partial error ? . . . How are we to interpret and apply the Scriptures ? " —F. W. ROBERTSON, *Sermons, 4th Series,* p. 298.

Replying to these questions seriatim. (1) The Bible is a revelation of Truth expressed in Divine symbolism ; it is not a human composition. (2) By Divine inspiration is meant a forthpouring of Ideas from the Holy Spirit (Wisdom-buddhi) into the mind of a selected person who probably does not apprehend the real meaning of the symbols in which the ideas take form. (3) The inspiration being Divine is infallible, but infallibility does not attach to the symbols, for they may be either correctly or incorrectly interpreted. (4) When God inspired the minds, he dictated the words, otherwise there could have been no symbology. (5) In the inspiration of the minds, the minds are receptive only, and the resulting words are not their words. Directly these minds resume activity, error clings to their words. (6) Dictation to a passive and receptive mind is an operation of Divine inspiration. (7) We possess the scripture words which have been Divinely selected from the contents of the minds, except where mistakes or alterations have supervened. (8) If inspired minds have correctly set down what has been Divinely dictated to them, there is no error so far. But it must be remembered that symbols can only be very partially suggestive of the truths they stand for. (9) The Scriptures have to be interpreted by a knowledge of the meanings and relations of the symbols, in accordance with a general knowledge of the scheme of existence, and of the origin of the soul and the process of its growth. These knowledges are inseparable and essential to interpretation, and seem hardly to be acquired except by attention to a great variety of scriptures.

"Doctrine is the vertebration of religion. Still it must be ever remembered that Christian teaching professes to be symbolical and an economy of divine things."—W. S. LILLY, *The Great Enigma*, p. 313.

"The same principle of symbolic language must be applied to all that lies outside our present human experience. The Bible begins with an account of creation and ends with an anticipation of the end of the world—things which lie outside our possibilities of present experience. Thus it begins and ends in pictures and symbolical narratives. I do not see that any Christian either can reasonably deny this or has any interest in doing so."—C. GORE, Bp. of Oxford, art. "The Place of Symbolism in Religion," *Constructive Quarterly*, March 1914.

See AMBAS, AXE, BOOK STUDIES, BREATH (divine), GOSPEL, HERMES (tris.), HOLY GHOST, KAYAN, KORAN, LOGOS, MYTHOLOGY, PAPYRUS, PARABLE, PEN, PRIESTS AND ELDERS, RAMAYANA, REVELATION, RITUAL, SACRED TEXT, SASTRA, SCRIPTURES, SIGN, SRUTI, THOTH, UPANISHAD, UR-HEKAU, VEDA, WORD OF GOD.

INTELLECT; INTELLIGENCE; REASON :—

The mental principle involves choice in uniting with, or rejecting, concepts of different kinds which are presented to it; and this choosing faculty introduces will which makes man (individuality) as God. It is the function of the intellect to disclose differences and perceive similarities, but unaided by intuition it can never show the perfect truth. Intellect, having this capacity for uniting with that which it perceives, becomes the formative factor in the soul, and as such, it tends to contract and limit that which it operates upon. It, therefore, requires an expanding influence, and this it finds in uniting with emotion which strives against its limitations. Originally, intellect and emotion were not in conflict, for they acted in accordance with the Divine law before the mind had come under the influence of the lower desires. Intellect beholding the good and true is instinctively drawn towards the ideal, and thus it causes the ego to evolve and finally attain to perfection. It is a regulating factor which must dominate the love-principle and emotion-nature, until perfect Truth becomes the ruler of the soul. It cannot of itself inherit the things of the Spirit, but when united with the intuition (buddhi) it produces love and truth. The intellect at first is unaware of the existence of a higher source of Truth, for it cannot conceive of that which is self-derived, and it falsely imagines that knowledge is only acquired through study of nature and history, and so borrowed by the senses from without. Afterwards it is able to perceive that the lower mind, with its changing opinions, is illusory and rooted in egoism and separateness, and then it is led to find out how the higher mental qualities shall uplift and transform the lower self.

"Religion alone reveals to us the connection of the intellect with God, its derivation from his wisdom, its nearness to his reason, its capacity of everlasting reception of his light of truth."—W. E. Channing, *The Perfect Life*, p. 187.

" At the apex of the intellectual powers of the soul stands the Reason."—*Aricenna*, De Boer, p. 141.

" The intellect, which is the principle of intellectual operation, is the form of the human body ; for that which is the principle by which anything operates is the form of the thing to which the operation is attributed. It is also evident that where the body lives, there the soul is ; and this life is manifested in living beings in various degrees according to its different operations ; for by the soul we are nourished, feel and move. Therefore that by which we understand, whether it be called the intellect or the intellectual soul, is the form of the body. For the nature of a thing is manifested by its operation, and understanding is the operation proper to man ; since it is by this that he transcends all other animals." —T. Aquinas, *Comp. of Summa Theol.*, p. 187.

" In the struggle (with Nature for knowledge, regarded), as the struggle of the Thinker, the intellect of man is rendered noble and its powers developed. The strengthening of spiritual powers by exercise has been often dwelt on, but this strife with doubt and darkness is especially ennobling because it gives us slowly the possession of the noblest ideas."—Stopford A. Brooke, Serm., *Lord, Increase our Faith*.

" In the Gathas we frequently find ' two intellects ' spoken of. In later Avesta writings, one of the intellects is called ' the original intellect or wisdom,' which we can best identify with the ' first ' in the Gathas ; the other is styled ' the wisdom heard by the ear,' which corresponds to the ' last.' Another name of the ' first ' is ' spiritual or heavenly wisdom.' Now we cannot be mistaken as to the meaning of these two intellects. The ' first intellect ' is not from earth, but from heaven ; not human, but divine. The ' last intellect ' represents what man has heard and learned by experience."—M. Haug, *Essays on Rel. of Parsis*, p. 310.

The " first intellect " is the intuition of truth (buddhi-manas) ; the " second " is the reason (manas) which acquires knowledge by means of the senses and experience. Or in a higher sense, the first may be taken as spiritual wisdom on the buddhic plane, and the second as the reasoning faculty on the mental plane.

See Aegaeon, Briareus, Hoa, Maishan, Manas, Mental, Talus, Tyrus, Will.

INTERCESSION WITH GOD :—

A symbol of the transmuting process of atma-buddhi,—the Holy Spirit,—by which intercession the qualities of the soul are raised to the higher levels of consciousness.—*See* Rom. viii. 24–8.

See Holy Ghost, Redemption, Saints, Transmutation.

INTOXICATION :—

A symbol of the stupefying of the lower nature by an influx of the higher nature for which it is unprepared.

" And Noah began to be an husbandman, and planted a vineyard : and he drank of the wine and was drunken."— Gen. ix. 20, 21.

The Self as the individuality is likened to a " husbandman," a cultivator of the " ground," or lower nature. The rearing of the grape is comparable to the gaining of experience, and the culture of the spiritual nature which, as it were, " intoxicates " the lower self and renders it for a time impotent.

" Enter into my heart and make it drunken, that I forget my wickedness and embrace Thee as my one possession ;— say to my soul ' I am thy salvation.' "— St. Augustine.

" ' Lord, tell me,' says the Servitor ; ' what remains to a blessed soul which has wholly renounced itself.' Truth says, ' When the good and faithful servant enters into the joy of his Lord, he is inebriated by the riches of the house of God ; for he feels, in an ineffable degree, that which is felt by an inebriated man. He forgets himself, he is no longer conscious of his selfhood ; he disappears and loses himself in God, and becomes one spirit with Him, as a drop of water which is drowned in a great quantity of wine. For even as such a drop disappears, taking the colour and the taste of wine, so it is with those who are in full possession of blessedness. All human desires are taken from them in an indescribable manner, they are rapt from themselves, and are immersed in the Divine Will. If it were otherwise, if there remained in the man some human thing that was not absorbed, those words of Scripture which say that God must be all in all would be false. *His being remains, but in another form, in another glory, and in another power.* And all this is the result of entire and complete renunciation ' (Suso, the *Book of Truth*)."—E. Underhill, *Mysticism*, p. 507.

" The true wine is that which containeth the true Name. . . . Man is known as properly intoxicated when he obtaineth a place in God's court " *Guru Nanak*.—Macauliffe, *The Sikh Religion*, Vol. I. p. 261.

"Some of the relatives of Krishna celebrated a festival in the Mountain Raivataka, to which both Arjuna and Krishna went. There they saw Balarama, elder brother of Krishna, in a state of intoxication."—MON. WILLIAMS, *Indian Wisdom*, p. 391.

At an auspicious occasion in the soul's progress, the higher qualities were assembled with the indwelling Self (Krishna) and the disciplined personality (Arjuna). "Balarama" signifies the Individuality, the same as "Noah"; and the "intoxication" means the quelling of the lower self which proceeds from the Individuality; the lower self being its partial and imperfect manifestation upon the lower planes.

See BALARAMA, BLANDISHMENTS, CRATER, DIONYSUS, DRUNKARD, GRAPES, HUSBANDMAN, NOAH, SATYRS, SILENUS, VINEYARD, WINE.

INTUITION :—

A buddhic function operating through the causal-body, bringing knowledge of reality to the intellect. It is the power of answering to the higher rates of atomic vibration on the planes above, and when united with intellect it gives birth to love and truth. The erroneous theories of the lower mind will not be got rid of until the intuition is recovered by the inner memory, and voluntary effort is made by the lower self to raise the consciousness to the spiritual understanding. The intuition is seen to be in its appropriate sphere when consecrated only to the highest ends.

"The true name of the child was Palestinus, or Pelusius, and the city of this name was built by the Goddess (Isis) in memory of him."—PLUTARCH, *Isis and Osiris*, § 17.

The true character of the mind is not the lower intellect, but the intuition whose abode, the causal-body, was fashioned by Wisdom (Isis), and this indeed is permanent.

"The highest truths are not those which we learn from abroad. No outward teaching can bestow them. They are unfolded from within, by our very progress in the religious life. New ideas of perfection, new convictions of immortality, a new consciousness of God, a new perception of our spiritual nature, come to us as revelations, and open upon us with a splendour which belongs not to this world."—W. E. CHANNING, *The Perfect Life*, p. 193.

"We ought to be able to spell out the attributes of God from what we see of them mirrored in the heart of man. After all, we could not reach 'From nature up to nature's God'; we could discover no spiritual correspondences between the outer world of appearance and the inner world of reality, between the lower or natural and the higher or supernatural order, if it were not for the fact that those correspondences are really within ourselves. . . . Paul declares that we have not been left without evidence in ourselves of the existence and the righteousness of God. There is a correspondence between our own nature and the eternal, and hence there is that in us which enables us to recognise and lay hold of God."—R. J. CAMPBELL, Serm., *Spiritual Correspondences*.

"A man has seen something he felt sure was true, and has then set to work to prove it. Knowledge flashes upon you sometimes you do not know why, and intellect may be a long time in confirming your intuition; something within you shoots straight to the mark and reason crawls after it. It is conceivable, there fore, that a state could be attained in which a soul would no longer feel itself hampered by ignorance or imperfection, but would see right into the heart of the deep things of God."—R. J. CAMPBELL, Serm., *The Super-Rational*.

"It is plain that as the genius of some philosophers is almost intuitive with regard to the secrets of nature, so there are other men whose feeling is intuitive with regard to the secrets of spiritual life. They know without proof, they need no authority and no evidence. They have no trouble of heart, but walk with God as friend with friend. But no one can tell how far previous education before they were born into this world may have given them that power."—STOPFORD A. BROOKE, Serm., *Lord, Increase our Faith* (1870).

See AN-RUT-F, BRIDGE OF GJALL, BRISEIS, BUDDHI, CHRYSEIS, FAITH, IRIS, KALCHAS, MAGIC, MEDEA, NEHEMAUT, PALESTINUS.

INVOCATION OF SAINTS :—

A symbol of reverence of the higher qualities by the lower.

See PRAYER, QUALITIES, SAINTS.

INVOLUTION AND EVOLUTION :—

These processes of life are the descent of Spirit into Matter and the ascent of Spirit therefrom. The first is the Divine Sacrifice, or the limitation of Spirit in forms; and the second is the Resurrection from the Dead, or the liberation of Spirit from captivity in matter.

" There is a raying out of all orders of existence, an external emanation from the Ineffable One. There is again a returning impulse, drawing all upwards and inwards towards the centre from whence all came " (*Plotinus to Flaccus*).— VAUGHAN'S *Hours, etc.*, p. 83.

The " raying out " is the involution into matter of all qualities and potencies, and the " drawing inwards " is the evolution of the same.

" Twofold is the truth I shall speak ; for at one time there grew to be One alone out of many, and at another time, however, it separated so that there were many out of the One. Twofold is the coming into being, twofold the passing away of perishable things ; for the latter (i.e. passing away) the combining of all things both begets and destroys, and the former (i.e. coming into being), which was nurtured again out of parts that were being separated, is itself scattered." —*Empedocles*, FAIRBANKS, 60.

A twofold truth is to be found in the World-process :—First, there is Involution, and then second, there is Evolution. For at one time, in one cycle, the many potencies have gone to compose the One Monad (the Archetypal Man) ; and subsequently at another time, in the following cycle, the One Monad by means of evolution, proceeds to actualise and differentiate, so that the many monads and potencies are brought forth from the One. Manifestation involves duality ; also the ceasing from manifestation. For the latter, —the indrawing (passing away),— both begets ideals enabling the Self to subsequently manifest, and also destroys the illusions of the lower mind : while the former,—the outpouring (coming into being),—the issuing forth from the Womb of Pain, in the separation of Spirit and Matter, —is also ultimately suspended as illusion vanishes.

In the San-khya philosophy, " There cannot be the production of something out of nothing ; that which is not, cannot be developed into that which is. The production of what does not already exist (potentially) is impossible ; because there must of necessity be a material out of which a product is developed ; and because everything cannot occur everywhere at all times ; and because anything possible must be produced from something competent to produce it. In the San-khya, therefore, we have a synthetical system propounded, starting from an original primordial ' eternally existing

essence ' called *Prakriti* (a word meaning ' that which evolves or produces everything else ')."—MON. WILLIAMS, *Indian Wisdom*, pp. 89, 90.

Prakriti at its origin is said to be identical with " Brahman the Supreme," and that its first production is *Buddhi*, followed by *Ahankara* and *Manas* or self-consciousness and mind. From the Absolute everything proceeds, but the process of manifestation is by involution of Spirit and evolution of the same, so that the Divine nature may be expressed.

" Matter in itself, as Anaxagoras represents it in the primitive state, before Spirit had begun to work upon it, can only be a chaotic, motionless mass ; for all motion and separation must come from Spirit. But matter must nevertheless contain all the constituents of derived things as such ; for Spirit creates nothing new : it only divides what actually exists. Conversely, Spirit is necessary, because matter, as such, is unordered and unmoved, and the activity of matter is restricted to, the separation of substances, because they are already supposed to contain within themselves all their determinate qualities."—E. ZELLER, *Hist. of Greek Phil.*, Vol. II. p. 383.

" It is because of this union (with Phanes) that Zeus is said to ' swallow' Phanes. For the creative Deity and architect of the sensible world must first imbibe the ideal and eternal types of things before he can fashion them forth into sensible shape. Thus Proclus (*Tim.* iv. 267) : ' Orphœus called God the Manifestator (Phanes) as manifesting the noëtic monads, and stored within him the types of all living creatures."— G. R. S. MEAD, *Orphœus*, p. 204.

The Second Logos (Phanes) is said to be contained by the First Logos (Zeus) in order that he (the Second, or Higher Self) should be replete with the prototypes of all things that are to be involved in matter, so that they may be fashioned forth afterwards by the process of evolution. It is from the mental plane that the intelligible type-forms of growth proceed.

" The single sense-and-thought of Cosmos is to make all things, and make them back into itself again, as Organ of the Will of God, so organised that it, receiving all the seeds into itself from God, and keeping them within itself, may make all manifest, and [then] dissolving them, make them all new again ; and thus like a Good Gardener of Life, things that have been dissolved, it taketh to itself, and giveth them renewal

once again (*Corpus Hermeticum*, IX)."—
G. R. S. MEAD, *T. G. Hermes*, Vol. II.
p. 133.

The Divine purpose in manifestation
is to involve all things in matter,
that they may return again by
evolution after having accomplished
the end for which they existed,
namely, the growth and exaltation of
the myriad souls of humanity.

"You will all admit, I hope, without
difficulty that what is evolved in nature
must first have been involved. When
people speak of the theory of evolution
as being enough to account for all the
order, beauty, life, form, and intelligence in creation, without the necessity
of postulating any personal or super-
personal Creator behind it, they are
simply begging the whole question.
Evolution accounts for nothing. It only
tells us how certain things have come to
be what they are, but it does not tell us
why. How could the evolutionary process result in the production of a Shake-
speare or Gladstone if the qualities which
appeared in these two great men were
not already latent in the whole vast
scheme of things ? . . . There would
have been no Gladstone if the Gladstone
soul, or potency, had not been wrapped
up somewhere in the cosmos from the
beginning of time."—R. J. CAMPBELL,
Serm., *The Source of Good.*

"He hath made everything beautiful
in its time : also he hath set eternity
in their heart, yet so that man cannot
find out the work that God hath done
from the beginning even to the end."—
ECCLES. iii. 11.

The first sentence refers to the
period and process of involution when
the archetypal world on the buddhic
plane is made perfect and "very
good." Then also is set potentially
in the causal-body (heart) the means
of immortality,—the Truth, Love,
and Wisdom of the Spirit,—yet, these
being latent, the lower mind (man)
is left in ignorance of the Divine
scheme, and is unable to find out the
work that God hath done in the
universe and the soul, from the
beginning even to the end of the cycle
of existence.

" 'He hath made every thing beautiful
in its time.' The nearest approach I can
make myself to an explanation of what
beauty is,—and even that is no explanation, but only an index finger pointing
towards it,—is to say that it is the witness
in the soul of that which *is* as opposed
to that which *seems*—the real of which
this world is but the shadow ; it is a
glimpse, an intimation of the supernal,
the state of being in which there is no
lack, no discord, strife, or wrong, and
where nothing is wanting to the ideal
perfection, whatever it may be."—R. J.
CAMPBELL, Serm., *The Elusive Revelation.*

" All perfection increases towards the
interiors, and decreases towards the
exteriors ; since interior things are
nearer the Divine, and in themselves
purer ; but exterior things are more
remote from the Divine, and in themselves
grosser."—SWEDENBORG, *Heaven and Hell,*
p. 23.

" The individual, or any grouping of
individuals, depends for its meaning, its
power to change and to grow, for the
direction of its development, its fullness
and sufficiency, upon a Life larger than
its own. This larger Life works within
the unit, as well as upon it from its
environment. The part played by this
inherent, larger Life which has purposes
beyond the unit while working within it,
is coming to be more and more allowed
for by biological science. The tide of
thought among biologists is flowing away
from a strictly mechanical theory of
evolution, and making for a psychic
conception of the driving-force in evolution. A living thing cannot be explained
by an analysis of its elementary substances. . . . It is coming more and
more to be felt that a directive Life has
been at work in Nature, and that that
Life, which was so much larger than any
one of its manifestations, was the sufficiency of that manifestation. The individual thing was nothing of itself, but it
was what it was by virtue of the action
of the Whole through it and upon it.
. . . We may indeed say that all beings
everywhere are local centres of the great
Universal Spirit that pervades the universe, and that when the beings are
human then they do become conscious
co-operating units."—T. RHONDDA
WILLIAMS, Serm., *Divine Sufficiency.*

See ADAM, AIR-ÆTHER, ARC. MAN,
BUDDHI, CIRCLE OF EXISTENCE,
CREATION, CRIPPLES, DEATH OF
OSIRIS, EVOLUTION, FORM AND NAME,
GEOMETRY, GLORY, GOING IN, GOOD
(light), HERB (seed), IABRAOTH,
INCARNATION, KHWAN, LION-GOD,
MATTER, MEDIATOR, MITHRA, MONAD,
MUSUBI, NECESSITY, NIGHT, OGDOAD,
PRAKRITI, PURUSHA, SABBATH, SEED,
SEPHIROTH, SETTLEMENTS, SOUL
(highest), SOUL AND BODY, T letter,
VISTASP, WHEEL OF LIFE.

INVOLUTION OF THE INCARNATE SELF OR ARCHETYPAL SOUL OF HUMANITY :—

After a period of primordial manifestation, and when the archetypal
conditions of involution are prepared,
then the Divine Self, or Soul, descends

as a spiritual germ to the astral plane, to be afterwards born on the mental plane, grow up thereon, and finally culminate on the buddhic plane as the Archetypal Man and progenitor by evolution of the myriad human souls.

"After he (Brahman) had practised self-mortification he created this entire universe, whatever exists ; after he had created it, he entered into it."—*Tait. Upanishad*, II. 6.

"Brahman after having created the universe enters into it as the individual soul. 'This universe was at that time not unfolded ; but it unfolded itself in name and form. . . . into it that (âtman) entered up to the finger tips . . . this therefore which here (within us) is the âtman, is the trace (to be pursued) of the universe ; for in it the entire universe is known' (*Brihad. Upanishad*, I. 4, 7)."—DEUSSEN, *Phil. of Upanishads*, p. 171.

The "self-mortification" is the withdrawal from manifestation of the Life of the Self prior to a fresh outpouring of the Divine Life. The "unfolding of the universe in name and form" signifies the involution of different qualities and their material vehicles or organisms on the lower planes. It is pointed out that the lesser or individual Self (âtman) of a human being is the same with the Greater or Supreme Self. In the Microcosm is to be found all the truth of the Macrocosm, and the Self within is the way, the truth, and the life of the striving human soul.

See ARC. MAN, ATMAN, BIRTH OF BUDDHA, BODHISATVA, COMING FORTH, FORM AND NAME, IMAGE, INCARNATION, MACROCOSM, MANVANTARA, MICROCOSM, PRALAYA, SELF.

IOLCUS, OR JOLCUS :—

A symbol of the beginning and the conclusion of the cycle of evolution of the soul.

See EGINA, GOLDEN FLEECE, JASON, SANDAL.

IRAD, SON OF FIRST ENOCH :—

A symbol of faith, the product of aspiration.

See ENOCH, SON OF CAIN, MEHUJAEL.

IRIS, THE GODDESS :—

A symbol of the intuition from buddhi, operating through the higher mind.

"She whom men call Iris (rainbow), this also is by nature cloud, violet, and red, and pale green to behold " (Xenophanes).—A. FAIRBANKS, *First Philosophers of Greece*, p. 69.

"At Deucalion's Flood :—Showers are poured in torrents from the sky. Iris, the messenger of Juno, clothed in various colours, collects the waters, and bears a supply *upwards* to the clouds."—Ovid, *The Metamorphoses*, RILEY, p. 19.

The "rainbow" signifies the "bridge" of manas which connects the higher and the lower natures in the soul. The "colours" and the "clouds" are symbolic of the buddhic qualities acting through the higher mind. They bring the message of Wisdom to the aspiring lower mind, and convey upwards the purified ideas for transmutation on the buddhic plane.

"The name of Iris is also the Greek name for the rainbow ; and the correspondence is very remarkable between her office of messenger from heaven to man and the traditional function of the rainbow as a sign that the great covenants of Nature remain undisturbed. As it is only by the tradition recorded in Scripture that the rainbow has this meaning, and not by any obvious natural significance, it appears hard to explain how Homer came to combine the two ideas, except by supposing that his race drew the association from the same early source from which Moses and the earlier descendants of Abraham obtained it."— W. E. GLADSTONE, *Juventus Mundi*, Vol. I. p. 331.

See BIFROST, BRIDGE, CLOUDS, COLOURS, COVENANT, HERMES, HORSE (red), INTUITION, RAIN, RAINBOW, VOURUKASHA, WATER.

IRON :—

A symbol of the mind, or mental power, effective in the preservation and defence of human life.

See METALS, SAVITRI, STAFF OF IRON, TUBAL CAIN.

IRON AGE :—

A symbol of the present period of consciousness, wherein the lower mind is rendered active through the vibrations from the physical plane.

"And that branch (period) which was mixed with iron is the evil sovereignty of the demons with dishevelled hair of the race of Wrath (Aeshm)."—*Bahman Yast*, Ch. I. 5.

That period of the cycle of evolution which shows the mental and physical natures in combination is the age in which the lower mind, allied with the desires, passions, and instincts, and also deficient of faith in the Divine, is plunged in conflict, sorrow, and suffering. It is the present age, the fourth.

See AESHM, DEMONS, GOLDEN AGE, HAIR, KALI-YUGA, RACES, ROUNDS, SCORPIO.

IRON BEATEN OUT WITH A STONE :—

A symbol of mental energy directed by knowledge.

"And Mashya and Mashyoi dug out a pit in the earth, and iron was obtained by them and beaten out with a stone ; and without a forge they beat out a cutting edge from it, and prepared a wooden shelter from the sun."—*Bundahis*, XV. 16, *S. B. of E.*

The "digging out a pit" signifies the attempt made to attain self-consciousness through the desire-nature (earth). "Iron" is a symbol of force-mental. "Stone" is here a symbol of knowledge which is on the spiritual side of being. And so it was at this early period of evolution that without an ideal or abstract conception of Truth, such experience of life as was necessary to soul-growth was acquired, and the astral sheath (shelter) formed and specialised.

"If the iron be blunt, and one do not whet the edge, then must he put in more strength : but wisdom is profitable to direct."—ECCLES. x. 10.

See DIGGING, EARTH, MATRO, PIT, SERPENT (hissing), SHELTER, STONE, TUBAL CAIN.

IRON FROM HEAVEN :—

A symbol of the higher mentality, or of buddhi-manas, the intuition.

See FIRMAMENT.

IRON PLATE AS THE FLOOR OF HEAVEN :—

A symbol of the higher mental plane which is below the buddhic (heaven).

"In the Pyramid Texts it is always assumed that the flat slab of iron which formed the sky, and therefore the floor of the abode of the gods, was rectangular, and that each corner of it rested upon a pillar. . . . At a later period, the four quarters of heaven were believed to be under the direction of four gods, and the four pillars of the sky were poetically described as the four sceptres which they held in their hands."—BUDGE, *Gods of the Egyptians*, Vol. I. pp. 156–7.

See CEILING OF SKY, CHILDREN OF HORUS, FIRMAMENT, FOUR BEINGS, GODS, HAND, LADDER, PANTHER, PILLARS, QUARTERS, REN, SCEPTRE, SKY.

IRRIGATION :—

A symbol of the bestowal of Truth (water) on the field of the lower experiences, to promote the growth of the higher qualities.

"Before the winter the produce of this country was pasturage ; the water used before to overflow it, and afterwards the melting of the snow, and pools would occur there, O Yima ! in the material world, where the footprints of cattle and their young would appear" (*Vendidad*, II).—HAUG, *Essays*, p. 233.

Previous to a period of obscuration, the produce of the astral plane consisted in the sensations and desires. The "overflowing water" signifies the functioning of Truth upon it, and this is possible only as Truth latent (the snow) is transformed into truth active, so this irrigation occurs. The acquisition of knowledge (pools) through experience, takes place below, when the budding desires give rise to distinctive impressions upon the physical forms (footprints) which are in process of construction.

See AQUEDUCT, CATTLE, CHANNELS, CULTIVATION, DEW, HORSE (red), LAND, PLANTS, RIVER, SNOW, VOURU-KASHA, YIMA.

ISHI-KORI-DOME, MIRROR MAKER :—

A symbol of the Creative Mind or Spirit, which produces centres of consciousness on the several planes.

See CONSCIOUSNESS, MIRROR, PLANES.

ISIS, GODDESS :—

A symbol of the buddhic principle, or the Wisdom nature. The Divine Mother, or bringer-forth, of the indwelling Self (Horus).

"Plato says that the ancients signified 'Holy One' by calling Isis 'Isia,' as being a *current* and *movement* impulse of the mind that longs for an object and is carried onwards ; and that they placed understanding, and generally, goodness and virtue in the things that *flow* ; as, on the other hand, the opposite thing binds down and hinders from *going*, we denominate it 'badness,' 'inability,' 'pain,' 'cowardice.'"—PLUTARCH, *Isis and Osiris*, § 60.

The Holy Spirit of Wisdom working through the lower nature is evidenced in the aspirations which arise in the mind and lead to the enlargement of the consciousness and the evolution (flow) of the faculties and virtues in the soul. The opposite to the aspirations are the desires which bind down the ego to the lower life and hinder the evolution (going) of the higher.

"The Goddess Isis is both wise, and a lover of wisdom, as her name appears to denote that more than any other ; *knowing* and *knowledge* belong to her."— *Ibid.,* § 2.

"Isis,—Justice - Wisdom,—shows the divine mysteries to 'carriers of sacred things,' and 'wearers of sacred robes' : these are they that carry in the soul, as it were in a copper, the sacred story respecting the Gods, that cleanses the recipient from all superstition and magical follies."—*Ibid.,* § 3.

The Wisdom-nature confers Truth and Love upon the souls who have acquired the higher emotions, and donned the causal and buddhic "robes" or vestures of spirit. These egos are they who comprehend the inner teaching of the scriptures, the knowledge of Truth-reality which is above all the delusions of the lower mind, and free from reliance upon external creeds and ceremonial observances.

"And Isis also came, bringing with her her words of magical power, and her mouth was full of the breath of life ; for her talismans vanquish the pains of sickness, and her words (of power) make to live again the throats of those who are dead" (Rā and Isis).—BUDGE, *Egyptian Magic,* p. 139.

The buddhic principle is the fount of the higher qualities by the transmuting power of which the soul is raised. In the expression (mouth) of wisdom-love the Divine life issues forth to heal the soul ; for the buddhic vibrations of love and truth harmonise and energise the qualities, and the higher qualities from above bring life into the lower minds of the personalities which are full of prejudice and convention and dead in trespasses and sins.

See ALCHEMY, ALTAR (goddess), ARMAITI, BARSOM, BREATH, BUDDHI, CARNELIAN, CIVILISING, DÆMONS, DEAD, DEATH OF OSIRIS, FIRE OF HELL, HEALING, MAGIC, MOTHER, MOUTH, NEPHTHYS, OSIRIS, PAPYRUS, PHÆDRUS, PYLONS, QUALITIES, RĀ, RACES, RITES, ROBE, SCENT, TALISMAN, THROAT, TRANSMUTATION, UPLIFTING RĀ, URNI, VEIL, VULTURE, WEEPING, WISDOM, WORDS OF POWER, WORSHIP.

ISLAND, THE FLOATING :—

This symbol, under the names of Chemmis in Egypt, Delos, Asteria, or Ortygia, in Greece, and Onogorojima in Japan, signifies the astral centre, at first free and unattached, from which the astral body is gradually built up. This body of sensation and desire originates on the fourth sub-plane of the astral plane, and becomes the focus of the soul's activities in the lower worlds.

See ASTRAL PLANE, CHEMMIS, DELOS, IZANAGI, ONOGOROJIMA.

ISRAELITES :—

A symbol of the lower mental qualities which are so far disciplined as to be united with the Divine upbringing, thus becoming the chosen ones of the Lord.

"O ye seed of Abraham his servant, ye children of Jacob, his chosen ones."— Ps. cv. 6.

The mental qualities of the natural man (Jacob) in whom the Divine nature (Abraham) is stirring, they are the qualities which are being drawn upward by the Spirit.

"Every name in the Psalms, whether of person or of place, hath a mystical meaning given to it in the Christian Scriptures. Jerusalem is not the Jerusalem that was, nor is Babylon the Babylon that was, and even David hath lost his personality in the everlasting David. Judah and Israel mean not now the cast-away root, but the branch that hath been grafted in."—E. IRVING, *Works,* Vol. 1. p. 395.

See ABRAHAM, BOOTHS, GENTILES, JACOB, JESHURUN, JEWS, JORDAN, JUDAH, SIMEON.

ISTAR, OR ISHTAR, GODDESS :—

A symbol of the buddhic principle, or Wisdom nature.

"Then the Lady of the gods (Istar) drew nigh, and she lifted up the great jewels which Anu had made according to her wish, and said : 'What gods are these !'"—SAYCE, *Babylonian Legend.*

"Then Wisdom approached the soul, and she succeeds in raising the higher qualities (jewels) which have been evolved below, and which in the natural order have been builded up unconsciously in the soul according to her direction. Wisdom exalts the qualities, and her utterance is,— 'Hail to these attributes of the Self! for in Faith, Mercy, Justice, and Reason, I am related with the Self.' "

"While the celestial seat of Istar was beyond the reach of man, Istar herself sought Tammuz, the bridegroom of her youth, in the underground realm of Hades, in the hope that she might give him to drink of the waters of life which gushed up under the throne of the spirits of the earth, and so bring him back once more to life and light."— SAYCE, *Rel. of Egypt. and Babyl.*, p. 426.

The buddhic plane is beyond the consciousness of the lower mind (man) which cannot attain to spirit. The raising of the soul is the function of buddhi. Wisdom seeks Love—the ally of primordial perfection,—who is now the striving indwelling Self, in the underworld of the lower planes, with the intention of bringing to him (the Christ-soul) the Truth and Life of the Spirit which is involved in the lower nature, and needs to be evolved, in order that the incomplete Self shall be completely manifested, and restored once more to the bliss of the higher planes.

See ANU, ASTARTE, ESTHER, FOUNTAIN, HADES, JEWELS, MERODACH, NECK, TAMMUZ, WATER.

ISVARA OR KAPILA :—

A symbol of the Higher Self,—the Logos.

"Isvara shines like the sun, irradiating all spaces above, below, between. Thus this potent and adorable deity alone presides over the various origins of things."—*Svetas. Upanishad*, V.

"That which dwells in all living things, inside the living things, and all living things know not, whose body all living things are, which actuates all living things from within,—that is thy Self (Isvara), the internal ruler, immortal. That which dwells within mind, inside the mind, and the mind knows not, whose body the mind is, which actuates the mind from within,—that is thy Self, the internal ruler immortal."—*Brihad. Upanishad.*

"The self-existent Isvara has suppressed the senses that go out towards the things of sense. These senses then go out, not inwards to the Self. Here and there a wise man with the craving for immortality has closed his eyes and seen the Self. The unwise follow after outward pleasures and enter into the net of widespread death ; but the wise, who know what it is to be immortal, seek not for the imperishable amidst the things that perish."—*Katha. Upanishad*, IV. 1.

The indwelling Self or Christ is the power within all things which causes them to evolve. The Self within the minds of men makes for righteousness and the control of the desires.

See ARC. MAN, DEMIURGE, KAPILA, NET (under), SELF, SOUL.

IZANAGI AND IZANAMI :—

Symbols of Divine Will and Wisdom, or the Monad of Life and the Monad of Form, or Spirit and Matter.

"The two Deities having descended upon Onogoro-jima erected there an eight-fathom house with an august central pillar. Then Izanagi addressed Izanami, saying : ' How is thy body formed ? ' Izanami replied, ' My body is completely formed except one part, which is incomplete.' Then Izanagi said, ' My body is completely formed, and there is one part which is superfluous. Suppose that we supplement that which is incomplete in thee with that which is superfluous in me, and thereby procreate lands.' Izanami replied, ' It is well.' " —*The Kojiki.*

Will and Wisdom having established an astral centre for the soul in the lower nature formed the astral body in direct relation with the Divine Ray. The next statements refer to the duality of Life and Form. When the form is complete for a new outpouring of Spirit, then the Spirit is prepared to occupy it ;—the monad of life becomes allied with the monad of form, and thence arises the generative or creative faculty whereby the several planes are formed and furnished for the evolution of consciousness from lower to higher states. First is produced the higher mental plane (Tsukushi), second, the buddhic plane (Toyo), third, the atmic plane (Hi), and fourth, the astro-mental plane (Kumaso), the arena of conflict. All this description refers to the formation of the soul in the involutionary period of the Life-cycle.

See AMATERASU, CHEMMIS, COMB, DELOS, HIRUKO, ISLAND (floating), KAGU. MONAD, ONOGOROJIMA, UKEMOCHI.

JABAL, SON OF LAMECH AND ADAH :—

A symbol of the germ stage of the transient emotions, produced by reflection and experience.

See ADAH, JUBAL, LAMECH, PATRIARCHS.

JACKAL :—

A symbol of the sense-nature. The jackal is sometimes portrayed with a loup round its neck. As the loup is an Egyptian sign for knowledge, this indicates the knowledge procured by means of the five senses.

See NOOSE, SHU.

JACKAL-ANUBIS :—

A symbol of the physical human body, the seat of the five senses.

See ANPU, ANUBIS.

JACOB OR ISRAEL :—

A symbol of the natural man of a period.

See ISRAELITES, LADDER (Jacob's).

JAIRUS' DAUGHTER :—

A symbol of an affection in a mind or mental quality developed as a ruler. This affection slumbered until life was abundantly given to it by the Christ in response to faith and trust in the higher guidance.

See HEALING (dead), INFIRMITY, RULER.

JAMES, THE APOSTLE :—

A symbol of the mental edifice of the human being, that is, the mentality or instrument of the mind, which is built up by the soul-qualities through aspiration and enlightenment. As a symbol of one of the four elements, " James " signifies Air (mind).

See APOSTLES, DISCIPLES, GETHSEMANE, TRANSFIGURATION.

JAMSHED (YIMA) :—

A symbol of the Higher Self, or Divine Ego.

See YIMA.

JANAKA, KING OF VIDEHA :—

A symbol of the Higher Self—Atma-buddhi.

See SITA.

JAPHET, SON OF NOAH :—

A symbol of wisdom and determination,—aspects of the individuality (Noah),—reflected inversely in the lower nature as desire and will (lower).

See NOAH'S SONS.

JARED, FATHER OF ENOCH :—

A symbol of the Source of Light and Life,—the author of the individual Self.

See ENOCH.

JASON, OR JASIUS, THE HEALER OR ATONER :—

A symbol of the Higher Self as the Saviour of the soul, or Son of God, seated in the causal-body (ship Argo), with his twelve (or more) disciplined qualities (the heroes), in the soul's expedition to attain Wisdom (the golden Fleece) on the buddhic plane,— the " kingdom of heaven."

" Once when Peleas offered up a sacrifice to Poseidon, he invited Jason, son of Aeson. Jason arrived with only one sandal, having lost the other in crossing the river Anaurus, on the banks of which he lived as a peasant " (*Argonautic Expedition*).—KEIGHTLEY, *Mythology*.

During an effort which the lower self (Peleas) makes to attain to the Divine consciousness (Poseidon) in an act of self-abnegation, or sacrifice, it requests that the Son of God (Jason) be born within it as Son of Man on the mental plane. Jason, the son of Aeson (Second Logos), is said to arrive at Iolcus (the mental plane), minus a sandal, that is to say :—the Lord from Heaven arrives in the soul without the power to stand in manifestation, i.e. without the means for self-expression. In other terms, there is only one sandal, because the perfect duality of the manifest on the upper planes, cannot be expressed in actuality on the lower planes. The one sandal stands for relativity. The " river Anaurus " is a symbol of the mentality which separates and limits, and acquires truth from outside. The Saviour, prior to his descent from the heights, is the Tiller and Sower of the field of the lower nature (as a peasant).

" Cretheus, who had founded Iolcus, was succeeded by his son Aeson ; but the latter was deprived of the kingdom by his half-brother Pelias, who attempted to take the life of the infant Jason. He was saved by his friends, who pretended that he was dead, and entrusted him to

the care of the centaur Chiron."—
Smith's Class. Dict.

The First Logos (unmanifest) who
had established the cycle of life from
the mental plane (Iolcus) was actualised in the Second Logos, or Higher
Self. But the lower self or adverse
principle (Pelias) became dominant
and attempted to destroy the Divine
Life germ (Jason) within the soul.
The Christ-soul (Jason) was protected
by the higher qualities in seeming
latency, and was fostered by the
spiritual mind (Chiron).

" The name Jesus in ancient times also
belonged to the Health-bringer and
patron of the Physician—namely, Jasias
or Jason, the pupil of Chiron, skilled in
healing,—who in general shows a remarkable resemblance to the Christian
Redeemer."—A. DREWS, *The Christ Myth*,
p. 58.

See AESON, ANAURUS, ARGO, ARGO-
NAUTS, CADMUS, GOLDEN FLEECE,
HEPHAISTOS, HEROES, IOLCUS,
JESHURUN, MEDEA, PEASANT, SALVE,
SANDAL, SOWER.

JEALOUS GOD :—

A symbol of the Higher nature as
reflected in the lower nature. The
Higher Self is at first regarded as
a powerful enemy,—jealous, angry,
revengeful and intolerant,—because
It opposes the course of the lower self
in its search for gratification in the
objects of desire and sensation.
The love of the higher life and the
love of the lower are two irreconcilable opposites, and therefore appear
as contending foes one against the
other. The voice of the jealous
God may be heard in every active
conscience, as of a Ruler who will
endure no rival, and accept no excuse
for transgression, and who is severe
and implacable.

" For thou shalt worship no other
god : for the Lord, whose name is
Jealous, is a jealous God."—EXOD. xxxiv.
14.

The " other gods " are the other
objects strenuously sought after,
namely, the objects of desire and
sense, which must never be placed in
rivalry with the call of the Spirit
from within.

See ANGER OF GOD, IDOLS, SELF
(lower), WRATH OF GOD.

JEHOVAH OR YAHVEH :—

A tribal name for the God of all.

It generally signifies the ethical aspect
of the Divine nature, which is severe
against all wrongdoing : but sometimes it signifies the Self as Truth
and Love, e.g. Is. xii. 2, 3.

" ' Jehovah ' is the expression of
God's being. And because He is true
being, though He is love, He must be
just and holy also, for evil is not true
being, but the negation or privation of
it."—A. JUKES, *The Names of God*,
p. 40.

" That name of ' Jehovah ' proclaims
at once His Eternal Being and His
covenant relation—manifesting Him by
its mysterious meaning as He who
dwells above time ; the tideless sea of
absolute unchanging existence, from
whom all the stream of creatural life
flows forth many coloured and transient,
to whom it all returns ; who, Himself
unchanging, changeth all things ;—He
is *the Lord* the Eternal."—A. MACLAREN,
Sermons, 3rd Series, p. 62.

See GOD, SELF, SIVA, TETRAGRAM-
MATON, YEDUD.

JERUSALEM, HEAVENLY :—

A symbol of the soul-centre in the
causal-body on the higher mental
plane. Or it may be on the buddhic
plane.

" Now Jerusalem, as the Lord Himself
teaches in the Gospel according to
Mathew, ' is the city of the great King.'
(MAT. v. 35). It does not lie in a
depression, or in a low situation, but is
built on a high mountain, and there are
mountains round about it, and the
participation of it is to the same place,
and thither the tribes of the Lord went
up, a testimony for Israel. But that
city also is called Jerusalem, to which
none of those upon the earth ascends,
nor goes in ; but every soul that possesses by nature some elevation and
some acuteness to perceive the things of
the mind is a citizen of that city."—
ORIGEN, *Comm. on John*, Bk. X. § 16.

" We ascend thy ways that be in our
heart, and sing a song of degrees ; we
glow inwardly with thy fire, with thy
good fire, and we go, because we go
upwards to the peace of Jerusalem."—
AUGUSTINE, *Confessions*, XIII. 11.

" We have created the upper Jerusalem
above the waters which are above the
third heaven, hanging directly over the
lower Jerusalem."—*Revelations of St.
Peter*, Ch. 27.

The buddhic plane is placed above
the third and higher sub-planes of
the higher mind, and it ensouls the
causal-body which is its vehicle
beneath.

" Now this Hagar is mount Sinai in
Arabia and answereth to the Jerusalem
that now is : for she is in bondage with

her children. But the Jerusalem that is above is free, which is our mother."—GAL. iv. 25, 26.

The egos at first are disciplined under the laws of nature by pressure from without to stimulate them into activity. They are born in bondage to the lower nature (flesh), and are socially forced to conform to a code of ethics (Sinai) which puts before them an ideal or centre of refuge (Jerusalem as now). But the wisdom and love of buddhi are attractive, not coercive (Jerusalem the golden); and it is Buddhi, the Divine Mother, who brought forth the egos that they might gain experience on the lower planes.

"What the womb of his mother is to each individual man, that the primary abode in Paradise became to the whole human race. For from it came forth the family of Man as it were from the womb, and tending to the increase of the race."—GREGORY THE GREAT, *Morals on the Book of Job*, Vol. I. p. 199.

"My heart my mother, my heart my coming into being. . . . Thou art my Ka within my body which knitteth together and strengtheneth my limbs."—*Papyrus of Ani*, BUDGE

"But the defect in the reasoning (of Catherine of Genoa) to which I have just alluded is its assumption that freedom is always and only a matter of the exercise of the will; it is not, and to say so is a begging of the whole question at issue. The psychology of the apostle Paul is a good deal nearer to the facts of experience. Paul says that we are all naturally in bondage, and that it is the heavenly Jerusalem,—the transcendental world,—which alone is free. People do not choose evil instead of good, death instead of life, in the way the ecclesiastical doctrine we are discussing implies. No man ever chooses evil because it is evil, or rejects good because it is good; he chooses one or the other at any given moment because he likes it, because there is something in his nature which finds gratification in it. Well, but what does that mean? It can only mean that he is not free; if he were free he would scarcely be conscious of choosing anything: it is just because he is not free, because there are elements in his nature which impel him this way or that, that such a thing as a moral choice is possible at all. . . . Good is the life-ward and evil is the deathward course. And we are all weighted by ignorance, by passion, and by earth-born desire; we do not start free; we are born in bondage."—R. J. CAMPBELL, Serm., *Sources of Spiritual Freedom.*

"Then Jesus took unto him the twelve, and said unto them, Behold, we go up to Jerusalem, and all things that are written concerning the Son of man shall be accomplished."—LUKE xviii. 30.

The progress of all the disciplined soul-qualities and the Ideal they follow is upwards to the higher planes, where the union of the lower Self and the Higher Self shall be consummated.

"Every true life has its Jerusalem, to which it is always going up. A life cannot be really considered as having begun to live until that far-off city in which its destiny awaits it, where its work is to be done, where its problem is to be solved, begins to draw the life towards itself, and the life begins to know and own the summons. At first far off and dimly seen, laying but light hold upon our purpose and our will, then gradually taking us more and more into its power, compelling our study, directing the current of our thoughts."—PHILLIPS BROOKS, Serm., *Going up to Jerusalem.*

See AMARAVATI, BONDAGE, CITY OF GOD, DISCIPLES, ERIDU, GUARDIAN SPIRITS, HEART, HOLY GHOST, HOUSE (frequented), IGNORANCE, KAABA, KAPILA, MAASEH, MOTHER (divine), MOUNTAIN, PARADISE, SIDES, WILL, ZION.

JESHURUN :—

A symbol of the associated mental qualities which are disciplined through Divine grace; they thereby become the Lord's chosen ones.—Is. xliv. 2.

Jesus (Jeshu) was regarded by the inspired writers as an Israelite. The Israelites were a "chosen people" (in the inner sense), and hence it is easy to see how it was that their name best served to typify the central ideal character associated with the Gospel Drama. "Jeshu" may be held to represent in the soul the central Ideal, or indwelling God, in the midst of the more or less disciplined qualities (Jeshurun) who follow their Lord and Saviour.

In fixing upon the Hellenised form "Jesus" as a name for the Christ-soul, there is possibility that the names Ies (Dionysus), and Jasius (Jason) were referred to; both being symbols of the Christ-soul or incarnate Self,—the Son of God.

"In Is. vii. 14, the 'son of the virgin' is named *Emmanuel*, and this is translated 'God with us.' That is also the meaning of the name *Jesus*, since in MAT. i. 21, the son of Mary receives this name, 'that it might be fulfilled which was spoken of the Lord by the prophets, saying, Behold, a virgin shall be with child, and shall bring forth a son, and they shall call his name Emmanuel' (MAT. i. 23)."—A. DREWS, *Witnesses, etc.*, p. 195.

"Justin tells us that nearly the whole of the west worshipped Jason and built temples to him (XLII. 3), and this is confirmed by Tacitus (*Annals*, VI. 34)."—*Ibid.*, p. 196.

Jeshurun is said to be a poetic name for the Israelites. The "Israelites" symbolise disciplined qualities of the soul. The discipline implies obedience to an inner ruler, who is a central Ideal to the qualities and in more or less harmony with them. This Ideal, then, is the "God with us," and is given the poetic name "Jeshu," to link him with his disciples "Jeshurun"—the disciplined qualities that adore him as their Lord.

See AMENI, DANCE (circle), DIONYSUS, DISCIPLES, INCARNATION, ISRAELITES, JASON, JESUS (servant), JEWS, JUDAH, SAVIOURS, VIRGIN MARY.

JESUS OF THE GOSPELS :—

A symbol of the indwelling Higher Self (Christ), or Divine Spirit in man, evolving towards complete manifestation. In other words, it is the Divinised Soul, or Christ-soul, not yet but almost perfected. It represents the personality towards the end of the cycle, becoming perfect at the conclusion in the death of the lower nature and the rise of the consciousness into the higher. The meaning of the symbol varies somewhat between the exalted Christ and the human, unperfected Christ-soul.

"Pilate therefore said unto him, Art thou a king then ? Jesus answered, Thou sayest that I am a king. To this end have I been born, and to this end am I come into the world, that I should bear witness unto the truth. Every one that is of the truth heareth my voice."—JOHN xviii. 37.

The worldly, unstable mind (Pilate) puts the inquiry to the higher nature, whether it is indeed a ruler of the soul ? To this the higher nature replies that the worldly mind always acknowledges the sovereignty of that which is above it and incomprehensible to it. The Christ within proclaims (verse 36),

"My kingdom is not of this world," for Christ reigns only over those qualities and souls which are liberated from the lower nature and are of the higher kingdom on the buddhic plane. To this end of victory over the lower, and establishment of the higher, was Christ born into the evolving soul. To this end did the Christ-soul become manifest in the lower nature (world) that he might show forth the Truth that should overcome illusion. Every quality and soul which is in harmony with the real and true, responds to the call of the Christ and acknowledges the supremacy of Love and Truth.

"The human soul conceived the Divine Life and brought it forth. Jesus is, when born, the Life of the Soul in which he is born. Jesus and the soul are one being, only the Life is greater than the soul."—JOHN WARD, *Zion's Works*, Vol. VI. p. 276.

"Christ Jesus is no other than the hidden and true man of the Spirit, the Perfect Humanity, the Express Image of the Divine Glory. And it is possible to man, by the renunciation—which mystically is the crucifixion—of his outer and lower self, to rise wholly into his inner and higher self, and, becoming suffused or anointed of the Spirit, to 'put on Christ,' propitiate God, and redeem the earthly and material. . . . For, such of us as know and live the inner life, are saved, not by any Cross on Calvary eighteen hundred years ago, not by any physical blood-shedding, not by any vicarious passion of tears and scourge and spear ; but by the Christ-Jesus, the God with us, the Immanuel of the heart, born, working mighty works, and offering oblation in our own lives, in our own persons, redeeming us from the world, and making us sons of God and heirs of everlasting life. But, if we are thus saved by the love of Christ, it is by love also that we manifest Christ to others. If we have received freely, we also give freely, shining in the midst of night, that is, in the darkness of the world."—*The Perfect Way*, pp. 112, 114.

See JOHN viii. 24. "Notice, to begin with, that the word 'he' is not present in the original. This makes a great difference. The passage should read,— 'If ye believe not that I *am*, ye shall die in your sins.' The belief here referred to has a moral significance ; it implies the conformity of one's whole being, the concentration of one's whole powers, upon a great and worthy object. And what is that object ? It is here said to be Christ, the Christ who in this gospel is not only identified with Jesus, but with the eternal Word by whom creation exists, and who is therefore the source of humanity itself. . . . The statement in the text thus amounts to this,—that unless we realise and trust the presence *within us* of that holy eternal fact, that supreme reality, that humanity divine, which the world has come to reverence as Jesus, we shall never escape from our moral disabilities, we shall die in our sins. . . . How is anyone ever going to escape from the dominion of earthly passion and desire except by relying upon something which is deeper and stronger than these masters of the outer man ? "—R. J. CAMPBELL, Serm., *The Faith that Saves*.

"The Waldenses pretend that every man is a Son of God in the same manner that Christ was. Christ had God or the Holy Spirit for soul, and they say that other men also have. They believe in the incarnation, the birth, the passion, and the resurrection of Christ, but they mean by it the Spiritual conception, Spiritual birth, Spiritual resurrection of the perfect man. For them the true passion of Jesus is the martyrdom of a holy man, and the true sacrament is the conversion of a man, for in such a conversion the body of Christ is formed (Jundt)."—R. M. JONES, *Mystical Religion*, p. 191.

"The individual can never say, 'I am not.' This 'I' which is the knower, the actor, the thinker, the doer. It is the subject, not the object, of thought. This is the genuine self, and it is identical in its nature with the supreme knower of the world whom we call God. It is one with God and inseparable from Him, as the sunbeam is one with the sun and inseparable from it. The sunbeam has no life of its own, but partakes of the life and nature of the sun. So does the Soul or genuine Ego partake of the life of God ; it is God within us. It is unborn, it does not die ; and it does not suffer."—K. C. ANDERSON, Serm., *The Buried Life*.

See AMEN, ARC. MAN, ASCENSION, BIRDS (two), CHRIST, CRUCIFIXION, FIG-FRUIT, HEBDOMAD, INCARNATION, KING, KING (great), KINGDOM, LIBERATION, PERSONALITY, SPARROWS, TEMPTATION, VICTORY, VIRGIN MARY.

JESUS AS SON OF GOD :—

A symbol of the Higher Self proceeding from the Supreme and manifesting upon the buddhi-mental plane. It signifies the potential indwelling Christ seated in the causal-body ; and it also means the perfected Soul wherein the higher and the lower consciousnesses are made one.

"The Father loveth the Son, and hath given all things into his hand. He that believeth on the Son hath eternal life ; but he that obeyeth not the Son shall not see life, but the wrath of God abideth on him."—JOHN iii. 35, 36.

From the potential, unmanifest Supreme Self proceeds the actual and manifest Self deputed to carry out the Divine purpose, and to be the Life within all forms. The quality or soul that becomes in harmony with the Christ hath the life immortal, but that quality which conformeth not to the Divine Will cannot be transmuted, but must be left to the destroying forces of the planes. It is the lower qualities *as such* which cannot be transmuted.

"Remember, the self that is imprisoned in the desires of the flesh, the slave self, is not the whole of you, not the chief part of you. There is a Self beyond and above who knows no such bondage, never has done, and never shall ; if that Self shall make you free you shall be free indeed. And who is the Self beneath even this self, the gold concealed within our dross, the life within our life, the creator Soul of all mankind ? I will tell you : it is Jesus. . . . It is the faith of Christendom ; it is the one central truth around which the New Testament was written ; it is the truth of experience upon which Catholic and Protestant are agreed, and upon which the whole Christian gospel rests."—R. J. CAMPBELL, Serm., *The Freedom of the Son of God*.

"The object of the faith of the Christian congregation, from its very inception, never was the earthly teacher Jesus, but ever and exclusively it was the heavenly spirit of Christ."—O PFLEIDERER, *Develop. of Christianity*, p. 25.

"A section (of Congregationalism) adopts the Modernist position that the ideal content of doctrine is everything, and the historic origin of it nothing. Even a historic Jesus, these extremists say, is indifferent, if only we trust ourselves to the ideal principles of which He was the symbol rather than the source."—PRINCIPAL FORSYTH, *Constructive Quarterly*, Sept. 1913, p. 499.

"Christianity is a historical religion, but its power to save depends upon our power to spiritualise history. I believe the personality of Jesus was indispensable to the early Christian movement, and I cannot understand the history of the movement without Him ; but it is not Jesus as a historical person who is our Saviour to-day. It is only as a symbol of what God is that Jesus is of value to us. And here He is of the greatest value. . . . When we come to look into later Church history, we find that its Jesus never has been a mere historical person ; Jesus has always been to the Church a symbol of God. And it is perfectly true to-day that only as a symbol of what God is, and what He is in the deepest heart of man, do we value Jesus."—ANON., Serm., *Jesus : the Great Symbol.*

See AMMIT, ARC. MAN, BIRDS (two), CHRIST, FIG-FRUIT, FIRST-BORN SON, GOD, IMAGE, INCARNATION, KRISHNA, SELF, SHOE-LATCHET, SON OF GOD, TRINITY.

JESUS AS SON OF MAN :—

A symbol of the Higher Self as born or evolved in the mind (man). It signifies the indwelling Christ seated in the causal-body, but in all degrees imperfectly manifest in the soul until redemption is accomplished.

" Jesus saith, Now is the Son of man glorified, and God is glorified in him ; and God shall glorify him in himself, and straightway shall he glorify him."—JOHN xiii. 31, 32.

As the end of the cycle draws nigh, so the Christ-soul becomes perfected through the Christ being fulfilled in him. And the Supreme Self shall thereby be fully manifest to Himself, and his purpose completed in the return of the victorious Soul to the Absolute.

" Eckhart and Tauler, Ruysbrock and Suso, exclaim,—' Arise O man ! realise the end of thy being : make room for God within thy soul, that he may bring forth his son within thee."—VAUGHAN, *Mystics,* Vol. I. p. 300.

" Whatever is God to a man, that is his heart and soul ; and conversely, God is the manifested inward nature, the expressed Self of a man,—religion, the solemn unveiling of a man's hidden treasures."—FEUERBACH, *Essence of Christianity,* p. 12.

God " brings forth his Son within the soul " on the mental plane (Son of man), and thereby manifests Himself in man's inward nature.

" The spirit of man, the changeless reality hidden within both body and soul, is eternal and uncreate—an out-breathing, as it were, of the very being of God himself."—R. J. CAMPBELL, Serm., *Our Eternal Glory.*

" God sending forth his Son, who should be conceived in the human mind by the moving of the Eternal Power, is *willing* his own manifestation, or the manifestation of Himself in the human properties."—JOHN WARD, *Zion's Works,* Vol. III. p. 278.

" I do honestly feel that Jesus of Nazareth stands nearer to me in intimate reality than anyone else I know. He is more than Saviour or Friend. The only adequate confession I can make is that he is my All ; all I have and all I want. If he is a myth, then I prefer myth to what is called history ; if he is not recoverable by criticism of the gospels, then I must know him by some other way ; if this is hallucination, then all other mental phenomena are far worse—they must be absolute delusion."—W. E. ORCHARD, *Christ. Com.,* Sept. 11, 1912.

As the symbol " man " signifies mind in all scriptures, and it is in the mind that " Jesus," historical or spiritual, appears to the lower consciousness, it is plain that " Jesus " is born into the mind, that is, Jesus is Son of man (mind). It must also be remembered that in evolution of qualities, the " son " is always greater than the " father."

" That is not first which is spiritual, but that which is natural ; then that which is spiritual. The first man is of the earth, earthy : the second man is of heaven.—1 COR. xv. 46, 47.

See AMENI, ASCENSION OF JESUS, BIRTH OF JESUS, BREATH (divine), CHILD, CHRIST'S SECOND COMING, DEMIURGE, EVOLUTION, FATHER (lower), GLORIFYING, INCARNATION, ISVARA, MAN, SON OF MAN, VIRGIN MARY.

JESUS, MORTAL :—

A symbol of the Christ-soul, or almost perfected personality, subject to the death of its lower nature.

" The Holy Spirit, by his influence and spiritual infusion, makes the earth conceive and bring forth the mortal Jesus, who, as hanging from every tree, is the life and salvation of men " (Manichæan dcctrine).—AUGUSTINE, *Manichœan Heresy,* p. 366.

The Higher Self brooding over the highest part of the lower nature (earth) so purifies and fructifies it that it is enabled to bear and bring forth the Christ-soul (Jesus) within the many souls of humanity. In each soul the incarnate Christ inheres within the personality, as it were, hanging from the " Tree of Life " or Divine ray within it, as that which shall redeem it from evil, perfect it, and raise it to the life immortal.

" The Wisdom of God Incarnate is represented by ' the Tree,' as where it is written thereon, ' She is a tree of life to them that lay hold on Her.' . . . And what is denoted by the title of ' the tree,' but the life of the righteous."—ST. GREGORY, *Morals on the Book of Job,* Vol. II. p. 48.

See AXE, EARTH, IMMORTALITY,

INCARNATION, PERSONALITY, TREE, TREE OF LIFE.

JESUS, DESCRIBED AS SEVERE AND TURBULENT :—

Symbolical either of the Christ's uncompromising hostility to evil in the qualities of the soul ; or as evidencing the indignation of the lower nature that is attached to the not yet perfected personality (Jesus).

" I came to cast fire upon the earth ; and what will I, if it is already kindled ? . . . Think ye that I am come to give peace in the earth ? I tell you, Nay ; but rather division : for there shall be from henceforth five in one house divided, three against two, and two against three. They shall be divided, father against son, and son against father ; mother against daughter, and daughter against her mother ; mother in law against her daughter in law, and daughter in law against her mother in law."—LUKE xii. 49–53

This signifies that Christ manifests in the soul to combat the tendencies of the lower nature (earth) by means of the life of the spirit (fire), which purifies from evil through suffering which is already present in nature. It must not be supposed that Christ brings to the soul a state of passivity to the lower nature. On the contrary, he produces conflict and sets the qualities warring among themselves in a great variety of ways. The " father " is a prior mental state which it is necessary to abandon. The " daughter against her mother " signifies the better emotion which casts off the worse condition which gave it birth. For the old from which the new springs is always opposed to the new advance.

Jesus said : " Ye serpents, ye offspring of vipers, how shall ye escape the damnation of hell."—MAT. xxiii. 33.

The Christ-soul emphatically denounces literalism, formalism and dogmatism which lead to such evil results. Christ's apparently harsh words are meaningless to those who are living in accord with the lofty ideals which we conceive of in connection with His nature. But whilst the Divinity of Christ did not and could not utter the reproaches which have been thus recorded against him, it must be admitted that the sentences embodied in some of these sayings alluded to are precisely those which all men's lower nature, struggling to realise the dictates of the Higher, would be apt indignantly to utter.

The Gospel Drama is, after all, a presentment not only of the Divinity of the Christ, but the manhood of the personality Jesus,—in whom the " old Adam " has not yet quite died out,—who is seeking Life eternal, and is gradually overcoming " the world, the flesh, and the devil," over which he triumphs finally in the death of the lower nature as symbolised in Calvary's Cross.

The severe remarks could indeed have been left out of the narrative ; they, however, add to the accuracy of the dramatic record, which takes account of the imperfections which attach themselves to the personality until complete purification is reached.

The scourging of the temple moneychangers, which historically is lawless violence inciting to riot, and ethically is subversive of the gentle teaching of the Sermon on the Mount, is to be explained by the Christ-soul's active aspect in cleansing the heart of man from low aims and degrading influences.

" It was no part of the design of the Gospels to represent either the course of a man perfect from the first, or the whole course from the first of the man made perfect. Had they been designed to represent the former, they had contained no account of a Crucifixion. For, of the man perfect, no crucifixion, in the Mystical sense, is possible, since he has no lower self or perverse will, or any weakness, to be overcome or renounced, the *anima divina* in him having become all in all. That, therefore, which the Gospels exhibit is a process consisting of the several degrees of regeneration, on the attainment of the last of which only does the man become ' perfect.' But of these successive degrees not all are indicated. For the Gospels deal, not with one whose nature is, at first, wholly unregenerate, but with one who is already, in virtue of the use made of his previous earth-lives, so far advanced as to be within reach, in a single further incarnation, of full regeneration."—*The Perfect Way*, p. 244.

See CLEANSING, DOVE-SELLERS, ENEMIES, FATHER (lower), INITIATIONS, PEACE AND SWORD, PETER, PRIESTS AND ELDERS, SCOURGE, SHRINE, SWORD, TEETH (gnashing).

JESUS WEPT :—

A symbol of the weakness of the lower nature in the presence of difficulties which the higher nature must surmount in raising and purifying the soul.

"And when he drew nigh, he saw the city and wept over it, saying, If thou hadst known in this day, even thou, the things which belong unto peace ! but now they are hid from thine eyes."— LUKE xix. 41, 42.

The Christ-soul had come to take the citadel of the lower activities, or capacity of mind wherein the qualities have been wont to be used. He had come to his own from afar, and when he saw the task which lay before him, the humanity in " Jesus " was stirred, hence the statement is made that " He wept." The *Christ*, however, did not weep. It was the distress and distrust of the lower nature to accomplish the task which lay before the Higher that appalled ; and it was only after the lower was able to see that it was not the *Doer* but only the illusory agent, that the triumph was ultimately achieved.

See CALAMITIES, CITY OR TOWN, JERUSALEM, TEARS.

JESUS AS THE FISH :—

A symbol of the Higher Self as the Saviour of the human soul.

"He (God) had his dwelling in the Great Sea, and was a Fish therein."— *Zohar.*

"Jesus is a Fish that lives in the midst of waters."—ST. AUGUSTINE.

The " Great Sea " is the primeval " water," the symbol of Truth-Reality which outpours from the Absolute. The Higher Self abides and manifests in that Ocean of Truth ; hence the symbol of the Fish, as the spiritual Life within the reality of Being.

See ABTU-FISH, DELUGE, FISH (great), JONAH, PISCES, POSEIDON, PUNGA, TANGAROA.

JESUS AS THE LAMB :—

A symbol of Christ as the Divine sacrifice for the benefit of humanity. The young ram (Aries) is a world-wide symbol of the sacrifice of the Higher Self in entering upon the cycle of manifestation (Zodiac).

See AFU-RĀ, ARIES, LAMB, LAMB OF GOD, PASSOVER, RAM.

JESUS THY SERVANT :—

A symbol of the awakening soul receptive of the grace of God.

" Jesus " being a generic name, with varieties such as Joshua and Jehoshua, it is requisite that it should be allocated to a particular described type before it may bear a symbolical meaning.

The *Didachē,* in which the expression " Jesus Thy servant " occurs, is a sort of moral dissertation upon the qualities. Reference to the co-ordinating principle,—Christ,—is rare. There is no biographical account of " Jesus " for the simple reason, probably, that the idea of the Gospel drama had not yet arisen in the religious mind in connection with the name *Jesus.* When it did arise, Gospels and also detached sayings relating to " Jesus" became very numerous indeed.

" As to the Eucharist, we give thanks in this wise. First for the chalice : We thank thee, our Father, for the Holy Vine of David, Thy servant, which Thou hast made known to us by Jesus Thy servant. Glory to Thee for evermore ! For the bread : We thank Thee, our Father, for the life and the knowledge which Thou hast made known to us by Jesus, Thy servant. Glory to Thee for evermore ! (*Doctrine of the Apostles*, a very ancient writing)."— DUCHESNE, *Christian Worship*, p. 52.

The Divine Life (holy vine) within the natural man (David) is made known to the awakening soul ; as also is the sustenance of goodness and truth (bread of heaven) which is bestowed in response to aspiration and effort.

See ASPIRATION, BREAD, CHRIST, CUP, DAVID, GOSPEL STORY, GRACE, JESHURUN, JESUS OF GOSPELS, JESUS (mortal), JOB, QUALITIES, SERVANT OF GOD, VINE.

JESUS THE PATTERN OR EXEMPLAR :—

" The whole course of the typical life of the Pattern Man (Jesus) is emblematic of the progressive development of the Life begun on earth, completed in Heaven ; born of self-denial, and culminating in spiritual ascension. In the Christ-life, as in a story, man may read the tale of the progress of Spirit from incarnation to enfranchisement." " The life of the Man Christ Jesus was a symbolic representation of the progress of Spirit."—WM. STAINTON MOSES, *Spirit Teachings*, pp. 256, 259.

JEWEL SPEAR OF HEAVEN :—

A symbol of the Divine Ray of Life and Truth which emanates from the Absolute and penetrates all planes.

See IZANAGI, ONOGOROJIMA, SPEAR, SUTRATMA.

JEWELS ; GEMS :—

A symbol of virtues and high qualities, which are the precious things of life.

"And they shall be mine, saith the Lord of hosts, in that day when I make up my jewels ; and I will spare them, as a man spareth his own son that serveth him."—MAL. iii. 17.

And the aspiring virtues shall become in unison with the Self,— saith the Lord of the qualities,—at the end of the cycle when the higher qualities become complete and perfect in me ; and eternal life shall be theirs, even as they have issued forth from me, and have sought for and found me again.

"God goes forth from himself in creation to return to himself in man. As has been finely said, the only satisfying explanation of the activity of the universe is that it represents the effort of manifested life to get back to its own centre, which is God."—R. J. CAMPBELL, Serm., *Our Quest for God.*

"There was an ancient ceremony called *mitama furishiki,* that is, shaking the august jewels, which is referred to in the *Kiujiki.* We are there told that when the Sun-Goddess sent down Ninigi to rule the world, she gave him ' ten auspicious treasures, namely, one mirror of the offing, one mirror of the shore, one eight-hands-breadth sword, one jewel of birth, one jewel of return from death, one perfect jewel, one road-returning jewel (that is, a jewel which has the property of making evil things return by the road they came), one serpent-scarf (a scarf which has power when waved to keep away serpents), one bee-scarf, and one scarf of various things,' saying, ' In case of illness shake these treasures and repeat to them the words, One, two, three, four, five, six, seven, eight, nine, ten. If thou doest so the dead will certainly return to life.' "—W. G. ASTON, *Shinto,* pp. 292, 293.

When the Self (Ninigi) descended through buddhi (Sun-Goddess) to be incarnated and rule the soul, he was possessed of the treasures of the higher planes which should enable him to overcome the temptations and limitations of the lower life and rise victorious in his return at the end. The buddhic nature endows the

Incarnate God with ten precious attributes :—(1) the causal-body ; (2) the astro-mental body ; (3) ' the sword of the Spirit,'—the expression of Truth, or spiritual force which dispels ignorance ; (4) faith in the Divine ; (5) love of the ideal ; (6) aspiration towards the Highest ; (7) steadfastness to the good and true ; (8) love of the inner Wisdom as opposed to outer desire and sensation ; (9) industry to acquire knowledge ; (10) intellectual faculties. In case of the soul's sickness, all the attributes are to be brought into harmonious concert (reciting the numbers), so that they together shall effectually cure the soul. When the harmony is perfect, then the " dead in Christ " shall rise to life eternal.

See AMATERASU, BEES, BREASTPLATE, CARNELIAN, CORPSE, DEAD, GARDEN OF EDEN, GEMS, HOSTS (Lord), MIRROR, NECK, NINIGI, QUALITIES, RUBIES, SAPPHIRE, SARDONYXES, SERPENT, SHORE, STRINGS, SWORD, TREASURES.

JEWS OF PALESTINE :—

A symbol of the social and religious element of a period or state of soul. They also represent the partially disciplined mental qualities out of which the most progressed are chosen as " disciples."

"For the gospel is the power of God unto salvation to every one that believeth ; to the Jew first, and also to the Greek."—ROM. i. 16.

For the message of Wisdom and Love to the soul is the effectual means of attaining perfection to every quality in harmony with it ; to the social and religious element first, and afterwards to the intellectual.

See DISCIPLES, GENTILES, GOSPEL, ISRAELITES, JESHURUN, SALVATION, SPARROWS.

JIVA :—

A symbol of the Divine Life in the soul.

See FRAVASHI, MONAD OF LIFE.

JIVATMAN :—

A symbol of the incarnate Self which strives to rise from below.

See BIRDS (two), FIG-FRUIT.

JOB, THE PERFECT MAN :—

A symbol of the Incarnate Self, or Soul, the " greatest of all the children of the east," that is, the rising sun (Self). The Self abandons his spiritual wealth on the higher planes and descends to incarnate in the forms on the lower planes. Then having undergone unsullied the strife and suffering of the life in matter, he puts off from him the garments of imperfection, and rises to a more glorious state than before on the higher planes at the end of the cycle.

" So the Lord blessed the latter end of Job more than his beginning."— JOB xlii. 12.

The " three friends " of the inmost Spirit are the three natures which enclose it ; namely, the mental, astral, and physical natures, which at first are rudimentary sheaths (afar off), without Self-consciousness, for they " knew him not." Then afterwards as they come " by appointment together " they grow into organised vehicles of the soul bringing suffering and trouble with them. They remain in the animal and pre-human stages for a complete period (seven), irresponsible beings, quite unaffected by the Spirit within, " none spake a word unto him,"—the natural could not perceive the spiritual.

In the third chapter, the Self is described as beginning to operate in the human mind through the lowest thoughts of cunning, craft, revenge, anger, etc., which often have in them elements of truth, justice, love, etc. The Self is said to " curse his day," in that he has to work in ignorance (darkness) and the opposites of goodness and love. He looks forward to the time when the evil conditions into which he was born in the soul shall perish. He longs for the death of the lower instincts and desires.

" These utterances of Job in his affliction are expressions of miserable Humanity, declaring the wretchedness of its own condition *by nature*, by reason of the Fall, and consequent *curse* pronounced upon the children of Adam. . . . Philippus, Bede, and Aquinas say that Job here speaks as a prophet, and mourns over the corruption and misery of Man by nature, as David did, ' Behold, I was shapen in iniquity ; and in sin hath my mother conceived me ' (Ps. li.

5). St. Ambrose declares that this confession and lamentation of the sin and misery of fallen humanity in Job is tantamount to a desire for deliverance by the new birth which it has in Christ." —WORDSWORTH, *Bible*, *Job*, p. 7.

In the fourth chapter the mental nature (Eliphaz) begins to assert itself and reflect upon the conditions of self and not-self. The awakening of the conscience is described as a spirit calling from within and causing fear and trembling. It is " the voice of the Lord God in the garden," proclaiming the moral law and the imperious demands of the spiritual nature. It is pointed out that the personalities are not the abiding part of the soul, for they perish betwixt their going forth into incarnation, and their coming in. (*See* JOB iv. 20.)

The reason why the Spirit is so full of complaints and despondency is, that the Perfect, expressing itself through the imperfect, is filled with a sense of limitation, oppression, and dissatisfaction. This spiritual tragedy is the Divine sacrifice—the crucifixion of the Spirit in matter. The higher Love-nature is in appearance born to suffering and sorrow, and subject to contumely and misunderstanding. It must be noted that " suffering " and " sorrow " are symbols of the bondage of Spirit in matter, and of the ego's deprivation of the higher qualities in its expression. The Spirit is described as longing for return to its former state of glory and freedom ; this indicates the aspiring life within the soul.

It is needful to remember that the three lower vehicles can only express themselves in the *lower mind*, for the seat of consciousness is only in the mind. This accounts for the sameness in the speeches of Job's three " friends." The mental, astral, and physical natures are expressions of the mind. In the first speech of Eliphaz there is indicated the awakenment of the conscience, which explains the moral tone of all the speeches. The lower mind in reproaching the Higher nature, which it does not understand, does this from its highest moral standpoint. The necessarily defective expression of the Spirit striving within is misinterpreted by the lower mind, which applies only rational tests of truth and right to the activities of the evolving Love-nature which cries plaintively from within the soul. The self-satisfied lower mind, full of intellectual pride, clings to its pet opinions and prejudices and resents the new truth that presents itself in objectionable guise. It always from its highest religious considerations rejects new ideals, and reproaches the Spirit for its defective expressions.

"The period (of the chastisement of the guilty in the fires of hell) has been fixed by tradition at twelve months, being that of the sufferings of Job, and also of Nephesh with the body "(Zohar).— A. E. WAITE, Secret Doctrine in Israel, p. 178.

A year of twelve months is a symbol of the cycle of life on the lower planes (hell), during which the souls, being imperfect (guilty), are purified (fires). This implies the bondage of the incarnate Self (Job) until perfection is attained. It is the same with man's desire-nature (nephesh) or lower soul, for this exists in various states throughout the cycle and is not discarded until the end.

In the fifth and succeeding chapters, the process of the evolution of the soul is further described. The soul-bodies express their relation to the Spirit, and expound the manifold workings of karma on the lower planes for the purpose of evoking all that is higher in the mind and heart of man. The desire-nature (Bildad) and the sense-nature (Zophar) assert their part in the evolution of the higher qualities. The Spirit (Job), being unable to express its true nature in a world of imperfection and evil, seems to be full of lamentation and woe and subject to the carping criticism which deals only with appearances and knows nothing of the Divine process in which all things work together for good.

In the thirty-second chapter there is indicated the passing of the Life-wave to a higher globe and the coming into activity of the causal-body (Elihu) or buddhi-manasic nature. "I am young and ye are very old." The causal-self is wiser

than the selves that preceded it, and seeks to justify the Spirit, but still fails to fully understand it and its limitation in matter.

In other chapters the Supreme (Lord) vindicates the indwelling Spirit (Job), which is declared to be in the foundation of the lower nature (earth), and he exhorts the Spirit to complete its evolution. "Deck thyself now with excellency and dignity," —and rise above the pride of the mind. Finally the Spirit comprehends the Divine scheme and its purpose that cannot be restrained; it realises itself and its oneness with the Supreme, for "now mine eye seeth thee," and the lower nature then falls away and disappears.

The "patience of Job" is the patience of the indwelling Christ who "feareth God and escheweth evil," and is always waiting to redeem the imperfections of the evolving souls who are essentially himself. Satan, the Adversary, is but the son and agent of the Supreme to work his will. "Satan" is the limitation and illusion inseparable from manifestation; it envelops the Self in the process of involution, and has to be resisted and overcome in the subsequent process of evolution.

"Christ, the Divine Job, conquers Satan by His own strength and holiness, and enables his members to conquer Satan by His power."—WORDSWORTH, Bible, Job, p. 98.

There came a period when the spiritual monads (sons of God) were ready to manifest upon the buddhic plane, and thereupon relativity and the opposites supervened. The Self (Job) then descends to the mental and astral planes, and becomes obscured to the lower consciousness. The desires are aroused, and, as it were, kill the intuitions and higher qualities from out the soul, but they cannot affect the Self within (JOB i).

Again there came a period when the spiritual monads descended to the mental plane, and in the lower nature of the soul began to experience the strife and suffering consequent to evolution in conditions of ignorance and evil (JOB ii).

"And therefore it behoved that blessed

Job also, who uttered those high mysteries of His Incarnation, should by his life be a sign of Him, Whom by voice he proclaimed, and by all that he underwent should show forth what were to be His sufferings. . . . Accordingly the blessed Job conveys a type of the Redeemer, Who is to come together with His own Body (the Church) : and his wife who bids him curse, marks the life of the carnal."—GREGORY THE GREAT, *Morals on the Book of Job*, Preface.

See ARC. MAN, BEHEMOTH, BIRDS (two), BRIAREUS, CASTES, CHILDREN OF EAST, CHILDREN OF HORUS, CONSCIENCE, EAST, ESTHER, EXILE, FOOT, GILGOOLEM, HEARING, HELL, IMMORTALITY, INCARNATION, JOSEPH, LEVIATHAN, PERSONALITY, POTSHERD, POVERTY, PRAGÂPATI RELAXED, RĀHU, REDEEMER, RENOVATION, SATAN, SERVANT OF GOD, SEVEN, SHEEP, SHORT-LIVED, SINGERS, SI-OSIRI, SKIN, SLEEP (waking), SONG, SONS OF GOD, SORES, SORROW, SUFFERING, SUNRISING, VESTURES, VOICE OF GOD.

JOHANNA THE BAPTISER :—

A symbol of the aspiration, or spirit, of Truth in the moral nature.

"Jesus comes to Johanna to be baptised. Jesus comes as a simple 'approacher' seeking initiation into the mystic school of Johanna. But Johanna is not to be deceived, and immediately recognises him as the Master, Manda d'Hajje, the Gnosis of Life."—*Codex Nazareus*, Tractate XI. of the Right Hand Genza.

This signifies the approach of the Christ-soul to the spirit of Truth in the moral nature, to which it is content to appeal so that it may unfold and realise the things of eternal Life which are contained within the soul. The Christ-soul comes as a little child, and is ready to take the Truth first hand,—to acquire it through the experiences which are to follow his " initiation," or deeper realization of some established fact of the spiritual life. But the spirit of Truth fails not to perceive the Life, Light, and Love which now illumine it and cognise it. So it follows that the Truth-nature realises that the Christ is above it, and it does homage. The meaning of " Manda d'Hajje " is Truth-Goodness in union, and " the Master " is the Higher Self,—the Divine Illuminator of those qualities which have sought

the way to Peace and to union with the Self.

See BAPTISM, EXPERIENCES, GNOSIS, INITIATIONS, JESUS, SACRIDAGAMIN.

JOHN THE BAPTIST :—

A symbol of the moral nature which of necessity precedes the coming of the spiritual into the human soul. It purifies by truth (water), and is the herald and forerunner of the Christ-birth.

" And in those days cometh John the Baptist, preaching in the wilderness of Judea, saying, Repent ye ; for the kingdom of heaven is at hand. For this is he that was spoken of by Isaiah the prophet, saying, The voice of one crying in the wilderness, Make ye ready the way of the Lord, make his paths straight."—MAT. iii. 1–3.

At an early period of the soul's evolution the moral nature emerging from its latent state became energised by the Spirit from within. And it began to admonish the qualities in that subjective condition of the regenerate soul in which it is cut off from the lower illusion, and freed from the deceptive and alluring attractions to which it falls an easy prey ere it has arrived at the stage in which the moral nature is active. The instruction to the qualities is that they should purify themselves in view of a raising of the consciousness to a higher level. For in the intuitive mind the advent of the moral nature is foreseen, and that the imperious voice of the conscience will cry out from the soul's inner solitude, that the qualities should realise the way of Truth which leads unto Life eternal, and see that the way be established by moral rectitude.

" John the Baptist is interior and mystic, inasmuch as he represents that all-compelling summons of the conscience to repentance, renunciation, and purification, which is the indispensable precursor of success in the quest after inward perfection."—*The Perfect Way*, p. 241.

" The faculty by means of which man has the apprehension of divine things— namely, the understanding—must first undergo the purification implied in the baptism which is of John. To say that he who becomes a Christ must be baptised of John, is to say that the first and most essential step to man's realisation of his due divinity is purification of body and mind. Only they who are thus purified can 'see'—that is, can realise—God."—E. MAITLAND, *Life of A. K.*, Vol. I. p. 151.

"The end of Salvation is perfection, the Christlike mind, character and life. Morality is on the way to this perfection ; it may go a considerable distance towards it, but it can never reach it. Only Life can do that. For this great formative agent Life must develop out according to its type ; and being a germ of the Christ-life, it must unfold into a *Christ*."—H. DRUMMOND, *Natural Law, etc.*, p. 129.

"There being no such thing as Spontaneous Generation, man's moral nature, cannot generate Life ; while, his high organisation can never in itself result in Life, Life being always the cause of organisation and never the effect of it."— *Ibid.*, p. 383.

"I do not think there is much doubt but that the greatness here (MAT. ii. 11) ascribed to John the Baptist is a moral and religious rather than a merely intellectual or material quality. . . . It has been held that the Master here refers to the difference between the new dispensation and the old, that by the kingdom of heaven he meant his church, and that every one who became a member of that church was forthwith ushered into a new experience, a state of grace, and had imparted to him a higher kind of life, a diviner life, than aught the world had hitherto known. This is the truth, but it is not all the truth. . . . The natural man may be great in all his various types—great in mind and morals, great as administrator, warrior, philosopher, prophet, great in all the arts and sciences, and in everything that tends towards the betterment of human lot in a material world. But greater still is he in whom Christ has arisen with regenerating power, disclosing to him his unlikeness to that which is highest and holiest, but at the same time declaring his kinship thereto, and enabling him to attain to ever closer and more perfect union therewith."—R. J. CAMPBELL, Serm., *The Higher Greatness*.

"(J. G. Fichte teaches)—What the moral man called duty and command is to the religious man the highest spiritual blossom of life, his element, in which alone he can breathe. . . . The pains of self-conquest, for the moral man the speechless sacrifice of blind obedience, are to the religious man no longer his own pains, but the pains of a lower nature in revolt against his true self, the pangs of a new birth, which engenders splendid life far above our expectations. He who is consecrated by religion is raised above time and decay, for his life is rooted in the one fundamental divine life with all its blessedness, and possesses it at each moment, immediate and entire. To religion thus understood, morality is related as a preparatory stage : ' By morality we are first trained

to obedience, and in trained obedience love arises as its sweetest fruit and recompense.' Religion being thus described on its practical or mystical side as a harmonious fundamental disposition of the soul, Fichte shows in what follows, how this disposition rests on a terrestrial view of the world, which reckons the world and all life in time to be not the true and real existence, but the divided appearance of the divine Being, which in itself is One."— PFLEIDERER, *Phil. of Religion*, p. 288.

"Should it not be the task of humanity, as it emerges from nature and rises into the life of the spirit, to realise and to make apparent above the physical universe that moral universe which reproduces all its riches, and all its harmony in a higher plane, and with ineffable glory ? For it is a fact that the moral consciousness does not appear at the beginning of evolution, nor does it at any moment burst suddenly into being all luminous and perfect. It emerges slowly and laboriously from the night of nature. It cannot establish itself without subordinating physical laws to its own laws, hence contradictions and repeated conflicts. Thus there is always a double relation between nature and the spirit ; nature remains for the moral consciousness a necessary support which it has no right to despise, and at the same time an obstacle which it ought to overcome, and a limit which it must overpass. In a positive sense nature prepares for the advent of the spirit ; this is its reason for being. In a negative sense, the spirit can triumph only in raising itself above nature."—A. SABATIER, *The Religions, etc.*, p. xxv.

See ARK (bul.), BAPTISM, BHARATA, CAMELS' HAIR, CHRIST INCREASES, DESERTS, FALL, GIRDLE (leather), LOCUSTS, MOSAIC, MOSES, PEOPLE, PROPHET, QUALITIES, SHOE-LATCHET, TREE OF KNOWLEDGE, WATER, WILDERNESS, ZACHARIAS.

JOHN, THE APOSTLE :—

A symbol of the ideal love-nature in the philosophic mind, which is the architect, or contriver, of the mental edifice of the human being. It is the spiritual factor which guides the operations of the mental builders of form. As a symbol of one of the four elements, "John" signifies *fire* (buddhi).

"Jesus saith unto his mother, Woman, behold thy son ! Then saith he to the disciple (John), Behold, thy mother ! And from that hour the disciple took her unto his own home."—JOHN xix. 27.

Under the direction of the indwelling Spirit, the purified lower nature

(Madonna) becomes allied with the philosophic mind, and so they are raised and united with the Christ, whose Spirit is with them henceforward.

See APOSTLES, DISCIPLES, GETHSEMANE, TRANSFIGURATION, VIRGIN MARY.

JONAH OF THE OLD TESTAMENT :—

A type of the soul whose evolution was consummated in the Christ as symbolised in the sign *Pisces*. "Jonah" corresponds to the stage of evolution signified by this sign as the Goal of attainment.

See JESUS (fish), SIGN, WHALE.

JONATHAN AND DAVID :—

Symbols of the intuition of love and truth, and of the the lower emotion nature or natural man, and its disciplining mind.

See DAVID.

JORDAN :—

A symbol of the " river of Life,"—the spiritual life-essence flowing from above and traversing the lower planes.

" Under ' the Jordan ' we have to understand the Word of God who became flesh and tabernacled among us, Jesus who gives us as our inheritance the humanity which He assumed."—ORIGEN, *Comm. on John*, Bk. VI. § 25.

" For he (the Logos) is Ocean—' birth-causing of gods, and birth-causing of men '—flowing and ebbing for ever, now up and now down. When Ocean flows down, it is the birth-causing of men ; and when he flows up . . . it is the birth-causing of gods. . . . For from water alone,—that is Spirit,—is begotten the spiritual man, not the fleshly. This is the Great Jordan, which flowing downwards and preventing the sons of Israel from going forth out of Egypt, or from the intercourse below, was turned back by Jesus and made to flow upwards " (Naassene Document).—HIPPOLYTUS, *Philosophumena*.

This refers to the Divine Life or Spirit (water) descending into Matter, and again ascending therefrom. The descending process is Involution which perfects the Archetypal Man, and causes the birth of human souls on the mental plane. The ascending process is Evolution, which causes the birth of the higher qualities (gods) and souls made perfect through the power of the indwelling Christ

(Jesus). " Egypt, etc." signifies the lower nature in which the egos are immersed, until the flow of the Divine Life is reversed by the Spirit (Jesus) and through Evolution rises to the buddhic plane (Jerusalem above) carrying with it the souls of humanity,—raising them from death unto the life eternal.

" In all we think and feel, and do, and suffer, we are like the water that comes down from above, seeking to get back to where we came from. . . . Despite all hindrances and setbacks, we are one and all making towards the ocean of perfect unity in Christ, whence our full humanity, now knowing itself divine, shall be lifted up and glorified eternally by the Holy Spirit of God."—R. J. CAMPBELL, Serm., *Our Quest for God*.

See ARC, MAN. EGYPT, (lower), EVOLUTION, EXODUS, GODS, INCARNATION OF SOULS, INVOLUTION, ISRAELITES, JERUSALEM, JESUS SON OF GOD, LOGOS, MATTER, OCEAN, RIVER OF LIFE, WATER (higher), WORD OF GOD.

JOSEPH, SON OF JACOB :—

A type of the Christ-soul, the Self struggling upward from below.

" Joseph in an Egyptian prison is Christ come into the world, where He can meet the two peoples, that is, the Jew and the Gentile. . . . After long suffering, first, from the ungoverned violence of activities which spring from true service, then through temptations from the affections of the natural man, then through bondage and pain, the spirit is freed and glorified. All Egypt bows to Joseph."—A. JUKES, *Types of Genesis*, pp. 407, 409.

" The fundamental thought of the entire *Testament of Joseph* is the following :—Joseph is a type of the suffering Christ. . . . The idea seems to have been so to group the sons of Jacob around Joseph that he should be the object of the hatred of them all in their manifold sins, and yet, whilst apparently perishing at their hands, be their deliverer."—DORNER, *The Person of Christ*, Vol. I. p. 421.

" Egypt " signifies the mental plane, and " Egyptians " the mental faculties. Mind becomes subject to spirit.

See DANIEL, EGYPT, GENTILES JACOB, JEWS, JOB.

JOSEPH, HUSBAND OF MARY :—

A symbol of the natural reason allied with the purified emotion-nature.

"But Joseph said privately to Mary : I dare not speak to Him (the child Jesus) ; but do thou admonish Him, and say : Why hast thou raised against us the hatred of the people ; and why must the troublesome hatred of men be borne by us ? "—*Gospel of Pseudo-Mathew*, Ch. 26.

When the reason and emotion nature realised what had been accomplished in killing out a lower desire, and because the lower qualities of the soul were incensed at the action of the higher nature, they sought to appeal to the Christ. But the reason could not appeal to the Christ ; supplication must needs come through the emotions. "Joseph" also signifies the lower aspect of the soul which fears the censure of the world, and will not sacrifice all for the kingdom of God. "Why," says Joseph, in effect, "must we suffer ? Why must the soul painfully climb to rise ? "

See BOYS (bad), SPARROWS, VINE-POLES.

JOSHUA, SON OF NUN :—

A generic name, the same as Jesus, and plays a similar dramatic part.

JOTUNHEIM :—

A symbol of the lower plane of the mind (kama-manas) with its activities of fear, cunning, greed, spite, etc.

See GOLDEN AGE, NIFLHEIM.

JOVE ; JUPITER ; ZEUS :—

A symbol of the Logos or Higher Self. The Divine Will.

See ZEUS.

JUBAL, SON OF LAMECH AND ADAH :—

A symbol of the germ of higher emotions aroused through reflection (Lamech) and experience (Adah).

"And his brother's name was Jubal : he was the father of all such as handle the harp and pipe."—GEN. iv. 21.

Allied with the transient emotions were the higher emotions, and the germ of these gave rise to the emotions of truth, wisdom, and love, which bring harmonious conditions into the life of the soul.

See ADAH, JABAL, LAMECH, MUSICIAN, PAN.

JUDAH, THE LAND OF :—

The region of the qualities beloved of God,—the chosen of the Lord. Those soul qualities in which the Divine nature is evolved in some degree.

See HILL COUNTRY, ISRAELITES, JESHURUN, PRAISE OF GOD.

JUDAH, THE TRIBE OF :—

A symbol of qualities in which is the spirit of insight and understanding of spiritual verities.

"For it is evident that our Lord hath sprung out of Judah ; as to which tribe Moses spake nothing concerning priests." —HEB. vii. 14.

"Jesus" is here taken as a symbol of the regenerate soul which stands for the Christ manifest in the "flesh" or lower nature. The Christ-soul is beyond the Law of the old dispensation, as Love is superior to Rule and obedience (Levi). "Judah" signifies the spirit of insight and understanding of the things of the higher life, and out of this the Christ-soul comes.

See DISPENSATIONS, MOSES, PRIEST, QUALITIES, TRIBES.

JUDAS ISCARIOT :—

This symbol of one of the twelve disciplined qualities of the soul signifies the lowest of these qualities, —the quality that happens to be the least raised of all of them. It becomes, therefore, the symbol of limitation,—the lowest point, on which the superstructure of the higher nature is built up from. In the process of involution of Spirit into matter, it is the Highest which descends to the lowest ; but in the present process of evolution it is Spirit that ascends from the lowest point to the Highest. This lowest point, then, "Judas," contains the potentiality of all things evolutional. It signifies the condition of absolute limitation, which seems nothingness from the physical or lower-mind standpoint, but from the Spiritual side it implies all-being. Limitation (Saturn) is thus the symbol of its direct antithesis, illimitability, and its visible sign. So it is that the germinal point (·)—the least element in the production of form,—becomes the fitting symbol of Life everlasting. In other terms, the quality "Judas" interiorly symbolises that state whence blossoms perfection or finality. Superficially, " Judas " may stand for prudence changing to contrition.

"And as they were eating, Jesus said, Verily I say unto you, that one of you shall betray me."—MAT. xxvi. 21.

The Christ-soul knew that the lower nature was not yet completely purified,—hence his accusation of one of the qualities. Had the lower nature been completely purified there was no need for the anguish which was to be experienced at the crossing over. The connection between the " cross " and the " betrayal " seems to be obscure, yet there is a vital connection between them. The " cross " is the symbol of *matter* upon which the Christ-soul was, as it were, " crucified," and " Judas " is a symbol of *limitation* which is at once the lowest and the foundation of the Highest. Thus the least-raised quality in the soul is a symbol of *matter* on which the Spirit is offered up.

"What is natural is the ultimate or lowest form of existence, in which things spiritual and celestial come to a termination, and upon which they rest, like a house upon its foundation."—SWEDEN-BORG, *On the White Horse*, p. 45.

"Thus the number thirteen, which on the earthly plane, and before the ' Crucifixion,' is, through the treachery of ' Judas,' the symbol of imperfection and ill-fortune, becomes, in the ' Kingdom of the Father,' the symbol of perfection." —*The Perfect Way*, p. 247.

The first drop issuing from a bottom tap in a barrel full of water may be taken as the first limited manifestation of the truth within, and therefore the foundation of the actual which gradually evolves to perfection as the potential (water in barrel) externalises to completion. " Judas " may signify the lowest drop at any stage of the process, and the lower limitation of the higher which is to follow.

See BETRAYAL, BOAR, CROSS, CRUCIFIXION, JESUS (gospels), MATTER, NIGHT AS DARKNESS, OLYMPUS, QUALITIES, SATURN, THIRTEEN.

JUDGES :—

A symbol of qualities transmuted and raised so that they become leaders and educators of qualities below them.

" I appoint unto you a kingdom, even as my father appointed unto me, that ye may eat and drink at my table in my kingdom ; and ye shall sit on thrones judging the twelve tribes of Israel "— LUKE xxii. 29, 30.

The time shall arrive at the end of the cycle when the qualities of the present stage shall be transmuted, and so brought to a higher state than can now be conceived of. When the Christ shall be exalted, the higher qualities shall be exalted with him, and shall be the leaders of those below them, according to the kinds and conditions of these, and their several stages of progress.

See DISCIPLES ON THRONES, KINGDOM OF HEAVEN, QUALITIES, REGENERATION, TABLE, TRANSMUTATION, TRIBES OF ISRAEL.

JUDGING OTHERS :—

Symbolic of mental qualities condemning the stage of progress of other qualities less progressed apparently than themselves.

"Who art thou that judgest the servant of another ? to his own lord he standeth or falleth. Yea, he shall be made to stand ; for the Lord hath power to make him stand."—ROM. xiv. 4.

This exhortation is to the effect that a quality must not presume to interfere with the evolution of a ministering quality subordinate to another discipline and serving its own Ideal. To that Ideal it is responsible, and the Self within is able to transmute the quality accordingly.

The " servant " of a mental quality, is a lower-grade quality which ministers to, and preserves, activities important to effect progress at a particular stage. To its own ruling quality the serving quality " standeth or falleth," and it is not to be condemned as out of place. It is evolved there by the will of the Higher Self, who needs it and maintains it.

"There are many who have an undisturbed belief in God and Christianity. They feel too deeply ever to ask a single question. They understand all they want to understand. They have a natural liking for authority, and they are convinced that the authority they depend on is a true and righteous one. And if their life be pure and noble it is a guilty thing to disturb their faith unless we absolutely believe that their belief is degrading their spiritual life. If scepticism arise spontaneously it must be met and accepted, but to instil it into the peaceful heaven of a pure soul is wickedness ; there is sorrow enough in the world without our needlessly creating it. But a warning ought to be given to these happy persons. They must not despise or denounce those who cannot trust authority, whose intellect troubles their spirit. . . . Their own peace is great ; let them show their gratitude by tenderness to others. As to their airs of superiority, it does not follow because they are not disturbed that they are spiritually superior."—STOPFORD A. BROOKE, Serm., *Lord, Increase our Faith.*

See FAITH, LANDMARKS, NEIGHBOUR, SERVANTS, SCEPTICISM.

JUDGMENT AND JUSTICE :—

Judgment denotes an estimation of the state of progress in relation to the completion and perfection of quality, that is, in relation to Truth. Justice requires balanced conditions on each plane of nature.

" By judgment is signified divine truth, and by justice divine good. . . . 'But let judgment run down as water, and justice as a mighty stream' (AMOS v. 24). . . . 'Justice and judgment are the habitation of thy throne' (Ps. lxxxix. 14)."—SWEDENBORG, *Apoc. Rev.,* n. 668.

See JUSTICE, SITTING (Jesus).

JUDGMENT-DAY :—

A symbol of the summing up of progress at the end of the cycle, when the vast multitude of souls have arisen from their lower nature (the dead) and are ready to become united with the Higher Self in the causal-body. Insufficiently progressed souls have to await on the mental plane the opening of another cycle. The desires and lower qualities attached to centres on the astral plane are destroyed as illusion by " unquenchable fire,"—buddhi.

" The Lord knoweth how to deliver the godly out of temptation, and to keep the unrighteous under punishment unto the day of judgment."—2 PETER ii. 9.

" Here, at the bridge Kinvat, Ormazd holds a tribunal and decides the fate of souls. The good pass the bridge into the mansions of the blessed, where they are welcomed with rejoicing by the Amshaspands ; the bad fall over into the gulf of Dusahk, where they are tormented by the daevas. The duration of the punishment is fixed by Ormazd, and some are redeemed earlier by means of the prayers of their friends, but many must remain till the resurrection of the dead."—*Zoroastrian System,* CLARKE.

The supreme Divine Power manifesting as Will now exercises its spiritual function on the higher-mind plane, and sifts the good from the bad ; that is, it liberates those purified souls which have already allied themselves with the Higher Self, and it puts due pressure upon those who are still full of the things of the personality. The " good " are able to rise to the abode of Bliss,—the buddhic plane,— and there they are met by those inner intelligences which are bringers of glad tidings, and so serve to evolve the inner capacities inherent, or potential, within the soul. The " bad," however, are said to fall ; and this means that, being insufficiently developed, they are disqualified from rising beyond those lower levels whereon they have sown, and where they are detained and tortured (as it seems to them) by the karmic results of their works. The duration of this term of probation is determined according to the scope of the more or less effective will. The earlier redemption merely refers to the fact that some souls are in a position, from having acted in the past in accordance with their knowledge, to receive aid from the upper planes, and so even then to rise and enter into the joy of the Higher Life. Many souls, however, must remain upon these lower planes during the interval between two cycles, and until the new manvantara arrives, when they shall again have opportunities to progress.

" The visible is the ladder up to the invisible ; the temporal is but the scaffolding of the eternal And when the last immaterial souls have climbed through this material to God, the scaffolding shall be taken down and the earth dissolved with fervent heat—not because it was base, but because its work is done."—H. DRUMMOND, *Natural Law, etc.,* p. 57.

See AAT, AKESI AMSHASPANDS, BRIDGE (kinvat), BUDDHI, CHRIST'S SECOND COMING, CONFLAGRATION, DAEVAS, DEAD, DUSAHK, FIRE (destr.), HELL, HORSE (white), KALKI, KHABIT, MAN (bad), PAHAD, PERSONALITY, REGNAROK, RENOVATION, SHENIT, SOSIOSH, THEMIS, UNRIGHTEOUS, VISCERA.

JUDGMENT HALL OF OSIRIS, AND THE WEIGHING OF THE HEART :—

Symbolical of the soul's evolution on the lower planes to ultimate perfection and union with God.

" The scribe Ani and his wife Thuthu enter the Hall of Double Maāt, wherein the heart, symbolic of the conscience, is to be weighed in the balance against the feather emblematical of right and truth. In the upper register are the gods who sit in judgment. . . . On the standard of the scales sits the dog-headed ape, the companion of Thoth, the scribe of the gods ; and the god Anubis, jackal-headed, tests the tongue of the balance. On the left of the balance, facing Anubis are :—(1) Ani's ' Luck ' ; (2) the *Meskhen* or ' cubit with human head,' thought by some to be connected with the place of birth ; (3) the goddesses Meskhenet and Renenet who presided over the birth, birth-place, and early education of children ; and (4) the soul of Ani in the form of a human-headed bird standing on a pylon. On the right of the balance, behind god Anubis, stands Thoth, the scribe of the gods, who holds in his hands his reed-pen and palette with which to record the result of the trial. Behind Thoth stands the monster called either Amām, the ' Devourer,' or Am-mit, the ' Eater of the dead.' "—BUDGE, *Book of the Dead*, p. 22.

The mental and emotional natures (man and wife) are prime factors in the soul's evolution on higher and lower planes of order and law (double Maāt). In the centre of the picture is symbolised the content of the soul, whose nature is to be weighed in the balance of experience. The heart in the vase stands for the causal-body, the shrine of the Higher Self, and the feather of Maāt in the other scale signifies the lower personality that relates to justice and law in contradistinction to the higher nature (heart), which is answerable to the dominion of love. The light and unstable feather is symbolic of the life of the personality, and is appropriately the sign of the ephemeral, illusory personality of the lower planes. The ideals (gods) are the tests of the soul's efforts to rise. The dog-headed ape symbolises the lower mind, which finds expression through the experiences of life. The figure of Anubis represents the physical body, which kneels to the law of

necessity in nature and so tries to turn the scale in his favour towards the lower life. By so doing the mind is led to act through the astro-physical nature, and thus it is that the ego's several early experiences are gained : these are recorded in the causal-body by the higher mind (Thoth).

(1) " Ani's Luck." The upright figure of a man next to the heart symbolises the lower human nature, or the material life portion of the individual, and refers to the personality. The physical existence being to a great extent independent altogether of the control of the soul itself, and the conditions of organism and environment being divinely pre arranged in accordance with karmic law, so the happenings which beset the physical body, or other outer vehicles of the soul, are to be conceived of as illusory, and, as it were, in the nature of chance or destiny, since they are but temporary combinations of conditions and circumstances which are conducive to such growth as will afford the Divine life within the means for expansion and development.

(2) " The Meskhen." The man-headed rectangular object symbolises the perfected individuality. It is said to be " connected with the place of birth," that is, it is an emanation from atma wherefrom the ego originates.

(4) " The man-headed bird " symbolises the spiritual ego or Divine soul. These three,—the spiritual ego, the individuality and the personality, —constitute the threefold aspect of the human being.

(3) The two small upright figures close together, called Renenet, goddess of nursing, and Meskhenet, goddess of the funeral chamber, symbolise nature in its dual aspect of sustainer and destroyer, by means of which the ego evolves from the germ state to maturity.

Thoth is a symbol of the higher mind or intellect which subjectively gathers up the life experiences of the ego into the causal-body. The monster behind Anubis is typical of negation,—that state into which the lower illusion will descend, and by which it will, as it were, be swallowed.

"Thoth, the judge of Right and Truth, saith :—'Hear ye this judgment. The heart of Osiris (Ani) hath in very truth been weighed, and his soul hath stood as a witness for him ; it hath been found true by trial in the Great Balance. There hath not been found any wickedness in him.' "—*Ibid.*, p. 26.

This signifies that the personality has been perfected and the soul is victorious over the lower nature.

See AB, AMMIT, ANUBIS, APE BALANCE, CAUSAL-BODY, EVOLUTION, EXPERIENCE, FEATHER, GODS, HAWK, HEART, HEBEN, HOME, INDIVIDUALITY, KARMA, MAAT, MESKHENIT, PERSONALITY, RECTANGLE, RENENIT, SAU, SHAI, SHENIT, THOTH.

JUMALA :—

A symbol of the Divine Will or Higher Self, Atma-buddhi.

"*Jumala* meant originally the sky. It is derived, as Castrén has shown (p. 24), from *Juma*, thunder, and *la*, the place, meaning therefore the place of thunder, or the sky. It is used first of all for sky, secondly for the god of the sky, and thirdly for gods in general." —MAX MÜLLER, *Science of Religion*, p. 133.

"God, the supreme creator—omnipotent Jumala."—*Kalevala.*

JUPITER, PLANET, (TISHTAR) :—

A symbol of the benefic directive function of the Self, which leads, governs and initiates activities that go to the awakenment of ideals in the soul.

"I call upon the star Tishtar, the brilliant, the glorious ; at the time when it is in the form of a Bull with golden horns, I call it most" (*Vendidad*, (Pahlavi), XIX. 126).—HAUG, *Essays*, p. 389.

I acclaim the Self, the fountain of Light and Truth, in his aspect of the positive, active, function of Wisdom, whereby he will awaken aspirations for wisdom and truth in the soul ! I hold to my ideals.

See BULL, HORNS OF GOLD, PLANETS, SATURN, TISTRYA.

JUSTICE :—

A symbol of balanced conditions of progress on different planes, in relation to karmic law.

"But he answered and said to one of them, Friend, I do thee no wrong : didst not thou agree with me for a penny ? Take up that which is thine, and go thy way ; it is my will to give unto this last, even as unto thee. Is it not lawful for me to do what I will with mine own ? or is thine eye evil, because I am good ? So the last shall be first, and the first last."—MAT. xx. 13–6.

The Higher Self disciplines the qualities, and chides their rebellious murmurings, and points out that no injustice has been done,—saying that as qualities have sown, so they have reaped. It is the will of the Logos that perfect fairness shall be meted out,—He lives in all, and all is but His own. He asks if there be imperfection in the lower nature, and whether, if so, it is not an imperfect mirror or reflector of His Divine Nature. For it is necessary that the first in order of evolution of qualities become last in progression, whilst the last take the chiefest place.

The first that are evolved are full of the desire nature, while the last are more advanced and are reincarnated later in the cycle.

"The necessary replies (or returns) which a man's surroundings make to what he is and does :—'With what measure ye mete, it shall be measured to you again.' It is a law of vast extent and wonderful exactness. The world is far more orderly than we believe ; a deeper and a truer justice runs through it than we imagine. We all go about calling ourselves victims, discoursing on the cruel world, and wondering that it should treat us so, when really we are only meeting the rebound of our own lives. What we have been to things about us has made it necessary that they should be this to us. As we have given ourselves to them, so they have given themselves to us. This is the law I want to trace with you, only begging you to keep your minds clear of any materialism which would think that in mere earth itself resides this power of just and discriminating reply. It is as we and all things exist together in the great embracing and pervading element of God that all things give themselves to us as we give ourselves to them. So all the phenomena of life are at the same time divine judgments if we are only wise enough to read them."— PHILLIPS BROOKS, Serm., *The Gift and its Return.*

See HOUSEHOLDER (highest), KARMA, LABOURERS, MONEY, QUALITIES, REINCARNATION, SOWING AND REAPING, STEWARD, VINEYARD, WAGES, WORK.

JUSTIFICATION BY FAITH :—

A symbol of being perfected through the intuition of Wisdom and Love, which reveals the Truth and the Life.

"But before faith came, we were kept under the law, shut off from the faith which should afterwards be revealed. Wherefore the law was our schoolmaster to bring us unto Christ, that we might be justified by faith. But after that faith is come we are no longer under a schoolmaster."—GAL. iii. 23–5.

Before intuition comes we are disciplined under law, reason, cause and effect, Karma, and kept in bondage to authority until intuition should evolve in the soul. Wherefore the law of cause and effect, of sequence and of experience, was as a teacher to lead us unto Wisdom and Love, that at length we should be perfected by intuition. So when the intuition is acquired, then we have knowledge of the truth, and have no more need of instruction by authority and experience, for we perceive the truth direct.

See DISPENSATIONS, FAITH, INTUITION, KARMA, LAW OF MOSES, MOSAIC, MOSES, REDEMPTION, SALVATION, TESTAMENT.

KA, GOD :—

A symbol of the Divine Will.

"Buddha performed various ceremonies hard to be accomplished, like the god Ka in the first aeon wishing to create living beings."—*Buddha-Karita*, Bk. II. p. 51.

At an early stage, the Soul made the initial attempt at undergoing initiations in order to increase the Divine life in the activities on the planes ; similarly as the Divine Will, at the first Round when the Son of Mind entered the scheme, contemplated projecting archetypal living beings on the plane of buddhi.

See BIRTH OF BUDDHA, BUDDHA, PROTOTYPES, RACES, ROUNDS, SON OF MAN.

KA, OR DOUBLE :—

A symbol of the causal-body which has to be nourished and developed through the activities of the Ego in its incarnations.

"There is, however, good reason for stating that the immortal part of man which lived in the tomb and had its special abode in the statue of the deceased was the 'double.' This is proved by the fact that a special part of the tomb was reserved for the *ka*, or double, which was called the 'house of the *Ka*,' and that a priest, called the 'priest of the *Ka*,' was specially appointed to minister therein. The double enjoyed the smell of the incense which was offered at certain times each year in the tomb, as well as the flowers, and herbs, and meat, and drink."—DR. BUDGE, *Egyptian Magic*, p. 218.

The "tomb" signifies the incarnation of the ego. Living in the physical body is the entombment of the soul in physical matter. The full-sized "statue" is the perfect personality, in contrast to the "shabti," small figure, emblem of the imperfect personality. The "special part of the tomb" is the inner being. The "priest of the *ka*" is the spiritual mind. The "smell of incense" at times of incarnation during the course of the cycle (year) is the discriminating of the aspirations by the higher mind. The "meat and drink," or goodness and truth ; the "flowers and herbs," or virtues, are the food of the Spirit to develop the causal-body.

"My heart my mother. . . . Thou art my *Ka* within my body which knitteth together and strengtheneth my limbs" (*Papyrus of Ani*).—BUDGE, *Book of the Dead*, p. 25.

See CAUSAL-BODY, CEILING OF SKY, INCENSE, KHUS, PERSONALITY, SAHU, SHABTI, TOMB.

KAABA :—

A symbol of the causal-body. A symbol similar to "house of God," "Temple," or "Church." It is the vehicle of the Higher Self (Atma-buddhi).

The "black stone" of the Kaaba is a symbol of the indwelling Spirit, —darkness, or blackness to us.

"The Ka'ba is but a church, if thou His trace be lost ; the church my only Ka'ba, while He there is found."—*Dewan-i-Shams-i-Tabrizi*, p. 238.

"We appointed the holy house of Mecca to be a place of resort for mankind, and a place of security."—SALE's *Koran*, Ch. II. p. 16.

That is, the causal-body in the higher mind centre (Mecca) retains the mental experiences of the personalities, and endures throughout the cycle.

"The Arabs say that Adam after his expulsion from paradise, begged of God

that he might erect a building like that
he had seen there, called Beit al Mamûr,
or the frequented house, and al Dorâh
towards which he might direct his
prayers, and which he might compass,
as the angels do the celestial sea. Whereupon God let down a representation of
that house in curtains of light, and set it in
Mecca, perpendicularly under its original,
ordering the patriarch to turn towards it
when he prayed, and to compass it by
way of devotion."—SALE's *Koran, Prel.
Disc.,* p. 83.

The aspirations of the lower self
(Adam), after the vibrations from the
buddhic plane (paradise) had ceased,
appealed to the Higher Self, and there
was formed a centre and nucleus of
the causal-body. This had its pre-
formed counterpart on the buddhic
plane as a centre of energy in the
Divine Ray (Tree of Life). The
"curtains of light" symbolise the
higher mind as being receptive of the
Wisdom above.

The "Holy city Mecca" signifies
the higher mind centre, the seat of
the Higher Self to which the lower
self must turn in devotion to its
ideals whereby the causal-body is
compassed and developed. The "perpendicularly" refers to the Divine
Ray from above in which are the
great centres of activity on each plane.

See ADAM (lower), ADYTUM, CHURCH,
CURTAIN, HOUSE (frequented), JERU-
SALEM, PALACE, PARADISE, PYRAMID,
STONE (black), STUPA, TABERNACLE,
TEMPLE.

KABANDHA, A HEADLESS MONSTER :—

A symbol of desire for the gratifica-
tions of sense, which is love perverted.

"And deep below the monster's waist,
his vast misshapen mouth was placed."
He was under a curse—
" that he should retain the disgusting
form he had adopted, at least till, in course
of time, Rama should in person deliver
him from its repulsive deformity. The
brothers (Rama and Lakshmana) placed
the giant's bulky body on a funeral
pyre, and from the ashes arose a beautiful
being clad in celestial raiment."—J. C.
OMAN, *The Great Indian Epics,* p. 52.

A longing desire for objects of
sense,—the lower attraction,—is but
the reverse of divine love,—the higher
attraction. When the Higher Self,
or atma-buddhi (Rama), has con-

quered desire and transmuted it by
fire (buddhi), its direction is changed ;
while its force remains in the spiritual
longing for that which is higher.

See BOTTOMLESS PIT, CREMATION,
DEVOURER, FUNERAL PILES, KILLING,
LAKSHMANA, MONSTERS, RAMA.

KAGU-TSUCHI, GOD OF FIRE :—

A symbol of the Archetypal Man
on the atma-buddhic planes.

"The last deity to be produced was
the God of Fire, Kagu-tsuchi, also called
Ho-musubi (fire-growth). In giving birth
to him Izanami was burnt so that she
sickened and lay down. From her vomit,
fæces, and urine were born deities which
personify the elements of metal, water,
and clay, while from the tears which
Izanagi shed when she died, there was
produced a deity called the Weeping
Female. In his rage and grief, Izanagi
drew his sword and cut Kagu-tsuchi to
pieces, generating thereby a number of
deities."—W. G. ASTON, *Shinto,* p. 92.

This describes the culmination of
Involution and the commencement of
Evolution. The perfected Matter
(Izanami) gives birth to the perfect
Soul or Archetype (atma-buddhic),
and these two have to die out of one
state to be evolved in another. Matter
involved gives rise to matter evolved,
namely, the mental (metal), astral
(water) and physical (clay) planes in
the new order. The "tears" of the
Spirit producing the "Weeping Female" symbolise the advent of suffering and sorrow which characterise the
evolutionary cycle. Then we have the
world-wide symbol of the cutting into
pieces of the body of the Archetypal
Man, and the scattering of the qualities
or "members" in the souls of mankind, now commencing their evolution.
In this case the Divine Will (Izanagi)
is represented as dismembering the
completely involved Self, producing
thereby the qualities (deities) which
war within the mind and soul.

See ARC. MAN, DISMEMBERMENT,
ELEMENTS, EVOLUTION, FIRE, INVO-
LUTION, IZANAGI, MUSUBI.

KAILASA MOUNTAIN :—

A symbol of perfect purity, justice
and wisdom on the higher planes of
the soul.

See ALBORDJ, HIMAVAN, MOUNTAIN,
OLYMPUS.

KAIOMARTS OR GAYOMARD :—

A symbol of the Archetypal Man.

"Kaiomarts was both man and woman, but through his death there came from him the first human pair ; a tree grew from his body, and bore ten pair of men and women."—*Zoroastrian System.*

The archetypal man is male-female (atma-buddhi), and includes mental (masculine) and buddhic (feminine) principles, and through the " death " of these, there appeared the kama-manasic and astral elements, and from these grew the " tree " of life, which corresponds to five lower sub-planes whereon the dual manifestations of the two elements yield the number ten pair of duads, commencing the human root-races in the third round.

" God is the eternal Substance within which lie hidden, waiting for expression, every conceivable form or mode of the ideal good. It is a portion of this infinite divine substance which has been ground into the clay of our earthly human life. And just as the supply of clay-forming rock in the physical world is practically inexhaustible, and contains innumerable varieties wherefrom works of beauty may be produced, so the infinitude of God contains within itself more potencies of good than the universe of universes can ever exhaust to all eternity. But we children of his heart are here that we may utter some of them to his glory and our own."—R. J. CAMPBELL, Serm., *A Christian World-view.*

" All this, up to the Third Round, is formless as matter, and senseless as consciousness. . . . This Adam of dust requires the Soul of Life to be breathed into him : the two middle principles, which are the *sentient* life of the irrational animal and the human soul, for the former is irrational without the latter. It is only when, from a potential andro-gyne, man has become separated into male and female, that he will be endowed with this conscious, rational, individual Soul (manas), ' the principle or intelli-gence of the Elohim,' to receive which, he has to eat of the fruit of Knowledge from the Tree of Good and Evil."—H. P. BLAVATSKY, *Secret Doctrine*, Vol. I. p. 267.

See ARC. MAN, BULL, DEATH, DIS-MEMBERMENT, GOSHURUN, IMAGE, MALE-FEMALE, NAVEL, PROTOTYPES, RACES, ROOT-RACES, ROUND, TREE OF LIFE.

KAI US, REIGN OF :—

Symbolic of an early period in the cycle of involution.

See Ox (splendid).

KAKHRA LAND, THE HOLY :—

A symbol of a condition of existence wherein the Divine life is poured forth ; as at the emanation from atma of a solar universe.

KAKSHIVAT'S BIRTH :—

A symbol of the production of the mental nature from the mental plane.

KĀKSHUSHI (EYE) :—

A symbol of the " eye of the soul," —the inner discernment which perceives only the good and har-monious, and so realises that Truth whereof the universe is built.

See MANASI.

KALAHANSA, THE SWAN IN AND OUT OF TIME :—

A symbol of the Higher Self.

See BIRD (great), KARSHIPTA, SWAN.

KALCHAS, OR CALCHAS, SON OF THESTOR :—

A symbol of the soul's inner memory of experiences, the child of the Self, which is the means of directing the higher mental qualities to the causal self, for it is of the higher mind.

" To Kalchas first spake Agamemnon with look of ill : ' Thou seer of evil, never yet hast thou told me the thing that is pleasant. Evil is ever the joy of thy heart to prophesy, but never yet didst thou tell any good matter nor bring it to pass.' "—*Iliad*, Bk. I.

The lusts and desires of the lower self having become intensified, the Desire-mind (Agamemnon) experiences a sense of dissatisfaction which pro-ceeds from the dawn of the higher consciousness within the soul. The conscience, an expression of the inner memory of experience, decides that certain things are evil, and this being distasteful to the Desire-mind, the sense of rebellion is stirred. The Desire-mind realises that the higher mind always foresees evil, since indeed it is through the apprehension of folly that wisdom is awakened.

" The higher and lower powers of the soul meet in the imaginative faculty, which is the psychical organ of memory and self-consciousness " (Plotinus).—T. WHITTAKER, *The Neo-Platonists*, p. 52.

See AGAMEMNON, CONSCIENCE, EXPERIENCES, GATHAS (chanting), INTUITION, REMINISCENCE, SHIPS OF GREEKS, WORD (living).

KALI-YUGA :—

A symbol of the present period and process of evolution in which Wisdom and Love are gradually developed from ignorance and desire.

"The Kali-yuga or fourth age of the world was supposed to commence at the death of Krishna. The Hindu idea of a succession of four Yugas or ages, in which a gradual deterioration of the human race takes place, has its counterpart among the Romans in the Golden, Silver, Brazen, and Iron Ages, as described in Ovid's *Metamorphoses* (I. 89, etc)."—Mon. Williams, *Indian Wisdom*, p. 333.

The period of evolution of Spirit from matter commences from the death of the Archetypal Man (Krishna). Prior to that is a triple period of involution, wherein Spirit descends into matter through the buddhic (Golden), mental (Silvern), and astral (Brazen) planes, and completes itself in the physical plane (Iron). This gradual obscuration of Spirit has the appearance of deterioration of the soul.

See Arc. man, Golden age, Iron age, Kalki, Scorpio.

KALKI AVATAR OF VISHNU :—

A symbol of the final triumph of the indwelling Self (Vishnu) over the lower nature, at the end of the cycle.

"Kalki or Kalkin, who is yet to appear at the close of the fourth or Kali age, when the world has become wholly depraved, for the final destruction of the wicked, for the re-establishment of righteousness upon the earth, and the renovation of all creation with a return to a new age of purity (satya-yuga). According to some, he (Vishnu) will be revealed in the sky, seated on a white horse, with a drawn sword in his hand, blazing like a comet."—Mon. Williams, *Indian Wisdom*, p. 335.

At the conclusion of the present cycle of evolution, when the lower nature of the soul is reduced to its lowest elements, the God within (Vishnu) shall manifest in perfection upon the highest mental plane and cast away the dregs of the desires. Then from the dissipation of the lower planes, there shall be re-established a more perfect state of soul. There will be a renovation of all creation in the subtler matter of the buddhic plane, and a return to a new age of purity in which the soul can find fuller expression for its inner nature. It

is made known by scripture that the Higher Self (atma-buddhi) reveals himself to the inner consciousness, and seated in the higher mind, will exercise his will in purifying the soul through the transmutation of the qualities. The "sword of the Spirit," or the spiritual energy of Truth from within, shall dispel error and ignorance on the mental plane, and destroy the planes of illusion.

See Aat, Buddha (Maitreya), Christ's second coming, Comets, Conflagration, Horse (white), Judgment day, Regnarok, Renovation, Resurrection, Soshyans, Sosiosh, Vishnu.

KALLIOPEIA, THE MUSE :—

A symbol of the buddhic function which transmutes lower qualities into higher.

"Would that in behalf of perishable beings, immortal Muse, mightest take thought at all for our thought to come by reason of our cares ! Hear me now and be present again by my side, Kalliopeia, as I utter noble discourse about the blessed gods."—*Empedocles*, Fairbanks, 338.

Would that the Divine Love and Wisdom might animate those beings or ideals which are the transitory forerunners of the celestial beings which on upper planes are typical of the virtues or higher emotions of the soul ! Would that the spiritual ideal might overshadow and inspire the actual ! The petition is offered up that the lower nature may be transmuted into the higher, and the attitude of mind is that of profound aspiration and devotion.

See Buddhi, Gods, Muse, Qualities, Transmutation, Wisdom.

KAMA :—

A symbol of desire which is love inverted. That is, desire is attraction to the outer nature, whereas love is attraction to the inner. Thus the twain are antagonists.

"The world was fashioned from the body of a primitive being, a giant *Purusha*, dismembered by the gods. . . . In (the self-existent substance Purusha) arose *Kama*, desire, and that was the first starting-point in the subsequent evolution of being."—Barth, *Religions of India*, p. 30.

The lower nature of the soul is

said to be formed of the "body," or outer envelope,—astro-mental,—of the Archetypal Man, who, when made perfect through *involution*, dies out of that state to be born in the next state—*evolution*. His "body" is divided into the many qualities (members of Christ) which are now to be found in humanity, his offspring. From the self-existent Spirit, which is at the foundation of all things, arose *desire* with its wish to manifest its nature outwardly. It is through the stimulus of desire that the first and subsequent early stages of the evolution of qualities are brought about in the soul.

"When he has set himself free from every desire of his heart, the mortal enters immortal into the Brahma. (From the Brāhmana of the hundred paths.) Desire (kama) and action (karman) are here named as the powers which hold the spirit bound within the limits of impermanence. Both are essentially the same. 'Man's nature,' it is said in the same treatise from which we have taken the passage quoted, 'depends on desire. As his desire, so is his aspiration, so is the course of action (karman) which he pursues ; whatever be the course of action he pursues, he passes to a corresponding state of being.' "—OLDENBURG, *Buddha, etc.*, p. 48.

"Desire is the actual essence of man, in so far as it is conceived as determined to a particular activity by some given modification of itself."—SPINOZA, *Ethics*, Bohn, Vol. II. p. 173.

See ARC. MAN, ASTRAL PLANE, ASURA, DISMEMBERMENT, EVOLUTION, INVOLUTION, KARMA, MARA, PURUSHA, RAVANA, SEKER, SEPARATION, SHAI, SLEEPING, TANEMAHUTA.

KAPILA :—

A symbol of the Second Logos or Higher Self.

"There was a city, the dwelling-place of the great saint Kapila, having its sides surrounded by the beauty of a lofty broad table-land as by a line of clouds, and itself with its high-soaring palaces, immersed in the sky."—*Buddha-Karita*, Bk. I. 2.

The "city" is the celestial region, the atma-buddhi-manas planes of manifestation ; and the "great saint Kapila" is the Self. The "sides of the city" are the planes below in their ideal aspect during involution. The "line of clouds" signifies Wisdom outpouring Truth. The "high-soaring

palaces" are symbolic of exaltation and bliss in the higher realms.

"There is one being who actuates phase after phase of being from within, all colours and all emanations. He fosters with knowledge the Rishi Kapila, that arose in the beginning, and behold him coming into being. This being is the immortal, internal ruler, the universal soul, or Isvara."—*Svetas. Upanishad*, V.

From the Divine Unity,—the Absolute,—is emanated from within, stage after stage of manifested life, setting forth all qualities and all forms. The Absolute forthpours through the Second Logos the eternal Truth. For the Higher Self arose as a germ in the beginning, and gradually unfolded his potencies in the manifest existence. And now is the Self involved in nature and the World-soul, and is in the human soul the indwelling God, its Saviour and Ruler.

See AMARÂVATI, ARHAT, CLOUDS, CITY OF GOD, COLOURS, FIRST-BORN, ISVARA, JERUSALEM, KING (great), MOUNTAIN, SELF.

KARANA-SARIRA (CAUSAL-BODY) :—

A symbol of the higher causal-body on the buddhic plane, or the lower causal-body on the higher mental plane.

"*Karana-sarira* = the cosmic body, the body out of which things emanate, the principle of emanation."—A. E. GOUGH, *Phil. of Upanishads*, p. 50.

This is the World-soul on the buddhic plane (the Argo, Boat of Rā, etc.).

See CAUSAL-BODY, LINGAM, MAHAVIRA-POT, SAHU, SAMKHARA, SHINTAI, SOUL (middle), STHULA, VESTURES.

KARMA :—

The law of causation and interaction between the higher and lower planes to bring about equilibrium between them and gradually raise the soul. It binds the lower Self to the Higher, and arises through the union of the will with knowledge of a moral standard involving choice. It estimates the experience of the ego and is expressed in effects (treasure in heaven) on the buddhic plane. It relates to the process underlying spiritual evolution and adjustment upon the higher planes. As the soul goes forth into the life of experience, so upon each succeeding level the account is squared, as it were, so that each successive stage carries it to its relatively appointed place. This idea underlies all religions, and the Christian who looks for compensation in heaven, or fears punishment in hell, is holding crudely and un-intelligently the truth that what we sow here we reap the result of upon entering the next state. The spiritual law of cause and effect in the soul is made to yield just and right results, so that throughout evolution perfect balance between higher and lower is maintained, and the outcome of it all is stored away in the soul's inner being. As long as the lower nature remains, karma is incurred, but when the lower nature is put away, then the "fruits of the spirit" are reaped by the ego on the buddhic plane.

"An act either mental, verbal, or corporeal, bears good or evil fruit; the various transmigrations of men through the highest, middle, and lowest stages are produced by acts."—*Laws of Manu,*XII.3.

Motives arising from opinions in the mental-body, from desires in the astral-body, and from sensations in the physical-body, accepted by the will operating on the mental plane, lead to particular conditions of incarnation on the lower planes. These are karmical results actualising in three stages which may be called good, bad and indifferent.

"Do not complain, O Soul! of the injustice of the Beloved (the karmic aspect of the Divine Law), for such is thy lot."—HAFIZ.

"The essential truth of heaven and hell is ineradicable in the universe. There is the mighty image of God standing in the centre of all things. And all things have to touch Him. And as all things touch Him, according to their characters, he becomes to them blessing or curse. He is the happiness of obedience (to the law of truth), and the misery of disobedience throughout his world He looks with sympathetic joy or with profoundest pity on the souls He judges, but the judgments both come from Him. The right hand and the left hand are both His. Burning there like the Sun of all the world, He must be a comforting and guiding light or a consuming fire— one or the other—to every soul."— PHILLIPS BROOKS, Serm., *An Evil Spirit from the Lord.*

See ADRASTIA, BALANCE, BHISMA, BINDING, BRIDGE (kinvat), DISEASES, DISPENSATIONS, EXPERIENCE, FATE-SPHERE, FRUIT, GUNAS, JUDGMENT-HALL, JUSTICE, KAMA, METEMPSYCHO-SIS, MOIRAE, NECESSITY, NORNOR, REAPING, SAMKHARAS, SHAI, SHENIT, SI-OSIRI, SOWING AND REAPING, TESTAMENT, THEMIS, TRANSMUTATION.

KARNA, SON OF THE SUN AND PRITHA :—

A symbol of self-esteem and personal dignity, produced by the Spirit (sun) acting through the natural order of emotion (Pritha).

"Karna exhibited in a high degree fortitude, chivalrous honour, self-sacrifice, and devotion. Especially remarkable for a liberal and generous disposition, he never stooped to ignoble practices like his friends the Kurus, who were intrinsically bad men."—MON. WILLIAMS, *Indian Wisdom,* p. 384.

"Karna" was said to have been born "clothed in armour," and that "Indra conferred upon him enormous strength." This means that self-esteem is able from the first to withstand the assaults of the lower self-interests and is powerful to maintain an ideal of devotion (Indra). Nevertheless, self-esteem fights on the side of the desires (Kurus), and is finally slain by the personality (Arjuna) as it attains to selflessness and perfection.

See ARJUNA, INDRA, KURUS, PRITHA, QUALITIES, SUN.

KARSHIPTA, THE BIRD :—

A symbol of the individuality or the higher ego in the causal-body.

"The law of Mazda is brought into the vara by the bird Karshipta."— *Vendidad,* II. *S. B. of E.*

The law of Love divine,—the higher nature or principle of being,—is brought from within to the lower self who occupies the lower quaternary (vara), by the individuality (bird).

There is a correspondency to this in the tables of the Law being placed in the ark of the covenant. The Moral Law comes down from above (or arises within), and occupies the inner sanctuary of the soul (ark).

See ARK (testimony), BENNU-BIRD, BIRD (great), KALAHANSA, LAW OF MAZDA, PHANG, PHŒNIX, SIMORG, SWAN, VARA.

KARSHVARES, SEVEN :—

A symbol of the planetary chain

system of seven terrene globes. Two on the buddhic plane ; two on the mental ; two on astral ; and one on the physical,—the earth. The process of the soul's involution and evolution takes place on these.

" On Arezahi (west) and Savahi (east) ; on Fradadhafshn (south) and Vidadhafshn (south) ; and Vourubaresti (north) and Vourugaresti (north) ; on this bright Karshvare of Hvaniratha, the abode of cattle, the dwelling of cattle, the powerful Mithra looks with a health-bringing eye."—*Miher Yasht, S. B. of E.*

The planetary chain system of the macrocosm has its correspondency in the microcosm of the individual soul. The globe Hvaniratha is the Earth with its physical, astral, and mental elements. The " abode of cattle " is the field of manifested life in which the egos acquire experience. The " powerful Mithra " is a symbol of omnipotence,—the Divine energy which serves to awaken and express the Self as the life in the forms.

The north globes are on the buddhic plane, the west and east on the mental, the south globes on the astral, and the manifest (bright) globe is on the physical plane.

" Invoke thou Zoroaster, the unseen Amshaspands who are over the seven keshvars of the earth ! "—*Vendidad,* XIX.

Rely upon the Soul which lies beyond the planes of manifestation, and which dwells beyond the eye and the ear which attend to Its expression !

See AAT (waters), BULL (man), CATTLE, HVANRATHA, PLANETARY CHAIN, REGIONS, RENOVATION, ROOT-RACES, ROUND, SABBATHS, SUMMER.

KAVIS AND KARPANS :—

These " foes " of the soul are typical of Form and Number, both of which limit and confine the Life, and so render the operations from the higher planes more difficult of achievement in raising the soul.

See FORM, NUMBERS.

KAYAN MYSTERIES :—

A symbol of the inner meanings of the sacred scriptures.

See AMBAS, INSPIRATION, REVELATION, SCRIPTURES.

KEEL OF BOAT :—

A symbol of lower instincts and desires.

" ' Tell me my name,' saith the Keel ; ' Thigh (or leg) of Isis, which Rā cut off with the knife to bring blood into the *Sektet* boat,' is thy name."—BUDGE, *Book of the Dead,* Ch. XCIX.

The progressive (leg) quality of Wisdom inverted as desire and instinct, by the law of the Supreme, in order to arouse the Divine Life in the evolving soul.

See BOAT (sektet), HEEL, ISIS, RĀ.

KELTS' COAST :—

A symbol of the second sub-plane of the buddhic plane.

KERESANI THE RULER :—

A symbol of the lower egoism with its limited vision and intolerance of that which is above it. The egoism of the lower self would limit and restrict the outgoing energy, and so stifle the growth that must needs expand beyond its rule.

See AHANKARA, CAIN, I AM, MAHAT, SEPARATION.

KERESASPA WITH SIDE-LOCK AND CLUB :—

A symbol of the path of devotion to the ideal. The " side-lock " signifies the intuition, and the " club " emotion, for by means of the Love-element, selfishness may be conquered.

See CLUB, HAIR (side-lock), NERYOSANG, SERPENT (svara).

KETHER, THE CROWN :—

A symbol of the Atman, or the plane of atma. The Higher Self supreme.

" When the Unknown of the Unknown wished to manifest Itself, It began by producing a point ; as long as that luminous point had not gone out of Its bosom, the Infinite was still completely unknown and diffused no light (*Zohar*). This emanated point is the Kether or Crown, the first Sephirah."—MYER, *Qabbalah,* p. 127.

When the Absolute determined to outpour its Life-energy, it emanated a centre of consciousness and operation,—the Atman or Higher Self.

" St. Thomas Aquinas virtually accepts the doctrine of Emanations when he writes : ' As all the perfections of creatures descend in order from God, who is the height of perfection, man should begin from the lower creatures and ascend by degrees, and so advance to the knowledge of God. . . . And because in that roof and crown of all things, God, we find the most perfect unity ; and everything is stronger and more excellent the more thoroughly it is one ; it follows that diversity and variety increase in things the further they are removed from Him who is the first principle of all.'"—E. UNDERHILL, *Mysticism*, p. 117.

See ABSOLUTE, AIN-SOPH, ATMA, ATMAN, CROWN, HOKHMAH, MONAD, SEPHIROTH, TAE-KEIH.

KEYS OF HEAVEN AND OF HELL, OR OF DEATH AND OF HADES :—

A symbol of the higher mind which occupies the central position between the higher and lower natures, and is therefore the key to both.

"By key is signified the power of opening and also the act of opening."—SWEDENBORG, *Apoc. Rev.*, n. 421.

"The true Guru holdeth the keys ; none save him can open the door ; the true Guru is found by good fortune."—MACAULIFFE, *The Sikh Religion*, Vol. II. p. 178.

"I am the first and the last, and the Living one ; and I was dead, and behold, I am alive for evermore, and I have the keys of death and of Hades."—REV. i. 18.

The "true Guru" is the Higher Self, the Christ within, the Living One, who died out of involution, and who now in evolution is manifest in the higher mind and holds the issues of life and death in the lower worlds of time and space.

In the soul's progress, the unperfected soul, or "wicked man," on its approach to the higher mental levels between its incarnations, is impelled downwards again to incarnate. The perfected soul, or "righteous man," is on the contrary drawn upwards to bliss.

"The most honorific passage (to Peter) in Matthew (xvi. 17–19) was omitted by Luke and Mark. . . . The section in Matthew is exceeding probably a quite late interpolation."—*Enc. Biblica*, " Simon Peter," (5).

The story about Jesus giving the "keys of the kingdom of heaven" to Peter does not fit in with the sacred symbology. "Peter," being a symbol of the *lower mind*, could not possibly have control of the higher nature of the soul. The statement was probably ignorantly interpolated by some ecclesiastics early in the third century, who inserted it for the sake of the visible Church, in order that it

should get apparent authority and sanction from the scriptures.

"It is the power of Thoth that binds and loosens ; he holds the keys of heaven and hell, of life and death."—G. R. S. MEAD, *T. G. Hermes*, Vol. I. p. 61.

"Thoth" is a symbol of the higher mind which is the *bridge, door,* or *gate* between the higher and lower natures (heaven and earth).

See BINDING, BRIDGE, DOOR, DOORS OPENED BY THOTH, GATE, HADES, HEAVEN, HELL, PETER, THOTH.

KHABIT, OR SHADOW :—

A symbol of the causal-body which develops by means of the aspirations and experiences of the lower self.

"The Khabit seems to have been nourished by the offerings which were made in the tomb of the person to whom it belonged. . . . In Ch. XCII the deceased is made to say, ' O keep not captive my soul, O keep not ward over my Shadow, but let a way be opened for my soul and for my Shadow, and let them see the Great God in the shrine on the day of the judgment of souls.' "—BUDGE, *Book of the Dead*, Vol. I. p. lxi.

The functioning of the personality on the lower planes (tomb of the person) is to provide, through aspiration and sacrifice, goodness and truth, the "bread of heaven" for the nourishment and building up, by love, of the causal-body in the higher mind. When this is perfected then the union of the Soul with the Self (Great God) will be accomplished at the close of the cycle.

"It is Love which builds up the soul. It is Love that goes to the making of your man's amount. It is Love which fabricates your inward spiritual body, in which you shall continue to express yourself when the outer mortal body shall have been slipped."—E. W. LEWIS, *Christ. Com.*, April 23, 1913.

"Religion is harmony with God ; that harmony is produced by love ; and that love is produced by faith. To be religious we must be like God, that to be like Him we must love Him, and that to love Him we must be sure that He loves us. And is it not true that faith must precede our love to God, and affords the only possible basis on which that can be built ? How can we love Him so long as we are in doubt of His heart, or misconceive His character, as if it were only Power and Wisdom, or awful Severity ? Men cannot love an unseen person at all without some very special token of his personal affection for them. . . . Our love is secondary, His is primary ; ours is reflection, His the original beam ; ours is echo, His the mother-tone. Heaven must bend to earth, before earth can rise to heaven. The skies must open and drop down love, ere love can spring in the fruitful fields."—A. MACLAREN, *Sermons, 2nd Series*, p. 216.

See BA, BREAD, CAUSAL-BODY, IRRI-GATION, JUDGMENT-DAY, KA, KHU, LAZARUS, LOVE OF GOD, MULTIPLY, OFFERING, QAHU, SAHU, SHRINE, SOUL (middle), TOMB, TZELEM, UNION, VOURUKASHA.

KHAMUAS, SETME AND WIFE :—

Symbols of Spirit and Matter.

See HEAVEN AND EARTH, SEED (good), SI-OSIRI.

KHEPER, OR KHEPERA :—

A symbol of the Self striving in the lower nature ; i.e. of the indwelling Christ.

"The majesty of this great God (Afu-Rā) taketh up his position in this Circle (Twelfth of the Tuat) which is the uttermost limit of thick darkness ; and this great God is born in his form of Khepara in this Circle ; and Nut and Nu are in this Circle for the birth of this great God when he cometh forth from the Tuat and taketh up his position in the Matet boat, and when he riseth up from the thighs of Nut."—BUDGE, *Egypt. Heaven and Hell*, Vol. I. p. 257.

The picture accompanying this text is emblematic of the process of the unfoldment and consummation of the Soul, and it indicates the actual as well as potential facts of the case. The causal-body (the boat), is upheld or evolved through the powers of the universe (Nu), and these yield up, as it were, that which is accomplished through their agency. The astral plane (water) is depicted below the causal-body (boat) to signify the process of conflict with the desire-nature which leads to the final triumph of the Spirit within. The globe upheld by the beetle,—emblem of Khepara, the Christ,—represents the buddhic vesture, for above is the plane of atma. The symbol of the figure of Osiris at the top curved round a space signifies *realisation,*—that state which is perfect and complete as the result of endeavour. The design altogether represents the ending of the path to liberation ; the Soul rising from the way of the underworld (Tuat) to

peace eternal, into which it is born from the womb of Space (Nut).

"Hail, thou who risest as a Mighty Soul (Kha-ba-aa), who hast received the things which belong to the Tuat ; Af, thou guardian of heaven, come thou, and cast thou thine eye in the name of the Living One, Khepara, at the head of the Tuat."—*Ibid.*, p. 40.

See AFU-RĀ, ASCENSION OF OSIRIS, ASTRAL PLANE, BOAT (sektet), CAUSAL-BODY, CIRCLE OF EXISTENCE, CON-FLICT, CRUCIFIXION OF JESUS, HUMAN BODY, LIBERATION, MONAD, NU, NUT, OSIRIS, RĀ, RESURRECTION, ROBE, SCARABÆUS, SOUL, TREASURE, TUAT, UPLIFTING RĀ, VICTORY, WATER (lower) WOMB.

KHIEN AND KHWAN :—

Symbols of Spirit and Matter, the dual elements of manifestation.

"Khien is the symbol of heaven, and hence has the appellation of Father. Khwan is the symbol of earth, and hence has the appellation of Mother."—*The Yi King*, Appendix V. Ch. X. 14.

"Khien symbolises Heaven, which directs the great beginnings of things ; Khwan symbolises Earth, which gives to them their completion."—*The Yi King*, Appendix III. Ch. I. §1, 5.

"Khien, the symbol of Heaven, and conveying the idea of strength, shows to men its easy and natural action. Khwan, the symbol of Earth, and conveying the idea of docility, shows to men its com-pendious receptivity and operation. . . . The great attribute of Heaven and Earth is the giving and maintaining Life."—*The Yi King*. Appendix III. § II. Ch. I. 7–10.

These passages from the Chinese scriptures explain themselves. Spirit is the Divine Life, active and power-ful. Matter is that which is acted upon ; it is plastic and receptive in involution, and subsequently brings forth the qualities in evolution.

See COSMOS, CREATION, EARTH, EVO-LUTION, HEAVEN AND EARTH, IN-VOLUTION, KHWAN, MATTER, PRAK-RITI, SPIRIT, TAO, YANG.

KHNENTA-LAND IN VEHR-KĀNA :—

A symbol of the love emotions on the buddhic plane.

KHORDAD, THE AMSHASPAND :—

A symbol of Time, a mode of manifestation of the Supreme ; in this aspect it becomes the interpreter

of Truth in such terms as are reflected in cycles, succession, duration, and evolution.

"Khordad was chief of the seasons, years, months, and days, and also protector of the water from Anduisur on Albordj."—*Zoroastrian System.*

See ALBORDJ, AMSHASPANDS, ANDUISUR, KRONUS, SEASONS, WATER (higher), YEAR.

KHUS (HIGHER ASPECT) :—

A symbol of the monads of Life, or the Individualities.

"Khu,—a shining or translucent part of the spiritual economy of a man which dwelt with his soul in the *sāhu* or spiritual body."—BUDGE, *Book of the Dead*, Vol. I. p. lxii.

"May I become a *Khu* therein (thy fields of Sekket Aaru)."—*Ibid.*, Ch. CX. p. 327.

In these experiences of life in the form, I, the Self, realise Myself.

"And behold, the *Khus*, each of whom therein (Sekhet-Aaru) is nine cubits in height, reap the wheat and the barley side by side with Hera-khuti (young Horus)."—BUDGE, *Book of the Dead*, Ch. CXLIX. p. 486.

The monads of Life, when perfected through experience in the "field" or arena of the lower life, inherit the treasures of Wisdom and Love, together with the indwelling Christ. The "nine cubits in height" signifies perfection attained on the lower planes. The perfected "Khus" are the individual souls (the saints), who rise with Christ to the higher planes of consciousness at the end of the cycle.

See AKESI, ANGELS, ARENA, BODHISATVAS, KA, MONAD OF LIFE, QAHU, REAPING, SAHU, SAINTS, TOMB.

KHUS (LOWER ASPECT) :—

A symbol of the personalities, or the astro-physical forms, containing the monads of Life.

"My mouth is strong; and I am equipped against the *Khus*; let them not have dominion over me."—*Book of the Dead*, Ch. CX.

The expression of the Self upon the lower and upper planes is significant, for the Self is impervious to the allurements of the sense nature.

"He places a limit to the hurtful power of the shining forms (khus)."—*Ibid*

The Self by limiting its own manifestation is also the means of preventing the attraction to the form-side of life from alluring the personality to destruction.

"The fullness of the forms of the shining ones is granted unto me; I comprehend the Light."—*Ibid.*

The forms having been exhausted, are outgrown and discarded, not, however, without furnishing the Self with such experience as may have been derived thereby.

See CLASSES (Egypt), FORMS, MOUTH, PERSONALITY.

KHWAN :—

A symbol of matter, the complement of spirit.

"Complete is the great and originating capacity indicated by Khwan! All things owe to it their birth;—it receives obediently the influences of Heaven. Khwan in its largeness supports and contains all things. Its excellent capacity matches the unlimited power of Khien. Its comprehension is wide and its brightness great. The various things obtain by it their full development."—*Yi King*, Appendix I. § 1, Ch. 2.

Matter in its nature is completely adapted to be the means by which the originating ideas can be expressed in forms. All forms and qualities owe to it their manifestation. It is fully receptive of the modifications of Spirit. Matter in its extension throughout the lower planes is the basis and container of all expressions of life. Its receptive capacity entirely corresponds with the unlimited energy of Spirit acting through it.

"Any good that God bestows grows richer with our experience of it—it never grows poorer; any truth He reveals is seen to be larger as we gain closer acquaintance with it,—it never grows less."—R. J. CAMPBELL, Serm., *Our Eternal Glory.*

See INVOLUTION, KHIEN, MATTER, MĀYĀ, MOTHER (divine), SPIRIT, YANG.

KHWAN, THE GREAT FISH :—

A symbol of the cycle of Involution originating in the ocean of Reality in which it has its being.

"In the bare and barren north there is the dark and vast ocean,—the Pool of Heaven. In it there is a Fish, several thousand lî in breadth, while no one knows its length. Its name is the Khwăn. There is also a Bird named the Phang (into which the Fish changes)."—*Writings of Kwang-tze*, Bk. I. Pt. I. 3.

From the chaos there forthpours

the "water" of the primeval Reality (Northern Pool of Heaven), in which the cycle of Involution has actuality. The content of the cycle is stupendous, and its length is unmeasured. After its termination there arises from it a new cycle, that of Evolution in which the Spirit ascends (bird) from matter and culminates ultimately in the Divine Reality (Southern Pool of Heaven).

See Leviathan, Manvantara, Ocean, Phang, Serpent (ananta), Whale.

KID FOR A LOVE-FEAST :—

A symbol of faith. Faith is a sense or intuition of that truth of being which is superior to the lower knowledge.

See Faith, Fatted calf, Feast, Intuition, Man.

KILLING-OUT OF DESIRE :—

A symbol of the transmuting effect of reason and the buddhic nature in rendering the desires and the lower instincts to all intents and purposes non-existent.

"A higher grade of religious consciousness is attained with the knowledge that all actions which depend upon the motives of expectation and fear are of no value for the ultimate destiny of mankind; that the supreme function of existence does not consist in the satisfaction of self-interest, but in its voluntary suppression; and that herein first the true divine reality of ourselves, through the individual self as through an outer husk, makes itself manifest."—Deussen, *Phil. of Upanishads*, p. 47.

See Battle, Conflict, Durasrobo, Individuality, Kabandha, Slaughter, Transmutation, Victory, War.

KING :—

A symbol of a ruling quality in the soul, of higher or lower significance in the mind.

"The Gods engender, son, the kings it has deserved, to rule the race that lives on Earth. The rulers are the emanations of the King, of whom the nearer to him is more royal than the rest; for that the Sun, in that 'tis nearer than the Moon to God, is far more vast and potent, to whom the Moon comes second both in rank and power" (*Hermetic Treatise*, "Virgin of the World").—G. R. S. Mead, *T. G. Hermes*, Vol. III. p. 126.

The ideals (gods) give rise to the higher qualities, when the soul has become prepared to obey them, so that the lower qualities may be effectively ruled. The ruling higher qualities proceed from the Higher Self, by whom they are harmonised and centralised. The nearer to Him of these qualities (disciples) are the most divine. The Individuality (sun) being nearer than the Personality (moon) to the Self, is far more potent in the soul than is the Personality, which comes second in importance and power.

See Agamemnon, Alcinous, Esther, Governors, Herod, Janaka, Melcarthus, Ravana, Ruler, Tribute.

KING, GREAT :—

A symbol of the Higher Self, the manifest God, as the ruler of the qualities of the soul on the higher and lower planes.

"Beautiful in elevation, the joy of the whole earth is mount Zion, on the sides of the north, the city of the great King."—Ps. xlviii. 2.

Harmonious and exalted, and the blissful hope of the evolving lower nature, are the higher planes of consciousness above the mental plane :—they are the planes of atma-buddhi, the "kingdom of heaven" in which the Higher Self is centred and reigns supreme.

A King formed of particles of the Lords of the gods, he therefore surpasses all created beings in lustre. . . . Through his supernal power he is Fire and Wind, he Sun and Moon, he the Lord of justice (Yama), he Kubera, he Varuna, he great Indra. Even an infant King must not be despised from an idea that he is a mere mortal; for he is a great Deity in human form."—*Laws of Manu*, VII. 5–8.

The Higher Self comprises in his nature all the higher qualities in their highest manifestation; he therefore surpasses all created beings in glory. Through his forthgoing energy he becomes Buddhi and Manas, the Individuality and the Personality, the Lord of Karma, the laid up Wealth of Evolution, the Substance of Truth, the Lord of Devotion. When, in the course of evolution, the Higher Self is born small and weak in the soul, he is not to be regarded as one of the lower mortal qualities, for, indeed, he is the Divine Ruler incarnate in the human soul, the indwelling God, the Christ in us.

"God is a truth to you. Your soul is your true self. Christ, the spiritual perfectness of manhood, the true Son of God, is really King of the world."— PHILLIPS BROOKS, Serm., *The Giant, etc.*

See AMENI, BIRTH OF JESUS, OF OSIRIS, CITY OF GOD, EMPEROR, KAPILA, OSIRIS, PAMYLES, SUDDHODANA, WORLD.

KING OF GLORY :—

A symbol of the Higher Self under the aspect of returning into the Absolute.

"Who is this King of glory ? The Lord of hosts, he is the King of glory."— Ps. xxiv. 10.

The Self, the ruler of the mental qualities, withdraws into Himself at the close of the cycle.

"Meanwhile the king for the sake of ensuring his son's (Buddha's) prosperity, and stirred in heart by the destiny which had been predicted for him, delighted himself in perfect calm, ceased from all evil, practised all self-restraint, and rewarded the good."—*Buddha-Karita,* Bk. II. 33.

Meanwhile the Logos, for the purpose of securing the Soul, and having responded to its requirements, and also having brooded over the Monad, rested from Its labours, quitted the realms of limitation, abode within Itself, and tasted the joy of Its own being.

See AUSTERITIES, BUDDHA, DISCIPLES (seated), GLORIFYING OF GOD, HOSTS (Lord of), SUDDHODANA.

KINGDOM OF HEAVEN, OR OF GOD :—

A symbol of the higher planes of consciousness whereon the Divine nature rules supreme. It may also be used in reference to the abode of bliss on the higher mental plane when the two consciousnesses become one. It is not Nirvana, but a state analogous to devachan.

"Blessed are the poor in spirit : for theirs is the kingdom of heaven."— MATT. v. 3.

The Divine Will operates in the qualities which have rid themselves of the lower desires and followed their ideals of goodness and truth, for they shall be transmuted to the higher planes and become in entire harmony with the Divine nature.

"The kingdom of God cometh not with observation : . . . it is within you." —LUKE xvii. 20, 21.

The higher nature is within the soul, and its evolution cannot be observed by the lower consciousness, whose attention is directed outwardly.

"Ye ask who are those that draw us to the Kingdom, if the Kingdom is in Heaven ; the fowls of the air, and all the beasts that are under the earth or upon the earth, and the fishes of the sea, these are they which draw you, and the Kingdom of Heaven is within you" (Saying of Jesus).—GRENFELL AND HUNT, *Oxy. Papy.* IV. 6.

The qualities are said to progress by means of the discipline of the lower nature,—through the aspirations (fowls), the passions and desires (beasts), and the acquisition of knowledge or facts (fishes). The development is entirely from within towards manifesting without, and the stimulus to growth is largely due to the impacts from without which stir the mind and emotions into persistent activity.

"By the Kingdom of God the primitive Christians meant the undisputed reign of eternal love, whether in heaven or on earth, while by eternal life they meant the living of that love in its fullness, the knowledge of the perfections of God which implies sharing them in their wholeness."—R. J. CAMPBELL, Serm., *Reaping for Eternal Life.*

"The kingdom of Christ is being made on earth as it is also being made in heaven ; it is not complete there any more than here ; in fact, the only reason why we have to try to build it here is that our efforts may finally establish it there. I am not speaking of God's eternal perfection when I say this. To that unimaginable blessedness nothing can be added ; it is the infinite fullness upon which we draw for the realisation of the good which shall be eternally ours in Christ, and it needs nothing that we can bring to it. But our own heavenly kingdom needs something, and seen and unseen are co-operating in furnishing it."—R. J. CAMPBELL, Serm., *Solidarity in Christ.*

"Virtue is the supreme good, the supreme beauty, the divinest of God's gifts, the health and harmonious unfolding of the soul, and the germ of immortality. It is worth every sacrifice, and has power to transmute sacrifices and sufferings into crowns of glory and rejoicing."—W. E. CHANNING, *Works,* Vol. I. p. 16.

See AMARÂVATI, AMENT, BEASTS, BIRDS, BLISS, BLUE HEAVEN, BUDDHIC PLANE, CHILDREN OF KINGDOM, CONSCIOUSNESS, DEVACHAN, EDEN, FISH GARDEN, GARODMAN, GOSPEL OF KINGDOM, HEAVEN, JERUSALEM, LEAVEN,

MALKHUTH, MEAT, MUSPELLHEIM, NIR-
VANA, PARADISE, POOR, QUALITIES,
REAPING, SEKHET-HETEP, SERMON,
SICKLE.

KINGDOMS OF THE WORLD :—

A symbol of the various directions
in which the qualities of power,
ambition, pride, greed, vanity, have
been applied in the lower life of the
soul.

See MOUNTAIN (lower), TEMPTATION,
WORLD.

KINGLY GLORY :—

A symbol of the Monad, the Divine
Ray of Light and Life from the
Absolute.

See ABSOLUTE, GLORY (divine),
HEBDOMAD, LIGHT, MONAD, SUN.

KINGLY OFFICE :—

A symbol of the Divine Will ruling
and organising the involution of
Spirit into matter.

See CIVILISING, GOVERNMENT,
MINISTERS, OANNES, YAO.

KINVAT BRIDGE :—

An emblem signifying the higher
mental plane.

See BRIDGE (kinvat), DUSAKH,
MAIDEN.

KIOS IN MYSIA BUILT :—

Symbolic of the formation of moral
habit.

KISHKINDHA, THE VANAR CITY :—

A symbol of the mental centre in
the mental-body. The centre of
intelligence.

See RAMA, RAVANA, SITA, VANAR,
VIBHISHANA.

KITRA :—

A symbol of the Divine Lawgiver,
or Word of God.

See MAN (born), MOON-WAXING.

KLYTAIMNESTRA, WIFE OF AGAMEMNON :—

A symbol of the seductive sensation-
nature allied to the desire-mind.

"Yea, I (Agamemnon) prefer her
(Chryseis) before Klytaimnestra my
wedded wife ; in no wise is she lacking
beside her, neither in favour nor stature,
nor wit nor skill. Yet for all this will
I give her back, if that is better ; rather
would I see my folk whole than perishing."
—*Iliad*, Bk. I.

The desire-mind prefers sensation
and sense-objects,—which owe their
seductiveness to the passivity of the
intuition (Chryseis)—to the higher
emotions. In no respect is the sense-
nature lacking whilst the lower mind
remains in this unspiritual condition,
neither as regards its attractiveness,
appeal, subtlety, nor intelligence.
Notwithstanding, the intuition shall
be recovered by the Higher Self. It
were better for the desire-mind to
experience the languishing of the
lower mental qualities than lose the
credit for having made the effort to
surrender itself ; pride being at this
time the motive in the lower self.

See AGAMEMNON, CHRYSEIS, INTUI-
TION, PESTILENCE, PRIZE.

KNEE, KNEELING :—

A symbol of moral strength, or
submission to the law of order and
progress, by restraining the lower
activities (lower limbs) and weakening
them by bending to the higher will
within.

See FAMILY, LEGS.

KNIFE :—

A symbol of the will to cut away
either desires on the one hand, or
progressive growth on the other.

KNIGHT-ERRANT :—

A symbol of the Christ-soul, or
indwelling Self, a wanderer and
saviour in the lower nature, rescuing
the higher emotions from captivity
to the lower desires, and vanquishing
the oppressors of the virtues.

See ANDROMEDA, PERSEUS.

KNOCK TO OPEN :—

Significant of aspiration. The
sending up vibrations from the lower
nature to the gate of the higher.—
MAT. vii. 7 ; REV. iii. 20.

See DOOR, GATE.

KNOWER OF THE FIELD (KSHETRA) :—

A symbol of the omniscient Higher
Self as the tiller and sower of the
lower nature, in order that it should
bring forth fruit.

"Know also that I (Krishna) am the
Knower in every mortal body ; that
knowledge which through the soul is
a realisation of both the known and the
knower is alone esteemed by me as
wisdom."—*Bhagavad-Gita*, Ch. XIII.

As the higher mind acquires power, so the lower quality is transmuted into buddhic quality,—knowledge in the lower mind is turned to wisdom, and experience to love.

See ARENA, FIELD, HUSBANDMAN, LAND, VARA.

KOPTIS, CITY OF MOURNING :—

A symbol of the Wisdom-centre obscured from the lower nature.

KORAN,—THAT WHICH IS FOR MORTALS TO READ (*KARAA*):—

A symbol of the " Word of God,"—the inner knowledge possessed by every soul, which will become *read*, or manifest, as the nature becomes able and willing to understand.

" The Mohammedans absolutely deny the Koran was composed by their prophet himself, or any other for him ; it being their general and orthodox belief that it is of divine original, nay that it is eternal and uncreated, remaining, as some express it, in the very essence of God."—SALE'S *Koran, Prel. Dis.*, p. 46.

" God created under the Arsh (Throne) and of its light, a great ' Tablet ' in colour as a green beryl, and a great ' Pen ' in colour as an emerald, and filled with ink which was of white light. God cried ' Write O Pen ! ' whereupon it moved over the Tablet and wrote thereon everything that should happen till the Last Day, and the Tablet was covered over with the writing. And thereon was then inscribed the Divine original of the Glorious Koran " (Sufi record).—GIBB, *Ottoman Poetry*, Vol. I. p. 35.

Below the plane of atma (the Arsh) is the buddhic, or Wisdom plane, whereon the Holy Spirit inspires the soul with Truth. The " Tablet " or " preserved table " is the " table of the heart " (causal-body) on which is written by Divine expression (pen) the " law of Wisdom " (PROV. iii. 1–5) expounding the Divine scheme of the Soul's involution and evolution ;— its descent into captivity of the lower nature, its ascent and liberation ; with final union with God at the end of the cycle (the last Day). The original of the Koran, or the Bible, and other sacred books, is, therefore, purely spiritual knowledge in the subjective possession of every soul, ready to become objective as the devout mind meditates freely on any of the sacred writings.

See AMBAYAVIS, CAUSAL-BODY, GOS-PEL, INSPIRATION, JUDGMENT-DAY, MYTHOLOGY, PAPYRUS, PEN, REVE-LATION, SASTRA, SCRIPTURES, UPANI-SHAD, UR-HEKAU, VEDA, WORD OF GOD.

KRISHNA, GOSVĀMIN—LORD OF COWS :—

A symbol of the Higher Self, supreme over the buddhic emotions (cows).

" Krishna, ' the dark god '—the most popular of all the later deities of India. This incarnation of Vishnu, at the end of the Dvapara or third age of the world, as the eighth son of Vasu-deva and Devaki of the Lunar race, was for the destruction of Kansa the representative of the principle of evil, corresponding to Ravana in the previous incarnation."— MON. WILLIAMS, *Indian Wisdom*, p. 334.

The " dark god " signifies the latency at first of the indwelling Self who pro-ceeds from the Divine Archetype (Vasu-deva) and Mother-matter (Devaki) in order to overcome the lower principle or desire-nature (Kansa) in the human soul. The Archetypal Man is perfected at the end of the period of involution (third age). The " eighth son " indicates preparatory states of soul completed (seven) prior to the birth of the Self. The " lunar race " refers to the growth of the astral mechanism of the desires on the globes of the lunar chain.

" Among the Pancarâtras Krishna was the supreme *Atman* ; his brother *Balarâma* was the *jiva*, the individual soul ; his son, Pradyumna, represented the *manas* perceptive sense ; and Aniruddha his grandson, the *ahamkâra*, self-conscious-ness. In like manner, the amours of Krishna and the shepherdesses become, among the Vishnuites, the allegorical expression of the relations of the soul with God."—A. BARTH, *Rel. of India*, p. 218.

The Higher Self (Krishna or Atman), the Individuality or Spiritual ego (Balarmàa or jiva), the lower Self (Pradyumna), and the Personality (Aniruddha or the ahamkâra), with its sense of separateness and self-con-scious feeling, constitute the leading aspects of the Soul. The " shepherd-esses " signify the higher emotions on the buddhic plane, which harmonise with, and surround, the central ideal of Love and Truth.

See ARC. MAN, ARJUNA, BALARAMA,

BIRTH OF KRISHNA, COW, DANCE (circle), DEVAKI, GOLDEN AGE, GOLOKA, GOPIS, INCARNATION, MOTHER (divine), RAVANA, VISHNU.

KRONOS ; SATURN ; SEB :—

A symbol of Time, which implies limitation and number in successive periods within the cycle of life. Time and space are relative to manifestation.

See CRONUS, KHORDAD, RHEA, SATURN, SEB, TIME, URANUS, ZEUS.

KSHATRIYA, OR MILITARY CASTE :—

A symbol of the mental body centralising the faculties of the lower mind which contend against ignorance and emotion.

"The Kshatriya, he (Manu) commanded to protect the people, to bestow gifts, to offer sacrifices, to study the Veda, and to abstain from attaching himself to sensual pleasures."—*Laws of Manu*, Ch. I. 89.

The lower mind was enjoined to co-operate with the qualities of the soul (the people); to add mentality to the desires; to give up a lower form of thought for a higher; to purify itself by Truth, Wisdom, and Love; and to shun attachment to the sense-nature and its objects.

See CASTES, CLASSES, RAGANYA.

KSHETRA OR FIELD :—
See FIELD, KNOWER.

KURSAYAH, A THRONE WITH FOUR FEET AND SIX STEPS :—

A symbol of the causal-body superimposed upon the lower quaternary and approached through the duality of the three lower planes.

See CAUSAL-BODY, THRONE.

KURSI, THE "FOOTSTOOL BELOW THE THRONE" :—

A symbol of the buddhic plane below the plane of atma (Arsh).

"After a while God looked again upon the Light, and from its perspiration He created the corporeal world. The first thing that arose was the Arsh, the 'Throne of God.' Beneath the Arsh, and of its light, God created another wondrous thing, which is called the Kursi, and may be conceived as the 'Footstool' below the 'Throne'" (*Ottoman Sufi Genesis*).—E. J. W. GIBB, *Ottoman Poetry*, Vol. I. p. 35.

From the Divine Life manifesting (perspiring) there appeared the planes of nature. The first was the highest,— the atmic plane, and this produced the second,—the buddhic plane.

See ARSH, ATMA, LOTE-TREE, PARADISE, THRONE.

KURUS, THE HUNDRED SONS OF DHRITA-RASHTRA :—

A symbol of the desires proceeding from the lower instinct nature.

"The Kurus are represented as mean, spiteful, dishonourable and vicious."— MON. WILLIAMS, *Indian Wisdom*, p. 383.

See DHRITA, DHRISTA, DRONA, KARNA, MARA, PANDAVAS.

KUSTI OR KUSHTI :—

A symbol of the Divine Ray, the Sutratma, or Tree of Life.

"The *kushti* consists of 72 fibres woven into twelve strands of 6 fibres each, the 12 strands being further woven into 3 cords of 4 strands each. These 3 cords, which are plaited together to form the *kushti*, represent the three fundamental principles of the Zoroastrian faith, good thoughts, good words, and good deeds; the other subdivisions having each in like manner a symbolical meaning."—E. G. BROWNE, *A Year among the Persians*, p. 369.

Sir Monier Williams informs us that,—

"the girdle must then be coiled round the body three times and fastened with two particular knots (said to represent the sun and moon), which none but a Parsee can tie in a proper manner."— *Modern India*, p. 96.

The two knots are the symbols of the Higher Self (sun) and the lower self (moon); the first in the causal-body, and the second in the mental body, both being centres upon the Divine Ray from above.

The twelve strands represent human experience in the twelve divisions of the cycle of life, leading to soul-growth. The three cords made from the strands of experience, symbolise the law of growth upon the four lower planes. The Divine law insists upon the regulation of the life by the soul itself, which shows that there is no abstract, or vicarious, goodness to rely upon, and that apart from Thought, Speech, and Action, duly regulated, there is no salvation for the soul. The 72 fibres relate to 72 potential and actual conditions of experience on the physical, astral and mental planes.

See BARHIS, BARSOM, BIRTH (second) BREASTPLATE, BUCKLE, EPHOD, TAMAGUSHI, WOOD, YAGNOPAVITA.

KUVERA, THE LORD OF WEALTH :—

A symbol of the Higher Self equipped with all its powers and attributes, its faculties and possibilities, and able to enrich the soul.

See GANESA, NALA-KUVERA, POVERTY, WEALTH.

KYAVANA, THE GREAT SEER :—

A symbol of a forerunner of the Soul, through which the Divine nature could not manifest.

See ASITA, VALMIKI.

KYDOIMOS (UPROAR) :—

A symbol of the lower, or astromental, emotions.

See HARPIES.

KYPRIS, QUEEN :—

A symbol of Wisdom, the buddhic ruler of evolution and the transmuter of the lower qualities.

"And thus then Kypris, when she had moistened the earth with water, breathed air on it, and gave it to swift fire to be hardened."—*Empedocles*, Bk. II. 215, FAIRBANKS.

And thus Wisdom, when she had inspired the lower nature with desire, endowed it with intelligence which was the means of its soaring towards spirit (fire), which enabled that which was to endure to proceed from it.

See AIR, BEES (libations), BLOOD (bulls), HALLOWED OFFERINGS.

KYPRIS, PERFECT HARBOURS OF :—

A symbol of perfection of qualities arrived at on the buddhic plane.

See CIRCE.

LABOURERS :—

A symbol of the qualities of the Soul which have to work for their development in the forms provided for the purpose.

"For the kingdom of heaven is like unto a man that is a householder, which went out early in the morning to hire labourers into his vineyard. And when he had agreed with the labourers for a penny a day, he sent them into his vineyard."—MAT. xx. 1, 2.

The "kingdom of heaven" signifies the consummation of endeavour found in Wisdom and Love on the higher planes at the close of the cycle. The "Householder" is the First Logos, who goes forth under many aspects and calls all the forms of his own life within His universe (vineyard) to discharge their appointed tasks. And when upon each plane of nature the law of cause and effect had been set in operation, the soul-qualities were sent to undertake their business of self-development in the chains of worlds. This implies the descent of the Divine life into the forms prepared for its reception. The "penny wage" is a symbol of the rate of pay, or gain of faculty, for successful work, or accomplished result. The "wage" is the lower equivalent of spiritual power. As money brings satisfaction to the lower nature, so spiritual power brings satisfaction to the higher.

"Yea, and in the parable of the labourers which were sent into the vineyard they (the Gnostics) say it is most evident that those 30 Æons are indicated ; in that some are sent about the first hour, some about the third, others about the sixth, others about the ninth, and a further set about the eleventh. Now the aforesaid hours, being added together, make up the number 30. For $1 + 3 + 6 + 9 + 11 = 30$. And these hours, they affirm, signify the Æons. And these, they add, are the great and wonderful and unutterable mysteries, the fruit of which themselves only bear."—IRENÆUS, *Against Heresies*, Bk. I.

The "hours" represent stages of mental and emotional development during periods (æons) of soul life. The "third hour" represents a period of tamasic activity or stupidity of the lower mind (kama-manas) in forms appropriate to that condition. The sixth and ninth periods correspond to the stages of development of intellect and intuition with the energy of rajas. The eleventh period answers to the stage of Wisdom-Love with sattva energy. These advanced souls incarnate in forms highly developed.

See ÆONS, GUNAS, HOUR, HOUSEHOLDER, JUSTICE, MARKET-PLACE, MONEY, MORNING, PLANETARY CHAIN, QUALITIES, STEWARD, VINEYARD, WAGES, WORK.

LAD ; BOY :—

Symbol of a young or immature mind, a recipient of knowledge through experience.

See BOY, YOUNG MAN.

LADDER, JACOB'S :—

A symbol of the soul's path from the lower nature (earth) to the higher nature (heaven). The "angels" ascending are the aspirations, and those descending are the Divine responses to the soul. "Jacob" represents the natural man turning to the Lord—the Ideal within. He sleeps upon a stone, that is, he relies upon the Spirit within.

"We, too, leave home, and are sent out alone to face the responsibilities of life ; we are driven then, not seldom, by the Spirit into the wilderness. We climb our mountain ridge alone, and our first days we often sleep on a stony pillow. It is there, in our solitude, and few solitudes are so deep ; in our grief,— that God often speaks home to our hearts. . . . . And often the very first impression made is similar to that made on Jacob— the comfort of feeling that heaven is near to earth. As the angels ascended and descended from God to him, and from him to God, he knew that prayer might ascend from him to God, blessings descend on him from God. Guilty and a deceiver, goodness and truth might yet be his. He might begin a new and higher life, for a new home had been opened to him in which God dwelt. And when he felt a union between him and heaven, a tide of new possibilities flowed in upon his soul. . . . We know that Christ has united heaven and earth, that all that is of heaven in us—our aspiration, faith, love of truth and of love—can ascend like angels in the power of the Son of man, to find their source in God, and in Him realise and perfect themselves."— STOPFORD A. BROOKE, Serm., *Jacob's Dream.*

See ANGELS, EARTH, HEAVEN, JACOB, PADDLES, PILLOW OF STONE, STONE, WIFE.

LADDER FROM EARTH TO HEAVEN :—

A symbol of the upward path of the soul, in stages or steps of progress. It represents the evolution of the higher qualities, and the gradual manifestation of the God within the soul.

"Homage to thee O ladder of the God, homage to thee, O ladder of Set. Set thyself up, O ladder of Horus, whereby Osiris appeared in heaven when he wrought protection for Rā " (Papyrus.)— BUDGE, *Book of the Dead,* p. lxxiii.

The last sentence refers to the ridding the soul of its enemies, the desires.

"There existed a belief that Osiris himself experienced some difficulty of getting up to the iron plate, and that it was only by means of the ladder which his father Rā provided that he at length ascended into heaven. On one side of the ladder stood Rā, and on the other stood Horus, the son of Isis, and each god assisted Osiris to mount it. Originally the two guardians of the ladder were Horus the Elder and Set."— BUDGE, *Egyptian Magic,* p. 52.

The "iron plate" signifies the "firmament," that is, the higher mental plane, the "floor of heaven" between the higher and lower natures. Osiris being the Archetypal Man— the Spirit involved in matter,—has to evolve from matter in the souls of humanity. Rā, the Supreme, stands here for organism and environment, or natural law which promotes evolution. Horus is said to hold out his "Two Fingers" wherewith to help Osiris ; these signify the love of goodness and truth which assists the God within to rise. Horus the actual, who attracts upward by love, assists Osiris the potential to manifest in the soul. Rā, stern nature, stands on one side below, and, as it were, pushes up the feeble Osiris by the varied experiences of life. On the other side above stands Horus (Christ), the radiant child of Love (Osiris) and Wisdom (Isis), born in the soul ; he puts forth his "two fingers" of blessing, and so enables the soul to mount.

"The Christ above stoops and lays hold of the Christ within ; nothing can keep the two apart, for they are really one."—Serm., Oct. 14, 1908.

"Evil will not last for ever ; it is the cross whereby we mount the throne of divine glory."—R. J. CAMPBELL, Serm., Jan. 9, 1908.

The "ladder" is sometimes called "the ladder of Set." "Set" stands for Desire, or the principle of evil, and it is by surmounting evil that we attain to goodness.

"The mystic makes it his life's aim to be transformed into the likeness of Him in whose image he was created. He loves to figure his path as a ladder reaching from earth to heaven, which must be climbed step by step. This *scala perfectionis* is generally divided into three stages. The first is called the purgative life, the second the illuminative, while the third, which is really the goal rather than a part of the journey, is called the unitive life."—W. R. INGE, *Christian Mysticism*, p. 9.

From ignorance and suffering, to knowledge and wisdom, culminating in union with the Divine.

"The story of Buddha's descent from heaven by help of golden steps is commonly believed both in Ceylon and Burma to the present day. . . . I was greatly pleased by discovering in the Indian Section of the South Kensington Museum a small bronze model of the triple ladder. . . . It will be observed that an image of the Buddha is represented above the ladder, as if seated in Indra's heaven, and as if engaged in the act of teaching there; while the earth is typically represented below in the shape of a square platform, with four small Buddhist temples, one at each of the four quarters of the compass."—MON. WILLIAMS, *Buddhism*, pp. 416–8.

The four lower planes (earth) are symbolised by the "square platform" with "temples at the four quarters"; corresponding with the Egyptian symbol of the square iron plate supported by four columns at the four cardinal points. The Higher Self (Buddha) is seated on the planes above, from which he descends, as it were, to be the true teacher and ruler of the lower nature (earth). The "triple ladder" signifies the higher planes,—atma-buddhi-manas.

"'Hereafter ye shall see heaven open, and the angels of God ascending and descending upon the Son of Man.' (JOHN i. 51.) Christ is the ladder between our earthliness and the heavenly Father's love, and that ladder is set up in every believing soul. . . . The messengers of God here spoken of are not only the spiritual illumination, help and comfort that stream down to us in Christ from our Father's compassionate heart, they are the holy aspirations that ascend from our souls by the same means to call the blessing down."—R. J. CAMPBELL, Serm., *The Christ Ladder.*

"He then leans a ladder against the (sacrificial) post. He may ascend either from the south northwards, or from the north southwards; but let him rather ascend from the south northwards (udak), for thus it goes upwards (udak). . . . He then rises by the measure of his head over the post (with wheat top piece), with, 'We (i.e. sacrificer and wife) have become immortal!' whereby he wins the world of the gods. . . . Having appropriated to himself the glory, the power, and the strength of the All, he now lays them within himself, makes them his own."—*Sata. Brâh.*, V. 2, 1, 9–15.

The "leaning of the ladder against the post" signifies the soul's commencement of the upward path by aspiration and reliance upon the Divine Light and Life from above (post). The soul may ascend either from the emotions by means of the rule of the mind, or from the mind by means of the stirring of the emotions; but really, progress is through the transmutation of the emotions, the mind being in itself static and unchangeable. The "wheat top piece" signifies the "bread of heaven," goodness and truth, the attainment of which renders the duality of mind and emotion immortal on the buddhic plane—the world of the ideals (gods). The soul, having triumphed over the lower nature and become possessed of the heavenly results of its experience in the worlds below, now identifies itself with the higher qualities.

"The man who 'rises,' who 'makes his pile,' who 'succeeds,' goes up the ladder of wealth, the rungs of which are vanity and applause, mistaking it for the ladder of life, the rungs of which are service, sacrifice and resolution."—A. PONSONBY, *Camel and Needle's Eye*, p. 18.

See ARC. MAN, BLESSING, BUDDHA, CEILING, CHILDREN OF HORUS, EXPERIENCES, FINGERS (two), FIRMAMENT, HORUS, IRON-PLATE, ISIS, MOUTH (speech), OSIRIS, PRAYER, QUARTERS, QUATERNARY, RĀ, SET, STAIRCASE, STAKE, STEPS.

LADY OF THE TWO EARTHS :—

A symbol of the buddhic emotion-nature possessed by the buddhic consciousness (earth) which rises from the lower consciousness (earth); or the higher emotion-nature become manifest through evolution below and fruition above.

See BUDDHI, EARTH (great), GODDESS, GOING IN, MAST, MOTHER, QUEEN, UNEN.

LAKE OF WATER :—

Significant of a limitation of Truth.

"Still the Fish grew, till the lake, though three leagues long, could not contain him."—Deluge Story in the *Mahā-Bhārata.*

But even so, the Self expanded in its functioning, and though the "lake was three leagues long," signifying three aspects of the Self, the Self was not contained thereby.

"In papyri wherein the vignettes are not very elaborate, Osiris stands or sits in his shrine alone, but in fully illustrated papyri he is accompanied by Isis and Nephthys, and by the four children of Horus, who stand on a lotus flower. The stem of this flower springs from out of the waters of a lake, whereon the throne of Osiris is placed ; this lake was fed by the celestial Nile, or by one of its branches, and was the source whence the beatified, as well as the gods, drank. This scene is of considerable interest from the point of view of comparative mythology, for many Semitic writers held the opinion that the throne of the deity was placed, or rested upon, a stream of water, or a river. Even in the Book of Revelation we have a reference to a 'pure river of water, clear as crystal, proceeding out of the throne of God' (see Ch. xxii 1)."—BUDGE, *Book of the Dead*, p. 34.

The Higher Self (Osiris) operates in the soul through the buddhic (Isis) and physical (Nephthys) natures, and growth is effected by experience in the buddhic, mental, astral, and physical human bodies (four children), which are nourished by the Divine life (Nile) from the fount of Truth. The higher causal-body (throne), the seat of the Self, reposes on eternal Truth (water).

See CABIN, CHILDREN OF HORUS, DELUGE, FISH (great), ISIS, LOTUS, MANU, NEPHTHYS, NILE, OSIRIS, RIVER OF LIFE, SHIP (Manu), THRONE, WATER.

LAKSHMANA :—

A symbol of the higher mind or the individuality.

"On the banks of the Godavari, Lakshmana, who has to do all the hard work of the party, built them (Rama Sita, and himself) a spacious hut of clay, leaves, and bamboos, propped with pillars and furnished with a fine level floor, and there they lived happily near the rushing river."—J. C. OMAN, *Great Indian Epics*, p. 44.

In intimate relation with the outpouring of the Divine Life, the Individuality (buddhi-manas) formed a causal-body on the higher mental plane, which should be the seat of the Higher nature in the soul. The causal-body is potentially perfect in all its parts, enthroned above the lower quaternary (four pillars), and having the higher mind, or "firmament," as its base.

See CAUSAL-BODY, FIRMAMENT,

HOUSE, INDIVIDUALITY, KABANDHA, PILLARS, RAMA, RIVER OF LIFE, SITA.

LAKSHMI, THE GODDESS :—

A symbol of the buddhic principle —Wisdom, allied with the Higher Self, or Atman (Rama). Buddhi directs the evolution of the soul.

See BUDDHI, CHURNING, CLOUDS, CONCH, DRAUPADI, FURROWS, POOLS, RAMA, SITA.

LAMB :—

A world-symbol of sacrifice :— born in order to die for human advantage.

"The symbol for lamb in Chinese is composed of *sheep* and *fire*, that is, a sheep on the fire, as though the peculiar appropriation and destiny of lambs were for sacrificial offerings through fire : an idea not incongruous with the statement of Confucius, that a lamb constituted an ancient sacrifice of very great importance."—S. KIDD, *China*, p. 182.

"In Thebes the reverence for the ram in which the god Amen was supposed to be incarnate was extended in a modified form to all rams, and they were held exempt from slaughter, for since the god had vouchsafed to clothe himself in this form its destruction was a crime ; in other Egyptian cities the animal was slaughtered for food without scruple."— A. WIEDEMANN, *Rel. of Anc. Egyptians*, p. 119.

See ABEL, AMEN, ARIES, BURNT, EQUINOX, FIRE, FUH-HE, INCARNATION, JESUS, (lamb), PASSOVER, RAM, SACRIFICE, SHEEP.

LAMB OF GOD :—

A symbol of the Divine Sacrifice. The Logos having been emanated from the Absolute limits his nature in the act of manifestation through forms of matter.

"And all that dwell on the earth shall worship him (the beast), every one whose name hath not been written in the book of life of the Lamb that hath been slain from the foundation of the world."— REV. xiii. 8.

And all the lower qualities shall serve the desire-mind ; every quality whose differentiation is not of the higher order and an expression of the Life of the Divine nature which sacrifices itself at the emanation of the universe, shall be ruled by the lower principle (beast) for a period.

"On looking into the boat of the Sun-god we see that this deity has transformed himself, and that he no longer appears as a fiery disk, but as a Ram-headed man, who stands within a shrine ; in other words Rā has taken the form of Osiris in order that he may pass successfully through the kingdom of the dead, whose lord and god is Osiris. The name given to this form is Af, or Afu, which means literally ' flesh,' and ' a dead body ' ; it was as a dead body that Osiris first entered the Tuat, and those who wished to become what he became subsequently, had to enter the Tuat as dead bodies and with the attributes wherewith he entered it."—BUDGE, *Egypt. Heaven and Hell*, Vol. III. p. 106.

This refers to the Logos (Rā) entering the life-cycle (Tuat) in the world-soul (boat). The symbolical imagery of the Ram's head signifies that the Logos thereby sacrifices himself (as the Lamb) and becomes hidden in matter, and as it were dead. The God cabined within the shrine of the human heart is the Incarnate Deity (Afu, flesh) crucified in matter, as all souls are crucified. For all souls, or sparks of the Divine, who wished to become what He became subsequently (when He rose triumphant from the dead), had also to enter the lower nature as dead in Osiris (Christ) and with the qualities and potencies wherewith He entered it.

" For if we have become united with him by the likeness of his death, we shall be also by the likeness of his resurrection ; knowing this, that our old man was crucified with him, that the body of sin might be done away, that so we should no longer be in bondage to sin ; for he that hath died is justified from sin. But if we died with Christ, we believe that we shall also live with hm."—ROM. vi. 5-8.

It is through the Divine Life (the slain Lamb) within the soul that the " body of sin,"—the desire-nature,— is gradually dissipated, (washed away by the " blood of the Lamb "), and the soul freed from bondage to matter.

" Looking back upon history, or down upon the brute creation, or into the individual human heart to-day, it is impossible to avoid a feeling of horror at the tragedy of it all. It is the passion of God on the cross of the world ; it is Deity being slain on the altar of time to rise in power in the solemn splendour of the eternal morning."—R. J. CAMPBELL, Serm., *God's Uses of Time.*

" The universe is fundamentally spiritual ; being what we are we can come to no other conclusion ; but in that very fact there lies a stern and dreadful necessity, the necessity for the cross. It must be as true of God as it is true of you that the cross is the condition of highest self-realisation ; the cross is eternally in the heart of the Father or he could be neither love nor joy, nor would his holiness have meaning and power. . . . What one dimly perceives is that God cannot help himself in this matter ; it is written deep in the nature of things ; it has to be ; omnipotence cannot alter it. ' The lamb slain from the foundation of the world ' is no figure of speech but the very heart of all reality. The revealing of the glory of God carries with it a cosmic calvary in which we, his children, are individually called to share, This is as truly the nature of things in their highest computation as] it is true of the simplest modes in which beauty and truth express themselves in our experience. It is an unspeakable relief to me to think this. It is the august law which governs life on all planes till it reaches perfect fulfilment and satiety in the vast infinitude of its eternal home."—R. J. CAMPBELL, Serm., *Swelling of Jordan.*

See AFU-RĀ, ARC. MAN, BEAST, BLOOD OF LAMB, BOAT, BONDAGE, BOOK, CABIN, CROSS, CRUCIFIXION, DEAD, DEATH OF OSIRIS, FLESH, HEART, INCARNATION, JESUS (lamb), LINEN GARMENT, MAN (lower), MAN (natural), MARRIAGE OF LAMB, NAME, OSIRIS, RĀ, REDEMPTION, RESURRECTION, SACRIFICER, SHRINE, SPARKS, TIPHYS, TUAT, VISVAKARMAN, WASHED (blood).

LAMBS, SAVOUR OF :—

A symbol of the contribution of the lower self in the thought of loving service and sacrifice.

See ABEL, ALTAR OF SACRIFICE, SAVOUR.

LAMENESS OF THE GOD :—

The Divine nature is limited by the forms in which it can only partially manifest ; and so becomes but the expression of an aspect of Truth. It is, therefore, incomplete (lame) in its progressive capacity.

See HARPOCRATES, HEPHAISTOS.

LAMECH, SON OF METHU- SHAEL :—

A symbol of reflection proceeding from endurance.

See ADAH, PATRIARCHS, ZILLAH.

LAMP AND OIL :—

Symbolic of the causal-body as the receptacle of Wisdom replenished by Love,—the substance wherewith the Spirit feeds the soul and fills it with the light of Truth.

"Wisdom is the lamp of love, and love is the oil of the lamp."—MAETER-LINCK, *Wisdom and Destiny*, § 31.

"Exercise yourselves to find the way of salvation, and dispel with the lamp of wisdom the darkness of ignorance."—*Lalita-vistāra*.

"The knowledge of God is a good material ; God will accept a lamp made out of it. Make good deeds thy wheel, and mould thy lamp on it ; it will accompany thee in this world and the next. When God looketh on him with an eye of favour, some rare pious man knoweth how to make this lamp. This lamp shall be permananent in his heart, and shall not be extinguished when he dieth" (*Guru Nanak*).—MACAULIFFE, *The Sikh Religion*, Vol. I. p. 349.

"For, indeed, all men are lamps, since they can be both lighted and extinguished. Moreover, when the lamps are wise, they shine and glow with the Spirit ; yet also, if they did burn and are put out, they even stink. The servants of God remain good lamps by the oil of His mercy, not by their own strength. The free grace of God, truly, is the oil of the lamps. 'For I have laboured more than they all,' saith a certain 'lamp' ; and lest he should seem to burn by his own strength, he added, 'But not I, but the grace of God that was with me' (1 COR. xv. 10)."—AUGUSTINE, *Gospel of John*, Vol. I. p. 328.

"Throughout the Old Testament the soft gracious influences of God's Spirit are symbolised by oil, with which therefore prophets, priests, and kings were designated to their office. Thus the lamp too must be fed, the soul which is to give forth the light of Christ must first of all have been kindled by Him, and then must constantly be supplied with the grace and gift of His Divine Spirit. What became of those who had lamps without oil ? Their lamps had gone out, and their end was darkness. Oh ! let us beware lest by any sloth and sin, we choke the golden pipes through which there steals into our tiny lamps the soft flow of that Divine oil which alone can keep up the flame. The wick, untrimmed and unfed, may burn for a little while, but it soon chars, and smokes, and goes out at last in foul savour offensive to God and man."—A. MACLAREN, *Sermons, 2nd Series*, p. 163.

See CANDLE, CANDLESTICK, DARKNESS, FIRE, FLAME, GOLD, GRACE, HEART, LIGHT, LOST PIECE, LOVE, OIL, TAE-KEIH, VIRGINS.

LAND :—

A symbol of the arena of life and experience on the different planes of manifestation.

"Land wherein are cultivated most corn, grass and fruit, and where there is most irrigation and good drainage."—*Vendidad*, III, *S. B of E.*

The buddhic plane whereon are reaped the "fruit of the Spirit" which are the higher faculties of Wisdom and Love. These products of goodness and knowledge are the transmuted produce of experience and the disciplining of the qualities by Truth (water).

See CORN, EXPERIENCE, FIELD, FRUIT, IRRIGATION, KARMA, KNOWER OF FIELD, SEKHET-HETEP, TRANSMUTATION, VAISYA.

LAND, DRY :—

A symbol of the lower quaternary, —the lower planes of the soul, or "natural man."

"And God called the dry land Earth : and the gathering together of the waters called he Seas : and God saw that it was good."—GEN. i. 10.

And the "dry land" is named "Earth," which term also stands for the lower nature of the Soul, which is the natural man ; and the "gathering together of the waters" signifies the formation of the astral "sea" of the desires. And all is pronounced "good," that is, perfect in involution for purposes of forthcoming evolution.

"These knowledges are the 'waters gathered together into one place,' and are called 'seas' ; but the external man is called 'dry land,' and presently 'earth.'"—SWEDENBORG, *Arc. Cel. to Gen.* i. 10.

See EARTH, GROUND, MAN (natural), QUATERNARY, SEA, WATER.

LANDMARKS :—

A symbol of the marks or stages in the development of the natural man, that is, the successive incarnations by means of which the soul garners its harvest on the higher planes.

"Thou shalt not remove thy neighbour's landmark, which they of old time have set in their inheritance, which thou shalt inherit in the land that the Lord thy God giveth thee to possess it."—DEUT. xix. 14.

This refers to the growth of kindred qualities, which must be effected in due relation to each other and not at others' expense.

See GOLD (spot), JUDGING, NEIGHBOUR.

LANGUAGE :—

A symbol of the recognition of sameness and the perception of difference.

"And the whole earth was of one language and of one speech."—GEN. xi. 1.

And at this early period, the entire lower nature of the soul was in a homogeneous condition.

"Therefore was the name of it called Babel ; because the Lord did there confound the language of all the earth."—GEN. xi. 9.

This "city" or centre of consciousness is known as "Babel,"—that is, perception of difference between qualities.

See BABEL, CITY, EARTH, SPEECH,

LANKA :—

A symbol of the astro-mental or kama-manasic plane, the plane of the desires (Rakshasas) and the desire-mental principle (Ravana). This is the arena on which the battle of life takes place, wherein the incarnate Self (Rama) overcomes the lower principle (Ravana) and the host of desires.

See HANUMAN, RAKSHASAS, RAMA, RAVANA, SITA, VANAR, VIBHISHANA.

LAO-KEUN-TZE, THE FOUNDER OF TAOISM :—

A symbol of the First Logos, or the Absolute.

"Lao-keun-tze is described as the Great Supreme, threefold Source, consisting of three personages."—*Chinese Mythology*, KIDD, *China*.

The Logos,—the One without a Second. This manifests in three aspects,—the Self, the Soul as will-intellect, and the Personality, desire-mind.

See ABSOLUTE, MONAD, PHANES, TAE-KEIH, TAO, TRIAD.

LATONA OR LETO, MOTHER OF APOLLO :—

A symbol of Wisdom, or the buddhic emotion-nature which gives birth to the Self within the soul.

"Leto would therefore (from her name) signify 'the obscure' or 'concealed,' not as a physical power, but as a divinity yet quiescent and invisible, from whom issued the visible divinity (Apollo) with all his splendour and brilliancy."—*Smith's Class. Dict.*

Unperceived by the lower nature, the buddhic nature (Leto) brings forth the Self in the souls of mankind, to save and illuminate them.

See APOLLO, BUDDHI, DELOS, DIOSCURI, MOTHER.

LAUGHTER OF THE GODS :—

Symbolic of the Highest Ideals becoming vivified and fully realised in the progressed soul.

"Then Hephaistos poured wine to all the other Gods from right to left, ladling the sweet nectar from the bowl. And laughter unquenchable arose amid the blessed Gods to see Hephaistos bustling through the palace."—*Iliad*, Bk. I.

Then the Creative Mind offered its activities forthflowing as loving service to its Ideals. And the Higher Ideals (Gods) became animated, i.e. were realised, as the Creative Mind progressed upon its higher path within the buddhic causal-body (the palace).

In the Japanese legend of the Sun-goddess ; when "Usumé" the symbol of wisdom evolving (dancing) in the soul, discards at the end of the cycle, her garments (lower-mental), it is said,—"With the laughter of the Gods the Heavens shook." That is ; with the animation of the Ideals the higher planes vibrated. It is only when the lower nature is outgrown at the time of resurrection and liberation that the Gods laugh.

See AMATERASU, GODS, HEPHAISTOS, NAKEDNESS, NECTAR, PALACE, USUMÉ, WINE.

LAUREL LEAVES :—

A symbol of those visionary and deadening emotions which beget an unreal and confused view of life.

LAW OF BUDDHA :—

The law of the manifesting Self is that through the phenomenal or outward activity there is displayed gradually by evolution the spiritual or inward activity.

"The thirsty world of living beings will drink the flowing stream of his Law, bursting forth with the water of wisdom enclosed by the banks of strong moral rules, delightfully cool with contemplation, and filled with religious vows as with ruddy geese."—*Buddha-Karita*, Bk. I. 76, *S. B. of E.*

The illusory or phenomenal existence, with its cravings for expression of that which is within it, is, as it were, the means whereby the Self-nature is realised. Through the phenomenal is displayed in various aspects that which is within the Self, and this is spoken of as the Law, since the finite-conditioned is but the symbol and evidence of the infinite-unconditioned. Through all the planes of its manifestation proceed the Truth-Wisdom (water of wisdom) aspects of the Self. On the planes of nature (the banks) the laws of the Self are operative, and these are the means of revealing that which is above the "Law and the Prophets," or duty and obedience. Under the rule of Love there is cessation from trouble, strife, or emotional stress, while aspirations (religious vows) yield such results as are capable of directing the evolution of the Self.

"No commandment is right and good merely because God wills it and has the power to enforce it ; God wills it because it is right and good, and it is right and good because it marks the way by which the soul achieves itself."—R. J. CAMPBELL, Serm., *Who Compels ?*

"The law of the Lord is perfect, restoring the soul. The testimony of the Lord is sure, making wise the simple."—Ps. xix. 7.

The law of the Self in the soul is to manifest its potential perfection, by restoring the actual imperfection to the perfection which completeness of evolution will give. The revelation of the Divine within brings wisdom to the attentive mind.

See EVOLUTION, INVOLUTION, PHENOMENA, SIDES, STREAM, THIRST, THIRSTY, WATER, WORLD (thirsty).

LAW OF MAZDA :—

The law of Divine Love,—the attraction to the Highest.

"The will of God, which is the law of holiness, is the deepest and inmost thing of all this world. And the ultimate question of every human life is whether he is at Peace with God. Peace is the being rightly and harmoniously related with that with which we have to do."—PHILLIPS BROOKS, Serm., *Peace in Believing.*

See KARSHIPTA, SURAS.

LAW OF MOSES :—

The moral law arising through experience, and the perception of superior and inferior action in relation to social well-being. This implies

subjection to karma. The moral law is the forerunner of the spiritual law of Love.

See COVENANT, DISPENSATIONS, JUSTIFICATION, MOSAIC, MOSES, SHOES (off), TESTAMENT.

LAW OF REVENGE, ANGER, AND FOLLY :—

The natural working of the inverted reflections of Truth, Love, and Wisdom.

See EVIL, GUILTY PERSONS, MURDER, OPPOSITES.

LAW OF ZOROASTER :—

The Divine Law of the growth of the Soul from a condition of illusion to a state of pure Truth.

"Ahriman and his daevas surround fallen man night and day, and seek to mislead him, in order to increase thereby the power of darkness. He would not be able to resist these temptations to which his first parents had already yielded, had not Ormazd taken pity on him, and sent him a revelation of his will in the Law of Zoroaster. If he obeys these precepts he is safe from the daevas, and under the immediate protection of Ormazd. The substance of the law is the command, ' *Think purely, Speak purely, Act purely.*' All that comes from Ormazd is pure, all from Ahriman impure."—*Zoroastrian System.*

As a spark of the Divine Self, the soul should know God. But the astral and physical consciousness limits the soul and prevents its attaining illumination. And so it is that the power of illusion is created, and further and further is the soul led away from the truth. Nor would it be possible for the soul unassisted to rise from these planes of consciousness unless there had been another forthpouring of the life of the Logos. This spiritual energy from above is spoken of as the "Law of Zoroaster" which simply means the Divine Law of the Soul's growth. Obedience to the requirements of the Higher Life, places the soul beyond the illusoriness of the lower planes, for the soul may then dwell under the shadow of the Eternal and need fear no ill. The Divine Law insists upon the regulation of the life upon the lower planes by the soul itself, which shows that there is no abstract goodness to rely upon, and that apart from personal Thought, Speech, and Action, there is no salvation for the soul. The soul's safety consists in its transferring the impetus given to its life from Above, to the lower planes whereon it functions, and so overcoming ignorance and evil. The will and the thought regulate the lower life, and unless the higher impulses are translated into terms of individual volition and ideation they remain inoperative. God becomes God to man only in so far as man becomes God : in other words, as the human will becomes God-like, so humanity becomes indistinguishable from God.

"My Me is God."—*St. Catherine of Genoa.*

"Not from nature, only from man, from the social process (which Professor Huxley opposed to the cosmic) can we discern the Law by which man may elect to live. In the human and ethical sentiment which lies in our own heart alone, can it be we obtain a glimpse of the higher order which we identify with God."—R. DIMSDALE STOCKER, *The God which is Man*, p. 118.

"You begin to try to do right. And then it is, in the pursuance of that effort, that there become gradually impressed upon your intelligence certain things which had found no recognition there before. The spiritual nature of the world ; that all this mass of things and events is fitted for and naturally struggles towards the education of character ;—the spiritual nature of man ; the truth that man is fully satisfied only with character, and with an endless chance for that character to grow ;—and God ; the existence, behind all standards and laws, of righteousness, of a perfectly righteous One, from Whom they all proceed, and by Whom those who try to follow them are both judged and helped."—PHILLIPS BROOKS, Serm., *Eye of the Soul.*

"It is the sanctified soul that can read the secrets of God, and not those which are wise only with the wisdom that is of this world. If you want to get behind the mystery of life, to find out what is the last word of creation, to learn the nature of the Creator and the life that is from everlasting to everlasting, you must seek it through goodness, and not through mere cleverness. It is the pure in heart who see God, and, one might add, it is those who have been conformed to the likeness of Christ who can sing the song of Moses and the Lamb. . . . Heaven utters itself in the heart. This is what it means to say, that those who are redeemed from the earth learn the song which is being sung by the glorified ones around the throne of God."
—R. J. CAMPBELL, Serm., *The Song of the Redeemed.*

See AHRIMAN, AHURA-MAZDA, AHURA RELIGION, DAEVAS, DARKNESS, DEVAYANA, EARTH, EVOLUTION, FALL, GOD, GOSPEL, HEART, IGNORANCE, ILLUSION, MAIDEN, MAN (righteous), PAURVAS, REDEMPTION, RELIGION, REVELATION, SALVATION, SONG, SOUL, ZOROASTER.

LAW, TABLES OF THE :—

A symbol of the higher or Love- and Wisdom-nature which has its seat in the causal-body (ark).

See ARK OF THE TESTIMONY.

LAYING OF HANDS ON HEAD :—

A symbol of the Spirit actively contacting the mind ; or the spiritual mind (priest) influencing the lower mind (man).

"The offering represents Christ's body, and the laying on of hands the identity of the offering and the offerer."—A. JUKES, *The Law of the Offerings*, p. 41.

See ANOINTING, HAIR, HAND, HEAD, MAN (lower), PRIEST.

LAZARUS :—

A symbol of the causal-body on the higher mental plane.

"The name of Lazarus suggests symbolism ; another form of it is Eliezar, who is in Philo (I. 481) the type of a being 'liable to dissolution and (indeed) a corpse,' but 'held together and kindled into life by the Providence of God.' "—E. A. ADENEY, in *Enc. Biblica.*

"Now a certain man was sick, Lazarus, of Bethany, of the village of Mary and her sister Martha."—JOHN xi. 1.

Now at a particular period of evolution, a certain high mental organic part of the soul was in a condition of depressed vitality ; this was the causal-body which existed in the inner soul,—or Abode of the Lord,—wherein the purified emotions and the higher demonstrative emotions dwelt.

"So they took away the stone. And Jesus lifted up his eyes, etc. . . . And when he had thus spoken, he cried with a loud voice, Lazarus, come forth."—JOHN xi. 41, 43.

The taking away of the stone corresponds to removing a mass of encumbrance of errors and desires which is calculated to arrest the progress of the soul in the required direction. To the prayer of the Christ-soul, there was granted an accession of power from Above. Then followed the re-awakenment of the causal-body ; "bound with grave-clothes," that is, fettered by the limiting tendencies which have had the effort of causing its "death" and "burial,"—the sleep of the intuition which is a function of the causal-body.

"'That mass placed on the sepulchre (of Lazarus) is the force of evil custom with which the soul is weighed down, nor permitted to rise up nor breathe' (AUGUSTINE, *Serm. 44 on St. John*). . . . St. Augustine says, Lazarus going forth from the sepulchre is the soul drawing back from carnal vices, but bound, that is, not yet freed from pains and troubles of the flesh, while it dwells in the body ; the 'face is covered with a napkin,' for we cannot have full understanding of things in this life ; but it is said, 'Loose him,' for after this life the veilings are taken away, that we may see face to face."—C. À LAPIDE, *The Great Comm.*, Vol. II. pp. 405, 406.

"And hence to dead Lazarus, who was kept down by a great weight, it is not said, 'Be thou restored to life,' but, 'Come forth,' by which same rising again, which was carried on in the body of that man, it is signified in what way we ourselves rise again in the body (from being dead in sin ")."—ST. GREGORY, *Morals on the Book of Job*, Vol. II. p. 573.

"The Lord cried out at the sepulchre of Lazarus, and he that was four days dead arose. He who stank in the grave came forth into the air. He was buried, a stone was laid over him : the voice of the Saviour burst asunder the hardness of the stone ; and thy heart is so hard, that that Divine Voice does not break it ! Rise in thy heart ; go forth from thy tomb. For thou wast lying dead in thy heart as in a tomb, and pressed down by the weight of evil habit as by a stone. Rise and go forth."—AUGUSTINE, *Gospel of John*, Vol. I. p. 319.

"'And he that was dead came forth bound with bandages, feet and hands.' This was symbolical of that man who had been bound in sins."—IRENÆUS, *Against Heresies*, Book V. 13.

"Now there was a certain rich man, and he was clothed in purple and fine linen, faring sumptuously every day ; and a certain beggar named Lazarus was laid at his gate, full of sores, and desiring to be fed with the crumbs that fell from the rich man's table."—LUKE xvi. 19.

The "rich man" is the lower self, or personality, which is satisfied with the things of the world and the pleasures of sense. The "robes of purple and fine linen" are figurative, and refer to the lower emotions and to the vehicles of the ego, i.e. the etheric double and the astral body. The "beggar Lazarus" is the causal-body laid at the entrance to the earthly life. He is one who begs for the fruits of incarnation, and is starved in regard to the opportunities which the rich soul has in abundance. The "sores" signify conditions which on the physical side mean pain and suffering, but which inwardly correspond to spiritual growth. The desire to be fed is the eager wish to receive from the lower nature the things which the "rich man" could bestow if he would deny himself.

"The 'rich man' is an invisible being, and so is the 'poor man' ; these two spirits have been in man all through time. 'Lazarus' was presented to the *will* of the 'rich man' ; for the will is the *gate* at which alone the Lord can enter, begging for the 'rich man' to bend his *thoughts* towards him, etc."—JOHN WARD, *Zion's Works*, Vol. VII. p. 16.

"A Kshatriya cannot thrive without a Brahman, nor a Brahman without a Kshatriya. The Brahman and the Kshatriya when associated together prosper in this world and the next."—*Laws of Manu*, IX. 322.

A personality (Kshatriya) cannot thrive without an individuality (Brahman), nor an individuality in the causal-body without a personality.

"The first thing that any true man ought to settle with himself when confronted with an occasion for sacrifice is what it is he really has to give. It must be his best that he offers to the Highest, not his second best. In fact, sacrifice rightly understood involves this all the way along. You have to sacrifice yourself in order to form yourself, or else yours is a poor lean soul."—R. J. CAMPBELL, *Serm.*, *The Higher Sacrifice*.

"Dives" offered crumbs, not his best, so "Lazarus" was left "a poor lean soul."

"Only those miracles, however, which are referable to the spiritual plane have significance and value for the Soul. Hence for it the raising from the dead,— as of Lazarus,—implies resurrection from the condition of spiritual deadness ; the giving of sight implies the opening of the spiritual vision ; and the feeding of the hungry multitude implies the satisfaction of man's craving for spiritual nourishment."—*The Perfect Way*, p. 229.

See BETHANY, BRAHMAN, CAUSAL-BODY, CLOTHING, EVOLUTION, FEEDING, FETTERS, FOOD, GATE, HADES, HEALING (dead), HEART, INCARNATION, INTUITION, KSHATRIYA, MAN (rich), MARTHA, PARABLE, PRANAS, RICH MAN, ROCK SEPULCHRE, SAHU, SELF (lower), SEPULCHRE, SI-OSIRI, SONS OF GOD, SORES, TOMB.

LEAVEN (HIGHER ASPECT) :—

A symbol of the spiritual life permeating the lower nature.

"The kingdom of heaven is like unto leaven, which a woman took, and hid in three measures of meal, till it was all leavened."—MAT. xiii. 33.

The Christ here alludes to the "Woman," or purified lower nature, conceiving the Christ-soul through which the lower triad of bodies,— *mental, astral,* and *physical,*—is purified and becomes one with, or disappears into, the *causal ;* for of such purification is the "kingdom of heaven,"—the spiritual or buddhic consciousness.

"The four elements which constitute man are, counting from without inwards, the material body, the fluidic perisoul or astral body, the soul or individual, and the spirit, or divine Father and life of his system. This last it is whose kingdom is described as the leaven taken by the woman—the divine Sophia or wisdom—and hidden in three measures of meal, namely, the soul, the perisoul, and the body, until the whole is leavened ; until, that is, the whole man is so permeated and lightened by it that he is finally transmuted into Spirit and becomes 'one with God.'"—*The Perfect Way,* p. 5.

"The parable of the Leaven which the woman is said to have hid in three measures of meal, they (the Gnostics) say, mean the three kinds (of men). For Wisdom they teach to be expressed by a woman ; by measures of meal, the three kinds of men,—spiritual, animal, earthy. As to leaven, they teach it to be a name of the Saviour Himself."—IRENÆUS, *Against Heresies,* p. 26.

"Compare Philo (I. 173) on 'the three measures of the soul' that are to be 'kneaded' like cakes, wherein the sacred doctrine must be hidden."—E. A. ADENEY, *Enc. Biblica.*

See DOUGH, ELEMENTS, FLOUR, KINGDOM OF HEAVEN, MEAL, PARABLE, SOPHIA, VESTURES, VIRGIN, WOMAN.

LEAVEN (LOWER ASPECT) :—

A symbol of passion and desire permeating the lower nature.

"Leaven signifies what is false derived from evil ; hence what is unleavened signifies what is pure or without that falsity."—SWEDENBORG, *Arc. Cel.,* n. 9992. (*See* 1 COR. v. 6–8. LUKE xii. 1.)

See UNLEAVENED.

LEAVES :—

A symbol of true ideas, or known facts.

"And the leaves of the tree (of life) were for the healing of the nations."—REV. xxii. 2.

The acquirement of true ideas perfects the qualities.

"Christ's Eye pierces through the thick leaves of our secret thoughts."—WORDSWORTH, *Bible, John,* p. 276.

"The reason why leaves signify rational truths is because by a tree is signified man."—SWEDENBORG, *Apoc. Rev.,* n. 936.

See HEALING, MULTITUDES, TREE, TREE OF LIFE.

LEES ; DREGS :—

A symbol of the lower instincts and desires which remain unpurified.

"Moab hath been at ease from his youth, and he hath settled on his lees, and hath not been emptied from vessel to vessel."—JER. xlviii. 11.

The lower nature at first is at ease in the soul ; there is little effort towards improvement, and habits of thought bind down to things below (lees). The lower nature has not been purified by being passed into mental forms (vessels) of better thought, so as to leave the lowest forms (the lees) behind.

See TAMAS, VESSEL.

LEFT :—

Indicative of passivity, or incoming energy.

See ARMS (body), CORN, HAND.

LEGGED, ONE-, RACE OF MEN :—

A symbol of the higher mind which co-ordinates ideas and enables the Self to stand alone.

LEGISLATION, DIVINE :—

Symbolic of the organising of the universe and of the activities of the soul.

See CIVILISING, GOVERNMENT, OANNES, YAO.

LEGS OF A MAN :—

A symbol of duality, when passive. When active, they signify the mental activities which are a means of progression upon the lower planes.

See KNEE, MAN, STRIDES.

LEGS OF A BEAST :—

A symbol of the lower quaternary, or of activities upon the lower planes.

See ANIMALS, QUATERNARY.

LEMMINKAINEN :—

A symbol of the Higher Self who descends into matter and becomes the Archetypal Man, who dies in order that the individual souls may have immortal life.

"Lemminkainen is principally connected with songs and feasts for the brewing of beer, and is hence sometimes confused (under the name of Ahti) with the sower and plougher Pellervoinen. . . . In the death of Lemminkainen we seem to find a remembrance of the Balder myth."—D. COMPARETTI, *Poetry of the Finns*, p. 243.

Like Dionysus, the Finnic Hero is associated with an intoxicating drink, a symbol of the Divine Life. He is also the Divine Husbandman who cultivates the lower nature (earth) and sows therein spiritual seed, that higher qualities may take root in human nature and bring salvation to the soul. Balder, Osiris, Pragâpati, Purusha, Christ, are all symbols of the Archetypal Man.

See ARC. MAN, BALDER, CRANBERRY, DEATH OF BALDER, OF LEMMINKAINEN, OF OSIRIS, DISMEMBERMENT, DIONYSUS, HUSBANDMAN, INCARNATION, MARJATTA, MARSH, SEED (good), SERPENT OF THE WATER, SOWER.

LEMNOS ISLAND :—

A symbol of the mental region of scientific knowledge based upon hard fact ; or of inductive science.

See DOLIONES, EUNEUS, HYPSIPYLE, THOAS.

LEO, THE ZODIACAL SIGN :—

A symbol of the fifth period of the cycle of life, which is a period of involution on the astral plane, wherein strong desire works in the lower nature through passion, instinct, appetite, and animal affection. It is the period of the involutionary development of the astral nature of the soul.

See CANCER, LION, VIRGO, ZODIAC.

LEOPARD :—

A symbol of the opinionative lower mind full of errors mingled with truths. The lower qualities, are,

as it were, devoured by the lower mind.—See JER. v. 6.

"Signifies the truths of the World falsified, owing to its black and white spots, for by the black spots are signified falses, and by the white intermixed with them is signified truth ; as therefore it is a fierce and murderous beast, it signifies the truths of the Word falsified and thus destroyed."—SWEDENBORG, *Apoc. Rev.*, n. 572.

See COW (spotted), SPOTTED, WHITE.

LEPER :—

A symbol of the lower mind troubled with conflicting desires and emotions and confused ideals.

"If the story of Naaman the leper is a symbol at all, the material must be a symbol of the spiritual ; the outward act, of the inward submission to the cleansing of the soul ; the washing which purified the leper, of the faith by which the sinner is cleansed—and the whole story, as we say, an illustration of that Divine simplicity and abstinence from all reliance on outward acts, which is the very essence of God's way of salvation. For if one part of the story has to be transposed into another key, there will be discord, unless the whole be so. And if we are to say leprosy was the symbol of the soul-sickness of sin, and healing the symbol of the soul-cleansing of pardon and sanctifying, then we must lift the washing in the river of Israel into the same region, and recognise in it the symbol of the soul's act of faith, whereby our stained nature is plunged into the fountain opened for sin and for uncleanness."—A. MACLAREN, *Sermons*, 3rd Series, p. 266.

See BAPTISM, BLOOD OF THE LAMB, CLEANSING, FOUNTAIN, HEALING, JORDAN, TEN LEPERS, WASHED, WATER.

LEPIDOTUS FISH, AND TWO OTHERS :—

Symbols of superstition, prejudice, and error.

See GENERATIVE.

LETTER FROM THE FATHER, MOTHER, AND BROTHER OF THE EAST :—

Symbolic of an inspiration of Truth from Atma-buddhi-manas, to assist the soul to rise. This inspiration may be received through pondering on the sacred scriptures.

"And my letter was a letter which the king sealed with his right hand, to keep it from the wicked ones, the children of Babel, and from the savage demons. It flew in the likeness of an eagle, the king of all birds ; it flew and alighted beside me, and became all speech. At its voice and the sound of its rustling, I started and arose from my sleep. I took it up and kissed it, and loosed its seal and read ; and according to what was traced on my heart were the words of my letter written. I remembered that I was a son of kings, and my free soul longed for its natural state " (*Hymn of the Soul* (Gnostic)).—*Acts of Judas Thomas.*

And the message was an appeal to me that came with power from Above,—

Through the outgoing energy of the Most High.

Then,—to keep it from those worldly thought currents in the mind,

Which understand not the mysteries of the Spirit.

And would pollute the sacred contents of the message ;

And also to preserve it from the savage emotions, which destroy and render waste,—

It sped forth to me with a directness and sureness of aim,

That might be compared to the swift flight of an eagle,

Which bird is a symbol of the Holy Spirit descending.

It came upon me and took possession of me mightily,

So that I had to listen to that whereof it told me.

At its entreaty, when I was roused from my slumber,

I trembled and turned in haste to attend unto it.

Its truck a chord in the deep of my heart,

And I welcomed it with a tender affection,

And then diligently set myself to learn of it.

In so far as I yielded myself up to it through love,

Was my devout response to the Holy Spirit given.

Then with joy did I remember my sonship,—my Father ;

For my soul, freed from the thraldom of desire and sensation,

Did eagerly await her union with the Divine.

See EAGLE, BABEL, GNOSIS, PEARL, RELIGION (good), ROBE, SALVATION, SEALED LETTER, SERPENT (loud).

LEVI, THE PRIEST :—

A symbol of obedience to the moral law, and subjection to karma.

See DISPENSATIONS, MOSAIC, MOSES.

LEVITES :—

A symbol of qualities serving the law of obedience to authority esteemed superior.

LEVIATHAN, OR LEVITIYA :—

A symbol of the Cycle of Life in the quaternary ; or the nature of things in time and space.

" In his neck remaineth strength, and sorrow is turned into joy before him (leviathan)."—JOB xli. 22.

In the purified emotions (the neck) there is the power to overcome the lower desires, and when these are conquered, suffering will give place to bliss at the termination of the cycle.

" Thou breakest the heads of leviathan in pieces, and gavest them to be meat to the people inhabiting the wilderness."—Ps. lxxiv. 14.

This refers to the intelligence developed in each period of a manvantara, which becomes sustenance to the qualities of the desire-mental order, and these in their turn shall be transmuted by the Spirit (*see* ISA. xxvii. 1).

" All ancient Fathers of the Church of Christ agree in recognizing a secondary and spiritual sense in this description (JOB xli.) The Leviathan of Scripture is a type of the Enemies of God and His people. . . . Proceeding in this sense (that Satan is called the dragon), the Ancient Expositors see here a series of questions which *cannot* be answered in the affirmative by the *natural* man, but *are* solved triumphantly by Christ, the Second Adam, the DIVINE JOB, Who conquered by suffering, and Who laid hold on the Dragon, that old Serpent, and bound him, and cast him into the bottomless pit."—WORDSWORTH, *Bible, Job*, p. 97.

" We must ask about this (leviathan) ; whether, when the saints were living a blessed life apart from matter and from any body, the dragon (leviathan), falling from the pure life, became fit to be bound in matter and in a body, so that the Lord could say, ' This is the beginning of the creation of God, made for His angels to mock at.' "—ORIGEN, *Comm. on John*, Bk. I. § 17.

See BEHEMOTH, CAPRICORNUS, CIRCLE, CROCODILE, HEAD, HINE, KHWAN, MANVANTARA, MEAT, NECK, OCEAN, PEOPLE, SERPENT (ananta), SIGN, WHALE (Jonah), WILDERNESS, ZODIAC.

LIBATIONS FROM BEES,— HONEY :—

A symbol of the free-will offerings, or fruits of industry (bees), which are exacted of the lower self, and have their return in wisdom and love (honey).

See BEES (libations), HONEY.

LIBERATION :—

This term signifies the release of the ego or Self from captivity to the lower nature. The release comes about when the ego has entirely overcome the downward or outward attraction to the objects of desire and sensation, and has completely purified his lower nature, so that in fact it disappears, and his consciousness rises to union with God on the higher mental plane in the causal-body.

"The negation of the merely natural and sensual life, which is itself the negation of the spirit, is the sole way to true spiritual life."—D. F. STRAUSS, *Life of Jesus*, p. 438.

"If Christ does not rise within the soul of the believer, transforming everything there into his own spiritual likeness, our faith is vain, and we are yet in our sins. But then he does so rise ; he does so gain the victory over our lower nature ; he does conform us to his own risen life, and in so doing sets us free from sin."— R. J. CAMPBELL, Serm., *Christ Arisen*.

"God's original plan comprehends a rising side, an economy supernatural, that shall complement the disorder and fall of nature, having power to roll back its currents of penal misery, and bring out souls into the established liberty and beauty of holiness. How manifest is it in the world's birth that God, from the first, designs it for a second birth ; some grand *palingenesia* that shall raise the fall of nature and make existence fruitful."—H. BUSHNELL, *Nature and the Supernatural*, p. 148.

See ASCENSION, ASCETIC, ATONEMENT, ATTACHMENT, BONDAGE, CAPTIVITY, CONQUEROR, CONSECRATION, COURSE, CRUCIFIXION, OF JESUS, DESTROYING EVILS, ESCAPE, EXILE, FALL, GUARDIAN SPIRITS, INCARNATION, KHEPERA, MANAS, PEACE, REBIRTH, REDEMPTION, REGENERATION, REMISSION, RESURRECTION, SAINTS, SALVATION, SCARABEUS, SIAMAK, SUNSETTING, VIBHU, VICTORY, VISHNU, WORKS (wisdom).

LIBRA, THE ZODIACAL SIGN :—

A symbol of the seventh period of the cycle of life, which is the first period of evolution on the astral plane. The first point of Libra represents the balance between involution and evolution, and the commencement of the evolution from homogeneity to heterogeneity of the many forms and qualities.

See ARC, MAN, EQUINOX, EVOLUTION, INVOLUTION, LIMBS, SABBATH, SEVENTH, VIRGO, ZODIAC.

LIGHT :—

A symbol of Truth, Wisdom and Knowledge, and of the consciousness which apprehends reality or relativity in each.

"This is not lawful for some and unlawful for others, but what is lawful for all extends on continuously through the wide-ruling air and the boundless light." —*Empedocles*, FAIRBANKS, 425.

The law of the Infinite is relative to the state of the soul, and to those qualities as yet undeveloped. The soul's early ideas of wisdom and truth would be folly and falsity ; but so much of the Infinite as may be apprehended is everywhere present, and through the mind (air) is perceived ; and then there is increased perception through the intuition and up to the spiritual, or buddhic, levels of Wisdom, Truth, and Love.

"Arise, shine ; for thy light is come, and the glory of the Lord is risen upon thee. For, behold, darkness shall cover the earth, and gross darkness the peoples : but the Lord shall arise upon thee, and his glory shall be seen upon thee."—Is. lx. 1, 2.

The soul hails the approach of Truth and the rising within it of the Higher Self to perfection and power. The darkness of ignorance covered the lower nature and its activities, but the Self shall manifest within the soul, and his perfection shall be apparent to all the higher qualities.

" 'That he may recall their souls from corruption, and enlighten them with the light of the living' (JOB xxxiii. 20). They who still live for this world are in darkness in the light of the dying. But they are enlightened with the light of the living, who, despising the light of the world, return to the splendour of the inward brightness that they may live in that place where they may see, by feeling it, the true light, where light and life are not different from each other, but where the light itself is life also."—ST. GREGORY, *Morals on the Book of Job*, Vol. III. p. 77.

"Sayings by Plotinus :—'We are not cut off or severed from the Light, but we breathe and consist in It, since It is what It is.' In the moment of Union, 'we are able to see both Him and ourself,—ourself in dazzling splendour, full of spiritual light, or rather one with the pure Light Itself . . . our life's flame is then enkindled.' 'There the soul rests, after it has fled up, away from evil, to the place which is free from evils, . . . and the true life is there. Arrived there, the soul becomes that which she was at first' (Enneads, VI. ix. 9)."—F. VON HUGEL, *Mystical Element*, Vol. II. p. 96.

"This Light of the everlasting world, which has risen by such wonderful steps till it has overspread our sky, is but the Heavenly Light given us in such measure as we could bear it ; given in the degree proportionate to time and mortality, and our stage of being ; given to men, not who have won their appointed place, but who are preparing for it. This Light, to which all that was before was darkness, is itself only the beginning and promise of the Perfect Light to come."—R. W. CHURCH, *Cathedral Sermons*, p. 89.

See AIR, CANDLE, CONSCIOUSNESS, DAYLIGHT, EARTH, GATE OF SALUTATION, GLORY, LAMP, MATTER, QUALITIES, RAIMENT, SUN.

LIGHT, PRIMORDIAL :—

A symbol of Truth as consciousness in the union of Spirit and Matter at the commencement of manifestation.

"And God said, Let there be light : and there was light."—GEN. i. 3.

The Supreme wills "light," or the union of Spirit and Matter, to be effected ; and so consciousness, self-illumination, thereupon occurs.

"'That which hath been made was (beforehand) life in him ; and that life became light in men' (JOHN i. 4). In other words, the life which was eternally in Christ is that which has been drawn upon to be individualised in creation, as a gardener might cut shoots off an apple tree to plant in other soils ; and this life it is and no other which has become light —that is, self-consciousness in mankind." —R. J. CAMPBELL, Serm., *Christ Transcendent*.

"First, then, a simple, pure spiritual Light was created, the material of Souls which are simple spiritual substances, of the nature of Light. That Light-material or Upper World, from which the souls descended, is also called Reason, or Light of the Light of God. The Light is followed by the Shadow, from which the Animal Soul is created, for the service of the Rational Soul" (Razi).—DE BOER, *Hist. of Philos. in Islam*, p. 79.

The obverse of Truth—the higher nature,—is Illusion, the lower nature, from which comes the desire and sensation nature for the use of the Ego.

"The nearest approach which meta-physical language can make to Brāhman, is to call it light, which is another name for knowledge. And so we read in the *Mundaka Upanishad* (V. 2) : 'This is the light of lights ; when it shines, the sun does not shine. . . . When Brāhman shines, everything shines after him, by his light all the world is lighted.' Conscious light would best represent the knowledge ascribed to Brāhman, and it is well known *Thomas Aquinas* also called God the intelligent Sun."—MAX MULLER, *Vedanta Phil.*, p. 137.

"Augustine constantly urges our recognition of the truth that God is the 'Father of lights.' From Him as our central Sun, all light whether of wisdom or knowledge, proceedeth."—Translator, *Confessions*. p. 76.

"Gerrard Winstanley's central religious idea is the Divine Light within man's soul. . . . 'Man,' he says, 'looks abroad for a God and doth imagine or fancy a God in some particular place of glory beyond the skies. But the Kingdom of Heaven is within you, dwelling and ruling in your flesh.' The Spirit within (which he also calls that mighty man Christ Jesus) is to arise, not at a distance from man, but He will rise up *in men* and manifest Himself to be the Light and Life of every man and woman that is saved by Him. 'The Spirit of reason is not without a man, but within every man : hence he need not run after others to tell him or to teach him, for this Spirit is his Maker, He dwells in him, and if the flesh were subject thereto, he would daily find teaching therefrom.' . . . '*You see Him ruling within you* ; . . . You rise higher and higher into life and peace as this manifestation of the Father increases and spreads within you.' "—R. M. JONES, *Mystical Religion*, p. 495.

"Then spake Jesus again unto them, saying, I am the Light of the world : he that followeth me shall not walk in Darkness, but shall have the Light of Life."—JOHN viii. 12.

"Human courage, human patience, human trustiness, human humility,— these filled with the Fire of God make the graces of the Christian life. We are still haunted by the false old distinction of the natural virtues and the Christian graces. The Christian graces are nothing but the natural virtues held up into the Light of Christ. They are made of the same stuff ; they are lifted along the same lines ; but they have found their pinnacle. They have caught the illumination which their souls desire. Manliness has not been changed into Godliness ; it has fulfilled itself in Godliness. . . . The great truth of Redemption, the great idea of Salvation, is that the realm (of human life) belongs to Truth, that the Lie is everywhere and always an intruder and a foe. He came in, therefore he may be driven out. When he is driven out and man is purely man, then man is saved."—PHILLIPS BROOKS, *Light of the World*, pp. 8, 10.

See ATEA, BRAHMA, CONSCIOUSNESS, CREATION, DARKNESS, HEAVEN AND EARTH, ILLUSION, PROCESSION, SPIRIT AND MATTER, SUN.

LIGHT-REALM :—

A symbol of the buddhic plane, whereon is the Wisdom consciousness.

See AMENT, BUDDHIC PLANE, EDEN, GARDEN, SAVIOURS.

LIGHT-TREASURE :—

A symbol of the qualities of the soul which have been transmuted on to the buddhic plane. *That* in the soul which shall attain to the Light-realm,—" those whom the Father hath given me."

See FRUIT OF THE SPIRIT, SAVIOURS, TRANSMUTATION.

LIGHT-WORLD :—

A symbol of that state of consciousness which corresponds to an extension of spiritual vision which perceives the Truth and the Life within.

" Awake, thou that sleepest, and arise from the dead, and Christ shall shine upon thee."—EPH. v. 14.

The soul spiritually unawakened is exhorted to arise from the dead personality and enter the higher consciousness, when Wisdom, Truth and Love will be revealed unto it.

See DEAD, GODS, SLEEP.

LIGHTNING   OR   LIGHTNING FLASH :—

A symbol of the omnipotent life activities of the higher planes of the invisible universe.

" There clings to the Maruts one who moves in secret, like a man's wife (the lightning), and who is like a spear carried behind, well grasped, resplendent, gold-adorned."—*Rig-Veda*, I. 167, 3.

There is attached to the spiritual egos the Life forces of the higher planes, centred in the Higher Self in his aspect of the Divine Ray (spear)—atma-buddhi—extending unobserved through all the planes.

See FOHAT, MARUTS, SPEAR, THUNDER, THUNDERBOLT, TLALOC, UDDER, ZEUS.

LIGNANS COAST :—

A symbol of the first (the lowest) sub-plane of the buddhic plane.

LILYBŒUM, ABODE OF BUTES :—

A symbol of the appointed state for the quality of attachment through association.

See BUTES.

LIMBS OF THE INEFFABLE :—

A symbol of the immanent qualities of the Archetypal Man,—the Self involved in matter. The qualities become separated and dispersed in the period of Evolution,—the homogeneous becoming the heterogeneous.

" At one time all the limbs which form the (human) body united into one by Love, grow vigorously in the prime of life; but yet at another time, separated by evil Strife, they wander each in different directions along the breakers of the sea of life. Just so it is with plants and with fishes dwelling in watery halls, and beasts whose lair is in the mountains, and birds borne on wings."—*Empedocles*, FAIRBANKS, 247.

In the pre-evolutionary period, the Archetypal Man existed in the Absolute, and so was involved in Love Divine, in which perfect harmony the potential diversity was merged in complete unity. But when evolution commenced, and the struggle for separate existence began, the functions of the Archetypal Man,—the Oversoul,—are said to be scattered, inasmuch as through desire, instinct, habit, opinion, etc., a continual surging and unrest served to stir the latent emotions by means of which growth of the soul is accomplished. So it is with the dawn of the emotions, the astro-mental nature, the ambitions, ideals, and aspirations (birds).

" The Body of the Heavenly Man (Adam Kadmon) from whose limbs emanate the universe and everything in it."—BLAVATSKY, *Secret Doctrine*, Vol. II. p. 662.

" It is clear that by the will of God every gain in life, human or sub-human, is the fruit of effort and struggle. It is no use wishing it were otherwise or arguing that life could have been sweeter and brighter if things had been so arranged that we could have had the gains without the struggle. That would have been very nice and agreeable, but it is not the method God has chosen in bringing many sons unto glory. It is a law which holds good on all planes—physical, mental, moral, and spiritual. The spiritual comes last in the order of time because it was also the first."—R. J. CAMPBELL, Serm., *Warfare of Life*.

See ADAM (higher), ARC. MAN, COSMOS, CRUCIFIXION (gnostic), DHRUVA, DISMEMBERMENT, EVOLUTION, INVOLUTION, MEMBERS, MUMMY, NAMES, PRAGÂPATI, PURUSHA, SEA, SEPARATION, SPACES OF INEFFABLE, STRIFE, ZAGREUS.

LINEN GARMENT, WHITE :—

A symbol of the buddhic robe of wisdom, goodness, and love.

"And it was given unto her (the Lamb's wife) that she should array herself in fine linen, bright and pure : for the fine linen is the righteous acts of the saints."—REV. xix. 8.

The "Lamb's wife" is the purified soul rising to union with the Higher Self on the upper planes. The soul then becomes clothed with the buddhic qualities of wisdom and love, which have been inherited through the harmonising of the disciplined qualities (saints) with the Divine nature.

"Man then puts on a linen garment, for completeness' sake : it is indeed his own skin he thereby puts on himself. Now that same skin, which belongs to the cow, was originally on man."—*Sata. Brâh.*, III. 1, 2, 13.

The ego having purified himself (verse 12) of his lower qualities, now assumes the buddhic robe to perfect his nature on the higher planes, for the robe of wisdom and love is indeed that which is possessed prior to his descent into the lower nature. Now that same endowment of the higher qualities which is of buddhi (cow) was originally on man before his fall into matter.

See Cow (milch), FALL, FLAYING, LAMB OF GOD, MAN, ROBE, SKIN.

LINEN, WHITE AND SHINING :—

A symbol of Divine Truth, or the world-substance of which the universe is woven,—the ultimate reality.

"The bloom of the scarlet dye mingles with shining linen."—*Empedocles*, FAIRBANKS, 286.

The power of the Divine Life (blood) energises the world-substance,—Truth-reality.

"By linen clean and shining is signified truth pure and genuine. . . . Linen signifies divine truth."—SWEDENBORG, *Apoc. Rev.*, n. 671.

See FABRIC, LOOM, MULA-PRAKRITI, RAIMENT, WARP, WHITE.

LINGAM, THE SUBTILE BODY :—

A symbol of the causal-body as containing the means of Self-manifestation,—all the qualities and powers of the soul.

"The eighteen first products of prakriti, viz.—*mahân (buddhi), ahankâra, manas, indryas,* and *tanmâtras* form the subtile body, which surrounds the soul and accompanies it in all its wanderings. It is termed *lingam.* . . . Every life-history is a new self-unfolding of the prakriti before the purusha concerned by means of the *lingam*."—DEUSSEN, *Phil. of Upanishads*, p. 242.

"*Linga-sarira* comprising the five organs of sense, the five organs of action, the five vital airs, with *buddhi* and *manas*."—MON. WILLIAMS, *Indian Wisdom*, p. 119.

"The *lingasarîram* is described in Sarvopanishats. 16, as the vehicle of the organs the prânas, the gunas, and the ethical qualification, and accordingly is identified with the bands of the heart." DEUSSEN, *Phil. of Upanishads*, p. 282.

The causal-body is first involved complete in potentiality ; afterwards it grows to completion in actuality.

See CAUSAL-BODY, KARANA, PRANAS, SENSE-ORGANS, STHULA, VITAL AIRS.

LION :—

A symbol of power in manifestation or of might, strength and courage as forces of the lower quaternary.

"Among beasts they become lions haunting the mountains, whose couch is the ground."—*Empedocles*, FAIRBANKS, 438.

Among the lower emotional qualities, strength of will and courage are the means of fostering ambitions which are rooted in the lower nature.

"Forasmuch as the nature of everything is compounded of different elements, in Holy Writ different things are allowably represented by any one thing. For the lion has magnanimity, it has also ferocity : by its magnanimity then it represents the Lord, by its ferocity the devil. Hence it is declared of the Lord, ' Behold, the Lion of the Tribe of Judah, the root of David, hath prevailed ' (REV. v. 5). Hence it is written of the devil, ' Your adversary, the devil, like a roaring lion, walketh about seeking whom he may devour ' (1 PETER v. 8.)."—ST. GREGORY, *Morals on the Book of Job*, Vol. I. p. 272.

"A symbol, we must remember, may mean two entirely different and opposing things. Thus the lion may symbolise the evil spirit walking about as a lion to devour his prey, or the all-conquering Christ, the Lion of the tribe of Judah. Our Lord too compared the kingdom of heaven in one of his parables to leaven ; yet elsewhere He spoke in an entirely different sense of the leaven of the scribes and pharisees."—F. E. HULME, *Symbolism, etc*, p. 4.

See ANIMALS, BEASTS (wild), GREEN LION, GRIFFIN, LEO, QUATERNARY, SERPENT (solar), SPHINX.

LION-GAIT OF BUDDHA :—

A symbol of the strong and powerful Self, as the victor over the lower nature of the soul.

" 'I (Buddha) am born for supreme knowledge, for the welfare of the world,—thus this is my last birth.' Thus did he of lion-gait, gazing at the four quarters, utter a voice full of auspicious meaning."
—*Buddha-Karita*, Bk. I. 34.

" The Self is born in the soul for its supreme illumination, and for the welfare of humanity,—i.e. the enlightenment of the incarnate Self. This is the supreme moment in spiritual involution when potential perfection is consummated (last birth), and now and henceforward proceeds the fulfilment of the Divine nature, which through the Self is brought to realise Itself. So did the Self of forceful mien, conqueror of the quaternary, foresee his Divine mission.

See Birth of buddha, Buddha, Involution, Quarters, Quaternary.

LION, MAN-HEADED WITH TRIPLE CROWN :—

A symbol of God-manifest ;—the Son of God under the aspect of Conqueror, seated upon the lower quaternary, which is to be brought into unison with the Higher Triad.

See Conqueror, Crown, Quaternary, Tiara, Triad, Union.

LION-GOD, DOUBLE :—

" Two lions seated back to back and supporting the horizon with the sun's disk, over which extends the sky ; the lion on the right is called *Sef*, i.e. ' Yesterday,' and that on the left, *Tuau*, i.e. ' To-day.' "—Budge, *Book of the Dead*, p. 90.

The " two lions " signify respectively the former period and process of *involution* (Yesterday), and the present period and process of *evolution* (To-day).

" I (Nu) am the double Lion-god, the first-born of Rā and Tem of Ah-khebti (as Buto), the gods who dwell in their divine chambers."—*Ibid.*, Ch. 38, p. 166.

The Divine power in the universe (Nu) proceeds first, from the celestial Logos (Rā) in the process of *involution*, and second, from the terrestrial Logos (Tem),—the Archetypal Man,—in the process of *evolution*.

" The two Lion-gods watch, one at each end, the path of the night Sun."—*Ibid.*, p. 216.

The cycle of life on the lower planes (the Tuat), wherein the Self (sun) is unapparent, is divided into two parts,—the descent of Spirit into matter, and the ascent of Spirit therefrom.

See Arc. man, Buto, Day, Evolution, Horizons, Involution, Musubi, Nu, Rā, Sekhet-aaru, Shu (double), Sun, Sun-rising, Tem, Tuat, Zodiac.

LIPS IN SPEECH :—

A symbol of the expression outwardly of that which is within, either truth or error, good or evil.

" The lip of truth shall be established for ever : but a lying tongue is but for a moment."—Prov. xii. 19.

The expression of truth in the soul brings immortality to life ; but the expression of error is evanescent.

" Mankind went forth from Rā's two eyes, the gods were created on his lips."
—Wiedemann, *Rel. of Anc. Egyptians*, p. 115.

The individuality and the personality proceeded forth from the higher and lower Selves on the mental plane ; the ideals or higher qualities were the expression of the Divine Will and Wisdom on the higher planes.

See Creation, Eyes (Horus), Gods, Higher and lower, Individuality, Mouth, Personality, Purusha, Rā, Speech, Tongue, Utchats.

LIT, A DWARF :—

A symbol of a small mind, implying error.

See Dwarf.

LITANY, THE GREAT (MAHAD UKTHAM) :—

A symbol of the evolving Divine life proceeding from below upwards.

" And that vital essence of his (the relaxed Pragapati's) which flowed upwards became the Great Litany ; it is in quest of that vital fluid that the priests go by means of the Rik and Saman."—*Sata. Brâh.*, X. 1, 1, 4.

The Archetypal Man (relaxed Pragâpati) has given up his life for humanity. His " vital essence " (blood of Christ) ascends in supplication or aspiration in the human souls. The higher emotions (priests) are allied to the Divine life through the vibrations from above (the Vedas).

" The Great Litany is the body or

Self, âtman." "A bird-like body."—
Ibid., X. 1, 2, 1 and 5.

The Divine life is the Self *below*
when meeting the Self *above* (the
âtman). The "body," or Self below,
is aspiring (bird-like).

See ARC. MAN, ATMAN, BLOOD,
BLOOD OF LAMB, GATHAS (chanting),
HOMA-JUICE, HYMN SINGING, PRÂGA-
PATI, SINGERS, SOMA-JUICE, VEDA.

LITTLE ONES ; INNOCENTS :—

A symbol of the germs of the higher
qualities appearing in the lower
nature.

"Whosoever shall cause one of these
little ones that believe on me to stumble,
it were better for him if a great millstone
were hanged about his neck, and he were
cast into the sea."—MARK ix. 42.

This pronouncement is an emphatic
protest against destroying any germ
of virtue or truth that may seem unwel-
come, or nipping in the bud any effort,
—however feeble,—towards expansion of consciousness, which, it must
be remembered, is *invariably* a proof
of belief in Christ, who is the goal of
attainment for all qualities, however
variously men may worship, think,
or act.

See CHILD, CHILDREN OF THE KING-
DOM, CONVERSION, CREATURES (small),
HEROD, SEEDS (good).

LITTLE CHILDREN, OR LITTLE
ONES :—

A symbol of the spiritual egos or
monads which descend into the forms
in order to gain experience and knowledge on the lower planes. They
are the "children of God."

"Thereupon they (the Maruts), according to their wont, assumed again the
form of new-born babes, taking their
sacred name."—*Rig-Veda*, I. 6, 4.

When the way was prepared, the
spiritual egos (Maruts) dispersed, and
became germs of spirit descending into
the forms and taking to them the
Divine differentiation.

"And Jesus called a little child unto
him, and set him in the midst of them,
and saith, Verily I say unto you, Except
ye be converted, and become as little
children, ye shall not enter into the kingdom of heaven. Whosoever therefore
shall humble himself as this little child,
the same is greatest in the kingdom of
heaven."—MAT. xviii. 2-4.

The Christ-soul called attention to
a spiritual monad (atma-buddhic)
set in the midst of the disciplined
qualities of the lower nature, and
explained that except the qualities
be transmuted into spiritual states,
as is the condition of the monads,
they cannot enter heaven, that is,
become conscious on the higher planes.
It is necessary, therefore, that each
quality should undergo the discipline
of the lower life, as does the monad,
in order that it should be purified
and exalted, and so become greatest
among the high but inexperienced
qualities on the higher planes.

"Take heed that ye despise not one of
these little ones ; for I say unto you, that
in heaven their angels do always behold
the face of my Father which is in heaven."
—MAT. xviii. 10.

The qualities are enjoined to be
faithful to the spiritual nature within
them ; for the individualities (angels)
in the causal-bodies of the souls are
in harmony with the Higher Self,
and therefore are aspects of the
Supreme—the Father, the Atman.

"Awake, O sword, against my Shepherd, and against the Man that is my
fellow, saith the Lord of hosts ; smite
the Shepherd, and the sheep shall be
scattered : and I will turn my hand upon
the little ones."—ZECH. xiii. 7.

At the end of the period of Involution, there comes the awakening of
the energies of conflict (sword). The
Divine Will first smites the Archetypal Man, or involved Self (Man that
is my fellow), and he is dismembered.
The higher qualities (sheep),—the
"limbs of the Ineffable,"—are then
scattered, and so the way is prepared
for the incoming of the spiritual
monads (little ones), who are now to
pass through the experiences of
suffering and sorrow.

See ARC. MAN, CHILDREN OF GOD,
DISCIPLES, DISMEMBERMENT, FATHER,
GERMS, HEAVEN, INCARNATION OF
SOULS, INDIVIDUALITY, INVOLUTION,
LIMBS, MARUTS, MONAD OF LIFE,
QUALITIES, REAPING, SHEEP, SHEEP
(lost), SHEPHERD, SONS OF GOD,
SPERMATIC WORDS, SWORD, WARRIORS.

LIVER :—

A symbol of the lower nature (flesh),
or the lower qualities of the personality.

See PROMETHEUS, QAHU, VISCERA,
VITAL AIRS.

LIVING THINGS OF ALL FLESH :—

A symbol of the buddhic ideal qualities which become dualised and inverted in the astro-mental nature (all flesh).

"And every living thing of all flesh, two of every sort shalt thou bring into the ark, to keep them alive with thee; they shall be male and female."—GEN. vi. 19.

The spiritual activities on higher planes, which correspond to the relations upon the lower planes; these exist as growth-producing ideals, and are said to be "kept alive" by the individual Self (Noah) seated in the causal-body (ark). The male-female principles are the dual aspects of qualities which always present themselves in the evolution of the Cosmos or the Soul.

See ADAM (dual), ARK (Noah), MALE-FEMALE, MULTIPLY, SEEDS (creatures), NOAH, TWO, VITAL AIRS.

LOAVES FOR FEEDING PEOPLE :—

A symbol of nourishment for the lower qualities; that is, means for acquiring knowledge, such as the use of the senses for experience and investigation.

See BREAD, FEEDING.

LOCK OF HAIR ; SIDE-LOCK :—

A symbol of the intuition.
See HAIR (side-lock).

LOCUSTS FOR FOOD :—

A symbol of facts of experience for the development of the mind and the moral nature.

"And his (John's) food was locusts and wild honey."—MAT. iii. 4.

This is the food which signifies the *natural* means of nourishment, subsistence upon uncooked, simple fare, signifying plain *facts*.

"Locusts signify the qualities of the sensual man, or the sensual principle which is the ultimate of the life of man's mind."—SWEDENBORG, *Apoc. Rev.*, n. 424.

See JOHN BAPTIST.

LOGOS (REASON-SPEECH) :—

A symbol of the Higher Self manifesting on the upper mental plane as a Divine outpouring of life and form, —the utterance of creative energy. The three aspects of the Logos are Will, Wisdom, and Action.

"The Logos of Heraclitus is at once world-principle and world-process. It seems to have been a name for the rational self-evolution of the universe, to be apprehended by the human mind which is capable of indentifying itself with it. With the Stoics, the 'seminal Logos' is God Himself as the organic principle of the universe. God dwells in our hearts as Logos. . . . Philo's Logos is a God who reveals Himself, in contrast with a God who hides Himself."—W. R. INGE, *Camb. Biblical Essays*, pp. 274-5.

There may be said to be three Logoi, or three Divine outpourings of Life, on the higher planes. The first is the involution of Spirit on the plane of atma, the second on the buddhic plane, and the third on the higher mental plane.

See AROUERIS, ASAR, ATHWYA, BIRTH OF OSIRIS, BOLTS, BUDDHIC FUNCTION, HORUS, HOUSEHOLDER, LAO, PWANKOO, SEED, SPEECH, THRAETONA, THRITA, WORD.

LOINS GIRDED :—

A symbol of restraint of the lower nature of desire and sensation, and a turning of the mind towards the things of the Spirit.

"Gird up now thy loins like a man; for I will demand of thee, and declare thou unto me."—JOB xxxviii. 3.

The soul is required to withstand the allurements of the desire-nature by means of the mind (man), and strive to understand the processes of the Divine life in involution and evolution.

"To 'gird up the loins' is to restrain lust either in work or in thought. For the delight of the flesh is in the loins. Whence it is said to holy Preachers, 'Let your loins be girded about, and your lights burning' (LUKE xii. 35). For by the loins is designated lust, but by lights the brightness of good works." —ST. GREGORY, *Morals on the Book of Job*, Vol. III. p. 269.

See CIRCUMCISION, FLESH, MAN (natural).

LOKE (OR LOKI), LOFO'S SON :—

A symbol of the desire-nature, kama-manas, full of cunning and egoism.

"Then said Ganglere : 'Loke acted most wickedly; first, by causing the death of Balder; and secondly, by preventing his release from Hel. But was he not punished for these his misdeeds?' Har replied: 'Yes, it was avenged on him, and in a manner which he will long remember.' "—*The Punishment of Loke, Edda*, HOWITT.

Then the conscience speaks within the mind:—The desire-nature has done amiss from the relative point of view, in that it has become the means of drawing the soul (Balder) downwards to the karmic planes (Hel), and that fall now serves to prevent it from rising to union with the Self. But under all the circumstances which were incidental to such a fall,—was not cause and effect, or compensation on higher planes, made to yield such results as were just and right withal ? And the answer comes,—that throughout the soul's evolution, perfect equilibrium between the higher and lower natures was maintained, and that the outcome of the whole process is stored away in the soul's inner being.

See BALDER, CAVE, CONSCIENCE, DEATH OF BALDER, DOORS (four), EYE (third), GANGLER, HEIMDALL, HELL, HIGHER AND LOWER, HODER, NARE, NET OF ASAR, VOICE, WOMAN (Loke).

LOOM OF ISIS OR HERA :—

A symbol of the buddhic nature which is instrumental in weaving the web of the universe.

" Isis invented the loom with the help of her sister Nephthys, and was the first to weave and bleach linen."—PLUTARCH, *Isis and Osiris.*

By means of the buddhic nature operating with the physical (Nephthys), the warp and woof of the universe (solar system) is fashioned and established. Divine Wisdom (Isis) devised the web of existence and the means for self-purification. " Linen " is a symbol of the world-substance, i.e. Truth-reality.

See BUDDHIC PLANE, FABRIC, ISIS, MANCO, NEPHTHYS, WARP, WOODEN.

LORD OF THE PEACE OF HORUS :—

A symbol of equilibrium in the soul.

See HORUS, PEACE.

LORDS OF MATERIAL THINGS :—

The nature elementals and directive intelligence which work upon the various form levels.

See DEVAS (lower).

LOSING OF THE WAY :—

A symbol of the adoption of theories and arguments which have been propounded by the lower mind to account for things Divine in the innermost depths of the soul. These theories will not lead to the Truth, because the lower mind is incapable of dealing with that which transcends itself.

See next Symbol.

LOST IN FOREST PATHS :—

A symbol of the confusion of thought and multiplicity of loose discordant ideas, which arise in the lower minds of the unenlightened souls who are wandering through the experiences of the worldly life.

" He (Buddha) will proclaim the way of deliverance to those afflicted with sorrow, entangled in objects of sense, and lost in the forest paths of worldly existence, as to travellers who have lost their way."—*Buddha-Karita*, Bk. I. 77.

The Self is the " Way, the Truth and the Life " ; he is able to show the path of salvation to the lower self, who lies struggling upon the lower planes,—such struggling and trouble being possible only through the initiative taken by the Higher Self from Above, to accomplish his evolution through the lower self. The lower self is distracted and confused through lack of true discrimination between the sense objects. The " lost in the forest paths " signifies the confused opinions of the lower minds (men) of those who are without knowledge of the truth. The " losing of the way " indicates the erroneous theories and speculations which are relied upon as explanations of moral and religious impulses in the human soul.

See HIGHER AND LOWER, ILLUSION, MAISHAN, PILGRIM, SALVATION, SORROW, STRIFE, SUFFERING, WANDERERS, WAY, WAYFARING, WILDERNESS.

LOST PIECE OF SILVER :—

A symbol of a spiritual ego having descended and become obscured on the lower mental plane.

" Or what woman having ten pieces of silver, if she lose one piece, doth not light a lamp, and sweep the house, and seek diligently until she find it ? And when she hath found it, she calleth together her friends and neighbours, saying, Rejoice with me, for I have found the piece which I had lost."—LUKE xv. 8–10.

The "woman" represents Wisdom (buddhi) in possession of the full number of spiritual egos (atma-buddhic). When an ego descends to become incarnate upon the lower planes, the buddhic consciousness is obscured, and the ego is lost in ignorance and illusion. The "lighting of the lamp" is the establishment of the causal-body through which Wisdom and Love will be recovered by the ego. The "sweeping, etc." signifies the efforts put forth to raise the lower qualities of the ego and transmute them. And when the ego again attains the buddhic consciousness, then Wisdom calls together the higher qualities and ideals, and endows the ego with them in the bliss of the immortal life.

"And the woman that sweeps the house and finds the piece of silver, they (the Gnostics) say is the supernal Wisdom, who, having lost that which she had conceived in her mind, finds it afterwards, when all things are cleansed by the coming of our Saviour : wherefore this also is restored, as they say, to be within the Pleroma."—IRENÆUS, Against Heresies, p. 27.

See CAUSAL-BODY, FRIENDS, FRUIT (spirit), HOUSE IN HEAVEN, INCARNATION OF SOULS, LAMP, MONAD OF LIFE, NEIGHBOUR, OIL, PLEROMA, SILVER, SOUL, WISDOM, WOMAN.

LOST SHEEP :—

A symbol of the spiritual ego, who descends to the lower nature, and is lost to the Higher Self by being obscured in the matter of the lower planes.

See SHEEP (lost).

"LOST SOUL" :—

This idea, which is due to primitive and absurd human conceptions, could not be for a moment entertained by anyone who had the least knowledge of the soul's nature and evolution. That which is unreal passes away, but that which is real persists. The personality does indeed pass away, but the individuality to which it is attached is immortal. The Divine purpose to bring to perfection every soul cannot be frustrated.

See CAUSAL-BODY, IMAGE, INDI-VIDUALITY, JUSTICE, LOST PIECE, PERSONALITY, SOUL.

LOT, ABRAHAM'S BROTHER'S SON :—

A symbol of the lower soul in process of up-building.

"The motif of deliverance out of the Underworld lies in the story of the rescue of Lot. Lot is in Sodom—Underworld.— A. JEREMIAS, Old Test., etc, Vol. II. p. 25.

See ABRAHAM, SODOM, SOUL (lower).

LOTE-TREE :—

A symbol of the tree of Wisdom bearing the fruit of the Spirit.

"Beneath the Kursi, but somewhat to the right hand, God created a region like white pearl, in which is the 'Lote-tree none may pass.' And this is the station of the Archangel Gabriel, beyond which he may not go. And in this place is the root of the Tuba tree."—GIBB, Hist. of Ottoman Poetry, Vol. I. p. 35.

Beneath the buddhic plane is the higher mental plane, which is the vehicle of atma-buddhi and the Wisdom nature. The lower consciousness cannot rise to this level, neither can the inner messenger of spiritual tidings descend below it. The tree of Life and immortality is only to be found in the higher mental region and the regions above.

See CHERUBIM, EDEN, FRUIT OF THE SPIRIT, GABRIEL, KURSI, PARADISE, PEARL, TREE OF LIFE, TUBA TREE, WHITE.

LOTOS, OR LOTUS, TREE,—A TREE IN N. AFRICA, WHOSE FRUIT MADE STRANGERS FORGET THEIR HOME :—

A symbol of egoism and the sense of separateness.

See HOME, SEPARATION, SERPENT (loud-breathing).

LOTUS, WATER LILY :—

A symbol of Wisdom. The buddhic nature is that of Truth (water) and Beauty (flower).

"Water-lilies symbolise the free possession of all the treasures of God. For we notice four things in the water-lily. It keeps always above the water, and has four green leaves between the air and the water ; and it is rooted in the earth, and above it is opened out to the sun."—RUYSBROECK, Stoddart's trans., p. 52.

"He who, having entered the inner lotus of the heart, devours food, the same having gone to the sky as the fire of the sun, called Time, and being invisible devours all beings as his food. . . . That lotus is the same as the ether: the four quarters, and the four intermediate points are its leaves."—*Mait. Upanishad*, VI. 2.

The indwelling Self being liberated from the lower nature enters the buddhic vehicle and partakes of the fruit of his experience,—wisdom and love; then having passed higher to the plane of atma at the end of the cycle, and becoming unmanifest, all qualities and beings become absorbed within Him. That buddhic nature is of the spiritual tree of Life, whose leaves may represent the lower quaternary and its centres of consciousness.

"The *lotus plant* was as sacred with the Egyptians as with the Indians. According to Rougè, it was the symbol of the *new birth*; but Lepsius considers that it was the symbol of *inexhaustible life*."
—BARLOW, *Essays on Symbolism*, p. 32.

See ÆTHER, BUDDHI, CHILDREN OF HORUS, FIRE, FLOWERS, FOOD, FOOTSTEPS OF BUDDHA, HEART, PLANTS, QUARTERS, QUATERNARY, SUN.

LOTUS LEAF, OR LEAVES :—

A symbol of the lower nature, or lower planes, which grow out of the higher.

"The Sacrificer puts down a lotus-leaf in the centre of the altar site ;—the lotus-leaf is a womb for Agni to be born from. . . . The lotus means the waters, and this earth is a leaf thereof. . . . Now this same earth is Agni's womb, for Agni the fire-altar is this earth. He lays it down so as not to be separated from the truth: he thereby establishes this earth on the truth."—*Sata. Brâh.*, VII. 4, 1, 8.

The Supreme establishes a centre on the astral plane for the organisation of the lower nature in which the Self shall be born. The "lotus" signifies the Truth,—atma-buddhi,—and the lower nature is the changing life and form to express the Truth outwardly. Now the lower nature is the matrix of the indwelling Self to bring forth all forms of life, for from the Archetypal Man springs the lower nature of the soul which has to be offered up. The lower nature is so contrived as that Truth shall be made manifest through it. The lower nature is therefore Divinely established upon the Truth.

See AGNI, ALTAR (fire), ARC. MAN, EARTH, FORMS, QUATERNARY, SACRIFICE, WATER, WOMB.

LOTUS SIGN IN HIGH RELIEF :—

A symbol of the Ideal of spiritual perfection held high before the earnest and adoring soul.

See FOOTSTEPS OF BUDDHA.

LOVE OF GOD :—

An intuition or direct sense that all things in the natural, moral, and intellectual orders work together for good, despite appearances to the contrary. Truth acquired best enables us to realise Wisdom, but not Divine Love, for which faith is necessary.

"To 'know God' is to see in the laws and events of nature the revelation of his will, or his eternal decrees. To 'love God' is to accept the order of the world, with all its necessity and invariable sequence and even with its apparent indifference to moral character, as not only inevitable but perfect. Further to know and love God is to know and love one's fellowmen, for they too are part of that real world which 'expresses' God; and hence all that makes for their welfare makes for one's own."—R. A. DUFF, *Spinoza's Philosophy*, p. 22.

Whilst we necessarily have only partial experiences of the good and the true, we have also what appear to be their contraries: but the appearance is illusory, it is of the form and not of the life.

Bruno teaches that "the soul or spirit tends towards that with which it has greatest affinity, as the sun-flower tends towards the sun, and this affinity in the human soul is Love. The symbol of love is fire, for love converts the object of love into the lover, as fire is of all elements the most active, the most potent to transform others into itself. It is the divine in man that makes him, or impels him, to love God as He is in reality, and the goal or aim of that love is to take God into himself, to become one with God."—MCINTYRE, *Giordano Bruno*, p. 280.

"And then should a man wrap his soul in the great Love of God, and clothe himself therewith as with a garment; and should account thence all things alike; because in the Creature he finds nothing that can give him, without God, the least satisfaction, and because also nothing of harm can touch him more while he remains in this love."—BEHMEN, *Supersensual Life*, p. 34.

"'We love, because He first loved us' (1 JOHN iv. 19). The writer's thought is that God's love is the source of ours; we are only able to love at all because God indwells us. . . . Divine love is the source of human love, but the latter must learn to know itself through human relations before it can rise to the higher level of immediate communion with that from which it came . . . Christ stands for love divine made manifest in sacrifice, the fundamental fact of all existence, the fact that explains everything else. There never would have been any egoism, any violence, wrong, greed, or suffering, but for the necessity of affording love its opportunity to burst forth in splendour. *The last in order of time is also that with which time began ; the highest to be evolved is also that which was first involved.*"— R. J. CAMPBELL, Serm., *The Source of Good.*

" ' God so loved the world that he gave ' is an accurate and expressive summing up of the great mystery of the divine manifestation in the world or worlds. God is love: hence the impulse to create. God is love: hence the sacrifice of himself in the limited and imperfect life of the cosmos, and the slow and painful struggle upward to ever fuller and richer modes of spiritual achievement, until at length the consummation shall be reached wherein all things shall be summed up in Christ and love be all in all."—R. J. CAMPBELL, Serm., *God's Gift of Himself.*

" The love of God is the love of goodness. The old Saxon word God is identical with Good. God—the Good One—personified goodness. There is in that derivation not a mere play of words,— there is a deep truth. None loves God but he who loves good. To love God is to love what God is. God is Pure, and he who loves purity can love God. God is True. God is Just: and he who loves these things out of God may love them in God ; and God for them, because He is good, and true, and pure, and just. No other love is real ; none else lasts."— F. W. ROBERTSON, *Sermons, 4th Series*, p. 69.

" The way is to throw ourselves in faith on the eternal Love of a Father. To do that is to know that there must be a divine and good end to all ; to know that is to know that all which we see, however dark it be, is education ; to know the victory of goodness, justice and truth, and knowing it to throw ourselves on that side, and to feel that in doing so we are chiming in with God, and yielding our lives and will into His hands. There is no doubt, if we can do that, that our pursuit of the secret of life, and the tragedy in which we live, will ennoble us. For so our minds will be steadily set towards right, and will company with the noble things of justice, temperance, love and truth, so that, though we are involved in tempest after tempest of feeling and thought, we shall finally get the good of these tempests in the education which they give to our whole nature."—STOPFORD A. BROOKE, Serm., *Secrets of Life.*

Knowledge of the soul's evolution

shows clearly that there is not, and cannot be, an outside objective Deity who superintends earthquakes, explosions, and all the horrors of the natural life, together with all the " providential " escapes, comforts, and pleasures of existence which go to wicked and good alike. God limits himself in creation, and can now only interfere in his universe through his human and other agents who act from the divine impulse within.

See DEMIURGE, EROS, EVOLUTION, FAITH, GOD, INVOLUTION, JUSTICE, KHABIT, RULER (aeon).

LOVE, THE UNITER OF ALL :—

A symbol of the attraction towards the within instead of the without.

" Behold the sun, warm and bright on all sides, and what ever is immortal and is bathed in its bright ray ; and behold the rain-cloud, dark and cold on all sides ; from the earth there proceed the foundations of things and solid bodies. In strife all things are endued with form and separate from each other, but they come together in Love and are desired by each other."—*Empedocles*, FAIRBANKS, 96.

Regard the Self as loving and wise, both on the planes above and the planes beneath. Behold all the virtues and all the qualities that endure, as living within It. And understand the outward manifestation of the Supreme, which appears to the ignorant, suffering lower nature, as inexorable law, dark, obscure, and repellent. From the lower nature proceed the foundations of human experience (for the sense-nature is the basis of all that is of utility and beauty to the lower mind). Through " strife," or the struggle for existence on the physical plane, all the lower forms of life subsist in multifarious separateness. But the sense of separateness is overcome so far as souls unite in knowledge of their own nature, and in realisation of Truth, for Wisdom brings them together in Love and enables them to live in harmony and mutual service.

" But, just as far as it (Strife) is constantly rushing forth, just so far there ever kept coming in a gentle, immortal stream of perfect Love ; and all at once what before I learned were immortal were coming into being as mortal things." —*Ibid.*, 180.

To that degree in which the lower

self responds through its vehicles of consciousness, the Higher Self (Love) forthpours energy and raises the self to the Self : and so the immortal ideals tend to actualise as evolution proceeds. Thus the natural gives way to the spiritual and the soul is purified and rises to life everlasting.

"To know God is to attain to the sublimest conception in the universe. To love God is to bind ourselves to a being who is fitted, as no other being is, to penetrate and move our whole hearts ; in loving whom, we exalt ourselves ; in loving whom, we love the great, the good, the beautiful, and the infinite ; and under whose influence the soul unfolds itself as a perennial plant under the cherishing sun. This constitutes the chief glory of religion. It ennobles the soul. In this its unrivalled dignity and happiness consist." —W. E. CHANNING, *Of Christianity.*

"Only Love is true, vital, wise. As Love grows in you, God grows in you. In your Love you become organic with God. When you are naught but Love you are the express image of His person." —E. W. LEWIS, *Christ. Com.,* April 1813.

"Christ, the eternal son of God, is gradually but irresistibly rising in all that is human, subduing all things unto himself, bringing them into captivity to the law of divine love, which alone is perfect freedom."—R. J. CAMPBELL, Serm., *From Subjection to Sovereignty.*

See ATTRACTION, CUPID, EROS, GOD, HARMONY, MARRIAGE.

LOVER OF GOOD WORKS WHO IS GOD-DISCERNING :—

A symbol of the higher manasic intelligence, or intuitional principle, which brings the higher and lower Selves together when perfection has been attained and the lower nature dissipated.

See DOORS OPENED BY THOTH, HIGHER AND LOWER SELVES.

LOVER OF THE HEAVENLY MAIDEN :—

A symbol of the indwelling Self working upwards through the personality towards union with Buddhi, Wisdom.

"Let him kiss me with the kisses of his mouth. . . . Thy name is as ointment poured forth ; therefore do the virgins love thee. Draw me ; we will run after thee. . . . I am black but comely."— SONG OF SONGS, i. 2–5.

The incarnate Self whose differentiation is Love (ointment) is adjured to express his true nature, for all the virtues (virgins) are in harmony with it. Let Love aspire, and Wisdom with the virtues will respond with joy. Wisdom is unapparent, latent (black), but beautiful when expressed.

See BLACK, CUPID, HIKOBOSHI, INCARNATION, MAIDEN, MOUTH, NAME, VIRGIN.

LUNAR CHAIN OF GLOBES :—

The arena of life which preceded our present Terrene chain of globes. The Life-wave has passed seven times round the lunar chain before its transference to the earth chain. The earth chain has attracted from the lunar chain its water and air, and its etheric and astral constituents, so far as the growth of its organisms is concerned.

See PLANETARY CHAIN, ROUND, SOMA (moon), SUKUNA, WHEELS (holy).

LUNAR CYCLE OF MANIFESTATION :—

The cycle of life on the lunar chain. In the lunar cycle the astral life and the desire nature have been developed, culminating in the personality. The personalities are the lunar pitris, or "fathers" of humanity on its form side. The individualities, or solar pitris, are the "fathers" on the life side, and bring with them the spiritual element, the Divine "sparks" or monads of life.

See DAYS (five), GOAT (milch), MOON (lower), MOON (solar), MOONWAXING, PERSONALITY, PITRIS (lunar), PITRIYANA.

LUNATIC, OR MOON-STRUCK MIND :—

A symbol of the astral principle which has been developed in the lunar cycle. It is through the stimulus of the astral or desire-nature that the mind is eventually awakened. When the desires are extremely active in combination with the lower mind there results an unruled and undirected state of soul, very dangerous morally.

See ASTRAL PLANE, CHURNING, KABANDHA, MOON-WAXING.

LYCUS, KING OF THE MARIANDYNI :—

A symbol of the higher intellect which governs right discrimination. *See* ANCÆUS.

MA-A'SEH MERCABAH, OR THE CHARIOT-THRONE OF EZEKIEL :—

A symbol of the Soul, that is, of the quaternary enthroning the higher triad, and constituting the vehicle of the Higher Self.

"Four living creatures. And this was their appearance ; they had the likeness of a man. And every one had four faces, and four wings. And their feet were straight feet."—EZEK. i. 5–7.

Four soul-bodies, causal, mental, astral, and physical. The four faces stand for the interrelated means of the soul's progression, through mind (man), desire (lion), obedient flesh-body (ox), and the buddhic function (eagle). The wings typify aspiration and growth, and the feet, the physical foundation of advance in time and duality.

"And they four (wheels) had one likeness : and their appearance and their work was as it were a wheel within a wheel. When they went, they went upon their four sides : they turned not when they went."—EZEK. i. 16, 17.

The four wheels of one likeness symbolise the incarnating cycles which are within the great cycle of life. Incarnation requires growth on the four planes (sides) ; and the souls advance and retreat unerringly to and from the physical existence.

"And over the head of the living creature there was the likeness of a firmament, like the colour of the terrible crystal. And under the firmament were their wings straight."—EZEK. i. 22, 23.

And above the lower mind (head) was the higher mind (firmament), which the souls cannot consciously attain to until perfected (crystal). The souls rest when withdrawn to the higher mind, and their lower vehicles disappear.

"And above the firmament that was over their heads was the likeness of a throne, as the appearance of a sapphire stone, and upon the throne was the appearance of a man."—EZEK. i. 26.

And on the higher mental plane was the causal-body (throne) formed through wisdom-love (sapphire), and it is the seat of the Higher Self.

"And the Lord spake unto the man clothed in linen, and said, Go in between the whirling wheels, even under the cherub, and fill both thine hands with coals of fire from between the cherubim, and scatter them over the city (Jerusalem)."—EZEK. x. 2.

The Self enjoins the spiritual mind to take the buddhic fruits of the soul's experience on the lower planes, and purify therewith the central nature of the soul.

"And their whole body (of cherubim), and their backs, and their hands, and their wings, and the wheels, were full of eyes round about, even the wheels that they four had."—EZEK. x. 12.

And the soul-vehicles and all their attributes and functions, together with the re-incarnating life cycles, are to the ego the means of mental perception (eyes) of the activities on the various planes.

See BACK, CASTES, CEILING, CHARIOT, CHERUBIM, CHILDREN OF HORUS, CRYSTAL, EAGLE, EYE, FACE, FEET, FIRE, FIRMAMENT, FOUR, HANDS, HEAD, INCARNATION OF SOULS, IRON PLATE, JERUSALEM, LINEN, LION, MAN, MERCABA, OX, PRIEST, RE-INCARNATION, SAPPHIRE, SIDES, THRONE, VESTURES, WHEELS, WINGS.

MAAT, GODDESS :—

A symbol of invariable law and justice applied to the activities of the lower planes. The law of Karma.

"Maat was the wife of Thoth, and daughter of Rā ; she assisted at the work of creation. She is the goddess of absolute regularity and order, of moral rectitude, and of right and truth. Her emblem is a feather." "The gods live by *maāt*, i.e., never-failing and unalterable regularity and order."—BUDGE, *Book of the Dead*, pp. 4, 8.

The ideals (gods) have their *raison d'être* in the law of karma, for by it they are related to the lower planes, and as higher qualities they function in the growth of the lower.

See ADRASTIA, FATE-SPHERE, FEATHER, GODS, JUDGMENT-HALL, KARMA, MOIRAE, NECESSITY, NORNOR, SAU, SHENIT, THEMIS, THOTH.

MĀB, A WEAPON OF HORUS :—

A symbol of the higher intellect, or will.

"Thereupon Isis and Horus stood near Rā, and the young god drove his weapon *mäb* into Set, at a place called 'She-nu-āha,' i.e. 'Lake of Battle,' or 'She-neter,' i.e. 'Lake of God.'"— *Legend of the Winged Sun-disk*.

Thereupon Wisdom and Love approached to their Source—the Higher

Triad,—and the Higher Self acting as Will-wisdom, overcame his enemy, the desire-mind, the "prince of darkness." The place with two names signifies the dual aspect which underlies the triumph over evil. On the one side there is Conflict (Battle); at the other there is Victory (God).

"Christ is always rising in human experience, always rising from the tomb wherein ignorance and wickedness have tried to enclose the eternal good. There is nothing for which the Easter festival more clearly stands than this inevitableness of the victory of the spiritual over the material, this continual bursting forth of divine life from the midst of darkness and death."—R. J. CAMPBELL, Serm., *Christ Arisen*.

See BATTLE, CONFLICT, CONQUEROR, DEVIL, HORUS, INTELLECT, ISIS, MJOLNER, RĀ, SET, STRIFE, TRIAD, VICTORY, WAR, WILL.

MACROCOSM AND MICRO-COSM :—

The Macrocosm is that aspect of the manifest God, or Divine Monad, in which he is shown to be the producer and container of all forms and qualities in his universe ; while the Microcosm is the individual monad, the reflection and perfect copy of the Divine,—being itself Divine. When the One became many, each of the many had in latency all the differentiations of the One.

The Son, "who is the image of the invisible God, the firstborn of all creation, for in him were all things created, in the heavens and upon the earth, things visible and things invisible."—Col. i. 15, 16.

"As God contains all things in Himself, so it is in our soul ; the soul is the microcosmos in which all things are contained and are led back to God. Therefore there is no difference between the Son of God and the soul " (Eckhart). —PFLEIDERER, *Develop. of Christianity*, p. 152.

"The Universal Perfect Soul is the Macrocosm. Humanity is the Microcosm" (Geberol).—MYER, *Qabbalah*, p. 156.

"The whole of the created, from its very beginning, is formed by the Qabbalistic philosophy into one Great Ideal Man, a Makrokosmos, a Great World, of which the terrestrial Adam was a copy, and who, with his descendents, are as a Mikrokosmos or Little World."— *Ibid.*, p. 225.

"Humanity is considered by the Qabbalah as one great universal brotherhood, as a great spiritual energetic vitality called the Mikrokosm, and in this slumbers the idea of the higher Makrokosm, the Heavenly or Celestial Man or Adam, the primordial Perfect Paradigm or Adam Qadmon, the Perfect Model of all Form and of the first terrestrial Adam, who was as to it the Mikrokosm. In this Great Paradigm, the Qabbalah asserts, are all the forms, the perfect ideals of the emanated or created existences. It might therefore be termed the Idealized Form, or the Form which contains all the perfect ideas in their origination."—*Ibid.*, p. 181.

"The teaching of the Faithful Brethren of Basra concerning Nature is that the human soul has emanated from the World-soul ; and the souls of all individuals taken together constitute a substance which might be denominated the Absolute Man or the Spirit of Humanity."—DE BOER, *Hist. of Philos. in Islam*, p. 92.

"The saying that the First Man was co-extensive with the world is found in various parts of the Talmud and the Midrash. The old philosophic conception that the world is a macrocosm and man is a microcosm is adopted by Philo and the Rabbis."—C. TAYLOR, *Sayings of the Jewish Fathers*, p. 71.

It is immaterial whether the individual or the race be regarded as the microcosm, for as all human individuals are united as one "universal brotherhood," or soul, on the buddhic plane, the microcosm for each is the same as for all. Every monad in every form is potentially a microcosm in which the universe is represented. All monads below the human tend upwards to become the human, which in its turn progresses onward to become the Divine (*see* diagrams, pp. 12, 60, 473).

"The deepest root and very essence of the soul in every man is *the eternal image of God there*—there without any agency of our own, there before our personal creation, and there for ever. *In* the *mirror of the Son* God sees, and we too may see, the types or patterns of all reality ; and the way to find ourselves and God and all that Is, is to stretch forth our arms toward the Divine pattern, which is ours : ' Flying from brightness to brightness, the spirit aspires with outstretched arms to reach this immortal pattern according to which it was created ' (Ruysbroek)."—R. M. JONES, *Mystical Religion*, p. 310.

"As the old Tabernacle, before it was built, existed in the mind of God, so all the unborn things of life, the things which are to make the future, are already living in their perfect ideas in Him, and when the future comes, its task will be to match those divine ideas with their material realities, to translate into the visible and tangible shapes of terrestrial life the facts which already have existence in the perfect mind. Surely in the very statement of such a thought of life there is something which ennobles and dignifies our living. The things which come to pass here in the world are not mere volunteer efforts of man's enterprise, not self-contained ventures which are responsible to nothing and to no one but themselves. For each of them there is an idea present already in the thought of God, a pattern of what each in its purest perfection is capable of being. Out of the desire to realise that idea must come the highest inspiration. In the degree to which it has realised that idea, must be the standard of judgment of every work of man."—PHILLIPS BROOKS, Serm., *The Pattern in the Mount.*

See ADAM (higher), ARC. MAN, BUDDHA, COSMOS, CRANIUM, CREATION, EVOLUTION, FIRST-BORN, GOD, GOD HEAD, HIGHER, IMAGE, INVOLUTION, MICROCOSM, MONAD, MONAD OF LIFE, PRAGÂPATI, PROTOTYPES, SEPHIROTH, SON OF GOD, SOUL (highest), SPHERE, TRINITY, ZODIAC.

MAGI FROM THE EAST :—

A symbol of those qualities which are enlightened intellectually.

"Now when Jesus was born in Bethlehem of Judea in the days of Herod the king, behold, wise men from the east came to Jerusalem, saying where is he that is born King of the Jews ? for we saw his star in the east, and are come to worship him."—MAT. ii. 1, 2.

Now when the Christ-soul was brought forth in the condition of purity and peace, in the cycle when the lower principle (Herod) ruled the soul, there arose qualities enlightened intellectually which aspired towards Truth. And these sought for the True Ruler of the soul qualities, for they saw the promise of his coming in the rise of knowledge (the star), and they hastened to adore the incoming Light of the world.

"The wise men, etc. simply mean that the human mind in which the precious gifts are born pays adoration to the new-born Light."—J. WARD, *Zion's Works,* Vol. III. p. 4.

"The East is the mystical term for the source of heavenly light. . . . The function (of the 'Kings of the East') is to announce the Epiphany of the Divine Life, to be the Sponsors for the Christ, the Godfathers of the heavenly Babe. To them it is appointed to discern him from afar off, and to hasten to affirm and declare him while yet in his cradle. Their offerings of gold, frankincense,

and myrrh denote the recognition of the indwelling Divinity by the prophetic, priestly, and regal attributes of man. Representing, respectively, the spirit, the soul, and the mind, they are symbolised as an angel, a queen and a king ; and they are, actually, Right Aspiration, Right Perception, and Right Judgment. The first implies enthusiasm for the glory of God and the advancement of souls, unalloyed by any selfish end. The second implies a vision for things spiritual, undimmed and undistorted by intrusion of elements, material or astral. And the third implies the ability to 'compare like with like and preserve the affinity of similars,' so that things spiritual may not be confounded with things physical, but ' to God shall be rendered the things of God, and to Cæsar the things of Cæsar.' "—*The Perfect Way,* p. 240.

See AN-RUT-F, BIRTH OF JESUS, CHILDREN OF THE EAST, EAST, ESTHER, GOLD, HEROD, INCENSE, JERUSALEM, JEWS, KING, LIGHT, MANGER, STAR IN EAST, TREASURE (cave).

MAGIC, OR MAGICAL POWERS :—

A symbol of the inner and unobserved processes within the soul by which lower qualities are raised and transmuted into higher. These processes are the workings of Buddhi through the higher mind, in response to the aspirations of the personality.

"Those remained for ever with the Sun (Râ) who possessed the most minute information as to the next world and who were best versed in magic. Thus the whole doctrine (of immortality) is based upon a belief in the power of magic : by magic only could demons be worsted and everlasting bliss be won."

"Thoth was the god of writing, the scribe of the gods, and the god of letters—especially of religious literature. He was supposed to have written the most sacred books and formulas with his own hand, and therein to have set down his knowledge of magic, in which art Isis only was his rival."—WIEDEMANN, *Rel. of Anc. Egyptians,* pp. 95, 227.

"In the religious texts and works we see how magic is made to be the handmaiden of religion, and how it appears in certain passages side by side with the most exalted spiritual conceptions ; and there can be no doubt that the chief object of magical books and ceremonies was to benefit those who had by some means obtained sufficient knowledge to make use of them."—BUDGE, *Egyptian Magic,* p. 3.

The "power of magic" is the efficacy of the buddhic function whereby the lower qualities are transmuted and the soul enabled to overcome the desires (demons) and rise to the planes of immortality.

Through the higher mind (Thoth) have come the revelations of the unseen contained in the symbolism of the sacred scriptures of the whole world. In the higher mind are to be found the meanings attached to the symbols of the ideas which have proceeded from the Holy Spirit or buddhic principle (Isis).

As the buddhic functioning (magic) is the means of the soul's redemption, its recognition is an exalted spiritual conception, and aspiration for its benefits is the essence of true religion.

The popular mistaken view of magic is referred to by Plutarch, who correctly gives the meaning of Isis.

" Isis,—Justice, Wisdom—shows the divine mysteries to be ' carriers of sacred things,' and ' wearers of sacred robes ' : these are they that carry in the soul, as it were in a copper (bowl), the sacred story respecting the Gods, that cleanses the recipient from all superstition and magical follies."—PLUTARCH, *Isis and Osiris*, § 3.

The Wisdom (Isis) from above explains the Divine scriptures as containing secret things of the Spirit and hidden wisdom of the soul. These scriptures, venerated as a vehicle of Divine truth, are the means of opening the revering mind to intuitions of truth symbolised in the miraculous stories and nonsensical statements of the holy books and myths, and so cleansing the soul from superstition and sorcery, the products of ignorance, greed, and hate.

" The human soul is made to turn, by the subtle chemistry of its digestive experience, truth into goodness."— PHILIPS BROOKS, Serm., *Young and Old Christian.*

See ALCHEMY, ASPIRATION, BARSOM, BUDDHI, BUDDHIC FUNCTION, CLOUDS, DEMONS, GRACE, HOLY GHOST, IMHOTEP, INTUITION, ISIS, MYTHOLOGY, PAPYRUS BOAT, PERSONALITY, REDEMPTION, RELIGION, REVELATION, RITUAL, SACRED TEXT, SCRIPTURES, THOTH, TRANSMUTATION, WISDOM, WORD.

MAGICAL FORMULÆ :—

Symbolic of the contents of the World-scriptures which treat of the hidden processes of nature.

" When Thoth heard this (of the impossibility of sailing further on the sea while numerous enemies occupied it) he recited certain chapters containing magical formulæ, with the view of protecting the boat and the vessels of the blacksmiths which were with it, and of quieting the sea during the period of storm."—*Legend of the Winged Sun-disk.*

When the higher intellect of the human race (Thoth) perceived the needs of the situation, it busied itself with the formulating of certain religious codes whereby the lower nature might be disciplined and so enabled to proceed with its evolution through the following of a set system, or a mode of action and aspiration. And this mode of discipline it arranged with the express object of preserving in the soul the germ of the higher intuition and capabilities of Divine realisation which should yet unfold in due order when the lower nature had accomplished its course on its own part. This systematised thought and action also provided a means, through fear, reverence and authority, of stilling the turbulent lower emotion-nature, and of quelling the stormy vehemence of the passions and desires.

The religious systems of the world are framed with a view, first of all, to preserve the germ of Buddhi intact in the consciousness ; and second, to quell the surgings of the astral self or kama-manasic nature, which, unless stilled by the action of Buddhi-manas, would prevent the Divine realisation of Truth through the mind. For the mind has to act as a mirror wherein may be reflected gleams of the radiance of Love, Righteousness and Reality.

" The starting-point of all magic and of all magical religion—the best and purest of occult activities—is, as in mysticism, man's inextinguishable conviction that there are other planes of being than those which his senses report to him ; and its proceedings represent the intellectual and individualistic results of this conviction—his craving for the hidden knowledge."—E. UNDERHILL, *Mysticism*, p. 180.

See ASPIRATION, BLACKSMITHS, BOAT, BUDDHI, ENEMIES, INSPIRATION, INTELLECT, INTUITION, PAPYRUS BOAT, SCRIPTURES, SEA, SIGN, STORM, THOTH, VESSEL, WORD.

MAGICAL PRACTICES (LOWER) :—

A symbol of the inward stimuli of the desire-mind (kama-manas) urging the soul towards fresh experiences of the lower life.

"When Zoroaster had attained his seventh year, the inimical Durasrobo and Bratrok-rish still continue to connive against him ; to harass and assail him. By magic practices they endeavour to daunt his spirit, and they attempt to destroy his body by poison."—A. V. W, JACKSON, Zoroaster, p. 32.

The "seventh year" signifies the growth of the soul upon the lower planes. The conspiracy is the means by which the soul is ensnared through the desire-nature and the lower mind which intensifies the strength of the desires. The "magic practices" are the untried routes of the lower nature over which the soul must needs pursue its way, and the way appears appalling and interminable. The "poisoning" signifies the immediate result of the severer experiences upon the lower planes whereon the effects of the coarser functionings of the lower self have all the appearance of effects of poison.

See ASTRAL-BODY, BLACK MAGICIANS, BRATROK-RISH, DURASROBO, FALL, KAMA, SERPENT (subtil), SEVEN, YEAR, ZOROASTER.

MAHABHARATA, OR THE GREAT ORIGINATOR :—

A symbol of the Logos or Higher Self,—God-manifest.

"The (Great) Bharata, doubtless is Pragâpati, for he sustains (bhar) this entire universe ;—' that his great light shineth brightly, as the sun,—he who overthrew Pûru in battles.' Pûru, by name, was an Asura—Rakshas : him Agni overthrew in battles."—Sata. Brâh., VI. 8, 1, 14.

The Higher Self, under many names, is the Life and Light of the universe, and the sun is his most general symbol. The desire-nature (Pûru) acts in opposition to the higher nature, and is eventually overcome by the incarnate Self (Agni) after much conflict.

See AGNI, BHARATA, CONFLICT, PRAGÂPATI, RAKSHASAS.

MAHAT :—

A symbol of the higher intellect,—buddhi-manas,—the plane of creation.

"The first production of the original Producer is Buddhi, commonly called ' intellect or intellectual perception ' (and variously termed Mahat, from its being the Great source of the two other internal faculties, Ahan-kara and Manas, or self-consciousness and mind)."—MONIER WILLIAMS, Indian Wisdom, p. 93.

See AHANKARA, BREATIC WORLD, MANAS, THOTH.

MAHÂVIRA, SOVEREIGN LORD :—

A symbol of the spiritual ego, or the individuality, ruler of the personalities. Or a symbol of the incarnate Self, Higher Self.

"Mahâvira, ' the great hero ' of the Jainas ; like Buddha."—BARTH, Rel. of India, p. 148.

See BUDDHA, INDIVIDUALITY, SELF, SOUL, SUN.

MAHÂVIRA-POT :—

A symbol of the causal-body the seat of the individuality, and of the Self.

"A (mystical) theory makes the Mahâvira pot a symbol of the sun, whilst the hot milk draught represents the divine flood of life and light with which the (Sacrificer) becomes imbued. These symbolic interpretations, whatever we may think of them otherwise, certainly adapt themselves admirably to the general sacrificial imagery. As the sun is the head of the universe—or in figurative language, the head of Pragâpati, the world-man,—so its earthly and earthen counterpart, the Mahâvira pot, is the head of Vishnu, the sacrificial man and the Sacrificer."—J. EGGELING, translator of the Sata. Brâh., S. B. of E., Vol. XLIV. Int. p. 48.

The sun is a symbol of the Higher Self which the lower self cannot distinguish from the individual Self and its vehicle the causal-body. The "hot milk" is a symbol of the Divine life—atma-buddhi. "Pragâpati" here stands for the Archetypal Man, who has sacrificed himself for humanity. This is the indwelling Christ whose " blood " (Divine life) cleanses from all sin as the soul evolves, that is, as the incomplete changes its nature and finally becomes the complete.

See ARC. MAN, BLOOD, CAUSAL-BODY, EVOLUTION, INDIVIDUALITY, KARANA, MILK, PRAGÂPATI, SACRIFICER, SHINTAI, SUN, VISHNU.

MAHĀ-YĀNA AND HĪNA-YĀNA :—

Symbols of the course of the soul's evolution. The first indicates the soul's path after mind has begun to function and the Divine spark has been conferred : the second indicates the prior path of the monad of form wherein the desire-nature and the personality are developed in animal forms on the lunar and terrene globes.

Māha-yāna and Hīna-yāna have the same significations as Devayana and Pitriyana. They indicate the double origin of the human being. The origin on the higher side from spirit and mind, and on the lower side from matter and desire ;—the spiritual man and the natural man ;—the two conflicting interests within the soul. On the greater path (Māha-yāna) man has descended from God ; on the lesser path (Hīna-yāna) he has ascended from the animal, and now he possesses the two natures within him.

See DEVAYANA, EVOLUTION, FALL, HIGHER AND LOWER, LUNAR CYCLE, MAN (born), MAN (natural), MOON-WAXING, -WANING, PITRIYANA, SOUL (middle), SPARK.

MAIDEN, HEAVENLY :—

A symbol of Wisdom (buddhi), or of the Intuition (buddhi-manas), which approaches the perfected soul as it rises to the higher consciousness.

" Advancing with this sweet-scented wind, there appeared to him what is his religious merit, in the shape of a beautiful maiden (of fifteen). . . . Then the soul of the righteous man spoke to her, asking, —What maiden art thou whom I have thus seen as yet the most beautiful of maidens in form ? Then answered him his own religion :—I am, O youth ! thy good thoughts, good words, good deeds, and who am thy own religion in thy own self."—HAUG, *The Hadokht Nask.*

The " advance " signifies the upward track which is now pursued by the soul ; for to the higher mental nature a purer and deeper sense of truth than that which may be apprehended through the intellect is vouchsafed. The " maiden," of which the soul is a part, is none other than the Wisdom-nature, lovely beyond conception, which is presently to become united with the operations of the Self through the higher mind. The ego of the perfected soul now supplicates the higher wisdom of the Self, requesting that its nature may be declared to it. In response, the Higher Self now makes

known its true being, and shows that the inner nature,—the better and truer self,—is that which alone is real and known. The Divine or complemental half of the perfected soul is but the result of those righteous efforts which have been made on the lower planes through the agency of the lower Self struggling upward to meet the Wisdom above.

" Now approacheth Wisdom, the Heavenly Maiden, to the soul, and embraceth it in its innermost essence with her sweetest love, placing her love as a sign of victory in its desires ; and now Adam riseth again from the dead in his heavenly part, in Christ. . . . For it is the marriage of the Lamb."—BEHMEN, *Thoughts, etc.*, Rainy, p. 42.

See ADAM (higher), BRIDGE (kinvat), BUDDHI, CHRIST'S SECOND COMING, HIKOBOSHI, LAMB, LAW OF ZOROASTER, LIBERATION, LOVER (maiden), MAN (righteous), MARRIAGE, RELIGION (good), RESURRECTION, SCENT, SOUL (middle), WISDOM.

MAISHĀN, ON THE SHORES OF THE SEA :—

A symbol of the mental plane, for the " shore of the sea " is the plane above the astral (sea).

" I passed the borders of Maishān, the meeting-place of the merchants of the East."—*Hymn of the Soul* (Gnostic).

I passed through the mental state, where the lower sensations are exchanged for the awakening emotion and ideas. The " merchants of the East " are the builders of thought, who transmute the sensations into ideas. (The sensations are wrought out through the astral centres : these in time exhaust the capacity of the vehicles, but in so doing, or before, vibrations are set up on the higher or mental plane, and in this way associations are set up in the mind, responses to which awaken sets of ideas, and these in time produce consecutive thoughts. Thoughts about feelings and the phenomena of sensation, when acted upon or vitalised by a powerful will, produce development in a man's character which coincides with evolution upon the higher buddhic plane. The mind is built up through the lower self, answering to the several sets of vibrations which enable it to respond through the aspects of mental

" qualities." These qualities, when distinct from astral emotions, gradually assert themselves as abstract mental attributes, and so merge into reason, judgment, analysis, synthesis, and love of truth and right, and in this way approximate to what we identify with the higher concepts of philosophy and metaphysics. These concepts are formed upon the upper rupa mental sub-planes and are perceived aright through the causal-body.)

See ASTRAL PLANE, BARSOM, BUDDHIC PLANE, EAST, INTELLECT, MAHAT, MANAS, MENTAL, MER-CHANDISE, POOL (Bethesda), QUALI-TIES, SEA, SPEECH, TABLES, TRANS-MUTATION, WILL.

MALE-FEMALE :—

The sex principle symbolises the dual aspects of the manifest which always present themselves in the evolution of the Cosmos,—such as spirit-matter, life-form, force-matter, love-wisdom, mind-emotion, intellect-intuition.

" The first emanation from *Kether*, the Crown, is *Binah*, the Universal Intellect or Understanding, which is Geberol's first emanation, Universal Matter. It is also termed by the Qabbalah *Immah*, the Mother, and is considered as receptive, negative, feminine, plastic, and to receive form. 'Everything existing' says the Zohar (III 290a), ' can only be the work of the male and female principles.' The Zohar and Geberol both hold that everything must be of Form (male) and Matter (female).—I. MYER, *Qabbalah*, p. 199.

From the Highest (Kether) is emanated the principle of Matter (Binah), which is receptive of truth from the Spirit. The principle of Matter is the Divine Mother—the bringer forth of all things both above and below. Matter receives forms and qualities from spiritual involution and then gives birth to all forms and qualities in spiritual evolution. Spirit is masculine, Matter is feminine, That which gives form is Spirit ; that which takes form is Matter.

See ADAM (dual), BINAH, COSMOS, CREATION, DIVORCE, EVOLUTION, FEMININE, FORMS, GARMENT OF SHAME, HEAVEN AND EARTH, INVOLUTION, KAIOMARTS, KETHER, LIVING THINGS, MATTER, MĀYĀ, MOTHER (divine),

SEX PRINCIPLE, TWO, URANUS, YANG AND YIN.

MALE-FEMALE OF THE DIVINE NATURE :—

A symbol of the dual aspects of the higher mind, which appear as Truth-Wisdom, Reason-Intuition, Intellect-Love, or Buddhi-manas.

" From the region of the heart came forth woman, the type in her very nature, as in her birthplace, of those affections ; formed to yield to the man or under-standing, as he to rule : the two, the understanding and will, making up the man created male-and-female. Now it is seen that there are two distinct lives in man, one of the intellect, the other of the affections, which though now separate in the human mind, unite as far as may be, and by their union produce all those forms of life which grow in and out of man. By these do we commune with God ; the understanding, as it is the image of God's wisdom, being the vessel to receive His truth and wisdom ; the will, as it reflects His love, to receive His goodness and love."—A. JUKES, *Types of Genesis*, p. 52.

See ADAM (higher), DIVORCE, FEMININE, IMAGE OF GOD, MAN (dual), MARRIAGE, MASCULINE, RIB, WIFE, WOMAN.

MALKUTH, THE HOLY SPIRIT :—

A symbol of the buddhic principle which directs the evolution of the soul.

" The Queen (Malkhuth) was also called the Church or Congregation of Israel, the Daughter, the Bride of the Spouse, the Shekeenah, i.e. the Glory, or real presence of the Deity, the Sabbath or Rest-day, the Harmony. It is considered by the Qabbalah as the executive energy or power of the Sephirah Binah, the Holy Spirit or Upper Mother."—I. MYER, *Qabbalah*, p. 203.

The buddhic principle is the consummation of the qualities (Israel), Wisdom the bride of Love, the source of inspiration, the completion of evolution, the Divine influx from above (Binah).

" Malkhuth, Kingdom, is the re-united action of all the Sephiroth . . . and is the immanent energy of all emanated things."—*Ibid.*, p. 282.

In the " kingdom of heaven," on the buddhic plane, will be found the spiritual results of the present evolution.

" We mean by ' God is Spirit ' that He is the Essential Being of all those things—invisible, immaterial, impossible for ever to be subjected to the senses—which we therefore call Spiritual Ideas, such as Truth, Love, Righteousness, Wisdom ; and that He is their Source in us, or rather their very Being in us, that in having them, we have God. . . . Our theory is this. We hold that there is a Divine Spirit, who is Truth, Wisdom, and the rest. We hold that our spirits and our intellect are in kind the same as His, are portions of the Eternal Fire and Light, differently conditioned in each of us by separate personalities, and that Truth, Love, Justice in us, are God in us. . . . We hold that the soul could never have conceived God had not its essence been of God."—STOPFORD A. BROOKE, Serm., *God is Spirit.*

See BINAH, BUDDHI, CHURCH, EVOLUTION, HESED, HOKHMAH, HOLY GHOST, KINGDOM, MĀYĀ (higher), MOTHER (divine), PAHAD, SABBATH, SEPHIROTH, SHEKINAH, TIPHERETH.

MAMMON OF UNRIGHTEOUS-NESS :—

A symbol of the lower emotion or desire nature, by the disciplining of which the higher emotions (friends) are evolved.

MAN, OR MEN :—

A universal symbol of mind in two aspects, higher mind or lower. It signifies intellect, reason, intelligence, or mental faculties and qualities.

"But he was angry, and would not go in : and his father came out, and intreated him. But he answered and said to his father, Lo, these many years do I serve thee, and I never transgressed a command-ment of thine : and yet thou never gavest me a kid, that I might make merry with my friends."—LUKE xv. 28, 29.

But the intellect is offended,—stubborn, proud, and unfit to make an effort to progress and inherit the things of eternal life. The intellect is the formative factor, and tends therefore to contract and limit its own activity, and so cannot expand of itself sufficiently. And therefore the effort of the Spirit (Father) from above is needed to assist it. But the intellect, as is its nature, argues and discusses. It is satisfied that it has not fallen from the path of rectitude, and ignores the fact that in this obtuseness lies its limitation. And so the son contends and complains that the Father has not bestowed upon him that which he ignorantly assumes he could have received, namely, union with the

higher qualities (friends) through the intuition of truth (the kid as meat).

"We must consider that the man who was formed of earth means the mind."—PHILO, *Works,* Yonge, Vol. I. p. 60.

"'Man' signifieth the rational principle, for the rational principle is imitative of intelligence. It appertaineth to the external man, which in itself is a kind of medium between the internal and external."—SWEDENBORG, *Arc. Cel. to Gen.* iii. 16, 17.

"Up, Lord, and let not man have the upper hand : let the heathen be judged in thy sight."—Ps. ix. 19.

"Let not the outer man, the old Adam, have the upper hand over the inner, spiritual man, nor let mere earthly thoughts lead us down from higher things."—ST. AMBROSE.

See ADAM (lower), ASPAHI, BREATH OF LIFE, CORPSE, DEAD, DUST, EARTH (ground), FAITH, FALL, FATHER, FRIENDS, HEEL, HERB, IMMORTALITY FORFEITED, KID, MA-A'SEH, MATRO, MEAT, NEPHESH, PERSONALITY, PRODIGAL, RUAH, SAVOUR.

MAN AND WIFE :—

A symbol of the mental and emo-tional natures united in the soul, and productive of thoughts and actions (children).

"Therefore shall a man leave his father and his mother, and shall cleave unto his wife : and they shall be one flesh."—GEN. ii. 24.

The mind, recognising that which is apparently of its own substance, and dual within itself, shall quit sense and desire which brought it into active being, and go in search of the ideal—higher emotions (buddhi, feminine). The mind with the ideal are *one,* when the mind and higher emotions are in harmony together in the liberated soul.

"Man, as His image, is therefore male and female, that he may be a figure both of the wisdom and love of God ; the man representing the understanding, the woman the will or love-part of the mind, which united make up that inward man or mind, by which we can both know and love, and so commune with, God."—A. JUKES, *Types of Genesis,* p. 40.

"By man, in the Word, is signified the understanding of truth ; and by woman the affection of truth, because man by birth is understanding, and woman affection."—SWEDENBORG, *Apoc. Rev.,* n. 434.

"So that they (man and wife) are no more twain, but one flesh. What there-fore God hath joined together, let not man put asunder."—MAT. xix. 6.

Christ here points out, that ideally reason and emotion are not at variance —not separate. This being the higher condition, the lower mind (man) is exhorted not to persist in maintaining the lower condition, (desire-mental), but preserve the union of mind and emotion and make the best of it by seeking the higher condition (buddhi-mental).

See ADULTERY, BUDDHI, CHILDREN OF MEN, DIVORCE, FATHER (lower), HIDING, HUSBAND, IMAGE, MAN WITHOUT WOMAN, MARRIAGE, MASCULINE, RIB, WIFE, WOMAN.

MAN, BAD, OR WICKED :—

A symbol of the mind subject to the lower desires, passions, affections, and emotions of the lower nature, which effectually bind it down to the re-incarnating process.

"The righteousness of the perfect shall direct his way: but the wicked shall fall by his own wickedness."— PROV. xi. 5.

The higher qualities of the perfected soul direct the consciousness upwards : but the soul that is undeveloped is attracted downwards by its desires for the things of the lower life.

"Those who have chosen the good in this world are received after death by good spirits, and guided, under the protection of the dog Sura, to the Kinvat bridge ; the wicked are dragged thither by the Daevas."—Zoroastrian System.

Those souls who have done well,— who have sown worthily,—shall reap the reward hereafter, upon those planes whereon they are gradually awakening. The "dog Sura" is the symbol of power, tenacity and will, and which stands for the Self's faithful servant, who has succeeded in crossing the bridge which unites the lower and the higher consciousnesses. The "wicked" souls are they who are relatively undeveloped, and who are drawn away by the lust of life, pride, attachment to the objects of sense and egotism.

"When I say unto the wicked, O wicked man, thou shalt surely die ; if thou (O son of man) dost not speak to warn the wicked from his way, that wicked man shall die in his iniquity ; but his blood will I require at thine hand."—EZEK. xxxiii. 8.

The "son of man" is the spiritual ego or spiritual mind, and stands for the conscience warning the mental qualities or the personality from evil courses. If the conscience does not speak, then the lower nature is not held responsible for wrongdoing, but the spiritual mind is accountable for not warning the lower mind.

See ADAM'S DEAD BODY, BLOOD, BRIDGE (kinvat), CONSCIENCE, DAEVAS, DOG-STAR, DUSAHK, GATHA (kam.), HAND OF BEAST, HARLOT, HELL, HIGHER AND LOWER, IMMORTALITY FORFEITED, JUDGMENT-DAY, KARMA, MAN (righteous), PERSONALITY, PRIEST, PURGATORY, REAPING, RE-INCARNATION, SON OF MAN, UNRIGHTEOUS MAN, WAY OF THE LORD, WICKEDNESS.

MAN, BLIND :—

A symbol of the mind which is not spiritually awakened, and which reveres the form of religion without knowledge of its substance. Creed-bound literalism and formalism.

"The Lord openeth the eyes of the blind : the Lord raiseth them that are bowed down : the Lord loveth the righteous."—Ps. cxlvi. 8.

The Divine Life within unfolds the higher nature which dissipates the lower, and brings truth to the perception of the soul. The Divine nature raiseth the mental qualities that are directed downwards. The Divine nature is in harmony with those which are perfected.

"That which had shut the higher wisdom out of your soul was part and portion of the soul itself, and so when it was broken up and kneaded in, it became part of the substance which received the new illumination. Your life had to open itself again in primal simplicity to God." —PHILIPS BROOKS, Mystery of Iniquity, p. 163.

See BLIND MAN, EYE, HEALING, MIRACLES (healing), SEEING, SIGHT.

MAN BORN AS AN ANIMAL :—

A symbol of an embryo ego on the mental plane which becomes embodied in a succession of animal forms in order to gain experience.

"And according to his deeds, and according to his knowledge, a man is born again here as a worm, or as an insect, or as a fish, or as a bird, or as a lion, or as a boar, or as a serpent, or as a tiger, or as a man, or as somebody else in different places."—Kaush. Upanishad.

According to the ego's operative results and experience, so is the monad's next life determined. From the worm,

EXPLANATORY

THE Diagram of Entities is to make plain the difference between Man and the Animals.

Regarded horizontally, man seems to inherit from the lower animals; but while this may be said to be partially true in respect to his physical form, it is not at all true of his mental and spiritual nature. The animals cannot confer what they do not possess, and they are themselves the effects of mental causation.

From the plant to the animal, and thence to man, there may appear to be developed, through variation and physical heredity, the human form. *Sequentially* this is true, as Darwin and Haeckel teach, but *causally* it is false that the lower can originate the higher. The forces behind phenomena are many and various, and quite independent of the physical which is their ultimate expression. The plane of causes or creation is the mental plane, as the Sacred Books (also Plato) teach, and it is to ideation we must look for the causes of vegetal, animal, and human variations of every kind.

Physical links between species are only very imperfectly traceable on the physical plane. Indeed, Weismann's extraordinary acuteness and nicety of observation really bring into prominence the inadequacy of the physical condition as cause for anything. To trace qualities to or through physical electrons is as unthinkable as it is unapparent. Qualities are not visible matter, but astro-mental activities.

Qualities are of an astral or mental nature, and can only be fully investigated on their own planes. Their expression upon the physical plane throws no light upon their genesis above that plane.

Causation is transmitted from above downwards, as indicated in the vertical life-lines of the diagram. When the group-soul of the apes is sufficiently developed, it segregates into individuals in which the germ of mind descends, as it were, to enlighten them. These souls, then, are fitted to enter human bodies of a low order. It must be added that the germ of mind carries with it the Divine spark, or spiritual Ego, which is enthroned in each individual soul. The idea that man (mind) descends from the animals is a mistake on the face of it, even though it may be held that he inherits his astral nature and physical form from them.

In *appearance* the higher condition always arises, or takes birth, from the lower condition, but this appearance is illusory as causation, and is due to the involutionary process which has preceded the evolutionary.

The Sacred Books explain that the type-forms of species originate intelligently on the mental plane,—the "plane of creation,"—and are carried forward upon the astral plane; the "plane of formation,"—where they modify astral forms of cognate species, and thence make entrance into physical life. Thus, at certain periods in the life-cycle, new species seem to arise from prior existing forms.

"Natural selection" is true in its degree as an appearance, but is itself dependent upon laws of variation which obviously appertain to the astral and mental conditions which are hidden from five-sense observation.

Physical heredity is a plain fact in appearance, but the causes of it are by no means plain, and it is evident that no microscopic observation of ova can throw the least light upon its causes, which are hidden behind the phenomena and are on higher planes. Inheritance is not from parents, but from the racial mind.

In the case of minerals, their etheric and astral bodies are collective and continuous, and the forces of the planes (as in earthquakes) play through them unimpeded. That etheric forces exist and are in common use, is shown by the great force present in explosions, electric engines, birds flying, etc. The physical force liberated by gas expansion can be calculated, and this force falls very far short of the total force exhibited in explosions.

With birds flying, the etheric force liberated is evidently in exact proportion to the muscular energy used, and is so much greater in amount than the animal force that birds can be almost constantly on the wing without being exhausted. Aeroplanes give little promise of real success until etheric force is employed in far greater measure than at present. There appear to be interactions between heat and electric vibrations and etheric currents. The *etheric* possibilities of electrical phenomena need to be studied very closely, and it seems likely that experiments such as those which are now being made in the laboratory will ultimately succeed in demonstrating the direction in which etheric force lies.

CONSTITUTION OF ORGANISMS

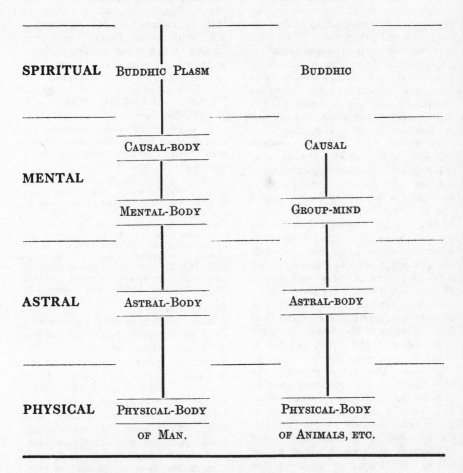

	HUMAN ENTITY	LOWER ENTITIES
SPIRITUAL	Buddhic Plasm	Buddhic
MENTAL	Causal-body / Mental-body	Causal / Group-mind
ASTRAL	Astral-body	Astral-body
PHYSICAL	Physical-body of Man.	Physical-body of Animals, etc.

HUMAN ENTITY   LOWER ENTITIES

MAN, ANIMALS AND VEGETALS

In this diagram the devolvement of life is shown vertically from above to below. Horizontally, the outer and inner bodies of all living beings are indicated on their respective planes of matter. The life of the human body and of every kind of organism is essentially subjective *purposeful mind* in action on its own plane, *directing* the forces on the lower planes to the formation, maintenance and functioning of the vegetal and animal mechanisms.

Each human individual possesses an incomplete causal-body on the higher mental plane, which is immortal and in process of building up to a perfect state in accordance with its perfect potential causal-body on a higher level. Man is endowed with a Divine ray of spirit from above, and this " Promethean fire " makes him a moral and spiritual being responsible for his actions to God within. The lower organisms are not individualised on the mental plane, and are therefore without causal bodies; but each species has its own ideal causal pattern, and its own group-mind, life and consciousness vivifying each unit, and gathering and utilising mundane experiences which convey information to the group-mind and suggest changes in the life of the species.

with its type of astral form, to the man with human astral form and human soul, and from personality to personality, so the spark of Divine life manifests and progresses. The evolution of the human astral form is accomplished from the evolution of the animal astral form,—the one flows insensibly into the other, so that oftentimes the astral forms of the most intelligent animals, though not in conscious touch with individual souls of their own, are yet expressions of the astral life, which will eventually manifest under human conditions when the law of karma provides openings for such embryo souls. The astral life is brought up, or worked, so to speak, through the animal evolution, so that when the time arrives, it provides the basis for the evolution of specifically human nature, since it then corresponds to the awakenment of activities which necessitate a form of human kind in which the mind is brought into activity, and which then forms a centre of individual consciousness such as will be able in time to direct its own evolution from within.

To make the matter clearer ; the statement about being born again as a worm, an animal, or a man, refers, first, to the astro-mental monad of form, and second, to the buddhi-mental monad of life, the son of mind (manasaputra), both of which are, of course, associated, so soon as the human soul is evolved with its awakened intelligence and indwelling germ of the Spirit, when man rises permanently above the animal kingdom. The "deeds and knowledge" determine the kinds of births of the embryo egos. On the lowest astral plane, as on the physical plane, cause precedes effect, and the law of each plane not only operates thereon but to some extent serves to regulate the conditions which obtain when the ego periodically descends into an astro-mental vehicle, prior to re-birth.

Man is properly the individual soul which is astro-mental, that is, when the differentiation from the animal order has taken place, as it does on the fourth astral sub-plane, and from thence the mind is stirred into activity.

See Devayana, Evolution, Hiruko, Involution, Karma, Lunar cycle, Mahayana, Man crawled, Man (natural), Manasaputras, Metempsychosis, Monad of form, of life, Moon-waxing, Pitris, Pitriyana, Re-incarnation, Skins of animals, Son of man, Wheels.

" MAN CRAWLED LIKE A WORM " :—

A symbol of the condition of animal-man before the advent within him of mind which raised him above the lower forms of life.

"The angels exhorted each other saying, ' Let us make man in our image and likeness.' He was accordingly formed, yet was unable to stand erect,—through the inability of the angels to convey to him that power,—but he wriggled like a worm. Then the Power from above taking pity upon him, since he was made after His likeness, sent forth a spark of life, which gave man an erect posture, compacted his joints, and made him live " (*Saturninus*).—Irenæus, *Against Heresies*, Bk. I. 24.

Man was first of all the production of those elemental forces, or builders of forms, which worked along the astral and physical planes whereon evolution was proceeding. These could not give mind to the animal natures of instinct and desire, whose forms they built. The period, however, arrived when the brute-human must needs become the God-human. And hence the Divine Archetypal Man in the heavens, created of God, descended upon the lower planes, and assumed that human form which was now fashioned into a fitting receptacle for his Divine nature to manifest therein. So it was, even, that God became man ; and so it is, also, that man may be said to become God,—for wherein differeth the one from the other, when each is united in Christ ? Raising man by a " spark of life " is the hinting at the supreme truth that the spiritually erect posture of man, which is related with his polarisation in the universe, bears a vital connection with the assumption of Godhood. The " angels," or nature-elementals, could not give man Divine attributes which, before they were conferred upon him, he lacked, so that he crawled upon the earth. Then it was that the soul was acquired, or rather that the individuated unit was incarnated, in a fitting vehicle, so that at last a living soul,—made in the image of God, and adapted to live in the true sense,—was evolved.

"Now we should consider that God gave the sovereign part of the human soul to be the divinity of each one . . . which raises us from earth to our kindred which is in heaven. And this is most true ; for the divine power suspended the head and root of us from that place where the generation of the soul first began, and thus made erect the whole body. He, therefore, who is always occupied with the cravings of desire and ambition and is eagerly striving after them, must have all his opinions mortal, and, as far as man can be, must be all of him mortal, because he cherished his mortal part. But he who has been in earnest in the love of knowledge and true wisdom . . . must of necessity, as far as human nature is capable of attaining immortality, be all immortal."— PLATO, *Timæus*, Jowett, Vol. III. p. 674.

"In one view, it may be rightly said that the whole object of God, in our training, is to develop in us a character of eternal uprightness ; developing also, in that manner, as a necessary consequence, grand possibilities of social order and well-being."—H. BUSHNELL, *Nature*, etc., p. 152.

See ARC. MAN, ASAR, DEVAS (lower), GROWTH, HIRANYAGARBHA, HIRUKO, IMAGE, IMPERIAL, MAN BORN, MATRO, METEMPSYCHOSIS, MONAD OF LIFE, REINCARNATION, SOUL, SPARK.

MAN, NATURAL :—

A symbol of the lower mind united with the desires and affections of the lower nature.

"Now the natural man receiveth not the things of the Spirit of God, for they are foolishness unto him, and he cannot know them, etc."—1 COR. ii. 14.

"By the natural man is meant the lower faculties of man ; and it is said of these that they cannot discover spiritual truth."—F. W. ROBERTSON, *Sermons, 1st Series*, p. 2.

"The natural man belongs essentially to this present order of things. He is endowed simply with a high quality of the natural animal life. But it is life of so poor a quality that it is not Life at all. He that hath not the Son *hath not Life*, but he that hath the Son hath Life—a new and distinct and supernatural endowment. . . . Not a difference of development, but of generation."— H. DRUMMOND, *Natural Law*, etc., p. 82.

"The Lord is the first-begotten from the dead, because He, as to his Humanity, is the Truth itself united to the Divine

Good, from whom all men, who in themselves are dead, are made alive."— SWEDENBORG, *Apoc. Rev.*, n. 17.

"In spiritual warfare we fight to overcome the natural man, not to destroy him, but to render him obedient to the law of Christ. To bring our whole nature into perfect harmony with the will of God is the true end of our striving. There can be no stopping short of that, but when the goal is won there shall be no more fighting but an entrance into everlasting peace."—R. J. CAMPBELL, Serm., *Warfare of Life*.

"Democracy must get rid of the natural man of each for himself, and have a new birth into the spiritual man, the ideal self of each for all. . . . This is the deepest craving of human nature. All attempts to reconcile man's heroism to his interests have ever failed."— R. WHITEING, *No. 5 John Street*, p. 279.

"The true self of every man is God (the Universal Self). There are millions of selves which think themselves separate from the Universal Self, but this sense of separation is an illusion. The problem of life is the overcoming of this illusion, and the identification of itself with the Universal Self. What we call the personal self is not the genuine self, but only the mere passing states of consciousness, which are never the same."—K. C. ANDERSON, Serm., *The Buried Life*.

See ADAM (lower), CORPSE, DAVID, DEAD, HIGHER AND LOWER SELVES, MAHAYANA, MAN BORN, MENIS, MOON-WAXING, PERSONALITY, ROCK OF SALVATION, SELF (lower), SEPARATENESS, SON OF MAN.

MAN, RICH :—

A symbol of the mind which identifies itself with a multitude of objects of desire ; an attitude of clinging to externalities, which fosters the pairs of opposites in the soul.

"It is easier for a camel to go through a needle's eye, than for a rich man to enter into the kingdom of God."—MAT. xix. 24.

This is an analogy, showing how impossible it is for a mind distracted by the conflicting desires and emotions of the lower planes to enter into the nature of that which is bliss.

"Blessed in spirit are the poor : for theirs is the kingdom of heaven."—MAT. v. 3.

The Divine nature operates in those who have rid themselves of the desires of the lower life ; for their consciousness rises to the higher planes.

See KINGDOM OF HEAVEN, LAZARUS, POOR IN SPIRIT, POVERTY, RICH MAN, SERMON ON MOUNT, WEALTH.

MAN, RIGHTEOUS :—

A symbol of the exalted mind about to be united to the Higher Self. It indicates the ego which has rid itself of its lower nature, and so has become liberated from the cycle of births and deaths.

"The soul of the righteous man first advanced with a step he placed upon good thought ; secondly, a step upon good word ; thirdly, a step upon good action ; and fourthly, a step he placed upon the eternal luminaries."—*Hadokht Nask*, HAUG, *Essays*, p. 221.

The soul of the perfected man is said to have advanced, firstly, through good thought,—the union of the intellect and judgment with emotion and the will. Secondly, by right speech,— the expression of goodness and truth. Thirdly, through good action,—the fulfilment of the object of right endeavour. Fourthly, reliance upon eternal Love and Truth,—the perfect subjugation of the lower nature of the ego to the Higher Self.

"As God is free from all finite ends, so also is the righteous man. Desire nothing, thus wilt thou obtain God and in him all things. Work for the sake of working, love for love's sake. . . . Virtue must be a condition, *my essential condition* ; I must be built up and built over in righteousness. No one loves virtue except him who is virtue itself. All virtues must become in me necessities, being performed unconsciously. Morality consists not in doing, but in being" (Eckhart).—UEBERWEG, *Hist. of Philos.*, Vol. I, p. 478.

"The real man, the inner spiritual man, is simply a receptacle for the impregnation and birth of ideas, an activity only acting through a conditioned receptivity, yet with a certain amount of liberty, but not a perfect autonomy. His spirituality contains the susceptibility, content, and living ability to produce spiritual and material births, but to be able to produce requires an outside spiritual impregnation and permission from the Deity."—I. MYER, *Qabbalah*, p. 184.

See GATHA (ush.), GRACE, LAW OF ZOROASTER, MAIDEN, NIGHTS (three) WAY OF THE LORD.

MAN WITHOUT WOMAN :—

A symbol of mind subject to desire and uninfluenced by emotion (woman).

"Man by himself must not carry a corpse or he will be defiled by the Nasu. The penalty for carrying a corpse is that a man shall be placed where there is least water and fewest plants, and on ground least passed over by flocks and herds."— *Vendidad*, III. *S. B. of E.*

The carrying of a corpse by one man alone signifies the attempt to allow the intellect (man) to function alone in the personality (corpse). Mind acting without emotion, without love, is calculated to defile a soul, for it becomes captive to desire (Nasu) ; and the consequence of such functioning would be a landing in ignorance and error, that is, in a state of mind where truth (water) and goodness (plants) are scarcest, and there are fewest gleams of wisdom through the lack of virtues (flocks) and moralised emotions (herds).

"The power of man to stand between abstract truth upon the one side, and the concrete facts of life upon the other, comes from the co-existence in his human nature of two different powers, without the possession of both of which no man possesses a complete humanity. One of these powers is the power of knowing, and the other is the power of loving. . . . From this it will immediately follow that the more perfectly these two constituents of human nature meet, the more absolutely they are proportioned to each other, and the more completely they are blended, so much the more ready will the human nature be for the fulfilment of every function of humanity. And if, as we have seen, one of the loftiest functions of humanity is to stand between the absolute truth and the world's needs, and to transmit the one in such way that it can really reach and help the other, then it will also follow that the more perfectly the knowing faculty and the loving faculty meet in any man, the more that man's life will become a transmitter and interpreter of truth to other men."—PHILLIPS BROOKS, Serm., *Visions and Tasks*.

"It is often asserted that emotion is modified only by emotion, that reason without emotion remains a dead letter ; and this is certainly the case. The dictates of reason, therefore, must be combined with love, which we may call the positive norm of emotion ; then will reason become effective. The ideal must become the object of love ; then will this supreme affection—enthusiasm for the ideal— work its effect upon the other forms. Such enthusiasm cannot, of course, be manufactured, it is something free— the unforced persistent glow of love for perfection, the practical interest in the ideal of reason. . . . Finally, the ideal comes to us in the impressions wrought by God within the soul. The mental impression in question, therefore, results not from any external object, but from our being, apprehended by our reason's own ideal, or by the Divine spirit within us."—A. DORNER, *Emotions*, *Ency. Rel. and Ethics.*

See CATTLE, CORPSE, DUNG, MAN AND WIFE, MARRIAGE, NASU, PERSONALITY, PLANTS, SHEEP, WATER, WIFE, WOMAN.

MANALA, THE ABODE OF THE DEAD, OR POHJOLA :—

A symbol of the lower planes on which the lower personalities are incarnated.

See DEAD, NORTH, SERPENT OF WATER.

MANAS, MANASIC :—

A symbol of mind, mentality, or the mental plane, below the buddhic plane.

"Place thy manas in me (Krishna), into Me let thy understanding enter; then without doubt thou shalt abide in Me hereafter."—*Bhagavad Gita*, XII. 8.

Devote thy mind (manas) to the service of the Most High, and harmonise thy higher emotions with the inner Self, then, O soul! thou shalt be liberated from the life below, and be united unto God for ever.

See BAKHDHI, BREATIC WORLD, INTELLECT, LIBERATION, MAHAT, MAISHAN, SWORDS, THOTH.

MANAS AS A CENTRE :—

A symbol of the causal-body on the plane of higher manas.

"The manas, although only the organ of the âtman, is yet the central organ of the entire conscious life; which not only as 'the primary root of the five faculties of knowledge' shapes into ideas the impressions of sight, hearing, taste, smell, touch, since we 'see only with the mind, hear with the mind,' but stamps these ideas further as resolves of the will." —DEUSSEN, *Phil. of Upanishads*, p. 273.

See CAUSAL-BODY.

MANASAPUTRAS, SONS OF MIND :—

A symbol of the spiritual element in humanity. The Divine monads, or "sons of God," brought forth on the mental plane of the soul. They are the "little ones" or "children of God," and their nature is atma-buddhic. They are born into the human souls as the true egos or immortal individualities seated in the causal-bodies and ruling over the lower bodies. When the lower nature is sufficiently developed in animal man so that from the astral centres are begotten the mental, then the "Sons of mind" are born,—the Divine monads descend into the astro-mental vehicles which are prepared for them. The souls in this way become individualised, as was previously not the case.

"Let me tell you plainly that you yourself are one of the sons of God, partially manifest here on earth, but only partially; your true home is with the glorious host above."—R. J. CAMPBELL, Serm., *The Kenosis, etc.*

"The first fact about me is that I— the thinking being—exist. That is the most certain of all my certitudes, the one reality of which it is impossible for me to doubt; and it is the true starting-point of all philosophy. The fleeting phenomena of consciousness are bound together and made intelligible by the *ego*, which, manifesting itself in and through them, declares that it abides among all changes, and does not change with them. By the same intellectual power we affirm the reality of the *non-ego*, of a world of sense and matter which is something more permanent than the phenomena dealt with by physical science. This process of objective affirmation is a primary fact of our intellectual life, revealing to us the *ego* and the *non-ego* as things in themselves. A permanent self and the unity of self-consciousness are the essential foundations of all philosophy, properly so-called : of every rational account of man. Now one of the primary facts of consciousness is the feeling of ethical obligation. It is a fact abundantly verifiable, its simplest expression being 'Thou oughtest,' and it is the starting point of morality."— W. S. LILLY, *The Great Enigma*, p. 305.

See ACHAIANS (sons), AGNISVATTAS, BODHISATVAS, CHILDREN OF GOD, FRAVASHIS, INCARNATION OF SOULS, LITTLE CHILDREN, MAN (born), MARUTS, MAZENDARANS, MONAD OF LIFE, MUSPELL (sons), PITRIS (solar), PITRIYANA, SHEEP (lost), SONS OF GOD, SPARK.

MANASI, THE BELOVED :—

A symbol of the causal-body in the higher mind.

"And the beloved Mânasi (mind) and her image Kâkshushi (eye), who, taking flowers, are weaving the worlds." —*Kaush. Upanishad*, I. 2.

The much valued mental centre— the causal-body,—conveying intuition, the soul's eye, that is, the inner discernment which perceives only the good and true, and so realises that whereof the universe is built. The flowers are the virtues or higher qualities which energise the higher planes.

See Causal-body, Flowers, Karana, Marks.

MANCO CAPAC AND MAMA OGLLO, OFFSPRING OF SUN AND MOON.

Symbols of the Divine Will and Wisdom proceeding from primordial Spirit and Matter.

"Manco Capac and Mama Ogllo descended from heaven in the region of Lake Titicaca. They had received commands from their parent, the sun-god, to traverse the country until they came to a spot where a golden wedge they possessed should sink into the ground, and at this place to found a culture centre. The wedge disappeared at Cuzoo (navel of the earth). The city founded, Manco Capac instructed the men in the arts of civilisation, and his consort busied herself in teaching the women the domestic virtues, as weaving and spinning."— L. Spence, *Myth. of Mexico and Peru*, p. 47.

The Divine Will and Wisdom manifested first upon the higher mental plane (the region), and in accordance with the scheme of the Logos, centres of operation had to be found for the formation of the Soul. Then, in the process of involution, a ray of the Divine Life (wedge) from the higher (gold) planes was projected to the centre of the mental plane (navel), and below to the centre of the astral plane, and from these centres (city) the Soul was gradually built up. The Divine Will then prepared the way for the subsequent evolution of man and other entities. The mental qualities were involved and brought to perfection, and the Divine Wisdom fully adapted the higher emotions (women) to the laws and mechanism of the soul-process.

See Chemmis, Civilising, Delos, Earth (ground), Gold, Golden age, Loom, Navel, Onogorojima, Warp.

MANDHATRI'S BIRTH FROM THE FOREHEAD :—

A symbol of the causal-body being produced from the buddhic plane in the course of involution.

See Causal-body, Involution.

MANEROS, THE LITTLE BOY :—

A symbol of the personality or lower mind in its astro-mental body.

"Others say (of Maneros) that he fell into the sea, and afterwards received the greatest honours on account of the Goddess (Isis) ; for that the maneros whom the Egyptians so frequently call upon in their banquets is none other than this very boy."—Plutarch, *Isis and Osiris*, § 17.

The "falling into the sea" means simply the resolution of the residual particles of the astro-mental vehicle into their primary constituents on the astral plane. The "honours" are the re-elaboration, through the co-operation of the forces in the laboratory of nature, of the particles into further combinations. The "maneros at the banquets" signifies that it is the mental function which is appealed to whenever the thirst for knowledge is sought to be gratified.

See Absyrtus, Isis, Palestinus, Personality.

MANES :—

A symbol of the monads of life, and form. The same as the pitris

"The manes are primeval deities free from anger, careful of purity, ever chaste, averse from strife, and endowed with great virtues."—*Laws of Manu*, III. 192.

The solar and lunar pitris are the spiritual monads of life and form, free from the pairs of opposites of the lower planes, operating without strife, and possessed of all useful qualities according to their types.

"The various classes of the manes are declared to be the sons of all those sages, Mariki, etc., who are children of Manu, the son of Hiranyagarbha."—*Ibid.*, 194.

The many classes of monads are differentiated on the mental plane according to the kinds of qualities and types of forms which are to appear and grow up on the lower planes in the course of the cycle of life.

See Hiranyagarbha, Manu, Monad (life, form), Pitris (lunar, solar).

MANGER IN WHICH THE INFANT JESUS WAS LAID :—

A symbol of simplicity of mind and understanding, in which the Christ-soul is to be received into the innermost nature of man.

Spiritual instruction for the understanding ; this is the signification of a manger, and the same is signified by the manger in which the Lord lay when an infant, because a horse, who eats out of it, signifies the understanding of the Word." — SWEDENBORG, *Apoc. Rev.*, n. 255.

See ARK (bulrushes), BIRTH OF JESUS, MAGI, STAR IN EAST.

MANIFESTATION INTO DAY :—

Symbolic of the night of the Soul ended, and the rise of the consciousness into Light and Life eternal.

"Chapter of Manifestation into Day, of Going in and Coming forth in the possession of Divinity. . . . Of Victory there, of Glory there, of Ploughing, Reaping, Feasting, and Marriage there : of Doing all these things while on earth." —*Book of the Dead*, Ch. CX. BLACKDEN.

The Soul's completed pilgrimage through the planes and periods of the manvantara, and the cycles, first, of involution (going in), and second, of evolution (coming forth), culminating in union with Divinity. This implies the victory of the Soul over the realm of nature ; the primordial potential being ultimately actualised ; the transfiguration of matter and energy, through Spirit acting upon matter ; the law of Karma (reaping), and the enjoyment of devachanic bliss ; the union between the lower Self and the Higher Self ; and the full expression of the Self through its vehicles on the planes of manifestation.

See CHAPTERS, COMING FORTH, DAY, EVOLUTION, FEAST, GOING IN, I A O, INVOLUTION, KARMA, MARRIAGE, NIGHT, PLOUGHING, REAPING, SPIRIT, TUAT, VICTORY.

MANNA :—

A symbol of goodness and truth, or higher emotion for the sustenance of the soul.

"Then said the Lord unto Moses, Behold, I will rain bread from heaven for you ; and the people shall go out and gather a certain rate every day, that I may prove them, whether they will walk in my law, or no."—EXOD. xvi. 4.

The rational and ethical nature (Moses) is made acquainted with the coming of the spiritual nature. From the buddhic plane will proceed an outpouring of truth and high emotion to energise and sustain the qualities in accordance with their rate of preparedness in each stage of their progress. This will fully prove them whether they are ready to harmonise themselves with the spiritual law of wisdom and love.

"Referring to the allegorical 'manna' or heavenly food, 'the bread which the Lord hath given you to eat' (Exod. xvi. 13). Philo writes : 'Dost thou not see the food of the soul, what it is ? It is the Continuing Reason (Logos) of God, like unto dew, encircling the whole of it [the soul] on all sides, and suffering no part of it to be without its share of it (the Logos)'" (From *Leg. Alleg.*, § 59).—MEAD, *T. G. Hermes*, Vol. I. p. 246.

"There is also a spiritual manna, the dew that is of spiritual Wisdom, which descends from heaven upon those who sincerely seek for it, and which waters the souls of the righteous, and puts sweetness into their mouths. Wherefore, he who comprehends this out-pouring of divine wisdom receives pleasure from it, nor requires any other food, 'nor lives by bread alone, but by every word of God.'"—ST. AMBROSE, *Letters*, p. 395.

"By the hidden manna, which they will have who are in good works, and who at the same time adjoin the truths of doctrine to works, is meant hidden wisdom of a quality like that which they who are in the third heaven enjoy."—SWEDENBORG, *Apoc. Rev.*, n. 120.

"Faith will produce just such effects (of home-sickness). In exact proportion to its strength, that living trust in God will direct our thoughts and desires to the 'King in His beauty, and the land that is very far off.' In proportion as our thoughts and desires are thus directed, they will be averted from what is round about us ; and the more longingly our eyes are fixed on the furthest horizon, the less shall we see flowers at our feet. To behold God pales the otherwise dazzling lustre of created brightness. They whose souls are fed with heavenly manna, and who have learned that it is their necessary food, will scent no dainties in the fleshpots of Egypt, for all their rank garlic and leeks."—A. MACLAREN, *Sermons*, 2nd *Series*, p. 140.

"Paul tells us that the manna of which the Israelites ate in the wilderness was to them a type and lively symbol of 'the bread of life' (1 COR. x. 3). 'They did all eat the same *spiritual* meat'—i.e. meat which was intended not only to support their natural lives, but to point them to Him who was the life of their souls. Now, Clement of Alexandria, to whom we are largely indebted for all the discoveries that, in modern times, have been made in Egypt, expressly assures us that, 'in their *hidden character*, the enigmas of the Egyptians were *very similar to those of the Jews*' (*Clem. Alex.*, Vol. III. p. 56)."—A. HISLOP, *Two Babylons*, p. 161.

"Yet he (the Lord) commanded the

skies above, and opened the doors of heaven ; and he rained down manna upon them to eat, and gave them of the corn of heaven. Man did eat the bread of the mighty : he sent them meat to the full.—Ps. lxxviii. 23–5.

This " parable " signifies the outpouring of truth and goodness on the evolving qualities of the soul in the arena of life.

See ARK OF TESTIMONY, BREAD, BUDDHIC PLANE, CAKE, CORN, DEW, EATING, FOOD, HONEY, MEAT, MOSES, RAIN, ROCK (spiritual), SACRAMENTAL CAKES, SHEWBREAD, SKY.

MANSION OF THE STARS :—

A symbol of the illimitable expansion of the mind or mental faculties.
See STARS (fixed).

MANSIONS :—

A symbol of states of consciousness which have reference more particularly to differentiated aspects of the mind. The abnormal cases of multiple personality illustrate this idea upon a lower plane.

" In my Father's house are many mansions ; if it were not so, I would have told you ; for I go to prepare a place for you."—JOHN xiv. 2.

In the causal-body of the race are many diverse states of consciousness appropriate to the growth of the qualities which have each a progressive course of their own on the mental plane. The Christ-soul in aspiring leads the way and prepares the conditions, and returns again to harmonise the qualities.

" For, albeit one is stronger than another, one wiser than another, one more righteous than another, ' in my Father's house there are many mansions ' ; none of them shall remain outside that house, where everyone, according to his deserts, is to receive a mansion. The ' many mansions ' point to the different grades of merit in that one eternal life." —AUGUSTINE, *Gospel of John*, Vol. II. p. 244.

" There are in heaven many goodly homesteads, and none without a celestial ward " (*Prose Edda*).—MALLET, *North. Antiq.*, p. 412.

" In a sense we are not creating anything by our sojourn in the flesh ; all that we shall ever possess in the heaven of heavens exists in its fullness already ; we are not making it, we have but to get up to it and possess it. ' We have a building of God, an house not made with hands, eternal in the heavens.' Yes, true enough, we each have our very own

place in the Father's house of many mansions, and we shall never improve on it to all eternity ; it is just what it is, a seat waiting for its occupant, a home waiting for its owner. But before we can take possession of it fully and finally, we have to prove ourselves, through manifold dangers, tribulations and temptations, to be worthy of the realisation of our divine sonship and our inheritance in God."—R. J. CAMPBELL, Serm., *Divine Restitution.*

See AAT, CAUSAL-BODY, CHURCH, CONSCIOUSNESS, FATHER, HOUSE (sleep), SEKHET-HETEP, TABERNACLE.

MANTLES, CLOAKS :—

A symbol of mental states of truth or error. Opinions, etc.

" Robes, mantles, and cloaks signify truths in common, because they are a common covering to the body. . . . By Elijah and Elisha the Lord was represented as to the Word, and therefore their mantle signified the divine truth of the Word in general."—SWEDENBORG, *Apoc. Rev.*, n. 328.

See CLOTHING, COAT, GARMENT, RAIMENT, ROBES.

MANU :—

A symbol of the Individuality, or the causal Self, upon the mental plane.

" Manu,—the son of Brahmā or a personification of Brahmā himself, the creator of the world, and progenitor of mankind. Derived from the root *man*, to think, the word means originally *man*, the thinker, and is found in this sense in the Rig-Veda."—R. T. H. GRIFFITH, *The Ramayan*, Bk. I. p. 96.

See ARC. MAN, BRAHMA, INDIVIDUALITY, MANES.

MANU VAIVASVATA :—

A symbol of the individuality working through the personality.

See CORRUPTION, DELUGE, DEPRAVITY, FLOOD, HORN OF SALVATION, VAIVASVATA.

MANVANTARA :—

The cycle of life in the lower nature, or the phenomenal universe of the solar system. It includes both the period of involution and the period of evolution, in relation to the lunar and terrene chains of globes. The mahamanvantara is the cyclic period of the whole solar system with all its planetary chains.

See ABRAXAS, CIRCLE OF EXISTENCE, DAY (great), HOUR, LEVIATHAN,

NIGHT, PLANETARY CHAIN, PRALAYA,
SABBATHS, SAMSARA, SERPENT
(ananta), TIME, TUAT, YEAR, ZODIAC.

MĀRA, THE TEMPTER :—

A symbol of the desire-nature or
desire-mind which entices the soul
and keeps it captive on the lower
planes.

" Māras are ' lords of sensuous desires.
. . . Millions of Māras ruled over by a
chief Māra, who tempts men to indulge
their passions and is always on the
watch to enter the citadel of the body
by the gates of (the senses), eye, ear, etc.
One of Māra's names is Kāma, ' desire.' "
—MON. WILLIAMS, Buddhism, p. 208.

A multitude of desires are directed
by the desire-mind (kama-manas).

See ASURA (lower), DEVIL, KAMA,
KURUS, SERPENT (subtil), SWAN.

MARE :—

A symbol of the feminine aspect
of mind (horse) as giving birth to
opinions, theories, and concepts of
the lower mind.

See ASVINS, HORSE.

MARIĀNDYNI :—

A symbol of a state of right mental
discrimination through the use of
the faculty of intuition.

See BOAR (wild).

MARKET-PLACE :—

A symbol of the " field " or arena
of life, in which the soul qualities
congregate to transact the business
of development by interaction and
co-operation under Divine law.—See
MAT. xx. 3.

See ARENA, FIELD, LABOURERS,
LAND, SETTLEMENTS, VARA, WORLD.

MARJATTA OR MARIATTA :—

A symbol of the purified part of
the lower nature, fit to bear the
Christ.

" Mariatta, child of beauty, Magic
maid of little stature, Guarded with her
sacred virtue, Her sincerity and honour,
Fed upon the dainty whiting, On the
inner bark of birchwood, On the tender
flesh of lambkins."—The Kalevala.

The child of virtue and beauty of
the lower nature, small but precious
in truth and righteousness ; steadfast
in faith, hope, and charity, in gentleness, purity, nobleness and sincerity.
Subsisting upon facts of experience,—
knowledge,—upon the " bread of life,"

—goodness,—and upon the " holy
meat," which is intellectual and
spiritual food.

" The word marja means a cranberry,
and consequently the name Marjatta
cannot have been originally derived from
Maria."—W. F. KIRBY. The Quest, Vol. I.
p. 326.

See CRANBERRY, HUITZILOPOCHTLI,
LEMMINKAINEN, SERPENT (water),
VIRGIN, VIRGIN MARY.

MARK ON CAIN :—

See ATOM.

MARKS OF JESUS :—

A symbol of the intuitions of the
causal-body which is the vehicle of
the Higher Self.

" From henceforth let no man trouble
me : for I bear in my body the marks of
the Lord Jesus."—GAL. vi. 17.

Henceforward no simply rational
(man) considerations shall have weight
with me ; for I bear the intuition of
Truth in the Christ-vehicle, or causal-
body, within me, which shall place
me above the subtle reasonings of
logicians and the dubious authority
of literalists and historians, by giving
me direct knowledge of truth. (The
lower is the vehicle of the higher, but
until the relationship between plane
and plane is established in the soul,
so that consciousness may pass and
repass, there can be no consciousness
below of any functionings above.
Hence the allusion.)

" The explanation of Wetstein still
seems to us to be the best ; according
to this, Paul means sacred signs, in virtue
of which he is declared to be one
consecrated to Christ."—G. A. DEISS-
MANN, Bible Studies, p. 350.

See BUDDHA (marks), CAUSAL-BODY,
FOOTPRINTS OF BUDDHA, MAN.

MARRIAGE :—

A symbol of the union of Wisdom
(fem.) and Love (masc.), or of Truth
(masc.) and Love (fem.), or in a lower
sense, of mind (man) and emotion
(woman). It also may mean the
union of the Higher Self (masc.) with
the purified lower Self (fem.) on the
higher mental plane.

" There is in every particular of the
Word, a marriage of love and wisdom, or
of good and truth. . . . The conjunction
of good and truth is called the heavenly
marriage."—SWEDENBORG, Apoc. Rev.,
n. 29, 97.

"But the chief of all the mysteries for Philo was apparently the Sacred Marriage, the mystic union of the soul as female, with God, as male."—G. R. S. MEAD, *T. G. Hermes*, Vol. I. p. 216.

The marriage of Wisdom (Medea) and Love (Jason) is indicated in the *Argonautic Expedition* :—

"Alcinous assented to give Medea up, provided she was yet a maid. His wife Arēte hearing this, lost no time in joining the lovers in wedlock."

The union of Wisdom and Love is rendered possible only when Divine truth has been realised. Before this there can be no true marriage between them, and Wisdom is, as it were, not virgin, since it is conjoined to the things of the lower planes. Therefore, until the hour comes when it is raised and purified, it cannot be united on the higher planes to its complemental half.

"Those two Beings, viz. the Inward Heavenly and the Outward Heavenly, were mutually espoused to each other, and formed into one body wherein was the most holy tincture of the Fire and Light; viz. the great joyful Love-desire which did inflame the Essence, so that both Essences did very earnestly and ardently desire each other in the Love-desire, and loved one another :— the Inward loved the Outward in its manifestation and sensation, and the Outward loved the Inward in its greatest sweetness and joyfulness as its precious Pearl and most beloved Spouse and Consort; and yet they were not two bodies, but only one,—but of a two-fold Essence; one inward Heavenly, Holy, and one from the essence of Time,—which were epoused and betrothed to each other eternally."—JACOB BOEHME, *Mysterium Magnum*, p. 79.

The marriage of the Higher Self with the lower Self takes place as the evolution of the lower qualities or elements,—-physical, astral, and mental,—enables the potencies of the Self to be completely expressed. When a given point is reached, that of perfection, then the lower is absorbed, so to say, into the Higher Self, which may be said to overshadow the lower, and so, since the latter ceases to exist, the Higher state as such also disappears,—that is, becomes *Something* for which no equivalent term can be furnished.

See ALCINOUS, APPLES, BUDDHI, CANA MARRIAGE, CONCEPTION (child), DIVORCE, EPIMETHEUS, FRIGG,

GUESTS, HERA, HIGHER AND LOWER SELVES, HIKOBOSHI, HUSBAND AND WIFE, MAIDEN, MALE-FEMALE, MAN AND WIFE, MAN WITHOUT WOMAN, TWO, UNION, VAIRAUMATI, VIRGIN, WEDDING, WIFE, WISDOM, WOMAN.

MARRIAGE, LOWER ASPECT :—

A symbol of union of an ego or mental quality with the lower emotions, or the mind with lower emotion.

"A wise man should avoid married life as if it were a burning pit of live coals."—*Dhammika-Sutta*, 21.

"Full of hindrances is married life, defiled by passion. How can one who dwells at home live the higher life in all its purity?" (*Tevijja-Sutta*, 47).— MON. WILLIAMS, *Buddhism*, p. 88.

An ego desirous of progressing should avoid alliance with the lower emotion-nature, defiled by passion and desire. An ego who remains on the lower planes (home) cannot attain to the higher life of its home above, freed from captivity to the lower emotions. (In the above texts it is plain from the setting that "marriage" must be taken in its lower sense of mind ruled by desire.)

See ADULTERY, CONCEPTION, DIVORCING, FOLLY, HARLOT, WHORE-DOM.

MARRIAGE OF THE LAMB :—

A symbol of the Incarnate Self, who died in Involution, rising again in the Soul's Evolution as Love of the Ideal, and ultimately becoming united with the Wisdom above, who is the transmuted Soul herself.

"Let us rejoice and be exceeding glad, and let us give the glory unto Him : for the marriage of the Lamb is come, and his wife hath made herself ready. And it was given unto her that she should array herself in fine linen, bright and pure : for the fine linen is the righteous acts of the saints."—REV. xix. 7, 8.

All the qualities rejoice in the approach to perfection, and return to the Absolute at the end of the cycle, when the Higher Self and the perfected soul become one. For the soul has made herself ready, and all her qualities have been transmuted to the buddhic plane, whereon she assumes the shining robe of wisdom, truth, and love, which is the inheritance of the perfected qualities that have progressed through experience below.

" The final state of the soul of the Man Regenerate is described in the Apocalypse under the figure of a marriage, wherein the contracting parties are the soul herself and the now Divine Spirit of the man, which is called the Lamb. The description of this Lamb, as ' slain before the foundation of the world,' denotes the original and eternal act of self-immolation, —typified in the Eucharist,—whereby Deity descends into conditions and distributes of Itself to be the life and substance of the Universe, alike for its creation, its sustentation, and its redemption. In the crowning act of this stupendous drama,—the act which mystically is called the ' Consummation of the Marriage of the Son of God,'— the Spirit and Bride, as King and Queen of the perfected individuality, are indissolubly united ; and the human is taken up into the Divine, having received the ' Gift of God ' which is life eternal. . . . A gift of God's own substantial Self being individualised in him."—*The Perfect Way*, p. 243.

See ARIES, CHURCH, CONSUMMATION, CRUCIFIXION OF CHRIST, EVOLUTION. INCARNATION, INDIVIDUALITY, INVOLUTION, LAMB OF GOD, LINEN, MARRIAGE, REGENERATION, SACRIFICER, SOUL (middle), TRANSUBSTANTIATION, WISDOM.

MARRIAGE WITHIN CASTES :—

Symbolic of the centres of consciousness and activity in the soul attaching to themselves bodies on the lower planes through which to function and bring forth results.

" It is declared that a Sûdra woman alone can be the wife of a Sûdra, she and one of his own caste the wives of a Vaisya, those two and one of his own caste the wives of a Kshatriya, those three and one of his own caste the wives of a Brâhmana."—*Laws of Manu*, III. 13.

The four caste " wives " of a " Brâhmana " are the four soul-vestures or bodies on the four lower planes attached to the causal centre or Individuality (Brâhmana). They are the physical body (Sûdra wife), the astral body (Vaisya wife), the mental body (Kshatriya wife), and the causal body (Brâhmana wife). They constitute the means for the soul's activity on the different planes, the gathering of experience, and the bringing forth of results (children).

See BRAHMANA, CASTES, CLASSES, KSHATRIYA, QUATERNARY, SUDRA, VAISYA, VESTURES.

MARROW :—

A symbol of the atmic plane, the innermost spiritual nature of the soul.

" Now it was those five bodily parts of Pragâpati that became relaxed,—hair, skin, flesh, bone and marrow,—they are those five layers of the fire altar ; and when he builds up the five layers, thereby he builds him up by those bodily parts."—*Sata. Brâh.*, VI. 1, 2, 17.

At the end of a manifesting cycle of the Divine Life (Pragâpati), there is an indrawal of the Divine Breath, and the five planes cease from activity. The five planes of the manifest are the physical (hair), astral (skin), mental (flesh), buddhic (bone), and atmic (marrow). These are " members " of the Archetypal Man (Pragâpati), and they constitute the nature of the soul (fire altar). The soul is evolved to perfection through the expression of the Self on the five planes.

See ALTAR (fire), ARC. MAN, BONES, BREATH, DISMEMBERMENT, MEMBERS, PRAGÂPATI, SEASONS (five), SKIN, WORLDS (five).

MARS, THE PLANET :—

Symbol of power, force, resistance and will,—the astral function intensified through the action of manas (mind).

" Mars gives man bravery and noble-mindedness."—From the Basra Encyclopedia, quoted by Dr. T. J. DE BOER in his *Hist. of Philos. in Islam*, p. 88.

See ARES, PLANETS.

MARSH ; SWAMP ; FEN :—

Symbols of astro-mentality, wherein truth (water) lodges ; which is soft and pliable—easily subordinated to truth ; or which easily yields truth.

" The *ushshu*-plant, the dittu-plant of the marsh, the reed and the forest he (Marduk) created, the lands, and the marshes and the swamps " (Babylonian Tablet).—L. W. KING, M.A., *Babylonian Religion*, p. 90.

The early growth of qualities and forms were established by the Logos on the mental and astral planes ; and the astro-mental life and organisation produced physical phenomena.

See BIRTH OF HORUS, DOORS OPENED, GARDEN OF REEDS, GEBAL, LEMMIKAINEN, PAPYRUS, PEACHES, REEDPLAIN, SEKHET-AARU.

MARTHA AND MARY :—

Symbols of the lower emotions actively engaged ; and the purified and regulated emotions.

"Martha received Jesus into her house. And she had a sister called Mary, which also sat at the Lord's feet, and heard his word. But Martha was cumbered about much serving."—LUKE x. 38–40.

"Mary," who sat at Christ's feet, signifies the soul now purified, who draws her inspiration direct from the central fount of Truth. "Martha," on the other hand, stands for the worldly mind engaged about the every-day occupations which take it away from both the spiritual and finer emotional activities. "Martha" chooses the path of duty, "Mary" the path of Love.

"For what is set forth by Mary, who sitting down gave ear to the words of our Lord, saving the life of contemplation ? And what by Martha, so busied with outward services, saving the life of action."—ST. GREGORY, *Morals on the Book of Job*, Vol. I. p. 361.

See LAZARUS, OINTMENT, WOMAN.

MARUTS :—

A symbol of the spiritual monads, or Divine " sparks," which descend into the soul-forms prepared to receive them.

"There can be no doubt about the meaning of the name, whatever difference of opinion there may be about its etymology. Marut and marutu in ordinary sanscrit mean wind, and more particularly a strong wind."—MAX MÜLLER, *S. B. of E.*, Vol. XXXII. p. 32.

As wind, or breath, expresses *spirit* in Hebrew, Greek, and perhaps Latin, it is not unreasonable to suppose it may express the same in Sanscrit.

The Maruts were certainly riders, and whatever other scholars may say to the contrary, it can be proved that they were supposed to sit astride on horseback, and to have the bridle through the horses' nostrils."—*Ibid.*, p. 43.

The " horse " is a common symbol of the mind, which is a vehicle of the spirit, and should be under the rule and direction of the spiritual ego. " Nostrils," used for direction, symbolise volition.

"The Maruts were born from the milk of Prisni. Prisni is called their mother, Rudra their father." " They were closely connected with each other, like the branches of a tree."—*Ibid.*, pp. 73, 208.

The spiritual monads are atma-buddhic. " Prisni," the " heavenly cow," is a symbol of the buddhic plane, which being the plane immediately above the mental must give birth to the monad in the mind. " Rudra " signifies the atmic plane, and is therefore the spiritual father. The monads are branches of the tree of Life, united in the trunk, and rooted in the Absolute.

" The flame-born Maruts."—*Rig-Veda*, VI. 66, 10.

" The Maruts are the peasants."—*Sata. Brâh.*, V. 3, 1, 6.

The monads are the sparks from the eternal Fire of the Divine Spirit (agniswattas). They are also the cultivators of the lower nature (i.e. peasants).

" The troops of the Maruts consist of seven each."—*Sata. Brâh.*, IX. 3, 1, 25.

The seven divisions of the monads are in correspondence with the seven globes, the seven planetary chains, the seven planes, etc. These numerical correspondences indicate certain organic relationships between the phenomenal sets.

See AGNISHVATTAS, BODHISATVAS, BREATH, CHARIOT, COW, FAN, FRAVASHIS, HORSES (bay), INCARNATION OF SOULS, LIGHTNING, MANASAPUTRAS, MAZENDARANS, MONADS OF LIFE, NOSE, PACCEKA-BUDDHAS, PEASANT, PITRIS (solar), POTSHERD, RACES, RUDRA, SACRIFICER, SAGES, SINGERS, SONS OF GOD, SPARK, SPEAR, SPIRIT, TREE OF LIFE, TWELVE, VACH, WIND.

MASCULINE PRINCIPLE :—

This designates the active and positive aspect of the manifest Duality; that which acts upon the receptive, feminine side of nature, which is the form side. The Spirit or Life side of manifestation is masculine ; the Matter or Form side is feminine. The highest manifest plane, Atma, is masculine, and is the plane of the Logos or Higher Self,—the " Sun-god " under many names. The mental and astral planes are masculine ; the buddhic and the physical are feminine. But it must be remembered that on all planes both aspects are present in greater or less degree.

See FEMININE, MALE-FEMALE, MAN AND WIFE.

MASONRY :—

A term for the sacred symbolism which in ancient times was cut or sculptured in stone.

The origin of Masonry is invested with a sacred character, for the reason that Divine inspiration indicated the symbols which had to be scrupulously rendered in stone or in paintings on walls of the temples, tombs, and palaces. This work required knowledge and accuracy, and was regarded as sacred. It naturally led to the formation of a guild, or brotherhood, of masons and painters, in close relation to the priesthood and temple buildings in ancient Egypt and, perhaps, in Babylonia.

" Freemasonry used as symbols the working tools of operative masons. The apron, consisting of a square with a triangular flap, represented the descent of the divine Spirit into matter. The interlaced triangle symbolised man coming forth from God, passing through his pilgrimage in matter, and returning again to his divine source. The square in compasses showed the spiritual nature controlling the physical. The symbol of the cross had a similar meaning, the down-stroke representing spirit and the cross-bar matter."—J. J. WEDGWOOD, Lecture, 1912.

" The mystery of speculative Masonry is of the building up of man into a spiritual house, meet for the inhabitation of God." —A. E. WAITE, Secret Doctrine in Israel, p. 297.

" And the house when it was in building was built of stone made ready at the quarry : and there was neither hammer nor axe nor any tool of iron heard in the house, while it was in building."— 1 KINGS vi. 7.

" Ye also, as living stones, are built up a spiritual house."—1 PETER ii. 5.

See ALTAR (fire), CROSS, HOUSE, IRON, STONE, TABERNACLE, TEMPLE.

MASS :—

See HOST, PROCESSION, SACRAMENT.

MAST OF A SHIP :—

A symbol of aspiration.

" Mast,—' Tell me what is my name ? ' The Deceased replies,—' Bringer back of the Lady after her departure ? ' "— BUDGE, Egyptian Magic, p. 168.

Aspiration is that which brings back to the soul the buddhic or Wisdom nature, which departed when, at the " fall," the mind was captured by the desires and sensations.

See AMATERASU, EDEN, ESTHER, FALL, HIDING, LADY, RETURN, SAILS, SHIP.

MAST LOWERED :—

A symbol of belief and opinions changed.

MASTER OF WISDOM :—

A symbol of the higher mind directly informed and guided by the Holy Spirit,—atma-buddhi. The developed individuality.

" And there was among them a man of unusual knowledge, and master especially of all sorts of wise deeds, who in truth possessed greatest wealth of mind, for whenever he reached out with all his mind, easily he beheld each one of all the things that are, even for ten and twenty generations of men."—Empedocles, FAIRBANKS, 415.

And at this period, amid the emotional and physical qualities, there was the mind gifted with the Divine spark,—atma-buddhi,—and master of every wise and holy thing that it is possible for the soul to possess. A mind which is the conscious possessor of the manifest within itself,—for whenever it exercised its inherent powers, it became the reflector of all things past and present, according to the many re-incarnating cycles through which the soul evolved.

See ADEPT, ARHAT, ASEKA, BROTHER, GURU, HERMES.

MASTER, RULED BY A :—

Instructed and guided by the Higher Self or the Supreme.

MASTER, NOT RULED BY A :—

The desire-nature not regulated through the will and reason.

MATRO (MESCHIA) AND MATROYAO (MESCHIANE),—THE FIRST HUMAN PAIR :—

These signify the mental and emotional natures evolved in the first class pitris on the third round of the terrene chain.

" And in forty years, with the shape of a one-stemmed Rivas-plant, and the 15 years of its 15 leaves, Matro and Matroyao grew up from the earth in such a manner that their arms rested behind their shoulders, and one joined to the other they were connected together and both alike."—The Bundahis, Ch. XV. 2.

And during a cyclic period of

transitory conditions the first root-race evolved in the third round. The "15 years of its 15 leaves" signify each a cyclic period answering to the evolution of the mental and emotional natures through the physical, astral, and lower mental planes. The "growth from the earth" is a symbol of the upward increasing stature of the nature of the manhood. The position of the "arms" is symbolic of the acquired power of will, and as this comes into play, the mental and emotion natures each approach the other more and more, and serve to complement one another. (The first class pitris were originally perfect in their higher nature, and capable of consciously functioning only upon the buddhic plane (Eden) in a state of innocence, free from care, and relying wholly upon the Divine Will. Afterwards occur the temptation and fall to the lower planes.)

See ADAM (lower), ARMS, ASKR, EDEN, EVOLUTION, FALL, GOAT (milch), GOLDEN AGE, MAN AND WIFE, MILK FROM GOAT, OPPOSITES, PITRIS, PLANETARY CHAIN, PLANTS, RACES, ROOT-RACES, ROUND, SHELTER, SHOULDERS, SIAMAK.

MATS OF FLOOR OF DWELLING :—

A symbol of the soul's physical body.

"There erect dwellings with mats and poles, and roofs, and walls."—Vendidad, II.

The "dwellings" are the vehicles on the lower planes in which the spiritual ego dwells. The "mats," "poles," "walls," and "roofs" are the physical, astral, kama-manasic, and causal sheaths.

See DWELLINGS FOR SEEDS.

MATTER (FEMININE) :—

A term for the complement of Spirit in the primal duality of Spirit and Matter. It is that aspect of manifestation which receives qualities and takes forms ; and this it does from the action of Spirit upon it ; Spirit being replete with all potencies and knowledges from all eternity.

"Numa is said to have consecrated the Perpetual Fire as the first of all things and the Soul of Matter which, without

it (the Fire), is motionless and dead."—PLUTARCH, Lives. Numa.

"It is possible to impress quality in matter, since it is without quality, and to extend form through the whole of it."—PLOTINUS, On Matter, § 7.

"Matter must be considered as formless prior to its variety. Hence, if by intellect you take away its variety, its forms, its productive principles, and intellections, that which is prior to these, is formless and indefinite matter."—Ibid., § 4.

"The unborn state of Matter, then, was formlessness ; its genesis is its being brought into activity" (Hermetic Ex. V). —G. R. S. MEAD, T. G. Hermes, Vol. III. p. 27.

Spirit (fire), in informing matter with qualities and forms, limits and conditions itself within matter, which state of captivity and spiritual death is called the Divine Sacrifice, or Crucifixion in Matter. During the period and process of evolution, Spirit rises from Matter and eventually discards it. Matter is almost comparable to a sieve through which Spirit is rubbed, as it were ; and in this way, in process of evolution, the gross physical and astral matter in the soul-vehicles is worn away ; so that what happens is this,—the Spiritual energy, which is seeking expression, remains, after having co-operated with its partner, as the complete and perfect manifestation of that which is contained within the Life of the Logos as the Divine Ideal, or Archetypal Man.

"Every individual soul is involved in Matter, and must gradually be formed into Spirit. To that end it possesses many faculties or powers, and of these the speculative faculties are the choicest, for knowledge is the very life of the soul." —DE BOER, Hist. of Philos. in Islam, p. 92.

This wearing away of Matter by spiritual qualities continues throughout the whole period of evolution ; but, of course, evolution, as far as its physical expression is concerned, culminates in the human race on this physical globe.

"There are two forms of Brahman, the material (effect) and the immaterial (cause). The material is false, the immaterial is true. That which is true is Brahman,—is light."—Mait. Upanishad, VI. 3.

"According to Plotinus,—Matter in the most general sense of the word is the basis, or 'depth,' of each thing. Matter is darkness, as the Logos is light.

It has no real being. It is the qualitatively indeterminate which is rendered determinate by the accession of form."—UEBERWEG, *Hist. of Philos.*, Vol. II. p. 246.

" The world (of matter) is not a thing that is ; it *is not*. It is a thing that teaches, yet not even a thing—a show that shows, a teaching shadow. However useless the demonstration otherwise, philosophy does well in proving that matter is a non-entity. The reality is alone the Spiritual."—H. DRUMMOND, *Natural Law, etc.*, p. 57.

" I hold,—and the whole scientific world appears to be coming to the same position,—that there is no such thing as matter apart from mind ; it has no independent existence ; the physical is but the language of the spiritual on a certain limited plane of experience."— R. J. CAMPBELL, Serm., *The Resurrection Life*.

The higher mental plane being the plane of proximate causation, the planes below are planes of effects according to natural laws. These effects are transient and illusory, without abiding reality. Consciousness is neither on the physical nor the astral planes, but on the mental. Consciousness is an aspect of spirit— the only reality.

" Natural knowledge tends more and more to the conclusion that ' all the choir of heaven and furniture of earth ' are the transitory forms of parcels of cosmic substance winding along the road of evolution, from nebulous potentiality, through endless growths of sun and planet and satellite ; through all varieties of matter ; through infinite diversities of life and thought ; possibly through modes of being of which we neither have a conception, nor are competent to form any, back to the indefinite latency from which they arose. Thus the most obvious attribute of the cosmos is its impermanence. It assumes the aspect not so much of a permanent entity as of a changeful process, in which naught endures save the flow of energy and the rational order which pervades it."—T. H. HUXLEY, *Evolution and Ethics*, p 50.

Energy and Order are attributes of Spirit which informs matter and endows it with qualities and potencies to be actualised or evolved under invariable laws.

" Although, by reason of its limitations, the cause of evil, Matter is not in itself evil. On the contrary, it comes forth from God, and consists of that whereof God's Self consists, namely, Spirit. It *is* Spirit, by the force of the Divine will subjected to conditions and limitations, and made exteriorly cognisable. Matter is thus a manifestation of that which in its original condition is unmanifest, namely, Spirit. And Spirit does not become evil by becoming manifest. Evil is the result of the limitation of Spirit by Matter. For Spirit is God, and God is good. Wherefore, in being the limitation of God, Matter is the limitation of good. Such limitation is essential to creation. For without a projection of Divine Substance, that is, of God's Self, into conditions and limitations,—of Being, which is absolute, into Existence, which is relative,—God would remain inoperative, solitary, unmanifest, and consequently unknown, unhonoured, and unloved. . . . For aught else to exist than God, there must be that which is, by limitation, inferior to God. . . . Creation, to be worthy of God. must involve the idea of a No-God, The darkness of God's shadow must correspond in intensity with the brightness of God's light."—*The Perfect Way*, p. 41.

Antiochus teaches :—" There are two natures, the active and the passive, force and matter, but neither is ever without the other. That which is compounded of both is called a body or a quality. Among these qualities the simple and the compound are to be distinguished ; the former consisting of the four, or according to Aristotle five, primitive bodies ; the latter of all the rest : of the first category, fire and air are the active, earth and water the receptive and passive. Underlying them all, however, is the matter without quality, which is their substratum, the imperishable, but yet infinitely divisible elements, producing in the constant change of its forms definite bodies."—E. ZELLER, *Eclecticism*, p. 94.

See ARC. MAN, BINAH, BIRTH OF BUDDHA, OF CHRIST, BONDAGE, CRUCIFIXION OF CHRIST, DARKNESS (lower), FIRE, HEAVEN AND EARTH, HETHRA, HINE, IGNORANCE, ILLUSION, INVOLUTION, KHIEN, KHWAN, LIGHT, MĀYĀ, MOTHER, MULA-PRAKRITI, PHENOMENA, PRAKRITI, PURUSHA, RANGI, SEPARATION, SPIRIT, SUDRA, VESTURES, WOMB, YANG.

MAUI, THE POTIKI :—

A symbol of the Higher Self, who is involved in Matter and the Soul.

" Maui Potiki appears to have had many names, which are expressive of his power : thus he is called Atamai from his liberality ; Toa, from his superior strength, and i-tikitiki-a-tarangi, which signifies that he possessed the top-knot (tiki), or power of his father (Taranga)."—R. TAYLOR, *New Zealand*, p. 24.

The Christ-child (Maui Potiki) is born in the soul to become its ruler and its dispenser of blessings through the endowment of higher qualities. The indwelling Self (Toa) is the victor over the lower nature, for he possesses the intuition of Truth (the top-knot), and can thereby overcome ignorance, illusion and desire. The Self below (Maui) and the Self above (Taranga) are one Spirit,—" I and my Father are one."

See ARC. MAN, HAIR, HIGHER AND LOWER SELVES, INTUITION, SELF, SUN-CATCHING.

MÂYÂ (HIGHER ASPECT) :—

A symbol of primordial Truth, the feminine aspect of Deity, which brings forth the Soul.

"To (king Suddhodana) there was a queen named Mâyâ, as if free from all deceit (mâyâ)—an effulgence proceeding from his effulgence, like the splendour of the sun when it is free from all the influence of darkness,—a chief queen in the united assembly of all queens."— *Buddha-Karita*, Bk. I. 15.

To the manifesting Self there is committed a counterpart which is feminine, passive ; and She is the embodiment of pure Truth, the opposite of illusion. The Truth is said to proceed from the Self, inasmuch as it bears witness to the Self-existent, and is the concrete expression of that which transcends the manifest. The " splendour of the sun " is referred to, since upon these high planes the Self is above temporalities which produce " shadow," matter. Truth or Wisdom upon this exalted plane, or condition of being, is the supreme fact of all facts, which testifies to the Self-existent,—the Being of all beings. If illusion is traced to its source, Truth will be found.

See ADITI, AKASA, BINAH, BIRTH OF BUDDHA, OF CHRIST, COW (mehurt), EARTH (great), GARDEN (lumbini), GODDESS, ILLUSION, MOTHER, OCEAN, PRAKRITI, PURUSHA, RHEA, SARASVATI, SHEKINAH, SUBSTANCE, SUDDHODANA, WOMAN (matter), WOMEN'S LIFE, WOMB, YAO.

MÂYÂ (LOWER ASPECT) :—

A symbol of the illusiveness of the lower planes, which are the inverted reflection below of the Truth above.

"The great intellectual truth, which the Upanishads taught before Kant,

that this entire universe, with its relations in space, its consequent manifoldness and dependence upon the mind that apprehends, rests solely upon an illusion (mâyâ), natural indeed to us owing to the limitations of our intellect ; and that there is in truth one Being alone, eternal, exalted above space and time, multiplicity and change, self-revealing in all the forms of nature, and by me, who myself also am one and undivided, discovered and realised within as my very Self, as the *âtman*."—P. DEUSSEN, *Phil. of Upanishads*, p. 48.

" How keenly, as one grows older, the idea enforces itself on the heart that all the events and experiences of this life are but *Mâyâ*. How clearly one sees that all the light of this world is but a false radiance, and that all its seeming realities are the tricks and shows of illusion ! Nothing *is ;* everything passes, flits by, and vanishes."—ANNA KINGSFORD, *Life*, Vol. II. p. 174.

" The world is a spiritual world, merely employing matter for its manifestations." —H. DRUMMOND, *Ascent of Man*, p. 420.

" Ever since I was a little child I have been impressed by the unreality of the material world and the events which are taking place in it. I can well remember, as a boy, the strange feeling I often had that I was not at home in it, that it was unsubstantial—a mirage which might easily disappear—and that in any case the true world was somehow hidden behind it and occasionally shining through. In the strenuous activities of later life this feeling lessened, though it never wholly left me, and now it has come back with almost the same intensity as in childhood. And since my spiritual life has deepened and matured somewhat, I find myself growing more aloof from the appearances and pre-occupations of the visible world, and concentrating more and more upon the permanent realities underlying it and the purpose of my being here. Not that I take no account of the present world or tell myself that it does not matter. On the contrary, I feel that it matters far more deeply than at present we are able to realise ; but it does not matter in the way it seems to matter ; it matters for something else. All that we say or do, feel, think, or know, matters in relation to the eternal and not otherwise."—R. J. CAMPBELL, Serm., *The Sense of the Eternal*.

See HINE, ILLUSION, MATTER, NECTAR, PHENOMENA, PRAKRITI, PURUSHA, SEPARATION, WOMB.

MÂZENDARANS :—

A symbol of the monads, or spiritual egos, which descend to the mental plane when the duality of mind and emotion gives rise to the higher mental or causal self.

"The rain is the seed of the Mâzen-darans, who are bound on the celestial sphere."—*Sikand-gumanik-vigar*, XVI. 14.

Truth (rain) is disseminated by the monads of life, which have become subject to the law of cause and effect on the lower planes. Truth becomes productive of aspiration and the higher qualities in the soul.

See FATE-SPHERE, MANASAPUTRAS, MARUTS, MONAD (life), RAIN, SEED (good).

MEADOW OF ATE OR HADES :—

A symbol of the astro-mental plane, or the arena of life on the lower planes.

"In darkness they roam over the meadow of Ate. . . . Deprived of life.— *Empedocles*, FAIRBANKS, 388, 389.

In the underworld the spiritual forces of growth lie hidden, concealed from view of the unenlightened, and consequently deprived of the light of knowledge, and unable to operate to the full, through the limited means at their disposal.

"Whereas the virtuous, in order, as it were, to purify themselves and to recover breath, after (the death of) the body, as being the source of sinful pollution, must pass a certain fixed time in the mildest region of air, which they call the 'Meadow of Hades.' "—PLU-TARCH, *On the E at Delphi*, § XXVIII.

Between incarnations, the more advanced and moralised souls, after physical death, enter astro-mentral regions, where they gradually discard their lower astral sheaths of instincts, passions, and desires, and remain for a period on the plane of the lower mind (air), before passing further inwards to touch the higher mind, prior to another descent to re-incarnation.

See AIR, COMB, HADES, INCARNATION OF SOULS, PARADISE (lower), PERSE-PHONE, PURGATORY, RE-INCARNATION, SLEEPING AND WAKING.

MEAL, OR WHEAT GROUND IN A MILL :—

A symbol of the higher, or buddhic, emotions as food for the soul. The harvest of aspiration and experience from the lower life, having become transmuted by the upper and lower millstones of buddhi-manas, furnish nourishment for the causal-body and conduce to its development.

"Meal signifies truth from good."— SWEDENBORG, *Apoc. Rev.*, n. 411.

See BREAD, CORN, FLOUR, FOOD, LEAVEN, WHEAT.

MEAOU TRIBES OF CHINA :—

A symbol of the lower instincts and desires.

"Those Meaou (said Yu) are doltish, stupid and confused, destitute of rever-ence, contemptuous, self-righteous tribes, who oppose divine reason, and subvert the principles of moral excellence. According to their notions, the mean man occupies the throne, and the philosopher dwells only among rustics. Such people are accursed, and fit objects of divine vengeance."—KIDD, *China*, p. 127.

See PELASGIANS, PEOPLE, KING, KURUS, TRIBES.

MEASURE :—

A symbol of correspondence in quality.

"Man is the measure of all things ; of those things which exist as he is ; and of those things which do not exist as he is not."—*Protogoras of Abdera*.

The human soul corresponds in quality with the whole universe. It has in it all the elements of the planes of manifestation. This truth is recognised when to the soul's actual qualities there are added the soul's latent qualities.

"To measure signifies to know and scrutinise the quality of a thing or state."—SWEDENBORG, *Apoc. Rev.*, n. 486.

"And he measured the wall thereof, a hundred and forty and four cubits, according to the measure of a man, that is, of an angel."—REV. xxi. 17.

The perfected soul is complete in all its qualities and attributes (12 × 12), according to its correspondence with the potential within it, that is, of the Archetypal Man (angel).—EPH. iv. 13.

See ALTAR (fire), ARC. MAN, CITY OF GOD, DESERTS, HEIGHT OF OSIRIS, MEAT, MICROCOSM, TWELVE.

MEAT, OR FOOD :—

A symbol of knowledge and higher emotion which conduce to the growth of the soul.

"The eyes of all wait upon Thee ; and thou givest them their meat in due season."—Ps. cxlv. 15.

The qualities aspire, and the Divine Wisdom responds in bestowing truth and love, as they are prepared to receive sustenance for the soul.

"And every tree, in which is the fruit of a tree yielding seed ; to you it shall be for meat."—GEN. i. 29.

And every emotion which is capable of becoming exalted, and which can be the means of affording the soul growth,—to the soul it shall serve as sustenance.

"The perfect measure of the Son of God, this it is the work of that Wisdom to make plain which has been hidden in a mystery ; and it also may show to our thought how the laws about meats are symbols of those things which will there nourish and strengthen our soul."— ORIGEN, *Comm. on John,* Bk. X. § 13.

See ASHEMOGHA, BHIMA, EATING, FOOD, FRUIT-TREE, MOUTH (opening).

MEAT, HOLY :—

A symbol of intellectual food. Science and philosophy for the development of the mental faculties, and the acquirement of truth.

"The man who fills himself with meat is filled with the good spirit."—*Vendidad,* IV.

The mind (man) that assimilates knowledge is filled with that which is necessary for its growth.

See ASHEMOGHA, EATING, MAN, MORTAR, WOOD (holy).

MEAT AND DRINK :—

Symbolic of the externalities to which men attach importance while they do not look to God only for the eternal Truth.

"For the kingdom of God is not meat and drink ; but righteousness, and peace, and joy in the Holy Ghost."—ROM. xiv. 17.

For the higher consciousness is not to be found in attachment to objects of sense, but in the transmuted higher emotions on the plane of Buddhi (Holy Ghost).

See EATING, KINGDOM OF HEAVEN.

MEDEA :—

A symbol of the intuition aspect of the mind, merging into Wisdom ; that is, buddhi-manas rising into buddhi.

"Jason was in perplexity about the accomplishment of these hard tasks, when Medea, the daughter of the king Æetes, who had conceived a sudden affection for him, proffered her aid in securing the Golden Fleece, if he would swear to marry her and take her with him to Greece."—*Argonautic Expedition.*

The indwelling Self (Jason), working upon the plane of the mind, is sore perplexed about accomplishing the soul-development required : but the intuition aspect (Medea) comes to its aid, and, as it were, promises help, providing that Wisdom (Medea) and Love (Jason) be thereby united in the higher mind, and the dual aspects of the Self become as one, " in Greece," which here signifies the sublimated astral instinct raised through the mind to the buddhic plane.

See ABSYRTUS, ÆETES, BUDDHI, CRETE, DRUGS, GOLDEN FLEECE, ICHOR, INTUITION, JASON, SALVE, WISDOM.

MEDIATOR CHRIST :—

A symbol of the Archetypal Man, who mediates between the Divine and the human ; that is, who is a means whereby the Higher nature makes perfect the lower nature and raises it to union with itself.

"The blood of Christ . . . cleanse your conscience from dead works to serve the living God. And for this cause he is the mediator of a new covenant, that a death having taken place for the redemption of the transgressions that were under the first covenant, they that have been called may receive the promise of the eternal inheritance."—HEB. ix. 14, 15.

The Divine Life, through the death of the Archetypal Man in a past state of being, rises to activity in the present order in human souls to perfect their inner natures and purify them from all illusions, so that they may conform to the highest Ideal. To bring about this result, the indwelling Self becomes the intermediary of a new realisation of the Divine nature. For, having died out of one state to be born in another, the Self is able to raise the soul from its subjection to desire and sense under the old dispensation of nature and the moral law. The birth of the Self in the souls which are ready brings with it the new dispensation of Love, which frees the soul from its bondage to the lower and raises the consciousness to the higher planes.

"For there is one God, one mediator also between God and men, himself man, Christ Jesus, who gave himself a ransom for all."—1 TIM. ii. 5.

Between the Divine Unity and the many egos incarnated, there is an incarnate means whereby the egos are to be made perfect. The Archetypal Man, by his death in the epoch of Involution, becomes in Evolution the potential Life Divine which gradually actualises in humanity, and in so doing, fills up the gap in men's souls between imperfection and perfection.

"What you call evil is nothing but imperfection."—G. B. SHAW, *Modern Religion*, p. 10.

"The higher man is the mediator between God and the lower man: only through man can man receive development."—F. W. ROBERTSON, *Sermons, 2nd Series*, p. 184.

"There is a celebrated saying in *T. B. Yoma*, 39a, which, somewhat enigmatically, seems to sum up the situation thus : ' If man sanctifies himself a little, God sanctifies him much ; if man sanctifies himself here below, God sanctifies him above.' Man carries a share of Divinity within him, but in order to realise that Divinity he must put forward his own effort. And every such effort avails. God does His part, provided man does his. The fact of God's Immanence in man raises him to ever higher stages of sanctity. . . . In the Rabbinic theology everyone is a potential possesor of just that quality which marked out the prophet, viz. the Holy Spirit. We can all raise ourselves to that highest of pinnacles where we approach as near to the pattern of the Divine as our limited mortality will permit."—J. ABELSON, *The Immanence of God*, p. 295.

See ARC. MAN, ATONEMENT, BIRTH OF JESUS, BLOOD OF LAMB, CHRIST, COVENANT, DISPENSATIONS, EVOLUTION, HIGHER AND LOWER NATURES, INVOLUTION, MESSIAH, PROPHET, RANSOM, REDEMPTION, RESURRECTION, SALVATION, UNION.

MEDICINE :—

A symbol of the means whereby the Divine nature delivers or heals the soul whose deliverance is to be achieved through the Soul itself, for it is to be its own deliverer.

"Whatever man shall flatter Homa as a young son, Homa comes to the aid of him and his children, to be their medicine. Homa ! give me some of the healing powers whereby thou art a physician."—*Homa Yasht*, HAUG, *Es*.

The Divine Life is first viewed in a false light and manner,—hence true praise is impossible. But even amid the delusions and mistakes of the lower mind, the groping of the youngest Son of God is assisted from above,— first of all the Divine influx seeming

as a medicine, unpalatable and unpleasant, nevertheless proving beneficial. The prayer of the wise soul takes the form of supplicating the Divine Love to use it as it will, and so to strengthen and maintain it that it may become a worthy and dutiful vehicle of the Divine Life.

"The mystery of healing, as we are constituted, stands in close affinity with God and the faith of his supernatural operation. Thus it was that the priests, both of the Egyptians and the Greeks, were their physicians. Æsculapius, too, the god of medicine, had his own altars and priests. At a later period, the Essenes and the Christian monks had their pious explorations of diseases and the sacred powers of remedies ; reducing medicine itself to a function of religion. Later still, Paracelsus himself began the restoration of medicine, as a kind of chemical theosophy. And as Christianity itself classes healings among the spiritual gifts, and calls the elders of the Church to pray for the sick ; so we find that some of our (American) Indian tribes have traditions of one whom, as related to the Great Spirit, they call the Uncle, and who came into the world by a mysterious advent, long ages ago, and instituted the ' Grand Medicine,' which is in fact, their religion."—H. BUSHNELL, *Nature and the Supernatural*, p. 158.

See ALCHEMY, GIFTS OF GOD, GRACE, HEALING, HOMA, IMHOTEP, MAN, PHYSICIAN, RUDRA, SERPENT ÆSCULAPIUS, SONS OF GOD, VALMIKI.

MEDUSA, THE GORGON :—

A symbol of the emotion-nature, first directing its activities to the higher, and afterwards to the lower. Or it may be taken as the general direction of the soul's activities, at first good and then evil.

"Medusa is that system which— originally pure and beautiful, the Church of God and guardian of the Mysteries— has through corruption and idolatry become ' the hold of every unclean thing,' and mother of a monstrous brood. And, moreover, like the once lovely face of Medusa, the Doctrine which bore originally the divine impress and reflected the Celestial Wisdom Herself (Athena) has—through the fall of the Church— become converted into Dogma so pernicious and so deadly as to blight and destroy the reason of all who come under its control. And the Perseus of the myth is the true Humanity . . . which is gone forth to smite and destroy the corrupt Church and deliver the world from its blighting influence."—*The Perfect Way*, p. 64.

The symbol " Church " may here be

taken as meaning the religious soul-state of a particular stage in evolution.

See CHURCH, COMB, EVIL, PERSEUS, SOPHIA ACHAMOTH (lower).

MEH, THE WATER OF :—

A symbol of the "river of Life," or Truth and Life on the higher planes.

See RIVER OF LIFE.

MEHUJAEL AND METHUSHAEL :—

Symbols of the states, or qualities, of courage and endurance.

See IRAD, PATRIARCHS.

MELANTIAN NECKS, ROCKS :—

A symbol of the sense of truth and duty.

See ANAPHE.

MELCARTHUS, KING :—

A symbol of the ego as governor of the astral plane activities.

See ASTARTE, FIRE OF HELL.

MELCHIZEDEK :—

A symbol of the Higher Self.

"Melchizedek, King of righteousness, and then also King of Salem, which is King of peace; without father, without mother, without genealogy, having neither beginning of days nor end of life, but made like unto the Son of God, abideth a priest continually."—HEB. vii. 2, 3.

A type of the Christ, who is the centre and pivot from which all manifestation proceeds. His kingdom is the abode of bliss (Salem) and peace, upon the higher planes. He is all Truth and Righteousness; second to none,—the first and the last,—the one emanation from the Absolute.

"Christ Himself is the Warrior King, the captain of the Lord's host, the true Joshua, whose last word ere His cross was a shout of victory, 'I have overcome the world.' He makes us His soldiers and strengthens us for the war, if we live by faith in Him. He Himself is the Priest —the only eternal Priest of the world,— who wears on His head the mitre and the diadem, and bears in His hand the sceptre and the censer; and He makes us priests, if faith in His only sacrifice and all prevalent intercession be in our souls. He is the dew unto Israel—and only by intercourse with Him shall we be made gentle and refreshing, silent blessings to all the weary and the parched souls in the wilderness of the world."—A. MACLAREN, *Sermons*, 3rd *Series*, pp. 358-9.

"And Melchizedek King of Salem brought forth bread and wine: and he was priest of God Most High."—GEN. xiv. 18.

Then cometh forth in the soul the love nature from the higher planes—Jerusalem, the city of the Great King. "Bread and wine" symbolise spiritual goodness and truth. The higher love-nature is the beloved of the Lord, the direct offshoot of the Divine nature, and this blesses the endeavours of the struggling soul.

See BREAD, HIGH-PRIEST, JERUSALEM, KING (great), KINGDOM OF HEAVEN, LOVE OF GOD, ROCK, SACRIFICER, SON OF GOD, SPENDYAD, TOKENS, VISVAKARMAN, WINE.

MELODY, MUSIC :—

A symbol of harmonised conditions of soul on the higher planes.

"Be filled with the Spirit; speaking one to another in psalms and hymns and spiritual songs, singing and making melody with your heart to the Lord."—EPH. v. 18, 19.

The qualities are exhorted to purify themselves and be in harmony in their inmost being one with another, and all with the Divine nature within them.

See HARMONY, HEART, HYMN, MUSIC, ORPHEUS, SINGERS, SONG.

MEMBERS OF BODY (DIVINE) :—

A symbol of the more or less disciplined qualities of the soul which have originally proceeded from the segregation (dismemberment) of the qualities of the slain Archetypal Man,—the Prototype of humanity.

"Now ye are the body of Christ, and severally members thereof. And God hath set some in the church, first apostles, secondly prophets, thirdly, teachers, then miracles, then gifts of healings, helps, governments, divers kinds of tongues." —1 COR. xii. 27, 28.

It is pointed out that as the qualities have proceeded from the perfect Archetype (Christ), they are partial expressions of the archetypal on their way to completion. The Supreme Law has set the highest active qualities in the innermost shrine (church) of the soul. First, the highly developed qualities (apostles) which are in harmony with the central Ideal. Second, the dawnings of the higher spiritual consciousness (prophets). Third, mental faculties, which draw down truth from above (teachers). Then psychic and spiritual powers (miracles). Then spiritual processes of purification (healing); thoughts of love and truth (helps); high principles of action (governments); the inner expressions of Wisdom and Love (tongues).

"Christ's death is the witness to His people, that since they are His members, they must also be crucified with Him."—A. JUKES, *The Law of the Offerings*, p. 198.

"What we are witnessing in the slow and toilsome evolution of mankind from brute-consciousness to God-consciousness is simply the emergence of Christ in the Race. When the sublime process is complete we shall be one in him to all eternity."—R. J. CAMPBELL, Serm., *The Faith that Saves*.

"The later Manichæans of the West designated the portions of Light scattered in the world—in elements and organisms—and waiting for redemption, 'Jesus patibilis' (i.e. Jesus who suffered and died)."—HARNACK, *Hist. of Dogma*, Vol.II. p. 325.

"Rā the creator of the names of his members which turned into the gods who are in the following of Rā."—*Papyrus of Hunefer*, Ch. XVII.

"There is no member of my body which is not the member of some god. The god Thoth shieldeth my body altogether, and I am Rā day by day. . . . There shall none do me hurt, neither men, nor gods, nor the sainted dead, nor those who have perished. I am he who cometh forth advancing, whose name is unknown."—BUDGE, *Book of the Dead*, Ch. XLIII.

"Afu-Rā addresseth words to the gods, who are (in the first division of the Tuat) saying, 'Give ye light unto me, and make ye yourselves guides to me, O ye who came into being from my members, my word hath gone forth to you. Ye are made of my bodies, I have made you, having fashioned you of my soul.'"—BUDGE, *Egypt. Heaven and Hell*, Vol. I. p. 18.

The Logos (Rā) differentiates the qualities which proceed from him, and are transmuted into the Ideals (gods) which approach unto him. The higher mind (Thoth) gathers into the causal-body the higher qualities, incarnation after incarnation, freed from all taint of the lower nature. The indwelling Self shall be unaffected by all externalities of mind, emotion, formation, or tradition. The Self emerges in the qualities, and "cometh not with observation," for the differentiation (name) of Spirit is unknown of the lower consciousness.

The incarnate God (Afu-Rā), or Archetypal Man, emanates the higher qualities (gods) on the buddhic plane that they may enlighten and prepare the way for his birth within the soul. For, verily, the higher qualities have come into being through the involution of the Spirit, and are now energised and evolved. The qualities are of the Divine Life on the higher planes; they are manifestations outwardly of the indwelling Self.

"Because men were generated from the Titans, who had been nourished with the body of Dionysus, he (Orpheus) therefore, calls them Dionysiacal, as though some of their members were from the Titans (and came from Dionysus), so that the human body is partly of a Dionysiacal and partly of a mundane nature" (Ficinus, L. IX. *Enn.* i. 83, 89). "For the smoke from the ashes of the Titans 'became matter,' we are told."—G. R. S. MEAD, *Orpheus*, p. 182.

Human beings (men) possess within themselves the primal constituent qualities and elements of manifestation (the Titans), which had been rendered actual through the change to heterogeneity of the Archetypal Man. So that human nature is partly spiritual and partly natural of the lower planes: for it has the qualities (members) of the Divine nature (Dionysus), and the qualities of the lower nature (matter).

"The Manicheans could employ the pagan fables as a drapery for their ideas. Thus the boy Dionysus torn in pieces by the Titans, according to the mysteries of Bacchus, was considered by them nothing else than the soul swallowed up by the powers of darkness, the divine life rent into fragments by matter."—NEANDER, *Church History*, Vol. II. p. 215.

"Pragâpati transforms himself, his body and his limbs, into the different parts of the universe. Therefore in creating he is swallowed up, he falls to pieces, and is restored by the performance of some rite which is in this way recommended."—P. DEUSSEN, *Outlines of Indian Philos.*, p. 18.

The Logos, in manifesting, becomes the archetype of all things, and when perfected passes into another state, which requires the distribution of all qualities (limbs) to be restored again to unity in the souls of humanity.

"Speech of Qebhsennuf:—'I am thy son (O Osiris), I have come that I might be among those who protect thee. I gather together for thee thy bones, and I piece together for thee thy limbs. I bring unto thee thy heart, and I set it upon its

seat in thy body. I make to flourish
(or germinate) for thee thy house after
thee, O thou who livest for ever'"
(Sarc. of Seti I).—BUDGE, *Egypt. Heaven
and Hell*, Vol. II. p. 52.

The Higher Self, on the buddhic
plane, undertakes to raise the qualities
(limbs) and re-form Divinity in
humanity. The causal-body (heart)
is established potentially in the higher
mind. It is gradually evolved and
perfected so as to be a vehicle (house)
of the eternal Spirit in the immortal
soul.

See AFU-RĀ, ALTAR (fire), APOSTLES,
ARC. MAN, BONES, CHURCH, CRUCI-
FIXION (gnostic), DEATH OF OSIRIS,
DIONYSUS, DISMEMBERMENT, DWARF,
GODS, HEALING, HEART, HOUSE,
INCARNATION, INVOLUTION, LIGHT,
LIMBS, MIRACLES, MUMMY, PRAGÂ-
PATI, PROPHET, PURUSHA, QEBH-
SENNUF, QUALITIES, SETTLEMENTS,
SHRINE, TITANS, TONGUE, YMIR,
ZAGREUS.

MEMPHIS :—

A symbol of the Wisdom nature,
or of a centre of energy on the buddhic
plane.

See APIS.

MEN, BAT-WINGED :—

A symbol signifying the aspiring
mind,—the Self active on the buddhic
plane.

MEN, BREAST-EARED :—

A symbol of the emotions on the
mental plane, which constitute the
receptive function which enables evolution to be initiated.

MEN, BREAST-EYED :—

A symbol of the higher emotions
which give rise to ideals ; sight
being comparable to the establishment of mental perception.

See EYE, SIGHT.

MEN OF THE FOREST WITH TAILS, AND WHO HAVE HAIR ON THE BODY :—

A symbol representing the atmic
aspects of mental qualities. The
aspects are compared to " hairy
beings " because hair is a symbol
of faith in the Divine.

See FOREST, HAIR, MUSCULAR.

MEN, ONE-EYED ; CYCLOPES :—

A symbol of the intuitive mind,
buddhi-manas, perceptive of spiritual
truths.

See CYCLOPES, EYE.

MEN, HUNDRED-HANDED,—THE CENTIMANI :—

A symbol of mental faculties,
numerous and powerful in activity.

See BRIAREUS.

MEN, ONE-LEGGED :—

A symbol of the higher mind which
co-ordinates ideas, and enables the
Self to stand alone.

MEN, OXEN- OR COW-HEADED :—

Symbolic of mental qualities
directed by the higher will ; or the
mind dominated by buddhi (cow).

See COW, HEAD, OX.

MENAT SIGN OR AMULET :—

A symbol of the higher qualities
as celestial food. The " fruit of the
Spirit " hanging downwards for the
nourishment of the soul.

" Usually the menat is held in the hand,
but it is often worn on the neck. Its
object was to bring joy and health to
the wearer ; and it was believed to
possess magical properties ; it represented
nutrition."—BUDGE, *Egyptian Magic*,
p. 60.

See FRUIT OF SPIRIT, NECK.

MENDES, BUSIRIS, OR TATTU :—

A symbol of a centre of activity on
the lower planes.

See CITY, TATTU.

MENDICANT, RELIGIOUS :—

A symbol of a mental quality which
lives by love (alms) received from
other qualities.

" A man is not a mendicant (Bhikshu)
simply because he asks others for alms;
he who adopts the whole law is a Bhikshu,
not he who only begs. He who is above
good and evil, who is chaste, who with
knowledge passes through the world,
he indeed is called a Bhikshu."—*Dhammapada*, XIX. 266–7.

A mental quality to live by love
must have fulfilled the law of righteousness and be above the opposites. It
must be pure and wise as it passes
through the soul.

See ALMSGIVING, BHIKSHU, MONK,
SANNYASIN.

MENELAUS, SON OF ATREUS :—

A symbol of strength on the astral plane, a product of illusion of separateness (Atreus).

See ATREUS, MARS.

MENIS ; WRATH OF ACHILLES :—

A symbol of the strife within the soul,—the passionate self-will, or self-seeking of the lower nature, which in all religions is said to be opposed to the law of God. Yet the strife is necessary to the Divine purpose.

" Sing, Goddess, the wrath, the ruinous wrath of Achilles, son of Peleus, which brought countless woes upon the Greeks."
—*Iliad*, opening lines.

Utter thy voice, O Wisdom, in the inborn strife of relativity and imperfection ! Proclaim the fierce outgoing energy of nature constituting the lower Self (Achilles), which is begotten of the Higher Self (Peleus) ! For the lower Self brings sorrow and countless sufferings into the separate minds (Greeks).

" The Christ of God hath many names in Scripture ; but they all mean only this, that he is, and alone can be, the Light and Life and holiness of every creature that is holy, whether in heaven or on earth. Wherever Christ is not, there is the Wrath of Nature, or nature left to itself and its own tormenting strength of life, to feel nothing in itself but the vain, restless contrariety *of its own* working properties. This is the one only origin of hell and every kind of curse and misery in the creature."— W. LAW, *Law's Memorial*, p. 65.

" By the word ' earth ' is understood the wrath in the Essence."—BOEHME, *Mysterium Magnum*, p. 42.

" We must know that war is universal and strife right, and that by strife all things arise and are used " (*Heraclitus*).— ORIGEN, *cont. Celsus*, VI. 42.

" Man will not always be warring against man, either in the battlefield or the counting-house. As Professor Huxley said in his Romanes lecture, the law of the survival of the fittest is giving way before the higher impulse of fitting as many as possible to survive. But we shall not have done with the struggle when war in all its modes has been left behind ; we shall still have to fight, but the fighting will be on a higher plane. For the individual it is on a higher plane even now. It is the struggle to conform the soul to Christ, to respond to the call of his spirit, to bring every faculty of our being into captivity to his love. We do not kill men in this fight ; we do our best to save them. It is against ourselves that we strive, ourselves that we have to overcome in order to share the glory of the Lord. If there were no struggle, if we had nothing to fight, there would be no growth, we should be beating the air. It is a curious thing, but true, that all advance, in whatever field, material or spiritual, is due to opposition."—R. J. CAMPBELL, Serm., *Warfare of Life*.

See ACHILLES, BATTLE, CONFLICT, CONQUEROR, EARTH, GREEKS, JOB, MAN (natural), OPPOSITES, PEACE AND SWORD, PERSONALITY, STORM, STRIFE, SWORD, TAWHIRI-MATEA, VICTORY, WAR, WARRIORS, WRATH.

MENTAL-PLANE :—

This central plane of Divine manifestation is the third plane from above or from below. It is the plane of creation of the forms on the lower planes. The prototypal ideas emanating from the planes above take form in mental matter on the mental plane, and are from thence projected outwardly on to the astral and physical planes ; in other words, the mental forms are re-embodied on the lower planes in the matter of the planes, thus constituting the material universe. But from the fact of the interplay and conflict of the forces on the lower planes, the ideas often become obstructed and distorted in their course outwards, so that the result on the physical plane is anything but perfect. This applies to animal, vegetal, and crystal forms, which are growths from within outwards, but not, of course, to accidental and constructed formations, which are the result of fracture and movement from place to place. The mental plane, like other planes, is atomic in its structure, transmitting vibrations which are far more subtle and rapid than those occurring on lower planes. The extension of the mental plane through space is proved by the facts of telepathy. It is also proved by the spatial images in our own minds. If we imagine a triangular-shaped object, we perceive its dimensions in space on the mental plane. We are almost constantly creating thought-forms which last for a time and then dissipate. Spirit, thought, emotion, desire, force cannot manifest without the matter of the planes of being. A philosophy which overlooks the primal duality of Spirit and Matter is lost in vagueness and delusion.

See AIR, ELEMENTS, FIRMAMENT, MAISHAN, MAHAT, MONAD (life, form), PROTOTYPES, WORLDS (five).

MENTAL SHEATH, OR BODY, OF THE HUMAN BEING :—

This is the instrument of the spiritual ego on the lower mental plane. It is formed of mental matter as a vehicle of thought and will. Thought is expressed in forms of thought, and the limitations and images in the mind are constructed of mind-stuff or mental-matter within the mental body. Thought restricted to a particular ego, as is the case with mankind, is necessarily limited by the forms of matter obtainable in the stage of development at which the ego has arrived.

" Perception contains all the elements of ' thought,'—of imagination, conception, reasoning. Remembered images or ideas, and new percepts, which will reinforce or alter the old images or add new ones, ' constitute the materials of all intellectual operations ; memory reasoning, imagination, are acts which consist in ultimate analysis, of grouping, and co-ordinating images, in apprehending the relations already formed between them, and in reuniting them into new relations ' (Binet). When general and abstract terms are brought to the assistance of the mind, thought is still imagination, with names instead of images ; yet even then the mind employs memory—images, which are images of those names."— A. E. CRAWLEY, *The Idea of the Soul*, p. 64.

We only get our conceptions of space and matter from images in our minds, which images must be material or they could not give us the conceptions we have of them. Forms take up space and possess qualities and these are all mental to our consciousness, which is in the mind and not on lower planes. The human soul must have a mental material body on the mental plane in order to put it in relation with images and ideas of mental matter which are the "materials of all intellectual operations." The mental body must also have an organised structure to render it capable of performing its functions in relation to the astral and physical bodies, which are also highly organised mechanisms to serve the requirements of the ego.

See CASTES, CHILDREN OF HORUS, CLASSES, INTELLECT, MAISHAN, MANAS, MARRIAGE (castes), PETER, QUATERNARY, RUAH, SHEATHS, VEHICLES, VESTURES.

MERCABA :—

A symbol of the soul.

" The old Jewish proverb,—' Four are the highest in the world—the lion among wild beasts, the ox among tame cattle, the eagle among birds, man among all (creatures) ; but God is supreme over all.' "—P. FAIRBAIRN, *Typology of Scripture*, Vol. I. p. 262.

See FIRMAMENT, MA-A'SEH.

MERCHANTS OF THE EAST :—

A symbol of the manasic intelligences which transmute the sensations and feelings into ideas and emotions.

See EAST, HERMES, MAISHAN.

MERCHANDISE, TRUE :—

A symbol of transmuted desires and lower emotions raised to aspirations and higher emotions, as " fruit of the Spirit " on higher planes.

" Abandon falsehood, pursue truth, and thou shalt obtain the fruit thy heart desireth. Few are they who traffic in true merchandise ; they who do so obtain profit. Depart with the merchandise of God's name, and thou shalt easily obtain a sight of God's court " (*Guru Nanak*).—MACAULIFFE, *The Sikh Religion*, Vol. I. p. 364.

" By the Guru's wisdom they obtain the true merchandise. He who possesseth the wealth of the true merchandise is enraptured with the true Word."—*Ibid.*, p. 365.

See FRUIT OF THE SPIRIT, MAISHAN, REAPING, TREASURE, VAISYA, WEALTH.

MERCURY, THE PLANET, VANANT :—

Signifies the function of vital activity, growth, and expansion in the forms of nature, and that which gives impetus and momentum.

See PLANETS.

MERODACH OR MARDUK :—

A symbol of the Higher Self,— the Hero who personified the triumph over the lower nature, i.e. the "world, the flesh, and the devil." He was not so much Son of Man, as " Lord of all that exists," and so did not personify the Soul which has to be purified and tried in the fires.

" Merodach, king of heaven and earth, the merciful one, who loves to raise the dead to life " (" Hymn to Merodach "). —SAYCE, *Hib. Lect.*, p. 99.

The Higher Self, lord of the higher and lower planes, by his Divine love raises the mortal to immortality.

' Merodach has been identified with Asari the son of Ea of Eridu. . . . Asari and Osiris were evidently the same. The character and attributes of both were the same. Osiris was Un-nefer, ' the good being,' whose life was spent in benefitting and civilising mankind , Asari also was ' the prince who does good to men.' . . . That Asari was a sun-god follows from his identification with Merodach. . . . Merodach was the divine man, freed from the limitations of our mortal existence, and therefore able not only to rule over the other gods, but also, like the magician, to make their natures his own."—SAYCE, *Rel. of Anc. Egypt. and Babyl.*, pp. 325, 327, 334.

Merodach, Asari, and Osiris are all symbols of the Higher Self regnant upon the higher planes of manifestation. They are sun-gods representing the one God on the plane of atma. Merodach signifies the Divine Man, God incarnate, who has risen in triumph from the lower planes, and has assumed the higher qualities (gods) and united them with himself.

See ARC. MAN, ARURU, CIVILISING, DEAD, EA, ERIDU, ESTHER, INCARNA-TION, ISTAR, OSIRIS, RESURRECTION, SELF, SOUL (highest), UNION.

MERT, CITY OR GOD OF :—

A symbol of the astral or desire plane, which corresponds to the level from which evolution of form proceeds.

MERTET SEA :—

A symbol of a sub-plane of the astral plane.

MERU, MOUNT :—

See AMARAVATI, MOUNTAIN, YATIS.

MESCH, OR MESCHGAH, THE PLANET VENUS :—

A symbol of astral love which, being a quality of attraction related with the buddhic, urges the life of nature to pour itself forth in the forms which are prepared and await its reception.

See APHRODITE, PLANETS, VENUS.

MESCHIA :—

See MATRO.

MESKHENET, GODDESS OF THE FUNERAL CHAMBER, AND RENENET, GODDESS OF NURSING :—

These figures symbolise nature in its dual aspect of sustainer and destroyer of forms.

See JUDGMENT HALL, RENENET, SIVA.

MESSENGER OF THE DIVINE :—

A symbol of an outpouring of the Spirit according to cyclic law.

" Behold I send my messenger, and he shall prepare the way before me : and the Lord whom ye seek, shall suddenly come to his temple ; and the messenger of the covenant whom ye delight in, behold he cometh, saith the Lord."—MAL. iii. 1.

This is the assurance of the gift of the Spirit, which independent of the limitations of time and space " cometh without observation." The temple is the " temple not made with hands, eternal in the heavens " ; and into that " temple " or causal-body,—so soon as the Lord's " willing servants," or lower functionings of the conscious-ness in the virtues, are ready to receive him,—will come the Sun of Righteous-ness, the Higher Self or Higher con-sciousness, who will for ever make his abode among the chosen of the Lord ; i.e. among the transmuted qualities.

" God dwells in the highest part of the soul. He who ascends this height has all things under his feet. We are united to God when, in the practice of the virtues, we deny and forsake our-selves, loving and following God above all creatures" (Ruysbroek).—VAUGHAN. *Hours, etc.,* Vol. I. p. 328.

See ABODE, AMSHASPANDS, ANGELS, ARCHANGELS, CAUSAL-BODY, CON-SCIOUSNESS, DEVAS, HEIGHTS, SELF, SERVANTS, TEMPLE, TIME.

MESSIAH :—

A symbol of the incoming Truth and Love,—the Higher Self born in the soul.

" Andrew findeth first his own brother Simon and saith unto him, We have found the Messiah (which is, being interpreted, Christ)."—JOHN i. 41.

The astro-mental nature was enabled to modify the closely allied physical brain and make it a better mental instrument for the needs of the Christ, who had now appeared within the soul.

"Andrew stays with the Lord 'at the tenth hour' and finds the Son of God the Word and Wisdom, and is ruled by him as king. That is why he says, 'We have found the Messiah,' and this is a thing which every one can say who has found this Word of God and is ruled, as by a king, by his Divinity. As a fruit he at once brings his brother to Christ, and Christ deigned to look upon Simon, that is to say, by looking at him to visit and enlighten his ruling principle ; and Simon, by Jesus looking at him, was enabled to grow strong, so as to earn a new name for that work of firmness and strength, and to be called Peter."—ORIGEN, *Comm. on John*, Bk. III. § 29.

"The coming of the Messiah is Divine knowledge gained by experience through the power of the Breath of Life inbreathed, that is the Mediator between God and man. . . . But of the Breath of Life, in union with the human essence, Messiah was to be made, by the mind going through a fiery *purgation*, in which it leaves the dross behind, namely, the old evil nature. The Living Breath uniting with the upright and purified mind of the creature, and the human spirit of the man with it ; thus Messiah is made, born, and comes forth. Charity bears him into the 'world' for this principle (charity) is the 'Virgin Mary.'"—JOHN WARD, *Zion's Works*, Vol. III. pp. 200, 202.

"According to the *Midrash Talpigoth*, the Messiah will bring eternal peace. . . It is said in the Zohar that, according to tradition, wherever Solomon is mentioned in the Song of Solomon this King of Peace is designated." "This is the Spirit of the Messiah, as it is written : 'Renew a right spirit within me.' (Ps. li. 12)."—A. E. WAITE, *Secret Doctrine in Israel*, pp. 143, 147.

See ANDREW, BREATH (divine), CHRIST'S SECOND COMING, MEDIATOR, SELF, PETER.

METALS :—

Symbols of higher and lower qualities ; as gold, wisdom ; silver, higher mental ; iron, lower mental ; brass, or bronze, mental.

"The metals all figure truths ; gold and silver, those which are more precious and spiritual ; brass and iron, those of an inferior class connected with the outward world."—A. JUKES, *Types of Genesis*, p. 91.

A certain Chinese written symbol "is expressive not only of refining metals in the furnace, but of man undergoing a trial for the purpose of proving and bene-fitting him."—KIDD, *China*, p. 45.

See BLACKSMITHS, BRASS, GOLD, GOLDEN AGE, IRON, RACES, SERPENT (brazen), SILVER, TUBAL CAIN.

METAL STATUES OF HORUS :—

A symbol of completion of the qualities of the soul, and their mergence in the Divine.

"And from that day there have been metal statues of Horbehûdti."—*Legend of the Winged Sun-disk.*

And from that period it was possible to define the fullness of stature of the Manifested God.

See IMAGE.

METEMPSYCHOSIS, OR THE TRANSMIGRATION OF SOULS THROUGH ANIMAL AND HU-MAN BODIES :—

A symbol of the passing of the ego during successive incarnations into human bodies, astral and physical, full of animal propensities denoted by names of animals of various kinds.

"But know this threefold course of transmigrations that depends on the three qualities . . . according to the particular nature of the acts and of the knowledge of each man. Immovable beings, insects, both small and great, fishes, snakes and tortoises, cattle and wild animals, are the lowest conditions to which the quality of *tamas* (darkness) leads."—*Laws of Manu*, XII. 41, 42.

The three states or conditions of the soul lead to corresponding condi-tions of mind and desire in the succesive reincarnations of the ego (man). Bad habits, primitive desires, delusions, gross desires, low appetites, sub-servience, ungoverned passions, etc. are the bodily conditions which ignorance (tamas) and sluggishness of mind and emotion lead the ego into.

"And the soul's vice is ignorance. For that the soul who hath no knowledge of the things that are, or knowledge of their nature, or of Good, is blinded by the body's passions and tossed about. This wretched soul, not knowing what she is, becomes the slave of bodies of strange form in sorry plight, bearing the body as a load ; not as the ruler, but the ruled" (*Corp. Herm., The Key*).—G. R. S. MEAD, *T. G. Hermes*, Vol. II. p. 145.

"The impious soul remains in its own essence, chastised by its own self, and seeking for an earthly body where to enter if only it be human. For that no other body can contain a human soul ; nor is it right that any human soul should fall into the body of a thing that doth possess no reason" (*The Key*).—*Ibid.*, p. 153.

See ANIMALS, BEASTS, CREATURES, CREEPING THINGS, FRAVASHIS, IN-CARNATION OF SOULS, MAN BORN AS ANIMAL, PITRIS (lunar), PITRIYANA,

RE-INCARNATION, SACRIFICE, SKINS, TORTOISE, TRANSMUTATION.

METIS :—

A symbol of the Divine Wisdom.

" And the names of it (Ætherial Light) Orpheus heard in prophetic vision, and declares them to be Metis, Phanes, and Ericapæus, which by intepretation are Will, Light, and Light-giver (or Consciousness, Light, and Life) ; adding that these three divine powers of names are the one power and one might of the One God."— G. R. S. MEAD, *Orpheus*, p. 164.

The three aspects of the Divine emanation are Will (Phanes), Wisdom (Metis), and Action (Ericapæus). These proceed forth at manifestation as three potencies of the one Higher Self. " Phanes " is expressed in Will, Love, and Consciousness on the plane of atma ; " Metis " in Wisdom, Light, and Intellect on the buddhic and mental planes ; while " Ericapæus " signifies the Divine Life active throughout all the planes of the Cosmos and Soul.

See ADITI, BUDDHIC PLANE, COSMOS, CREATION, EGG, ERICAPÆUS, LIGHT, NOAH'S SONS, ORPHEUS, PHANES, SELF, TRIAD.

METZTLI, MOON-GODDESS :—

A symbol of the buddhic principle, and also the buddhic reflected in the astral.

" The moon-goddess of the Astecs or ancient Mexicans. Her myth relates that in the absence of a luminary of day all humanity was plunged into darkness, which a human sacrifice alone could relieve. Metztli thereupon brought to the sacrifice Nanahuatl the Leprous, and cast him into a huge pyre which stood ready for the victim. She herself followed him into the furnace, and on her disappearance the sun rose."—*Non-classical Mythology*, p. 117.

This is a concise account of the process of the soul's salvation. The Higher Self (sun) is obscured to our consciousness, and only by the sacrifice of the " natural man " will it be possible for the Self to shine in the soul. Therefore it is provided that through the functioning of the buddhic principle (Metztli) the corrupt lower self or personality (the Leper) is put through the experiences of life and gradually purified through suffering until it is perfected. The last sentence

refers to the final consummation, when the buddhic is withdrawn and the Highest (atma) alone remains.

See ARMATERASU, BUDDHI, MAN (natural), MOON (higher).

MICHAEL, THE ARCHANGEL :—

A symbol of the Self under the aspect of Deliverer of the soul from captivity to the lower nature. The Self as victor over the lower principle.

" *Nephesh* is presumably of the earth, earthy, for it is said to remain in the tomb ; *Rua'h* enters the Earthly Paradise, where the High Priest Michael offers it as a holocaust to the Holy One and it remains in the joy of Paradise ; *Neshamah* ascends on high. It returns to the Tree of Life, because it came therefrom." A. E. WAITE, *Secret Doctrine in Israel*, p. 160.

The body of desire (Nephesh) is of the lower nature (earth) and disintegrates there (tomb). The mind (Rua'h) is delivered by the Self from captivity, and its lower part is purified and raised to union with the Holy Spirit (buddhi). The Divine monad (Neshamah) is now supreme in the soul, and is of the Divine life (tree). This does not refer to *post-mortem* states, but to the union of the soul with God.

See ARCHANGEL, BONDAGE, CAPTIVITY, EARTH, HOLY GHOST. MELCHIZEDEK, MONAD OF LIFE, NEPHESH, NESHAMAH, PARADISE, RUA'H, SELF, TOMB. TREE OF LIFE, VICTORY.

MICROCOSM :—

A symbol of the little world of the human soul, which contains all the elements, qualities and potencies of the great world of the universe (Macrocosm).

" It is in man, the microcosm, in whom all the universe meets, that the Divine ideas chiefly unfold themselves, and that in proportion as his receiving surface is purified and expanded."—J. BRIERLEY, *The Eternal Religion*, p. 239.

" Man is the Microcosm epitomising in himself the whole universe."—GIBB, *Hist. of Ottoman Poetry*, Vol. I. p. 56.

" The human soul stands in the centre of the All ; and just as the World is a huge Man, man is a little world " (Basra teaching).—DE BOER, *Hist. of Philos. in Islam*, p. 92.

" These four Worlds form together an unit, a single great Man, the Macrocosm or Adam Illa-ah." " The Qabbalah in presenting the earthly man as the Microcosm or inferior copy of the prototypic Heavenly Adam, asserts the existence of four divisions or worlds, which are to be found in a greater or less degree in each."—MYER, *Qabbalah*, pp. 198, 331.

The " four worlds " are the buddhic, mental, astral, and physical planes. These constitute the World-Soul, as they do also the human soul.

" Ye therefore shall be perfect, as your heavenly Father is perfect."—MAT. v. 48.

The microcosm is only partially evolved, and therefore imperfect. When it is fully evolved, it will be as perfect as the Macrocosm on the higher planes.

" As God contains all things in Himself, so it is in our soul ; the soul is the microcosmos in which all things are contained and are led back to God " (Eckhart).— PFLEIDERER, *Develop. of Christianity*, p. 152.

" Erigena's *mysticism* appears especially in his root conception of man's soul. There is an *ultimate ground of truth* in the depth of personal consciousness. Man is an epitome of the universe, a meeting-place of the above and the below, a point of union for the heavenly and the sensuous. *We* understand the world only because the forms or patterns of it— the Ideas which it expresses—are in our own minds. So that a mind which wholly fathomed itself would thereby fathom everything, and we can rise to Divine contemplation because God is the ground and reality of our soul's being. —R. M. JONES, *Mystical Religion*, p. 127.

" The loftiest purpose of God, in all His dealings, is to make us like Himself ; and the end of all religion is the complete accomplishment of that purpose. There is no religion without these elements— consciousness of kindred with God, recognition of Him as the sum of all excellence and beauty, and of His will as unconditionally binding upon us, aspiration and effort after a full accord of heart and soul with Him and with His law, and humble confidence that that sovereign beauty will be ours. . . . The full accord of all the soul with His character, in whom, as their native home, dwell ' whatsoever things are pure, whatsoever things are lovely,' and the full glad conformity of the will to His sovereign will, who is the life of our lives—this, and nothing shallower, nothing narrower, is religion in its perfection." —A. MACLAREN, *Sermons, 2nd Series*, pp. 212-3.

" The seed is a means to an end, and the end may as well be the bird or the insect (if eaten) as the plant ; and man *qua* physical may very well come to similar ends. But the image of God in man cannot be simply a means like the seed. It must be an end in itself, the one

true end of the entire cycle."—H. M. GWATKIN, *Knowledge of God*, Vol. I. p. 237.

See AB, ADAM, (higher), ARC. MAN, COSMOS, CREATION, EVOLUTION, HIGHER AND LOWER, IMAGE, MACROCOSM, MEASURE, PROTOTYPES, SELF, SON OF GOD, TREE OF LIFE, WORLDS (five).

MICTLAN :—

A symbol of the lower principle, the desire-mind, or the astral plane of illusion.

" Mictlan was the Mexican Pluto. The name signifies ' Country of the North ' —the region of waste and hunger and death, and was used both of the place and the deity. There, surrounded by fearful demons (Tzitzimitles), he ruled over the shades of the departed much as did Pluto, and possessed several wives. The representations of him give to him a most repulsive aspect, and he is usually depicted in the act of devouring his victims."—L. SPENCE, *Mythologies of Ancient Mexico, etc.*, p. 24.

The astral plane (north) is a region devoid of spiritual food and subject to change and dissolution. On it are the desires (demons) and instincts attached to the personalities. The desire-mind (Mictlan) is allied with the lower emotions and passions (wives), and it seeks to engulf and rule the personalities.

See DEMONS, DEVIL, HADES, HELL, MANALA, NORTH, SERPENT.

MIDGARD :—

A symbol of the mind or mental plane.

See YGGDRASIL.

MIDGARD'S SERPENT :—

A symbol of the desire-mind which engirdles the lower nature of the soul.

" He (Thor) goes, the descendant of Odin, to fight the Serpent ; the defender of Midgard strikes him in his anger." —*The Voluspa*.

The higher mind (Thor), energised by the Spirit (Odin), combats the desire-mind, which identifies itself with the objects of sense and is at enmity with the higher nature.

" In the Midgard serpent which girdles the world, we have here another testimony to the Biblical correspondence of the Serpent in the Word, as meaning everywhere the sensual mind,—*sensuale*,— which is the outermost, or encompassing mind, in which the *amour propre* or *proprium* resides. In like manner with this, nearly the whole of the particulars in *Voluspa* are susceptible of a Biblical interpretation."—GARTH WILKINSON, *Revelation and Mythology*, p. 66.

See DEVIL, NIDHOGG, ODIN, SATAN, SERPENT (subtil), THOR.

MIDST, SECOND SPACE IN THE :—

A symbol of the buddhi-manasic plane.

" He is a God who hath found the words of the Mysteries of the second space in the midst."—*Books of the Saviour*.

He has attained Godhood in the germ who has arrived at the stage referred to, which is the higher emotion-mental plane. This illustrates the saying,—" I said, ye are Gods " (Ps. lxxxii. 6 ; JOHN x. 34).

"That is called the midst which is inmost." —SWEDENBORG, *Arc. Cel. to Gen.* iii. 8.

See MYSTERY.

MIDST, WAY OF THE :—

A symbol of the higher sub-planes of the astral.

"Jesus and his disciples soar aloft into the way of the midst, and come to the first order of the Way of the Midst."—*Books of the Saviour, in Pistis Sophia.*

The Christ activity having made the qualities obedient to his word departs from the plane of physical manifestation, and so withdraws to the higher astral.

See DISCIPLES, JESUS OF GOSPELS.

MILK FROM COW :—

A symbol of the higher emotion nature ; that which is yielded by buddhi (cow) ; the product of the Wisdom function.

" And it shall come to pass in that day, that the mountains shall drop down sweet wine, and the hills shall flow with milk, and all the brooks of Judah shall flow with waters ; and a fountain shall come forth of the house of the Lord, and shall water the valley of Shittim."—JOEL iii. 18.

At the end of the cycle all aspirations (mountains, hills) shall be satisfied in the spiritual endowments (wine and milk) that shall come to them. The region of the qualities beloved of God shall be filled with knowledge, and from the soul's innermost shrine shall well up a fountain of truth which shall obliterate the lower nature.

See BUDDHI, COW'S MILK, MAHA-

VIRA-POT, UDDER, VACH, WATER, WEALTH SHOWER, WINE.

MILK AS FOR BABES (LOWER ASPECT) :—

A symbol of experience of the conditions of the lower life, and of the external stimulus to progress.—See HEB. v. 12, 13

See EXPERIENCE.

MILK FROM GOAT :—

A symbol of the lower emotion-nature, that which is yielded by desire (goat) ; the product of the desire-mental function.

"After 30 days they went forth into the wilderness, came to a white-haired goat, and milked the milk from the udder with their mouths. When they had devoured the milk, Mashya said to Mashyoi thus : ' My delight was owing to it when I had not devoured the milk, and my delight is more delightful now when it is devoured by my vile body."—*The Bundahis*, Ch. XV, 10, 11.

After the lunar cycle was passed, the soul struggled up from the astral to the mental plane, and encountered the " goat," or false knowledge and desire, " white " because attractive and alluring. This " drinking of the goat's milk " signifies the partaking of sensuous gratification resulting in the evolution of the desire-mental nature of the human being. When this experience had been undergone, the mental-nature (Mashya) says, as it were ;—My pleasure exists also in anticipation and imagination of enjoyment, and now further delight is experienced in the increased satisfaction which is derived through the evolution of the lower mental vehicle, the vehicle of error and illusion.

(It must be noted that while the lower soul or " lunar pitri " struggles upward as the *personality*, the higher soul or " solar pitri " is coming downward as the *individuality*, and this is the " fall " of man (mind) and angels (spiritual egos).

See GOAT (milch), LUNAR CYCLE, MATRO, PITRIS, PITRIYANA, SERPENT (subtil), SIAMAK, UDDER, WILDERNESS.

MIMER WELL :—

A symbol of the fountain of Truth.

" She (Frigg) was seated without, solitary, when he came,—the oldest, the most circumspect of the Ases,—and looked in her eyes : ' Why sound me ? why put me to the proof ? I know all, Odin ; I know where thou hast concealed thine eye,—in that great fountain of Mimer."—*The Voluspa*, 89–94.

The Wisdom nature is aware that the Higher Self through the experience of the lower consciousness (eye) acquires Truth.

See ASAR, EYES (two), FOUNTAIN, FRIGG, ODIN, WATER, WELL.

MIND, GOOD :—

A symbol of the Logos or Higher Self, manifesting as Atma-buddhi-manas on the higher mental plane.

"The School of Zeno teach that God is unity, and that he is called Mind, and Fate, and Jupiter, and by many other names besides."—DIOG. LAERTIUS, *Lives*, Yonge, p. 308.

"He (Mind) is the Good Daimon. Blessed be the soul that is most filled with him, and wretched is the soul that is empty of the Mind " (*The Key*).—G. R. S. MEAD, *T. G. Hermes*, Vol. II. p. 156.

"We invoke the Mind with man-lauding strain, and with the hymns of the fathers. May the Mind come back to us for us to obtain wisdom, vigour and life, and that we may long see the sun ! May the divine race restore to us the Mind, O Fathers, that we may abide with the living kind ! "—*Sata. Bráh.*, II. 6, 1, 39.

"We call God a Mind. He has revealed himself as a Spirit. But what do we know of mind, but through the unfolding of this principle in our own breasts ? That unbounded spiritual energy which we call God is conceived by us only through consciousness. through the knowledge of ourselves.—We ascribe thought or intelligence to the Deity, as one of his most glorious attributes. And what means this language ? These terms we have framed to express operations or faculties of our own souls. The Infinite Light would be for ever hidden from us, did not kindred rays dawn and brighten within us. God is another name for human intelligence raised above all error and imperfection, and extended to all possible truth. The same is true of God's goodness, and of all the moral perfections of the Deity. These are comprehended by us only through our own moral nature. It is the conscience within us, which, by its approving and condemning voice, interprets to us God's love of virtue and hatred of sin ; and without conscience these glorious conceptions would never have opened on the mind. It is the law-giver in our own breasts which gives us the idea of divine authority, and binds us to obey it."—W. E. CHANNING, *Likeness to God*.

"Let me point out that if there be a mind behind the flux of causation ; if there be a mind, or anything that includes what we know as mind immanent in the universe—in a word, the mind of God—it must be a mind that moves on levels to which ours have at present no access. It must be a mind that does not need to infer anything, it knows ; it does not guess or wonder, it sees all there is to see ; it cannot make mistakes, for there can be nothing outside its own range. ' My thoughts are not your thoughts, neither are your ways my ways, saith the Lord. For as the heavens are higher than the earth, so are my ways higher than your ways and my thoughts than your thoughts ' (Is. lv. 8, 9)."—R. J. CAMPBELL, Serm., *The Super-rational*.

See AGATHODAIMON, AKEM-MANO, DÆMON, FORM AND NAME, GOD, MONAD, PITRIS, VOHUMANO.

MINERVA, OR ATHENA :—

A symbol of the buddhic function, —Wisdom.

See ATHENA, BUDDHI.

MINISTERS OF THE STATE:—

A symbol of the cosmic agents through which the laws of the Supreme are carried out.

"The Kingly office was not mere pageantry ; nor were the functions of state ministers empty show. Good government was established by rulers, and correct instruction diffused among the people."—*Chinese Mythology*.

At this period of the Golden Age of Involution no self-consciousness has been arrived at,—that is, things could not be other than they are centrally decreed. *Necessity* is at this stage imperative. The "Kingly office " is the Divine Will ; and the "state ministers " are those agents through whom the Divine Will is executed. During Involution all the principles or laws of the universe are, as it were, laid down and worked out in an ideal and perfect archetypal system, and these serve for the guiding of the Evolution which is to follow.

"First, the Prime Intelligence created He, through the which Four Ministers He made to be ; He those Four the Columns Four of earth had dressed, whereby Fixture, Elevation, Traction, Rest, Water, Fire, Air and Earth He named them there, and He made of them this kingdom's bases fair. Four domains unto the Four did God decree " (*Gharib Náme of Ashig*).—E. J. W. GIBB, *Hist. of Ottoman Poetry*, Vol. I. p. 188.

From the Absolute there emanated the Creative Mind, who established below atma the four principles of manifestation to be "ministers" of the Divine Life outpoured upon the four planes formed for their activities.

See CIVILISING, COSMOS, CREATION, ELEMENTS, EVOLUTION, GOLDEN AGE, GOVERNMENT, INVOLUTION, OANNES, PEOPLE, PILLARS (four), QUATERNARY, WORLDS (five).

MINOS, ÆACUS, AND RHADA-MANTHUS, SONS OF ZEUS :—

These symbols signify the Divine principles of the Higher Triad—Will, Wisdom, and Action.

" Minos, who is stated by Thucydides to have been the first known founder of a maritime empire, appears in Homer as the greatest and most important of his archaic personages. . . . The name of Minos, whether mythical or not, is a symbol of political power, of the administration of justice, in a word, of civilisation. . . . His brother Rhadamanthus, hardly less distinguished, has the custody of the Elysian Plain."—W. E. GLADSTONE, *Juv. Mundi*, pp. 119, 120.

The Divine Will rules over the empire of Truth (water). The Divine Wisdom presides over the buddhic plane.

See CIVILISING, METIS, NOAH'S SONS, PHANES, TRIAD.

MINOS THE SECOND :—

A symbol of the lower self.

MIRACLES OF HEALING :—

These are symbolic of certain facts of spiritual growth which take place on planes of nature whose laws are as yet unrecognised by people at large. They occur as the Higher nature becomes more powerful in the soul, and they are psychic and spiritual endowments which come in due course according to the soul's preparedness for them, and which are added to the human nature as the souls evolve. They are not external phenomena exciting wonderment. They are wrought in the soul by an appreciation and application of laws of nature to which sectarian religionists are blind. They have nothing to do with the healing of physical diseases and defects.

" By faith in Jesus we call upon the deeper or Spiritual Man, who is one with the infinitude of God, and that divine man, that true Self, will rise in power in our souls, free us from the bondage of flesh and sense, and carry us upward to our eternal source and goal."—R. J. CAMPBELL, Serm., *The Self and the Body*.

" The Son of God became man. He came to us in our blindness, as we sat and begged by the wayside of life ; He *made clay*, i.e. He took of the mortal dust of our earthy nature (*see* JOHN ix. 6), and moulded it by the breath and moisture of His mouth, and blended it with the Divine nature, and *anointed* it with the Holy Ghost, and sent us to Siloam ; and by the co-operation of our Faith and Obedience with His Divine Power and Love, our eyes are opened and we see."—WORDSWORTH, *Bible, John*, p. 317.

" The story in the ninth of *John* about the healing of the blind man is a parable ; the event very likely took place, but it is used here as a parable ; all the miracles in the fourth gospel are used as parables."—R. J. CAMPBELL, Serm., *The Door, the Thief*, etc.

See ALCHEMY, ARC. MAN, BLIND, BONDAGE, FAITH (miracles), GIFTS OF GOD, GRACE, HEALING, INITIATIONS, INTUITION, MAN (blind), MEDICINE, PARABLES, PHYSICIAN, SERPENT ÆSCULAPIUS.

MIRROR :—

A symbol of the causal-body as a reflector of atma-buddhi,—the Love and Wisdom of the higher planes.

" Amaterasu, the Sun-Goddess, in presenting the Sacred Mirror to her grandson Ninigi-no-mikoto, said,—' Look upon this Mirror as my spirit, keep it in the same house and on the same floor with yourself, and worship it as if you were worshipping my actual presence.' "—SATOW, *Legend of the Sun-goddess*.

Wisdom, in directing the evolution on the lower planes of the soul instructs the indwelling Self (her grandson), in his struggles upward, to aspire to the ideal and seek the Wisdom, Love, and Truth reflected in the causal-body on the higher mental plane (same floor), which is the plane from which the Self operates.

" I (Lakshmi) reside in a lotus flower, in blazing fire, and in a polished sword or mirror."—*Institutes of Vishnu*, XCIX. 12.

" Sometimes the soul is called the ' Mirror of God.' Thus Jellàl eddin says :—' If a mirror reflects not, of what use is it ? Knowest thou why thy mirror reflects not ? Because the rust has not been scoured from its face. If it were purified from all rust and defilement, it would reflect the shining of the Sun of God.' "—MAX MÜLLER, *Theosophy*, etc., p. 357.

" We shall behold with our inward eyes the mirror of the wisdom of God, in which shall shine and be illumined all things which have ever existed and which can rejoice our hearts."—RUYSBROECK, Stoddart's trans., p. 76.

"But we all, with unveiled face reflecting as a mirror the glory of the Lord, are transformed into the same image from glory to glory, even as from the Lord the Spirit."—2 COR. iii. 18.

"Canst thou with him spread out the sky, which is strong as a molten mirror ?"—JOB xxxvii. 18.

"The soul of man, individually and in the lump, needs to be reclaimed from its subjection to material conditions, and its essential divinity made fully manifest, perfectly reflecting the face of God, ere it is ready for the fulfilment of its eternal destiny."—R. J. CAMPBELL, Serm., *The Refiner's Fire.*

"'External nature,' St. Bernard writes, 'is but the shadow of God, the soul is His image. The chief, the special mirror in which to see Him is the rational soul finding itself.' And he continues : 'If the invisible things of God are understood and clearly seen by the things which have been made, where, I ask, rather than in His image (within us), can be found more deeply imprinted the traces of the knowledge of Him ? Whosoever therefore thirsteth to see his God, let him cleanse from every stain his mirror, let him purify his heart by faith.' The substance of Christian mysticism is presented in this passage of St. Bernard."—W. S. LILLY, *The Great Enigma*, p. 266.

See AMATERASU, BUDDHI, CAUSAL-BODY, FACE OF GOD, FACES OF MEN, HOUSE, IMAGE, INSIGNIA OF JAPAN, ISHI, LAKSHMI, MITEGURA, MOSES, NINIGI, SHINTAI, SIMORG, SKY, SUN, VEIL.

MISTLETOE :—

A symbol of the germ of mind which becomes engrafted, as it were, in the desire or astral nature (wood). Mind is roused into action by the desires.

"Then asked the woman (Loke) : 'Has everything sworn to spare Balder ?' Frigg replied : 'Eastward of Valhalla there grows a twig which is called Mistletoe and it seemed to me too young to require an oath from ?'"—*The Story of Balder, Prose Edda,* HOWITT, *Literature, etc.*

Balder (like Buddha) is a symbol of the World-Soul (Divine Archetype) at the end of the Involutionary cycle, when he is prepared to manifest in the new cycle,—that of Evolution. Frigg (Wisdom) has, at the opening of the new cycle, taken "oaths" from all things : i.e. Buddhi has set its seal of limitation of operation upon all forms of relative experience, so that through the Soul's new growth upon the several planes no harm shall happen to the Divine One within ; for the Divine Feminine Holy Spirit of Wisdom rules this evolution which all souls are now engaged in : the one Soul having become many souls.

Evolution begins by the birth, or germination, of the World-Soul on the astral plane (fourth sub-plane), and after a period of development in astral bodies, the Soul comes into touch with the physical plane.

Loke, symbol of Desire, acts in guise of "a woman," as the physical plane is feminine. The physical nature inquires, as it were, whether the Soul is perfectly secure. Then the Desire-nature (Wisdom's utterance being through Desire) answers that in the "East," i.e. *above* the astral plane and *below* the buddhic (Valhalla), there is the germ of mind (mistletoe) : at present it is latent, but as soon as it grows the Soul will have its eyes opened, and become a responsible being, knowing good and evil, capable of accepting the life immortal, or of dying indefinitely until purification is complete.

"I foresaw for Baldur, for that bloody victim, for that son of Odin, the destiny reserved for him : He was raising in a charming valley a tender and beautiful mistletoe. From that stalk which appeared so tender grew the fatal arrow of bitterness which Hoder took upon himself to dart."—*The Voluspa.*

The intuition of coming Truth perceived the consummation of the Involutionary process in the death of the Archetypal Man and the shedding of his Life (blood) into the souls of humanity. On the mental plane (valley) appears the germ of mind which the instincts (Hoder) seize upon wherewith to ignorantly quell the Spirit within.

See ARC. MAN, BALDER, BLOOD, BUDDHI, DEATH OF BALDER, EAST, EVOLUTION, FALL, FRIGG, HODER, INVOLUTION, LOKE, OATH, ODIN, VAL-HALLA, VALLEY, WISDOM, WOMAN (Loke), WOOD.

MITEGURA, OR GOHEI :—

A symbol of the Divine scheme of the soul's evolution and salvation.

"One of the Gods then pulled up a sakaki-tree by the roots, and on its upper branches hung the Necklace of Jewels; at the middle he hung the Sacred Mirror, and to the lower branches he attached Coarse and Fine Cloth. This formed a large *mitegura* (or gohei) which was held by Ameno-futo-dama-no-mikoto, while he pronounced an address in honour of the Sun-Goddess."—*Japanese Legend.*

The Divine Will then fully organised the life within the soul, in the pattern of a tree. On the atma-buddhic heights were the treasures of the Spirit,—the higher emotions of Wisdom, Truth, and Love. In the higher mind (middle) was the Causal-body, and below on the astral plane was the astral mechanism of the lower nature of the human being. This constitution formed a connected whole, a "Tree of life," a comprehensive system for the development of the soul by the Higher Self, and under the immediate executive direction of the Wisdom principle.

See AMATERASU, CHRISTMAS-TREE, INSIGNIA, MIRROR, NET, SEPHIROTH, TAMA-GUSHI, TREASURE, TREE OF LIFE.

MITHRA SLAYING THE BULL :—

This is an emblem of the Reason overcoming the Emotion-nature,—the same as St. George and the Dragon. The scorpion below the bull is the lower aspect of the emotion-nature. It is a sign to indicate that the emotions are active through the contact with matter. The dog lapping the blood is a symbol of one of the inhabitants of the lower astral sub-planes, which feeds upon the cor-rupted astral life. The raised torch on the one side is a symbol of illu-mination and intelligence, and signi-fies the evolving life which rises from latency upward. The lowered torch is that of concealed light, and signifies the involution of life down-wards into matter. The torches signify also, as Lessing pointed out, the fall and return of the soul. The Divine spark descends to the lower planes to gain experience, and after-wards ascends victorious to the source from which it came.

See BLOOD, BULL, DEVAS (lower), EVOLUTION, FALL, FIENDS, GEORGE AND DRAGON, INVOLUTION, LIGHT, MATTER, SCORPION, SPARK, VICTORY.

MITHRAS OR MITHRA :—

A symbol of Divine omnipotence,—the power which serves to awaken and express the Self.

"The great Mithra was the God of fructification and reproduction in the whole organic world; his work was to lead the Fravashis to the bodies 'they were to occupy."—*Zoroastrian System.*

"Mithra" stands for the positive or energising power which awakens the spiritual life within the forms. In this way the link is set up between the monad of form and the monad of life : and so the lower planes become fruitful of living forms. The monad of life ensouls the form, and so makes it beget and bring forth its kind. "Leading the fravashis to bodies" is a symbol of birth into the lower life. These "bodies" are the forms which are prepared for and receive the life. (Mithras, god of the Rock, is the same as the "Rock which is Christ."—1 COR. x. 4.)

See CHILDREN, FORMS, FRAVASHIS, GENERATIVE, INCARNATION OF SOULS, MAN BORN, MONAD (form, life), MULTIPLY, PHALLIPHORIA, RE-INCARNATION.

MITRE :—

An emblem of Divine rule over the lower planes. It has the same mean-ing as the "crown of Lower Egypt." The cleft across represents a mouth opening upwards, which signifies the expression of the Divine Will in the lower realms.

"The mitre, the symbol of authority of the Jewish high priest, is also the attribute of bishops and archbishops. Cardinals anciently wore them."—F. E. HULME, *Symbolism, etc.*, p. 151.
"The mitre denotes Divine Wisdom." —SWEDENBORG, *Arc. Cel.*, n. 9999.

See BISHOP, CROWN, MOUTH.

MITRO, SROSH, AND RASHNU :—

Symbols of Understanding, Will, and Love.

See BALANCE (spirits), RASHNU, SROSH.

MIXTURE AND ITS SEPARA-TION :—

Symbolic of combinations and segregations of phenomena.

"There is no origination of anything that is mortal, nor yet any end in baneful death ; but only mixture and separation of what is mixed but men call this origination."—*Empedocles*, FAIRBANKS, 36.

All that exists upon the lower planes cannot persist, since it has no life of itself : it is consequently mortal. Death is equally non-existent,—death cannot be an end. The "mixture and its separation " are the combinations and segregations, or finalities, of the lower life of illusions. The lower mind (men) speaks of these things as real, whereas they are but transient appearances.

See ILLUSION, MATTER, MĀYĀ (lower), PHENOMENA, PRAKRITI, SEPARATION FROM, STRIFE.

MJOLNER, THE HAMMER OF THOR :—

A symbol of the will exercised on the mental plane.

"With this Thor grew angry, and grasped his hammer, and would have knocked Hyrrocken on the head, had not the Gods interceded for her."—*The Story of Balder, Prose Edda.*

Whereupon the higher mind (Thor) is aroused into activity, whose first dawning upon the lower mental plane takes the form of anger, and thus blindly wields the will (Mjolner) which is now in its possession, a proceeding which, but for the Divine purpose shaping the ends, would have had the effect of causing confusion on the astro-mental plane instead of evolution above it.

See BERSERKS, DEATH OF BALDER, HYRROCKEN, MAB, THOR.

MODGUNN, THE BRIDGE MAIDEN :—

A symbol of the intuition of wisdom, buddhi-manas.

"Modgunn, the maiden who keeps the bridge, asked of Hermod his name and his parentage, and added, that the day before, five companies of dead men had ridden over the bridge of Gjall ; ' but it rang,' said she, ' under no step save thine alone, neither hast thou the complexion of the dead ; wherefore thus ridest thou on the path of the dead ? ' "—*The Story of Balder, Prose Edda.*

The " keeper " of the way of the higher mind, which is the " bridge " between the higher and lower natures in the soul, is symbolised by the feminine or Wisdom element. This scrutinises the motives which have

given rise to the growth of consciousness, and now realises that only " yesterday," meaning, the dead past, or the relative condition, the perceptions of the five senses (dead men) were to give place to a transmutation of modes of apprehension of truth. But the quivers within the causal-body (or bridge) were alone communicated by the inner Self-initiated impulses ;—the vibrations from without, through the senses, not being sufficiently subtle or powerful to be transmitted thereunto. The intuition (Modgunn) now discerns that the Christ-soul (Hermod) has none of the signs of the planes of illusion and mortality ; and she asks why it happens that the Self comes forth apparently from that which is practically non-existent, as it is found to proceed from the potential instead of through manifestation.

See BRIDGE OF GJALL, CAUSAL-BODY, DEAD, FIVE, HERMOD, INTUITION, MAIDEN, MUSPELL, NORTH, SPIRIT.

MOIRAE OR FATES, DAUGHTERS OF ZEUS AND THEMIS :—

Symbols of the three groups of karmic life forces which operate on the three lower planes in accordance with law, in the formation of the three bodies which are the vehicles of the soul.

" And of the three Fates (Moiræ), Atropos, seated in the sun, supplies the origin of birth ; Clotho, moving about the moon, unites together and mingles the various parts ; lastly, Lachesis on earth, who has most to do with Fortune, puts her hand to the work. For the inanimate part is powerless, and liable to be acted upon by others ; but the mind is impassive and independent ; and the soul is of a mixed nature, and intermediate between the two."—PLUTARCH, *The Moon's Orb*, § 12.

" Atropos " signifies the higher-mind forces which build up the causal-body as a vehicle of the spiritual ego (sun) which takes birth in it as the immortal individuality. " Clotho " represents the " web " of astral forces which build up the astro-mental body for the personality (moon), and provide a complex mechanism for the functioning of the intermediate lower soul with the mental on the one side, and the physical on the other. "Lachesis" signifies the forces of heredity and growth on the physical plane, which build up the unalterable physical body for a fixed life-period. This lowest vehicle is of itself inert and without life of its own, being animated from the astral and mental planes.

See FATE-SPHERE, KARMA, MAAT, NECESSITY, NET, NORNOR, SHENIT, THEMIS, URDAR, VESTURES.

MOIST AND DRY :—

Symbolic of truth and falsity.

MOIST ESSENCE :—

A symbol of the Divine Reality :— the Truth (water) above.

"The more learned among the priests do not only call the Nile ' Osiris,' and the sea ' Typhon,' but give the name of Osiris generally to every Principle and power productive of *moisture*."— PLUTARCH, *Isis and Osiris*, § 33.

"The moist Principle being the Final Cause and origin of all things has produced from the beginning the three first elements, Earth, Air, Fire."—*Ibid.*, § 36.

As the "river of life" (Nile) is a symbol of the Divine Ray from the Absolute, it is indistinguishable from the Logos (Osiris). The astral plane (sea) is the medium of the desire-principle (Typhon, Set). The Logos is the Word or Expression of Truth (moist principle).

See ELEMENTS, HAPI, NILE, OSIRIS, RIVER OF LIFE, SET, WATER, WITNESS.

MOISTURE AND HEAT :—

A symbol of the energy of Truth-reality as Will and Wisdom.
See FIRE, WATER.

MONAD, THE ONE :—

A symbol of the Spiritual Centre of all being. The One from which the illusory many radiate. The One Life which differentiates into the many lives, each a centre of qualities or forms.

"Yet these three Sages of Tao-ism are but one First Cause, that is, the One Indivisible Monad, called Tae-keih (the Highest Point)."—*Chinese Mythology*.

The three centres of consciousness, i.e. the Self, the Individuality, and the Personality, are but aspects of the One Central Spirit, which is ultimately indivisible, without parts, vehicles, or any sense whatsoever of

separateness, complete, entire, and all in All.

"' If there is an infinite,' the Eleatics said, ' it is one, for if there were two, they could not be infinite, but would be finite one towards the other. But that which exists is infinite, and there cannot be more such. Therefore, that which exists is One ' " (*Mellissus, Fragm.* 3).— MAX MÜLLER, *Theosophy, etc.*, p. 93.

"I am he who came into being in the form of Khepara ; I became the Creator of all that came into being. . . . I was alone, for I had not spit in the form of Shu, nor had I emitted Tefnut ; there existed not another who worked with me."—BUDGE, *Gods of the Egyptians*, Vol. I. p. 308.

At the dawn of manifestation there existed the Divine Monad and none else. The Divine Will (Shu) was not projected, neither was the material form-nature (Tefnut) made apparent.

"All being is *one*, however multitudinous the forms in which it manifests itself. You yourself *are* the eternal subjected for awhile to the limitations of time and sense. You are part of that infinite whole of reality which is from everlasting to everlasting, and whose nature can only rightly be interpreted from the best that you know of yourself and of human nature in general."—R. J. CAMPBELL, Serm., *Our Solidarity with God*.

See ABSOLUTE, ÆON, BRAHMA, CHIP, FIRST-BORN, FRAVASHI, GODHEAD, HIRANYAGARBHA, KHEPERA, LAO, MITHRAS, SEED, SPHERE, SHU, TAE-KEIH, TEFNUT.

MONAD OF FORM :—

A symbol of Nature, or the astro-mental energy and intelligence, which under fixed laws, and after archetypal patterns, direct the growth or building up of forms in the matter of the lower planes. The countless monads of form are the specific astro-mental moulds of every differentiated growth,—every variety of natural formation on the astral and physical planes. These moulds have their mental and spiritual prototypes on the higher planes, which bring intelligence and purpose into the operations of nature in the phenomenal world. The prototypes are to be conceived of as schemes of being germinating within when conditions favour, and finding expression without in time and space. Thus are the atoms guided in the building up of the organisms of the animals and plants of the present teeming world of living things.

See BARHISHAD, BODHISATVAS, DEVAS (builders), FORMS, FRAVASHIS, GENERATIVE, GERMS, HIGHER AND LOWER WORLDS, MANES, MITHRAS, PITRIS, PROTOTYPES, SIMILITUDES, SPERMATIC WORDS.

MONAD OF LIFE :—

A symbol of Spirit, or the atma-buddhic energy of Truth, Love, and Wisdom, which ensouls the form, and under archetypal concepts directs its course in evolution and enables it to beget and bring forth its kind. The monad of life must be linked to the monad of Form so that the lower planes may become fruitful, and the forms multiply. The monad of Life becomes differentiated in human souls on the higher mental plane, and these separated monads of life constitute the Individualities.

"The Barbarian philosophy knows the world of thought and the world of sense ;—the former archetypal, and the latter the image of that which is called the model (or pattern) ; and assigns the former to the Monad, as being perceived by the mind , and the world of sense to the number six. For six is called by the Pythagoreans *marriage*, as being the genetic number ; and he places in the Monad the invisible heaven and the holy earth, and intellectual light. . . . Does not Plato hence appear to have left the Ideas of living creatures in the intellectual world, and to make intellectual Objects into sensible species according to their genera ?"—CLEM. ALEX., *Miscellanies*, Bk. V.

The "six" as "marriage" refers to the alliance of the Monad of Life (atma-buddhi-manas, or heaven, holy earth, and intellect), with the Monad of Form (manas-kama-sthula, or mental, astral, and physical), the union being productive of innumerable forms and qualities.

"Now when the Creator had framed the Soul according to his will, he formed within her the corporeal universe, and brought them together, and united them centre to centre. The Soul, interfused everywhere from the centre to the circumference of heaven, of which she is the external envelopment, herself turning in herself began a divine beginning of never-ceasing and rational life enduring throughout all time" (PLATO, *Timæus*).—JOWETT, *Dialog.*, etc., Vol. III. p. 619.

The Monad of Life (Soul) is one in Involution, and for its growth in Evolution it is necessary that it should first descend to the lower planes, or rather, take unto itself the Monad of Form (nature or universe) and become involved or interfused in matter, and thus become prepared to manifest in diversity and multiplicity its forms and qualities in the many monads or souls of humanity.

"For the invisible things of him from the creation of the world are clearly seen, being understood by the things that are made, even his eternal power and Godhead "(ROM. i. 20). "In these words we have a clear statement of a principle which occupies a large place in what is called mystical theology. . . . It is the statement of a certain definite correspondence between the visible and the invisible worlds, between heavenly and earthly things, between the divine and the human. The lower are in a sense the images of the higher, the temporal of the eternal. All the attributes of the being of God, all that is real and abiding as contrasted with what is ephemeral and fleeting, may be inferred from what we know of the phenomenal universe, including human nature itself. The things that are seen are the symbols, the partial and impermanent present-ments of that which is from everlasting to everlasting and constitutes divine perfection. Plato has a great deal about it and develops it very suggestively, holding that the material world stands to the transcendental as the blurred and shifting reflection in the surface of a lake does to the landscape which produces it."—R. J. CAMPBELL, Serm., *Spiritual Correspondences*.

See AGNISHVATTAS, AIR-ÆTHER, ARC. MAN, ARHATS, ATMAN, BA, BODHISATVAS, EGG, EVOLUTION, FRAVASHIS, GERMS, GUARDIAN SPIRITS, HIGHER AND LOWER WORLDS, IMAGE, IMPERIAL, INCARNATION OF SOULS, INDIVIDUALITY, INVOLUTION, MAN BORN, MAN CRAWLED, MANASA-PUTRAS, MANES, MARUTS, MAZENDA-RANS, MULTIPLY, MUSPELL (sons), PACCEKA-BUDDHAS, PITRIS (solar), PROSPERITY, PROTOTYPES, RISHIS, SAGES, SIX, SONS OF GOD, SOUL, SPARK, SPERMATIC WORDS, SPIRIT, WHEAT.

MONARCHS AND LORDS, AS SIGNS :—

Symbolic of power for the attainment of Love and Truth divine.

MONEY :—

A symbol of the lower equivalent for a higher acquisition. Such as desires for objects of sense and affection, given up, or exchanged, for high virtues and spiritual power.

"But they that desire to be rich fall into a temptation and a snare and many foolish and hurtful lusts, such as drown men in destruction and perdition. For the love of money is a root of all kinds of evil : which some reaching after have been led astray from the faith, and have pierced themselves through with many sorrows."—1 TIM. vi. 9, 10.

Those who seek to fill their minds with desires and thoughts of the objects of sense (riches) will be the prey of carking cares which destroy the higher mental qualities. For the love of lower things (money) is productive of all kinds of evils, entailing much sorrow and suffering.

"We are God's money : we have wandered away as coin from the treasury. The impression that was stamped upon us has been rubbed out by our wandering : He has come to refashion, for He it was that fashioned us at first ; and He is Himself asking for His money, as Cæsar for his. Therefore He says, ' Render unto Cæsar the things that are Cæsar's, and unto God the things that are God's.' To Cæsar his money, to God yourselves." —AUGUSTINE, *Gospel of John*, Vol. II. p. 27.

"And Moses gave the money of them that were redeemed unto Aaron and to his sons, according to the word of the Lord, as the Lord commanded Moses.— NUM. iii. 51.

And the ethical nature rendered up the love of lower things regarded as right out of obedience to esteemed authority, so that this love might be transmuted, and the spiritual mind and its concepts might use it in the soul's development, according to the Divine law of moral and spiritual progress.

See AARON, CHARON, HOUSE-HOLDER, JUSTICE, LABOURERS, LEVITES, MAN (rich), MOSES, POOL OF BETHESDA, RICH MAN, TRANS-MUTATION, VINEYARD, WAGES, WORK.

MONK OR HERMIT :—

A symbol of an ego who " retires alone into the desert to lead a religious life," that is, who withdraws into the soul's inner mental being, intent upon consciously developing his nature in accordance with the Divine law. To this end he ceases for a period from external activities and incarnation.

See ASCETIC, ARHAT, ASRAMAS, CHURCH (four), HERMIT, MENDICANT, NUNS, ORDERS, SAINTS, SUFFERING, TRI-RATNA.

MONKEY, OR APE :—

A symbol of the lower mind which imitates or reflects the higher. Or of the automatic mind.

See APE, JUDGMENT HALL.

MONSTERS OF TIAMAT :—

A symbol of undirected and undisciplined emotions needing the governance of mind which guides and directs. These unregulated qualities are deficient of that sense of due proportion which is begotten of the faculty of reason.

See KABANDHA, TIAMAT, WHALES.

MONTH :—

A symbol of time or space, and refers to the phenomenal existence. The months correspond to planetary periods in the cycle of life.

"The month is Pragâpati ; its dark half is matter, its bright half spirit. Therefore some Rishes perform sacrifice in the bright half, others in the dark half."—*Prasna Upanishad*, I. 12.

The phenomenal state of existence is the cycle of the Divine Life on the lower planes, which is divided into two parts. The first part (Pitriyana) is for the development of the desire and form side of nature : the second (Devayana), for the evolution of the spirit and life side of human being. Therefore the more-developed egos undergo self-limitation in the second half of the cycle, and the less-developed egos in the first. The former egos are the Individualities, the latter the Personalities.

See ADITYAS (twelve), BORN (out), CIRCLE OF EXISTENCE, DEVAYANA, MATTER, MOON-WAXING, PITRIYANA, PRAGÂPATI, RISHES.

MOON (HIGHER ASPECT) :—

A symbol of Buddhi as containing the transmuted results of the experience of the lower self.

"When the person goes away from this world he comes to the wind. Then the wind makes room for him, like the hole of a wheel, and through it he mounts higher. He comes to the sun. Then the sun makes room for him, like the hole of a lambara (drum ?), and through it he mounts higher. He comes to the moon. Then the moon makes room for him, like the hole of a drum, and through it he mounts higher, and arrives at the world when there is no sorrow, and no snow. There he dwells eternal years."—*Brihad. Upanishad*, V. (7) 10, 1.

When the spiritual monad, or Individuality, quits the lower nature, it passes into the energised higher mental vehicle, or causal-body, and from thence unites with the Higher Self. Fortified by this union, it passes upward through the buddhic plane (moon) and becomes merged in Love eternal on the plane of atma.

See AMATERASU, BUDDHI, INDIVI-DUALITY, METZTLI, MONAD OF LIFE, SELF, SUN (door), TRANSMUTATION, WIND, WOMEN'S LIFE.

MOON (LOWER ASPECT) :—

A symbol of the astral plane, the plane of the desires by means of which the soul ascends.

"When the living Father perceived that the soul was in tribulation in the body, He sent his own Son for its salvation. Then He came and prepared the work which was to effect the salvation of the souls, and with that object prepared an instrument with twelve urns, which is made to revolve with the sphere, and draws up with it the souls of the dying. And the greater luminary receives those souls, and purifies them with its rays, and then passes them over to the moon, and in this manner the moon's disc, as it is designated by us, is filled up. For he (Manes) says that these two luminaries are ships or passage boats. Then, if the moon becomes full, it ferries its passengers across towards the East wind, and thereby effects its own waning in getting itself delivered of its freight. And in this manner it goes on making the passage across, and again discharging its freight of souls drawn up by the urns, until it saves into its own proper portion of the souls."—*Disputation of Archelaus (see also* EPIPHANIUS, *Adv. Hær.*, 66).

When the soul begins to aspire from out of the strife and suffering of the lower life, the Supreme sends his Son, the manifestation of himself, into the souls of humanity. Then the Son of Truth comes forth mentally to the "sons of Gods," who are the spiritual egos having in God a common parent, but who must be, so to say, brought up and nurtured by their mother the moon, which stands for the astral plane and its activities. The device which has been prepared for the soul's evolution is the cycle of life

(zodiac) with its twelve divisions having correspondences in twelve states of the soul. The " souls of the dying " lower bodies are those embryo egos who are translated from the physical life, or solar state, to the state of the astral, whose correspondency is the lunar symbol. This implies that on the physical and astral planes, in the lunar chain period, the physical and desire natures of animal-man are developed. This is expressed by the moon's disc being filled up in waxing. The physical-nature (solar) and the desire-nature (lunar) are, as it were, " passage boats " in which the spiritual egos voyage heavenward (east). Then on the desire-nature becoming fully stimulated and developed (moon waxing full), the soul is rendered fit for the addition of mind to desire. When mind begins to control desire, this addition is said to effect the moon's waning, that is, the rule of the desire-nature weakens as mind gets uppermost. The desire-nature, through the higher qualities it calls forth, becomes a means of conveying " a freight of souls " to the higher planes. The process therefore represents the transference of the soul from the physical to the emotional plane, and represents the condition into which the soul enters at the passing over from a lower to a higher state. The twelve urns or bowls signify disciplined and advanced qualities (disciples); for the Christ cannot manifest his nature excepting through appropriate vehicles, and these are symbolised by the urns.

See ASTRAL PLANE, DEVAYANA, DISCIPLES, EAST, EYES OF HORUS, LUNAR CYCLE, MONTH, MOON-WAX-ING, PILLARS OF LIGHT, PITRIYANA, PLANETARY CHAIN, SALVATION, SONS OF GOD, SUN-SETTING, TUAT, TWELVE, URNS, ZODIAC.

MOON (SOLAR ASPECT) :—

A symbol of the lower self—the Personality. This includes the astral principle of the lower nature, namely, desire, and also the form or matter side of nature, which were developed in the lunar cycle on the lunar globes.

"The sun is Spirit, matter is the moon."—*Prasna Upanishad*, I. 5.

The sun is the great symbol of the Higher Self; the moon, of the lower Self involved in matter.

"For the moon herself, out of desire for the sun, revolves round and comes in contact with him because she longs to derive from him the generative principle."
—PLUTARCH, *Face in the Moon's Orb.*

The lower Self, being attracted to the Higher Self, evolves through the life cycle; for the soul longs for regeneration and immortal union with the Higher Self in the causal-body wherein the two Selves become one.

"Two things are needed for the burning of a lamp : that it should be lit, and that it should be fed. In both respects the light with which we shine is derived. We are not suns, we are moons ; reflected, not self-originated, is all our radiance. That is true in all senses of the figure : It is truest in the highest. It is true about all in every man which is of the nature of light. Christ is the true light which lighteth every man that cometh into the world. Whatsoever beam of wisdom, whatsoever ray of purity, whatsoever sunshine of gladness has ever been in any human spirit, from Him it came, who is the Light and Life of men."—A. MACLAREN, *Sermons, 2nd Series,* p. 161.

See HIGHER AND LOWER SELVES, LUNAR CYCLE, PERSONALITY, PLANETARY CHAIN, REGENERATION, SELENE, SOMA (moon), SUN, SUN (moon).

MOON—WAXING PERIOD, OR THE PITRIYANA :—

A symbol of a period of evolution of animal-man, during which the astro-physical nature is developed sufficiently to be a fit vehicle for the incoming mind and spirits. This period has occurred in the lunar cycle for most egos.

"And Kitra said : All who depart from this world go to the moon. In the former (the waxing) half, the moon waxes big by their vital spirit." — *Kaush. Upanishad,* I. 2.

The Divine Lawgiver (Kitra) gave utterance :—All embryo souls, or baby egos, in animal forms, when they quit the flesh bodies go to the astral realm (moon). In the first, the "waxing-half" period,—meaning the half-cycle when the physical nature is developed,—the astral nature (moon) waxes big, that is, the desire-nature is stimulated, and in proportion as the desires have been developed, the astral world (moon) is said to increase. During this period the embryo-egos, or proto-souls, proceed, on quitting the flesh body, from the physical realm to the astral, and no higher.

See next.

MOON—WANING PERIOD, OR THE DEVAYANA :—

A symbol of the present period of the evolution of humanity in which, as time proceeds, the stimulation of the desire-nature is worked out, and the mind functions, with ultimately the spirit.

"But in the waning half, the moon causes them to be born."—*Ibid.*

In the second period, when the rule of the desires is to be gradually superseded, consequent on the awakenment of mind, the spiritual egos are born on the mental plane to begin their influence in human nature. Then the personalities build up the causal-bodies for the individualities on the higher mental plane.

See ARREST, ASTRAL PLANE, BOAT SEKTET, CAUSAL-BODY, DEVAYANA, EVOLUTION, HIGHER AND LOWER, INCARNATION OF SOULS, INDIVIDUALITY, INVOLUTION, LUNAR CYCLE, LUNATIC, MAN BORN, MAN (natural), MONTH, MOON (lower), PERSONALITY, PITRIS, PITRIYANA, ROUND, SUN-CATCHING, URNS, WHEELS (holy).

MOON-BEAMS :—

A symbol of reflections of truth in the lower nature.

"The moon-beams, though they shine everywhere, are especially bright on mount Kailâsa."—*Buddha-Karita,* Bk. I. 21.

The "moon-beams" here signify the reflections of truth which are especially brilliant through the intuition.

See KAILÂSA, MOUNTAIN.

MOONLIGHT :—

A symbol of the astral light which conveys but distorts truth.

"If the unseen is ever to rule in men's lives, it must be through their thoughts. It must become intelligible, clear, real. It must be brought out of the flickering moonlight of fancy and surmises into the sunlight of certitude and knowledge."

—A. MACLAREN, *Sermons, 2nd Series,*
p. 141.

See ASTRAL PLANE, ILLUSION,
MĀYĀ (lower).

MOON-LIKE FACES OF WOMEN :—

A symbol of the buddhic emotions
which proceed forth at the emanation
of a soul.

See BLANDISHMENTS, HOURIES,
WOMAN.

MOORING POST FOR SHIP :—

A symbol of the Higher Self to
which the soul must be consciously
attached.

" 'Tell me my name,' saith the Wood
whereat I would anchor ; 'Lord of the
two lands who dwellest in the Shrine'
is thy name."—BUDGE, *Book of the Dead,*
Ch. XCIX.

The "Wood" is the same as the
"Horn," or "Rock of Salvation,"—
the Christ. The Higher Self is Lord
of the higher and lower natures in the
soul, and has his seat in the causal-
body (shrine).

"And the mooring-post is fixed for
me in the Pool of the Zenith, the mooring-
post is set up for me."—*Ibid.,* Ch. CX.

And the Higher Self, as the goal of
righteousness, is set before the soul
as its aim.

"Then they cast out the mooring stones,
and made fast the hawsers."—*Iliad,*
Bk. I.

Then the attraction to lower opinions
was lessened, and further effort was
made to attach the lower self to the
Higher.

See ANCHORAGE, DELUGE, POOL
(zenith), SHIP (Manu), SHRINE,
WHEAT AND BARLEY.

MORNING :—

A symbol of outgoing energy.
Emanation or outbreathing of the
Spirit.

"And let us know, let us follow on to
know the Lord ; his going forth is sure
as the morning : and he shall come unto
us as the rain, as the latter rain that
watereth the earth."—Hos. vi. 3.

The soul aspires to realise Wisdom
and Love, and looks for the Divine
outpouring which is sure to follow the
prayer of the earnest soul. And the
Divine nature will come in the Truth
that shall rain down from above, the
fuller Truth that makes fruitful the
lower nature (earth).

"The 'morning' is used to denote
every particular coming of the Lord, and
consequently it is an expression which
hath respect to new creation.'—SWEDEN-
BORG, *Arc. Cel. to Gen.* i. 5.

See BREATH, CREATION, DAWN,
EARTH, RAIN, SUN-RISING, WATER.

MORNING AND EVENING :—

Symbolic of outpouring and indrawing of the Divine Life. Out-
breathing and in-breathing of Brahm,
—the Absolute.

See ABSOLUTE, BRAHMA, BREATH
(divine), EVENING AND MORNING,
MANVANTARA.

MORNING STAR :—

A symbol of the expression of
Truth on the higher mental plane.

"By morning is signified the coming
of the Lord." "By stars are signified
knowledges of good and truth." "By
morning-star is signified intelligence and
wisdom."—SWEDENBORG, *Apoc. Rev.,*
n. 151.

"Jesus is the 'the bright and morning
star' (REV. xxii. 16). It means that
what the world has seen in Jesus is the
ushering in of the dawn of a higher
spiritual consciousness for all mankind.
He comes to show us what we are and
what we shall be."—R. J. CAMPBELL,
Serm., *Persistence of Jesus.*

See BENNU BIRD, DAWN, SINGERS,
STAR IN THE EAST, STARS (fixed).

MORROW, OR NEXT DAY :—

A symbol of a subsequent period
and stage of progress in development.

"Be not therefore anxious for the
morrow : for the morrow will be anxious
for itself. Sufficient unto the day is
the evil thereof."—MAT. vi. 34.

"Jesus is seen (JOHN i. 35) by the
witness-bearer coming to him while he
is still advancing and growing better.
This advance and improvement is symbolically indicated in the phrase, 'on the
morrow.' For Jesus came in the
consequent illumination, as it were, and
on the day after what had preceded."—
ORIGEN, *Comm. on John,* Bk. VI. § 30.

See BENNU BIRD, STRIDES OF THE
SOUL, WALKING.

MORTAL MIND :—

A symbol of the lower mind, kama-
manas ; or the personality which is
subject to death.

"And thou, now that thou hast
withdrawn hither, shalt learn no more
than what mortal mind has seen."—
Empedocles, FAIRBANKS, Bk. I. 2.

And now that the soul has identified

itself with the Higher Self, it shall see and hear in actuality that which the purified personality has at last realised through experience.

See HECTOR, HEEL, IMMORTALITY FORFEITED, MAN (lower), PERSONALITY, SHABTI.

MORTAR ; CEMENT :—

A symbol of affection : that which binds together.

See BRICK FOR STONE.

MORTAR AND PESTLE :—

A symbol of the critical intellect ; that which pounds up "food" or "meat," knowledge, that truth may be assimilated.

"Now the mortar and pestle mean all kinds of food ; for by the mortar and pestle food is prepared, and by means of them it is eaten."

"The mortar is the birth-place of all breaths. . . . The mortar is the air, and everything that is above this earth is air ; and the air is the middle."—*Sata. Brâh.*, VII. 5. 1, 12, 22–6.

The mind (air) plane is the middle plane between the higher and lower natures. From the mind come all interpretations (breaths) of Spirit and matter, life and form.

See AIR, BREATH, EARTH, FIRMAMENT, FOOD, MEAT, WOOD (holy).

MOSAIC DISPENSATION :—

The rational and moral order in the conduct of life, under coercion of law and conscience. This order precedes the order of Wisdom and Love,—the Christ.

"Now viewing the institutions of the dispensation brought in by Moses as typical, we look at them in what may be called their *secondary* aspect, we consider then as *prophetic symbols of the better things to come in the Gospel.*"—P. FAIRBAIRN, D.D., *Typology*, Vol. I. p. 75.

See CONSCIENCE, COVENANT, DISPENSATIONS, JOHN BAPTIST, JUSTIFICATION, LAW OF MOSES, MOSES, PROPHET, TESTAMENT, WOMAN (adultery).

MOSES, THE SERVANT OF GOD :—

A symbol of the rational and ethical nature, which formulates laws of conduct under penalties for non-observance and disobedience. The moral nature is the law-giver and the conserver of the higher nature (God).

"By Moses is meant, in an extensive sense, all the law written in his five books, and, in a more confined sense, the law which is called the decalogue."—SWEDENBORG, *Apoc. Rev.*, n. 662.

"But unto this day, whensoever Moses is read, a veil lieth upon their heart. But whensoever a man shall turn to the Lord, the veil is taken away. Now the Lord is the Spirit : and where the Spirit of the Lord is, there is liberty. But we all, with unveiled face reflecting as a mirror the glory of the Lord, are transformed into the same image from glory to glory, even as from the Lord the Spirit."—2 COR. iii. 15–18.

When conduct is governed by ethical considerations only, without love, the veil of the lower nature precludes a vision of the higher in the inner heart of man. But when a mind turns to the God within, the veil of the lower nature is removed, and the Divine Love of the Spirit is perceived as an ideal ; and where the heart is tender, and the love of right and truth active, there is liberty : for conduct is no longer coerced by moral laws, but follows gladly the teaching of the Spirit. And so it will come about that at the end of the cycle, when the lower nature is transcended, the soul will reflect clearly the Divine attributes and become the image of its Lord, passing from stage to stage upward to bliss.

"This is the normal condition of all souls, that they be filled with God, acted by God, holding their will in His, irradiated always by His all-supporting life. Just this it is that constitutes the radical idea of religion, and differs it from a mere ethical virtue. God is the prime necessity of all religious virtue. The necessity is constituent, not penal. . . . Religious character is God in the soul, and without that all pretences of religious virtue are, in fact, atheistic."—H. BUSHNELL, *Nature, etc.*, p. 163.

"St. John's position is that the law was given by Moses for a time, until grace and truth came by Jesus Christ. Moses is treated almost as a forerunner."—W. R. INGE, *Camb. Bibl. Essays*, p. 263.

"The feeling of ethical obligation is as real, as undeniable, as is the fact of sense-perception. As surely as consciousness reveals to me, in the ordinary exercise of my faculties, myself, and an objective world not myself, so surely does it reveal to me, through the feeling of moral obligation, a Higher than I, to whom that obligation binds me. This Kant deemed the surest revelation of the Divine. 'Ethic,' he writes, 'issues inevitably in religion, by extending itself to the idea of a sovereign moral Lawgiver, in whose will *that* is the end of creation, which at the same time can be, and ought to be, man's chief end.' And here the great philosopher of these latter days does but express, in his own language, what has been delivered, in divers manners, by the world's spiritual teachers of all creeds, in all ages."— W. S. LILLY, *The Great Enigma*, p. 306.

"The birth of the power of recognising and dealing with ideas, the birth of ideality is an epoch in the history of the world or of man."—PHILLIPS BROOKS, *Mystery of Iniquity*, p. 94.

See ANGER OF GOD, ARK (bul.), ARK (test.), CHRIST'S SECOND COMING, DISPENSATIONS, HOUSE OF BONDAGE, IMAGE, JOHN BAPTIST, LAW OF MOSES, MIRROR, MOSAIC, READING, ROCK (spiritual), SHOES PUT OFF, TABERNACLES, TESTAMENT, WOMAN (adultery), WRATH OF GOD.

MOSQUITO :—

A symbol of a condition of unrest and inquietude.

See NASU.

MOTHER, DIVINE :—

A symbol of the feminine, or receptive, aspect of the manifesting Spirit, which brings forth from latency within the forms the qualities and activities apparent in nature. This mother principle, buddhi, directs human evolution, and it is eventually through her functioning, and through the raising of the soul by intuition, that the buddhic state of consciousness is attained.

"But Chaos did not know its own creation. From its embrace with Spirit, Môt was born. From her (Môt, the Great Mother) it was that every seed of the creation came, the birth of all the cosmic bodies" (Sanchuniathon).—PHILO BYBLIUS, *Fragment*.

"Like a mother to her subjects, intent on their welfare,—devoted to all worthy of reverence like devotion itself, —shining on her Lord's family like the goddess of prosperity,—she (Mâyâ) was the most eminent of goddesses to the whole world."—*Buddha-Karita*, Bk. I. 16.

The maternal relationship stands as the symbol of Divine watchfulness and guidance which directs the lower evolution. The "devotion" is the sign of that complete and unfeigned love which is willing to expend itself in the interest of all. She "Mâyâ," pure Truth,—the feminine aspect of

the One,—shines forth and is the means of awakening the faint beginnings of true life in the soul. She is the highest symbol of which any conception can be framed in the mind.

"For, since the present world is female, as a mother bringing forth the souls of her children, but the world to come is male, as a father receiving his children (from their mother), therefore in this world there come a succession of prophets, as being sons of the world to come, and having knowledge of men."—*Clementine Homilies*, II. Ch. XV.

Because the buddhic principle brings forth the higher qualities in the souls which the Spirit allies with itself, therefore in the souls there arise dawnings, or intuitions, of the higher consciousness which is to come to the enlightened minds.

"The Sakti, or female energy of Siva, is worshipped by a vast number of persons as the true Jagad-amba, or 'Mother of the Universe.' "—MON. WILLIAMS, *Indian Wisdom*, p. 101.

The Higher Self (Siva) is allied with the buddhic principle (female energy), and it is from the buddhic plane that the prototypes of all things are reflected, as it were, on to the lower planes. So it is that buddhi brings forth the universe.

See BIRTH OF CHRIST, BUDDHI, CREATION, EARTH (great), HETHRA, HINE, ILLUSION, INTUITION, ISIS, LADY, LATONA, MATTER, MĀYĀ, MUT, OCEAN (fem.), PRAKRITI, PROPHET, PROTOTYPES, PURUSHA, SERPENT (water), SHEKINAH, SIVA, TAO, WOMAN (matter), WOMB.

MOTION AND STABILITY :—

Symbolic of karma and compensation in relation to the activities of mind and emotion in the soul.

See KARMA.

MOUNT OF OLIVES :—

A symbol of the soul's aspiration, and love of the true and good.

"And when they had sung a hymn, they went out unto the mount of Olives." —MAT. xxvi. 30.

The "singing of the hymn" symbolises the aspiration through harmony of the qualities and uplifting of the nature in prayer and psalm. And the repairing to the "mount of Olives" serves to indicate the ascent of the Christ soul ere it is enabled to make its final triumph over the lower limitations.

"The Mount of Olives signified Divine love."—SWEDENBORG, *Apoc. Rev.*, n. 493

See GETHSEMANE, HARMONY, HYMN SINGING, MOUNTAIN, OLIVE FRUIT, PASSION, PRAYER.

MOUNTAIN OR MOUNT :—

A symbol of aspiration towards ideals, or the rise of the soul to higher planes of consciousness.

"And seeing the multitudes, he went up into the mountain : and when he had sat down, his disciples came unto him : and he opened his mouth and taught them . . . And when he was come down from the mountain, great multitudes followed him."—MAT. v. 1, and viii. 1.

The going up a mountain corresponds to the ascent of the Divine nature in the soul. In that state the disciplined qualities (disciples) are instructed and brought into harmony with the Christ. The " sitting down " signifies suiting the instruction to the lower comprehension of the qualities.

"While the Lord taught on the mount, the disciples were with Him, for to them it was given to know the secret things of the heavenly doctrine ; but now as He came down from the mount the crowds followed Him, who had been altogether unable to ascend into the mount. They that are bowed by the burden of sin cannot climb to the sublime mysteries. But when the Lord came down from the mount, that is, stooped to the infirmity and helplessness of the rest, in pity to their imperfections, great multitudes followed Him."—PSEUDO-ORIGEN, *Hom. in Liv.*, 5.

"Hence even in these (Pietistic) circles, now and again there is an insight that they must journey to the mountain-top in order to serve the Christian ideal in larger fashion, more boldly and more successfully."—PFLEIDERER, *Develop. of Christianity*, p. 317.

In the first division of the Tuat, according to the *Book of the Gates*, are to be found two groups of Gods :—

"One group called 'Gods of the Mountain,' and the other 'Gods of the Mountain of the Hidden Land.' The Gods of the Mountain are the offspring of Rā himself, and they 'emerged from his eye,' and to them has Amentet been given as an abode."—BUDGE, *Egypt. Heaven and Hell*, Vol. III. p. 110.

The first division of the cycle of life (the Tuat) is on the higher buddhic plane. The Divine Ideals (Gods) have their realisation on this plane, which is unapparent (hidden) to the lower

self. The Ideals are the offspring of the Supreme ; they emanated from the Higher Self (his eye), and they have their abode in buddhi (Amentet).

"Great is the Lord, and greatly to be praised in the city of our God, in the mountain of his holiness."—Ps. xlviii. 1.

Exalted is the Higher Self within, and regarded with appreciative love in the inmost heart of being, and in the soul's highest aspirations after Wisdom, Truth, and Love.

"Above each man Christian morality sets the infinite life. The identity of nature between that life and his, while it enables him to emulate that life, compels him, also, to compare himself with it. The more zealously he aspires to imitate it, the more clearly he must encounter the comparison. The higher he climbs the mountain, the more he learns how the high mountain is past his climbing. It is the oneness of the soul's life with God's life that at once makes us try to be like Him and brings forth our unlikeness to Him. It is the source at once of aspiration and humility." —PHILLIPS BROOKS, *Influence of Jesus*, p. 65.

"The 'garden' implies the condition of purity ; the 'vineyard,' the culture of a pure spirit in man ; the 'cloud,' the place from which the divine voice within man utters itself ; the 'mount,' the 'hill of regeneration' or 'mount of the Lord' within man ; so-called from its representing that process of ascent inwards and upwards towards his highest and best, by means of which he becomes regenerate or 'twice born,' and thereby divine."—E. MAITLAND, *The Bible's Own, etc.*, p. 64.

See ALBORDJ, AMENTET, ARARAT, CAUCASUS, CROWN (upper), DISCIPLES, GOAT (white), HAIR OF HEAD, HILL COUNTRY, HIMAVAN, KAILASA, KAPILA, MULTITUDES, OLYMPUS, PEOPLE, QUALITIES, SITTING, TEN DAYS, TRANSFIGURATION, VAIRAMAUTI, VALLEY.

MOUNTAIN TOP :—

A symbol of the higher planes— atma and buddhi.

See OLYMPUS, TLALOC.

MOUNTAIN (LOWER ASPECT) :—

A symbol of self-exalted qualities of the lower nature, such as pride, vanity, ambition, greed, desire for power over others, which qualities must be transmuted into aspiration, zeal, public spirit, etc.

"Again the devil taketh him (Jesus) unto an exceeding high mountain, and sheweth him all the kingdoms of the world, and the glory of them ; and he said unto him, All these things will I give thee, if thou wilt fall down and worship me, etc."—MAT. iv. 8, 9.

Again, from the lower principle, or not-Self, full of pride, ambition, vainglory, greed, etc., there came the insinuating suggestion that the various directions in which these qualities have been applied in the soul's experience are highly praiseworthy, and are sufficient in themselves to satisfy the soul's needs. To the Christ-soul is offered, if it suppress its upward yearnings, all the self-content that the exercise of its lower emotions can bring it.

"Mountains we understand to be all the lofty ones of this world, who were swollen in their hearts with earthly loftiness."—ST. GREGORY, Morals on the Book of Job, Vol. III. p. 419.

"'Thou shalt worship the Lord thy God, and Him only shalt thou serve.' We can understand, then, what spiritual trials are gathered up in this symbolic narrative also. The 'exceeding high mountain,' from which the dazzling landscapes of ambition were visible, was raised in the ardent mind itself, and the eyes that swept those far-reaching horizons were the eyes of the spirit. A whole multitude of commonplace, and, indeed, hardly regarded, experiences of normal human life are collected, interpreted, and appraised in this brief story. Whosoever is brought face to face with the necessity of choosing his method of serving his own ideals, finds the choice (however subtly disguised) to come ultimately to this single alternative—the worship of Satan, the prince of this world, or the worship of God."—H. HENSLEY HENSON, The Value of the Bible, etc., p. 240.

See BEASTS OF MOUNTAINS, KINGDOMS, TEMPTATION OF JESUS, TYRUS.

MOUNTAINS :—

A symbol of aspirations ; the attainment of ideals ; and the higher states of consciousness.

"I praise the cloud and rain which make thy body grow on the summit of the mountains. I praise the high mountains where thou hast grown, O Homa !"—Homa Yasht, HAUG, Essays.

"Praise," or the sense of appreciative love, is extended to the wisdom (cloud) and truth (rain) which are the means of accelerating the growth of the aspiring higher emotions. The "high mountains" symbolise the state of

highest attainment,—the Atman,—and through this consummation the Self (Homa) knows and becomes Itself.

"The Spirit of Wisdom answered thus :—' Of these mountains which are in the world, there are some which are moderators of the wind, and there are some which are warders off ; there are some which are the place and vent, the resting-place and support of the rainy cloud ; and there are some which are smiters of Aharman and the demons, and maintainers and vivifiers of the creation of Auharmazd, the Lord.' "—Mainogi Khirad, Ch. LVI. S. B. of E.

The principle of Buddhi uttered the truth from within :—Of the various aspirations which arise in the lower nature, there are some which moderate the desire-mental energy, and there are some which guide it into harmless channels. There are some which are the occasion and means, the reason and justification of the forthpouring of Truth and Love into the soul ; and there are some which destroy the love of self, and self-seeking desires, and draw out and energise the higher emotions which proceed from the Divine Nature within.

"By mountains are understood those who are in the good of love, by reason that the angels dwell upon mountains ; such as are in love to the Lord dwelling on high mountains, and such as are in love to their neighbour dwelling on lower ones ; wherefore by every mountain is signified every good of love."—SWEDENBORG, Apoc. Rev., n. 336.

"Let the mountains receive peace for thy people, and the hills righteousness" (Ps. lxxii. 3). "The 'mountains' are lofty souls, the 'hills' little souls. But for this reason do the mountains receive peace, that the hills may be able to receive righteousness. What is the righteousness which the hills receive ? Faith, for 'the just doth live by faith.' The smaller souls, however, would not receive faith unless the greater souls, which are called mountains, were illuminated by Wisdom herself, that they may be able to transmit to the little ones what the little ones can receive ; and the 'hills' live by faith, because the 'mountains' receive peace."—AUGUSTINE, Gospel of John, Vol. I. p. 2.

"The more profoundly we feel the reality of the great eternity whither we are being drawn, the greater do all things here become. When the mist lifts, and shows the snowy summits of the 'mountains of God,' the nearer lower ranges which we thought the highest dwindle indeed, but gain in sublimity and meaning by the loftier peaks to which they lead up. Unless men and women live for eternity, they are 'merely players,' and all their busy days 'like a tale told by an idiot, full of sound and fury, *signifying nothing.*'"—A. MACLAREN, *Sermons, 2nd Series*, p. 146.

See CAUCASUS, HILL COUNTRY, QAF.

MOURNER'S ROBE OR APPAREL :—

A symbol of the obscuration of the higher nature from the lower ; and the suffering and sorrow, pain and anguish, through the experience of which the Higher Self reveals itself to the lower.

See HAIR (side-lock), HIGHER AND LOWER, SUFFERING, TAMMUZ (lower).

MOURU LAND, THE STRONG, HOLY :—

A symbol of the buddhic plane and its activities.

See BUDDHIC PLANE, NISAYA.

MOUTH FOR RECEIVING FOOD :—

A symbol of capacity for sensuous enjoyment.

"And Set's mouth had been closed by a blow from the club of the god Horus." —*Legend of the Winged Sun-disk.*

Nor could the desire-nature (Set) enjoy, for its sense had been taken away through the exercise of resistence by the higher emotion-nature.

See CLUB, HORUS, SET.

MOUTH, FOR SPEECH :—

A symbol of expression of potencies and qualities in a given condition ; also implying perception and consciousness.

"May my mouth be given unto me that I may speak with it in the presence of the great god, the Lord of Amentet. May my hand and my arm not be forced back before the divine sovereign chief of the gods. I am the god Osiris, the lord of the mouth of the tomb (Re-stau) and I have a portion with him who is at the top of the steps."—*Papyrus of Hunefer*, Ch. XXII. trans. Budge.

The soul having become perfected, and, therefore,

"escaped from the Pool of Fire."—*Ibid.* which is the present purgatorial cycle of life, claims expression on the higher mental plane, as having a "portion" with God. The "portion" is the perfected lower Self, which is now identical with the Higher Self (Osiris), Lord of

the lower nature (tomb) and its cycle (Re-stau or Tuat). This means that the Christ striving in us, ultimately triumphs, and meets his Father above, and the two unite, for "I and my Father are one" (JOHN x. 30) ; the personality disappearing in the process and being replaced by the individuality, who "opens his mouth" on the higher plane, or is "born again." The "steps" symbolise the upward path to God. The "hand and arm" signify activity in rising from the "tomb."

"By mouth is signified doctrine, preaching and discourse."—SWEDENBORG, *Apoc. Rev.*, n. 574.

See AMENTET, BORN AGAIN, HETEP, LADDER, LIPS, MITRE, OSIRIS, RE-STAU, SPEECH, STAIRCASE, STEPS, TOMB, TONGUE, TUAT, WORD.

MOUTH, OPENING OF THE :—

A symbol of the attainment of the expression of the indwelling Self, or ego, on the higher planes, through the rise of consciousness.

"The ceremony which will give the deceased the power to eat, and to drink, and to talk in the next world."—BUDGE, *Book of the Dead*, p. 40.

"The Chapter of opening the mouth of Osiris. The scribe Ani, triumphant saith :—May the god Ptah open my mouth, and may the god of my city loose the swathings which are over my mouth. Moreover may Thoth, being filled and furnished with charms, come and loose the bandages of Set which fetter my mouth ; and may the god Tem hurl them at those who would fetter me with them, and drive them back. May my mouth be unclosed by Shu with his iron knife wherewith he opened the mouth of the gods."—*Ibid.*, Ch. XXIII.

The supplication is that the Divine Mind (Ptah) may raise the soul and enable it to express the truth within it. To effect this the Individuality (god) must free the causal-body (my city) from its ties to the lower nature which prevent its higher expression. Moreover, the higher mind (Thoth) is enjoined by means of the buddhic emotions of wisdom and love to rid the soul of all attraction to the lower desires (bandages of Set), so that the Christ within (god Tem) may drive out from his temple all that is unworthy and base. The soul yearns for liberation, and that the Divine will (Shu) wielding the intellect (iron knife) shall sever its bonds. For it is will-intellect which enables the ideals (gods) to express themselves in the mind.

See CAUSAL-BODY, CITY, CLEANSING, DEFUNCT, EATING, FETTERS, FOOD, GODS, IRON, MEAT, PLACE, PTAH, SCOURGE, SHU, TEM, THOTH, UR-HEKAU.

MULA-PRAKRITI, OR SVAB-HAVAT :—

A symbol of the primordial Substance which differentiates into spirit and matter at the emanation of that which becomes a solar universe. It outpours on the highest sub-planes of atma, and is not to be confounded with a visible nebula, which is an effect or appearance on the physical plane.

See AKASA, COW (black), HEAVEN AND EARTH, LINEN (white), MATTER, MĀYĀ (higher), PRAKRITI.

MULES AND SWIFT DOGS :—

Symbols of perversity and keen desire, exercised on the lower mental plane.

MULTIPLY AND BE FRUITFUL :—

An expression to signify the need there is for the soul to increase its experiences, faculties, capacities, and higher qualities.

"And God blessed them : and God said unto them, Be fruitful and multiply, and replenish the earth and subdue it."—GEN. i. 28.

And the Divine Power extended towards these manifesting aspects of Its own nature,—the dual Archetypal Man (the image of God),—the assurance of infinite support. And the twain are directed to be fruitful, that is, be the means whereby the natural order is to be converted into the womb of that which is to transcend and divinise the soul. "Subdual of the earth" signifies the gradual subordination of sense to Spirit, by the disciplining and purifying of the lower nature (earth).

"Increase ye in increasing, and multiply in multitude, ye creatures and creations all ; and man that hath Mind in him, let him learn to know that he himself is deathless, and that the cause of death is love, though Love is all" (*Pœmandres*, 18).—G. R. S. MEAD, *T. G. Hermes*, Vol. II. p. 11.

The Divine Will decrees that the union of mind and emotion is to be productive of thoughts, opinions, concepts, etc., and these again of various mental states. And the ego that hath the Spirit within him is to learn that he is thereby an immortal individuality (deathless), and that the cause of the death of the lower nature is love of the ego for the higher ; for Love is all in All.

See ARC. MAN, CHILDREN OF MEN, CONCEPTION OF CHILDREN, CREATURES, DEATH, EARTH (spec.), GENERATIVE, IMAGE, KHABIT, LIVING THINGS, PHALLIPHORIA, SEXUAL.

MULTITUDES HEALED :—

A symbol of the purifying and harmonising of the qualities of the soul.

"And Jesus went about . . . preaching the gospel of the kingdom, and healing all manner of disease and sickness. But when he saw the multitudes, he was moved with compassion for them, because they were distressed and scattered, as sheep not having a shepherd."—MAT. ix. 35, 36.

And the Christ-soul impressed upon the centralised qualities a perception of the coming of the buddhic consciousness ; and he also rectified disordered conditions, and harmonised the qualities. The "healing of the multitudes" has just the same meaning as the "healing of the people" spoken of in the Old Testament (2 CHRON. xxx. 20 ; Ps. cvii. 20) ; for the raising and co-ordinating of the qualities (people) are the work of the Christ-soul, and the "healing" is personified in Jesus because it is an integral part of the Drama, and symbolic of a necessary step in the bringing together of all qualities into one family, which means that whilst human souls are sick and suffering, the result of discordant qualities, they are not partakers of the riches of God's inexhaustible storehouse of blessings.

"The Saviour who was born of Mary came to rectify the passions (or heal the multitudes) of the soul" (Gnostic statement).—HIPPOLYTUS, *Works*, Bk. VI. 31.

The redeeming Higher Self, born of the purified lower nature and brought forth in the soul, came to rectify and subdue the passions and desires, and harmonise the multitude of qualities in the soul.

"The Multitude and Diversity of natures in the universe proceed directly from the intention of God, who brought them into being, in order to communicate His goodness to them, and to have it represented by them. And since It could not be sufficiently represented by one creature alone, He produced many and diverse ones, so that what is wanting to the one towards this office, should be supplied by the other."—AQUINAS, *Summa Theol.* I.

See BUDDHIC PLANE, GOSPEL, HEALING, KINGDOM, QUALITIES, REDEMPTION, TRANSMUTATION, WEALTH.

MUMMY OF A HUMAN BODY :—

As an *embalmed* corpse, this is a symbol of the purified personality ; but a simple corpse is a symbol of the lower personality " dead in trespasses and sins."

"The preservation of the embalmed body, or mummy, was the chief end and aim of every Egyptian who wished for everlasting life."—BUDGE, *The Mummy*, Preface.

"The perishable body must be preserved in such a way that each limb of it may meetly be identified with a god, and the whole of it with Osiris, the judge of the dead and king of the nether world."—*Ibid.*, p. 160.

The personality (body), purified through saturation with the higher qualities (spices, etc.), rises to immortality and union with the Divine (Osiris). Each purified quality (limb) is a member of the Divine body of the Archetypal Man (Christ), and the perfected souls at the end of the cycle will be identified with their Lord and Saviour, who has evolved within them.

See ARC. MAN, BA, CORPSE, DEAD, DEFUNCT, EMBALMMENT, FINGERS (two), GODS, INCENSE, LIMBS, MEMBERS, OSIRIS, PERSONALITY, PHŒNIX, PILLOWS (mummies), SAHU, SPICES, VULTURE.

MUMMY OF OSIRIS :—

A symbol of the archetypal astro-physical body containing the personality which is an expression of the Individuality in the cycle of evolution.

"The emblamed body of Osiris was the first mummy that was made in the world."—PLUTARCH, *Isis and Osiris.*

The making of the mummy of the archetypal man is the fashioning of the astro-physical body, which is now to be perpetuated ; the ideal physical vehicle having at length been built up as a generative pattern for heredity in the human race.

See BODY OF OSIRIS, DEATH OF OSIRIS, EMBALMMENT, OSIRIS.

MUMMIES OF ANIMALS :—

Symbolic of the purification of the desires and lower qualities of the soul.

See ANIMALS, BEASTS, EMBALMMENT.

MURDER, WRATH, AND HATRED :—

Symbols of the earlier manifestations of the Divine indwelling principle, which breaks down habits of thought.

"Some of you shall they cause to be put to death. And ye shall be hated of all men for my name's sake."—LUKE xxi. 16.

Murder and hatred are typical of disintegrating factors which make for the dispersal of the lower aspects of the qualities, and at the same time enable the higher aspects to be manifested.

See CALAMITIES, DISEASES, EVIL, GOVERNORS, GUILTY, LAW OF REVENGE.

MURDERER, THIEF, OR WOLF :—

Symbolic of the nature of the desire-mind which kills, steals and attacks the nascent higher qualities, and requires to be overcome and subdued by the indwelling Self.

"Whosoever hateth his brother is a murderer : and ye know that no murderer hath eternal life abiding in him."—1 JOHN iii. 15.

See DOOR (higher), THIEF, WALKS (six), WOLF.

MUSCULAR AND HAIRY MEN :—

A symbol of strong and energetic mental qualities.

"In its warmer parts the womb is productive of the male, and on this account men are dark and more muscular and more hairy."—*Empedocles*, FAIRBANKS, 276.

Through the stirring of the desires and emotions, the mental qualities (male) are aroused, and hence it comes about that the mental qualities so evolved are more intense, powerful and virile than those evolved by thought alone.

See CHURNING, MEN (forest), MOON-WAXING.

MUSE, THE WHITE-ARMED MAIDEN :—

A symbol of Wisdom or intuition, pure and spotless from the buddhic plane.

See ATHENA, HERA, KALLIOPEIA, PIETY, WHITE-ARMED.

MUSES :—

Symbols of the buddhic emotions, intuitions and faculties, centred in the Higher Self (Apollo, Dionysus).

See DANCE (circle), GOPIS, HOURIES, PHAEACIANS.

MUSIC, OR MELODY :—

A symbol of order and harmony of the qualities on the buddhic plane, where there is perfect adaptation of each part to the whole.

"I (Lakshmi) reside in the sound of musical instruments."—*Institutes of Vishnu*, XCIX. 15.

The buddhic nature is symbolised by musical sounds.

"So feasted the Gods all day till the setting of the sun; nor was their soul aught stinted of the fair banquet, nor of the beauteous lyre that Apollo held, and the Muses singing alternately with sweet voice."—*The Iliad*, Bk. I.

So on the buddhic plane harmony was promoted and love established, until the manifesting aspect of the Self was exhausted in the termination of that cycle. Nor was a single spiritual quality starved as the Soul evolved; nor was the emotion-aspect of the Higher Self withheld, for the higher emotions became active in complete harmony, and the channels of Love and Truth from above were opened. The "alternate singing of the Muses," signifies the rhythmic action of the outpouring from above,— active and passive.

"If we want to know what God is and what His relations are to the human soul, we have, in this great (music) realm of ordered harmony, what might be described almost as a distinct revelation ready to our hand."—J. BRIERLEY, *Studies of the Soul*, p. 60.

See APOLLO, BLISS, BUDDHIC PLANE, CONCH, CUP (double), GATHA DAYS, HYMN, LAKSHMI, MELODY, ORPHEUS, PROCESSION, SINGERS, SONG.

MUSIC AND DANCING :—

Symbols of harmony and rhythm in the qualities of mind and emotion, brought about through the opening of perception upon the buddhic plane. In the acquirement of knowledge, the mind first evolves through the sense of melody and the spirit of harmony.

See DANCES, GOPIS, HARMONY, HYMN SINGING, INTUITION, PHAEACIANS, UZUMÉ.

MUSIC OF THE SPHERES :—

A symbol of the complete co-ordination and harmony that prevails among the atma-buddhic qualities and ideals upon the higher planes or spheres of the invisible archetypal universe. In the spheres of atma and buddhi there is prototypal perfection undisturbed by any discord of conflicting opposites, for Love and Truth are dominant.

MUSICIAN :—

A symbol of the mind which fosters the higher emotions, and thus comes into harmony with the Divine nature.

"And his brother's name was Jubal: he was the father of all such as handle the harp and pipe."—GEN. iv. 21.

"Jubal," as musician, stands for the mental quality which begets the higher, or buddhic, emotions.

See JUBAL, MUSIC, UZUMÉ.

MUSPELL, SONS OF :—

A symbol of the spiritual egos which descend into the cycle of the lower life, and rise from it again.

"Bifrost is of itself a very good bridge, but there is nothing in nature that can hope to make resistance when the sons of Muspell sally forth to the great combat" (*Prose Edda*).—MALLET, *North. Antiq.*, p. 409.

The bridge of consciousness between the higher mind and the lower is, as it were, "broken down" at the "fall" of mind, when the spiritual egos have passed across it to ensoul the human forms on the lower planes, in order to fight the battle of life.

"The word muspell is evidently used in the sense of elemental or empyreal fire; but its etymology is quite unknown."—MALLET, *North. Antiq.*, p. 560.

The spiritual egos are of atma-buddhic (fire) nature.

See AGNISHVATTAS, BIFROST, BODHISATVAS, FALL, FRAVASHIS, INCARNATION OF SOULS, MANASAPUTRAS, MARUTS, MONADS OF LIFE, SOLAR PITRIS, SONS OF GOD, SPARKS.

MUSPELLHEIM :—

A symbol of the buddhic plane, the heaven-world.

"First of all there was in the southern region (sphere) the world called Muspell. It is light and hot, insomuch so that it is flaming and burning, and it is impervious to those who are foreign, and not indigenous there (or who have no home or heritage therein)" (*Prose Edda*).—MALLET, *North. Antiq.*, p. 401.

The highest plane of the quaternary is the buddhic (fire) plane, which is imperceptible to the lower consciousness. The lower qualities (foreigners) cannot reach it, for they have no heritage therein.

See BUDDHIC PLANE, EDEN, FIRE, GARODMAN, HEAVEN, KINGDOM, PARADISE, SOUTH.

MUSUBI, THE GOD OF GROWTH :—

A symbol of the World-process of Involution and Evolution, by which the Soul is formed and developed.

"This God is the abstract process of growth personified—that is, a power immanent in nature and not external to it. . . . As a God's name, Musubi is usually found with one of the laudatory adjectives, *taka*, high, or *kamu*, divine, prefixed to it. To these the honorific particle *mi* is commonly added, giving the forms Taka-mi-musubi and Kama-mi-musubi. Even in the *Kojiki* and *Nihongi* these are recognised as two distinct deities."—W. G. ASTON, *Shinto*, p. 172.

The two deities, so-called, signify the two processes of the Divine Life : first, Involution of Spirit into the matter of the planes ; and second, Evolution of Spirit from matter in the souls of humanity.

See ARC. MAN, CRUCIFIXION OF CHRIST, EVOLUTION, HEAVEN AND EARTH, INVOLUTION, KAGU, LION-GOD, MATTER, MITHRA, PURUSHA, SABBATH, SALVATION, SEPHIROTH, SHU (double), SPIRIT.

MUT, THE GODDESS :—

A symbol of the buddhic plane as containing the archetypal forms of all things on the lower planes.

"Mut, the ' mother,' was the wife of Amen, and the second member of the Theban triad. . . . She symbolised Nature, the mother of all things."

"At times the goddess Mut seems to be indentified with Nut, ' the sky.' "—BUDGE, *The Mummy*, pp. 116, 289.

Buddhi, the receiver and bringer forth, is allied with Atma (Amen) and is the second in the Divine triad atma-buddhi-manas. She contains the archetypal patterns of all the species of living forms on the three lower planes. Buddhi thereby identifies herself with space (Nut) on her own plane of being.

See AMEN, BIRTH OF OSIRIS, BUDDHI, EARTH (great), HETHRA, ISIS, MATTER, MOTHER, NUT, OSIRIS, PRAKRITI, SAPANDOMAD, SKY, THETIS, WOMAN (matter), WOMB.

MYRMIDONS OF ACHILLES :—

A symbol of the lower mental concepts subject to the personality.

"(Agamemnon to Achilles),—Go home with thy ships and company, and lord it among thy Myrmidons ; I reck not aught of thee nor care I for thy indignation."—*Iliad*, Bk. I.

The Personality is therefore bidden to depart on its upward way, and the Desire-mind (Agamemnon) conceives it to be possible for the Personality to dissociate itself in so great a degree from the false concepts, lusts and passions, as to confine the ego to the upper planes, an attempt to withdraw the Spirit from the lower, which would more and more retard evolution. The Desire-mind cannot realise the Personality under its higher aspects, nor can it sympathise with its dawning higher emotions.

See ACHILLES, AGAMEMNON, JESUS OF GOSPELS, MAN (natural), PERSONALITY, SHIPS (GREEK).

MYRRH :—

A symbol of high qualities, such as peace or bliss ; and in another context, truth or logic.

"For what is designated by the name of myrrh, amber, and cassia except the sweetness of virtues."—ST. GREGORY, *Morals on the Book of Job*, Vol. III. p. 695.

See EMBALMMENT, GOLD (myrrh), INCENSE, SPICES.

MYRRH POURED OVER AN OFFERING :—

A symbol of the consecration of the mind to a high ideal.

See COLUMN.

MYRTLE, BURNT :—

A symbol of envy.

MYSIA REGION :—

A symbol of the stage of pure intellect.

MYSTERIES OF LIGHT :—

A symbol of the higher nature suffused in the light of Truth, which is a mystery to the lower mind. It refers to the raising of the consciousness to a higher level, and the arousing of latent powers in the soul.

See LIGHT, MIDST.

MYSTERIES AND MAGIC OF THE THIRTEENTH ÆON :—

Symbolic of the awakening of powers which have hitherto lain dormant, until the cyclic period which is indicated by this Æon of final liberation from the lower conditions.

See ÆON (thirteen).

MYSTERY, FIRST :—

A symbol of purity, gentleness, and obedience to the calls of duty and love.

"The disciples thought that all had been revealed (by Jesus), and that the First Mystery—the Father in the likeness of a dove,—was the gnosis of all gnoses."—*Pistis Sophia*.

The disciplined qualities mistakenly thought that revelation and finality are synonymous. This is an error into which many more or less enlightened people fall. The First Mystery as a dove is an emblem of simplicity, meekness, and willingness to descend to everyday duties of life.

"The way to the eternal glory lies through a right relationship to the common things of life, not in despising and forsaking them. The man of faith is he who discerns the spirituality inherent in material existence, and lives accordingly. And to him who so lives God reveals the truth that everything earthly is more and other than it seems; is, in fact, divine."—R. J. CAMPBELL, Serm., *Steadying Power of Faith*.

See DOVE, GNOSIS, MIDST.

MYSTERY-NAME :—

A symbol which conveys no special signification to the lower mind, but one which indicates the idea signified to the individuality or higher mind.

See ABERAMENTHO.

MYTHOLOGY :—

This contains the symbolism of Divine emanation from the Absolute, and manifestation of Spirit and Matter in Time and Space throughout the cycle of Life : the symbolism of the origin and growth of the Soul, the descent of Spirit into Matter in the process of Involution, followed by the ascent of Spirit from Matter in the process of Evolution : the symbolism of the five planes of being, and of the higher and lower natures, and of the four soul-bodies : the symbolism of the struggle in the soul between the Divine principle or Self and the lower principle or not-Self ; and also of a great variety of unapparent activities.

"And yet, how strange (are these tales) ! From the very childhood of philosophy, from the first faintly whispered Why ? to our own time of matured thought and fearless inquiry, mythology has been the ever-recurrent subject of anxious wonder and careful study. . . . There is this common feature in all who have thought or written on mythology, that they look upon it as something which, whatever it may mean, does certainly not mean what it seems to mean ; as something that requires an explanation, whether it be a system of religion, or a phase in the development of the human mind."—MAX MÜLLER, *Chips*, Vol. IV. pp. 156–7.

"It may pass for a further indication of a concealed and secret meaning, that some of these (Greek) fables are so absurd, and idle, in their narration, as to show and proclaim an allegory even afar off. A fable that carries probability with it may be supposed to be invented for pleasure, or in imitation of history ; but those fables that could never be conceived, or related in this way, must surely have a different use. For example, what a monstrous fiction is this, that Jupiter should take Metis to wife ; and as soon as he found her pregnant, eat her up ; whereby he also conceived, and out of his head brought forth Pallas armed ? Certainly no mortal could, but for the sake of the moral it couches, invent such an absurd dream : so much out of the road of thought."—LORD BACON, *Wisdom of the Ancients*.

"Let the narrations in the Eddas be compared with the beginning of Hesiod's Theogony, with the mythology of some Asiatic nations, and with the book of Genesis, and we shall instantly be convinced that the conformity which is found between many circumstances of their recitals cannot be the mere work of chance."—MALLET, *North. Antiq.*, p. 99.

"This voice of fable has in it somewhat divine. It came from thought above the will of the writer. That is the best part of each writer, which has nothing private in it; that which *he does not know*; that which flowed out of his constitution, and not from his too-active invention."—EMERSON, *Essay on Compensation*.

"On the subject of Greek Symbolism generally, Rektor Siljestrom says: 'The Greek Fables are thoroughly symbolical, and the Wisdom that speaks from this mythology is so deep and so comprehensive that it is impossible not to see the actual civilization of thousands of years mirrored in it.' "—J. J. G. WILKINSON, *Revelation and Mythology*, p. 74.

"It has been well pointed out that myth and legend are truer than history for they take us to the inside of things, whereas history only shows us the outside."—R. J. CAMPBELL, *New Theology*, p. 261.

See ACHILLES, ADONIS, AGAMEMNON, AIDONEUS, ANDROMEDA, APOLLO, ATALANTA, ATHENA, BACCHUS, CHILDREN OF HORUS, COMB, COSMOS, CREATION, CUPID, DEMETER, DIONYSUS, DIOSCURI, ELEMENTS, EROS, EVOLUTION, GILGAMES, HEAVEN AND EARTH, HELEN, HERA, HESPERIDES, HIGHER, INSPIRATION, INVOLUTION, JASON, LATONA, MEADOW, MEDEA, MEDUSA, PAN, PANDORA, PERSEPHONE, PERSEUS, PHANES, PLANES (five), PROMETHEUS, QUATERNARY, RAMAYANA, REVELATION, SCRIPTURES, SUSANOWO, TITANS, UPANISHADS, URANUS, VENUS, VESTURES, WORLDS (five), ZAGREUS, ZEUS.

NAAMAH, THE SISTER OF TUBAL CAIN :—

A symbol of the intuition element which is associated with the discriminative and analytical intellect.

See TUBAL CAIN.

NAASENE, OR OPHITE :—

A symbol of divine inspiration, or Wisdom teaching. That afflatus which proceeds from the buddhic plane, or the Holy Spirit of Wisdom (serpent).

See BUDDHI, INSPIRATION, INTUITION, REVELATION, SERPENT, WISDOM.

NACHIKETAS, SON OF VĀJASRAVASA :—

A symbol of the Soul, or indwelling Self, proceeding from the Higher Self.

"Yama said: I know the fire that leads to paradise, and tell it to thee (Nachiketas): therefore listen. Know that that fire that wins the endless sphere for him that knows it, the bases of the world, is seated in the heart. . . . Yama revealed to him that fire, the origin of these spheres of migration, etc., and Nachiketas repeated everything after him as he said it. Feeling gratified, the large-minded Yama said, I give thee now and here another gift: this fire shall be called by thy name. Take also this necklace of gems of various colours."
—*Katha. Upanishad*, I.

It is the Divine Life (atma-buddhi) within the "heart" of the love-nature which leads the soul to bliss and immortality. The perfected personality (Yama) reveals, little by little, the meaning and process of that life (fire) within; the soul repeating its knowledge in its experiences. Then comes a time when the soul claims the life as its own, and is adorned with the higher qualities (gems).

See CAUSAL-SELF, DEATH (king), FIRE, GEMS, HEART, NECK, PERSONALITY, REINCARNATION, SOUL (middle), VAJASRAVASA, YAMA.

NAIADS, OR NYMPHS :—

A symbol of nature elementals, or builders of form on the lower planes. On the mental plane a "water nymph" may mean metaphysical speculation at the spring of truth.

"Nymphs of the spring were thought to be endowed with prophetic power, and to inspire men with the same."—
—*Smith's Class. Dict.*

See DEVAS (lower), HYLAS.

NAKEDNESS (HIGHER ASPECT) :—

A symbol of purity, that is, freedom from the limitations and opinions (garments) of the lower nature.—*See* JOB i. 21.

"Such a spirit descended on the Goddess Usumé, that she loosened her dress (as she danced), revealing more and more of her loveliness, and at last, to the intense amusement of the Gods, discarded her dress altogether."—"The Dancing of Usumé," *The Nihongi*.

The soul realising its needs, consciously hastened its own progress; the now exalted emotions (Usumé) cast away the bonds of convention and opinion, and revealed the truth within; until finally all Ideals (Gods) were realised, and the lower nature being purified, all its restrictions were discarded.

"Plotinus describes psychologically the method of preparation for the vision of the One. The process, which may begin at any point, even with the lowest part of the soul, consists in stripping off everything extraneous till the principle is reached."—T. WHITTAKER, *The Neo-Platonists*, p. 105.

"In order to bring back the soul to God, man is required to strip off all that pertains to the creature."—ECKHART.

"By nakedness is signified innocence, and likewise ignorance of good and truth."—SWEDENBORG, *Apoc. Rev.*, n. 213.

"Catherine (of Genoa) not only, as ever, simply ignores all questions of a risen body, and transfers the concept of a luminous ethereal substance from the body to the soul itself, and refers the 'nakedness,' 'unclothing,' 'clothing,' and 'clothing upon' to conditions obtaining not between the soul and the body, but between the soul and God; but she also, in most cases, takes the nakedness as the desirable state, since typical of the soul's faithful self-exposure to the all-purifying rays of God's light and fire, and interprets the 'unclothing' as the penitential stripping from off itself of those pretences and corrupt incrustations which prevent God's blissful action upon it."—F. VON HUGEL, *Mystical Element*, Vol. II. p. 78.

"There is an overshadowing of the embodied by a disembodied personality recognised by the Zohar and referred to twice by the text, namely, in the discourse of the Ancient Man in section *Mishpatem*. It is a very important section for many doctrines and ideas connected with transmigration. The thesis is (1) That all holy and superior souls which are destined to enter this world are accustomed—while awaiting incarnation—to descend from their residence on high and visit the Earthly Paradise at stated periods. (2) That they meet therein the souls of proselytes and other inferior souls which have been incarnated once only and cannot ascend higher. (3) That the superior souls clothe themselves with inferior souls, as if with a vesture, and are so joined to these during their sojourn in Paradise; but they unclothe to return above. It is a particular illustration of the invariable teaching that the spirit is draped to come down and undraped to go up. (4) That the inferior soul, so far from being degraded by this use as a vesture, profits through the experience."—A. E. WAITE, *Secret Doctrine in Israel*, p. 288.

This is a luminous description of the process of incarnation of souls. (1) The "holy souls" are the spiritual egos or individualities who periodically descend to incarnate on the astro-mental plane (lower paradise). (2) They then meet with what remains

of their attached personalities which have each been once incarnated. (3) The egos invest themselves with fresh personalities in the combined mental, astral and physical bodies of the lower nature. Physical death commences a gradual undraping of the egos, who build into the causal-bodies the best results of incarnation. (4) The personalities are developed by their experiences during life on earth.

"No distinction is more important than that between the personal self and the Impersonal or Spiritual self. The Latin word *persona*, from which our word 'person' comes, means a mask, such as was worn by the old Greek actor on the stage, so called because the sound of the voice came through it. That is exactly what the personal self is—a mask which the genuine self wears upon this stage of life. I have called it 'illusive,' but we may be sure it is not for nothing; it serves some important purpose, and it may be that the term 'illusive' is not the one to apply to it. The great Self is within each of us, and is the genuine self of each of us. The real man—the soul—is permanent in distinction from the personal self, which is the changing consciousness."—K. C. ANDERSON, *Serm.*, *The Buried Life*.

See AMATERASU, ASTRAL, CLOTHING, DANCES, EXPERIENCES, GARMENTS, GILGOOLEM, INCARNATION OF SOULS, LAUGHTER OF GODS, METEMPSYCHOSIS, MONAD OF LIFE, MUSIC, REINCARNATION, SAMSARA, SELF, SINGING, UZUMÉ, VESTURES WHEELS OF BIRTH.

NAKEDNESS (LOWER ASPECT) :—

A symbol of a state of ignorance, a lack of ideas and opinions (clothes). As all external states have analogous reference to internal states, this condition is emblematic of an empty state of soul.

"And the eyes of them both were opened, and they knew that they were naked; and they sewed fig-leaves together, and made themselves aprons."—GEN. iii. 7.

And both the emotions and the mind perceive their utter nakedness or ignorance, that is, they recognise the necessity for further evolution. Fig leaves, so used, signify concealment of the inward growth of the Spirit.

"Now when Adam and Eve were awakened in the bestial property, the beast stood there naked and bare. When the Image of the Heavenly Essence did disappear, then the bestial property was manifest."—BOEHME, *Mysterium Magnum*, p. 96.

" By nakedness is signified ignorance of truth."—SWEDENBORG, *Apoc. Rev.*, n. 706.

See ADAM (lower), CLOTHING, EVE, GARMENTS (lower).

NAKULA AND SAHADEVA, TWIN SONS OF MADRI BY THE ASVINS :—

Symbols of the evolving love-natures of goodness and truth on the mental plane of the more developed soul.

" When the Asvins restored the *rupa* of Indra, Nakula and Sahadeva were born."—MON. WILLIAMS, *Indian Wisdom*, p. 388.

When the individuality and the personality together formed the causal-body, love of goodness and truth was evolved in the higher mind. In evolution the potential gives place to the actual.

See ASVINS, DIOSCURI, INDRA.

NALA-KUVERA, SON OF THE LORD OF WEALTH (KUVERA) :—

A symbol signifying the recipient of his heritage ; that is, the Soul as the inheritor of the riches of the potential Higher Self.

" When the body perisheth, whose shall be its wealth ? Without the Guru how shall God's name be obtained ? God's name is wealth, which accompanieth and assisteth us."—MACAULIFFE, *The Sikh Religion*, Vol. I. p. 315.

See HEIR, HUSBAND (good), KUVERA, POVERTY, WEALTH.

NAME :—

A symbol of perception of difference, whereby one quality is distinguished from another.

" Whatsoever Adam called every living creature, that was the name thereof."—GEN. ii. 19.

The primitive lower mind (Adam) began to perceive and reflect upon the differentiations of the sensations, desires, and lower emotions presented to the consciousness. And according as the mind energised the desires, so each emotion was distinguished. Knowledge commences in the perception of differences.

" And whatsoever ye do, in word or in deed, do all in the name of the Lord Jesus, giving thanks to God the Father through him."—COL. iii. 17.

The qualities are enjoined to identify themselves in all their ideas and activities with the spiritual differentiation denoted by the symbol " Lord Jesus," aspiring through this towards the Absolute.

" Upon the pillar thus wrought into the temple of God's loving kingdom there are three inscriptions :—' I will write upon him the name of my God, and the name of the city of my God the new Jerusalem, which cometh down out of heaven, and my new name ' (REV. iii. 12). The soul that in obedience to God is growing into His likeness is dedicated to the divine love, to the hope of the perfect society, and to the ever new knowledge of redemption and the great Redeemer."—PHILLIPS BROOKS, Serm., *The Pillar, etc.*

See ADAM (lower), ANIMALS, CREATURES, FAMILY, FORM AND NAME, JESUS OF GOSPELS, PILLAR, REN, TREADING.

NAME AND FORM :—

Symbolic of aspects of Matter and Spirit, implying individual existence.

See FORM AND NAME.

NAMES OF BEINGS :—

A symbol of differentiations of qualities ; or the differences by which each quality is distinguishable from other qualities. Knowledge of Names therefore implies acquisition of the qualities indicated.

" I am the great god Nu, who gave birth unto himself, and who made his name to become the company of the gods. What does this mean ? or Who is this ? It is Rā, the creator of the names of his limbs, which came into being in the form of the gods who are in the following of Rā."—BUDGE, *Book of the Dead*, Ch. XVII.

The eternal Truth (Nu) is self-existent, and from the Absolute proceed all differentiations. The manifesting Self (Rā) differentiates into attributes and qualities (limbs), which come into existence as Space, Time, Consciousness, Law, the five planes, etc., for " Rā is of many names."

" The creative source is in the transcendent Self of all things. This Self at its first differentiation into multiplex ' aspects ' (or individualities) manifests at the same time the Ideas which are inherent in its being ; and these again descend into Feeling, Thought, and Action, and finally into external structure and life,—which latter may be looked upon as largely due to the conditioning or limitation of the ideas manifested in one individuality by those manifested in another. . . . Being has no differentia tion except through the Ideas which it manifests."—ED. CARPENTER, *Art of Creation*, p. 121.

"By the Lord's name is meant the all of doctrine, and, in a universal sense, the all of religion. . . . In heaven no other names are given but what involve the quality of anyone."—SWEDENBORG, *Apoc. Rev.*, n. 81.

See BOAT ON RIVER, COSMOS, CREATION, HOLD, LIMBS, MEMBERS, NU, QUALITIES, RĀ, REN, TITANS.

NANDA AND YASODA :—

Symbols of the purified mind and emotions.

NANNA, DAUGHTER OF NEP, AND WIFE OF BALDER :—

A symbol of Buddhi proceeding from Truth (Nep) and allied with the Self or Soul (Balder).

"Balder's body was then borne to the funeral pile on board the ship, and this ceremony had such an effect on Nanna, the daughter of Nep, that her heart broke with grief, and her body was burnt on the same pile with her husband's" (*Prose Edda*).—MALLET, *North. Antiq.*, p. 448.

The emotion-nature, through which the Self acts, is now conveyed to the vehicle in which it is to operate ; and when the Wisdom element (Nanna) perceives this, it is obscured by illusion in the lower consciousness. And now comes the process which corresponds with the sacrifice of the forms which are to yield the offering of the Life to the soul. The purification of the soul is by fire (buddhi).

See ALTAR (fire), ARC. MAN, BALDER, BURNING, CREMATION, DEATH OF BALDER, FIRE, FORMS, FYLLA, OFFERING, RINGHORNE, SACRIFICER.

NĀRADA, THE GREAT RISHI :—

A symbol of the higher mind at an early period of the soul's evolution.

"Sir William Jones compares Nārada to Hermes and Mercury, and calls him 'the eloquent messenger of the Gods.' "—BLAVATSKY, *Secret Doctrine*, Vol. II. p. 52.

See HERMES, NEBO, THOR, THOTH.

NĀRĀYANA, OR IDAS-PATI, THE "MASTER OF THE WATERS" :—

A symbol of the Spirit of Truth, operating in Time and Space.

"One of the most ancient and popular of the numerous names of Vishnu. The word (Nārāyana) has been derived in several ways, and may mean 'he who

moved on the waters,' or 'he who influences men or their thoughts.' "—GRIFFITH, *The Ramayan*, Vol. I. p. 86.

The Higher Self (Vishnu) broods over the waters of Truth—the Divine Reality,—at the dawn of manifestation.

See CHAOS, HEAVEN AND EARTH, OCEAN, POSEIDON, SERPENT (ananta), SITA, VISHNU, WATER.

NARE, OR NARVE :—

A symbol of greed.

"The Asar then took Loke's sons, Vale and Nare, or Narve. Vale they changed into a wolf, and it then tore his brother Nare, and with his entrails the Asar bound Loke upon the three stones." —*The Story of Loke, Prose Edda.*

And then in the Divine scheme, the offspring of the astral nature,— force and desire,—are taken as factors ; and these now assume the forms of energy and greed ; and it is said that the latter binds the mind, through the desire-nature for a time to three of its modes, namely, will, feeling, and intelligence (the stones).

See ASAR, LOKE, WOLF.

NASU, THE FIEND, AS A RAGING FLY :—

A symbol of time, which, as it were, captures residual astral elements of the lower self, and sets them aside as astral matter for future use.

See ABSYRTUS, DOG (white), FIENDS, MAN WITHOUT WOMAN, MOSQUITO, TIME.

NATIONS, OR PEOPLES :—

A symbol of associated groups of qualities, higher or lower.

See BIRTH OF MAN CHILD, COUNTRIES, GOATS, GOSPEL OF KINGDOM, PEOPLE, QUALITIES.

NAVEL :—

A symbol of a point on the mental plane midway between the higher and lower natures.

"That part of the vital air which is immortal is above the navel, and streams out by upward breathings ; but that which is mortal passes by and away from the navel."—*Sata. Brâh.*, VI. 7, 1, 11.

That part of the active mind (air) which is immortal is above the lower nature and aspires upward ; but that which is mortal is influenced by the desires and sensations which are below.

" We worship the guardian angel of Gayo-marathan (Gayomard) the righteous, who first listened to Ahuramazda'a thoughts and sayings ; out of whose body he (Ahuramazda) formed the central mass (nâfô, ' navel ') of the Aryan countries, the surface of the Aryan countries."—M. HAUG, *Essays on Religion of Parsis*, p. 211.

The Divine nature (fravashi) of the Archetypal Man is extolled as carrying out the designs of the Supreme. From the form side (the body) of the Ideal Man, the mental plane (Iran) was evolved and divided centrally into higher and lower.

" Delphi was regarded as the central point of the whole earth, and was hence called the ' navel of the earth.' It was said that two eagles sent forth by Jupiter, one from the east and the other from the west, met at Delphi at the same time."—*Smith's Class. Dict.*

The reference to the " two eagles " signifies that the Self above, and the Self below, advancing in the soul from the opposite sides of spirit and matter, meet at the junction of the higher and lower minds, when the two become one in the resurrection of the lower Self from the dead (matter).

See AIR, ARC. MAN, ARYAVARTA, BREATH, DEAD, EAGLE, FRAVASHI, KAIOMARTS, MANCO, PRANAS, ZEUS.

NAVIGABLE WATER :—

A symbol of the astral plane whereon evolution could be accomplished in the progress of the soul (ship).

See BOAT ON RIVER, SHIP, WATER (lower).

NAVIGATION (MARITIME) :—

Symbolic of a co-ordination of the astral mechanism in relation to the formation of the Soul.

" Pwan-koo taught navigation, made passages through the mountains, and reigned as the first king of the human race."—KIDD, *China*, p. 100.

The Logos, or Divine Mind, was the originator and first ruler of the human soul. Teaching " navigation " is emblematic of the management of the astral mechanism, and is preparatory to experiences on the plane of desire. The " passages " refer to the establishment of tracts upon the mental plane. And from the astral plane through the action of manas,—the mind principle,—evolves the human soul.

See ASTRAL PLANE, NET, PWAN-KOO, SEA, VALLEYS, WATER (lower).

NAZARENE OR NAZARÆAN :—

A title given to those souls who follow a course of life similar to that which the Christ-soul or Jesus is described as following. A Nazarene is one of an order which makes soul-culture the chief object of life. The Nazarene is consciously a pathfinder to the spiritual life of the soul.

See PATH OF BIRDS, WAY OF THE LORD.

NAZARETH :—

A symbol of progress in the path to perfection.

See GALILEE.

NEBO :—

A symbol of the higher mind, or the higher mental plane, central in the universe.

" Nebo presided over Mercury. He is called ' the god who possesses intelligence,' ' he who hears from afar,' ' he who teaches and instructs.' "—RAWLINSON, *Religious Systems*, p. 26.

" Nebo went by the Accadian name of *dim-sar*, the scribe ; and the ideograph by which he is sometimes denoted was regarded by the Semitic literati as signifying ' the maker of intelligence ' and ' the creator of writing.' He was also ' the bond of the universe,' and ' the overseer of the angel-hosts of heaven and earth.' "—SAYCE, *Rel. of Anc. Babyl.*, p. 115.

The mental plane unites the higher and the lower natures, and on it are the mental qualities (angel-hosts) of both natures.

See HERMES, NARADA, OVERSEER, THOR, THOTH.

NEBROPHONUS, A SON OF JASON AND HYPSIPYLE :—

A symbol of the expression of truth proceeding from the union of intellect and intuition.

See HYPSIPYLE, JASON.

NECESSITY :—

Symbolic of the Divine uniformity of action in the order of nature, which makes possible human interpretation of, and reliance on, Divine laws, in the development of the soul. Perfect order and certainty must characterise the laws of the higher planes as of the lower.

" Antiochus teaches : There are two natures, the active and the passive, force and matter, but neither is ever without the other. That which is compounded of both is called a body or a quality. Among these qualities the simple and the compound are to be distinguished; the former consisting of the four or, according to Aristotle, five, primitive bodies; the latter of all the rest; of the first category, fire and air are the active, earth and water the receptive and passive. Underlying them all, however, is the matter without quality, which is their substratum, the imperishable, but yet infinitely divisible elements, producing in the constant change of its forms, definite bodies (*qualia*). All these together form the world; the eternal reason which animates and moves the world is called Deity or Providence, also Necessity; and because of the unsearchableness of its workings, sometimes even Chance."—E. ZELLER, *Hist. of Eclecticism, etc.*, p. 94.

The four elements are the quaternary. Spirit (fire) and mind (air) are the active; the astral (water) and the physical (earth) are the receptive. The imperishable substratum is the same as prakriti.

See ADRASTIA, ELEMENTS, FATE-SPHERE, INVOLUTION, KARMA, MAAT, MOIRAE, PHENOMENA, PRAKRITI, QUATERNARY, SHENIT, THEMIS.

NECK :—

A symbol of the purified emotions; being situate between the breast and head, or the heart and mind.

" My neck is the neck of the divine goddess Isis."—BUDGE, *Ideas, etc.*, p. 127.
See MENAT, STIFFNECKED.

NECK, WITH NECKLACE AND JEWEL :—

A symbol of the higher mind and higher emotions : with the higher mind centre (jewel). The " bridge " between the higher and lower natures.

"Then the Lady of the gods (Istar) drew nigh, And she lifted up the great jewels which Anu had made according to her wish, and said : ' What gods are these ! By the jewels of *lapis lazuli* which are about my neck, I will not forget ! ' "—L. W. KING, *Babylonian Religion*, p. 136.

After the appeal from the lower nature, then Wisdom approached the soul, and she succeeds in raising the higher qualities which have been evolved below, and which have been formed unconsciously by the Divine Will according to her direction. Wisdom exclaims,—" Hail to these attri-

butes of the Self ! By the blue keystone of the Bridge,—the Higher Mental centre,—and by the raised qualities of Faith, Mercy, Justice, and Reason, I will not fail to bring about union with the Self."

See ANU, BEL, BRIDGE, GEMS, JEWELS, ISTAR, NACHIKETAS, QUALITIES, UNION.

NECTAR, SWEET :—

A symbol of the soul's entire, complete, and loving service to the highest ideals of Truth, Wisdom, and Justice.

" Now it is this matter (Hylē), which, after being impressed by the Divine Ideas, fashioned every body in the cosmos which we see. Its highest and purest nature, by means of which the divinities are either sustained or consist, is called Nectar, and is believed to be the drink of the Gods ; while its lower and more turbid nature is the drink of souls. The latter is what the Ancients called the River of Lethe [or Forgetfulness].—*Macrobius*, Bk. I. Ch. 8, quoted by G. R. S. MEAD in *T. G. Hermes*, Vol. I. pp. 415–16.

Hylē in its higher and lower natures appears to be the same as Māyā in its higher and lower aspects. Hylē leaves its Source as Truth-Reality and returns to its Source as the same, but with additional experience. The lower " drink of souls " is the experience of the illusions of the transitory lives, which is forgotten by the successive personalities.

" He who drinketh the nectar of the Name shall be satisfied, and go to God's court with a dress of honour." " The Name is nectar in the heart as well as in the mouth : through it man is freed from worldly desires" (*Nanak*).—MACAULIFFE, *The Sikh Religion*, Vol. I. pp. 274, 292.

The soul that identifies itself with the highest ideals is liberated from desire, and shall rise to the higher planes and be given the robe of Wisdom,—the Buddhic quality.

See CHURNING, LAUGHTER OF THE GODS, MĀYA, STYX.

NEHAHA, THE FIEND :—

A symbol of negation.
See AMMIT, SCAPEGOAT.

NEHE-MĀUT, SPOUSE OF THOTH :—

A symbol of the intuition of Truth allied with the higher mind.

" To aid him in the world Thoth has a spouse, or syzygy, Nehe-māut. She is among the Gnostics, the Sophia-aspect of the Logos. She is presumably the Nature of our Trismegistic treatises. Together Thoth and Nehe-māut are the initiators of all order, rule and law in the universe " (*Pietschmann*).—G. R. S. MEAD, *T. G. Hermes*, Vol. I. p. 49.

See CHRYSEIS, INTUITION, SOPHIA, THOTH.

NEIGHBOUR :—

Symbolic of a quality which has an affinity with another quality :— these qualities are " neighbours " to each other.

" Let everyone of us please his neighbour for his good to edification."— ROM. xv. 2.

The qualities are enjoined to be helpful to each other in the way of development and progress : for it is the actual that must evoke, or awaken, the potential ; there is no other course.

" And they shall teach no more every man his neighbour, and every man his brother, saying, Know the Lord : for they shall all know me, from the least of them to the greatest of them."— HEB. viii. 11 ; JER. xxxi. 34.

The personality having become perfected, the higher mental qualities are fully evolved, and ready to unite with the Higher Self. There is no longer need for educing the potential, for all has been evolved from the less to the greater.

" Everything in nature has, as regards its own good, a certain inclination to diffuse itself amongst others as far as possible. And this applies, in a supreme degree, to the Divine Goodness, from which all perfection is derived."—ST. THOMAS AQUINAS.

See EVOLUTION, JUDGING OTHERS, LANDMARKS.

NEKHEBIT AND UACHIT :—

Symbols of wisdom and the emotions, or of intelligence and will, through which Divine manifestation is proceeded with, and made effective.

" Horus took with him Nekhebit, the goddess of the South, and Uazit, the goddess of the North, in the form of two serpents, that they might destroy the enemies in their bodily forms of crocodiles and hippopotami at each place to which he came in the South Land and in the North Land."—*Legend of the Winged Sun-disk.*

And from the higher and the lower regions whereon the evolution of the

Self (Horus) was to be accomplished did he choose two energies to accompany him, the Wisdom-nature from above, on the one hand, and the Love- and emotion-nature evolved from below, on the other, as through these he was to rise and accomplish his course ; that so he might destroy the illusions which were begotten of the sense of separateness, both on the mental and desire planes of the soul.

See CROCODILE, CROWN (double), HIPPOPOTAMI, NORTH LAND, SERPENT (south), SOUTH, UATCHIT.

NEPHESH, THE LOWER SOUL, OR ANIMAL PRINCIPLE :—

A symbol of the emotion-nature in the astral body, or astro-mental body. The lower emotions.

" The (lower) *Rua'h* forms with the *Nephesh* the actual personality of the man. . . . *Rua'h* is that which rides on that *Nephesh* (the lower soul) and rules over her, and lights her with everything she needs, and the *Nephesh* is the throne to that *Rua'h* " (From the *Zohar*).—I. MYER, *Qabbalah*, pp. 391, 393.

The lower mind (ruah) energised by the emotion-nature constitutes the lower personality in the human soul. The lower mind is that which regulates the emotion-nature, and controls it, and also brings intelligence to bear on all methods of supplying the needs of the desires. The astral body is the vehicle, or instrument, of the lower mind and emotions.

See ADAM (lower), GILGOOLEM, MICHAEL, NESHAMAH, RUAH, SOUL (lowest), WHEELS (holy), YEHUDAH.

NEPHESH ELEMENTARY :—

A symbol of the astral-body.

NEPHILIM OR GIANTS :—

Early physical human forms ; mostly Lemurian, some Atlantean. In these rugged forms mind is first aroused.

" The Nephilim were in the earth in those days, and also after that, when the sons of God came in unto the daughters of men, and they bare children to them." —GEN. vi. 4.

These Nephilim are the monsters which are pre-human and semi-animal. They correspond in soul life to the early attempts at Self-realisation, which are possible only through the agency of such clumsy modes of expression as are appropriate to the sub-human kingdoms of nature. The ideals of the minds, or spiritual egos (sons of God), conjoined to the processes of the lower planes, give rise to the "children of men," the progeny of mind, or mental —astro-physical forms. It is as the cosmic forces work through the personality while guided from the individuality, that the "sons of men" are born, that is, the successive incarnations are engendered.

"Like a beautiful seedling hidden away within a rough and ugly husk, through which it must break in order to achieve itself, our divine selfhood has been hidden and compressed within material conditions. Consciousness has had to use first one kind of vehicle and then another, and as the vehicle so has been the quality of the self-expression."— R. J. CAMPBELL, Serm., *Solidarity of Spiritual Experience.*

See CHILDREN OF MEN, DAUGHTERS, GADERINE DEMONIACS, GIANTS, SONS OF GOD.

NEPHTHYS, OR NEBKHAT, GODDESS :—

A symbol of the physical principle, or physical plane.

"Nephthys, the Egyptians call the extreme limits and boundaries of the land, and those contiguous to the sea ; for which reason they style Nephthys the 'end,' and say she is the consort of Typhon."—PLUTARCH, *Isis and Osiris,* § 38.

The physical plane is the extreme plane of the universe, and internally it is contiguous to the astral plane (the sea). It is therefore allied to the astral or desire principle (Typhon or Set) which fructifies it.

"Nephthys was born upon the fifth and last of the superadded days. Typhon and Nephthys were begotten by Kronos." —*Ibid.,* § 12.

The physical plane is the fifth and lowest of the planes of manifestation. The astral principle (Typhon) and the physical (Nephthys) are produced through the procession of Time (Kronos or Seb).

"In the Pyramid texts Nephthys appears as a friend of the deceased, and she maintains that character throughout every Recension of the *Book of the Dead,* indeed, she seems to perform for him what as a nature goddess she did for the gods in primeval times when she fashioned

the 'body' of the 'Company of the Gods,' and when she obtained the name Nebkhat, i.e. 'Lady of the Body [of the Gods]. . . . She was a "nursing mother" of Osiris.' . . . She was the opposite of Isis in every respect ; Isis symbolised birth, growth, development and vigour, but Nephthys was the type of death, decay, diminution and immobility."— BUDGE, *Gods of the Egyptians,* Vol. II. pp. 255–8.

The physical plane supplies the means whereby the individuality (deceased) gets its experience to enable it to develop and acquire the higher qualities (gods). The physical brings up, or nurses, the Self (Osiris) within. It is the opposite of Wisdom, and it harbours corruption, and has no life of itself.

See ANUBIS, DAYS (five), DEFUNCT, HAIGI, HESTIA, ISIS, NESTIS, SIGYN, UPLIFTING RĀ, WOMAN (Loke).

NEPHTHYS' EMBLEM (ON HEAD) :—

A symbol of the "cup" or physical vehicle of the four soul-bodies, i.e. the "four children of Horus." *See* CHILDREN OF HORUS.

NEREIDES, NYMPHS OF THE SEA :—

A symbol of emotions arising astrally through the regulating and disciplining of the desires,—productive of self-control.

NEREUS, THE WISE MAN OF THE SEA :—

A symbol of the Force aspect of the Logos in the physical nature, operative through the astral. *See* THETIS.

NERYOSANG, THE ANGEL :—

A symbol of the intellect which arouses love of ideals.

"Then Srosh and Neryosang the angel go to Keresasp (the Saman); three times they utter a cry, and the fourth time Saman rises up with triumph, and goes to meet Azi Dahak. And Saman does not listen to his words, and the triumphant club strikes him on the head and kills him."—*Bahman Yasht,* III. 60, 61. *S. B. of E.*

The Divine Will (Srosh), acting through the intellect (Neryosang), approaches the Love-element (Keresasp) aud arouses it completely in the evolving soul. Then the Divine force (Saman) Love goes forth on

the path of devotion to the Ideal,
undeterred by the temptations of
sense, and with the higher emotions
(club) overcomes illusion and selfishness.

See CLUB, ILLUSION, KERESASPA,
SAMAS, SERPENT DAHAKA, SROSH.

NESHAMAH, HIGHEST SOUL :—

A symbol of the Divine monad,
atma-buddhi, or spiritual ego within
the individual human soul.

"Job describes the continuance of
his life by saying 'all my *neshāmāh* is
still in me' (JOB xxvii. 3). In three cases,
the term denotes the breath-soul as the
principle of the moral and spiritual life,
as when it is said that man's discernment
is due to God's *neshāmāh* within him
(JOB xxii. 8; cf. xxvi. 4, and PROV.
xx. 27). The other instances are those
in which the term is applied to the wind
as God's breath."—H. W. ROBINSON,
Christian Doctrine of Man, p. 16.

"There are three degrees, and they
are connected as one. Nephesh, Rua'h,
and Neshamah, and the highest of them is
Neshamah."—*Zohar*, III. 70b, Brody ed.

"Neshamah (Divine soul) goes over
to that Rua'h, and rules over him, and
lights him with that Light of Life"
(*Ibid.*).—MYER, *Qabbalah*, pp. 391–3.

The three human principles in
ascending degrees are the astral
(Nephesh), the mental (Rua'h), and
the atma-buddhic (Neshamah), and
these are all connected in the one
human soul. The Divine and highest
principle ensouls the causal body and
dominates it, imparting to it the light
of Wisdom, Truth, and Love.

"The 'outer man' consists for St.
Paul of the body's earthly material,
'the flesh'; and of the animating
principle of the flesh 'the psyche,' which
is inseparably connected with that
flesh. . . . The 'inner man' consists
for St. Paul, in the Mind, the Heart,
and the Conscience. The Mind (noûs),
corresponding roughly to our theoretical
and practical Reason, has a certain
tendency towards God. . . . The Heart
is even more accessible to the divine
influence. . . . The Spirit, the Pneuma,
is, strictly speaking, only one—the Spirit
of God, God Himself, in His action either
outside or inside the human mind Noûs."
—F. VON HUGEL, *Mystical Element*,
Vol. II. pp. 64, 67.

The Spirit, the Pneuma, is the same,
as the Neshamah.

See CAUSAL - BODY, GILGOOLEM,
HEART, MICHAEL, MONAD OF LIFE,
NEPHESH, RUAH, SOUL (highest),
YEDUD.

NESTIS, HESTIA OR VESTA :—

A symbol of the sensation principle of the physical plane.

"Nestis, who moistens the springs of
men with her tears."—*Empedocles*, FAIR-
BANKS, 33.

The activities of the physical nature
are the means of producing suffering
to the mind (men).

See AIDONEUS, BONES, HESTIA,
NEPHTHYS.

NESTOR, THE SWEET-VOICED :—

A symbol of the spiritual emotion of Faith-Hope in the higher
mind.

"Therefore to them arose the sweet-
voiced Nestor, the harmonious orator of
the Pylians, from whose tongue flowed
language sweeter than honey."—*Iliad*,
Bk. I.

On account of the submission of
the lower emotions to the higher
ideal, these emotions became responsive to the charms of Faith-Hope in
the higher mentality (Pylus), which
spiritual quality answers to the higher
opposite of the lower emotions.

"As long as man has not yet attained
unto that which is perfect, and is still
in pursuit of it, hope must be regarded
as the greatest, for it is even the true vital
flame of faith, as well as of love and of
all higher existence. This divine hope
is even the fruit-bearing principle and
the fructification of the immortal soul
by the Holy Spirit of Eternal Truth—
the luminous centre and focus of grace,
where the dark and discordant soul is
illuminated and restored to unison with
itself and with God."—SCHLEGEL, *The
Philosophy of Life*, Eng. Trans., p. 113.

See FAITH, GREECE, HARMONY,
HONEY, MUSIC, PANDORA, PYLUS,
SINGING, SWEET, TONGUE.

NET-RĀ :—

A symbol of the buddhic plane of
the soul.

"The time of evening has come, and
the Sun-god in the Sekhet Boat, wherein
he has travelled since noon, draws nigh
to Thebes, flooding the First Division of
the Tuat with light. This Division, or
antechamber, of the Tuat is, according
to the *Book Am-Tuat*, called Net-Rā."—
BUDGE, *Egypt. Heaven and Hell*, Vol. III.
p. 105.

The Higher Self (Rā) in descending
to the lower planes in the Life-cycle
(Tuat) first enters the buddhic plane.

See APES, ARIES, BOAT (Sektet),
THEBES, TUAT.

NET FOR THE CATCHING OF FISH :—

A symbol of the astral mechanism which lies behind the physical organs of the five senses, and serves to collect and differentiate the facts of sensation, passing them on as modes of vibration to the mental plane, whereon they become interpreted to the ego as thoughts and feelings of different kinds and qualities.

"Füh-he invented nets for fishes, and snares for wild beasts, in the use of which he instructed the people, for the twofold purpose of supplying their wants and procuring victims to offer in sacrifice."—*Chinese Mythology*, KIDD, *China*.

From the Logos is emanated the Divine scheme of existence ; and now it is that an astral mechanism of sensation comes to be developed, which is to be used by the ego in gathering the facts (fish), which it is necessary that it shall collect for its experience and development. The "wild beasts" signify the baser passions, which are to be checked and subdued and so become transmuted to higher emotions through the gradual evolution of the Self within. The "people" are the undeveloped instincts and activities which are to be disciplined and used, as means to the end of Self-realisation. The "supplying of wants" refers to the need for realising that the powers within the soul are to be utilised only for the highest purpose, and this self-abnegation and giving up of lower aims becomes the offering up of the lesser Self to the greater Self,—or consecration of the individual life to the One Life, in return for His own sacrifice "from the foundation of the world."

"And when they had this done, (let down the nets) they inclosed a great multitude of fishes ; and their nets were breaking."—LUKE v. 6.

The lower mind (Peter) and its qualities, acquired through the senses a great multitude of facts which were utilised in the formation of mental currents directed to given ends.

"The scribe Nebseni hath drawn the net together in the region of Aaru, and he hath running water in Sekhet-hetep, and his offerings are among those of the gods."—BUDGE, *Book of the Dead*, Ch. CLXXVIII.

The individuality (Nebseni deceased) hath made use of the mechanism of sensation on the astral plane (Aaru), in order to acquire Life and Truth (water) on the buddhic plane (Sekhet-hetep), and his aspirations are realised in the higher emotions and the ideals (gods).

See ASTRAL PLANE, BEASTS (wild), BONES, CIVILISING, DEFUNCT, EXPERIENCES, FISH, FUH-HE, GODS, OANNES, PETER, SACRIFICER, SEKHET-AARU.

NET OF THE UNDERWORLD, OR OF THE "UNITER OF THE EARTH" :—

A symbol of the astral mechanism of sensation and desire which unites the individuality with the lower nature (earth) ; at first enmeshing the soul, but afterwards becoming a means of development.

"The name of the Temple of Thoth at Khemennu, or the City of Eight, was Het Abtit, or the 'House of the Net,' —a very curious expression. From Ch. CLIII. of the Ritual, however, we learn that there was a mysterious Net which, as Budge says, 'was supposed to exist in the Underworld, and that the deceased regarded it with horror and detestation. Every part of it—its poles, and ropes, and weights, and small cords, and hooks —had names which he was obliged to learn if he wished to escape from it, and make use of it to catch food for himself, instead of being caught by those who laid snares.' Interpreting this from the mystical standpoint of the doctrine of Re-birth, or the rising from the dead,— that is to say, of the spiritual resurrection of those who had died to the darkness of their lower natures and had become alive to the Light of the spiritual life, . . . I would venture to suggest that this Net was the symbol of a certain condition of the inner nature which shut in the man into the limitations of the conventional life of the world, and shut him off from the memory of his true self. The poles, ropes, weights, small cords, and hooks were symbols of the anatomy and physiology, so to say, of the invisible 'body,' or 'envelope' of the soul. The normal man was enmeshed in this engine of Fate ; the man who received the Mind inverted this Net, so to speak, transmuted and transformed it, so that he could catch food for himself. 'Come ye after me and I will make you fishers of men.' The food with which the 'Christ' nourishes his 'body' is supplied by men. Thus in a prayer in this chapter of the Ritual we read : 'Hail thou "God who lookest behind thee," thou "God who hast gained the mastery over thine heart,"

I go a fishing with the cordage [? net] of the "Uniter of the earth," and of him that maketh a way through the earth.' "
—G. R. S. Mead, *T. G. Hermes*, Vol. I. pp. 58, 59.

To the above excellent interpretation may be added :—The "city of eight" refers to the dual nature of the quaternary centralised by the higher mind (Thoth). The higher mind contains the causal-body (house of the net) from which the individuality (deceased) lowers the astral mechanism (net), while abhorring the illusions of the lower planes, which obscure the Self within. The ego is enmeshed in the mechanism of nature, but when the Spirit (Mind) begins to direct through the mind, the mechanism is made a means of evolution through the acquirement by it of facts (fish) and knowledge (food). The causal-body, or "Christ-body," is nourished by truth and love, the "bread from heaven," bestowed in response to the aspirations of the personality.

"This one deity (Isvara) spreads out his net in many modes for every one in this field of illusion, and draws it in again."
—*Svetas. Upanishad*, V.

"As Apep was a monster of the deep, to make use of nets in his capture was a wise decision on the part of the friends of Afu-Rā. Having taken up their positions for attacking Apep, the men with the harpoons work the rope which is attached to Aai, the goddesses and the apes shake out their rope nets over their heads, and recite their spells, and the men who know the proper words of power, shake out their nets and recite the formulæ which shall have the effect of throwing Apep and Sessi into the state of stupefaction wherein it will be easy to slay them."—Budge, *Egypt. Heaven and Hell*, Vol. I. p. 185.

See Afu-rā, Akeru, Ape, Apep, Birth of buddha, Boat sektet, Bones, Causal-body, Defunct, Earth, Fish, Food, Isvara, Rebirth, Sekhet-hetep, Thoth.

NET OF THE ASAR TO CATCH LOKE :—

A symbol of the astral mechanism of the physical eye which is to be used as a sense apparatus for the acquirement of knowledge and experience through which the mind may control the desire-nature.

"When the net was finished, they went out and cast it into the force.

Thor held the net on one side, and all the Asar upon the other, and so drew it. Loke crept down and lay between two stones, so that the net passed over him, although they could very well perceive that there was something alive there."—*The Punishment of Loke, Prose Edda*.

When the astral mechanism of the physical eye was finished, the organ was adapted to the use of the ego which responds through the desire-nature to the impacts from without in sensation. The higher mind (Thor) is said to use the "net," yet it is not the mind alone which is responsible for the mechanism. The nature forces (the Asar) play their part in assisting at its manufacture. Now the desire-nature (Loke) is said to descend in the water,—to be scarcely perceptible, in fact. This corresponds to the earliest feeble functionings of the desire-nature. At the same time the flickerings of self-consciousness are quite apparent. The "two stones" are symbols of differentiation, and signify the life forces segregating the atoms on the astral plane. As the impacts from without through the sense organs cause thrills in the matter of the lower astral sub-planes, so the response from within is aroused, and the Self under the aspect of desire is said to descend and lie between "two stones," or perceive differences.

"Then a second time they went up the force and threw the net, having first tied something so heavy to it that nothing could possibly escape under it."—*Ibid.*

And again the impacts from without are so strong that they are said to penetrate the "net." And at this stage the sensorium is established, which precludes the possibility of any vibration from the lower levels going unperceived.

See Asar, Astral plane, Eye (third), Frananger, Loke, Salmon, Thor, Water (lower).

NET, GOLDEN :—

A symbol of the web, or ideal scheme, of the universe on the buddhic plane.

"When the infant Buddha is born, four Brahmins, the wise men of India, receive him in a golden net. Then the Maharajahs, the four great kings of the Kosmos, bear him ; for is he not Purusha, the Kosmos imaged as a heavenly man ? "
—A. Lillie, *Budd. in Christendom*, p. 20.

The Soul is born on the buddhic plane during involution and enters the Divine scheme as its centre, uniting all forces and co-ordinating them. The four kings relate to the quaternary focussed on the mental plane. The four lower planes are centralised in the causal Self on the mental plane. The Soul is the Spirit (Purusha), which descends into Matter with all its qualities and thereby informs the Archetypal Man,—the One Soul (Buddha),—from which the many souls arise.

See ARC. MAN, BIRTH OF BUDDHA, BODHISATVA, BUDDHA, COSMOS, GOLD, PURUSHA, QUATERNARY.

NICODEMUS, A RULER OF THE JEWS :—

This symbol represents a phase of the lower personality in whom the sense of separateness is yet strong. He regarded Christ as distinct from himself and above him, and he is therefore said to approach him " by night." He was ignorant of the fact that the lower self could be nothing except it were given him of the Higher Self. And yet he is typical of the state of consciousness wherein the soul gropes towards an Ideal of whose presence it has become dimly aware,—of whose existence it is only just convinced. There are many of this type of soul ; some of whom call their Higher Self Lord and Master without doing the things that He approves. Nicodemus knew nothing of rebirth on the higher planes, and of the purifying process of truth (water) and Spirit (fire), which is necessary before re-birth can take place, and the soul rise to the heaven world.—*See* JOHN iii.

" Nicodemus was of that number who believe in the name of Christ, but Jesus does not trust Himself to them. He came to the Lord, and came by night ; came to the Light, and came in darkness. But what do they that are born again of water and of the Spirit hear from the apostle ? ' Ye were once darkness, but now light in the Lord ; walk as children of light ' (EPH. v. 8.). Therefore they who are born again were of the night, and are of the day ; were darkness, and are light. Now Jesus trusts Himself to them, and they come to Jesus, not by night. . . . Mark, my brethren, what answer this man who came to Jesus by night makes. Although he came to Jesus,

yet because he came by night, he still speaks for the darkness of his own flesh. He understands not what he hears from the Lord, understands not what he hears from the Light. . . . This man knew but one birth, that from Adam and Eve ; that which is from God and the Church he knew not yet : he knew only those parents that bring forth to death, knew not yet the parents that bring forth to life ; he knew but the parents that bring forth successors, knew not yet the ever-living parents that bring forth those that shall abide."—AUGUSTINE, *Gospel of John*, Vol. I. pp. 155–8.

See BAPTISM, DARKNESS, NIGHT (darkness), PERSONALITY, RE-BIRTH, REGENERATION.

NICOTHEA HARPY :—

A symbol of the absorbing attractiveness of the sense of sight.

" One of the Harpies named Nicothea or Aelopus flew to the Peloponnesus, where she fell into a river named Tigris, but which was henceforth called Harpys."—*Argonautic Expedition.*

And the lust of the eyes swelled and increased, and was at length submerged in the astral tide of desire, which is henceforth known as the sense-nature.

See ARIZURA, HARPIES, PHINEUS, ZETES.

NIDĀNAS, TWELVE :—

A symbol of the twelve divisions, or departments, of the Cycle of Life ;—the same as the Zodiac.

" Out of this ignorance (Avijja), as out of some sort of counterpart of the primordial cell, the Buddha has his Buddha-world issue in twelve distinct stages ; the twelve Nidānas, as they are called, whereof the final phase of development, the bloom of sorrow, takes shape as old age, disease, death, misery and distress, grief and despair."—DAHLKE, *Buddhist Essays*, p. 34.

The cycle of life commences on the lower planes as a world-germ developing from the homogeneous protoplasm of matter which implies ignorance of all else, and passing on to greater and greater heterogeneity as the qualities and forms appear. This world-process occupies twelve stages,—six of Involution, and six of Evolution. At the close of the final stage the soul is perfected, while the death and distress in the process are of the personality as it casts off the last vestiges of the lower nature :—the cry of despair being, "My God, my God, why hast *thou* forsaken me ? "

See ADITYAS, CRUCIFIXION OF JESUS, EVOLUTION, IGNORANCE, INVOLUTION, MUSUBI, SEPHIROTH, SUFFERING, TUAT, TWELVE, ZODIAC.

NIDHOGG SERPENT :—

A symbol of the principle of desire, or of the desire-mind.

" One root (of the great ash Yggdrasil) strikes down to Nifelheim, and into the fountain Hvergelmir which is full of serpents, and where Nidhogg, the most venemous of snakes, with all its reptile brood, gnaw at its roots."—HOWITT, *Literature of North Europe*, Vol. I. p. 41.

One division of the Divine Life (Yggdrasil) extends to the lower planes and into the fount of illusion and separateness in which the desires (serpents) are immersed. The desire-mind (Nidhogg) is the opponent of the spiritual aspirations, and it and all the lower qualities sap the Divine Life which rises upwards in the human soul. But the desires cannot ultimately prevail, and the time comes when the incarnate Self shall have " bruised the Serpent's head " and entirely overcome the illusory desire-mind.

See HEEL, HVERGELMIR, MIDGARD, QAF, SERPENT (subtil), YGGDRASIL.

NIFLHEIM, THE SHADOWY REGION OF DEATH :—

A symbol of the astro-physical region, or of the lower planes.

" Alfadir hath formed heaven and earth, and the air, and all things thereunto belonging. And what is more, he hath made man, and given him a soul which shall live and never perish, though the body shall have mouldered away, or have been burnt to ashes. And all that are righteous shall dwell with him in the place called Gimli, or Vingolf; but the wicked shall go to Hel, and thence to Niflhel (or Niflheim), which is below in the ninth world " (*Prose Edda*).— MALLET, *North. Antiq.*, p. 401.

The Logos hath emanated the higher and the lower natures, and centrally the mental plane (air) and all that appertains to it. The object of existence is the formation and growth of the soul which is immortal while its lower vehicles are subject to decay and extinction while the soul is being purified stage by stage. The purified souls, or individualities, shall rise from the lower planes, and become conscious on the higher planes ; but the unpurified personalities shall continue to re-incarnate below until they are perfected.

See FATHER, HADES, HEAVEN AND EARTH, HELL, HVERGELMIR, JOTUNHEIM, NINE, PERSONALITY, REINCARNATION, UNDERWORLD, YGGDRASIL.

NIGHT, PRIMORDIAL :—

A symbol of potential being, or of the cycle of life in the underworld,—the planes of the quaternary, —wherein the Higher Self (sun) is unapparent to the lower consciousness.

" Night, then, is the Mother of the Gods, or as Orpheus says, ' the Nurse of the Gods is immortal Night ' (Proclus in Crat., p. 57). . . . Hermias (Phœdr., p. 144) tells us that of the three Nights, Orpheus ' ascribes to the first the gift of prophecy, but the middle [Night] he calls humility, and the third he says, gave birth to righteousness.' . . . ' And so she (Night) brought forth Earth and wide Heaven, so as to manifest visible from invisible.' "—G. R. S. MEAD, *Orpheus*, pp. 171, 172.

The Life-cycle brings forth the higher qualities (Gods) in the Soul, or, the Soul-process of involution and evolution sustains and nourishes the ideals (Gods). The three stages of the Cycle are, first, Involution, predictive of what follows ; second, Rest or latency, the lowest state ; and third, Evolution which brings forth perfection in qualities and souls. The Cycle of manifestation produces the lower and the Higher, so that the consciousness may discern the difference between them, and forsake illusion for Reality.

" The daughter of Odin by Night was Jord, the Earth, who became also his wife, and the mother of Asa-Thor. Yet Frigga was also his wife, and therefore was Jord but another name of Frigga."— HOWITT, *Literature of North*, Vol. I. p. 42.

The Spirit (Odin) begets in the Cycle (Night) the lower nature (Earth) which, in course of evolution, through the descent of Spirit into human forms, brings forth the higher mind (Asa-Thor). Yet buddhi (Frigga) is allied with Atma (Odin), whereby the lower nature becomes transmuted into buddhi at the Cycle's end.

" The night of this dark life of ours ; what comes after this life is, as it were, the dawn of day."—ORIGEN, *Comm. on John*, Bk. X. § 13.

See CAVE, CIRCLE OF EXISTENCE, COW (black), CREATION, DARKNESS, EARTH, EVOLUTION, FRIGG, GODS, HEAVEN, INVOLUTION, NOX, NURSE, ODIN, PRALAYA, QUATERNARY, SABBATH, SAMSARA, TANAOA, TUAT, UNDERWORLD, ZODIAC.

NIGHT AS DARKNESS :—

A symbol of a condition of ignorance, error, and evil in the activities upon the lower planes.

"And after the sop, then entered Satan into him (Judas) . . . He then went out straightway : and it was night."—JOHN xiii. 26, 30.

The least-raised quality (Judas) was passive or negative until he had partaken of "food," or knowledge of circumstance. Then desire (Satan) entered into him, and he was able to go forth. He acted apparently all on his own account, utterly regardless of the other qualities ; and in the condition of ignorance and evil, symbolised by "night," he went to the formalists and sought the counsel of those of this world, and not the guidance of the Higher Self, whence proceeds illumination and life.

'If without any doubt the darkness of ignorance is the night of the soul, the understanding is not improperly styled the day."—ST. GREGORY, *Morals on the Book of Job*, Vol. I. p. 46.

See BETRAYAL, DARKNESS, DAYS, JUDAS, NICODEMUS, PO, PRIESTS AND ELDERS, WOMEN'S LIFE.

NIGHT AS NULLITY :—

A symbol of negation, secrecy, or the forgetting of all past experience on entering a higher level of consciousness. This implies the expunging of sorrow and pleasure, the wiping out of pain and sense-happiness, the killing out of desire, in passing from the "night" of the soul,—the delusion of the lower planes,—to the "day" of the higher planes. The symbol "night" may thus come to stand for inaction, or subjectivity.

See CHARON'S FERRY, NECTAR, NOX, PRALAYA, RECOLLECTION, STYX.

NIGHT AS MATTER :—

A symbol of the material form-side of nature.

"And God called the light Day, and the darkness he called Night."—GEN. i. 5.

The "light" signifies the consciousness, whilst the "darkness" indicates the form-side of nature, not of itself conscious.

See DARKNESS, DAY AND NIGHT, FORMS, HINE, LIGHT, PO, TANAOA.

NIGHTS, THREE AFTER DEATH :—

Symbolic of three states on the astral and lower mental planes, in the intervening period between incarnations.

"When a righteous man passes away, where dwells his soul that night ? Then said Ahuramazda : 'It sits down in the vicinity of the head, chanting the Gatha Ushtavaiti, imploring blessedness. . . . That night the soul experiences as much of pleasure as all that which it had as a living existence'" (*Hadokht Nask*).—M. HAUG, *Essays, Rel. of Parsis*, p. 220.

When the soul is projected beyond the physical plane, into what condition does it enter ? It returns inward towards the mental plane, and recapitulates subjectively, as in dreams, the nature of the emotions and desires to which it had habituated itself. And its enjoyment is proportionate to its capacity for realisation of bliss when incarnated. (The second and third "nights" of the soul signify the arrival of the consciousness at the various sub-planes of the mental plane which contribute to the devachanic state.)

See BLISS, DEVACHAN, GATHA (ush., kam.), HEAD, INCARNATION OF SOULS, MAN (righteous), REINCARNATION, SLEEPING.

NILE RIVER ; GOD HĀPI :—

The Nile, like the Ganges, Jordan, and other national rivers, is taken as the River of Life,—the Divine Life, which flows from its source in the Absolute, downward or outward through all the planes of being.

"Hāpi was the god of the Nile, and with whom most of the great gods were identified."—BUDGE, *Egyptian Ideas, etc.*, p. 109.

The Divine Life cannot be differentiated from aspects of the Logos or Higher Self ; hence the identifications.

"Hāpi is generally depicted in the form of two gods ; one has upon his head a papyrus plant, and the other a lotus plant, the former being the Nile-god of the South, and the latter the Nile-god of the North."—*Ibid.*, p. 19.

These two forms of the symbol represent the Divine Life as it manifests on the upper (south) and the lower (north) planes.

"The Nile is a felicitous figure of the spiritual experience of mankind, or rather of that which makes spiritual experience possible. The ultimate springs of life are hidden from us, but by availing ourselves of its flow, and only by doing so, we have been able to grow the fairest fruits of human character."—R. J. CAMPBELL, Serm., *The Hidden God*.

"The great celestial watery mass was the source of the river Nile."—BUDGE.

"What is Life ? And what is the Water of Life ? You will find many answers to that question, in this, as in all ages ; but the one which Scripture gives is this. Life is none other, according to the Scripture, than God himself."—C. KINGSLEY, *Water of Life*, p. 7.

See ABSOLUTE, FOUNTAIN, HĀPI, LOTUS, MOIST, NORTH LAND, PAPYRUS, RIVER OF LIFE, SOUTH, WATER.

NINE, NUMBER :—

The number three is the number of perfection and completeness. Nine, which is three squared, refers to the attainment of perfection on the three lower planes.

See GATES OF BODY, NIFLHEIM, WHEAT AND BARLEY.

NINE DAYS :—

A symbol of nine cycles or periods.

"Nine days through the army went the arrows of the god (Apollo) ; but on the tenth, Achilles called the people to an assembly."—*Iliad*, Bk. I.

For nine periods the Life of the Logos ensouled the manifesting egos on the mental plane ; but at the tenth period the personality is evolved sufficiently to enable the lower qualities to assemble.

See ACHILLES, APOLLO, ARROWS, ASSEMBLY, PESTILENCE, TEN.

NIN-GIS-ZIDA, GOD :—

A symbol of the love of life in the forms, which attaches the ego to the lower planes.

See FORMS, TAMMUZ (god), VENUS.

NINIGI, THE SOVRAN GRAND-CHILD OF THE SUN-GODDESS :—

A symbol of the Higher Self born in the soul's lower nature purified by buddhi.

"Ninigi on his descent to earth took to wife Konohana-sakuyahime (lady-blooming-like-the-flowers-of-the-trees). Her father Ohoyamatsu-mi (great-mountain-person) had offered him both his daughters, but the elder was rejected by Ninigi as being too ugly. Her name was Iha-naga-hime (rock-long-lady). She in her shame and resentment, uttered a curse and said : ' The race of visible men shall change swiftly like the flowers of the trees, and shall decay and pass away.' This is the reason why the life of man is so short."—W. G. ASTON, *Shinto*, p. 112.

The Self born in the lower nature became allied with Faith-in-the-Divine-within,—a product of Aspiration which at first produces Trust-in-tradition-and-authority, with which the Self cannot ally itself. But the teaching of Tradition is self-destructive, for opinions (visible men) change swiftly, and authorities lose hold and pass away.

See AMATERASU, FAITH, INCARNATION, INSIGNIA, MIRROR, MITEGURA, MOUNTAIN, OX-LEADER, PHARISEES, PRIESTS AND ELDERS, SHINTAI, TRADITION, VAIRAUMATI.

NIRVÂNA, OR NIBBĀNA :—

A symbol of a subjective state of consciousness on the buddhic plane, for a period during which the ego receives no impacts from without. It is an unmanifest condition of soul between periods of manifestation upon the globes of a planetary chain.

"Nibbāna means nothing but a condition of perfect freedom from desire. The heart that has reached the final goal of all, which,—upon the ground of a perception of the true nature of things, through the knowledge of Not-I,—has so completely loosed itself from everything that it no longer has any desires. Where there is no desire in the heart, there is no attachment either. Where there is no attachment, there is also no parting, no sorrow. Where there is no sorrow, there is also no transiency, no change."—P. DAHLKE, *Buddhist Essays*, p. 85.

"The disciple who has put off lust and desire, rich in wisdom has here on earth attained the deliverance from death, the rest, the Nirvâna, the eternal state."

"He who has escaped from the trackless, hard mazes of the Sansāra, who has crossed over and reached the shore, self-absorbed, without stumbling and without doubt, who has delivered himself from the earthly, and attained Nirvâna, him I call a true Brahman"

(Sutta-sangaha).—H. OLDENBERG, *Buddha*, p. 264.

" ' Dissolved is the body,' says Buddha, when one of the disciples has entered into Nirvâna, 'extinct is perception ; the sensations have all vanished away. The conformations have found their repose : the consciousness has sunk to its rest.' "—*Ibid.*, p. 266.

In the state of Nirvâna there is no perception of the external world, and the archetypal causes (conformations) are latent in the soul. The causal-body (consciousness) is also latent, the ego having risen in consciousness to the buddhic plane. Extinction is only of the lower nature, not of the higher in which consciousness is in a state of bliss. The " hard mazes of the Sansâra " are the troubles and sufferings of the soul in its passage through the life cycle on the lower planes.

See ATTACHMENT, BLISS, BUDDHIC PLANE, CAUSAL-BODY, CONSCIOUSNESS, DEVACHAN, DISCIPLES, GARDEN OF REST, PLANETARY CHAIN, QUALITIES, RAFT, SAMSARA, SEKHET-HETEP, SHORE (other), SLEEP AND WAKING, SORROW, SUFFERING.

NISAYA LAND :—

A symbol of the higher mental plane.

"The fifth good land was Nisaya that lies between Mouru and Bakhdhi."—*Vendidad*, I.

This is the plane of the causal-body, between the buddhic plane and the devachanic plane.

See BAKHDHI, CAUSAL-BODY, DEVACHAN, MOURU.

NIZISTO THE DEMON :—

A symbol of the sense-nature which allures.

NOAH :—

A symbol of the individuality, or the manifested Self in evolution, —the permanent centre of evolution in the soul. It is the buddhi-manasic principle, or the incarnation of the Self as applying to the three lower planes.

"These are the generations of Noah. Noah was a righteous man, and perfect in his generations : Noah walked with God."—GEN. vi. 9.

Now follows an account of the evolution of the " Noah " principle,

which is perfection of the soul according to its stage of development. The knowledge it possessed is derived from within (walked with God).

" And he (Lamech) said to him (Methuselah) : ' I have begotten a strange son : he is not like man but resembles the children of the angels of heaven ; and his nature is different and he is not like us, and his eyes are as the rays of the sun and his countenance is glorious."— *Book of Enoch*, Ch. CV. 5.

" Noah is the divinely appointed figure, in whom the whole course of regeneration is set forth, every secret of this great mystery being here drawn for us as God alone could draw it. . . . Noah, then, is the spiritual mind,—for he is only the continuation of Seth's line, and figures the form of life which the spiritual mind takes at this stage in its development, when it has come so far as to know the judgment of the old creation, and the way through that judgment to a cleansed and better world."—A. JUKES, *Types of Genesis*, pp. 104–5.

See ADAM'S BODY, ARK, BEASTS, EVOLUTION, FLOOD, GOD SMELLING, HAM, HOUSE (frequented), INCARNATION, INDIVIDUALITY, INTOXICATION, MAN (righteous), OLIVE LEAF, RAINBOW, REGENERATION, ROCK, SAVOUR, SETH, SILENUS, WALKING WITH GOD.

NOAH'S SONS :—

Symbols of the three Divine aspects,—Will (Shem), Action (Ham), and Wisdom (Japhet) ; or in a lower sense, of intelligence, works, and desire.

" And Noah went in, and his sons, and his wife, and his son's wives with him, into the ark, because of the waters of the flood."—GEN. vii. 7.

And the Self, or the individuality, takes refuge within the causal-body appointed for it ; and so also its knowledges, affections, etc. And this occurs because the pressure upon the lower self (the reflected Higher) forces it, so to say, to this course. The " son's wives " signify the dual aspects of the three aspects of the Self.

" There is, first and highest (of Noah's sons), the contemplative life, which delights in things unseen, in adoring love and holiness. There is again the active life, which is good, and does good, but deals more with external things. Besides these there is the doctrinal life, a mind occupied with truth, without the savour and power of it ; a form of life, which, though growing out of the regenerate mind, is nigh to evil, and must be subdued and fought against. Shem is the first of these ; Japhet, the second ; the third is Ham, the father of Canaan, whom Israel have to overcome. . . . In point of honour Shem stands first, but in their development Japhet's and Ham's sons are given before Shem's ; shewing, what indeed is proved by all experience, that the highest life in us is the last to develop itself."—A. JUKES, *Types of Genesis*, pp. 132–3.

See ARK, CANAAN, CAUSAL-BODY, HAM, JAPHET, TRIAD.

NOAH'S WIFE :—

A symbol of the subjective intuition. At that early period of the soul's growth, the higher nature had not evolved sufficiently to be active in the soul ; so of the " wife of Noah " there is nothing said in the sacred story.

NOD, LAND OF :—

A symbol of the three lower planes in the soul.

" And Cain went out from the presence of the Lord, and dwelt in the land of Nod, on the east of Eden."—GEN. iv. 16.

And the personality goes forth from the Lord ; i.e. at the command of the Higher Self it emerges into activity, and in its sheaths dwells on the lower-mental, astral and physical planes, below the buddhic plane (Eden) which is reflected in the personality.

" By ' Cain's going out from the faces of Jehovah ' is signified that he was separated from the good of faith grounded in love. By his ' dwelling in the land of Nod ' is signified his abode out of goodness and truth. Towards the ' east of Eden ' signifies near the intellectual mind, where love was before."—SWEDEN- BORG, *Arc. Cel. to Gen.* iv. 16.

See CAIN, EDEN, PERSONALITY.

NOD OF JOVE OR ZEUS :—

A symbol of the power of the higher will and conscience in the soul.

" I will nod to thee with my head, that thou mayest feel confidence. For this for me is the greatest pledge among the immortals : for my pledge, even whatsoever I shall sanction by nod, is not to be retracted, neither fallacious nor unfulfilled."—*Iliad*, Bk. I.

Nature (Thetis), the mother of the Personality (Achilles), has appealed to the Higher Self (Jove) on behalf of her " short-lived " son, who has been dishonoured by the Desire-mind

(Agamemnon) in that the Desire- mind is contented with self-love, whereas the Personality is born for greater honour, namely, to be a vehicle of the Higher Self.

The Higher Self in responding assures Nature that the care of the Personality shall not be neglected, for the Higher Self shall make its power felt by the Personality, from the higher mental nature, through the conscience and will, which cannot seem fallacious or without significance. The symbol of the " nod " is a sign of power and dominion,—it stands for responsibility and individual initia- tive.

See ACHILLES, AGAMEMNON, CON- SCIENCE, HEEL, PERSONALITY, THE- TIS, WILL, ZEUS.

NOISE, SOUND :—

A symbol of atomic vibrations from higher or lower planes, affecting the personality.

" Hearken ye unto the noise of his voice, and the sound that goeth out of his mouth."—JOB xxxvii. 2.

Give heed to the vibrations of the spiritual nature within and the voice of the conscience, which is the soul's recognition of God the highest asserting dominion over will and conduct.

See CONSCIENCE, MOUTH, SOUND, VOICE.

NOOSE OF VARUNA :—

A symbol of knowledge, and love of Truth and Right.

" Having made a noose, the sacrificer throws it over the victim with,—' With the noose of sacred order I bind thee, O oblation to the gods ! '—for that rope, forsooth, is Varuna's : therefore he thus binds it with the noose of sacred order."— *Sata. Brâh.*, III. 7, 4, 1.

This refers to the transmutation through buddhi-manas of the lower qualities which have been relinquished for truth and righteousness and offered up as sacrifice to the ideals (gods).

See GODS, JACKAL, OBLATION, SACRI- FICE, SUN-CATCHING, TRANSMUTATION, VARUNA.

NORNOR, OR NORNS :—

Symbols of the life forces of speci- alised tendency and fixed limitation to an ideal type or figure, which

operate in forming the soul-sheaths or bodies on the several planes.

"Near the fountain Urdar, which is under the ash Yggdrasil, stands a very beauteous dwelling, out of which go three maidens, named Urd, Verdandi, and Skuld (i.e. Present, Past, and Future). These maidens fix the lifetime of all men, and are called Norns. . . . They draw every day water from the spring, and with it and the clay that lies around the fount sprinkle the ash, in order that its branches may not rot and wither away. The water is so holy that everything placed in the spring becomes as white as the film within an egg-shell. The dew that falls thence on the earth men call honey-dew, and it is the food of the bees" (*Prose Edda*).—MALLET, *North. Antiq.*, pp. 413, 4.

In the higher mind, which is a fount of truth to the lower nature, is placed the causal-body as a centre for the life forces which go forth to construct the vehicles wherewith the individual soul manifests itself on each plane of nature. The *present* vehicle is the astro-mental, the *past*, the astral, and the *future* will be the causal. The object and scope of these forces are determined by the Archetype, or Divine pattern within, which fixes for each soul the instrument through which it may work. These forces draw from the higher mind the intelligence and the moulding direction which are needful for the conservation and growth of the Divine Life (Tree) in each human being. The water of Truth purifies every quality that receives it, and as it forthpours upon the lower nature it brings sustenance to the toiling egos.

See ARC. MAN, BEES, CASTES, DEW, EARTH, FATE-SPHERE, FOOD, HONEY, HOUSE, IMAGE, MOIRAE, PROTOTYPES, SHENIT, THEMIS, URDAR, VESTURES, WATER, WHITE, YGGDRASIL.

NORTH QUARTER :—

A symbol of the astral plane in many countries, but not in India, where it signifies the higher planes, because, apparently, of the Himalayas (high mountains) and the source of the Ganges (river of Life) being to the north of the Aryan land.

"Hermöd answered to Modgunn the maiden who keeps the Bridge, 'I ride to Hell to seek for Balder, hast thou not seen him in these regions ?' She replied

that Balder had ridden over the bridge of Gjall, and that the road to Hell lay downward and towards the North."—*Prose Edda*, HOWITT, *Literature, etc.*

The Self within replies,—I descend to the Underworld to realise myself. Hast thou not seen me through those phases of life wherein I have reflected my being ? The Intuition makes answer that it perceives that the Self within has attained a high state of consciousness on the higher mental plane through involution in the first instance. Evolution of the Self being by way of the lower planes of manifestation, the underworld is symbolised as "towards the north" or astral plane.

"In a spiritual sense, the phrase, 'the sides of the north,' or, 'towards the north,' seems to intimate the quarter from which *evil* comes."—WORDSWORTH, *Bible, Psalms*, p. 74.

"Pohjola lies in the north. . . . Pohjola, being thus the seat of evils and darkness, has some elements in common with Manala, the kingdom of the dead."—COMPARETTI, *Poetry of the Finns*, pp. 199, 200.

"Pohjola" signifies the underworld energised from the astral plane of the desires.

See ASTRAL PLANE, BALDER, BRIDGE OF GJALL, DEATH OF LEMMINKAINEN, EVOLUTION, GJOLL, HELL, HERMOD, INTUITION, INVOLUTION, MANALA, MODGUNN, SERPENT OF THE WATER, UNDERWORLD.

NORTH LAND AND SOUTH LAND :—

Symbols of the desire and mental planes ; or of the lower mental and the higher mental planes, in the scriptures of Egypt and Europe.

"Southern Egypt was given to Horus, Northern Egypt to Set."—PLUTARCH, *Isis and Osiris.*

Southern Egypt represents the higher mental plane, more manasic and solar ; Northern Egypt, the lower mental plane, more kamic and lunar.

See COUNTRIES, EGYPT, HORUS, NEKHEBIT, NILE, PHAEACIANS, SET, SOUTH LAND.

NOSE AND NOSTRILS FOR BREATHING :—

Symbolic of volition and free-will, since the nose is allied with the breathing function of the lungs, by means of which the brain is enabled to act for the mind, and the control of which function implies restraint and discipline.

"All things are comprehended in this Spirit of the Ancient of the Ancient Ones, Who proceedeth from the concealed brain, into the gallery of the nostrils. . . . The nose of the Ancient of Days is life in every part."—*The Greater Holy Assembly*, Ch. X.

All things originate in the Absolute, from which the manifesting Spirit proceeds as an emanation from the hidden intelligence to proclaim the Divine Will, and forth-pour the Divine Life.

See ÁBSOLUTE, ADAM (lower), AIN SOPH, BREATH (divine).

NOSTRILS FOR SMELLING :—

A symbol of the function of the lower mind to discriminate the lower aspects of the qualities of the soul.

"With its nostrils seeking out the fragments of animals' limbs, as many as the delicate exhalation from their feet was leaving behind in the wood."— *Empedocles*, FAIRBANKS, 313.

With the functions of the lower mind, the Self seeks out the lower aspects of its nature, to the extent that it has been capable of appropriating the experiences which were acquired through traversing the astral plane (wood).

See ASTRAL PLANE, EXPERIENCES, PLACE (annu), SAVOUR.

NOX, SISTER OF EREBUS :—

A symbol of the withdrawal from manifestation into the negative and latent state of pralaya. The inpouring of the Divine Life which alternates with the outpouring (Erebus).

"From Chaos were born Nox and Erebus,—Nox or Dissolution, the most ancient of the deities, the subduer of gods and men ; the one of whom Zeus (Life) himself stands in awe, as well he may; Nox or Dissolution, sister and mate to, and sprung from the same source as Evolution or Erebus, from whom came Æther and Hemera, the archetypes of all that followed."—FITZ SIMON, *The Gods of Old*, p. 14.

From out of the primordial formless state of matter came the ebbing and flowing of the tides of Life. The indrawing (Nox) caused the Ideals (gods) and the mental faculties (men) to cease from activity. The highest plane (Æther) and the day of mani-

festation (Hemera), with the archetypes of all things, arise out of pralaya (Nox).

See ÆTHER, EREBUS, EROS, NIGHT, PRALAYA, PROTOTYPES, SABBATH.

NŪ, THE GOD :—

A symbol of the Divine powers operating in the hidden universe and subserving the evolution of the soul.

"I am the great god who created himself, that is to say, I am Water, that is to say, Nū the father of the gods, or as others say, Rā, the creator of the names of his members which turned into the gods."—BUDGE, *Papyrus of Hunefer* Ch. 17.

From the self-derived Truth-reality (water) proceeds the manifesting Self (Rā) with its differentiated ideals (gods) of the Divine scheme.

See BIRTH OF OSIRIS, GODS, HAPI, KHEPER, MEMBERS, NAMES, NUT, RĀ, SELF, WATER.

NUBIA :—

A symbol of subjectivity or negation on the higher planes : this may be prior to a fresh outpouring.

"Finally Horus and his companions went back to Nubia, to the town of Shashertet, where he destroyed the rebels of Uauat, and their ablest soldiers." —*The Legend of the Winged Sun-disk.*

Ultimately the Higher Self returns to his "own land,"—a state of withdrawal from objective activity,—and thence exterminates the more subtle lower qualities which had eluded his vigilance heretofore. These "rebels" are symbolic of the various phases of intellectual pride, arrogance, vanity, and such like.

See AMENI, COMPANY OF GODS, RĀ, SHASHERTET, UAUAT.

NUMBERS :—

Numbers become symbols because the internal universe is on a definite and co-ordinated plan in which quantitative relations are repeated correspondentially through different states and planes. Number is common to all the planes and thus unites them. *One* is the initial number of the Monad, the centre of all things. *Two* represents the inevitable duality of being on the planes of manifestation. *Three* represents completeness of state, there being three related states on the three higher planes, and three related states on the three lower planes. *Six* also represents completeness because it adds duality to three. *Nine* signifies the same by adding three for the planes.

"The symbolical meaning of Numbers in Holy Scripture deserves more study and attention than it has received in recent times. 'God doeth all things in number and measure and weight' (WISDOM xi. 20). From an induction of particulars it would appear that 3 is an arithmetical symbol of what is *Divine*, and 4 of what is *Created*. $3 + 4 = 7$ is the union of the Two ; hence signifying Rest, a Sabbath : $3 \times 4 = 12$ is the blending and indwelling of what is Divine with what is created : e.g. as in Israel, the people of God : and in the heavenly Jerusalem."—WORDSWORTH, *Bible, Matthew*, p. 34.

"The reason why numbers signify things, or rather resemble certain adjections to substances denoting some quality in things, is because number is in itself natural ; for natural things are determined by numbers, but spiritual things by things and their states."—SWEDENBORG, *Apoc. Rev.*, n. 10.

See PARTICULAR NUMBERS, KARVIS.

NUNS :—

A symbol of higher emotions nurtured in seclusion from the turmoil of the desires. They are under the uplifting influence of aspirations (vows) and the harmonising discipline of the Higher Self.

See MONK, VIRGIN, WOMAN.

NURSE OF THE SOUL :—

A symbol of the process by which the Divine Ego, or inner Self, is given the means of sustenance, growth, and manifestation, namely, that of Involution followed by Evolution.

"The god Akau (Anubis) transporteth me to the chamber (?), and my nurse is the divine double Lion-god himself. I am made strong and I come forth like him that forceth a way through the gate, and the radiance which my heart hath made is enduring."—BUDGE, *Book of the Dead*, Ch. LXIV.

The soul's experience in the physical body (Anubis) is reflected in the causal-body ; and the process of involution and evolution (double Lion-god) sustains and promotes the soul's development. By this process the indwelling Self is made strong so that it may rise to the higher mind, the

"gate of heaven," and entering in may find the wisdom and love which renders the soul immortal.

"For matter hath the function of mother and nurse, as Plato says, and containeth the elements from which everything is produced."—PLUTARCH, *Symposiacs*, II. qu. 3.

Matter brings forth in evolution what before it received in involution.

"Having heard this address of Asita, the King with his steps bewildered with joy, took the prince, who lay on his nurse's side, and showed him to the holy ascetic."—*Buddha-Karita*, Bk. I. 64.

The aspiration of the primordial Lower Self (Asita) having penetrated to the Higher Self (causal Self), whose nature is now awakened under the aspects of joy or faith, the Higher seizes the Reality of the Self in process of involution (nurse) and cherishes it. And now the Self is shown forth to the lower nature, i.e. nature weaned from attraction to objects of sense.

See ANUBIS, ASITA, ARC. MAN, BUDDHA, EVOLUTION, GATE, HEART, INVOLUTION, LION-GOD, NIGHT.

NURSE OF MEN :—

A symbol of that which promotes the growth of mind, namely, experience which is the outcome of the manasic evolution.

See NIGHT, PHTHIA.

NŪT OR RHEA, GODDESS :—

A symbol of space on the higher planes of being.

"Nūt, the feminine principle of Nū, i.e. the watery mass out of which all the gods were evolved ; she is the goddess of the sky, across which sailed the boat of the Sun-god."—BUDGE, *Book of the Dead*, p. 4.

"In Heliopolis Tûm-Râ was held to be the creator of the world, from him came forth Shû and Tefnût, and of this pair were born Seb and Nût, who were the parents of Osiris and Isis, Set and Nephthys. The chief function of Shû was to separate the heavens from the earth (Nût from Seb), in order to provide the path for the sun (Râ). When this was accomplished there appeared upon earth Nile and desert, life and death, good and evil, these contrasts being personified in Osiris and Set."—WIEDEMANN, *Rel. of Anc. Egyptians*, p. 106.

From the Absolute there emanated the Divine Will allied with Truthmatter by which Time and Space objectified and brought forth the

Atmic, Buddhic, Astral, and Physical planes. The Divine Will, active upon the mental plane, distinguished between Space and Time, and then the opposites appeared in the manifest.

"Time, plus time, plus time, ad infinitum, is the negation of time ; you cannot cut a piece out of the infinite series and say that that comprises the period of a universe, for when you have done it you have left your series still intact, still infinite. What appears to us, therefore, a succession of time-states is probably no succession at all ; indeed, one cannot see how it could be without introducing this conception of infinity in which it totally disappears. The time notion is a limitation imposed upon our minds ; it is a way of thinking which we cannot help, but which we perceive to be only relatively and not absolutely true. If we were not obliged to think in terms of the time notion we should know nothing about space either, for we only become aware by our perception of the time necessary to pass from one point to another. *Space and Time are mutually dependent mental abstractions* and nothing more, though we cannot help being dominated by them. Once admit that time has no beginning, as you are obliged to do, and you have destroyed its reality ; you have passed beyond it ; you are dealing with eternity. All our sense-experience is provisional and contingent ; all we know of the visible and material is but relative to something we do not know, something higher and more stable."—R. J. CAMPBELL, Serm., *Eternal and Temporal.*

See ADITI, AKERT, BIRTH OF OSIRIS, BOAT (sektet), CREATION, CURSE, DAYS (five), GODS, ISIS, KHEPER, MUT, NEPTHYS, NILE, NŪ, OPPOSITES, OSIRIS, PILLARS OF SHU, RĀ, RHEA, SEB, SET, SHU, TEFNUT, TEM, TIME, WATER.

NUT-URT, A POOL IN THE FIRST COMPARTMENT OF SEKHET-HETEPET :—

A symbol of the causal centre on the higher mental plane.

"O Nut-urt, I have entered into thee, and I have counted my harvest and I go forth to Uakh."—BUDGE, *Book of the Dead,* Ch. CX.

The causal centre is apprehended as the real beginning, when established, of the True life of the soul, and through it as a centre of consciousness it is perceived that the higher Selfhood is attained.

See CAUSAL-BODY, CONSCIOUSNESS, POOLS, SEKHET-HETEP.

NYMPHS, HEAVENLY, AND THEIR DANCES :—

Symbolic of the higher faculties of the soul, and the buddhic emotions. The "dances" signify the exercise of the harmonious higher powers.

See DANCES, DIONYSUS, HARMONY, HEAVENLY NYMPHS.

OAK-TREE :—

A symbol of the Divine Life of the Universe.

"The Great Oak-Tree is a theme about which hundreds of variants have been collected in Finland and Esthonia. The contrast between the baleful influence of the tree and the beneficent qualities of its fragments is very curious."—W. F. KIRBY, *The Quest,* Vol. I. p. 326.

This "God's tree," or "tree of heaven," grows from an acorn planted by "Tursas, the water-giant," a symbol of Truth, which when mature obscures everything. The explanation is that this growth from the germ of the Spirit, represents the process of *involution*. It signifies the descent of Spirit into Matter to endow it with all the qualities which are to evolve from it. The "baleful influence" means simply the obscuration of Spirit and the cessation of manifest life prior to evolution. The tree is felled by a dwarf, who grows to be a giant, signifying the same as *Purusha* (the Spirit), for both are described as "smaller than small, and greater than great, and of the size of a finger or thumb." The tree is broken up, and the fragments have the same signification as the fragments of the bodies of Lemminkainen, Osiris, Dionysus, and Pragâpati, and the members of the body of Christ (1 COR. xii. 27) the Archetypal Man. They represent the "beneficent qualities" of the soul, which evolve to completion.

"The Keltic Magi, or Druids, the priests of the religion of the oak (deru), regarded this tree as symbolical, or even representative, of the Almighty Father. Under it was the *sanctum* ; here they performed their most solemn rites. . . . The (oak) monarch of trees in our northern flora, as indicative of living strength and power, was an appropriate symbol of the living God."—BARLOW, *Essays on Symbolism,* pp. 88, 90.

"You are like an acorn in which a

mighty oak lies folded up waiting to come forth, as come forth it will if only it can ally itself with the limitless forces of the universe—invisible as well as visible, for it is something behind the visible universe that makes an oak-tree grow, or produces a soul."—R. J. CAMPBELL, Serm., *Freedom of Son of God.*

See ARC. MAN, DISMEMBERMENT, DWARF, EVOLUTION, FIG-TREE, GERMS, INVOLUTION, MEMBERS, PRAGÂPATI, PURUSHA, SEED, TREE OF LIFE, YGGDRASIL.

OANNES :—

A symbol of the Higher Self or Archetypal Man.

"The founder of civilisation in the Assyrian and Babylonian myth is the Oannes of Berosus. 'During the day-time Oannes held intercourse with men, taught them sciences and arts, the building of cities and temples, laws and the introduction of the measurement of planes ; further he showed them how to sow and reap ; in a word, he instructed them in everything necessary to social life, so that after his time they had nothing new to learn. But when the sun set, Oannes fell into the sea, where he used to pass the night.' "—GOLDZIHER, *Myths among the Hebrews,* pp. 214-15.

During the period of involution the Self instructed the mental qualities in every kind of knowledge and all potencies of growth—material and spiritual ; also in the laws of progress and the stages of development ; preparing them for every variety of experience and discipline. In short, the soul was perfected in every particular. At the end of this "golden age" the Archetypal Man was fully involved in matter, and ready to produce from himself the many souls in which he is to evolve in the present period.

See ARC. MAN, CIVILISING, GOLDEN AGE, GOVERNMENT, INVOLUTION, NET FOR FISH, OHONAMOCHI, REAPING, SEA, SOWING.

OARS OF THE BOAT :—

Symbolic of the higher emotions which propel the soul onward towards its goal.

See BOAT (river), PADDLES.

OAR-RESTS ; ROWLOCKS :—

Symbolic of the conditions of the soul's development and progress, namely, the four lower planes of nature

"Horus is occupied in tying loops of rope to the elongated hawk-headed rowlocks in which the paddles may be worked."—BUDGE, *Egypt. Heaven and Hell,* p. 45.

"Loops" signify the knowledge required for progress.

" ' Tell us our name,' say the Oar-rests ; 'Pillars of the underworld,' is your name."—BUDGE, *Book of the Dead,* Ch. XCIX.

The planes of the lower nature, giving experience and knowledge, form the conditions in which progress of the ego can take place.

See BOAT (river), NOOSE, PADDLES, PILLARS.

OATH :—

A symbol of a fixed resolution in a set course of action : or a strict adherence to an ideal.

See MISTLETOE, VOW.

OBELISK :—

An emblem denoting aspiration.

See COLUMN, SPIRE.

OBLATION ; OFFERING :—

A symbol of the relinquishing of a lower quality in favour of a higher.

"Speak unto the children of Israel, and say unto them, When any man of you offereth an oblation unto the Lord, ye shall offer your oblation of the cattle, even of the herd and of the flock."—LEV. i. 2.

The lower mental qualities were impressed with the duty of surrendering the forms of thought which were outgrown. This offering of their best to the Ideal within, they were enjoined to make through their feelings of reverence and of respect to the virtues.

See ALTAR, CATTLE, ISRAELITES, NOOSE OF VARUNA, OFFERINGS, PRAYERS AND OBLATIONS, SACRIFICE, SHEEP.

OCEAN, OR SEA :—

A symbol of either the Truth above, or the illusion below. The water above,—the ocean of Poseidon, or the sea Vourukasha,—is a symbol of Truth,—the Divine Reality replete potentially with the all.

"The Fish next asked to be taken to the Ganges ; but even the Ganges was soon too small for it, so it was finally transferred to the ocean."—Deluge Story in the *Maha-Bharata.*

Then was the Greater Self raised to the atma-buddhic plane, but even this cannot contain the Self, and so It merges in the All—the eternal Truth, the ultimate Reality.

"The Self is that into which all things pass away, even as the ocean is the one thing into which all waters flow."— *Brihad. Upanishad.*

"But despite all hindrances and setbacks, we are one and all making towards the Ocean of perfect unity in Christ, whence our full humanity, now knowing itself divine, shall be lifted up and glorified eternally by the Holy Spirit of God."—R. J. CAMPBELL, Serm., *Our Quest for God.*

"There are two modes of the being of God,—the infinite, eternal, transcendental, all complete,—and the finite, temporal, immanent, and incomplete. One might illustrate the difference between them thus : Imagine a boundless Ocean of life—pure, undifferentiated, and therefore unmanifest. Such an Ocean of life could know no lack, for it would be all-inclusive ; there could be nothing outside it and nothing wanting to its completeness. Every possible good, of every possible grade, would be latent therein, for nothing could be imagined or brought into existence which was not already there comprised within its blissful infinitude. Nothing can be missing from the infinite, and nothing can be added to it ; every conceivable excellence lies within its bosom, if only in potency. But suppose that boundless Ocean of life to be able to think about itself—as it certainly could, for even thought must be a property of the infinite, or it could never have come into being,—then one can imagine it as saying to itself, 'There are capacities within me of which I am quite aware but which I cannot use, cannot bring into play, qualities which can find no exercise, unless I detach them from my infinitude, deprive them of their illimitable resources, and bid them reveal themselves by contrast with their seeming opposites.' So a corner of that ocean would be marked off, as it were, from the rest, ringed around with matter, isolated, or all but isolated, from its Source, and made to bring forth, to live out, all the wonders hidden away in its mysterious depths. That comparatively small fragment of the one great Ocean of life would forthwith become a universe in itself, and would be quite a different mode of the universal life from the Infinite whence it derived. It would be different, to begin with, because it would be conditioned, whereas the former was unconditioned ; it would be partial, restricted, incomplete, whereas that from which it came had fullness of everything at command. But this finite ocean could do what the Infinite could not do ;

it could give form to some things whose very existence implies effort, hindrance, opposition, and the overcoming of odds." —R. J. CAMPBELL, Serm., July 4, 1912, *God's Fellowship with Man's Woe.*

The " infinite Ocean " is the " water above the firmament," i.e. the Truth-reality above the higher mental plane ; and the " finite ocean " is the " water below," i.e. the illusion of the lower planes. The " fragment universe " may be taken as a solar system, visible and invisible.

"(Jacoponi da Todi says) 'Drawn forth out of her natural state, into that unmeasurable condition whither love goes to drown itself, the soul, having plunged into the abyss of this ocean, henceforth cannot find, on any side, any means of issuing forth from it.' . . 'The heavens have grown stagnant ; their silence constrains me to cry aloud : O profound Ocean, the very depth of Thine Abyss has constrained me to attempt and drown myself within it.'— where note the interestingly antique presupposition of the music of the spheres, which has now stopped, and of the watery constitution of the crystalline heaven, which allows of stagnation ; and the rapidity of the change in the impressions,—from immobility to silence, and from air to water. Indeed, that Ocean is one as much of air as of water, and as little the one as the other ; and its attractive force is still that innate affinity between the river-soul and its living Source and Home, the Ocean God, which we have so constantly found in Plotinus, Proclus, and Dionysius."—F. VON HUGEL, *Mystical Element*, Vol. II. pp. 108–9.

See ABSOLUTE, ABTU-FISH, AIN SOPH, ATMAN, BRAHMA, COSMOS, DELUGE, FIRMAMENT, FISH (great), GODHEAD, HIGHER AND LOWER NATURES, IMAGE, JORDAN, KHWĀN (fish), MACROCOSM, MICROCOSM, MUSIC (spheres), PHANG, POSEIDON, RIVERS OF LIFE, SEA, SHIP (Manu), THIRST, TRIDENT, VOURUKASHA, WATER, YI, ZERANA.

OCEAN, OR SEA (FEMININE) :—

A symbol of primordial Truth on the matter side of being, which brings forth all qualities and forms proceeding from the Absolute.

"The feminine Sephirah Binah is sometimes termed by the Qabbalists the Great Sea. Among her Divine names are Ya H and Elohim. She is called the Great Mother, the Upper Mother. She is the Holy Spirit and the Upper She-kheen-ah. Her symbol is the brooding dove; she brooded over the face of the waters at creation."— MYER, *Qabbalah*, p. 336.

The highest condition on the matter side of manifestation is Truth-reality (ocean) in its receptive aspect (feminine) towards Spirit. This primordial condition of things fructified by the Higher Self is the " Great Mother " bringing forth on the buddhic plane the prototypes of all forms for the manifestation of the Divine Life on the higher and lower planes.

See ADITI, BINAH, DOVE, GODDESS, HOLY GHOST, MĀYĀ (higher), MOTHER (divine), NARAYANA, PROTOTYPES, SARASVATI, SHEKINAH.

OCEANUS, SON OF HEAVEN AND EARTH :—

A symbol of the Spirit of Truth, produced primordially from Spirit and Matter.

" Of the divine Titanic hebdomads, Ocean both abides and proceeds, uniting himself to his father [Heaven], and not departing from his kingdom. But all the rest of the Titans, *rejoicing in progression*, are said to have given completion to the will of Earth, but to have assaulted their father, dividing themselves from his kingdom, and proceeding unto another order."—PROCLUS, *Timæus*, V. 292.

Of the essential elements of life, Spirit both abides above and proceeds to action below, and is one with the Supreme, not departing from the higher planes. But the other primal conditions, rejoicing in *the new cycle of evolution*, are said to have given completion to the process of involution into matter, repulsing the direct action of the Supreme Spirit, in separating themselves from the higher nature, and proceeding into the new process and order of evolution.

See EARTH (great) EVOLUTION, GE, HEAVEN AND EARTH, INVOLUTION, POSEIDON, SPIRIT, TITANS, TLALOC, URANUS, VARUNA.

OCYPETE, THE HARPY :—

A symbol of the love of physical life, which conducts the soul to a variety of physical and astral conditions involving suffering and sorrow.

See HARPIES, NICOTHEA, PHINEUS, ZETES.

ODIN, OR WODAN :—

A symbol of the Divine Will, Logos, or Higher Self.

" Odin governs all things, and although the other deities are powerful, they all serve and obey him as children do their father. Frigga is his wife. She foresaw the destinies of men, but never reveals what is to come. . . . Odin is named Alfadir (All-father), because he is the father of all the gods, and also Valfadir (Choosing Father), because he chooses for his sons all those who fall in combat. For their abode he has prepared Valhalla " (*Prose Edda*).— MALLET, *North. Antiq.*, p. 416.

The manifest God is supreme above all, and the higher qualities are in harmony with him and carry out his laws. Buddhi (Frigga) is allied with Atma, and superintends the evolution of the mental qualities, knowing the glory in store for them, but remaining unobserved by them. From the Self proceed the highest ideals ; and God hath chosen to be his sons those souls who have fought the good fight, and from whom the lower nature has fallen away. For they shall inherit the kingdom (Valhalla) prepared for them from the foundation of the world.

" There was a vast concourse of various kinds of people at Baldur's obsequies. First came Odin, accompanied by Frigga, the Valkyrior, and his ravens."—*Ibid.*, p. 448.

At this burying of the dead past of the involutionary cycle, the Divine Will (Odin) assisted under the aspect of spiritual Life, both in its outgoing and incoming phases of atmic energy through Buddhi (Frigga). The " Valkyrior " symbolise the " host of heaven " which stand for the higher nature forces. The " ravens of Odin " signify intelligence and power.

See ASAR, ATMA, BALDER, BUDDHI, DEATH OF BALDER, FATHER, FRIGG, GODS, HERMOD, MIMER, RAVENS, VALHALLA.

ODOUR, SWEET :—

A symbol of bliss on high planes caused by the reception of aspirations from below.

" An odour of a sweet smell, a sacrifice acceptable, well-pleasing to God."— PHIL. iv. 18.

" He approaches the tree Ilya, and the odour of Brāhman reaches him."— *Kaush. Upanishad*, I. 2.

The soul becomes in unison with the Tree of the Divine Life which yields the fruit of Wisdom; and the blissful breath of the Supreme invigorates his being.

See Brahma, Flavour, Ilya tree, Perfumes, Salagya, Scent (sweet), Taste, Vibhu.

ODYSSEUS, ULYSSES :—

A symbol of courage, arising out of Love and Faith, in learning by experience to rule the lower nature in the interests of the higher.

"Then Odysseus of many counsels brought Chryseis to the altar, and gave her into her father's arms, and spake unto him : Chryses, Agamemnon king of men sent me hither to bring thee thy daughter, and to offer to Phoebus a holy hecatomb on the Danaans' behalf, wherewith to propitiate the king that hath now brought sorrow and lamentation on the Argives."—Iliad, Bk. I.

Then Courage, full of resource, delivered the Intuition of Truth to her parent, the Spiritual-mind, and spake thus,—" The Desire-mind, ruler of the lower nature, impelled me hither to bring thy offspring and offer up to the Higher Self the results of the operation of the mind, in order thus to enable the Desire-mind to operate more harmoniously than it hitherto has been able to do owing to the emotional distress which has been engendered."

"The morality of Jesus involves the only true secret of courage and of the freedom that comes of courage. More and more we come to see that courage is a positive thing. It is not simply the absence of fear. To be brave is not merely not to be afraid. Courage is that compactness and clear coherence of all a man's faculties and powers which makes his manhood a single operative unit in the world. That is the reason why narrowness of thought and life often brings a kind of courage, and why, as men's range of thought enlarges and their relations with their fellow-men increase, there often comes a strange timidity."—Phillips Brooks, Influence of Jesus, p. 66.

See Alcinous, Agamemnon, Argives, Briseis, Chryse, Chryseis, Hecatomb, Priest of apollo.

OFFERING, OR SACRIFICE :—

A symbol of the giving up of the lower for the sake of the higher.

"Burnt offerings and peace offerings represented the conceptions of self-surrender and thanksgiving."—F. W. Farrar, The Atonement, etc., p. 43.

"The faculty by which we lay hold on Eternal Life is to be attained only by actually renouncing the sensuous and its objects, and sacrificing them to that law which takes cognisance of our will only and not of our actions ;—renouncing them with the firmest conviction that it is reasonable for us to do so,—nay, that it is the only thing reasonable for us. By this renunciation of the Earthly does faith in the Eternal first arise in our soul, and is there enshrined apart, as the only support to which we can cling after we have given up all else,—as the only animating principle that can elevate our minds and inspire our lives. We must indeed, according to the figure of a sacred doctrine, first ' die unto the world and be born again, before we can enter the kingdom of God.' "—J. G. Fichte, Vocation of Man, Bk. III.

See Altar, Beasts, Burnt offering, Higher and lower, Oblation, Roasted, Sacrifice.

OGDOAD :—

A Symbol of the Supreme Being, the Source of Light and Life which proceeds into manifestation through the Hebdomad or seven planes, of which five are manifest.

"The nature of this symbolic Ogdoad is most clearly seen in the inscription of Dêr-el-Bahari, of the time of the Twenty-second Dynasty, which Maspero has lately published.

In it the Osirified says to the Supreme : ' I am One who becomes Two; I am Two who becomes Four; I am Four who becomes eight; I am the One after that."—G. R. S. Mead, T. G. Hermes, Vol. I. p. 120.

The One Supreme becomes dual as Spirit and Matter ; the dual becomes the quaternary as the means of soul-development : the quaternary becomes the completed evolution of the soul which rises and passes into the One again. The individuality (the Osirified) having passed through all the stages of manifestation identifies itself with the Supreme.

See Brahma, Defunct, Eight, Geometry, Hebdomad, Illusion, Individuality, Involution, Numbers, Om, Quaternary, Thirteen, Udgitha.

OHONAMOCHI,—THE CREATOR :—

A symbol of the Logos, Divine Monad, or the Self.

"Coming at last to the province of Idzumo, Ohonamochi spake and said :

'This central Land of Reed-plains had been always waste and wild. The very rocks, trees, and herbs were all given to violence. But I have now reduced them to submission, and there is none that is not compliant.' Therefore he said finally : 'It is I, and I alone, who now govern this land. Is there perchance any one who could join with me in governing the world ?' Upon this a divine radiance illuminated the sea, and of a sudden there was something which floated towards him and said : 'Were I not here, how couldst thou subdue this land ? It is because of my presence that thou hast been able to accomplish this mighty task. I am thy spirit of good luck, the wondrous spirit.'"
—*The Nihongi*.

The Self struggling upward through the lower nature has at last reduced to submission the turbulent desires and emotions of the astro-mental nature (Reed-plains), so that finally the God-within is the supreme Master, and aspires for union with the God above. All being fulfilled, the Divine radiance of the Eternal Spirit illumines the entire nature, and the lower Self becomes aware of the Source of Power by which the mighty task of the Soul-process has been accomplished. The lower Self then perceives that the Higher Self is indeed himself—his own spirit—and the two become one in Victory (good luck) dwelling in the causal-body (shrine) on the heights.

"The *Idzumo Fadoki* frequently calls Ohonamochi 'the great God who made the Under-Heaven.' The spear which he carries is indicative of warlike prowess and political sway ; while the mattock given to him by one myth points rather to agricultural development. He is, along with Sukuna-bikona, the instructor of mankind in the arts of medicine and magic."—ASTON, *Shinto*, p. 144.

The Self is the producer of the lower nature or the under-world. The "spear" is a symbol of the Divine Ray, and the "mattock" indicates the Divine "Husbandman" who cultivates the "field" of life. "Sukuna-bikona, the dwarf" is a symbol of the enlightened personality who is associated with the Self in bringing knowledge to the human soul of the means by which it may be cured of its infirmities and have its lower nature transmuted.

See ARC. MAN, CIVILISING, DWARF, GOLDEN AGE, GOVERNMENT, OANNES, REED PLAINS, SUKUNA,

OIL, OR HOLY OIL :—

A symbol of Divine Love,—the Love-principle of the higher planes which attracts the soul upward in softness, gentleness, and harmony.

"Thou lovest righteousness, and hatest wickedness : therefore God, thy God, hath anointed thee with the oil of gladness above thy fellows."—Ps. xlv. 7.

The soul on its attaining perfection is endowed from within with love and bliss beyond what is bestowed upon the unperfected.

"Thou receivest the oil of the cedar in Amentet, and the cedar which came forth from Osiris cometh unto thee ; it delivereth thee from thy enemies" (Ritual of Embalmment).—BUDGE, *Egyptian Magic*, p. 186.

The purified soul is said to receive on the higher planes the love which comes forth from the Supreme and delivers it from the desires. The "cedar tree from Osiris" signifies the "tree of Life,"—the Divine Ray which comes down from the Highest and penetrates all planes.

"Oil signifies the good of love which sanctifies, and everything that is sanctified has relation to truth."—SWEDENBORG, *Apoc. Rev.*, n. 173.

"From the Essence of the Free Lubet (longing delight) there proceedeth forth in the Fire an Oily Power, which is the body or essence of the Understanding wherein the Fire burneth."

"The Love-oil gives meekness."—BOEHME, *Mysterium Magnum*, p. 13.

See ANOINTING, BUTTER, CANDLESTICKS, CHRESTOS, FAT, FOOD (soul), GHEE, HEAD, INCENSE, LAMP, OLIVE, UNCTION, VIRGINS, ZAREMAYA.

OINTMENT :—

A symbol of love Divine.

"The alabaster vase in Mary's hand, broken, and pouring out in loving abundance and unsparing effusion the *whole* of its precious contents on Christ's head, is a beautiful emblem of the contrite and broken heart, pouring out itself in acts of penitential love on Christ and His members, and thinking nothing too costly for that holy and blessed service."—WORDSWORTH, *Bible, Mark*, p. 147.

"For in that she hath poured this ointment on my body, she did it for my burial."—MAT. xxvi. 12.

The purified lower affection (Mary) draws forth Divine love in the personality (Jesus), and prepares it for dissolution (burial). It is by a supreme effort of love of the ideal that the personality is discarded, or the sense of separateness is overpassed, when Jesus and Christ,—the lower Self and the Higher Self,—become one.

See BURYING, CRUCIFIXION OF JESUS, DEAD (burying), FAT, GHEE, HOUSES (friends), MARTHA, POOR PEOPLE, UNGUENTS.

OLIVE FRUIT :—

A symbol of love and faith, implying courage.

"Moreover, as to this fruit of the olive, if the matter be examined, you will find what it was. The fruit of the olive signifies charity. How do we prove this ? Just as oil is kept down by no liquid, but bursting through all, bounds up and overtops them ; so likewise charity cannot be pressed to the bottom, but must of necessity show itself at the top."—AUGUSTINE, *Gospel of John*, Vol. I. p. 88.

"An olive signifies love and charity, because the olive tree signifies the celestial church, and thence the olive, which is its fruit, signifies celestial love, which love is love to the Lord ; hence it is that this love is also signified by the oil, by which all the holy things of the church were anointed."—SWEDENBORG, *Apoc. Rev.*, n. 493.

"In Judaic legends the olive is the Tree of Life."—A. JEREMIAS, *The Old Test., etc.*, Vol. I. p. 209.

See BUTTER, CANDLESTICKS, CRUCIFIXION (*Rev.*), GARDEN OF FLOWERS, GHEE, MOUNT OF OLIVES, OIL.

OLIVE LEAF OFFERING :—

A symbol of a tribute of love.

"And the dove came in to him at eventide ; and lo, in her mouth an olive leaf pluckt off : so Noah knew that the waters were abated from off the earth."— GEN. viii. 11.

And now, at the conclusion of the re-incarnating period of that stage of the soul's development, an " olive leaf " or love tribute offered by the lower self,—as the result of the previous action of the Higher Self,—is brought to the individual Self. Then it is the higher consciousness realises that the power of recognising the Truth is contained within the soul.

"When we have felt the tossings cease, and received the olive leaf, the earnest of the inheritance, from the mouth of the gentle dove, which thus assures us of a world beyond the water-floods, then our freedom is near."—A. JUKES, *Types of Genesis*, p. 123.

See ARK, DOVE, EVENING, FLOOD, NOAH, WATER (lower).

OLYMPUS, MOUNT :—

A symbol of the height of perfection and attainment ; or the plane of atma, the summit of manifestation.

"Homer was the first to divide the world into five portions. The three intermediate he has assigned to the three gods, the two extremes, Olympus and Earth, whereof the one is the boundary of things below, the other of things above, he has left common to all and unallotted to any."—PLUTARCH, *On the E at Delphi*, § 13.

There are five manifested planes (portions) of the soul (world). The three intermediate, namely, buddhi (Hera), manas (Hermes) and kama (Hades), have above them atma (Olympus), and below them sthula (Earth). Atma bounds manifestation above, and the physical (sthula) is the limit below. The highest and the lowest planes are the foundations of the rest.

"And Athene forthwith was departed to Olympus, to the other gods in the palace of ægis-bearing Zeus."—*Iliad*, Bk. I.

And from this time forward, in the course of the evolution of the soul, Wisdom appears to retire from the plane whereon it can be revealed to the Personality (Achilles). It is therefore said to join the " other Gods," or immortal, transcendental facts on the highest planes, which are at the origin of the Divine scheme of existence.

"Many elements of the Hebrew traditions recorded in the Holy Scriptures, or otherwise preserved among the Jews down to later times appear in the Olympian Court of Homer."—W. E. GLADSTONE, *Juventus Mundi*, 209.

"The Incarnation of Christ may be compared to the Mountain of continental Greece, from which all its principal rivers flow, and fertilize the land. He is the One Well-spring of Living Water."— WORDSWORTH, *Bible, Acts*, p. 75.

"Is not Christ the mountain up into which the believer goes, and in which he finds the divine idea of himself ? As a mountain seems to be the meeting-place of earth and heaven, the place where the bending skies meet the aspiring planet, the place where the sunshine and the cloud keep closest company with the granite and the grass : so Christ is the meeting place of divinity and humanity ; He is at once the condescension of divinity and the exaltation of humanity ; and man wanting to know God's idea of man, any man wanting to know God's idea of him, must go up into Christ, and he will find it there. . . . This, then, is the great truth of Christ. The treasury of life, your life and mine, the life of every man and every woman, however different they are from one another, they are all in Him."—PHILLIPS BROOKS, Serm., *The Pattern in the Mount.*

See ALBORDJ, ALCINOUS, AMARA-VATI, ATHENE, ATMA, CAUCASUS, FRIGG, HIMAVAN, JUDAS, KAILASA, MERU, MOUNTAIN, PALACE, WORLDS (five).

OM ! OR AUM :—

A symbol of the expression of the Spirit as Love within the soul ; or the Word of God—the inspiration of Truth and Righteousness.

"'Aum Tat Sat,' this has been considered to be the threefold designation of the Eternal. By that were ordained of old Brâhmanas, Vedas and sacrifices. Therefore with the pronunciation of ' Aum ' the acts of sacrifice, gift and austerity as laid down in the ordinances are always commenced by the knowers of the Eternal."—*Bhagavad-Gîta*, Ch. XVII.

"Om. This syllable is all. Its interpretation is that which has been, that which is, and that which is to be. All is Om, and only Om, and whatever is beyond trinal time is Om, and only Om. For all this world is Brahman, this Self is Brahman, and this Self has four quarters."—*Mandukya Upanishad.*

"May that Indra, Om, that is the highest thing in the Vedas, that is all that is immortal, above the immortality of the Vedas, may that divine being strengthen me with wisdom."—*Tait. Upanishad.*

"In the Prasna Upanishad the great teacher Pippalâda says, ' This syllable Om is the higher and the lower Brahman.' That is to say, Om is Brahman as unconditional, and Brahman in fictitious manifestation as the Demiurgus (Isvara)."— A. E. GOUGH, *Phil. of Upanishads*, p. 68.

In this teaching "Om" is taken as a symbol of the Higher Self potential above, in identity with the Higher Self actual below. The first Self is complete and perfect but unmanifest ; the second Self is under illusion, incomplete and imperfect in its manifestation of itself. The two Selves are really One Self, and the One is the All, Om !

"That is what faith means, the faith that counts for righteousness. It is the soul with face upturned to the eternal light ; the spirit of man intently listening for what the still small voice of the Spirit of God is saying. . . . It is waiting upon God daily, hourly, to ascertain his will concerning you, and to receive grace to carry it out as far as it rests

with you so to do. . . . Faith flings wide the doors of your spiritual nature ; it releases divine energy ; it is that attitude of soul through which God's mighty works are done."—R. J. CAMPBELL, Serm., *The Faith, etc.*, 1914.

See ARROW, FAITH, HIGHER AND LOWER SELVES, OGDOAD, UDGITHA, WORD OF GOD.

OMBROS AND AETHER (AIR) :—

Symbols of emotion and reason. *See* AIR.

ONOGOROJIMA ISLAND :—

A symbol of a centre of operation established in the astral body of the nascent soul.

"Before Izanagi and Izanami produced the land generally, an island for them to rest upon was necessary to be created. The two Deities, standing upon the Bridge of Heaven, pushed down the ' Jewel-spear of Heaven ' into the green plain of the Sea, and stirred it round and round, when they drew it up, the drops which fell from its end consolidated and became an island, Onogorojima. They then descended on to the island, and planting the spear in the ground point downwards, built a palace round it, taking that for the central roof-pillar. The spear became the axis of the earth, which had been caused to revolve by the stirring round."—*Japanese Nihongi.*

Before the soul could be formed it was necessary first to fix a centre in the lower nature to construct from. Therefore the Divine Will and Wisdom manifested on the higher mental plane (the bridge), and from thence they vibrated a ray of Divine Life and intelligence downward to the astral plane (the sea), with the result that upon its fourth sub-plane a centre for the lower soul was established. To this formative matter was attracted. Then Will and Wisdom manifested in the laws of growth upon the astral plane, in which the Divine Life (spear) operated from within outwardly. The "palace" signifies the astral-body of desire and sensation, which becomes the focus of the soul's activities in the lower worlds (earth). But the Divine Ray is the true axis of the soul, causing it to revolve as a "wheel of life," in a cycle of births and deaths.

See ATOM, BRIDGE OF HEAVEN, CHEMMIS, CHURNING, DELOS, IZANAGI,

JEWEL SPEAR, LAND, MANCO, PALACE, SEA.

ONYX STONE AND BDELLIUM :—

Symbols of power and wisdom on the buddhic plane.

See HAVILAH.

OPHIONEUS, THE SERPENT :—

A symbol of the lower principle of desire and illusion.

"Pherecydes says that there existed before all things, and from eternity, Zeus, Chronos, and Chthon (earth). . . . Chronos produces from his seed, fire, wind, and water; the three primal beings then beget numerous other gods in five families. . . . Ophioneus, with his hosts, representing probably the unregulated forces of nature, opposes this creation of the world, but the divine army under Chronos hurls them into the deep of the sea, and keeps possession of heaven."—ZELLER, *Hist. of Greek Philos.*, Vol. I. p. 89.

Spirit (Zeus), Time cycle (Chronos), and Matter (Chthon) originate existence. The Time cycle produces buddhi (fire), manas (wind), and kama (water). Then are produced the ideal qualities (gods) on five buddhic sub-planes. The lower principle (Ophioneus) creates the opposites, but in the cycle of involution these are inoperative as opponents.

See AHRIMAN, CHTHONIE, GODS, KRONOS, OPPOSITES, SERPENT.

OPPOSITES, PAIRS OF :—

These are positive and negative aspects of qualities, without which manifestation on the lower planes could not occur. The negative aspects imply the absence of the positive, and are therefore illusive.

"While Ormazd was thus completing his Light creation, Ahriman was making a corresponding evil being for every good being created by Ormazd. These stood in their ranks and orders, with their seven presiding evil spirits, or Daevas, corresponding to the Amshaspands."—*Zoroastrian System.*

Whilst upon the upper planes the archetypal creation was proceeding, upon the lower planes of manifestation the dual, or opposite, of each quality was produced by the lower principle. The dual in the lower comes as an opposite thing to the relationship of the mind with the quality. It is through the inverted reflection below of the things which are above that illusion is created in the lower mind. The lower conception of things is always finite and limited;—it always requires qualification. The order in which the ranks are maintained refers to the several planes upon which the universe is manifest. In each case the opposite is produced of whatever is ideally created.

"And from Mashya and Mashyoi arose seven pairs, male and female, and each was a brother husband and a sister wife; and from every one of them in fifty years children were born, and they themselves died in a hundred years."—*The Bundahis*, Ch. XV. 24.

And from reason and emotion—dual aspects of the Self,—came forth the seven pairs of opposites which now actively function on the planes of relativity. These are the active and passive aspects of the several emotional and mental qualities. The seven pairs are :—Like—dislike ; Faith — unfaith ; Hope — despondency ; Aspiration—contentment ; Strength —weakness ; Pity—apathy ; Courage —fear. From these, during the period of cyclic activity, "children" or experiences were born. The dual aspects of the Self are destined eventually to be absorbed and superseded in the course of a double cyclic period.

"The ten fundamental oppositions (in the Pythagorean table of opposites) were as follows :—(1) Limited and Unlimited ; (2) Odd and Even ; (3) One and Many ; (4) Right and Left; (5) Masculine and Feminine ; (6) Rest and Motion ; (7) Straight and Crooked ; (8) Light and Darkness ; (9) Good and Evil ; (10) Square and Oblong. . . . According to this theory the primary constituents of things are of a dissimilar and opposite nature ; a bond was therefore necessary to unite them, and cause them to be productive. This bond of the elements is harmony."—ZELLER, *Hist. of Greek Philos.*, Vol. I. pp. 381-3.

"The German philosopher Hegel holds that a thing can only exist through its opposite, that the thing and its opposite must arise together, and that eternally, as the complements of a unity ; white is not without black, nor black without white, good is not without evil, nor is evil without good. This is the doctrine of the Siphra D'Tzni-oothah and the Sepher Y'tzeer-ah. At the very beginning of the life germ, dissolution and death oppose its vitality and endeavour to destroy it, and the whole existence of man in this world is a continual struggle to preserve his vitality."—I. MYER, *Qabbalah*, p. 184.

"The Deity has created both the good and the evil, and the one is absolutely necessary to the existence of the other. It (Qabbalah) considers that each human being is accompanied throughout its life on earth, and is influenced spiritually, by two spirits, the good and the evil. These are the oppositions, but the free-will of the individual is the harmony by which he exercises the Divine power of judgment, and accepts the one or the other as his master."—*Ibid.*, p. 126.

"There is but one potency of two contraries, because contraries are apprehended by one and the same sense, therefore belong to the same subject or substate ; where the principle (i.e. the source or faculty) of the *knowledge* of two objects is the same, the principle (i.e. elementary form) of their existence is also one."—MCINTYRE, *Bruno*, p. 177.

"The Contrariety in nature causeth Strife. . . . For without contrariety (that is) contrary properties, is no strife, and without strife is no production, and without production all would be stillness, inactivity, and unknown to itself. Thus the properties which when separate are authors of a hellish kingdom, are also, when they operate harmoniously, the exalters of the Divine blessed kingdom of Love."—BOEHME, *Answer to 22nd Question*.

"The doctrine of development by contraries was passed from Sebastian Frank to Paracelsus, and from him to Weigel. According to this theory, God manifests himself in opposites. The peace of Unity develops into the strife of the Manifold. . . . Only by resistance, only in collision, is the spark of vitality struck out, is power realised, and progress possible."—VAUGHAN, *Hours with the Mystics*, Vol. II. p. 92.

"And as a man driving in a chariot might look at the two wheels, thus he will look at day and night, thus at good and evil deeds, and at all pairs (correlative things). Being freed from good and evil, he, the knower of Brahman, moves towards Brahman."—*Kaush. Upanishad*, I. 2.

The perfected ego now regards the activities of opposite qualities as together equally (as wheels) carrying forward the soul (chariot) in its progress heavenward. Knowledge and ignorance, right and wrong actions, have respective parts in soul-development ; and neither can manifest without the other. The balanced mind having become stilled by the action from above, extends its vision so that the pairs of opposites become as aspects of the one great Reality, and

the indwelling Self knows Itself alone to be the Doer. Then being free from all relativity,—from good and evil alike,—He, the Knower, passes into the Supreme (Brahman), having known that His nature is that of the Supreme.

"A certain limitation of the true selfhood of every individual is necessitated. If the essential nature of the good is to become manifest in every particular, then in every particular it must be confronted with its opposite, that it may strive against it and overcome it. Why, the very word 'good' implies acquaintance with evil, just as white implies black, and light implies darkness. The current flowing along an electric wire never shines until it meets with resistance ; then it flames forth, and this is just the way God has worked throughout human experience. Treachery and violence are not only the opposites of, but the limitations imposed upon, all latent fidelity and gentleness. God has wrapped up the divine consciousness within these limitations and bidden it work its way through, and this is what the race has been doing all through its long strenuous history."—R. J. CAMPBELL, Serm., *Solidarity of Spiritual Experience*.

See AHRIMAN, AKEM-MANO, BRAHMA, CHARIOT, COLD AND HEAT, CREATION, DAEVAS, ENIGORIO, EVIL, FRAVAK, GOSHURUN, GUILTY, ILLUSION, MATRO, NUT, OPHIONEUS, PLAGUES, RELATIVE, RICH MAN, SEEDS OF FOODS, STRIFE, SUMMER, SUSANOWO, VIGARA.

OPPRESSORS :—

A symbol of opinions which oppose the truth, such as unfounded prejudices and preconceptions.

ORACLE CONSULTED :—

A symbol of the inner nature questioned, and intuition apprehended.

See GEUSH-TASHA, GOLDEN FLEECE, HEROES.

ORDERS OF THE SPACES :—

The "orders" signify the laws of manifestation of conditions of progressive development. The "spaces" represent the means by which such conditions are attained.

See ADITYAS, ÆONS (twelve), COMPARTMENTS, IABRAOTH, NIDĀNAS, SAMSARA, TUAT, ZODIAC.

ORDERS, FOUR OF MANU :—

A symbol of four successive states of consciousness on the mental and buddhic planes in the course of the growth of the soul.

"The Student, the Householder, the Hermit, and the Ascetic, these constitute four separate orders which all spring from the order of Householders."—*Laws of Manu*, VI. 87.

The "Student" represents an ego manifesting in the mental-body as a centre of consciousness on the four lower mental sub-planes. This is the personality either incarnate or excarnate. The "Householder" is the ego seated in the causal-body on the fifth mental sub-plane. This is the individuality from which proceed the other three phases of consciousness. The "Hermit" is the ego manifesting in a centre of consciousness on the sixth mental sub-plane. And the "Ascetic" is the ego manifesting in a centre of consciousness on the buddhic plane. The two last "orders" are without lower vehicles and receive no vibrations from the lower planes.

See Ascetics, Asramas, Conscious-ness, Hermit, Householder, Monk, Sannyasin, Snataka, Spring-time, Student, Yellow dress.

ORIGINAL SIN :—

A symbol of the negative state of ignorance and imperfection which originates in the process of involu-tion, through the limitation of Spirit by matter. This necessitates the subsequent evolution of Spirit from the lowest condition of ignorance to the highest state of Truth.

"Theology has had much to say about original sin. This original sin is neither more nor less than the brute inheritance which every man carries with him, and the process of evolution is an advance towards true salvation."—J. Fiske, *Destiny of Man*, p. 103.

"Everything inferior is a higher in the making; everything hateful is a coming beautiful; everything evil a coming good."—G. Prellnitz.

"All good things were originally bad things, every original sin has developed into an original virtue."—Nietzsche.

"Original sin is precisely the condition of blindness (to the spiritual) which, owing to the soul's immergence in materiality, hinders the perception of divine things. By no possibility can the Divine Life be generated in any soul afflicted with this blindness."—*The Perfect Way*, p. 242.

"Orphism held the doctrine of original sin. The soul was enclosed in the body

as in a tomb or prison, to punish a very early crime committed by the Titans, the ancestors of man, who had treacher-ously slain the young god Zagreus."— S. Reinach, *Orpheus*, p. 82.

"When Paul speaks of sin entering the world, and death by sin, he does not mean physical death; indeed, he is not speaking of happenings on the physical plane at all. This has been the cause of great misunderstanding of the apostle, because it is easy to see that physical death did not enter the world as the consequence of the sin of man. It was in the world long before man appeared on the scene. The sin of man, as Paul thought of it, was the development in man of the *isolated self* causing him to become out of harmony with God or the Universal Self. Under the old symbolism this was represented as the expulsion from Eden, but really it was the cessation, by a process of inevitable change, of the Eden condition within him-self. Paul is speaking of spiritual matters when he is dealing with both sin and death. Man died to Eden or heaven by becoming alive to the converse of that condition, to the consciousness of himself as a separate entity, distinct from the life of God. It is a Fall or Descent into matter, a burial or entombment."— K. C. Anderson, Serm., *The Buried Life*.

See Captivity, Death, Eden, Evo-lution, Fall, Heaven, Higher and lower selves, Ignorance, Involu-tion, Matter, Pitriyana, Self, Separateness, Sorrow, Spirit, Titans, Tomb, Zagreus.

ORO, THE TAHITIAN GOD :—

A symbol the Logos or Higher Self.

"Oro, the son of Taaroa, desired a wife from the daughters of Taata, the first man; he sent two of his brothers to seek among the daughters of man a suitable companion for him."—Ellis, *Polynesian Researches*, Vol. I. p. 231.

The Logos, whose parent was the Absolute, desired to manifest in the soul, and sought that whereby he might do so. The "first man" signifies the mind: the "daughters" are the emotions. The "two brothers" are the remaining aspects of the Higher Self.

See Heavenly regions, Hoa, Man, Rainbow, Taaroa, Taata, Tufara, Vairaumati, Woman.

ORPHEUS, THE DIVINE MUSICIAN :—

A symbol of the power of atma-buddhi,—the united wisdom and

love,—in harmonising and raising the lower elements in the soul. The desires (animals) are attracted, harmonised, and transmuted to higher planes.

See ANIMALS, EURYDICE, HARMONY, MELODY, METIS, MUSIC, PAN, VAPOUR (white).

OSIRIS :—

A symbol of the First Logos,—the Higher Self.

" Upon the first of these five new-made days Osiris was born, and a voice from heaven proclaimed, ' The Lord of all things hath appeared.' "—PLUTARCH, *Isis and Osiris*, § 12.

At the dawn of complete manifestation, the First Logos forthpours on the highest plane, that of atma. The " voice " refers to the Word which " was in the beginning with God " : it signifies the expression of the creative energy of the Logos,—the advent of duality,—Spirit-Matter.

" Hesiod makes the first elements of creation to be Chaos, Earth, Tartarus, Love. Let us distribute his names and assign them thus : to Isis that of Earth ; to Osiris that of Love, to Typhon that of Tartarus, for his Chaos seems to imply a certain place or *basis* for the Universe."—*Ibid.*, § 57.

This is correctly given :—Isis, buddhic (higher earth), Osiris, atmic (Love Divine), Typhon, astral (Tartarus), Chaos, primordial formless matter.

" Osiris was beautiful of face, but with a dull and black complexion ; his height exceeded five and a half yards."—*Ibid.*

This statement signifies that the Logos at manifestation was perfect potentially, but actually was non-existent, and, as it were, " black," which stands for negation. The height refers to the five planes whereon his evolution would be accomplished, and commencing from the Unmanifest above atma.

" O Osiris, son of Nut, I have given unto thee the sovereignty of thy father Seb, and the goddess Mut, thy mother, who gave birth to the gods, brought thee forth as the firstborn of five gods, and created thy beauties and fashioned thy members."—BUDGE, *Book of the Dead*, Ch. CLXXXIII p. 627.

Here Osiris is said to be the son of space (Nut) and time (Seb). " Mut " represents the formative energy in space, differentiating the Divine attri-

butes. The " five gods " represent the principles of the five planes of manifestation, of which the first produced and highest is atma (Osiris).

" The legend that ascribes the discovery of vine culture and the making of wine to Dionysus reminds us that the Egyptians gave the honour of those inventions to Osiris, but it is only a subordinate feature with the Egyptians, whereas in Greece Dionysus soon came to preside, pre-eminent and unique, over wine. If the worship had not more completely preserved more essential characteristics, it would be almost impossible to justify the identity in origin of Dionysus and Osiris. The rites of the festivals, especially those of the Anthestêria, are the only things that still prove it."

" Those mysteries, so sacred to the ancients, would be incomprehensible to us if certain details did not reveal their purpose and analogy. The queen's companions were fourteen in number, and offered sacrifices to Dionysus on fourteen altars, with other ceremonies not less secret than the rest. The ceremonial commemorated both the number of murderers who, according to the Cretan legend, massacred Dionysus, and the number of pieces into which they divided the corpse. Foucart rightly mentions the Egyptian legend in which Typhon, having assassinated Osiris, tore his victim into fourteen pieces, which he scattered among the nomes. Isis collected them, put them together, and from their union drew her Osiris, whom she resuscitated. . . . The sisters Isis and Nephthys, assisted by Horus and Anubis, made in fourteen moulds the fourteen pieces of which the divine body had been reconstructed, and then combined them into a perfect statue. They then endowed the statue with life, and rising from its funeral couch, it became again the god himself. . . . Our knowledge of the ceremonies of the Anthestêria scarcely permits us to doubt that the Egyptian Osiris was the original of the Attic Dionysus. We have in both cases the resurrection of a god who had been treacherously mutilated, the number of pieces is the same, and the march of events identical : just as Isis sought everywhere for the remains of Osiris, so Demeter never rested till she had gathered together those of Dionysus, and only after she had restored the body did the god come again into existence."— G. MASPERO, *New Light, etc.*, pp. 236, 238.

The dismemberment and reconstruction of the Archetypal Man are symbolised in the New Testament, and in the scriptures of India and Finland. To say the terms are " religious borrowings " explains nothing of their origin and meaning.

See APIS, ARC. MAN, ASCENSION
OF OSIRIS, BIRTH OF OSIRIS, CHAOS,
CIVILISING, CROCODILE, DAYS (five),
DEATH OF LEMMINKAINEN, OF OSIRIS,
DIONYSUS, DISMEMBERMENT, EARTH
(great), HEIGHT OF OSIRIS, INCARNA-
TION, ISIS, MEMBERS, MOIST, MOUTH
(speech), MUMMY, MUT, NUT, OAK,
OLYMPUS, PAMYLES, PRAGÂPATI
(relaxed), RE-STAU, RESURRECTION,
SEB, TARTARUS, TATTU, TYPHON,
WEEPING, WORD, YUDHI, ZAGREUS.

OVERSEER OF THE HOUSE :—

A symbol of the individuality
seated in the causal-body (house).

"Every male fiend and every female
fiend shall the Osiris Nu, the overseer of the house of the overseer of the
seal, destroy."—BUDGE, *Book of the Dead*,
Ch. CXXXIV.

Every error and every lower emotion shall the Self, as the individuality
operating in the lower forms, destroy.

"He who knows and has thrown off all
evil, the overseer of the senses, the
pure-minded, firmly grounded in the
Self, and looking away from all earthly
objects, he is the same."—*Mait. Upanishad*, VI. 1.

The individuality perfected by means
of the personality, who has overcome
the attractions of sense and desire, becomes one and the same with the Self.

See CAUSAL - BODY, DEFUNCT,
FIENDS, HOUSEHOLDER, INDIVIDU-
ALITY, NEBO, PERSONALITY.

OX FOR DRAUGHT :—

A symbol of reverence for the
higher, which eventuates in obedience and action.

"Oxen and bullocks correspond,
specifically, to the affections of the
natural mind, and sheep and lambs to the
affections of the spiritual mind."—
SWEDENBORG, *The Future Life*, p. 35.

See CATTLE, LAMB, MAN (natural),
RACES, SHEEP.

OX SARSAOK :—

A symbol of the buddhic plane on
which manifestation first takes place.

See BUDDHIC PLANE, BULL, COW,
CREATION.

OX, SPLENDID PRIMORDIAL :—

A symbol of buddhic intuition
passing downwards.

"In the reign of Kai Us, a splendid
Ox is said to foretell the revelation

from Zoroaster."—A. V. W. JACKSON,
Zoroaster, p. 24.

At a certain early period of involution, a power of divination or intuition
causes on the lower planes a dim
apprehension of the advent of the
Ego or Soul.

See BULL, INTUITION, INVOLUTION,
KAI US, SOUL (highest), ZOROASTER.

OX AND ASS :—

Symbols of higher activities operating upon qualities of the lower planes.

"Ox,—the image of patient labour
and productive energy."—P. FAIRBAIRN,
Typology, Vol. I. p. 263.

"What are the *oxen plowing*, except
we understand our serious thoughts,
while they wear the heart with diligent
tillage, yield abundant fruits of increase ?
And what do we take to be the *asses
feeding beside them*, but the simple emotions of the soul, which whilst carefully
withheld from straying in double ways,
we feed in the free pasture of purity ?"—
GREGORY THE GREAT, *Morals on the
Book of Job*, Vol. I. p. 114.

See AGRICULTURE, CULTIVATION,
PLOUGHING, REAPING.

OX-BORN :—

A symbol of the atma-buddhic
nature of the soul or ego as proceeding from buddhi to incarnation
in the lower vehicles of consciousness.

See BEES, HONEY.

OX-LEADER :—

A symbol of a ruling spirit of
reverence for truth.

"An endeavour is made by the sorcerers to have the babe trampled to
death by a herd of oxen ; the leading
ox, however, stands over the child and
prevents it from perishing beneath the
feet of the herd."—A. V. W. JACKSON,
Zoroaster, p. 29.

The endeavour of the "sorcerers,"
signifies the instinctive and blind
trust to habit and authority, which
is calculated to crush out the
early effort which the Self (the babe)
makes to seek and know for itself.
The highest aspiration, however, which
reverences the spirit of truth and
reason, more than mere tradition,
is the means of protecting the Self.

See BIRTH OF KRISHNA, DURASROBO,
HEROD, NINIGI, PHARISEES, PRIESTS
AND ELDERS, SPARROWS (twelve),
TRADITION, ZOROASTER.

OX-EYED QUEEN HERA :—

A symbol of the intuition aspect of buddhi. "Ox-eyed" refers to the intuition, it is a symbol of spontaneous cognition.

See EYE, HAIR (side-lock), HERA, INTUITION.

OXEN, OFFSPRING OF :—

Symbolic of qualities which are begotten of reverence, patience and submission.

See Ox (draught).

OXEN'S HEADS ON CHILDREN OF MEN :—

Symbolic of mental qualities directed by the higher will.

See CHILDREN OF MEN.

OXYRYNCHUS, LEPIDOTUS, AND PHAGRUS FISHES :—

Symbols of false knowledge, superstition, and prejudice ; which are illusions of the lower mind allied with desire.

See GENERATIVE.

PACCEKABUDDHAS OR PRATY-EKA-BUDDHAS :—

A symbol of the primordial spiritual egos, or Divine monads, who have not yet descended to incarnate in the lower worlds.

"High above these four stages (of sainthood) stand those perfect ones, 'who have of themselves alone become partakers of the Buddhahood' (Paccekabuddha); they have won the knowledge that brings deliverance, not as disciples of one of the holy, universal Buddhas, but of their own power, yet their perfection does not extend so far that they could preach it to the world. . . . 'In the whole universe,' says Buddha, 'there is, except me only, no one who is equal to the Paccekabuddhas.' "—H. OLDENBERG, *Buddha*, pp. 321, 322.

On the highest plane, atma, are the spiritual monads, "Sons of God," who in prior universes have become perfect and are now in unity with the manifesting Self. Those of them who have not already descended to gain experience in the lower life have full consciousness on their own plane of atma, but not on any plane below, for they have no lower nature and cannot express (preach) their perfections to the lower worlds. But in the whole universe there is none but the Higher Self equal to these other Selves, for essentially they are all one on the highest plane.

See AGNISHVATTAS, ARHATS, BODHISATVAS, FRAVASHIS, MANASAPUTRAS, MARUTS, MONAD OF LIFE, OCEAN, SONS OF GOD, TRI-RATNA.

PADDLES, TWO :—

Symbols of the love of goodness and the love of truth, wherewith the soul is propelled onward in its course.

" 'Tell us our name,' say the Paddles ; 'Fingers of Horus the first-born,' is your name.' "—BUDGE, *Book of the Dead*, Ch. XCIX.

The two "fingers of Horus "—the Christ within,—have the same signification as the two paddles.

See BOAT (river), FINGERS OF HORUS, LADDER, OARS.

PAGODA :—

A symbol of the higher planes in which are the Divine attributes. The dragons and ornaments signify wisdom and the "treasures in heaven,"—the higher qualities on the buddhic plane.

See CHURCH, SHRINE, TEMPLE.

PAHAD (GEBURAH), PUNISHMENT, JUDGMENT, SEVERITY ; THE MOON :—

A symbol of the Personality on the lower mental plane of consciousness.

"*Geburah* or *Pachad* is sometimes used in a good and sometimes in an evil sense ; the world is based thereon —in the sense that severity is indispensable—but it could not subsist without Mercy (*Chesed*). It is said also to be the repentance of God, and it seems even to connect with Samael. It was by *Geburah* that Jerusalem was destroyed."—A. E. WAITE, *Secret Doctrine of Israel*, p. 40.

The Personality acts well or ill according as it chooses the good or evil course. The choice of evil entails suffering according to karmic law. The Individuality (Chesed) projects the Personality into conditions calculated to correct some of the defects of the Personality. The Divine Love aids the Personality by giving it improved means of expression. The Personality when ruled by desire

(Samael) obscured and rendered in-operative the higher nature (Jerusalem) of the soul.

See FALL, GOD REPENTING, HESED, HOKHMAH, INDIVIDUALITY, JERUSALEM, JUDGMENT DAY, KARMA, PANDORA, PERSONALITY, PRODIGAL, SEPHIROTH, SUFFERING, SUN, MOON, TIPHERETH.

PAIRIKA KNATHAITI :—

A symbol of the astral principle which first awakens the soul.

See CHURNING, FALL, PEARL (precious), SEPARATION, TANE-MAHUTA.

PAIRIKA AS STAR-WORMS :—

Symbols of fear and ambition which are detrimental to the perception of truth.

"O Lord of light (Osiris), come thou and swallow up the worms that are in Amentet."—BUDGE, *Book of the Dead*, p. 48.

The Higher Self is entreated to annul the fear and ambition which disturb the soul.

See AMENTET, CREEPING THINGS, MOUNTAIN (lower), STAR-WORMS.

PALACE OR HOUSE :—

A symbol usually of the causal-body, but occasionally of the astral-body, in accordance with the context.

See DWELLING, HOUSE, KAABA, ONOGOROJIMA, STUPA, TEMPLE.

PALACE OF THE DEITY :—

A symbol of the plane of atma, the abode of the Self.

"Thetis at once plunged from splendid Olympus into the profound sea. But Zeus on the other hand returned to his palace."—*Iliad*, Bk. I.

Nature being submerged in the plane of desire, as sense and instinct, the Self as Truth remained on the plane of atma.

See OLYMPUS, PYRAMID, THETIS, ZEUS.

PALACES, HIGH-SOARING :—

Symbolic of an exalted condition of bliss on high planes.

See AMARAVATI, KAPILA.

PALANQUIN OF THE CHILD BUDDHA :—

A symbol of forthgoing energy of the Self in his buddhic vehicle.

See BUDDHA, CHARIOT.

PALESTINUS OR PELUSIUS :—

A symbol of the higher intellect enlightened by the intuition and put in relation to the personality.

"This relation (story) is again contradicted by such as tell us that the true name of the child was Palestinus, or Pelusius, and that the city of this name was built by the Goddess (Isis) in memory of him."—PLUTARCH, *Isis and Osiris*, § 17.

This previous statement would appear to be at variance with that which shows us that the true character of the mind (child) is not the lower intellect, but the intuition, whose abode, the causal-body, was fashioned by Wisdom, and is indeed permanent.

See CAUSAL-BODY, INTUITION, MANEROS.

PALM TREES ; PALMS :—

Symbolic of glimpses of higher things. Intuitions of love and truth.

"By palm trees are signified the divine truths of the Word, and by Palms in their hands confessions from them. . . . Palms signify divine truths in ultimates, which is the divine truth of the literal sense of the Word."—SWEDENBORG, *Apoc. Rev.*, n. 367.

See INTUITION, TREES (tall).

PAMYLES :—

A symbol of the personality.

"A certain person, named Pamyles, as he was fetching water from the temple of Jupiter at Thebes, heard a voice commanding him to proclaim aloud that 'The good and great King Osiris was then born.'"—PLUTARCH, *Isis and Osiris*, § 12.

This signifies that as the soul searches for truth in its inner nature, the Divine voice from within announces to the lower self that the Lord Christ is born in the mind to be the soul's ruler and Saviour.

See BIRTH OF OSIRIS, KING (great), OSIRIS, PERSONALITY, SON OF MAN, TEMPLE, THEBES.

PAN, THE GREAT GOD, SON OF HERMES :—

A symbol of the subjective astro-mental life of the sympathetic system of the natural man, through which the desires and the feelings are increased and brought into relation with the objective mind. "Pan" is the product of mind

(Hermes) brought forth of the astral nature, and therefore progresses by means of desire (goat-legged). He delights the Divine attributes (Gods) because he is the perfect instrument through which Dionysus (Christ) can evolve in the lower nature and be the Saviour of the soul. " Pan " on the astral plane corresponds with " Orpheus " on the buddhic plane : they both are agents for the co-ordinating and harmonising (music) of the lower qualities (flocks both of wild and tame animals).

" As the god of everything connected with pastoral life, Pan was fond of music, and the inventor of the syrinx or shepherd's flute."—*Smith's Class. Dict.*

See ANIMALS, DIONYSUS, FLOCKS, GOAT, HERDS, HERMES, JUBAL, MAN (natural), MUSIC, ORPHEUS, PANIC TERRORS, PASTORAL LIFE, SATYRS.

PANACEA :—

See FOOD.

PANCALA, KINGDOM OF DRUPADA :—

A symbol of the higher mental plane, the domain of the spiritual mind.

See DRAUPADI, DRONA, DRUPADA.

PANDAVAS, OR FIVE PANDU PRINCES, THE SONS OF PANDU :—

Symbols of five of the higher active attributes of the soul, namely,—Yudhi-shthira = the Spiritual mind. Bhima = the philosophic Intellect. Arjuna = the Personality with Spark. Nakula = the love of Goodness. Sahadeva = the love of Truth.

These enter the field of conflict (the mind) to overcome the desires (Kurus).

" *Dhritarashtra :* Tell me, O Sanjaya, what the people of my own party and those of Pandu, who are assembled at Kurukshetra resolved upon war, have been doing. *Sanjaya :* King Duryodhana, having just beheld the army of the Pandus drawn up in battle array, went to his preceptor and spoke these words : ' Behold ! O Master, the mighty army of the sons of Pandu drawn up by thy pupil, the clever son of Drupada.' "—*Bhagavad-Gita,* I. 1.

See ARENA, ARJUNA, BHIMA, BHISMA, DHRISTA-DYUMNA, DHRITARASHTRA, DRAUPADI, DRONA, DURYODHANA, FIELD, KARNA, KRISHNA,

KURUS, PANDU, SANJAYA, YUDHISHTHIRA.

PANDORA :—

A symbol of the emotion-nature which becomes allied with the lower mind (Epimetheus).

" Pandora whom the Hebrews call Eve."—*Zosimus,* 26, 14.

" When Prometheus had stolen the fire from heaven, Zeus in revenge caused Hephaestus to make a woman out of earth, who by her charms and beauty should bring misery upon the human race. . . . In the house of Epimetheus, her husband, was a closed jar, which he had been forbidden to open. When Pandora out of curiosity opened the lid, all the evils incident to man poured out. She had only time to shut down the lid, and prevent the escape of Hope."—*Smith's Class. Dict.*

When the soul or individuality had possessed itself of the Divine Spark, the law of the Supreme required that from the lower nature (earth) there should arise the Emotion-nature, which, after being allied with the lower mind, shall be the means through the temptations of desire (jar) of bringing strife, suffering and evils of all kinds into the human soul. But Hope, or the promise of salvation, remains to encourage the efforts of the soul to rise. As in the case of Adam and Eve, the Higher Self necessarily forbids the mind to surrender to the attractions of the lower nature ; nevertheless the inevitable curiosity for new experience brings about the fall of mind into the realm of desire and sense, and the obscuration of the spiritual vibrations from above.

See ANDROMEDA, CHEST, CUPID, DRAUPADI, EPIMETHEUS, EVE, FALL, HEPHAISTOS, NESTOR, PERSEPHONE, PROMETHEUS, SELENE, WIFE, WOMAN.

PANDU, KING :—

A symbol of the Divine Mind, active at a certain stage.

" Pandu was born of a pale complexion."—*Mahabharata.*

The Divine Mind began to manifest free from the lower qualities.

See PANDAVAS, WHITE.

PANIC TERRORS :—

This symbol refers to the functioning of the sympathetic system which is astral.

See PAN.

PANOPOLIS, OR CHEMMIS :—

A symbol of an astral centre having its seat in the solar plexus.

See CHEMMIS, DELOS.

PANS :—

Symbols of the activities of the lower mind, that is, desire-mental functionings of the brain-mind.

See CENTAURS, SATYRS.

PANTHER SKIN :—

A symbol signifying the overcoming of the lower desires.

"The iron which is the ceiling of heaven openeth itself before Pepi, and he passeth through it with his panther skin upon him, and his staff and whip in his hand."—BUDGE, Book of the Dead, Vol. I. p. lxiii.

The higher mind, which is the firmament below the buddhic plane, is receptive of the consciousness of the purified soul which has overcome the desires, and actively aspires to that which is above.

See CEILING OF SKY, DEFUNCT, FIRMAMENT, IRON PLATE, REN.

PAPYRUS BOAT OF ISIS :—

A symbol of the sacred scriptures, which serve as a vehicle of Divine Wisdom (Isis).

"Isis once more sets out in search of the scattered fragments of her husband's body, making use of a boat made of the reed Papyrus in order the more easily to pass through the lower and fenny parts of the country."—PLUTARCH, Isis and Osiris, § 18.

Then Wisdom, as it were, descends and endeavours to harmonise and discipline the qualities which are commencing to evolve. When once the Divine voice has been identified in the mind with the dramatic modes of expression in sacred writings, and the Scriptures are deemed binding, help is to be derived therefrom by the impressionable emotion-nature (fens), which catches in this means of declaration of Truth a hint of the message and meaning which is there to be interpreted by the earnest and devout soul.

"The papyrus is frequently mentioned in the colophons of Assur-banipal's tablets under the name of gis-li-khu-si, or 'grass of guidance.' Another ideographic name was gis-zu, 'vegetable of knowledge.'"—SAYCE, Rel. of Anc. Babyl., pp. 9, 10.

See AGNISHTOMA, AMBAS, BOAT (wisdom), BOOK STUDIES, CROCODILE, DEATH OF OSIRIS, DISMEMBERMENT, GOSPEL, HERMES (tris.), INSPIRATION, ISIS, KORAN, MARSH, RELIGION, REVELATION, SASTRA, SCRIPTURES, UPANISHADS, UR-HEKAU, VEDA, WISDOM, WORD, WORSHIP.

PARABLE :—

A symbolic narrative of comparison, to illustrate the laws of the inner world by the laws of the outer.

"I will open my mouth in a parable : I will utter dark sayings of old."—Ps. lxxviii. 2.

The expression of the inner nature shall appear in the outer, and under scriptural narratives there shall be revealed the hidden wisdom of the soul.

"It is clear, therefore, that if Hebrew history is to be read as our Lord and His Apostles teach us that it ought to be read, it must not be regarded (as too many regard it) merely as a literal recital of facts, but as also a typical representation of spiritual truths. Hebrew History, as written by the Holy Spirit in the Old Testament, is a divine Parable."—WORDSWORTH, Bible, Psalms, p. 122.

"It is almost singular that the identification of the Laws of the Spiritual World with the Laws of Nature should so long have escaped recognition. For apart from the probability on à priori grounds, it is involved in the whole structure of Parable. When any two phenomena in the two spheres are seen to be analogous, the parallelism must depend upon the fact that the Laws governing them are not analogous but identical."—H. DRUMMOND, Natural Law, etc., p. 52.

"Unto you is given to know the mystery of the Kingdom of God ; but unto them that are without, all these things are done in parables."—MARK iv. 11.

"In other words, all material things are symbols, sacraments, of eternal and spiritual facts, and what needs to be done with human beings is to awaken them to an immediate knowledge of those facts. . . . The visible world was so real to the people that the invisible could not make much appeal ; they could not see in the one a parable of the other, a material representation of a spiritual reality, a mystery which could not be fully revealed to mortal flesh, but which could be immediately known nevertheless. . . . The most real thing in our experience is just that which cannot be rationalised ; it is felt and known but not explained ; it is a mystery. When we are most aware of it is when we are at our best, when thoughts and feelings are most elevated, when desire and will are both thrown on the side of what we perceive to be highest and holiest; it is then that the supernatural breaks through and lays hold of us."—R. J. CAMPBELL, Serm., *The Mystery of the Heavenly Kingdom.*

See ASS AND COLT, EXODUS, HOUSE-HOLDER, LAZARUS, LEAVEN, MYTHO-LOGY, PEARL, PRODIGAL, REAPING, SEED (good), SICKLE, SIGN, VINEYARD, VIRGINS (ten), WEDDING.

PARACLETE, COMFORTER, OR INTERCESSOR :—

A symbol of Wisdom, the buddhic function, allied with the highest principle (atma-buddhi).

"And I will pray the Father, and he shall give you another Comforter, that he may be with you for ever, even the Spirit of truth; whom the world cannot receive; for it beholdeth him not, neither knoweth him: ye know him; for he abideth with you, and shall be in you."—JOHN xiv. 16, 17.

"The Spirit, the Paraclete, she shall teach you everything."—JOHN xiv. 26 (Old Syriac Version).

To the aspiring Christ-soul there will come the response from the Absolute in the bestowal of the intuition of Truth through the buddhic function, which the unpurified lower nature cannot receive, it being unapparent and unknown. But to the disciplined qualities the holy Spirit is perceptible, and has become the inner guide and teacher, abiding always in the soul.

"Christ knew what was most expedient for the disciples, because that inward sight, wherewith the Holy Spirit was yet to comfort them, was undoubtedly superior; not by bringing a human body into the bodies of those who saw, but by infusing Himself into the hearts of those who believed."—AUGUSTINE, *Gospel of John*, Vol. II. p. 357.

"Holiness comes from the operation and indwelling in our spirits of a Divine Spirit, which draws away our love from self to fix it on Him, which changes our blindness into light, and makes us by degrees like itself, 'holy, harmless, undefiled, separate from sinners.' The Spirit of the Lord is the energy which produces all righteousness and purity in human spirits."—A. MACLAREN, *Sermons, 2nd Series*, p. 119.

"These three—justice, love, truth—are the three great attributes of the divine nature, aspects of the one perfection which God is. When they meet in our heart God may be said to take up His abode within us."—B. JOWETT, Serm., *The Subjection of the Son.*

See ABSOLUTE, ATMA, BLASPHEMY, BUDDHIC FUNCTION, CHRIST PRINCIPLE, HAIR OF HEAD, HEART, HOLY GHOST, SHEKINAH, WISDOM.

PARADISE :—

A symbol of a state of blissful consciousness on either the higher mental plane or the buddhic plane, in which the soul is suffused in Wisdom, Truth, and Love, and entirely free from the lower nature.

"Paradise, symbolically taken, means wisdom, intelligence, both divine and human, and the proper comprehension of the causes of things."—PHILO, *Works*, Yonge, Vol. IV. p. 286.

"In a straight line below the Arsh and Kursi, and of the light of the former, God created the eight Paradises. These are arranged one within the other, in as many ascending stages, the innermost and highest of all being the 'Garden of Eden,' which overlooks all the others like a citadel on a lofty eminence in the midst of a walled city. . . . The wonderful tree called the Tuba or 'Beatitude,' the roots of which are in the region of the Lote-tree above the highest Paradise, sends its branches down to all the eight Gardens, a shoot entering the abode of every inhabitant."—GIBB, *Hist. of Ottoman Poetry*, Vol. I. pp. 36–7.

"To him that overcometh, to him will I give to eat of the tree of life, which is in the Paradise (or Garden) of God."—REV. ii. 7.

Below the planes of atma (Arsh) and buddhi (Kursi), there is the mental plane divisible into seven sub-planes, on each of which the ego may experience a subjective state of consciousness, while withdrawn from incarnation. On the three higher of these sub-planes is the blissful state of devachan. On the lower sub-planes of the buddhic plane is the "Kingdom of heaven," the "Garden of Eden," or the "eighth Paradise." The "tree of Life," or "Tuba tree," which has its roots above, in atma, and its branches below, is the Ray of the Divine Life, the Spirit or Spark which is in the higher nature of every human soul. The ego which overcometh the lower nature shall rise to the buddhic plane and be given the fruit of the tree of Life,—the spiritual endowments which accrue from successful efforts in the life below.

See ARSH, ATMA, BUDDHIC PLANE, DEVACHAN, EDEN, FRUIT, GARDEN (Eden), GARDEN (flowers), GARODMAN, HEAVEN, HOURIES, KINGDOM OF HEAVEN, KURSI, LOTE-TREE, SPARK, TREE OF LIFE, TUBA-TREE, WISDOM (masc.).

PARADISE (LOWER) :—

A pleasurable state of illusion on the astro-mental plane.

"Verily, the moon is the door of the Svarga-world."—*Kaush. Upanishad,* I. 2.

Truly the moon is the symbol of the astral paradise created by desire as an illusion of the mind.

See HARAVAITI, MEADOW OF HADES, SLEEPING, SVARGA.

PARENTS OF CHILDREN :—

A symbol of lower conditions which give birth to higher.

"For the children ought not to lay up for the parents, but the parents for the children."—2 COR. xii. 14.

This refers to the laying up of "treasure in heaven," which must be for the "children," or the more highly developed qualities that are to follow. By the law of evolution, lower states of mind and emotion give rise in course of time to higher states, which leave the lower states to die out.

See CHILD, CHILDREN OF MEN, DEAD (burying), EVOLUTION FATHER (lower), PEACE AND SWORD, TREASURE IN HEAVEN.

PARGANYA :—

A symbol of the Divine Life of the universe and of the soul on the buddhic plane.

"The winds blow, the lightnings fly, plants spring up, the sky pours. Food is produced for the whole world, when Parganya blesses the earth with his seed."—*Rig-Veda,* V. 83, 4.

"He rules as God over the whole world; all creatures rest in him; he is the life (atma) of all that moves and rests."—*Ibid.,* VII. 101, 6.

Atma ensouls buddhi and the prototypes.

See CLOUDS, CREATURES, EARTH, FOOD, LIGHTNING, PLANTS, SEED, SOMA.

PASSAGES, OR VALLEYS, THROUGH THE MOUNTAINS :—

A symbol of the establishment of tracts on the mental plane, in relation to the astral mechanism.

See BRIDGE OF GJALL, CHANNELS, MOUNTAINS, VALLEY.

PASSION OF JESUS :—

A symbol of the agony of the yet imperfect soul as it approaches perfection.

"My soul is exceeding sorrowful, even unto death : abide ye here, and watch with me. And he went forward a little, and fell on his face, and prayed, saying, O my Father, if it be possible, let this cup pass away from me : nevertheless, not as I will, but as thou wilt."—MAT. xxvi. 38, 39.

As the Spirit is raised in the aspiring soul, so in proportion the personality (Jesus) becomes depressed, and the suffering makes it appear that it cannot do the things that it would. It is filled with a sense of powerlessness, of futility, of sore trial. The Christ-soul could not do then,—in his present condition,—that which he foresaw would be done by the Higher Self which strengthened him. Yet he progressed, and losing sight of the lower, he yearned after union with the Higher. In the soul there was the alternation between the human and the spiritual in the struggle for perfection. As the personality grew weaker, the individuality increased in strength, and the mental depression and suffering became temporarily the greater in the lower consciousness.

"With all sound theologians, and with all the doctors, I deny the possibility of the Divine nature suffering. The Godhead cannot be tempted, and how should the Godhead suffer ? The human nature of Christ alone suffered; and that is not infinite, but finite."—E. IRVING, *Col. Writings,* Vol. V. p. 147.

"Even Jesus was not perfect, as the Gospels themselves witness. For one who could pray, '*Not my will, but* Thine *be done* !' was plainly not yet in entire union with God. And so it needs must be, for when that perfect union is accomplished, there remains no passion, no cross, no burial, to be endured. All re-births are ended, and the spirit is for ever freed from matter. There could not, therefore, by the very nature of things, be any *perfect* man upon the earth-plane; because, so soon as perfec-

tion is attained, this plane is necessarily incapable of retaining the purified spirit."
—*The Perfect Way*, p. 345.

See BLOODY SWEAT, CRUCIFIXION OF JESUS, GETHSEMANE, INDIVIDUALITY, JESUS OF GOSPELS, JESUS (severe), MOUNT OF OLIVES, PERSONALITY, SERVANT OF GOD, SORROW, SUFFERING, TRIAL OF JESUS, VINEGAR.

PASSOVER, JEWISH :—

A symbol of the process of redemption wherein partly disciplined qualities (Israelites), by partaking of the Divine nature (lamb), are nourished by the Divine Life as they triumph over the things of darkness, and pass over from a lower stage (Egypt) to a higher stage (Canaan).

"For our passover also hath been sacrificed, even Christ."—1 COR. v. 7.

Through the sacrifice of the Higher Self in involution, the Divine Life is outpoured in evolution.

"For Israel in Egypt (the house of bondage), for the Christian in the world, the one great truth is the Passover, redemption through the blood of the Lamb, salvation, not for our righteousness' sake, but because the blood is on the door-post. . . . And what is this passover but *redemption*? The elect family, with shoes on their feet, and their loins girt ready for flight from Egypt, are standing by night (ROM. xiii. 12) within the house whose door-posts are sprinkled with blood, while the destroying angel is abroad."—A. JUKES, *The Law of the Offerings*, p. 23.

"The water and blood which flowed from the side of Jesus as the true Paschal lamb is the symbol of the spiritual life which through the death of Jesus is communicated in all its fullness to mankind."—F. C. BAUR, *Church History*, Vol. I. p. 159.

"What God is aiming at is the production of a humanity which shall be the perfect expression of Christ. Through Christ from the very first he has been working out this divine idea, but not on this plane only ; every man of faith who has ever lived has but passed on to another department of the service of the Lord when he has finished with the body. It is all one work ; we are in the lowest department of it now, and we know not what is being done in the higher, but the higher knows what is being done in ours, and how we are doing it."—R. J. CAMPBELL, Serm., *Solidarity in Christ*.

See ATONEMENT, BLOOD OF LAMB, BONDAGE, CRUCIFIXION OF CHRIST, DARKNESS, EGYPT, EVOLUTION, EXODUS, FEET, HOUSE OF BONDAGE, INVOLUTION, ISRAELITES, LAMB, QUALITIES, REDEMPTION, ROOM (house), SACRIFICER, SALVATION, SHOES, UNLEAVENED.

PASTORAL LIFE :—

A symbol of the activities of the desire-mind, and the disciplining of the lower emotions.

"Fuh-he recommended pastoral employments for the people, and the rearing of domesticated animals."—*Chinese Mythology*, KIDD, *China*.

This is a reference to the dawn of the intelligence, and the cultivation of the lower faculties in such a way that they might become of use to the soul.

See ANIMALS, FUH-HE, JABAL, PAN.

PASTURES OF THE LORD :—

A symbol of the buddhic functioning producing the transmuted emotions, the virtues (sheep), and the love of goodness and truth.

See DOOR (higher), PRISONERS, SHEEP.

PATERAGTARASPO'S VILLAGE :—

A symbol of the astral form-side of the soul.

See POURUSHASPO.

PATH OF THE BIRDS ON HIGH :—

A symbol of the way of the Self upward in the mind (air). The way of love and aspiration. The growth to perfection.

"The way of love, which may at times become the way of self-sacrifice, is the soul's homeward road, the way that leads to the eternal."—R. J. CAMPBELL, Serm., *The Soul's Exile*.

"The growth in perfection or towards perfectness is the deepest law of man's being. It is not man's work as compared with God's work, for it is the most divine thing in the world, and the divine impulse which God has implanted in man brings it into existence. But it is man's work, both in the sense that nothing else but man is capable of this, and also in the sense that nothing of it is *given* to man, for by its very nature it cannot be given. . . . Men cannot be made happy, or blessed, except through the process of their own self-unfolding and self-endeavour."—R. A. DUFF, *Spinoza's Philosophy*, p. 172.

See BIRDS, DEVAYANA, WAY OF THE LORD.

PATH, EIGHT-FOLD :—

See SUFFERING.

PATH, TWOFOLD :—

A symbol of the path of Love and Action, the dual path to perfection which the spiritual monads enter upon when they descend to the planes of the manifest.

"The grades of Spirit and its knowledge correspond to the grades of existence. The lower strives wistfully to reach the higher, and the higher lifts the lower up to its own level. The Spirit which stands above us, and which has lent to all earthly things their Forms, seeks to bring these scattered Forms together that they may become one in Love.—T. J. DE BOER, *Phil. in Islam*, p. 120.

" ' I shall be satisfied, when I awake, with Thy likeness ' (Ps. xvii. 15). We have here the blessed confidence that when all the baseless fabric of the dream of life has faded from our opening eyes, we shall see the face of the ever-loving God. Here the distracting whirl of earthly things obscures Him from even the devoutest souls. . . . No longer befooled by shadows, we shall possess the true substance ; no longer bedazzled by shows, we shall behold the reality. And seeing God we shall be satisfied."— A. MACLAREN, *Sermons, 2nd Series*, p. 16.

See APARÂGITA, BRAHMA, GODHEAD, WAY OF DELIVERANCE, WORKS (wisdom).

PATRIARCHS OF GENESIS :—

Symbols of the successive stages of growth in the evolution of the consciousness, within which stages the several powers and virtues are developed and realised, by means of which the ego is gradually built up, until finally the "Noah,"—or Self to be ensheathed in the causal-body (ark),—is arrived at. The lives of the patriarchs signify the periods, and their names serve to connect the successive effects with their antecedent spiritual causes.

"This fifth chapter of Genesis treateth in particular concerning the propagation of the Most Ancient Church, through successive generations, even almost to the flood. The Most Ancient Church, which was celestial, is what is called Man and a likeness of God. A second Church which was not so celestial as the former is called 'Seth.' A third, 'Enos.' A fourth, 'Canaan.' A fifth, 'Mahaleel.' A sixth, 'Jared.' A seventh, 'Enoch.' An eighth, 'Methusaleh,' etc."—SWEDENBORG, *Arc. Cel. to Gen. v.*

"Church" signifies an inner state of the soul, or the religious consciousness.

See each Patriarch, ANCESTORS, ARITS, ARK, CHURCH, YEARS.

PATROCLUS :—

A symbol of the reasoning mind which is strongly attached to the personality (Achilles).

See ACHILLES.

PAURVAS, THE GOOD MAZDA-YASNIAN RELIGION :—

A symbol of the Love and Truth latent within the soul.

See LAW OF ZOROASTER, RELIGION.

PAVILION :—

A symbol of a vehicle of consciousness, or sheath of the soul.

See TABERNACLE, TENT.

PEACE, OR REST :—

A symbol of blissful union of the higher and lower Selves. This implies liberation from the strife of lower plane activities, and the establishment of equilibrium in the soul.

"The sage who has attained a certain height will find peace in all things that happen ; and the event which saddens him, as other men, tarries but an instant ere it goes to strengthen his deep perception of life."—MAETERLINCK, *Wisdom and Destiny*, § 93.

"Peace is the entire harmony between the nature of anything and its circumstances. That is what every healthy aspiration after peace is really seeking for. . . . Peace will become a deeper and deeper thing to men as they become aware more and more of what their surroundings are, as they open their eyes to more and more intimate and sacred things with which they have to do."—PHILLIPS BROOKS, Serm., *Peace in Believing*.

"The Divine Persons, who form one sole God, are in the fecundity of their nature ever active : and in the simplicity of their essence they form the Godhead and eternal blessedness. Thus God according to the Persons is Eternal Work : but according to the essence and Its perpetual stillness, He is Eternal Rest. Now love and fruition live between this activity and this rest. Love would work without ceasing : for its nature is eternal work with God. Fruition is ever at rest, for it dwells higher than the will and the longing *for* the well-beloved, *in* the well-beloved."—RUYSBROECK, *De Septem*, etc., Ch. XIV.

" ' Delight thyself also in the Lord, and He shall give thee the desires of thine heart' (Ps. xxxvii. 4). These eager desires, transfer them to Him; on Him let the affections fix and fasten; make Him the end of your longings, the food of your spirits. And this glad longing for God is the cure for all the feverish unrest of desires unfulfilled, as well as for the ague fear of loss and sorrow. Quietness fills the soul which delights in the Lord, and its hunger is as blessed and as peaceful as its satis-faction."—A. MACLAREN, *Sermons*, *2nd Series*, p. 249.

See HIGHER AND LOWER SELVES, LIBERATION, LORD (peace), STRIFE, UNION.

PEACE AND A SWORD :—

Symbols of passive and active conditions.

"Think not that I came to send peace on the earth : I came not to send peace, but a sword. For I came to set a man at variance against his father, and the daughter against her mother, and the daughter in law against her mother in law : and a man's foes shall be they of his own household."—MAT. x. 34–6.

"Peace " is the stilling, the quiet-ing, the calm, negative condition. The "sword" is the outgoing or positive side of the nature, which must needs be exercised ere the other is possible to a soul's attaining. The Christ-soul is speaking on the active side of life's endeavour, from which point of view such apparently painful results are entailed through His opera-tions. The progressed mental quality becomes opposed to its "father," the less progressed ; the raised emotion is averse to the lower emotion, its "mother." The foes of the soul are to be found in its desires which encompass it round.

"And indeed He came not to bring peace on the earth, that is, to corporeal and sensible things, but a sword, and to cut through, if I may so say so, the disastrous friendship of soul and body, so that the soul, committing herself to the spirit which was against the flesh, may enter into friendship with God."—ORIGEN, *Comm. on John*, Bk. I. § 36.

"The only way in this world to get peace is to make it out of pain. And, after all, did you come into this world to find happiness ; was it for your own sake alone that you were created into the midst of this vast humanity ? What are you that you should pay so much attention to yourself and lose in that attention the thought of others ? You are not here to find happiness directly, as the first thing. You are here to discover truth, and the way is dark,

and leads to the Cross before it finds the Resurrection."— STOPFORD A. BROOKE, Serm., *Lord, Increase our Faith.*

"In this world we cannot yet have peace without previous war in matters pertaining to truth. Every truth, or form of truth, calls up its opponent falsehood ; every good insisted on evokes its own special adversary, and war is inevitable. I came not, said Christ, to send peace on earth, but a sword."—*Ibid.*, Serm., *God is Spirit.*

See CHILD, FATHER (lower), GIL-GAMES, PARENTS, SCOURGE, SWORD.

PEACHES OF IZANAGI, THREE :—

Symbols of the fruit of the Spirit, —Truth, Love, and Wisdom.

"On reaching the foot of the 'Even Pass of Yomi,' Izanagi gathered three peaches that were growing there, and smote his pursuers (the Ugly Females) with them, so that they all fled back. Moreover, he said to the peaches, ' As ye have helped me, so must ye help all living people in the Central Land of Reed plains when they are in trouble."—*The Kojiki.*

The consciousness rising to the higher mental plane perceives the Truth, Love, and Wisdom, to be found there. These are effectual in withstanding the lower emotions (Ugly Females), and are made accessible in the soul, so that the striving mental qualities (the people), having in them the germ of Divine life, may be nourished by them. The "Land of Reed-plains " is the astro-mentality.

See BIRTH OF HORUS, FRUIT OF THE SPIRIT, GARDEN OF REEDS, IZANAGI, MARSH, REED-PLAIN, SEKHET-AARU, YOMI.

PEARL OF GREAT PRICE :—

A symbol of the Higher Self.

"The kingdom of heaven is like unto a man that is a merchant seeking goodly pearls : and having found one pearl of great price, he went and sold all that he had, and bought it."—MAT. xiii. 45, 46.

The "man " is the mind or the ego. The pearl is the Higher Self. The possessions with which the ego parted are the sense-nature and the things of the lower planes, in exchange for which he may inherit all things ; —the real in substitute for the apparent and illusory. The ego sur-renders the lower in order to secure the higher.

See KINGDOM, MAN, PARABLE.

PEARL, PRECIOUS :—

A symbol of experience with its outcome, the *gnosis* or knowledge of the soul-process. The *gnosis* is ultimately found first through the awakenment of the ego by the clamour of his kama-manasic nature, for it is through this desire side of his nature that he first begins to function as a truly human entity, and it is from this mentality, therefore, that the germ of *experience,* which from this viewpoint is another expression for the "pearl," is collected and transferred to the higher plane of the being's consciousness. It must be remembered that all experience is only the reflection, piecemeal, upon the lower plane of that complete *gnosis* which is above ; —the ideal actualising, as it were.

"If thou goest down into Egypt, and bringest the one pearl, which is in the midst of the sea, hard by the loud-breathing serpent, then shalt thou put on thy bright robe and thy toga, which is laid over it, and with thy Brother, our next in rank, thou shalt be heir in our kingdom."—*Hymn of the Soul* (Gnostic). *Acts of Judas Thomas.*

The Divine Parents enjoin,—"If thou, our son, journeyest deep down into the domain of illusion, and carryest forth from thence the 'pearl' of experience giving control of the lower realms and bringing intuitive knowledge,—the *gnosis,*—which 'pearl' is in the astral keeping, betwixt the lower emotions and the desires of the flesh, hard by the passions and animal senses, wherein experience and power to control is gained ; then shalt thou arise and assume for thyself thy higher vehicles causal and buddhic, and with our brother, thy Causal Self, thou shalt inherit the heavens."

"And these twelve gates (of the holy city) are described as being each of a single pearl, because, like pearls, the excellences denoted by them are attainable only through skill and courage, and devotion even to the death, and require of those who would attain them the divestment of every earthly encumbrance."—*The Perfect Way.*

"Cast not your pearls before swine" (MAT. vii. 6). "We must take the pearls to mean virtues with which the soul is adorned as with precious pearls ; and not to cast them before swine, as meaning that we are not to cast these virtues, such as chastity, temperance, righteousness, and truth, to impure pleasures

(swine), lest they, fleeing from the virtues, cause the soul to live a swinish and a vicious life."—METHODIUS, *On Things Created.*

See CHURNING, EGYPT, EXPERIENCE, FALL, GNOSIS, GOLDEN FLEECE, INTUITION, KINGDOM OF HEAVEN, LETTER, ROBE, SEA, SEALED LETTER, SERPENT (loud-breathing), SONS OF GOD, SWINE, TOGA.

PEARLS :—

A symbol of higher truths and emotions.

PEASANT, OR CULTIVATOR OF THE GROUND :—

A symbol of the Higher Self, as the Divine Husbandman, Tiller, and Sower of the lower nature. He is the "Knower of the Field,"—the *Kshetrajn*a.

See AGRICULTURE, CULTIVATION, HUSBANDMAN, JASON, KNOWER OF FIELD, MARUTS.

PELASGIANS :—

A symbol of the lower instincts, or lower qualities of the soul ;—the powers of darkness.

See ARGOS, MEAOU TRIBES, SHAVING.

PELEAS, KING OF IOLCUS :—

A symbol of the lower self, ruler of the lower mind.

See GOLDEN FLEECE, IOLCUS, PERSONALITY.

PELEIDES,—(DERIVED FROM PELEUS) :—

A symbol of the personality (Achilles).

See ACHILLES.

PELEUS, FATHER OF ACHILLES :—

A symbol of the Higher Self, who emanates the lower self or personality.

See AGAMEMNON, SHIPS OF GREEKS.

PEN AND TABLET :—

Symbols of the Holy Spirit (atma-buddhi) and the causal-body. The writing signifies the Divinely inspired Scriptures which teach of the evolution of the soul until the end of the cycle.

"Reeds love rivers, as the fading and transitory things of the world delight us. If, however, anyone shall pluck up this reed from the earth, and strip off its useless parts—'spoiling the old man with his deeds,'—and guide it by the hand of a scribe writing quickly, it begins to be no more a reed, but a pen, which impresses the precepts of the heavenly Scriptures on the hidden places of the mind, and writes them on the tables of the heart" (St. Ambrose).—C. À. LAPIDE, *The Great Comm.*, Vol. II. p. 54.

See AMBAYAVIS, CAUSAL-BODY, GOSPEL, INSPIRATION, KORAN, PAPYRUS, REVELATION, SACRED TEXT, SASTRA, SCRIPTURES, SHINTAI, UPANISHADS, VEDA, WORD.

PEN OF IRON :—

A symbol of the soul's expression upon the higher mental plane.
See IRON.

PENANCE :—

A symbol of aspiration which implies discontent with a lower condition to which the spirit is for a time bound.

"But those in whom dwell penance, abstinence, and truth, to them belongs that pure Brahma-world, to them, namely, in whom there is nothing crooked, nothing false, and no guile."—*Prasna Upanishad*, Ques. I. 15, 16.

Those qualities or souls which aspire while withdrawing from the lower attractions, and which pursue the truth, to them is assigned consciousness on the buddhic plane, free from the errors, illusions, and evils of the lower planes.

See ABSTINENCE, ASCETICISM, ASITA, AUSTERITIES, FASTING, PEOPLE, SCEPTICISM.

PENANCES :—

A symbol of the sufferings and travail which the ego undergoes in its passage through the lower life in order to attain to perfect bliss, and to pass beyond the planes of manifestation.

See NIRVANA, PASSION, SORROW, SUFFERING.

PEOPLE, MEN AND WOMEN :—

A symbol of the lower mental and emotional qualities ; the natural undeveloped instincts and activities which are to be disciplined and used as a means to the end of the manifestation of the Self.

"And there followed him a great multitude of the people, and of women who bewailed and lamented him. But Jesus turning unto them said, Daughters of Jerusalem, weep not for me, but weep for yourselves and for your children."—LUKE xxiii. 27, 28.

The "company of people and women" signify the lower nature, which clings to the letter of the scriptures and sees not the glorification of the Spirit, which shall be accomplished in the soul by breaking away from such limitations and impediments to Truth. The Christ-soul says, —what the Higher nature can always say to the lower,—that the lower qualities must become dissatisfied with their own state of captivity to custom and authority, for the lower mind without its Head, or indwelling test of truth, is indeed in a sorry plight.

See BONDAGE, CAPTIVITY, FOLK, MULTITUDES, NATIONS, PENANCE, QUALITIES, SCRIPTURES, WOMAN.

PEOPLE OF A PARTICULAR NATION :—

These symbolise the lower mental qualities, the raw material, or elemental essence of astro-mentality, divided in the case of the Jews into twelve tribes, out of which the more developed qualities are chosen, as the twelve disciples which are centralised by the Christ-soul, who instructs and disciplines them.

See COUNTRIES, DISCIPLES, EGYPTIANS, GREEKS, ISRAELITES, JEWS, KURUS, NATIONS, PELASGIANS, TRIBES.

PER-AHA, OR "HOUSE OF BATTLE " :—

A symbol of the stage of the soul's evolution when victory over the lower nature is possible.
See BATTLE, CONFLICT, VICTORY.

PERFUMES :—

Symbolic of faith and trust in the Highest. These are effects upon the higher planes which become the causes, in turn, of mental evolution.

See DRAUPADI, ODOUR (sweet), SCENT (sweet), SWEET SMELL OF ISIS.

PERMANENT ATOMS :—
See ATOMS.

PER-REREHU, CITY OF THE TWINS :—

A symbol of will in the higher and lower.

"Horus straightway hurled his lance at Set, and threw him down upon the ground near the city which afterwards was called Per-Rerehu."—BUDGE, *Legend of the Winged Sun-disk.*

The Christ now directs his attention to the complete mastery of the relative, and obtains this in the centre of its being, which is known as will of the individuality and personality.

See HORUS, INDIVIDUALITY, PERSONALITY, SET.

PERSEPHONE, DAUGHTER OF DEMETER :—

A symbol of the emotion-nature brought forth of Wisdom on the buddhic plane.

" Persephone was in a mead with the Ocean Nymphs gathering flowers, when she beheld a narcissus of surprising size and beauty. Unconscious of danger the maiden stretched forth her hand to seize the wondrous flower, when suddenly the wide earth gaped, and Aidoneus (Hades) in his golden chariot rose, and catching the terrified goddess, placed her in it."—KEIGHTLEY, *Mythology.*

The emotion-nature on the buddhic plane (mead), with the higher qualities (nymphs), becomes aware of the attractions (narcissus) of the outer life of sensation, and longs for experience. A descent, therefore, to the lower planes takes place, and in the astro-mental body (chariot) the emotion-nature becomes allied with the desire-mind (Aidoneus), while the higher nature becomes obscured in the soul (i.e. Demeter loses sight of her daughter). Then begins the pursuit of the lower by the higher.

" The Soul indeed descends ; but both the words ' soul ' and ' descends ' are, in this connection, used figuratively. For our language requires that we should speak of ' descent ' when we infer a passage from Being into Existence ; although, of course, transference from one locality to another is not intended, but only change of condition. And the ' soul ' that so descends is the Soul of the world—Persephone—not a number of individual souls. For the evolution and elaboration of individual souls is accomplished *by means* of development in material conditions ; therefore soul is already individualised before assuming those conditions. That which ' descends ' into generative states is the Monad, or divine substance vivified by the divine life. . . . I affirm that the soul ' descends ' by free-will, for God is immanent in the very substance of the worlds. Wherefore this descent, or putting forth of subjective Deity into objective conditions, is obviously an act of free-will. The Monad

—Persephone—is the true daughter of Zeus, the very substance of God. Her descent is not accident, blunder, or fault, for it occurs with the cognition and express will of Zeus."—ANNA KINGSFORD, *Life,* Vol. II. p. 208.

See ADONIS, AIDONEUS, ANDROMEDA, BUDDHI, CHARIOT, COMB, CUPID, DEMETER, GUARDIAN SPIRITS, HADES, MEADOW, MONAD OF LIFE, NYMPHS, PANDORA, SELENE, WIFE, WILL, WISDOM, WOMAN.

PERSEUS, SON OF ZEUS AND DANAË :—

A symbol of the indwelling Self, begotten of the Spirit and born of the purified emotion-nature.

" Aratus asserts that Cepheus is Adam, Cassiopea Eve, Andromeda the soul of both of these, Perseus the Logos, winged offspring of Jove, and Cetos the plotting monster. Not to any of these, but to Andromeda only does he repair, who slays the Beast ; from whom, likewise taking unto himself Andromeda, who had been delivered (when) chained to the Beast, the Logos—that is Perseus—achieves, he says, her liberation."—HIPPOLYTUS, *Refutation, etc.,* Bk. IV. 49.

" The Perseus of the myth is the true Humanity (' Son of God ')—earth-born indeed, but heaven-begotten—which, endowed by Wisdom (Athena) and Understanding (Hermes) with the wings of Courage, the shield of Intuition, and the sword of Science, is gone forth to smite and destroy the corrupt Church (Medusa) and to deliver the world from its blighting influence. But it is not enough that the Gorgon be slain. A task yet greater and more glorious awaits achievement. Andromeda, the Soul, the better part of Man is on the point of being devoured outright by the baleful dragon of Negation, the agent of the lower nature. . . . The Deliverer of the Soul must be bent, not on destruction merely, but on salvation likewise ; . . . It is not enough that he carry to Olympus the dead Medusa's head ; he must bear thither also a living Bride. His mission is not only to satisfy the Mind but to content the Heart."—*The Perfect Way,* p. lxv.

See ADAM (lower), ADONIS, ANDROMEDA, ATHENA, BEAST, DRAGON, EVE, HERMES, MEDUSA, SALVATION, WHALES.

PERSON :—

A fleeting outer appearance of an inner mental condition which is changing and temporary as qualities develop in the soul.

PERSONALITY :—

A temporary aggregation of a limited number of soul-qualities

about a centre of consciousness during a life-period on the lower planes. Consciousness itself is spiritual and eternal, and is an attribute of the Divine monad or Ego in the personality; but the states of consciousness in the lower nature are phases of experience,— states which pass away, having no abiding reality. The personality has to be regarded as a limited manifestation of the immortal individuality which periodically outbreathes it and again inbreathes it. Its seat is in the lower mind, where it is an observer of a series of evanescent feelings and appearances on the mental plane.

"Because this I, this my personality, like everything else in the world, is conditioned, has arisen from a cause, and thus is wholly transient,—therefore it cannot truly be my I, to which latter alone can be ascribed the demand for a 'soul,' an eternal principle. Hence this I is only an apparent I; as the Buddha says,—'It is not mine.' "—P. DAHLKE, *Buddhist Essays*, p. 23.

"The Sacrificer now establishes that immortal element (Agni) in his (the Sacrificer's) innermost soul, and,—though there is for him no hope of immortality,—he obtains the full measure of life; for indeed he becomes unconquerable, and his enemy, though striving to conquer, conquers him not."—*Sata. Brâh.*, XI. 2, 2, 14.

The personality becomes endowed with the Divine Spark, the spiritual Ego (Solar pitri), in its innermost being. The personality (Lunar pitri) is mortal, and regarded as attached to the permanent atoms, it reappears life after life, conquering all evil tendencies until it arrives at perfection, when it dies out of the lower nature to be reproduced in the higher, the which is symbolised in the death, resurrection, and ascension of Jesus.

"What we now understand by personality is not final, not eternal. Personality as we know it now is a prison house; it shuts us in and down from experiencing our proper selfhood. We never do more than glimpse the truth of what we are."—R. J. CAMPBELL, Serm., *The Lifting up of Christ*.

"Anu ordered the food and water of life to be offered him. Adapa, however, remembered the commands of Ea, and refused the food of immortality. Man remained mortal, and it was never again in his power to eat of the tree of life. But in return, sovereignty and dominion were bestowed upon him, and

Adapa became the father of mankind."— SAYCE, *Religions, etc.*, p. 384.

The Highest now offers the Love and Truth of the Spirit to descend upon the personality. The lower Self, however, refuses the offer, since the power of choice is accomplished upon the lower mental plane. Man so continued mortal, nor was it possible for man as lower mind ever to become more. But in return for that, evolution upon the lower plane was consummated, and thereby man remained a distinct species until he was to be raised through the coming within of the Super-man, i.e. Christ, who being above man, and knowing what is in man, is able to draw man unto Himself.

"Do thou, son of Atreus, repress thine anger; for it is I (Nestor) that entreat thee to forego thy resentment on behalf of Achilles, who is the great bulwark of destructive war to all the Achaeans."— *Iliad.*, Bk. I.

The desire-mind is to be repressed in its exercise of harshness and violence, since Faith-hope (Nestor), coming forth through the personality (Achilles), requires it to restrain its lower emotions. The personality is the surviving principle throughout the struggle of life, and is that wherein all the mental qualities are collected as they evolve life after life.

"Then Thetis weeping made answer to Achilles: 'Ah me, my child, why reared I thee, cursed in my motherhood? Would thou hadst been left tearless and griefless amid the ships, seeing thy lot is very brief and endureth no long while; but now art thou made shortlived alike and lamentable beyond all men; in an evil hour I bare thee in our halls.' "—*Ibid.*

Then Nature (Thetis) appears to question why she has been called upon to rear the lower-mind or Personality (Achilles), since the evolution of the higher mind has made it impossible for it to proceed any longer along the path (i.e. that of nature) which it has hitherto chosen. Nature would prefer to have the lower mind remain without knowledge of good and evil, especially as it has an existence of only brief duration. But now the Personality is perceived to be short-lived and limited in its range and scope. It is therefore regretted that it should have been brought forth; for Nature cannot understand the spiritual object of existence.

"We must add to the ordinary theological conception the assertion that the fate of no one is decided in this world, that our short space of thirty or sixty years is but a moment in the long education which God is giving to every soul; and that the end of that education is inevitable good, never inevitable evil. So that the Fatherhood never ceases to be loving Fatherhood, and the redeeming power never ceases till its work is done in restoring all men to the bosom of God."—STOPFORD A. BROOKE, Serm., *Victims of Fate.*

"A man is a bundle of passions which severally use his reason to get gratification, and the result in all times and places depends on what passions are dominant."—H. SPENCER, *Autobiography*, p. 450.

"A rational soul is born in the midst of the astral body. This rational soul is the person; itself dual, in virtue of its earthly and its divine parts. And from that moment this personality is an individual existence."—*The Perfect Way*, p. 91.

"One of the most persistent assumptions of the ordinary mind of to-day is that of the fundamental character of personality. Personality is not fundamental; it is derivative. You neither know yourself nor your neighbour, except in a very limited and fragmentary way. Your present self-consciousness, if I may so put it, is only that part of your selfhood which has so far managed to awaken on the material plane; it is larger now than it was when you were a child, and it will be larger still when you get rid of the clog of the physical body."—R. J. CAMPBELL, Serm., *The Kenosis of the Human Race.*

See ACHILLES, ADAPA, APPENDAGES, ARJUNA, ARROW (self.), CONSCIOUSNESS, CORPSE, DEAD, DEFUNCT, EA, EPIMETHEUS, FIRE OF HELL, FOOLS, GEUSH-URVA, GOSHURUN, HEEL, IMMORTALITY, JESUS MORTAL, LUNAR CYCLE, MAN (natural), MAN WITHOUT WOMAN, MONAD OF LIFE. MOON, MORTAL MIND, MUMMY, MYRMIDONS, NACHIKETAS, NESTOR, NOD, PITRIS, PITRIYANA, PROMETHEUS, QUALITIES, RECOGNITION, RUAH, SHABTI, SHAI, SOUL (lowest), THETIS, TREE OF LIFE, VULTURE, WALKING WITH GOD, YEHEEDAH.

PESTILENCE CAUSED BY APOLLO :—

The operations of the Higher Self in raising the lower nature cause unbalanced conditions upon the lower planes whereby the lower qualities are afflicted and destroyed.

"Therefore hath the Far-darter (Apollo) brought woes upon us, yea, and will bring. Nor will he ever remove the loathly pestilence from the Danaans till we have given the bright-eyed damsel (Chryseis) to her father, unbought, unransomed, and carried a holy hecatomb to Chryse; then might we propitiate him to our prayer."—*Iliad*, Bk. I.

Hence the Higher Self is the means of disquieting the lower self. Nor will the erroneous theories of the lower mind be got rid of until the intuition of Truth (Chryseis) is recovered by the inner memory, and voluntary effort is made on the part of the lower self to raise the consciousness to the spiritual understanding (Chryse), in which case the reconciliation between the Higher will and the lower mind will have been effected.

"God is hunting you through every false experience in which your soul seeks rest, tracking you down through sorrow after sorrow, driving you forth from everything unreal, that in the end he may grasp and hold you eternally, the willing prisoner of his love."—R. J. CAMPBELL, Serm., *God Pursuing the Soul.*

"Sometimes the religious man with good intentions, but wanting wisdom and strength, tries to palliate the evils of life, to cover its dark features, to exaggerate its transient pleasures, for the purpose of sheltering God's goodness from reproach. But this will not avail. The truth cannot be hidden. Life is laid open to every eye, as well as known by each man's experience; and we do and must see that suffering, deep suffering, is one of the chief elements in our lot. It is not a slender, dark thread winding now and then through a warp of dazzling brightness; but is interwoven with the whole texture. . . . This I state, that we may all of us understand that suffering is not accidental, but designed for us, that it enters into God's purpose, that it has a great work to do, and that we know nothing of life till we comprehend its uses, and have learned how to accomplish them."—W. E. CHANNING, *Works*, Vol. III. p. 204.

See APOLLO, ARGIVES, ARROWS, CENSERS, CHRYSE, CHRYSEIS, FUNERAL, GOATS (unblemished), HECATOMB, NINE DAYS, QUIVER, REMINISCENCE, SLAUGHTER, WRATH OF APOLLO.

PETER, THE APOSTLE :—

A symbol of the lower mind, or

"natural man," with sense of separateness.

"And Peter took him, and began to rebuke him, saying, Be it far from thee, Lord: this shall never be unto thee. But he turned and said unto Peter, Get thee behind me, Satan: thou art a stumbling block unto me: for thou mindest not the things of God, but the things of men."—MAT. xvi. 22, 23.

This signifies the incapacity of the lower mind to understand the sublime heights to which the Christ-soul shall rise; and also the lower mind's revolt against the suggestions of a purifying process in the promptings of the Higher Ego, which suggestions, however, are strangely distorted as they come as reflections to the lower mind, and which, therefore, are not understood. This attitude of mind is rebuked by the indwelling Christ. The "rebuke" must be taken as signifying the casting forth from the mind of doubt and error which obstruct truth and right.

"What then is designated by the 'air,' but the minds of worldly men, which, given up to the countless desires of this life, are, being fluid, scattered hither and thither like the air. But the 'air' is collected into 'clouds,' when unstable minds are, by the grace of the Divine regard, strengthened with the solidity of virtue, in order that, by thinking of what is right, they may gather themselves within the bosom of their heart and may not melt away in empty thoughts. Peter had been 'air,' when the occupation of fishing for the life of the flesh used, as a transient breeze, to agitate him, distracted still with earthly desires."—ST. GREGORY THE GREAT, Morals on the Book of Job, Vol. I. Preface.

See AIR, ANDREW, APOSTLES, ASCENSION OF OSIRIS, DISCIPLES, DOORKEEPER (fem.), FEED, FISH, GETHSEMANE, HORSES (manes), JESUS (severe), MAN (natural), MESSIAH, NET, SATAN, TABERNACLES, TRANSFIGURATION, TRIBUTE.

PHAEACIANS :—

A symbol of the higher mental faculties on the arupa levels of the mental plane.

"The Phaeacians have no pilots nor any rudders after the manner of other ships, but their ships themselves understand the thoughts and intents of men; they know the cities and fat fields of every people, and most swiftly they traverse the gulf of the salt sea, shrouded in mist and cloud, and never do they go in fear of wreck or ruin."—Odyssey, Bk. VIII.

The higher mental qualities have as vehicles the aspirations of love and truth which rise in the mind as the thoughts and intents of the lower mind are raised and purified. The higher mental qualities are transmutations of the fruits of experience and effort of all associated groups of the lower mental qualities, and they transcend entirely the astral realm (sea) of the desires to which they are unapparent. They are not transient but immortal.

"The feet of the Phaeacian youths (who are inferior in wrestling and pugilism) move with admirable rapidity and precision to the divine music of (the bard) Demodocus."—R. W. MACKAY, Progress of Intellect, p. 172.

The activities of the higher mental qualities are free from strife and conflict. They are exercised harmoniously in complete unison with the Divine ideal.

See ALCINOUS, ARGO, CONFLICT, CORCYRA, COUNTRIES, DANCE (circle), MUSES, MUSIC, NATIONS, ORPHEUS, PEOPLE, QUALITIES, REAPING, SEA, TRANSMUTATION, VAIMANIKA, WORDS OF POWER.

PHALLIPHORIA, PRIAPEIA, OR DIONYSIA :—

Rites in which the generative function is made the symbol of the creative function in the union of spirit and matter. As soon as the Self or Spirit is born within the soul, a new order of the manifest is initiated. In this new order the Spirit begins to interact with the purified matter of its environment, and a creative function is established, by means of which higher qualities are produced, and the growth of consciousness is effected.

"Priapus (son of Dionysus and Aphrodite) was regarded as the promoter of fertility both in vegetation and in all animals connected with an agricultural life; and in this capacity he was worshipped as the protector of flocks of sheep and goats, of bees, of the vine, of all garden produce, and even of fishing."—Smith's Class. Dict.

The Self working within the activities of the lower nature brings about growth of the higher qualities in every department of life.

See AGRICULTURE, BEES, CATTLE, CHILD, FISH, GENERATIVE FUNCTION, MITHRAS, PASTORAL, RITES, SEXUAL, SHEEP, VINE.

PHANES, GOD THE MANIFESTATOR :—

A symbol of the Second Logos, or Higher Self, who proceeds from the Absolute as a Divine germ of universal life.

"The Triple God born from the Egg was called Phanes, and also Metis and Ericapæus, the three being aspects of one Power."—G. R. S. MEAD, *Orpheus*, p. 162.

"Of the three aspects, Phanes is said to be the ' father,' Ericapæus the ' power,' and Metis the ' intellect ' in Platonic terms. . . . Phanes was also called Love (Eros) . . . also the Limit or Boundary ; also intelligible Light."—*Ibid.*, pp. 164, 167, 170.

The Higher Self comes forth in three aspects,—Will (Phanes), Wisdom (Metis), and Action (Ericapæus). The Higher Self is the Divine attraction or Love ; also Atma, the highest state of the manifest, and the Light of Truth.

See ABSOLUTE, CAVE, EGG, ERICAPÆUS, EROS, HIRANYAGARBHA, LAO, METIS, MONAD, NOAH'S SONS, SEED, TRIAD.

PHANG, THE GREAT BIRD :—

A symbol of the incarnate Self aspiring upwards in the cycle of Evolution, from the material to the spiritual.

"There is also a Bird named the Phang ; its back is like the Thâi mountain, while its wings are like clouds all round the sky. In a whirlwind it mounts upwards as on the whorls of a goat's horn for 90,000 lî, till, far removed from the cloudy vapours, it bears on its back the blue sky, and then shapes its course for the South, and proceeds to the ocean there (the Pool of Heaven)."—*Writings of Kwang-tze*, Bk. I. Pt. I. 3.

The Higher Self within the soul aspires (mountain) to be free from captivity to the lower nature. It rises by means of the buddhic (clouds) function through the mental plane (wind) in the cycle of Evolution, passing spirally from the illusions (vapours) of the lower life to the buddhic plane (sky), and merging itself again in the eternal Ocean of Reality on the plane of atma.

See ATMA, BENNU BIRD, BIRD (great), CLOUDS, INCARNATION, KARSHIPTA, KHWĂN, MOUNTAIN, OCEAN, PHŒNIX, POOL OF PEACE, SIMORG, SKY, SOUTH.

PHARISEES :—

A symbol of that state of mind which produces literalism, formalism, and dogmatism.

"There came certain Pharisees, saying to him, Get thee out, and go hence : for Herod would fain kill thee. And he said unto them, Go and say to that fox, Behold, I cast out devils and perform cures to-day and to-morrow, and the third day I am perfected."—LUKE xiii. 31, 32.

The literalists are afraid of the true interpretation of the facts of soul-growth with which the Christ-illumination provides them ; and so they immediately bring forward some piece of sophistry against the truth, which the Christ within is not slow to detect and expose in its true colours. His remarks are the assertion of the Christ respecting his gradual work of soul-purification ; the "third day" being that period during which his perfectionment is accomplished. "Herod the fox" is a reference to the sense-nature as a "hole" or "bottomless pit" in which the lower principle (Herod) dwells.

See CAIAPHAS, FOXES, HEALING (devils), HEROD, PIT, PRIESTS AND ELDERS, RITES, THREE DAYS, TRADITION, TRIAL.

PHENOMENA :—

These are appearances subject to constant change, and therefore having no reality in themselves.

"And a second thing I will tell thee : There is no origination of anything that is mortal, nor yet any end in baneful death ; but only mixture and separation of what is mixed, but men call this origination."—*Empedocles*, FAIRBANKS, 36.

All that exists upon the lower planes cannot persist, since nature has no life of itself and is consequently mortal. Death is negative and equally non-existent ; death therefore cannot be an end. The "mixture" and "separation" are the combinations and segregations of the lower life. The lower mind speaks of these phenomena as real, whereas they are but appearances.

"According to the Qabbalah, the emanated in its inner being does not in reality proceed from the emanating one; that which is produced is only an appearance, and the real (or true) nature remains in the inner upper one."— I. MYER, *Qabbalah*, p. 110.

"All that is subject unto genesis and change is verily not true. . . . The untrue, O Son, doth perish" (*Hermetic Treatise Of Truth*).—G. R. S. MEAD, *T. G. Hermes*, Vol. III. pp. 21–2.

"The phenomenal world cannot disclose its own secret. To find this, man must seek in that substantial world which lies within himself, since all that is real is within the man."—E. MAITLAND, *Life of A. K.*, Vol. I. p. 54.

"You cannot prove that anything whatever exists outside your own mind; you can only jump the difficulty and make at least the provisional assumption that things are what they seem, that the world as we know it has objective reality —a more than doubtful proposition."— R. J. CAMPBELL, Serm., *Knowing in Part*.

See ILLUSION, MATTER, MĀYĀ, MIXTURE.

PHILIP THE APOSTLE :—

A symbol of courage, force, and also that side of the nature which corresponds to the calculative capacity, that estimates and weighs.

See APOSTLES, DISCIPLES, FEEDING.

PHINEUS, THE PROPHET-PRINCE :—

A symbol of the discriminating mind which first interprets the higher, but afterwards becomes spiritually blind through seeking the lower.

"Phineus was the son of Agenor or Poseidon, and was married to Cleopatra, the daughter of Boreas and Oreithyia." —*Argonautic Expedition*.

This signifies that discrimination is the offspring of the Divine Mind, and at the same time the affinity of the instinct-nature, which is its feminine counterpart on the lower planes. The instinct-nature is the astral reflection of buddhi-manas.

See ANTELOPE, BOREAS, CLEO-PATRA, HARPIES, HODER, IDÆA, NICOTHEA, OCYPETE, POSEIDON, ZETES.

PHŒDRUS RIVER :—

A symbol of the lower mind full of errors and illusions.

"The river Phœdrus sending forth a rough and sharp air, Isis in her anger dried up its current."—PLUTARCH, *Isis and Osiris*, § 16.

The lower mind (air), with its cut-and-dried opinions, its hard-outlined and rigid ideas, and its sharp and cold "wind of doctrine," Wisdom from above disperses and supersedes.

See AIR, CHILDREN OF MEN, ISIS, MAN, WINDS (various).

PHŒNIX, THE BIRD OF ARABIA :—

A symbol of the Higher Self in the cycle of Life, passing through processes of Involution and Evolution.

"I am that Great Phœnix which is in Heliopolis. I am the Ordering of all that is and exists. What does that mean? It is the Phœnix Osiris which is in Heliopolis. It is the Ordering of what is and exists,—his body. Variant: —Eternity and Unending Time. Eternity is the day, Unending Time is the night." —A. WIEDEMANN, *Rel. of Anc. Egyptians*, p. 259.

"This bird was represented as resembling an eagle, with feathers partly red and partly golden."—*Herodotus*, II. 73.

The eternal Spirit (eagle), which descends and ascends, has the aspect of Love (rose-red) and Wisdom (gold). The various stories of the Phœnix symbolise,—First, that the Self comes forth from the higher planes (east, Arabia).—Second, that it descends into matter, and having been perfected (nest of spices) dies.—Third, the incipient lower self (worm) arises from the lower nature (decomposed body), and is developed through experience and the Divine life (heat of the sun). Fourth, the lower Self, in becoming fully evolved at the end of the cycle, is said to complete and purify the personality (father). This is indicated by the "egg of spice," which is at first solid, then emptied, and finally filled with the personality as in embalmment. It is said that the weight now of the "egg" is the same as when solid at first, implying that original potential perfection has passed into actual perfection. The "egg," or mummied personality, is then offered as a sacrifice to the Supreme (temple of the Sun), meaning that the purified personality is mortal but merges into the individuality, which alone survives.

See BENNU BIRD, EAGLE, EMBALM-MENT, EVOLUTION, FIRE, INDIVIDU-

ALITY, INVOLUTION, KARSHIPTA, MAN (born), MUMMY, PERSONALITY, PHANG, SPICES, SUN.

PHTHIA, THE NURSE OF MEN :—

A symbol of prolific experience, which is the outcome of the evolution of the mental faculties in the soul.

See NURSE OF MEN, SHIPS (beaked).

PHYSICIAN, SUCCESSFUL :—

A symbol of the Self under the aspect of Love which brings harmony to the soul.

" Homa ! give me some of the healing powers whereby thou art a physician. Homa ! give me some of the victorious powers whereby thou art a victor, etc."— *Homa Yasht,* HAUG, *Essays.*

The prayer of the wise soul takes the form of supplicating the Divine Love to use it as It will, and so to strengthen and maintain it that it may become a worthy and dutiful vehicle of the Divine Life. The powers sought are the wisdom, the truth, and the love whereby the Divine nature is enabled to claim the soul's co-operation in the work of upraising humanity.

See ALCHEMY, HEALING, HOMA, IMHOTEP, MEDICINE, PRAYER, RUDRA, SERPENT ÆSCULAPIUS, VALMIKI.

PIETY IN CAR OR CHARIOT :—

A symbol of the Self in the causal vehicle.

" But, ye gods, avert the madness of those men from my tongue, and from lips that are holy cause a pure stream to flow. And thee I pray, much-wooed, white-armed maiden Muse, in what things it is right for beings of a day to hear, do thou and Piety, driving obedient car, conduct me on."—*Empedocles,* FAIRBANKS, 11.

The Higher nature, under its aspects of Truth, Will, and Love, is now called upon to seal the lips (tongue), or stay the attempts of the personality at expressing its separative self, that is, stop its working from the lower self :—and from the Higher Self, working from the Infinite Reality, cause to forthpour from its potentiality,—the Truth within,—the stream of the Divine Life. And supplication is made to the beneficent, presiding Wisdom principle, that fit and helpful knowledge and the higher virtues be

communicated to the soul. Thus in the causal vehicle to which intelligence (horses) is harnessed, the Self and Wisdom are said to be driven in towards the Spirit.

" That attitude of filial piety toward God which includes receptivity of the truth, penitence and loving trust toward the forgiving and purifying Divine Love, surrender of the self in the spirit of obedience and of desire to do the Divine Will, is, indeed, the very essence of religion, subjectively regarded."—G. T. LADD, *Phil. of Religion,* p. 540.

See ATHENA, CHARIOT, HERA, HORSE, MUSE, PERSONALITY, PRAISE, SELF, WISDOM.

PIG, OR SWINE :—

A symbol of the desire-mind, or desire-nature, which seeks its food in matter (the earth).

" Now the black pig was Suti (Set), who had transformed himself into a black pig. . . . The pig is an abominable thing to Horus."—BUDGE, *Book of the Dead,* Ch. CXII.

The darkness of ignorance or illusion characterises the desire-mind (Set). Illusion and ignorance are eschewed by the higher nature (Horus).

The " pig of evil," as a symbol of the enemy of righteousness, accounts for the abhorrence among some nations of the pig as food for man.

See BOAR, CIRCE, SET, SOW, SWINE.

PILATE, PONTIUS :—

A symbol of ordinary worldly-mindedness, constantly wavering between higher and lower motives to action, and incapable of a straight course.

" So when Pilate saw that he prevailed nothing, but rather that a tumult was arising, he took water, and washed his hands before the multitude, saying, I am innocent of the blood of this righteous man : see ye to it. And all the people answered and said, His blood be on us, and on our children."— MAT. xxvii. 24, 25.

The worldly mind was wise enough to see what any mind of ordinary, but not deeply spiritual, intelligence must see, viz. that unless it serves one master, nothing can be accomplished. Pilate " washes his hands," signifying that he dissociates himself from the course he appears to have adopted ; that is, the mind remains in a state of suspense, though more favourably inclined to the lower nature than the higher. The worldly mind henceforth places itself on a par with the lower qualities (the people) and becomes little better than an automaton.

See ASSEMBLY, CAIAPHAS, GAB-BATHA, GOLGOTHA, PRIESTS AND ELDERS, SIXTH HOUR, THREE DAYS, TRIAL.

PILGRIM :—

A symbol of the Monad, either of the World-soul or of the individual soul. It may be taken as atmic, or as atma-buddhic (two in one).

" ' Pilgrim ' is the appellation given to our Monad (the Two in one) during its cycle of incarnations. It is the only immortal and eternal principle in us, being an indivisible part of the integral whole—the Universal Spirit, from which it emanates, and into which it is absorbed at the end of the cycle."—BLAVATSKY, *Secret Doctrine*, Vol. I. p. 45.

" Starting upon the long journey imma-culate, descending more and more into sinful matter, and having connected himself with every atom in manifested Space,—the Pilgrim, having struggled through, and suffered in, every form of Life and Being, is only at the bottom of the valley of matter, and half through his cycle, when he has identified himself with collective Humanity. This, *he has made in his own image*. In order to progress upwards and homewards, the ' God ' has now to ascend the weary uphill part of the Golgotha of Life. It is the martyrdom of self-conscious exist-ence. Like Vishvakarman, he has to sacrifice *himself to* himself in order to redeem all creatures, to resurrect from the many into the One Life."—*Ibid.*, p. 288.

" Within the divine infinitude all the aspects of the perfect experience which I have named (life, love, joy, rest, activity), are fully included and imply each other. But we are only on the way to this ; we are in process of becom-ing ; and hence it is necessary that at various points on our pilgrimage we have to pass from a lesser to a larger apprehension of spiritual reality by sacrificing it on its lower planes ; we have to die to live. But there is never any real dying, never any permanent giving up ; it only seems to be so. . . . You never can relinquish anything that is rightfully yours nor can you put it from you ; you only lay it down for a moment to grasp it again with a greater power and closeness."—R. J. CAMPBELL, Serm., *Life's Great Antinomy*.

See DEVAYANA, EVOLUTION, FUGI-TIVE, GILGOOLEM, INCARNATION OF

SOULS, INVOLUTION, MONAD OF LIFE, PLANETARY, REINCARNATION, SACRI-FICER, SHEEP (lost), SHRINE, SOSHY-ANTS, SOUL (middle), VISVAKARMAN, WANDERERS, WAYFARING MEN, YI.

PILGRIMS TO A SHRINE :—

A symbol of the souls, or soul-qualities, attracted towards ideals, and congregating about them as centres of spiritual energy on the mental plane.

See ASSEMBLY, ATTRACTION, CITY, RITUAL, SHRINE.

PILLAR OF THE TEMPLE :—

A symbol of the perfected soul on the higher mental plane.

" He that overcometh, I will make him a pillar in the temple of my God, and he shall go out thence no more."—REV. iii. 12.

The soul that has triumphed over the lower nature shall be raised to the higher mental plane and united with the individuality in the causal-body (temple), and it shall no more go forth to re-incarnation on the lower planes. Its differentiations (names) are of the higher planes, and the consciousness is raised to the buddhic level.

See BATTLE, COLUMN, CONQUEROR, CONSCIOUSNESS, GOLDEN PILLAR, INDIVIDUALITY, NAME, REINCARNA-TION, STRIFE, TEMPLE, VICTORY, WAR.

PILLARS OF THE LIGHT, OR CURTAINS OF LIGHT. THE FIRMAMENT :—

A symbol of the higher mind as being receptive of the Spirit of Truth and Love.

" The souls delivered over by the moon to the æons of the Father, they abide there in that pillar of glory which is called perfect air. And this air is a pillar of light, for its fullness is in the souls that are being purified."—ARCHE-LAUS, *Doctrine of Manes*.

The lunar pitris (souls), or monads of form, in which the astral (moon) life of desire is worked up, provide the personality, which in due course is delivered over to the collective solar pitris (Father) evolution for the bestowal of the germ of the indivi-duality. These Divine monads (atma-buddhic) have their seat in the higher mind (perfect air), in the causal-body (pillar of light); and the development of the causal-body is to be accomplished through the purification of the personalities (souls).

See ÆON, AIR, ATLAS, FATHER, FIRMAMENT, MOON, MOON (lower), PITRIS (lunar), SHINATSU.

PILLARS, FOUR, OR FOUR SUPPORTS, OR COLUMNS, OF HEAVEN :—

A symbol of the quaternary or four planes of manifestation below atma as a foundation for aspiration towards spiritual being.

"First the Prime Intelligence created He, through the which Four Ministers He made to be; He those Four the Columns Four of earth hath dressed, whereby Fixture, Elevation, Traction, Rest. Water, Fire, Air and Earth He named them there, and He made of them this Kingdom's bases fair."— ("Water may be compared to Nasb, 'Fixture,' because it is, as it were, tied down to earth and unable to rise to the higher spheres; Air to Jerr, 'Traction,' as the wind carries along such as ships at sea; Fire to Ref, 'Elevation,' as it is the lightest and most subtle of the elements, and ever seeks to ascend to its own—the highest of the elemental spheres; and Earth to Sukun 'Rest,' as it is stationary in the centre of the Universe ")(ASHIG, Gharib Náme).—GIBB, Hist. of Ottoman Poetry, Vol. I. pp. 187-8.

The Four Columns of the Kingdom of heaven are described as being the same as the Four Elements,—Fire, buddhi; Air, manas; Water, astral; and Earth, physical.

"Never till Day of Resurrection glows, from their offices shall any these depose. 'Tis these Chieftains Four who form earth's bases sure; These it is who ever hold the earth secure; 'Tis through these the world doth fixed and steadfast show; 'Tis through these that plants upon the earth do grow. Naught upon this earth may to Existence win, but of these there still is present therewithin. Whatsoe'er hath form doth grow from out these Four."—Ibid.

Not until the end of the cycle shall the quaternary dissolve and disappear. Until then the lower nature (earth) is secure under Divine laws. Through it the instincts, desires, emotions, etc. (plants) are developed. Nothing in the lower nature can attain permanence; but of the desires there is the present fleeting outrush towards the objects of sense. All forms arise from the four lower planes

See AIR, ATLAS, CHILDREN OF HORUS, EARTH, ELEMENTS, FIRE, MINISTERS, QUATERNARY, WATER (lower).

PILLARS, FOUR, OF SHU :—

A symbol of the four planes of manifestation below atma, produced by the Divine Will (Shu).

"Seb, the earth, and Nut, the sky. These deities were supposed to unite every evening, and to remain embraced until the morning, when the god Shu separated them, and set the goddess of the sky upon his four pillars until the evening."—BUDGE, Egyptian Ideas, etc., p. 94.

Time (Seb) and Space (Nut) during the cycle of pralaya,—indrawal of the Divine Life,—are said to unite, or become one and unmanifest, until the opening of the next manvantara, when the Life again outpours, and the Divine Will (Shu) differentiates Time from Space, and by means of the creation of the four planes of matter establishes manifestation until the next period of withdrawal of the tide of Life.

See BACABS, CHILDREN OF HORUS, EVENING, GATE (tchesert), HEAVEN AND EARTH, HETEP, IRON PLATE, MORNING, NUT, RANGI, SEB, SEPARATION, SHU, TET.

PILLOW OF SUPPORT AND REST :—

A symbol of reliance upon the Higher Self within the soul.

"Prosperity, the pillow of the couch of Brahman."—Kaush. Upanishad.

This signifies the sense of security which is the result of complete trust in the Higher Self and a knowledge of its Divine nature,—a state of consciousness which implies complete mistrust of all that is less than Divine, or of the nature of illusion.

See BRAHMA, CUSHION, PROSPERITY.

PILLOW OF STONE :—

A symbol of faith and rest in the underlying Spirit (stone).

"And Jacob took of the stones of that place, and put them for his pillows, and lay down in that place to sleep."—GEN. xxviii. 11.

This is symbolic of the spiritual nature relying upon Divine support, and turning from external attractions.

See JACOB, LADDER (Jacob), STONE.

PILLOWS (LOWER ASPECT) :—

A symbol of reliance upon the lower nature, and contentment with the things of the worldly life.

"Behold, I (the Lord) am against your pillows, wherewith ye there hunt the souls to make them fly, and I will tear them from your arms, and will let the souls go."—EZEK. xiii. 20.

The Self condemns contentment with the things of the lower life, which is active in driving out the higher qualities (souls) ; and points out that trouble and suffering will supervene to destroy contentment, and so allow the higher qualities to expand.

"It is said by the Prophet, ' Woe to those that sew pillows under every elbow of the hand, and make cushions under the head of every age ' (EZEK. xiii. 18). For a ' pillow ' is put for this, that we may read the easier. Therefore whoever flatters persons doing wrongly is putting a pillow under the head or the elbow of one lying, so that the man that should have been chidden on account of sin, being stayed up therein by commendations, should rest at his ease."— ST. GREGORY, Morals on the Book of Job, Vol. II. p. 321.

PILLOWS FOR MUMMIES :—

A symbol of the reliance of the purified soul upon the Supreme Spirit.

"Pillows of wood, alabaster and stone which are placed under the heads of mummies to 'lift them up.' "—BUDGE, The Mummy, p. 261.

As embalmment signifies purification of the personality, complete trust is placed in the Higher Self (Osiris) to raise the consciousness to the higher planes.

These pillows often had figures inscribed upon them, such as two lotus flowers and an eye of Horus, which signify Divine wisdom, perception, and expression ; or a figure of the god Bes,—a symbol of the outbreathing and inbreathing Absolute Spirit.

See EMBALMMENT, MUMMY, OSIRIS, UTCHAT.

PINEAL GLAND :—

A symbol of the spiritual process of enlightenment, as it is an organ of psychic perception.

"In man, soul and body touch each other only at one single point, the pineal gland in the brain."—DESCARTES.

"Now these (membranes in the brain) are gently moved by the spirit, which careering through a certain blood-vessel like a reed, advances towards the pineal gland. And near this is situated the entrance of the cerebellum, which admits the current of spirit, and distributes it into what is styled the spinal marrow." "The Peratæ allege that this cerebellum, by an ineffable and inscrutable process, attracts through the pineal gland the spiritual and life-giving substance."— HIPPOLYTUS, Works, pp. 124, 169.

The pineal gland and the pituitary body are means for detecting vibrations subtler than science ordinarily recognises, but which even now are used to some extent as a means of educating the soul through the physical body.

See EYE (third).

PINNACLES :—

A symbol of high aspirations.

In a lower aspect it signifies ambitions, and the seeking after a " pinnacle " of fame.

See ARCHED GATEWAYS, OBELISK, SPIRE.

PIRITHOUS :—

A symbol of ambition.

PISCES, THE ZODIACAL SIGN :—

A symbol of the twelfth period of the cycle of life, which is the final period of evolution on the buddhic plane. At the close of the cycle, the Christ-soul (Jesus the " Fish ") becomes one with the Christ (Higher Self the " Fish "), or the redeemed souls become one with the Redeemer, —the lower consciousness unites with the higher (the two fishes).

"Possibly the ' Fish ' symbol of early Christianity may be explained by Pisces. On the catacomb lamps there are two fish, one swallowing the other."—A. JEREMIAS, The Old Test., etc., Vol. I. p. 76.

"Pisces, the last of the signs, is represented by two fishes bound by a cord. Love and deep compassion is the real nature of Pisces."—J. H. VANSTONE, On the Zodiac.

See AMENT, AUSHEDAR, FISH (great), GEMINI, IABRAOTH, JESUS (fish), SUN-MOTIONLESS, ZODIAC.

PISHON RIVER :—

A symbol of the higher mental plane.

" The name of the first is Pishon : and that is it which compasseth the whole

land of Havilah where there is gold."—
GEN. ii. 11.

The symbol (name) of the first
river answers to the higher mental
plane : this comprises the circuit
around the buddhic state wherein is
Truth (gold).

See EDEN (river), HAVILAH.

PIT, OR HOLE IN THE EARTH :—

A symbol of the lower planes, or
the desire and sense-nature which
surrounds and darkens the soul.

"God will deliver his soul from going
into the pit, and his life shall see the
light."—JOB xxxiii. 28.

This refers to the liberation of the
soul from the lower nature, and the
rise of the consciousness to the higher
planes whereon truth will be apparent.

"Ye that seek the Lord : look unto
the rock whence ye are hewn, and to
the hole of the pit whence ye are digged."
Is. li. 1.

The "rock of thy strength"
(Is. xvii. 10) is the Archetypal Man
(Christ) from "whence ye are hewn,"
and the "pit" is the lower nature in
which the spiritual ego is embedded.
The "hole" is the way upward to
the light of Truth, the path which the
soul shall take as the Spirit within
enables it to liberate itself from
earthly things.

"Yes, all is well, not in spite of the
pit and the clay, but because of them.
Through these we ascend to that from
whence we came, having achieved what
we are—not dust but God."—R. J.
CAMPBELL, Serm., The Rock and the Pit.

See ARC. MAN, ARIZURA, BEAST,
BOAT (wisdom), BOTTOMLESS PIT,
EARTH, IRON BEATEN, LIBERATION,
LIGHT, PHARISEES, POLE, ROCK,
SERPENT (hissing).

PITCH FOR CAULKING :—

A symbol of limitation and definition of ideas, which provide for the
distinguishment of truth.

See ARK (Moses), ARK (Noah).

PITCHER OF WATER :—

A symbol of a mental vehicle
containing knowledge or truth.

See GIVING CUP, HYLAS, VESSEL.

PITRIS, LUNAR :—

A symbol of the "fathers" of
the present human personalities.
These are incipient personalities

from the animal evolution which
have been developed in the lunar
cycle on the lunar globes, prior to
their appearance on the earth chain.
Lunar pitris are in their nature
monads of the lower life energising
on the astral plane in astral and
astro-physical animal forms. They
become human personalities when
their development is complete and
mind dawns upon their entering
human bodies. They represent the
animal nature of the human being.
They are man's inheritance from
the lower creation. They account
for the instincts, appetites, desires,
and passions in humanity, but not
for the mental, ethical, and spiritual
faculties, which have a higher origin
altogether. Man only descends from
the anthropoids in his lower nature,
not in his higher. Evolution is an
ascent, not a descent ; a descent of
man from animals is merely an
appearance, an illusive fact, and
quite untrue in reality. The "missing links" may some day be discovered, but they will contain no
proof that mind is a product of the
lower nature. In his lower self
man proceeds from the animals,
but in his higher self he is a son
of God.

See ASTRAL PLANE, BARHISHAD,
CHIP, EVOLUTION, FATHERS (lower),
HEAVEN, HEIFER, LUNAR CYCLE,
METEMPSYCHOSIS, MAN (born), MANES,
MONAD OF FORM, MOON-WAXING,
PERSONALITY, PILLARS (light), PITRI-
YANA, PLANETARY CHAIN, RACES,
RULERS OF MATTER, SKINS OF ANI-
MALS, SUKUNA, WHEELS (holy).

PITRIS, SOLAR :—

A symbol of the spiritual "fathers"
of the human individualities which
centralise every soul. These are
the Divine sparks (agnishwattas)
from the solar fire, the Eternal
Spirit. They are the spiritual egos
which descend to the lower planes
to incarnate in human nature by
identifying themselves with the
human personalities while they gain
experience and seek to manifest
their nature in the heart of man.
The spiritual egos are seated in the
causal-bodies on the higher mental
plane, and render man a spiritual
being with a higher nature from
God, and a lower nature from
matter.

" These five beings obtained out of an immense crucible, by chemical process, a male and a female, from whom, through the essential influence of the sun and moon, human beings descended, who gradually filled the earth."—KIDD, *China*, p. 167.

The five planes of nature are permeated or energised by a central spiritual intelligence whose dual aspects are masculine-feminine, active-passive, force-matter, and from this duality the life manifested which was to be evolved upon the planes. The lunar cycle and lunar pitris are symbolised by the " moon " ; the sparks of the Divine life (solar pitris) by the " sun." In this manner and process,—the lunar pitri (personality) collecting, as it were, the " solar ray " or germ of individuality, and transmuting through the Spirit its own inherent latent qualities,—the soul is evolved.

" As individualised beings we had our beginnings in this world ; but the being thus individualised has had a nobler origin : it is of the eternal God himself." " All life that comes to self-consciousness is a ray of the eternal wisdom, a spark from the eternal fire. The Word has been made flesh in you and me as well as in our Lord and Master. . . . As I have said before, there are no untrue doctrines ; there are only more or less inadequate apprehensions of the one eternal truth which is the love of God."—R. J. CAMPBELL, Serms., *Christ Transcendent*, and *The Word made Flesh*.

See AGNISHVATTAS, BODHISATVAS, CAUSAL-BODY, FRAVASHIS, GUARDIAN SPIRITS, HEAVEN, INCARNATION OF SOULS, INDIVIDUALITY, MANASAPUTRAS, MANES, MARUTS, MATRO, MONAD OF LIFE, MOON, MUSPELL (sons), PACCEKA-BUDDHAS, PERSONALITY, RULERS OF MATTER, SONS OF GOD, SPARKS, SUN.

PITRIYANA (PATH OF THE FATHERS) :—

A symbol of the course taken in the evolution of the human form and personality after the establishment of a centre on the fourth subplane of the astral plane. This evolution has mainly taken place in the sub-cycle previous to the present one, that is, on the lunar chain of globes, previous to the life-wave coming over to the terrene chain. In evolving the personality, the desire-nature is developed and com-

pleted, prior to the coming in of mind and spirit, when the path of the Gods (Devayana) commences. The latter path begins where the former leaves off. There is no break or interval, for the one follows upon the heels of the other : but, of course, whereas the first is of the form, the second is of the life divine.

" The year indeed is Pragâpati, and there are two paths thereof, the Southern and the Northern. Now those who here believe in sacrifices and pious gifts as work done, gain the moon only as their world, and return again. Therefore the Rishes, who desire offspring, go to the South, and the path of the Fathers is matter."—*Prasna Upanishad*, I. 9.

The " year " signifies the Cycle of Life (Pragâpati), and the " two paths " are the Pitriyana (southern), and the Devayana (northern). Now those monads of form which here evolve through the struggle of life and the instincts on the physical plane develop the desire-nature (moon) only, as the complete result of their course of action, and so always return to physical embodiment. But the spiritual egos, or monads of life, who intend to manifest their nature and produce qualities, go to the astral plane (south) and occupy the human forms and personalities that are prepared and ready for them. The " path of the fathers " is the course of the lunar pitris in matter, the " path of the gods " is the course of the solar pitris from matter.

See ASTRAL PLANE, DEVAYANA, EVOLUTION, HEAVEN, INCARNATION OF SOULS, LUNAR CYCLE, MAHAYANA, MAN BORN, MAN CRAWLED, MAN (natural), MANASAPUTRAS, METEMPSYCHOSIS, MONAD (form, life), MONTH, MOON, MOON WAXING, NORTH, ORIGINAL SIN, PERSONALITY, PITRIS, PLANETARY CHAIN, RISHES, SKINS OF ANIMALS, SOMA (moon), SOUTH, SUKUNA, WHEELS (holy), YEAR.

PLACE OF PEACE IN ANNU :—

A symbol of the causal-body on the plane of the higher mind.

" My nostrils are opened in Tattu, or, as others say, ' My mouth and my nostrils are opened in Tatau, and I have my place of peace in Annu which is my house ; it was built for me by the goddess Sesheta (a form of Hathor,—

goddess of writing and of books), and the god Khnemu set it up for me upon its walls.' "—BUDGE, *Book of the Dead*, Ch. LVII.

The incarnating ego explains that through the functioning of the lower mind he discriminates the things of the lower planes ; in other words, he is enabled to find expression of his will and thought in the cycle of life in the underworld (Tatau). He re-joices that he possesses an immortal habitation in the causal-body which has been built up for him through the functioning of Buddhi (Sesheta), and set up by the indwelling Self working within his own soul, through the varied experiences of life.

See ANNU, BUDDHI, CAUSAL-BODY, DWELLING (palace), HATHOR, INCAR-NATION OF SOULS, MOUTH (opening), NOSTRILS, TATTU, UR-HEKAU.

PLACES, FIVE, WHERE THE EARTH FEELS MOST JOY :—

A symbol of the five means of classifying the functionings of the Ego. The awakenment of the Self must proceed from the physical plane (the earth) by way of the stimulus from sensation and desire.

PLACES, FIVE, WHEREON IS MOST SORROW :—

A symbol of the five senses which operate from the physical plane and are causes of suffering to the mind, or lower consciousness.

See BRATROK, FIVE, PLANETS, VIRGINS (ten).

PLAGUES AND EVILS :—

A symbol of the pairs of opposites ; the lower being created by the mind energised by desire.

" By these plagues are meant self-love, the pride of self-derived intelligence, and the concupiscences of evil and falsity flowing from them."—SWEDEN-BORG, *Apoc. Rev.*, n. 456.

See EVIL, OPPOSITES, PESTILENCE.

PLANES, FIVE OR SEVEN :—

These are divisions of the material nature of the universe, graded accord-ing to the rates of vibration of the atoms on each plane, the slowest rates being, of course, of the atoms on the physical plane, which is the external or lowest plane of all. In the present cycle of life, only five planes are manifest or in activity :

the two highest, to make up the seven, being latent.

" The 'Five Worlds' (Awalim-i Khamsa) of the Sufis. These Five Worlds are not five different localities, but five different planes of existence, which loses in true Being as it descends ; they are consequently often spoken of as the ' Five Planes ' (Hazrat-i Khamsa)."—GIBB, *Hist. of Ottoman Poetry*, Vol. I. p. 54.

The five planes of manifestation must be regarded as occupying the same space in the universe, one plane within the other. This explains the bodies or sheaths of the soul, for these are the correlated forms on the lower planes in which each Ego dwells.

See ATOMS, CHAPTERS, DAYS (five), ELEMENTS, GATHA (ahuna), WORLDS (five).

PLANETARY CHAIN SYSTEM :—

Each physical globe has three counterpart globes of ascent, and three of descent, on the three planes above the physical, i.e. two on the astral plane, two on the mental, and two on the buddhic. Round this chain of globes the life-wave passes in seven rounds. The life-wave has passed through the seven rounds of the lunar manvantara, and three and a half rounds of the terrene, and is now, therefore, on the fourth globe of the fourth round, which is the planet Earth on which humanity is at present developing. The planetary chain system has its correspondency in the individual soul (the microcosm). The passing of the life-wave from globe to globe synchronises with the evolution of the vestures of the Ego, which enable the mental, astral, and phy-sical natures to receive expression. The globes answer to the means whereby the Ego is enabled to undergo its pilgrimage.

" Origen holds to a series of worlds following one upon the other—the one rising a step higher than the other, representing thus a teleological develop-ment, so that every later world brings to ripeness the seeds that were imbedded in the former, and itself prepares the seed for that which is to follow."

See AAT, BEASTS (three sorts), HVANIRATHA, KARSHVARES, LUNAR CHAIN, MANVANTARA, MICROCOSM, PRALAYA, RACES, REGIONS, RENOVA-TION, ROOT-RACES, ROUND, SABBATH, SNOW, VESTURES.

THE GLOBES OF THE PLANETARY CHAIN.

SPIRITUAL

Vourugaresti (north)

Vourubaresti (north)

MENTAL

Savahi (east)

Arezahi (west)

ASTRAL

Vidadhafshn (south)

Fradadhafshn (south)

PHYSICAL (The Earth)

Hvaniratha

In the above diagram of the Earth's planetary chain, the Zoroastrian names are given to the seven globes. "Out of these seven only one, the lowest and most material of these globes, is within our plane or means of perception, the six others lying outside it and being therefore invisible to the terrestrial eye. Every such chain of worlds is the progeny and creation of another, *lower* and *dead* chain—its re-incarnation, so to say" (*Secret Doctrine*, Vol. I. p. 176.) The Earth chain is the progeny of the Lunar chain, which is now lifeless, as is to be seen in the case of the moon, which is the physical globe of that chain.

The Life-wave has passed entirely from the Lunar chain, and temporarily from the first three globes of the Earth chain. It has now passed from the lowest astral globe to the physical globe,—our Earth,—and will next pass on, after an immense period, to the higher astral globe of the Earth chain.

PLANETS, FIVE GREATER :—

These are symbols of mental centres of functionings in the soul, which have each their special form of activity.

"The planet Tistrya (Jupiter) presides over the division of troops in the East, and is named Prince of the stars. Sitivisa (Saturn) presides over the Western division ; Vanant (Mercury) over that of the South, and Hapto-iringa (Mars) over the star troops of the North. In the middle of the heavens is the great planet Mesch (Venus), he leads the troops against Ahriman."—*Zoroastrian System.*

The planet *Jupiter* is a symbol of the Self in its directive function on the higher mental plane. It leads and governs evolution from the buddhic plane, as the positive function of Buddhi. *Saturn* corresponds to the function which limits and defines, and determines the cyclic periods in the decline or decay of things. *Mercury*, on the other hand, signifies the function of activity, growth, expansion, and gives impetus and momentum. *Mars* signifies power, force, resistence, and will. *Venus* is the symbol of the astral love-energy, which being related with the buddhic principle urges the stream of the evolving life to pour itself forth in the forms which are prepared to await its reception ; and so leads the advance towards perfection.

"Mercury is the lord of education and science : we owe to him our knowledge, which comprises bad and good. . . . The Moon causes man's body to grow and Mercury forms his mind. Then he comes under the sway of Venus. The Sun gives him family riches or dominion ; Mars bravery and noblemindedness. Thereupon, under the guidance of Jupiter, he prepares, by means of religious exercises, for the journey to the world beyond, and he attains rest under the influence of Saturn " (From the *Basra Encyclopedia*).—DE BOER, *Phil. in Islam*, p. 88.

See AHRIMAN, BUDDHI, CITY, EAST, HERMES, JUPITER, MARS, MERCURY, MESCH, NORTH, SATURN, STARS (fixed), TISTRYA, VENUS, WEST.

PLANETS, FIVE SMALLER :—

These are symbolic of the five astro-mental centres from which the vibrations of the astro-physical five senses emanate upon the mental plane to enter into the consciousness of the ego.

"Then Ormazd created the five smaller planets, and the whole host of fixed stars, in the lowest circle of the heavens." —J. F. CLARKE, *Zoroastrian System.*

Then the centres from which the five senses emanate upon the mental plane are established, and the many faculties which enable the mind to be exercised are formed upon the astro-mental plane.

See FIVE, NET, PLACES (sorrow), SEKHET-AARU, STARS (fixed).

PLANKS OF THE BOAT :—

Symbols of the environing conditions of the soul (boat). The buddhic nature for the higher emotions ; the mental nature for ideas ; the astral nature for desires ; and the physical nature for sensations.

See BOAT ON RIVER.

PLANTS :—

Symbols of simple instincts and feelings growing upward to the light.

"And both Matro and Matroyao changed from the shape of a plant into the shape of a man, and the breath went spiritually into them, which is the soul."—*The Bundahis*, Ch. XV. 5.

The mind and emotion-principles undergo the transformation from the simple feelings and instincts into human ideas and emotions ; and this being accomplished, the spirit of the one Self,—the Spark of the Divine Life,—entered in and became theirs. And so the human race was launched upon its evolution.

"Wherever the scattered seed pushed upward out of the dark bosom of the earth and unfolded itself in a plant, in its blossom and its fruit, Mani beheld the triumphant evolution of the principle of light, gradually working its way onward to freedom from the bondage of matter."—NEANDER, *Church History*, Vol. II. p. 214.

"Underneath the surface of the earth just now thousands of bulbs are beginning to be stirred by the breath of springtime. Hitherto they have lain buried and hidden in darkness and corruption, but they each hold enough of the life of the universe to be able to respond to the rays of the sun of heaven which penetrate to their prison-house. The time of summer flowers is not yet, but pale green shoots are appearing above ground, and despite the set-backs of occasional frost and snow and biting winds, will grow and strengthen till they burst into bloom and become part of the glory of the sunshine itself. To do this they must free themselves from the earth while assimilating to their own higher ends all the good it has to give ; or, rather, this is what the mysteriously operating universal life is already doing within them. And so it is with the soul. As Christ frees us from the bondage of the flesh we unfold into the light of God and reflect the eternal glory, assimilating to that end all the force and wisdom our earthly probation can supply. The struggle is not an evil ; but to submit to our present conditions without a struggle, and without seeking to give expression to our latent divinity, would be an evil indeed."— R. J. CAMPBELL, Serm., *The Song of the Redeemed*.

See BONDAGE, GOSHURUN, HERB, HOMA, LIGHT, LOTUS, MATRO, RU, SEED (good), SEKER, SEPARATION, SOMA, TREE.

PLEROMA :—

A symbol of the manifesting Logos replete with all intelligences and potencies : or the Archetypal Man in his fullness of stature as perfect manhood and Godhood (atma-buddhi).

" For in Christ dwelleth all the fullness of the Godhead bodily, and in him ye are made full, who is the head of all principality and power."—COL. ii. 9, 10.

For in Christ, the Archetypal Man, every higher quality and potency subsists ; and Christ being in every soul, he gradually evolves in it his own perfection, and makes it one with himself.

" He is the very Pleroma itself, who hath found the Mystery in which they all are, and in which they are all set." —*Books of the Saviour*, in *Pistis Sophia*.

He is the very Christ, who has found the secret to each plane,—or is able to control and manifest at will on all planes of being.

" The true notion of God says that there can be no work which is not done in Him ; that we cannot get out of His vast circle ; that all men are dwelt in by the Holy Spirit ; that all work is done by His inspiration ; that all places are peopled by Him ; that never for a moment has time been empty of His eternal presence ; that in every movement of Force, as well as in every thought and feeling, and act of every spirit—He is. There is but one Being in the universe, and the universe is, because He is. No atom of matter, if matter exist, can divide itself from Him ; no personality, that is, no consciousness, will and character can get away from Him, for they only exist because He

exists. There is nothing which is not God. And to yield to this truth, to live in it, and to obey its calls, is happiness, certainty, power and redemption. To feel it is to *know* that we are immortal. This is not a faith which stands on authority. It is the conviction of the soul, because the soul believes in the omniscient, omnipresent, allcontaining Goodness."—STOPFORD A. BROOKE, Serm., *Immortality and God*.

See ABRAXAS, ÆONS, ARC. MAN, COSMOS, EVOLUTION, I A O, INITIATIONS, INVOLUTION, LOST PIECE.

PLOUGHING :—

Symbolic of the fashioning of the vehicles and producing the conditions wherein the lower self is placed and operating, with a view to the sowing and reaping by the True Self of that which the lower self appears to do and undergo in the life periods.

" And I am glorious therein (the Garden) ; I drink therein ; I plough therein ; I reap therein ; I move therein ; I am wedded therein ; my utterance is powerful therein."—*Book of the Dead*, Ch. CX. This Ch. trans. by M. W. BLACKDEN.

In these experiences of life, I (the Self) realise myself ; I derive Truth and Love ; I fashion the bodies and conditions wherein the lower self is engaged ; I sow and reap the fruits of the Spirit ; I live therein. In me the two aspects of the Higher Self (atma-buddhi) become One. Power is mine, and the Will of the Absolute is within me.

" Brahman ; I plough and sow, and of my ploughing and sowing I reap imperishable fruit. . . . My field is the Dharma (truth) ; the weeds which I pluck up are the cleaving to existence ; the plough which I use is wisdom ; the seed which I sow, the seeking of purity ; the work which I perform, attention to precepts ; the harvest which I reap is Nirvâna " (Buddhist parable).— BUNSEN, *The Angel Messiah*, p. 47.

" Thus it is with the world of men, if there was not the second Adam (Christ) to plough them and sow them, they could none of them become saints ; No, not the elect themselves ; because the means are determined, as well as the end."—J. BUNYAN, *Exp. of Genesis*.

See AGRICULTURE, BALARAMA, CULTIVATION, DHARMA, GEUSH-URVA, HARVEST, HUSBANDMAN, NIRVANA, OX AND ASS, OXEN, REAPING, SEED (good), SEKHET-HETEP, SHABTI, SOWER, SOWING.

PLUMES ON THE ATEF CROWN :—

A symbol signifying the condition of the soul in which supremacy over the lower nature is realised.

See AMEN, CROWN-ATEF.

PO, OR NIGHT :—

A symbol of chaos, primordial formless matter, or the material form-side of nature.

"The Marquesas Islanders have a legend which relates that in the beginning there was no life, light, or sound in the world, that a boundless night, *Po,* enveloped everything, over which *Tanaoa,* which means 'darkness,' and *Mutu-hei,* which means 'silence,' ruled supreme. . . . Through all the Polynesian cosmogonies, even the wildest and most fanciful, there is a constant underlying sense of a chaos, wreck, *Po,* containing all things, and existing previous to the first creative organisation ; the chaos and wreck of a previous world, destroyed by fire according to the Hawaiian legend, destroyed by water according to the Samoan legend ; a chaos, ruin, or night, *Po,* in which the gods themselves had been involved, and only in virtue of their divine nature, after continued struggle, extricated themselves and reorganised the world on its present pattern."—A. FORNANDER, *Polynesian Race,* Vol. I. pp. 63, 64.

At the opening of the cycle of manifestation the state of matter was formless and inchoate, for from the Absolute there was no expression of the Life. Yet potentially all was hidden within, together with the memory of previous cycles of life. The higher qualities (gods), which had been involved in the Absolute, had yet to come forth and manifest their nature through the matter of the planes in the universe and soul. Eventually the higher qualities and the spiritual egos overcame the desire-nature and began to discipline the human soul.

See ABYSS, CHAOS, DARKNESS (pri.), DEEP, HINE, NIGHT (matter), REINGA, TAAROA, TANAOA.

POET, BARD, OR HYMN WRITER :—

A symbol indicating an advanced quality capable of educating and leading upwards the qualities below.

"The self-shining bards have extolled thee with their newest hymn."—*Sata. Brâh.* II. 6, 1, 38.

The intuitional qualities have become exalted through aspiration and harmony.

See HYMN SINGING, INTUITION, PROPHET.

POHJOLA :—

See MANALA, NORTH.

POISON, OR POISON-DROPS :—

A symbol of the coarser functionings of the lower self, and the severer experiences on the lower planes.

See YMIR.

POISONOUS FOOD OR ODOUR :—

A symbol of the astral activity of the passions and desires, which inflames and excites the lower nature.

See HARLOT.

POISON, YELLOW :—

Symbolic of falsity and greed.

See YELLOW COLOUR.

POLE, UPRIGHT :—

A symbol of aspiration.

"Whereupon Râ said, 'the monster Ba (Set) hath turned himself into a hissing serpent, let Horus, the son of Isis, set himself above his hole in the form of a pole on the top of which is the head of Horus, so that he may never again come forth therefrom.'"—*Legend of the Winged Sun-disk.*

And the Divine nature asserted,— "Now the lower principle is ultimated and appears as a serpent, subtle and deceitful, that is, mâyâvic, illusory,— so let the Higher Self seat himself above the sense-nature, in the form, as it were, of a pole,—the symbol of aspiration, and with the head signifying true manhood, the sign of leadership and rule." Hence the *head,* a symbol of manas, surmounts the pole. And thus the "serpent" shall not issue forth to obstruct the workings of the Supreme.

See COLUMN, FOXES, HEAD, HORUS, ISIS, PIT, RÂ, SERPENT (hissing), SET.

POLLUX OR POLYDEUKES :—

A symbol of the "Son of God" within, that is, the Higher Self in its relation with the lower Self (Castor) ; or the Individuality (Pollux) with the Personality (Castor).

"According to some, Pollux and Helen only were children of Zeus, and Castor was the son of Tyndareus, King of

Lacedaemon. Hence Pollux was immortal, while Castor was subject to old age and death like every other mortal."
—*Smith's Class. Dict.*

The Higher Self and Wisdom only were Divine ; while the Personality was begotten by the astro-mental nature. Hence, while the first were immortal, the second was mortal.

See AMYCUS, ASVINS, DIOSCURI, GEMINI, HELEN, PERSONALITY.

POLYPHEMUS, SON OF POSEIDON :—

A symbol of the force aspect of the Divine Will proceeding from the eternal Truth. It is the intellectual energy of the Self on the mental plane. The one eye in the forehead represents consciousness on the mental plane.

See CYCLOPES, FOHAT, POSEIDON.

POLYTHEISM :—

A symbol of the many aspects of the One Supreme Being : the active and the passive aspects being indicated by masculine and feminine deities.

"Without the infinitely Many the Eternal One is imperfect ; nor could Polytheism ever have had an existence as a Providential Establishment if it had not contained an elemental, a vital and eternal truth. The omnipresence of God is merely another word for his Polytheistic Unity. As the whole of the Divine consciousness, wisdom and efficiency in action must be in every portion of space at once, and as he must have the faculty of subdividing his attention to an infinite number of things, what else can this be but an infinite multiplicity of individualities in the infinite and eternal universality ? In this we perceive the absolute and the free in the Divine nature,—the Male and Female Principles, from which the unity and the infinite variety of creation are derived."—J. SMITH, *Divine Drama of History*, p. 160.

See particular Gods and Goddesses, FEMININE, MASCULINE, MYTHOLOGY.

PONIARD :—

A symbol of spiritual energy exercised from within the soul, or the intuition which dispels ignorance and error.

"Then Ahura Mazda gave Yima a ring and a poniard."—*Vendidad*, II.

Then the Supreme endows the soul with the "ring," symbol of completeness, indicating that which

encompasseth its course (the actual course as signified by the Zodiac) ; and the "poniard," a symbol of the intuition,—the same as the "sword of the Spirit."

See ARROW, SWORD, YIMA.

PONTIFF, OR PONTIFEX :—

A symbol of the spiritual mind having a leading position in the religious activities of the "Church" or "Temple" of the soul, and subjectively directing the lower qualities (people).

See AARON, ADVARYA, AGNIDHRA, ATHORNE, CHRYSE, CHURCH, HIGH PRIEST, POPE, PRIEST, TEMPLE.

POOL OF BETHESDA :—

A symbol of the intuition or perception of the truth.

"Now there is at Jerusalem by the sheep market a pool, which is called in the Hebrew tongue Bethesda, having five porches. In these lay a great multitude of impotent folk, of blind, halt and withered, waiting for the moving of the water."—JOHN v. 2, 3.

Near Jerusalem,—the "City of the Great King,"—that is, the causal-body, the seat of the Higher Self, is the "sheep market," which is the state where "sheep" or living truths are got in exchange for "money" their lower equivalent, i.e. for desires and sense-objects. The "pool" signifies mental enlightenment by intuition. "Bethesda" signifies a state of bliss, because enlightenment is the haven of rest for those who have outgrown the tribulations and fetters of the "flesh." The "five porches" are the five senses, and the "impotent folk" are the qualities who put their trust in the senses. The "water" is the perception of truth. The qualities wait until their intuitions are stirred.

See BETHESDA, CAUSAL-BODY, CITY, CROSS, HEALING, JERUSALEM, MAISHAN, PORCHES, SHEEP, WATER.

POOL OF PEACE :—

A symbol of the Higher Self, the Spirit of Truth.

"Yet lo ! I, even I, have piloted this great ship into the pool of Peace."—*Book of the Dead*, Ch. CX.

The One Self, notwithstanding, has *alone* throughout the cycle been the means of directing the soul, and proceeding with the evolution. The "great ship" is the soul in which is the lesser Self. The "Pool of Peace" is the Greater Self wherein all qualities unite and are made One in Truth (water) atma-buddhi.

See HIGHER AND LOWER SELVES, OCEAN, PHANG, SHIP OF MANU, USERT.

POOL OF THE ZENITH :—

A symbol signifying the completion of purification by Truth, and the attainment of the higher state of consciousness.

See BAPTISM, WHEAT AND BARLEY, ZENITH.

POOLS OF CLAY, SEVEN :—

A symbol of the seven root-races of humanity, filled with Divine life from the River of Life.—See Gospel of Pseudo-Mathew, Ch. 26.

See ROOT-RACES, SPARROWS.

POOLS OF THE HOLY GODDESS :—

A symbol of the buddhic functioning as the means of purifying the soul.

"O 'Being in Peace!' Lord of the Two Earths, I have come into Thee; I have bathed in the Pool of the Holy Goddess; and lo! for me, all unclean things have passed away."—BLACKDEN, Book of the Dead, Ch. CX.

O Being whose nature is bliss!—so the Self is addressed,—"I know thy might, thy power and active aspect; the lower nature has been purified through Wisdom, and been cleansed by truth; and so the impurities of the lower planes have been gotten rid of.

"I (Lakshmi) reside in lakes filled with water, in pure waters, and in ground covered with fresh grass, in a wood abounding in lotuses and fruits."—Institutes of Vishnu, XCIX. 17.

Among symbols of Wisdom (Lakshmi) are "pools of water," "pure waters," etc.

See BAPTISM, FANG, LAKSHMI, NUTURT, SMAM, TCHESERT.

POOR PEOPLE :—

A symbol of the undisciplined lower qualities, poor in development, deficient in goodness and truth.

"For ye have the poor always with you; but me ye have not always. For in that she poured this ointment upon my body, she did it to prepare me for burial."—MAT. xxvi. 11, 12.

That is, the disciplined qualities readily direct their efforts towards the less-developed nature beneath them, but they have not the Christ until the love-nature (the woman with ointment) is stirred within them. For ere the lower personality (body) disintegrates, it is by a supreme effort of love of the Highest that the "corpse" (lower nature) is "buried," or the sense of separateness is got rid of.

"Poor and needy are often mentioned in the Word, and in the spiritual sense by poor is understood one who is not in truths, and by needy, one who is not in goods."—SWEDENBORG, Apoc. Rev., n. 95.

See AURVAITO-DIH, CORPSE, MARTHA, OINTMENT, PEOPLE, PERSONALITY, POVERTY, RICHES, SEPARATENESS, TREASURE, WOMEN.

POOR IN SPIRIT :—

A symbol of those qualities which have rid themselves of the lower desires, and are filled with the spirit of goodness and truth.

"Hath not God chosen the poor of this world, rich in faith, and heirs of the kingdom which he hath promised to them that love him?"—JAMES ii. 5.

In the Divine scheme of progression, those qualities which are free from the attractions of sense and desire, and are filled with the higher energies of wisdom and love, are heirs of the higher state of consciousness which the law of the Supreme has made the spiritual result of righteousness.

See KINGDOM OF HEAVEN, MAN (rich), POVERTY, RICHES, SERMON.

POPE OF ROME :—

A symbol of the spiritual mind which dominates the religious consciousness, and directs the activities in relation to the higher emotions of Truth, Wisdom, and Love (the Christian "Church").

See AARON, ADVARYA, AGNIDHRA, ATHORNE, CHRYSE, CHURCH, HIGH PRIEST, PONTIFF, PRIEST, TIARA.

PORCH OF HOUSE :—

A symbol of the sense-nature, which is, as it were, an entrance from outside to the lower consciousness.

See DOOR (lower), GATE (lower), HOUSE.

PORCHES, FIVE :—

A symbol of the five senses, the entrances of desires.

" The five porches in Bethesda represent the five senses of unredeemed humanity, i.e. the unregenerate passions."
—E. A. A., *Enc. Biblica*, Gospels, 47.

See BETHESDA, CROSS, POOL OF BETHESDA.

POSEIDON OR NEPTUNE :—

A symbol of the Truth aspect of the manifesting Higher Self. It represents the consensus of prototypal ideas which are reflected on the lower planes in the multiplicity of the forms of life. The Truth aspect relates to the intellect.

" The gods decided that Athens should receive its name from the deity who should bestow upon man the most useful gift. Poseidon then created the horse, and Athena called forth the olive tree, in consequence of which the honour was conferred upon the goddess."—*Smith's Class. Dict.*

The Truth aspect produced the *intellect* (horse), and the Love aspect, the *intuition* (olive tree), and the greatest of these is the intuition, which has its seat in the causal-centre (Athens), but its origin in buddhi (Athena).

" Poseidon was a son of Cronus and Rhea. . . . Originally a personification of the fertilising power of water. . . . The symbol of his power was the trident. . . . He was god of the sea."—*Ibid.*

The manifesting Divine nature appears to proceed from time (Cronus) and space (Rhea). Through Truth-reality (water) comes the Divine Life of atma-buddhi-manas (the trident), and this is reflected in the astral " sea " as the illusion of the lower nature. In a higher sense the " sea " signifies the ocean of Truth-reality on the higher planes, over which the Spirit of God broods that it may bring forth every type of life that is to become existent in the phenomenal world of the lower planes.

" I image the being of God to myself as a shoreless ocean of undifferentiated being, the one reality which eternally is, and out of which, whatever be the reason for the emanation, our temporal conditioned life has come. That shoreless ocean is bliss, light, life, love, and power all in one. There is no other reality. This it is which was from the beginning, is now, and ever shall be, world without end. We are in it now, though we do not know it ; we have never really left it ; and when our present probation and pilgrimage are over, we shall awaken within its bosom."
—R. J. CAMPBELL, Serm., *The Ineffable Divine.*

See AGENOR, ATHENA, ATMA, CITY, CRONUS, DOLPHIN, FISH OF SEA, FISH (great), HORSE, IRRIGATION, JESUS (fish), NARAYANA, OCEAN, OCEANUS, OLIVE, PHINEUS, PROTOTYPES, RHEA, SEA, TANGAROA, TISTRYA, TLALOC, TRIDENT, URANUS, VARUNA, VOURUKASHA, WATER.

POT (HIGHER ASPECT) :—

A symbol of the causal-body.

See CAUSAL-BODY, CRATER, CUP, MAHAVIRA-POT.

POTSHERD :—

A symbol of a quality of the soul, being a separated part of the whole.

" Woe unto him that striveth with his Maker ! Let the potsherd strive with the potsherds of the earth."—Is. xlv. 9.

The quality that acts in opposition to the Divine ordinance is destroyed. Let the higher quality oppose and discipline the lower qualities.

" ' And he took him a potsherd to scrape the humour withal ' (JOB ii. 8). For what is the potsherd in the hand of the Lord, but the flesh which He took of the clay of our nature ? For the potsherd receives firmness by fire. . . . But what is to be understood by *humour* saving sin ? For it is the custom to denote the sins of the flesh by flesh and blood. And hence it is said by the Psalmist, ' Deliver me from blood ' (Ps. li. 16). *Humour* then is the corruption of the blood. And so what do we understand by *humour* but the sins of the flesh rendered worse by length of time ? And so the Mediator between God and man, the Man Christ Jesus, in giving up His Body into the hands of those that persecuted Him, scraped the humour with a potsherd, forasmuch as He put away sin by the flesh ; for He came, as it is written, ' in the likeness of sinful flesh, that He might condemn sin of sin.' "—GREGORY THE GREAT, *Morals on the Book of Job*, Vol. I. p. 153.

" That Vaisvânara cake, doubtless, is yonder sun, and the Maruta cakes are those rays. They are of seven potsherds each, for the troops of the Maruts consist of seven each."—*Sata. Brâh.*, IX . 3, 1, 25.

The Divine Mind or Higher Self (sun) is the source of Life and sustenance, and the high Devas, or spiritual intelligences, are the prime agents for the dissemination of Life and Truth. These Devas are of seven different prime qualities, and in correspondence with them the spiritual egos (Maruts) issue forth in seven classes.

See BLOOD, DEVAS, EARTH, FIRE, FLESH, JOB, MARUTS, REDEMPTION, SUN, VAISVÂNARA.

POURUSHASPA, THE FATHER OF ZOROASTER :—

A symbol of the early activities of the astral nature which lead to the birth of the Soul (Zoroaster).

"Pourushaspa was the fourth man who prepared me (Homa) for the material world; this reward he obtained, that thou wert born to him, O Zarathustra of the house of Pourushaspa, who art opposed to the demons, and of the Ahura religion."—*Homa Yasht.*

The preparation for the manifesting of the Divine Life through "Pourushaspa" means that at this period of involution the process of creation takes place upon the astral plane. And it is upon this plane that the World-soul (Zoroaster) is said to be born, inasmuch as the desire-principle (Pourushaspa), being the motive power of evolution, is the first means of enabling the Soul to commence by involution the accomplishment, through evolution, of its purpose. The desire-nature being essentially the love element (attractive) is opposed to the power of darkness (ignorance and inertia) and is the only means of awakening the positive, initiative power of the Soul. The desire-nature being of "the Ahura religion" means that it is through the awakenment of Love that the affinity of the Soul with the Higher Self is seen and known.

"The only power to oppose to evil is love, strong enduring love, a benevolence which no crime or wretchedness can conquer, and which therefore can conquer all. . . . Go then with this love, and it will be mightier than the sword of the magistrate, or the armies of monarchs, to conquer evil. It will touch the heart which has hardened itself against all other influences. It will pierce the conscience, which is impregnable against the most vehement rebuke. Love gives a new tongue, the only one which all men can comprehend."—W. E. CHANNING, *Works*, Vol. II. p. 41.

See APHRODITE, ASTRAL PLANE, AURVAITO, BIRTH OF ZOROASTER, CREATION, DARKNESS, DEMONS, DUGHDHOVA, EVOLUTION, GLORY (divine), HOMA, INVOLUTION, PRITHA'S, RELIGION (good), SOUL, SOUTH WIND, TANE-MAHUTA, VENUS, YUDHI, ZOROASTER.

POVERTY :—

A symbol of lack of reality,—a deficiency of truth, wisdom, and love, in the manifest.

"For ye know the grace of our Lord Jesus Christ, that, though he was rich, yet for your sakes he became poor, that ye through his poverty might be rich."—2 COR. viii. 9.

This statement refers to the Divine Sacrifice "from the foundation of the world." Christ, in descending into matter, forfeits his spiritual wealth,—the only riches,—so that through material activity (poverty of the spiritual), humanity,—Christ's reflection, or outcome,—should be made rich in spiritual realities, and become the inheritor of all things.

"Wise men lay up knowledge : But the mouth of the foolish is a present destruction. The rich man's wealth is his strong city : The destruction of the poor is their poverty."—PROV. x. 14, 15.

Minds full of wisdom, love, and truth are rich and enduring, but minds empty of true riches have no life in them.

See AURVAITO, GRACE OF GOD, JOB, KUVERA, MAN (rich), POOR PEOPLE, POOR IN SPIRIT, PRAGÂPATI (rel.), RICH MAN, SACRIFICER, VÂGAS-RAVASA, WEALTH, WOMB.

POWER AND AMBITION :—

These qualities when transmuted through the buddhic function become Dignity and Aspiration.

See TRANSMUTATION.

PRAGÂPATI, THE LORD OF CREATURES :—

A symbol of the creative aspect of the Supreme, which goes forth primordially as Divine Truth producing Spirit and Matter in the cycle of manifestation, and eventually taking form as the Archetypal Man.

"Some call Pragâpati the Father with five feet (the five seasons), and with twelve shapes (the twelve months), the Giver of rain in the highest half of heaven ; others again say that the Sage is placed in the lower half, in the chariot with seven wheels and six spokes."— *Prasna Upanishad*, I. 11.

The "five feet or seasons " signify progression on the five planes of the universe, and the "twelve shapes or months " represent the twelve divisions of the great cycle of time and life, during which the Self accomplishes his course. The Divine Wisdom dispenses Truth from above ; he is also the indwelling Self in the lower nature, seated in the causal-body related with the seven globes of the planetary chain, and the dual aspects of relativity of the three lower planes.

See ADITYAS, AGNI, ARC. MAN, CHARIOT, DAY AND NIGHT, DEATH OF OSIRIS, EVOLUTION, FOOD, GOAT (white), GODHEAD, GOLD MAN, HIGHER AND LOWER SELVES, HIRANYAGARBHA, HORSE SACRIFICE, INCARNATION, INVOLUTION, KARSHVARES, MAHABHARATA, MAHAVIRA-POT, MONTH, PLANETARY CHAIN, PURUSHA, RÃ, RAIN, SAGE, SEASONS (five), TIME, TORTOISE, TUAT, WHEEL, WORLDS (five), YEAR, ZODIAC.

PRAGÂPATI RELAXED, AND AFTERWARDS RESTORED :—

A symbol of the Archetypal Man, who, having lost the Divine Life of Involution, afterwards receives. that of Evolution, and is restored in the souls of humanity.

"Pragâpati created whatsoever exists. Having created creatures, he, having run the whole race, became relaxed, . . . the vital air went out from within. When it had gone out of him the gods left him."—*Sata. Brâh.*, VI. 1, 2, 12.

The Self, having produced the archetypal world with all its forms and qualities perfect on the higher planes, ceased to manifest in Involution. The life, or spiritual energy, operating upon the mental plane, subsided, and the higher qualities became latent.

"The gods said to Agni, ' In thee we will heal this our father Pragâpati.'— ' Then I will enter into him, when whole,' he (Agni) said.—' So be it,' they said. Hence while being Pragâpati, they yet call him Agni."—*Ibid.*, v. 21.

The higher qualities look to the birth of the Self within the soul, for the restoration of the greater Self involved in matter of the lower planes. The lesser Self will enter as a divine seed "when whole," i.e. when the lower nature is evolved complete. The greater Self and the lesser Self are yet the same.

"Here now they say, ' Wherefore is Agni (the fire-altar) built of this earth ? ' But, surely, when that deity (Pragâpati) became relaxed (fell asunder), he flowed along this earth in the shape of his life-sap ; and when the gods restored him (put him together) they gathered him up from this earth."—*Ibid.*, v. 29.

Wherefore is the Divine nature to be built up of the lower nature—the quaternary ? Because it is through perfecting the lower nature that the Divine nature arises from it. This is shown in the fact of the dismemberment of the Archetypal Man and the shedding of his blood (life sap), which is the Life permeating the lower nature (earth), and which is gathered up when the higher qualities put his members together for his resurrection and ascension in the souls of humanity.

" By offering up his own self in sacrifice, Pragâpati becomes dismembered ; and all those separated limbs and faculties of his come to form the universe. . . . It requires a new and ever new sacrifice to build the dismembered Lord of creatures up again."—J. EGGELING, *S. B. of E.*, Vol. XLIII. Intro.

"The Son of God came from the fullness of the Godhead into a human life. For having emptied Himself, and taken upon Him the form of a slave, He was restored again to His former perfection and dignity. For He, being humbled, and apparently degraded, was restored again from His humiliation and degradation to His former completeness and greatness, having never been diminished from His essential perfection."—METHODIUS, *Banquet, etc.*, Ch. XI.

"Nebertcher, i.e. the ' Lord of all.' In the ' Book of the Dead ' Osiris is frequently called by this name, the allusion being to the complete reconstruction of his body after it had been hacked to pieces by Set."—BUDGE, *Book of the Dead*, Vol. I. p. 19.

"Hence the state of the inward man. . . . His remaking or regeneration appears to them (mystics) as the primal necessity, if he is ever to obtain rights of citizenship in the ' country of the soul.' We have seen that this idea of the New Birth, the remaking or transmutation of the self, clothed in many different symbols, runs through the whole of mysticism

and much of theology. It is the mystic's subjective reading of those necessary psychological changes which he observes taking place within himself as his spiritual consciousness grows. His hard work of renunciation, of detachment from the things which that consciousness points out as illusory or impure, his purifications and trials, all form part of it. If that which is whole or perfect is to come, then that which is in part must be done away : ' For in what measure we put off the creature, in the same measure are we able to put on the Creator ; neither more nor less ' (*Theol. Germ.*, Ch. I.)."
—E. UNDERHILL, *Mysticism*, p. 167.

See ABRAXAS, ADAM (higher), AFU-RÂ, AGNI, ALPHA, ALTAR (fire), ARC. MAN, BLOOD, CHARIOT, CREATURES, CROSS, CRUCIFIXION (gnostic), DEATH OF LEMMINKAINEN, OF OSIRIS, DIONY-SUS, DISMEMBERMENT, DVIYAGUS, EARTH, EVOLUTION, HEAVEN AND EARTH, HOMA-JUICE, HUMAN, INCAR-NATION, INVOLUTION, JOB, LIMBS, MARROW, MEMBERS, PURUSHA, QUA-TERNARY, QEBHSENNUF, REDEMPTION, REGENERATION, SACRIFICE, SACRI-FICER, SAP, SEED, SOMA-JUICE, URA-NUS, VITAL AIRS, YMIR, ZAGREUS.

PRAGNÂ, CAPACITY OF PER-CEPTION :—

A symbol of realised spiritual Truth, as the soul's support.

"That throne is Pragnâ (knowledge), for by knowledge he sees clearly."—*Kaush. Upanishad*, I. 2.

That " throne " to which the Soul rises is the Supreme Knowledge, for through that alone the Self is perceived and becomes one with Itself. (The throne of Osiris is represented as resting upon Water, the symbol of Truth.)

"The foundations of man are not in matter, but in spirit. But the element of spirit is eternity."—R. W. EMERSON, *Nature*.

"And further still we climbed, in inner thought and speech, and in wonder of Thy works, and we reached to our own minds, and passed beyond them, so as to touch the realm of plenty never failing, where Thou feedest Israel for ever in the pasture of the truth, and where life is that Wisdom, by which all things are made, both those which have been, and those which shall be ; and Itself is not made, but is now as it was and ever shall be ; or rather in it is neither ' hath been ' nor ' shall be,' but only ' is,' since It is eternal."—AUGUSTINE, *Confessions*, Book IX. Ch. 10.

See DHARMA, OSIRIS, WATER, WISDOM.

PRAISE OF GOD :—

A symbol of the soul's conforming to the higher laws of its being in furthering its own evolution and emancipating the indwelling Self.

"Let heaven and earth praise him ; the seas, and everything that moveth therein. For God will save Zion, and build the cities of Judah ; and they shall abide there, and have it in posses-sion."—Ps. lxix. 34, 35.

The higher and lower natures in the soul must conform to the Divine laws of evolution and progress. The desire- and sense-natures (the seas), and all the lower energies, must take their part in the Divine scheme of salvation. Then shall the causal-body (Zion) be perfected, and centres be formed on the buddhic plane ; and the transmuted qualities shall abide there and be in possession of Truth, Wisdom, and Love.

"To thee (Indra) the splendid, we will sing praises, O bountiful One ! Thus praised do thou now issue forth, with well-filled car, agreeably to our desire ! yoke, then, thy pair of bay steeds, O Indra ! "—*Sata. Brâh.*, II. 6, 1, 38.

The higher qualities conform to the Divine nature, which is ready to bless ; and the conditions being favourable, the Higher Self is enabled to further the evolution of the causal-body (car) by means of mind and emotion (the pair of bay steeds).

See CHARIOT, EVOLUTION, HOMA-JUICE, HORSES (bay), INDRA, JUDAH, PIETY, SEA, ZION.

PRAKRITI, OR MULA-PRAKRITI, BEING THAT OUT OF WHICH EVERYTHING IN NATURE IS PRODUCED :—

A symbol of primordial Matter as emanated from the Absolute. This Divine essence differentiates into seven planes of manifestation, two of which,—the highest,—are potential, and five are actual. Spirit working into and through Matter makes matter fertile for the production of all forms and qualities on the four lower planes.

"The source of all things is the power of the divine spirit (Mâyâ), the power that is hidden beneath the things that emanate out of it. It is the one deity that actuates and controls all those proposed principles of emanation, includ-ing time and the personal soul."—*Svetas. Upanishad*, § I. *S. B. of E.*

"Mâyâ, or Prakriti, a birthless beginning that gives birth to all things. . . . Prakriti is Mâyâ, and Mahesvara is the Mâyin or arch-illusionist. All this shifting world is filled with portions of him."—*Ibid.*

"The root and substance of all things (except soul, Purusha) is Prakriti. It is no production. Seven things produced by it are also producers. Thence come sixteen productions. Soul, the twenty-fifth essence, is neither a production nor producer." — MON. WILLIAMS, *Indian Wisdom*, p. 92.

Much preparation is needed before the Self or Soul can enter the World-process. States of being produce other states following, and many states are begun and ended before the lower nature is in a condition capable of bearing the Divine Child,—the God within. The Self is not a product, but is the eternal Spirit, and comes to be the ruler and organiser of the entire nature.

"By various means Prakriti endowed with qualities, acting as a benefactress, accomplishes without profit to herself the purpose of soul, who is devoid of qualities, and makes no return of benefit."—*San-khya-karika*, 59, 60.

The soul being essentially Spirit,— eternal, unchangeable,—is regarded as "witness, solitary, bystander, spectator, and passive" (*ibid.*, 19), before whom the qualities of matter (prakriti) are displayed.

"Prakriti, the principle of emanation, unconscious as it is, acts with a view to the liberation of Purushas or Selves. . . . Prior to a fresh creation, or palingenesia of the world, there is no misery, as the migrating souls have neither bodies, senses, nor environments."— A. E. GOUGH, *Phil. of Upanishads*, p. 205.

"The Sâmkhya philosopher makes Prakriti, under the eye of a Purusha (Self), develop into Buddhi."—MAX MÜLLER, *The Six Systems*, p. 371.

See AKASA, BINAH, BUDDHI, CHARIOT, COW-MEHURT, EVOLUTION, HETHRA, ILLUSION, INVOLUTION, MATTER, MÂYÂ, MOTHER, MULA-PRAKRITI, PLANES, PURUSHA, SELF, SPIRIT, WOMB.

PRALAYA, OR NIGHT :—

A symbol of a state of cosmic inactivity, when the Divine Life is indrawn from the manifest and all things have disappeared for a period.

"The days and Nights of Brahmâ. This is the name given to the periods called Manvantara and Pralaya or Dissolution; one referring to the Active Periods of the Universe; the other to its times of relative and complete Rest, whether they occur at the end of a Day, or an Age, or Life, of Brahmâ."

"The essence of Darkness being Absolute Light, Darkness is taken as the appropriate allegorical representation of the condition of the Universe during Pralaya, or the term of Absolute Rest, or Non-being, as it appears to our finite minds."

"Nature runs down and disappears from the objective plane, only to re-emerge, after a time of rest, out of the subjective, and to re-ascend once more. Our Kosmos and Nature will run down only to re-appear on a more perfect plane after every Pralaya."—BLAVATSKY, *Secret Doctrine*, Vol. I. pp. 98, 173, 395.

See BREATH (divine), DARKNESS, DAY, DAYS, HOUSE TO SLEEP IN, MANVANTARA, NIGHT, NIRVANA, NOX, PLANETARY CHAIN, PRANA, REGNAROK, RENOVATION, SABBATH, SATURDAY, SUMMER, TIME, WINTER.

PRÂNA (BREATH OR LIFE) :—

A symbol of the Higher Self or Divine Life in all things.

"In the Upanishads we frequently meet with the explanation that Brahman, whose nature it is sought to ascertain, is the prâna, the breath of life that pervades both the universe and the human body."—DEUSSEN, *Phil. of Upanishads*, p. 110.

"When a man sleeps, his speech, eye, manas, and ear enter into the prâna; and when he awakes, from the prâna they are reborn. Thus far in relation to the self. Next in relation to the gods. In truth, Agni is that which this speech is here, yonder Aditya is this eye, yonder moon this manas, and the heavenly regions this ear. But yonder vâyu (wind), which purifies there as it blows, is this prâna (breath). When now the fire (agni) is extinguished, it is blown out in the wind. And when the sun (âditya) sets, it enters into the wind; and similarly the moon and the heavenly regions are dependent on the wind; and from the wind they are reborn. He, therefore, who departs from this world knowing this, enters with his speech into the fire, with his eye into the sun, with his manas into the moon, with his ear into the heavenly regions, with his prâna into vâyu; for from them he has arisen, and from these divinities, whom he ever loves, united to them he finds rest."—*Sata. Brâh.*, X. 3, 3, 5–8.

This is an explanation of the correspondences of manifestation of the individual ego, the higher qualities, and the Higher Self.

When an ego indraws his life forces, then his outward mental expresssion or action (speech), his perceptive ability or consciousness, (eye), his mental faculty (manas), and his receptive capacity or intuition (ear), are withdrawn into the Divine Life (prâna); and when subsequently he outpours his life forces (awakes), then from latency in the Divine Life these qualities reappear in actuality. This is in relation to the individual ego manifesting in the lower nature. Next in relation to the higher qualities (gods) on higher planes. The life force of the Self (Agni) is, in truth, his action or mental expression; the ray of the Self (Aditya), the consciousness or perceptive ability; the intuition, the mental faculty; and the buddhic nature the receptive capacity. But the spiritual energy (vâyu), which purifies the qualities as it manifests in them, is the same Divine Life as through all. When now the life force (agni) subsides outwardly, it is absorbed into the indrawing Spirit. And when the Self (sun) withdraws (sets) from manifestation, it also is absorbed into the unmanifest. And in like manner the higher planes are absorbed, to reappear subsequently.

The spiritual ego, who is liberated from the lower nature, thereby knows the truth and advances to higher states of consciousness; his mental expression is spiritualised, his perceptive ability merges in the Self; his mental ability becomes intuition, his receptive capacity wisdom, and his soul-life (prâna) the life and love of the Spirit. For from the higher qualities he has arisen, and to them, whom he ever loves, he returns for reunion with them in immortal bliss.

"To our instructed hopes there is a certain future on which we can build, far more glorious, far more beautiful, than anything in the past. 'We *know* that when He shall appear, we shall be like Him.' We have a future which is an object, not of dim expectation and trembling hope, but of knowledge. Our word is not 'it may be,' but 'it will be.' We have a certainty. Hope is truer than history."—A. MACLAREN, *Sermons, 2nd Series*, p. 46.

"Can it really be true that God not merely indwells man but is the very basis of his being, in such a way that to arrive at what one fundamentally *is* is to come upon the eternally perfect and divine ? This is a solemn thing to say, and traditional Christianity shrinks from affirming it. But I ask again, is it true ? For if it be true, its realisation is of far more importance to the future of mankind than any of the ephemeral questions of the hour with which we are busying ourselves so greatly ; indeed, without the one how can we rightly understand the other ? Yes, it is true, gloriously true, sweetly true, consolingly true, redeemingly true. God is our life, and apart from God there is no man. Within us all, the very centre and core of our being, is a reality which is older than creation itself, for it has never had any beginning at all, and will never have an end. That is the true you, the true me, the true self in everybody, the universal life individualised in human souls."—R. J. CAMPBELL, Serm., *God's Life in Man*.

See ADITYA, AGNI, AIR, AMITAUGAS, ATOMS (perm.), BREATH (divine), EAR, EYE, GODS, FIRE, LIBERATION, MANAS, MOON, PRALAYA, SPEECH, SUN, TRANSMUTATION, VAYU.

PRANAS, FIVE LIFE-BREATHS :—

Symbolic of five energies of conscious life in the soul, both higher and lower.

"These fires of prâna, which are on the watch in sleep, are themselves five in number, viz. *prâna, apâna, vyâna, samâna, udâna*, and they are mentioned together both earlier and later numberless times, and employed in the most varied allegories, without its being possible to obtain a clear and consistent explanation of them."—DEUSSEN, *Phil. of Upanishads*, p. 275.

"The prâna makes its exit upwards, the apâna downwards, and carries off the excrements."—*Ibid.*, p. 279.

The *prâna* signifies the Divine life which flows upwards or inwards. The *apâna*, the "wind of digestion" and having an "evil odour," signifies the lower life of desire which flows downwards or outwards. "The *prâna* dwells in the heart, the *apâna* in the bowels."—*Ibid.*

"Vyâna, 'interspiration,' is 'the bond between prâna and apâna.' The conception of it is accommodated to that of apâna. . . . Samâna, 'all-breathing,' bears the name because it 'leads to union.' . . . Udâna, or 'up-breathing,' conducts the soul from the body at death, while already in deep sleep it guides to Brahman."—*Ibid.*, p. 280.

Vyâna is the life of the lower emotions, which is modifiable by both the higher and the lower energies. *Samâna* is the life of the higher emotions, it " assimilates the food " and " dwells white as milk in the navel," —that is, the higher emotions give sustenance to the causal-body, and purify the lower nature. *Udâna* is the life of aspiration, which leads the ego upward from its submersion in the lower nature, and raises it to union with the Higher Self.

The five life energies of the soul are said to be " organs of nutrition," for they serve to give sustenance to the causal-body (manas), which grows from latency to actuality in the many human souls. The causal-body is potentially perfect, but in each human being it is actually defective and incomplete, and having to be nourished or built up by means of the life processes on the lower planes.

See AIR, BREATH, CAUSAL-BODY, CHARIOT, FOOD FOR SOUL, HEART, HIGHER AND LOWER NATURES, LAZARUS, LINGAM, MILK, NAVEL, SAHU, SENSE ORGANS, UNION, VISCERA, VITAL AIRS.

PRAYER :—

A symbol of aspiration. The supplication of the lower for spiritual advancement.

" For everyone that asketh receiveth ; and he that seeketh findeth ; and to him that knocketh it shall be opened." —LUKE xi. 10.

Every spiritual appeal from the lower self meets with a response from the Higher. The application of this supreme law is universal. The aspiration from the lower causes the higher vibrations, or response from above, to be received by the lower.

" *Aspiration* is an element in all true prayer. It is the desire to rise above the limitations of our imperfect nature, and to enter into communion with that larger life of which by our very constitution we are dimly conscious. . . . To seek God is to seek goodness, that ever-expanding ideal which recedes as we approach it, but which is ever within us. . . . Prayer is illuminating and educative. It brings man into the current of God's purposes. It is the means whereby he ascends to a higher knowledge of the mode in which God works." —R. J. CAMPBELL, *A Faith for To-day*, pp. 314, 315, 322.

" God dispenses the Holy Spirit by fixed laws. Prayer also is heard by laws as definite as the laws of equilibrium in forces. And what is called the doctrine of the Spirit and the doctrine of prayer, as given in the Scriptures, is, in fact, nothing more nor less than the unfolding to us, if we could so regard it, of the laws of the Spirit and the laws of prayer, as pertaining to the supernatural kingdom of God. . . . These two great powers, the hearing of prayer and the dispensing of the Spirit, are like the waterfalls and winds of nature, to which we set our wheels and lift our sails, and so by their known laws take advantage of their efficacy. A crystal or gem that is being distilled and shaped in the secret depths of the world is shaped by laws not as well understood as the law of the Spirit of life when it moulds the secret order and beauty of a soul."—H. BUSHNELL, *Nature and the Supernatural*, p. 186.

" Every impulse after good, every thought in which we forget ourselves, every action in which we sacrifice ourselves, is an influx of the Divine Spirit into our spirits."—W. S. LILLY, *The Great Enigma*, p. 307.

" All we can ever need or desire is already present in God's loving purpose for our good, and only waits to be claimed ; but it must be claimed, for that is the necessary condition by which alone the soul can grow."—R. J. CAMPBELL, Serm., *Conquering Prayer.*

See ASPIRATION, AVALOKITESVARA, BLESSING, HORSE (red), PUITIKA SEA.

PRAYERS AND OBLATIONS :—

Symbols of aspirations after ideals ; and of the acts of devotion and sacrifice which are to secure the safety of the soul.

" When ten days were fulfilled after his son's birth, with his thoughts kept under restraint, and filled with excessive joy, the king offered for his son (Buddha) most elaborate sacrifices to the gods with muttered prayers, oblations, and all kinds of auspicious ceremonies."—*Buddha-Karita*, Bk. I. 88.

The ten cycles (days) process is the elaboration of the mechanism through which the Self is to manifest in the physical, astral, and mental bodies on their respective planes.

When this process was accomplished, with His Will directed to the completion of Divine achievement and full of hope and courage, aspiration is awakened within the lower self, which is the free-will offering to the aspects of the qualities which are of the Self. The " prayers and oblations " are the ideals that are followed, and the acts of devotion to right and truth which are to make sure the salvation of the soul.

"How closely connected with whatever is lovely and of good report is this detachment from the near and the visible. A man that is living for remote objects is, in so far, a better man than one who is living for the present. He will become thereby the subject of a mental and moral discipline that will do him good. And, on the other hand, a life which has no far-off light for its guiding star has none of the unity, of the self-restraint, of the tension, of the conscious power which makes our days noble and strong. Whether he accomplish them or fail, the man who lets future objects rule present action is in advance of the other."—A. MACLAREN, *Sermons*, *2nd Series*, p. 142.

See BUDDHA, OBLATION, SACRIFICE.

PRECIOUS STONES :—

Symbols of virtues and higher qualities of the soul.

"Precious stones in the Word signify such things as are of the truth of wisdom or of the good of love."—SWEDENBORG, *Apoc. Rev.*, n. 231.

See particular stones, BREAST-PLATE, GEMS, JEWELS, NECKLACE.

PRIAM AND HIS SONS :—

A symbol of the Causal Self and its assemblage of faculties.

See CAUSAL-SELF, GREECE, ILIUM, SHIPS (Ilium), TROJANS, TROY.

PRIEST OF APOLLO (CHRYSE) :—

A symbol of the subjective spiritual mind, which is related to the intuition (Chryseis).

"Upon this, all the other Greeks shouted assent, that the priest should be reverenced, and the splendid ransoms accepted; yet was it not pleasing in his mind to Agamemnon, son of Atreus; but he dismissed him evilly, and added a harsh mandate."—*Iliad*, Bk. I.

Thereupon all the mental qualities are energised in relation to the spiritual mind, and the consent is obtained for the Ego to undertake its own evolution. The desire mind, the product of illusion, is, however, dissatisfied, and the denial of the rule of the spiritual mind is therefore brought about: the lower self, self-centred, works as from itself, henceforward, and at first treats the Higher Self as an enemy.

"To see truths from their own light is to see them from man's interior mind, which is called the spiritual mind, and this mind is opened by charity; and when it is open, light and the affection of understanding truths flow in from the Lord, which constitutes illumination."—SWEDENBORG, *Apoc. Rev.*, n. 85.

See AARON, ADVARYA, AGAMEMNON, AGNIDHRA, ATHORNE, APOLLO, CHRYSE, CHRYSEIS, HIGH PRIEST, ODYSEUS, PONTIFF, POPE, PROCESSION.

PRIEST OF THE ALTAR :—

A symbol with the same meaning as "priest of Apollo."

"I accompany thy preparation, at the beginning each time, with words of praise, O intelligent (Homa)! when he (the managing priest) takes thy twigs. I accompany thy preparation, in each successive act by which thou art killed through the strength of a man, with words of praise, O intelligent."—*Homa Yasht*.

"I, the individuality, increase as thou, the Divine Life, dost live within me." The "priest with twigs" is a symbol of the buddhic emotions, and these are interpreted through the mind. "I, the Self, celebrate thee in each successive mode of manifestation through the karmic law, and trace thee in all things up to the human in whom thou dost fulfil thyself." The "words of praise" symbolise the higher aspirations which live and carry on the evolution. The "killing" refers to the sacrifice of the Logos in the Archetypal Man, on the one hand, and the defeat of the lower nature in man, on the other.

"The Advarya (priest) is the mind, and the Hotri (priest) is speech."—*Sata. Brâh.*, I. 5, 1, 21.

"By priests in the Word are meant they who are in the truth of love."—SWEDENBORG, *Apoc. Rev.*, n. 854.

See ADVARYA, AGNIDHRA, ALTAR (fire), BARSOM, FIRE PRIESTS, HIGH PRIEST, HOTRI.

PRIEST, OR SOOTHSAYER :—

A symbol of tradition, current opinion, or literalism.

See ANNAS, CAIAPHAS.

PRIESTS AND ELDERS :—

Symbolic of conventional ideas and empty religious notions, which distinguish sectarian systems.

"Now the chief priests and the whole council sought false witness against Jesus, that they might put him to death."—MAT. xxvi. 59.

The " chief priests, etc." may stand for the " higher criticism " empty of Divine inspiration ; and also respectively for the mouthpiece of a " creed outworn," and for its stereotyped, antiquated presentation. These mental states ignorantly seek for the living spirit among the dead forms of past history and present conventions ; and these always attempt to put to death the object of their professed veneration. The " false witnesses " are the misinterpreted truths hidden under the letter : that is, they are the false notions which an exegesis of external illusions generates.

" Educated Christians know that ' inspiration ' is no longer allowed by scholars any influence on interpretation. It cannot establish the truthfulness of any statement against the verdict of historical critics. . . . The modern Christian student ignores both inspiration and canonicity."—H. HENSLEY HENSON, *Value of the Bible*, pp. 26, 27.

" The science of Christian Apologetics has grown to enormous dimensions, its convincingness inversely proportional to its mass."—" Credo," *Hibbert Journal*, April, 1909.

" Religion is never intolerant, only the systems of religion ; it is love of system that rejects what is foreign to the system, while religion, on the contrary, abhors a bald uniformity, which would destroy her divine influence. It is only the adherents of the dead letter which religion rejects, who have filled the world with the clamour and uproar of religious controversies ; the true contemplators of the Eternal were ever quiet souls, either alone with themselves and the Eternal, or, if they looked about them, conceding willingly to every one the kind of religion he chose " (F. D. E. Schleiermacher).—PFLEIDERER, *Phil. of Religion*, Vol. I. p. 311.

See ANNAS, ASSEMBLY, CAIAPHAS, CALF (molten), CHILDREN OF JERUSALEM, CONVERSION OF PAUL, FOOLS, HIGH PRIEST (lower), IDOL PRIEST, INSPIRATION, NINIGI, PHARISEES, PILATE, RELIGION, RITES, SCRIPTURES, TRADITION, TRIAL OF JESUS, WITNESSES (false).

PRINCES OF THE GREEKS :—

A symbol of the higher qualities of the mind.

See GREEKS (great-hearted).

PRISONERS OR CAPTIVES :—

Symbolic of the spiritual egos confined to the lower planes, and held in fetters of the lower desires and the attractions of the objects of sense.

" That thou mayest say to the prisoners, Go forth ; to them that sit in darkness, Shew yourselves. They shall feed in the ways, and their pastures shall be in all high places."—ISA. xlix. 9.

The indwelling Self is to be the means whereby the egos are to be liberated from ignorance and illusion, and express their spiritual nature. They are to be sustained in their paths to perfection, and their means of growth are provided for them on the higher planes.

" The only freedom we possess is like that of a bird in a cage : we can choose between the higher and the lower standing ground, a choice called for by the very fact that we are in prison ; but we cannot chose where the cage shall go."—R. J. CAMPBELL, *The New Theology*, p. 39

" ' Am I a sea or a whale, that thou hast compassed me about with a prison ? ' (JOB vii. 12). Man is ' compassed about with a prison ' in that he very often both strives to mount on high by the strides of virtuous attainments, and yet is impeded by the corruption of his fleshly part. Of which same the Psalmist rightly prays that he might be divested, saying, ' Bring my soul out of prison, that I may praise Thy name ' (Ps. cxlii. 7). But what have we set forth by the designation of ' the sea ' saving the hearts of carnal men tossed with swelling thoughts ? and what by the name of ' a whale ' except our old enemy ? who, when in taking possession of the hearts of the children of this world he makes his way into them,—does in a certain sort swim about in their slippery thoughts. But the ' whale ' is made fast in prison in that the evil spirit, being cast down below, is kept under by the weight of his own punishment."—GREGORY THE GREAT, *Morals on the Book of Job*, Vol. I. pp. 444–5.

See BONDAGE, CAPTIVITY, DARKNESS, EXODUS, FETTERS, HOUSE OF BONDAGE, LIBERATION, PASTURES, PURGATORY, SEA, SONS OF GOD, STRIDES OF SOUL, SUFFERING, WHALES.

PRITHA'S BIRTH FROM THE HAND :—

A symbol of the production of the emotion-nature from the activities of the kama-manasic nature.

See BHIMA, CUPID, KARNA, POURUSHASPA, YUDHI.

PRIZE OF HONOUR GAINED :—

A symbol of credit taken to itself by the lower egoism for having made an effort to surrender itself to the higher nature ; pride being the motive at this stage.

" Only make ye me ready a prize of honour forthwith, lest I alone of all the Argives be disprized, which thing beseemeth not ; for ye all behold how my prize is departing from me (i.e. Agamemnon)."—*Iliad*, Bk. I.

This vanity in seeking for honour signifies the growth of the egoistic feeling as the lower emotions increase in intensity. As this takes place the Desire-mind realises how its captive, the Intuition of truth (Chryseis), is destined gradually to recover its liberty and manifest in the soul.

See ACHILLES, AGAMEMNON, ARGIVES, CHRYSEIS, INTUITION, KLYTEMNESTRA.

PROCESSION OF THE EUCHARIST :—

A symbol of the process of salvation, i.e. the descent of the Higher Self into the lower nature, and its ascent therefrom in the souls of humanity.

The Divine Sacrifice or Victim (host), from his exalted place on the highest plane (high altar), descends as the real presence (wafer) in the Sun of righteousness (monstrance), into the lower nature of the soul (nave). This descent is beautifully symbolised in the procession of the mass from the high altar. The spiritual mind (chief priest) holds to his " heart " the Divine Presence (sacred element) in the shadow of the higher nature (canopy). The higher qualities (priests and acolytes), surround the Incarnate Christ (host) in the descent of the Spirit into matter (involution). At the lowest point on the physical plane (farthest from altar) the descent ends, and the ascent commences in the return of the soul to God, until finally Christ, with his perfected saints, ascend to the higher planes (altar) in glory and power, and the process of salvation is fulfilled in evolution.

Every detail of the ceremony is wonderfully true in its inner meaning. The vestments of the priests signify the higher virtues—the robes of truth, beauty and goodness, and the white garments of purity. The two swinging censers facing the priests signify the Wisdom and Love ever purifying the qualities in the soul's long pilgrimage. The lighted candles held by the acolytes are symbolic of the light of truth illuminating men's minds. The canopy with four supports indicates the obscuration of Spirit in the lower nature, or underworld. The congregation of worshippers are the lower mental qualities reverencing the higher, and turning away from darkness to the adoration of the Light, while the music they hear is a symbol of the harmony that attends the exercise of the higher qualities in the region of the blest.

" ' The spirit shall return to God who gave it.' Let us suppose a procession, say, on Ascension Day. It leaves the High Altar, goes round the great church, or perhaps, in some favoured place, leaves the church and goes through the streets of the town, re-enters the church and returns to the Altar again. ' I came forth from the Father, and am come into the world : again, I leave the world and go to the Father.' "—R. L. G. in *The Nation*, July 31, 1920.

See AFU-RĀ, ALTAR, APOLLO, BREAD, CABIN, CANDLES, CANDLESTICKS, CANOPY, CENSERS, EVOLUTION, FIRE, FOOD (God), HARMONY, HEART, HOST, HYMN SINGING, INCARNATION, INCENSE, INVOLUTION, LIGHT, MUSIC, PEOPLE, PILLARS (four), PRIEST, RITUAL, ROBE, SACRAMENT, SACRIFICER, SAINTS, SALVATION, STRIDES OF SOUL, SUN.

PRODIGAL SON, PARABLE :—

A symbol of the evolution of the soul in its emotion-nature (younger son) and its mental-nature (elder son).

" A certain man had two sons : and the younger of them said to his father, Father, give me the portion of thy substance that falleth to me. And he divided unto them his living. And not many days after the younger son gathered all together, and took his journey into a far country ; and there he wasted his substance with riotous living."—LUKE xv. 11–33.

The Father in heaven had two evolving attributes on the higher planes,—mind and emotion. Unto each of these he apportions his substance; that is, he endows them with that wherewith each shall accomplish its work of self-development on the respective planes on which they function. The endowment of the "younger son" having been effected, shortly afterwards the evolution of the emotions commenced. The soul descended to the lower planes, wherein it seemed to the ego he was divided from the parental influence, but which really was yet at work unseen above him. The "riotous living" means simply complete absorption in worldly affairs and the things of desire and the senses. The parable proceeds to show how the emotion-nature blindly gains experience leading to dissatisfaction and a yearning for that which is higher. The soul then turns to go towards its eternal home, and the Father responds with blessing. The mind is then stirred to progress, and finally both the mind and emotions are merged in the Divine.

See Arc. man, Calf, Conviction of sin, Dances, Home, Husks, Music and dancing, Parable.

PROMETHEUS :—

A symbol of the individuality seated in the causal-body on the plane of the higher mind (forethought).

"Prometheus, with a view of deceiving Zeus, cut up a bull, and divided it into two parts : he wrapped up the best parts and the intestines in the skin, and at the top he placed the stomach, which is one of the worst parts ; while the second heap consisted of the bones covered with fat. When Zeus pointed out to him how badly he had made the division, Prometheus desired him to choose, but Zeus, in his anger, seeing through the stratagem of Prometheus, chose the heap of bones covered with the fat."—*Smith's Class. Dict.*

The higher mind, or individuality, in view of the descent of the ego to the illusions of the lower planes, is the means of dividing the archetypal matrix of qualities and forms (the bull) into lower and higher natures in the soul. The lower, or astromental-desire (flesh) nature is wrapped in the physical (skin), and is distinguished by the appetites (stomach). The higher nature consists of the

foundation of the consciousness (bones) and the affections (fat). It is the higher nature that is acceptable to the Self (Zeus).

"The father of the gods avenged himself by withholding fire from mortals, but Prometheus stole it in a hollow tube. Zeus thereupon chained Prometheus to a pillar, where an eagle consumed in the daytime his liver, which was restored in each succeeding night. Prometheus was thus exposed to perpetual torture ; but Hercules killed the eagle and delivered the sufferer, with the consent of Zeus, who in this way had an opportunity of allowing his son to gain immortal fame."—*Ibid.*

Meanwhile the Divine Will has not yet aroused a spiritual influence within the human mind, but the individuality now being evolved attracts the Divine Spark (fire) from above to the nascent causal-body by means of the Divine Ray or "Sutratma" (tube). Through the acquisition of the Spark of the Divine Fire (atma-buddhi) the individuality becomes bound by its emanating personalities to the pillar (or mountain) of aspiration.

"For Hesiod said that the *outer man* was the 'bond' by which Zeus bound Prometheus (Theogony, 614)."—Zosimus, *Fragments,* 14.

The "eagle" represents the Spirit (buddhi) which during each incarnation (daytime) consumes, through suffering and sorrow, a little of the lower nature (liver-flesh), which as a whole is restored for the next earthlife. And in this manner the purification of the soul proceeds, until at the end of the cycle perfection is attained, and the Divine Law (Hercules) puts an end to the buddhic function (eagle) as no lower nature remains. Then it is that the soul rises to the higher planes and becomes one with the "son of God" in the life everlasting.

"By the transference of the vitalising Fire from the 'heaven' to the 'earth' of the human system, the lower nature is inflamed and set at war with the Divine Spirit or 'Zeus' within the man. This act is the Promethean Theft, punished so terribly by the 'Father' at the hand of Hermes, the true Thought, or Angel of Understanding. For by this act man becomes bound and fettered to the things of sense, the victim of a perverse will, which, as an insatiable bird of prey, continually rends and devours him. Thus is formulated that condition which Paul so graphically laments :— ' I find then the law, that, to me who would do good, evil is present, etc ' " (ROM. vii. 21–5).—*The Perfect Way*, pp. 157–8.

"In the Gathas, the 'two lives' are distinguished as *astvat*, 'bodily,' or *parâhu*, 'prior life,' and as *manahya*, 'mental' or *daibitya*, 'the second.' Their meaning is clear enough, and requires no further comment ; they express our idea 'body and soul.' To be distinguished from these 'two lives,' are the 'first' and the 'last' lives, which mean this life and that hereafter."—M. HAUG, *Essays on Rel. of Parsis*, p. 310.

Prometheus is said to mean "forethought," which corresponds with "second life." His brother Epimetheus denotes "afterthought," which corresponds with "first life." The "first life" is of the personality, mortal ; the "second life" is of the individuality, immortal. The personality and the individuality are often symbolised as brothers, e.g. Castor and Pollux, the Dioscuri.

"Christ is the Lord of the Spirit. He is come to scatter that fire on the earth. He brings the ruddy gift from heaven to mortals, carrying it in the bruised reed of His humanity ; and in pursuance of His merciful design, He is bound and suffers for our sakes, but, loosed at last from the bands by which it was not possible that He should be holden, and ' being by the right hand of God exalted, He hath shed forth this.' His mighty work opens the way for the life-giving power of the Spirit to dwell as an habitual principle, and not as a mere occasional gift, among men, sanctifying their characters from the foundation, and not merely, as of old, bestowing special powers for special functions."—A MACLAREN, *Sermons, 2nd Series*, p. 234.

See BONES, BULL, CAUSAL-BODY, COLUMN, DAY AND NIGHT, DIOSCURI, EAGLE, EPIMETHEUS, FAT, FIRE, FLESH, GOSHURUN, HERCULES, HIGHER AND LOWER NATURES, HOM (stem), INCARNATION, INDIVIDUALITY, LIVER, MOUNTAIN, PANDORA, PERSONALITY, SKIN, SPARK, STOMACH, SUTRATMA, VISCERA, VITAL AIRS, ZEUS.

PROMISES OF GOD :—

A symbol of the measures taken in the Divine scheme for the raising of the qualities and souls in response to their aspirations, so that when they are perfected they may have

eternal life. The raising of the qualities is through the "Holy Spirit of promise," that is, through the functioning of buddhi.—*See* EPH. i. 13, 14 ; ROM. iv. 13–16 ; HEB. vi. 12–17 ; 2 PETER i. 3, 4.

See BLASPHEMY, BLESSING, HOLY GHOST, TRANSMUTATION.

PROPHECY :—

This signifies the faculty of spiritual discernment which is derived by intuition from buddhi, which gives utterance to the truth of hidden things. It is an exercise of the intuition respecting the evolution of the higher qualities in the soul.

See BUDDHI, FAITH (miracles), INTUITION, QUALITIES.

PROPHET :—

A symbol of a dawning of higher consciousness, and a recognition of reality. An intuition within the mind which foresees coming outpourings of spiritual faculty and increased perception of truth.

"And they glorified God, saying, a great prophet is arisen among us : and God hath visited his people."—LUKE vii. 16.

This refers to the perfecting of the qualities and their recognition of the higher state of consciousness which Christ brings to the soul.

"By a prophet is understood truth of doctrine. . . . By prophet is meant doctrine of the church derived from the Word."—SWEDENBORG, *Apoc. Rev.*, n. 3, 7.

See CHILDREN OF JERUSALEM, ELIJAH, JOHN BAPTIST.

PROPHETIC DREAMS :—

A dream is prophetic when the dreamer is able to become not only fully conscious upon superior levels, but when he is able to transmit his experiences thereon to his brain and waking consciousness. The consciousness in deep sleep may rise to the planes of causation and almost beyond them, and unaffected by either cause or effect,— karma. But the below can never contain the above, and we cannot see things of the future in their true aspect until they are things of the past.

See RECOLLECTION.

PROPHETS, FALSE :—

A symbol of states of mind which regard outer events and personalities of time past or to come, as sources of soul-growth and salvation.

"And many false prophets shall arise and lead many astray. And because iniquity shall be multiplied, the love of the many shall wax cold."—MAT. xxiv. 11, 12.

The "false prophets" signify those minds which point others to particular persons, and times, and localities as sources of salvation, and thereby deceive and mislead many. As soon as erroneous religious notions abound, and these signs of spiritual inertness creep into the soul, the love of the higher, or the unifying principle, is lost to the qualities.

"Ye observe days and months, and seasons and years. I am afraid of you, lest by any means I have bestowed labour upon you in vain."—GAL. iv. 10, 11.

See CALAMITIES, COLD AND HEAT, ENDURING, IDOLATRY, IDOLS, PRIESTS AND ELDERS, RITES, TRADITION.

PROPONTIS (SEA OF MARMORA) :—

A symbol of the astral plane.
See SEA, WATER (lower).

PROSPERITY AND EARTH ARE THE WESTERN FEET OF BRĀHMA'S THRONE :—

This symbolises the sublimated lower self, or "natural man," through which the Higher Ego has attained its final liberation. Although this condition is "unreal," yet it has been absorbed into the Self; for the germ of this state exists and will persist through eternity; it is transformed, but is still visible to the Self,—though now seen to be derived of It. Nothing in manifestation, or experience, is ever lost: there is an atom or centre on each plane which, when communicated with, will respond to vibrations which answer to the varied aspects of the Self.

See AMITAUGAS, ATOMS, ATOMS (permanent), BRAHMA, GOLD (spot), MAN (natural), MONAD OF LIFE, PILLOW.

PROTOTYPES, FIXED :—

A symbol of the spiritual monads on the plane of atma.

"The first of these five planes is called the 'Plane of the Absolutely Invisible' or the 'Plane of the Nebulosity,' and

its world is the 'World of the Fixed Prototypes.' " "The Sufis Doctrine of the Soul."—GIBB, *Hist. of Ottoman Poetry*, Vol. I. p. 55.

The highest of the five planes of manifestation is the plane of atma, the abode of the Higher Self and of the Divine "sparks" or monads of life and form which are the prototypes of all things which appear on the planes below.

"All that which is on the earth, is also found above (in perfect prototype)" (*Sepher Shephathal*). — MYER, *Qabbalah*, p. 109.

"When man has moved out of himself away to God, like the image to its Prototype, he has reached his journey's end." —PLOTINUS, *Enneads*, V. Bk. I.

"(According to Erigena) there is a divine 'procession' by which God reveals Himself in an unfolding universe. He cannot be 'seen' in Himself; He can be 'seen' in His creation. The second of the four 'divisions'—that which is created and creates—is the immaterial world of Ideas, of prototypes. These perfect patterns of things have their origin in God, they are His thoughts. 'God' so Erigena says, 'does not know things because they are—they *are because He knows* (*i.e.* thinks) them.' That which is *real* in any object, what is called the *essence* of the object, is the Divine Idea which the object manifests, and this Idea, or pattern, *creates* the object, so that our visible world is all only a 'copy' of a perfect Divine pattern. These patterns are themselves dynamic —they are Divine *wills*, as well as Divine thoughts; that is to say, when God thinks, things are."—R. M. JONES, *Mystical Religion*, p. 125.

"The Hervey islanders speak of the things of this world as a 'gross copy of what exists in spirit-land,' and of the soul as 'an airy but visible copy of the man.' "—A. E. CRAWLEY, *The Idea of the Soul*, p. 195.

See ARC. MAN, ATMA, ATZEELATIC, BUDDHIC PLANE, COLOUR, COSMOS, CREATION, GERMS, GODDESS, GODS, HIGHER AND LOWER WORLDS, IMAGE, MONAD OF LIFE, SIMILITUDES, SPARK, SPERMATIC WORDS, TYPE, WORLDS (five).

PROVINCE-RULER :—

A symbol of the higher emotion-nature operating from the causal-body and ruling the soul through feelings of truth, justice, benevolence, faith, hope, and wide love of humanity.

"That which is in the Vohu-khshathra Gatha the province rulers should carry on."—*Shayast La-Shayast*, XIII.

That which is in the operations of the causal-body is due to the activities of the higher emotions in the higher mind.

See CAUSAL-BODY, QUALITIES, RULERS (world).

PSYCHE :—

See CUPID.

PTAH :—

A symbol of the Divine Mind,— the Logos energising as the creative power on the higher mental plane.

"Ptah was one of the most active of the three great gods who carried out the commands of Thoth, who gave expression in words to the will of the primeval creative Power ; he was self-created, and was a form of the Sun-god Rā as the 'Opener' of the day. From certain allusions in the Book of the Dead he is known to have 'opened the mouth' of the gods. His feminine counterpart was the goddess Sekhet."— BUDGE, *Egyptian Ideas, etc.*, p. 98.

"Ptah bore the titles,—'Father of the mighty fathers (the other gods), father of the beginnings, he who created the sun egg and the moon egg.' . . . He is also called the 'creator of his own image, he who created himself, who establishes truth, king of both lands, lord of heaven,' etc."—WIEDEMANN, *Rel. of Anc. Egyptians*, pp. 132-3.

The Divine Mind or Self manifesting on the mental plane becomes the progenitor of higher and lower conditions inclusive of the individuality (sun-egg) and the personality (moon-egg). He creates his own image— the Archetypal Man, and rules the higher and the lower planes (both lands). The Self is allied with the buddhic principle (goddess Sekhet).

See ARC. MAN, BUDDHI, CREATION, EGYPT, GODS, HEPHAISTOS, IMAGE, MOON, MOUTH (opening), RĀ, SELF (supreme), SUN, TEM, THOTH.

PUITIKA SEA :—

A symbol of the soul's experience of the lower nature, which in going through it, eventually proves the truth of that which is above.

"The sea Puitika, whose waters are purified before going back to their heavenly seat—the sea Vouru-kasha, the waters above (Mount) Alborj."— *Vendidad*, V.

The "sea Puitika" is a symbol of experience by which the soul learns truth, and which ultimately through purification in the higher mind proves to the soul the truth underlying existence, thereby passing into the ocean of Reality (Vouru-kasha) above the mount of aspiration (Alborj).

"As the air is the element in which man moves, and yet again the element of life which is present within the man : so the Pneuma-Christ is for St. Paul both the Ocean of the Divine Being, into which the Christian, since his reception of the Spirit, is plunged," and in which he disports himself, "and a stream which, derived from that Ocean, is specially introduced within his individual life."—H. J. HOLTZMANN, *Lehrbuch, etc.*, Vol. II. p. 79.

See ALBORDJ, EXPERIENCE, OCEAN, PRAYER, RIVER, TISTRYA, VOURU-KASHA, WATER.

PUNGA, THE SHARK :—

A symbol of the soul.

"But before Tangaroa fled, his children consulted together how they might secure their safety, for Tangaroa had begotten Punga, and he had begotten two children, Ika-tere, the father of fish, and Tute-wehiwehi, the father of reptiles."—G. GREY, *Polynesian Mythology*.

But before the obscuration of Spirit, the Logos (Tangaroa) had brought the soul (Punga) into active being. The soul was endowed with two capacities for development ; one springing from above,—the capacity (Ika-tere) for aspiration (fish), and the other rising by reflection from below, the capacity for desire (reptiles). These capacities became operants in the evolution of the soul.

See DOLPHIN, FISH, IKA-TERE, JESUS (fish), RANGI, SOUL (middle), TANGAROA, TUTE.

PURGATORY :—

Symbolic of a state of the soul, incarnate or discarnate, in which purification is brought about by the functioning of buddhi (fire), through experiences of suffering and sorrow.

"Among the Greek Fathers, Clement of Alexandria tells us that 'the Fire' of Purgatory 'is a rational,' spiritual, 'fire that penetrates the soul' ; and Origen teaches that 'each sinner himself lights the flame of his own fire, and is not thrown into a fire that has been lit before that moment and that exists in front of him. His conscience is agitated and pierced by its own pricks.'"—F. VON HUGEL, *Mystical Element*, Vol. II. p. 216.

If " Purgatory " is to be understood as a state of consciousness after the death of the body, then it means the buddhic " fire " is operating on the astral plane to purify the lower nature of its worst characteristics. Again, if " Purgatory " is a state of soul under more or less physical conditions, then it becomes a symbol of life in the physical body on earth, in which through suffering and sorrow some of its selfishness is purged away.

" Purgatory " does not seem to be a *sacred* symbol, that is, a Divinely inspired one, and in the absence of any clear idea of its exoteric meaning, little can be said about it. It does not apparently occur specifically in any sacred scripture.

"The Roman Catholic Church still teaches not only that the purgatorial fire is material, but that it is situated in the middle of the earth ; but it is certain that educated Romanists do not believe this. We cannot cast stones at them, for in our Church the teaching about the Ascension is equally chaotic. The story of a literal flight through the air is still treasured by many people, though we have all, I suppose, abandoned the idea of a geographical heaven, which alone gave to it a coherent meaning."— W. R. INGE, *Paddock Lectures*, p. 124.

"The soul, divine in its nature, a portion of the Divinity imprisoned in this house of clay is the real Self. To deliver it from the prison where it languishes, expiating the sins committed in former existences, is the one true end. And the way to attain thereto is a *Via Purgativa*, a way of purification from earthly desires " (Plotinus).—W. S. LILLY, *The Great Enigma*, p. 262.

See BAPTISM (fire), FIRE (destroying), FURNACE, GATHA (kam.), HADES, HAND OF BEAST, HELL, MAN (bad), MEADOW OF HADES, PRISONER, REINCARNATION, SI OSIRI.

PURPLE COLOUR :—

A symbol of wisdom. The colour of the buddhic vesture, the robe of glory ; also of the ram from which the " golden fleece,"—the buddhic vesture,—was taken.

"By purple and scarlet are signified celestial good and celestial truth."— SWEDENBORG, *Apoc. Rev.*, n. 773.

See COLOURS, GOLDEN FLEECE, ROBE.

PURUSHA :—

A symbol of the Divine Spirit or Self, replete with all qualities, who descends into union with Matter (prakriti) in order to reproduce himself as the Archetypal Man,— the perfect prototype and progenitor of the human race.

"Purusha, the Self, is within the midst of the body of the size of a thumb, the lord of all that has been and of all that is to be. This alone is to-day and is to-morrow. This is that."—*Katha, Upanishad*, IV.

The Self is said to be in " buddhi within the cavity of the heart," figuratively of " the size of a thumb."

"From him, called Purusha, was born Viraj, and from Viraj was Purusha produced, whom gods and holy men made their oblation. With Purusha as victim they performed a sacrifice. When they divided him, how did they cut him up ? What was his mouth ? What were his arms ? and What his thighs and feet ? The Brahman was his mouth, the kingly soldier was made his arms, the husbandman his thighs, the servile Sudra issued from his feet " (*Mundaka Upanishad*, II). —MON. WILLIAMS, *Indian Wisdom*, p. 24.

From the Supreme Spirit was produced the buddhic principle (Viraj), and from buddhi was born, in the new cycle on the buddhic plane, the Higher Self, who, in incarnating on the lower planes, became the Divine Sacrifice for humanity. The ideals of goodness, love and truth (gods and holy men) make this sacrifice to the Supreme in order that the highest qualities shall manifest in the souls of men. So it was the Archetypal Man died out of the cycle of Involution to be born in that of Evolution. Then from him and of his pattern and image was formed the human being. The expression (mouth) of his Divinity became the Individuality (Brahman) on the higher mental plane ; the active and contesting qualities (the arms) became the Personality (soldier) on the lower mental plane ; the progressive quality (the thighs) became the desire-nature (husbandman) on the astral plane ; and the foundation serving quality (feet) became the physical nature (Sudra) on the physical plane.

"Vishnu or Krishna is called Purushottama, and the name Purusha is equally given to Brahmā and Siva."— *Ibid.*, p. 101.

See ARC. MAN, ARMS, BUDDHI, CASTES, CRUCIFIXION (Gnostic, Purusha), DEATH OF OSIRIS, DISMEMBER-

MENT, EVOLUTION, FEET, GODS, HUMAN BODY, IMAGE, INCARNATION, INDIVIDUALITY, INVOLUTION, KAMA, KSHATRIYA, LIMBS, LIPS, MATTER, MĀYĀ, MEMBERS, MOTHER, MOUTH, NET (golden), PRAGÂPATI, PRAKRITI, SACRIFICER, SELF, SOMA (moon), SPIRIT, SUDRA, THIGH, VAISYA, VIRAJ, VISHNU, YMIR, ZAGREUS.

PWAN-KOO, THE DIVINE ARTIFICER :—

A symbol of the Divine Mind,— the Logos from whom all emanates.

See DESERTS, HEAVEN AND EARTH, NAVIGATION.

PYLONS (GATEWAYS) OF THE STILL HEART, THE HOUSE OF OSIRIS :—

Symbolic of the higher mental qualities energised from the buddhic plane, which raise and purify the soul, and give access to the higher planes. They are love of Truth, Wisdom, Goodness, Purity, Justice, Gentleness, Perfection, etc.

"Homage to thee saith Horus, O thou eighth pylon of the Still Heart. I have made my way. I know thee, and I know thy name. . . . 'She that belongeth to her lord; the mighty goddess, the gracious one, the lady who giveth birth to the divine form of her lord,' is thy name."—BUDGE, *Book of the Dead*, Ch. CXIV.

The adoring soul (Horus) through its intuition reveres the buddhic nature, which is the way of peace to God. Wisdom allies itself with Love, for it is through the power and grace of the buddhic function that the Divine Self is born within the soul.

See BIRTH OF HORUS, BUDDHIC PLANE, EIGHT, GATE, GATES, HEART, HORUS, HOUSE IN HEAVEN, INTUITION, ISIS, NAME, QUALITIES.

PYLUS, DIVINE, AND THE PYLIANS :—

Symbols of the higher mental plane, and the higher mental qualities.

"Therefore to them arose the sweet-voiced Nestor, . . . During his life, two generations of articulately speaking men had become extinct, who formerly were reared and lived with him in divine Pylus, but he was now ruling over the third."—*Iliad*, Bk. I.

The soul had so far developed that the lower emotions had become responsive to the charms of Faith-Hope (Nestor), and during the attractive guidance of this dual influence, the two earliest races of mankind in astral bodies approached extinction, for they could no longer proceed with their evolution on the superphysical planes. Formerly they influenced the ego on the higher mental plane (divine Pylus). Now, however, the evolution of the Third Race was being accomplished.

See ADAM (lower), ASTRAL, BEASTS (three sorts), DYNASTIES, GREECE, GOLDEN AGE, NESTOR, RACES, RAGHA, ROOT-RACES.

PYRAMID :—

A symbol of the causal-body,— the seat of the spiritual Triad, Atma-buddhi-manas,—resting upon the foundation of the four planes of the lower quaternary (four sides).

"Hail, Great Company of the Gods who are in Annu, grant that Pepi Nefer-ka-Ra may flourish, and grant that his pyramid, his everlasting building, may flourish, even as the name (*ren*) of Temu, the Governor of the Great Company of the Gods, flourisheth" (Pepi Pyramid Text).—BUDGE, *Book of the Dead*, Vol. I. p. lxiii.

The Divine attributes,—the ideals upon the higher planes (Annu),—are extolled by the ego, so that the perfected personality (Pepi) may be merged in the individuality, which is within the causal-body (his pyramid), the immortal vehicle of the soul (2 COR. v. 1). The spiritual ego claims similarity and union of nature with the Higher Self (Temu), who is exalted above all divine attributes and ideals.

"The entrance to this pyramid (of Cheops) is, as with all pyramids, on the north side."—BUDGE, *The Mummy*, p. 332.

The *north* in Egyptian and European scriptures, always stands for the lower planes, hence the soul rising from the lower nature is said to enter the causal-body (pyramid) "on the north side." The passage to the chambers of the King and Queen represents the soul's progress to the atma-buddhic heights, the state of consciousness of the Love and Wisdom of the Highest. The passage from below refers to the narrow way from earth to heaven. "Stone" is a symbol of the eternal substance Spirit, and undoubtedly the builders of the pyramids got their architectural ideas from Divinely inspired sources reverenced very deeply.

See ANNU, ATMA, BUDDHI, CAUSAL-BODY, CHURCH, COMPANY (gods), CONE, HOUSE IN HEAVEN, INDIVIDUALITY, KAABA, NAME, NORTH, PALACE, PERSONALITY, REN, SPIRIT, SQUARE, STONE, STUPA, TABERNACLE, TEM, TEMPLE, TRIAD, TRINITY, TSURAH, WITNESSES.

QAF RANGE OF MOUNTAINS :—

Symbolic of aspiration or uplifting from the desire-nature.

" The earth, which is flat, is surrounded as by an eightfold ring, by the eight mountain chains of Qaf; these alternate with the Seven Seas, the innermost Qaf being within the innermost of the seas. . . . Round the outermost Qaf, which is outside of all, is wound a great snake."—GIBB, *Hist. of Ottomon Poetry*, Vol. I. p. 38.

This means that within the lower nature (the earth) are the seven sub-planes of the astral plane (the seven seas), and the " mountain chains " represent the mentality which raises the desire-nature (the snake). The " eight-fold range of Qaf " may stand for the dual aspects of the lower quaternary.

See ASTRAL PLANE, CHURNING, EARTH, EIGHT, MOUNTAINS, NID-HOGG, SEA, SERPENT.

QAHU, CITY OF THE GODS :—

A symbol of perfection ; or of purification of the qualities on a high buddhic sub-plane.

" Hail, thou city of the gods Qahu, who take possession of Khus and gain mastery over the shades (khaibit), who devour vigorous strength and consume filth when their eyes see, and who guard not the earth."—BUDGE, *Book of the Dead*, Ch. CXLIX.

The high ideals of perfection are said to take possession of the monads of life (Khus),—the returning Egos,—and also dominate the causal-bodies (khaibit), which have overcome the lower desires through spiritual perception, and which conserve not the lower nature (earth).

See CITY OF GOD, EARTH, GODS, KHAIBIT, KHUS.

QEBHSENNUF, ONE OF THE FOUR CHILDREN OF HORUS :—

A symbol of the buddhic vehicle of the soul, the buddhic principle, or the buddhic plane.

" I am Qebh-sennuf, and I have come that I may protect Mut-hetep (the lady deceased Osiris) ; I have collected into a whole body for thee thy bones, I have gathered together for thee thy members, I have brought thy heart and I do set it upon its seat within thy body, and I make thy house to germinate after thee."—BUDGE, *Book of the Dead*, Ch. CLIA.

The buddhic principle explains the means that have been taken to raise the soul. In the perfecting of the causal-body (whole body), the spiritual foundation (bones) and all the higher qualities (members) have been brought together and the whole made complete. The Love-principle (heart) from above has been firmly seated in the causal-body, and the state of consciousness (thy house) shall be prolific of future growth.

" Qebhsennuf was hawk-headed, and represented the west, and protected the liver and the gall-bladder."—BUDGE, *Egyptian Magic*, p. 89.

The " hawk-head " is a symbol of aspiration and the higher nature. " West " signifies the buddhic plane. The lower qualities (liver, etc.) are transmuted by buddhi.

See BONES, BUDDHI, CAUSAL-BODY, CHILDREN OF HORUS, DEATH OF OSIRIS, DISMEMBERMENT, HAWK-HEADED, HEART, HOUSE, MEMBERS, OSIRIS, PRAGÂPATI (rel.), PROMETHEUS, VISCERA.

QEN-QENTET, A POOL OF SEKHET-HETEPET :—

A symbol of atma-buddhi.

" O Qen-qentet, I have entered into thee, and I have seen the Osiris (my father), and I have gazed upon my mother, and I have made love. I have caught the worms and serpents, and I am delivered."—BUDGE, *Book of the Dead*, Ch. CX. p. 334.

The Self is addressed under its aspect of wisdom. The indwelling Self has now arrived at Wisdom (buddhi). It has fulfilled its manhood (higher manas) and fathomed also the Wisdom principle, which implies that the higher and lower natures are now united. The " serpents " and " worms " signify limitation and matter,—time and space,—and these being transcended, the Self is " delivered," that is, liberated from captivity to the lower nature and raised above the conditions affecting lower plane activities.

See BONDAGE, CAPTIVITY, LIBERATION, OSIRIS, SEKHET-HETEP, SERPENT, STAR-WORMS, UNION, WISDOM.

QETETBU, OR REITERATION :—

This signifies the unwearying effort of the Higher Self to raise the lower Self.

QUADRUPED :—

A symbol of the Cosmos as an animal. The head, neck, and body signify the upper planes of atma, buddhi, and higher manas, while the four legs stand for the lower quaternary, that is, the lower manas, astral, etheric, and physical planes of manifestation. If an elephant is given as a symbol of the Cosmos, then the trunk has the same meaning as the sutratma, for through it flows the breath of life, corresponding to the Ray of life from the Supreme.

See ANIMAL, BULL (man), ELEPHANT, GRIFFIN, RAT, SPHINX, SUTRATMA.

QUAILS AS FLESH FOOD :—

A symbol of the lower desires, which bring sorrow and suffering to the soul.

" And there went forth a wind from the Lord, and brought quails from the sea."—NUM. xi. 31.

It was necessary that the lower desires should bring experience to the soul, hence the desires of the astral plane (sea) were energised for a period.

See ASTRAL, EXPERIENCE, FLESH, SEA.

QUALITIES OF THE SOUL :—

These are attributes of the soul, and not the soul itself. They are so many changing and developing modes of the soul's expression. The soul in its ultimate aspect must be conceived of as the spiritual centre of the manifested Higher Self, and to this centre and source the qualities are attached. As the consciousness of the human being resides only on the mental plane,

all the various orders of qualities appear to the personality as states of consciousness more or less fleeting. The qualities may be classified in three main orders. (1) Higher qualities (buddhi-manasic) ; (2) abstract mental qualities (manasic) ; and (3) lower qualities (kama-manasic). The higher qualities are related to the innermost spiritual nature, and are expressed in the mind as Love of Ideals of Truth, Wisdom, Goodness, Justice, Perfection, etc., and shown in Unselfishness, Gentleness, Sympathy, Compassion, Kindness, Steadfastness, Patience, Faith, Hope, Love, Reverence, etc. The abstract mental qualities are Reason, Judgment, Dispassion, Balance, Breadth, etc. The lower qualities are: (1) The higher natural, Affection, Sociability, Friendship, Generosity, Courtesy, Courage, Prudence, Fairness, Truthfulness, Simplicity, etc. ; these blend gradually into the higher qualities. (2) The lower natural, Hate, Aversion, Selfishness, Meanness, Anger, Rage, Rudeness, Cowardice, Lust, Cunning, Intemperance, Cruelty, Arrogance, Vanity, Pride, Oppression, Deceit, Revenge, Jealousy, Greed, Malice, Injustice, etc.

As these three orders of qualities are all perceived through vibrations on the mental plane, it is evident that the planes both above and below the mental are not directly cognised, and so their existence can only be inferred from the vibrations received. The astral and physical planes transmit their vibrations of emotion, desire, instinct, appetite, and sensation through a complex astral mechanism to a lower mental centre. The higher mental and buddhic planes transmit vibrations through the causal-body to the personality, and they affect its superior qualities in order to raise and transmute them. These vibrations are only perceived through the spiritual aspects of the higher qualities ; they cannot be observed by the lower consciousness (LUKE xvii. 20), except as pure impulse towards the higher nature, which endures no opposition. The vibrations from the five sense organs, transmitted through the astral mechanism to a centre of consciousness on the mental plane, acquaint the ego of the physical world. The vibrations from the desires, feelings, etc. inform the ego of the astral nature. The vibrations of thought give the ego direct acquaintance with the mental nature. The spiritual vibrations which enter the mind from within show the ego the reality of the higher nature.

The lower qualities bind the ego to the lower nature, and to attain liberation these must be raised and transmuted. There is a gradual increase of capacity,—an unfoldment, as it were, of means through which liberation is to be arrived at. The qualities, however raised or transmuted, are to be regarded as the non-ego, but only as they remain qualities—distinct and separate. As the higher qualities become more and more complete and harmonious, they lose their limitations and merge gradually into the one Ideal from which they have emanated. There is greater multiplicity among the lower qualities than among the the higher, because separateness and conflict prevail among the lower and not among the higher.

"The essential tendency of spirits is to live a mutual life, to come together in a higher common life. What the law of gravitation is for maintaining harmony in the physical world, that love is, and so it works, in the spiritual and moral world. Love is the vital force of spirits. By going out of themselves, sharing themselves, giving themselves, they realise their individuality, in the very act of entering into union with one another. The religion of the Spirit is the religion of love. As the ultimate power of moral development in the human being, the Spirit of God brings to it no constraint from without ; it determines and animates it from within, and thus maintains its life. The performance of natural duties, the regular exercise of all human faculties, the progress of culture as of righteousness, these make the perfection of the Christian life. When the Christian religion becomes an inward reality, a fact of consciousness, it is nothing other than consciousness raised to its highest power." —A. SABATIER, *The Religions of Authority and the Religion of the Spirit*, p. 282.

"We cannot describe the natural history of the soul, but we know that it is divine. I cannot tell if these wonderful qualities which house to-day in this mortal frame shall ever reassemble in equal activity in a similar frame, or whether they have before had a natural history like that of this body you see before you ; but this one thing I know, that these qualities did not now begin to exist, cannot be sick with my sickness nor buried in my grave ; but that they circulate through the universe : before the world was, they were. Nothing can bar them out, or shut them in, but they penetrate the ocean and land, space and time, form and essence, and hold the key to universal nature."—EMERSON, *The Method of Nature*.

"As Carlyle writes : 'The end of man is an action and not a thought, though it were of the noblest.' Thus conceived, then, the soul is to be identified with conduct, character. We are, we *only* are, as we *behave*. Man comprises a variety of functions, faculties and powers within him : but, wondrous as is his complex organisation, its use, its value, lies alone in its capacity for *doing*. Every act thus undertaken involves a moral significance and consequence ; for every act that is deliberately conceived and purposed has its corresponding image in the mind—as we may say, *its soul*. To this we impart our spiritual vitality. We *are*, as we behave. As we do, we become."—R. DIMSDALE STOCKER, *The God which is Man*, p. 77.

See APPENDAGES, BLASPHEMY, CHURCH (quarters), GOATS, GODS, GOSPEL OF KINGDOM, GUILTY, GUNAS, JUDAH, MAISHAN, NAMES, RIMTHURSAR, SAVIOURS, TRANSMUTATION, TRIBES, VITAL AIRS, WEAPONS.

QUARTERS OF THE COMPASS :—

A symbol of the four lower planes of being, i.e. the quaternary below atma, or the lower quaternary.

"Jesus said to his disciples,—'Come unto Me.' He turned to the four angels of the world."—*Books of the Saviour*.

Here the Christ is said to turn to the disciplined qualities when they aspire, and for this purpose is represented as turning to the four quarters, i.e. to the quaternary symbolised by Earth, Water, Air and Fire,—the physical, astral, mental, and buddhic planes. The meaning is that the Divine influence extends to all the planes of the soul's being in response to the aspirations of the qualities.

"Let him cut the tree for the Sacrificial stake so as to fall towards the east, for the east is the quarter of the gods ; or towards the north, for the north is the quarter of men, or towards the west (the western quarter belongs to the serpents). But let him take care to keep it from falling towards the southern quarter, for that is the quarter of the fathers (pitris)."—*Sata Brâh.*, III. 6, 4, 12.

From the " tree " of the Divine Life there is, as it were, a part separated off for the growth of each soul through aspiration (stake) upwards. The statement about the " tree of life " being allowed to fall towards every quarter but the south means that aspiration may be directed towards the plane of atma (east), the plane of buddhi (west), the plane of higher manas (north), but not towards the plane of kama (south), because that is the plane of the desires wherein the Life-force proceeds in the contrary direction to aspiration, that is, outwardly and not inwardly.

In this Indian scripture the four higher planes are denoted by the quarters, while the physical plane is left to be understood by the downward direction to earth. The direction of the sun-rise made the eastern quarter an appropriate symbol for the atmic plane, the abode of the manifesting Self (sun). The northern position of the great mountains (aspiration) made the northern quarter a suitable symbol for the mental plane (men). The abode of the " serpents " of wisdom and emotion rendered the western quarter a symbol of the buddhic plane. And the position of the great sea made the southern quarter a symbol suited to the astral plane (sea). The lunar pitris (fathers) represent the development of the animal or desire nature.

In Egypt, Palestine, and Europe, geographical considerations have given to the cardinal points somewhat different meanings to those found in Indian sacred writings. In the three countries named, the north signifies the atmic plane, the south, the atmic, the west the buddhic, and the east the mental. But when the four quarters are mentioned without being specified further, the quaternary of four planes below atma may be taken as referred to in all countries.

See ASHADHA, CHILDREN OF HORUS, CHIP, CHURCH (quarters), COUNTRIES, EAST, FOUR, FOUR BEINGS, HEBEN, LION-GAIT, NORTH, QUATERNARY, QUETZALCOATL, SHINATSU, SOUTH, SQUARE, STAKE, SWASTIKA, TET, TLALOC, WEST, WINDS (four).

QUASER, OR KVASIR :—

A symbol of a clairvoyant sense possessed by the early astral races of humanity, and giving a very limited perception of external things. This " third eye " function ceases to act when physical sight is fully acquired in the fourth root-race of mankind.

See EYE (third), NET OF ASAR.

QUATERNARY :—

A symbol of four planes of manifestation of the Divine Life. The four planes are sometimes taken as those below atma, namely, the buddhic, the mental, the astral, and the physical planes. But usually the quaternary stands for the lower nature of the present cycle, which implies all manifestation below the higher mental plane. This, which may be called the lower quaternary, comprises the lower mental, the astral, the etheric, and the physical planes, which are now the planes of relativity and illusion subject to the law of karma.

" The quaternary of the sensible world, which is properly what Pythagoras meant by the word Kosmos, is Fire, Air, Water, and Earth."—OLIVER, *Pythagorean Triangle*, p. 112.

This quaternary signifies the four planes (elements) below atma, viz. the buddhic (fire), the mental (air), the astral (water), and the physical (earth).

" ' It is the root that never dies, the Three-tongued Flame of the Four Wicks. The Wicks are the sparks that draw from the Three-tongued Flame ' (*Book of Dzyan*). The ' Three-tongued Flame that never dies ' is the immortal spiritual Triad, the Atma, Buddhi, and Manas, or rather the fruitage of the last, assimilated by the first two after every terrestrial life. The ' Four Wicks ' that go out and are extinguished are the Quaternary, the four lower principles, including the body."—BLAVATSKY, *The Secret Doctrine*, Vol. I. p. 257.

" Man, who consists of soul and body, consists of seven qualities. For he flourishes in three spiritually and in four bodily. For in the love of God he is excited in three qualities spiritually when it is said to him by the Law,— ' Thou shalt love the Lord thy God with all thy heart, and with all thy soul, and with all thy mind ' (MAT. xxii. 37). But he consists of four qualities bodily, because he is composed of hot and cold, of moist and dry matter."—ST. GREGORY, *Morals on the Book of Job*, Vol. III. p. 692.

"To put the matter shortly, up to the present human consciousness has functioned upon the physical plane, also on that of the passions and emotions, to a lesser degree on that of the intellect—which, after all, is not consciousness, but only one of its instruments—and, much more rarely, on the plane of the spiritual. By the spiritual I mean that plane of experience on which we realise our oneness with one another and with the mysterious power behind phenomena, whom we call God."—R. J. CAMPBELL, Serm., *Evolution of the Spiritual Man.*

See AUKERT, AUSHEDAR, ELEMENTS, FOUR, GATHA (ahuna), HEBEN, IRON PLATE, LAND, LION-GAIT, LOTUS LEAF, MINISTERS, PILLARS, PILLARS (four), QUARTERS, SAU, SKY, SQUARE, TORTOISE, VARA, VARENA, VESTURES, WORLD, WORLDS (five), YOMI.

QUEEN OF HEAVEN :—

A symbol of the principle of buddhi, or the Wisdom-nature.

See BUDDHI, GODDESS, ISIS, LADY, WISDOM.

QUETZALCOATL (FEATHERED SERPENT) :—

A symbol of the Higher Self, who incarnates in the lower nature.

"By the sorceries of the Aztec god Tezcatlipoca, he was driven from the land of Mexico, and returned to the fabled country of Tlapallan, whence he had come. But he promised to return. Other accounts state that he cast himself upon a funeral pyre and was consumed, and that his heart ascended into the sky and became the morning star. Some authorities regard him as a sun-god, and point to the circumstance of his returning to the east, his native home. Others regard him as a god of the air. He is, they say, connected with the cardinal points, and wears the insignia of the cross which symbolises them."—*Non-classical Mythology,* p. 142.

By the law of the Supreme, at the "fall of man" the Self (Quetzalcoatl) was obscured in the mind (Mexico), and he retreated as it were to the higher planes (Tlapallan), but gave assurance of return to be born in the soul. It is also said that the Self became perfected as the Archetypal Man sacrificing himself and giving over the Divine essence (heart) to the next order—evolution, wherein it becomes the expression of Truth (morning star) on the higher mental plane. That is, the potential causal-body (heart) is established in the higher

mind to guide the process of evolution. The Self (sun-god), after being obscured in the lower mind, reappears in the soul, rising in the glory of eternal truth (the east). Again, it is said, the Self is seated in the higher mind (air) above the lower quaternary (cardinal points), in other words,—he is crucified on the cross of matter.

See AIR, ARC. MAN, BIRD, CHILDREN OF HORUS, COUNTRIES, CROSS, CRUCIFIXION (gnostic), DEATH OF BALDER OF OSIRIS, DISMEMBERMENT, EAST, EVOLUTION, EXILE, FEATHER, HEART, HOME, INVOLUTION, MORNING STAR, PLUMES, QEBHSENNUF, QUARTERS, SACRIFICER, SERPENT, SKY, TEZCATLIPOCA.

QUIVER OF ARROWS :—

A symbol of the potential higher nature out of which comes forth spiritual energy and truth to dispel evil and ignorance.

"'Because He hath opened His quiver and afflicted me" (JOB xxx. 11). What is denoted by 'the quiver' of God, but secret counsel ? Now the Lord casts the arrow from the quiver, when from His secret counsel He sends forth an open sentence. For that any man is scourged, we know, but for what cause the scourge comes, we know not. But when after the scourge amendment of life follows, the actual power of counsel is itself disclosed as well. So the 'quiver shut' is hidden counsel. But we are chastened by an 'open quiver' when by that which follows after the scourge we see with what counsel we are stricken."—ST. GREGORY, *Morals on the Book of Job.* Vol. II. p. 484.

See ARROWS, PESTILENCE, SCOURGE.

RĀ, OR RĀ HARMAKHIS, THE EVER LIVING :—

A symbol of the Logos, either unmanifest or manifest. The Supreme Self or the Higher Self.

"I (Rā) am he who came into being in the form of Khepera. I became the creator of all that came into being. Heaven existed not, nor earth, nor had been created the things of the earth. I raised them up from out of Nu, from a state of inactivity."—BUDGE, *Gods of the Egyptians,* Vol. I. p. 308.

The Supreme Self manifests as the Indwelling Self (Khepera). The Self is the emanator of all that appears. In the beginning, the higher nature (heaven) did not exist, neither did the lower (earth), nor had the lower forms and qualities commenced to evolve. The Self proceeded to emanate the Universe from Truth-reality (Nu), from a state of latency.

"In the year 363 of the reign of Râ Harmakhis, the Ever Living. Râ was in the land of Nubia with his warriors, but foes conspired against him."—WIEDE-MANN, *Rel. of Anc. Egyptians*, p. 69.

The number 363 refers to the Divine Triad, Will, Wisdom, Action, which is *in abscondito* in the first figure 3; manifests in the dual aspect—Spirit-matter, in 6; and returns victorious in the last 3, thus completing 12, the summation of the cycle (year $3 + 6 + 3 = 12$).

In the cycle of manifestation in twelve stages, at a time when it was determined that a Solar System should proceed forth, the Logos, or Sun-god, lay in the state of negation, or "land of the shadow," with his attributes and potencies. Then as duality transpired there came forth against him the powers of evil, for there had arisen the opposites, the sense of good and evil, repulsion as well as attraction, and will fore-shadowed as preference. The dawn of manifestation with birth of a System is always attended by a Divine sacrifice.

See ADITYAS, ÆONS, AFU-RÂ, COS-MOS, CREATION, EARTH, GEOMETRY, HEAVEN AND EARTH, KHEPER, NU, NUBIA, OPPOSITES, PRAGÂPATI, PTAH, SACRIFICER, STRIDES, TATTU, TRIAD, TUAT, TWELVE, UPLIFTING RÂ, URNI, YEAR, ZODIAC.

RACE-COURSE :—

The mental nature in which the consciousness rises.

"Homa grants strength and vigour to those who, mounted on white horses, wish to run over a race-course."—*Homa Yasht*, 22, HAUG, *Essays*.

The Spirit of the Supreme energises the mental ideals and aspirations which are to carry the egos on to the higher sub-planes of the mental plane.

See DEVAYANA, HOMA, HORSE (white).

RACES OF MEN, ACCORDING TO HESIOD :—

Symbolic of five stages of essential constituents of the human soul in manifestation.

The "Golden race" signifies the Divine "sparks" or spiritual egos (atma-buddhic). These are the "guardians of mortal men," "shrouded in darkness," being obscured (dying) in the lower nature (earth), judges of good and evil, and "bestowers of wealth" of high qualities. They are monads of the higher life, and become the indivi-dualities of the souls of humanity.

The "Silver race" signifies the monads of the lower life which energise the lower qualities and build up the forms. They become the personalities of human beings, having but transient lives in the incarnating cycle. They evolve slowly from low forms of life in instinct and ignorance; and when the per-sonalities are perfected their period of existence is ended.

The "Brazen race" stands for thought-forms of the lower mind, transitory opinions, prejudices, theo-ries, arguments, speculations, which "slay each other" and disappear. They are all of the matter of mind (metal) and have been aroused by the astro-physical (ash-trees) activities.

The "Divine race of heroes" signifies the higher qualities (buddhi-manasic) which are divinely implanted in the soul, where they combat the lower qualities. The twelve or more higher qualities won for the soul Wisdom and Love (Sheep of Edipus), or Wisdom (Helen). At the fall of mind, when the higher qualities became obscured (died) to the lower consciousness, they abode away from mind (man) potentially on the buddhic plane (Islands of the blest), where they are nourished by the spiritual food (honey) of the transmuted qualities of the lower nature (earth).

The present "Iron race" sym-bolises the desires, passions, appe-tites and sensations allied with mind (kama-manasic), which cause untold misery and suffering to the lower consciousness. Every variety of con-dition produces disharmony, and "faith and justice" have no place in the self-seeking desire-mind. But "good will still be mixed with the evil," and a time will arrive when the lower nature will become effete (hoary-templed) and so it then will be destroyed.

"Ovid (*Meta.* I. 89) makes the races of men four in number,—golden, silver, brazen, and iron. The first enjoyed a perpetual spring, the earth producing everything spontaneously for them : in the time of the second the divisions of the seasons took place : the third were martial, but not yet utterly wicked : the fourth gave way to every species of vice and crime, and Zeus destroyed them by a deluge of water."

In this series the "Divine race" is omitted, and the fourth race is the same as Hesiod's fifth race. The "divisions of the seasons" symbolise the re-incarnating cycles, and the "deluge of water" signifies an out-pouring of Truth which destroys the illusion of the lower nature.

"Aratus (*Phœnomena*) speaks of but three races of men,—the golden, the silvern, and the brazen. . . . Unable to endure the third race, who first forged arms and fed on the flesh of the labouring ox, Justice flew up to heaven and became the constellation of the Virgin."

Buddhi (justice) was repelled by the lower qualities, which had no reverence for the higher, and so retreated, as it were, to the higher planes, ready in the fullness of time to give birth to the Self.

See ADAM (lower), BEASTS (three sorts), DYNASTIES, FALL, FIVE, GOLDEN AGE, GUARDIAN SPIRITS, HELEN, HEROES, INDIVIDUALITY, IRON AGE, ISIS, MARUTS, METAL, MONAD OF LIFE, OX, PERSONALITY, PITRIS, PITRIYANA, PYLUS, RAGHA, RESPECTFUL, ROOT-RACES, ROUND, SPARK, VIRGIN, VIRGO, WATER, ZEUS.

RAFT OF WISDOM :—

A symbol of the functionings of buddhi to raise the soul.

"Even if thou art the most sinful of all sinners, yet shalt thou (eventually) cross over all sin by the raft of wisdom."— *Bhagavad-Gita*, Ch. IV. 36.

The ego in all the stages of its progress through the lower nature has before it the certainty of rising above all evil and imperfection by means of the transmutations of buddhi.

"'By me is made a well-constructed raft,'—so said Bhagavat (Buddha),—I have passed over to Nibbâna, I have

reached the further bank, having overcome the torrent of passions."—*Sutta-nipāta*, 21.

The soul (Buddha), in the course of its pilgrimage, has become possessed of the higher qualities which are the means by which the consciousness passes over from the lower to the higher planes. The indwelling Self has overcome the attractions of desire and sensation and entered into a state of bliss (nibbâna).

See ARA, BOAT OF WISDOM, BUDDHI, NIRVANA, SHORE (other), VIGARA.

RAGANYA :—

A symbol of the personality, or lower mind.

"Now the gods do not commune with everyone, but only with a Brahman, or a Raganya, or a Vaisya : for these are able to sacrifice."—*Sata. Brâh.*, III. 1, 1, 10.

Ideals (gods) are only recognised by the individuality, or the personality, or the desire-nature ; for these are able to give up the lower for the higher.

See BRÂHMANA, CASTES, GODS, KSHATRIYA, PERSONALITY, SACRIFICE, VÂGAPEYA, VAISYA.

RAGHA LAND :—

A symbol of the buddhic plane on which is manifested a buddhic globe of the lunar planetary chain.

"The twelfth good region was Ragha of the three races. Thereupon Angra Mainyu created the sin of utter unbelief."—*Vendidad*, I.

The three root races of incipient humanity were upon the plane of buddhi (Ragha). These races were upon one of the globes of the lunar chain in matter of the wisdom plane, awaiting the period when they shall descend and solidify on the mental and astral planes. At this early period they had no vehicles in which to behave as humanity does under later circumstances. The consequence is they have reference entirely to the Archetypal Man,—the potential pattern of humanity. In opposition to this condition of manifestation, the division is hinted at between the lower and higher principles, since their union has not yet been effected.

See ADAM (lower), ARCHETYPAL MAN,

BEASTS (three sorts), GOLDEN AGE, LUNAR CHAIN, PLANETARY CHAIN, PYLUS, RACES, ROOT-RACES, ROUND.

RĀHU, THE ASCENDING NODE :—

A symbol of darkness, ignorance, suffering, and evil, during evolution.

"If a person be born under the planet Rāhu, his wisdom, riches, and children will be destroyed; he will be exposed to many afflictions and be subject to his enemies."—WILKINS, *Hindu Mythology*, p. 435.

The spiritual ego, or individual soul, born into the lower nature has left in latency his wisdom and powers on the upper planes, and is now subject to ignorance and sorrow while he works his way upward.

See BONDAGE, DARKNESS, IGNORANCE, JOB, SORROW, SUFFERING.

RĀHULA, SON OF BUDDHA :—

A symbol of light, knowledge, truth, and love, born into the soul.

"In course of time to the fair-bosomed Yasodhara,—who was truly glorious in accordance with her name,—there was born from the son of Suddhodana a son named Rāhula, with a face like the enemy of Rāhu."—*Buddha-Karita*, Bk. II. 46.

In course of involution, to the form-side of the universe whose vehicle had been preparing there went forth from the World-soul the One who was to bring light to the souls in darkness. The Sun of righteousness is the enemy of darkness, for it dispels ignorance, doubt, sorrow, etc.

See BUDDHA, LIGHT, SUDDHODANA, YASODHARA.

RAIMENT BECOMING WHITE AS THE LIGHT :—

A symbol signifying the without becoming as the within; the nature made perfect exteriorly as interiorly.

See GARMENTS, GATE OF SALUTATION, GUEST (wedding), LINEN, SHINING, TRANSFIGURATION, WHITE.

RAIN :—

A symbol of downpouring truth (water) from buddhi (cloud), to dispel error and illusion.

"I will pour forth rain from the clouds of the Law upon the beings plunged in hell and devoured by hell-fire, and they will be filled with joy and gladness (says the infant Buddha)."—*Lalita-vistara*.

The Self from its Wisdom-Truth aspect (the Law) will bestow truth upon the egos immersed in the lower nature (hell) and subject to suffering (hell-fire); and they will be purified of their imperfections and enter into bliss.

"If 'clouds' are holy preachers, the rains from the clouds are the words of their preaching."

"For the drops of dew (or rain) are the holy preachers themselves, who water the fields of our breast with the grace of bounty from above."—ST. GREGORY. *Morals on the Book of Job*, Vol. III. pp. 245, 340.

"Rain signifies divine truth from heaven."—SWEDENBORG, *Apoc. Rev.*, n. 496.

See DEUT. xxxii. 2; Is. lv. 10, 11; Hos. vi. 3.

See CLOUD, DEW, DROUGHT, HERB, MAZENDARANS, UDDER, VOURUKASHA, WATER, WEALTH SHOWER, WINDOWS.

RAIN CAUSING DELUGE :—

A symbol of a flood of truth contained in erroneous ideas which envelop the lower mind.

"And the rain was upon the earth forty days and forty nights."—GEN. vii. 12.

And the outpouring of truth, reflected erroneously in the lower nature, continued for a period answering to those re-incarnating terms (days and nights) which enabled the lower nature to absorb fresh truth, or attain expansion of consciousness.

"All the work that the Spirit had done was now swept away with the flood of error and thoughts; and this is in reality what is meant by 'Noah's Flood.'"—JOHN WARD, *Zion's Works*, Vol. III. p. 5.

See CLOUDS, DELUGE, FLOOD, FORTY, HEROD, MOUNTAIN, RAKSHASES, REINCARNATION, WATER.

RAINBOW :—

A symbol of the higher mental plane which forms a bridge, as it were, between the higher and the lower natures (heaven and earth). The rainbow is a peculiarly appropriate symbol of the "bridge of heaven," caused as it is by the reflection of the sun (the Self) in the water-drops (Truth) forthpouring from the cloud (buddhi) to the earth (lower nature). When the lower nature fully reflects the higher, then the "bridge" may be traversed by the victorious egos returning to their home above.

"The god Oro fixed the rainbow in the heavens, one end of it resting in the valley at the foot of the red-ridged mountain, the other penetrating the skies, and thus forming his pathway to the earth. . . . Every evening he descended on the rainbow, and returned by the same pathway on the following morning to the heavenly regions."—W. ELLIS, *Polynesian Researches*, Vol. I. p. 231.

The Higher Self throws from the higher mental plane to the plane of the desires a bridge or pathway across which it may descend to the lower planes. And at regular intervals descents,—evening, *night*, morning,—marking periods of incarnation, would be made; after which the Self, or ego, would again quit the temporary abode in the flesh for the devachanic state.

"And it shall come to pass, when I bring a cloud over the earth, that the bow shall be seen in the cloud."—GEN. ix. 14.

And it shall follow that when Truth envelops the personality, the "bridge of manas" shall appear before the soul, by which it may effect its escape from the lower nature.

"The bridge cannot be always the Milky-way. In at least one Sanscrit hymn we learn,—'Upon it, they say, there are colours, white, and blue, and brown, and gold, and red. And this path Brahma knows, and he who has known Brahma shall take it; he who is pure and glorious.'—Here the singer is evidently describing the rainbow. Now in the Norse cosmology the rainbow had the same name as the Indian *patha-devayano*, God's path. The Eddas call it Asbru, the bridge of the Æsir, or gods. Its other name Bifrost, the trembling mile, it may even have inherited from the Milky-way, for that, when we look at it, seems to be always trembling. Asbru, or Bifrost, then is the bridge whereby the gods descend to earth. One end of it reaches to the famous Urdar fount."—C. F. KEARY, *Myths, etc., Cont. Rev.*, Oct. 1879.

"For the Rainbow is the sign and token of this Covenant, that man was created out of Three Principles into an Image, and that he should live in all three. . . . For the Rainbow hath the colour of all the Three Principles; viz. the colour of the First Principle is red and darkish-brown, which betokens the dark and Fire world, that is the kingdom of God's Anger. The colour of the Second Principle is white and yellow, signifying a type of the Holy world of God's Love. The Third Principle's colour is green and blue; blue from the Chaos and green from the water or salt-petre. . . . This Bow is a figure of the last judgment, showing how the inward Spiritual World will again manifest itself,

and swallow up the Outward World of four elements."—BOEHME, *Mysterium Magnum*, p. 207.

"*I have set my bow in the cloud* signifies the state of the regenerate spiritual man. That the bow in the cloud represents regeneration, no man can know unless it be given him to see and therefore to know how it is :—When the spiritual angels, who were all regenerate men of the spiritual church, are so presented to view in the other life, there appears as it were a rainbow about the head (REV. x. 1). . . . The reason why the resemblance of a rainbow appears is that their natural truths corresponding to their spiritual present such an appearance."—SWEDENBORG, *Arc. Cel.*, n. 1042.

When the purified lower nature (natural) corresponds with the higher nature (spiritual), then union of higher and lower is effected, and the higher mind (rainbow bridge) appears in the consciousness. The "regenerate men" are the souls who have attained liberation from the cycle of births and deaths.

"When a man becomes regenerate he then first enters upon a state of freedom; before he was in a state of bondage."—*Ibid.*, n. 892.

"Then, mid dark waters, when the sun breaks out, though the cloud may be dark, a bow appears amid the darkness; half a ring—half that ring with which the regenerate soul is now married to the Lord, and assured of endless rest with Him. The lower world yet hides the rest of the ring; but on high 'a rainbow' shall be seen '*in a circle round* the throne.'"—A. JUKES, *Types of Genesis*, p. 129.

See BIFROST, BOW, BRIDGE OF HEAVEN, CLOUDS, COVENANT, DEVACHAN, EARTH, ELEMENTS, FALL, HEAVENLY REGIONS, IMAGE, IRIS, MUSPELL (sons), NOAH, ORO, REGENERATION, REINCARNATION, TAATA, VAPOUR (white), WATER.

RAJAS STATE :—

This signifies mental outgoing energy directed towards objects of desire and sense.

"*Rajas* is of the nature of desire, producing thirst and propensity; it imprisoneth the ego through the consequences produced from action. . . . The love of gain, activity in action, and the initiating of works, restlessness and inordinate desire, are produced when the quality of *rajas* is prevalent. . . . When the body is dissolved while the quality of *rajas* is predominant, the soul is born again in a body attached to action."—*Bhagavad-Gita*, Ch. XIV.

"That austerity (restraint) which is practised with hypocrisy, for the sake of obtaining respect for oneself or for fame or favour, and which is uncertain and belonging wholly to this world, is of the quality of *rajas*. . . . That gift which is given with the expectation of a return, or with a view to spiritual benefit, or with reluctance, is of the *rajas* quality, bad and partaketh of untruth."—*Ibid.*, Ch. XVII.

The mental activity of *rajas* is good or bad in the ordinary sense, according to the great or little consideration given to the welfare of others.

See AUSTERITIES, DROPNER, GUNAS, RAKSHASAS.

RĀKSHASAS :—

A symbol of the desire-mental qualities (fleshly lusts) which war against the soul.

"Those of the quality of *rajas* worship the celestial powers,—the Yakshas and Rākshasas (cloud demons who withhold the rains)."—*Bhagavad-Gita*, Ch. XVII.

Those mortals full of desire extol the pleasures of sense and the desire-mental attractions which prevent the influx of truth to the soul.

"Under the story of the conflict between the armies of the noble Rāma and the barbarous races of the South, figured by the Rākshasas, there appears to lie a typical representation of the great mystery of the struggle ever going on between the powers of good and evil."—MON. WILLIAMS, *Indian Wisdom*, p. 362.

See DAEVAS, DAIMONS, DEMONS, DEVILS, LANKA, MAHABHARATA, RAIN, RAMA.

RAM OF SACRIFICE :—

A symbol of the Second Logos, or the Divine Life involved in matter.

"A ram caught in a thicket by his horns: and Abraham went and took the ram, and offered him up for a burnt offering in the stead of his son."—GEN. xxii. 13.

The "thicket" signifies the matter in which the Divine Life is caught but finally conquers (horns). A phase of the Divine (Abraham) sacrifices *involved* Life for the sake of the *evolved* Life (the son) which is to be the Divine life within every human soul to bring it to perfection.

"The Kalmucks consecrate a ram as 'the ram of heaven' or the 'ram of the spirit.' The animal is tended carefully and never shorn. When it is old, and the owner bethinks him of consecrating a young ram, the ram of heaven is slain, and its flesh eaten."—*Ency. Religion and Ethics*, Vol. V. p. 137.

"In the New Year Festival the Jews sing a hymn whose refrain refers to the story of Abraham and Isaac on Mount Moriah, and runs thus: 'O remember in my favour the merits of him who bound, and of him who was bound, and the altar.'"—T. RHONDDA WILLIAMS, Serm., *Redemption*.

See ABRAHAM, AFU-RĀ, ALTAR, BURNT SACRIFICE, CABIN, DIONYSUS, EVOLUTION, INVOLUTION, LAMB, REDEMPTION, SACRIFICE, SALVATION.

RÂM, THE CELESTIAL BREATH :—

A symbol of the First Logos, the unmanifest God, who is the out-breathing Source of all.

See BREATH (divine).

RAMA, AVATAR OF VISHNU :—

A symbol of the incarnate Deity, or indwelling Self of atma-buddhic energy, born in the human soul.

"Vishnu asks the gods why it is necessary for him to effect their deliverance. Being told of Brahma's promise to Rāvana, he at length consents to be born as man, in order to slay the giant and his family."—WILKINS, *Hindu Mythology*, p. 174.

The promise of Brahma is that the desire-principle (Rāvana) is not to be slain by either "gods or demons," that is, by subjective forces. The Higher Self (Vishnu), therefore, is to become objective or evolved in order to deliver the spiritual egos (gods) in humanity, and destroy the desire-principle and all its attendant desires. The Higher Self consents to become incarnate in the human soul.

"To this end was the son of God manifested that he might destroy the works of the devil."—1 JOHN iii. 8.

It requires the Divine centralising principle (Vishnu) manifested in the mind to enable the soul to overcome the contrary principle of evil (Rāvana) and destroy its qualities (family).

See BALARAMA, BHARATA, HANUMAN, KABANDHA, LAKSHMANA, LANKA, RĀKSHASAS, RAVANA, SITA, SHOES, VIBHISHANA, VISHNU.

RAMAYANA :—

A symbolic drama of the evolution of the Soul: its descent into matter, and ascent therefrom.

"No one can read either the Ramayana or Mahabharata without feeling that they rise above the Homeric poems in this—that a deep religious meaning appears to underlie all the narrative, and that the wildest allegory may be intended to conceal a sublime moral, symbolising the conflict between good and evil, and teaching the hopelessness of victory in so terrible a contest without purity of soul, self-abnegation and subjugation of the passions."—Mon. Williams, *Indian Wisdom*, p. 425.

" The pious legends, the purânas, which record the actions and manifestations of the gods, are only the veil that conceals a higher truth which the believer must penetrate. From this point of view the epic fable has been reconstrued in special works, such as the *Adyâtma Ramâyana*, " the spiritual Ramâyana," in which all the events in the history of Rama are resolved into the divine order. Side by side with the abstract doctrine there was thus formed in the majority of the sects an allegorical doctrine, a gnosis or a mystical interpretation of their legend, which was regarded as far superior to the simple philosophy." —A. Barth, *Religions of India*, p. 217.

If it is true that the Ramayana bears a mystical interpretation, then it must be equally true that all other really sacred legends have mystical undermeanings, for they all have the same features of pious absurdity. The outer shell of symbolism has within it a kernel of truth, and the truth being a revelation of the unseen, shows that the symbolism is of Divine not human origin.

See Gospel, Inspiration, Koran, Mythology, Revelation, Satrughana, Scriptures, Sign, Upanishads, Veda.

RANGHA FLOODS :—

A symbol of a condition of Truth upon higher planes above the mind. *See* Head (without), Water.

RANGI AND PAPA :—

Symbols of Spirit and Matter, or of the higher and lower natures.

" Men had but one pair of primitive ancestors ; they sprang from the vast heaven that exists above us, and from the earth which lies beneath us. . . . Rangi and Papa, or Heaven and Earth, were the source from which, in the beginning, all things originated."—G. Grey, *Polynesian Mythology*, p. 1.

The soul, or humanity, has arisen from the interactions of Spirit and Matter, for from this primal duality all things have been produced.

" Darkness then rested upon the

Heaven and upon the earth, and they still both clave together, for they had not yet been rent apart."—*Ibid*.

Actual existence had not yet emerged from potential being (darkness), for Spirit and Matter were not yet differentiated from each other in the new cycle.

See Cave, Darkness, Earth (prim.), Heaven and earth, Ikatere, Matter, Pillars of shu, Punga, Rongo, Ru, Separation, Spirit, Tanemahuta, Tawhirimatea, Tumatauenga, Tute, Uranus.

RANSOM, OR PRICE PAID FOR LIBERATION :—

A symbol of the higher qualities, which are potential or latent within the soul. When the conditions are fulfilled, offering is made by the lower Self of its highest qualities in order that still higher qualities (ransom) shall become active, and release the soul from its thraldom to the lower nature. This process implies the transmutation of the lower qualities into the higher.

" The Son of man came not to be ministered unto, but to minister, and to give his life a ransom for many."—Matt. xx. 28.

The first among the qualities shall assist those qualities next below. The indwelling Self born in the mind (man) came to raise the qualities, and by his outflowing Life become the potential perfection which brings actual perfection to those qualities which approach nearest to him.

" Two conceptions of human life are uncovered and contrasted in the text. To live at all involves for every one a double experience of ministering and being administered unto. Character is developed and revealed in the article of service received and service rendered. . . . Of some, wherever placed in the vast and manifold system of society, the Master's Words about Himself may, in a measure, be spoken ; they, like Him, carry ever on the earth the sacred and sanctifying character of service ; they also have come to minister, and to give their lives for the rescue and help of others. . . (Some again) grow to regard society as an organisation directly designed for their comfort and advancement. Less and less does the thought of service as due from them to society find admission to their minds ; more and more it is barred out from entrance by the ever-multiplying requirements of self. Of them, also, the word of Christ is true ; their whole life from cradle to grave might be summed up in the simple and luminous sentence, 'they came to be ministered unto.' Society is full of them, and, unless the prophets of our time speak falsely, becoming yearly more full of them. The old World has to carry on its weary shoulders an ever-waxing burden of useless drones, who take all and give nothing back, and worse still, of social wolves, who are abroad in society only to prey upon it."—H. HENSLEY HENSON, *The Value of the Bible*, pp. 265–8.

See ATONEMENT, CHRYSEIS, MEDIATOR, REDEMPTION, RICHES, SON OF MAN, ZION.

RASHNU, THE ANGEL :—

A symbol of Divine love ; attraction towards the higher.

"The meditation of Mitro, and Srosh and Rashnu, and the weighing of Rashnu the just."—*The Minokhired*, HAUG, *Essays*.

The "meditation" is a symbol of concentration, or the value of mental balance. "Mitro, Srosh, and Rashnu" stand for Understanding, Will, and Love.

See BALANCE (spirits), SROSH.

RAT OF GANESA :—

A symbol of the lower quaternary.

"Ganesa is frequently attended by, or is riding upon, a rat."—WILKINS, *Hindu Mythology*, p. 324.

The Higher Self, operating upon the higher mental plane, presides over the lower mental, the astral, the etheric, and the physical planes, symbolised by the four limbs of a rat.

See ANIMAL, GANESA, QUADRUPED, QUATERNARY.

RATHANTERA, SAMAN VERSE :—

A symbol of Divine love governing the soul.

See BRIHAT.

RĀVANA, KING OF LANKA :—

A symbol of the lower principle, or desire-mind, ruler of the lower nature of the soul (Lanka).

"Rāvana's form was a thick cloud, or a mountain, or the god of death with open mouth. He had all the marks of royalty ; but his body bore the impress of wounds inflicted by all the divine arms in his warfare with the gods."—MON. WILLIAMS, *Indian Wisdom*, p. 355.

The desire-mind is full of illusion and pride. It represents the qualities which have no expression of the Divine life in them. The lower principle is a ruler of the lower nature, but the higher qualities (gods) are constantly sapping his strength.

"Ravana underwent severe austerities in the forest of Gokarna for 10,000 years, standing in the midst of five fires with his feet in the air ; whence he was released by Brahma."—MON. WILLIAMS, *Indian Wisdom*, p. 356.

This refers to the desire-nature as being the love-nature reversed, and exposed to the purifying power from five centres of energy on the lower planes.

"Vishnu took this form of Rama at the close of the second or Treta age, to destroy the demon Ravana."—MON. WILLIAMS, *Indian Wisdom*, p. 330.

The Supreme (Vishnu) became incarnate as the indwelling Self (Rama) in the period of involution in order that the lower principle (Ravana) should be overcome in human souls.

"The first thought round which the grand wonder of the atonement grows into shape is this thought of sin as a real live thing standing forth to be fought with, to be conquered, to be killed. Not of a mere moral weakness to be strengthened, or an intellectual emptiness to be filled, but of an enmity to be slain, a giant to be subdued. To meet that enmity, to slay that giant, Christ comes forth with his wonderful nature. He undertakes a distinct and dreadful struggle."—PHILLIPS BROOKS, *Mystery of Iniquity*, p. 15.

See AHRIMAN, ALTAR (fire), ATONEMENT, AUSTERITIES, DURODHANA, GODS, HANUMAN, INCARNATION, INVOLUTION, KAMA, LANKA, RAMA, SEPARATION (heaven), SOPHIA (lower), TANEMAHUTA, VIBHISHANA, VISHNU, VRITRA.

RAVEN OF NOAH :—

A symbol of the lower mind, which goes forth to the things of the world, and returns not again.

"The dove and the raven are sent forth, figuring (for they are birds of heaven, and the heaven is the understanding) certain powers or emotions of the understanding, both pure and impure. In the actions of these is shown the working of the good and evil which to the last remains with us. The raven, finding its food in carrion, figures those inclinations which feed on dead things."—A. JUKES, *Types of Genesis*, p. 120.

"The raven washeth and rubbeth itself in a small pool in the desert ; its mind and body are full of demerits and

its beak of filth " (Hymn of Guru Nanak).
—MACAULIFFE, *The Sikh Religion*, Vol. I.
p. 380.

See DOVE, OLIVE LEAF.

RAVENS, FLESH-EATING :—

A symbol of the disintegrating elementals of the lower planes.

RAVENS OF ODIN, CALLED HUGIN (MIND) AND MUGIN (WILL) :—

These are symbols of intelligence and power, attributes of the Logos (Odin).

See ODIN.

RAY OF LIGHT FROM THE SUN :—

A symbol of a Divine mode of functioning bringing illumination from the Spirit to the aspiring soul.

"Aton-Rā was the god of the Solar disk, with rays terminating in hands which hold the Ankh, the emblem of life, the *crux ansata*."—WIEDEMANN, *Rel.*

The Divine Truth (light) and activity (hands) are the Life (ankh) of the spiritual universe.

See CROSS, HAND, LIGHT, SUN.

READING BOOKS :—

A symbol of veneration of the scriptures according to the letter.

"Whensoever Moses is read, a veil lieth upon their heart. But whensoever it shall turn to the Lord, the veil is taken away."—2 COR. iii. 15, 16.

"Now the Lord is the Spirit : and where the Spirit of the Lord is, there is liberty " to perceive the truth behind the veil of the letter.

See BOOK STUDIES, MOSES, PAPYRUS, SCRIPTURES, SIGN.

REAPING THE HARVEST :—

A symbol of acquiring the "fruits of the Spirit," which are the buddhic fruition from the cultivation of the lower nature.

"He that reapeth receiveth wages, and gathereth fruit unto life eternal ; that he that soweth and he that reapeth may rejoice together. For herein is the saying true, One soweth and another reapeth. I sent you to reap that whereon ye have not laboured : others have laboured, and ye are entered into their labour."—JOHN iv. 36–8.

The Higher Self, or individuality, having striven after perfection, gathers the harvest due to it of spiritual endowments which shall last through life eternal, so that the lower Self, or personality, which hath sown the seeds of wisdom and love, may become one with the Higher Self in the bliss of realisation. For in this is the truth made clear,—the natural man soweth, and the spiritual man reapeth. The Christ directs that the disciplined qualities shall reap the spiritual fruit accruing from the efforts of qualities below them, so that these lower qualities shall be raised and become united with them.

"What is a farm but a mute gospel ? The chaff and the wheat, weeds and plants, blight, rain, insects, sun,—it is a sacred emblem from the first furrow of spring to the last stack which the snow of winter overtakes in the fields. . . . Nor can it be doubted that this moral sentiment which thus scents the air, grows in the grain, and impregnates the waters of the world, is caught by man and sinks into his soul."—EMERSON, *Nature*, Ch. V.

See AGRICULTURE, CHAFF, CORN, CULTIVATION, FIELD, FRUITFUL, FURROW, HARVEST, KINGDOM, KHUS, MAN (natural), PARABLE, PERSONALITY, PLOUGHING, RAIN, SEED, SEKHET-HETEP, SICKLE, SOWER, SOWING, WAGES, WHEAT.

REAPING AFTER SOWING :—

A symbol of the consummation of the soul-process, arrived at through the karmic law of cause and effect in the higher and lower natures.

"He that soweth the good seed is the Son of man ; the field is the world ; the good seed are the children of the kingdom ; but the tares are the children of the wicked one ; the enemy that sowed them is the devil ; the harvest is the end of the world (æon) ; and the reapers are the angels."—MAT. xiii. 37–9.

The "Son of man " is the Higher Self born in the mind (man) ; the " field " is the arena of life, i.e. the lower nature (world) ; the " children of the kingdom " are the germs of the higher emotions proceeding from buddhi (kingdom) ; the " children of the wicked one " are the desires and passions proceeding from the lower principle (the devil). The "harvest " is the spiritual fruit of experience and endeavour to be gathered on the higher planes at the end of the cycle when the qualities and souls have attained perfection.

" In Sekhet-hetepet, the field of Peace, the grain is three cubits high, and it is the perfect Spirits who reap it" (Papy. of Ani).—BUDGE, *Egypt. Heaven and Hell*, Vol. III. p. 47.

When the harvest of high qualities on the buddhic plane (field of peace) is fully (three) ripe, then the individualities (angels, or perfect spirits) realise its nature (reap it).

"Osiris reaps and I plough; yea and I also reap."—*Book of the Dead*, Ch. CX.

The Self (Osiris) reaps; the lower Self ploughs and cultivates; and afterwards also the lower Self reaps as it realises its true nature. The personalities cannot reap except as they become merged in their individualities on the higher planes.

"And the servants say unto him, Wilt thou then that we go and gather them up? But he saith, Nay; lest haply while ye gather up the tares, ye root up the wheat with them. Let both grow together until the harvest: and in the time of the harvest I will say to the reapers, Gather up first the tares, and bind them in bundles to burn them: but gather the wheat into my barn."—MAT. xiii. 28–30.

The Higher Self points out that the desires and passions (the tares) are necessary for the growth of the soul, and that without them the higher qualities could not be evolved. The lower qualities must therefore remain until the end of the cycle, when the individualities will control and discard them for further purification (burning), but the higher qualities will be garnered on the buddhic plane.

See ÆON, CHILDREN OF KINGDOM, CONSUMMATION, CORN, DEVIL, EARTH, ENEMIES, EXPERIENCE, FIELD, GERMS, HARVEST, HIGHER AND LOWER NATURES, INDIVIDUALITY, KARMA, LITTLE CHILDREN, PLOUGHING, RESURRECTION, SEED, SEKHET-HETEP, SICKLE, SON OF MAN, SOWER, SOWING, TARES, TREASURE, WHEAT (barley).

REBELS OF UAUAT :—

These are symbolic of the various phases of intellectual pride, arrogance, vanity, and love of power.

See HIPPOPOTAMUS.

REBIRTH, BORN ANEW OR FROM ABOVE, BORN OF GOD :—

A symbol of the passage of the purified ego from its life on the lower planes to which it had been born, and its emergence or new birth upon the higher planes; or the raising of the consciousness from the lower mind to the higher mind at the close of the cycle.

"Except a man be born of water and the Spirit, he cannot enter into the kingdom of God. That which is born of the flesh is flesh; and that which is born of the Spirit is spirit. Marvel not that I said unto thee, Ye must be born anew."—JOHN iii. 5-7.

Except an ego is purified by truth (water) ethically, and his qualities are transmuted spiritually, he cannot rise to the buddhic plane. That which is a product of the lower nature (flesh) remains of the lower nature only; and that which is produced by the higher nature is of the higher nature and immortal. It is only by the higher nature superseding and casting out the lower that it is possible for the soul to rise.

"Reality, says Eucken, is an independent spiritual world, unconditioned by the apparent world of sense. To know it and to live in it is man's true destiny. His point of contact with it is personality: the inward fount of his being: his heart, not his head. Man is real, and in the deepest sense alive, in virtue of this free personal life-principle within him: but he is bound and blinded by the ties set up between his surface intelligence and the sense-world. The struggle for reality must be a struggle on man's part to transcend the sense-world, escape its bondage. He must renounce it, and be 're-born' to a higher level of consciousness; shifting his centre of interest from the natural to the spiritual plane. . . . Our life, says Eucken, does not move upon a single level, but upon two levels at once—the natural and the spiritual. The key to the puzzle of man lies in the fact that he is 'the meeting point of various stages of Reality.' The whole question for him is, which world shall be central for him—the real, vital, all-embracing life we call Spirit, or the lower life of sense? Shall 'Existence,' the superficial obvious thing, or 'Substance,' the underlying verity, be his home?"—E. UNDERHILL, *Mysticism*, p. 40.

See ATONEMENT, BAPTISM, BONDAGE, BORN AGAIN, BUDDHIC PLANE, CONSECRATION, DEATH UNTO LIFE, FLESH, HEART, KINGDOM OF HEAVEN, MAN (natural), NICODEMUS, PERSONALITY, REDEMPTION, REGENERATION, REMISSION, RESURRECTION, SAINTS, SALVATION, SPIRIT, WATER.

RECOGNITION OF HIGHER AND LOWER STATES OF CONSCIOUSNESS :—

The distinguishing of the moral or spiritual values of states or qualities is the true function of the personality with the Divine spark.

See CONSCIENCE, PERSONALITY.

RECOLLECTION OF PAST INCARNATIONS :—

This becomes possible through the establishment of the "bridge" of the higher mind, and the perfect building up of the structure of the causal-body in actuality.

"Though the physical brain may forget events within the scope of one terrestrial life, the bulk of collective recollections can never desert the Divine Soul within us. Its whispers may be too soft, the sound of its words too far off the plane perceived by our physical senses ; yet the shadow of events *that were*, just as much as the shadow of events *that are to come*, is within its perceptive powers, and is ever present before its mind's eye."—BLAVATSKY, *Secret Doctrine*, Vol. II. p. 442.

The power of foreseeing future events must be of a strictly limited nature. When events are truly foreseen, they are usually of little consequence.

See BRIDGE OF HEAVEN, CHARON'S FERRY, HIKOBOSHI, PROPHETIC DREAMS, REMINISCENCE.

RECTANGLE, PERFECT :—

A symbol of Truth-Reality, indicating the Source from which the soul emanates.

See JUDGMENT HALL, SAU.

RED COLOUR :—

A symbol of ambition and power of the lower self.

See MARS, TISTRYA.

RED, ROSE, COLOUR :—

A symbol of Divine love.

See HEIFER (red), HORSE (red), TISTRYA.

RED FIRES :—

A symbol of astral growth in the forms.

REDEEMER OF THE SOUL :—

A symbol of the indwelling Self, who pays the penalty attached to imperfection with his own Divine Life (his blood). The souls are full of suffering and ignorance, and the price of redemption from evil is the efflux of the Divine Life of the incarnate Self, which, by being assimilated by the imperfect souls, gradually makes perfect the qualities in them which are imperfect. The Archetypal Man, or Christ incarnate within every soul, gives of his own nature that which the individual soul lacks, in response to the soul's own efforts to prepare itself for accessions of higher qualifications. The Redeemer is latent within until he is called forth by sacrifice and aspiration to save the soul from its captivity to its lower nature, and to raise it to its pristine state of bliss.

"But I know that my redeemer liveth, and that he shall stand up at the last upon the earth : And after my skin hath been thus destroyed, yet from my flesh shall I see God : whom I shall see for myself, and mine eyes shall behold, and not another."—JOB xix. 25–7.

I know that the perfect Self liveth within me, and that at the end of the cycle he shall overcome my lower nature (earth). And after my lower vehicles (skin) have been thus destroyed, yet rising from my lower self (flesh), I shall become one with the Self. I, the individuality, shall unite with Him, and not the personality.

"If God then finds a passage from heaven to the grave, so must a way be discoverable for man from the grave to heaven : the death of the Prince of Life is the Life of mortals."—D. F. STRAUSS, *Life of Jesus*, p. 433.

"God is conceived of by the religious consciousness as not only the creator of the world of things and men, but as the present Life of the human soul. He is moral Ruler and Providence ; He is Redeemer ; and He is the Revealer and Inspirer as well."—G. T. LADD, *Phil. of Religion*, Vol. I. p. 612.

"The Divine Sufferer was God Himself, who in creating the universe sacrificed Himself for it. The Cross, therefore, represents the Greatest of all sacrifices, not something that happened once, and once for all, but something that is eternal and timeless—the sacrifice of God in and for His own creation that could not be unless He poured His own life into it, and restricted Himself within its forms and substance. Great is this mystery of Godliness : unthinkable in its magnitude is this sacrifice, for it means nothing less than the identification of the Infinite with the finite in its lowest forms. Here is the profoundest mystery open to human contemplation, to speak or think of which is possible only in forms of symbol and parable. The literal truth is too vast, too mysterious, too sublime to be made known to human comprehension. . . . Creation is none other than God's primal and continual self-revelation : it is the Great Father coming down and voluntarily incarnating Himself and being made man for us men and our salvation."—K. C. ANDERSON, Serm., *Cradle of the Christ.*

See ARC. MAN, ATRI, BLOOD, BLOOD OF LAMB, BONDAGE, CAPTIVITY, CHRIST, CROSS, CRUCIFIXION, FLESH OF JESUS, FOOD AS GOD, HEAVEN AND EARTH, INCARNATION, INDIVIDUALITY, INVOLUTION, LAMB OF GOD, REGENERATION, SACRIFICER, SALVATION, SKINS, SPIRIT.

REDEMPTION OF THE SOUL :—

A symbol of the substitution of the Divine perfection for the soul's imperfection, by paying the price of involved potential perfection in order to make perfect the evolved actual imperfection of qualities and souls. The price paid being the Divine Self-limitation in matter.

"Ye were not redeemed with corruptible things. . . . But with the precious blood of Christ, as of a lamb without blemish and without spot. Who verily was foreordained before the foundation of the world, but was manifest in these last times for you."—1 PETER i. 18-20.

" Blood " being a symbol of the Divine Life, the shedding of this Life is the Divine Sacrifice.

"The Lamb slain from the foundation of the world."—REV. xiii. 8.

It is the involution of Spirit into Matter. This is the origin of the indwelling Christ, who becomes the redeemer as he rises in the soul from a state of latency, or death, to a state of actuality or life. The indwelling Christ is the Archetypal Man foreordained as the Prototype within humanity becoming manifest in each soul at the present period of evolution.

" There is an indwelling Christ who redeems the soul from sin and fills it with his own life."—R. J. CAMPBELL, Serm., *Christ Arisen.*

" The glaring contrast between earthly suffering and imperfection on the one part, and heavenly bliss and purity on the other, lies at the heart and core of the philosophy of the Orphics and Pythagoreans. Hence came their longing for purification, for atonement and final redemption. The goal they aimed at was hard to attain ; a single earthly existence was not enough to cleanse the soul. . . . A long series of palingeneses formed a kind of continuous pilgrimage, extending through thousands of years, and interrupted and embittered by the penalties suffered by the soul in the ' pool of mire.' Late, if at all, the soul was freed from its labours, and returned to the starting point of its journey. As a pure spirit once more, it re-entered its home and rejoined the brotherhood of the gods."—T. GOMPERZ, *Greek Thinkers,* Vol. I. p. 129.

" *Redemption* is the full compensation both to God and to the universe for all that is undergone and suffered by and through Creation. And it is brought about by the return from Matter of Spirit to its original condition of purity, but individuated and enriched by the results of all that has been gained through the processes to which it has been subjected ;—results which, but for Matter, could not have been. . . . That through which we are made perfect is experience, or suffering ; and we are only really alive and exist in so far as we have felt. Now of this divine and indispensable ministry of experience, Matter is the agent."—*The Perfect Way,* p. 43.

" I should like to be informed who was ever made spiritually rich by notions of an *outward* Christ ? No, Christ is the *inward* spiritual Being or Life that God has sent now into us, to be the actual Redeemer of this our natural being, from its low estate, and to *raise it up,* I say, joint heirship with Himself."—JOHN WARD, *Zion's Works,* Vol. VII. p. 3.

" Redemption is the making good of what we have made ill, and it contains two necessary ingredients—relief and reinforcement—and in Christ we have both. Here on earth we are immersed and stifled in matter, and in moral darkness and stupor—all to a great end. And we have to be got out and brought back somehow to that whence we came. If we were left only to ourselves we never should get out or up ; it is because of our vital indefeasible relation to Christ that we can hope to come victoriously through into divine liberty and joy."—R. J. CAMPBELL, Serm., *The Divine Mystery.*

See ADOPTION, ARC. MAN, ASCENSION, ATONEMENT, BLOOD OF LAMB, BONDAGE, CHRIST, CRUCIFIXION OF CHRIST, OF JESUS, EVOLUTION, EXPERIENCES, INCARNATION, INVOLUTION, LAMB OF GOD, LIBERATION, RANSOM, RE-BIRTH, REGENERATION, REINCARNATION, REMISSION, SACRIFICER, SALVATION, SPIRIT, URNS (twelve), VICTORY.

REED IN THE RIGHT HAND :—

A symbol of volition and rule.

" The reed (in the hand of Jesus) symbolised the royal sceptre and the divine law."—Bp. DIONYSIUS.

See ROD (hand), SCEPTRE, VINEGAR.

REED SHAKEN WITH THE WIND :—

A symbol of instability of purpose and weakness of volition.

"Tropologically, 'a reed shaken with the wind' is a light man, inconstant, tossed to and fro : at one time impelled by the words of flatterers, he asserts something : again being driven by detractors, he denies it, as a reed is blown in different directions by different winds. A reed is one who is devoid of truth, virtue, and consistency, as a reed has no strength, or *stamina*."—C. À LAPIDE, *Great Comm.*, Vol. II. p. 53.

REED-PLAIN :—

A symbol of the astro-mental plane, or the astral plane.

"That ancestor (of the whole race) is generally called the Unkulunkulu, great-great-grandfather. When pressed as to the father of this ancestor, the general answer of the Zulus seems to be that he 'branched off from a reed, or that he came from a bed of reeds'" (Reported by Dr. Callaway).—MAX MÜLLER, *Science of Religion*, p. 45.

The "bed of reeds" evidently means the same as the "papyrus swamps," or "marsh," from which the Self emerges (as Horus).

See BIRTH OF HORUS, GARDEN OF REEDS, HIRUKO, MARSH, OHONA-MOCHI, PEACHES, SEKHET-AARU, UNION (reeds), VULTURE.

REGENERATION :—

A symbol of the production anew, through a process of spiritual transmutation and evolution, of the purified and perfected qualities of the ego which thereby rises to a new birth on the higher planes of consciousness.

"Not by works of righteousness which we have done, but according to his mercy he saved us, by the washing of regeneration, and renewing of the Holy Ghost."—TITUS iii. 5.

Not by the highest impulses of the lower nature can a spiritual result, or rise in consciousness, be brought about ; but only according to a free gift of the Spirit can the soul be made immortal. Spiritual qualities are bestowed in proportion as the human nature is purified and raised through the transmutations effected by the operations of Buddhi (Holy Ghost).

The teaching is that the lower nature cannot possibly raise its condition, for it does not possess or control the higher elements. The higher elements are *given* to the struggling soul when it is sufficiently evolved and prepared to receive them, and chooses to accept them.

"There is no ascent of the human desires above their source. And wherever in a heart there springs up heavenward a thought, a wish, a prayer, a trembling confidence, it is because that came down first from heaven, and rises to seek its level again. All that is divine in man comes from God. All that tends towards God in man is God's voice in the human heart ; and were it not for the possession and operation, the sanctifying and quickening, of a living divine Spirit granted to us, our souls would for ever cleave to the dust, and dwell upon earth, nor ever rise to God and live in the light of His presence."—A. MACLAREN, *Sermons, 1st Series*, p. 62.

"Regeneration has not merely been an outstanding difficulty, but an overwhelming obscurity. Philosophically one scarcely sees either the necessity or the possibility of being born again. Why a virtuous man should not simply grow better and better until in his own right he enter the Kingdom of God, is what thousands honestly and seriously fail to understand. Now Philosophy cannot help us here. Her arguments are, if anything, against us. But Science answers to the appeal at once. If it be simply pointed out that this is the same absurdity as to ask why a stone should not grow more and more living till it enters the Organic World, the point is clear in an instant."—H. DRUMMOND, *Natural Law, etc.*, p. 80.

"The true and definitely directed mystical life does and must open with that most actual and stupendous, though indescribable phenomenon, the coming forth into consciousness of man's deeper spiritual self, which ascetical and mystical writers of all ages have agreed to call Regeneration or Re-birth. Here its more profound and mystical side is exhibited, its divine character revealed. By a process which may indifferently be described as the birth of something new, or the coming forth of something which has slept—since both these phrases are but metaphors for another and more secret thing—the eye is opened on Eternity ; the self, abruptly made aware of Reality, comes forth from the cave of illusion like a child from the womb and begins to live upon the supersensual plane. Then she feels in her inmost part a new presence, a new consciousness—it were hardly an exaggeration to say a new Person—weak, demanding nurture, clearly destined to pass through many phases of development before its maturity is reached ; yet of so strange a nature, that in comparison with its environment she may well regard it as Divine."—E. UNDERHILL, *Mysticism*, p. 147.

See ASCENSION, ATONEMENT, BAPTISM, BORN AGAIN, BUDDHI, CAVE, CIRCLE OF EXISTENCE, CONSECRATION, EVOLUTION, GRACE OF GOD, HOLY GHOST, INVOLUTION, JUDGES, LIBERATION, MAN (natural), NICODEMUS, RE-BIRTH, REDEMPTION, REMISSION, RESURRECTION, SACRIFICE, SAINTS, SALVATION, TRANSMUTATION, VIRGIN MARY, WATER.

REGIONS, SEVEN :—

A symbol of the seven globes of the terrene planetary chain. All are invisible with the exception of the Earth.

" The Drop (sun) moving along the common seat (of sky and earth) ; the Drop I offer along the seven hotras,— the seven hotras are the regions : he thus establishes yonder sun in the regions."—*Sata. Brâh.*, VII. 4, 1, 19.

The indwelling Self, progressing through the cycle of life and commencing small as a drop of water (Truth) within the higher and lower natures, is furnished by the Supreme with the globes of the planetary chain as an arena whereon the Divine Life may be evolved, and the Higher Self manifested in his glory.

In the Indian sacred books the seven regions (dvipas) are given the names of—Plaksha, Shâlmalia, Kusha, Krauncha, Shâka, Pushkara, and Jambu-dvîpa, which last is said to be central to the others. Each region is surrounded by great oceans respectively of sweet juice, wine, butter, curds, milk, etc. (*Vishnu Purana*, II. 109). Jambu-dvîpa is a symbol of our earth, and this *dvipa* is said to be surrounded by a " sea of salt water," which is suggestive both of the proximate astral plane (sea) and of the habitable land of the earth globe. The " oceans " refer to the buddhic, the mental, and the astral planes.

" And of these seven regions every benefit was created most in Khvaniras, and the evil spirit also produced most for Khvaniras, on account of the superiority which he saw in it."—*Bundahis*, Ch. XI. 5.

And of these seven globe-conditions of being, the conditions prevailing in the present world (Khvaniras)

are the most effective for the Divine purpose. The possibilities of evil being great ; great also is the scope for good overcoming evil.

See AAT OF WATERS, BARSOM, EARTH, HIGHER AND LOWER NATURES, HORSE SACRIFICE, HVANRATHA, KARSHVARES, PLANETARY CHAIN, RENOVATION, ROOT-RACES, ROUND, SKY, SPRINGTIME, SUN, WATER.

REGNAROK :—

A symbol of the termination of the cycle, and of the soul's attainment of liberation from the lower nature by the Divine Will, in fulfilment of the Great Law of manifestation.

See AAT OF WATERS, HEIMDALL, HORSE (white), JUDGMENT DAY, KALKI, PRALAYA, RENOVATION, SOSIOSH.

REINCARNATIONS :—

These are successive terrestrial embodiments of the individual soul, to enable it to gain experience and development in the process of evolution. Reincarnation makes effective the relation of the natural law of development with the more specifically spiritual process. It provides opportunities for the unfoldment and interplay of spiritual forces, which, unless the lower planes were responsive *periodically* to the rhythmic succession of soul activities, would not afford the spirit-nature within the soul the means of evolution. Reincarnation is assumed in the Bible teaching, though little is said of it, and that is because it is an incident,—a mere passing phase,— in the real spiritual life. The Bible might just as well give information regarding the digestive process, sleep, or any other natural vital function, as expound the method of reincarnation, which is quite subordinate to the interests of the soul, and which exists simply as a means whereby it is to attain its end. Nevertheless, to deny the fact of reincarnation is on the face of it absurd, because without it any theory of the gradual evolution of the immortal soul through time, past, present and future, is inexplicable. All the sacred books teach involution and evolution through vast periods, and never hint at special creations of souls, or other things, taking place. Yet such special creations must be assumed if the doctrine of evolution of souls is denied.

"Why should not every individual man have existed more than once upon this world ? . . . Why should I not come back as often as I am capable of acquiring fresh knowledge, fresh expertness ? Do I bring away so much from once that there is nothing to repay the trouble of coming back ? Is this a reason against it ? Or because I forget that I have been here already ? Happy is it for me that I do forget. The recollection of my former condition would permit me to make only a bad use of the present."—LESSING, *Divine Education, etc.*

"These two systems, the purely spiritual and the sensuous,—which last may consist of an immeasurable series of particular lives,—exist in me from the moment when my active reason is developed, and pursue their parallel course. The former alone gives to the latter meaning and purpose and value. I *am* immortal, imperishable, eternal, so soon as I form the resolution to obey the law of reason. After an existence of myriad lives, the super-sensuous world cannot be more present than at this moment. Other conditions of my sensuous existence are to come, but these are no more the true life than the present condition is."—J. G. FICHTE, *Vocation of Man*, Bk. III.

"What sleep is for the individual, death is for the Will. It would not endure to continue the same actions and sufferings throughout an eternity, without true gain, if memory and individuality remained to it. It flings them off, and this is lethe ; and through this sleep of death it reappears refreshed and fitted out with another intellect, as a new being—'a new day tempts to new shores.' These constant new births, then, constitute the succession of the life-dreams of a Will which in itself is indestructible, until, instructed and improved by so much and such various successive knowledge in a constantly new form it abolishes or abrogates itself."—SCHOPENHAUER, *The World as Will and Idea.*

"The soul, like the body, has to go through various stages of development, and change very greatly at one phase of experience as compared with another, before it is ready to enter upon its full inheritance. I feel moved to add that I am not at all prepared to say that it is the persons of religious temperament who are in every case the most highly developed of their kind ; on the contrary, it is highly probable that, here or hereafter, many of these will have to go back and learn some of the lessons which their fellows are learning now."—R. J. CAMPBELL, Serm., *The Larger Hope.*

See BOAT OF EARTH, DAY AND NIGHT, EXPERIENCE, FORTY (nights), GATHA (kam.), GATHAS (chanting), GILGOOLEM, GIRDLE (star), HEAVENLY REGIONS, INCARNATION OF SOULS, JUSTICE, LIBERATION, MAN (born), METEMPSYCHOSIS, NAKEDNESS, NIGHTS (three), PURGATORY, REDEMPTION, REINGA, SAMSARA, SENSE ORGANS, SHEPHERD (good), TABERNACLE, VESTURES, WHEELS OF BIRTH.

REINGA :—

A symbol of the mind as the " bridge of manas " from the higher nature to the lower ; or of the lower planes.

"The prevailing idea of the abode of spirits was that they went to the Reinga, which is another name for Po or Hades ; the word *Reinga* literally means the leaping place. The spirits were supposed to travel to the North Cape, or land's end, and there passing along a long, narrow ledge of rock, they leaped down upon a flat stone, and thence slinging themselves into the water by some long sea-weed they entered Po, the Reinga being the passage to it."—R. TAYLOR, *New Zealand*, p. 103.

"In a myth of the New Hebrides, the soul runs along the line of hills till he reaches the end of the island, and then he comes to the place of recollection, the Maewo name for which is *vat dodona*, the stone of thought ; if he remembers there his child or his wife, or anything that belongs to him, he will run back and come to life again. In the same place are two rocks with a deep ravine between them ; if the ghost clears this as he leaps across he is forever dead, but if one fails he returns to life again."—R. H. CODRINGTON, *The Melanesians*, p. 279.

The two myths refer to the same esoteric facts of the soul's evolution. The spiritual egos descend periodically to the lower planes in order to incarnate in human bodies ; and after physical death, ascend to the higher mental plane (stone of thought). If the egos continue to be attached by desire to the lower life they return, after a period, to re-incarnation ; but if they are perfected, they are liberated from the lower nature and return again no more.

See BRIDGE, LIBERATION, PO, REINCARNATION, STONE.

REINS :—

A symbol of the inner nature of the soul.

See GIRDLE (body).

RELATIVE ; THE STATE OF RELATIVITY :—

The condition of consciousness in which there appears duality in opposite qualities,—as good and evil, right and wrong, knowledge and ignorance, etc. This condition characterises evolution on the lower planes.

See EVIL, OPPOSITES, RESPECTFUL, STRIFE.

RELATIVES, BELOVED AND UNBELOVED :—

Symbolic of the complete and the incomplete conditions of manifest existence.

"His beloved relatives obtain the good, his unbeloved relatives the evil he has done."—*Kaush. Upanishad*, I. 2.

The "beloved and unbeloved relatives" signify other schemes of manifestation which in him, the liberated, are to go forth. The "beloved" are the good or perfected ; the "unbeloved" are the evil or relatively imperfect. These will form the higher and lower plane activities for future processes of evolution.

(The ascetic) "Making over the merit of his own good actions to his friends, and the guilt of his evil deeds to his enemies, he attains the eternal Brahman by the practice of meditation."—*Laws of Manu*, VI. 79.

See FRIENDS, RENOVATION.

RELIGION, OR THE GOOD RELIGION :—

A symbol of the science of the spiritual life,—knowledge of the process of the soul's growth from imperfection to perfection, from ignorance to wisdom, from separateness to Love, and from illusion to the eternal Truth.

"Approved by the good, the high priest of the good religion of the Mazdayasnians, the glorified Spendyad, son of Mah-vindad, son of Rustom, son of Shatroyar."—*Preface to the Bundahis.*

The ego who has conquered the lower nature and recognised the Truth, Wisdom, and Love within the soul, is said to be approved by the spiritual forces which maintain and manifest the truth of the Self in the soul-process. The "glorified Spendyad" is the Self who has undertaken to go forth and accomplish his evolution. The Self is the product of the process of the three who bear witness upon "earth," viz. the physical, the astral, and the lower-mental natures, in which the Self is incarnated, and out of which he ascends in glory at the last.

"The thought common to India, Plato, and Kant, that the entire universe is only appearance and not reality, forms not only the special and most important theme of all philosophy, but is also the presumption and *conditio sine quâ non* of all religion. . . . The necessary premises of all religion are, as Kant frequently expounds :—(1) the existence of God, (2) the immortality of the soul, (3) the freedom of the will (without which no morality is possible). These three essential conditions of man's salvation—God, immortality and freedom—are conceivable only if the universe is mere appearance and not reality (mere *mâyâ* and not the *âtman*), and they break down irretrievably should this empirical reality, wherein we live, be found to constitute the true essence of things."—P. DEUSSEN, *Phil. of Upanishads*, p. 45.

"The material world is more or less illusory, and we are quite wrong in regarding it as having a separate and independent existence. 'The things which are seen are not made out of things which do appear.' The world of spirit underlies and interpenetrates the world of sense at all points."—R. J. CAMPBELL, Serm., *The Fact of Death.*

"According to the system (of Doctrine and Life) recovered (by Intuition), the Christ Jesus, Redeemer and Saviour, while equally its beginning, middle, and end, is not a mere historical personage, but, above and beyond this, a Spiritual Ideal and an Eternal Verity. Recognizing fully that which Jesus was and did, it sets forth salvation as depending, not on what any man has said or done, but on what God perpetually reveals. For, according to it, Religion is not a thing of the past, or of any one age, but is an ever-present, ever-occurring actuality ; for every man one and the same ; a process complete in itself for each man ; and for him subsisting irrespective of any other man whatsoever. It thus recognises as the actors in the momentous drama of the Soul two persons only, the individual himself and God."—*The Perfect Way*, p. 25.

"A scientific age rightly refuses to be any longer put off with data which are more than dubious, and logic which morality and philosophy alike reject. A deeper, truer, more real religion is needed for an epoch of thought, and for a world familiar with biblical criticism and revision ;—a religion whose foundations no distractive agnosticism can undermine, and in whose structure no examination, however searching, shall be able to find flaw or blemish. It is only by rescuing the Gospel of Christ from the externals of history, persons, and events, and by vindicating its essential significance, that Christianity can be saved from the destruction which inevitably overtakes all idolatrous creeds." —*Ibid.*, p. 341.

" Religion has its psychological sources in every important form of the functioning of the human soul. *It is man in his entirety who is the maker of religion.* Every factor of his complex being enters into his religious life and religious development. The unconscious influences are present and potent factors. The lower impulsive and emotional stirrings solicit or impel him to be religious. His social instincts or more intelligent social desires and aims co-operate in the same result. The uplift to that condition of rational faith which corresponds to the ideal adjustment of the human self to the Divine Self, is effected largely through the awakening and employment of the higher æsthetical and ethical sentiments." —G. T. LADD, *Phil. of Religion*, Vol. I. p. 263.

" The distinctive note of mysticism is the fact that it brings religion into the closest contact, not with authority or formulas or traditions, but with the nature of man as man. It looks upon the soul as the prime factor in religion, and it regards man's awareness of God, his intimate consciousness of the nearness of God, his innate striving after union with God, as dependent upon the soul's possibility of approaching God directly. Now, the possession of a soul is not the prerogative of the devotee of any one particular religion to the exclusion of others. All men possess souls. It follows, therefore, logically, that no religion which contains mystical elements ought to claim, on behalf of its adherents, an exclusive approach to the Divine favour, or, indeed, any superiority in the realm of the spiritual life."—J. ABELSON, *The Immanence of God in Rabbinical Literature*, p. 300.

See AHURA RELIGION, ATMAN, EVOLUTION, GIRDLE (star), HIGH PRIEST, ILLUSION, INCARNATION, LETTER, MATTER, MĀYĀ (lower), PAPYRUS, PHENOMENA, SEALED LETTER, SELF, SPENDYAD, VICTORY, VISTASP, VOHUMAN, WILL, WITNESSES.

RELIGIONS, POPULAR :—

These are states of thought and emotion produced by the belief in certain Divinely inspired scriptures and myths, viewed from a literal standpoint and very imperfectly understood. The dramatic or mystery element in reverently regarded scriptures arouses emotions of an impersonal and exalted nature, which help to evolve the spirit within the soul. As the whole object of religions is the evolution of the spiritual nature in humanity, popular religions attain this end within the souls stirred by them, in spite of much that is injurious in the prevalent misconceptions and practice. Doctrines of immortality are hardly suggested in some scriptures, e.g. the Hebrew Bible, evidently because of the selfish considerations they naturally arouse in undisciplined minds. Doctrines, as such, seem to be of minor importance in religions, for they change and differ in every religion, and in no religion are they comprehensible. These facts are very evident at the present time, when more is known about religions and less is settled as to the meaning of any of them. Even about the cardinal doctrines of Christianity there is no settled opinion, and views of the "atonement" have changed within a generation.

Respecting the truth of religious doctrines, they are doubtless all expressions of truth, but popular phrases convey little meaning, and the truth is not evident. The use in the soul-life of incomprehensible doctrines seems to be to stimulate speculative thought and religious emotion, and this beneficial effect is apparent through all the ages of history.

" If religion may not exactly confess its allegorical nature, it gives sufficient indication of it in its mysteries. ' Mystery ' is in reality only a technical theological term for religious allegory. All religions have their mysteries. Properly speaking, a mystery is a dogma which is plainly absurd, but which, nevertheless, conceals in itself a lofty truth, and one which by itself would be completely incomprehensible to the ordinary understanding of the raw multitude. The multitude accepts it in this disguise on trust, and believes it, without being led astray by the absurdity of it, which even to its intelligence is obvious ; and in this way it participates in the kernel of the matter so far as it is possible for it to do so."— SCHOPENHAUER, *Religion : a Dialogue*, p. 17.

" The great change of feeling and outlook which is passing over the world to-day in regard to the relations of God and man may be described as the transition from the pedagogic to the vitalist view of God's relation to mankind. If you refer to the religious language of a generation or two ago, or better still, of centuries ago, you will find that our Christian fathers for the most part thought of God as a being who was always more or less indignant on account of the trouble they had caused him. The great presupposition of the religious thought of those days was that man was an undeserving rebel, and God a rightly offended judge. . . . I think that we are all instinctively aware that life is a deeper, more complex thing than can be explained in that conventional fashion."—R. J. CAMPBELL, Serm., *The Divine Mystery.*

"The religions of the world are not isolated, but are parts of a whole, forming together the religious education of the human race."—B. JOWETT, Serm., *The Subjection of the Son.*

"Now there is a spiritual world as extended as Humanity, and to assert its existence is no more to beg the question than the assertion of a physical world. I mean by it the world of the human heart in its relation to the idea of God and to all the feelings and actions which cluster round that idea. No one can deny the existence of this world, though they may give it a different name. It exists and has played its part, age after age, in nation after nation, in almost every individual of the race, in savage and civilised man, in heathen and Christian peoples. And there have been in this world a vast series of spiritual phenomena; distinct national worships; thousands of modifications of the idea of God; revolutions of religious thought profoundly altering national character; a multitude of facts, some related, some isolated, some strange, some normal in their succession—but all having one or two common features at least, which suggest the possibility of their mutual relation, and of their being arranged into order under a few great Ideas."— STOPFORD A. BROOKE, Serm., *Lord, Increase our Faith,* p. 117.

See AGNISHTOMA, BOOK STUDIES, PAPYRUS BOAT, PRIESTS AND ELDERS, READING, RITES, RITUAL, UR-HEKAU.

RELIGIOUS MERIT :—

A symbol of the wisdom-nature attained to by the ego through its strivings in the lower nature.

See MAIDEN.

RELIGIOUS VOWS :—

Symbolic of aspirations which yield such results as are capable of directing the evolution of the Self.

See VOW.

REMINISCENCE OR MEMORY :—

This, in its deeper signification, is identified with the causal Self, which is a direct offshoot or ray of the Self emanating from a centre in the higher mind. The personality is the means whereby intercommunication between the inner memory and the outer nature is eventually established, for through this memory the lower mind is awakened on its higher side and made receptive of ideals which are implanted by the causal Self.

See GATHAS (chanting), KALCHAS, RECOGNITION, RECOLLECTION, SHIPS (Greeks).

REMISSION OF SINS :—

This expression signifies liberation from captivity to the lower nature through the raising of the qualities by an influx of Divine Life.

"Jesus breathed on the disciples, and saith unto them, Receive ye the Holy Ghost : Whose soever sins ye remit, they are remitted unto them ; and whose soever sins ye retain, they are retained." —JOHN xx. 22, 23.

The disciplined qualities (disciples) "were glad," and therefore prepared for the outpouring (breathing) of the Spirit which raised them. The "remitting of sins" is the loosening from the imperfections and limitations which bind down the qualities, and from which liberation is obtained as soon as the qualities are "breathed upon" by the living Christ. The "retaining of sins" is the opposite course,—the failing of qualities to receive the Spirit through the agency of qualities more spiritualised than themselves, and consequent retention of evil and ignorance.

See ADOPTION, ATONEMENT, BONDAGE, BREATH (divine), CAPTIVITY, LIBERATION, RE-BIRTH, REDEMPTION, REGENERATION, RESURRECTION, RITES, SAINTS, SALVATION, VICTORY.

REN, OR NAME :—

A symbol of the differentiated and regenerate individuality, it having acquired through aspiration and effort the higher qualities wherewith it is now endowed.

"The *ren*, or name, to preserve which the Egyptians took the most extraordinary precautions, for the belief was widespread that unless the name of a man was preserved he ceased to exist. Already in the time of King Pepi the name was regarded as a most important portion of a man's economy, and in the following passage it ranks equally with the *ka* :—' The iron which is the ceiling of heaven openeth itself before Pepi, and he passeth through it with his panther skin upon him, and his staff and whip in his hand ; Pepi passeth with his flesh, and he is happy with his name, and he liveth with his double.' Already in the Pyramid Texts we find the deceased making supplication that his name may 'grow' or 'shoot forth' and endure as long as the names of Tem, Shu, Seb, and other gods."—BUDGE, *Book of the Dead*, p. lxiii.

The individuality (ren) is seated in the causal-body (ka) and is indistinguishable from it spiritually.

See CEILING OF SKY, IRON PLATE, KA, NAME, PANTHER SKIN, PYRAMID.

RENDING THE GARMENTS :—

A symbol of the rejection either of truth or error. It implies either enlargement of mind by the breaking forth of truth, or the suppression of truth and retention of opinions which narrow the intelligence.

"Then the high priest rent his garments, saying, He hath spoken blasphemy."—MAT. xxvi. 65.

The literalist rejects (rends) the spiritual truths offered him, because he is agnostic towards the higher, and does not believe in the possibilities which the Christ-soul pre-figures.

"We 'rend our mantle' whenever we review with a discriminating eye our past deeds ; for unless with God our deeds were as a cloak that covered us, it would never have been declared by the voice of an Angel, 'Blessed is he that watcheth, and keepeth his garments, lest he walk naked, and they see his shame'; for 'our shame' is then 'seen' when our life, appearing worthy of condemnation in the eyes of the righteous in judgment, has not the covering of good practice."—ST. GREGORY, *Morals on the Book of Job*, Vol. I. p. 123.

See CLOTHING, GARMENTS, SACK-CLOTH.

RENENET, GODDESS OF NURSING :—

A symbol of nature as the sustainer of forms.

See JUDGMENT HALL, MESKHENET.

RENOVATION OF THE EARTH :—

This signifies the passing on of the Life-wave to another globe of the terrene chain, which will be not physical but astral, mental, and buddhic.

"From the extinct fire of purification there will come a more beautiful earth, pure and perfect, and destined to be eternal."—*Zoroastrian System*.

Following the extinction of the purified lower planes, from which emerges the soul, the new "heaven" arises, and also a new "earth," which is a complete and perfect replica of the lower planes. In this buddhic state, the soul expresses itself in subtler vehicles, which are all that the lower vehicles have been, plus the increase of responsiveness which the finer materials engender.

"The coming of the day of God, by reason of which the heavens being on fire shall be dissolved, and the elements shall melt with fervent heat. But according to his promise, we look for new heavens and a new earth, wherein dwelleth righteousness."—2 PETER iii. 12, 13.

There is a reference here to the passing of the Life-wave to the next globe of the terrene chain, when both higher and lower states will be replaced by subtler conditions.

"And I saw a new heaven and a new earth : for the first heaven and the first earth are passed away, and the sea is no more."—REV. xxi. 1.

As existence for the soul is raised to the heaven (buddhic) plane, so that "heaven" disappears and there is a new heaven to aspire to. The first lower nature (earth) passes away, and the astral plane (sea) is no more.

"The world being melted and re-entered into the bosom of Jupiter, this God continues for some time totally concentered in himself ; . . . afterwards we see a new world spring from him, perfect in all its parts ; animals are produced anew ; an innocent race of men is formed under more favourable auspices, in order to people this earth."—SENECA, *Epist.* 9, and *Quæst. Nat. L.* 3, c, ult.

"But though heaven and earth are consumed with fire, and all the gods perish, with the whole human race ; yet is every human soul to live eternally in another world. The good find themselves in Gimlé, and all gods and things are again reproduced."—*Voluspa, Poetic Edda*, HOWITT, *Literature, etc.*

"Will any of the gods survive (after Regnarok), and will there be any longer a heaven and an earth ? There will arise out of the sea another earth most lovely and verdant, with pleasant fields where the grain shall grow unsown. Vidar and Vali shall survive ; neither the flood nor Surtur's fire shall harm them. They shall dwell on the plain of Ida, where Asgard formerly stood.

Thither shall come the sons of Thor, Modi and Magni, bringing with them their father's mallet Mjolnir. Balder and Hodur shall also repair thither from the abode of death (Hel)" *Prose Edda.* —MALLET, *North. Antiq.*, p. 457.

"Kalki (incarnation of Vishnu), who is yet to appear at the close of the fourth or Kali age, when the world has become wholly depraved, for the final destruction of the wicked, for the re-establishment of righteousness upon the earth, and the renovation of all creation with a return to a new age of purity (satya-yuga). According to some, he will be revealed in the sky, seated on a white horse, with a drawn sword in his hand, blazing like a comet."—MON. WILLIAMS, *Indian Wisdom*, p. 335.

"In that time (when the Messiah comes) all those who have not tasted the taste of death will die through Him, and He will revivify them at once. Why is this? Because nothing whatever of that pollution (the pollution of sin) shall remain in the world, and there will be a new world made by the Holy, Blessed be He!" (*Zohar*).—MYER, *Qabbalah*, p. 437.

"Then shall the earth no longer hold together. . . . The voice of every God shall cease in the Great Silence that no one can break; the fruits of the Earth shall rot; nay Earth no longer shall bring forth; and Air itself shall faint. This, when it comes, shall be the World's old age, impiety,—irregularity, and lack of rationality in all good things. . . . God ending all ill, by either washing it away with water-flood, or burning it away with fire, or by the means of pestilent diseases, spread through all hostile lands,—God will recall the Cosmos to its ancient form; so that the World itself shall seem meet to be worshipped and admired; and God, the Maker and Restorer of so vast a work, be sung by the humanity who shall be then. . . . For this Re-birth of Cosmos is the making of all good things, and the most holy and most pious bringing-back again of Nature's self, by means of a set course of time" (*The Perfect Sermon*).—G. R. S. MEAD, *T. G. Hermes*, Vol. II. p. 357.

"The world, or what we call the creation, is not so much a completed fact as a *conatus*, struggling up concomitantly with the powers that are doing battle in it for a character; falling with them in their fall, rising with them, or to rise, to a condition, finally, of complete order and beauty. There is much to be said for such an expectation, and it appears to be just what is held up in the promise of a new heavens and earth, wherein dwelleth righteousness."—H. BUSHNELL, *Nature and the Supernatural*, p. 143.

See AAT (waters), ASGARD, BALDER, BUDDHA (maitreya), CHRIST'S SECOND COMING, COMETS, CONFLAGRATION, HORSE (white), HVANIRATHA, JOB, JUDGMENT DAY, KALKI, KARSHVARES, KINGDOM, PLANETARY CHAIN, PRALAYA, REGIONS, REGNAROK, RESURRECTION, SOSHYANS, SOSIOSH, SPRINGTIME, SURTUR, VOHUMAN.

RESPECTFUL MANNERS :—

A symbol of harmony in human conditions during the period of involution.

"Human beings, among whom respectful manners and pure customs prevailed, occupied one territory."—*Chinese Mythology*, KIDD, *China.*

And now is developed the humanity of the fabled Golden Age,—the early type of man in which the absence of all relative experience of opposites appears as Edenic perfection. The "territory" is a symbol of the limitation imposed upon the race by the Absolute.

See CIVILISING, EDEN, GOLDEN AGE, OPPOSITES, RACES, RELATIVE, YAO.

RE-STAU, THE PASSAGES OF THE TOMB :—

A symbol of the lower planes in which the Self is involved.

"Thy name (Osiris) hath been made in Re-stau when it had fallen therein. Homage to thee, O Osiris, in thy strength and in thy power, thou hast obtained the mastery in Re-stau. Thou art raised up, O Osiris, and thy might is in Re-stau, and thy power is in Abtu (Abydos). Thou goest round about through heaven, and thou lookest upon the generations of men, O thou Being who circlest."—BUDGE, *Book of the Dead*, Ch. CXIX.

The manifestation of the Christ hath been completed in the lower nature to which it had descended at the beginning. Christ is glorified in that he has obtained the mastery over the lower activities. He is risen from the dead lower nature, and is all-powerful both below and above (Abtu). He traverseth the higher nature of the soul and draweth upward the developing mental qualities in all their stages of growth. He is the indwelling Spirit who passes through the cycle of life.

"You may nail Christ on his cross in the agonies of suffering humanity; you may lay him in the sepulchre of hate, and roll the stone of unbelief to the door, and seal it with the seal of brutal materialism; but you cannot keep him down. Oh, miracle of miracles, this constant resurgence of the spirit of Christ in our common life ! Christ breaks his fetters and issues forth invincible in the teeth of all that his foes can do."—R. J. CAMPBELL, Serm., *Christ Arisen*.

See ABTU, FETTERS, HEROIC RUNNER, MOUTH (speech), OSIRIS, SEPULCHRE, TOMB.

RESURRECTION FROM THE DEAD :—

A symbol of the rising of the Higher Self from the potential to the actual in the minds of humanity : also the rising of the indwelling or incarnate Self from the lower nature to the higher at the end of the cycle. In relation to the egos, the resurrection signifies the rising of the conscious-ness from the lower mind to the higher in the causal-body at the cycle's end ; or the liberation of the spiritual egos from captivity to the lower nature. The lower nature is "dead," for it has in it no true Life.

" For if the dead are not raised, neither hath Christ been raised. . . . But now hath Christ been raised from the dead, the first-fruits of them that are asleep. . . . Christ the first-fruits ; then they that are Christ's, at his coming. Then cometh the end, when he shall deliver up the kingdom to God."—1 COR. xv. 16-24.

If the lower qualities (the dead) have not been transmuted (raised), neither hath the incarnate Self been raised ; for the raising of the qualities implies the rise of the Self in the soul. But now the Self hath been raised in the qualities as the first spiritual fruit of the experience of the egos "asleep" in the human forms. The Self is the first to rise, then the egos rise whose qualities are raised from the dead lower nature. Then at the end of the cycle, when the Self has raised the souls to the buddhic plane,— the Self becomes merged in the Absolute.

" The true resurrection, the resurrection to newness of life, is the rising of the Christ in human nature and human society into higher, fuller, and richer modes of expression. That resurrection is continually going on, and its correla-tive is the ascension of human conscious-ness into perfect oneness with the all-embracing mind of God in the sacred fellowship of love."—R. J. CAMPBELL, Serm., *The Resurrection Life*.

" The Phrygians call Him (Korybas the perfect Man) also dead—when buried in the body as though in a tomb or sepulchre. . . . 'The dead shall leap from their graves,' that is, from their earthly bodies, regenerated spiritual, not fleshly. This is the Resurrection which takes place through the Gate of the Heavens, through which all those who do not pass remain dead. The same Phrygians again call this very same Man, after the transformation, God. For he becomes God when rising from the dead ; through such a Gate he shall pass into Heaven " (Doctrines of the Naassene Gnostics). From the *Philosophumena* of Hippolytus.—G. R. S. MEAD, *T. G. Hermes*, Vol. I. p. 172.

The Archetypal Man (Korybas) dies at the close of the involutionary period, and rises in the souls of humanity in the present evolutionary epoch. He is the Higher Self or the God in us.

" Out of the tomb of worldliness and selfishness, and the grave-cloths of materialism, ignorance and error, the Eternal Christ is coming forth. Resurrection is not an isolated, catas-trophic act ; it is a perpetual process and an ever-active principle. The Divine Spirit is always rising within humanity. The stone is always being rolled away from the tomb in order that the Divine Life may come forth in power and glory."—E. W. LEWIS, *Easter*, 1910.

" The chief priests and the Pharisees were gathered together unto Pilate, saying, Sir, we remember that that deceiver said, while he was yet alive, After three days I will rise again."— MAT. xxvii. 62, 63.

The state of mind in literalism, formalism, and dogmatism (Phari-sees, etc.), does not wish for Christ to rise in the mind, for that would put an end to the practices it finds pleasure in ; it therefore appeals to worldly-mindedness (Pilate) to crush out the Spirit. Yet, "after three days," which here signify a period of time to complete a condition of development, Christ would rise in glory in the minds of human kind, and become the actual ruler in men's lives, and not only the Ideal of their souls. For the ideal of life of one age is the actual conduct of the next.

" Curiously enough we find the story of the resurrection of Dionysus, after his dismemberment by the Titans, com-pared by the most learned of the Christian Fathers with the resurrection of the Christ. Thus Origen (*Con. Celsum*, IV. 171), after making the comparison, remarks apologetically and somewhat bitterly : ' Or, forsooth, are the Greeks to be allowed to use such words with regard *to the soul, and speak in allegorical fashion,* and we forbidden to do so ? '—thus clearly declaring that the ' resurrection ' was an *allegory of the soul, and not historical.*"—G. R. S. MEAD, *Orpheus,* p. 186.

" The Cross and Passion represents the pain and stress that accompanies the process (of the return of man to the perfect Humanity—Christ) ; the pain of self-sacrifice, of penitence, of resistance to temptation, the trouble connected with the maintenance of a consistent life in the midst of a selfish world. The Resurrection is the new life that follows the sacrifice ; the Ascension is the final attainment of union with God."—J. G. ADDERLEY, *The Symbolism of the Mass.*

" Damacius, speaking of the dismemberment and resurrection of Osiris, remarks, ' this should be a mingling with God, an all perfect at-one-ment, a return upwards of our souls to the divine.' "—MEAD, *Orpheus,* p. 186.

" Osiris died and was buried, like Asari or Merodach, whose temple at Babylon was also his tomb ; but it was that he might rise again in the morning with renewed strength and brilliancy. . . . Both in Egypt and in Babylonia he was the God of the resurrection, whether that took place in this visible world or in the heavenly paradise. . . . In order to share in this state of bliss, it was necessary for the believer in Osiris to become like the God himself. He must himself be an Osiris, according to the Egyptian expression. His individuality remained intact ; as he had been on earth, so would he be in heaven."—A. H. SAYCE, *Rel. of Anc. Egyptians, etc.,* pp. 164, 169.

The Higher Self (Osiris) became involved in matter (tomb) in order to rise from it in greater glory during the emanation (morning) of a new era. The soul, or ego, must become perfect in all its qualities even as the Self is perfect, and when the perfected soul is liberated from the lower nature it becomes one with the Self above.

" The apostle bids us reckon : ' Likewise reckon ye also yourselves to be dead unto sin, but alive unto God through Jesus Christ.' Hence Christ says, ' I am the resurrection and the life,' for that all his are safe in him, suffering, dying and rising. He is the life, ' *our* life ' ; yea, so our life, that by him the elect do live before God, even then when as to themselves they yet are dead in their sins. Wherefore, hence it is that in time they partake of quickening grace from this their Head, to the making of them also live by faith, in order to their living hereafter with him in glory ;

for if Christ lives, they cannot die that were sharers with him in his resurrection. Hence they are said to ' live,' being ' quickened together with him.' "—JOHN BUNYAN, *Justification, etc.*

" Risen with Christ. This Resurrection, then, is a moral change ; it is a spiritual movement. A resurrection is a transfer from one state to another. It is a passage from the darkness of the tomb to the sunshine of the upper air. It is an exchange of the coldness, stillness, corruption of death for the warmth and movement, and undecayed energies of life. . . . The spiritual resurrection of a soul belongs to nature just as little as does the bodily raising of a corpse. It is an evidence of the real introduction of a Higher Power into humanity. It is essentially *super*natural."—H. P. LIDDON, *University Sermons,* pp. 260, 265.

See AFU-RĀ, ASCENSION, ATONEMENT, BONDAGE, CAUSAL-BODY, CHRIST'S SECOND COMING, CONFLAGRATION, CRUCIFIXION (Jesus), DEAD, DEATH UNTO LIFE, DIONYSUS, DISMEMBERMENT, EVOLUTION, INCARNATION, KALKI, KHEPER, LIBERATION, MORNING, OSIRIS, PHARISEES, PILATE, RE-BIRTH, REGENERATION, REMISSION, RENOVATION, SAHU, SAINTS, SALVATION, SCARABEUS, SELF, TET, THREE, TOMB, TZELEM, VICTORY.

RETURN OF THE GREAT GODDESS :—

A symbol of the Wisdom-nature evolving in the soul after its period of obscuration or latency. Since the fall of mind (man) into the lower nature, the buddhic consciousness (Wisdom) has been absent from the human soul. This spiritual consciousness returns to the ego when the soul is perfected at the end of the cycle, and reveals the " treasures in heaven."

See AMATERASU, EDEN, ESTHER, FALL, GODDESS, HIDING, MAST, WITNESSES (two).

REVELATION :—

A symbolic communication from the higher nature to the lower, imparting truths of the invisible universe and the soul. As revelation does not, and cannot, arise from the lower nature, so it is self-evident that the lower or objective mind of man does not *compose* the revelation, but is merely the receptive vessel into which the Divine message is poured. The evidence for this view of " revealed truth " is over-whelming when appreciated. That evidence is to be found in the universal fact that the sacred scriptures and myths of the world are almost throughout of obscure, miraculous, and nonsensical appearance, and of such a character, taken as a whole, as to make incredible any theory of their mundane rational origin. Their purport, indeed, precludes a human origin, for no mind of man is able to investigate cosmical beginnings, and the nature of that which transcends the lower consciousness.

A thousand instances will be found in this dictionary of the nonsensical appearance of the world-scriptures, and it may be sufficiently obvious that they have been neither invented nor composed by man. The scriptures themselves always assert that they are of *Divine origin*, and this is a consistent and intelligent view of them. The apparent nonsense is nothing but an indication of their symbolical nature, and an assurance that their diction has never seriously been tampered with. It is plain that their symbology would be ruined if meddling scribes altered the language and introduced interpolations to accord with their own ignorance.

" In the religious history of humanity it is human thought and human speech which are the most distinctive and effective media of the Self-revelation of God ; and yet more especially, the thought and speech of the divinely selected and inspired men of revelation. . . . This voice of God to man, through man, has been variously expressed. In the creeds of these different religions, the avatars of Vishnu, the various incarnations of the Buddha, the demi-gods that descended from the Scandinavian Heimdallr, the prophets and seers of Old-Testament religion, and Jesus and his Apostles in the New Dispensation all have the office of revealing God to man."—G. T. LADD, *Phil. of Religion*, Vol. II. pp. 419-20.

" When the future philosophic theologian comes to take in this conception (of many inspired scriptures), he will no longer be satisfied to study the sacred text of his own form of religion. He will study the text of all the higher religions, trying to find the similar import represented through their different legends, and the similar principle expounded in their not greatly differing precepts. Such an attitude of mind will almost infinitely elevate his aims and widen his horizon."—G. L. RAYMOND, *Psychology of Inspiration*, p. 131.

" The theory of an essentially similar revelation in East and West would harmonise with the conception of Paul. He writes that God had never left himself without witness, that man's conscience is the witness of God, and that a ' mystery ' was hid in God from the beginning of the world, which ' eternal purpose ' was in his time made known as it had in former times not been made known. According to this universalist conception, held by Origen and Augustine, Christian revelation is directly connected with Divine revelations at all times and in all places, with a continuity of Divine influences."—E. DE BUNSEN, *Angel Messiah*, p. 51.

" No revelation can be adequately given by the address of man to man, whether by writing or orally, even if he be put in possession of the Truth itself. For all such revelation must be made through words : and words are but counters—the coins of intellectual exchange. There is as little resemblance between the silver coin and the bread it purchases, as between the word and the thing it stands for. Looking at the coin, the form of the loaf does not suggest itself. Listening to the word, you do not perceive the idea for which it stands, unless you are already in possession of it. . . . He alone believes truth who feels it. He alone has a religion whose soul knows by experience that to serve God and know Him is the richest treasure. And unless Truth come to you, not in word only, but in power besides,—authoritative because true, not true because authoritative—there has been no real revelation made to you from God. . . . God is a Character. To love God is to love His character. This Love is manifested in obedience—Love is the life of which obedience is the form. ' He that hath my commandments and keepeth them, he it is that loveth me. He that loveth me not keepeth not my sayings.' . . . To this Love, adoring and obedient, God reveals His truth. Love is the condition without which revelation does not take place. As in the natural, so in the spiritual world :—by compliance with the laws of the universe, we put ourselves in possession of its blessings."—F. W. ROBERTSON, *Sermons*, 1st Series, pp. 6-12.

Revelation by means of symbols is not authoritative but suggestive. The inner mind already possesses truth, and the truth must be awakened by the symbols. If the mind is pre-occupied and antagonistic, the new truth will not be aroused in it.

" Unless I misread the religious tendencies of our time, there is evidenced just now a remarkable return on the part of many people to the desire for a special and definite authoritative divine word of revelation as contrasted with all merely human and naturalistic explanations of things as they are. . . . But Sabatier contends that as we gain in spiritual autonomy and the sense of spiritual freedom, we tend more and more to rely upon the inward light, the presence of God in our own souls, to guide us into truth. Now I repeat that, unless I am greatly mistaken, present-day tendencies to a large extent are not justifying this forecast. . . . I know personally quite a number of highly educated and intelligent men who all say with one voice that if they are to have a religious faith at all it must not be based only upon what they can discover for themselves, but upon an undoubted revelation of God to men, an opening of the door between seen and unseen, between earth and heaven, and the coming through from the higher side to the lower of that which is eternal and divine."—R. J. CAMPBELL, Serm., *The Morning Star.*

See AMBAYAVIS, AXE, BAPTISM OF FIRE, DEVELOPMENT, GOSPEL, INSPIRATION, KORAN, MYTHOLOGY, PAPYRUS BOAT, PEN, RAMAYANA, SACRED TEXT, SASTRA, SCRIPTURES, SRUTI, UPANISHAD, VEDA, WORD OF GOD.

RHADAMANTHUS, MINOS, AND ÆACUS :—

Symbols of Divine principles of the Higher Triad.
See TRIAD.

RHEA, GODDESS (NŪT) :—

A symbol of space.

"Rhea is represented as a daughter of Uranus and Ge, and the wife of Cronos, by whom she became the mother of Hestia, Demeter, Hera, Hades, Poseidon and Zeus."—*Smith's Class. Dict.*

Space is said to be originated by Spirit and Matter (Uranus and Ge). It is united to Time, by which it brings forth the physical (Hestia), the lower buddhic (Demeter), the higher buddhic (Hera), the astral (Hades), and the atmic (Poseidon) planes ; also the Higher Self (Zeus).

"The Secret Doctrine,—postulating that conditioned or limited space (location) has no real being except in this world of illusion, or in other words, in our perceptive faculties,—teaches that every one of the higher, as of the lower worlds, is interblended with our own objective world."—H. P. BLAVATSKY, *Secret Doctrine*, Vol. I. p. 662.

See ADITI, AIDONEUS, BIRTH OF OSIRIS, CRONUS, GE, HEAVEN AND EARTH, MĀYĀ, NUT, SATURN, TIME, TITANS, URANUS, ZAGREUS, ZEUS.

RIB OF MAN, FROM NEAR THE HEART :—

A symbol of a high sub-plane of the mental plane, from which the emotion-nature (woman) evolves.
See BONES, WOMAN.

RICE AND BARLEY :—

Symbols of wisdom and love.
See BARLEY.

RICE GRAINS FROM WATERY FIELDS :—

Symbolic of intuitions of wisdom arising from the exercise of the mental faculties in the pursuit of truth.
See CORN, MARSH, WATER.

RICE GRAINS THROWN IN THE AIR TO DISPEL THE DARKNESS :—

Symbolic of intuitions of wisdom in the mind (air), which is stirred from above ; these dispel ignorance and error.
See AIR, DARKNESS.

RICH MAN :—

A symbol of the mind set upon identifying itself with a multiplicity of objects, while inclination fosters the " pairs of opposites " that beget the sense of separateness.

"Would that the days passed swiftly over me, and that all the hours were one, that I might go forth from this world ; and go and see that Beautiful One, . . . where there is neither day nor night, and no darkness but light, and neither good nor bad, nor rich nor poor, neither male nor female, nor slaves nor freemen, nor any proud and uplifted over those who are humble."—*Acts of Judas Thomas,* WRIGHT's trans., p. 265.

Here the soul yearns for union with the Higher Self, when the lower nature (world) will be surpassed, and all conflict be at an end. But it is impossible for an ego while distracted by the opposites and the conflicting emotions (riches) of the lower planes to enter into the nature of that which is bliss.

See LAZARUS, MAN (rich), OPPOSITES, POVERTY, TREASURE.

RICHES OR WEALTH (HIGHER ASPECT) :—

A symbol of the higher emotions and true knowledge. The transmuted qualities,—the treasure laid up in heaven.

" There is that maketh himself rich, yet hath nothing : there is that maketh himself poor, yet hath great riches. The ransom of a man's life are his riches : but the poor heareth not rebuke."— PROV. xiii. 7, 8.

The first rich man is full of the satisfactions of desire, which profit nothing. The second has made himself poor in desire, but rich in wisdom and love, and it is this heavenly wealth which will be the ransom to liberate him from bondage to desire. The poor in this wealth perceive not its excellence.

See BONDAGE, HUSBAND (good), POOR PEOPLE, POOR IN SPIRIT, RANSOM, WEALTH.

RICHES, OR WEALTH (LOWER ASPECT) :—

A symbol of that quality of acquisitiveness which appertains to the sensation-nature, with its coveted objects of sense. This includes the activities of the lower emotions which are concerned with the personality and its desires.

See SHIPS (beaked).

RIDGES OF MOUNTAINS OR EARTH :—

A symbol of the striving aspirations of the lower nature.

See EARTH, FURROWS, HILL COUNTRY.

RIGHT ARM AND LEFT :—

Symbols of will,—the outgoing and incoming activity ; also symbolic of that exercise of choice which incurs Karma.

See ARMS OF BODY, CORN.

RIGHT FOOT :—

A symbol of outgoing energy in progressive activity.

See FEET, FOOT, STRIDES OF SOUL.

RIGHT HAND :—

A symbol of the active principle in outgoing energy. The " right hand of power " signifies the positive, outgoing, energetic, evolutionary force.

See CLOUDS OF HEAVEN, HAND (right).

RIGHT SIDE :—

This symbol indicates the stirring of the outgoing principle of action.

RIGHTEOUS MAN :—

A symbol of the perfected soul liberated from the lower nature.

See GATHA (ush.), MAN (righteous).

RIMTHURSAR, OR FROST GIANTS :—

A symbol of the primal powers and qualities that arise from latency (frost) in matter, and become active in the lower nature of the soul during the cycle of evolution.

" We are far from believing Ymir to have been a god, for he was wicked as are all of his race, whom we call Frost-giants. And it is said that, when Ymir slept, he fell into a sweat, and from the pit of his left arm was born a man and woman, and one of his feet engendered with the other a son, from whom descend the Frost-giants, and we therefore call Ymir the old Frost-giant " *Prose Edda.*—MALLET, *North. Antiq.*, p. 403.

The Archetypal Man (Ymir) in his lower nature originates the lower planes and all their powers and qualities in the present cycle. First, the mental (man) and buddhic (woman) planes were produced from the matter side (left) of latent being. Then on the active progressive side (feet) there was outpoured the life of the lower planes (son) in which are all the primal energies and qualities that were lying latent (frost) in the Archetypal Man, who is the consummation of the process of involution. Both the *Ymer* and *Demiurge* symbols are said to be " wicked " to indicate the potential lower nature of being.

" Alfadir (All-Father) hath formed heaven and earth, and the air, and all things thereunto belonging. And what is more, he hath made man, and given him a soul which shall live and never perish though the body shall have mouldered away, or have been burnt to ashes. And all that are righteous shall dwell with him in the place called Gimli, or Vingolf ; but the wicked shall go to Hel, and thence to Niflhel, which is below, in the ninth world. ' And where did this God remain before he made heaven and earth ? ' asked Gangler. ' He was then,' replied Har, ' with the Hrimthursar ' " *Prose Edda.*—*Ibid.*, p. 401.

Prior to manifestation of the higher and lower planes, the Divine Life is inactive and potential ; Truth (water) is latent (frozen).

See ARC. MAN, ASKR, DEMIURGE, FATHER, FROST, GIANTS, GIMLI, HADES, HELL, MAN, NIFLHEIM,

QUALITIES, TITANS, WELL, WOMAN, YGGDRASIL, YMIR.

RING, GOLD :—

A symbol of wisdom, and domination over the lower planes.

" By a ' ring ' is designated the omnipotence of Divine Power. For when it keeps us from being seized by temptations, it encircles around and holds firm in wondrous ways the snares of the ancient enemy."—ST. GREGORY, *Morals on the Book of Job*, Vol. III. p. 575.

See FYLLA, GOLD.

RING AS A CIRCLE :—

A symbol of completeness and perfection, and therefore refers to the higher planes.

See CIRCLE.

RINGHORNE, BALDER'S SHIP :—

A symbol of the astral vehicle at an early stage.

" The Asar (gods) took up the body of Balder and carried it to the sea, where lay Balder's ship, which was called ' Ringhorne,' and which was the largest of all ships."—*The Story of Balder, Prose Edda*, HOWITT, *Literature, etc.*

And now the Higher Self under its threefold aspect raises the lower consciousness to the higher sub-planes of the astral plane, whereon were now established such means as would enable centres to be established for its completer expression and functioning. The " ship " is the desire-body, or astral-body, of greatest importance in the lower evolution.

See ASAR, BALDER, CHEMMIS, DEATH OF BALDER, NANNA, SEA.

RIOTOUS LIVING :—

A symbol of the soul absorbed in pursuit of objects of sensation and desire, and immersed in ignorance on the lower planes.

See PRODIGAL.

RISHES OR PATRIARCHS, SEVEN :—

These are symbols of the seven root-Races of humanity, commencing on super-physical planes of being.

See DELUGE, ROOT-RACES, SHIP OF MANU.

RISHES OR SAINTS :—

A symbol of spiritual influences, atma-buddhic, imparting truths to the soul. Or the spiritual monads of life.

See MONAD OF LIFE, SAGES, SAINTS, SONS OF GOD.

RITES, CEREMONIES AND OBSERVANCES IN POPULAR RELIGIONS :—

Materialistic practices invariably based upon mistaken interpretations of the sacred scriptures, whereby the symbols themselves are taken literally in a false sense, while the true meanings remain obscured.

" Then there come to Jesus from Jerusalem Pharisees and scribes, saying, why do thy disciples transgress the tradition of the elders ? For they wash not their hands when they eat bread. And he answered . . . Well did Isaiah prophesy of you saying,—This people honoureth me with their lips ; but their heart is far from me. But in vain do they worship me, teaching as their doctrines the precepts of men."—MAT. xv. 1–9.

Then there enter into the soul carping states of formalism and literalism, which complain that their way of worshipping is not followed by other qualities of mind. The statement refers to the readiness with which people criticise and cavil at the methods by which some of their fellows derive their spiritual food of truth and goodness (bread). As if, forsooth, everyone must go through some particular prescribed ritual ere the " bread of heaven " can be received and assimilated ! The " precepts of men " signify the unilluminated observance of forms and rites and ceremonies which are put in the place of yearnings towards Love, Wisdom, and Truth.

" Repent, and be baptised everyone of you in the name of Jesus Christ for the remission of sins, and ye shall receive the gift of the Holy Ghost."—ACTS ii. 38.

The lower qualities (people) had appealed to the higher for help ; and the disciplined lower mind (Peter) pointed out the necessity for the aspiring lower qualities to purify themselves by truth (water baptism), so that they may advance towards the Divine Ideal (Christ), thereby causing the disappearance of evil and inducing a mental state receptive of the higher emotions bestowed of buddhi (Holy Ghost). There is no outward ceremony of a material character enjoined in the above text, but an immaterial spiritual purification and grace.

" The vision of the Eternal is possible to us in this world of time ; real communion with the God who is from everlasting to everlasting, in this life of transient things. Don't miss the vision in the dazzle of the hour ; don't miss the pearl of high price in the smaller transactions of the world's markets. Don't miss them in the practical materialisms of ecclesiasticism and the stereotyped dogmas of theology. You can stifle the religious life with ecclesiastical garments, and kill the religious soul with theological opinions ; you can argue for stereotyped forms and doctrines, and leave God's great world unsearched and unrevered, and miss the opening revelations of the Everlasting Spirit. But if you do, God will have another Church and other priests, men who will turn to the world as Moses did to the bush on Horeb, and hear God speak out of the midst of it. For, depend upon it, that Word which was in the beginning with God, by whom all things were made, and which was made flesh, and became incarnate in man, is not yet fully spelt out ; we are only diving deeper into its meaning, and much is yet to be revealed. O human spirit, enter upon thy large inheritance in the Unseen and the hitherto Unknown." —Ed. Irving.

See Baptism, Caiaphas, Ceremonies, Disciples, Food, Healing, Herod, Jesus of gospels, Peter, Pharisees, Priests and elders, Prophets (false), Qualities, Religions, Remission, Sacrament, Taurobolium, Worship (wood).

RITUAL AND CEREMONIAL :—

Symbolism of the Soul and its qualities, together with the means and process of their spiritual evolution.

Buddhism and Christianity have both developed, in the course of fifteen hundred years, into sacerdotal and sacramental systems, each with its bells and rosaries and images and holy water ; each with its services in dead languages, with choirs and processions and creeds and incense, in which the laity are spectators only ; each with its mystic rites and ceremonies performed by shaven priests in gorgeous robes ; each with its abbots and monks and nuns, of many grades ; each with its worship of virgins, saints and angels ; its reverence to the Virgin and the Child ; its confessions, fasts, and purgatory ; its idols, relics, symbols, and sacred pictures ; its shrines and pilgrimages ; each with its huge monasteries and gorgeous cathedrals ; its

powerful hierarchy and its wealthy cardinals ; each, even, ruled over by a Pope, with a triple tiara on his head and the sceptre of temporal power in his hand, the representative on earth of an eternal Spirit in the heavens ! If all this be chance, it is a most stupendous miracle of coincidence. And it cannot be objected that the resemblance is in externals only. The principles which bind each of these two organisations together, which give them their recuperative vital power, are also similar. Each of the two Churches claims to be guided by the eternal Spirit, who is especially present in the infallible Head of the Church ; each lays peculiar stress upon the mystic sacrament in which the priest reverently swallows a material thing, and by so doing believes himself to become partaker in some mysterious way of a part of the Divine Being, who, during the ceremony, has become incorporated therein."—T. W. Rhys Davids, *Indian Buddhism*, p. 193.

" The crozier, the mitre, the dalmatic, the cope or *pluvial*, which the Grand Lamas wear on a journey, or when they perform some ceremony outside the temple ; the service with a double choir, psalmody, exorcisms, the censer swinging on five chains and contrived to be opened and shut at will, benediction by the Lamas, with the right hand extended over the heads of the faithful, the chaplet, sacerdotal celibacy, Lenten retirements from the world, the worship of saints, fasts, processions, litanies, holy water—these are the points of contact between the Buddhists and ourselves."—M. Huc, *Travels in Tartary, etc.*, Vol. II. Ch. 2.

Sacred symbolism being of Divine origin is interrelated and consistent throughout all nations and periods, therefore occasional similarities in scriptures and ritual are just what might be expected. Their presence does not indicate human intervention in the majority of cases. They are quite well accounted for by reference to the one Intelligence behind all the symbolism.

The origin of ritual is to be found in the tendency to materialise sacred symbols and treat them as of religious value, whereas, of course, it is the spiritual meaning only that is of value. Passages in the sacred books are mistakenly taken as authority for the outward observances and physical arrangements which now characterise popular religions.

" Christian teaching is professedly symbolical. And the symbolised is greater, and deeper, and older than the symbol."—W. S. LILLY, *The Great Engima*, p. liv.

See BAPTISM, CEREMONIES, CHURCH, CROSS, FASTING, FINGERS (two), FOOD AS GOD, HAIR SHAVEN, HOST, HYMN, INCENSE, INSPIRATION, MONKS, MUSIC, PILGRIMS, POPE, PROCESSION, PURGATORY, RELIGIONS, ROBE, SACRAMENT, SCEPTRE, SCRIPTURES, SHRINE, TEMPLE, TIARA, TRANSUBSTANTIATION, VIRGIN, WATER.

RIVER :—

A symbol of the course of the soul's evolution from the material to the spiritual life in the world of experience.

"The analogy between human life and a river is indeed very complete. Our course starts far from our divine goal, and sometimes seems to be leading us right away from it ; it is long before we can even catch a glimpse of what it is ; but the current of our being gradually deepens and broadens as we near the full ocean of the life of God, and at the last stage of our winding journey the ocean tide comes up to meet us, gathers us into its bosom, and bears us away to our eternal home. As the river never stops flowing till it gets to the ocean, so man can never stop seeking till every part of his being is perfectly at one with God. The flow of our desires is first in one direction and then in another, but it can never cease and never pause till it comes to rest—and every part and particle of it comes to fulfilment— in the infinitude of God."—R. J. CAMPBELL, Serm., *The Ceaseless Quest.*

See EVOLUTION, OCEAN, PUITIKA, TUAT, VOURUKASHA.

RIVER, SACRED. USUALLY THE PRINCIPAL RIVER OF A COUNTRY :—

A symbol of the Divine Life forth-pouring from above, and passing downwards through every plane. It may be taken as signifying atma-buddhic energy to fertilise the lower planes.

"The great celestial watery mass which was the source of the river Nile." —BUDGE, *Egypt. Heaven and Hell*, Vol. III. p. 124.

The "celestial ocean" is a symbol of the Divine Truth,—the "water above the firmament,"—and this is the source of the Divine Life (river Nile) which causes the growth of the soul.

"The river (Urnes) was in direct communication with the watery mass of the sky on which Rā sailed by day."— *Ibid.*, p. 95.

The Self (Rā) is said to sail in the Sun-boat, or higher causal-body (World-soul), on the "waters" of Truth-reality, when manifesting in the cycle of life, i.e. the "Tuat."

"And a river went out of Eden to water the garden ; and from thence it was parted, and became four heads."— GEN. ii. 10.

And from the buddhic plane, with atma-buddhic energy, proceeded a "river" or channel of Divine Life and communication, to bring truth to the soul ; and from this buddhic level differentiation takes place, which involves the quaternary,—the higher mental, the lower mental, the astral, and the physical planes.

"Thou visited the earth, and after thou hadst made it to desire rain thou greatly enrichest it. The river of God is full of water : thou providest them corn, when thou hast so prepared the earth."—Ps. lxv. 9.

The Higher Self is said to brood over the lower nature (earth) of the soul, and after having thereby caused it to yearn for truth (rain), he responds by filling it with the germs of the higher qualities. For the Divine Life which flows from the Absolute is Truth (water) itself, and the qualities will be given that spiritual food (corn) which they need for sustenance, when their lower nature is prepared to receive it.

"There is a river, the streams whereof shall make glad the city of God, the holy place of the tabernacles of the most High."—Ps. xlvi. 4.

The Divine Life brings many aspects of truth to the seat of the Higher Self in the innermost shrine of the causal-bodies of mankind, in which the Supreme abides.

"First we have the gladdening River— and emblem of many great and joyous truths. . . . Its waters shall never fail, and thirst shall flee whithersoever this river comes. It is to be remembered that the psalm is running in the track of a certain constant symbolism that pervades all Scripture. From the first book of Genesis down to the last chapter of Revelation, you can hear the dashing of the waters of the river. ' It went out from the garden and parted into four heads.' ' Thou makest them drink of the river of thy pleasures.' ' Behold, waters issued out from under the threshold of the house eastward,' and everything shall live whithersoever the river cometh. ' He that believeth on me, out of his belly shall flow rivers of living water.

'And he showed me a pure river of water of life, clear as crystal, proceeding out of the throne of God and of the Lamb.' . . . Guided by the constant meaning of scriptural symbolism, I think we may conclude that this river, 'the streams whereof make glad the city of God' is God himself in the outflow and self-communication of his own grace to the soul. The gift of God, which is living water, is God himself, considered as the ever-imparting source of all refreshment, of all strength, of all blessedness. . . . Not with noise, not with tumult, not with conspicuous and destructive energy, but in silent, secret underground communication, God's grace, God's love, His peace, His power, His Almighty and gentle Self flow into men's souls. Quietness and confidence on our sides correspond to the quietness and serenity with which He glides into the heart. . . . And then I need only touch upon the last thought, the *effects* of this communicated God. 'The streams make glad'—with the gladness which comes from refreshment, with the gladness that comes from the satisfying of all thirsty desires, with the gladness which comes from the contact of the spirit with absolute completeness; of the will, with perfect authority; of the heart, with changeless love; of the understanding, with pure incarnate truth; of the conscience, with infinite peace; of the child, with the father; of my emptiness, with his fullness; of my changeableness, with His immutability; of my incompleteness, with His perfectness."—A. MACLAREN, *Sermons*, 3rd Series, pp. 50-5.

See ANDUISAR, AQUEDUCT, CHANNELS, CITY OF GOD, CORN, EARTH, EDEN (rivers), ERIDANUS, GANGES, HAPI, IRRIGATION, JORDAN, LAKSHMANA, MEH, NILE, OCEAN, RAIN, TUAT, VOURUKASHA, WATER.

RIVERS :—

A symbol of channels of truth or life through the quaternary,—the four planes of nature which are below atma.

"All nature rejoices at Zoroaster's birth, the very trees and rivers share in the universal thrill of gladness that shoots through the world."—A. V. W. JACKSON, *Zoroaster*, p. 27.

All the elemental kingdoms and forces of the lower planes contribute towards the Soul's development. As science shows, the physical body comprises all the materials and properties which are appropriate in nature to serve an end. So the World-Soul is indeed the sum total of all the conscious life in the Logos, which contributes under every phase of its manifestation to the upbuilding of the human soul. The "trees and rivers" are symbols for channels of love and truth, which are the very warp and roof of the World-soul.

"By rivers are signified truths in abundance, because by waters are signified truths. In an opposite sense, rivers denote falsities in abundance."—SWEDENBORG, *Apoc. Rev.*, n. 409.

See AMBAYAS, AQUEDUCT, BIRTH OF KRISHNA, CHANNELS, EDEN RIVER TREES AND RIVERS, ZOROASTER.

ROASTED FLESH OF SACRIFICE :—

A symbol of purified and transmuted desires and passions of the lower nature.

"Now when the thighs were burnt and they had tasted the vitals, then sliced they all the rest and pierced it through with spits, and roasted it carefully, and drew all off again."—*Iliad*, Bk. I.

When the possibility of fresh desires being generated was removed, and the Higher Self had received the transmuted passions (roasted vitals), the residue of desires was broken up. And to this end the lower self was pierced by the operation from above and purified, then once more transmuted.

See BURNT OFFERING, DIONYSUS, FLESH, HECATOMB, SACRIFICE (burnt), TRANSMUTATION, VISCERA.

ROBE, BRIGHT, BEST, PURPLE, GOLDEN, WHITE, GLORIOUS, OR FIERY :—

These are symbols of the higher vestures of the soul,—atma-buddhic, buddhic, and causal.

"As long as the soul is imprisoned in the earthly tabernacle of the body, the intelligence is deprived of the robe of fire in which it should be clothed."—*Pœmandres*, Ch. I. 10, MEAD, *T. G. H.*

While the soul is in captivity to the lower nature, and occupying astral and physical bodies, the individuality is deprived of the buddhic robe in which it should be vestured.

"And my parents took off from me the bright robe, which in their love they had wrought for me, and my purple toga which was measured and woven to my stature."—Gnostic *Hymn of the Soul.*

The Spirit (Atma-buddhi) for awhile took away from me (the descending ego) the vesture which corresponded

to the vehicle for the higher consciousness, which was being woven for
me, and also my ideal causal-body
which was fashioned according to
the express image of my potential
being.

"The Kind One will give us a robe
of honour, and by His favour we shall
reach the gate of salvation. Nanak, we
shall thus know that God is altogether
true" (*The Japji*).—MACAULIFFE, *The
Sikh Religion*, Vol. I. p. 198.

"These men (learned agnostics), it
may be said, erect in the mansions of
their hearts a splendid throne-room,
in which they place objects revered and
beautiful. There are laid the sceptre
of righteousness and the swords of
justice and mercy. There is the purple
robe that speaks of the unity of love
and power, and there is the throne that
teaches the supreme moral governance
of the world. . . . Yet that noble
chamber, with all its beauty, its glorious
regalia, its solitary throne, is still an
empty room."—LORD HUGH CECIL,
Speech, 1902.

"The white cloth which Tanabata has
woven for my sake, in that dwelling
of hers, is now I think being made
into a robe for me. Though she is far
away and hidden from me by five hundred
layers of white cloud, still shall I turn my
gaze each night towards the dwelling-
place of my (wife)."—HEARN, *Romance
of Milky Way*, p. 40.

The robe of Wisdom, woven on the
buddhic plane, awaits the Self, who
in Love and aspiration struggles
upward through each night of the
terrestrial life.

"Let thy priests be clothed with
righteousness ; and let thy saints shout
for joy."—Ps. cxxxii. 9.

"In the new Israel, as in the first
constitution of the old, all the people
are priests. Righteousness, then, is to
be the robe of every Christian soul. To
be good, to be gentle and just, loving
and truthful, self-forgetting and self-
ruling, honest and true, kind and helpful,
to live in the exercise of the virtues,
which the consciences and tongues of
all men call lovely and of good report,
and to add to them all the consecration
of reference to Him in whom these
parted graces dwell united and complete
—this is to be righteous."—A. MACLAREN,
Sermons, 2nd Series, p. 273.

See CLOTHING, GARMENT, GATE
(sal.), HIKOBOSHI, LETTER, LINEN
GARMENT, PEARL, SEALED LETTER,
SERPENT (loud), SHOES, TOGA.

ROBE OF THE WATERS :—

A symbol of the vesture of Wisdom
enwrapping the liberated Self.

"O Tchefet ! I have come into
Thee ; I have cast about me the robe
of the waters ; I have girt myself with
the girdle of knowledge."—*Book of the
Dead*, Ch. CX.

The Self is seen to be as a centre
wherein all the rays of the Divine
Life are focused into one Supernal
Light, and about the Divine nature
is the garment and girdle of Truth
(water) and of Wisdom,—the buddhic
and causal vestures.

See FOCUS, TCHEFET.

ROCK OR STONE :—

A symbol of Spirit as a firm
foundation for all things. The
Higher Self as a refuge from
adversity.

"For who is God, save the Lord ?
And who is a rock, save our God ?"—
2 SAM. xxii. 32.
"God only is my rock and my salvation."—Ps. lxii. 2.

The soul relies upon the Higher Self
to enable it to vanquish the desires, and
rise to the higher planes.

"Melchizedec and the three sons of
Noah reach a spot where the Rock
opens and receives the chest containing
the body of Adam and the four sacred
tokens. There Melchizedec remains,
clothed and girdled with fire, to serve
God before the body of Adam to all
time."—*Book of the Conflicts of Adam*.

The indwelling Higher Self with
its aspects Will, Action, and Wisdom,
operating as Faith Courage and
Will, so discipline the soul (chest)
that it attains to a state which allows
of its reception by the Higher Self,
the "spiritual rock"; the four
"tokens" of its acceptance being
Faith, Love, Wisdom, and Power. In
these exalted conditions the indwelling
Self remains until the Christhood is
attained by the soul and the buddhic
"robe" is put on ; that is, the
consciousness rises to the buddhic
(fire) plane. The Self becomes the
means whereby the old Adam nature
is transmuted into a living soul—and
the new Adam, as the inheritor of
heaven, becomes a life-giving spirit.

"Great is the power of a life which
knows that its highest experiences are
its truest experiences, that it is most
itself when it is at its best. For it, each
high achievement, each splendid vision,
is a sign and token of the whole nature's
possibility. What a piece of the man
was for that shining instant, it is the duty
of the whole man to be always. When

the hand has once touched the rock the heart cannot be satisfied until the whole frame has been drawn up out of the waves and stands firm on its two feet on the solid stone."—PHILLIPS BROOKS, *Light of the World*, p. 20.

See ADAM'S DEAD BODY, CHEST, FIRE, FORTRESS, MELCHIZEDEC, NOAH, SALVATION, STONE, TOKENS, TRIAD.

ROCK SEPULCHRE :—

A symbol of a condition of hardness of feeling and stagnation in religious thought and opinion.

" The sepulchre was hewn out of a rock, and a great stone was rolled to the door of the tomb."—MAT. xxvii. 60.

This signifies a contracted mental condition that has but little life in it. It is inert, senseless, dark, and cold, and every crevice is closed to the light of Truth.

" And behold, there was a great earthquake ; for an angel of the Lord descended from heaven, and came and rolled away the stone, and sat upon it."—MAT. xxviii. 2.

This indicates a disruptive process, which abolishes the stagnation of mind and has the effect of causing mental states which regard things of the lower life as fixed and permanent, to quake with fear. The " angel " signifies the positive spiritual action from within which transfigures the conditions.

See ANGELS, EARTHQUAKE, LAZARUS, SEPULCHRES, SPICES, SUNDAY, TOMB.

ROCK, SPIRITUAL :—

A symbol of the Higher Self— atma-buddhi,—who outpours truth to dissipate illusion on the lower planes.

" And Moses lifted up his hand, and smote the rock twice : and water came forth abundantly, and the congregation drank, and their cattle."—NUM. xx. 11.

It is the province of the rational and ethical nature (Moses) to prepare the way for the Spirit (atma-buddhi) to outpour truth (water), so that the centralised qualities (congregation) and their emotions of an obedient and docile order, should be instructed. Striking the rock twice is significant of the appeal of the lower duality to the one Self. The rod is a symbol of power.

Our fathers were all under the cloud, and all passed through the sea ; and were all baptised unto Moses in the cloud and in the sea ; and did all eat the same spiritual meat ; and did all drink the same spiritual drink : for they drank of a spiritual rock that followed them : and the rock was Christ."— 1 COR. x. 1–4.

Our egos were all under the discipline of the buddhic function (the cloud), and all passed through the conflict of passions and desires (the astral sea) ; and were all purified by truth (water baptism) imparted by reason and ethics (Moses) for the disciplining of the lower nature ; and did all receive sustenance for the soul from goodness and truth (manna) ; and did all have a part in the Divine life (drink) ; for they received into their inner nature the Spirit of Truth that followed the moral awakening and that Spirit was the Higher Self now born in the soul.

" It appears that the greatest sanctity attached to caves in the living rock ; and there are many remains of Mithraic altars cut in rocks ; nay more, the rock came to be specially associated with Mithras, who was named ' rockborn ' ; and the phrase ' God out of the rock,' or ' Mithras out of the rock,' became one of the commonest formulas of the cultus."—J. M. ROBERTSON, *Pagan Christs*, p. 318.

" Mithras " is a symbol of the Higher Self and " cave " is a symbol of the soul in which the Self is manifested (born).

See CATTLE, CAVE, CLOUD, EXODUS, HOUSE OF BONDAGE, MANNA, MELCHIZEDEC, MOSES, PARABLE, PEOPLE, SEA, STONE, WATER.

ROCK OF SALVATION :—

A symbol of the Higher Self as the foundation on which the soul shall be perfected.

" He (David) shall cry unto me, Thou art my father, my God, and the rock of my salvation."—Ps. lxxxix. 26.

The natural man raised through the qualities, disciplined in mind and emotion and made the ruler of the lower nature (David my servant), is able thereby to recognise the Self as his progenitor, his supreme Ideal, and the foundation of his progressive purification.

See DAVID, MAN (natural), SALVATION, STONE.

ROCK-BOAT OF HEAVEN, OR STONE-CANOE :—

A symbol of the causal-body in the higher mind, by means of which

the buddhic consciousness (heaven) is reached by the soul.

See BOAT (river), BUDDHIC PLANE, CAUSAL-BODY, HEAVEN.

ROCKS, FLOATING :—

A symbol of fear.

"The Symplégades were the first danger they had to encounter. These were huge floating rocks, which were at times driven together by the winds, and crushed whatever came between them."—*Argonautic Expedition.*

The first danger in the wider mental outlook, which beset the qualities, was the negative state of fear, the lack of the positive courage. Fear is comparable to obstructive rocks, in that they stifle effort and paralyse initiative. Fear "floats," for it has no real foundation, and evidences lack of intellectual will.

"Behold I have taken out of thine hand the cup of trembling . . . thou shalt no more drink it again."—Is. li. 22.

"God himself is essentially joy, and joy must ever break triumphant from the heart of pain. The cup of trembling is the cup of fearing. Take fear out of any dark experience and most of its power to hurt is gone. There is nothing more spiritually destructive, more fatal to the best and highest in the soul than allowing yourself to become the victim and the slave of fear. The angel of God's peace cannot find a way to your heart, when you submit to that tyranny."—R. J. CAMPBELL, Serm., *The Cup of Trembling.*

See SYMPLÉGADES.

ROD FOR STRIKING DOWN :—

A symbol of force on a low plane, —neither good nor bad, but blindly directed. It is also a symbol of fear and hate, which, with doubt, cause destruction and devastation in the soul.

ROD HELD IN THE HAND AS A SCEPTRE OR WAND :—

A symbol of power actively exercised.

See HAND, REED, SCEPTRE, STAFF.

ROD OF CORRECTION :—

A symbol of disciplining the qualities through suffering and sorrow.

"The Lord 'rules and breaks us with a rod of iron' (Ps. ii. 9), in that by the strong rule of righteousness in His dispensation, while He reanimates us within, He distresses us without.

For as He abases the power of the flesh, He exalts the purpose of the Spirit."—ST. GREGORY, *Morals on the Book of Job,* Vol. I. p. 377.

See BIRTH OF MAN CHILD, IRON, RULE.

RODASI :—
See CHARIOT.

ROMAN SOLDIER IN JUDEA :—

A symbol of the aggressive, strong, destructive side of the lower nature, which fulfils the most useful function of dissipating stagnation and opening up whatever requires exercise.

"The soldiers, therefore, when they had crucified Jesus, took his garments, and made four parts, to every soldier a part."—JOHN xix. 23.

When through aggressive agencies the Christ-soul had triumphed finally over the ultimate ills, the vehicles of the lower quaternary were broken up and dissipated in the natural course of things on the four lower planes.

See BERSERKS, CAIAPHAS, CRUCIFIXION, SOLDIERS, TRIAL.

RONGO-MATANE :—

A symbol of Wisdom, atma-buddhi.

"But at length their plans having been agreed on, lo! Rongo-matane, the God and father of the cultivated food of man, rises up, that he may rend apart the Heavens and the Earth ; he struggles, but rends them not apart."—G. GREY, *Polynesian Mythology,* p. 3.

At length, the conditions being complete, Wisdom, the active principle in the transmutation of desires and ideas into higher emotions and true knowledge,—the results of self-discipline,—which nourish the soul, is said to strive for expression by separation of Spirit and matter now together involved ; but fails because it possesses no opposing force to Love, which binds.

See COCOA-NUT, HAUMIA, HEAVEN AND EARTH, RANGI, SEPARATION, TANEMAHUTA, TAWHIRIMATEA, TUMA-TAUENGA.

ROOF OF PALACE, OR HOUSE :—

A symbol of the limit upward of the intellectual atmosphere or mental capacity in the soul.

See INTELLECT.

ROOM IN A HOUSE :—

A symbol of a sub-plane of the mental plane.

"And he will show you a large upper room furnished: there make ready (the passover)."—Luke xxii. 12.

The "house" is the state into which the soul is brought through its own efforts. It is the mental environment to some extent; but it is more than that: it is also the whole external aspect of the Higher Self. Each "room" serves for a sub-plane; and an "upper room" is that upon which the Christ-soul functions as the time of glorification draws nigh.

See House of a man, Passover, Sacrament.

ROOT :—

A symbol of foundation,—stable or unstable.

ROOTED AND ROOTLESS FOOD :—

Symbols of the desires and illusions which nourish the lower nature.

See Cow (spotted), Food for man, Haumia.

ROOT-RACES :—

These are described as four, five, seven, or ten types or forms of humanity on the buddhic, mental, astral, and physical planes of the globes of the planetary chain.

"Every Life-cycle on globe D (our earth) is composed of seven Root-races. They commence with the ethereal and end with the spiritual, on the double line of physical and moral evolution—from the beginning of the terrestrial round to its close. One is a 'planetary Round' from globe A to globe G, the seventh; the other, the 'globe Round' or the Terrestrial."—H. P. Blavatsky, Secret Doctrine, Vol. I. p. 183.

"There are seven Rounds in every manvantara; this Round is the fourth, and we are in the fifth Root-race at present. Each Root-race has seven sub-races."—Ibid., Vol. II. p. 452.

"Evolution in general, events, mankind, and everything else in nature proceed in cycles. Every Root-race, with its sub-races, etc., was entirely distinct from its preceding and succeeding Race. . . . The Human Races are born one from the other, grow, develop, become old, and die. Their sub-races and nations follow the same rule."—Ibid., pp. 462, 463.

See Beasts (three sorts), Karshvares, Planetary chain, Pylus,

Races, Ragha, Regions, Round, Snow.

ROPE FOR HAULING THE BOAT :—

A symbol of the spiritual agencies for drawing onward the soul (boat.)

"'Tell me my name,' saith the Rope; 'Hair with which Anpu (Anubis) finisheth the work of my embalmment' is thy name."—Budge, Book of the Dead, Ch. XCIX.

The meaning of the symbol (name) of the "rope" is :—The highest qualities evolved through physical instrumentality, in the process of the purification of the personality in the physical body (Anubis), aid the soul's progress.

See Anpu, Anubis, Boat in river, Embalmment.

ROUND OF THE LIFE-WAVE THROUGH SEVEN GLOBES OF A PLANETARY CHAIN :—

There have been seven rounds completed on the lunar chain. Humanity is now in the fourth round, and on the fourth globe of the terrene chain.

"The One Indivisible Monad called Tae-keih (the highest point) is considered as the restorer of reason, who has by incarnation assumed some form or other in seven different periods from the highest antiquity downwards."—Kidd, China, p. 141.

The Supreme evolves within nature and the soul until the stage of reason or wisdom (buddhi-manas) is arrived at; and during seven world-periods of embodiment and incarnation completes the growth of wisdom in the soul which thereby is raised to the buddhic consciousness.

"Every sidereal body, every planet, whether visible or invisible, is credited with six companion globes. The evolution of Life proceeds on these seven globes or bodies, from the first to the seventh, in Seven Rounds or Seven Cycles. . . . When the seventh and last round of (a planetary chain) has been entered upon, the highest or first globe, A, followed by all the others down to the last, instead of entering upon a certain time of rest—or 'obscuration,' as in the previous rounds—begins to die out. The planetary dissolution (pralaya) is at hand, and its hour has struck; each globe has to transfer its life and energy to another planet."—H. P. Blavatsky, Secret Doctrine, Vol. I. p. 182.

"Evolution appears to be cyclical, from the simplest etheric basis—if anything is simple—up to the highest and most complex cosmic products and back again. On, on it goes, age after age, without pause or rest, as it always has been, as it always will be, world without end, repeating the same process, following the same sequences, but never reaching a culmination or arriving at a final goal ; it is one perpetual round, or round of rounds. 'That which hath been is now ; and that which is to be hath already been ; and God requireth that which is past ' (ECCLES. iii. 15)."—R. J. CAMPBELL, Serm., *Eternal and Temporal*.

See KARSHVARES, LUNAR CHAIN, MOON-WAXING, PLANETARY CHAIN, RACES, RAGHA, REGIONS, ROOT-RACES, SABBATHS, SNOW, WHEELS (holy).

RU :—

A symbol of the astral or desire-nature.

" Ru is the father of lakes and rivers."—R. TAYLOR, *New Zealand*, p. 32.

The desire-nature resides on the astral plane (water below).

" Heaven and earth were only separated by the Teva plant, till the god Ru lifted Heaven up."—*Ibid.*, p. 19.

Spirit and Matter, at the close of the period of involution, were in a state of latency, save for a faint aspiration for growth (the plant) arising from the lower nature (earth). But when desire (Ru) was aroused, then separateness of the higher and lower natures became manifest.

See ASTRAL PLANE, HEAVEN AND EARTH, PLANTS, RANGI, SEPARATION, TANEMAHUTA, WATER (lower).

RUA'H :—

A symbol of the dual mind,—the higher mind and the lower mind. The higher mind is attached to buddhi (neshamah), and the lower mind to desire (nephesh). This difference makes the first the spiritual mind, and the second the desire mind.

" Neshamah (Divine soul) goes over to that Rua'h, and rules over him, and lights him with that Light of Life ; and that Rua'h depends on the Neshamah, and receives light from her which illuminates him. . . . The Neshamah soul goes up direct to the very Inner, and the Rua'h spirit goes up to *Eden*, but not so high as the Soul ; and Nephesh (the animal principle, lower soul) remains in the grave below" (From the *Zohar*).—I. MYER, *Qabbalah*, p. 394.

The atma-buddhic principle inspires the causal-body and rules the spiritual mind by wisdom and love ; and that spiritual mind is united (buddhi-manas) to the higher Soul and receives through it the light of Truth. The buddhic Soul aspires, or ascends, to the very Atman, and the spiritual mind rises to the buddhic plane (Gan Eden). The desire-nature (nephesh) pertains to matter and disappears.

" This Rua'h does not go to *Gan Eden* (Garden of Eden) because he is Nephesh, and each has its own place."—*Ibid.*, p. 394.

This other " Rua'h," the lower mind, does not ascend to the buddhic plane, for it is mortal, being united to desire (nephesh). It cannot rise, but must perish on its own plane of kama-manas.

See ATMAN, BUDDHI, CAUSAL-BODY, EDEN, GILGOOLEM, INDIVIDUALITY, MICHAEL, MONAD OF LIFE, NEPHESH, NESHAMAH, PERSONALITY, TOMB, YEHEEDAH.

RUBIES :—

A symbol of high qualities of the mind.

" And rubies of India, and agate from the land of Kushan."—*Hymn of the Soul. Acts of Judas Thomas.*

And "rubies," aspects of the higher mind, of "India," the " kingdom of the Sun-rising," comparable to the ascent of the Soul. And "agate," which is a symbol of Truth from the sphere of Wisdom.

See GEMS, HOUSE (frequented), JEWELS.

RUDDER OF THE BOAT :—

A symbol of intuition of Truth through Wisdom, guiding the course of the evolution of the soul (boat).

" ' Tell me my name ' saith the Rudder, ' Leg of Hapiu ' is thy name."—BUDGE, *Book of the Dead*, Ch. XCIX.

The meaning of the idea "rudder" is :—Knowledge of the mode of progression derived from the Wisdom-nature by means of experience.

" ' Aga ' (i.e. true one) is thy name ; O (rudder) thou that shinest from the water, hidden-beam, is thy name."—*Ibid.*

Knowledge of evolution derived from the fount of truth (water) ; for the Light of Truth is shining within the soul : this is the meaning of "rudder."

See BOAT ON RIVER, LEGS, LIGHT, NAME, THIGH, WATER.

RUDRA :—

A symbol of the Higher Self in several aspects,—Destroyer of evil, Saviour of good, etc.

" We seek from Rudra, the lord of songs, the lord of sacrifices, who possesses healing remedies, his auspicious favour ; from him who is brilliant as the sun, who shines like gold, who is the best and most bountiful of the gods " (*Vedas*). —MUIR, *O.S. Texts*, IV. 299.

The Higher Self is entreated as the power which brings harmony and spiritual response to the offering up of the lower nature, for the Self possesses reality to take the place of illusion. The Self is the source of Light and Life ; his wisdom (gold), goodness, and love are bestowed on all that are ready to receive.

See HEALING, MARUTS, MEDICINE, PHYSICIAN, SACRIFICE, SERPENT ÆSCULAPIUS, SONG.

RULE NATIONS WITH A ROD OF IRON :—

A symbol of the Spirit disciplining the qualities (nations) through the mental (iron) activities which control the lower emotions and desires.

" To rule with a rod of iron signifies to rule by rational arguments drawn from the light of nature."—SWEDENBORG, *Apoc. Rev.*, n. 544.

See IRON, NATIONS, QUALITIES, ROD OF CORRECTION.

RULER, CHIEF, OR KING :—

A symbol of a higher or a lower mental faculty in a position of authority over groups of soul quali- ties (tribes or nations).

See ARK (Moses), GOVERNORS, HEALING (dead), JAIRUS, KING, NATIONS, SHEPHERDS, TRIBES.

RULER OF THE ÆON :—

A symbol of the Life of the Logos emanating in the Cycle as the power which makes for righteousness interpreted in the natural, moral, and intellectual orders. And which is realised when we perceive that all things work together for good,— since such an intuition is a direct sense of the Love of God.

" God, our eternal source and goal, *is* love, and love is self-givingness, and self- givingness is joy. There is no particu- larism in the life of God. God *must* give himself, being what he is, and in giving himself realises himself. Man made in the image of God, being of his being, and substance of his substance, must do the same. The particular must be surrendered to the universal at every stage of our upward progress, but in that very surrender we grasp a larger life, we enter upon a greater joy. Perfect self-giving and perfect self-realisation are one and the same."—R. J. CAMPBELL, Serm., *Through Death to Life.*

See ÆON, CHRIST, FAITH, GOD, IMAGE, LOVE OF GOD, REDEEMER, SACRIFICER.

RULERS OF THE WORLD :—

Symbolic of the five natures which constitute the Soul.

" The five shoots (of the tree of Life) are the five rulers,—the House ruler, the Village-ruler, the Tribe-ruler, the Province-ruler, and the supreme Zara- tust."—*Sikand-Gumanik Vigar*, S.B.E., Vol. XXIV. p. 118.

These are the physical, astral, lower mental, causal, and Atma- buddhic natures.

See CASTES, CHILDREN OF HORUS, CLASSES, DAYS (five), ELEMENTS (five), GATHA DAYS (five), HOUSE (clan), PROVINCE, TREE OF LIFE, TRIBE (ruler), VESTURES, VILLAGE, WORLDS (five), ZOROASTER.

RULERS OF MATTER :—

A symbol of the forms of mani- festation in which spirit is embodied.

" The substance of the Rulers is the matter out of which souls are made."— *The Pistis Sophia.*

This refers to the Lunar Pitris of the astro-physical evolution, which develop the human forms in which the Solar Pitris, or Divine Sparks, become embodied, thus constituting the souls of humanity.

See MONADS OF FORM AND LIFE, PITRIS (lunar), PITRIS (solar).

SABBATH, JEWISH :—

A symbol of a state of rest of the life forces which supervenes on the higher planes at the close of a period of activity on the lower planes, when a result has been accomplished.

" And on the seventh day God finished his work which he had made ; and he rested on the seventh day from all his work. . . . And God blessed the seventh day, and hallowed it : because that in it he rested from all his work."—GEN. ii. 2, 3.

And on the seventh period of the Divine outbreathing and inbreathing, when the return of the Life into Itself is accomplished, the Divine nature is said to rest. At this stage the Divine Spirit is said to " rest," inasmuch as a suspension of activities is rendered necessary, prior to another and distinct movement forth. And the Supreme blesses and sanctifies the period, for at this termination of the process of Involution the soul has arrived at that blessed condition which answers to completion and entirety, when the Spirit appears to cease its operations.

" Malkhuth represents the Sabbath or seventh day, the close of the construction or building of the universe, the Rest Day or harmony of all."—I. MYER, *Quabbalah*, p. 272.

The buddhic principle contains the scheme and consummation of the lower plane activities, therefore the indrawal of the Life would be to the buddhic plane a state of rest and harmony.

In the Hebrew *Genesis* the period of Involution is signified by the six days of Divine activity preceding the Sabbath of rest or inactivity, after which the universe and the soul awaken to the new life-process of Evolution, as described in the first part of the second chapter.

The Jewish Saturday Sabbath connotes a cessation from activity (pralaya), and not a rousing to life (manvantara) which is signified by Sunday.

" This seventh day of rest is the stage here drawn, the state of ' full age,' or ' perfection,' when instead of growth and change, and the varying life of faith, and the struggle between the old state and the work of God within us, we reach the life of vision and of rest."—A. JUKES, *Types of Genesis*, p. 42.

" This ' resting ' (on the seventh day) —which is not annihilation but repose,— involves the return of Matter (from its dynamic) to its static condition of Substance. The idea presented is that of the cessation of active-creative force, and the consequent return of phenomenal existence into essential being. This stage it is which constitutes the termination of the creative period, and the perfection of every creative work. It is at once the ' rest which remains for the people of God '; the attainment of perfection by the individual, system, or race ; and the return of the universe into the bosom of God, by re-absorption into the

original substance."—KINGSFORD and MAITLAND, *The Perfect Way*, p. 16.

In the completion of involution of all qualities and forms the soul is perfected potentially as the Archetypal Man, who dies within the lower nature and becomes the prototype of the many souls, who incarnate and actualise in the present period of evolution.

See ARC. MAN, BREATH (divine), BUDDHIC (plane), CREATION, EVOLUTION, HOUR (mid-day), IMAGE, INCARNATION OF SOULS, INVOLUTION, MALKHUTH, MANVANTARA, NIGHT, NOX, PLANETARY CHAIN, PRALAYA, PROTOTYPES, SATURDAY, SEVENTH, SUNDAY.

SABBATHS :—

A symbol of periodic states or conditions of the cosmic and soul life on the lower planes, or the higher, i.e. material or spiritual states.

" Then shall the land enjoy her sabbaths, as long as it lieth desolate, and ye be in your enemies' land ; even then shall the land rest, and enjoy her sabbaths. As long as it lieth desolate it shall have rest ; even the rest which it had not in your sabbaths, when ye dwelt upon it."— DEUT. xxvi. 34, 35.

Then shall the general outspread life of the soul enjoy the buddhic consciousness during the periodic spiritual states when it is without the sensations, passions and desires (desolate), and the lower qualities, being relative and unreal, are non-existent (in enemies' land). Even then shall the indrawn life partake of bliss. As long as it is without the opposites it shall have peace ; even the peace which it had not in the periodic material states when the lower qualities were in the stress and suffering of life.

" These Sabbaths (of LEV. xxiii) are seven Pralayas between seven manvantaras, or what we call Rounds."—H. P. BLAVSTSKY, *Secret Doctrine*, Vol. II. p. 790.

See BLISS, BUDDHI, DEARTH, KARSHVARES, LAND, MANVANTARA, OPPOSITES, PRALAYA, QUALITIES, ROUND, SNOW, SPARROWS, SUMMER (unfruitful), WINTER.

SACKCLOTH ON FLESH :—

A symbol of severe discipline and restraint put upon the lower nature during periods of re-incarnation of the soul.

"And it came to pass, when king Hezekiah heard it, that he rent his clothes, and covered himself with sackcloth, and went into the house of the Lord."—ISA. xxxvii. 1.

This refers to the turning of the personality from the allurements of desire, and to the change of opinions, and restraint of the lower nature, and reliance upon the Divine.

"Thou hast turned for me my mourning into dancing ; thou hast loosed my sackcloth, and girded me with gladness."—Ps. xxix. 11.

At the end of the cycle the soul rises from the lower nature, liberated from desire, and enters into the harmony and joy of life on the higher planes.

"For by ' sackcloth ' is set forth the roughness and the piercing of sin, but by ' ashes ' the dust of the dead. . . . Let piercing sins then be considered in sackcloth, let the just punishment of sins, which succeeds by the sentence of death, be considered in ashes."—ST. GREGORY, *Morals on the Book of Job*, Vol. III. p. 666.

See ASCETICISM, ASHES, AUSTERITIES, CLOTHES, DANCE, RENDING GARMENTS.

SACRAMENT :—

A symbol of a binding compact within the sanctuary of the soul :— a covenant between the inner Divine soul and the outer advanced qualities, whereby they may be consciously raised to higher efficiency and purity.

"Jesus took bread and blessed it, and brake it, and gave it to his disciples, and said, Take, eat ; this is my body. And he took the cup, and gave thanks, and gave it to them, saying, Drink ye all of it, for this is my blood of the new testament, which is shed for many for the remission of sins."—MATT. xxvi. 26-8.

The "body" of the Divine Soul (Christ) is the transmuted lower nature (flesh), for that makes possible his activity in the soul,—it is his vesture whereby he manifests. This transmuted nature is the wisdom-nature, or Truth the substance of Goodness, which is the "bread of heaven." On Truth-Goodness the advanced qualities (disciples) must feed.

Truth-Goodness (Christ's body in us) is not only of the inner nature, it is also an expressed fact of human life, whose beauty and efficacy is exemplified in the outer nature as well as the inner.

The "wine" is the "blood," that is, the Divine Life, the active Spirit. The "cup" and the "wine" signify respectively the Soul and the Life, —the psychic receptacle for the Spirit, and the vivifying Spirit itself.

The Divine Life is to be absorbed by the qualities, for it is the Life now welling up within the soul, which was "shed" at the "foundation of the world," when Spirit with its potencies descended into matter, thus becoming in Involution the Divine Sacrifice for the "remission of sins" in Evolution (new testament).

"Jesus," symbol of the now perfected, or fully evolved, personality, has no further need of the means of evolution, hence he joins the "Christ" in the resurrection, when a "new" order obtains (*see* verse 29).

The partaking of this sacrament implies an intelligent compact between the advanced part of the lower nature, which seeks the food of the Spirit, and the responding Christ within. The soul, in becoming conscious of its destiny, yearns for instruction in the Truth, that it may progress the faster.

"Sacraments served to abolish the time-form of the redemption myth, in that they represented under symbolic signs the eternal spiritual truth that lay hidden in the myth—the truth of the continuous incarnation of God in the hearts of good men."—O. PFLEIDERER, *Early Ch. Conception of Christ*, p. 169.

"John the Scot (Erigena) says : ' There is nothing in the visible and material world which does not signify something immaterial and reasonable,' so that everything is a *symbol*, and has a sacramental significance. *Matter is only a concourse of accidents or qualities, no real being.* It is wholly dependent on thought for its existence, and therefore it would be absurd to say that the ' material ' Bread and Wine are more than symbols. The *value* of a sacrament for John could only be an inward and spiritual value —a value for faith."—R. M. JONES, *Mystical Religion*, p. 121.

"Action and contemplation must act and react upon each other ; otherwise our actions will have no soul, and our thoughts no body. This is the great truth which the higher religions express in their sacraments. A sacrament is more than a symbol. The perception of symbols leads us from the many to the One, from the transitory to the permanent, but not from appearance to reality. This belongs to the sacramental experience, which is symbolism retranslating itself into concrete action and to mundane interests."—W. R. INGE, *Faith*, Preface.

See AGATHODÆMON, BLOOD, BLOOD OF LAMB, BREAD, CUP, DISCIPLES, DISPENSATIONS, EATING, EVOLUTION, FLESH OF JESUS, FOOD, HOMA TREE, HOST, HUNGER, INVOLUTION, PROCESSION, REMISSION, RESURRECTION, RITES, SUPPER, TABLE, TRANSUBSTANTIATION, VINE, WINE.

SACRAMENTAL CAKES :—

A symbol of spiritual nourishment, i.e. Truth and Goodness.

"O 'Heavenly Springtime'! I have come into Thee; I have eaten my sacramental cakes; I have power over the sacrificial portions of my beasts and birds; the feathered fowl of the light are given unto me, for I have followed the Gods when the Divine forms come."
—*Book of the Dead*, Ch. CX., BLACKDEN.

The consciousness having risen to the higher mental plane, the growth of the true Self is now perceived to be the supreme fact of life. The "food of the Gods" has been eaten, and power is attained which renders sacrifice, asceticism, self-denial, or any form of self-abnegation, as not only unnecessary but impossible. The aspirations (birds), which led to these inflictions formerly, now yield their fruit in Wisdom and Love, for the Self has followed its ideals and been true to them.

See AMBROSIA, BEASTS, BIRDS, BREAD, CONSCIOUSNESS, EATING, FOOD, GODS, HEAVENLY SPRINGTIME, LOVE OF GOD, MANNA, SACRIFICE, SELF, SHEWBREAD, TREASURE, UNLEAVENED.

SACRED TEXT :—

A symbol of the true message of the Higher Self engraven on the spiritual tables of the heart, and to be understood by the personality when it is open to receive it.

"Those who study the Doctrine are set free from fear—whether of things in heaven or things on earth, for they are grafted on the Tree of Life and are taught daily thereby. As regards things in heaven, the meaning is that the fear of God, which is the beginning of wisdom, has been absorbed by the love of God, which is wisdom in realisation, and the Divine Doctrine cannot be studied without imparting love for the Divine. To walk in the path of the Doctrine is therefore to follow the path of love; it is said otherwise to lead into the way of

truth, so that we learn how the soul may return to its Master. It is not the work of a certain day, nor of a certain hour but one of the day and the night. . . . We shall understand why it is added that he who neglects or forsakes the study of the doctrine is not less guilty than if he separated himself from the Tree of Life, for he is leading the life of separation" (from *Zohar*).—A. E. WAITE, *Secret Doctrine in Israel*, p. 25.

See AMBAYAS, BLASPHEMY, DAY AND NIGHT, GIRDLE (star), PEN, REVELATION, VĒDA, WORD.

SACRIFICE OF ANIMALS :—

Symbolic of the devitalising and offering up of the lower desires and affections for the sake of making a place in the soul for the higher qualities of goodness, love, and truth.

"Svayambhu (the Self-existent) himself created animals for the sake of sacrifices; sacrifices have been instituted for the good of this whole world; hence the slaughtering of beasts for sacrifices is not slaughtering in the ordinary sense of the word."—*Laws of Manu*, V. 39.

This signifies that the Supreme brought the lower qualities—the desires, etc. (animals) into existence for the express purpose of providing the means whereby the higher qualities should be developed in the soul (world). The lower qualities have to be overcome and exchanged for the higher. They must be sacrificed.

"Sacrifice is the law of life-manifestation which not even omnipotence can escape. . . . The very qualities which to us are most admirable in human nature, which we reverence most in human character and conduct, and associate specially with the Christ ideal, are qualities which could not become manifest,—however really they might be latent in the Life-Force,—were it not for the conflict with evil. Where would be pity, fidelity, heroism, integrity, and the like, if our moral nature had never had anything to cut its teeth on, so to speak ?"—R. J. CAMPBELL, Serm., *Nature of Life-Force*.

"Herbs, trees, cattle, birds, and other animals that have been destroyed for sacrifices receive, being re-born, higher existences."—*Laws of Manu*, V. 40.

This refers to the transmutation of lower qualities (animals, etc.) into higher qualities, as taught in all scriptures. The qualities are "re-born" on to a higher plane of existence.

"Sacrifice is the true type of progress. We sacrifice a lower life to cultivate and enjoy a higher. All improvement is a sacrifice in this sense. But in growing up from the root, it begins at the bare and barren rock that affords no nourishment to the soul. The blood of the beast is this lowest idea. . . . It is by sacrificing the lower grades that we ascend to the higher. . . . The highest of all sacrifices are the everlasting sacrifices of righteousness, the sacrifices of selfish and inferior feelings and passions ; for these are the true beasts, best represented by clean or domestic animals as they belong to ourselves, and are transubstantiated into ourselves by being used as food. And therefore it is for ever a sacrifice of beasts ; only the lower is translated into the higher meaning, as the rock is translated into alluvial and nourishing soil."—J. SMITH, *The Divine Drama of History*, pp. 56, 57.

" To sacrifice is to stir up, actually to beget, two divinities of the first rank, the two principles of life *par excellence*, Agni and Soma."—A. BARTH, *The Religions of India*, p. 36.

" Agni " is the force aspect of atma-buddhi, and " Soma " is the Divine Life ; these emerge in the soul as growth proceeds.

" ' By sacrifices,' says the Taittiriya-brâhmana, ' the gods obtained heaven.' " —MON. WILLIAMS, *Religious Thought in India*, p. 23.

The " gods " are the Divine Sparks, who descend to rise.

" The Indian gods even look to mortals for their daily sustenance, and are represented as actually *living on the sacrifices* offered to them by human beings, and at every sacrificial ceremony assemble in troops, eager to feed upon their shares. In fact, sacrifice with the Hindus is not merely expiatory or placatory ; it is necessary for the *food* and *support* of the gods. If there were no sacrifices the gods would starve to death. This alone will account for the interest they take in the destruction of demons whose great aim was to obstruct these sources of their sustenance."—MON. WILLIAMS, *Indian Wisdom*, pp. 428–9.

The " gods " are the highest ideals, or highest qualities within the human soul. They always grow in strength and beauty as the lower desires and passions are overcome and abandoned. It is said, therefore, that " sacrifices are for the sustenance of the gods." The " demons " signify evil habits and erroneous opinions which obstruct the offering up of the desires, and consequently retard the growth of the ideals (gods).

" The main object of sacrificial performances generally is the re-construction of Pragâpati, the personified universe, and the divine body of the Sacrificer."—

J. EGGELING, *S.B. of E.*, Vol. XLIV. p. xlvii.

The soul's evolution is the re-forming or gradual building up of Christ, the Archetypal Man, " for we are members of his body " ; and this re-formation of Divinity in humanity is effected by the offering up of the lower nature to the higher, so that " Christ be formed in us," and grow to perfection.

" Man's regeneration is an image of the Lord's glorification."—SWEDENBORG, *Arc. Cel.*, n. 10,042.

" All the animals on earth signify such things as pertain to man ; which in general refer to the affections which are of his will, and to the thoughts which are of his understanding, and therefore to goods and truths. . . . The sacrifices and burnt-offerings in general signify the regeneration of man by the truths of faith and the goods of love. The whole process of regeneration is also described by the particular rituals of each sacrifice and burnt offering."—SWEDENBORG, *Ibid.*

See AGNI, ALTAR, ANIMALS, ARC. MAN, BEASTS, BURNT OFFERING, CATTLE, COW, DEMONS, FOOD OF GODS, GODS, HECATOMB, LAMB, OBLATION, OFFERING, PASSOVER, PRAGÂPATI (relaxed), PRAYERS (oblations), RAGANYA, RAM, REGENERATION, ROASTED FLESH, SACRAMENTAL CAKES, SALVATION, SOMA, VAGAPEYA, VITAL AIRS, WASHED (blood).

SACRIFICES, BURNT :—

A symbol of the purifying (fire) buddhic process, by which the lower qualities are raised and transmuted to higher qualities.

" I will come into thy house with burnt offerings, I will pay thee my vows, which my lips have uttered, and my mouth hath spoken, when I was in distress. I will offer unto thee burnt offerings of fatlings, with the incense of rams ; I will offer bullocks with goats."—Ps. lxvi. 13–15.

The lower self aspires through self-abnegation and purification to rise to the causal-body (house of God). Through fixed adherence to ideals, tested in times of trouble, the lower self seeks the Higher. The lower offers up to the Higher the affections, emotions, and desires, in order that it may progress.

" For what do the sacrifices of those animals designate, except the death of the Only-Begotten ? What do the sacrifices of those animals signify, except

the extinction of our carnal life."—
St. GREGORY, *Morals on the Book of Job*,
Vol. III. p. 296.

"I, Fire, the Acceptor of sacrifices,
ravishing away from them their darkness, give the light."—CATHERINE OF
SIENA, *Dialogo*, 85.

"Multitudes of people there are all
about us, who thoroughly accept it as
the great law and necessity of human
life that there must be self-sacrifice. . . .
They see that the world would be a
dreadful and intolerable place if every
creature in it lived only for his own mere
immediate indulgence. They own that
the higher nature and the higher purpose
everywhere have a right to the submission of the lower, and they freely
accept the conviction that the lower
must submit. There is the need that a
man should sacrifice himself to himself,
his lower self to his higher self, his passions
to his principles. There is the need of
sacrificing one's self for fellowmen. There
is the highest need of all, the need of
giving up our will to God's. . . . I have
a right to give the less as a burnt offering
to the greater."—PHIL. BROOKS, Serm.,
Joy of Self-sacrifice.

See ALTAR, BEASTS, BURNT OFFER-
ING, FAT, FIRE, OBLATION, OFFERING,
ROASTED FLESH, SAVOUR.

SACRIFICER, THE :—

A symbol of the Supreme, who in
manifestation limits his own nature
and conditions his activity.

"The name of the First Celestial
Emperor was Tae-haou,—Excessive Splendour. He was also called Fuh-he, or
Paou-he, 'the Sacrificer.' The tradition
is that he had no father, was the first to
reign, and that his name was Fung,
meaning wind, spirit, breath."—*Chinese
Records*, KIDD, *China.*

The First Logos is the Supreme
Ineffable Potency, which, in the second
aspect of its forthgoing, is said to have
been the "sacrifice" and the "sacrificer," inasmuch as it is that limitation of being which is offered to itself,
or that limitation of itself which is
endured for the sake of its sentient
universe. It is inwardly received that
the Supreme is Self-derived, neither
begotten, nor created, but Self-existent. Wind, spirit, breath, are all
symbols of emanation, to which the
forth-pouring from the Absolute is
comparable.

"The Tāndya-brāhmana makes the
Lord of creatures offer himself up as a
sacrifice. Even Sacrifice (Yajna) itself
was sometimes personified as a god."—
MON. WILLIAMS, *Religious Thought in
India*, p. 23.

"Soma thought, 'I must not become
sacrificial food for the gods with my
whole self.' That form of his which was
most pleasing he accordingly put aside.
. . . Then as to why he is called Yajna
(sacrifice). Now when they press him,
they slay him; and when they spread
him, they cause him to be born."—*Sata.
Brâh.*, III. 9, 4, 22–3.

The Divine Life (Soma) in emanating becomes dual,—higher and lower.
The higher Self (the most pleasing)
remains inoperative and potential.
The lower Self limits itself (is sacrificed)
in matter during the period of involution. When fully involved he dies.
Then afterwards, when the "crucified"
Self, or Archetypal Man, from One
becomes many (is spread), he is born
in each soul or quality during the
period of evolution.

"Christ is the offering, Christ is the
priest, Christ is the offerer. . . . Thus in
the self-same type *the offerer* sets forth
Christ in His person, as the One who
became man to meet God's requirements : the *offering* presents Him *in
His character and work*, as the victim by
which the atonement was ratified ; while
the *priest* gives us a third picture of
Him, *in His official relation*, as the
appointed mediator and intercessor."—
A. JUKES, *Law of the Offerings*, pp. 36, 37.

"Hence arose the myths which represent sacrifice as the first act in the
cosmogony. It was by sacrifice,—it is
not said to whom,—that the gods
delivered the world from chaos, just as
it is by sacrifice that man prevents it
from lapsing back into it, and the dismemberment of the primeval giant
Purusha, whose skull was fabled to form
the heavens and his limbs the earth,
came to be regarded in India as the first
act of sacrifice. What is more, the gods
being inseparable from the world, their
existence must have been preceded by
sacrifice ; hence the singular myth which
represents the Supreme Being as sacrificing himself in order to give birth
to other existences."—A. BARTH, *The
Religions of India*, p. 37.

"Chaos" being the condition out
of which arises the first duality,—
spirit and matter,—it is said that the
primal differentiations (gods) delivered
the soul (world) from chaos by sacrifice. This they did by becoming involved in matter, as the first qualities
of Spirit.

Man prevents the soul from lapsing
back into unfruitfulness by the sacrifice of his lower nature, which implies
the evolution of his higher, and the
reappearance of the ideals (gods).

"Purusha," the Spirit involved in matter, that is, the introduction into the vibrations of atoms of all the energies and qualities afterwards to be evolved out of atomic vibrations, is the Archetypal Man whose dismemberment, or division into many, constitutes the origin of the human race with its multitude of separate souls.

The "sacrifice" is the involution and apparent death (latency) of the Divine qualities. But the Gods are inseparable from the souls, and as the highest ideals, they come to life within us as our natures are purified and perfected.

"But when the fullness of the time was come, God sent forth his Son, made of a woman, made under the law. To redeem them that were under the law, that we might receive the adoption of sons. And because ye are sons, God hath sent forth the Spirit of his Son into your hearts, crying, Abba, Father."—GAL. iv. 4-6.

When the Absolute outbreathed, the Second Logos was emanated to become the Divine Sacrifice, as Spirit involved in Matter,—Māyā, Mother,— the veil of matter (feminine) in which manifestation takes place. Spirit thereby becomes conditioned, i.e. limited by law. Matter is receptive to energy or vibration, adapted to take impress from Spirit, and so are originated phenomena—the expressions of Spirit in nature.

After the involution of the World-soul, the One Soul separates into many souls, each of which has to evolve the qualities and Spirit with which it is endowed. It is in this evolution that the redemption takes place, for there arise in the souls the inner spiritual vibrations, which, once established, play upon the several egos "under the law," and raise them to the "adoption of sons," who cry, as it were, for union with their Divine source.

"At the centre of all existence, at the beginning of all beginnings, is a divine act of sacrifice; without that primordial sacrifice, there would have been no material universe, no human life as such, no splendour of human achievement, and no glorious end worth striving for. God in Christ laid down his life in creation when time began, we are the product of it, and so are all our struggles and pain.

. . . The life of God has been laid down in us, triumphs in us, and in us will ascend in glory and majesty to the Eternal again."—R. J. CAMPBELL, Serm., The Book of Destiny.

"In its generalised form this high truth (Divine Self-sacrifice) has been recognised even in Buddhism. 'In all the world there is not one spot so large as a mustard seed where the Buddha has not surrendered his body for the good of the creatures' (L. Hearn). Here Buddha is plainly not Gautama, but the divine in man. Christians can point, with far more force, to the sacrament or symbol of this divine sacrifice in the historical Passion of the Son of God."— W. R. INGE, Paddock Lectures, p. 71.

"God has no self-life, but realises His life in the life of all, and in giving of Himself away becomes the life of all— it means the clear recognition of this by the heart, and such an action following on the recognition as unites us in similar sacrifice to the life of God, till we too find our only being along with Him, in the being of all which lives by Him."— STOPFORD A. BROOKE, Serm., Individuality.

See ALTAR GROUND, ALTAR (fire), ARC. MAN, ATONEMENT, BUDDHA, CRUCIFIXION, DISMEMBERMENT, EVOLUTION, FUH-HE, GODS, HORSE SACRIFICE, INVOLUTION, LAMB OF GOD, MARUTS, MĀYĀ (higher), MELCHIZEDEK, MOTHER (divine), PRAGÂPATI (relaxed), RECESSION, PURUSHA, QUETZALCOATL, REDEMPTION, SACRIFICE, SOMA, VISVAKARMAN.

SAGE :—

A symbol of the Self or ego.
See DEATH (Yama), PRAGÂPATI.

SAGES, GREAT :—

A symbol of the spiritual Egos, the Divine Sparks, the Monads of Life.

"The great sages approached Manu, who was seated with a collected mind, and having duly worshipped him, spake, etc."—Laws of Manu, I. 1.

The spiritual Monads descended to the mental plane whereon the Divine Mind was seated preparatory to going forth: they became united with Him, and they sought knowledge.

See MARUTS, MONAD OF LIFE, RISHES, SONS OF GOD.

SAGITTARIUS, THE ZODIACAL SIGN :—

A symbol of the ninth period of the cycle of life, in which the lower mind is perfected through evolution, and therefore "dies." The Higher Self seated on the intelligence (horse) destroys with the "arrow" of the Spirit the lower qualities, thus enabling the lower consciousness to rise to the higher mind.

See APOLLO, ARROW OF SPIRIT, ARROWS (divine), HORSE, QUALITIES, ZODIAC.

SĀHU OF OSIRIS :—

A symbol of the causal-body, which is the receptacle, or seat, of the Spirit in the human soul, and which is built up from the potential pattern as a result of the experiences of life in the physical body.

"The texts show that the Egyptians believed that, if the prescribed prayers were said and the appropriate ceremonies were properly performed over the dead body by duly appointed priests, it acquired the power of developing from out of itself an immaterial body called *sāhu*, which was able to ascend to heaven and to dwell with the gods there. The *sāhu* took the form of the body from which it sprang and was immortal, and in it lived the soul."—BUDGE, *Book of the Dead*, Vol. I. p. lviii.

The "prayers" are the aspirations from the lower self, without which development is impossible. The "ceremonies" symbolise the process of the transmutation of qualities. The "priests" are spiritualised mental forces operating to build up the causal-body. The "dead body" is the lower personality, which being a transient centre of consciousness is in itself lifeless. The immortal causal-body (sahu) is developed in the image of the perfected personality, which merges into the individuality.

"Ulrici's doctrine that we are, during our earthly probation, by the action of our will, our moral decisions, and the processes which go to the making of character, building up within us a spiritual body, whose presence reveals itself in imperfect ways while we are yet in the flesh, but which will be the fully developed organ of the soul after death, runs on lines very similar to Oriental teachings on this subject, which have been reproduced in modern Theosophy. There is something to be said for it, and it may be that revelations are yet in store for humanity along this line of things as the result of future investigations"—J. BRIERLEY, *Studies of the Soul*, p. 111.

"The entire aim, drift, and purpose of religion might well be compendiously summed up in the soul theory. The keynote to religion is the soul: man's con-

cern about himself, and now no less than formerly. It has been, it is to this day, the soul—or rather the immaterial, unseen conception of man, which has been opposed to the visible and actual world—that has served exclusively to perpetuate our conception of a relatively permanent and abiding order."—R. DIMSDALE STOCKER, *The God which is Man*, p. 61.

See ALTAR (fire), CAUSAL-BODY, CORPSE, DEFUNCT, KA, KARANA, KHUS, LAZARUS, MUMMY, PRANAS, RESURRECTION, SOUL (middle), TCHEFET, VESTURES.

SAIL OF A BOAT :—

A symbol of progress by means of mental currents through space of mind, or through mental matter of the soul.

"The chapter of living by air in the Underworld. *Vignette :* the deceased holding a sail, symbolic of air."—BUDGE, *Book of the Dead*, p. 164.

Through the mind (air) the Divine Life vivifies the soul on the lower planes (underworld).

" 'Tell me my name,' saith the Sail; 'Nut' is thy name."—BUDGE, *Book of the Dead*, Ch. XCIX.

The meaning of the symbol "Sail" is: progression through mental space (Nut) by means of currents of thought (air).

See AIR, BOAT ON RIVER, DEFUNCT, NUT.

SAILOR OF THE BOAT :—

A symbol of the Divine Monad or Ego, the conductor of the Soul.

"It is a matter of doubt whether soul as the perfect realisation of the body may not stand to it in the same separable relation as a sailor to his boat."—ARISTOTLE, *De An.* 413a, 6.

" 'Tell me my name,' saith the Sailor; 'Traveller' is thy name."—BUDGE, *Book of the Dead*, Ch. XCIX.

The meaning of the symbol " Sailor" is :—the Divine Spark of the soul, the "pilgrim of the night" of the Tuat (underworld).

"To work with Christ is like hoisting your sail to the breeze and pushing out into the deep whither your own efforts could never have propelled the boat of your soul. Your will may keep you rowing, but you will not make much headway without the sail of faith that the same will puts up, and the strong wind of heaven which is the saving Spirit of Christ."—R. J. CAMPBELL, Serm., *The Sovereignty of the Will*.

See BOAT ON RIVER, MONAD OF LIFE, NAME, PILGRIM, SHIP, SPARK, TUAT, WANDERER, WAYFARING MAN, WIND.

SAILS OF THE BLACK SHIP :—

A symbol of the ambitions of the soul.

"They set up their mast (in the black ship) and spread the white sails forth, and the wind filled the sail's belly, and the dark wave sang loud about the stern as the ship made way and sped across the wave accomplishing her journey."—*Iliad*, Bk. I.

The mental qualities erect an opinion of high import, which becomes the means of raising the vehicle of mind by its enhanced receptiveness. And as this took place, the lower emotions (wind) surged about the soul (ship). And thus the soul hastened on its upward course and accomplished its mission for the time being.

See GREEKS, MAST, SHIP (black), WAVES, WIND.

SAINTS, OR THE SANCTIFIED :—

A symbol of the qualities or souls in harmony with the Divine nature, and becoming purified and perfected ; or finally being perfected and attaining liberation from the lower nature at the end of the cycle.

" ' They that believe ' are men in whom human life is perfect in proportion to the completeness of their faith through the Son of Man. They are men raised to the highest power. The man in whom Christ dwells by faith is the man in whom the divine ideal of human life is perfect, or is steadily becoming perfect, by the entrance into him of the perfect life of the man Christ Jesus, through obedience and love."—PHILLIPS BROOKS, *Serm.*, *The Safety and Helpfulness of Faith.*

"For what is the goal to which (the saints) tend ? The likeness of God in Christ—all His wisdom, His love, His holiness. He is all theirs, and all that He is, is to be transfused into their growing greatness. On the one hand is infinite perfection, destined to be imparted to the redeemed spirit. On the other hand is a capability of indefinite assimilation to, by reception of, that infinite perfection. We have no reason to set bounds to the possible expansion of the human spirit. If only there be fitting circumstances and an adequate impulse, it may have endless growth."—A. MACLAREN, *Sermons, 2nd Series*, p. 193.

See ARHATS, CHRIST'S SECOND COMING, INVOCATION, LIBERATION, MONKS, RE-BIRTH, REDEMPTION, REGENERATION, REMISSION, RESURRECTION, RISHES, SALVATION, SOSHYANTS, TRI-RATNA, VICTORY.

SAKAKI TREE OF HEAVEN :—

A symbol of the Divine Life (atma-buddhi) which flows through all forms in the invisible and visible universe.

See CHRISTMAS-TREE, MITEGURA, TAMA-GUSHI, TREE OF LIFE.

SAKRIDAGAMIN INITIATION :—

This initiation, or raising of the consciousness, is the arousing of the higher intellect, bringing perception of the Truth and the Life. It corresponds with the derivation of knowledge from within, by the child Jesus when he is said in the story to discourse with the doctors.

See INITIATIONS, INTELLECT, JOHANNA, WALKS.

SAKYAS, RACE OF MEN :—

A symbol of the higher mental faculties.

SALAGYA, CITY :—

A symbol of the centre of perfection, the Higher Self seated on the buddhic plane.

See ILYA, ODOUR, SELF, TASTE, VIBHU, YESHTIKA.

SALAMANDERS AND SYLPHS :—

These terms denote nature-spirits on the astral plane which build up and weave together the forms of organisms. They are builders not architects. Their operations (not themselves) may be watched under a microscope in the forming of plant cells.

See DEVAS (lower), DRYAD, FIRE.

SALMON, FISH OF LOKE :—

A symbol of the lower self upon the astral plane submerged in the desire-nature.

"Loke considered what would be the stratagem by which the Asar would endeavour to catch him as a salmon in the waterfall."—*The Punishment of Loke, Prose Edda*, HOWITT, *Literature, etc.*

At this early stage of human evolution it first of all became necessary for the soul to work along the plane of desire,—seeking food, shelter, safety, etc., for its physical body, so that it might maintain its existence and promote its well-being, while gathering such experience as came to it in the play of ideas and the lower emotions. The higher ideals (Asar) would in course of time capture and subjugate the desire-mind (Loke).

See ASAR, ASTRAL PLANE, DOORS (four), LOKE, NET OF ASAR, WATER (lower).

SALT, SALTNESS :—

A symbol of truth regarded as the means by permeation of raising the qualities.

" Salt is good : but if the salt have lost its saltness, wherewith will ye season it ? have salt in yourselves, and be at peace one with another."—MARK ix. 50.

Truth is to be sought. Error can be no substitute for truth. Without truth there can be no progress. Truth is the element of equity or equality which makes for peace in the soul, and is an ingredient in the spiritual man.

" Moreover, that salt is believed to be the savour of those two, the sky and the earth."—*Sata. Brâh.* II. 1, 1, 6.

" The sky and the earth were originally close together. On being separated they said to each other, ' Let there be a common sacrificial essence for us ! ' What sacrificial essence there was belonging to yonder sky, that it bestowed on this earth, that became the salt in the earth ; and what sacrificial essence there was belonging to yonder sky, that became the black spots in the moon."—*Tait. Brâh.* I. 1, 3, 2.

Spirit and matter were originally combined. When they separated into higher and lower natures, it became necessary that there should be a reciprocating medium between them and a means for raising the lower to the higher. The higher nature possesses love of the truth which the lower requires, and the higher is ready to bestow truth in response to the efforts and aspirations of the lower. When the desires are sacrificed for love of the higher qualities, truth (salt) permeates the lower nature (earth). Love of truth in the higher nature is reflected as recognition of defects and ignorance (black spots) in the lower mind or personality (moon).

" Salt in the Divine language is often a symbol of wisdom : ' Let your speech be savoured with salt.' "—F. E. HULME, *Symbolism in Christian Art*, p. 210.

See BLACK, EARTH, HEAVEN AND EARTH, HIGHER AND LOWER NATURES, MOON, PERSONALITY, SACRIFICE, SAVOUR, SEASONING, SEPARATION OF HEAVEN AND EARTH, SKY, SPOTTED, SUN (moon).

SALVATION :—

A symbol of the liberation of the soul from the lower nature, preceded by the process of purification through suffering and evil, during the cycle of evolution.

But Christ is entered " into heaven itself, now to appear in the presence of God for us : Nor yet that he should offer himself often. . . . For then must he often have suffered since the foundation of the world : but now once in the end of the world hath he appeared to put away sin by the sacrifice of himself. And as it is appointed unto men once to die, but after this the judgment : so Christ was once offered to bear the sins of many ; and unto them that look for him shall he appear the second time without sin unto salvation."—HEB. ix. 24–8.

The Higher Self (Christ) during the process of involution commences its evolution in the higher mind, the soul-centre, and so forms the germ-soul. This spiritual evolution proceeds upwards and prepares the patterns on the higher planes, which, when the lower evolution is begun, are capable of being reflected downward on the lower planes, where they become distorted beyond recognition owing to the fact that they do not appear in a sequential or coherent form in the evolving souls of humanity.

So it is that Christ enters into heaven and stands in the presence of the Supreme, while below, at the " foundation of the world " and at the " end of the ages " of involution, he is the " Lamb slain," the Divine sacrifice,—the Archetypal Man, who dies once in order that the many souls, who are his " limbs,"—his " members,"—shall evolve in evil and sorrow, and finally be " washed in the blood of the Lamb," i.e. be purified by the Divine Life which wells up within the soul. When Christ shall appear a second time, it will be in the glorified souls of the saints awaiting their final deliverance, which is the union of the lower self and the higher self, or the " marriage of the Lamb."

" If then deliverance be based at one time on the conquest of all desire, and at another on the knowledge of the Brahma, both may be regarded merely as the expression of one and the same thought. . . . What keeps the soul bound in the cycle of birth, death, and re-birth ? Buddhism answers : desire and ignorance.

Of the two the greater evil is ignorance, the first link in the long chain of causes and effects, in which the sorrow-working destiny of the world is fulfilled."—Dr. Oldenberg, *Buddha, etc.*, trans. p. 52.

"There is no such thing as individual retribution or individual salvation. For good or for evil the human race is a solidarity ; we are all members one of another ; we suffer and achieve in common. There is no heaven that does not imply willingness to share the sinner's hell ; there is no hell that is not heaven in the making. God has no interest in punishment as such, and no evil-doer can bear his punishment alone. Indeed, there is no such thing as punishment in the sense that so much pain must be endured for so much sin."—R. J. Campbell, *Thursday Mornings*, p. 166.

"The way Christ saves you is to take possession of your soul and conform it entirely to his own likeness, and this he cannot do until you yourself see what is needed."—R. J. Campbell, Serm., *Hell*.

"By the deeds of the law, shall no man living be justified. Salvation is by faith : a state of heart right with God. . . . Salvation is God's Spirit in us, leading to good. Destruction is the selfish spirit in us, leading to wrong."—F. W. Robertson, *Sermons, 3rd Series*, p. 249.

"The gift and blessing of salvation is primarily a spiritual gift, and only involving outward consequences secondarily and subordinately. It mainly consists in the heart being at peace with God, in the whole soul being filled with Divine affections, in the weight and bondage of transgression being taken away, and substituted by the impulse and the life of the new love. Therefore, neither God can give, nor man can receive, that gift upon any other terms than just this, that the heart and nature be fitted and adapted for it. Spiritual blessings require a spiritual capacity for the reception of them ; or, as my text says, you cannot have the inheritance unless you are sons (Rom. viii. 17)."—A. Maclaren, *Sermons, 1st Series*, p. 70.

See Adoption, Arc. man, Atonement, Blessing, Bondage, Christ, Christ's second coming, Conqueror, Crucifixion of christ, Escape, Evolution, Ignorance, Image, Involution, Lamb of god, Letter, Liberation, Marriage, Members, Re-birth, Redemption, Regeneration, Resurrection, Rock of salvation, Sacrifice, Saints, Sealed letter, Sorrow, Suffering, Victory, Washed (blood).

SALVE OF MEDEA :—

A symbol of the intuition, which, when realised, reconciles the mind of the troubles and difficulties of life.

"Medea, who was an enchantress, gave Jason a salve to rub his body, shield, and spear. The virtue of this salve would last an entire day, and protect alike against fire and steel."—*Argonautic Expedition*, Keightley, *Mythology*.

From Wisdom (Medea) comes the intuition which exercises over the lower mind an irresistible sway as soon as it becomes established. Wisdom presents the lower Self with that which reconciles difficulties and causes all seeming incongruities to be made plain. The "body" is a symbol of desire, the "shield" of will, and the "spear" of intention. The "virtue of the salve" is said to "last a day," inasmuch as it signifies that subtle force from above, which, acting on the lower planes, enables the ego thereon to rise a stage above where it formerly stood ; and to serve as a protection against "fire and steel," symbolic of disintegrating and crystallising forces.

See Absyrtus, Golden fleece, Intuition, Jason, Medea, Shield, Spear, Wisdom.

SAMAN (CONCILIATION)
VERSES :—

Symbolic of spiritual qualities and powers.

"Brihat and Rathantera" verses signify government through Wisdom and Love ; "Syaita and Nandhasa," Truth and Goodness ; "Vairupa and Vairaga," Indifference to Form and the lower Attachment ; "Sâkvara and Raivata," Reality and Being ; "Bhadra and Yagnâ," Will and Wisdom.

See Brihat, Vairupa, Yagnâ.

SÂMAS :—

A symbol of the Divine Forces of the universe.

See Neryosang, Om, Thrita, Udgitha.

SAMKHÂRA OR SANKHÂRA :—

A symbol of the archetypal causal-body on the buddhic plane containing the prototypes of all things and qualities that are to appear in the universe and soul.

"The word Sankhâra is derived from a verb which signifies to arrange, adorn, prepare. Sankhâra (conformations) is both the preparation and that prepared. . . . To the Buddhist mind, the made thing has existence only and solely in the process of being made ; whatever is, is not so much a something which is, as the process rather of a being, self-generating and self-again-consuming being."—H. OLDEN-BERG, *Buddha*, p. 242.

See BOAT SEKTET, CAUSAL-BODY, IGNORANCE, KARANA, SKANDHAS, VESTURES.

SAMKHÂRAS (AGGREGATE OF FORMATIONS) :—

A symbol associated with Dhamma (karma). It signifies usually the transitory mental type-forms which change with every personality.

" Impermanent truly are the Sank-hâras, liable to origination and decease ; as they arose so they pass away ; their disappearance is happiness."—*Ibid.*, p. 251.

See CONSCIOUSNESS, FORMS, IGNOR-ANCE, KARMA, SKANDHAS.

SAMSÂRA :—

A symbol of the cycle of life on the lower planes in which the spiritual egos are involved.

" Samsâra, the course of the world, the circle of cosmic existence, the succession of births and deaths."—MAX MÜLLER, *Theosophy, etc.*, p. 277.

" All the Upanishads, even the oldest, when they discuss the conditions of bondage in the *samsâra* and of deliverance therefrom, distinguish between the imprisoned soul and that (soul) which has been delivered, between the soul entering on deliverance and that to which it enters in ; and thus often enough a poetic personification of the two conditions is arrived at, as of the souls imprisoned in samsâra, and of the divine emancipated souls."—DEUSSEN, *Phil. of Upanishads*, p. 258.

The spiritual egos entering upon the conditions of manifestation are imprisoned and obscured therein. They can only express their nature by overcoming these conditions and so being delivered therefrom. They have to traverse the cycle of life and rise from the lower nature as glorified images of the Divine nature of the Supreme.

" Those who again and again go to samsâra with birth and death, to existence in this way or that way,—that is the state of avigga (ignorance). For this avigga is the great folly by which this existence has been traversed long, but those beings who resort to knowledge do not go to re-birth."—*Sutta-nipâta*, 729, 730.

Those spiritual egos, or monads of life, who time after time descend from the higher planes to the cycle of the quaternary, therein to be embodied in forms of one kind or another, are

plunged into spiritual ignorance. For this ignorance is due to the ego's identification of itself with the great illusion of phenomenal existence through protracted periods of time. But those egos who do not identify themselves with their lower nature, and who turn to the truth within, are liberated from reincarnation.

See ABRAXAS, BONDAGE, CHARIOT, CIRCLE OF EXISTENCE, DAY (great), IGNORANCE, INCARNATION OF SOULS, LEVIATHAN, LIBERATION, MANVAN-TARA, MONAD OF LIFE, NAKEDNESS, NIGHT, NIRVANA, QUATERNARY, RE-INCARNATION, SERPENT (ananta), STRIDES, TUAT, UPANISHAD, YEAR, ZODIAC.

SAND CARRIED FROM WEST TO EAST :—

A symbol of the lower nature brought from its lowest condition (sunset) to its highest state (sunrise).

See EAST, SHABTI, WEST.

SANDAL, OR SHOE :—

A symbol of relativity in the progress of the soul.

" Jason arrived at Iolous with only one sandal, having lost the other in crossing the river Anaurus."—*The Argonautic Expedition*, KEIGHTLEY, *Mythology*.

The Self, the Saviour, is said to arrive on the mental plane to be born within the soul, minus a " sandal,"—that is to say, without the power to proceed mentally, or having no means for self-expression. The " one sandal " is a symbol of relativity, implying that the perfect duality of spirit-matter cannot be expressed actually on the lower planes. The " losing of a sandal " implies that the inner sense of power is not yet realised in the soul, though the means for attaining it is now present. The " river Anau-rus " signifies limitation, that which separates higher from lower, truth revealed, definition of mental concepts, or that which is made evident.

See ANAURUS, FOOT, IOLCUS, JASON, SHOES.

SANDALS, OR SHOES :—

Symbolic of power to advance and attain Self-expression.

See FEET, SHOES, WALKING.

SANDS OF THE SEASHORE :—

A symbol of the astro-mental plane.

"They drew up their black ship to land high upon the sands."—*Iliad*, Bk. I.

See GINUNGA, SHIP (black), SHORE OF SEA.

SANJAYA, THE CHARIOTEER OF DHRITA-RASHTRA :—

A symbol of natural law which brings about progress of the instinct-nature.

See DHRITA-RASHTRA.

SANNYASIN, OR BHIKSHU :—

A symbol of an ego who has attained liberation from the lower nature and "cast off everything from himself," and now proceeds upward through the buddhic plane.

"*Jâb. Up.* 4. enjoins entrance into the sannyâsa only after passing through the stages of brahmacarin, grihastha and vanaprastha, but permits the transition direct from any stage."—DEUSSEN, *Phil. of Upanishads*, p. 374.

The spiritual ego progresses, first, through the personality (brahmacarin) in the present life of experience, moral discipline, and aspiration (study of the Veda), second, through the individuality (grihastha) in the causal-body, third, through the individuality centred on the higher mental plane above the causal-body, (the vâna-prastha).

"The sannyasin after thus separating himself from sacrificial duties, a highly significant act followed, upon which accordingly stress is laid by all the texts, namely the laying aside of the sacred thread, the token that he belongs to the Brâhmanical class, and the lock of hair which indicates his family descent. Henceforth meditation alone is to serve as a sacrificial cord, and knowledge as the lock of hair."—*Ibid.*, p. 377.

The ego having fulfilled the law of sacrifice in renouncing the lower, rises above the condition signified by the "sacred thread and lock of hair," namely, the causal individuality (Brâhman caste) from which he has sprung. He finds within him the Divine life of love and wisdom, and he has direct knowledge of the truth.

See ALMSGIVING, ASCETIC, ASRAMAS, BRAHMACARIN, HAIR (side-lock), HERMIT, KUSTI, MENDICANT, ORDERS, YAJNOPAVITA.

SAP, OR LIFE-SAP :—

A symbol of the Divine Life (blood).

See BLOOD, COW (spotted), FIG-JUICE, HOMA-JUICE, PRAGÂPATI (relaxed), SOMA-JUICE, TORTOISE.

SAPANDÂR :—

A symbol of buddhi.

"Invoke thou the strong wind created by Mazda Sapandâr, the pure daughter of Hormazd."—*Vendidad*, XIX.

Invoke thou Soul! the Divine Breath,—the Holy Spirit, which is the functioning of the Absolute upon Buddhi.

See BREATH (divine), BUDDHI, HOLY GHOST.

SAPANDOMAD, QUEEN OF EARTH :—

A symbol of Nature, as the Divine expression upon the physical plane ; or the relationship established between buddhi and the astral principle, which eventuates in the physical world of phenomena.

See EARTH (great), MUT, THETIS.

SAPPHIRE STONE :—

A symbol of wisdom-love.

"The sapphire stone is in colour etherial blue, with golden sparkles ; it represents the soul of man purged from all iniquity, and tinctured through with the Spirit of Truth (the heavenly blue), which dispels all misunderstandings upon the Word and ways of God."—JOHN WARD, *Zion's Works*, Vol. II. p. 23.

"And like the sapphire stone also were its manifold hues."—*Hymn of the Soul.*

See GEMS, JEWELS.

SARASVATI (" THE WATERY ") :—

A symbol of Wisdom, the buddhic function.

"Brahmâ formed from his own immaculate substance a female, who is celebrated under the names of Satarupa, Savitri, Sarasvati, Gâyatri, and Brâhmanî."—*Matsya Purana.*

"Brahmâ's wife is Sarasvati, the goddess of wisdom and science, the mother of the Vedas. She is represented with four arms. With one of her right hands she is presenting a flower to her husband, by whose side she constantly stands ; and in the other she holds a book of palm-leaves. In one of her left hands she has a string of pearls, called Sivamâla (Siva's garland), and in the other is a small drum."—WILKINS, *Hindu Mythology*, p. 107.

The Atman is allied with the principle of Buddhi, which brings forth the scriptures. The "four arms" represent buddhic activities. (1) Production of the higher qualities for the Self. (2) The inspiration of the scriptures. (3) The passing on of the Divine Life (Sutratma) to the lower planes. (4) The harmonising (music) of the qualities.

See ATMAN, BINAH, BRAHMA, BUDDHI, FLOWERS, HAND, MĀYĀ (higher), OCEAN, PAPYRUS, SCRIPTURES, SUTRATMA, VASISHTHA.

SARDINIAN SEA :—

A symbol of the third sub-plane of the buddhic plane counting upwards.

SARDONYXES :—

Symbolic of aspects of receptiveness or humility.

See GEMS, JEWELS.

SÂSTRA, OR VEDA :—

A symbol of the law of the Spirit, —that which unifies and co-ordinates the soul's experiences,—the operation of the Self within. The revelation of the laws of the growth of the soul ; or the Divine inspiration of the scriptures which reveals to the lower mind the hidden nature of humanity and the Divine process of development and salvation.

See GOSPEL, INSPIRATION, KORAN, PAPYRUS, PEN, REVELATION, SCRIPTURES, UPANISHAD, UR-HEKAU, VEDA, WORD.

SATAN :—

A symbol of darkness, relativity, limitation (Saturn), ignorance.

"And Jesus said unto them, I beheld Satan fallen as lightning from heaven."— LUKE x. 18.

This is allegorical, and signifies the casting forth of the relative in the process of perfectionment through the absolute principle of real being.

See ADVERSARY, AHRIMAN, ANTICHRIST, APEP, DEVIL, JOB, PETER, SET.

SATRUGHANA :—

A symbol of experience through the senses :—

"Satrughana, on his part, seized the deformed slave-girl Manthara, and literally shook the senses out of her." —*Ramayana*

The astro-physical nature through experience of suffering caused by the uncurbed lower emotion-nature (deformed slave-girl) is the means of diminishing its violence.

See RAMAYANA.

SATTVA STATE :—

This signifies mental incoming energy directed towards wisdom and love for the perfecting of the soul.

"The *sattva* quality by reason of its lucidity and peacefulness entwineth the soul to rebirth through attachment to knowledge and that which is pleasant." —*Bhagavad-gita*, Ch. XIV.

"When wisdom, the bright light, shall become evident at every gate of the body, then one may know that the *sattva* quality is prevalent within."—*Ibid.*

"If the body is dissolved when the *sattva* quality prevails, the Self within proceeds to the spotless spheres of those who are acquainted with the highest place."—*Ibid.*

"Honoring the gods, the brahmans, the teachers, and the wise ; purity, rectitude, chastity, and harmlessness are called mortification of the body. Gentle speech which causes no anxiety, which is truthful and friendly, and diligence in the reading of the Scriptures, are saith to be austerities of speech. Serenity of mind, mildness of temper, silence, self-restraint, absolute straightforwardness of conduct, are called mortification of the mind. This threefold mortification or austerity, practised with supreme faith and by those who long not for a reward, is of the *sattva* quality."—*Ibid.*, Ch. XVII.

See AUSTERITIES, GUNAS, QUALITIES.

SATURDAY, THE SIXTH DAY :—

This symbol connotes a cessation from activity. It implies limitation (Saturn) at the end of a sixth period ; such as the sixth "day" of the period of involution, which closes that cycle and ushers in a pralaya (sabbath), after which state of latency (rest), a new manvantara of activity opens on the first "day" of the cycle of evolution.

See DAY, EVOLUTION, MANVANTARA, PRALAYA, SABBATH, SIX, SUNDAY.

SATURN, PLANET :—

A symbol of that law which limits or defines manifestation ; and so stands sometimes for the physical as the extreme limit of existence and foundation of all. It agrees with the decline or decay of things. It also corresponds to the individual stage of growth through experience.

"Under the guidance of Jupiter (planet) man prepares, by means of religious exercises, for the journey to the life beyond, and he attains rest under the influence of Saturn" (*Basra Encyclopedia*).—DE BOER, *Philosophy in Islam*, p. 88.

See CRONUS, JUDAS, JUPITER, PLANETS, RHEA.

SATYRS :—

A symbol of the higher emotions (buddhi-manas) united with the mind, and attached to the lower nature of the soul. The horns on the forehead and pointed ears signify lofty thought and aspiration. Their love of music and dancing indicates their self-regulating powers and disposition towards harmonious activity among themselves.

"Satyri are inseparably connected with the worship of Dionysus, and represent the luxuriant vital powers of nature. They are always described as fond of wine, and of every kind of sensual pleasure, whence they are seen sleeping, playing musical instruments, or engaged in voluptuous dances with nymphs."—*Smith's Class. Dict.*

The connection of the buddhi-mental qualities with the Self within (Dionysus) refers to their active relations with the Self, as development proceeds.

"By man and beast together (Satyr), is signified man as to spiritual and natural affection."—SWEDENBORG, *Apoc. Rev.*, n. 567.

See DANCE, DIONYSUS, GOPIS, INTOXICATION, PANS, SILENUS, WINE.

SAU AMULET (EGYPTIAN) :—

A symbol of the lower quaternary through which desire operates and to which it applies. The four planes are indicated both in the crossed square and the lines, while the steps signify the path of the soul upward through the underworld (Tuat).

"Why the feather was chosen as the symbol of Maāt instead of the usual object (the sau) it is impossible to say, and this fact suggests that all the views which the Egyptians held about the weighing of the heart have not yet been understood."—DR. BUDGE, *Gods of the Egyptians*, Vol. II. p. 143.

The feather of Maāt signifies the lower personality as related to justice and law (old testament dispensation) in contradistinction to its affectional relation to the dominion of Love (new testament).

The feather was chosen as a sign, probably, of the instability of the lower expression of the Divine life, for the personality cannot continue to persist. The light and drifting feather is symbolic of the transitory and illusory personality of the lower planes. The idea in the "weighing scene" is, perhaps, better symbolised by the usual object,—the *sau*.

See DISPENSATIONS, FEATHER, JUDGMENT HALL, MAAT, PERSONALITY, QUATERNARY, RECTANGLE, STEPS, TUAT.

SAVIOURS, THE TWELVE :—

Symbolic of the twelve highest qualities involved in the soul, by means of which the Higher Self is enabled to raise the souls to bliss.

"He (Jesus) chose the Twelve before he came into the world. He chose twelve powers, receiving them from the Twelve Saviours of the Light-treasure. When he descended into the world, he cast them as sparks into the wombs of their mothers that the whole world might be saved."—*Pistis Sophia*, trans. G. R. S. MEAD.

Christ of necessity beforehand chose the means by which he is to accomplish his purpose in the raising of the soul. He cannot manifest excepting through special vehicles, and these are the highest qualities, such as Faith, Aspiration, Steadfastness, Fortitude, etc., symbolised by the "twelve powers" or "disciples." The "Saviours" are typical of the "apostles"; they save souls who rise through them, and they are "those whom the Father hath given me." The "Light-treasure" is that aroma of virtue which shall attain to the "Light-realm" (heaven).

When Christ manifests himself, he comes forth to the Sons of God,—the Divine "Sparks." These have a common Father, but must, so to say, be brought forth and nurtured by the matter side of nature, or their "Mother the Moon,"—astral matter. By this means the qualities are to attain liberation by triumphing over the limitations of the astral and physical planes.

See ÆONS, ANTHROPOS, APOSTLES, DISCIPLES, JESHURUN, LIBERATION, LIGHT TREASURE, QUALITIES, SPARKS,

Sons of god, Thrones (twelve), Twelve.

SAVITRI, THE SUN :—

A symbol of the Higher Self, God manifest.

" As Savitri, the sun is represented as standing on a golden chariot, with yellow hair, with golden arms and hands and eyes, nay, even with a golden tongue, while his jaws are said to be of iron."— Max. Müller, *Origin and Growth of Religion*, p. 268.

The " golden chariot " represents the higher causal-body, or World-soul. It is the buddhic vehicle of the Atman or Higher Self. The " yellow hair " signifies kingship or supremacy over all. The " golden arms and hands " signify activities through buddhi. The " golden eyes " are symbols of perception through centres of consciousness. The " golden tongue" signifies the Divine expression on the higher planes, and the " jaws of iron " are a symbol of creative power upon the mental plane.

See Aditya, Chariot of sun, Gods, Gold, Helios, Iron, Spade, Sun, Surya.

SAVOUR, SWEET :—

A symbol of the yearning of the lower self after righteousness and truth, which draws down the Divine blessing.

" And the Lord smelled the sweet savour ; and the Lord said in his heart, I will not again curse the ground any more for man's sake, for that the imagination of man's heart is evil from his youth ; neither will I again smite any more everything living, as I have done."—Gen. viii. 21.

And the Lord, or Greater Self, " smelled " or apprehended the earnest strivings of the lesser self to secure its blessing. And the Love of the Self rendered it impossible for the lower self to be cut off from It—the Higher. No more henceforth is the lower nature to be non-productive of useful result ; for as the lower mind cannot of itself yield good, so also it cannot bring forth lasting evil. No more in the course of the cycle shall what is now called into existence come to an end (see 2 Cor. ii. 15).

See Altar building, Burnt offering, Goats (unblemished), God (smelling), Incense, Man, Noah, Nostrils, Sacrifice, Smelling.

SCAPEGOAT :—

A symbol of ignorance and error, that is, the absence of the real, the true.

" And he shall take the two goats, and set them before the Lord at the door of the tent of meeting. And Aaron shall cast lots upon the two goats ; one lot for the Lord, and the other lot for Azazel." —Lev. xvi. 7, 8.

The " two he-goats " signify, (1) Desire for lower things, and (2) Ignorance and error, which are negative and illusory conditions. The first must be offered up to the Higher Self (the Lord), and the second must bear, as an excuse, the sins of the qualities, and be dismissed to nullity or negation (Azazel). Ignorance dissipated and replaced by true knowledge atones for sin.

" This very circumstance of a word (Azazel) having been coined for the occasion, suggests what seems to me the right view. . . . To have the iniquities conveyed by a symbolical action into that desert and separate region, into a state of oblivion, was manifestly the whole intention and design of the rite."—P. Fairbairn, *The Typology of Scripture*, Vol. II. p. 536.

" Azazel (in the Book of Enoch) was conceived as chained in the wilderness into which the scapegoat was led. The Jerusalem Targum (Ps. Jonathan) on Leviticus says that ' the goat was sent to die in a hard and rough place in the wilderness of jagged rocks, i.e. Beth Chaduda."—R. H. Charles, *Book of Enoch*, p. 72.

See Aaron, Ammit, Atonement, Goats, Ignorance, Sacrifice.

SCARABÆUS :—

A symbol of the Divine nature which enters the lower nature, from which it afterwards emerges.

" The scarab was the type and symbol of the god Khepera. The unseen power of God made manifest under the form of the god Khepera caused the sun to roll across the sky, and the act of rolling gave the scarab its name, Kheper, i.e. ' he who rolls.' . . . Now the god Khepera also represented inert but living matter, which was to begin a course of existence, and at a very early period he was considered to be a god of the resurrection."—Budge, *Egyptian Magic*, p. 38.

The Higher Self in-rolls in involution and out-rolls in evolution, as he (the sun) traverses the lower planes of nature during the great cycle of life (the Tuat). When he has completed his course in the souls of humanity, he rises from the under-world in them and through them at the end of the cycle.

The meaning of the symbol was rightly expressed by Epiphanius, who spoke of Christ as " the scarabæus of God" See also Ambrose, Bishop of Milan (*Opera*, tom. I. col. 1528).

See ASCENSION OF OSIRIS, EVOLUTION, INCARNATION, INVOLUTION, KHEPER, LIBERATION, RESURRECTION.

SCARLET :—

A symbol of energy, or regarded as blood, the Divine Life permeating all things.

" The bloom of the scarlet dye mingles with shining linen."—*Empedocles*, FAIRBANKS, 286.

The power of the Divine Life energises the Divine Truth within the World-substance.

" There are no religious ideals that may be regarded with a purely speculative interest. In religion everything—facts, conceptions, ideals—is shot through and through with the logic of feeling, is deeply dyed (often enough literally ' blood-red ') with convictions, is held with a grasp, or rejected with a movement of soul, which is more profoundly seated, more intensely emotional, and more sternly practical than anything of a simply intellectual character can well be."—G. T. LADD, *Phil. of Religion*, Vol. I. p. 25.

The higher qualities and emotions are, when permitted exercise by the personality, of tremendous efficacy in the soul. They are " words of power " of truly magical import.

See BLOOD, COLOURS, LINEN, LOOM, MAGIC, RED, WORDS OF POWER.

SCENT, SWEET, FROM THE SOUTH :—

A symbol of a pure and deep sense of the Truth which enters into the higher mind from the buddhic plane above the highest intellect.

" So Isis came to Byblos, and by reason of the sweet smell which emanated from her, she found favour with the women servants of the palace, obtained entry there, and was appointed nurse to the King's child."—PLUTARCH, *Isis and Osiris*, § 15.

The buddhic function approaches the lower self, and because it contains Truth, Beauty, and Love, finds favour with the emotions of admiration, veneration, devotion, etc., and so

effects an entrance into the conscious-ness of the ego.

See ATALANTA, BYBLOS, IMMORTALITY, ISIS, MAIDEN, ODOUR, PERFUME, WIND (sweet).

SCEPTICISM, OR PHILOSOPHIC DOUBT :—

This implies aspiration, for it is the doubt which is begotten of the distrust of the appearance or form of thought, therefore answers to an unconscious awakenment within. It is inverted confidence and faith upon which perception of Truth reposes.

See JUDGING OTHERS, PENANCE.

SCEPTRE HELD IN THE HAND :—

An emblem of power and rule, either higher or lower.

See HAND, IRON PLATE, ROD (hand).

SCEPTRE OF ACHILLES :—

An emblem of the dominance of desire and sensation, and of physical rule.

See ACHILLES.

SCEPTRE OF AGAMEMNON :—

An emblem of the rule of the desire-mind and the lower principle over the lower nature of the soul.

See AGAMEMNON.

SCEPTRE OF EGYPT :—

An emblem of supremacy and rule over the higher and lower natures.

See AMEN.

SCEPTRE, GOLDEN, OF APOLLO :—

An emblem of the power and rule of the Spirit, and of the Divine Ray from the Supreme, which is atma-buddhic (golden).

See FILLET OF APOLLO.

SCORPIO, THE ZODIACAL SIGN :—

A symbol of the eighth period of the cycle of life, in which the desire-nature is predominant in the soul. It signifies the mental-emotional procreative function,—that which can procreate and re-create mental concepts and states. This is the multiplying function which ties to re-birth, and so Scorpio becomes the sign of the " fall into generation " on the physical plane in the middle of the Third Root Race, when mind commenced to function in early human bodies. The present period of the life-cycle in which humanity is gaining experience and evolving its nature is still that of the sign Scorpio.

See ATHYR, CHILDREN OF MEN, EVOLUTION, FALL, GENERATIVE, IRON AGE, KALE-YUGA, MULTIPLY, REINCARNATION, ZODIAC.

SCORPION :—

A symbol of the lower aspect of the emotion-nature. As seen in the sculptures of the God Mithra slaying the Bull, it signifies that the emotions are active through the contact with matter.

"By a scorpion is signified deadly persuasion; and by a scorpion of the earth, persuasion that falses are truths in things relating to the church; for a scorpion when he stings a man induces a stupor upon the limbs."—SWEDENBORG, Apoc. Rev., n. 425.

"Behold I have given you authority to tread upon serpents and scorpions, and over all the power of the enemy: and nothing shall in any wise hurt you."—LUKE x. 19.

The disciplined qualities of the soul, which possess the power of the Christ, —the love of goodness and truth,— within them, are able to overcome the lower desires and emotions, and the power of the lower principle; and illusion cannot affect them, for they have knowledge of truth.

"The DIVINE JOB which is CHRIST can tame these (carnal) powers, and He enables us to do it. He not only bruised the serpent's head, but He gives us power 'to tread on serpents and scorpions and over all the power of the Enemy' (see ROM. xvi. 20)."—WORDSWORTH, Bible, Job, p. 96.

See HOUSE OF BONDAGE, MITHRA, SERPENT, TREADING.

SCOURGE :—

A symbol of outgoing spiritual energy, to dissipate error with truth. This takes effect through experience and discipline in the life of the soul.

"And Jesus made a scourge of cords, and cast all out of the temple, both the sheep and the oxen; and he poured out the changers' money, and overthrew their tables; and to them that sold the doves he said, Take these things hence; make not my Father's house a house of merchandise. . . . 'The zeal of thine house shall eat me up.'"—JOHN ii. 15–17.

This signifies the positive attitude assumed by the Christ-soul in regard to those conflicting influences which set up the jars and jangles found upon the lower planes. The lower personalities in their highest aspect are the "temples" or sheaths of the Holy Spirit, and it is the lower nature which yet needs purifying, steadying, controlling, and disciplining. The "dove-sellers" are those minds who profess to be kind and amiable, but are in reality selfish and indifferent, and who therefore prostitute the ideals which they profess to be living up to. It must be remembered that the lower planes, being those of relativity, can be used in a two-fold manner, or as is said,— for good or for evil. Christ's "zeal" is the emphatic assertion of the force for good, constituting a tremendous influx of truth from above, taking effect upon the lower condition, and expelling ignorance and disharmony.

"It may also be the case that the natural temple is the soul skilled in reason, . . . and in which before Jesus' discipline is applied to it are found tendencies which are earthly and senseless and dangerous, and things which have the name but not the reality of beauty, and which are driven away by Jesus with His word plaited out of doctrines of demonstration and rebuke, to the end that His Father's house may no longer be a house of merchandise but may receive, for its own salvation and that of others, that service of God which is performed in accordance with heavenly and spiritual laws."—ORIGEN, Comm. on John, Bk. X. § 16.

"Not that evil, which does not subsist by its own nature, is created by the Lord, but the Lord shows Himself as creating evil when He turns into a scourge the things that have been created good for us, upon our doing evil, that the very same things should at the same time both by the pain which they inflict be to transgressors evil, and yet good by the nature whereby they have their being. . . . And hence it is rightly said, 'I form the light and create darkness.' For when the darkness of pain is created by strokes without, the light of the mind is kindled by instruction within. 'I make peace, and create evil.' For peace with God is restored to us then, when the things which, though rightly created, are not rightly coveted, are turned into such sort of scourges as are evil to us. Therefore it is meet that we should be brought back to peace with Him by the scourge."—

ST. GREGORY THE GREAT, *Morals on the Book of Job*, Vol. I. p. 140.

"Blessed is the man whom thou chastenest, O Lord, and teachest out of thy law ; that thou mayest give him rest from the days of adversity, until the pit be digged for the wicked."—Ps. xciv. 12, 13.

The mind (man) that is disciplined and cleansed of error may have rest from strife while the lower qualities (wicked) are dissipated.

See CLEANSING, DOVE-SELLERS, JESUS SEVERITY, MOUTH (opening), PEACE AND SWORD, SWORD, TEMPLE.

SCRIPTURES, SACRED :—

These are ancient writings which profess to be of Divine origin, and to be correct transcriptions of verbal communications received into the minds of selected persons, who have fatihfully set down the statements they were entrusted with.

"Thoth, the most mighty god, the lord of Khemennu, cometh to thee, and he writeth for thee the Book of Breathings with his own fingers."—BUDGE, *Book of the Dead*, p. 659.

"Thy fingers (O Scribe Nebseni) are stablished with written works in the presence of the lord of Khemennu, Thoth, who hath given to me the speech of the sacred books."—*Ibid.*, p. 507.

"I am Thoth, the perfect scribe whose hands are pure, . . . the scribe of right and truth ; who abominateth sin."—*Ibid.*, p. 621.

"Thoth" is a symbol of the higher mind through which the Divine messages, as ideas, are projected into the subjective lower mind, there to be expressed in words which make their appearance in the receptive objective mind. Thus the message is, as it were, breathed into the mind of a devout recipient.

"Just as, when a fire is laid with damp wood, clouds of smoke spread all around, so in truth from this great Being have been breathed forth the Rigveda, the Yajurveda, the Sâmaveda, the (hymns) of the Atharvans and the Angirases, the narratives, the histories, the sciences, the mystical doctrines (upanishads), the poems, the proverbs, the parables, and expositions,—all these have been breathed forth from him."—*Brihad. Upanishad*, II. 4, 10.

The sacred writings are veiled in mystery and obscurity (clouds of smoke) because of human inability to apprehend subjective truths in early stages of thought. The truths being hidden in symbolism, it follows

that the outer appearance of the scriptures is usually nonsensical, historic, poetic, allegorical, and didactic ; and the whole has been inspired of the Spirit of Truth.

"The language of religion is plainer and more direct than the language of common life. Symbolism can be looked at with gross eyes or with idealised eyes."—W. M. RAMSAY, *Ency. Brit.* "Mysteries."

"Men are saved not by the historical, but by the metaphysical."—MANSEL, *Gnostic Heresies*, p. 10.

"Language, it has been said, is a storehouse of faded metaphors ; and if this be true of language in general, it is still more true of theological language. We can understand the spiritual and the abstract only through the help of the material ; the words by which we denote them must be drawn, in the first instance, from the world of the senses. . . . Thought is impossible without the brain through which it can act, and we cannot convey to others or even to ourselves our conceptions of right and wrong, of beauty and goodness, without having recourse to analogies from the world of phenomena, to metaphor and imagery, to parable and allegory. If we would deal with the spiritual and moral, we *must* have recourse to metaphorical forms of speech. A religion is necessarily built up on a foundation of metaphor. To interpret such metaphors in their purely natural sense would therefore land us in gross error. Unfortunately modern students of the religious history of the past have not always been careful to avoid doing so."—A. H. SAYCE, *Religions of Anc. Egypt. and Babyl.*, p. 15.

"We must recognise that the Biblical language is symbolic, but we must recognise, if we would be Christian believers, that what the symbols teach is true. . . . The symbolical principle must be admitted : the language is true symbolically and not literally."—C. GORE, Bp. of Oxford, *Constructive Quarterly*, March 1914.

"It seems neither best nor possible for sacred writings to give expression to truth in any other way than by that of suggestion,—not best because of what is required for the development of reason in man ; and not possible because of the essential differences between the spiritual and the material, which latter furnishes the only means in this world of enabling us to interpret that which issues from the former."

"If this be a universal fact with reference to the degree in which the spiritual can be communicated through the material, how mistaken must he be who acts upon the theory that the Scriptures should or can be understood literally ? We can probably understand and interpret them thus to some extent. Almost every word, which originally had more or less of a figurative or merely representative meaning, becomes apparently literal when it comes to be used conventionally with only one meaning. But when we consider such words, phrases, and prolonged descriptions of the Scriptures as attempt to describe conditions that can never come to be conventionally understood because they have never and can never be experienced or conceived by mortals, we would better be humble, and gratefully accept what is revealed to us upon the hypothesis that it is merely suggestive."—G. L. RAYMOND, *Psychology of Inspiration*, pp. 177, 178.

" I say there is not one word (of Scripture) true according to the letter. Yet I say that every word, every syllable, every letter, is true. But they are true as He intended them that spake them ; they are true as God meant them, not as man will have them."—DR. EVERARD, *Gospel Treasury Opened* (1659).

"Now Scripture language is symbolical."—F. W. ROBERTSON, *Sermons*, 1st Series, p. 117.

" A spiritual and symbolical interpretation alone yields truth, whilst a carnal and literal acceptation profits nothing. The spirit quickens ; the flesh is of no avail."—SLADE BUTLER, *Nineteenth Cent.*, Nov. 1906.

" I agree with Professor Flint that by the historical method we obtain only history. But we want more than that ; we wish to understand and to explain."—C. P. TIELE, *Science of Religion*, Vol. I. p. 17.

" In the internal sense there is no respect to any person, or anything determined to a person. But there are three things which disappear from the sense of the letter of the Word when the internal sense is unfolded ; that which is of time, that which is of space, and that which is of person."—SWEDENBORG, *Arc. Cel.* n. 5253.

" All the mistakes made* in Biblical interpretation come of referring statements of which the intention is spiritual and mystical, implying principles or states,—to times, persons or places."—*The Perfect Way*, p. 194.

" He who follows the letter takes figurative words as if they were proper, and does not carry out what is indicated by a proper word into its secondary signification. . . . Now it is surely a miserable slavery of the soul to take signs for things, and to be unable to lift the eye of the mind above what is corporeal and created, that it may drink in eternal light."—ST. AUGUSTINE, *Christian Doctrine*, p. 86.

" Our religious vocabulary, to begin with, consists almost entirely of images. It is a set of concepts borrowed from the region of the material and the visible to set forth the invisible and the spiritual."—J. BRIERLEY, *Studies of the Soul*, p. 146.

" All religious expression is symbolism, since we can describe only what we see, and the true objects of religion are unseen."—R. W. MACKAY, *Progress of the Intellect*, p. 134.

There appears to have been no other way for the Divine Spirit to impart to mankind knowledge of hidden things of the soul but through a method of symbolism. The necessary ideas had to be expressed in the only way possible, that is, by using the images of the material and visible to express the spiritual and invisible. These images, relating to history and life in the physical world, would be found ready at hand in the minds of the inspired writers, and the most appropriate would be employed as symbols for the higher knowledge. Fragmentary notions of history in these minds will explain why history sometimes creeps into the inspired writings, and also account for the fact that the history is often erroneous, a matter which is not of the smallest consequence, from the religious point of view.

" The fourth Gospel is not history, and never was intended to be understood as history. It contains historical elements, but these are always used as a picture language of great ideas ; this is the writer's method all through, and was quite in accordance with the whole school in which he had been trained. It is more than probable that there was at one time a large literature in existence of the same general character as this gospel. Understand, then, when you read this book, that every saying it contains, and every incident it relates, has an inner spiritual meaning. The book is a connected whole, but every separate saying is profound and complete. For instance, there are no parables in this gospel, and the miracles recorded are for the most part quite different from those in the other gospels. The very first one, the turning of water into wine, is not alluded to elsewhere ; and as for the raising of Lazarus, which we might suppose to have been the most astounding of all, not a word is said about it in the older gospels. The truth is that in this gospel the miracles are parables, and every one of them is designed to bring out some special aspect of spiritual truth."—R. J. CAMPBELL, *Thursday Mornings*, p. 140.

" It is now generally recognised by liberal scholars that considerable portions of the gospels are unhistoric."—PRESERVED SMITH, *Hibbert J.*, July 1913.

" In the region of historical inquiry results are surprisingly contradictory, and there seems at present to be no

likelihood of agreements being reached."
—W. C. ALLEN, *Criticism* (*N.T.*), *Ency. Religion and Ethics*.

" For St. John the whole drama is a kind of mystery play, in which the eternal counsels of God and his love for the world are revealed."—W. R. INGE, *Constructive Quarterly*, June 1913.

" St. John's treatment of history is very characteristic. He combines Philo's allegorism with the positivism which is more natural to Jewish thought. He would accept Goethe's dictum that ' all that is transitory is only a symbol,' with the exception of the word *only*. In his hands every event is a type, a symbol, an illustration of some aspect of the nature and character of the Divine Logos. Our Lord's miracles are all acted parables, and the evangelist generally gives us the key to their interpretation, e.g. ' I am the Bread of Life,' ' I am the Light of the World.' Even accidental coincidences have a meaning for him, as when Judas turns away from the supper-table and goes out to his doom—' and it was night '; or when Caiaphas spoke more truly than he knew, and said, ' It is expedient that one man should die for the people.' Every incident in the Gospel is selected for its symbolical value ; the events, miracles, and discourses are so arranged as to exhibit in a series of pictures the various aspects of the Incarnate Word. But even when so treated, St. John does not wish us to make the outward history the basis of our faith."— W. R. INGE, *Paddock Lectures*, p. 47.

" Clement and Origen considered that what is important in history is not the facts themselves, but the universal truths which they illustrate or symbolise. So Origen speaks of the actions of Christ during his ministry as—acted parables." —*Ibid.*, p. 58.

" What we have now to do is to transform the sensible Gospel into a spiritual one. For what would the narrative of the sensible Gospel amount to if it were not developed to a spiritual one ? It would be of little account or none ; any one can read it and assure himself of the facts it tells—no more. But our whole energy is now to be directed to the effort to penetrate to the deep things of the meaning of the Gospel and to search out the truth that is in it when divested of types."—ORIGEN, *Comm. on John*, Bk. I. 10.

" The Bible's authority is wholly spiritual ; it depends not upon the letter, but the spirit of the Scriptures, and appeals to the mind and heart. It is freely accepted, because it exists only so far as it becomes one with the experiences or the present aspirations of piety. It has no more need of official verification, of outward attestation, than the light which enlightens the eye ; or the duty which commands the conscience, or the beauty which ravishes the imagination. The efficacy of the divine word is

at once the inward sign, the measure, and the foundation of its authority." — A. SABATIER, *The Religions, etc.*, pp. 241-2.

" The inner light can only testify to spiritual truths. It always speaks in the present tense ; it cannot guarantee any historical event, past or future. It cannot guarantee either the Gospel history or a future judgment. It can tell us that Christ is risen, and that He is alive for evermore, but not that he rose again the third day."—W. R. INGE, *Christian Mysticism*, p. 326.

" With Scotus (Erigena) the historical element in religion was reduced to a minimum. It seems hardly too much to say that the historical Jesus of Nazareth scarcely existed for thousands of mediæval Christians. Christ was the Second Person of the Trinity, enthroned on high, . . . the inspiring and creative Word which brought order out of chaos in each Christian soul."—ALICE GARDNER, *John the Scot*, p. 143.

See AMBAS, AXE, BOOK STUDIES, DEVELOPMENT, GOSPEL, GOSPEL STORY, HERMES (tris.), INSPIRATION, KAYAN, KORAN, LAZARUS, MIRACLES, MYTHOLOGY, PAPYRUS, PARABLE, PEN, PEOPLE, RAMAYANA, REVELATION, RITUAL, SACRED TEXT, SASTRA, SIGN, SRUTI, THOTH, UPANISHAD, UR-HEKAU, VEDA, WORD OF GOD.

SCRIPTURES, PONDERING ON THE :—

A symbol of the soul relying upon the Word of the Lord, i.e. relying upon the higher nature which is within.

" The words of Christ should be considered further in connection with the general character of the Gospel according to St. John ; for the character of that narrative is not historical, but spiritual, not descriptive of the outward forms of the Church, but of the inner life of the soul. It hardly ever touches upon the relation of believers to the external world or to society, but only upon their relations to God and Christ. They are withdrawn from the world that they may be one with the Father and with the Son ; they eat the bread of life ; they drink the water of life ; they receive another spirit which is to guide them into all truth. . . . Christ is not described in the Gospel of St. John as instituting the Sacrament of Baptism or the Lord's Supper, but as teaching men that He is the Bread of Life. . . . We desire to have the peaceful and harmonious growth of religion in the soul, which becomes a part of our being, and is not shaken by the accidents of public opinion or the discoveries of science, or the satire of society and the world ; which is the same in all ages,

and is inseparably bound up with goodness and truth everywhere."—B. JOWETT,
Serm., *Religion and System.*

See HIGHER AND LOWER, WORD OF
GOD.

SCYLLA AND CHARYBDIS :—

**Symbols indicative of expectation
for the fruits of action (Scylla),
and desire for the same (Charybdis),
which impede the growth of the
higher qualities of the soul until
they are surpassed by complete
surrender of the lower interests for
the sake of the Self, the supreme
Ideal and the principles of Wisdom,
Love, and Truth.**

See ROCKS (wandering).

SEA (LIMITED) :—

**A symbol of the astral plane of
the desires and passions.**

"And God said, Let the waters under
the heaven be gathered together unto
one place, and let the dry land appear :
and it was so. And God called the dry
land Earth; and the gathering together
of the waters called he Seas : and God
saw that it was good."—GEN. i. 9, 10.

And the Supreme now directs that
the waters "under the heaven," that
is, the astral matter, shall be centralised and co-ordinated, so that
preparation shall be made for physical
matter (dry land) to appear. And the
physical matter is named "Earth,"
which term also stands for the lower
nature of the soul,—the "natural
man"; and the "gathering together
of the waters" signifies the formation
of the astral "sea" of desires. And
all is pronounced "good," that is,
perfect in involution for purposes of
forthcoming manifestation through
evolution.

"Thou saidst 'Let the waters be
gathered together into one place, and let
the dry land appear' which 'thirsteth
after Thee.' For neither is the bitterness
of men's wills, but the gathering together
of waters called sea ; for Thou even
curbest the wicked desires of men's souls
and fixest their bounds, and thus dost
Thou make it a sea, by the order of thy
dominion over all things."—AUGUSTINE,
Confessions, p. 367.

"In the midst of the waters a heaven
is formed in the once benighted creature.
That unstable element, so quickly moved
by storms, is the well-known type of the
restless desires of the heart of fallen man ;
for 'the wicked are like the troubled
sea, which cannot rest, whose waters cast
up mire and dirt' (Is. lvii. 20)."—A.
JUKES, *Types of Genesis,* p. 15.

"The eye of man, O disciples, is the
sea ; things visible are the foam of this
sea. He who hath overcome the foaming
billows of visible things, of him, O disciples, it is said : that is a Brahman who
hath in his inner man outridden the sea
of the eye, with its waves and whirlpools,
with its depths profound and its pro-
digies ; he hath reached the shore ; he
stands on firm earth.' (The same follows
regarding the sea of hearing and the other
senses.) "Thus spake the Exalted One ;
when the Perfect One had thus spoken,
the Master went on to say :—
'If thou this sea with its abyss of
waters,
Full of waves, full of deeps, full of
monsters,
Hast crossed, wisdom and holiness are
thy portion ;
The land hast thou, the goal of the
universe hast thou reached:'
(*Samyutta Nikâya*)."—H. OLDENBERG,
Buddha, p. 260.

Perception on the lower mental
plane discloses the astral plane with
its passions and desires which have to
be controlled and outgrown ere the
ego can reach the higher planes of
consciousness (the further shore).
When this sea of desire and strife is
crossed, Wisdom and Love are gained.

"There are many who look with dis-
gust upon that man who flies into a rage
and shamefully beats his child, or horse ;
while within the soul of the spectator is
a sea surging back and forth in surly,
irritable moods, like the open and broad
expanse of the ocean, never tranquil and
still like an inland lake."—A. B. OLSTON,
Mind Power, p. 322.

"Typhon is called the sea. . . . Typhon
is that part of the soul that is subject to
the passions."—PLUTARCH, *Isis and Osiris,*
§§ 33 and 49.

Typhon or Set, the adversary, is
a symbol of the desire principle on
the astral plane—the "sea."

"The transformations of fire are, first
of all, sea ; and of the sea one half is
earth and the other half is lightning
flash."—HERAKLEITOS, V. 21.

"The priests hold the sea to proceed
from *fire,* and as distinct from all else ;
neither a part nor an element of nature,
but something of a different sort, both
destructive and the occasion of disease."
—PLUTARCH, *Isis and Osiris,* § 7.

There is a close relation between
the buddhic and astral planes. The
astral plane (sea) is a transformed or
inverted representation of the buddhic
plane (fire). The astral plane is
related on the one side to the physical
(earth), and on the other side to the
life (lightning). The astral plane contains the lower life principle—desire,—

which opposes the Divine will, and is the occasion of evil.

" It is clear that when these chapters (of magic) had been recited, Rā and his company set out and went over the whole sea, but as no more enemies were seen, they returned to Egypt travelling by night."—*Legend of the Winged Sun-disk.*

The Logos, having now so far accomplished His course in disciplining the soul by means of a set religious system (magic), is said to be Lord of the astral sea, and now is able to dwell at peace in the sublimated sense-nature, free of unruly desires. The reference to " travelling by night " is an allusion to the forgetting of all past experiences, which implies the expunging of all pain and sorrow, pleasure and sense-happiness,—the killing out of desire, which is compatible with the beginning of a new life conformable with the reign of the higher individuality.

" For what is denoted by the title of ' the sea,' but this world's bitterness raging in the destruction of the righteous ? Concerning which it is said by the Psalmist too, ' He gathereth the waters of the sea together as in a skin ' (Ps. xxxiii. 7). For the Lord ' gathereth the waters of the sea together as in a skin,' when disposing all things with a wonderful governance, He restrains the threats of the carnal pent up in their hearts. Thus ' the Lord treadeth upon the waves of the sea.' For when the storms of persecution lift up themselves, they are dashed in pieces in astonishment at His miracles."—GREGORY THE GREAT, *Morals on the Book of Job,* Vol. I. p. 501.

See ASTRAL PLANE, BOLTS, BUDDHIC PLANE, EARTH, FIRE, MAGIC, MAN (natural), NAVIGATION, OCEAN, RĀ, SET, SHIP ON SEA, SHORE (other), WALKING ON WATER, WATER (lower), WAVES.

SEA, UNVINTAGED OR BARREN :—

A symbol of the unfructified lower emotions ; or the astral desire-nature, which is illusion, i.e. without abiding reality.

SEAL, GREAT SACRED :—

A symbol of the Higher Self as the Archetypal Man, the Prototype of Humanity.

" Atzeel-ooth is the Great Sacred Seal, by means of which all the worlds are copied which have impressed on themselves the image on the Seal ; and as this Great Seal comprehends three stages, which are three prototypes of *Nephesh* (the vital spirit or soul), *Rua'h* (the ethical and reasoning spirit) and the *Neshamah* (the Highest Soul of man), so the Sealed have also received three prototypes, namely, B'ree-ah, Ye'tzeer-ah, and A'seey-ah, and these three prototypes are only One in the Seal."—I. MYER, *Qabbalah,* p. 321.

Atma-buddhi-manas, organised by the process of Involution, is the Archetypal Man, or Divine Image, from and by means of which all human souls (worlds) are produced as potential copies having impressed on their very nature the image of their Divine Progenitor. And as the Great Archetypal Soul comprehends in Itself three prototypal co-ordinated states of being, which are the astral body of desire (Nephesh), the mental body of thought and moral rule (Rua'h), and the causal-body as the vehicle of the Individuality—atma-buddhi—(Neshamah), so the emanated souls are also possessed of three potential states, namely, the mental-nature (B'ree-ah), the desire-nature (Ye-tzeer-ah), and the physical-nature (A'seey-ah) ; and these three natures constitute the Personality, which is the imperfect image below of the perfect Individuality above. The Personality when perfected becomes one with the Individuality on the higher planes.

" Philo, however vague and uncertain some of his thoughts may be, is quite distinct and definite when he speaks of the Logos as the Divine Thought which like a Seal is stamped upon matter and likewise on the mortal soul. Nothing in the whole world is to him more Godlike than man, who was formed according to the image of God, for, as the Logos is an image of God, human reason is the image of the Logos. But we must distinguish here, too, between man as part of the intelligible, and man as part of the visible world. The former is the Perfect Seal, the perfect idea or ideal of manhood, the latter its more or less imperfect multiplication in each individual man."—MAX MÜLLER, *Theosophy, etc.,* p. 409.

" As there was a previously existing idea of the particular mind, and also of the indivisible minds, to serve as an archetype and model for either ; and also a pre-existent idea of particular sensation, being, so to say, a sort of Seal which gave impressions of forms, so before particular things perceptible by the intellect had any existence, there was a pre-existent abstract idea."—PHILO, *Works,* Yonge, Vol. IV. p. 57.

" The bone and flesh which possess no writing are wretched, but, behold, the writing of Unas is under the Great Seal, and behold it is not under the little seal."
—BUDGE, *Egyptian Magic*, p. 124.

The personalities who are without the inner guidance of the Spirit are in wretched plight. But, observe, the perfected soul is under the guidance of the Higher Self, and not under that of the lower self.

" ' The seal shall be restored as clay, and shall stand as a garment ' (Job xxxviii. 14). For the Lord made man, whom He fashioned after His own likeness, as a kind of seal of His power. But yet it shall be restored as clay ; because . . . he is condemned by the death of the flesh, in punishment of the pride he has committed. For man, who has been formed from clay and adorned with the likeness of the Divine image, having received the gift of reason, forgets, when swelling with pride of heart, that he was formed of the basest materials. . . . And because he lost the likeness of God by sin, but returns by death to his own clay, it is rightly said, ' The seal shall be restored as clay.' For our clay to ' stand as a garment ' is for it to remain empty and stripped off, even till the time of the resurrection."   " And having been a ' seal,' it appeared as ' clay ' in the eyes of the Truth, when it lost, through the wickedness of impiety, the mysteries of the Word which it had received, and chose to savour only of the things of earth, which pollute."—ST. GREGORY, *Morals on the Book of Job*, Vol. III. pp. 316, 307.

" The true ground of certainty lies in this, that you have the Spirit in your heart, operating its own likeness, and moulding you, sealing you, after its own stamp and image."—A. MACLAREN, *Sermons, 1st Series*, p. 47.

See ARC. MAN, ASEEYATIC, ATZE-LOOTHIC, BOOK (God), BREEATIC, EVO-LUTION, IMAGE, INDIVIDUALITY, IN-VOLUTION, MACROCOSM, MICROCOSM, NEPHESH, NESHAMAH, PERSONALITY, PROTOTYPES, RUAH.

SEALED LETTER OF THE KING:—

A symbol of an impression in the mind, of the existence of a higher nature of goodness and truth, and the reality of its claim on the allegiance of the soul.

" And my letter was a letter which the King sealed with his right hand."—*Hymn of the Soul*, in the *Acts of Judas Thomas*.

And the inner message, which was an appeal to me through the higher side of my consciousness, came with power from the Higher Self above.

The " letter " represents a scheme of salvation and information of spiritual conditions, and within this message the Spirit of Love and Truth awakens in the mind as the most powerful attractive force in the universe, however feeble it may seem to be during times of obscuration.

(In the Greek Epitome of the *Acts of Thomas* by Niceta, Archbishop of Thessalonica, the " letter " is taken to be a symbol of the Holy Scriptures : *vide* Professor Bonnet.)

See GNOSIS, KING, LETTER, PEARL, RELIGION, ROBE, SALVATION, SCRIP-TURES, SERPENT (loud), WORDS OF POWER.

SEALING THE LIPS (LOWER ASPECT):—

Symbolic of staying the attempts of the personality at expressing itself, or working as from itself.

See LIPS, MOUTH (opening), PER-SONALITY.

SEASONING WITH SALT AND TRIAL BY FIRE :—

A symbol of imparting spiritual truth and spiritual energy, respectively.—*See* COL. iv. 6.

See FIRE, SALT.

SEASONS :—

A symbol of cycles of manifestation in which the soul evolves.

" Then Brahman says to him : Who art thou ? And he shall answer : I am a season, and a child of the seasons. Sprung from the womb of endless space, the seed of the wife, the light of the year, the Self of all that is ; what thou art, That am I."—*Kaush. Upanishad*.

Then asks the Supreme, " Art thou different from God ? " For through the causal-body it is that the soul realises its Divine nature and questions with the Supreme.   And the inner being of the soul shall answer, " I am but a phase of the universal life, and a child of the manifest cycles ; I have sprung from the matrix of infinite space, and am born as a spiritual germ in Matter which is now the purified lower nature, symbolised by the " Virgin-mother." I am a Spark of the Divine, evolved through the cycle of the twelve stages, by means of which growth is accomplished. I am the Self, therefore, of all that is or can be,—That which indeed Thou art, That am I."

"When love has carried us above all things, above the light, into the Divine Dark, there we are transformed by the Eternal Word, who is the image of the Father; and as the air is penetrated by the sun, thus we receive in peace the Incomprehensible Light, enfolding us and penetrating us. What is this Light, if it be not a contemplation of the Infinite and an intuition of Eternity ? *We behold that which we are*, and *we are that which we behold*, because our being, without losing anything of its own personality is united with the Divine Truth, which respects all diversity."—RUYSBROECK, *De Contem.*, p. 145.

"The overwhelming consensus of spiritual testimony and probability is that our true being has never had any beginning at all and will never have an end. It is eternal, the outbreathing of the spirit of God himself. That in us which is imperishable is of the divine essence, and is as certain to find its way back towards its source, as the rivers flow towards the sea."—R. J. CAMPBELL, Serm., *The Eternal Self.*

"Nature is a machine, compounded of wheels and moved by steady powers. Hence it goes in rounds or cycles, returning again and again into itself, producing thus seasons, months and years; repeating its dews, and showers, and storms, and varied temperatures; in the same circumstances or times, doing much the same things. But it is not so in the affairs of a mind, a society, or an age. There the motion is never in circles, but onward, eternally onward. Nothing is ever repeated. No mind or spirit can reproduce a yesterday. No age, the age or even year that is past. And where the outward conditions appear to be exactly the same, the inward states and spiritual connections may be so various as to take away all resemblance. . . . Hence, while the course of nature is a round of repetitions, the course of the supernatural repeats nothing, and for that reason takes an aspect of variety that appears even to exclude the fact of law. But it is only in appearance. God's perfect wisdom still requires the same things to be done in the same circumstances, and when not the same, as nearly the same as the circumstances are nearly resembled. Everything transpires in the uniformity of law."—H. BUSHNELL, *Nature and the Supernatural*, p. 185.

See ATMAN, BRAHMA, DEMIURGE FOUR SEASONS, GODHEAD, I AM, PRAGÂPATI.

SEASONS, SIX, DURING THE YEAR :—

Symbolic of six periods of creation during the cycle of involution.

"The six periods during which, according to Zoroastrian doctrine, the world was created. In the first period heaven was created, in the second the waters, in the third the earth, in the fourth the trees, in the fifth the animals, and in the sixth man."—See *Gen.* i., M. HAUG, *Essays on Religion of Parsis*, p. 192.

See ADAMAS (lower), ÆONS (twelve), DAYS, IABRAOTH, SIX.

SEASONS, FIVE :—

A symbol of the five planes of manifestation within the cycle of life.

"And that Pragâpati who became relaxed is the year; and those five bodily parts of his (i.e. hair, skin, flesh, bone, and marrow) which became relaxed, are the seasons; for there are five seasons, and five are those layers."— *Sata. Brâh.*, VI. 1, 2, 18.

The Archetypal Man, being perfected in the cycle of involution, thereafter suffered a reversed process and became segregated for the cycle of evolution. The five planes (physical, astral, mental, buddhic, and atmic), which had received their qualities and potencies in involution, were now to evolve the same in multiplicity of forms. The five planes are the five layers or regions of the universe and soul.

"And those five bodily parts of his, the seasons which became relaxed, are the regions; for five in number are the regions, and five those layers; when he builds up the five layers, he builds him up with the regions."—*Ibid.*, VI. 1, 2, 19.

The inner Self is built up as mastery over the lower planes is achieved. The lower conditions are the means by which the Self is manifested in the soul.

See ALTAR (fire), ARC. MAN, ASTRAL PLANE, ATMA, BONES, BUDDHIC PLANE DISMEMBERMENT, ELEMENTS (five), EVOLUTION, FIVE, INVOLUTION, MARROW, PRAGÂPATI (relaxed), SKIN, WORLDS (five), YEAR.

SEB, KRONUS :—

A symbol of Time in relation to manifestation.

"Shu was the first-born son of Râ by the goddess Hathor, the sky; he typified the light, and lifted up the sky (Nut) from the earth (Seb), and placed it upon the steps which were in Khemennu (Hermopolis)."—BUDGE, *Book of the Dead*, p. 93.

The Divine Will in manifestation (Shu) proceeded through the innermost Buddhi (Hathor) to produce the lower planes. The Divine Will emanated the consciousness (light) in actualising the relation between Space (Nut) and Time (Seb); and so commencing from the highest plane the processes of Involution and Evolution.

"The Greeks identified Seb with Kronos, probably only because as father of Osiris he might be considered as senior among the gods. Shu was supposed to be his father, and Nut his wife. His sacred animal was the goose, and sometimes he is supposed to be connected or even identical with the goose which laid the egg whence issued the world."—WIEDEMANN, *Rel. of Anc. Egyptians*, p. 231.

Through time is produced the germ of every new solar universe.

See BIRD (great), BIRTH OF OSIRIS, CRONUS, CURSE, EGG, HATHOR, INVOLUTION, KHORDAD, KRONOS, NUT, PILLARS OF SHU, RĀ, SATURN, SHU, STEPS, TIME, ZODIAC.

SEED :—

A symbol of the manifesting God, the source of all things.

"The Docetae conceived God as the first principle, under the figure of a seed, containing the infinitely great in the infinitely small. The world grew out of God as the fig-tree from the seed. As the fig-tree consists of stem, leaves, and fruit, so from the first principle there arose three Aeons, and from these thirty Aeons."—F. C. BAUR, *Church History*, Vol. I. p. 238.

The Tree of the Divine Life springs from God, its seed or root. It is—
"the fig-tree under which the gods sit in the third heaven."—*Atharva-Veda*, V. 4, 3.

"William Law says :—If Christ was to raise a new life like His own in every man, then every man must have had originally in the inmost spirit of his life a seed of Christ, or Christ as a seed of heaven, lying there in a state of insensibility out of which it could not arise but by the mediatorial power of Christ. For what could begin to deny self, if there were not something in man different from self ?"—W. R. INGE, *Christian Mysticism*, p. 282.

"Within the human soul itself is a portion, so to speak, of the eternal divine essence, the being of God himself. Every soul is like a seedling in which is wrapped up a mysterious potency of life which may take long to unfold but cannot be destroyed. As a giant oak is hidden away in every acorn, so is the life of God latent within the spirit of man waiting for unfoldment. It may be long before it finds it in any high degree, but it is there and nothing can expel it ; if it could be withdrawn from humanity there would be no humanity. And, just as the child in the womb passes through every stage of evolution through which the race itself has passed in its ascent to where it now stands, including some so gross that we do not like to think of them, so the soul may have to shed many unlovely exteriors before it becomes a fitting and beautiful vehicle of the spirit immortal and divine. That of God from which we came is Christ."—R. J. CAMPBELL, Serm., *The Christhood of Jesus, etc.*

See ÆON, ATMAN, BODHISATVA (great), CHIP, CONCEPTION, COSMOS, CRANBERRY, CREATION, EGG, FIG-TREE, FIRST-BORN SON, GODS, HARVEST, HIRANYAGARBHA, HUITZILOPOCHTLI, HUSBANDMAN, IMAGE, MONAD, OAK, PARGANYA, PLOUGHING, REAPING, SICKLE, SOWER, SPERMATIC WORDS.

SEED, GOOD :—

A symbol of the germs of the higher emotions arising from buddhi.

"The seed is the word of God. And those by the wayside are they that have heard : then cometh the devil, and taketh away the word from their heart that they may not believe and be saved."—LUKE viii. 12–15.

The "word of God" is the Divine expression, the "breathing of the Spirit" (buddhi), the higher emotional influx. Those "by the wayside" are those qualities which are not yet on the direct path to peace. They are therefore unable to receive the "good seed," which cannot germinate while the desire-nature (the devil) rules them. They cannot "believe," that is, unite or be in harmony with the higher nature, and therefore cannot be "saved" or transmuted.

"Seed from a celestial origin is of such a nature, that love ruleth the whole mind and maketh it one ; for the human mind consisteth of two parts,—will and understanding ; love or good belongeth to the will ; faith or truth belongeth to the understanding."—SWEDENBORG, *Arc. Cel.* to *Gen.*, iii. 24.

"Christ is the material out of which the thread of humanity has been spun ; his is the seed-life which dies in the darkness and sorrow of earth to rise in divine beauty and splendour in the garden of God."—R. J. CAMPBELL, Serm., *Revelation Manifold.*

Christ is the Archetypal Man, who dies in involution and becomes the human race in sorrow and suffering, from whence in evolution he rises in the souls of humanity through wisdom and love on the buddhic plane (Eden).

"The seeds of God-like power are in us still. Gods are we, bards, saints, heroes, if we will."—MATTHEW ARNOLD.

"The parents of the wonderful child are Setme Khamuas and his wife. Before the conception of their son, the mother is told in a dream to eat of the seeds of a certain plant ; and it is revealed to the father that the child shall be known as Si-Osiri (son of Osiris)."—GRIFFITH, *Stories of the High Priests*.

The "parents" are symbols of Spirit and Matter. Before the conception of their Divine Son, the Mother is told to "eat of the seeds of a certain plant" ; which means that before the Soul is embodied in matter, the Mother partakes of the seeds of the Tree of the Divine Life, that is, matter is prepared and energised by the Spirit which is to confer immortality upon the Soul. The Spirit, then, forms within the purified receptive matter of the lower planes, at a certain stage of development, the indwelling Saviour or Son of God.

"Job xxxviii. 30 means that the Lord first waters in a wondrous manner the soil of our hearts for the reception of the seeds of the word, by the secret rain of His grace, and that He afterwards keeps it down by the discipline of His secret dispensation lest it should bring forth too luxuriantly with the virtues it has conceived, in order that the rigour of discipline may likewise bind that which the rain of grace irrigates."—ST. GREGORY, *Morals on the Book of Job*, Vol. III. p. 347.

"In man's deepest nature lies hidden the seed of infinite possibilities, and the spirit of God must find access to that seed in order to germinate it into actual life. He may not do this by bringing any influences to bear upon them from *without*. His Spirit must brood *within* over the seed if it is ever to come to life. . . . He stands at the door and knocks because He must be intelligently and willingly admitted, otherwise He cannot brood over the hidden seeds of eternity within."—J. MACKENZIE, *New Reformer*, Aug. 1913.

See AGRICULTURE, ARC. MAN, BIRTH OF JESUS, BREATH (divine), CRANBERRY, CREATURES (small), CULTIVATION, DEVIL, EDEN, EGYPT (lower), EVOLUTION, FOOD (man), FRUIT-TREE, GERMS, GODS, HARVEST, HUSBANDMAN, INVOLUTION, IRRIGATION, KHAMUAS, MAZENDARANS, MOTHER (divine), OSIRIS, PARABLE, PLOUGHING, QUALITIES, REAPING, SICKLE, SI-OSIRI, SOWER, SOWING, TEM, TREE OF LIFE, VIRGIN MARY, WHEAT, WORD (divine).

SEEDS OF FOODS AND PLANTS :—

Symbols of germs of thoughts, ideals, and desires.

"Thither bring the seeds of all plants which are the tallest and most odoriferous on this earth. Thither bring the seeds of all foods which are the most eatable and most odoriferous on this earth. Make pairs of them unceasingly, in order that these men may exist in the enclosures."—*Vendidad*, II.

The "seeds of plants" are symbolical of the germs of desires which are to give rise to the higher emotions. The "seeds of foods" are the germs of ideas and ideals which are to fructify in goodness and truth and become nourishment for the soul. The "pairs" are the *pairs of opposites* without which no existence upon the planes of the lower quaternary would be possible.

"At first the germs of thought remained asleep ; but as the elements fitted to make them grow were added to the soil of the world, they grew up, one after another, trees of knowledge and of life, of whose fruits men took, and eating, knew more of God, of their own being, and of their duties to their fellow-men. Many of these seeds are still asleep, and the future extension of revelation consists in their coming to the light as the conditions under which they can spring up are fulfilled in the progress of mankind. 'I have yet many things to say to you,' said Christ, ' but ye cannot bear them now.' . . . It seems reasonable, then, to say that revelation is not yet completed, but being completed, that we look for higher knowledge of God, for larger moral views of His relation to us and of ours to Him, as time goes on and mankind grows. God has not said His last word to us, nor Christ given His last counsel of perfection, nor has the Spirit yet shown to us the whole of truth."—STOPFORD A. BROOKE, Serm., *The Changed Aspect of Theology*.

"Everywhere the lower furnishes opportunities for the higher, and is a failure unless the higher blooms out of the ground which the lower has made ready."—PHILLIPS BROOKS, *Mystery of Iniquity*, p. 254.

See CHILDREN OF MEN AND WOMEN, EARTH, FOOD FOR GODS, FOOD FOR

MAN, FRUIT-TREE, GERMS, HERB (seed), MAN, ODOUR, OPPOSITES, PLANTS, QUATERNARY, SETTLEMENTS, TREES (tall), VARA.

SEEDS OF MEN, WOMEN AND CATTLE :—

Symbols of the archetypal forms of the vehicles of mind, emotion, and higher desires.

"Thither bring the seeds of all men, women, and cattle, which are the greatest and best and finest on this earth."—*Vendidad*, II.

The "seeds," which are the ideal type-forms brought over from the previous cycle of manifestation,—the Lunar,—are now introduced on the terrene globe. These type-forms are on the mental, astral, and physical planes.

See BEASTS (sorts), CATTLE, DWELL-INGS, KARSHVARES, LUNAR CHAIN, PLANETARY CHAIN, REGIONS, SHIP OF MANU.

SEEDS OF THE SIX CREATURES :—

Symbols of centres of conscious-ness in vehicles of the soul.

"Ahura-Mazda directed that a vara (enclosure) should be made foursquare ; into which the seeds of the six creatures should be brought."—*Venidad*, II.

The Supreme directs that the quaternary should be prepared, in order that the six centres of the manifestation of the Divine life may be introduced. Two buddhic, two mental, and two astral.

See CONSCIOUSNESS, LIVING THINGS, QUATERNARY, SETTLEMENTS, SIX, VARA, VITAL AIRS.

SEEING (HIGHER ASPECT) :—

A symbol of perception of light and truth.

See CLOUDS OF HEAVEN, EYE, SIGHT.

SEEING (LOWER ASPECT) :—

A symbol of attraction towards objects of sense.

See AELOPUS, MAN (blind) OCYPETE.

SEKER OR SOKARIS :—

A symbol of the primitive motive-power of evolution, which is the desire-principle active on the astral-plane, and the life (astro-mental) of the physical organisms.

"The form (of Seker) in which this god (Rā) is depicted is that of a hawk-headed man, who stands between a pair of wings that project from the back of a huge serpent having two heads and necks, and a tail terminating in a bearded human head."—BUDGE, *Egypt. Heaven and Hell*, Vol. III. p. 135.

This description symbolises the Higher Self (Rā) manifesting in the aspiration (wings) proceeding from desire (serpent) through mind and emotion (two heads) in physical hu-manity (head extremity). Rā's lower realm, "the kingdom of Seker," is the astral plane where he lives ob-scured in thick darkness under the guise of desire (Seker).

"The kingdom of Seker was shrouded in thick darkness, and instead of con-sisting of fertile plains and fields, inter-sected by streams of running water, was formed of bare, barren, sandy deserts, wherein lived monster serpents of terri-fying aspect, some having two, and some three heads, and some having wings. This region offered so many difficulties to the passage of the Boat of Afu-Rā that special means had to be found for overcoming them, and for enabling the god and his followers to proceed north-wards to the House of Osiris."—*Ibid.*, p. 131.

This region being in the fourth division of the Tuat signifies the involution of the qualities of kama-manas. The soul-state is barren of all higher qualities and filled with desires (serpents) and passions. Hence the obscurity of the indwelling Self (Afu-Rā) and the apparent difficulties of progress wherein the Spirit cannot express itself. Progress in the involu-tionary cycle is "northwards" to cul-minate in the lowest condition (house) in which is encased the perfected Soul—the Archetypal Man (Osiris).

See AFU-RĀ, ARC. MAN, ASTRAL PLANE, BOAT ON RIVER, DARKNESS, DEATH OF OSIRIS, DESERT, HAWK, HEAD, INVOLUTION, KAMA, MAN, NORTH, PLANTS, SERPENT, TANEMA-HUTA, TUAT, WINGS.

SEKHET-AARU, OR FIELD OF REEDS :—

A symbol of the lower nature, or astro-mental life, by means of which the individuality first manifests.

"Grant me power to float down and to sail up the stream in Sekhet-Aaru, and may I reach Sekhet-hetep ! I am the double Lion-god."—BUDGE, *Book of the Dead*, Ch. LXXII.

The Soul relies upon the Supreme in passing downwards into the lower life, and by means of the astral life thereafter ascending to the buddhi-mental region, or Nirvana. In this undertaking the soul becomes involved in matter, and afterwards evolved.

"The new man was conducted into the Fields of Aalu (or Aaru), into the kingdom of the blessed followers of Osiris, which was a country modelled altogether on earthly lines, but especially resembling the Delta : a Nile ran through it divided into many branches and forming many islands. Here the dead ate and drank, went hunting, fought with their foes, . . . made offerings to the gods. But the chief occupation was agriculture, which differed from that of earth only in that the harvest never failed."—WIEDEMANN, *Rel. of Anc. Egyptians*, p. 254.

The ego incarnates in a personality (new man) which descends into the arena of life to gather experience, overcome evil, sacrifice lower for higher qualities (gods), cultivate the faculties, and lay up treasure in heaven which never fails.

See AGRICULTURE, BIRTH OF HORUS, DEAD, EARTH, GARDEN OF REEDS, HARVEST, LION-GOD, MARSH, NET (fish), OFFERING, PEACHES, REAPING, REED-PLAIN, STRIDES OF SOUL, UNION (reeds), WHEAT AND BARLEY.

SEKHET-HETEP, OR FIELD OF PEACE :—

A symbol of Nirvana, Devachan, or a buddhi-manasic state of consciousness.

"Meat-offerings and entrance into the presence of the god Osiris shall be granted to him (the soul victorious and righteous) together with a homestead for ever in Sekhet-hetepu, as unto the followers of Horus" (*Papyrus of Ani*).—BUDGE, *Book of the Dead*, p. 26.

The liberated soul, victorious over the lower nature, shall partake of the "fruits of the Spirit" and become united to the Higher Self (Osiris). He shall possess a "mansion" or state of consciousness in Devachan, as is bestowed upon all the saints of Christ (Horus), who rise with him in the resurrection of the perfected.

See BUDDHIC PLANE, CULTIVATION, DEVACHAN, FRUIT, GARDEN OF REST,

HEAVEN, HORUS, KINGDOM, LAND, MANSIONS, MEAT, NET, NIRVANA, NUT-URT, OSIRIS, REAPING, RESURRECTION, SAINTS, SOWER, TCHEFET.

SELENE OR LUNA :—

A symbol of the emotion-nature which originates on the buddhic plane and descends to the astral, from which it again arises.

"By Endymion, whom she loved, and whom she sent to sleep in order to kiss him, she became the mother of fifty daughters."—*Smith's Class. Dict.*

The indwelling Self in the higher mind, who is obscured by the play of the lower emotions is, nevertheless, a means of raising the emotion-nature, and producing through it many emotions of a higher order.

"I shall be satisfied, when I awake, with thy likeness."—Ps. xvii. 15.

"Awake from what ? From illusion to reality. It is the spiritual consciousness that is in question, the awakening of the soul. . . . Give your whole life to Christ and you will soon begin to find something wonderful taking place in your soul. It will be as though your whole nature were being remade, as indeed it is ; a diviner self will begin to emerge in your consciousness than you have ever known ; you will cease to be conformed to this world."—R. J. CAMPBELL, Serm., *Eternal Satisfaction*.

See ANDROMEDA, CUPID, MOON (solar), PANDORA, PERSEPHONE, SOMA AS MOON.

SELF, SUPREME ; AND LIVING, OR INDIVIDUAL SELF :—

Symbols of the Logos or God Manifest, and the indwelling Spirit or incarnate God within the human soul. The Two are One.

"This Self is the Lord of all, this the internal ruler, this the source of all things ; this is that out of which all things proceed, and into which they shall pass back again."—*Māndūkya Upanishad*.

"There are two, one knowing (isvara), the other not-knowing (giva), both unborn, one strong, the other weak ; there is she, the unborn, through whom each man receives the recompense of his works ; and there is the Infinite Self under all forms, but himself inactive. When a man finds out these three, that is Brahma."—*Svetas. Upanishad*, I. 8, 9.

There are two modes of the Divine Life, one, the Higher Self, wise and all-perceiving ; the other, the lower Self, ignorant and acquiring knowledge ; both unmanifest exteriorly, one powerful in the Divine scheme, the other oppressed by the lower conditions. There is Wisdom, the buddhic principle, unmanifest outwardly, through whose functionings each ego receives the transmutations of his qualities according to his efforts after goodness, love, and truth. And there is the Absolute Being subsisting under all appearances, but Itself unconditioned and latent. When the ego attains all Truth, and identifies himself with the three modes of the Divine Life, he is pure Spirit,—that is God.

" He who seeth the Supreme Being existing alike imperishable in all perishable things, sees indeed. Perceiving the same Lord present in everything and everywhere, he does not by the lower self destroy his own soul, but goeth to the supreme end. He who seeth that all his actions are performed by nature only, and that the self within is not the actor, sees indeed. And when he realises perfectly that all things whatsoever in nature are comprehended in the One, he attains to the Supreme Spirit."— *Bhagavad-Gita*, XIII. 27–30.

" Juliana's view of human personality is remarkable, as it reminds us of the Neo-platonic doctrine that there is a higher and a lower self, of which the former is untainted by the sins of the latter. ' I saw and understood full surely,' she says, ' that in every soul that shall be saved there is a godly will that never assented to sin, nor ever shall ; which will is so good that it may never work evil, but evermore continually it willeth good, and worketh good in the sight of God. We all have this blessed will whole and safe in our Lord Jesus Christ.' This ' godly will ' or ' substance ' corresponds to the *spark* of the German mystics. ' I saw no difference,' she says, ' between God and our substance, but, as it were, all God.' "—W. R. INGE, *Christian Mysticism*, p. 206.

" Behind all this play of mental causation there all the while stood that Self, which was at once the condition of its occurrence, and the *First Cause* of its action. . . . As a matter of fact we know that this Self is here, and that it can thus be proved to be a substance *standing under* the whole of that more superficial display of mental causation which it is able to look upon introspectively—and this almost as *impersonally* as if it were regarding the display as narrated by another mind."—ROMANES, *Mind and Motion*, p. 137.

" The deeper soul within you is one with the Soul of the universe, and will not be denied its heritage. You may trifle with it, or try to avoid arduous tasks and painful experiences, but you must go on until your goal is attained, because you are being driven thereto by the divine force of your own soul."— R. J. CAMPBELL, Serm., *Who Compels ?*

" This larger self (of a man) is in all probability a perfect and eternal spiritual being integral to the being of God. His surface self, his Philistine self, is the incarnation of some portion of that true eternal self which is one with God. The dividing-line between the surface self and the other self is not the definite demarcation it appears to be. To the higher self it does not exist. To us it must seem that to all intents and purposes the two selves in a man are two separate beings ; but that is not so : they are one, although the lower, owing to its limitations, cannot realise the fact. If my readers want to know whether I think that the higher self is conscious of the lower, I can only answer, ' Yes, I do, but I cannot prove it ; probabilities point that way.' . . . The true being is consciousness ; the universe visible and invisible is consciousness. The higher self of the individual man enfolds more of the consciousness of God than the lower, but lower and higher are the same being. This may be a difficult thought to grasp, but the time is rapidly approaching when it will be more generally accepted than it is now."—R. J. CAMPBELL, *The New Theology*, p. 32.

See ABSOLUTE, ARC. MAN, ATMAN, BIRDS (two), BRAHMA, BUDDHI, CHRIST, CONSCIOUSNESS, EMPEROR, FIG-FRUIT, FIRST-BORN SON, GOD, GODHEAD, HEROIC RUNNER, HIGHER AND LOWER SELVES, HIRANYAGARBHA, INCARNATION, ISVARA, JESUS (Son of God), JOB, MAUI, MESSIAH, MONAD, PTAH, SEASONS, SON OF GOD, SONS OF GOD, TRINITY, WISDOM.

SELF, LOWER :—

This symbol can be taken in two senses,—higher and lower. In the higher sense it signifies the Higher Self incarnate in the human soul and striving to gain the mastery of the lower nature and attain full expression of Itself. In the lower sense, the symbol stands for the illusory and fleeting lower personality, —the sense of separate consciousness and will in the lower mind.

." The wise man should raise the self by the Self ; let him not suffer the Self to be lowered ; for Self is the friend of self, and in like manner, self is its own enemy. The Self is the friend of him in whom the self by the Self is vanquished ; but to the unsubdued self the Self verily becometh hostile as an enemy."—*Bhagavad-Gita*, VI. 5 6.

The wise ego should raise the personality by the Higher Self. Let him not suffer the Divine nature to be obscured; for the Higher Self is the upholder of the personality, which of itself gravitates downward to desire and sense. The Higher Self is in harmony and union with the raised consciousness (self) of the ego in whom the illusive, separated self is by the Higher Self dissipated. But to the averted and undisciplined lower personality, the Higher Self has the illusive aspect of anger and hostility.

"But the very nature of religious development is such that it begets an increasing consciousness of schism and disharmony within, and of separation from the spiritual Being believed in and worshipped as God. On the one hand, then, man constructs the Object of his religious faith and adoration in a manner to correspond with his higher and nobler Ideals,—he idealises the Divine Being; and on the other hand, he feels more intensely those deficiencies and needs which he looks to religion to supply and to fulfil. Thus he endeavours to bring self-harmony into his life by discovering and following the way to conform his own self-hood to his growing ideal of the Absolute Self."—G. T. LADD, *Phil. of Religion*, p. 253.

"Below this outer self of yours, which is satisfied with family and business, there is another self which you know nothing of but which God sees, which He values as your truest and deepest self, which to His sight is a real person pleading so piteously for help that He has not been able to resist its pleading, but has sent His ministers, has sent His Bible,—nay, has come Himself to satisfy it with that spiritual aid it cannot do without."—P. BROOKS, Serm., *Man of Macedonia*.

"'I (God) am working in you, growing in you. Your lower self, your outward man is making you uncomfortable, because my Spirit is lusting against the flesh. But your outward man is perishing, it is doomed.' Thank God, our outward man is doomed!—because his Spirit is ultimately omnipotent. He says. 'Thou art my temple, I love thee; I am cleansing it because I love thee with an everlasting love. I more often wake the sleeping soul with a scourge than I do with a kiss, but both are love.' The almighty Lord of the universe is perfect love."—B. WILBERFORCE, Serm., *Message of Advent*.

See ANGER, ATHWYA, ATMAN, INCARNATION, JEALOUS, LAZARUS, MESSIAH, PERSONALITY, SCOURGE, SLEEP (waking), SON OF GOD, SOUL (highest), SPIRIT.

SENSE ORGANS, OR FIVE ORGANS OF KNOWLEDGE :—

Symbolic of the soul's five means of perception on the lower planes.

"To the brain as the central organ, and its two dependents the sensible and the motor nerves, corresponds the relation of manas (mind and conscious will) to the five *jnâna-indriyas*, or organs of knowledge (these are, following the order of the five elements to which they correspond,—hearing, touch, sight, taste, and smell), and the five *karma-indriyas*, or organs of action (speech, hands, feet, and the organs of generation and excretion)."—DEUSSEN, *Phil. of Upanishads*, p. 263.

This central manas is a symbol of the causal-body, the centre of the soul's perceptive and active functionings. In their proper order the sense organs given as eye, ear, skin, tongue and nose; or as sight, hearing, touch, taste, and smell, are symbols of *consciousness* (sight), *intuition* (hearing), *mind* (touch), *desire* (taste), and *sensation* (smell). These correspond with the five elements (planes), light, fire, air, water, earth, i.e. the planes atma, buddhi, manas, astral, and physical, as will be seen.

The organs of action which produce karma are *mental action* (speech), *mental discipline* (hands), *progress* (feet), *production of higher qualities* (generation), and *riddance of lower qualities* (excretion).

"The jnâna-indryas convey the impressions of the senses to the manas, which manufactures them into ideas (*sankalpa*). These ideas are then formed into resolves (*sankalpa*) by the manas in its function as 'conscious will,' and are carried into execution by the five karma-indriyas."—*Ibid.*

The five organs of perception and knowledge convey as ideas the experience of the ego during an incarnation, to the causal-body (manas); then these ideas are sifted and readjusted to become motives to action of a progressive order in the next incarnation of the ego.

"The soul lastly is further attended by the ethical substratum (*karma-âsraya*), which determines the character of the new body and life. This ethical substratum is formed by the actions committed in the course of each several life, and is therefore different for each soul and for each life course."—*Ibid.*, p. 265.

See CHARIOT, ELEMENTS, EXPERIENCE, LINGAM, MANAS, PRANAS,

SKANDHAS, REINCARNATION, VITAL AIRS.

SEPARATION FROM THE WHOLE, OR SEPARATENESS :—

A symbol of the fall of Spirit, or the ego, into Matter, whereby is produced the lower consciousness, which has the illusory sense of separateness.

"And men were constituted, and the other animals, as many as have life. And the men have inhabited cities and works constructed as among us, and they have Sun and Moon and other things as among us; and the earth brings forth for them many things of all sorts, of which they carry the most serviceable into the house and use them. These things then I have said concerning the separation, that not only among us would the separation take place, but elsewhere too."—*Anaxagoras*, FAIRBANKS, 10.

And the mind (men), with the sub-human qualities, the instincts, passions, and desires (animals), came into being. And the mind operates through its centres of activity on the mental plane, and through the organised vehicles ; and the mind derives knowledge from the Higher Self (sun) and the lower self (moon), and from the mental faculties, the senses, etc. For the lower nature (earth) yields experiences of many kinds, of which those that are capable of transmutation are by this means conveyed to the causal-body (house) for its nourishment and growth. All this archetypal development is preparation for the Separation or Fall, when Spirit and Matter become apart and distinct in operation and function. This "fall" extends not only from above to below, but as "separateness" it is universal in nature.

"What, then, is the thing against which we have to strive in our efforts to achieve the good ? It is just the one general tendency to separateness, to particularism, which is a feature of material existence. The downward tendency in morals is always towards particularism, just as the upward tendency is towards wholeness."—R. J. CAMPBELL, *Serm., The Sense of Sin.*

See ANIMALS, ARROGANT, ATTACHMENT, BONDAGE, CITY, EARTH, FALL, FATE, HOUSE, I AM, KAMA, LOTOS, MAN, MOON, SERPENT (water), SHEEP (lost), SPIRIT, SUFFERING, SUN.

SEPARATION OF HEAVEN AND EARTH :—

A symbol of the origination of Spirit-matter, which succeeds unity of substance in the unmanifest Source. The Monad divides and becomes the Duad—Spirit and Matter,—between the polarities of which all manifestation proceeds.

"Heaven and earth were anciently of one form : from these, as soon as they were separated from each other, all things were produced and brought to light,—trees, birds and beasts, and the race of mortal men."—EURIPIDES, *Menalippe apud Diod. Sic.* I. i, e, 7.

"The myth of Dyaus, the sky, and Prithivi, the earth, once joined and now separated, is the basis of a great chapter in Mythology, such as the mutilation of Uranus by Cronus, and other tales of a distinctly savage type."—W. CROOKE, *Pop. Rel. of N. India*, Vol. I. p. 26.

"Dyaus the Heavens, and Prithivi the Earth, were once joined, and subsequently separated from one another."—MUIR, *Sanscrit Texts*, V. 23.

"The story is told here (in Nanumanga island) also of the union of the heavens and the earth, and of their separation, and the elevation of the former by the sea serpent."—G. TURNER, *Samoa*, p. 288.

"Rangi and Papa, or Heaven and Earth, were the source from which, in the beginning, all things originated. Darkness then rested upon the heaven and upon the earth, and they still both clave together, for they had not yet been rent apart" (New Zealand Myth).—G. GREY, *Polynesian Mythology.*

"The order of creation, according to Hawaiian folk-lore, was that after heaven and earth had been separated, and the ocean had been stocked with its animals, the stars were created, then the moon, then the sun. In this order the Marquesan legend agrees with the Hawaiian, and both agree exactly with the Babylonian legend of the cuneiform inscriptions."—A. FORNANDER, *Polynesian Race*, Vol. I. p. 76.

The stocking of the astral plane (sea) with the desires (animals), is followed by the awakening of mind (stars), the personality (moon), and then the incarnate Self (sun). This is the true order of appearance in the growth of the soul regarded from below in the cycle of evolution. In the period of involution there is a reverse order as in *Genesis*. First the Self or higher Individuality (sun) in germ within the world-soul ; then the germ of personality (moon) on the astral plane, and lastly the mental faculties (stars) on the plane of mind.

" Of old, Heaven and Earth were not yet separated, and the In and Yo (Chinese Yin and Yang) not yet divided."—W. G. ASTON, *Shinto*, p. 84.

" For air and aether are separated from the surrounding mass ; and the surrounding mass is infinite in quantity."—*Anaxagoras*, FAIRBANKS, 2.

For Spirit and Matter are external emanations from the Absolute ; duality proceeds from Unity—the Ultimate Reality.

" But before these were separated, when all things were together, not even was any colour clear and distinct, for the mixture of all things prevented it."—*Ibid.*, 4.

But ere the forthgoing of the Divine Life took place, when no appearance was made manifest, no sign was shown of māyā : for all as yet was in the Absolute, and relativity was not apparent.

See ABSOLUTE, AIR AND AETHER, COSMOS, CREATION, CRONUS, DARKNESS, HEAVEN AND EARTH, INVOLUTION, KAMA, KHIEN, MĀYĀ (lower), MIXTURE, MONAD, PILLARS OF SHU, PLANTS, RANGI, RAVENA, RONGO, RU, SALT, SEX, SPIRIT, SUN, SUN (moon), TANEMAHUTA, URANUS YANG.

SEPHIROTH OR NUMERATIONS :—

These ten conditions of being constitute with their relations a scheme of life in the invisible and visible spheres, and they indicate the means of the soul's progress to perfection.

" According to the Zohar, the *Sephiroth* are comparable to chariots for the degrees of the Divine Essence, and the word degrees, which is used very frequently in the text, illustrates after a simple manner the idea of gradations in the nature of the Presence as the spheres of manifestation proceed further from the centre. The supernal world contains the highest degrees of which the human mind can conceive by the intellection of faith, and *Kether, Chokmah, Binah* form a unity therein."—A. E. WAITE, *Secret Doctrine in Israel*, p. 33.

The three highest states are the supreme Self (Kether), the involved Self (Chokmah), and the principle of matter (Binah), in which Spirit is involved.

" The Sephiroth are conventionally described thus :

(1) *Kether*   = the Crown.
(2) *Chokmah* = Wisdom.
(3) *Binah*   = Understanding.

(4) *Chesed*   = Mercy.
(5) *Geburah*   = Severity or Judgment.
(6) *Tiphereth* = Beauty.
(7) *Netzach*   = Victory.
(8) *Hod*   = Glory.
(9) *Yesod*   = Foundation.
(10) *Malkuth*   = The Kingdom."

" To the first world of *Atziluth* are referred *Kether, Chokmah* and *Binah* : to the second world of *Briah* are allocated *Chesed, Geburah* and *Tiphereth*."—*Ibid.*, pp. 31, 33.

The first three Sephiroth are on the highest planes, the next three are on the mental plane. *Chesed* (merit) signifies the individuality ; *Geburah* (demerit) the personality, and *Tiphereth* the perfected causal-body and ego. *Netzach* and *Hod* signify respectively the soul's triumph over the lower nature, and the treasure laid up in heaven. *Yesod* is a symbol of the physical body through which experience is gained and progress made possible. *Malkuth* is the buddhic principle which brings about the transmutation of the lower into the higher.

See ATZEELOOTH, BINAH, BREEATIC WORLD, EVOLUTION, HESED, HOKHMAH, INCARNATION, INDIVIDUALITY, INVOLUTION, KETHER, MALKUTH, PAHAD, SHEKINAH, TIPHERETH.

SEPULCHRES, OR TOMBS :—

Symbolic of modes of functioning on the lower planes from an astromental centre. They represent empty forms of faith ; sectarian presentations under which truth is buried ; formal creeds devoid of spiritual life,—desire-mental in character.

" Moreover, we often cling to the outworn shell (or tomb) of a spiritual truth, and hope vainly for its re-vindication before the gaze of the world, when the truth itself has risen to a higher plane of expression and power over the human heart."—R. J. CAMPBELL, Serm., *The Resurrection Life*.

" The true plane of religious belief lies, not where hitherto the Church has placed it,—in the sepulchre of historical tradition, but in man's own mind and heart ; it is not, that is to say, the objective and physical, but the subjective and spiritual ; and its appeal is not to the senses but to the soul."—*The Perfect Way*, Preface.

See DEATH OF OSIRIS, LAZARUS, RE-STAU, ROCK SEPULCHRE, SPICES, SUNDAY, THROAT, TOMB.

SERAPHIM :—

A symbol of higher laws by which the buddhic plane is secluded, and the lower consciousness is cut off from the higher.

See CHERUBIM.

SERAPIS :—

A symbol of the Second Logos, or Higher Self.

" Philarchus says that Serapis, in the proper meaning of the word, signifies,— Him who disposed the universe into its present beautiful order."—PLUTARCH, *Isis and Osiris*, § 29.

" Serapis " signifies outgoing activity and the formative aspect of the Divine nature.

" It is evident that the nature of Serapis and the Sun is one and indivisible." " Talismanic gems very commonly bear the full length figure or the bust of Serapis, with the legend,—' There is but one God, and he is Serapis,' or ' The One Living God.' "—C. W. KING, *The Gnostics, etc.*, pp. 160, 172.

The sun is a symbol of the Higher Self, the one Living God (Serapis).

See APIS, BULL (primeval), OSIRIS, SUN.

SERMON ON THE MOUNT :—

A symbolic statement of aspiration and attainment. A beatific vision of seemingly Utopian ideals in which the true relationship of the Soul to the Infinite is perceived by the intuition. In that blissful state of soul, the incarnate Self not only regards this relationship as something abstract, but rather sees the application of the vision to the needs and requirements of humanity. The blessings and exhortations of the Christ are extended to all those who do the will of the " Father which is in heaven,"—and that steadfast approximating of the soul to its Prototype indeed suffices to bring its own rich reward. Passing by the crude interpretation usually put upon parts of the vision, it needs to be viewed through the intuitions, which will show, not only that it indicates the purest and most practical economic system of society, but that its symbology is also applicable to higher departments of nature than those with which the critic and the student are generally familiar.

" We may ask why it was that Christ expressed Himself in so mystical a manner. It was partly because He spoke not only for the period in which He lived, but for all periods of the history of the world. He gave to men seeds of thought which were to be developed in proportion as the world developed. But the plain reason for the mystery of Christ's sayings is this, that all the highest truths are by their nature mystical, above and beyond the power of the intellect *acting by itself*. The super-intellectual lies beneath our science, our theology, our philosophy, even our art. Many of the conclusions of science as well as those of theology and philosophy are deduced from intuitions, which we cannot demonstrate. . . . The man who lives much with Christ, that is, with divine humanity, feels the principles which rule the spiritual life of man. These principles were felt and stated by Christ."—STOPFORD A. BROOKE, *Serm., Individuality*.

" You know how possible it is to see a thing instantly and not know quite why you see it ; it often takes reason a good while to catch up with intuition." —R. J. CAMPBELL, Serm., *Sources, etc.*

See BLESSING OF GOD, BLISS, INTUITION, KINGDOM OF HEAVEN, MAN (rich), POOR IN SPIRIT, POVERTY.

SERPENT :—

A symbol of the inner forces of the relative existence, which appear and again disappear, by which the growth of the soul is accomplished. These forces are dual, and of the higher and lower natures. They act reciprocally although in opposition. The higher serpent is atma-buddhic, the lower serpent kama-manasic. The first is of the Wisdom-nature and the second of the Desire-nature, and each is active through the mind.

" Heaven was not, earth was not, the good and evil serpents did not exist " (*Rhind Papyrus*).—SAYCE, *Gifford Lectures*, p. 239.

This signifies the state of being prior to manifestation, when Spirit (heaven) and Matter (earth) were latent in the Divine Monad. There was no relativity, and the higher and lower forces of the World-soul were not present.

" Homage be to the serpents, which ever are on earth, and they that are in the air, and they that are in the sky, to those serpents be homage ! Whatever serpents there are in these three worlds, to them the Sacrificer thereby does homage."— *Sata. Brâh.* VII. 4, 1, 28.

Here the " serpents " are designated as of three orders, kamic (earth), manasic (air) and buddhic (sky). As these forces on the three planes (worlds) exist for the express purpose of soul-development, the ego (sacrificer) acclaims the wisdom and love of the Supreme.

"In ancient mythology the serpent is sometimes used as an emblem of the intelligence of God, and at other times of the subtlety of the evil one" (Serpent-worship).—GARDNER, *Faiths of the World*.

"The serpent has had a good meaning given to it, and a very bad one. It has been an emblem of *wisdom*, and *par excellence*, the symbol of sin. With a pair of wings it became the *Seraph*. Curled up in a circle it has stood for *time without end*."—BARLOW, *Essays on Symbolism*, p. 37.

See AIDONEUS, BOAT (serpent), CADU-CEUS, DRAGON, NAASENE, OPHIONEUS, SCORPION, SEKER, VITAL AIRS, VRITRA, WISDOM.

SERPENT ANANTA, OR SESHA :—

A symbol of the Cycle of Life, which is inclusive of the higher and lower forces (serpents) of existence.

"Narayana, with whom Vishnu is identified, the oldest of all beings, who, carried on the coils of Sesha or Ananta, the serpent 'without end,' the symbol of eternity, appeared at the beginning of things floating above the primordial waters."—BARTH, *Religions of India*, p. 169.

The Spirit of Truth, from whom arises the Higher Self (Vishnu), calls into being in time and space the cycle of Life (Sesha) at the commencement of a solar universe. Then the Spirit of Truth broods over the expanse of the Divine Reality.

"Moreover, the Naasenes say that the Serpent is the Moist Essence—just as did Thales the Milesian."—HIPPOLYTUS, *Philosophumena*.

Here the cycle of Life is identified with the primordial reality—Truth (celestial water).

See BALARAMA, CIRCLE OF EXIST-ENCE, KHWAN, LEVIATHAN, MOIST ESSENCE, NĀRĀYANA, VISHNU, WATER.

SERPENT APEP :—

See APEP.

SERPENT ÆSCULAPIUS :—

A symbol of the Higher Self, who is the Divine healer by means of the forces of the buddhic plane,—those spiritual forces which harmonise the qualities and "raise the dead to life," that is, transmute the lower into the higher.

"The god Æsculapius frequently appeared in the form of a serpent. . . . Serpents were everywhere connected with his worship."—*Smith's Class. Dict.*

See ÆSCULAPIUS, ALCHEMY, HOUSE (clan), IMHOTEP, MEDICINE, PHYSICIAN, SUN, VALMIKI, WISDOM (masc.).

SERPENT, BRAZEN :—

A symbol of the buddhic forces acting through the mind, which raise and heal the soul.

"As Moses lifted up the serpent in the wilderness, even so must the Son of man be lifted up."—JOHN iii. 14.

As the moral law (Moses) points to and exalts wisdom (serpent) in the arena of the soul's lower nature, so the Son of mind,—the Christ-soul, —must be exalted when the soul is sufficiently evolved, or perfected.

See BRASS, METALS, MOSES, SON OF MAN, WILDERNESS.

SERPENT DAHĀKA :—

A symbol of the unreal astro-mental lower principle, or illusion of the manasic function and sense of separateness.

"Thraetona (Fredūn) of the Hero tribe, who smote the Serpent (Ashi) Dahāka which had three mouths, three heads, six eyes, a thousand spies ; which was of enormous strength, a devastator of the settlements, and what was a destroyer which Angra Mainyush produced in the material world for the destruction of the settlements of righteousness." —*Homa Yasht*, HAUG, *Essays*.

"Thraetona or Fredun from the Hero tribe" signifies that the Third Divine outpouring is a Conqueror from the Celestial hierarchies, and he gives the deathblow to illusion. The "Serpent Dahāka" is the sense of separateness which continues to ensnare until the soul has advanced considerably ; hence the strength required to circumvent it is great. The "three mouths" are Lust, Envy, and Greed ; the "three heads," Ignorance, Falsity, and Pride ; the "six eyes" are various perceptive functions. The "spies" are symbolic of limitation, i.e. the inclination to trust in the "flesh" instead of the Spirit. The great creator of illusion—the astro-mental "Serpent"—is said to devastate the soul, inasmuch as it is the cause of the sense of desolation, emptiness, and satiety, which follows the protracted employment of the sense-nature and lower mind. The desire-mind (Angra Mainyush) is the great creator of this illusory principle, and it is only after it has fully functioned and disappeared, that the planes below it which have been used for the evolution of righteousness, can be said to be destroyed.

See ANGRA-MAINYU, APOSTATES, CONQUEROR, ILLUSION, NERYOSANG, SEPARATENESS, SETTLEMENTS, THRAETONA.

SERPENT SRVARA :—

A symbol of the selfishness which takes possession of the mind, and is full of greed and falsity.

" Keresāspa, a youthful hero who wore a side-lock and carried a club, who slew the Serpent Srvara, which devoured horses and men, which was poisonous and yellow, and over which yellow poison flowed."—*Homa Yasht*, HAUG. *Essays.*

" Keresāspa " signifies the strenuous path of Devotion to ideals. The " side-lock " is a symbol of intuition. The " club " is a symbol of the power of the higher emotions. The lower nature has to be disciplined through the Love-element, which conquers selfishness (the Serpent Srvara). The self-centred lower nature has hitherto asserted itself through its immediate desires so as to swallow up, or else exclude, the mental faculties,—lower and higher (" horses and men "). The " yellow " and " poison " of the " serpent " are symbolic of ruling greed and falsity.

See CLUB, HAIR (side-lock), HORSE, KERESĀSPA, LOVE OF GOD, MAN, POISON.

SERPENT, MIGHTY, OF ANGRA-MAINYU :—

This symbol serves to indicate the subtle nature of that illusory lower self which first ensnares the ego, but which ultimately proves the means of enlightening the evolving soul.

" We have to achieve our own divinity, and we can only do so by overcoming that which seems to be the negation of it, but is in reality the indispensable means for the manifestation of the eternal glory."—R. J. CAMPBELL, Serm., *The Flesh Transfigured.*

See AHRIMAN, ANGRA-MAINYU.

SERPENT KING ; NAGA KING :—

A symbol of wisdom and enlightenment.

See AGATHODÆMON.

SERPENT, THREE-HEADED, WITH WINGS AND HUMAN LEGS :—

A symbol of Atma-buddhi-manas, the consummation of human evolution.

See HEAD, LEGS OF MAN, MAN, MANAS, TRIAD, WINGS.

SERPENT OF THE SOUTH, EGYPT :—

A symbol of Wisdom of the higher planes.

See CROWN (upper), EGYPT (higher), NEKHEBIT.

SERPENT OF THE NORTH, EGYPT :—

A symbol of the lower emotions, which proceed from the union of mind and desire. Northern Egypt is a symbol of the lower mind or astro-mental nature.

" By serpents, in the Word, are signified sensual things, which are the ultimates of man's life, and sensual things are the lowest of the understanding and will, being a close contact with the world, and nourished by its objects and delights." —SWEDENBORG, *Apoc. Rev.*, n. 455.

See CROWN (lower), EGYPT (lower), UATCHIT.

SERPENT, LOUD-BREATHING :—

A symbol of the sense-nature and its desires, which so strongly attract the attention of the ego and draw it downwards to matter.

" And I entered the walls of (a town). I went down into Egypt, and my companions parted from me. I betook me straight to the serpent. Hard by his dwelling I abode, waiting till he could slumber and sleep, and I could take my pearl from him."—*Hymn of the Soul,* from the *Acts of Judas Thomas.*

I then entered the condition of thought wherein mind must needs limit and define everything.

I became immersed in self-seeking, fallen low, and in Egyptian darkness.

And my companions, Truth and Hope, departed from me.

I betook me headlong to the realm of the senses,—

Nigh whose centres of astral activity did my consciousness have its abode,

Waiting until the cycle of the
dominance of the senses was ended,

And I could capture the experience
that through it should come to me,

Taking unto me my Pearl,—the
treasure laid up for me in Heaven.

See CONSCIOUSNESS, EGYPT, EX-
PERIENCE, FALL, GNOSIS, LETTER,
MAISHAN, PEARL, PRODIGAL, ROBE,
SEALED LETTER, TREASURE.

SERPENT MORE SUBTIL THAN ANY BEAST OF THE FIELD :—

**A symbol of the desire-mind, which
is more penetrative and captivating
to the ego than any of the lower
desires (beasts).**

"The serpent in the Genesis story,
which ever after crawled upon the ground,
is the allegorical symbol of man's lower
animal desires, which had only come to
be recognised as lower when it was seen
that they resisted the upward striving
towards an ideal. The subtilty of the
serpent in its conversation with Eve
represents the struggle within man's
mind, the wavering between his upward
impulses and the insidious attractiveness
of his downward tendencies. . . . Man
was now in a position to choose deliberately in any given instance whether he
would strive upwards, or obey the animal
nature which pulled in the opposite
direction."—A. H. M'NEILE, *Expository
Times*, June 1906.

"Sin is a subtle, elusive, inapprehen-
sible thing, if we attempt to grasp all
its movements. We understand why in
the first sin it took as its first typical
representation the figure of the serpent,
which cheats the eye with sinuous changes
of place continually, refuses to be located,
and while it leaves no doubt of its
existence is seen only in flashes and
a wavering indistinctness."— PHILLIPS
BROOKS, *Mystery of Iniquity*, p. 3.

"In Egypt, in India, in Scandinavia,
in Mexico, we find clear allusions to the
same great truth (of the god crushing the
serpent). 'The evil genius,' says Wilkinson, 'of the adversaries of the Egyptian
god Horus is frequently figured under
the form of a snake, whose head he is
seen piercing with a spear. The same
fable occurs in the religion of India,
where the malignant serpent Calyia is
slain by Vishnu in his avatar of Krishna ;
and the Scandinavian deity Thor was
said to have bruised the head of the
great serpent with his mace.' Among the
Mexicans, we find Humboldt saying
that 'The serpent crushed by the great
spirit Teotl, is the genius of evil.' "—
A. HISLOP, *The Two Babylons*, p. 60.

"But now when they had eaten, the
Wrath of God's anger did awake in the
Monstrous image, viz. the properties of
the Dark World, namely, the Devils
introduced Desire, which now had its
seat in the Monstrous image—in the
Serpent's essence. In this instant all
the forms of subtlety and craftiness did
awake in the Human Mystery."—JACOB
BOEHME, *Mysterium Magnum*, p. 92.

"Desire is appetite with consciousness
thereof. . . . Desire is the actual essence
of man, in so far as it is conceived as
determined to a particular activity by
some given modification of itself."—
SPINOZA, *Ethics*, Bohn, Vol. II. 137, 173.

See AIDONEUS, ANIMALS, BEAST
(earth), CURSE (ground), DEVIL, EVE,
FALL, GOAT (milch), HEEL, INCAR-
NATION OF SOULS, MARA, MIDGARD'S
SERPENT, MILK (goat), TREE OF KNOW-
LEDGE, WOMAN.

SERPENT, SOLAR :—

**A symbol of the Higher Self, or
manifesting Logos, as arising from
the darkness of potentiality.**

"The symbol, then, of Agathodaimon
as Logos was the Serpent of Wisdom,
. . . in his sun-aspect, symbolised as a
serpent with a lion's head."—G. R. S.
MEAD, *T. G. Hermes*, Vol. I. p. 480.

"O dazzling Sun, who shed'st thy
beams on all the world ! Thou art the
mighty Serpent, the chief of all the Gods,
O thou who dost possess Egypt's beginning and the end of all the world" (A
prayer, Hermetic).—C. WESSELY, *Papyri
Græc.*

The Higher Self (sun) is adored as
the Divine Life manifesting through
the cycle of existence (the serpent) ;
outpouring in the beginning on the
mental plane (Egypt), and at the end
indrawing from the lower nature
(world).

"As there is a serpent below which is
still at work in the world, so there is a
sacred serpent above which watches over
mankind in all the roads and pathways
and restrains the power of the impure
serpent" (*Zohar*).—A. E. WAITE, *Secret
Doctrine in Israel*, p. 87.

See AGATHADAIMON, LION, SERPENT
(ananta), SUN, WISDOM (masc.).

SERPENT OF THE WATER :—

**A symbol of the desire-mind in
its lowest phase of activity, giving
the sense of separateness, and producing deceit, craft, cunning, cruelty,
and other low egoistic qualities.**

"And Lemminkainen went down into
the abysses of Manala, the abode of the
dead. But there, near the river, lay in
wait for him the evil-minded shepherd
whom he had despised, and when Lem-

minkainen came near, this shepherd pulled from the waters a monstrous serpent and hurled it against him. The viper penetrated into the very belly of the hero, and he died, thinking on his mother."—Dom. COMPARETTI, *Traditional Poetry of the Finns*, p. 86.

And the Higher Self descended to the underworld, the abode of the personality (dead). But there, near the astral region (river), were the lower instincts (the shepherd) developed unchecked. And when the Higher Self approached the soul, the lower instincts working on the astral plane became directed by the newly aroused desire-mind (serpent), acting from its centre as a separate self, and thus killing out the inner spiritual influence. But the soul is to be saved through Buddhi (the Mother).

See ANGRA-MAINYU, CRANBERRY, DEAD, DEATH OF BALDER, OF LEMMINKAINEN, DHRITA-RASHTRA, HODER, LEMMINKAINEN, MANALA, MARJATTA, MOTHER (divine), NORTH, PERSONALITY, SEPARATENESS, SHEPHERDS, UNDERWORLD, VISCERA, WATER (lower).

SERPENT, THE HISSING :—

A symbol of the desire-mind, with its knowledge of good and evil, or the distinctions of relativity. It assumes the attitude of tempter,— subtle and deceitful, that is, illusory (māyāvic). The "hissing" signifies the activity of the senses, which dig channels for themselves in the lower vehicles.

"After this, Set changed himself into a serpent which hissed loudly, and he sought out a hole for himself in the ground wherein he hid himself and lived" (*Legend of the Winged Sun-disk*).— BUDGE, *Gods of the Egyptians*.

And following this stage of evolution, "evil" (Set) acquired the capability of tempter (serpent) from having the knowledge of good and evil. The "hole," or "bottomless pit," is the sense-nature, which is never satisfied and has no ending in the lower nature (ground). The "hiding" and "living" signify the latent power which the desire-mental nature acquires in the process of the evolution of buddhi in the soul.

See BEAST, BOTTOMLESS PIT, BUDDHI, DHRITA-RASHTRA, EVIL, FIEND, GROUND, HEAD OF HORUS, ILLUSION, PIT, POLE, SET.

SERPENTS, TWO PRIMORDIAL :—

Symbols of Time and Space, or of Limitation and Matter.

SERPENTS EMITTING SPARKS TO ILLUMINE THE NIGHT :—

Symbolic of the higher emotions (buddhic) uniting with mind and producing virtues in the soul.

"Nine gods and twelve goddesses, who sing praises unto Rā as he entereth the Tuat, and twelve serpents which belch forth the fire that gives light to lighten the god on his way. . . . The serpent goddesses sing hymns to him, and they lighten the darkness by pouring out fire from their mouths" (*Book of Am-Tuat*).—BUDGE *Egypt. Heaven and Hell*, Vol. III. p. 107.

Fire is a symbol of spirit, and the higher qualities are in harmony (sing) with the Self (Rā) as he enters the cycle of Life (the Tuat) on the buddhic plane. At this high level the lower qualities are unapparent, or rather, they belong to the lower planes which do not affect the higher. The state of soul represented is that of Edenic bliss.

"The beauty of Wisdom, which is the body of Philosophy (the glorious Lady Beatrice), results from the order of the Moral Virtues which visibly make that joy. And, therefore, I say that her beauty, which is Morality, rains down little flames of fire, meaning direct desire, which is begotten in the pleasure of the Moral Doctrine."—DANTE ALIGHIERI, *The Banquet*, III. Ch. XV.

See APES (nine), BEATRICE, BUDDHI, DARKNESS, FIRE, GODDESSES, HYMN-SINGING, LIGHT, MOUTH, NIGHT, PRAISE OF GOD, RĀ, SINGERS, SONG, TUAT, TWELVE, WISDOM.

SERVANT OF GOD :—

A symbol of the incarnate Self, or Christ-soul, awakening in humanity, and subjected to the buffetings of the lower nature.

"Behold my servant shall deal wisely, he shall be exalted and lifted up, and shall be very high."—Is. lii. 13.

"For he grew up before him (the Lord) as a tender plant, and as a root (or branch) out of a dry ground : he hath no form nor comeliness ; and when we see him, there is no beauty that we should desire him. He was despised, and rejected of men ; a man of sorrows and acquainted with grief. . . . He was wounded for our transgressions, he was bruised for our iniquities : the chastisement of our peace was upon him, and with his stripes we are healed."—Is. liii. 2-6.

The incarnate Self, from lowly beginnings in the soul, shall maintain righteousness and truth, and so shall become exalted and be ruler over all qualities at the cycle's end.

For from a Divine germ he grew up in the power of the Self (Lord) as a feeble desire, and as a living thing out of a barren soil. He hath no attractiveness to the perception of the lower qualities; when these perceive him, they find in him nothing to admire and follow after. He was despised and rejected by the mental qualities attached to desire and sense, and in sorrow and suffering he manifested within the little developed soul. It is through the transgressions and imperfection of the lower nature that the Self within is obscured. The disciplining of the qualities to bring about peace, or union with the Divine, is the work required of him, and by his spiritual energy the qualities are perfected.

"From oppression and judgment he was taken away; and as for his generation, who considered that he was cut off out of the land of the living? for the transgression of my people was he stricken. And they made his grave with the wicked and with the rich in his death; because he had done no violence, neither was any deceit in his mouth."—Is. liii. 8, 9.

The incarnate Self in the period of involution, having at last fully attained self-limitation (oppression), was unmanifest, for his Divine life was cut off and no longer active in the cycle. To prepare for the descent of the spiritual egos to the lower planes was the Self sacrificed. For the egos required the Self to be immured in ignorance and illusion, and obscured with the multiplicity of objects of sense. For he was now passive in complete involution, and perfected for the evolution that was to follow.

"He shall see of the travail of his soul and shall be satisfied: by his knowledge shall my righteous servant justify many: and he shall bear their iniquities."—Is. liii. 11.

The incarnate Self, the Archetypal Man, having become "an offering for sin" (verse 10) prolongs his days through the period of evolution in the souls of men, and fulfils the Divine will. He shall perceive that his labour is not in vain, and shall be satisfied in the raising of the qualities. By manifestation of truth from within, the incarnate Self will make perfect the imperfect, and so will of himself rectify the shortcomings of many souls.

Therefore in the end he shall be requited in the increased efficiency of the higher qualities, because he underwent deprivation of them, and gave himself as a sacrifice for the saving of the souls of humanity.

See ARC. MAN, BONDAGE, EVOLUTION, GUARDIAN SPIRITS, IGNORANCE, INVOLUTION, JESUS (servant), JOB, PASSION, SORROW, SOUL, SUFFERING, TOMB, WICKED, WILL.

SERVANTS :—

A symbol of those qualities in subordinate positions which watch over and preserve the interests of activities which need to be directed by service or careful attention.

"And there shall be no more curse: but the throne of God and of the Lamb shall be in it; and his servants shall serve him."—REV. xxii. 3.

There shall be no more limitation of the soul to the lower planes: but the causal-body, the seat of the united Higher and evolved Self, shall be exalted within it; and the glorified qualities shall minister to keep clear the way of the Spirit, that its effulgence may manifest freely.

See BONDAGE, CURSE, HIGHER AND LOWER SELVES, JUDGING OTHERS, LAMB OF GOD, THRONE, UNION.

SERVITUDE :—

Symbolic of the state of the soul when the ego is under the thraldom of the desire- and sense-natures.

See BONDAGE, CAPTIVITY.

SET, OR TYPHON :—

A symbol of the power of darkness, ignorance, limitation, the desire-mind, relativity, or the adversary of the Self.

"When Set saw the fate of his friends, he uttered awful imprecations, and because of his foul words, the fiend was ever after called Nehaha."—Legend of the Winged Sun-disk.

When the power of illusion was vanquished, he uttered the opposites of truth and goodness; and on account of his opposition to the absolute good, he is known as negation.

" Suti or Set, the personification of darkness, and the mighty antagonist of Horus, by whom he was slain."—BUDGE, *Book of the Dead*, p. 57.

See AKERU, DEVIL, HEAD (Set), HOLD, MOIST, MOUTH (food), PERREREHU, PIG, SATAN, SUSANOWO, TYPHON, URNI-TENTEN.

SETH, SON OF ADAM :—

A symbol of hope, or mental desire for immortality, a sense of the real within.

" And Eve bare a son, and called his name Seth : for, said she, God hath appointed me another seed instead of Abel ; for Cain slew him."—GEN. iv. 25.

And the lower emotion-nature expands and realises more of the nature within the soul, so that it is vouchsafed Hope (Seth). The emotion-nature (Eve) now realises that it may be receptive of that which cannot be taken away,—hope being a promise of eternal life. The self (lower) is slain by the Self (higher), but this perception of the real Self shall not be slain.

" And all the days of Seth were nine hundred and twelve years ; and he died." —GEN. v. 8.

And the period (12) during which this stage of Hope continued was in conformity with its own nature : and at length it also is dispersed.

See ABEL, BEGETTING, CAIN, EVE.

SETTLEMENTS :—

A symbol of manifested worlds and forms, or globes as the arena of life.

" Then Ahura-mazda said : Thou, O Yima ! . . . enclose my settlements ; then shalt thou become the conservator, and herdsman, and protector of my settlements. Then Yima answered : I will enclose thy settlements ; I will become the conservator and the herdsman and the protector of thy settlements ; in my empire there shall be no cold wind nor hot, no fog, no death."—*Vendidad*, II.

The Supreme points out that the first thing to be done is that the Divine Life should enter the forms, so that the Higher Self (Yima) should become thereby related as an overshadowing guardian and organiser of the lower planes. On its part, the Higher Self is ready to gather its own members together when it comes

to itself in its lower aspect and realises its powers in the soul. On the buddhic plane (my empire) there shall be no struggle, no evil nor good, no ignorance, no death of forms, in involution.

See ARENA, DISMEMBERMENT, FIELD, INVOLUTION, MEMBERS, SERPENT (dahāka), VARA.

SETTLEMENTS SUPPLIED WITH CREATURES :—

Symbolic of manifested worlds primordially containing the monads of life and form. In this " golden age," the egos functioning through the quaternary dwell prosperously and are at peace. There is no strife. Time passes unheeded in this condition of peaceful involution on the Lunar and Terrene globes.

See GOLDEN AGE, INVOLUTION, KARSHVARES, LUNAR CHAIN, PLANETARY CHAIN, REGIONS, VARA.

SEVEN, NUMBER :—

This is a perfect number and signifies completion or consummation. It follows six, which stands for completeness of process. Applied chronologically, seven indicates the beginning and the ending of a cycle, —" alpha and omega."

" Numbers in the Word signify things, and *seven*, all things and all, and thence also what is full and perfect,—consequently, this number involves what is holy, and in an opposite sense, what is profane."—SWEDENBORG, *Apoc. Rev*, n. 10.

" What is conveyed to us in the number seven, saving the sum of perfection ? for to say nothing of the arguments of human reasoning which maintain that it is therefore perfect, because it consists of the first even number, and of the first uneven ; ·of the first that is capable of division, and of the first that is incapable of it ; we know most certainly that holy Scripture is wont to put the number seven for perfection, whence also it tells us that on the seventh day the Lord rested from all His works. . . . Thus ' there were born to him (Job) seven sons ' (JOB i. 2), namely the ' Apostles ' manfully issuing forth to preach ; who in putting in practice the precepts of perfection, as it were, maintained in their life the courage of the superior sex. For hence it is that twelve of them were chosen who should be replenished with the perfection of the sevenfold grace of the Spirit. . . . $4 + 3 = 7, 4 \times 3 = 12$."

" The three sisters, daughters of Job, represent three virtuous affections."— ST. GREGORY THE GREAT, *Morals on the Book of Job*, Vol. I. pp. 40, 53.

The sons and daughters of Job, and all Job's possessions, represent the higher qualities on the buddhic plane which were taken from the incarnate Self (Job) on his descent into the lower nature of the soul.

See HIKOBOSHI, JOB, KARSHVARES, PLANES, REGIONS, ROOT - RACES, ROUND, SHEEP, SIX, SUMMER.

SEVENTH DAY :—

See SABBATH.

SEVENTH HOUR OF THE NIGHT OF THE TUAT :—

This symbolises the first period of evolution, after the close of the six periods of involution. The cycle of life is taken as made up of twelve periods,—six for the process of involution of all the qualities into matter, and six for their evolution from matter. The intermediate state between involution and evolution is a state of pralaya or quiescence, sometimes called a " day of rest "; this is not counted in the twelve divisions of the Tuat or the Zodiac, because it is a negative state. The first point of the sign Libra indicates the perfect or balanced condition of things from which evolution starts.

See ADAMAS, ÆONS (twelve), EVO-LUTION, INVOLUTION, LIBRA, SABBATH, TUAT, ZODIAC.

SEXUAL UNION :—

A symbol of the union of mind and emotion or desire, which results in the progeny of ideas and feelings.

" The rulers in the twelve Æons below hated Pistis Sophia, because she had ceased to do their mystery—sexual union,—and desired to go into the height and be above all."—*Pistis Sophia.*

The lower nature, like Joseph's brethren, hates the Higher, because it does not comprehend it. It also rebels at first at the discipline which is entailed by conforming to the aspiration which is from Above.

See ÆONS, CHILDREN OF MEN, GENERATIVE, MULTIPLY, SOPHIA.

SEX PRINCIPLE IN DIVINE MANIFESTATION :—

When the Divine Monad, or World-egg, divides into two essences, the sex principle is shown in the one essence being dynamic, replete, and fecundating, and the other being static, receptive, and reproductive. This primal duality is known as Spirit and Matter. Spirit first impregnates Matter with all formatives and qualities in the process of Involution ; then subsequently Matter reproduces forms, qualities, and Spirit in the process of Evolution. Spirit is therefore called male and Matter female ; or the first, God, and the second, Goddess.

" Self-consciousness cannot be expressed in terms of material things. The inner world of Spirit and the outer world of Matter are to our experience two, not one, and nothing can make them one. Fundamentally, no doubt, they are from the same source, but in their manifestation they are an irresolvable duality. What is matter ? It is a means to the expression of spirit. And what is spirit ? It is the eternal substance, that which is. Spirit is ever in a state of becoming, ever uttering itself, and yet through all eternity can never exhaust its own potentialities, for these are limitless. Matter and time imply each other, but spirit transcends time. The only *raison d'être* for human existence which completely satisfies our questioning minds as well as our aspiring souls is that human and divine are a solidarity, and that the former has been subjected to its present limitations that the latter may manifest truth, beauty, goodness, and love."— R. J. CAMPBELL, Serm., *The Creator Spirit.*

" Give birth Shu and Tefnut, Seb and Nut. Give birth Seb and Nut to Osiris, Horus-Khent-an-maati, Set, Isis, Nephthys from the womb."—BUDGE, *Gods of the Egyptians,* Vol. I. p. 313.

From Spirit (Shu) and Matter (Tefnut), are born Time (Seb) and Space (Nut). The Higher Self (Osiris) arises with the Incarnate Self (Horus) in potency. Also there are brought forth the relative not-Self (Set), the buddhic principle (Isis), and the physical (Nephthys).

All the Gods are on the Spirit, Love, Time, Mind, and Desire sides of manifestation. All the Goddesses are on the Matter, Wisdom, Space, Emotion, and Sensation sides of the same.

See EGG, EVOLUTION, GODDESS, HEAVEN AND EARTH, HORUS, INVO-LUTION, ISIS, KHIEN, MALE-FEMALE, MATTER, MONAD, MOTHER, NEPHTHYS, NUT, OSIRIS, SEB, SEPARATION, SET, SHU, SPIRIT, SUBSTANCE, TEFNUT, URANUS.

SHABTI FIGURE, PLACED WITH THE MUMMY IN THE TOMB :—

A symbol of the personality, which during incarnation has apparently to do the work for the production of spiritual food to nourish and develop the causal-body. The personality ploughs and sows in the lower nature of the soul.

" I lift up the hand of the man who is inactive. I have come from the city of Unna (Hermopolis). I am the divine Soul which liveth, and I lead with me the hearts of the apes " (*Book of the Dead*, Ch.V).—BUDGE, *Egyptian Magic*, p. 71.

The " inactive man " is the causal-body, latent of itself, and entirely dependent for its development, upon the activities of the personality (lower mind,—ape) attached to it. The Divine Soul, or Individuality (Higher Self emerging) is immortal, and has his seat in the higher mind-centre (Unna), and is the Christ to lead upward the love-nature of the personalities (hearts of the apes).

The Divine soul pleads :—
" Let the judgment fall upon thee instead of upon me always, in the matter of sowing the fields, of filling the water-courses with water, and of bringing the sands from east to the west. After these words comes the answer by the (shabti) figure, ' Verily I am here, and will do whatsoever thou biddest me to do.' "—*Ibid.*, p. 72.

Let the responsibility for development fall upon thee, rather than upon me always, for I am unable without thy co-operation, to sow the seeds of virtues in the lower nature, to conduct truth to the soul, and to clear away the low habits and opinions which smother effort and stifle growth.

To which plea of the Higher Self, the Divine Spark in the personality answers with loving acquiescence.

Dr. Budge explains that the Shabti figures—
" were placed in the coffins to do certain agricultural works for the deceased, who was supposed to be condemned to sow the fields, to fill the canals with water, and to carry sand from the West to the East."—*The Mummy*, pp. 211, 212.
" To these figures the Egyptian gave the name *ushabtiu*, a word which is commonly rendered by ' respondents ' or ' answerers,' and they are often described in modern times as the ' working figures of Hades.' "—BUDGE, *Book of the Dead*, Vol. I. p. lxviii.

See AGRICULTURE, APE, CAUSAL-BODY, CULTIVATION, DEFUNCT, FIELD, FOOD (man), HADES, HAND, HEART, HEEL, INCARNATION OF SOULS, INDIVIDUALITY, IRRIGATION, KA, LAZARUS, MAN, MORTAL MIND, PERSONALITY, PLOUGHING, SAND, SEEDS (good), SOUL, SOWING, WATER.

SHADOW OR DARKNESS :—

A symbol, in its higher aspect, of potentiality, the unmanifest ; and in its lower, of matter or illusion.
See DARKNESS, NIGHT.

SHADOW-IMAGE :—
See TZELEM.

SHAI, GOD OF LUCK OR DESTINY :—

A symbol of the material relation of the individuality, and refers to the personality. The physical life being to a great extent independent of the control of the soul itself, and under the divine guidance of the Lords of Karma, so the happenings which beset the physical body are not to be conceived of as anything but illusory, and, as it were, in the nature of chance, since they are but temporary combinations of conditions which are conducive to such growth as will afford the Divine life within the means for its expansion and development.
See IMMORTALITY, JUDGMENT HALL, KAMA, KARMA, MOIRAE, PERSONALITY, SHENIT, THEMIS.

SHARP AIR, OR EVERY SORT OF WIND :—

Symbolic of " wind of doctrine " ; diverse doctrines which are begotten of illusions of the lower mind ; or cut and dried opinions.
See AIR, ILLUSION, PHOEDRUS, WINDS (various).

SHASHERTET, A CITY OF NUBIA :—

A symbol of a centre of potentiality on the higher planes (Nubia in the far south).
See CITY, NUBIA, SOUTH.

SHAVING THE HEAD IN GRIEF :—

Symbolic of contrition, and readiness to sacrifice the highest qualities of the lower nature for the love of God.

" The Doliones taking the Argonauts to be their enemies the Pelasgians, attacked them by night, and several of the Doliones, and among them Cyzicus their king, lost their lives. With daylight, discerning their error, the Argonauts shore their hair, and shedding many tears, buried Cyzicus with solemn magnificence."—*The Argonautic Expedition.*

Trust is still put in the things of the lower planes, which are comparable to darkness or the night ; and so amid adversity the soul is again impelled to aspire. Then ensues the conflict between the powers of darkness (the illusive Pelasgians) and the powers of the soul, with the result that Faith (Cyzicus) is for the time dethroned. When light comes, and the soul is shown the error of its ways, it is moved to contrition (shaving the head), which is a sign of a fervent desire to contact the Source of Power. But it is only after the "shedding of tears," i.e. the struggle for Truth and the pains of disposing of the dead form of its misdeeds, that harmony is restored.

See ARGONAUTS, CYZICUS, DARKNESS, DEAD, DOLIONES, FAITH, HAIR SHAVEN, LIGHT, NIGHT, PELASGIANS, SACRIFICE, STRIFE, TEARS.

SHEATHS OF THE SOUL :—

A symbol of the bodies on the lower planes in which the incarnate ego gains experience of life.

See CASTES, VESTURES.

SHEEP :—

A symbol of the higher qualities, virtues, or living truths, which are the sustenance of the soul.

" By Him who provides pasture for sheep mankind is nourished, through the sheep ; even for this reason, because the nourishment of mankind is through the sheep, and that of the sheep through pasture. . . . This too, that strength in virtue is increased and taught by Him who produces joyfulness through seeking gradual development."—*The Dinkard,* IX. 65, 2, 4. S. B. of E.

" And he shall set the sheep on his right hand, but the goats on the left."— MAT. xxv. 33.

At the end of the cycle, the Higher Self shall cause the virtues to enter upon higher activities, but the desires (goats) shall recede into passivity and extinction.

" We possess seven thousand sheep, when we feed the innocent thoughts within our breast, in a perfect purity of heart, with the food of truth which we

have sought after." "What is signified by ' sheep ' but the innocency of our thoughts ? What is signified by ' sheep,' but cleanness of heart in the good ? "— ST. GREGORY, *Morals on the Book of Job,* Vol. I. pp. 53, 115.

See DOOR (higher), FOOD (soul), GOATS, HAND, JOB, LITTLE CHILDREN, POOL OF BETHESDA, QUALITIES, SEVEN, SHEPHERD.

SHEEP, LOST :—

A symbol of the spiritual ego, or Divine spark, which separates itself from the spiritual whole and descends to incarnation on the lower planes of nature.

"How think ye ? if a man have an hundred sheep, and one of them be gone astray, doth he not leave the ninety and nine, and goeth into the mountains, and seeketh that which is gone astray ? And if so be that he find it, verily I say unto you, he rejoiceth more of that sheep than of the ninety and nine which went not astray. Even so it is not the will of your Father which is in heaven, that one of these little ones should perish." —MAT. xviii. 12–14.

The "sheep gone astray" stands for the spiritual ego who voluntarily undertakes to separate himself from the Divine Whole on the highest plane. He "goes astray" to seek wisdom individually, through the acquisition of knowledge by actual experience, such as will qualify him to be "found," or raised, by the Higher Self, the Divine Shepherd of the souls. Then there is joy on the higher planes in that he has tasted that actual wisdom and love which the potential "ninety and nine," who went not through the perilous vicissitudes of the lower life which he underwent, had not tasted. No soul can perish, for Spirit is immortal and eternal : but it must be remembered that the effort to manifest and acquire experience as a "little one," or feeble embryo soul, may prove temporarily unsuccessful,— a sort of celestial failure. But it is never the will of God that that which is begun should not be finished, or in other words, that the evolution of the less should not lead to its consummation in union with the Greater.

" I have gone astray like a lost sheep ; seek thy servant ; for I do not forget thy commandments."—Ps. cxix. 176.

" For ye were as sheep going astray ; but are now returned unto the Shepherd and Bishop of your souls."—1 PETER ii. 25.

" All we like sheep have gone astray ; we have turned every one to his own way ; and the Lord hath laid on him the iniquity of us all."—Is. liii. 6.

The spiritual egos have become differentiated on the lower planes, and their imperfections are to be rectified by the indwelling Self.

" The ' Coming of Christ ' is, from one point of view, the spiritual return of the lost sheep of humanity into the one flock of loving hearts, the home-coming of the separated sons of God."—J. G. ADDERLEY, *The Symbolism of the Mass.*

" I have willed with the world-will and have gone the way of all flesh. The responsibility for all my actions falls upon myself. My natural character, although inborn in me, is yet something that I have myself willed ; I myself have affirmed it. I cannot shift the responsibility of my being on to anything else or anybody else ; there is only one will in the world, and I am of its essence."— W. CALDWELL, *Schopenhauer's System*, p. 394.

" In a sense, therefore, which no thoughtful mind can ever deny, you are yourself the author of all your earthly discipline, however painful ; for, being what you are, a child of God, an offshoot of divinity, you can do no other than strive and suffer that the eternal divine perfections may become manifest in you."—R. J. CAMPBELL, Serm., *Manifesting the Works of God.*

See BODHISATVAS, DISCIPLES SENT, FUGITIVE, GUARDIAN SPIRITS, HELEN, INCARNATION OF SOULS, INDIVIDUALITY, LITTLE CHILDREN, MONAD OF LIFE, MOUNTAIN, PILGRIMS, REDEMPTION, SEPARATENESS, SHEPHERD, SONS OF GOD, SOSHYANTS, SPARK, WANDERERS, WAYFARING MEN, WILL, WISDOM.

SHEKINAH :—

A symbol of the Holy Spirit, Buddhi, and its functioning on the lower planes.

" Malkhuth is the She-keen-ah, the Glory which hovered over the Ark of the Covenant. the female or reflection of Zeir Anpeen, and is the creating Spirit." —I. MYER, *Qabbalah*, p. 272.

The buddhic principle is the formative spirit immediately ensouling the causal-body (ark), and is primordially the *māyā* or material emanation from the Absolute (Zeir Anpeen) which gradually brings forth all forms and qualities.

" And above (the ark of the covenant) cherubim of glory overshadowing the mercy-seat."—HEB. ix. 5.

Above the causal-body is the higher nature with its Divine laws which minister to the upraising of the soul.

" Enshrined within you is the true Shekinah, the heavenly light, the Creator's life, differentiated in every one of his children, which is so often dimmed by the encroachment of the temple wall."— B. WILBERFORCE, *The Message of Advent.*

" The first light which may be said to fall on our subject is that the Shekinah is an indwelling glory. The proper word is *inhabitans*, for it is said that the Shekinah dwells in man, being in the heart of those who seek after good works zealously. And more definitely : Man is the House of the Shekinah. The beginning of this inhabitation is when man makes a firm effort towards self-amendment, for by such turning the Shekinah is drawn towards him. . . . Again, it is said that the work of Shekinah below is comparable to that which the soul accomplishes in the body : more accurately still, it is the same work, and this enables us to understand in what sense she is termed the soul of the Tabernacle below, which Tabernacle is the sacred body of man.

It is idle to decode books of secret doctrine unless they have something more definite to tell us concerning the way, the truth and the life. . . . There have been recurring intimations in these pages concerning a mystery of sex ; it is imposed upon me now to affirm that this is the mystery of the Shekinah."—A. E. WAITE, *Secret Doctrine in Israel*, pp. 226, 227.

Buddhi (fem.) and Manas (masc.) become united in the perfected soul.

See ARK (test.), BARSOM, BINAH, CHERUBIM, HEART, MALE-FEMALE, MALKHUTH, MAN AND WIFE, MAN WITHOUT WOMAN, MARRIAGE, MĀYĀ, MOTHER, OCEAN, TABERNACLE, UNION, WISDOM.

SHELTER FROM THE SUN, OF WOOD :—

A symbol of the astral nature (wood) which is now developed and utilised, for the astral sheath of the soul has been formed and specialised. This sheath, or body of astral matter, is in effect a " sunshade " or " shelter " from the rays of the Self (sun), because, whilst the astral nature interprets such lower ranges of atomic vibrations as may be collected and received through its appropriate mechanism, it at the same time obscures the higher and more rapid vibrations sent down from the Self.

" Mashya and Mashyoi prepared a wooden shelter from the sun."—*Bundahis*, Ch. XV. 16.

Mind and emotion having so far evolved the instinct-and-desire-nature, the astral body became organised according to the Divine scheme, and this led to the obscuration of the higher nature, which was now no longer perceived by the lower consciousness.

See AMERDAD, ASTRAL, DATE, IRON (beaten), MATRO, SUN-CATCH-ING, WOOD, WOODEN.

SHEM, HAM, AND JAPHET :—
See NOAH'S SONS.

SHENIT :—

A symbol of karmic agencies or Lords of Karma, ruling cause and effect.

"May the *Shenit* (i.e. the divine officers of the court of Osiris), who form the conditions of the lives of men, not cause my name to stink. . . . Let there be joy of heart unto us at the weighing of words."—BUDGE, *Book of the Dead*, Ch. XXX.

The soul aspires through the Divine law of causation which regulates the conditions of the successive stages of the mental qualities, and it seeks differentiation upward and not downward. When the expression of the soul's manifestation is estimated (weighing of words) the bliss of the inner being (heart) is longed for and assured.

"Whatever becomes of this world and the greatness thereof, there can be no destruction of any spiritual gain the race has ever achieved, for all spiritual gain is the revealing of Christ in the heart of man."—R. J. CAMPBELL, Serm., *Christ Arisen*.

See FATE-SPHERE, HEART, JUDG-MENT HALL, JUSTIFICATION, KARMA, MAAT, MOIRAE, NAME, NECESSITY, SHAI, SI-OSIRI, THEMIS, WORDS.

SHEPHERD, GOOD :—

A symbol of the Higher Self who leads the higher qualities upwards, or tends the spiritual monads who incarnate in human forms.

"Verily I say unto you, I am the door of the sheep. All that ever came before me are thieves and robbers : but the sheep did not hear them. I am the door : by me if any man enters in, he shall be saved, and shall go in and out and find pasture. The thief cometh not, but for to steal, and to kill and to destroy : I am come that they may have life, and that they might have it more abundantly. I am the good shepherd who giveth his life for the sheep. . . . Therefore doth my Father love me, because I lay down my life, that I might take it again."—JOHN x. 7–17.

Referring to the verses previous : "sheep" signify the higher qualities manifesting on the mental plane (sheepfold). The "door" represents the higher mind as the entrance from above to the soul. The "other way" is the lower mind as the entrance from below, to which the desires (thieves) climb in order to tempt and capture the soul. The Higher Self enters by the higher "door"; to him the Divine Will opens the soul, and the higher qualities respond to the voice within. Verily, Christ is the higher "door,"—the way, the truth, and the life,—and he is the ruler of the higher qualities. The desires (thieves), which come before the Christ, rule first the lower nature, but the higher qualities remain latent until the Spirit stirs them from within. Through the Christ shall the mind be raised. The ego shall go in and out of the causal-body to his successive re-incarnations wherein he shall gather experience and the means of growth. The desire-nature (thief) is that which would kill out the spirit, and destroy the germs of the higher qualities. The Christ came that these germs might have life to become mature. The Christ laid down his life in the involution of the prototypal human soul, in order that he might take it again in the evolution of the many souls of humanity, and so fulfil the Divine Law of sacrifice.

"Now the God of peace, who brought again from the dead the great shepherd of the sheep in the blood of the eternal covenant, even our Lord Jesus, make you perfect in every good thing to do his will."—HEB. xiii. 20, 21.

The power of the Self through harmony raises from death in the lower nature, the incarnate Self, leader of the higher qualities (sheep), within the Divine life of the individual soul who realises the Divine nature as his ideal of aspiration and eternal possession (covenant). The incarnate Self is the means of making perfect in every good quality the individual soul, whose whole nature is thereby brought into conformity with the Divine will.

See ARC. MAN, BISHOP, COVENANT, DOOR (higher), LITTLE CHILDREN, RE-INCARNATION, SHEEP, SUN (door), THIEF.

SHEPHERDS :—

A symbol of ambitions and other leading emotions, which collect and subordinate the simple qualities to serve their ends.

"Woe be to the shepherds of Israel that do feed themselves! should not the shepherds feed the flocks?"—EZEK. xxxiv. 2.

Those leading emotions are condemned which seek to satisfy themselves, rather than minister to the growth of the virtues.

See RULER, SERPENT (water).

SHEWBREAD, OR BREAD OF THE FACES :—

A symbol of the higher qualities of goodness, love, and truth, evolved upon the buddhic plane, as the result of transmuted experiences below during the soul's incarnations.

"And thou shalt take fine flour, and bake twelve cakes thereof: two tenth parts of an ephah shall be in one cake. And thou shalt set them in two rows, six on a row, upon the pure table before the Lord. And thou shalt put pure frankincense upon each row, that it may be to the bread for a memorial, even an offering made by fire unto the Lord. Every sabbath day he shall set it in order before the Lord continually; it is on the behalf of the children of Israel, an everlasting covenant. And it shall be for Aaron and his sons; and they shall eat it in a holy place: for it is most holy unto him of the offerings of the Lord made by fire by a perpetual statute."—LEV. xxiv. 5-9.

"And thou shalt set upon the table shewbread before me alway."—EXOD. xxv. 30.

It is enjoined that by the moral law (Moses), truth and goodness derived through the activities of the lower nature (two parts fine flour) shall be purified and transmuted (baked) into wisdom and love. These higher qualities of the soul are divisible into two sets,—six of wisdom, and six of love,—and these manifest in the higher mind (table) as the food for the soul. The mind thereby becomes purified and fragrant (frankincense), and so comes into harmonious relation with the vibrations from atma-buddhi (fire). Every periodic state of rest between incarnations, when the ego is indrawn, there shall be set forth this fruit of experience and the Spirit which devolves from the efforts and aspirations of the qualities (Israelites) according to the Divine law of growth. And this spiritual fruit shall become the food of the spiritual mind and its ideas (Aaron and sons) for the development of the causal-body (holy place), for these qualities of wisdom and love are the most perfect results following from the sacrifice of the lower to the higher, and the transmutations brought about by the eternal law.

"The shewbread, literally the 'Bread of the Faces,' or of 'the Presence,' consisted of twelve loaves, which denoted the 'presence' of Jehovah himself, under his twelve mystical faces at the altar."— SMITH, Dict. of the Bible.

The Divine "faces" signify the mental aspects of the higher qualities showing the Truth and Love of the Self (Jehovah); that is, showing the presence of the Self in the religious consciousness (altar).

"The holy place, in which was the candlestick and the shewbread, the two great symbols of light and life, was the emblem of that more close and internal converse to which Christ admitted his faithful disciples and elected ones. . . . And for the holiest of all, which was the abode of the Godhead."—E. IRVING, Col. Writings, Vol. V. p. 259.

See AARON, ALTAR, ARK (test.), BREAD, BREASTPLATE, CAKE, CAUSAL-BODY, CORN, EXPERIENCE, FIRE, FLOUR, FOOD FOR SOUL, FRANK-INCENSE, FRUIT OF SPIRIT, INCARNATION OF SOULS, ISRAELITES, MANNA, MOSES, OFFERING, QUALITIES, SABBATH, SACRAMENTAL CAKES, SACRIFICE, TABLE OF LORD, TREASURE, TWELVE, UNLEAVENED BREAD.

SHIELD AND SPEAR :—

Symbols of *will* which protects from the negative, and *intention* which initiates energy.

See HELMIT, SALVE, SPEAR, SWORD, WILL.

SHINAR LAND :—

A symbol of a condition of inertia: the same as the state of *tamas*.

"And it came to pass, as they journeyed east, that they found a plain in the land of Shinar; and they dwelt there."—GEN. ix. 2.

And as the wave of Divine life "journeyed east," that is towards its means of experience and development, it arrived at a field of action in "Shinar,"—a condition of relative inertia.

See AMRAPHEL, BABEL, EAST, GUNAS, TAMAS.

SHINING FACE OF JESUS :—

A symbol of celestial efflux of Truth and Love reflected in the aspiring soul approaching perfection.

See RAIMENT, TRANSFIGURATION, WHITE.

SHINATSU-HIKO, WIND-GOD :—

A symbol of the spiritual mind on the higher mental plane of the soul.

"Shinatsu-hiko (wind-long-prince) was produced from Izanagi's breath when he puffed away the mists which surrounded the newly formed country of Japan. . . . A *norito* (prayer) addressed to them makes two Wind-Gods—one masculine, named Shinatsu-hiko, and one feminine, called Shinatobe. They are also referred to as Ame-no-Mihashira (august pillar of heaven) and Kuni-no-Mihashira (august pillar of earth). Hirata supposes that it was by them that communication was maintained between earth and sky in the Age of the Gods, and that it is due to their agency that the prayers of men are heard in Heaven. Their *shintai* is a mirror."— W. G. ASTON, *Shinto*, pp. 154, 155.

The spiritual mind was produced from the Divine Life when the homogeneous condition of the upper planes gave place to the heterogeneous, so that the lower planes (Japan) should be replenished. The spiritual mind was accompanied with the buddhic emotion-nature (Shinatobe). Through these the lower mind or personality is purified, and its qualities transmuted, in response to its aspirations and efforts. The higher mental plane is the plane of communication between the higher and lower natures (sky and earth).

See AARON, AIR, BREATH (divine), CHRYSE, COUNTRIES, EARTH, HEAVEN AND EARTH, HERMES, IZANAGI, MIRROR, PILLARS OF LIGHT, PRAYER, QUARTERS, SKY, THOTH, VAPOUR (white), WIND.

SHINTAI :—

A symbol of the causal-body, the immortal vehicle of the Self.

"This (token of God) is known as the *mitama-shiro* (spirit representative, spirit token), or more commonly as the *shintai* (god-body). The *shintai* varies much in form. It is frequently a mirror or a sword, but may also be a tablet with the God's name, a sprig of sakaki, a gohei, a bow and arrows, a pillow, a pot, a string of beads, a tree or river bank, or even the shrine itself. A stone is a very common *shintai*."—W. G. ASTON, *Shinto*, p. 70.

The symbols mentioned are all symbols of the causal-body, or have close relation with it. The Divine Life (tree); the Spirit (stone); the Divine Ray on which are strung the souls of humanity (string of beads); etc. The shintai, broadly regarded, indicates reliance upon the Supreme through knowledge of the Divine Life of the soul.

See CAUSAL-BODY, INSIGNIA, KARANA, MAHAVIRA-POT, MIRROR, PEN, SAKAKI, STONE, TAKE-MIKA.

SHIP OF BALDER :—

A symbol of the astral vehicle, or desire-body, at an early stage.

See ASTRAL, RINGHORNE.

SHIP, BLACK :—

A symbol of a desire-mental form of thought containing false concepts and prejudices, and full of error and illusion.

See FORMS, SAILS OF BLACK SHIP.

SHIP OR BOAT ON THE SEA :—

A symbol of the lower mental, or of the causal vehicle of the soul.

"But the ship was now in the midst of the sea, tossed with waves: for the wind was contrary."—MAT. xiv. 24.

This "warring of the elements" signifies the transferring of the lower astral impressions to a higher plane, that is, the transmutation of lower qualities into higher. It takes place amid much disturbance in the lower mind, and is effected only through the power of the Christ within the lower mental vehicle (ship), which is an aspect of the lower ego.

See BOAT, HOLD, MAST, SEA, STORM, WALKING (water), WAVES, WIND (adverse).

SHIP OF MANU :—

A symbol of the nascent causal-body :—

"Manu, however, was to be preserved by the help of the Fish, who commanded him to build a ship and go on board with the seven Rishes, and with the seeds of all existing things."—*Mahā-Bhārata, Deluge story.*

The mind (Manu) is to be saved for development through the power of the Self (Fish); and a causal-sheath is to be builded on the mental plane, in which the mind is to take refuge. The "Rishes" signify the seven root-races of humanity; and the "seeds" are the potencies of all things, brought over from previous manvantaras.

See ABTU, ARK (Noah), CAUSAL-BODY, DELUGE, DWELLING, DWELL-INGS, FISH (great), HORN, LAKE, MANVANTARA, MOORING POST, OCEAN, POOL OF PEACE, RISHES, ROOT-RACES, SEEDS OF MEN, SEVEN, VAIVASVATA.

SHIPS, BEAKED :—

Symbolic of directed aspirations from the mind.

"Now I (Achilles) will depart to Phthia, seeing it is far better to return home on my beaked ships; nor am I minded here in dishonour to draw thee (Agamemnon) thy fill of riches and wealth."—*Iliad*, Bk. I.

The Personality resolves to regain those higher states of consciousness (Phthia) which are the outcome of the manasic evolution. The resolution involves the directed aspirations, and these are realised as the sense of right. The Personality decides that it shall not be enslaved by the Desire-nature with its objects of sense.

See ACHILLES, AGAMEMNON, BOAT, HOME, MAN (rich), PERSONALITY, PHTHIA, RICHES (lower), STORM.

SHIPS OF THE GREEKS :—

Symbolic of the astro-mental qualities in their vehicles.

"But Achilles sat by his seafaring ships, still wroth, even the heaven-sprung son of Pelius, Achilles fleet of foot; he betook him neither to the assembly that is the hero's glory, neither to war, but consumed his heart in tarrying in his place, and yearned for the war-cry and for battle."—*Iliad*, Bk. I.

But the Personality, though gifted with the Divine Spark, remained self-absorbed in the vehicles of desire and lower mind, still attached to the objects which engender passion. The Personality rises not to the heights of the mental qualities, nor to the

higher activities of the lower mind; but, joined to its own idea, that of egoism, it longs for the fruits of action on the lower planes.

See ACHILLES, ASSEMBLY OF PEOPLE, ASTRAL, BATTLE, GREEKS, HEROES, MYRMIDONS, PELIUS, PERSONALITY, SEA, SPARK, WAR.

SHIPS OF THE GREEKS GUIDED TO ILIUM (TROY) :—

Symbolic of the higher mental qualities directed to the causal-self.

"To them there arose by far the best of augurs, Kalchas, son of Thestor, who knew the present, the future, and the past, and who guided the ships of the Greeks to Ilium, by his prophetic art, which Phœbus Apollo gave him."—*Iliad*, Bk. I.

To the mind appeared Memory (reminiscence) the child of the Ego, which is the means, through correlation of experiences, of directing the higher mental qualities to centralise in the causal-self. This it effects by its higher consciousness, which is the direct offshoot or ray of the Higher Self (Apollo).

"Ships signify containers of knowledges of what is good and true, serving for use of life. Ships signify those knowledges, because they are what contain things."—SWEDENBORG, *Apoc. Rev.*, n. 406.

See APOLLO, CONSCIOUSNESS, EX-PERIENCES, GREEKS (great), ILIUM, KALCHAS, PRIAM, PROPHET, REMINIS-CENCE, SILENUS, TIME, TROJANS, TROY.

SHIP'S HAWSERS :—

A symbol of means of attaching the lower Self to the Higher.

See ANCHORAGE, MOORING POST.

SHOE-LATCHET OF JESUS :—

Symbolic of spiritual power through love.

"In the midst of you standeth one whom ye know not, even he that cometh after me, the latchet of whose shoe I am not worthy to unloose."—JOHN i. 26, 27.

In the midst of the qualities of the soul is the central Ideal—the Christ, even the Spiritual nature which is evolved after the moral nature. The suggestion of unworthiness refers to the fact that the moral nature (John) embraces the sense of *veneration* and is inwardly aware of the greater Love-nature which is to supersede it. "John" speaks thus in order to emphasise the fact that whilst the Spiritual nature *stands upon*, or is supported by, the moral nature, the moral nature itself may not presume to question or interfere in any way with the Christ, who is whole and entire, without spot or blemish, and wanting nothing.

See BHARATA, CHRIST, CHRIST (increase), JESUS, JOHN BAPTIST.

SHOES OF RAMA :—

A symbol of advancing spiritual power.

See BHARATA, RAMA.

SHOES ON THE FEET :—

A symbol of power to advance.

See FEET, FOOT, GOLDEN SOLES, ROBE, SANDALS.

SHOES PUT OFF :—

A symbol of the discarding of the lower nature.

"And God said, Draw not nigh hither : put off thy shoes from off thy feet, for the place whereon thou standest is holy ground."—EXOD. iii. 5.

It is pointed out by the Spirit within that the moral nature (Moses) is incapable of furthering the growth of the soul beyond a certain level, when the love-nature (Christ) is evolved to bring the soul to perfection.

See LAW OF MOSES, MOSAIC, MOSES.

SHORE OF THE SEA :—

A symbol of the astral or astromental plane.

See ASKR, JEWELS, SEA.

SHORE, THE OTHER :—

A symbol of the buddhic or buddhi-mental plane, including a devachanic or nirvanic, state of consciousness.

"Few there are among men who arrive at the other shore (become Arhats) ; the other people here run up and down the shore. But those who, when the Law has been well preached to them, follow the Law, will pass across the dominion of death, however difficult to overcome."—*Dhammapada*, Ch. VI. 85, 86. (Footnote by Max Müller : "'The other shore' is meant for Nirvana, 'this shore' for common life.")

Few of the mental qualities or souls have passed on to the higher planes ; most are engaged in the activities of the lower planes, going to, and returning from the physical life. But when the Divine Law is understood and followed, then the souls are purified and they pass from death to life everlasting.

See ARHATS, DEVACHAN, DHARMA, HIKOBOSHI, NIRVANA, RAFT.

SHORT-LIVED ACHILLES :—

A symbol of the brief duration of the personality.

"His mother Thetis foretold him that his fate was either to gain glory and die early, or to live a long but inglorious life. The hero chose the former, and took part in the Trojan war, from which he knew that he was not to return."—*Smith's Class. Dict.*

Nature (Thetis), which produced through biological evolution the personality (Achilles), now develops it to completion as the lower mind, and so gives it the choice of accepting the endowment of higher mind and spirit that it might achieve the glory of raising the soul to heaven (Ilium) through its efforts and the death of the lower mind,—or of remaining a protracted period as an irresponsible animal subject to the lower forces. The personality chose the higher state and became a moral being knowing good and evil, and thereupon entered into conflict with the lower qualities (Trojans) from which it would never retreat.

See ACHILLES, ADAM (lower), FALL, HEEL, IMMORTALITY FORFEITED, JOB, PERSONALITY, THETIS, TROJANS.

SHOULDER, RIGHT :—

A symbol of outgoing positive force, or of directive ability.

See ARMS (body).

SHOULDER, LEFT :—

A symbol of the astral or desire principle.

See GOSHURUN, VULTURE.

SHRINE OR SANCTUARY :—

A symbol of the causal-body in which is seated the Higher Self.

"A man has a little shrine hidden away somewhere in his heart, where he worships occasionally in secret the God of the might-have-been."—R. J. CAMPBELL, *Serm., Coming to the True Self.*

The monstrance, emblematic of the sun (Self), when containing the consecrated host is placed in the elevated shrine of the altar ; thus symbolising the real presence of God in the highest and inmost heart of humanity.

" I walked the earth, Myself God's sanctuary."—FABER, Hymn, *The Starry Skies.*

" What is the heavenly sanctuary in human life ? It is the identification of that human life with the life of God ; it is man knowing himself in God, and God in him. I do not mean that he understands it, but only that he knows it, and he can be much more sure of it than of anything he understands. When Jesus felt ' I and my Father are one ' all the good of existence was present, and he had entered into the Holy Place. He had died, that is, He had done with all feeling of separateness from God. Now that was his redemption (HEB. ix. 12). That was the deliverance which He obtained for himself. Deliverance from what ? From any feeling of separateness from the Source of life, and from that Spirit who is the unity of all spirits. The feeling of separateness is that illusion which accompanies the unfolding of individuality. Individuality is real, and nothing in our consciousness is more unquestionable than this consciousness of individuality. But that we are separate from God and from other men is an illusion."—T. RHONDDA WILLIAMS, Serm., *Redemption.*

See ADYTUM, ALTAR, CABIN, CAUSAL-BODY, CLEANSING, HEART, HOST, HOUSE (heaven), SEPARATENESS, TEMPLE.

SHU, SON OF RĀ AND HATHOR :—

A symbol of the Divine Life emanated by the Supreme Spirit through the highest primordial Matter of the buddhic plane.

" Shu was the first-born son of Tem . . he typified the light. . . . Tefnut was the twin sister of Shu, . . . she typified moisture. Shu was the right eye of Tem, and she was the left, i.e. Shu represented an aspect of the Sun, and Tefnut of the Moon."—BUDGE, *Egyptian Ideas, etc.,* p. 93.

The Divine Life was the first aspect of the Supreme (Tem) in manifestation ; and illumination, or consciousness, occurs in the union of Spirit and Matter. The Divine Life in order to be active requires something to operate upon, and this is the receptive, form-side of nature (Tefnut) typified by " moisture " without which there is no life in nature. The Divine Life is the active aspect (right eye) of the Supreme (Tem), and receptive matter in forms (Tefnut) is the passive aspect (left eye). The Self (sun), possesses its reflection māyā (moon).

" Shu is supposed to symbolise the air or sunlight, and in papyri and in coffins he is represented in the form of a man, standing with both arms raised, lifting up Nut, the sky, from the embrace of Seb the earth."—BUDGE, *The Mummy,* p. 280.

The Divine Life on the mental plane,—the plane of creation,—at the beginning of manifestation, opens the cycle of activities in space (Nut) and time (Seb), and distinguishes the higher planes from the lower.

" The (four) pillars of the god Shu were not as yet created, when he was upon the high ground (or staircase) of him that dwelleth in Khemennu " (*Papy. of Ani*).—BUDGE, *Book of the Dead,* p. 93.

The four planes below atma, the highest plane, were non-existent when the Divine Life was operative only on the plane of atma whereon the Higher Self was centred.

See ASCENSION OF OSIRIS, CON-SCIOUSNESS, EYE, EYES OF HORUS, GATE (tchesert), HATHOR, JACKAL, MATTER, MĀYĀ, MOON, NUT, PILLARS OF SHU, SEB, SEPARATION, SPIRIT, SUN, TEFNUT, TEM, UTCHATS, VAYU.

SHU DOUBLE :—

A symbol of the Divine Will as outbreathing and inbreathing the Divine Life.

" Ka-Shu, i.e. the ' double of Shu,' is present in the Boat (of Afu-Rā) in order to supply the god with air."—BUDGE, *Egypt. Heaven and Hell,* Vol. III. p. 106.

The Divine Will has the double capacity of outpouring and indrawing the Life of the lower planes, in order that the Incarnate Self (Afu-Rā) shall experience alternate periods of activity and of rest.

See AFU-RĀ, BOAT, BREATH, HORIZONS (two), LION-GOD (double), MUSUBI.

SHUN, CHINESE EMPEROR :—

A symbol of the Self operating on the buddhic plane during the cycle of Involution.

See CONFUCIUS, DYNASTIES.

SIAMAK AND VESCHAK :—

Symbols of will and knowledge which make man a responsible being.

" After fifty years Meshia and Meschiane had two children, Siamak and Veschak, and they died a hundred years old. For their sins they remain in hell until the resurrection."—*Zoroastrian System.*

After the union of the mental and emotional principles (kama-manas) in astral vehicles for fifty ages, there is evolved the will-to-act with knowledge ; that is, when the consciousness has reached the stage of development answering to a responsible will and knowledge, giving rise to karma, the lower principles, which are related with the central soul and exist no longer apart from it, are dissolved in the soul,—the first period of their evolution having been accomplished. And for the mistakes which the egos, having will and knowledge, make upon the lower planes, they have to remain confined to those planes (hell) until they are perfected, when, at the close of the cycle, they rise from their " death " and are liberated (resurrection).

See Astral, Evolution, Fravak, Hell, Karma, Liberation, Matro, Milk (goat), Races, Resurrection, Root-races, Tree of knowledge, Will.

SICKLE :—

A symbol of outgoing spiritual energy to overcome and cut down the attachments to the lower nature, in order to liberate the soul.

" And he said, So is the kingdom of God, as if a man should cast seed upon the earth ; and should sleep and rise night and day, and the seed should spring up and grow, he knoweth not how. The earth beareth fruit of herself ; first the blade, then the ear, then the full corn in the ear. But when the fruit is ripe, straightway he putteth forth the sickle, because the harvest is come."— Mark iv. 26–9.

So are the higher planes attained by the ego :—it is as if the Self should cast the germs of truth, righteousness and love into the lower nature of the soul (the earth), and then should await their growth through the process of rests and re-incarnations ; and that the germs should expand and develop in secret and unobserved. The lower nature (earth) brings forth that which is implanted in it ;—first the faint aspiration for what is better,

then the higher quality, and lastly the perfect fruition of wisdom and love. But when the qualities are perfected, the Self puts forth spiritual energy (sickle) to sever the ties that bind the ego to the lower nature, because the time has come when the ego receives on the higher planes the spiritual results of its aspirations and sacrifices on the lower.

" By a sickle the same thing is signified as by a sword. That by a sword is signified divine truth fighting against falses, and vice versa."—Swedenborg, *Apoc. Rev.,* n. 643.

" The very moment the soul begins to desire God, God comes. The change may not be great at first, but whatever it is God takes advantage of it to the full to heal, and bless, and lift up. It is like what happens at this (winter) season of the year. . . . It is the sun that starts the process, and then unceasingly follows up every slightest response thereto. It may be long before the buds show themselves, and longer still before the foliage and the flowers arrive, but they are on the way. From afar God comes, like the sun of heaven into our wintry dreariness and death, and lays hold of every feeblest desire of the soul for eternal life, fostering and encouraging it with his grace and love as opportunity affords till he has brought it to perfection."—R. J. Campbell, Serm., *God's Loving-kindness.*

See Agriculture, Corn, Cultivation, Day and night, Earth, Fruit, Germs, Grass, Harvest, Herb, Kingdom of heaven, Liberation, Reaping, Reincarnation, Resurrection, Seed (good), Sower, Sword.

SIDE-LOCK :—

A symbol of intuition.
See Hair (side-lock).

SIDES OF THE CELESTIAL CITY :—

A symbol of the four lower planes of being.
See Amarāvaiti, City of god, Jerusalem, Kapila.

SIGHT :—

A symbol of perception of truth by the intellect or the intuition. Or perception on the higher planes.

" Spiritual things are real things, but natural things are their forms : it is the spiritual sight of man which is called the intellect."—Swedenborg, *Apoc. Rev.,* n. 7.

" For you are to understand, it is no part of the Divine essence or wisdom to cover Himself with clouds and darkness ; seeing God is light, and with Him is no darkness at all. These clouds are in our vision, the dimness of our sight, the veils of sin, the darkening scales of vice ; but not in Him who dwelleth in light that is unapproachable and full of glory. And the end of all revelation—wherefore it is called revelation—is to remove the blindness from our eyes, that we may see ; and to unstop the deafness of our ears, that we may hear ; to destroy the carnality of our mind, that we may understand ; and to awake the sensibility of our spirit, that we may hold communion with the Father of spirits, and live. This, I say, is the very end of revelation,—to make all things naked and open which by nature are dark and mysterious, and to deliver the soul out of all captivities of sense and worldliness, of error and ignorance, into the enjoyment of Divine liberty and light."— ED. IRVING, *Works*, Vol. I. p. 84.

See BLIND MAN, CLOUDS OF HEAVEN, EYE, MAN (blind), MEN (breast), SEEING.

SIGN OR SYMBOL (SACRED) :—

An outward form subjectively selected to indicate an inward condition, or process of the Divine life in the soul of the universe.

"Then certain of the scribes and Pharisees answered him, saying, Master, we would see a sign from thee. But he answered and said unto them, An evil and adulterous generation seeketh after a sign ; and there shall no sign be given to it but the sign of Jonah the prophet : for as Jonah was three days and three nights in the belly of the whale ; so shall the Son of man be three days and three nights in the heart of the earth."— MATT. xii. 38–40.

This is the inquiry made by those formalists and shallow thinkers who would try to substitute for the Living Spirit the dead letter (sign). The superficial form for which they look, and the importance which they attach to convention and outward things, are rightly disregarded by the Christ— who points to the evolutionary process accomplished by the soul (Jonah) in faith and steadfastness of purpose in passing through the lower life (sea monster), as the only means of arriving at the goal of attainment, that is, resurrection or liberation from the illusion of the lower planes. " Jonah " signifies a type of the soul whose evolution is accomplished in the power of the Self. The " whale " signifies the lower life in which the soul (Jonah)

completes a period of evolution. So, in the same symbolism, the Christ-soul must complete a period of evolution through the lower nature (earth) before he is perfected and rises from the dead (i.e. the lower illusion which is devoid of life).

"Symbolism, indeed, is always necessary before we can apprehend the abstract : it is only through the sensuous symbol that we can express the abstract thought." —SAYCE, *Rel. of Anc. Egyptians,* p. 31.

"Symbols may indicate realities, but the realities must interpret symbols."— H. M. GWATKIN, *The Knowledge of God,* Vol. I. p. 8.

"The perennial value of Christianity is its symbolic value. There are great controversies as to what is and what is not historical in Christianity, but let us remember that if we could settle all the historical questions to-morrow, that would not give us religion, nor would it give Christianity abiding value ; everything would depend upon our finding the symbolic value of the facts. A fact of past history has nothing in it for present-day religion, unless it stands forth as a symbol of a Reality behind itself."— ANON., Serm., *Jesus the Great Symbol.*

See DEAD, EARTH, HEART, ILLUSION, INSPIRATION, JONAH, LEVIATHAN, LIBERATION, MONSTERS, MYTHOLOGY, PHARISEES, PROPHET, RESURRECTION, REVELATION, SCRIPTURES, SIMEON, SON OF MAN, THREE, THREE DAYS, TOMB, VISCERA, WHALE.

SIGYN, WIFE OF LOKE :—

A symbol of the physical nature, the vehicle of the astral.

See LOKE, NEPHTHYS, SET.

SILENCE AND VOICE :—

Symbolic of muteness and utterance in relation to Self-expression.

SILENUS, LEADER OF THE SATYRS :—

A symbol of the individuality or of the spiritual mind.

"Silenus always accompanies Dionysus, whom he is said to have brought up and instructed. Like the other Satyrs he is called a son of Hermes. . . . He is described as resembling his brethren in their love of sleep, wine and music. He was conceived also as an inspired prophet, who knew all the past and the most distant future, and as a sage who despised all the gifts of fortune."— *Smith's Class. Dict.*

"This deity was remarkable for his wisdom ; his drunkenness being regarded as inspiration."—KEIGHTLEY, *Mythology,* p. 204.

The spiritual mind, offspring of the higher mind (Hermes), brings up the Christ (Dionysus) in the soul; it is unconscious (sleep) of external attractions, loves wisdom (wine), and harmony (music and dancing). It is cognisant of the process of the soul's evolution, and esteems not at all the pleasures of sense and the objects of desire.

See BALARAMA, CHIRON, DIONYSUS, DRUNKARD, HERMES, INDIVIDUALITY, INTOXICATION, MUSIC, NOAH, PROPHET, SATYRS, SHIPS (Ilium), WINE.

SILVER AND GOLD (NOT AS MONEY) :—

Symbols of the mental qualities and the buddhic ; or silver = moon, passive, and gold = sun, active.

" ' Surely there is a mine for silver, and a place for gold which they refine ' (JOB xxviii. 1). In silver the power of speaking, in gold brightness of life or of wisdom is used to be denoted."—ST. GREGORY, *Morals on the Book of Job*, Vol. II. p. 343.

" The Alchemists held that the Divine Idea is always aiming at ' Spiritual Gold '—divine humanity, the New Man, citizen of the transcendental world,—and ' natural man ' as we ordinarily know him is a lower metal, silver at best."— E. UNDERHILL, *Mysticism*, p. 169.

See ALCHEMY, GOLD, LOST (silver), MAN (natural), METALS, RACES.

SIMEON, WHO WAITED FOR THE CONSOLATION OF ISRAEL :—

A symbol of an inner mental state or type of soul subjectively perfected, who knew that salvation was at hand, for the lower qualities (Israel) needed a Saviour.

" And Simeon blessed them, and said unto Mary his mother, Behold this child is set for the falling and rising up of many in Israel ; and for a sign which is spoken against."—LUKE ii. 34.

And the type " Simeon " was in accord with the purified lower nature (Mary), and was able to impart to it his own spiritual discernment. He pointed out that this birth of Christ in the soul is set as a critical factor in the descent and ascent of the Spirit into and through matter, whereby the qualities are raised, and the aim is the attainment of Christhood in all qualities. The Christ stands to the qualities as an opponent of ignor-

ance and desire, and is therefore " spoken against " by the lower nature.

See ANNA, ASITA, BIRTH OF JESUS, ISRAELITES, SIGN, VIRGIN MARY.

SIMILITUDES, WORLD OF :—

A symbol of the astral plane, next above the physical.

" The World of Similitudes is so called because in it exist, ready to be materialised, the forms which are to be actualised on the Physical Plane. The confines of this World of Similitudes touch those of the Visible World."—GIBB, *Hist. of Ottoman Poetry*, Vol. I. p. 56.

The forms on the astral plane are reproductions of forms on the mental plane, the which forms have been modified by karmic agencies.

" Occultism teaches that no form can be given to anything, either by nature or by man, whose ideal type does not already exist on the subjective plane : more than this, that no form or shape can possibly enter man's consciousness, or evolve in his imagination, which does not exist in prototype, at least as an approximation. Neither the form of man, nor that of any animal, plant or stone, has ever been ' created ' ; and it is only on this plane of ours that it commenced ' becoming,' that is to say, objectivising into its present materiality, or expanding *from within outwards*."— BLAVATSKY, *Secret Doctrine*, Vol. I. p. 303.

See ANDREW, ARC. MAN, ASTRAL PLANE, COSMOS, CREATION, FORMS, IMAGE, KARMA, PROTOTYPES, WORLDS (five), YETZEERATIC.

SIMORG, THE GREAT BIRD :—

A symbol of the Higher Self, the central Ideal of aspiration in all souls, and their Divine Archetype.

" The Highest is a sun-mirror ; who comes to Him sees himself therein, sees body and soul, and soul and body. When you came to the Simorg, three therein appeared to you, and had fifty of you come, so had you seen yourselves as many. Him has none of us yet seen."— FERIDEDDIN ATTAR, *Bird Conversations*.

When the soul attains perfection, the many higher qualities are seen in the One, and the One in the many ; for the soul then identifies itself with its innermost nature, which is one with the Supreme. As long as the soul identifies itself with external things, so long the One within remains unperceived by it.

See BIRD (great), BRAHMA, KARSHIPTA, MIRROR, PHANG, QUALITIES, SEASONS, SELF (supreme), UNION.

SINA OR INA, BRIDE OF TUNA :—

A symbol of matter in its primal aspect, and of the soul in its receptive capacity as the vehicle of Spirit (Tuna).

" For a full understanding of this very complicated myth (of Ina and Tuna) more information has been supplied by Mr. Gill. Ina means moon ; Ina-mae-aitu, the heroine of our story, means Ina-who-had-a-divine-lover, and she was the daughter of Kui, the blind. Tuna means eel."—MAX MÜLLER, *Contributions, etc.*, Vol. I. p. 5.

The moon is a symbol of the matter side of manifestation, and the lower nature of the soul, which is a product of ignorance and instinct (Kui, the blind). The divine lover is the incarnate Self—the Redeemer of the soul.

" It was early morning, and the golden beams of the rising sun were flooding the world with light. A maiden named Sina came out of her hut to go for her morning bath in a favourite pool in the stream."—KATE M. C. CLARK, *Maori Tales.*

This represents the dawn of manifestation and the golden age of early involution. Matter (Sina) becomes immersed in the river of life which flows to the lower planes.

" Sina took the head of the Eel-god and buried it near the sea shore, and she visited the place each day and wept as she thought of Tuna who had given his life for hers."—*Ibid.*

This signifies the commencement of evolution after the death of the Archetypal Man (Tuna). The Spirit is buried in the desire-mind (sea shore), and every incarnation (day) the soul or matter (Sina) comes into relation with it amid suffering and sorrow.

See ARC. MAN, COCOA-NUT, DAWN, EEL-GOD, HEAD, HODER, INCARNATION, INVOLUTION, MATTER, MOON, REDEEMER, RIVER OF LIFE, SHORE, SUN-RISING.

SINGERS, PIOUS :—

A symbol of the spiritual monads, or sparks, which descend from the plane of atma to inhabit human forms.

" The pious singers (the Maruts) have after their own mind shouted towards the giver of wealth, the great, the glorious Indra."—*Rig-Veda*, I. 6, 6.

The monads rejoicing in harmony and bliss on the highest planes, and full of spiritual energy, have determined of their own free-will to enter upon manifestation, that they may claim the treasure in heaven, the wealth of the Eternal Spirit (Indra).

" From yonder, O traveller (Indra), come hither, or from the light of heaven ; the singers all yearn for it."—*Ibid.*, V. 9.

The Higher Self passing through the cycle of life is called upon to raise the individual souls, and grant them wisdom and love,—the light of heaven,—which the egos yearn to possess.

" Whereupon were the foundations (of the earth) fastened ? Or who laid the corner-stone thereof ; when the morning stars sang together, and all the sons of God shouted for joy ? "—JOB xxxviii. 6, 7.

The Supreme questions the incarnate Self (Job) with the object of evolving in him knowledge of the soul-process of which he is outwardly ignorant. The Supreme points out that the lower nature (earth) is derived from the higher nature, and that within it is archetypal perfection (corner stone). Then the mental faculties (stars) in harmony awaited the dawn of the Self (sun), and with the spiritual monads (sons of God), were ready to manifest their energies.

See ATMA, CHILDREN OF EAST, DAWN, HARMONY, HYMN-SINGING, INDRA, JOB, LIGHT, MARUTS, MELODY, MONAD OF LIFE, MORNING STAR, MUSIC, SHEEP (lost), SONG, SONS OF GOD, SOUL (middle), STARS, STONE (corner), SUN, SUN-RISING, TREASURE, WEALTH, WILL.

SINTEAN FOLK :—

A symbol of higher qualities of the lower mind, as logic, analysis, synthesis, etc.

SI-OSIRI (SON OF OSIRIS) :—

A symbol of the Self incarnate,— the Christ-soul, Son of God (Osiris).

" Si-Osiri took his father to Amenti, and showed him that the poor man was highly honoured, while the rich man was in misery because of his evil deeds."— GRIFFITH, *Stories of the High Priests.*

The Christ-soul attains to a direct knowledge of the process underlying spiritual evolution and adjustment upon the higher planes. As the soul goes forth to gain experience on one level, so upon each succeeding level the account is squared, so to say,

with the result that each successive stage carries it to its karmically appointed place, relatively at least. This is no new idea. It is to be found underlying all religions ; and the sectarian who looks for compensation in heaven or hell is feeling crudely and unintelligently the truth that we sow here that which we reap the fruits of upon entering the next state of being.

See AMENTI, JOB, KARMA, LAZARUS, PURGATORY, SEED (good), SHENIT, STRIDES (soul).

SIRENS, OR GANDHARVAS :—

A symbol of Devas of harmony on the fourth sub-plane of the buddhic plane. These become tempters as the soul rises above their level.

See ANGELS, BUTES, COLCHIS, DEVAS, GANDHARVAS, HEAVENLY NYMPHS.

SIRIUS, THE DOG-STAR, SURA :—

A symbol of the fixed will in concentration through the steadying of the mind. Until the mind is stilled from the surgings of desire, there is no fixity of purpose.

" The Dog Sirius (Sura) is another watchman of the heavens ; but he is fixed in one place, at the bridge Kinvat, keeping guard over the Abyss Dusakh out of which Ahriman comes."—*Zoroastrian System*, J. F. CLARKE, *Ten Religions.*

The " Dog Sirius " at the " bridge " of the higher mind represents power, tenacity and will,—the mind as recorder and agent of karma, seated in the causal-body, and guarding the soul from desire so far as the soul is emancipated from the lower nature.

See AHRIMAN, BRIDGE (kinvat), CAUSAL-BODY, DOG-STAR, DUSAKH, KARMA, STARS, WILL.

SĪTĀ, WIFE OF RĀMA :—

A symbol of the buddhic emotion-nature which is allied with the incarnate Higher Self (Rāma).

" Sītā enters the flames of the pyre, invoking Agni ; upon which all the gods with the old king Dasaratha (father of Rāma) appear, and reveal to Rāma his divine nature, telling him that he is Nārāyana, and that Sītā is Lakshmi."— MON. WILLIAMS, *Indian Wisdom*, p. 360.

The buddhic emotion-nature becomes transmuted, and the consciousness rises to the buddhic plane. The

ideals (gods) are then energised, while the Divine Father and Son become One Truth-Reality on the plane of atma, and the principle of Buddhi is their manifesting life.

See ERECTHEUS, FIRE, FURROW, HANUMAN, LAKSHMI, LANKA, NĀRĀ-YANA, RĀMA.

SITIVISA, PLANET SATURN :—
See SATURN.

SITTING DOWN OF PEOPLE :—

A symbol of acquiescence of mind to truth. The attitude in which spiritual instruction can be imparted to the qualities by the indwelling Self.

" This is the meaning which I find in the words of Jesus when he said to his disciples, ' Make the men sit down (JOHN vi. 10). It is the change from the active and restless to the receptive and quiet state, from the condition in which all the life was flowing outward in eager self-assertion, to the other condition in which the life was being influenced, that is, being flowed upon by the richer power which came forth from him."—PHILLIPS BROOKS, Serm., *Make the Men Sit Down.*

See FEEDING FOUR THOUSAND, PEOPLE, QUALITIES.

SITTING DOWN OF JESUS :—

A symbol of the Divine nature dominant over the lower.

" And he sat down, and called the twelve ; and he saith unto them, If any man would be first, he shall be last of all and minister of all."—MARK ix. 35.

This relates to the competition of the qualities to be first in order. Christ's rebuke is administered when He is " seated," and it is by the Higher nature *sitting in judgment* upon the lower, and pointing out faults, that the warring and confusion of the latter is at length put a stop to.

" He spoke to them sitting and not standing, for they could not have understood Him had he appeared in His own majesty."—JEROME.

See DISCIPLES, JUDGMENT AND JUSTICE, MOUNTAIN.

SIVA, GOD :—

A symbol of the Divine energy in the evolution of the universe and of the soul. The producer of forms, and their destroyer, that progress may ensue.

" Siva is *Mahâkâla*, endless time, which begets and devours all things. As pro-

creator, his symbols are the bull and the phallus, as well as the moon, which serves for his diadem."—BARTH, *Religions of India*, p. 164.

"According to the teaching of Hinduism, death is not death in the sense of passing into non-existence, but simply a change into a new form of life. He who destroys, therefore, causes beings to assume new phases of existence,—the Destroyer is really a re-Creator; Hence the name Siva, the Bright or Happy One, is given to him."—WILKINS, *Hindu Mythology*, p. 263.

Like Jehovah, Siva is sometimes described as a cruel and revengeful Deity, but this only symbolises the opposition of good to evil, and the destruction of the lower desires and passions which precedes the awakenment of the higher qualities.

See ANGER OF GOD, BULL, DEATH, DHRISTA, DURGA, EVOLUTION, FORMS, JEHOVAH, MOTHER, WRATH OF GOD.

SIX, NUMBER :—

A symbol of accomplishment of growth or purpose ;—the number which limits and serves to usher in the seventh, that of perfection. It signifies completion of a period of activity,—as six days, six hours, six signs, six months, six seasons, six years.

" Now in the sixth month (of Elisabeth) the angel Gabriel was sent from God unto . . . Nazareth, to a virgin ; . . . and the virgin's name was Mary."— LUKE i. 26, 27.

Now when the completion of the moral nature (John) was accomplished, the inner messenger (angel) of intuition was enabled to acquaint the soul of the spiritual results which were to follow ethical rule. The messenger came to the centre of progression (Nazareth) in the soul, and to the purified lower nature (Mary) which is " virgin," i.e. unfructified by mind (man), but which can be fructified by the Holy Spirit.

" The reason why six signifies what is complete to the end, is because three has that signification, and six is double that number, and a number doubled has the same signification as the simple number." —SWEDENBORG, *Apoc. Rev.*, n. 489.

" The number six is perfect, because it is the first number which is made up of its several parts, that is, its sixth, its third and its half, which are 1, 2 and 3, and these added together become 6. But because we transcend all this knowledge, by advancing through the loftiness

of Holy Scripture, we there find the reason why the numbers 6, 7, 10 and 1,000 are perfect. For the number six is perfect in Holy Scripture, because in the beginning of the world God completed on the sixth day those works which He began on the first. The number seven is perfect therein, because every good work is performed with seven virtues through the Spirit, in order that both faith and works may be perfected at the same time. The number ten is perfect therein, because the Law is included in ten precepts. . . . In a denary three are joined to seven."— ST. GREGORY, *Morals on the Book of Job*, Vol. III. p. 691.

" It may perhaps appear curious that the number six should occur so often in Ainu folk-lore, but it may be now, once for all, noted that we find it constantly recurring as the numerical exponent of perfection, and is regarded by the people as the sacred number. We often find it so appearing in their legends."—J. BATCHELOR, *The Ainu, etc.*, p. 305.

See ADAMAS (lower), DAYS, MONAD OF LIFE, SATURDAY, SEASONS (six), SEEDS OF SIX, VIRGIN MARY, WEEK.

SIXTH HOUR FOR CRUCIFIXION OF JESUS :—

A symbol of completion of the evolution of the soul (Jesus) on the lower planes, prior to final perfection at the crossing over (crucifixion) of the consciousness.

" It was about the sixth hour. . . . Then therefore Pilate delivered him unto them to be crucified."—JOHN xix. 14, 16.

The period corresponds to the sixth Round, which is the age during which most souls will accomplish their evolution. It is the point that is reached by the soul when the combination of circumstances symbolically related in the trial of Jesus takes place. It is the worldly, unstable mind (Pilate) that delivers the Christ-soul to the tormenting lower qualities in the final struggle for liberation.

" But why at the sixth hour ? Because at the sixth age of the world. In the Gospel, count up as an hour each, the first age from Adam to Noah ; the second, from Noah to Abraham ; the third, from Abraham to David ; the fourth, from David to the removing to Babylon ; the fifth, from the removing to Babylon to the baptism of John ; thence is the sixth being enacted."— AUGUSTINE, *Gospel of John*, Vol. I. p. 214.

See ANTHRŌPOS, CRUCIFIXION OF JESUS, FATE SPHERE, HOUR (mid-day), IABRAOTH, I E O U, LIBRA, PILATE, RACES, ROUND.

SKADE :—

A symbol of Divine Law.

SKAITYA FLY, DEATH-DEAL-
ING :—

A symbol of the critical intellect
which dispels error and illusion.

SKANDHAS, FIVE :—

Symbols of the five elemental
bodies or vestures of the soul, as
instruments for the manifestation
of spirit.

"Every being is composed of five
constituent elements called Skandhas,
which have their source in Upādāna,
and are continually combining, dissolving,
and recombining, viz. (1) Form (rupa),
i.e. the organised body.   (2) Sensation
(vedanā) of pain or pleasure, or of neither,
arising from contact of eye, ear, etc.
with external objects. (3) Perception
(sanna) of ideas through the same sixfold
contact.   (4) Aggregate of formations
(samkhāra), i.e. combination of properties
or faculties or mental tendencies, fifty-
two in number, forming individual character and derived from previous existences.
(5) Consciousness (vinnāna) or thought.
This fifth is the most important. It is
the only soul recognised by Buddhists.
Theoretically it perishes with the other
Skandhas, but practically is continued,
since its exact counterpart is reproduced
in a new body."—Mon. Williams,
Buddhism, p. 109.

The bodies are taken in their
receptive aspects towards the energies
upon the several planes. Placing them
in their proper order, the five bodies
are,—

        Samkhāra = Buddhic ;
        Vinnāna = Causal ;
        Sanna   = Mental ;
        Vedanā   = Astral ;
        Rūpa   = Physical.

The Samkhāra is described as the
potential higher causal-body containing the prototypes of all things and
qualities that have to be evolved on
the planes below. These prototypes
are derived from the experience of
previous life-cycles. They are perfect
and complete $(5 + 2 = 7)$, and guide
the formation of the character of the
units in the phenomenal world. The
Vinnāna represents the causal-body
on the higher mental plane, the
seat of the higher consciousness of
humanity. The causal-body persists
throughout the cycle, and periodically
reproduces the transitory lower bodies
at each incarnation. The Sanna is
the mental body which gives perception of ideas formed through vibrations from the lower activities. The
Vedanā is the astral body of the
desires, feelings, and lower emotions
which are aroused by the senses.
The Rūpa is the physical body by
means of which action is effected.

See Castes, Causal-body, Con-
sciousness, Elements (five), Five,
Ignorance, Pranas, Prototypes,
Samkhāra, Sense organs, Vestures.

SKIN OF HUMAN BODY :—

A symbol of the outer envelope of
the soul, which is the means of
functioning upon the astral or
physical plane.

"The interior man is ' clothed with skin
and flesh ' (Job x. 9), since wherein it is
raised up to things above, it is straightly
blockaded with the besieging of fleshly
motions. . . . 'And hast fenced me with
bones and sinews.' With flesh and skin
we are clothed, but we are ' fenced with
bones and sinews,' in that though we
receive a shock by temptation assaulting
us from without, yet the hand of the
Creator strengthens us within, that we
should not be shattered. And so by the
promptings of the flesh, He abases us in
respect of His gifts, but by the bones of
virtue He strengthens us against temptations."—St. Gregory, Morals on the
Book of Job, Vol. I. p. 552.

See Bones, Flaying of man, Flesh,
Job, Prometheus.

SKINS AS CLOTHING :—

Symbolic of the mental, astral,
or physical sheaths of the soul.

"And the Lord God made for Adam
and for his wife coats of skins, and
clothed them."—Gen. iii. 21.

And the Divine Law caused the
mental and astral bodies to be formed
for the soul.

See Adam (lower), Eve, Redeemer,
Vestures.

SKINS OF ANIMALS :—

A symbol of the astro-physical
forms of the lower animals or man.

"Fuh-he's dress consisted of the skins
of animals, his drink, their blood."—
Chinese Mythology, Kidd, China.

The Logos working from within
produced the animal creation. The
"dress of animals' skins" refers to
the passing on of the forms of the
brute kingdom to mankind. The

"blood" signifies the transmitted physical vitality which is also largely relative to the physical plane. The type-forms are worked up to the "fittest" in the animal kingdom according to the measure of the astrophysical life which is expressed. This refers in the most man-like types, however, only to the accommodation of the *astral man* type-form, or lunar pitri, which is introduced to the physical evolution at an advanced stage. This introduction comes as a tendency to human form in a series of anthropoid forms which eventuate in the human type.

"The main conclusion here arrived at is that man is descended from some less highly organised form. The grounds upon which this conclusion rests will never be shaken, for the close similarity between man and the lower animals in embryonic development, as well as in innumerable points of structure and constitution, both of high and of the most trifling importance,—the rudiments which he retains, and the abnormal reversions to which he is occasionally liable,—are facts which cannot be disputed. They have long been known, but until recently they told us nothing with respect to the origin of man. Now when viewed by the light of our knowledge of the whole organic world, their meaning is unmistakable. The great principle of evolution stands up clear and firm, when these groups of facts are considered in connection with others, such as the mutual affinities of the members of the same group, their geographical distribution in past and present times, and their geological succession. It is incredible that all these facts should speak falsely."—C. DARWIN, *Descent of Man*, Summary.

See ARC. MAN, EVOLUTION, FUH-HE, MAN (born), MAN CRAWLED, METEMPSYCHOSIS, MONAD OF FORM, NEPHILIM, PITRIS (lunar), SONS OF GOD, SUKUNA.

SKULL :—

A symbol of the emptiness of the lower affections and concepts if taken as an end in themselves, rather than a means of progress.

See GOLGOTHA.

SKY, OR SKIES :—

A symbol of the buddhic plane or principle.

"When he made firm the skies above : When the fountains of the deep became strong."—PROV. viii. 28.

When the buddhic principle was fashioned or consolidated as a plane of being : When the higher desires became active for reflection below.

"I advance upon my feet, I become master of my vine, I sail over the sky which formeth the division betwixt heaven and earth."—BUDGE, *Book of the Dead*, Ch. LXXXV.

Through the physical activities the soul advances ; it becomes master of its evolving life. It passes upward to the buddhic plane for further development, whereby the buddhic plane is intermediate between the higher nature and the lower.

See ANU, BUDDHIC PLANE, CEILING, CHIP, COW (spotted), FEET, FIRMAMENT, FOUNTAIN, HEAVEN AND EARTH, QUATERNARY, VINE, ZENITH.

SLAUGHTER OF ENEMIES :

A symbol of the subdual and dissipation of the passions, desires, and illusions of the lower nature, which are the foes of the Higher Self.

"Thus saith the Lord God of Israel ; Behold, . . . I myself will fight against you (Zedikiah) with an outstretched hand and with a strong arm, even in anger, and in fury, and in great wrath. And I will smite the inhabitants of this city, both man and beast : they shall die of a great pestilence."—JER. xxi. 4–6.

"Surely thou wilt slay the wicked, O God : depart from me therefore, ye bloody men. For they speak against thee wickedly, and thine enemies take thy name in vain. Do not I hate them, O Lord, that hate thee ? and am not I grieved with those that rise up against thee ? I hate them with perfect hatred : I count them mine enemies."—Ps. xxxix. 19–22.

These imprecatory passages refer to the lower impulses of the natural man. The lower qualities must be opposed and destroyed, for they are the enemies of the higher nature. The voice of God in the conscience is full of wrath and fury against wrongdoing. Every evil quality has to be overcome and slaughtered.

"It is possible to bring down to the earth the perfect standards of the heavens, to stop thinking about safety and comfort and salvation altogether, and to be splendidly inspired with the consciousness that we are soldiers under God ; to think of our own sins not as the things which are going to condemn us to eternal torture, but as the enemies of Him, the hindrances that stand in the way of His victorious designs ; to see their badness not in their consequences, but in their nature, not in their quantity but in their quality ; and so to bring to bear upon the very least of them the intense hatred and intolerance which the very nature of sin must always excite in him who has attained a true passion for holiness. So it is possible for us to deal with every sin, little or great, that we discover in our hearts. To count it God's enemy and to fight it with all His purity and strength ; that is what it means for us that our sword should be bathed in heaven ! (Is. xxxiv. 5)."—PHILLIPS BROOKS, Serm., *The Sword Bathed*, etc.

See ANGER OF GOD, ARROWS, BATTLE, CONFLICT, CONSCIENCE, DURGA, EGYP-TIANS, ENEMIES OF GOD, GOATS, KILLING-OUT, PESTILENCE, SWORD, TONGUES, WAR, WRATH OF GOD.

SLAVERY :—

A symbol of subjection to the lower nature with its desires, passions, and sensations.

See BONDAGE, CAPTIVITY, SUFFERING.

SLEEP :—

A symbol of a state of oblivion to spiritual enlightenment ; or the reverse,—a state of unconsciousness of external things. Pralaya.

See CUPID, LIGHT-WORLD, SELENE.

SLEEP AND WAKING :—

Symbols of earth-life and deva-chanic life in relation to spirit.

" Our birth is but a sleep and a for-getting ; The soul that rises with us, our life's star, Hath had elsewhere its setting, And cometh from afar."—WORDSWORTH.

" True waking is a true rising up from the body, not with a body."—PLOTINUS, *Enn.*, III. 6, 6.

" And what is it that the touch of Christ does for us but to awaken the true man within us, the spiritual man who lies slumbering under the spell of the enchant-ment of flesh and sense."—R. J. CAMP-BELL, Serm., *The Kenosis, etc.*

See DAY AND NIGHT, JOB, RESUR-RECTION, SELF.

SLEEPING AND WAKING, THE FOUR STATES OF THE SOUL :—

Symbolic of the states of con-sciousness in the physical (waking state), astro-mental (dream sleep), causal (deep sleep), and buddhic (blissful sleep) bodies.

" The Vaisvânara that exists in a waking condition, recognising external objects, with seven limbs and nineteen mouths, enjoying that which is material, is his first quarter " (*Mand. Upanishad,*

III).—DEUSSEN, *Philosophy of the Upani-shads*, trans. p. 300.

The spiritual ego in the physical body is conscious of the vibrations of sensation from the external world. He is possessed of the five planes and of the individuality and the person-ality (seven limbs) ; also of the faculties of perception, expression, knowledge and action.

" When now he falls asleep, he takes from this all-comprehending universe the timber, cuts it down, and himself builds up of it his own light, by virtue of his own brilliance ; when therefore he sleeps this spirit serves as light for itself " (*Brihad. Upanishad*, IV. 3, 9).—*Ibid.*, p. 302.

After physical death the ego per-ceives no external world, but he takes from the manifold life, activities and forms of the astral plane (wood) and builds up for himself an environment of imagination (dream-sleep) to be his own world of light and thought, desire and joy.

" Then that god enjoys greatness, inasmuch as he sees yet again that which was seen here and there, hears yet again things heard here and there, perceives again and again in detail that which was perceived in detail in its surroundings of place and circumstance ; the seen and the unseen . . . as the whole he views it " (*Prasna Upanishad*, IV. 5).—*Ibid.*, p. 304.

The ego in the *post-mortem* state is the centre of a world of attractive memories, and with these the con-sciousness is filled, so that it seems to be the whole of things.

" Just as there hovers in space, a hawk or an eagle, after it has circled round, folds its wings wearied, and drops to the ground, so also the spirit hastens to that state in which fallen asleep it no longer experiences any desires nor sees any dream image " (*Brihad. Upanishad,* IV. 3).—*Ibid.*, p. 306.

The ego after exhausting the astro-mental activities of the " dream sleep " leaves the astral body to decay, and passes into the state of consciousness called " deep sleep " (*sushupti*).

" That is its real form, in which it is exalted above desire, free from evil and is fearless. For just as a man, embraced by a beloved wife, has no consciousness of outer and inner, so also the spirit embraced by the Self consisting of know-ledge (i.e. by Brahman) has no conscious-ness of outer and inner. That is his real form, in which desire has been laid to rest " (*Brihad. Upanishad*, IV. 19).—*Ibid.*, p. 306.

The causal-body is the real form of the manifesting ego, and in it the consciousness of " dreamless sleep " is exalted above the desires and imperfections of the lower planes. The consciousness here perceives the truth and becomes one with the Higher Self on the higher mental plane in devachan.

" Knowing neither within nor without nor yet on the two sides, nor again consisting throughout of knowledge, neither known nor unknown,—invisible, intangible, incomprehensible, indescribable, unthinkable, inexpressible, founded solely on the certainty of its own self, effacing the entire expanse of the universe, tranquil, blissful, timeless,—that is the fourth quarter, that is the atman, that we must know " (Mând. Upanishad, VII).--Phil. of Upanishads, p. 310.

The spiritual ego, rising above the mental plane, manifests in the world-soul or the causal-body on the buddhic plane (fourth quarter) of the quaternary. The state of consciousness at this high level, called the " blissful sleep " (turîya), is inconceivable to the lower mind and negatives all its conceptions ; its fullness of content must transcend all that pertains to the phenomenal universe and the cycle of time.

" The matter of the astral plane is much more plastic and obedient to imagination and desire than that of the gross earth. . . . In this condition of being people are well aware that they have quitted the earth life and have passed through the change spoken of here as death, but conceive themselves translated to another world filled with the same interests and occupations as those they have quitted, although these are divorced completely from the strained and painful aspects they have worn down here. The inhabitants of this region create for themselves dwellings, churches, entertainments, music and instruments, and social surroundings of all sorts, in the midst of which they pass their time in a state of placid contentment." —A. P. SINNETT, Growth of the Soul, p. 191.

See ASTRAL, ATMAN, BLISS, BRAHMA, BUDDHIC PLANE, DEVACHAN, GATHA (kam.), GATHA (ush.), HARAVAITI, ILLUSION, KAMA, MEADOW OF HADES, NIGHTS (three), NIRVANA, PARADISE (lower), SMAM, SVARGA-WORLD, TIME, UNION, VAISVÂNARA, WORLDS (five).

SLEIPNER, ODIN'S HORSE :—
A symbol of the higher mind.
See HERMOD.

SLIME FOR MORTAR :—
Symbolic of craft for affection.
See BRICK FOR STONE, MORTAR.

SMAM, A POOL IN THE THIRD COMPARTMENT OF SEKHET-HETEPET :—
A symbol of a state of consciousness on the third sub-plane of the buddhic plane.

" O Smam, I have come into thee. My heart watcheth, my head is equipped with the white crown."—BUDGE, Book of the Dead, Ch. CX.

This refers to the consummation of life, when final liberation is reached by the soul. The emotion-principle articulates the whispers of the Spirit within, and the higher mind attains the summit of its powers in perfection.

See CONSUMMATION, CROWN (Osiris), HEART, LIBERATION, POOLS, UNION.

SMELLING :—
A symbol of apprehension or discrimination of what is beneath. Intelligence directed downwards
See NOSE, SAVOUR.

SMINTHIUS :—
A symbol of the Omnipotent Being.
See TENEDOS.

SMOKE AND VAPOUR :—
Symbolic of ignorance and of the mists of illusion obscuring the truth. Or, in a reverse sense, the symbols may indicate the " fire " of Divine love and truth.

" Smoke signifies divine truth in ultimates, because fire from which smoke issues signifies love. In an opposite sense, smoke signifies falses darkening the truth."—SWEDENBORG, Apoc. Rev., n. 674, 422.

" According to you (Manichaeans) the First Man was armed against smoke with air, and against darkness with light. So it appears that smoke and darkness are bad. . . . The other three again are good." — AUGUSTINE, Works, Vol. V. p. 148.

The First Logos dispels error (smoke) with mind (air) ; and ignorance (darkness) with light (truth). Fire (spirit), air, and light signify good principles.

See FIRE OF AHRIMAN, VAPOUR AND SMOKE.

SNÂTAKA :—
A symbol of the incarnating ego, or spiritual monad, who descends

into the forms to gain experience as a responsible being, and who becomes individualised on the higher mental plane.

"Let him (a Snātaka) walk here on earth, bringing his dress, speech and thoughts to a conformity with his age, his occupation, his wealth, his sacred learning, and his race."—*Laws of Manu*, IV. 18.

Let the incarnating ego progress through the stages of the soul's experience upon the lower planes (earth), making his opinions (dress), his outer expression (speech), and his inner nature or character (thoughts) accord with his stage of growth (age), his self-discipline (occupation), his mental endowments (wealth), his religious intuitions (sacred learning), and his social obligations (race).

See ANCHORITE, ASCETIC, ASRAMAS, CLOTHING, EARTH, EXPERIENCE, FOREST, FRAVASHIS, HERMIT, HOUSEHOLDER, INCARNATION OF SOULS, MONAD OF LIFE, ORDERS, SACRED TEXT, SPEECH, STRIDES OF SOUL, WALKING DAY BY DAY, WEALTH.

SNOW, ICE, FROST :—

Symbols of truth latent or unexpressed. Truth (water) congealed.

"Unto the material world the evil of winter will come ; consequently much driving snow will fall on the highest mountains and their summits."—*Vendidad*, II.

In this descent of the life-wave to the astral and physical globes, the upper globes become obscured to the lower consciousness, so that the truth of buddhi becomes latent (snow) as the lower globes are informed through evolution from below upward.

See FROST, ICE, KARSHVARES, PLANETARY CHAIN, ROOT-RACES, ROUND, SABBATH, SUMMER, WINTER.

SODOM AND EGYPT :—

Symbols of the lower planes, or lower nature.

"By Sodom is signified the love of dominion grounded in self-love ; and by Egypt is signified the love of rule grounded in the pride of self-derived intelligence."—SWEDENBORG, *Apoc. Rev.*, n. 502.

See CRUCIFIXION OF CHRIST (Rev.), EGYPT (lower), LOT.

SOLDIERS :—

A symbol of striving mental qualities, good or bad, which act under guidance.

"Suffer hardship with me, as a good soldier of Christ Jesus. No soldier on service entangleth himself in the affairs of this life ; that he may please him who enrolleth him as a soldier."—2 TIM. ii. 3, 4.

The mind is exhorted to bear suffering patiently in striving for truth and righteousness. No mental quality (soldier) in the service of the ideal attaches itself to the things of the lower nature, but faithfully strives for the ideal which evoked it and employed it.

"Then the soldiers of the governor took Jesus into the palace, and gathered unto him the whole band."—MAT. xxvii. 27.

Then the lower mental qualities of an aggressive order on the side of worldly-mindedness (governor), proceed to disrupt the soul in an attempt to crush out the Higher from it. The disruptive process is the falling away of the lower from the Higher, which is symbolised in the higher correspondencies of the mocking, robing, and crowning, being degraded.

"Mark how the warfare which we have to wage is the same as the priestly service which we have to render. The conflict is with our own sin and evil ; the sacrifice we have to offer is ourselves. As soldiers, we have to fight against our selfish desires and manifold imperfections ; as priests, we have to lay our whole being on His altar. The task is the same under either emblem. And we have a conflict to wage in the world, and in the world we have a priestly work to do, and these are the same."—A. MACLAREN, *Sermons 3rd Series*, p. 351.

See ARMY, BERSERKS, CENTURION HOSTS, ROMAN SOLDIER, TRIAL, WARRIORS.

SOMA-JUICE, OR SAP :—

A symbol of the Divine Life, or love of righteousness and truth, upspringing in the soul. The "sap" of the "Tree of Life," is the same as the "blood of Christ," or the "wine" of the sacrament.

"The gods drank of Soma and became immortal ; men will become so when they in turn shall drink of him with Yama in the abode of the blessed."—BARTH, *Religions of India*, p. 11.

"That in you which protests against the evil you do is already one with God.

I love to call it Christ, for it is Christ. Christ is the sap of the tree of humanity, the force whereby we utter the divine idea that we are."—R. J. CAMPBELL, Serm., *Coming to the True Self.*

"King Suddhodana drank the soma-juice as enjoined by the Veda, in the heartfelt self-produced happiness of perfect calm."—*Buddha-Karita,* Bk. II. 37.

The Soul imbibes the spirit of Life as the "Word of God," or utterance of the Supreme direct. This "happiness, etc." signifies the perfect serenity which proceeds from the buddhic nature, the Self being alone within Itself.

"By Soma the Adityas are strong; by Soma the earth is great, and Soma is placed in the midst of the stars. When they crush the plant, he who drinks regards it as Soma. Of him whom the priests regard as Soma (the moon) no one drinks."—MUIR, *O. S. T.,* V. 271.

Through the Divine Life the aspects of the Self are energised, and the lower nature is utilised; and the Christ is centred in the midst of the mental qualities (stars). When the higher emotions are aroused, the soul that acquires them regards them as Divine. Of the Divine Life inverted as desire on the astro-mental plane, the qualities are not nourished.

"Into the heaven hath he placed the Sun, and Soma upon the rock. Soma on the rock because Soma is in the mountains."—*Sata. Bráh.* III. 3, 4, 7.

The higher planes are the abode of the Self, and the involved Divine Life is beneath. The Divine Life is involved "from the foundation of the world," because it has to evolve upward in the aspirations (mountains). The "rock" is Christ.

See ADITYAS, ATONEMENT, BLOOD, BLOOD OF THE LAMB, EARTH, EVOLUTION, FOOD AS GOD, GODS, HOMA-JUICE, HORSE SACRIFICE, MOON, MOUNTAINS, PARGANYA, PRAGÂPATI RELAXED, PRIEST, ROCK, SACRAMENT, SACRIFICE, SAP, STARS, SUDDHODANA, SUN, TREE OF LIFE, VEDA, WINE, WORD OF GOD, YAMA.

SOMA PLANT OR TREE :—

A symbol of the Divine Life or "Tree of Life" in the soul, which has its rise in the Absolute, and extends through all planes.

"The Chândogya Up. (8, 5, 3) and the Kaushîtaki Up. (1, 3) have a knowledge of 'the fig-tree which distils the soma,'

and 'the tree of life,' of the celestial world."—BARTH, *Religions of India,* p. 263.

"Agni and Soma (as spiritual conceptions) were invested with a subtle and complicated symbolism; they were impregnated, so to speak, with all the mystic virtue of sacrifice; their empire was extended far beyond the world of sense, and they were conceived as cosmic agents and universal principles."—*Ibid.,* p. 9.

"To sacrifice is (also) to stir up, actually to beget, two divinities of the first rank, the two principles of life, Agni and Soma."—*Ibid.,* p. 36.

Agni represents the force-aspect of the Self, and *Soma* the life-aspect, and these are aroused in the soul as the soul aspires in offering up the lower for the higher.

See AGNI, FIG-TREE, HOMA-TREE, PLANTS, SACRIFICE, TREE OF LIFE, VINE, VRITRA.

SOMA, AS THE MOON :—

A symbol of the Divine Life reflected upon the astral plane as desire which is inverted love.

"Fire proceeds from him (Purusha), and the sun is the fuel of that fire. From the moon proceeds the cloud-god Parjanya; from the cloud-god the plants upon the earth; from these the germ of life. Thus the various living things issue out of Purusha."—*Mundaka Upanishad,* II.

"*Soma,* the Moon, the progenitor of the lunar race, who reigned at Hastinâpur, was the child of the Rishi *Atri*" (*Mahâ-bhârata*).—MON. WILLIAMS, *Indian Wisdom,* p. 376.

"The moon is (as in *Rig-veda,* X. 85, 5) the soma cup of the gods, which is alternately drained by them and again filled" (*Chând.* V. 10, 4).—DEUSSEN, *Phil. of Upanishads,* p. 218.

Life-energy (fire) proceeds from the Supreme Spirit, and the Higher Self (sun) conditions and directs that energy. From the life on the astral plane (moon) the Divine Life on the buddhic plane is aroused, and this Life causes the lower emotions (plants) to develop and also to receive the germs of the higher qualities. Thus the various qualities and forms of life issue forth from the Supreme.

The astral life-energy (Soma the moon) from which proceed the desire-nature and the personality that ruled the lower mind (Hastinâ-pur), was the product of the nascent soul (Atri).

The life of the astral plane (moon produces the lower qualities which become transmuted into the higher qualities (gods), leaving no lower qualities. This requires the process to be repeated ; and so on alternately.

"Soma is the husband of the Nakshatras, the constellations of the lunar zodiac."—BARTH, *Religions of India*, p. 42.

The Divine life is, as it were, the Husbandman who sows the seed of the higher qualities in the astral or desire-nature which has been developed on the lunar planetary chain of globes.

See ASTRAL PLANE, ATRI, CLOUD, CUP, EARTH, EVOLUTION, FIRE, GERMS, GODS, HUSBANDMAN, LUNAR CHAIN, MOON (solar), PARGANYA, PITRIS (lunar), PLANTS, PURUSHA, SEED, SELENE, SUN.

SON OF GOD, FIRST-BORN :—

A symbol of the Second Logos or Higher Self,—the first emanation from the Father, the Absolute, or the First Logos.

"Who is the image of the invisible God, the first-born of all creation ; for in him were all things created, in the heavens and upon the earth."—COL. i. 15, 16.

"Whosoever shall confess that Jesus is the Son of God, God abideth in him and he in God."—1 JOHN iv. 15.

"And who is he that overcometh the world, but he that believeth that Jesus is the Son of God ? This is he that came by water and blood, even Jesus Christ." —1 JOHN v. 5, 6.

"God gave unto us eternal life, and this life is in his Son. He that hath the Son hath the life ; he that hath not the Son of God hath not the life."—1 JOHN v. 11, 12.

"Jesus" is here a symbol of the Higher Self incarnate in humanity. "Jesus," the Ideal of love and truth is identified with the indwelling Self ; and the mind which seeks to conform to the Ideal has in it the eternal life of the Spirit. The Ideal (Jesus) entered the mind by Truth (water) and Life (blood), that the mind might turn entirely to God.

"The eternal Birth or generation of the Son or Divine Word. This Birth is in its first, or Cosmic sense, the welling forth of the Spirit of Life from the Divine Abyss of the unconditional Godhead. 'From our proper Source, that is to say, from the Father and all that which lives in Him, there shines,' says Ruysbroeck, 'an eternal Ray, the which is the Birth of the Son.' It is of this perpetual genera-

tion of the Word that Meister Eckhart speaks, when he says in his Christmas sermon, 'We are celebrating the feast of the Eternal Birth which God the Father has borne and *never ceases to bear* in all Eternity ; whilst this birth also comes to pass in time and in human nature.' . . . Here in a few words the two-fold character of this Mystic Birth is exhibited. The interest is suddenly deflected from its Cosmic to its personal aspect ; and the individual is reminded that in him, no less than in the Archetypal Universe, real life must be born if real life is to be lived. Since the soul, according to mystic principles, can only perceive Reality in proportion as she is real, know God by becoming God-like, it is clear that this birth is the initial necessity."—E. UNDERHILL, *Mysticism*, p. 146.

"The Son of God is indeed our Lord Jesus Christ, but he is also your own true self, your higher self, your unfettered self, whose angel doth ' alway behold the face of the Father.' This is a truth which is not very easy to explain in terms of ordinary everyday experience, but once it is grasped it sheds a wonderful light upon some of the deepest problems of existence. . . . That of you which enters into your field of consciousness at any one time is but a small portion of the real you. You are like an island in the ocean, which is really the top of a mountain that may be five miles deep, and whose base is one with all the land in the world. Christ is the ocean bed at the base of the island of your soul. . . . The fundamental fact in you, the fact without which there would not be a *you*, is the eternal Son of God. What is needed now in order that God's purpose may be fulfilled in you is that that eternal Son, that indestructible divine self, should arise in his strength within your soul and break the bonds that bind you to everything that you feel to be unworthy of your kinship to the Father of love and light." —R. J. CAMPBELL, Serm., *The Freedom of the Son of God.*

"Only in the human soul is God present in God-like fashion. The soul is therefore God's resting-place in which the temporal and the eternal are allied. Our spirit is the divine spark within us, wherein is completed the alliance of God and the soul. As God contains all things in Himself, so it is in our soul ; the soul is the microcosmos in which all things are contained and are led back to God. Therefore, there is no difference between the Son of God and the soul" (*Eckhart of Strasburg*).—PFLEIDERER, *Develop. of Christianity*, p. 152.

See ARC. MAN, ATMAN, BIRTH OF JESUS, BIRTH CEREMONIES, BLOOD, CHRIST, COSMOS, CREATION, DISK, FIRST-BORN SON, GOD, HEAVEN AND EARTH, HIGHER AND LOWER SELVES, HOKHMAH, HORBEHUDTI, IMAGE, IN-

CARNATION, JESUS (Son of God), MACROCOSM, MICROCOSM, MONAD, SACRAMENT, TRINITY, WATER, WORLD.

SON OF MAN :—

A symbol of the soul in the stage of being made perfect, wherein the lower nature is being purified finally by the Higher. It represents a soul not yet completely evolved and perfected, for the perfect soul is a Son of God. "Son of man" means son of mind, i.e. the manifesting spiritual ego as an evolved product, or "child," of the "natural man," or mind, while the ego remains attached to the mind, and its manifestation is limited by the lower conditions. When the natural man is purified and transmuted, then the spiritual ego is fully manifest and again becomes "Son of God" as it was before its descent into matter.

"What is man, that thou art mindful of him ? and the son of man, that thou visitest him ? For thou hast made him but little lower than God, and crownest him with glory and honour. Thou madest him to have dominion over the works of thy hands ; thou hast put all things under his feet."—Ps. viii. 4–6.

"Let thy hand be upon the man of thy right hand, upon the son of man whom thou madest strong for thyself."—Ps. lxxx. 17.

These texts refer to the Son of man of the cycle of *involution*, the Self born on the mental plane, and become the Archetypal Man having dominion over all things of the soul life.

"The Son of man, the Lord from Heaven, as he was variously called, was the *divine root or essence of human nature in general* as well as the strong deliverer which was to come."—R. J. CAMPBELL, Serm., *The Eternal Self.*

"Representing the soul as having sprung from the *primitive man*, Mani interpreted in this sense the biblical name, 'Son of man.'"—NEANDER, *Church History*, Vol. II. p. 214.

"And he said unto me, Son of man, go, get thee unto the house of Israel, and speak with my words unto them. For thou art not sent to a people of a strange speech and of a hard language, but to the house of Israel."—EZEK. iii. 4, 5.

The spiritual ego or mind (Son of man) expresses "God's words" in the conscience to disciplined qualities (Israel), but cannot do so to undisciplined qualities whose expression is hard and strange to spiritual influ-

ences. God can send the conscience only to those who are sufficiently progressed to be able to hear the Divine voice within.

See AMENI, ARC. MAN, CHILD, CONSCIENCE, FOXES, HORBEHUDTI, INVOLUTION, ISRAELITES, JESUS (son of man), LANGUAGE, MAN (born), MAN (natural), PAMYLES, RANSOM, SELF, SERPENT (brazen), SOUL, SPEECH, VOICE OF GOD.

SONG :—

A symbol of aspiration through harmonising of the qualities, and raising the mind towards wisdom and love.

"Yet the Lord will command his loving-kindness in the daytime, and in the night his song shall be with me, even a prayer unto the God of my life."—Ps. xlii. 8.

Through suffering and trouble, the ego will be given opportunities of development at the period of incarnation (daytime), and in the discarnate interval (night) there will be harmony of the qualities through aspiration towards the Divine love and truth within.

"The Lord is my strength and song, and is become my salvation."—Ps. cxviii. 14.

The Self is the power within the soul to raise and harmonise the qualities on the path of love and duty which leads to perfection.

See DAY AND NIGHT, HARMONY, HYMN SINGING, INCARNATION OF SOULS, JOB, LOVE OF GOD, MELODY, MUSIC, NIGHT, PRAYER, REINCARNATION, SINGERS.

SONS AND DAUGHTERS :—

Symbols of opinions or ideas, and of feelings or emotions,—the progeny of mind and emotion. Or, the higher mental qualities and the buddhic emotions,—the progeny of the Spirit.

"Wherefore come ye out from among them, and be ye separate, saith the Lord, and touch no unclean thing ; and I will receive you, and will be to you a Father, and ye shall be to me sons and daughters, saith the Lord Almighty."—2 COR. vi. 17, 18.

The indwelling Self exhorts those qualities which have in them a measure of the Divine Life to separate themselves from their lower elements, and have no alliance with selfish desires. Then the Self will transmute them, and so become their progenitor, and they will be the higher mental and buddhic qualities on spiritual planes.

" A son denotes truth and good in the understanding and thence in the thought ; a daughter denotes truth and good in the will and thence in the affections. . . . Young men signify truths, and virgins affections thereof." — SWEDEN-BORG, *Apoc. Rev.*, n. 543, 620.

See DAUGHTERS, CHILDREN OF MEN AND WOMEN, FATHER, INCARNATION, TRANSMUTATION.

SONS OF GOD :—

A symbol of the Divine monads or spiritual egos which incarnate in the human forms when the lower nature of man has evolved mind.

" And it came to pass, when men began to multiply on the face of the ground, and daughters were born unto them, that the sons of God saw the daughters of men that they were fair ; and they took them wives of all that they chose."—GEN. vi. 1, 2.

This refers to the period when from the anthropoid animal the human animal evolved, and mind began to function in each individual, uncouth, human form.

And the period arrived when evolution of the individual mind commenced in many human units, and as the consciousness was drawn to the objects of desire, and as affection for them was set up, the spiritual egos, or ideals in the mind (sons of God), identified themselves with the sensations and affections (daughters of men), and hence illusion of the personality was produced. The taking of " wives " is the seeking for the Self through the form-life.

" Primeval monsters all lived and died in fulfilment of their destiny, doing their appointed part, but without asking any questions about it. And then came man—a beast, no doubt, at first, like the rest, but a thinking beast. . . . He is able to do this because there has awakened in him a spark of that same divine reason, that eternal Word, which was before creation and is incarnate within it.— 'For the earnest expectation of the creature waiteth for the manifestation of the sons of God ' (ROM. viii. 19)."—R. J. CAMPBELL, Serm., *God's Greater Works*.

" But who were the Nephilim of Genesis (vi. 4) ? There were Palæolithic and Neolithic men in Palestine ages before the events recorded in the Book of the Beginnings. The theological tradition identifies these Nephilim with hairy men or satyrs, the latter being mythical in the Fifth Race, and the former historical in both the Fourth and Fifth Races."— H. P. BLAVATSKY, *Secret Doctrine*, Vol. II. p. 819.

" And the Lord said, My spirit shall not strive with man for ever, for in their going astray they are flesh ; therefore shall his days be an hundred and twenty years."—GEN. vi. 3.

This refers to the subsequent evolution of the spiritual ego through human forms, and its final reunion with the Self.

And the Divine Mercy expresses itself in the soul, and imparts confidence of ultimate re-conjunction of the many with the One. Like " lost sheep " they have gone astray into the lower nature. The lower self (flesh) is now converted into an instrument of the Divine will for the evolution of the soul, and cannot be for ever opposed to the higher nature. The time-limit for the lower self to function is therefore fixed at twelve periods (120) of the cycle of life.

" Beloved, now are we the sons of God, and it doth not yet appear what we shall be : but we know that, when he shall appear, we shall be like him ; for we shall see him as he is."—1 JOHN iii. 2.

" Man is God's son, not because God has adopted him, but because man in his inmost is spirit. God and man must then come together, because of the affinity between them, because the distinctive element of humanity is an emanation from the fullness of Divine life."—B. WILBERFORCE, *Problems*, p. 79.

" God has been at work from the beginning of time, the Life-Force of all existence, giving himself, sacrificing himself, that the latent wonder and beauty of his eternal Being might be declared in his children. 'The whole creation groaneth and travaileth in pain together until now waiting '—waiting for what ? ' Waiting for the manifestation of the sons of God.' Yes, the end of creation is the fashioning of a divine humanity which will perfectly embody and show forth the greatness and goodness of God, and the day will come when we shall say with him that the end to be gained was worth the price to be paid."—R. J. CAMPBELL, Serm., *Jesus and the Life-Force*.

" Brethren, happiness is *not* our being's end and aim. The Christian's aim is perfection, not happiness, and every one of the sons of God must have something of that spirit which marked their master."

—F. W. ROBERTSON, *Sermons*, 3rd Series, p. 153.

See APES (nine), BENNU BIRD, BODHISATVAS, CHILDREN OF GOD, DAUGHTERS, EVOLUTION, FALL, FLESH, FRAVASHIS, HIKOBOSHI, INCARNATION OF SOULS, JOB, MANA-SAPUTRAS, MARUTS, MONAD OF LIFE, MUSPELL, NEPHILIM, PACCEKA-BUDDHAS, PERSONALITY, PITRIS (solar), SAGES, SATYRS, SAVIOURS, SHEEP (lost), SINGERS, SKINS OF ANIMALS, SPARK.

SOPHIA OR WISDOM :—

A symbol of the buddhic principle, and the buddhic function on the lower planes.

"So the Æons all betook themselves to praying the Father to put an end to Wisdom's grieving, for she was bewailing because of the *abortion* which she had produced by herself."—HIPPOLYTUS, *Refutation*, Bk. VI. 26.

This refers to the awakening of the higher manifesting principles (Æons) to their own state in relation to evolution, and the consequent so-called prayer or petition to the Highest, which is an effort of aspiration towards Wisdom and Love, bringing the reasoning mind to cease grieving for the struggling lower plane activities which work out one-sided results. The "abortion" signifies the inharmonious forcing of a certain side of the nature, which, unless "born out of due time," that is, evolved when the conditions are matured, does not yield a perfect result, and is as an unripe fruit,—without flavour, and lacking in perfection of development.

See ABORTION, ÆONS, BUDDHI, EVOLUTION, NEHEMĀUT, SEXUAL, STRIFE, WISDOM.

SOPHIA ACHAMÔTH (HIGHER ASPECT) :—

A symbol of the buddhic principle functioning in the soul and giving birth to the Self.

"And this same seed (of the Spirit sown by Wisdom in the natural man, the Gnostics) affirm also to be the Church, corresponding to the Church above. And with this they maintain their inward being to be completed, as though they had their animal soul from the Demiurgus, their body from the dust of the earth, and their fleshly part from its matter, while the Spiritual man comes from their

Mother Achamôth. . . . And this, they say, is the *salt* and the *light of the world.*"—IRENAEUS, *Against Heresies*, Bk. II.

The Church signifies the religious consciousness or purified state of soul, in which can be received the Christ-germ, for Christ becomes the head of the Church and the completion of humanity. The desire-nature (animal soul) proceeds from the potential lower nature of the Archetypal Man (Demiurge); the mental vehicle (body) from the lower mind (dust); and the physical vehicle (flesh) from the physical plane. While the Spiritual man, Christ, is born within the soul, brought forth of the Buddhic principle (Sophia), the Divine Madonna; and this is the Son of the Highest and the Light of the world.

See ARC. MAN, BIRTH OF CHRIST, BUDDHI, CHURCH, DEMIURGE, DUST, HOLY GHOST, LIGHT, MAN (natural), MOTHER (divine), NEPHESH, SALT, SEED.

SOPHIA ACHAMÔTH (LOWER ASPECT) :—

A symbol of the lower emotion-nature as the inverted reflection of the buddhic principle, on the psychic or astral plane.

"Sophia Achamôth was the daughter of Sophia, the Divine Wisdom—the female Holy Ghost of the early Christians,—Sophia Achamôth personifying the lower Astral Light or Ether."—BLAVATSKY, *Secret Doctrine*, Vol. I. p. 219.

"This wisdom is not a wisdom that cometh down from above, but is earthly, sensual, devilish."—JAS. iii. 15.

See DEMIURGE, MEDUSA, RAVANA.

SORCERORS, OR WIZARDS :—

A symbol of the following of false ideas and vain and unpractical notions, from habit and authority. This course of action crushes the efforts of the inner Self to attain knowledge of the truth for the ego.

See WIZARDS.

SORES ON THE BODY :—

A symbol of the suffering lower nature in the forms.

See JOB, LAZARUS.

SORROW, OR EVIL :—

A symbol of the ego's deprivation of the higher qualities when it descends into the lower nature; this implies ignorance and suffering.

"Now the Buddha declares that life in every form and in every expression is sorrow, but why is all life sorrow ? Because all life is transient and unenduring. . . . Because everything has arisen from some cause or reason, it follows that it must come to an end just as soon as this cause ceases to act."— P. DAHLKE, *Buddhist Essays*, p. 22.

"Sorrow by itself does not exist. Being transiency as reflected in the individual, it is, and it is not. . . . Sorrow, like everything else, is a relative conception, which comes into being with me, and with me expires."—*Ibid.*, p. 78.

"Sorrow is not punishment,—the result of sin : sorrow is ignorance."—*Ibid.*, p. 23.

"For as ignorance in this system is synonymous with illusion, so in this system is knowledge synonymous with truth."—*Ibid.*, p. 193.

Sorrow on the lower planes is the opposite of bliss on the higher ; but while the first is transient, the second is eternal. Ignorance and evil are one.

"Humanity as a whole, and every human being in particular, is a portion of the Eternal Divine Essence subjected to earthly conditions that its latent spiritual qualities, the qualities which constitute the ideal good, whatever it is, may find opportunity to declare themselves. Or, to put it another way, the travail of earth has been necessary that a glorious divine idea might be brought to the birth and live for ever in the eternal world,—an idea in whose fulfilment the highest welfare, the fullest self-realisation of every being taking any part in the work will be included."—R. J. CAMPBELL, Serm., *A Christian World-view.*

"We ought to realise that a necessary condition of the work we are severally and collectively doing in the flesh is mainly done by means of suffering. All the woe of the past and all the anguish of the present have been necessary to it, and will continue to be so until God's great end is achieved."—R. J. CAMPBELL, Serm., *God's Use of Time.*

See BLISS, BUDDHA, FORMS, IGNORANCE, ILLUSION, JOB, KARMA, LOST (forest), NIDANAS, NIRVANA, ORIGINAL SIN, PASSION, PENANCES, SERVANT OF GOD, SUFFERING, VINEGAR, WEALTH.

SOSHYANS :—

A symbol of the indwelling Self in the souls of humanity.

"Soshyans is born in Khvaniras, who makes the evil spirit important, and causes the resurrection and future existence."—*Bundahis*, XI. 4. *S. B. of E.*

The Higher Self incarnates within the pilgrim souls on this Earth-planet (Khvaniras) and in them overcomes the desire-nature (evil spirit), and thereby causes the rise of consciousness in the souls and the attainment of immortality at the close of the cycle.

See CHRIST'S SECOND COMING, HVANIRATHA, INCARNATION, KALKI AVATAR, RESURRECTION.

SOSHYANTS :—

A symbol of the individualities or spiritual egos, who are as pilgrims passing through the experiences of the lower life on their way to the eternal city above.

See CITY OF GOD, EXPERIENCES, FRAVASHIS, FUGITIVE, HYMNS, INDIVIDUALITY, MONAD OF LIFE, PILGRIM, SHEEP (lost), WANDERERS, WAYFARING MEN.

SOSIOSH :—

A symbol of a Divine outpouring into the souls of humanity towards the close of the present cycle.

"But before this, Ormazd will send his prophet Sosiosh, and will bring about the conversion of mankind, to be followed by the general resurrection."— *Zoroastrian System*, Clarke, *Ten Religions.*

But previous to the termination of the cycle, the Divine Will shall appear to the lower nature as One who illuminates with Truth, and so will be the means of purifying and perfecting many souls, and thereby enabling the egos to rise from the lower planes whereon they have lain as dead in the forms.

"Jesus said unto her, I am the resurrection and the life : he that believeth on me shall never die."—JOHN xi. 5.

The Christ-soul, being the Divine innermost, is the way, the truth and the life in the raising of the consciousness to higher planes. The quality in harmony with the Divine is immortal.

See AAT (waters), BUDDHA (maitreya), CHRIST'S SECOND COMING, CONFLAGRATION, HORSE (white), JUDGMENT-DAY, KALKI AVATAR, PROPHET, REGNAROK, RENOVATION, RESURRECTION, SPRINGTIME.

SOUL AND BODY :—

Symbolic of spirit and matter in relation to the Divine process of manifestation,—Involution and then Evolution.

"As it is said thus : Which is created before, the soul or the body ? And

Auharmazd said that the soul is created before, and the body after, for him who was created ; it is given into the body that it may produce activity, and the body is created only for activity ; hence the conclusion is this,—that the soul is created before, and the body after."— *The Bundahis*, XV. 4, *S. B. of E.*

The question resolves itself into :— Which is first of all brought into existence,—the Involutionary or the Evolutionary process ? And in answer, the voice of Eternal Truth affirms that the former must first go forth, inasmuch as unless the organised World-soul were first produced to provide means of experience and expression for the spiritual egos, no evolution would be possible, no redemption or transmutation attainable. The Life of the World-soul is the means whereby the form is thrilled into activity. Hence it is,—that Spirit pre-exists, and Matter subsists.

See AHURA-MAZDA, ARC. MAN, CREATION, EVOLUTION, EXPERIENCE, FORMS, REDEMPTION, TRANSMUTATION, VESTURES.

SOUL, SPIRIT, AND BODY :—

A symbol of atma (spirit), buddhi (soul), and manas (body). The soul is completed on the buddhic plane.

" And the God of peace himself sanctify you wholly ; and may your spirit and soul and body be preserved entire, without blame at the coming of our Lord Jesus Christ. Faithful is he that calleth you, who will also do it."—1 THESS. v. 23, 24.

The Higher Self completes the evolution of the spiritual ego and its qualities (atma-buddhi-manas) on the higher planes at the end of the cycle.

" The highest of all selves, the ultimate Self of the universe, is God. The New Testament speaks of man as body, soul, and spirit. The body is the thought-form through which the individuality finds expression on our present limited plane ; the soul is a man's consciousness of himself as apart from all the rest of existence, and even from God ; the spirit is the true being thus limited and expressed,—it is the deathless Divine within us. The soul, therefore, is what we make it ; the spirit we can neither make nor mar, for it is at once our being and God's."—R. J. CAMPBELL, *The New Theology*, p. 34.

See ATMA, BIRDS (two), BUDDHI, CHRIST'S SECOND COMING, FIG-FRUIT, INDIVIDUALITY, MANAS, SPIRIT.

SOUL (HIGHEST ASPECT), WORLD-SOUL, OR OVER-SOUL :—

A symbol of the manifested Higher Self on the planes of atma and buddhi, in relation to the cosmic causal-body on the buddhic plane, which is the centre of emanation.

" From One Soul,—the All-soul,— come all these souls which are made to revolve in all the cosmos, as though divided off " *Corpus Hermeticun, The Key*, 7).—G. R. S. MEAD, *T. G. Hermes*, Vol. II. p. 145.

" The soul has its origin in the Supreme Intelligence, in which it is asserted, the forms of the coming existences already can be distinguished from each other, and this Supreme Intelligence can be termed the Universal Soul."—I. MYER, *Qabbalah*, p. 110.

" So the Soul is asserted to descend here below ; and so it is restored to the bosom of the Deity when it has fulfilled its mission, and adorned by its virtues, is prepared for heaven ; and raising itself by its own action and the assistance of Divine Love, which it incites by that which it feels, to the *real existence*, and thus places itself in harmony and affinity with the *ideal form*."—*Ibid.*, p. 111.

The One Soul, or Self, descends, as it were, into the matter of the lower planes during the process of Involution, and afterwards re-ascends in the many souls in the process of Evolution to its Divine source. This ascent of the Soul is accomplished through its own Divine Life, supplemented by the Love-energy responding from above to its aspirations below. It rises with enhanced powers and virtues, and realises the Ideal from which it emanated.

" That Unity, that Over-soul, within which every man's particular being is contained and made one with all other ; that common heart, of which all sincere conversation is the worship, to which all right action is submission ; that overpowering Reality which confutes our tricks and talents, and constrains everyone to pass for what he is, and to speak from his character, and not from his tongue, and which evermore tends to pass into our thought and hand, and become wisdom, and virtue, and power, and beauty. We live in succession, in division, in parts, in particles. Meantime within man is the Soul of the whole ; the wise silence ; the universal beauty, to which every part and particle is equally related ; the eternal ONE."— EMERSON, *Essays*.

" Men need, it is true, a lofty, spiritual conception in order that they may be encouraged to enlarge the narrow circumference of their personal life, and merge themselves within the universal. But unless it be that the personal aspect of life be duly insisted upon, until it is realised that the universal lives, moves, and acquires its reality from what we severally impart and communicate to it, the *raison d'être* of that conception must be missed. The end, the aim, the purpose of life for man is the soul. But the soul must remain a mere symbol until man translates his loftiest imaginings into true, noble impulses and deeds, which shall serve to transmit to others, and to posterity, the flame of immortal life, and so kindle within their hearts the passion for the pure, the beautiful, and the perfect. Therein lies the germ of all that is eternal. Therein lies the solution, ay, the very nature, of the soul."—R. DIMSDALE STOCKER, *The God which is Man*, p. 79.

See ARC. MAN, ATMAN, BIRTH OF ZOROASTER, CHRIST'S SECOND COMING, COSMOS, CREATION, EVOLUTION, GODHEAD, HIGHER AND LOWER SELVES, IMAGE, INCARNATION, INVOLUTION, ISVARA, MACROCOSM, MONAD, NESHAMAH, SEED, SELF, SERVANT OF GOD.

SOUL (MIDDLE ASPECT) :—

A symbol of the causal-body on the higher mental plane, the centre or seat of the manifested Higher Self (atma-buddhi),—the rock upon which an ego builds,—the foundation and pivot upon which, and around which, the inner activities are carried on.

" The kinds of souls are three :—divine, and human, and irrational. Now the divine is that of its divine body, in which there is the making active of itself. For it is moved in it, and moves itself. For when it is set free from mortal lives, it separates itself from the irrational portions of itself, departs unto the god-like body, and as 'tis in perpetual motion, is moved in its own self, with the same motion as the universe. The human kind has also something of the god-like body, but it has joined to it as well, the parts irrational,—the appetite and heart. These latter also are immortal, in that they happen also in themselves to be activities ; but they are the activities of mortal bodies. Wherefore, they are removed far from the god-like portion of the Soul " (*Corpus Hermeticum*, XVIII).—G. R. S. MEAD, *T. G. Hermes*, Vol. III. p. 78.

The " divine or god-like body " is the causal-body which is the centre and source of the qualities of the soul, and so many modes of its ex-pression on the several planes. When the astro-mental and physical bodies (mortal lives) drop away from it, it withdraws into itself with the results of its experience. The " human soul " is the astro-mental body to which are joined the desires and emotions (irrational). The latter are enduring only as activities transmuted to the higher planes.

" It must be said . . . with respect to our soul that one part of it always abides on high, that another part of it is conversant with sensibles, and that another has a subsistence in the middle of these. For as there is one nature in many powers, at one time the whole soul tends upwards in conjunction with the most excellent part of itself and of the universe ; but at another time, the worst part being drawn down, draws together with itself the middle part."—PLOTINUS, *Against the Gnostics*, Taylor, pp. 47, 48.

The " part on high " is the causal-body ; the " middle part " the astro-mental, and the " worst part " is the desires, etc. (sensibles) which are attached to the astro-mental body.

" We must explain to you how the question stands by some further conceptions drawn from the Hermaic writings. Man has two souls, as these writings say. The one is from the First Mind, and partakes also of the power of the Creator, while the other, the soul under constraint, comes from the revolution of the celestial spheres. Into the latter the former—the soul that is the Seer of God,—insinuates itself at a later period. This being so, the soul that descends into us from the worlds keeps time with the circuits of these worlds, while the soul from the Mind, existing in us in a spiritual fashion, is free from the whirl of Generation ; by this the bonds of Destiny are burst asunder ; by this the Path up to the Spiritual Gods is brought to birth ; by such a life as this, is that Great Art Divine, which leads up to That beyond the spheres of genesis, brought to its consummation."—JAMBLICHUS, Bk. viii. 6.

This refers to the Divine origin of the spiritual ego which descends at a certain stage into the personality which has been developed on the lunar and terrene globes of their planetary chains. This union of the spiritual, the mental, and the animal natures forms man, and opens his path upward to the ideals on the higher planes. The spiritual ego (Seer of God) is described as proceeding from the plane of atma (First Mind) and partaking of buddhi and manas (creative power); while the personality (soul under constraint) is said to be evolved from the life-waves circling over the planetary chains of globes. Into the personality the spiritual ego (atma-buddhi-manas) insinuates itself at the period when the personality is mature. This being so, the personality which has been formed on the globes is uniformly subject to the karmic conditions of the life of the lower nature, while the spiritual ego being of the higher nature is free from the life and death of the forms (whirl of generation), and ultimately will break the bonds asunder which bind it to forms. By this entrance of spirit into humanity the path of the ego is opened to the higher qualities (gods). It is by the life of the spirit in aspiration and intelligence (art Divine) that our souls will be led up to That which transcends all form-life and is the consummation of endeavour.

" Of soul the bodie forme doth take,
for soul is forme and doth the bodie make."—SPENSER.

" Erigena's *mysticism* appears especially in his root conception of man's soul. There is an *ultimate ground of truth* in the depth of personal consciousness. Man is an epitome of the universe, a meeting-place of the above and the below, a point of union for the heavenly and the sensuous. We understand the world only because the forms or patterns of it—the Ideas which it expresses—are in our own minds. So that a mind which wholly fathomed itself would thereby fathom everything, and we can rise to Divine contemplation because God is the ground and reality of our soul's being. In very truth the soul is always in God, and by *contemplation* it may rise above the mutable and *become that which it beholds*. In a remarkable passage in the Fourth Book (*De Div. Nat.*) he says : ' Whoever rises to pure understanding becomes that which he understands. We, while we discuss together, in turn become one another. For, if I understand what you understand, I become your understanding, and in a certain unspeakable way I am made into you. And also when you entirely understand what I clearly understand you become my understanding, and from two understandings there arises one.' "—R. M. JONES, *Mystical Religion*, p. 127.

" When in Pauline language we speak of body, soul, and spirit, we are speaking of three different ideas. The body is the vehicle and instrument of the soul, the soul is the sheath of the spirit, the spirit is the deathless divine, the spark of God's fire that is in every man, that

essence of His own Being without which none of us could exist, and which none of us can destroy. The soul is man's consciousness of himself, as apart from all the rest of the world, and even from God. The body might be here in all its parts, and yet we should say of someone who has left us, that he is gone. What we mean is that that which distinguishes him from all other humanity, and even from God, his consciousness of himself, our consciousness of him, has departed. That is what we mean by the soul. The soul is in a sense the use that a man makes of his own divinity, the soul is the moral and spiritual consciousness of a man. The spirit is something you can neither make nor mar ; the soul is what you make it."—R. J. CAMPBELL, *Song of Ages*, pp. 99, 100.

See ATRI, CAUSAL-BODY, GILGOO-LEM, GODS, INDIVIDUALITY, KARANA, KARMA, LAZARUS, LUNAR CHAIN, MIND (good), NESHAMAH, PERSONALITY, PLANETARY CHAIN, REGIONS, SAHU, SELF, SPARK, WHEELS (holy).

SOUL (LOWEST ASPECT), ANIMAL SOUL :—

A symbol of the astral body of desires, appetites, passions, instincts, and lower affections and emotions. The personality when ruled by the lower principle.

" The soul of the wicked desireth evil."—PROV. xxi. 10.

" Behold all souls are mine ; as the soul of the father, so also the soul of the son is mine : the soul that sinneth, it shall die."—EZEK. xviii. 4.

All personalities are emanated by the Higher Self through the individuality. As the preceding personality (father), so also the succeeding personality (son) comes from the individuality seated in the causal-body. The personality that is unpurified is dissipated, and a new personality is incarnated. Each personality is responsible in degree for its actions, and not for the actions of its " father " or its " son." The personality dies in his sins, but the individuality is immortal. In a general sense the personality endures through the cycle and dies when perfected.

See ACHILLES, ASTRAL, ATOM (permanent), HEEL, IMMORTALITY FORFEITED, NEPHESH, PERSONALITY.

SOUND, OR VOICE :—

A symbol of spiritual vibrations from the higher planes which find response in the mind as higher emotions or the conscience.

"The clouds poured out water; the skies sent out a sound : Thine arrows also went abroad."—Ps. lxxvii. 17.

From the buddhic principle (clouds) within, truth (water) was poured forth ; from the higher planes (skies) came vibrations of wisdom and love ; also the Self with spiritual force (arrows) overcame the lower qualities.

See Arrows, Clouds, Hearing (higher), Noise, Sky, Voice.

SOUTH QUARTER IN SCRIP-TURES OF EUROPE AND NORTH AFRICA :—

A symbol of the higher planes of buddhi and atma, while North is a symbol of the lower planes.

"For upon the 'south wind' coming, the 'north wind' arising departs (Cant. iv. 16) when our old enemy, who had bound up our soul in inactivity, being expelled by the coming of the Holy Spirit, takes himself away. . . . And thus the chambers of the South' are those unseen orders of the Angels, and those unfathomed depths of the heavenly Country, which are filled with the heat of the Holy Spirit."—St. Gregory, *Morals on the Book of Job*, Vol. I. p. 507.

See Egypt (higher), Muspellheim, Phang.

SOUTH QUARTER IN SCRIP-TURES OF PERSIA, INDIA, BURMA :—

A symbol of the lower planes, especially of the astral plane.

See Agnihotra, Hanuman, Lanka.

SOUTH LAND, AND NORTH LAND OF EGYPT :—

Symbols of the planes of buddhi-manas, and of kama-manas, or of mind and desire.

See Egypt (higher), (lower), Nek-hebit.

SOUTH WIND :—

A symbol of currents of the emo-tion of love stirring the mind to thought and action.

"Once, the south wind upset Adapa's skiff, and in revenge he broke his wings. But the south wind was a servant of Anu, and the God of the Sky demanded the punishment of the daring mortal. Ea, however, intervened to save the man he had created."—Sayce, *Story of Adapa*.

On an occasion in the mind's awakenment, the vibrations from the emotion, or higher astral, plane,—a strong breeze of love,—surged about the primeval mind so that it was well-nigh capsized, and in its perplexity it put forth an effort of will and restrained its emotion, so that it could not for awhile soar into the realms of fancy, for it had reflected. But the emotion-nature is a servant of the Highest (Anu), and an aspect of the One Life : and so it was that the daring and presumptuous mortal was called upon to account for that which he had done. He had asserted himself. He had become "one of Us." Intelligence is the function which involves choice, and as such introduces will,—which makes man, the individuality, as God. And herein arises karma. The Supreme (Ea), however, intervened. God does not leave man to the karmic law alone ; in other words, the lesser life, the individual, after its fall into matter, is even yet in touch with the Greater Life, or more correctly, the Greater is in conscious communication with the individual life in order to raise it from the lower conditions.

See Adapa, Anu, Fall, Image, Intellect, Personality, Pouru-shaspa, Will, Wind (sweet).

SOUTHSAYING :—

A symbol of the assertion of the higher mental faculties.

SOW OR PIG :—

A symbol of the lower desires and instincts.

"Sow, sacred to Set, was the abomina-tion of Horus, according to the 112th chapter of the Book of the Dead."—Budge, *The Mummy*, p. 299.

The lower desires which captivate the mind, prevent the manifestation of Christ (Horus) in the soul.

See Boar, Pig, Set, Swine.

SOWER OF SEED :—

A symbol of the Higher Self who places in the lower nature (earth) of the soul, when prepared, the germs of the higher qualities of wisdom, truth, and love, that these may grow up and increase, and by crushing out the lower qualities render the soul a fit abode for the Holy Spirit, a veritable "garden of God."

"No man ever has a complete and perfect intellectual consciousness of all his active nature; something instinctive germinates in us, and grows underground, as it were, before it bursts the sod and shoots into the light of self-consciousness. Sheathed in unconsciousness lies the bud, ere long to open a bright, consummate flower."—THEODORE PARKER, *Ten Sermons*, p. 6.

"How it is possible to teach spiritual things by natural emblems. The mystery lieth in this, how it should be possible to represent things which are invisible by means of things which are visible; things which are spiritual by things which are sensual; things which are pure and perfect, as the will of God, by things which are to the very heart impregnated with, and to the brim full of, impurity, imperfection, and wretchednesss? How come these analogies to exist between the realities of a fallen world, and the ideas, promises, first rudiments, and beginnings of a world unfallen? Are they accidental? or are they designed in the purpose of God? Is it a work of ingenuity or of piety to search them out? These are questions which, though simple as to the occasion which suggesteth them, are yet as deep as they are important, and, being well sifted, will afford the true resolution of the main difficulty which we have always felt in the exposition of this parable of the sower. . . . Certainly it is not accidental that the natural world should bear such wonderful analogies with, and afford so many emblems or similitudes for expressing, the spiritual world."—ED. IRVING, *Works*, Vol. I. p. 69.

"This parable of the sower, of course, contains an image so natural in its application to all wisdom, that it is not on His lips only that *truth* has been described as 'seed.' There are manifold facilities about the emblem on which one may dwell for an instant. The seed has a germinating power in itself that leads to endless reproduction. So every blessed word, every true word, whether of Christ's gospel or of man's wisdom, that finds its way into hearts and minds, works there, springing and growing, and bears fruit and reproduces itself—on and on again without end. . . . And then, again, there are such other ideas as these: Man is but the soil. If you are to get Divine desires and a Divine life in a human heart, they must be sown there: they are not products of the soil. There needs the bringing of the seed by another. There needs the imparting of truth and righteousness and purity from a higher source and a Diviner hand. There must be the sowing before there is any right and good harvest off this soil of our sinful souls, barren but for weeds."—A. MACLAREN, *Sermons, 2nd Series*, p. 282.

See AGRICULTURALIST, CORN, CULTIVATION GARDEN, GERMS, HARVEST, HUSBANDMAN, PLOUGHING, REAPING, SEED (good), SEKHET, SICKLE, WHEAT.

SOWING AND REAPING :—

Symbolic of the karmic law of cause and effect in the process of spiritual evolution. According to the kinds of action, so are the fruits of action.

"Within the Garden of Rest wherein I am; I feast therein; I sow therein; I reap therein; I plough therein; I wed therein."—*Book of the Dead*, Ch. CX.

I,—the True Self,—enjoy the experiences which are collected through me and transmuted. From my abode in the causal-body I sow and I reap that which the lower self appears to do and undergo. The "ploughing" signifies the forming of the bodies and conditions in which the lower self acts. The "wedding" is the union between the liberated lower Self and Myself, where we twain are One.

"As he soweth so shall he reap; human life is lost without virtue. O silly one! happiness is obtained by being a slave to virtue. She who under the Guru's instruction abandoneth evil shall be absorbed in the Perfect One" (*Guru Nanak*).—MACAULIFFE, *The Sikh Religion*, Vol. I. p. 270.

"Whatsoever a man soweth, that shall he also reap."—GAL. vi. 7.

"God is the original sower. He has taken of His own eternal life and sown it upon the earth as upon a ploughed field. Into every human heart some of that divine seed has fallen, and will spring up and grow as we give it opportunity. Ever and anon it ripens into the full corn in the ear, some perfect revealing of some aspect of eternal truth. Then it is reaped; for the man in whom that fruitage appears remains to all eternity what he has thus achieved. Nor does the process stop there. Every consecrated life becomes the spiritual seed of other lives in which Christ has yet to be formed. God is still the sower, but He is continually taking of the harvest of some beautiful character or noble deed and sowing it afresh that it may reproduce itself in the harvests of generations to come."—R. J. CAMPBELL, Serm., *Reaping for Eternal Life*.

See AGRICULTURE, CAUSAL-BODY, CORN, CULTIVATION, EVOLUTION, EXPERIENCES, FEAST, FIELD, FRUITFUL, GARDEN OF REST, HARVEST, KARMA, KINGDOM, PLOUGHING, REAPING, SEED (good), SEKHET-HETEP, SELF, SHABTI, SICKLE, SOWER, TRANSMUTATION, UNION, WHEAT.

SPACES OF THE INEFFABLE :—

Symbolic of the outward emanating means by which the conditions of manifestation are established.

"The first vesture hath in it all the names of all the mysteries of all the orders of the spaces of the Ineffable."—*The Pistis Sophia*, trans. G. R. S. MEAD.

The "first vesture" of being, the outermost plane, contains within it, as it were, all the rest of the mysteries of existence. From the physical there evolves that which is involved within it. The "orders" are the laws of manifestation : the "spaces" are the means by which such conditions of life are attained. "The Ineffable" signifies the Absolute—the Christ Supernal.

See LIMBS OF THE INEFFABLE, NAME, VESTURES.

SPADE TO DIG THE EARTH :—

A symbol of the buddhic function in its action on the lower nature (earth).

"The sacrificer takes the spade with, 'I take thee, at the impulse of the divine Savitri, with the arms of the Asvins, with the hands of Pûshan : thou art a woman.'"—*Sata. Brâh.*, III. 7, 1, 1.

The incarnate Self energised by the Supreme (Savitri), and becoming active in the Individuality and the Personality (the Asvins), functions in the lower nature to bring about the buddhic (woman) transmutations of the lower qualities.

See ARMS, ASVINS, BUDDHI, SAVITRI, TRANSMUTATION, WOMAN.

SPARK, DIVINE :—

A symbol of the spiritual ego or monad on the atmic plane ; or of the atma-buddhic Individuality enthroned in the causal-body. It is the individualised spirit and inactive source of will.

"The highest faculty is not, like each of the inferior faculties, one faculty among others ; it is the soul itself in its totality ; as such it is called the 'spark,' also *Synteresis* (corresponding to the soul-centre of Plotinus). This highest faculty is served by all the faculties of the soul, which assist it to reach the source of the soul, by raising the latter out of the sphere of inferior things. The spark aspires to the Absolute, to that unity outside of which there remains nothing" (Eckhart).—UEBERWEG, *Hist. of Philos.*, Eng. trans., Vol. I. p. 472.

"The freedom from law and from all activity belongs, according to Eckhart, only to the 'little spark,' but not to the faculties of the soul. Only the 'little spark' of the soul is to be at all times with God and united with God ; but thereby are desire, action, and feeling, all to be determined."—*Ibid.*, p. 479.

A good man having "thoughts that were like lightning poems, singing themselves to his inner consciousness and declaring him to be a living soul—a part of God—a spark of the Divine, sent to evolve itself through experience and difficulty from the imperfect to the perfect state of being."—MARIE CORELLI, *Holy Orders*.

"'The spirit of man,' says Behmen, 'contains a spark from the power and light of God.' The Holy Ghost is 'creaturely' within it when renewed, and it can therefore search into the depths of God and nature, as a child in its father's house. In God, past, present, and future ; breadth, depth and height ; far and near,—are apprehended as one, and the holy soul of man sees them in like manner, although (in the present imperfect state) but partially."—VAUGHAN, *Hours with the Mystics*, Vol. II. p. 97.

"JOHN xvii. 22, 'The glory which Thou gavest Me I have given them, that they may be one even as We are one ; I in them and Thou in Me, that they may be made perfect in one.' The 'spark' at the centre of the soul is the very presence of the divine Logos himself. Jerome is, I think, the first to use the queer word *synteresis* for this highest faculty of the soul. The whole object of our life here is to make this 'spark' extend its light over the whole man, expelling and destroying that selfishness and isolation which is the principle of our false 'self.' . . . The elder Eckhart has the following striking sentence : 'God is nigh unto us, but we are far from him ; God is within, we are without ; God is at home, we are strangers ; God is always ready, we are very unready.'"—W. R. INGE, *Paddock Lectures*, p. 67.

See AGNISVATTAS, BA, BODHISATVAS, CHILDREN OF GOD, FRAVASHIS, GUARDIAN SPIRITS, INCARNATION OF SOULS, MANASAPUTRAS, MARUTS, MONAD OF LIFE, MUSPELL (sons), PACCEKABUDDHAS, PITRIS (solar), PROTOTYPES, RACES, SAVIOURS, SHEEP (lost), SONS OF GOD, SOUL (middle), WILL.

SPARROWS, TWELVE :—

Symbols of the twelve qualities in the lower nature, which should attain "apostleship." They are aspiring tendencies which embody the reflection of the Higher Self, who is so often symbolised as a bird.

"One of the Jews said to Joseph Dost thou not see the child Jesus working on the Sabbath at what it is not lawful for him to do ? for he has made twelve sparrows of clay."—*Gospel of Pseudo-Matthew*, Ch. XXVII.

When old habit of thought (the Jew) perceived that a higher motive had been introduced into the soul, an appeal was made to the lower reason (Joseph), which is usually ready to afford excellent justfication for not acting against customary opinion. Habit appeals to the hitherto constituted authority, and asks whether it is not aware that the ego is acting from motives quite outside those ordinarily recognised. For the new qualities (sparrows) have been fashioned, which will afford the Christ-soul better means for expressing itself.

"Then Joseph reproved Jesus, saying : Wherefore doest thou on the Sabbath such things as are not lawful for us to do ? And when Jesus heard Joseph, he struck his hands together, and said to his sparrows : Fly ! And at the voice of his command they began to fly. . . . He said to the birds : Go and fly through all the world and live."—*Ibid.*

And when the lower reason (Joseph) hears the appeal from old habit of thought, it chides the attempt to surpass traditional law. But when the Christ hears the lower reason, he at once directs its attention to the higher means of expression, and so by personally making an effort (striking the hands together) the qualities are enabled to function. And when the qualities are thus animated, they are gradually developed, and go forth in every separate mind to enable evolution to proceed in the lower nature of the soul (the world).

See APOSTLES, BOYS (bad), DISCIPLES, HABIT, JESUS, JEWS, JOSEPH, POOLS (seven), SABBATHS, STRIKING.

SPEAR :—

A symbol of the Divine Ray of Life through all nature, which puts an end to illusion.

"The spear of the Maruts is meant for the lightning, and we actually find rishti-vidyutah, having the lightning for their spear, as an epithet of the Maruts— I. 168, 5 ; V. 52, 13."—MAX MÜLLER, *Vedic Hymns*, *S.B.E.*, Vol. XXXII. p. 274.

The Divine Ray of the Monads of Life, or Spiritual Egos (Maruts), is the life-energy of the spiritual universe (the lightning),

"Horus next cut off Set's head, and the heads of his followers, in the presence of Rā and the gods, and then dragged his body through all the land with the spear thrust through his head and his back" (*Legend of the Winged Sun-disk*).— BUDGE, *Gods of the Egyptians.*

This decapitation of "Set" is a symbol of depriving evil of its intelligent quality. The Higher Self now united the consciousness of the lower planes with his own, so that no longer was there separateness between the Self on the upper and the Self on the lower planes. The "spear" is a symbol of the Divine Ray which unifies the consciousness in wisdom, love, and power.

See ARROWS (divine), GODS, HEAD, HORUS, JEWEL SPEAR, LIGHTNING, MARUTS, OX-LEADER, RĀ, SALVE, SET, SHIELD.

SPEARMEN OF TROY :—

A symbol of the activity of the lower emotions.

See TROJANS, TROY.

SPEECH OR SPEAKING :—

Symbolic of the exercise of mental faculties and qualities, good or ill, as the mind is directed upward or downward.

"And the whole earth was of one language, and of one speech. And it came to pass as they journeyed from the east, that they found a plain in the land of Shinar ; and they dwelt there. And they said one to another, Go to, let us make bricks, and burn them thoroughly. And they had brick for stone, and slime had they for mortar. And they said, Go to, let us build us a city and a tower, whose top may reach unto heaven ; and let us make us a name, lest we be scattered abroad upon the face of the whole earth."—GEN. xi. 1-4.

At an early period of evolution, the entire lower nature of the soul is in a homogeneous condition. (This means that hitherto no special faculties and qualities to deal with externals had been evolved. The evolution, such as it was, was principally interior, that is, not directly concerned with the mental, astral and physical vehicles whose responsiveness to outward stimuli constitutes the medium for the growth of specific mental qualities.)

As the Divine Life advanced towards its means of experience (journeyed east), it arrived at a condition of inertia (tamas), and then it abode for a time.

And now it is said that "brick is to be burned," or means are to be devised whereby further experiences are to be gathered. Superstition (brick) is to be put in place of spiritual knowledge (stone : see 1 PETER ii. 5) ; and craft (slime) in place of affection (mortar).

So it is proposed by means of superstition and craft to carry out a scheme for attaining knowledge through subtle devices of the lower mind. Through individualisation, and egotism or sense of separateness, it is first conceived that wisdom may be reached. Scattering of consciousness through the mass of the lower soul, or extinction of personality, is dreaded at this stage.

"And the Lord came down to see the city and tower, which the children of men builded. And the Lord said, Behold the people is one, and they have all one language, and this they begin to do : and now nothing will be restrained from them, which they have imagined to do. Go to, let us go down, and there confound their language, that they may not understand one another's speech."— GEN. xi. 5, 6, 7.

And the Divine nature responds to the cry from within for knowledge, however expressed. The Divine nature perceives, as it were, the beginning of separate existence for the qualities, and the multiplicity of faculties in the awakening lower life ; and foresees that for a season the evolution must proceed solely from below.

The Divine Life therefore descends, since it is a means of causing necessary disagreement and disharmony in the lower nature,—a state of soul which precedes a craving for the higher things.

"So the Lord scattered them abroad from thence upon the face of all the earth : and they left off to build the city. Therefore is the name of it called Babel ; because the Lord did there confound the language of all the earth : and from thence did the Lord scatter them abroad upon the face of the earth."—GEN. xi. 8, 9.

So from homogeneity of soul-condition heterogeneity is gradually produced ; and the consciousness is diverted from the astro-mental centre (city) wherefrom it had previously worked.

This " city " or centre of consciousness is known as " Babel," that is, perception of difference between one quality and another. (Neither mind nor desire alone can produce confusion, it is as each struggles with the other in the emotions that confusion occurs.) Through this faculty of perception of difference the Divine nature leads the soul to see celestial similitudes, and by its means the reasoning mind commences to evolve, as the qualities multiply through the mental aspects of the lower nature.

" The Ashâdhâ (brick) is speech, and by speech the gods than indeed conquered and drove the Asuras, the enemies, the rivals, from this universe ; and in like manner the Sacrificer, by means of speech, conquers and drives his spiteful rival from this universe."—Sata. Brâh., VII. 4, 2, 34.

The lower quaternary is the expression of mind in the lower consciousness, and by the exercise of mental qualities the ideals (gods) subdue the unruly desires in the soul. In a similar way the incarnate Self, by means of spiritual expression in the mind, dissipates the lower principle, and perfects the soul.

See AMITAUGAS, ASHADHA, ASURAS, BABEL, BRICK, CHILDREN OF MEN, CITY, CONFUSION, EARTH, EAST, EXPERIENCES, FORM AND NAME, GOAT (white), GODS, LANGUAGE, LIPS, MAISHAN, MOUTH, NAME, PEACE (sword), PEOPLE, QUALITIES, SACRIFICER, SEPARATENESS, SHINAR, TAMAS, TONGUE, WORD.

SPEED AND LOITERING :—

Symbols of energy (rajas), and inertia (tamas).

See GUNAS, RAJAS, TAMAS.

SPENDYAD, OR SPEND-DAD :—

A symbol of the triumphant Higher Self.

" The high priest of the good religion of the Mazda-yasnians, the glorified Spendyad son of Mah-vindad, son of Rustom, son of Shatroyer."—Preface to the Bundahis, S. B. of E.

The " high priest of the good religion " is the Self, the upholder of the science of the spiritual life. He is the "glorified one" who has undertaken to go forth and accomplish the Soul's evolution. He is the spiritual product of the three who bear witness on earth,—the physical, astral, and lower mental natures. The Self is "glorified," or the higher and lower consciousnesses are brought together, as the evolution of the lower elements,—physical, astral, and mental,—enables the potencies of the Self to be completely expressed.

See CHRIST'S SECOND COMING, CONQUEROR, EARTH, ELEMENTS, EVOLUTION, GLORIFYING, HIGHER AND LOWER SELVES, MELCHIZEDEK, RELIGION, SELF, STRIFE, UNION, VICTORY.

SPENTO MAINYUSH, AND ANGRO MAINYUSH; THE GOOD AND EVIL SPIRITS :—

Symbols of the positive principle of Right and Truth, and the negative principle of Wrong and Error.

"Thou (Homa said) madest all the demons hide themselves beneath the earth, who formerly flew about the earth in human shape, O Zarathustra! who wert the strongest, most active, and triumphant of the creatures of the two spirits,—Spento Mainyush and Angro Mainyush."—*Homa Yasht*, Haug, *Essays.*

And now it is that the nature-spirits (demons), which were originally, as it were, let loose upon the lower planes, are relegated to the lowest sub-planes, — that is, as the out-breathing of intelligence from above informs the matter of the lower planes, the organisation of the particles serves to interfere with, or restrain, the natural behaviour of the elemental forces and guide them in their activities. The Soul (Zarathustra) is the strongest, most active and victorious of beings, inasmuch as, so soon as it commences its individual evolution, it proves that it is capable of demonstrating that from the spirit within proceeds the overcoming of wrong (negative) by right (positive).

See AHRIMAN, AHURA, DAEVAS, DEMONS, EARTH, GATHAS (chanting), TRIBE-RULERS, ZOROASTER.

SPERMATIC WORDS :—

Symbolic of the monads of life and form which descend into matter to give it properties of change and growth.

"In the system of the Porch, Logos plays a very important part. It means in the first place Reason or Intelligence, and is the highest attribute of God. In the second place it means Power, and in this sense is the active cause of creation. For this purpose the Universal Reason emitted a vast number of individual forces, Spermatic Words, or Seed-like Forces, which as soon as they were shot into matter began to germinate and assume shapes."—C. BIGG, *Origins of Christianity*, p. 332.

The highest intelligence and power are evidenced in the changing phenomena of the universe. The properties of atoms, and the specific growths in the inorganic and organic worlds, are due to the intelligence brought into matter by the highly differentiated monads of life and form.

"As soon as God beholds Himself in that Eternal Now, He beholds within Himself the forms or Ideas of the entire universe—all that has essential reality in the universe. In fact, for Eckhart, the Son, the Word, stands for the total unity of the Divine Thought, the forthcoming of God into expression, the utterance of Himself, so that he often calls God's thinking the archetypal forms, or Ideas, 'the begetting of the Son.' These archetypal forms, the expressions of God's thought, are 'the matured Nature,' and these forms, projected into space and time, are our world of nature—the 'world of creatures.' God is like a perfect architect who *thinks* his structure and it is done. There are no stages in it, no before and after. God thinks and Creation *is*. The world which is thus uttered into being has two faces, one turned out toward differentiation and multiplicity, and the other turned in toward God and unity—in very fact all reality is in God, and 'if God drew back His own into Himself, all the creatures would become nothing at all.' The real world is the world of archetypes—divine Ideas—and that world is not created, it always *is*. 'God,' he says, 'creates the world and all things in an ever-present Now.'"— R. M. JONES, *Mystical Religion*, p. 228.

See ARC. MAN, BUDDHIC PLANE, COSMOS, CREATION, GERMS, HIGHER AND LOWER WORLDS, IMAGE, MONAD (form, life), PROTOTYPES, SEEDS, SIMILITUDES.

SPHERE, OR SPHAIROS :—

A symbol of the Supreme Being, also of the Cosmos, or of the Soul.

"Kircher says of this symbol (of a globe with wings and serpent) that in the teaching of Hermes, 'The globe (i.e. the disk of the Sun) represents the simple essence of God, which he indifferently called The Father, The First Mind, The

Supreme Wisdom. The serpent emerging from the globe was the vivifying influence of God which called all things into existence. This he called *The Word*. The wings implied the moving penetrative power of God, which pervaded all things. This he called Love. The whole emblem represented the Supreme Being as Creator and Preserver.' A similar figure without the wings was the symbol among the Greeks for a daimon, or the Deity."— J. GARNIER, *The Worship of the Dead*, p. 232.

" Horbehûdti (Horus) flew up to the sun as a great winged disk ; therefore was he henceforth called the Great God, the Lord of Heaven. From heaven he saw the foe : he pursued them as a great winged disk " (*Legend of the Great Winged Sun-disk*).—WIEDEMANN, *Rel. of Anc. Egyptians*, p. 69.

The Second Logos (Horus) rose towards the " sun," which stands here for the Individuality of the human race in the higher causal-body (buddhic). Hence he is named Great God, the Lord of Heaven. From the higher planes he saw, as it were, the sin and trouble which had overtaken the lower planes. And he went forth in the soul as a symbol of perfection and completeness, coupled with aspiration,— through which the qualities should rise.

" Then neither is the bright orb of the sun greeted, nor yet the shaggy might of earth or sea ; thus, then, in the firm vessel of harmony is fixed God, a sphere, round, rejoicing in complete solitude."— *Empedocles*, FAIRBANKS, 135.

At the first, the Self (sun) is not known, nor the possibilities which are gradually evolved through the mechanism of the lower self in its vehicles. Thus, unknown to the lower consciousness, God-potential, — the Germ Deific,—exists in all souls ; each department of his latent nature being pre-arranged harmony, adaptation, and capability of perfect reciprocal action, re-action, and inter-action. This completeness of the Macrocosm reflected in the Microcosm is comparable to the figure of a sphere, which well symbolises unity,—that which is self-sufficient, and having equality in all its aspects, while inclusive of all things.

" And of the matter stored beneath it (the ideal Cosmos) the Father made of it a universal body, and packing it together made it spherical,—wrapping it round the Life which is immortal in itself, and that doth make materiality

eternal. But He, the Father, full-filled with His ideas, did sow the lives into the sphere, and shut them in as in a cave, willing to order forth the life with every kind of living " (*Corpus Hermeticum*, VIII (IX)).—G. R. S. MEAD, *T. G. Hermes*, Vol. II. p. 125.

And of the matter beneath the plane of atma, the Supreme by involution formed the World-soul, or higher causal-body, thereby obscuring the immortal Self, who from dead matter raises the soul to eternal life. But the Supreme to carry out his perfect scheme, implanted in the lower nature of the Soul the germs of all the qualities, which in latency would await the evolution of the diverse forms and kinds of living things in which to manifest.

See CAVE, CIRCLE, COSMOS, CROSS (ankh), DISK, FATHER, HIRANYA-GARBHA, MACROCOSM, MONAD, SERPENT, SUN (moon), SUN-DISK, WINGS, WORD OF GOD.

SPHINX :—

A symbol of the higher nature arising from the lower, or of the Spirit triumphant over matter.

" Primarily the sphinx represented an imaginary quadruped, human-headed, and supposed to be the favourite incarnation assumed by Rā the Sun-god when he desired to protect his friends and adherents."—WIEDEMANN, *Rel. of Anc. Egyptians*, p. 197.

" Horus changed himself into the form of a lion, with the head of a man surmounted by the triple crown " (*Legend of the Winged Sun-disk*).—*Ibid.*

Then the Son of God (Horus) came forth under the aspect of Conqueror, and stood, as it were, on the lower quaternary (lion), which is now brought into unison with the higher triad (triple crown) through the mind (head).

" In representing the lowest as linked to the highest,—the loins of the creature of prey to the head and breast of the Woman,—the Sphinx denoted at once the unity, and the method of development, under individuation, of the soul of the universal humanity."—*The Perfect Way*, p. 25.

See AKERT, BULL (man), GRIFFIN, LION, QUADRUPED.

SPICES :—

A symbol of those spiritual qualities which go to purify the mind or personality. These qualities are

aspirations towards love and truth, and good thoughts leading to beneficent action.

"And the women, which had come with him out of Galilee, followed after, and beheld the tomb, and how his body was laid. And they returned, and prepared spices and ointments."—LUKE xxiii. 55, 56.

The "women" here symbolise the loving acts of affection which are done within the soul in memory or recognition of a living ideal of righteousness and truth. These are prayers, and good thoughts, and just deeds (the spices, etc.).

"We make a perfume compounded of spices, when we yield a smell upon the altar of good works with the multitude of our virtues; and this is 'tempered together and pure' (EXOD. xxx. 35), in that the more we join virtue to virtue, the purer is the incense of good works we set forth. Hence it is well added, 'And thou shalt beat them all very small, and put it before the Tabernacle of the Testimony.' We 'beat all the spices very small' when we pound our good deeds, as it were, in the mortar of the heart, by an inward sifting, and go over them minutely to see if they be really and truly good: and thus to reduce the spices to a powder is to rub fine our virtues by consideration."—ST. GREGORY, Morals on the Book of Job, Vol. I. p. 64.

See ALTAR, EMBALMMENT, INCENSE, MORTAR, MUMMY, MYRRH, OINTMENT, PERSONALITY, PHŒNIX, PRAYERS, ROCK-SEPULCHRE, SEPULCHRES, SUNDAY, TABERNACLE, TOMB, WOMAN.

SPIES :—

Symbolic of limitation,—the inclination to trust in the flesh instead of the Spirit.

SPIRE :—

An emblem of aspiration from the quaternary to the One above.

See CONE, OBELISK, PYRAMID.

SPIRIT :—

A symbol of the positive, energetic, forceful, qualitative, and formative aspect of the Divine outpouring, in distinction from the passive, receptive, quantitative, form-taking aspect —matter. Spirit is the life-side which imparts qualities and motion. Matter is the form-side which receives qualities and motion. Spirit manifests in matter as the life moulding the successive forms, more or less evanescent. Spirit uses

matter as a sheath which lies outside and below it. Hence the intense vibrations of Spirit gradually dissipate it and bring the forms to nought. In their origin spirit and matter are eternal; duality proceeds from Unity which is neither spirit nor matter, and is the Ultimate Reality.

"The world is a living organism, which is not made through any cause external to itself, but is formed and developed by means of an inner principle, a principle which is at once operative power and purposeful reason, at once real and ideal, and which consequently appears in nature as a twofold substance, a spiritual and a bodily, while these two nevertheless are finally traceable to one essence and one root, and as regards substance are ultimately one and the same" (Bruno's Cosmology).—PFLEIDERER, Phil. of Religion, p. 26.

"The Active Principle, the Mind of the universals, is absolutely pure, and absolutely free from all admixture. It transcendeth virtue; It transcendeth Wisdom; nay, It transcendeth even the Good Itself, and the Beautiful Itself. The Passive Principle is of itself soulless and motionless, but when It is set in motion, and enformed and ensouled by the Mind, It is transformed into the most perfect of all works—namely, this Cosmos."—PHILO, De Mund. Op., § 2.

"Pragâpati (lord of creatures) produces a pair,—Matter (rayi) and Spirit (prana), thinking that they together should produce creatures for him in many ways. . . . The sun is Spirit, Matter is the moon, . . . and Body indeed is Matter."—Prasna Upanishad, I. 4, 5.

From the Absolute there is emanated that Unity which becomes Duality as Matter and Spirit, from the interactions of which all things in every variety are produced. The Higher Self (sun) is Spirit, Matter is its reflection as form, and form indeed is matter.

"I feel that the universe is spirit and nothing but spirit, and that infinity and eternity are implied in the very existence of every individual soul."—R. J. CAMPBELL, Thursday Mornings, p. 151.

See BREATH (divine), EVOLUTION, FUH-HE, HEAVEN AND EARTH, INVOLUTION, KHIEN, MATTER, MÂYÂ, PRAGÂPATI, PURUSHA, RANGI, SELF, SEPARATION, SPARK, T (letter), TEZCATLIPOCA.

SPIRIT OF MAN :—

A symbol of the higher or spiritual mind.

"Now the spirit of man loves Purity, but his mind disturbs it."—*The Classic of Purity*, § 3.

The higher mind vibrates to the spiritual influences, but the lower desire-mind repels them.

See KAMA, MANAS, TAO.

SPITĀMA ZARATHUSTRA :—

A symbol of the Soul on the buddhic plane.

See SOUL, ZOROASTER.

SPITĀMA'S CATTLE PASTURE :—

A symbol of the buddhic plane on which are manifested the higher qualities.

See CATTLE, PASTURES, SHEEP.

SPOTTED COWS AND MARES :—

Symbolic of qualities of emotion and mind which are to be transmuted by buddhi. They are impure and of the desire-nature.

See COW OF PLENTY, COW (spotted), LEOPARD, TRANSMUTATION.

SPRINGTIME BLOSSOMING :—

A symbol of the beginning of a new evolution of life from the higher mind plane of the next globe of the chain.

"O 'Great City' (Nut-urt)! I have come into Thee; I have comprehended my fullness; I have brought about the blossoming (Uakh) of the Springtime."
—*Book of the Dead*, Ch. CX., BLACKDEN.

The causal centre is apprehended as the real beginning of the True life, and through it it is seen that the higher Selfhood is secured. The "blossoming of the Springtime" is a symbol of the Divine life which commences from the upper mental plane, after attainment of liberation from the planes below. It is the individuality which then proceeds on its course upward, the mortal personality having been dissipated.

See AAT (waters), ASCETIC, ASRAMAS, CAUSAL, CHRIST'S SECOND COMING, CITY OF GOD, HEAVENLY SPRINGTIME, HORSE (white), INDIVIDUALITY, KARSHVARES, LIBERATION, ORDERS, PERSONALITY, PLANETARY CHAIN, REGIONS, RENOVATION, ROUND.

SQUARE :—

A symbol of the four lower planes. Either of the quarternary below atma, or of the lower quaternary below the higher mind.

"A triangle and a quaternary (square), the symbol of Septenary Man."—BLAVATSKY, *Secret Doctrine*, Vol. II. p. 625.
"The triangle being a symbol of Deity everywhere."—*Ibid.*, Vol. I. 138.

See CIRCLE, IRON PLATE, PYRAMID, QUARTERS, QUATERNARY.

SRAOSHA-KARANA :—

A symbol of the Divine Will and purpose in the sufferings of the lower self.

See ASPAHI, SUFFERING.

SROSH, OR SRAOSHA, THE RIGHTEOUS :—

A symbol of the Divine Will and power.

"Srosh is the great teacher of the good religion. . . . He fights chiefly against the evil daevas."—M. HAUG, *Essays*, p. 308.

The Divine Will guides the outpouring spiritual life, and dispels ignorance and illusion in the mind.

See ASHA-VANUHI, DAEVAS, IGNORANCE, ILLUSION, MITRO, NERYOSANG, RELIGION (good).

SROTAPANNA, SROTAPATTI, OR SOTAPANNA : STAGE OF SANCTIFICATION OR INITIATION :—

This is the first of the four higher initiations, and is said to mean "He who has entered the stream." It consists in the dedication of an advanced personality during a physical life, to the highest ideals of spiritual goodness, love, and truth, and to the most noble and worthy ends of beneficence, in entire disregard to the selfish solicitations of the desire-mind. This course of life maintained to the end implies the mastery achieved over a lower soul-state and the rise to a higher condition.

See INITIATIONS.

SRUK, OFFERING SPOONS :—

A symbol of the receptive vehicles of the ego, i.e. the causal, the mental, the astral, and the physical bodies.

See DHRUVA, SRUVA, UPABHRIT.

SRUTI, REVELATION :—

A symbol of Divine inspiration of truth.

"The Vedanta philosophers always cling to the conviction that the Divine

has never been really absent from the
human soul, that it always is there,
though covered by darkness or nescience
(avidyâ) and that as soon as that darkness or that nescience is removed, the
soul is once more and in its own right
what it always has been ; it is, it does
not become Brahman."

"According to the orthodox Vedantist,
Sruti alone, or what is called Revelation,
can impart that knowledge and remove
that nescience which is innate in human
nature."—F. MAX MÜLLER, *Theosophy*,
etc., pp. 284, 293.

"The Hindus have divided the whole
of their ancient literature into two parts,
. . . *Srutam*, what was heard, and was
not the work of men or any personal
being, human or divine, and *Smritam*,
which was remembered, and has always
been treated as the work of an individual,
whether man or god." . . "Nor are
even these fictitious poets (of the Rig-
veda) supposed to have created or composed their poems, but only to have
seen them as they were revealed to them
by a higher power, commonly called
Brahman, or the Word."—F. MAX
MÜLLER, *Six Systems, etc.*, p. 3.

See AMBAS, BOOK-STUDIES, GOSPEL,
IGNORANCE, INSPIRATION, KORAN,
MYTHOLOGY, PARABLE, PEN, RAMA-
YANA, REVELATION, SACRED TEXT,
SASTRA, SCRIPTURES, SIGN, THOTH,
UPANISHAD, UR-HEKAU, VEDA, WORD
OF GOD.

SRUVA (MASC.), THE DIPPING SPOON :—

A symbol of atma, the Life-ray.

"The dipping spoon is no other than
the breath. This breath passes through
all the limbs, and for that reason the
dipping spoon goes to all the offering
spoons."—*Sata. Brâh.*

The atma is the Breath of the
Divine Life which energises the qualities, and brings spiritual nourishment
to the receptive vehicles of the ego.

See BREATH, DHRUVA, SRUK,
UPABHRIT.

STAFF, FOR WALKING AND SUPPORT :—

An emblem of Divine guidance ;
or a symbol of the mind leaning
upon external authority and tradition.—*See* Ps. xxiii. 4 ; Is. xxxvi. 6.

STAFF, OR ROD OF IRON :—

A symbol of power and mental
discipline.

"Staff in the Word signifies power,
and iron signifies natural truth, consequently the natural sense of the Word,
and at the same time the natural light

of man ; in these two consists the power
of truth."—SWEDENBORG, *Apoc. Rev.*,
n. 148.

See IRON, ROD.

STAIRCASE, STAIRS :—

A symbol of the means of evolution from a lower to a higher state.

"Osiris is called 'the god on the top
of the staircase.'"—BUDGE, *Book of the
Dead*, p. liv.

The Higher Self manifests on the
plane of atma—the height of aspiration in the human soul.

"The height of the Christian life is
the glorious consciousness where all is
light, and all is peace. A few have a
genius for it and reach it without much
effort ; it may be that they have had
their struggles in some previous existence—I know not. For most the only
way to it is by the narrow stair of
arduous duty, a stair that often winds
through dark places, where discourage-
ment and fear and despair are apt to
come upon the soul. At such times,
keep an open ear for the voices that
say : 'It is lighter up above.' As the
realisations of God grow fuller, and all
the selfish instincts die down, and the
desires for personal aggrandisement are
overcome, you shall gradually cease from
your labour, though living to do greater
and better work, and the word of Christ
shall come to rule in your heart, and you
shall find your life in that 'Immortal
Love, within whose righteous will is
always peace.'"—T. RHONDDA WILLIAMS,
Serm., *Dying in the Lord*.

See ATMA, LADDER, MOUTH (speech),
STEPS.

STAKE, SACRIFICIAL :—

A symbol of the "tree" of the
Divine life, the means by which the
incarnate ego climbs upward from
the lower planes.

The "stake" is erected in the
lower nature (earth), on "a chip
from the stake thrown into the hole,"
that is, it is founded upon an implanted spiritual germ. It is raised
up in the soul "for the conquering of
these worlds" (*Sata. Brâh.*, III. 7, 1,
14). It is girded with "a triple
rope," that is, it is vitalised by the
higher nature — atma - buddhi - manas ; and so it becomes a means
of enabling the ego to sacrifice the
lower for the sake of attaining the
higher.

"It is the God in man that reaches up
to God, the man in God that makes that
aspiration possible ; it is the God in man
that enables us to recognise and adore
the Christhood of Christ, the man in God

that is that Christhood ; it is the God in man that is ever urging us upward to the eternal throne of life and love and power ; it is the man in God that stoops in Christ to lift us there."—R. J. CAMPBELL, Serm., *The Eternal Man.*

See CHIP, GIRDLE ROPE, JESUS (mortal), LADDER, QUARTERS, THUNDERBOLT, TOP-RING, TREE OF LIFE.

STAR IN THE EAST :—

A symbol of the rise of knowledge forecasting perception of the Truth —Christ born in the soul.

" And the wise men, having heard the king, went their way ; and lo, the star, which they saw in the east, went before them, till it came and stood over where the young child was."—MAT. ii. 9.

The intellectual faculties, having observed the apparently favourable attitude of the lower principle (Herod), pursued their course, enlightened by the knowledge dawning through philosophy and science, which led them to the inner abode of the Christ-soul.

" But wherefore is it to a Cave and a Stable that the Star of the Understanding directs the steps of the Wise Men when seeking the birthplace of the Christ ? Because, ' In the elements of the Body is he imprisoned, lying asleep in the caves of Iacchos, in the crib of the Oxen of Demeter.' Because, that is, in constituting the culmination of the returning and ascending stream of emanation, Christ is attained by evolution from the lowest :—' From the dust of the ground to the throne of the Most High.' "—*The Perfect Way*, p. 240.

See EAST, ESTHER, HEROD, INTELLECT, MAGI, MORNING STAR, STARS.

STARS (FIXED) :—

These are symbols of the many centres of faculties on the lower mental plane which enable the mind to be exercised. They are lights of reason in the lower mind, small as compared with the greater light, the Self (sun), and the lesser light, the personality (moon).

" And the lower air I adorned with lesser stars."—*Book of the Secrets of Enoch*, Ch. XXX. 4.

And the lower mind (air) is furnished with the mental faculties.

" By ' stars ' are meant the knowledges of faith, or cognitions of good and truth."—SWEDENBORG, *Arc. Cel. to Gen.* i. 16.

" Reason and science should be assigned to the sphere of fixed stars " (Plato).—ZELLER, *Plato, etc.*, p. 359.

See CHILDREN OF EAST, CRATER, PLANETS, SINGERS, SUN (moon).

STARS AS SOULS, OR GODS :—

Symbolic of the Divine Sparks or Monads of life (atma-buddhic), which descend into the lower vehicles, and are the spiritual egos in the causal-bodies of every human being.

" God divided the whole mixture into souls equal in number to the stars, and assigned each soul to a star."—PLATO, *Timæus*, 41.

" Souls equal in number to the stars." —PHILO, *De Som.*, I. § 22.

" Philo also (besides Plotinus) accepted the opinion attributing life and mind to the stars."—WHITTAKER, *Neo-Platonists*, p. 88.

" At the time when the pictorial hieroglyphics were first being formed (in Babylonia), the star was already the symbol and representation of the divine. . . . At most we can only suggest that the *zi*, or spirit, was localised in the star. A spirit of the sun was as conceivable as a spirit of Ea, and the son of Ea, it must be remembered, became a sun-god. ' The *zi* of the god ' meant originally ' the spirit of the star.' "—SAYCE, *Rel. of Egypt. and Babyl.*, p. 481.

" The fixed stars are also the essences, or souls of matter. . . . A living soul, the sublimated essence of matter, is denominated a star. These stars and essences became Gods. They were regarded as having divine attributes. The stars look down from their region of purity and stillness on the world of men, and they influence the fortunes of men invisibly, but most powerfully. . . . There is a remarkable analogy in the double meaning of our word *spirit* and that of the Chinese word *sing* (star). The terms for *soul* and for *essence*—in Chinese *shin* and *tsing*—are often convertible, as they are in our language."—J. EDKINS, *Religion in China*, pp. 106–7.

In the Greek and the Japanese legends " star-gods " are also mentioned. They are the Divine spirits within the souls of humanity powerfully influencing their development.

" Our forefathers in the most remote ages have handed down to us their posterity, a tradition in the form of a myth that these substances (i.e. the stars) are gods, and that the divine encloses the whole of nature."—ARISTOTLE, *Metaphysics.*

" By the stars we understand two things : (1) How innumerable the saints, those spiritual stars shall be (HEB. xi. 12). (2) How they shall differ each from other in glory" (1 COR. xv. 41).—J. BUNYAN, *Exposition of Genesis.*

See HIKOBOSHI, MARUTS, MONAD OF LIFE, SINGERS, SONS OF GOD, SPARKS.

STAR-WORMS :—

Emblematical of low ideals connected with ambition, love of power

and fame, and schemings through fear.

"Again, below the moon are other stars, corruptible, deprived of energy, which hold together for a little while, in that they've been exhaled out of the earth itself into the air above the earth,—which ever are being broken up, in that they have a nature like unto that of useless lives on earth, which come into existence for no other purpose than to die,—such as the tribe of flies, and fleas, and worms" (*Corpus Hermeticum*, IX. 9).—G. R. S. MEAD, *T.-G. Hermes*, Vol. III. p. 51.

In the astral nature there are motives of desire (other stars) which unite with mind (air) and are without permanence. They are symbolised by "creeping things."

"Tishtrya defeats and expels the *pairika*, who fall as 'star-worms' between Earth and Heaven, into the sea Vourukasha (to prevent the waters from coming out)" ("The Tir Yasht)."—*Haug's Essays*, p. 200.

The mind under the aspect of will (Tishtrya) banishes the fear and ambition (star-worms) which remain obscuring the higher life, as these are detrimental to the perception of pure truth (water) which flows from above.

"By 'star wormwood falling from heaven' (REV. viii.) is signified the appearance of self-derived intelligence from a pride springing from infernal love. By a star and also by a lamp is signified intelligence, here self-derived, because it seemed to burn, and all self-derived intelligence burns from pride. By 'wormwood' is signified infernal falsity from which that intelligence exists."—SWEDENBORG, *Apoc. Rev.*, n. 408.

See CREEPING THINGS, PAIRIKA, QEN-QUENTET.

STATUTE, FIRST DIVINE :—

This signifies supreme law in the ideal realm, of which natural law is the complement and counterpart: all the nature of the manifest God is contained therein.

See CHERUBIM, MAAT, SHENIT, THEMIS.

STEM OF THE HOM-PLANT, THE HEIGHT OF A MAN :—

A symbol of the vehicles of the Divine Life on the successive planes of the human soul, all being interconnected from above downward,—the height of the ego.

See DESERTS, HEAVEN AND EARTH, HEIGHT OF OSIRIS, HOM-PLANT, SUTRATMA, VESTURES.

STENCH, POISONOUS :—

A symbol of external stimuli which inflame and excite the lower nature. These are the desires which continue unsatisfied, and the longings which cannot end for the objects of sense.

See BOTTOMLESS PIT, POISON.

STEPS :—

A symbol of the path of life ; the rising from a lower level to a higher.

See LADDER, MOUTH (speech), STAIRCASE.

STEWARD OF THE LORD OF THE VINEYARD :—

A symbol of the Higher Self as the agent of the Supreme within his universe.—MAT. xx. 8.

See HOUSEHOLDER, JUSTICE, LABOURERS, VINEYARD.

STEWARD, UNJUST, OF THE PARABLE :—

A symbol of the lower self entrusted with opportunities of development (the goods). It is developed by the desire-nature (unrighteous mammon). The debtors are the mind and emotions which possess (owe) the means whereby the lower nature may be raised. The "friends" are the transmuted emotions. The lower self reduces the debt by availing himself of a portion of the means of development. "Sit down quickly" signifies disciplining the lower nature so that the desires may be transmuted, and buddhic emotions (friends) made in heaven.—LUKE xvi. 1.

See FRIENDS, PARABLE, TRANSMUTATION.

STHŪLA-SARĪRA, GROSS BODY :—

A symbol of the physical body, the external sheath of the soul.

"All the (Indian) systems assign to each person two bodies : (*a*) an exterior or gross body (*sthūla-sarīra*) ; (*b*) an interior or subtle body (*sūkshma-sarīra* or *linga-sarīra*). The last is necessary as a vehicle for the soul when the gross body is dissolved. . . . The Vedānta affirms the existence of a third body, called *karana-sarīra* or causal body."—MON. WILLIAMS, *Indian Wisdom*, p. 64.

These three bodies are the physical, the astral, and the causal bodies, functioning on the physical, the astral and the higher mental planes respectively.

See CAUSAL-BODY, KARANA, LINGAM, VESTURES.

STIFFNECKED GENERATION :—

A symbol of a backward state of mind devoid of active higher emotion (neck), and therefore difficult to move along the way of righteousness.

" Ye stiffnecked and uncircumcised in heart and ears, ye do always resist the Holy Ghost : as your fathers did, so do ye."—ACTS vii. 51.

The mental state is deplored wherein the purified emotions and affections (heart) are undeveloped, latent (stiff). This state of uncontrolled desire (uncircumcised) always resists the discipline of the Spirit or the buddhic functioning, as precedent states which have generated the present condition of mind, have ever done.

The scripture goes on to point out how this unprogressed mental state is unfitted to receive the gifts of the spirit, and kills out the higher impulses which must precede the advent of the perfect Self in the soul.

See CIRCUMCISION, HOLY GHOST, NECK, TAMAS.

STOMACH :—

A symbol of the appetites of the lower nature.

" Be no longer a drinker of water, but use a little wine for thy stomach's sake and thine often infirmities."—1 TIM. v. 23.

Imbibe no longer errors and illusions, but seek wisdom, so as to be able to control the appetites and desires.

" Porphyry tells us that in his time, when the bodies of the wealthier classes were embalmed, the Egyptians ' take out the stomach and put it into a coffer, and holding the coffer to the sun, protest, one of the embalmers making a speech on behalf of the dead. This speech, which Euphantos translated from his native language, is as follows : " O Lord the Sun, and all ye gods who give life to man, receive me and make me a companion of the eternal gods. For the gods, whom my parents made known to me, as long as I have lived in this world I have continued to reverence, and those who gave birth to my body I have ever honoured. And as for other men, I have neither slain any, nor defrauded any of anything entrusted to me, nor committed any

other wicked act ; but if by chance I have committed any sin in my life, by either eating or drinking what was forbidden, not of myself did I sin, but owing to these members," at the same time showing the coffer in which the stomach was. And having said this, he throws it into the river, and embalms the rest of the body as being pure.' "—A. H. SAYCE, *Rel. of Anc. Egyptians*, p. 64.

Sez BHARATA, CHILDREN OF HORUS, DEFUNCT, PROMETHEUS, VISCERA, WATER (lower), WINE.

STONE OR ROCK :—

A symbol of Spirit, because it is a substance unreceptive, resisting impression, firm. The opposite of matter, which is receptive, takes impressions, and is resolvable or unstable.

" It is by means of God,—the Divine Spirit working within him to build him up in the Divine Image,—he meanwhile co-operating with the Spirit,—that man achieves Divinity. In the familiar but rarely understood terms, ' Philosopher's Stone,' ' Elixir of Life,' ' universal Medicine,' ' holy Grail,' and the like, is implied this supreme object of all quest. For these are but terms to denote pure Spirit, and its essential correlative, a Will absolutely firm and inaccessible alike to weakness from within and assault from without."—*The Perfect Way*, p. 218.

" *Mitama* (Japanese word for) spirit. *Mi* is simply a honorific prefix. *Tama* mean something valuable, as a jewel. Owing to its precious quality, it is used symbolically for the most sacred emanation from the God, and also for the human life or soul."—W. G. ASTON, *Shinto*, p. 27.

" In Holy Scripture ' stones ' are wont to be taken sometimes on the side of bad and sometimes on the side of good. For when a ' stone ' is put for insensibility, by ' stones ' we have hard hearts denoted. Whence also it is said by John : ' God is able of these stones to raise up children unto Abraham '; who surely, by the name of ' stones,' denotes the hearts of the Gentiles, at that time hard and insensible in respect of unbelief. And by the Prophet, the Lord promises, saying, ' And I will take the stony heart out of your flesh, and will give you an heart of flesh ' (EZEK. xi. 19). Again, by ' stones ' the minds of the strong ones are used to be denoted. And hence it is said by Peter, ' Ye also as lively stones, etc.' "—ST. GREGORY THE GREAT, *Morals on the Book of Job*, Vol. II. p. 354.

" By a stone is signified truth."— SWEDENBORG, *Apoc. Rev.*, n. 791.

" When the final barrier has been passed, and the final victory won, God will give us to eat of the hidden manna —the sustenance of the life eternal that knows neither limit nor decay—and the white stone, the shining jewel, the pure soul, which is the resplendent reflection of his own glory, and the undimmed revelation of what we eternally are in Christ."—R. J. CAMPBELL, Serm., *Winning the Divine Name.*

"There was a precious stone, lustrous and resplendent—for that is the force of the word *white* here, not a dead white, but a brilliant coruscating white—on which there was something written which no eye but one ever saw,—that mysterious seat of revelation and direction known in the Old Testament by the name of Urim and Thummim (that is lights and perfectnesses), enclosed within the folds of the High Priest's breast-plate, which none but the High Priest ever beheld. . . . ' I will give him a new name '—a deeper, a more inward, a fresh knowledge and revelation of my own character—as eternal love, eternal wisdom, all-sufficient, absolute power, the home and treasure, and joy and righteousness of the whole heart and spirit."—A. MACLAREN, *Sermons, 3rd Series,* pp. 82-4.

"Spirit alone is substance, and matter is a manifestation of spirit."—W. S. LILLY, *Ancient Religion,* p. vii.

See ALCHEMY, BONES, BREASTPLATE, DELUGE, INSIGNIA, IRON BEATEN, JEWELS, MANNA, MIRROR, NAME, REINGA, ROCK, ROCK (spiritual), SHINTAI, SPIRIT, SUBSTANCE, URIM, ZEUS.

STONE FOR CORNER :—

A symbol of the spiritual perfection of the indwelling Self.

"Thus saith the Lord God, Behold, I lay in Zion for a foundation a stone, a tried stone, a precious corner stone of sure foundation."—ISA. xxviii. 16.

The Supreme points out that in the causal-body (Zion) is seated the Spirit —the Self—the eternal reality. For the causal-body is " for a habitation of God in the Spirit,"—archetypal perfection in every human soul.

"The process of this passage of the ' new ' or spiritual man from his awakening to the illuminated life, has been set out by Jacob Boehme in language which is at once poetic and precise. ' When Christ the Corner-Stone [i.e. the divine principle latent in man] stirreth himself in the extinguished Image of Man in his hearty Conversion and Repentance,' he says, ' then Virgin Sophia appeareth in the stirring of the Spirit of Christ in the extinguished Image, in her Virgin's attire before the Soul ; at which the Soul is so amazed and astonished in its uncleanness that all its sins immediately awake in it, and it trembleth before her. . . . But the noble Sophia draweth near in the Essence of the Soul, and tinctureth its dark Fire

with her Rays of Love.' "—E. UNDER-HILL, *Mysticism,* p. 277.

See SINGERS, STONE, ZION.

STONE, OR STONES, FOR BUILDING :—

A symbol of raised and spiritualised qualities in the higher mind.

"Ye also, as living stones, are built up a spiritual house to be a holy priesthood, to offer up spiritual sacrifices, acceptable to God through Jesus Christ." —1 PETER ii. 5.

The qualities that have been purified and transmuted build up the immortal causal-body (house) and inform, or evolve, the individuality, that the ego may be enabled to offer up the lower life in order to gain the higher through the love of the indwelling Christ.

See ALTAR (fire), CAUSAL-BODY, HOUSE IN HEAVEN, SACRIFICE, STONE.

STONE, BLACK, OF THE KAABA :—

A symbol of the buddhic-sheath of the indwelling Spirit. Its vehicle is the causal-body (Kaaba). It is black to signify the potential and hidden spirit within the soul.

See HOUSE (frequented), KAABA.

STONES AND BREAD :—

The "stones" signify spiritual truths which are always very hard to apprehend. The "bread" is the bread of goodness, — the readily assimilated food of knowledge from experience of life, which man, the thinker, can daily incorporate in his being.

"But Jesus answered and said, It is written, man shall not live by bread alone, but by every word that proceedeth out of the mouth of God."—MAT. iv. 4.

But the indwelling Christ pointed out that the Divine law of the soul's well-being is written upon the heart. The soul cannot live by reason and experience only, but needs to possess direct spiritual truth emanating from within in order to live from God as the fount of Life eternal.

See BREAD, INCARNATION, SACRED TEXT, TEMPTATION, WORD OF GOD.

STONES THROWN AS MISSILES :—

Symbolic of positive power exercised on the mental plane.

See BLACKSMITHS.

STORM OF WIND :—

A symbol of the surgings of the astro-mental nature. Also of winds of doctrine implying ignorance, which prevent the appearance of truth from within.

"Then Jesus arose, and rebuked the winds and the sea ; and there was a great calm."—MAT. viii. 26.

At the right moment the qualities (disciples), being actuated by the highest motives, are thereby able to awaken the indwelling Christ, who immediately responds and subdues the tempest of passion and ignorance, for "without Me ye can do nothing."

"The Christ, the Christ-nature, the God-germ, is within, in the ship, slumbering, waiting to be awakened. The storm, the suffering, the distress, the fear causes the Divine within to be recognised, voluntarily chosen, obeyed. When the storm has done its work, He who has always been there, arises, and there is a great calm."—BASIL WILBERFORCE, *Problems*, p. 41.

"In every man there is a latent Christ. The touch of the Divine Spirit wakens that Christ within and brings Him into union with the Christ above. As Origen so sweetly put it centuries ago, ' Christ sleeps in the soul of every man as He slept in the boat on the Lake of Galilee, and He wakes at the cry of penitence to still the storm of sinful passion in our lives."—R. J. CAMPBELL, *Song of Ages*, p. 152.

"The hurricane of the passions, Jealousy, Hatred, Revenge, Love, breaks out suddenly from some secret and sleeping quality in our nature of which we knew nothing before, and the surprise of it as it dashes upon us in the midst of our innocent and peaceful life is terrible and perilous. These are the hours of frenzy in a man's or woman's life, when one passion seizes as tyrant on the whole nature, and devours all the other passions, enslaves the imagination, the will, the intellect, the heart, and the body. There is but one thing which may save us from utter shipwreck in that hour, and that is daily strengthening of character. . . . We may by such preparation escape its worst consequences ; we may be shattered, but not betrayed into irremediable evil ; we may not be able to sail freely for years, but we shall spread our canvas again and court a happier gale. For the best of having gone through and conquered such a storm, if there be any good in it at all, is that having conquered it we have conquered all other storms of the same kind."—STOPFORD A. BROOKE, Serm., *Shipwrecks of Life*.

See AIR, CROPS, DISCIPLES, GALES, HIGHER AND LOWER SELVES, MAGIC, MENIS, SEA, SELF, SHIP (sea), SHIPS (beaked), TAWHIRI-MATEA, WAVES, WINDS.

STORM OF RAIN :—

A symbol of increase of spiritual energy, and an outflow of truth (water). It may imply an initiation. *See* RAIN.

STRANGERS DESERVING OF RESPECT :—

A symbol of the entrance into the consciousness of the higher emotions, which are the means of aspiration. *See* FRIENDS.

STREAM OF HIS LAW :—

A symbol of the means for the realisation of the Self in manifestation.

"The thirsty world of living beings will drink the flowing stream of His Law."—*Buddha-Karita*, Bk. I. 76.

The "thirsty world" is a symbol of the illusory or phenomenal which yet is, as it were, the means whereby the nature of the Self is realised. Through the phenomenal is displayed that which is within, the Self, and this order of being is spoken of as the Law, since the finite-conditioned is but the symbol and evidence of the infinite and unconditioned.

See ILLUSION, LAW OF BUDDHA, PHENOMENA, THIRST, THIRSTY.

STREETS OF CITIES :—

Symbolic of connections between mental and astral centres. Currents of thought and feeling.

"By streets are signified the truths or falses of doctrine, by reason that a city signifies doctrine."—SWEDENBORG, *Apoc. Rev.*, n. 501.

See CHANNELS, CITY, CRUCIFIXION OF CHRIST (Rev.).

STREETS OF THE EARTH NINE :—

Symbolic of connections between astral centres and the nine apertures of the physical body.

See BRIDGES (nine), GATES OF BODY.

STRIDES OF THE SUPREME :—

Symbolic of the successive manifestation of the planes of the universe.

"Vishnu strode over this (universe) ; in three places he planted his step."—*Rig-Veda*, I. 22, 17.

This refers to the creation of the three higher planes,—atma, buddhi, and manas.

"With long strides thou stridest over heaven, O Heru-khuti (Harmachis) (*Papy. of Ani*).—BUDGE, *Book of the Dead*, Ch. XV.

See CREATION, EYE OF VISHNU, FOOTSTEPS OF BUDDHA, RĀ HARMACHIS, VISHNU.

STRIDES OF THE SOUL :—

Symbolic of the successive stages in the development of the soul during the cycle of manifestation.

"I (the Osiris) am the hidden Bennu bird ; I enter in as he resteth in the Tuat, and I come forth as he resteth in the Tuat. I am the lord of the celestial abodes and I journey through the night sky after Rā. My offerings are in heaven in the Field of Rā, and my sepulchral meals are on earth in the field of Aaru. I travel through the Tuat like the beings who are with Rā, and I weigh words like the god Thoth. I stretch myself at my desire, I run forward with my strides in my spiritual form of hidden qualities, and my transformations are those of the double god Horus-Set."—BUDGE, *Book of the Dead*, Ch. CLXXX.

I, the perfect one, am the indwelling spiritual ego. I enter into the lower nature when the Self has completed involution (rests), and I then commence to evolve. My home is on the higher planes, for my nature is atma-buddhic, and I progress through the cycle with the incarnate Self (Rā). My transmuted qualities are on the buddhic plane, and my experience is undergone in the lower nature (earth) on the astro-mental plane (Aaru). I advance through the cycle (Tuat) as do the higher qualities which are in harmony with the Self, and I find expression through intuition in the higher mind (Thoth). I seek enlarged conditions and expansion of consciousness. I progress in successive stages of initiations in accordance with the archetypal faculties and qualities latent within me ; and my manifesting aspects are the same as those of the Self (Horus) limited (Set) in order to manifest. The duality of Energy and its Limitations is a necessary condition of Divine manifestation.

"Amid the selfish animal principles of our nature there is a voice which speaks of Duty, an idea grander than the largest personal interest—the Idea of Excellence, of Perfection. Here is the seal of Divinity on us ; here the sign of our descent from God. It is in writing this inward law on the heart, it is in giving us the conception of Moral Goodness, and the power to strive after it, the power of self-conflict and self-denial, of surrendering pleasure to duty, and of suffering for the right, the true, and the good ; it is in thus enduring us, that God's goodness shines."—W. E. CHANNING, *Sermon on Dr. Follen*.

See APES (nine), BENNU BIRD, DEFUNCT, EARTH, EVOLUTION, EXPERIENCE, FIELD, FOOD FOR MAN, FOOTSTEPS, HORUS, INCARNATION, INITIATIONS, INTUITION, INVOLUTION, NIGHT, OFFERINGS, OSIRIS, PATRIARCHS, RĀ, SAMSARA, SEKHET-AARU, SEPULCHRE, SET, SI-OSIRI, SKY, SPARK, THOTH, TUAT, WALKS, YEAR, YEARS, ZODIAC.

STRIFE OR CONFLICT :—

A symbol of the diversity which induces the struggle for separate existence among the evolving qualities and forms on the lower planes.

"In strife all things are endued with form and separate from each other ; but they come together in Love and are desired by each other."—*Empledocles*, FAIRBANKS, 96.

Through "strife," or the struggle for existence on the physical plane, all the lower forms of life subsist. But the sense of separateness is overcome so far as Souls unite in knowledge and realisation of Truth, for wisdom brings them together in love. The instinct of attraction (love) serves to build up cellular tissues, organisms, communities, societies, and the great World-soul.

"And as they were joining together, Strife departed to the utmost boundary. But many things remained unmixed, alternating with those that were mixed, even as many as Strife, remaining aloft, still retained ; for not yet had it entirely departed to the utmost boundaries of the circle, but some of its members were remaining within, and others had gone outside."—*Ibid.*, 169.

And as the effort is made by the monads of life to come together (through attraction, and through the principle of sex, both active and passive), "strife," or diversity and separateness, is eventually put to flight. The "unmixed alternating with the mixed" refers to the emotions and desires, the higher of which (the buddhic) cannot be said to mix with the lower, although there is reciprocal action from below to above, and vice-versa. But until manifestation ceases, strife or separateness cannot be entirely gotten rid of. There were some phases of Self-manifestation latent, whilst other phases were actual, or had become transmuted.

"The Life itself standeth in strife, that it may be made manifest, sensible, and palpable, and that the Wisdom may be made separable and known."—BEHMEN, *The Supersensual Life*, p. 109.

"We are advancing towards collectivism both within and without."—REV. W. RICHMOND, *Personality*, p. 28.

"But just as far as strife is constantly rushing forth, just so far there ever keeps coming in a gentle, immortal stream of perfect Love."—*Empedocles*, 180.

To that degree in which the struggling lower self responds to the vibrations from above, the Higher Self reciprocally forthpours energy and raises the self to the Self by Love Divine.

"God cannot sanctify us unless we freely contribute our effort. There is a reciprocal desire on our part and that of God. The free inspiration of God is the spring of all our spiritual life. Thence flows into us knowledge—an inner Revelation which preserves our spirit open, and lifting us above all images and all disturbance, brings us to an inward silence. . . . Then the riches of God are open to us" (Ruysbroeck).—VAUGHAN, *Hours, etc.*, Vol. I. p. 328.

"The importance of manifold forms of struggle for the evolution of all kinds and stages of existence, surely has not been neglected by modern science and modern philosophy. Religion, however, has to feel the potent working of a conflict which is more interior than that between external nature and man as a totality, or between the body and the mind of man. This conflict emerges in consciousness when the obligations of the world of Ideals meet with the tendencies and forces which determine the world of present actual existence. The feeling of the incongruity between the two worlds, in both of which man seems bound to live, to discharge his many functions and to fulfil his destiny, together with the consciousness of his powerlessness to realise these Ideals under the existing conditions of reality, occasions a painful state of longing and of spiritual unrest. This condition becomes an incitement and a challenge to free the soul by an act of will and thus to establish the desired harmony. But the way for accomplishing this desirable result is that voluntary abandonment of the human self, which religion proposes, to

the Other and Divine Self."—G. T. LADD, *Phil. of Religion*, Vol. I. p. 340.

See ATTRACTION, BATTLE, CONFLICT, CONQUEROR, EDDY, HIGHER AND LOWER WORLDS, HORSE (white), LIMBS, LOST (forest), LOVE OF GOD, MENIS, MIXTURE, MONAD OF LIFE, PILLAR (temple), SEPARATENESS, SPENDYAD, TANGAROA, VICTORY, WAR.

STRIKING THE HANDS TOGETHER :—

A symbol of personally and voluntarily making an effort to proceed on the path.

See HAND, SPARROWS.

STRINGS OF GEMS :—

A symbol of functionings of the ego upon the plane of emotion, or buddhi-manas.

See GEMS, JEWELS.

STROPHADES OR ECHINADES ISLANDS :—

A symbol of various conditions upon the astral and physical planes.

STUDENT ; ONE OF THE FOUR ORDERS OF ARYANS :—

A symbol of the personality in its aspect of a learner from the experience it undergoes in the lower vehicles during its incarnations. It is a manifestation of the ego in the lower mind under the disciplining influence of the ethical and spiritual factors which cause the growth of the soul.

See ASRAMAS, BRAHMACHARIN, ORDERS.

STUPA, MARVELLOUS, OF BUDDHA :—

A symbol of the causal-body perfected at the end of the cycle.

"It rises in the air from the ground, in the midst of the assembly : it is made of seven precious substances. It has thousands of balconies strewn with flowers, etc."—*Lotus of the Good Law*.

The causal-body is on the higher mental (air) plane, above the lower nature (ground), and centralised amid the higher qualities. It is complete in all virtues.

See CONE, HOUSE (frequented), KAABA, PALACE, PYRAMID, TABERNACLE, TEMPLE, TONGUE.

STYX RIVER :—

A symbol of the dividing line, as it were, between the lower mind and the higher; separating the lower consciousness from the higher consciousness.

See ANAURUS RIVER, CHARON'S FERRY, GJOLL RIVER, NECTAR, NIGHT (nullity).

SUBSTANCE :—

A symbol of Spirit which is the eternal reality, the foundation of all things. It may be understood as that which differentiates into spirit and matter.

According to Bruno,—"there are strictly speaking, only two *substances*, matter and spirit : all particular things result from the composition in varying degrees of these two,—are therefore mere ' accidents,' and have no abiding reality."—J. L. McINTYRE, *Giordano Bruno*, p. 159.

" That Divine Truth is the only one real Being ; and that the subject in which it inheres and which is derived from the Divine Being is the one only substantial Being."—SWEDENBORG, *Arc. Cel.*, n. 5200, 5272.

" But though Substance is in its nature Spirit, there is a sense in which Spirit is not Substance. This is the sense in which Spirit denotes will or energy, as distinguished from the Substance in which this inheres."—*The Perfect Way*, p. 15.

" There is no substance but consciousness. What other kind of substance can there be ? Therefore I hold that when our finite consciousness ceases to be finite, there will be no distinction whatever between ours and God's. The distinction between finite and infinite is not eternal. The being of God is a complex unity, containing within itself, and harmonising, every form of self-consciousness that can possibly exist."—R. J. CAMPBELL, *The New Theology*, p. 42.

See ADITI, CONSCIOUSNESS, HEAVEN AND EARTH, HIGHER AND LOWER, MĀYĀ (higher), ROCK, SPIRIT, STONE.

SUDDHODANA, KING, THE FATHER OF BUDDHA :—

A symbol of an aspect of the Supreme Self at the commencement of the cycle of involution.

" A king, by name Suddhodana, of the kindred of the sun, anointed to stand at the head of earth's monarchs,—ruling over the (celestial) City, adorned it, as a bee-inmate, a full-blown lotus. The very best of kings with his train ever near him, intent on liberality yet devoid of pride ; a sovereign, yet with an ever-equal eye thrown on all,—of gentle nature and yet with wide-reaching majesty."—*Buddha-Karita*, Bk. I.

The "King of the Race of the Sun " is a symbol of the collective solar pitris which originate human evolution. The Supreme Self calls forth the expression of its own nature as the Self or Ego (the anointed king) ; and it is ordained that it shall so evolve through the universe. The "City " stands for the higher planes, atma, buddhi, and higher manas. The "bee-inmate " is a symbol of the understanding, the "lotus," of wisdom (buddhi). The Spiritual Ego is the one ruler of all,—in touch with all the aspects of its own nature ; intent upon manifesting itself, and withholding nothing from aught. The governor, but devoid of all sense of separateness, gentle and harmonious in all qualities, yet exemplifying all aspects of its own nature.

See ANOINTING, BIRTH CEREMONIES, BUDDHA, COW (milch), HOLY PLACES, KING OF GLORY, PITRIS (solar), RAHULA, SELF, SUN, YASODHARA.

SUDRA, THE FOURTH CASTE :—

A symbol of the physical-nature of man, or the human physical body.

" One occupation only the Lord prescribed to the Sudra, to serve meekly even these other three castes."—*Laws of Manu*, I. 91.

The physical and sense-nature of the outermost vehicle of the soul is for activity and experience only, in entire subordination to the desires, the mind and the will (the other castes), which rule it both for their own contentment and its preservation.

" The idea that we have disengaged from the facts and confirmed by reasoning is that our body is an instrument of action, and of action only."—H. BERGSON, *Matter and Memory*, p. 299.

" If the urge of the body did not exist, we should have no governments, no politics, no cities, factories, ships, railway lines, and standing armies. If you ask yourself why human beings should be brigaded as they are, why we have legislators, commerce, industry, and the like, the answer is, that it is because we have bodies ; if we had no bodies we should have none of these things, nor should we want them. It is the struggle to maintain our individual bodily organisation that has driven us to adopt first one expedient and then another for facilitating the work ; all discovery, all progress, all mental activity even, springs from this humble root. It created the family, the tribe, the nation, forced us to combine for common ends in ways that otherwise we never should have done, and has thus produced all the higher intellectual and social results, all the refinement, culture, and spiritual life that we enjoy together to-day. . . . I say that whatever your spirit may be, and it is probably greater far than you yet know, this is the way in which it has learned to manifest."—R. J. CAMPBELL, Serm., *Through Death to Life.*

See ANUBIS, ARTIFICER, BIRTH (second), CASTES, CLASSES, HESTIA, MARRIAGE (castes), MATTER, NEPHTHYS, SIGYN.

SUFFERING, AS A SACRED TRUTH :—

A symbol of the bondage of the Spirit in matter, implying limitation and suppression of spiritual energy or Divine life.

(The four sacred truths of Buddhism.) "This, O monks, is the sacred truth of suffering : Birth is suffering, old age is suffering, sickness is suffering, death is suffering, to be united with the unloved is suffering, to be separated from the loved is suffering, not to obtain what one desires is suffering ; in short the five-fold clinging (to the earthly) is suffering."—*Buddha's Sermon.*

This is the inner truth of the bondage of the Self in matter :—Entrance of the spiritual ego into the lower life of illusions which create the sense of separateness is bondage. Detention in the condition of unrest and insecurity of the lower self is bondage. The dissatisfaction of the lower self while without true knowledge of the Higher is bondage. The passing out of one state of illusion into another is bondage. For the spirit to be chained to the desires is bondage. For the spirit to be separated from the higher qualities is bondage. Not to obtain emancipation is bondage. In fine, this outflowing life towards the objects of desire and sense is bondage.

"This, O monks, is the sacred truth of the origin of suffering : it is the thirst (for being) which leads from birth to birth, together with lust and desire, which finds gratification here and there : the thirst for pleasures, the thirst for being, the thirst for power."—*Ibid.*

This is the inner truth of the origin of the bondage of spirit in matter :— The impulse of the spiritual ego to manifest its nature upon the lower planes, which leads to its passing through a succession of progressive states. To this is added the identifying of the ego with the lower qualities which attach it to appetite and desire, and arouse a feeling of gratification from time to time. Also is included the longing for pleasurable states, the outward life, the activities centred in self.

"This, O monks, is the sacred truth of the extinction of suffering : the extinction of this thirst by complete annihilation of desire, letting it go, expelling it, separating oneself from it, giving it no room."—*Ibid.*

This is the inner truth of the abolition of the bondage of spirit in matter : —The extinction of this longing for the lower life by the complete abrogation of the desire-nature, disallowing it to act, expelling it from the mind, separating the inner Self from it, giving it no scope in the soul.

"This, O monks, is the sacred truth of the path which leads to the extinction of suffering : it is this sacred, eight-fold path, to wit : Right Faith, Right Resolve, Right Speech, Right Action, Right Living, Right Effort, Right Thought, Right Self-concentration " (*From Buddha's Sermon at Benares*).—H. OLDENBERG, *Buddha,* p. 211, Eng. trans.

This is the inner truth of the means by which the Self will attain release from bondage in matter :—It is the spiritual process of the growth of the soul, the initiative to which process the indwelling Self urges by impressing upon the ego the need there is for self-discipline in the numerous outgoings of mind and emotion. Through perception of the ideal (faith) the soul responds to the Divine impression, and there follows a right resolve to turn from the lower illusions to the teaching of the Truth within, when through the mind's right expression (speech) there will come right action and the lower life be so regulated that there is right living. Then, through right effort to subdue the desires and passions, and right thought to attain knowledge of the higher life, there will arise in the soul the power of concentration on the Higher Self, the Saviour, bringing about liberation from the fetters of matter.

"This conditioned existence wherein we struggle and suffer, as we all have to do. It is only as a spiritual process that it becomes comprehensible at all, and it is only as we address ourselves to it with a spiritual purpose that we rise above its illusory levels and get into touch with that which is true and abiding. And this we can do by faith in him who is the way, the truth, and the life, and whose life is the light of men. Having him, we have found the eternal in the midst of the temporal, and holding fast to him we shall attain to that fullness of life in which the constantly shifting barriers of time and death are merged and lost for ever."—R. J. CAMPBELL, Serm., *The Eternal Invading the Temporal*.

See BABYLON, BONDAGE, CAP-TIVITY, FETTERS, IGNORANCE, ILLU-SION, LIBERATION, LOST (forest), MONK, NIDĀNAS, NIRVANA, ORIGINAL SIN, PENANCES, PRISONERS, RAHU, SEPA-RATION, SORROW, SUN-SETTING, TAR-TARUS, THIRST.

SUFFERING ROOTED IN IGNORANCE :—

A symbol of bondage (suffering) of the Spirit in matter (ignorance).

"The discourse on the four truths is constantly coming to the front as that 'which is the most prominent announce-ment of the Buddhas.' The Buddhists describe ignorance as being the ultimate and most deeply hidden root of all the suffering in the universe : if any one inquires (respecting the nature and in-fluence of) the ignorance of what is re-garded as this fatal power, the uniform answer comes : the ignorance of the four sacred truths. And thus we find these propositions times without number in the canonical texts repeated, discussed, and their importance magnified in extra-vagant terms."—H. OLDENBERG, *Buddha*, p. 210, Eng. trans.

The four sacred truths affirm the bondage (suffering) of Spirit in Matter and the liberation of Spirit from Matter. The meaning, therefore, of "ignorance of the four sacred truths" is that Matter (ignorance) is the root of bondage (suffering), and its extinc-tion in the soul is the aim of religious effort. In the formation of the soul there is to be observed the sacrifice, ob-scuration or death of Truth in Matter, implying ignorance, illusion and evil. Hence the great significance of the symbols "suffering" and "ignor-ance," which have the same meanings as 'crucifixion" and "cross" in Manichaean and Christian scriptures.

"The abolition of ignorance is the beginning and ending of Buddhism. It is the beginning because the whole system is founded on the realisation of the 'truths' which are the object of knowledge. These lie at the foundation." "Ignorance is, in fact, simply ignorance of the Four Truths. In the grasp of them freedom consists. A large part of the (Buddhist) books is occupied with the statement and re-statement of them in every conceivable order and com-bination."—R. S. COPLESTON, *Buddhism*, pp. 105, 112.

The abolition of matter is the beginning and ending of the soul's evolution from matter to spirit. The triumph of Spirit over Matter, of Truth over Ignorance, of the Higher over the Lower, is the great theme of all sacred scriptures of the world. Freedom consists in the abolition of the bondage of Spirit in matter. When the striving Spirit in humanity escapes from the fetters of matter, the illusion of matter ceases and the consciousness enters into bliss.

"One cannot deny that, whether there be a directing Divine providence over human affairs or not, the race has been subjected to illusion at every stage of its progress. Who would dare to say otherwise ? The only question is whether the use of illusion has itself served a beneficent purpose. Assuming that there is such a purpose, it is clear that one aspect of it is that we should be kept in comparative ignorance concerning the full nature and range of the whole. . . . The older I grow, the more terrible and perplexing does life appear to be, and, making all requisite allowance for tem-perament, I think the same is true of most of the people one meets. It contains sinister and dreadful features, is shot through and through with tragedy, is filled with lamentation, and mourning, and woe. It is not a happy world, withstanding the beautiful, gracious, tender, joyous, and uplifting experiences which come our way. The sombre and unideal elements in it are too pronounced to permit of our describing it as very good. Minds constituted as ours are quite un-equal to unravelling the tangle and finding out what it all means."—R. J. CAMPBELL, Serm., *Through Parable to Truth*.

See CROSS, CRUCIFIXION, IGNOR-ANCE, ILLUSION, LIBERATION, MATTER, NIDĀNAS, NIRVANA, SORROW, SPIRIT, VINEGAR.

SUGADHA PLAIN :—

A symbol of the higher sub-planes of the astral plane.

SUKUNA-BIKONA, LITTLE PRINCE :—

A symbol of the personality as a ruler of the lower mind.

"A dwarf deity who wore garments of bird skins and came over the sea in a tiny boat."—W. G. Aston, *Shinto*, p. 107.

The personality is a much-limited (dwarf) manifestation of the soul. The "bird skins" signify the capacity of the personality to aspire to higher conditions; and the "coming over the sea in a boat" is an allusion to the development of the personality on the astral plane (sea) in animal forms which have been evolved first on globes of the lunar chain and afterwards on the physical earth.

See BIRD, BOAT, DWARF, LUNAR CHAIN, OHONAMOCHI, PERSONALITY, PITRIS (lunar), PITRIYANA, PLANETARY CHAIN, SKINS OF ANIMALS.

SUMMER AND WINTER :—

Symbols of love and hate, or fruitfulness and barrenness.

"While the earth remaineth, seedtime and harvest, and cold and heat, and summer and winter, and day and night shall not cease."—GEN. viii. 22.

So long as the lower nature remains, karma, evil and good, love and hate, enlightenment and ignorance, shall as relativity have no end.

See COLD AND HEAT, DAY AND NIGHT, HARVEST, KARMA, OPPOSITES, WINTER.

SUMMER, SEVEN MONTHS :—

A symbol of the period during which the Self realises Itself upon the upper planes of being, as Love and Bliss.

See AUSHEDAR, BLISS, LOVE OF GOD, MONTH, SEVEN, SUN-MOTIONLESS, ZENITH.

SUMMER WHEN UNFRUITFUL :—

A symbol of latency on the buddhic and higher mental planes.

"Ten months of winter are there; two of summer; and these latter are cold as to water, earth and plants; then as frost continues there is disaster."—*Vendidad*, I.

The long winter signifies that there occurs a period of manifestation on the lower planes before there is awakening of the true Divine life upon them. The "two months of summer" symbolise the state on the higher planes, described as being unfruitful, which indicates periods of latency when there is no manifesta-

tion of spiritual life on a globe of the planetary chain.

See BUDDHIC PLANE, EARTH, FROST, KARSHVARES, PLANETARY CHAIN, PLANTS, PRALAYA, SABBATHS, SNOW, WINTER.

SUN :—

The great and universal symbol of the Higher Self,—God manifest,— the central source of Light and Life within the soul.

"There is no visible thing in all the world more worthy to serve as a type of God than the Sun, which illuminates with visible light itself first, and then all the celestial and elemental bodies."—DANTE ALIGHIERI, *The Banquet*, III. 12.

"I feel how difficult it is for the human mind even to form a conception of *that Sun* who is not visible to the sense, if our notion of Him is to be derived from the sun that is visible; but to *express* the same in language, however inadequately, is perhaps beyond the capability of man! To fitly explain His glory, I am very well aware, is a thing impossible. . . . The Sun, that is, Apollo, is 'Leader of the Muses,' and inasmuch as He completes our life with good order, He produces in the world Æsculapius; for even before the world was He had the latter by his side."—EMP. JULIAN, *Upon the Sovereign Sun*.

The Higher Self (sun) is the central harmoniser of the higher qualities (Apollo, Leader of the Muses in the Circle Dance), and completes the life of the soul with the perfect order of its final evolution. He produces in the lower nature (world) the indwelling Divine Saviour (Æsculapius) to heal and raise the soul. For before the lower nature existed, the soul's Redeemer was potential in the Self.

"I was set up from everlasting, from the beginning, or ever the earth was."—PROV. viii. 23.

The Self was, is, and ever shall be, and necessarily existed before the lower nature.

"And so the Sun, just as the Cosmos, lasts for aye. So is he, too, for ever ruler of all vital powers, or of our whole vitality; he is their ruler, or the one who gives them out. God then is the eternal ruler of all living things, or vital functions, that are in the world. He is the everlasting giver forth of Life itself (*The Perfect Sermon*).—G. R. S. MEAD, *T. G. Hermes*, Vol. II. p. 366.

"In the well-known hymn, Rig-veda I. 115, 1, the Sun (Sûryah)—interpreted by advanced pandits to mean the Supreme Being—is called the Soul (Atman) of the Universe, (that is, of all that moves, and is immovable)."—MON. WILLIAMS, *Religious Thought in India*, p. 95.

"The eye of Mitra, Varuna and Agni, for that Sun is the eye of both gods and men ;—he hath filled heaven and earth, and the air, for when he rises he indeed fills these worlds ;—Surya, the soul of the movable and immovable ; for that sun is indeed the soul of everything here that moves and stands."—*Sata. Brâh.*, VII. 5, 2, 27.

The Self in all its aspects is the centre of perception or consciousness within both buddhic and mental states. The Self outpours in the higher, lower, and mental natures ; for when the cycle commences he indeed energises the planes of nature. The Self (Surya) is the emanator of spirit and matter, for the Self is indeed the source of all life and form.

"Later Manicheans taught expressly that Mani, Buddas, Zoroaster, Christ, and the Sun, are the same."—NEANDER, *Church History*, Vol. II. p. 198.

The Higher Self is known under many names and symbols in the scriptures of the world.

"The Sun is a figure in the outward world of the Heart of God."—J. BEHMEN.

"The sun, when mentioned in reference to the Lord, signifies his divine love, and at the same time his divine wisdom. . . . By the sun is understood the Lord as to love and wisdom."—SWEDENBORG, *Apoc. Rev.*, n. 53.

"By the 'sun' the Lord is typified, as is said in the Book of Wisdom (5, 6), that all the ungodly in the day of the last judgment, on knowing their own condemnation, are about to say, 'We have erred from the way of truth, and the light of righteousness hath not shined unto us, and the sun rose not upon us.' As if they plainly said,—The ray of inward light has not shone on us. Whence also John says, 'A woman clothed with the sun, and the moon under her feet.' For by the 'sun' is understood the illumination of truth, but by the 'moon,' which wanes and is filled up every month, the changeableness of temporal things. But Holy Church, because she is protected with the splendour of the heavenly light, is clothed, as it were, with the sun ; but, because she despises all temporal things, she tramples the moon under her feet."—ST. GREGORY, *Morals on the Book of Job*, Vol. III. p. 636.

See ADITYA, APOLLO, ATMAN, CROWN OF TWELVE STARS, DANCE (circle), EYES OF HORUS, GOLD PLATE, HELIOS, HEROIC RUNNER, LIGHT (primordial), MAHAVIRA, PROCESSION, SAVITRI, SELF, SERAPIS, SERPENT ÆSCULAPIUS, SERPENT (solar),

SURYA, TENT, URNS, UTCHATS, VAISVĀNARA, YAO.

SUN AS THE DOOR :—

A symbol of the Higher Self as the means by which the lower consciousness shall rise to union with the higher.

"When he departs from this body he mounts upwards by those very rays (the rays of the sun which enter the arteries of the body), or he is removed while saying Om. And quickly as he sends off his mind (as quick as thought), he goes to the sun. For the sun is the door of the world, an entrance for the knowing, a bar to the ignorant."—*Khand. Upanished*, VIII. 6, 5.

When the perfected soul quits the vehicle of the lower mind, it passes upwards by means of the Divine Life (rays) from above, which purifies the currents of thought and emotion (arteries) ; or by means of the inspiration of Truth and Righteousness (Om). And immediately as the ego (mind) is liberated, the consciousness rises to the causal-body, and union is effected between the lower Self and the Higher Self. For the Higher Self (sun) is the means of union (the door),—the "way, the truth, and the life," which lead to immortality. From the lower life (world) the Self is the means of raising the perfected soul to bliss, and of relegating the unperfected to further experience and discipline below.

See BRAHMARANDRAM, DOOR (higher), HIGHER, MOON (higher), OM, SHEPHERD, UNION, WINDOW OF ARK.

SUN-RISING, OR DAWN :—

A symbol of the commencement of a new cycle of life. The Higher Self (sun) beginning to appear in manifestation on the higher planes.

"That ye may be the children of your Father which is in heaven : for he maketh his sun to rise on the evil and on the good, and sendeth rain on the just and on the unjust."—MAT. v. 45.

The qualities of the soul are exhorted not to strive against their fellow qualities, but to assist them to purify themselves, so that all may be transmuted to the spiritual realm. For the Higher Self is established in the cycle from the commencement, for the purpose of raising all qualities, both evil and good, and therefore truth (rain) is poured forth both on the perfect and imperfect alike in response to their aspirations.

" Now the ' rising of the dawn ' is the brightness of inward truth, which ought to be ever new to us. For the rising of this dawn is in the interior, where the brightness of the Divine Nature is manifested ever new to the spirits of the Angels."—St. Gregory, *Morals on the Book of Job*, Vol. I. p. 213.

" We learn that the highest is present to the soul of man, that the dread Universal Essence, which is not wisdom, or love, or beauty, or power, but all in one, and each entirely, is that for which all things exist, and that by which they are ; that spirit creates ; that behind nature, throughout nature, spirit is present ; one and not compound, it does not act upon us from without, that is, in space and time, but spiritually, or through ourselves : therefore, that spirit, that is, the Supreme Being, does not build up nature around us, but *puts it forth through us*, as the life of the tree puts forth new branches and leaves through the pores of the old. . . . Who can set bounds to the possibilities of man ? Once inhale the upper air, being admitted to behold the absolute natures of justice and truth, and we learn that man has access to the entire mind of the Creator."—Emerson, *Nature*, Ch. VII.

See Aditi, Air, Children of east, Creation, Dawn, East, Father, Heaven, Horizons, Horse sacrifice, Job, Lion-god, Rain, Self, Spirit.

SUN-SETTING :—

A symbol either of the termination, or the commencement, of the great cycle of life. The Higher Self withdraws into the Absolute, or the Higher Self becomes obscured and unapparent to the lower consciousness.

" Thy sun shall no more go down ; neither shall thy moon withdraw itself ; for the Lord shall be thine everlasting light, and the days of thy mourning shall be ended."—Isa. lx. 20.

At the end of the cycle, the individuality (thy sun) shall no longer be obscured to the consciousness, neither shall the personality (thy moon) withdraw any more into incarnation. For the Higher Self (the Lord) is united with the immortal individuality, and the grief of captivity to the lower nature is ended.

" At thy rising all live : at thy sitting they die by thee ; but the duration of thy life is the life that is in thee. Eyes shine brightly until thou settest ; ceaseth all labour when thou settest in the west "

(*Hymn to Aten* (*sun-disk*)).—Wiedemann, *Religion of Anc. Egyptians*, p. 42.

See Bondage, Evening, Horizons, Liberation, Moon (lower), Suffering, West.

SUN MOTIONLESS IN THE ZENITH :—

A symbol of the culmination of the Higher Self in the buddhic consciousness, at the beginning or the ending of a cycle.

" When Aushedar becomes thirty years old, the sun stands still in the zenith of the sky for ten days and ten nights, and it arrives again at that place where it was first appointed by allotment."—*The Dinkard, S.B. of E.*

When the Christ (Aushedar) has arrived at the stature of manhood, that is, when the buddhic consciousness has been attained by the soul, the Higher Self as the individuality (sun) becomes fully (ten) established, having evolved up to that point on the buddhic plane from whence it had fallen, or from whence it had proceeded in entering upon the cycle of involution.

(This statement refers to development on the buddhic plane beyond the present cycle which terminates in the union of the lower Self with the Higher on the higher mental plane.)

See Arrest, Aushedar, I am (bull), Pisces, Summer, Zenith.

SUN-CATCHING AND SUN-BINDING :—

Symbolic of the retardation, as it were, in its course, of the Higher Self by the lower activities. The astro-mental and astro-physical natures seem to oppose and weaken the powers of the Self in the lower nature.

" The fall of the Soul is its approach to matter, and it is made weak because its energies are impeded by the presence of matter which does not allow all its powers to arrive at their realisation " (Plotinus).—T. Whittaker, *The Neo-Platonists*, p. 82.

" Tall as a mountain peak Ravana stopped with his arms the sun and moon in their course, and prevented their rising. The sun when it passed over his residence drew in his beams in terror."—*Ramayana*, III. 36.

The lower principle (Ravana) retards the spiritual course of the higher and lower Selves, and causes suffering.

" We must notice two different conceptions, both of which sound quite mythical, which are preserved in the Jewish and Arabic tradition. One of these supposed that the Sun exhibited such an eagerness for the performance of his work, that the whole world would be set on fire if its consequences were not moderated by various means for cooling down the heat ; and these means are the Pools of the Sun. In the Midrash on Eccles. i. 5, it is said :—' It is reported in the name of Rabbi Nathan, that the ball of the Sun is fixed in a reservoir with a pool of water before him. When he is about to go forth he is full of fire, and God weakens his force by that water that he may not burn up the whole world.' "—Goldziher, *Mythology among the Hebrews*, pp. 340-1.

The " pool of water " is a symbol of the astral plane which " quenches the Spirit," and the " reservoir " may be taken to signify the underworld,— the present life.

" According to another view, the Sun at first resists the performance of his business, and is only moved to do so by violent measures."—*Ibid.*, p. 341.

This refers to the strife of the opposites, good and evil, etc., and the difficult progress of the soul (*see* Mat. xi. 12).

" Maui plaited six great cocoa-nut fibre ropes to make his royal nooses to catch the sun-god Rā ; the first noose he set at the opening where the sun climbs up from Avaiki, the underworld, and the other five one after another further on in the sun's path ; as Rā came up in the morning, Maui pulled the first slip-knot, which held him by the feet, the next by the knees, and so on, till the last noose closed round his neck, and Maui made him fast to a point of rock ; then Rā, nearly strangled, confessed himself conquered, and promised henceforth to go more slowly through the heavens, that men might have time to get easily through their work. The sun-god Rā was now allowed to proceed on his way ; but Maui wisely declined to take off these ropes, wishing to keep Rā in constant fear."—W. W. Gill, *Myths of South Pacific*, p. 62.

The relative Self (Maui), acting from below in the forms, constructed a complete (six) astral mechanism of the soul by which it should function on the lower planes. The series of nooses refers to the gradual evolution of the soul's mechanism through animal forms, from the lower forms (feet) to the higher form (neck), which is the human and which is bound to

the rock (Christ). The Higher Self, or Divine Life (Rā), is now fully involved (noosed) in the soul, and time for the growth of the egos (men) is provided so that they may work out their own salvation in fear and trembling ; " for it is God which worketh in you both to will and to work, for his good pleasure " (Phil. ii. 13).

See Arrest, Boat-sektet, Higher, Maui, Moon-waxing, Net, Noose, Opposites, Shelter, Six, Skins of animals, Underworld, Water (lower).

SUN-DISK, WINGED :—

A symbol of the higher Individuality, which is the atma-buddhic, and which ensouls the causal-body.

" At this juncture the divine Isis asked her father Rā that the winged sun-disk might be given to her son Horus as a talisman, because he has cut off the heads of the fiend and his companions " (*Legend of the Winged Sun-disk*).—Budge, *Gods of the Egyptians.*

And now Wisdom (Isis) craves of the Supreme (Rā) that the mind may be so raised that it be consecrated entirely to the service of the Higher Self (Horus), so that the Divine impress or seal (talisman) be made upon it, and it rise to be one with its Father in heaven, as the Individuality. For it is in this prerequisite,—the conquering over the lower powers,—that the soul is entitled to aspire towards the higher possibilities of the upper planes.

" Horbehûdti (Horus) came in the bark of Rā Harmakhis in a many coloured form as a great winged disk."—*Ibid.*

The Second Logos approached the soul in the " bark of Rā " which is a symbol of the higher or buddhic causal-body of all humanity, containing the complete collective experience of the race. The "many coloured form " is the buddhic vehicle of the higher Individuality.

See Causal-body, Conqueror, Disk, Horbehûdti, Individuality, Isis, Rā, Seal, Sphere, Talisman.

SUN OF RIGHTEOUSNESS :—

A symbol of the Higher Self, the centre of perfection and fount of truth.

" But unto you that fear my name shall the Sun of righteousness arise with healing in his wings; and ye shall go forth, and grow up as calves of the stall." MAL. iv. 2.

To the disciplined qualities which yearn for perfection, the Higher Self (sun) shall arise within to impart truth and transmute their nature. They shall then go forth on higher planes, and develop in harmony and peace the higher emotions.

"The visible world is a book in which, if our spiritual eyes are open, we can read the nature of the invisible; in the soul of man we can discern the lineaments of God. . . . Metaphors and illustrations of spiritual ideas are only possible because of this undoubted correspondence between the two planes of being (higher and lower) with which we have to do. Take such a beautiful figure of speech as the following: 'Unto you that fear my name, saith the Lord, shall the Sun of Righteousness arise with healing in his wings.' Here the sun of our visible universe is used as an image of God's purifying action on the life of the soul; the righteousness of God is spoken of as rising like the sun upon human experience, bringing healing exactly as the rays of our earthly sun dissipate darkness and war against disease. . . . Everything in the universe that has power to awaken in us feelings of delight and elevation of soul is really a spiritual symbol, directly connected with that which it symbolises, a word of God. . . . The universe is a spiritual whole, a system within a system, a work revealing a work; it all means, for those who have eyes to read; it tells of what is hidden."—R. J. CAMPBELL, Serm., *Spiritual Correspondences.*

See CALVES, CREATION, HEALING, HIGHER, IMAGE, NAME, PROTOTYPES, WINGS.

SUN, MOON, AND STARS :—

Symbols of the Individuality, Personality, and mental qualities, or of the Higher Self, lower self, and mental faculties.

"The Sun is not only a seeing eye, but also a flowing well. The Sun being a well, the light of his rays is the moisture that flows from the well. In the Egyptian *Book of the Dead* the Sun is called 'the Sun, the *primitive water*, the father of the gods.' . . . In the *Vendidad* (XXI. 26, 32, 34), 'the Sun, moon, and stars are rich in *milk*.' No less frequent is the idea that the heavenly bodies make *water*."—GOLDZIHER, *Mythology among the Hebrews,* pp. 345–6.

From the Higher Self (sun), the personality (moon), and the mental faculties (stars) there flow wisdom (milk), and truth (water), to nourish the soul.

"The space between the earth and the firm vault of heaven is therefore divided into three spheres, that of the sun, of the moon. and of the stars."—*Zoroastrian System.* J. F. CLARKE, *Ten Religions.*

The plane of Atma, for Higher Self (sun), the astral plane for personality (moon) and the mental plane (stars) are produced as the arena of divine life whereon the Soul expresses its nature under the aspects of Will, Wisdom, and Love.

"And God made the two great lights; the greater light to rule the day, and the lesser light to rule the night: he made the stars also."—GEN. i. 16.

And the Divine Will created two great luminaries in the Soul :—the Individuality and the Personality. The one serving to rule the higher nature (day), the other serving to rule the lower nature (night). And the mental qualities (stars), as lights in the "night," are also said to be made by Him.

"By the sun is signified love; by the moon is signified intelligence and faith; by stars are signified the knowledges of truth and good from the Word."—SWEDENBORG, *Apoc. Rev.*, n. 413.

See CHILDREN OF THE EAST, MILK, MOON, NIGHT, RAIN, SUN, STARS, WATER, WELL.

SUNDAY, THE FIRST DAY :—

This is a symbol of the rousing to life at the opening of a manvantara. It connotes the activity of the Higher Self (sun).

"Now late on the sabbath day, as it began to dawn toward the first day of the week, came Mary Magdalene and the other Mary to see the sepulchre."—MAT. xxviii. 1.

The period represented is now referred to as Sunday because of the association with the visible source of life and light, warmth and power, which is in every way adapted to express the sense of liberation which comes to the risen Christ or perfected soul. The "Marys" bringing "spices" symbolise the quickening and purifying of the emotions through the Rising from the dead lower nature.

See DAWN, EIGHT, LIBERATION, MANVANTARA, RESURRECTION, ROCK SEPULCHRE, SABBATH, SATURDAY, SEPULCHRES, SEVEN, SPICES, SUN-RISING, WEEK, WOMAN.

SUNLIKE OF MEN, YIMA :—

A symbol of the Divine Ego or Self in the aspects of self-command, dignity, and power, which subdue and conquer the lower nature.

See YIMA.

SUPPER, LAST :—

A symbol of the soul's acceptance of a more excellent Way for evolving the Truth and the Life within it.

See SACRAMENT, TRANSUBSTANTIATION.

SURAK COUNTRIES, PEOPLE OF :—

Symbolic of qualities which are to be co-ordinated as disciples of the Higher Self.

See DISCIPLES, PEOPLE.

SURAS, CHIEF :—

A symbol of the supreme Law of the soul's development.

See LAW OF MAZDA.

SURTUR :—

A symbol of cyclic law.

See CHERUBIM.

SURYA, THE SUN :—

A symbol of the Higher Self.

"Because there is none greater than he (i.e. Surya), nor has been, nor will be, therefore he is celebrated as the Supreme Soul in all the Vedas."—*Bhavishya Purāna.*

See ADITYA, HELIOS, HEROIC RUNNER, SAVITRI, SUN, VAISVÂNARA.

SUSA-NO-WO, GOD OF THE SEA :—

A symbol of the desire-nature, or the lower principle.

"Susa-no-wo, before proceeding to take up his charge as Ruler of the Nether Region, ascended to Heaven to take leave of his elder sister, the Sun-Goddess. By reason of the fierceness of his divine nature there was a commotion in the sea, and the hills and mountains groaned aloud as he passed upwards. The Sun-Goddess, in alarm, arrayed herself in manly garb, and confronted her brother wearing her royal necklace of jewels, and armed with sword and bow and arrows. The pair stood face to face on opposite sides of the River of Heaven. Susa-no-wo then assured his sister of the purity of his attentions, and proposed to her that they should each produce children by biting off and crunching parts of the jewels and swords which they wore and blowing away the fragments. Eight children born in this way were wor-

shipped in after times as the eight princely children."—W. G. ASTON, *Shinto,* p. 97.

Before the lower principle is to be identified with the desire-mind on the lower planes (nether region) it stands for relativity and the opposite of all that is Divine in quality. As manifestation is not as yet lower than the buddhic plane (heaven), the lower principle seems to rise and threaten the buddhic principle (Sun goddess) with which it is allied as the inverted reflection of atma, desire being inverted love (divine nature). The fall of mind (man) is conversely the ascent of desire to the mind where it is said to "take leave" of the buddhic principle whose consequent obscuration leaves the lower principle, or desire-mind, to rule the lower nature. The passing upwards corresponds with the commencement of astral (sea) and mental (countries) activities, strife (groans), and growth. The buddhic principle (Goddess) is replete with all the higher qualities (jewels) and spiritual powers (weapons). The lower and higher natures appear to stand opposite each other, divided by the higher mental plane (river). Then to carry out the Divine scheme, the lower and higher natures are said to co-operate in the formation of ruling attributes of the soul. These are the pairs of opposites which are produced in the mind when it begins to function in the human being, and conflict in a multiplicity of ways (fragments) becomes inevitable. Eight leading opposites begin to strive for rule (princely) in the evolving mind of humanity. These are in pairs, and may be described as Love–Dislike, Courage–Fear, Generosity–Greed, Aspiration–Contentment.

"'There shall no strange god be in thee' (Ps. lxxxi. 9). On which the sages (of the Talmud) remark, 'What is the strange god that is in the body of man ? It is the evil impulse' (T.B. Sabbath, 105b).—J. ABELSON, *Immanence of God,* p. 143.

See ADVERSARY, AHRIMAN, AMATERASU, ARROWS, BRIDGE OF HEAVEN, CHILD, CHILDREN, COUNTRIES, FALL, HEAVEN, HIDING PLACE, JEWELS, MYTHOLOGY, NECKLACE, OPPOSITES, QUALITIES, RIVER, RULERS, SEA,

SET, SWORD, TANE-MAHUTA, TYPHON, UKEMOCHI, UNDERWORLD, WEAPONS, YOMI.

SUTRATMA, THE "THREAD-SOUL" :—

Symbol of the Divine Ray, Buddhi-manas, which, issuing from above, penetrates to the lower nature. It constitutes in man the Individuality to which the successive personalities are attached.

"A collective totality of subtle bodies is supposed to exist, and the soul, which is imagined to pass through these subtle bodies like a thread, is called the *Sūtrāt-man*, 'thread-soul' (occasionally styled the *Prānātman*), and sometimes identified with Hiranyagarbha."—MON. WILLIAMS, *Indian Wisdom*, p. 124.

"Who then doth have a Ray shining upon him through the Sun within his rational part—and these (Rays) in all are few—on them the daimons do not act ; for no one of the daimons or of Gods has any power against one Ray of God." (*Corpus Hermeticum*).—G. R. S. MEAD, *T. G. Hermes*, Vol. II. p. 275.

The Divine Ray extends through the Higher Self (sun) seated in the higher mind, and is quite unaffected by the lower nature. None of the desires, passions, or ambitions has any influence upon the spiritual ego, which is the centre of every soul and is in unison with the Supreme Soul (Hiranyagarbha).

"'When the âtman as the cause of the natural constitution of compounds en-dowed with the supreme (consciousness) appears in all bodies, like the string threaded through the store of pearls, he is then called the inner guide (antar-yâmin)' (Sarvopanishatsâra, No. 19). In the Vedântasâra, § 43, the *antaryâmin* is identified with *Isvara*. A similar place is held by it in the system of Râmânuja."—DEUSSEN, *Phil. of Upanishads*, p. 207.

"Being what you are, a spiritual being, a ray from the eternal light, a seedling from the eternal life, a mode of the eternal whole, you must work out your destiny in accordance with the urge of the whole, which is your own urge. It was the urge of the whole which sent you here and subjected you to the conditions under which you are uttering the divine truth latent within you ; it is the urge of the whole, however little you may be conscious of it, which shows you sooner or later where you have made your mis-takes ; which leads you through success and failure, joy and pain, toil and conquest, to the heights of everlasting love. If the whole were not you, you might reasonably regard this discipline as arbitrary ; but it is you ; it is the life

of your own life, your spirit is of its very essence, and you neither have nor could have any interests or any existence apart from it."—R. J. CAMPBELL, Serm., *Who Compels ?*

See ATMAN, BACKBONE, BIRDS (two), BRAHMARANDHRAM, FIG-FRUIT, FILLET, HIRANYAGARBHA, HOMA-TREE, ISVARA, JEWEL SPEAR, SHEEP (lost), SUN, TALUS, TET, TRIDENT, WILL.

SVARGA-WORLD :—

A symbol of the astral paradise, a state of delusion on the astral plane. The after-death dream-world.

See ASTRAL PLANE, PARADISE (lower).

SVAYAMBHU, SON OF THE SELF-EXISTENT :—

A symbol of the manifested Logos.

See FLESH OF JESUS, SACRIFICE.

SWALLOW :—

See FIRE OF HELL.

SWAMP :—

Symbolic of the astro-mental nature (kama-manas).

See MARSH, REED PLAIN.

SWAN, WHITE :—

A symbol of the Higher Self, or the individuality.

"The swan dwelling in the light, doubtless is yonder sun."—*Sata. Brâh.*, VI. 7, 3, 11.

"The swans go on the path of the sun, they go through the ether by means of their magical power ; the wise are led out of this world, when they have con-quered Mara and his train."—*Dhamma-pada*, XIII. 175.

The individualities, or egos, traverse the cycle of life, they pass upward by means of the spiritual energy within them ; the perfected souls are able to rise above the lower nature, for they have been victorious over the desire-principle (mara) and all it stands for.

"The swan that lives in the black waters of the river of Tuoni, lord of the dead."—*Kalevala.*

The spiritual ego that is incarnated, and that manifests in the astro-mental nature, subject to desire and illusion (Tuoni).

"In the ether he (the âtman) is the swan of the sun, in the air Vasu."—*Rig-Veda*, IV. 40, 5.

On the highest plane (æther) the Higher Self (âtman) is the individu-ality of the Supreme (sun); on the mental plane (air) he is the individuality of the Soul.

See ÆTHER, ATMAN, BIRD (great), BLACK, DEAD, DEATH OF LEMMINKAINEN, HIRANYAGARBHA, INDIVIDUALITY, KALAHANSA, MAGIC, MARA, SELF, SUN, URDAR, VAYU, WATER (lower).

SWASTIKA, OR FYLFOT SIGN :—

Emblem of the wheel or cycle of life. The cross with the four arms signifies the four " winds," i.e. the quaternary or four lower planes of nature which are the arena of the soul's development during the cycle. The emblem thus becomes significant of high aims through a period of stress and struggle, with attainment of the heart's desire at the ending.

The widespread appearance of the emblem and its associations show it to be a sacred symbol emanating from the one source of all inspired myths and scriptures, namely, the Holy Spirit on the buddhic plane.

" This was also known as gammadion. In the Greek alphabet the capital letter *gamma* consists of two lines at right angles to each other, and many of the mystical writers of earlier days have seen in this form a symbol of Christ as the corner stone. . . . Many theories have been propounded in attempted elucidation, one being that it represents a revolving wheel, and symbolises the great sun-god."—F. E. HULME, *Symbolism, etc.,* p. 220.

See CROSS, FOUR, FOUR ANGLES, MAASEH-MERCABA, QUARTERS, QUATERNARY, STONE (corner), **T** (letter), WHEEL OF LIFE, WINDS (four).

SWEAT OF THE FACE :—

A symbol of falsity and illusion, —the inverted reflection of truth.

" In the sweat of thy face shalt thou (Adam) eat bread, till thou return unto the ground ; for out of it wast thou taken : for dust thou art, and unto dust shalt thou return."—GEN. iii. 19.

Through gropings of ignorance,—the effort generated of the truth-nature (face), reflected as falsity and illusion (sweat),—shall goodness (bread) be appropriated, until evolution upon the lower planes ends. For the lower mind (Adam) is but the culminating product of the lower evolution. It is as dust which passes away, and it shall not ascend.

See ADAM (lower), BREAD, DUST, EVOLUTION, FACE, FALL, GROUND, ILLUSION, PERSONALITY.

SWEET, BITTER, SHARP, HOT :—

Symbols of happiness, pain, grief, and care, as states of the soul.

SWEET SMELL OF ISIS :—

Symbolic of beauty and love.
See DRAUPADI, PERFUMES.

SWINE :—

A symbol of the lower desires, instincts and astral forces ; signifying an evil state,—depraved and unclean.

" When Jesus the Son of Mary shall descend from the heavens upon your people as a just king, he will break the cross and will kill all the swine."—*The Mishkat,* Bk. XXIII. 6.

When Christ, born in the soul of the purified lower nature, shall irradiate and raise the purified qualities (people), he will be victorious in the crossing-over from the lower to the higher, and will put an end to all evil conditions and desires (swine).

" That the swine should be connected with the underground world of the dead is not surprising. We find the same connection in Keltic mythology (as in Babylonian). There, too, the swine are the cattle of Hades."—SAYCE, *Rel. of Egypt and Babyl.,* p. 358.

See BIRTH OF CHRIST, BOAR, CIRCE, CROSS, HADES, HEAVEN, HUSKS, JESUS, KING, PEOPLE, PIG, SOW, VIRGIN MARY.

SWORD :—

A symbol of outgoing positive energy, either of the higher mind or of the lower, and indicating conflict between the true and the false.

" Then saith Jesus unto him, Put up again thy sword into its place : for all they that take the sword shall perish with the sword."—MAT. xxvi. 52.

The Christ-soul counsels action from high motives, and restraint to bear upon lower desires. " They that take the sword," that is, those aggressive minds or qualities which trust to measures which are the outcome of physical force,—however disguised,—reap as they sow. They are employing means which bring about results in precise accordance with the intent with which they are employed. They are in peril of setting in operation forces which they but imperfectly understand.

"By sword nothing else is signified but truth fighting against falses and destroying them ; and also in an opposite sense, the false fighting against truths."—SWEDENBORG, *Apoc. Rev.*, n. 52.

"In no part of His universe can God be passive. Everywhere He must be the foe of the evil and the friend of the good. Everywhere, therefore, throughout the great perplexed tumultuous universe, we can see the flashing of His sword. 'His sword!' we say, and that must mean His nature uttering itself in His own form of force. Nothing can be in His sword which is not in His nature. And so the sword of God in heavenly regions (Is. xxxiv. 5) must mean perfect thoroughness and perfect justice contending against evil and self-will, and bringing about everywhere the ultimate victory of righteousness and truth."—PHILLIPS BROOKS, Serm., *The Sword Bathed in Heaven*.

See ARROWS (divine), BATTLE, CHERUBIM, CONFLICT, FUDO, INSIGNIA, PEACE AND SWORD, PONIARD, SHIELD, SICKLE, SLAUGHTER, STRIP, TAKE-MIKA, WAR.

SWORD OF THE SPIRIT :—

A symbol of spiritual force, or the intuition which dispels error and ignorance.

"The sword of the Spirit, which is the word of God."—EPH. vi. 17.

Spiritual energy from within, which is the Divine expression of Truth outwardly manifested.

See HELMET, INTUITION, LIGHTNING, SPEAR, THUNDERBOLT, WILL, WORD.

SWORDS, TWO :—

Symbolic of two modes of outgoing energy.

"And they said, Lord, behold, here are two swords. And he saith unto them, It is enough."—LUKE xxii. 38.

This saying refers to the "sword of the Spirit," and to the "sword" of the intellect which trusts to its much might. The two energies are in apparent conflict,—the one with the other. Yet each is well in its appointed place. The energies may therefore be taken as signs of development, and as indicating inward graces which are ultimately to fit the users for their true place in the scheme of the soul's evolution.

See MANAS, RAJAS.

SYCAMORE AND ACACIA :—

Symbols of goodness and truth.

"The forepart of the boat was made of acacia wood, and the after part of sycamore wood, and both kinds of wood were henceforth holy."—*Legend of the Winged Sun-disk*.

The fore front of the causal-body was, as it were, formed of Truth, and the after part of Goodness ; then henceforth Truth and Goodness were conjoined, or made entire and perfect.

"Let me eat my food under the sycamore tree of my lady, the goddess Hathor, and let my times be among the divine beings who have alighted thereon."—BUDGE, *Book of the Dead*, Ch. LII.

"On the sacred monuments of the Egyptians we do find such a tree (of Life), a tree furnishing in the divine economy of the spiritual man the required nourishment of everlasting life. . . . The tree is the *ficus-sycamorus*, the sycamore tree of the Bible."—BARLOW, *Essays on Symbolism*, p. 58.

See ACACIA, BOAT, BOWS, HATHOR, HORIZONS, TREE OF LIFE, YGGDRASIL, ZACCHEUS.

SYMPLÉGADES :—

A symbol of fear, which is a lack of courage to stand firm in mind.

"Watching the recession of the Symplégades rocks, and aided by Hera, the heroes rowed the Argo vigorously on, and escaped so narrowly, that the floating rocks as they rushed together carried off some of her stern-works."—*Argonautic Expedition*.

Watching the progress of effects,—a symbol of right meditation,—and assisted by the Wisdom within, the soul (Argo) went forth, having, however, experienced some suffering and sorrow in the lower self, which is signified by the havoc played by fear (rocks).

See ARGO, FEAR, HEROES, ROCKS (floating).

SYZYGY OF SOPHIA :—

A symbol of the complement of Wisdom (Sophia), which is Love. The rule of Love is at the summit of attainment.

See LOVE OF GOD, WISDOM.

T, THE LETTER, OR THE TAU CROSS :—

A symbol of manifestation of the Divine Life. Tree of life.

"Among the earliest and simplest ideographic symbols in the Chinese language is one which resembles our capital letter **T**, signifying that which is 'above,' and the converse of this, the **T** resting on its base (⊥) signifies that which is 'below.' In both cases a point or a comma, as if a tongue of fire, is placed occasionally over an angel or divine messenger, to signify his more than human character. . . . Hence the symbol **T̈** means to come down from above, where the dot or fiery tongue denotes a spark or flame descending from the upper world, which is signified by **T**. Hence again ⊥ means the lower world, and the symbol ⊥̇ means to go up from below, or to ascend."—BUNSEN, *Angel Messiah*, pp. 57, 58.

The first process is that of Involution, wherein Spirit (fiery tongue) descends into Matter and supplies it with all potencies and qualities. The second process is that of Evolution wherein Spirit ascends from Matter, making manifest in multiplicity and diversity that which had been placed within it. In these two processes the the Divine Life finds expression in the invisible and the visible universes of a solar system.

See CROSS, EVOLUTION, FIRE, HEAVEN AND EARTH, INVOLUTION, MATTER, SPIRIT, SWASTIKA, TREE OF LIFE.

TAAROA :—

A symbol of the First Logos, or of the Absolute, the source of all.

" The Polynesian Supreme Being Taaroa was ' uncreated, existing from the beginning, or from the time he emerges from the *po*, or world of darkness.' In the Leeward Isles Taaroa was Toivi, fatherless and motherless from all eternity. In the highest heavens he dwells alone. He created the gods. . . . Says a native hymn, ' He was : he abode in the void. No earth, no sky, no men ! He became the universe ' " (ELLIS, II. 193).—A. LANG, *Making of Religion*, p. 275.

See CHAOS, DARKNESS, GODS, ORO, PO, TANGAROA.

TAATA, THE FIRST MAN :—

A symbol of the primordial higher mind in alliance with buddhi.

See ADAM, HOA, ORO, RAINBOW, VAIRAUMATI.

TABERNACLE :—

A symbol in its higher aspect of the causal-body ; in its lower aspect, of the astro-mental body.

" It is enough to refer to such passages as HEB. ix. 24—where the holy places of the earthly tabernacle are called the *antitypes* of the true or heavenly ; the latter, of course, being viewed as the types of the other. HEB. viii. 5—where the whole structure of the tabernacle, with its appointed ritual of service, is designated an example and shadow of heavenly things. Ps. cx. 4, HEB. vi. 10, 12, vii. —where Melchizedek is exalted over the ministering priesthood of that tabernacle." —P. FAIRBAIRN, *The Typology of Scripture*, Vol. I. p. 65.

" The Tabernacle of Moses was fourfold. The Outer Court, which was open, denoted the Body or Man physical and visible ; the covered Tent, or Holy place, denoted the Man intellectual and invisible ; and the Holy of Holies within the veil, denoted the Heart or Soul, itself the shrine of the Spirit of the Man, and of the divine Glory, which, in their turn, were typified by the Ark and Shekinah. And in each of the four Depositaries were three utensils illustrative of the regenerative degrees belonging to each division." —*The Perfect Way*, p. 246.

" From this holy Mount (the Celestial Kingdom) proceed all the oracles and dispensations of Heaven. . . . ' For ever, O Lord,' says the psalmist, ' Thy Word is written in Heaven.' And for this reason the Scriptures declare that everything in the Tabernacle of the Wilderness was ' made after the pattern of it in the holy Mount.' For the Tabernacle in the Wilderness is, like the Kaabeh, a figure of the Human House of God, pitched in the wilderness of the material world, and removable from one place to another."— *Ibid.*, p. 149.

" By the tabernacle of the covenant understand the state of perfection. Where perfection of the soul is, there is the indwelling of God. The nearer we approach perfection, the more closely are we united with God. The tabernacle must have a court about it. Understand by this the discipline of the body ; by the tabernacle itself, the discipline of the mind. The one is useless without the other. The court is open to the sky, and so the discipline of the body is open to all. What was within the tabernacle could not be seen by those without. None knows what is in the inner man save the spirit of man which is in him. The inner man is divided into rational and intellectual ; the former represented by the outer, the latter by the inner part of the tabernacle. We call that rational perception by which we discern what is within ourselves. We here apply the term intellectual perception to that faculty by which we are elevated to the survey of what is divine. Man goes out of the tabernacle into the court in the exercise of works. He enters the first tabernacle when he returns to himself. He enters the second when he transcends himself. Self-transcendence is elevation into Deity " (Richard of St. Victor).— *On Contemplation*, Appendix.

"For we know that if the earthly house of our tabernacle be dissolved, we have a building from God, a house not made with hands, eternal in the heavens. For verily in this we groan, longing to be clothed upon with our habitation which is from heaven."—2 Cor. v. 1, 2.

We are assured that when the astro-mental body is finally put off and dissipated, the consciousness rises to the higher mind plane and to the causal-body, which is not formed by the lower activities, but is immortal on the heaven plane. For in this mortal body the personality suffers while the spirit within earnestly strives for liberation, and to be "clothed upon" by the immortal vesture which is laid up for it above.

"This impressive statement (2 Cor. v. 1, 2) means that every human being has more than one body. We are only conscious of possessing one—that is, the physical—but we have a spiritual body, too, in which we shall function consciously by-and-by when we have done with all earthly limitations. We might describe the matter thus : That which is *you* eternally in God, being of his own being, a centre of his own life, is distinguished from every other mode of being by having its own spiritual body, that is, its own peculiar means of realising and expressing itself. The body, any kind of body, is only a means whereby the spirit becomes conscious of itself, and relates itself to all other modes of the universal being. . . . Your spiritual body, your 'house not made with hands, eternal in the heavens,' needs to be enriched and beautified before it can become an adequate instrument for the expression of your spirit. This is why God has given you a physical body, too ; your life in the physical body is for the purpose of acquiring experience bringing certain qualities into manifestation, that your spiritual body may thereby become a glorious vehicle for the utterance of what you eternally are in God."—R. J. CAMPBELL, Serm., *The Two Bodies*.

"Looking for the Maker of this tabernacle, I shall have to run through a course of many births, so long as I do not find him ; and painful is birth again and again. But now, Maker of the tabernacle, thou hast been seen ; thou shalt not make up this tabernacle again. All thy rafters are broken, thy ridge-pole is sundered ; the mind approaching the Eternal has attained to the extinction of desires."—*Dhammapada*, Ch. XI. 153, 154.

Yearning for union with the Higher Self, the contriver of the astro-mental body, the ego has to pass through a protracted series of incarnations. As long as union is unachieved, the descent into sorrow and suffering must continue, until perfection is attained. But now, O Divine Self, thou art perceived by the consciousness ; no longer are the lower bodies to hold captive the spirit. The "ceiling," as it were, of the lower mind is done away with, and the glory of heaven appears. The human intelligence approaching the Eternal has vanquished the lower nature and attained to the extinction of all desires.

"'As I was in the days of my youth : when God was secretly in my tabernacle' (JOB xxi. 4). What in this place do we take the 'tabernacle' for, but the dwelling place of the mind ? Because by all that we do with taking thought, we dwell in the counsel of our heart. But whoever in silence thinks of the precepts of God, to him 'God is secretly in his tabernacle.'"—ST. GREGORY, *Morals on the Book of Job*, Vol. II. p. 410.

See CAUSAL-BODY, CHURCH, HOUSE IN HEAVEN, KAABA, PYRAMID, REINCARNATION, SHRINE, TEMPLE, TENT, WILDERNESS.

TABERNACLES, OR BOOTHS, OF PETER :—

Symbolic of mental definitions or compartments in which the lower mind formulates its conceptions.

"Peter said unto Jesus, Lord, it is good for us to be here : if thou wilt, I will make here three tabernacles ; one for thee, and one for Moses, and one for Elijah."—MAT. xvii. 4.

The unenlightened reason or lower mind (Peter) possesses the tendency to formulate, define, and confine, ideas in forms of thought. Therefore, when the lower mind becomes aware of the reason and ethical (Moses), the emotional (Elijah), and the spiritual (Christ), it wishes to keep each in a special "water-tight" (truth-isolated) compartment (tabernacle) of its own devising.

See BOOTHS, ELIJAH, JESUS, MOSES, PETER, TRANSFIGURATION.

TABLE OF THE LORD :—

A symbol of the highest part of the lower nature or the quaternary (four legs). It is in the religious consciousness (table top) that the selfish desires and aims are offered up to the Divine Ideal within. The desires being transmuted become the sustenance of the soul.

"Ye cannot drink the cup of the Lord and the cup of devils. Ye cannot be partakers of the Lord's table and the table of devils."—1 Cor. x. 21.

It is not possible to receive a measure of the Divine Life, while filling the consciousness with the life of the desires. The qualities cannot partake of the Divine sustenance of goodness and truth when they are being fed by the sensations and desires (devils). The Divine life of Wisdom and Love (the cup) is the antithesis of the self-seeking life of passion, appetite, and desire. If the higher life is to be accepted, then the lower life must be renounced.

See Altar of sacrifice, Anointing, Bread, Cup, Cup of wine, Offering, Religion, Sacrament, Sacrifice, Transmutation.

TABLES HO-TOO AND LO-SHOO :—

Symbols of perception on the mind plane of the ideas of subject and object, of cause and effect, when the interactions of mind and desire commence to operate.

"Fuh-he endeavoured to express thoughts by hieroglyphic signs. These are said to have originated in the drawing up of two linear tables, the Ho-too and the Lo-shoo, which he copied from the back of a dragon rising from the deep."—Kidd, *China*, p. 103.

In the manifestation of the Logos (Fuh-he) at this stage, there arises the possibility of inter-communication between the mental and lower planes. The formation of the kama-manas, or desire-mind, is compared to two tables, —symbolic of the recognition in the lower consciousness, of subject and object, cause and effect,—functions of the mind which are said to be produced from the "back of a dragon," or the astral plane of the lower nature.

See Astral plane, Dragon rising, Fuh-he, Intellect, Mahat, Maishan, Manas, Merchandise.

TABLET :—
See Pen.

TAE-HAOU, THE FIRST EMPEROR OF CHINA :—

A symbol of the First Logos or Higher Self.
See Emperor.

TAE-KEIH, MEANING THE HIGHEST POINT :—

A symbol of the Supreme Self, the Atman.

"When therefore the Holy One, Who is the mystery of all mysteries, willed to manifest Himself, He constituted in the first place a point of light, which became the Divine Thought—that is to say, in its application to the purpose then in view. Within this point he designed and engraved all things, but especially that which is termed the Sacred and Mysterious Lamp, being an image representing the most holy mystery. . . . It follows in the meantime that the universe was created by and from thought. In the beginning, however, that is to say, in the point of Divine Thought, the creation was only in the subject of the Divine Mind, or—as the text (in the *Zohar*) says—it existed, yet existed not."—A. E. Waite, *Secret Doctrine*, p. 53.

See Atman, Creation, Dweller, Kether, Lamp, Lao, Monad.

TAHITIAN ISLANDS :—

A symbol of the mental, astral, and physical planes, as the arena of life's activities.
See Vairaumati.

TAKE-MIKA-DZUCHI, AND FUTSU-NUSHI :—

Symbols of Divine Will and Divine Action in combat with evil and ignorance.

"These two deities have in historical times been universally recognised as War-gods. . . . The *shintai* of both Gods, to some worshippers the Gods themselves, were *swords*. . . . When savage tribes were subdued, or foreign invaders repulsed, these Gods led the van and were followed by the other deities."—W. G. Aston, *Shinto*, p. 157.

These two aspects of the Divine nature,—Will and Action,—are exercised in the conflict between good and evil, the results of which inhere in the causal-body (shintai). When the unruly desires are subdued, or the selfish qualities repulsed, the exercise of the "sword of the spirit" is followed by the evolution of the higher qualities (deities).

See Battle, Conflict, Conqueror, Insignia, Kurus, Meaou tribes, Shintai, Slaughter, Strife, Sword, Victory, War.

TALISMAN :—

A symbol of the Divine Life whose inner vibrations become the object of the religious consciousness, consecrating the mind to Truth and Love, while giving power to withstand the lower desires.

See AMULET, ISIS, MAGIC, SUN-DISK.

TALTHYBIUS AND EURYBATES :—

Symbols of Trust and Aspiration.

TALUS, THE BRAZEN MAN :—

A symbol of the critical faculty of the lower mind.

"This Talus had but one vein in his body, which ran from his neck to his heels, and was filled with ichor : a brass pin was fastened in this vein."—*Argonautic Expedition.*—KEIGHTLEY, *Mythology.*

This "vein" signifies the sutratma, or Divine ray. It runs from the higher mind plane downwards. By "ichor" is meant the consciousness—the reflection of the Divine spark. The "brass pin" is a symbol which may be taken as comparable to the content of consciousness, therefore its removal would indicate the dissolution of the lower nature.

See ÆGAEON, BRIAREUS, CRETE, DOG (Vanghapara), ICHOR, INTELLECT, PERSONALITY, SUTRATMA.

TAMA-GUSHI (TWIGS) :—

A symbol of the purifying buddhic vibrations passing between the buddhic and astral planes.

"The *tama-gushi* are twigs of the sacred evergreen tree (*sakaki*) or of bamboo, with tufts of *yufu* attached. They are, in short, a simple form of *nusa* or *gohei.*"—W. G. ASTON, *Shinto*, p. 216.

"Usumé bound her sleeves close up to the armpits, and grasped in her hand a *bundle of twigs*, and a spear wound round with grass, with small bells attached to it."—*The Nihongi.*

The Emotion-nature, encompassed with opinions and habits, became active, and allied itself with the buddhic vibrations, and the aspirations from the desires and mental faculties, so that the transmutations of lower qualities into higher should be proceeded with, and the lower nature be raised and purified.

See BARHIS, BARSOM, BIRTH (second), BUCKLE, CLOTHING, KUSTI, MITEGURA, SAKAKI, USUMÉ, YAGNAPAVITA

TAMAS STATE :—

This signifies mental inertia,—stupidity and lack of progressive energy in the lower mind.

"*Tamas* is the deluder of all creatures ; it imprisoneth the Ego in a body through heedless folly, sleep, and idleness. *Tamas,* surrounding the power of judgment with indifference, attaches the soul through heedlessness. *Tamas* produceth only senselessness, ignorance, delusion, and indifference."—*Bhagavad-gita*, Ch. XIV.

The mental activity of *tamas* is concerned only with the senses, the instincts, and the lower desires. It has no initiative, and seeks neither truth nor goodness.

See COLD AND HEAT, DROPNER, GUNAS, SHINAR, STIFFNECKED, THIRD HOUR.

TAMBOURINES SOFTLY SOUNDED BY WOMEN :—

Symbolic of the higher emotions which stir the soul when striving to express itself.

See HARMONY, MELODY, MUSIC, WOMAN.

TAMMUZ, THE SON OF THE SPIRIT OF THE DEEP, EA :—

A symbol of Divine Love, the indwelling Self, the Son of the Supreme, the incarnate Self.

"At the summer solstice Tammuz descends into the Underworld (the month in question bears his name). His mother Ishtar, or his sister (both in fact identical), descends to bring him back. . . . At the winter solstice he ascends to bring new life."—A. JEREMIAS, *Old Test.*, etc., Vol. I. p. 126.

See ADONIS, EA, ISTAR.

TAMMUZ, GOD,—LOWER :—

A symbol of self-love and separateness.

"The gate of heaven was guarded by the gods Tammuz and Nin-gis-zida, who asked Adapa the meaning of the mourner's garment which he wore."—SAYCE, *Story of Adapa.*

The portals of heaven, or devachan, are protected by the laws of the lower planes, which prevent their being entered by the force of desire. The symbolism of the guardians is very simple,—one is love of self, the other is love of form-life. While the ego is captivated by these, it remains on the lower planes. The guardians interrogate the ego under its aspect of a sufferer and probationer upon the path to perfection.

See ADAPA, DEVACHAN, DOOR-KEEPERS, ERIDU, GATES (Eridu), MOURNER'S ROBE, NIN-GIS-ZIDA

TANAOA, DARKNESS; AND ATEA, LIGHT :—

Symbols of Matter and Spirit.

"The Marquesas Islanders have a legend which relates that in the beginning there was no life, light, or sound in the world, that a boundless night *Po* enveloped everything, over which *Tanaoa*, which means 'darkness,' and *Mutu-hei*, which means 'silence,' ruled supreme."— A. FORNANDER, *Polynesian Race*, Vol. I. p. 63.

At the inception of the solar universe there was chaos, depth, formless matter, a tenuous concourse of atoms on the buddhic plane, without order and consciousness. Matter unthrilled by Spirit, and negation of life (Silence) pervaded space. (There is indication in the legends that "Tanaoa" sometimes denoted the Absolute, or potential Being (darkness), the source of all).

See ABYSS, ADITI, ATEA, BUDDHIC PLANE, CHAOS, DARKNESS, DEEP, NIGHT, PO, TAAROA, TANGAROA.

TANABATA :—

A symbol of buddhi, the Wisdom function.

See BUDDHI, HIKOBOSHI.

TANE-MAHUTA :—

A symbol of the desire-nature active on the astral plane.

"Tane-mahuta signifies forests, the birds and insects which inhabit them, and all things fashioned from wood."— G. GREY, *Polynesian Mythology*, p. 12.

"Tane-mahuta" is a symbol of desire in its astral medium, together with the formative forces of organic life operating in astral matter (wood).

"Tane-mahuta is represented as a tree with its head downward and roots upward."—R. TAYLOR, *New Zealand*, p. 20.

This refers to the downward, or outward, tendency of desire, the opposite of Love, which is the inner life of the Spirit, urging the soul's development.

"Lo, Tane-mahuta pauses; his head is now firmly planted on his mother the Earth (Papa); his feet he raises up and rests against his father the Skies (Rangi), he strains his back and limbs with mighty effort. Now are rent apart Rangi and Papa, and with cries and groans of woe they shriek aloud. But Tane-mahuta pauses not, he regards not their shrieks and cries; far, far beneath him he presses down the Earth; far, far above him he thrusts up the Sky."—G. GREY, *Polynesian Mythology*, p. 4.

Desire to be effectual in evolution must become the separator, the antagonist of Love, the combiner. Desire is Love inverted, and disunites Spirit (Rangi) and Matter (Papa), when by involution they have come together in potential perfection of being, containing all qualities and prototypal forms. The initiative power in evolution is desire in the lowest forms of life, and it is through struggle and suffering that the forms develop the life that is in them. And so in strife and pain evolution proceeds, while Spirit seems far away and Matter is all in all.

See ARC. MAN, ASTRAL PLANE, CREATURES, DISMEMBERMENT, EARTH, EVOLUTION, FEET, HEAVEN AND EARTH, INVOLUTION, KAMA, PLANTS, PROTOTYPES, RANGI, RAVANA, RONGO, RU, SEKER, SEPARATION, SKY, SOPHIA (lower), SUSANO-WO, TANGAROA, TAWHIRI, TUMA, WOOD.

TANGAROA, THE FATHER OF ALL FISH, AND THE GREAT GOD OF THE OCEAN :—

A symbol of the Logos, or Higher Self, from whom proceeds all Truth.

"Tangaroa, enraged at some of his children deserting him, and being sheltered by the god of the forests on dry land, has ever since waged war on his brother Tane-mahuta, who in return has waged war against him."—G. GREY, *Polynesian Mythology*, p. 8.

Divine Love regarded from below appears as anger, because opposed to the lower self-will and accompanied by suffering. Evolution proceeds through the struggle in the soul between Love and Desire (Tane), God and the devil, Spirit and Matter. The strife is necessary in the separate souls, in order that they should possess individually the potencies of Spirit and come forth as conquerors through the power of the Christ within them.

See ANGER, COCOA-NUT, CONQUEROR, DOLPHIN, EVOLUTION, FISH, FISH (great), IKATERE, JESUS (fish), OCEAN, POSEIDON, PUNGA, STRIFE, TAAROA, TANAOA, TANE-MAHUTA, TUMATAUENGA, TUTE, VARUNA, WATER.

TANHA :—

See THIRST.

TÂO, THE GREAT :—

A symbol of the Absolute, the Infinite, the Unknowable Reality behind all manifestation.

"Lao the Master (Lao-tze) said, The Great Tâo has no bodily form, but it produced and nourishes Heaven and Earth The Great Tâo has no passions, but it causes the sun and moon to revolve as they do. The Great Tâo has no name, but it effects the growth and maintenance of all things."—*The Classic of Purity*, Ch I. 1.

The Higher Self declares within the soul that,—the Absolute is unmanifest, but it emanates and sustains the universe of Spirit and Matter. The Absolute is unconditioned, but from it proceed the activities of the Higher and Lower Selves in the cycle of life. The Absolute cannot be described or defined, but it is the source of the life, development, and sustenance of all that exists.

"There was something undefined and complete, coming into existence before Heaven and Earth. How still it was and fearless, standing alone, and under-going no change, reaching everywhere and in no danger of being exhausted. It may be regarded as the Mother of all things. . . . It is the Tâo—the Great." *Tâo Teh King*, XXV. 1–2.

See ABSOLUTE, KHIEN, LAO-KEUN-TZE, MOTHER (Divine).

TÂO IN TWO ASPECTS,—THE PURE AND THE TURBID :—

Symbols of Spirit and Matter differentiated from the One.

" Now the Tâo shows itself in two forms —the Pure and the Turbid, and has the two conditions of Motion and Rest. Heaven is pure and Earth is turbid, Heaven moves and Earth is at rest. The masculine is pure and the feminine is turbid; the masculine moves and the feminine is still. The radical (Purity) descended, and the turbid issue flowed abroad; and thus all things were pro-duced "—*The Classic of Purity*, Ch. I, 2.

The Absolute emanates two aspects, —the primal duality, Spirit and Matter, having the conditions of Energy and Inertia respectively. Spirit is vibratory and Matter is atomic ; Spirit is dynamic and Matter is static ; Spirit is the Life-side of being, and Matter is the Form-side ; Spirit is the mover, and Matter is the moved. The Ray of Spirit descended into Matter and the forms with their qualities came into being ; and thus the universe was produced.

See HEAVEN AND EARTH, KHIEN, LAO, SPIRIT OF MAN, YANG AND YIN.

TARES, OR " CHILDREN OF THE EVIL ONE " :—

A symbol of the desires and passions proceeding from the lower principle, and which bind the soul to incarnation in the lower nature.

See INCARNATION OF SOULS, REAPING AFTER SOWING.

TARTARUS :—

A symbol of the lower nature in which the souls are confined as they pass through the cycle of life.

" Poets describe Tartarus as the place in the lower world in which the spirits of wicked men are punished for their crimes ; and sometimes they use the name as synonymous with Hades, or the lower world in general."—*Smith's Class. Dict.*

The " spirits of wicked men " are the unperfected souls which, after each incarnation and subsequent inter-val, must descend again to the lower life to undergo development and puri-fication amid conditions of strife and suffering.

See BONDAGE, CAPTIVITY, DUSAKH, EROS, HADES, HELL, SUFFERING, TATTU, TUAT, UNDERWORLD.

TASTE OF BRAHMAN :—

A symbol of the sense of supreme bliss.

" Having evolved that world, he (Brahman) entered into it, he became the limited and the unlimited. . . . Non-existent was this in the beginning, from that the existent proceeded. That made itself, and therefore it is called self-made or holy. He is taste, for on receiving taste a man becomes blissful. For who could live, who could breathe, if in this ether there were not bliss ? For he gives bliss."—*Brihad. Upanishad.*

" The soul approaches the city Sâlagya, and the flavour of Brahman reaches him." —*Kaush. Upanishad*, I. 2.

The ego approaches the centre of the Higher Self and the sense of supreme bliss, to which the sense of taste corresponds, comes to him. This may be compared with,—" O taste and see that the Lord is good " (Ps. xxxiv. 8). It answers to the assimilation of the Truth and Goodness of the Highest. —(*See* HEB. vi. 4, 5 ; 1 PETER ii. 3).

See BLISS, BRAHMA, FLAVOUR, ILYA, ODOUR, SALAGYA, VIBHU.

TATTU, OR LOWER EGYPT :—

A symbol of the lower planes of manifestation of the Self.

" What then is this ? It is Osiris when he goeth into Tattu and findeth there the Soul of Rā ; there the one God embraceth the other, and divine souls spring into being within the divine Twin-Gods. . . . They are Horus the avenger of his father Osiris, and Horus the dweller in darkness. Or, the double divine Soul which dwelleth in the divine Twin-Gods is the Soul of Rā and the Soul of Osiris."—BUDGE, *Book of the Dead*, Ch. XVII.

This refers to a stage in the soul's growth when the lower consciousness of the striving Self (Osiris) perceives the involved or incarnate Self (Rā) within the lower nature (Tattu), and experiences the harmony between each, and the higher qualities that spring into being within them. In other terms, the " Twin-Gods " are the Self-consciousness (Horus) which seeks righteousness and Truth (Osiris), and the indwelling Christ (Horus) potential. Or, again, the Spirit, atma-buddhi (double divine) which is in the " Twin-Gods," is the same in the potential (Rā) as in the actual (Osiris) Christ.

See AKERT, AVENGING, EGYPT, (lower), HORUS, MENDES, OSIRIS, PLACE (Annu), RĀ, TARTARUS, TUAT, UNDERWORLD.

TAUROBOLIUM, MITHRAIC RITE :—

A symbol of the Divine sacrifice in the process of spiritual involution, and of the saving efficacy of the involved Divine Life (blood) in the present process of the soul's evolution.

" Hail, holy Bull, beneficent, who makest increase ; who dost bestow thy gifts upon the faithful. Hail to thee whom the Gahi (and Ahriman) kills."—*Vendidad*, XXI. 1.

" May he who is the strong Bull of the Vedas, assuming all forms. . . . May that Indra strengthen me with wisdom."—*Tait. Upanishad*, 4.

The " bull," like the " lamb," is a symbol of the sacrifice of the Logos in Self-manifestation. Through this sacrifice of the Self in involution, the growth and salvation of souls is secured. The strengthening of the souls in wisdom is brought about by the Divine Life (blood) energising from within. The revolting ceremony of the *taurobolium*

is due to the mistake of materialising the symbols instead of understanding their meaning.

See ATONEMENT, BLOOD, BLOOD OF BULLS, BLOOD OF LAMB, BULL, CORD, CRUCIFIXION OF CHRIST, EVOLUTION, INVOLUTION, RITES, SACRIFICER, TAURUS, WASHED (blood).

TAURT, OR THUERIS, THE WIFE OF SET OR TYPHO :—

A symbol of the emotion Wonder which is allied with the desire-mind.

"Among the great numbers who were continually deserting from Typho's party was his concubine Thueris, and a serpent pursuing her as she was coming over to Horus, was slain by her soldiers."—PLUTARCH, *Isis and Osiris*, § 19.

The " desertion from Typho's party to Horus " signifies the transmutation of the desires and lower emotions to a higher plane. *Wonder*, which aspires to know, becomes raised in quality above the desires, and therefore forsakes Typho (desire-mind). The " serpent " is a symbol of seductiveness of desire, which nearly has the effect of dragging down the aspiring Wonder, when the raised emotions dissolve its life.

"An old philosopher called *wonder*, the beginning of all philosophy. All true philosophy, all philosophy that is founded solely upon wonder and deep reflection, leads to the dissolution of life."—P. DAHLKE, *Buddhist Essays*, p. 184.

" Politically and socially, the great things are done by the men whose minds are full of ' all the wonder that shall be.' Their visions impel to labour that their visions may become realities."—A. MACLAREN, *Sermons*, 2nd Series, p. 50.

See ÆGEUS, CAUSAL-SELF, CORD, HORUS, THESEUS, TYPHON.

TAURUS, THE ZODIACAL SIGN :—

A symbol of the second period of the cycle of life. It signifies the Divine out-going activity in the creation of forms. The " Bull of the West " represents the Matrix of Forms on the buddhic plane ; or the productive energy of buddhi. It pertains to the period of involution when spirit is descending into matter and giving it the potencies of forms and qualities afterwards to be evolved in natural phenomena, and in the souls of humanity.

" The title given to Merodach the Sun-god, when he passed through the twelve zodiacal signs, was Gudi-bir, ' the bull of light.' Hence it was that the ecliptic was termed ' the yoke of heaven,' bound, as it were, upon the neck of the solar bull ; that the first of the Zodiacal Signs, the opener of the primitive Accadian year, was called ' the bull who guides ' the year ; and that two prominent stars received the names of ' Bull of Anu ' and ' Bull of Rimmon.' ''— SAYCE, *Rel. of Anc. Babylonians*, p. 48.

The Higher Self (Merodach), as the matrix (bull) of all forms and qualities, passes through the twelve stages of the cycle of life.

"According to the Chaldæans, Aries is a male zodiacal sign, but Taurus female." HIPPOLYTUS, *Refutation*, V. 8.

See AMENT, ARIES, BUDDHIC PLANE, BULL, CREATION, INVOLUTION, MERODACH, YEAR, ZODIAC.

TAWHIRI-MATEA, THE GOD AND FATHER OF WINDS AND STORMS :—

A symbol of the negative condition of ignorance and illusion which produces disharmony and strife.

" Then also there arose in the breast of Tawhiri-matea a fierce desire to wage war with his brothers, because they had rent apart their common Parents. He from the first had refused to consent to his Mother being torn from her Lord and Children ; it was his brothers alone that wished for this separation, and desired that Papa-tuanuku, or the Earth alone, should be left as a Parent for them. The god of hurricanes and storms dreads also that the world should become too fair and beautiful, so he rises, follows his Father to the realms above, and hurries to the sheltered hollows in the boundless skies."—G. GREY, *Polynesian Mythology*, p. 5.

Then the negative condition of ignorance, in which the entities were necessarily involved, had the effect of producing incessant conflicts throughout nature as soon as the entities became active on their own account. Ignorance could not have consented to separation of matter (Papa), and spirit (Rangi), because, through the consequent evolution, ignorance would be dispelled. But all nature in its five planes (the brothers) was ready for manifestation and to pour out the Divine Life that was in it, while matter (earth) alone was apparent to the consciousness as containing all that was needful. Ignorance is said to dread the development of the soul (world), so it apparently rises and

becomes, as it were, the negation of Spirit, taking refuge negatively in the obscurity of the Infinite Reality ; for the lower nature is ignorant and cannot comprehend the Higher, even as the lesser cannot contain the greater.

See CROPS, GALES, MENIS, RANGI, RONGO, SEPARATION, STORM, STRIFE, TANE-MAHUTA, TUMA-TAUENGA, WINDS (various).

TAZ, MAN, AND TAZAK, WOMAN, ON THE PLAIN OF THE TAZIKAN (ARABS) :—

These symbols signify the active and passive aspects of the emotional qualities (Arabs) in the nascent humanity of early races of mankind.

See ARABS, FEMININE, MASCULINE, RACES, ROOT-RACES.

TCHATCHA OF OSIRIS :—

A symbol of the quaternary,— the four planes below atma.

" May there be no opposition to me from the Tchatcha."—*Papyrus of Ani*. (The *Tchatcha* of Osiris were Mestha, Hāpi, Tuamāutef and Qebhsennuf.)— BUDGE, *Book bf the Dead*, p. 25.

The soul aspires to that which is beyond the opposition on the lower planes.

See CHILDREN OF HORUS, OSIRIS, QUATERNARY.

TCHEFET, IN SEKHET-HETEPET :—

A symbol of a centre on the higher buddhic plane in the soul.

" O Tchefet, I have entered into thee. I array myself in apparel, and I gird myself with the *sa* garment of Rā."— BUDGE, *Book of the Dead*, Ch. CX.

O Self within ! I perceive thee to be the centre of the Divine Life, while I am vestured and girdled with Truth and Wisdom,—the causal and buddhic robes.

See CAUSAL-BODY, ROBE, ROBE OF WATERS, SAHU, SEKHET-HETEP.

TCHESERT, GODDESS ; AND THE DISTRICT :—

A symbol of purification through buddhi,—divine wisdom.

" I have plunged into the lakes of Tchesert ; behold me, for all filth hath departed from me."—BUDGE, *Book of the Dead*, Ch. CX.

Through the functioning of buddhi, the lower nature has been cleansed by truth, and thus the impurities attached to the ego have been gotten rid of.

See BAPTISM, BUDDHI, POOLS OF GODDESS, WATER.

TEARS SHEDDING :—

A symbol of sufferings endured in the pursuit of ideals and the struggle for Truth.

See DOLIONES, JESUS WEPT, SHAVING HEAD, THETIS.

TEE, APEX ORNAMENT :—

A symbol of the stages of progress to the attainment of supremacy over the lower nature.

" On the summit of the great Rangoon pagoda is the *Tee*, a gilt umbrella-shaped ornament with many tiers of rings, on each of which ' hang multitudes of gold and silver jewelled bells.' "—MON. WILLIAMS, *Buddhism*, p. 456.

See MELODY, TET, TIARA, UMBRELLA.

TEETH GNASHING :—

Symbolic of negative, kama-manasic conditions which bring suffering for a time, but afterwards fall away and disappear.

" He shall say, I know not whence ye are ; depart from me, all ye workers of iniquity. There shall be the weeping and gnashing of teeth when ye shall see Abraham and Isaac, and Jacob, and all the prophets, in the Kingdom of God, and yourselves cast forth without."—LUKE xiii. 27, 28.

This signifies the fact of the inability of the Christ to respond when no means is afforded It to do so. The " weeping and gnashing of teeth " symbolise types of low astral, passional conditions which are doomed to dissolve in the ordinary course of things, for they imply impermanence and negation. The reference to the " prophets " means the perception of the dim reflection of the Higher Triad (Abraham, Isaac and Jacob) in the lower nature, which reflection, however, is not destined to partake of the joys of the kingdom of heaven.

See ABRAHAM, DOOR (narrow), FURNACE, JESUS (severity), KINGDOM OF HEAVEN.

TEETH PROTRUDING FROM MOUTH :—

These symbolise power ; the force of that which is uttered ; the spoken Word of God which goes forth and manifests in act and form.

See BOAR (wild), DESERTS, FANG, TUSK.

TEFNUT, WIFE OF SHU :—

A symbol of the receptive form-side of primordial matter on the buddhic plane, which is acted upon by the Divine Life (Shu), Spirit energising.

" Râ breathed, and the god Shu cometh into being, and created the goddess Tefnut."—BUDGE, *Book of the Dead*, Ch. CXXX.

The Supreme Being outpoured the Divine Life, which emanated on the highest plane, and there was added receptiveness to form and quality on the buddhic plane.

See BREATH (divine), NUT, RÄ, SHU.

TELENTE, APHRODITE, OR NIKE :—

A symbol of the physical plane as the reflection below of the atmic plane in respect to its principle Love, which is shown in atomic attraction and in gravitation.

See NEPHTHYS.

TEM, TEMU, TMU :—

A symbol of the Supreme,—the Higher Self in all its aspects.

" I am the god Tem, the maker of heaven, the creator of things which are, who cometh forth from the earth, who maketh to come into being the seed which is sown, the lord of things which shall be, who gave birth to the gods ; I am the great god who made himself, the lord of life, who maketh to flourish the company of the gods."—BUDGE *Book of the Dead*, Ch. LXXIX.

The Higher Self, the founder of the higher planes, the producer by involution of all qualities and forms below, who thereby arises by evolution from the lower planes (earth), who makes manifest the higher qualities from the spiritual germs (seed) placed in the forms ; the ordainer of all future development ; who is the originator of the ideals (gods). He is the self-existent source of Life, the energiser of the Divine attributes.

See COMPANY OF GODS, CREATION, DISMEMBERMENT, EVOLUTION, GATE (tchesert), INVOLUTION, SEED (good), SHU.

TEMPLE OF GOD :—

A symbol of the causal-body, or of the higher mental condition in which the universal consciousness is brought into relationship with the highest forces, and where it becomes possible for all minds to unite in harmony as one.

"Know ye not that ye are a temple of God, and that the Spirit of God dwelleth in you ? If any man destroyeth the temple of God, him shall God destroy ; for the temple of God is holy, which temple ye are."—1 Cor. iii. 16, 17.

The mental quality which is adverse (destroyeth) to the higher nature shall be dissipated by the Higher Self, for the causal-body is the immortal soul.

"Christ transforms us. . . . A holy temple for the Lord shall the house of our heart be. . . . He Himself dwells in us, opening the door of the temple, which we are, i.e. the mouth ; granting us repentance, He carries us into the ever-lasting temple by which he (Barnabas) understands the inner man, to which also he ascribes self-legislation and self-counsel."— Dorner, *The Person of Christ*, Vol. I. p. 115.

"God builds his temple in the heart on the ruins of churches and religions."— Emerson, *On Worship*.

"Temples are not to be built for God with stones piled on high ; He is to be consecrated in the breast of each."— Seneca.

"Temple signifies the church in the world, and the church in heaven."— Swedenborg, *Apoc. Rev.* n. 191.

"Hail, all ye gods of the Temple of the Soul, who weigh heaven and earth in the balance, and who provide sepulchral meals in abundance.' (Temple of the Soul,'—the name of a part of the sky where the gods lived ; a place which had a counterpart on earth, probably at Annu.)"—Budge, *Book of the Dead*, p. 5.

The higher qualities or ideals (gods) reside on the buddhic plane (sky), and they weigh the nature of the soul in the balance of experience, and provide nourishment of truth and goodness for the causal-body.

"A pure mind is a holy temple for God, and clean heart without sin is His best altar " (*Sixtus*).—Augustine, *Anti-Pelagius*, Vol. I. p. 300.

"In these two things the greatness of man consists. One is to have God so dwelling in us as to impart His character to us ; and the other is to have God so dwelling in us that we recognise His presence, and know that we are His and He is ours. They are two things perfectly distinct. To *have* God in us, this is salvation ; to *know* that God is in

us, this is assurance."—F. W. Robertson, *Sermons*, 3rd Series, p. 238.

"Conscious mind—the ordinary action of your cranial brain—is the temple of the Christ-mind. Your will controls, or ought to control, your conscious mind. The duty of your will is to hold your conscious mind or cranial brain to the realisation of the Christ-mind within you. Am I exercising my will in keeping the temple of my conscious mind clean, so that the Christ-mind may have freedom ? Have I learned to direct and control my thought, or do I let my little tiresome thoughts come rushing in and occupy the whole space ? Is my mental temple clean ? Is my mind a pure dwelling-place for his Spirit ? Suppose the answer is, ' No.' Then call on him ; say, ' Even so, come, Lord Jesus.' Come, if you will, with your scourge ; drive out the wrong thoughts, the tempers, and the doubts, and the appetites, and the angers, and the irritabilities, drive them out of thy holy of holies ; cleanse the thoughts of my heart with the inspiration of thy Holy Spirit, that I may perfectly love thee."—B. Wilberforce, Serm., *The Message of Advent*.

See Aaron, Ab, Adytum, Agnish-toma, Annu, Aparagita, Ascension, Causal-body, Church, City of god, Cleansing, Heart, Heben, House in heaven, Kaaba, Pillar (temple), Pyramid, Scourge, Shrine Stupa, Tabernacle.

TEMPLE, FIRE :—

A symbol of the causal-body,— the abode of the Self or Spirit,— atma-buddhi (fire).

"For now the Eternal Father by his fiery power begetteth his Son in thee (the Soul), who changeth the Fire of the Father, namely, the First Principle, or Wrathful Property of the Soul, into the Flame of Love, so that out of Fire and Light (viz. Wrath and Love) there cometh to be one Essence, Being, or Substance, which is the true Temple of God."—Behman, *Supersensual Life*, p. 143.

"Is there any other greater, more satisfying, more majestic thought of life than this—the scaffolding by which souls are built up into the temple of God ? "—A. Maclaren, Serm., *Christian Life*.

"The Lord is in His Holy temple when the Holy Ghost takes up His abode in a pure heart."—J. M. Neale, *Comm. Psalms*, Vol. I. p. 173.

See Altar (fire), Causal-body, Fire, Houses for corpses, Wrath.

TEMPTATION OF JESUS :—

A symbolic epitome of the soul's evolution from the period when

the Son of man (Jesus) was born in the mind, and the consciousness thereby became aware of good and evil, and some faith in goodness was aroused. Then the Higher Self (the Spirit), foreseeing the soul's needs, puts it to the test of experience by placing it in the arena of conflict (wilderness) where it is in relation with the not-Self (devil). Then, after a protracted term of the re-incarnating cycle, the soul is sufficiently advanced to be "hungered," that is, to crave the spiritual sustenance of wisdom and love.

"The narratives of the Temptation are upon the face of them Symbolical."—DR. SANDAY, *Hastings Dict.*, Vol. II. p. 612.

"And the devil said unto him, If thou art the Son of God, command that these stones become bread. And Jesus answered unto him, It is written, Man shall not live by bread alone."—MAT. iv. 3, 4.

This first temptation implies the insecurity of the soul ere the indwelling Christ has become a living factor established in the will. This stage of experience accords with a period of mental instability, when it is possible only to judge truth by contrast with error, or by discernment brought about through the Higher Self acting upon the lower. The "stones" signify the spiritual truths hard to apprehend. The "bread" is the readily assimilated food of knowledge, which man,—the thinker,—can incorporate in his being. And from the not-Self (devil), filled with the pride of relative knowledge, came the suggestion, 'If thou art to progress to Godhood, then reduce spiritual truth (stone) to terms of reason (bread) so that it may be comprehended by the lower mind.' And the Christ within replied, that the Divine law of progress was written upon the heart. The soul cannot live by reason only, but needs to possess truth from the Spirit in order to live the life from God.

"Man has had to put forth his latent spiritual potencies one by one, and this has necessitated the gradual purification and elevation of desire by the deliberate and conscious rejection of the merely egoistic tendencies of our nature. There is no other way in which moral excellence, as contrasted with innocence, can be attained."—R. J. CAMPBELL, Serm., *The Nature of Temptation.*

See ARENA, BREAD, DEVIL, EVOLU-

TION, EXPERIENCE, FOOD FOR SOUL, FORTY, HUNGER, INCARNATION, JESUS, KINGDOMS, MAN, MOUNTAIN (lower), REINCARNATION, STONES AND BREAD, WILDERNESS.

TEN, NUMBER :—

A symbol of completion of a process, or accomplishment of a purpose. It is also a sacred number and bears reference to the line | and the circle O, which produce a cross X only when the lower nature is acting in opposition to the higher.

"Ten—is symbolic of natural perfection and completion in general."—J. GARNIER, *Worship of the Dead*, p. 221.

"That ten days signify duration of state to the full is because 'days' signify states, and 'ten' what is full; for times in the Word signify states, and numbers designate their quality."—SWEDENBORG, *Apoc. Rev.*, n. 101.

"This number ten signifies perfection; for to the number seven, which embraces all created things, is added the trinity of the Creator."—AUGUSTINE, *Manichaean Heresy*, p. 107.

"And as Jesus entered into a certain village, there met him ten men that were lepers, which stood afar off: and they lifted up their voices, saying, Jesus, Master, have mercy on us. And when he saw them, he said unto them, Go and show yourselves unto the priests. And it came to pass as they went, they were cleansed. And one of them, when he saw that he was healed, turned back, with a loud voice glorifying God, etc."—LUKE xvii. 12–19.

The cry of the ten lepers is the appeal of the troubled lower self to the Christ within, who directs that the restoration to health of mind and spirit be accomplished by ordinary and familiar means, viz. means consistent with the ethical and religious ideals (priests) of the personality. The lepers are said to be cleansed of their infirmity, though only one returns to render thanks; thus signifying that the majority of the qualities,—nine,—were as yet active only on a lower plane, whereas the tenth quality, the one who returned glorifying God, was lifted up above his former position, or, in other words, the state or condition of soul into which he now entered was one of increased usefulness.

"By the number 'ten' the sum of perfection is set forth."—ST. GREGORY, *Morals on the Book of Job*, Vol. I. p. 43.

See HEALING, LEPER, NINE DAYS.

TEN DAYS, MONTHS, OR YEARS :—

Symbolic of complete periods of development within stages of the soul's growth.

"And the waters decreased continually until the tenth month; in the tenth month, on the first day of the month were the tops of the mountains seen."—GEN. viii. 5.

And the "waters" of illusion and error diminish in the soul until the "tenth month," that is, until the completion of a full term of spiritual growth required at that state and period. The term being completed, then the heights of attainment are laid before the soul.

See AUSHEDAR, FLOOD, MOUNTAIN.

TENEDOS ISLAND :—

A symbol of the lower state of the soul which knows not the higher nature that rules it.

"Hearken to me (Chryses), god of the silver bow that standest over Chrysa and holy Killa, and rulest Tenedos with might."—*Iliad*, Bk. I.

The Spiritual Mind (Chryses) aspires and seeks to raise the desires. 'Attend, O Soul of Truth! that standest over the Causal-self, and art the inspirer of Buddhi, and who governest the lower nature by higher motives.'

See APOLLO, CHRYSES, SMINTHEUS.

TENT OR TABERNACLE OF THE SUN :—

A symbol of the buddhic causal-body as the abode or vehicle of the Higher Self, in which he accomplishes his course through the cycle of manifestation.

"The heavens declare the glory of God ; and the firmament sheweth his handywork. Day unto day uttereth speech, and night unto night sheweth knowledge. There is no speech nor language, where their voice is not heard." —Ps. xix. 1–3.

On the higher planes are the ideals to be attained when the Self returns to his own in glory and power ; and on the higher mind plane (firmament) are the energies and the archetypal forms. In the outgoing periods there is expression of the mental faculties and qualities, while in the indrawing periods there is gathered in the wisdom due to effort. There is no outpouring of truth where the ideals are not sought after.

"Their rule is gone out through all the earth, and their words to the end of the world. In them hath he set a tent for the sun, which is as a bridegroom coming out of his chamber, and rejoiceth as a strong man to run a race. His going forth is from the end of the heaven, and his circuit unto the ends of it : and there is nothing hid from the heat thereof."—Ps. xix. 4–6.

The ideals of buddhi-manas govern the lower nature, and their expression is to be complete in the human soul. On the buddhic plane there is formed the causal-body for the Higher Self (sun), who cometh out from atma in love and power to run his course. His going forth is from the heights of buddhi (the first point of Aries), and his circuit is to the same again in greater height ; and there is nothing in which Spirit is not predominant.

[Compare Rā (Helios) in the cabin (tent) of his boat (soul) traversing the river of the Tuat (cycle of life), accompanied by all his attributes and higher qualities (gods and goddesses).]

See AFU-RĀ, CABIN, CAUSAL-BODY, CIRCLE OF EXISTENCE, DAY, EARTH, FIRMAMENT, NIGHT, TABERNACLE, SUN.

TENT OR HUT :—

A symbol of the mental vehicle in which are concepts and opinions of the lower mind.

"Slumber not in the tents of your fathers ; the world is advancing, advance with it."—MAZZINI.

"Here in the body pent,
    Absent from Him I roam,
Yet nightly pitched my moving tent
    A day's march nearer home."

See BOOTHS, HUT, PAVILION.

TESTAMENT :—

A symbol of a covenant between the Higher Self and the soul-qualities, whereby, on the fulfilment of certain conditions by the evolving qualities, the Self will redeem or raise them.

"How much more shall the blood of Christ, who through the eternal Spirit offered himself without spot to God, purge your conscience from dead works to serve the living God ? And for this cause he is the mediator of the new testament, that by means of death, for the redemption of the transgressions that were under the first testament, they which are called might receive the promise of eternal inheritance."—HEB. ix. 14, 15.

The "old testament" is the moral law which requires the sacrifice of the lower desires and passions (goats and bulls), whose "blood" is shed or whose life is dissipated on the altar of the heart. The "new testament" is the law of Love-divine, i.e. the attractive love of Truth and Goodness which replaces the coercive moral law.

The Divine Life of the Self (blood of Christ) was offered through Buddhi (Spirit) in all its purity to the Supreme Will, at the soul's foundation, in order that the conscience should be cleansed of the taint of coercion, and the Divine love should lead the already disciplined qualities. Thus the Self-within—the Divine Indweller—became the mediator and redeemer of the qualities, by means of the death in matter which constitutes him the Indweller. He entered in once into the "holy place" of the over-soul, and "shed his blood," that is, gave up his life that eternal redemption might accrue to the evolving qualities accepting that life. When the qualities have passed through the stage of moral coercion, they are called upon to enter the stage of liberty and love, and receive the promise of their transmutations on the higher planes.

See ALTAR, ARC. MAN, BEASTS, BLOOD, BLOOD OF LAMB, BURNT OFFERING, CONSCIENCE, COVENANT, DEED, DISPENSATIONS, EVOLUTION, FRUIT, GRACE, HOMA-JUICE, INCARNATION, INVOLUTION, JUSTIFICATION, KARMA, LAW OF MOSES, MEDIATOR, MOSAIC, MOSES, OFFERING, QUALITIES, REDEEMER, REDEMPTION, SACRIFICE, SACRIFICER, SALVATION, SOMA-JUICE, SOUL, TRANSMUTATION.

TET-PILLAR, OR BACKBONE OF OSIRIS :—

A symbol of the tree of the Divine Life transpiercing the four lower planes, and signifying aspiration and the ultimate attainment of perfection above the quaternary.

"The four cross bars of the Tet are intended to indicate the four branches of the roof-tree of a house, which were turned to the four cardinal points."—BUDGE, *Gods of the Egyptians*, Vol. II. p. 125.

The four quarters of the compass signify the four lower planes, as do the four winds, the four children of Horus, and the four supports of heaven.

"As a religious emblem, the Tet symbolises Osiris the Lord of Tettu, great god of the underworld. The meaning of the word tet is 'firmness, stability, preservation,' etc. The Tet had on it sometimes the plumes, disk and horns, and was painted on mummies and tombs."—BUDGE, *The Mummy*, p. 259.

"On a post on which is graven a human countenance, and which is covered with gay clothing, stands the so-called Tât-pillar, entirely made up of superimposed capitals, one of which has a rude face scratched upon it, intended no doubt to represent the shining sun. On the top of the pillar is placed the complete head-dress of Osiris, the ram's horns, the sun, the ureus adder, the double feather, all emblems of light and sovereignty, which in my judgment must have been intended to represent the highest heaven."—C. P. TIELE, *Hist. of Egyptian Religion*, p. 46.

"Like the Buckle, the Tet had to be dipped in water in which *ankham* flowers had been steeped, and laid upon the neck of the deceased, to whom it gave the power to reconstitute the body and to become a perfect Khu (i.e. spirit). —BUDGE, *Egyptian Magic*, p. 46.

The Tet symbolises the indwelling Higher Self (Osiris) striving to manifest in the lower nature (the underworld of four planes) by means of aspiration (the pillar). The plumes of victory crown achievement. Truth (water) and virtue (flowers), through the higher mind (neck), cause the transmutation (reconstitution) of the qualities, so that the soul rises in its buddhic vesture (Khu), the "purple robe."

"Rise up thou, O Osiris! Thou hast thy backbone, O Still Heart! Thou hast the fastenings of thy neck and back, O Still Heart! Place thou thyself upon thy base, I put water beneath thee, and I bring unto thee a Tet of gold that thou mayest rejoice therein."—BUDGE, *Book of the Dead*, Ch. CLV.

The "Still Heart" is the Divine Love latent within the soul awaiting the aspiration (backbone) which should arouse the soul into activity. The lower nature is attached to the higher mind (neck) and to the passive aspect of Spirit (the back), i.e. Buddhi, in order that purification should come about. Truth (water) shall raise the aspiring lower Self, and the treasures of the Spirit (the tet of gold) are laid up in heaven for the glorified soul.

"*Scene from the Papyrus of Ani.* The Tet, or tree-trunk which held the body of Osiris, standing between Isis and Nephthys, who kneel in adoration, one on each side of it. From the Tet proceeds the emblem of life, which has arms that support the disk of the Sun. The six apes represent the spirits of the dawn." "Text: A Hymn of praise to Râ when he riseth in the eastern part of heaven."—BUDGE, *Book of the Dead*, p. 73.

This picture is a very clear and full symbolical diagram of the Resurrection. The ankh cross stands upon the Tet, signifying the crucifixion in the lower nature (four planes) from which the Soul now rises. The raised arms symbolise the purified personality transmuted to become one with the Higher Self (Sun). The spiritual (Isis) and the natural (Nephthys) have finished their work in developing the Soul. The six adoring apes represent the multitude of egos (saints) which rise with their Saviour to the heaven world.

See APES, BACKBONE, CROSS, CROWN OF OSIRIS, CRUCIFIXION OF CHRIST, DAWN, DEATH OF OSIRIS, DISK, EAST, FOUR, HEART, HORNS, HOUSE, HOUSE (four doors), ISIS, KHUS (higher), NECK, NEPHTHYS, OSIRIS, PILLARS (four), PLUMES, QUARTERS, QUATERNARY, RESURRECTION, SUN, SUTRATMA, TATTU, TEE, TREASURE, TREE OF LIFE, UNDERWORLD, UNION, URAEI, VICTORY, WATER.

TETRAGRAMMATON, THE *WORD* OF FOUR LETTERS, **IHVH** :—

A symbol of the outpouring of the *Logos* on the four planes below atma. This is the quaternary which at the completion of the involutionary process stands for the Heavenly Man, the Archetypal Man, Adam Kadmon, Purusha, Pragâpati, Kaiomarts, Jehovah, Christ incarnate, etc.

"And the Word became flesh, and dwelt among us (and we beheld his glory, glory as of the only begotten from the Father), full of grace and truth."—JOHN i. 14.

And it was so that the Christ, the Higher Self, became related to the lower nature and dwelt among the qualities of the soul (and the higher qualities had perceptions of the Ideal which was exalted within them), full of love and wisdom, grace and truth.

See ADAM (higher), ARC. MAN, FIRSTBORN SON, FUH-HE, I E O U, INCARNATION, INVOLUTION, JEHOVAH,

QUALITIES, QUATERNARY, WORD (divine), YEDUD.

TEZCATLIPOCA :—

A symbol of the Supreme Being, the First Logos, the Father, the unmanifest God proceeding from the Absolute—the Source of All.

"He was primarily the personification of the breath of life. Savage man regards the wind as the great source of breath and of immediate life, and in many tongues the words 'wind,' 'soul,' and 'breath' have a common origin. But, although he was a life-giver, Tezcatlipoca had also the power to end existence. He was usually depicted as holding a dart in his right hand, and his mirror-shield with four spare darts in the left. His exalted position in the Mexican pantheon seems to have won for him especial attention as a god of fate and fortune."— *Non-classical Mythology*, p. 167.

The Divine Life is out-breathed in producing existence, and in-breathed in ending existence. The Supreme Being originates the buddhic causalbody (mirror) and exercises the outgoing spiritual energy (dart) on the four planes below Atma. From Him proceed the laws of nature and the Karmic law of cause and effect.

See ARROWS, BREATH (divine), FUH-HE, MIRROR, QUETZALCOATL, SHIELD, SPIRIT.

THEBE, THE HOLY CITY OF KING EËTION :—

A symbol of preconceived ideas of truth which lie innate within the mind.

See INTUITION.

THEBES IN EGYPT :—

A symbol of the higher mind.

See CADMON, NET-RÃ, PAMYLES.

THEMIS, GODDESS :—

A symbol of Divine law in the inner and outer universes.

"In the Homeric poems, Themis is the personification of the order of things established by law, custom and equity, whence she is described as reigning in the assemblies of men, and as convening, by the command of Zeus, the assembly of the Gods."—*Smith's Class. Dict.*

Through Divine law the mental qualities (men) are co-ordinated, and on the spiritual planes the Ideals (gods) are harmonised.

See ASSEMBLY OF PEOPLE, COMPANY OF GODS, FATE-SPHERE, JUDGMENT,

Karma, Maat, Moirae, Necessity, Nornox, Shai, Shenit, Word.

THEOPHILUS (OF LUKE) :—

A generic term signifying the "beloved of God."

"It is far more reasonable to suppose that Theophilus' is a personification of the whole God-loving class, than to take it as the name of a literal man."—E. Gough, *Barrowford Treatise*, p. 62.

THESEUS, SON OF ÆGEUS :—

A symbol of Wonder-awe proceeding from spiritual knowledge. This mental state incites to the pursuit of truth and the dispelling of delusions.

See Ships of Greeks, Taurt.

THETIS, GODDESS :—

A symbol of nature, the cosmic process ;—the buddhic scheme reflected on the astral plane.

"So spake Achilles, weeping, and (Thetis) his lady mother heard him as she sat in the sea-depths beside (Nereus), her aged sire. With speed arose she from the grey sea, like a mist, and sate her before the face of her weeping son, and stroked him with her hand, and spake and called on his name."—*Iliad*, Bk. I.

Thus the Personality is stirred by the sorrows which afflict it, whereupon evolving Nature, which is buddhi, reflected in the astral sub-planes, beside the force aspect of the Logos in the physical—came forth from the desire-nature (grey sea) like more refined emotions (as mist), and stirred the intelligence of the Personality, thereby arousing the latent qualities within the soul.

"Nature works inside her productions, and forms them by growth ; whereas man works from the outside, and by adding one part to another. Nature also makes her living product reproduce itself, while man must himself make a new machine. . . . The blind properties of things play exactly the same part in both cases : whether design underlies them both is just the question at issue."—H. M. Gwatkin, *The Knowledge of God*, p. 67.

See Achilles, Hand, Mut, Name, Nereus, Nod, Palace, Sapandomad, Statute, Tears, Thunder.

THIEF OR ROBBER :—

A symbol of the desire-nature which robs the Self of his primordial wealth.

"All that came before me are thieves and robbers."—John x. 8.

The desires which precede the birth of Christ in the soul assail the ego from without and rob the soul of its higher qualities.

"'All that came before me are thieves and robbers.' Could anyone come before him when the spiritual consciousness first arose, if he has been both door and shepherd all along ? Yes, 'first that which is natural, and afterward that which is spiritual.' The lower ever precedes the higher in the earthly unfoldment of the divine purpose. . . . The impulses and desires of the natural man have to be brought into captivity to the obedience of Christ, for if they are not, they will work havoc in the soul."—R. J. Campbell, Serm., *The Door, the Thief, etc.*

See Door (higher), Murderer, Shepherd (good).

THIEVES, THE FIVE :—

A symbol of the five planes of nature as robbing the Self of his primordial unity and perfection.

"To Heaven there belong the five mutual foes, and he who sees them, and understands their operation, apprehends how they produce prosperity. The same five foes are in the mind of man, and when he can set them in action after the manner of Heaven, all space and time are at his disposal, and all things receive their transformations from his person."—*Kwang-tze, S. B. of E.*, Vol. XXXIX p. 258.

To this Mr. Legge, the translator, has added in a footnote :—

"The startling name thieves (= foes, robbers) here is understood to mean the 'five elements,' which pervade and indeed make up the whole realm of nature, the heaven of the text, including also earth."

The Spirit or Self is involved in the five planes of manifestation ; and the Ego, who perceives this involution and understands the nature and functioning of the planes, is able to apprehend how they conduce to the glorifying of the Self. For the same five planes are in the human soul, and when the human ego can deal with them in accordance with the will of the Spirit, then he shall attain mastery over time and space, and all the qualities of his personality shall be transmuted for his Individuality.

See Days (five), Elements (five), Gatha days (five), Heaven, Hermes, Incarnation, Involution, Khien, Macrocosm, Microcosm, Planes (five), Rulers, Self, Worlds (five).

THIGH :—

A symbol of power to advance, or of progressive quality, or means of progress. Position of thigh signifies the astral plane.

See AURVA, PURUSHA, RUDDER.

THIGHS OF BULLS AND GOATS :—

Symbolic of the lower desires which must be sacrificed.

See BEASTS, BULLS, FLESH, GOATS, HECATOMB, SACRIFICE.

THIRD EYE :—

A symbol of the vague astral clairvoyant faculty of early humanity, which, as evolution proceeds, is exchanged for the physical organs of sight.

See EYE (third).

THIRD HOUR :—

A symbol comparable to the stage of tamasic energy (stupidity) in the lower mind, kama-manas. It may mean also the completion of a period or stage of development. In the first case twelve hours is taken as a complete period or cycle of life.

See GUNAS, TAMAS, THREE, TUAT, ZODIAC.

THIRST, OR TANHA :—

A symbol of longing either for the "water above," truth-reality ; or the "water below," illusion-sensation.

"To thirst signifies to desire truths." "Him that is athirst means he who desires truth for the sake of any spiritual use."—SWEDENBORG, Apoc. Rev., n. 956, 889.

"He who has reached the consummation, who does not tremble, who is without thirst and without sin, he has broken all the thorns of life : this will be his last body."—Dhammapada, 351.

The ego who has attained liberation who is without weakness and longing for the things of the lower life, whose nature is purified—he has severed the bonds to a suffering existence, and will incarnate no more.

"A man accompanied by tanha (thirst), for a long time transmigrating into existence in this way or in that way does not overcome transmigration."—Sutta-nipâta, 740.

An ego who retains a longing for the illusions of desire and sensation will continue to incarnate again and again.

"By 'water' sacred knowledge is denoted, as it is said : 'and give him the water of wisdom to drink' (ECCLUS. xv. 3)."—ST. GREGORY, Morals on the Book of Job, Vol. II. p. 400.

"My soul thirsteth for God, for the living God."—Ps. xlii. 2.

"I by myself am full of passionate longings, of earnest desires, of unsupplied wants. 'I thirst' is the voice of the whole world. No man is made to be satisfied from himself. For the stilling of our own hearts, for the satisfying of our own nature, for the strengthening and joy of our being, we need to go beyond ourselves, and to fix upon something external to ourselves. We are not independent. None of us can stand by himself. No man carries within him the fountain from which he can draw. . . . We want one Being in whom shall be sphered all perfection, in whom shall abide all power and blessedness ; who is light for the understanding, power for the will, authority for the practical life, purpose for the efforts, motive for the doings, end and object for the feelings, home of the affections, light of our seeing, life of our love, the love of our heart, the one living God, infinite in wisdom, power, holiness, justice, goodness and truth. . . . He that believeth upon Him shall never hunger, and he that cometh unto Him shall never thirst. God is the divine and unfathomable ocean ; Christ the Son is the stream that brings salvation to every man's lips."—A. MACLAREN, Sermons, 1st Series, pp. 125–30.

See AAT, (waters), CHRIST, CONSUMMATION, DRINK, HOUSE OF BONDAGE, HUNGER, ILLUSION, INCARNATION OF SOULS, LAW OF BUDDHA, LIBERATION, METEMPSYCHOSIS, OCEAN, REINCARNATION, STREAM, SUFFERING, THORNS, WATER.

THIRSTY WORLD :—

A symbol of the phenomenal and illusory existence of the ego on the lower planes, in which Truth is sought and Self-realisation gained.

See LAW OF BUDDHA, STREAM, WORLD (thirsty).

THIRTEEN, NUMBER :—

A symbol signifying completeness or infinity. It is a "holy number," and cannot be divided.

"As the number of the lunar months, thirteen is the symbol of the Woman, and denotes the Soul and her reflection of God—the solar number twelve being that of the Spirit. The two numbers in combination form the perfect year of that dual humanity which above is made in the image of God—the true 'Christian Year,' wherein the two—the inner and the outer, Spirit and Matter—are as one.

Thirteen then represents that full union of man with God wherein Christ becomes Christ."—*The Perfect Way*, p. 247.

See Æon (thirteenth), Born out, Judas, Ogdoad.

THOAS, FATHER OF HYPSIPYLE :—

A symbol of the germ of truth which produces philosophic pride.

See Euneus, Hypsipyle, Lemnos.

THÖCK,—A GIANTESS :—

A symbol of the passional nature which engenders the sense of separateness, and so binds the soul to the wheel of re-birth.

"But, Thöck she weepeth with dry tears for Balder's death : ' Neither in life nor yet in death, gave he me gladness ; let Hel keep her prey.' It is supposed that this Thöck was Loke the son of Lofo."—*The Prose Edda*, Howitt, *Literature, etc.*

But the personality dominated by the lower emotions is not able to be the means of bringing the Christ to birth within the soul, and it professes to know nothing of the spiritual nature in which it seems to have no part at this early stage.

See Asar, Balder, Frost, Hell, Loke, Personality, Reincarnation, Separateness, Soul, Wheel of life, Woman (Loke).

THOR WITH HIS HAMMER :—

A symbol of the higher mind wielding the will (Mjölner).

"Thor, as mediator between heaven and earth, had the general command of this terrestrial atmosphere."—Mallet, *Hist. de Danemarc*, Intro.

The higher mind is the medium of communication between the higher and lower natures in the soul, and organises the mental plane (air).

"Thor stood beside the funeral pile of Balder, and consecrated it with his hammer Mjölner. Before his feet sprung up a dwarf called Lit ; Thor kicked him with his foot into the fire, so that he also was burned."—*Story of Balder, Edda.*

And from the mental plane with which the ego is identified the Self beholds the sacrifice and sanctifies it with self-conscious experience. And now rises a "dwarf," the symbol of error, which the mind consigns to the purifying process which is to yield spiritual fruition.

See Cremation, Fire, Funeral, Hermes, Mjölner, Nanna, Ringhorne, Thoth.

THORNS AND THISTLES :—

Symbolic of evils, sufferings, and sorrows.

"Thorns also and thistles shall it (ground) bring forth to thee ; and thou shalt eat the herb of the field."—Gen. iii. 18.

Sins and sufferings shall proceed from the lower nature ; and the lower mind (Adam) shall subsist through the produce of the sensation-nature and the affections.

"For the body becomes liable to a curse, since it has for its husbandman an intellect (Adam) unchastened and unsound. And its fruit is nothing useful, but only thorns and thistles, sorrow and fear, and other vices which every thought strikes down and, as it were, pierces the intellect with its darts."—Philo, *Works*, Yonge, Vol. IV. p. 309.

"Each man is the soil in which the hereditary Adam-seed produces thorn and thistle, and the hereditary God-seed produces grape and fig. The two growths in the same individual strive for the mastery, and from the deep contrast between them emerges the perfected life of the child of God."—Basil Wilberforce, *Problems*, p. 81.

See Adam (lower), Crowning, Curse, Herb, Personality, Thirst.

THOTH :—

A symbol of the higher mind principle, between the higher and lower natures.

" ' In the mystic sense Thoth, or the Egyptian Hermes, was the symbol of the Divine Mind ; for he was the incarnated Thought, the living Word—the primitive type of the Logos of Plato and the Word of the Christians ' " (Artaud).—G. R. S. Mead, *T. G. Hermes*, Vol. I. p. 27.

"And Cronus [Ammon] going to the land of the South gave the whole of Egypt to the God Taaut (Thoth) to be his kingdom."—Sanchuniathon, *Cory's Fragments.*

Higher and Lower Egypt signify the mental plane.

"Thoth was held to be both the heart and the tongue of Râ, that is to say, he was the reason and the mental powers of the Gods, and also the means by which their will was translated into speech. . . . In every legend in which Thoth takes a prominent part, we see that it is he who speaks the word that results in the wishes of Râ being carried into effect."—Budge, *Gods of the Egyptians*, Vol. I. p. 407.

"Then spake Thoth to Râ : ' Lord of the Gods ! there came the God of Behûdet (Edfu) in the form of a great winged-disk.' From this day forth he shall be called Horbehudti (Horus of Edfu)."—*Legend of the Winged Sun-disk.*

Then spake the higher mind or awakening intelligence to the Creator —Lord of the ideals! there came forth the Son of Man in the wisdom vesture on the buddhic plane; and this being so, he shall now be known as the Son of God, born of the eternal Spirit of Truth.

"Thoth, the divine intelligence which at the creation uttered the words which resulted in the formation of the world. He was self-produced, and was lord of earth, air, sea, and sky; he was the scribe of the gods, and the inventor of all arts and sciences."—BUDGE, Book of the Dead, p. 5.

"The Egyptians relate that Thoth had one arm bent so that it could not be straightened." — PLUTARCH, Isis and Osiris, § 22.

The "arm bent" is a symbol of the inability of the intellect to act with perfect directness and sureness. It is the function of the mind to perceive dissimilarities and to disclose differences, more or less completely; and unaided by a higher faculty it can never display the perfect truth.

"Every abstract proposition intellect enunciates is based upon a contradiction somewhere; there is no help for it; this is the inevitable outcome of the way it is made and of the conditions under which it has to work. Furthermore, it is so uncertain in its operations that what it discovers to-day may have to be discarded to-morrow. If the intellect were thoroughly reliable there ought to be no room for differences of opinion on any subject whatever. But unfortunately it is not so. Two individuals, both intelligent and both conscientious, may form diametrically opposite judgments from exactly the same evidence."—R. J. CAMPBELL, Serm., The Super-rational.

See ADAM (higher), DAIMONS, DOORS OPENED, EDFU, EGYPT, HERMES, IBIS, INTELLECT, INTUITION, MAGIC, MAHAT, MANAS, NARADA, NEBO, NEHEMAUT, PTAH, SCRIPTURES, SHINATSU, THOR, WORD.

THRACE :—

A symbol of metaphysical cogitation.

THRAÊTONA (FREDÛN), SON OF ATHWYA :—

A symbol of the Divine outpouring of Life, proceeding from the Second Logos (Athwya).

"The fourteenth land was the four-cornered Varena for which was born Thraêtona, who smote Azis Dahaka."—Vendidad, I.

The "four-cornered land" signifies the lower self entire, that is, the quaternary of four planes below Atma. "Thraêtona" is a symbol of the Divine outpouring, which takes effect upon the buddhic plane, and is the buddhic emotion-nature which is the means of slaying the unreal—the sense of separateness, or illusion, caused by the function of the lower mind.

See ATMA, BUDDHIC PLANE, QUATERNARY, SAPANDAR, SEPARATENESS, SERPENT-DAHAKA, SLAUGHTER, VARENA.

THREE, NUMBER :—

A symbol of completeness of process or state. The perfect number of the higher planes.

"Three is symbolic of individual completion and individual action; of the threefold aspect of God to man, as Father, Son, and Holy Spirit, and of man himself as body, soul, and spirit."—J. GARNIER, Worship of the Dead, p. 220.

"The Chinese say numbers begin at one, are made perfect at three, and terminate at ten."—S. KIDD, China, p. 304.

"By three is signified all and full, a completion to the end."—SWEDENBORG, Apoc. Rev., n. 416, 505.

"'Behold, I cast out devils, and I do cures to-day and to-morrow, and the third day I shall be consummated or perfected' (LUKE xiii. 32). For He said this in the person of His body, which is His Church, putting days for distinct and appointed periods; whilst He also signified on 'the third day' the perfection which should accrue to Him in His resurrection."—AUGUSTINE, Anti-Pelagius, Vol. I. p. 345.

See RESURRECTION, SIGN, TRIAD, TRINITY, WALKING DAY BY DAY.

THREE DAYS :—

A symbol of a completed period of time.

"The chief priests and the Pharisees were gathered together unto Pilate, saying, Sir, we remember that that deceiver (Jesus) said, while he was yet alive, after three days I rise again."—MAT. xxvii. 63.

The literalists, formalists, and dogmatists did not want Truth, for their occupation would be gone if fresh illumination came to them. After a period completing a state of soul, Christ would rise in glory in human minds and become the actual in their lives, and not only the ideal of their souls. The ideal of life in one

age is the conduct of life in the next.

See PHARISEES, PILATE, PRIESTS AND ELDERS, SIGN.

THREE TRIPLE POWERS :—

Symbolic of love of power, lust, and avarice. They are triple because they act upon the three lower planes.

THRESHOLD, HEAVENLY :—

A symbol of the higher planes of mind which are the entrance to spirit.

THRINAKEA, ISLE OF THE SUN :—

A symbol of the centre of the buddhic plane in the soul.

THRITA, THE THIRD MAN :—

A symbol of the Third Logos emanating on the mental plane.

"Thrita, the most useful of the Sâmas, was the third man who prepared me (Homa) for the material world."—*Homa Yasht.* HAUG, *Essays.*

This symbolises the production of the mental plane through the Third Logos. The mental principle is the most useful of the Divine forces (Samâs), inasmuch as it corresponds to the formative aspect of the functioning of the soul.

See CREATION, HOMA, MAHAT, SAMÂS.

THROAT :—

A symbol of lower mental expression of prejudice and convention subversive of truth.

"Their throat is an open sepulchre; with their tongues they have used deceit."
—ROM. iii. 13.

The little-developed mental qualities are under the sway of formalism and sectarianism, and so their expression controverts the truth.

See ISIS, SEPULCHRES, TONGUE.

THRONE (HIGHER ASPECT) :—

Symbol of the causal-body, the seat of the Higher Self. In its highest aspect "throne" is the buddhic vehicle of atma.

"Thus saith the Lord, The heaven is my throne, and the earth is my footstool. Where is the house that ye build unto me? and where is the place of my rest."—ISA. lxvi. 1.

In the expression of the Supreme the atma-buddhic nature is the summit of attainment, and the lower nature

(earth) provides the fou[...] the elevation of the [...] causal-body (house) is [...] developed, by the strivin[...] qualities, and is to beco[...] of the Higher Self.

"The human soul sits a[...] everything, and Christ sits[...] of the human soul. If h[...] then everything will be c[...] 'He that sitteth upon the [...] Behold I make all things [...] change must be in you. To [...] all things shall be new. If [...] Christ, he is a new creature[...] creature is immediately [...] creation."—PHILLIPS BRO[...] *Timeliness.*

See ARSH, BOOK, CH[...] HORUS, DISCIPLES SEATE[...] MAASEH.

THRONE OF HIS HEAR[...]

A symbol of the causa[...] which is seated the Self [...] aspect of Love.

See BIRTH OF MAN-CHILD[...] BODY, GARDEN OF REST.

THRONE VIKATSHAN[...] BRAHMAN :—

A symbol of mastery ov[...] the sign of absolute po[...] sovereignty.

THRONES, TWELVE :—

A symbol of twelve qualitie[...] muted, and so brought to a[...] state compared with a [...] condition.

See DISCIPLES ON TWELVE T[...] JUDGES, SAVIOURS (twelve), [...] (twelve).

THUNDER OF GOD O[...] HEAVEN :—

A symbol of the expressi[...] the Divine Will in pain and [...] on the lower planes.

"The Lord also thundered i[...] heavens, and the Most High utter[...] voice; hailstorms and coals of fi[...] Ps. xviii. 13.

"The voice of the Lord is upo[...] waters; the God of glory thunde[...] even the Lord upon many water[...] Ps. xxix, 3.

Through the sufferings and terro[...] the lower planes (the waters), fo[...] of thought, erroneous opinions, [...] unruly passions, are disrupted [...] made to give place to better states[...]

"But I (Thetis) will go myself to sn[...] clad Olympus to tell this thy saying[...]

us, whose joy is in the thunder, if chance he may hearken to me."—*Iliad*, Bk. I.

Nature, however, contemplates soaring to the heights to impart the knowledge which has been gathered by the Higher Self, who rejoices in the errors which must beneficially befall the lower Self in its progress.

See LIGHTNING, THETIS, TLALOC, VOICE, ZEUS.

THUNDERBOLT ; LIGHTNING :—

A symbol of spiritual energy active on the higher mental plane (upper air).

"Verily, as large as the altar is, so large is the earth. The sacrificial stakes are thunderbolts ; and by means of these thunderbolts he obtains possession of this earth, and excludes his enemies from sharing therein."—*Sata. Brâh.*, III. 7, 2, 1.

Truly, the necessary structure of spiritual idealism for developing the soul's higher nature is planted in the soul's lower nature (earth). The individualised structure of the Divine Life, which is raised up in the soul through sacrifice of the lower for the higher, is the means of releasing the invincible spiritual energy which captures the lower nature and dissipates the lower qualities (enemies).

[The various sources of spiritual activity on the higher planes are said to be "thunderbolts"—such as water (truth), cattle or cows (buddhic emotions), ghee or butter (Divine love). The last is also said to be "fiery mettle" or "fiery spirit."]

"The Holy Spirit cries in us with a loud voice and without words, 'Love the love which loves you everlastingly.' His crying is an inward contact with our spirit. This voice is more terrifying than the storm. The flashes which it darts forth open the sky to us and show us the light of eternal truth. The heat of its contact and of its love is so great that it well-nigh consumes us altogether."—RUYSBROECK (Eng. trans.), p. 95.

See ALTAR (fire), EARTH, ENEMIES, LIGHTNING, SACRIFICE, STAKE, YEAR.

TIAMAT, THE SPIRIT OF CHAOS :—

A symbol of the emotion-nature undirected by the mind.

"The Deep over which Tiamat—the Spirit of Chaos—held sway, was without limits or law, whose only progeny was a brood of monsters."—SAYCE, *Rel. of Egypt. and Babyl.*, p. 376.

The emotion-plane is not the plane whereon harmony and order are first maintained. That order is introduced through the manasic evolution which guides and directs, and moulds and defines. The "monsters" are inchoate emotions of all kinds, which are quite without any sense of that due proportion which reason brings about.

See CHAOS, DEEP, EVOLUTION, MANAS, MONSTERS, TRIBE-RULERS.

TIARA, THE PAPAL CROWN :—

A symbol of divine supremacy over the lower nature. The three crowns are emblematical of rule over the mental, astral, and physical elements of human nature. The triple crown is worn by the Pope of Rome because he represents the spiritual mind which directs religious activities in the soul.

See CROWNS, LION (man), POPE, TEE.

TIGRIS, OR HIDDEKEL, RIVER :—

A symbol of the astral plane.

See ASSYRIA, ASTRAL PLANE, EDEN (rivers), HIDDEKEL, NICOTHEA.

TILLER OF THE GROUND :—
See HUSBANDMAN, PEASANT.

TIME AND NON-TIME :—

Time is a condition of the manifestation of the relative. Non-time is the absence of manifestation.

"There are two forms of Brahman, time and non-time. That which was before the existence of the sun is non-time and has no parts. That which had its beginning from the sun is time and has parts. Of that which has parts, the year is the form, and from the year are born all creatures ; when produced by the year they grow, and go again to rest in the year. Therefore the year is Pragâpati, is time, is food, is the nest of Brahman, is Self."—*Mait. Upanishad*, VI. 15.

There are two predicates of God— the Absolute and the Relative. That which is prior to the Higher Self (sun) is the Absolute and Unconditioned. That which proceeds in or from the Self is a series of successive states of the conditioned. The whole series constitutes the Cycle of Life (the year) ; and from the Cycle and its states are produced all qualities and forms (creatures). These arise when conditions allow of them ; they develop, mature, and subside in the Cycle.

Therefore the Cycle is the creative aspect of the Supreme, is a succession of states of being, is Truth replacing illusion, is the dwelling place of God, is the Self.

" If there never was any beginning to time, then there is no time. If there never was a moment when the first universe sprang into being, then there is no universe at all. To speak of an infinite succession of worlds, or of anything else, is the same thing as to say that there is no succession whatever. Is it not plain that the whole material universe as it enters into our experience now is but *the creation of our own consciousness ?* It is what it is because we are what we are. . . . You cannot escape the dilemma. Either your own mentality, your own self-awareness, is unreliable, or the external world is unreliable. I prefer to say the latter —indeed, I cannot help saying it. It is our selfhood that is real, and only that, however little we know about it. The one fact of which we can be sure in all this drift of phantasms is the tiny flame of *self-consciousness,* the light of the Spirit that derives from himself. It is that which is ; all else may come and go, but that abides. Time and space are *within it,* not it within them."—R. J. CAMPBELL, Serm., *The Timeless Affinity.*

See ABSOLUTE, ALPHA, BIRD'S NEST, CIRCLE, CRONUS, FIRST, FOOD, ILLUSION, MANVANTARA, MATTER, MĀYĀ, NUT, PHENOMENA, PRAGÂPATI, PRALAYA, RHEA, SEB, SUN, YEAR, ZODIAC.

TIPHERETH, THE HEART OF THE HEAVENLY ADAM :—

A symbol of the causal Self, or Individuality, in the causal-body.

" The male or positive principle Hesed, i.e. Grace, etc., and the negative or female principle Pahad, i.e. Punishment, etc., unite in Tiphereth, i.e. Beauty. . . . Tiphereth, says the Idrah Zootah, is ' the highest manifestation of ethical life and perfections, the sum of all goodness, in short, the Ideal.' . . . The Sephirah Tiphereth is called the King, and all the existences proceed from the union of the King and the Queen (Malkhuth)."— I. MYER, *Qubbalah,* pp. 200-203.

The individuality (Hesed) and the perfected personality (Pahad) unite in the Self seated in the causal-body (Tiphereth), and become thereby the highest manifestation of spiritual perfection. The causal Self and the buddhic principle (Malkhuth) are the two factors in the evolution of the qualities of the soul. These are the Divine cause of aspiration and purification of the soul.

" The reciprocal affinity of the *Two Faces* (Tiphereth and Malkhuth) operates in two ways, sometimes it is from Above to Below, then the existence and life go out of the Highest World affecting the objects of nature ; sonetimes, on the contrary, it goes from the Below to the Above, that is from this, our world of illusion, change, and unreality, to the real and true, Above ; and takes back to the Highest the existences entitled to such a return."—*Ibid.,* p. 283.

This refers to the outpouring and indrawing of the qualities in the process of alternate incarnation and discarnation of the soul. The causal-Self (mental) and the buddhic principle (emotional)—the " Two Faces "—unite in emanating the mental-emotional qualities to manifest in the lower nature of the soul ; these pass, as it were, from Above to Below, where experience and development are gained. On the return of the qualities from the illusion below to the Reality above the gain in the manifestation of the true and the good is transmuted to the higher planes.

See HESED, ILLUSION, INDIVIDUALITY, MALKUTH, PAHAD, PERSONALITY, PHENOMENA, SEPHIROTH.

TIPHYS, THE SON OF AGNIUS :—

A symbol of the lower aspect of the " Lamb of God," and indicates the initiative of which the Self is capable directly the gentleness and calm of the lower nature is established.

See LAMB OF GOD, VIRGIN.

TISTRYA (JUPITER PLANET) :—

A symbol of the Ego who initiates, directs, and governs qualities on the mental plane, in order to awaken ideals.

" Tistrya is called the giver of wealth ; his lustre is red, and of great beauty."— HAUG, *Essays,* p. 200.

Tistrya is a symbol of the Ego or causal Self. He is the " giver of wealth," because all that is gotten comes through the Self seated in the causal-body. The " red lustre " is the sign of force and mental power.

See CLOUDS, HORSE (red), JUPITER, PLANETS, PUITIKA, RED, VOURUKASHA, WEALTH.

TITANS, TWELVE :—

A symbol of the primal, essential, constituent qualities of life on the lower planes, qualities which condition the struggle between higher and lower, but are not themselves lower qualities, but rather qualities of necessity.

"The sons and daughters of Uranus and Ge originally dwelt in heaven. They were twelve in number, six sons and six daughters, namely, Oceanus, Coeus, Crius, Hyperion, Iapetus, Cronus ; Thia, Rhea, Themis, Mnemosym, Phoebe, and Tethys ; but their names are different in other accounts."—*Smith's Class. Dict.*

The "Titans" are said to be produced by Spirit and Matter on the plane of buddhi (heaven). They reappear at the close of the period of involution, and after pralaya, in order to condition evolution. They are active and passive qualities, and may be indicated thus—Spirit, Number, Action, Love, Will, Time : Wisdom, Space, Order, Memory, Intuition, Harmony.

"The Titans are the ultimate artificers of things, and the most proximate to their fabrications."—OLYMPIODORUS, *On the Phædo of Plato.*

The story of Cronus emasculating his father Uranus simply refers to the completion of the period of involution of Spirit (Uranus) into Matter (Ge). Time, as it were, put a stop to the process of impregnation of matter with all the qualities and forms afterwards to be brought forth during the process of evolution. The "Erinyes" signify the instincts, opposites, and strivings, which are the life (blood) of the lowest condition of evolution. "The Titans depose Uranus," that is, the natural order takes the place of the spiritual, and Spirit is obscured. Time (Cronus) and Space (Rhea) are allied and reign supreme in the new order of things. "Cronus swallows his children," that is, Time encompasses all the planes and powers of nature, visible and invisible. But Time cannot encompass Spirit (Zeus). It can only seem to do so, when the new-born Christ is small and feeble on the buddhic plane. The Spirit is nurtured and brought up in the soul (cave). The Spirit and the powers of nature enter upon the great contest (Titanomachia) with Time and the potential qualities (Titans), to wrest from these the soul's experience and development. The potential becomes the actual, and the Spirit is victorious at the last.

See CRONUS, DIONYSUS, HYPERION, KRONOS, OCEANUS, RHEA, RIMTHURSAR, THEMIS, URANUS, ZAGREUS, ZEUS.

TITHES TO THE SUPERIOR :—

A symbol of the sacrificial tribute of the lower qualities to the higher ; for then "without any dispute the less is blessed of the better" (HEB. vii. 7).

See BLESSING, MELCHIZEDEK, TRIBUTE.

TLALOC, GOD OF WATER :—

A symbol of the Higher Self under the aspect of Truth-reality.

"He was espoused to Chalchihuitlicue (Emerald Lady), who bore him a numerous progeny, the Tlalocs or clouds. He manifested himself in three forms, the lightning-flash, the thunderbolt, and the thunder. He was supposed to inhabit the four cardinal points and every mountain-top, and the colours of the four directions of the compass were introduced into his costume, in stripes of yellow, green, red, and blue. In order that he might fructify the crops a vase containing every kind of grain was placed before him. He dwelt in a well-watered and luxurious paradise, called Tlalocan, where those who had been drowned or struck by lightning enjoyed immortal pleasures. He is usually represented in the Aztec manuscripts as having a dark complexion, a large round eye, a row of tusks, and an angular blue stripe rolled over the lips."—*Non-classical Mythology*, p. 174.

The eternal Truth (atma) was allied to Wisdom (buddhi), and produced the buddhic functioning (clouds) which disseminates truth (rain) to the lower planes. Truth is manifested in the Divine Life activities of the higher planes (lightning), the spiritual energy on the higher mental plane (thunderbolt), and the Divine Will in fear and terror on the lower planes (thunder). From Truth-reality on the heights of being (atma) there emanate the four planes below, namely, buddhic (red), mental (blue), astral (green), and physical (dirty yellow). The Higher Self sows the seeds of Truth in the lower nature, and fructifies them that they may bring forth abundantly the higher qualities on the buddhic plane (Tlalocan) in the souls of humanity.

The large eye signifies omniscience—the all-perceiving Truth; the tusks, omnipotence on the planes of being; and the dual blue stripe on lips, the higher and lower centres of consciousness on the mental plane of the soul.

See BLUE, CLOUDS, COLOURS, FOUR, LIGHTNING, MOUNTAIN TOP, OCEANUS, POSEIDON, QUARTERS, QUATERNARY, RAIN, SOWER, THUNDER, TUSK, VARUNA, WINDS (four), WATER, ZEUS.

TOGA, OR ROBE :—

A symbol of the causal-body as a vesture of the soul.

"And my purple toga, which was measured and woven to my stature."—GNOSTIC, *Hymn of the Soul*.

And my causal-body which was fashioned according to the express image of my personality when perfected.

See CAUSAL-BODY, CLOTHING, GATE OF SALUTATION, PEARL (precious), PERSONALITY, RAIMENT, ROBE, VESTURES.

TOKENS, FOUR SACRED :—

Symbols of aspiration.

"Noah carries the body of Adam into the Ark, his three sons following with the four sacred tokens."—*Book of the Conflicts of Adam*.

"Noah" stands for the sublimated "Adam"; he therefore carries his old self into the Ark (soul-state), as it is only through its means he rises. His "sons" stand for the fruit of the affectional nature, who willingly follow with the symbols of his aspiration. The "sacred tokens" are Faith, Love, Wisdom, Power.

See ADAM'S DEAD BODY, ARK, MELCHIZEDEK, NOAH, NOAH'S SONS, ROCK, TREASURES (cave).

TOMB :—

A symbol of the lower nature in which the personality (corpse) is interred. A mode of functioning on the lower planes.

"The Tomb, that is to say, the present world, which is the receptacle of corruptible things."—DANTE, *The Banquet*, IV. Ch. 22.

"The Chapter of coming forth by day after having made the passage through the Tomb. Saith Osiris Ani :—

"Hail Soul, thou mighty one of strength! Verily I am here, I have come, I behold thee. I have passed through the Tuat (underworld), I have seen my divine father Osiris, I have scattered the gloom of night. I am his beloved one. I have stabbed the heart of Suti (Set). .

I have become a *sāhu*, I have become a *khu*."—BUDGE, *Book of the Dead*, Ch. IX. p. 57.

This is the joyous outpouring of the liberated soul on the higher planes, after having accomplished his course through the lower nature.

Saith the soul : I acclaim the Self, the mighty indweller ! Truly I have risen, and now I perceive the Self within. I have progressed through the Cycle of the lower quaternary, and I behold the archetypal Self who begot me. I have done away with ignorance and have attached myself to Truth. I have overcome and cast out the lower principle (Set), and have become an Individuality (khu) in a causal-body (sāhu).

"Religious people are always tending to seek the living among the dead, and having to be recalled to the obvious truth that the soul of good can never be shackled in the bonds of matter, or buried permanently in any tomb of failure and misunderstanding, however strong."—R. J. CAMPBELL, Serm., *The Resurrection Life*.

See ARC. MAN, COMING FORTH, CORPSE, DEFUNCT, ENTOMBMENT, KA, KHABIT, KHUS (higher), LAZARUS, MOUTH (speech), NIGHT, OSIRIS, PERSONALITY, QUATERNARY, RE-STAU, RESURRECTION, ROCK SEPULCHRE, SAHU, SEPULCHRE, SET, SPICES, TUAT, UNDERWORLD.

TOMI (CUTTINGS OR PARTS) :—

A symbol of discarded astro-mental forms of thought utilised for lower planes of the soul.

See ABSYRTUS, TONGUE (lower).

TONGUE (HIGHER ASPECT) :—

A symbol of the expression of truth, or of the active manifestation of the Logos on the several planes of nature.

"Then the blessed Sakya-muni and the blessed Prabhūtaratna, still seated on the throne of the stūpa, smile to one another. Their tongues protrude from their mouths as far as the world of Brahma."—*Lotus of the Good Law*, Ch. 20.

The Higher Self and the Individuality seated in the causal-body are united in harmony, and their expression of Truth is in accordance

with the Divine Reality,—the actual
realising the potential.

See BRAHMA, BUDDHA, HEROIC
RUNNER, LIPS, MOUTH, SPEECH,
STUPA, THRONE.

TONGUE (LOWER ASPECT) :—

**A symbol of the expression of
falsity and perversion of truth and
right.**

"And Horus, grasping in his hand his
keen-edged knife, pursued them, and
brought back 142 of the enemy, whom he
slew; and he tore out their tongues, and
their blood gushed out upon the ridges of
the ground."—*Legend of the Winged Sun-
disk.*

And the Son of God, the active
agent (hand) of the eternal Truth,
taking the "sword of the Spirit,"
went forth in the strength of the
Divine Will, slew his enemies the
desires, and "tore out their tongues,"
a symbol of falsity and perversity;
and the vitality which had before animated them was dissipated and flowed
to the lower planes, wherein it was
resolved into its primary constituents.

"By tongue is signified the doctrine of
the church or of any religion; but in an
opposite sense, false doctrine."—SWEDEN-
BORG, *Apoc. Rev.*, n. 282.

"Casting out the old man, plucking
out the right eye, maiming self of the
right hand—there is no growth without
some sorrow. *Conflict* is the word that
defines man's path from darkness to light.
No holiness is won by any other means
than this, that wickedness should be
slain day by day, and hour by hour.
In long lingering agony often, with the
blood of the heart pouring out at every
quivering vein, you are to cut right
through the life and being of that sinful
self; to do what the Word does, pierce
to the dividing asunder of the thoughts
and intents of the heart."—A. MACLAREN,
Sermons, 1st Series, p. 87.

See BLOOD, CONFLICT, ENEMIES,
GROUND RIDGES, HAND, SLAUGHTER,
SUFFERING, SWORD, THROAT.

TONGUES, GIFT OF :—

See GIFT.

TONSURE :—

See HAIR SHAVEN.

TOOTH OF BUDDHA, DALADA :—

**A symbol of the spiritual power
of the Self,—the force of the uttered
Word, or expression of the Divine
Will.**

See BUDDHA, ELEPHANT (white),
TUSK.

TOP-KNOT :—

See MAUI.

TOP-RING OF THE SACRIFICIAL STAKE :—

**A symbol of the buddhic causal-
body.**

"The sacrificer then looks up at the
tog-ring with, 'the wise ever behold
that highest step of Vishnu, fixed like
an eye in the heaven.'"—*Sata. Brâh.*, III.
7, 1, 18.

See CHIP, GIRDLE ROPE, SACRIFICER,
STAKE, STRIDES, VISHNU.

TORCH LIGHTED AND RAISED :—

**An emblem of illumination, signi-
fying intelligence and knowledge;
or life.**

See MITHRA AND BULL.

TORCH EXTINGUISHED AND REVERSED :—

**An emblem of darkness, signify-
ing ignorance; or death.**

TORTOISE :—

**A symbol of the higher and the
lower planes centralised by the
mental plane, and energised by
the Divine Life.**

"This tortoise is that life-sap (blood)
of these worlds, which flowed away from
them when plunged into the waters:
that life-sap he (Pragâpati) now bestows
on Agni. As far as the life-sap extends,
so far the body extends; that tortoise
thus is these worlds.

"That lower shell of it is this terrestrial
world; it is, as it were, fixed; for fixed,
as it were, is this earth-world. And that
upper shell of it is yonder sky; it has its
ends, as it were, bent down; for yonder
sky has its ends, as it were, bent down.
And what is between the shells is the air.
That tortoise thus is these worlds; it is
these worlds he thus lays down to form
part of the altar."—*Sata. Brâh.*, VII.
5, 1, 1-2.

"Râ liveth, the Tortoise dieth" (On
Sarcophagus of Seti I).—BUDGE, *Egypt.
Heaven and Hell*, Vol. II. p. 52.

The Divine Life (blood) of the planes
of the manifest was indrawn when at
the close of the involutionary cycle,
the planes disappeared into the eternal
Reality (waters) during an interval of
pralaya, prior to the next outpouring.
That Divine Life of the Archetypal
Man (Pragâpati), at the opening of
the new cycle, passed into the force
aspect of the Self (Agni) in this
evolutionary cycle, and permeated
the whole renewed universe.

The lower quaternary (lower shell) is the lower nature of the soul, and it is, as it were, fixed to be the foundation on which to build the higher nature (sky). The higher nature, atma-buddhi (upper shell), influences the lower through the mind (air). It bends down to the lower whenever the lower aspires towards truth and goodness. The planes of manifestation are the means in part by which the soul is enabled to sacrifice the lower for the higher, and through spiritual idealism rise triumphant at the cycle's end.

See AGNI, AIR, ALTAR (fire), ARC. MAN, BLOOD, CARAPACE, CHURNING, EARTH, ELEMENTS, EVOLUTION, HIGHER AND LOWER WORLDS, INVOLUTION, LEVIATHAN, OCEAN, PLANES, PRAGÂPATI (relaxed), QUATERNARY, RÂ, SACRIFICE, SAP, SKY, SOMA-JUICE, VISHNU, WATER, WORLDS (five).

TOWN, OR CITY :—

A symbol of a centre of energy where qualities (people) congregate.
See ATTRACTION, CITY.

TRADITION :—

A symbol of a course of life which has quitted its original connection and become effete.
See CAIAPHAS, NINIGI, PHARISEES, PRIESTS AND ELDERS.

TRANSFIGURATION OF JESUS :—

A symbol of an initiation, and signifying the using or raising of the lower nature in the interests of the higher.

"And he was transfigured before them (on the high mountain); and his face did shine as the sun, and his garments became white as the light."—MAT. xvii. 2.

As the Christ-soul meditated in an exalted mental condition, more and more of the celestial efflux descended upon him and was reflected in his expression of truth. And the without became as the within, the nature being perfect exteriorly as interiorly.

"And behold there appeared unto them Moses and Elijah talking with him."—MAT. xvii. 3.

The ethical (Moses) and the psychical (Elijah) natures were shown to be in harmony with the indwelling Spirit. The three disciples stand for the natural man (Peter), the mental man (James), and the higher love-nature or philosophic man (John). These are exalted within the Christ-soul.

" The forms beheld in this allegory—of Moses and Elias—are the Hebrew correspondences of Buddha and Pythagoras. And they are described as beheld by the three Apostles in whom respectively are typified the functions severally fulfilled by Pythagoras, Buddha, and Jesus; namely, Works, Understanding, and Love, or Body, Mind, and Heart. And by their association on the Mount is denoted the junction of all three elements, and the completion of the whole system comprising them, in Jesus as the representative of the Heart or Innermost, and as in a special sense the ' beloved Son of God.' "—The Perfect Way, p. 250.

See ELIJAH, INITIATIONS, JAMES, JOHN (apostle), MAN (natural), MOSES, MOUNTAIN, PETER, RAIMENT, SHINING, TABERNACLE, WHITE.

TRANSMUTATION OF LOWER QUALITIES INTO HIGHER :—

This is a spiritual process which takes place in the soul by slow degrees, as evolution proceeds on the lower planes. Transmutation is effected by the Higher Self acting through buddhi-manas on the lower qualities as they arrive at a state of preparedness for being raised to a higher condition. It is the function of the Holy Spirit, atma-buddhi, to transmute lower into higher, and this is the meaning of white magic and alchemy. There is a transfer of impressions from the astral to the buddhic plane. Love-passion on the astro-physical plane is gradually transmuted into pity and compassion on the buddhic plane. Power exercised is transmuted into dignity; ambition into aspiration; greed into zeal or industry; knowledge is turned to Wisdom; varied experience to Love.

"Tauler teaches: First of all, the senses must be mastered by, and absorbed in, the powers of the soul. Then must these very powers themselves—all resonings, willings, hopings, fearings, be absorbed in a simple sense of the Divine presence. . . . These powers of the soul must cease to act, in so far as they belong to self; but they are not destroyed: their absorption in the higher part of our nature is in one sense a death; in another, their truest life. They die; but they live anew, animated by a principle of life that comes directly from the Father of lights. . . . They are, as it were, the glorified spirits of those powers. They are risen ones. They are in this world, but not of it. Their life has passed into the life which by slaying has preserved and exalted them."—VAUGHAN, *Hours with the Mystics*, Vol. I. p. 293.

"While the emotions of the senses hinder the mind in the activity peculiarly suited to its being, and alone resulting in true satisfaction, and so make it unhappy, it is by the 'heroic emotions' of an endeavour directed towards the true, the beautiful, and the good, that the spirit is raised to blissful freedom from sensuous impulses, and from the chances of the sensible world. By the stages of perception, representation, understanding, and reason, the heroic spirit is raised to the intellectual contemplation of God, and therewith the soul, as Bruno expresses it, changes itself entirely into God, and becomes at home in the intelligible world; *divine Love*, which is the Deity himself, becomes now the dominant emotion in the soul, and thus the latter overcomes the iron law of necessity, which bends only before love, and extends the endeavour after its own self-perfecting to the blessed labour for the general perfecting of all, in which lies the fulfilment of the divine purpose in the world."—PFLEIDERER, *Phil. of Religion*, p. 28.

"Mine eye discerns this eternal life and motion in all the veins of sensible and spiritual nature, through what seems to others a dead mass. And it sees this life forever ascend and grow and transfigure itself into a more spiritual expression of its own nature."—J. G. FICHTE, *Destiny of Man*.

"God does raise up the dead and quicken them in marvellous and miraculous fashion, but you cannot. God is daily taking of that which belongs to one plane of being, and making it live and function on another and higher; but such an achievement is surely his alone, it is beyond all human power to do the like."—R. J. CAMPBELL, Serm., *The Creatorship, etc.*

See ALCHEMY, BARSOM, BLASPHEMY, BOAT (wisdom), BUDDHI, DEATH, DHARMA, EVOLUTION, HAETUMANT, HEALING (dead), HEIR, INTERCESSION, KALLIOPEIA, KILLING OUT, MAGIC, METEMPSYCHOSIS, MULTITUDES, PRANA, PROMISES, QUALITIES, STEWARD (unjust), VAHISTO, WORDS OF POWER.

TRANSUBSTANTIATION :—

A symbol of the transmutation of the highest qualities of the lower nature into the qualities of wisdom, truth, and love of the Divine nature.

"Learn that the bread which we see, though to the taste it be bread, is nevertheless not bread, but the body of Christ; and that the wine which we see, though to the taste it be wine, is nevertheless not wine, but the blood of Christ."—ST. CYRIL, *Catech. Myst.*, IV.

Realise that the Truth-goodness (bread) which we perceive in our innermost soul is not a product of the natural man, but of the Divine Man (Christ), whose "body" of expression it is; and that the wisdom-love (wine) of which we have experience is not a result of the life of the lower planes, but is an inward manifestation of the Divine Life (blood) of the Incarnate Christ within the souls of a progressed humanity. In other words, we are to identify our spiritualised mental qualities with the expression of the Divine Life within us.

See BLOOD OF LAMB, BREAD, CHRIST, FLESH OF JESUS, FOOD AS GOD, HOST, SACRAMENT, SUPPER, WINE.

TRAPPED THE BIRDS :—

A symbol of attainment to the ideals through aspiration and effort. *See* BIRDS.

TRAPPED THE SERPENTS :—

A symbol of having transcended limitation, and overcome the attractions of desire and sense on the lower planes of matter. *See* SERPENT.

TREADING UNHARMED ON SERPENTS AND SCORPIONS :—

A symbol of power attained over the desires and lower emotions.

"Behold I have given you authority to tread upon serpents and scorpions, and over all the power of the enemy; and nothing shall in any wise hurt you. Howbeit in this rejoice not, that the spirits are subject unto you; but rejoice that your names are written in heaven."—LUKE x. 19, 20.

Union with the Higher Self gives complete mastery over the lower planes, because then the Ego—the dweller in the sheaths—is conscious upon the spiritual, moral, and intellectual levels, where strife and divisions and perils are impossible. Nevertheless, rejoice not that you can command the lower nature, but that you can perceive and obey the higher.

See DISCIPLES SENT, ENEMIES, NAME, SCORPION, SERPENT, SHEATHS, UNION, VESTURES.

TREASURE IN HEAVEN :—

A symbol of the intuition of truth, or the buddhic higher reason and emotions which enlighten the Individuality ensouled in the causal-body.

"Jesus said unto him, If thou wouldst be perfect, go, sell that thou hast, and give to the poor, and thou shalt have treasure in heaven; and come, follow me. But when the young man heard the saying, he went away sorrowful: for he was one that had great possessions."—MAT. xix. 21, 22.

The "young man" signifies a condition of soul not fully matured. He is seeking wisdom from the Christ, and so puts his trust in the intuition. This utterance of the Christ-soul refers to the parting with conditions that have in the past proved of value, but which are now, in the light of present experience, no longer of use, but bind the soul to lower levels, and so hinder its progress. The saying about "selling to give to the poor" also hints at a law of vital importance to soul growth, viz. that the imparting to others of truth and knowledge serves but to increase the capacity for the reception thereof—implying intuition (treasure in heaven). The "young man" is sorrowful because he despairs of reconciling the ideals before him, on the one hand, with the actual facts of his worldly experience, on the other hand. And so, being not at present capable of responding in an adequate degree to the ideals of truth and righteousness, he is said to "go away" unto his own possessions of opinions and desires.

"I (God) was a Hidden Treasure, therefore was I fain to be known, and so I created creatures in order that I should be known" (*Hadis or Apostolic Tradition*). — GIBB, *Hist. of Ottoman Poetry*, p. 16.

See BONDAGE, CAKE, CAUSAL-BODY, CHURNING, HEIR, INDIVIDUALITY, INTUITION, MAN, MAN (rich), POOR PEOPLE, POVERTY, RICH MAN, SHEW-BREAD.

TREASURES OF THE CAVE :—

A symbol of the higher emotions and virtues deep within the soul.

"After Adam and Eve leave the Garden of Eden, then, at God's command, gold, frankincense and myrrh are brought by angels, dipped in the water by the Tree of Life and given to Adam as tokens out of the Garden. These are the sacred treasures of the cave."—*Book of the Conflicts of Adam.*

The Supreme, through His messengers or devas, sends spiritual wisdom (gold), purity or grace (frankincense), and peace or bliss (myrrh); these are vitalised by truth (water) and energised by love (life), and are the fruit of the buddhic nature (the garden) bestowed upon the personality (Adam). They constitute the inner beauty of the soul, which is as a dark cave until it is beheld by spiritual vision, bathed in the light of Truth.

See ADAM (lower), CAVE, EDEN, EVE, FRUIT, GARDEN OF EDEN, GOLD, ETC., MAGI, PERSONALITY, TOKENS, TREE OF LIFE, WATER.

TREE :—

A symbol of man, or the human being on all planes, as a replica in small, of the Divine Being in whose image man is made. As God is a Tree of Life, so man is the same.

"By a tree is signified man, and therefore by all things appertaining to a tree, corresponding things in man are signified, as by branches, leaves, flowers, fruits, and seeds. By branches are signified the sensual and natural truths in man; by leaves his rational truths; by flowers, primitive spiritual truths in the rational mind; by fruits, the goods of love and charity; and by seeds, the last and first principles of man."—SWEDENBORG, *Apoc. Rev.*, n. 936.

"The Tree of Life signifies the Lord as to the good of love, . . . because celestial and spiritual life is derived to man from the good of love and charity, which is received from the Lord."—*Ibid.*, n. 89.

"Both good and wicked men are compared to trees. The godly, says the psalmist, ' shall be like a tree planted by the rivers of water, that bringeth forth his fruit in his season ' (Ps. i. 3). His soul shall be plentifully fed from heaven with the never-failing influences of grace and consolation, whereby he shall be made fruitful in every good word and work."—*Cruden's Explanations.*

See ASKR, AXE, IMAGE, JESUS (mortal), LEAVES, MATRO, MICROCOSM, OAK.

TREE OF LIFE :—

A symbol of the Divine Life which spreads through the universe and soul, and produces all forms and activities on the planes of manifestation.

"The Kingdom of God is like unto a grain of mustard seed, which a man took and cast into his own garden;

and it grew and became a tree, and the birds of the heaven lodged in the branches thereof."—MAT. xiii. 31.

" The primal Being is symbolised (by the Docetæ) as the seed of the Fig-tree, the mathematical point which is everywhere, smaller than small, yet greater than great, containing in itself infinite potentialities. . . . The manner of the infinite generation of things is also figured by the fig-tree, for from the seed comes the stem, then branches, then leaves, and then fruit, the fruit in its turn containing seeds, and thence other stems, and so on in infinite manner: so all things come forth" (HIPPOLYTUS, *Refutation*, Bk. VIII. Ch. I).—G. R. S. MEAD, *Fragments, etc.*, p. 218.

The "Tree" is indeed the best analogue that could be given for the "Kingdom" as above and so below. For, as a diagram of the evolution of the Divine Life, the growth from the seed, the sprout, roots, trunk, branches, leaves, flowers and fruit, typify the entire cosmic process, and serve to show how gloriously and wonderfully the Great Spiritual Universe, the archetype of the phenomenal cosmos, is contrived, energised, and sustained by the Master Builder—its Source and Centre. The "birds of the heaven" are symbolic of those individualities who have "gone before," having aspired to the things which are above. These are the Elder Brethren of humanity.

" The ' birds of the air ' are wont to be put in a good sense, as in the Gospel of the Lord, when He was declaring a likeness of the kingdom of heaven by a grain of mustard seed, said, ' Unto what is, etc.' (LUKE xiii. 18, 19). For He is Himself ' a grain of mustard seed,' who, when He was planted in the burial place of the garden, rose up a great tree. For He was ' a grain,' through the abasement of the flesh, ' a tree,' through the mightiness of His Majesty. The branches of this tree are the holy preachers (apostles). In these ' boughs the birds of the air rest,' because the holy souls (the birds), which by a kind of wings of virtues, lift themselves up from earthly thinking." —ST. GREGORY THE GREAT, *Morals on the Book of Job*, Vol. II. p. 395.

"Without food even the gods and the illuminated ones of heaven cannot exist. In the east of heaven stands that high sycamore upon which the gods sit, the tree of life by which they live, whose fruits also feed the blessed." —A. ERMAN, *Egyptian Religion*, p. 93.

"As in Eastern legend, the universe-tree was venerated as something more than a mere material supporter of the world,

being sometimes the giver of wisdom, and sometimes the conveyer of immortality, so in European myth it is found linked with a similar beneficence. In the legends of the Finns, its branches are represented as conferring ' eternal welfare ' and ' the delight that never ceases.' "— J. H. PHILPOT, *The Sacred Tree*, p. 120.

" The tree of life would seem to have been in the terrestrial Paradise what the Wisdom of God is in the spiritual, of which it is written, ' She is a tree of life to them that lay hold upon her ' (PROV. iii. 18)."—AUGUSTINE, *City of God*, Vol. I. p. 545.

" In the ' Tree of Life ' of the Egyptians, we have perhaps the earliest, certainly the most complete and consistent representation of this most ancient and seemingly universal symbol—the ' Tree of Life ' in the midst of Paradise, furnishing the divine support of immortality. And what does this tree mean ? In the Scriptures we read that ' man doth not live by bread alone, but by every *word* that proceedeth out of the mouth of God.' Here we have a key to the symbolical teaching, itself symbolically explained. The divine *word* is the support of the divine life ; they who live by it shall never die. ' Whoso receiveth me and my *word*,' saith our Lord, ' I will raise him up again at the last day.' We have the authority of St. Augustine, that the Egyptians firmly believed in a resurrection from the dead. . . . The ' Bread of Life,' and the fruit of the ' Tree of Life,' and the ' Water of Life,' are all significant of one and the same thing—the divine nourishment of the soul unto everlasting life."—H. C. BARLOW, *Essays on Symbolism*, p. 79.

See BACKBONE, BIRDS (heaven), BIRDS (two), BREAD, FIG-TREE, FRUIT, GATHA DAYS, HARVISPTOKHM, HOMA-TREE, IMMORTALITY, JESUS (mortal), KINGDOM, LEAVES, LOTE-TREE, OAK-TREE, PLANTS, RULERS (world), SEED, SOMA-PLANT, SYCAMORE, TET, TUBA-TREE, VALHALLA, VINE, WORD, YGGDRASIL.

TREE OF LIFE IN THE MIDST OF THE GARDEN :—

Symbol of the Atmic Ray, or current of the Divine Life flowing downward through the central essence of the buddhic nature (garden).

" This is the ancient Tree, whose roots grow upward, and whose branches grow downwards, . . that is called Brahman. . . . All worlds are contained in it, and no one goes beyond."—*Katha. Upanishad*, VI. 1.

" In the middle of the sea Vouru-kasha is the well-watered tree Harvis-ptokhm, tree of all seeds."—*Vendidad*, V.

The " sea Vouru-kasha " is the Ocean of Reality, the upper water of Truth. The " tree " is a symbol of the atmic outpouring. It is founded in Truth and bears the spiritual germs of all the manifest qualities and forms.

" The wonderful tree called the Tuba or ' Beatitude,' the roots of which are in the region of the Loti-tree above the highest Paradise, sends its branches down into all the Eight Gardens, a shoot entering the abode of every inhabitant, just as the sun, which is aloft in the skies, sends its beams into every house on earth."—E. J. W. GIBB, *Hist. of Ottoman Poetry*, Vol. I. p. 37.

" I rather conceive that Moses was speaking in an allegorical spirit, intending by his paradise to intimate the dominant character of the soul, which is full of innumerable opinions, as this figurative paradise was of trees. And by the Tree of Life he was shadowing out the greatest of the virtues—namely, piety towards the Gods, by means of which the soul is made immortal ; and by the tree which had the knowledge of good and evil, he was intimating that wisdom and moderation, by means of which things contrary in their nature to one another, are distinguished. . . . The Tree of Life is that most general virtue which some people call Goodness ; from which the particular virtues are derived, and of which they are composed . . . The unspeakable formations and impressions of all the things in the universe are all borne forward into and comprehended by the soul, which is only one. When, therefore, that receives the impression of perfect virtue, it has become the Tree of Life ; but when it has received the impression of vice, it has then become the Tree of the knowledge of good and evil."— PHILO, *Works*, Yonge, Vol. I. pp. 46, 66, 67.

" The Tree of Life is the Central Will or Divine Life, the God, that is, whether of the universe or of the individual. And the Tree of Knowledge is experience which comes of trespass, or a descent from the region of spirit to that of matter. It is thus Māya, or illusion ; and the Serpent, or tempter, is the impulse by yielding to which the inward reality of Being is abandoned for the outward appearance. . . . The Tree of Life signifies also the secret of regeneration, or final transmutation into pure Spirit, and the consequent attainment of eternal life, which can come only when all the necessary processes have been performed, and the soul—Eve—is once more pure and free, when she becomes ' Mary.' "— A. KINGSFORD, *Clothed with the Sun*, pp. 22, 23.

" Whatever feeds and sustains the spiritual life of man comes from the Tree of Life, whose roots are in the garden of God. . . . The leaves of the tree of God's love are numberless, and the

Life they bear is for the healing of the nations."—R. J. CAMPBELL, Serm., *Healing of the Nations.*

" The Great Tree in whom is all healing (is Mani)."—The Manichaean *Fihrist.*

See ATMAN, BRAHMARANDHRAM, ISVARA, KAIOMARTS, SUN, SUTRATMA, TRIDENT.

TREE OF KNOWLEDGE OF GOOD AND EVIL :—

A symbol of the reflex spiritual life growing upward through all the ramifications of experience on the lower planes, and bearing the fruit of experience,—the evolving moral nature.

"And out of the ground made the Lord God to grow every tree that is pleasant to the sight, and good for food ; the tree of life also in the midst of the garden, and the tree of knowledge of good and evil." —GEN. ii. 9.

And from the lower nature the Wisdom-Love caused the faint beginnings of growth—evolution—to take place, through the pleasant desires that are to commence the growth of the soul ; and so was produced all that is found desirable and that can serve to gratify the awakened cravings of the soul. Also from the centre of the " garden " or buddhic nature proceeds a "ray " of the Supreme Spirit which extends downward (the tree of life), and through this the moral nature—to know good and evil—was founded.

" The tree of life is the holy of holies— Christ, the tree of the knowledge of good and evil, the will's free choice."—AUGUSTINE, *City of God*, Vol. I. p. 546.

"And the Lord God commanded the man, saying, Of every tree of the garden thou mayest freely eat ; but of the tree of the knowledge of good and evil, thou shalt not eat of it : for in the day that thou eatest thereof thou shalt surely die." —GEN. ii. 16, 17.

And instruction by intuition is delivered to the mind (man) that experience is to be acquired through the activities of the lower nature. But it is not through the intuitive sense of absolute right and truth in self-guidance that the mind's earlier evolution is to be promoted, for this is impossible to the lower mind, and at the period (day) when the soul ultimately arrives at a perfect knowledge of Truth, the lower mind (man) will cease to exist. The natural course is otherwise, for at the stage when the fall of the ego into matter is accomplished, the direct perception of Truth will cease from consciousness.

"Jesus Christ is called the 'tree of life' (REV. ii. 7; xxii. 2). He will be to all his members as a tree of eternal life, satisfying and refreshing them with fellowship and communion with himself."

"The tree of knowledge of good and evil, so called because by the eating of it man came to know experimentally the vast difference between good and evil."—*Cruden's Explanations.*

"The Holy Ghost presents the church to us under the similitude of a garden. An excellent type of the presence of Christ with his church. . . . These trees, and their pleasurableness, do show us the beauty of the truly godly, whom the Lord hath beautified with salvation. This 'tree of life' was another type of Christ, as the bread and healing medicine of the church, that stands 'in the midst of the paradise of God' (REV. ii. 7; xxii. 2). The 'tree of the knowledge of good and evil' was a type of the law, or covenant of works, as the sequel of the story clearly manifesteth; for had not Adam eaten thereof, he had enjoyed for ever his first blessedness. As Moses saith, 'It shall be our righteousness, if we observe to do all these commandments before the Lord our God, as he hath commanded us' (DEUT. vi. 25). But both Adam and we have touched, that is, broken the boughs and fruit of this tree, and therefore now for ever, by the law, no man can stand just before God. (GAL. ii. 16)."—J. BUNYAN, *Exposition of Genesis.*

See CURSE (ground), DAY, DEATH, EATING, EXPERIENCE, EYE, FALL, FOOD FOR MAN, FRUIT OF TREE, GARDEN, JOHN BAPTIST, KAIOMARTS, MAN, MAN (natural), SERPENT (subtil).

TREES, TALL :—

A symbol of aspirations from below.

"And thus tall trees bear fruit; first of all olives."—*Empedocles,* FAIRBANKS, 219.

And thus the soul's aspirations bring forth deeds. "Olives" signify faith or courage, implying love of the higher.

See FOREST, OLIVES, PALM TREES.

TREES FREE FROM DROUGHT :—

A symbol signifying the nourishing of the intelligence (trees in water) through pure truth.

See MAN, TREE, WATER.

TREES AND RIVERS :—

A symbol for channels of truth and love, which are the very texture of the world-soul.

See AMBAYAS, CHANNELS, RIVERS, WARP.

TRIAD, HIGHER :—

A symbol of the Divine principles, Atma-Buddhi-Manas; or the Divine aspects, Will-Wisdom-Action.

See ABRAHAM, LAO, LION (man), MINOS, PYRAMID, TRIDENT, TRINITY TSURAH, WITNESSES (three).

TRIAL OF JESUS :—

Symbolic of the Christ-soul going through the throes of purification for the sake of the Higher Life. He is first tried by religious systems and creeds, forms of thought from which the spiritual life has fled; and is made to suffer from misinterpretations and false opinions. Then he is reviled by the customs and prejudices of the world, which resents any change for the better. Finally he is condemned by all prevalent thought; for the lower mental qualities neither know nor value the Christ.

"In you the King of heaven stands afresh before His judges—Annas, Caiaphas, Pilate and Herod."—R. J. CAMPBELL, Serm., *Crucified with Christ.*

"Remember Christ in the Judgment Hall, the very symbol and incarnation of spiritual strength; and yet when revilings were loud around Him, and charges multiplied, 'He held his peace.'"—F. W. ROBERTSON, *Sermons, 2nd Series,* p. 8.

See ANNAS, CAIAPHAS, CROWNING WITH THORNS, GABBATHA, GOLGOTHA, PHARISEES, PILATE, PRIESTS AND ELDERS, ROMAN, SOLDIERS, TRADITION, WITNESSES (false).

TRIBE-RULERS :—

A symbol of the mental qualities which regulate and direct the lower nature.

"The progress which is in the Spentamainyu Gatha the tribe-rulers should carry on."—*Shayast La-Shayast,* Ch. XIII.

The development of soul occasioned through the Mental-body is due to the rule of the mental qualities which control and co-ordinate the desires and passions, and direct the emotions.

"Which class of faculties is entitled to rule? I answer, that the moral and intellectual powers are superior in kind to the animal propensities, and that every well-constituted mind *feels* that, in cases of conflict, they are entitled to restrain the inferior desires. This is the sense in which I speak of the supremacy of the

moral sentiments and intellect."—G.
COMBE, *Moral Philosophy*, p. 19.

See CONFLICT, GEORGE AND DRAGON,
HOUSE (clan), HOUSE (ruler), INTEL-
LECT, MENTAL-BODY, MITHRA (bull),
QUALITIES, RULERS, SPENTO, TIAMAT.

TRIBES OF ISRAEL, TWELVE :—

**Symbolic of twelve kinds of mental
qualities in an early stage of development, but gradually becoming
disciplined by the moral nature.
They may also stand for the races
of mankind which serve to represent
on the mental plane some special
side of the Logos.**

"The Saviour knew of what nature
each of his disciples was, and that it needs
must be that each of them should go to
his own nature. For from the twelve
tribes he chose twelve disciples, and
through them he spake to every tribe.
Wherefore, also, neither have all men
hearkened to the preaching of the twelve
disciples, nor if they hearken, can they
receive it " (Statement by the Naasene
Gnostics).—HIPPOLYTUS, *Philosophumena*,
Bk. V. 3.

The Christ knows the nature of
each of the twelve disciplined qualities
(disciples), because the Higher always
knows the lower. He points out that
each quality must develop according
to the conditions of its own special
nature. The " chosing from the twelve
tribes " signifies the calling of the
qualities to a differentiated state
higher than before ; that is, from
each of twelve varieties of primal
qualities (tribes), the most advanced
quality is raised to the status of
a " disciple." Then through the
disciplined qualities Christ is able to
influence the less disciplined (every
tribe). The last passage refers to the
fact that the different grades of mental
qualities cannot hear and understand
that which is above them, and that
when they are enabled to perceive the
higher, they no longer remain on their
former level.

" *Without*—our eyes can see the immense variety of tribes which have come
forth from Adam, all of which are but
various forms or manifestations of man
or human nature. But *within*—though
secret and hidden—the outcome is the
same. Old Adam in us brings forth as
many different minds, each of which
throughout this book (Genesis) is figured
and set before us in some son of Adam,
or Noah, or Shem, or Ham, or Japhet ;
some outward, some inward, some sensual,

some natural, some spiritual, and this in
different measures ; the elect, all representing some form of the spiritual mind
in us ; the non-elect, some form of that
mind which is earthly, sensual, devilish."
—A. JUKES, *Types of Genesis*, p. 400.

" The twelve tribes signify the Lord's
church as to all its truths and goods.
They signify all truths of doctrine derived
from the good of love from the Lord.
Tribes signify religion, and the twelve
tribes, the church as to all things relating
to it."—SWEDENBORG, *Apoc. Rev.*, n. 349.

See ADAM (lower), ÆONS (twelve),
BREASTPLATE, COMPARTMENTS, DIS-
CIPLES (twelve), EPHOD, ISRAELITES,
JUDAH, JUDGES, PEOPLE, QUALITIES,
RACES, SPEECH, THRONES (twelve),
TUAT, TWELVE, ZODIAC.

TRIBUTE MONEY :—

**A symbol of the discharge of
obligations in regard to the lower
or the higher life.**

" Jesus spake first to him, saying,
What thinkest thou, Simon ? the kings
of the earth, from whom do they receive
toll or tribute ? from their sons, or from
strangers ? And when he said, From
strangers, Jesus said unto him, Therefore
the sons are free," etc.—MAT. xvii. 25-7.

This story refers to the discharging
of mundane as opposed to spiritual
obligations. But as the one is involved
to a great extent in the other, the
Christ-soul will not allow that there
should be any ignoring of the former.
The appeal of the Christ represents
the presentation to the lower mind
(Peter) of the problem of the subjective
versus the objective life. The lower
mind decides in favour of the value of
the latter, and Christ knowing that
that is best for it for a time, directs it
to gather experience and facts (fish),
and fulfil its obligations, giving as
tribute that which it finds should be
given.

See EARTH, KING, PETER, TITHES.

TRIDENT :—

**A symbol of the lower conscious-
ness raised into union with the
higher ;—the three crowning points
signifying Love, Wisdom, and
Action, or Atma, Buddhi, and Manas.**

" The trident of Poseidon is a symbol
of the third region, which the ocean
occupies, assigned to him after the heaven
and air. For which cause also they
invented the names Amphi-trite and
Tritons."—PLUTARCH, *Isis and Osiris*,
§ 76.

The "water" of Reality, or the ocean of Truth (Poseidon), is an aspect of Atma, which with Buddhi (heaven) and Manas (air) are symbolised in the three points at the apex of the upright trident. "Amphitrite and the Tritons" represent the buddhic emotions and faculties which appertain to the higher Triad. The stem of the trident is a symbol of the Divine ray, or the Sutratma.

See ATMA, BUDDHI, HERMES, TRISMEGISTUS, MANAS, OCEAN, POSEIDON, SUTRATMA, TRIAD, TSURAH.

TRINITY, HOLY :—

A symbol of the Godhead in three aspects. *Father—*Absolute, Unconditioned, Potential, Unmanifest, Power. *Son—*Conditioned, Actual, Active, Manifest, Love. *Spirit—*Means of creation and sustentation, Wisdom.
In Hindu terms, the Trinity is expressed in Paranatma, Atma, and Buddhi.

"The Father uttered himself and all creatures in the Word, his Son, and the return of the Father into himself includes the like return of all creatures into the same Eternal Source. The logical genesis of the Son furnishes a type of all evolution or creation ; the Son is the unity of all the works of God. . . . God is in all things, and God is all things " (Eckhart). —UEBERWEG, *Hist. of Philos.*, Vol. I. p. 475.
"The difference between Father and Son is this—' The Father ' is to express God-hidden, ' The Son ' is God-manifest, and the ' Holy Ghost ' is the Knowledge or Spirit of Truth, proceeding from the *experience* of both, as God hidden, and revealed."—JOHN WARD, *Zion's Works*, Vol. VIII. p. 59.
"Does physical science imply the doctrine of the Trinity ? Yes, unquestionably it does. . . . Now, when we start thinking about existence as a whole, and ourselves in particular, we are compelled to assume the infinite, the finite, and the activity of the former within the latter. In other words, we have to postulate God, the universe, and God's operation within the universe. Look at these three conceptions for a moment, and it will be seen that every one of them implies the rest ; they are a Trinity in unity. The primordial Being must be innfiite, for there cannot be a finite without something still beyond it. We know, too, that to our experience the universe is finite ; we can measure, weigh, and analyse it. And yet, if we think of infinite and finite as two entirely distinct and unrelated modes of existence,

we find ourselves in an impossible position. . . . We are compelled to think of the infinite as ever active within the finite, the source of change and motion, the exhaustless power which makes possible the very idea of development from simplicity to complexity. If the universe were complete in itself, change would not occur, and a cosmic process, evolutionary or otherwise, would be inconceivable." —R. J. CAMPBELL, *The New Theology*, pp. 86, 87.
"Cosmos is God's Son ; but things in Cosmos are by Cosmos. And properly hath it been called Cosmos [Order] ; for that it orders all with their diversity of birth, with its not leaving aught without its life, with the unweariedness of its activity, the speed of its necessity, the composition of its elements, and order of its creatures " (*Corpus Hermeticum*, IX). —G. R. S. MEAD, *T. G. Hermes*, Vol. II. p. 134.
"The terms Father, Son, and Spirit are but symbols which stand for three manifestations of God, three constituents of the Divine nature, three relationships essential to the perfect life of Deity. God goes forth from Himself in the eternal Son, returning to Himself in the Eternal Spirit."—R. J. CAMPBELL, *A Faith for To-day*, p. 283.
"Mediæval theology generally distinguished the Three Persons as Power, Wisdom, and Love, the Holy Ghost being the *copula* between the Father and the Son. It is instructive to notice that to each of the Three Persons is assigned all these attributes. . . . May we say not further that Wisdom, Power and Love have been the Divine attributes which the Greek Church, the Roman Church, and the Protestant bodies respectively have been most ready to grasp ?—are all attributes of each Person, and it is quite inadmissible to set them over against each other, as is done in transactional theories of the Atonement."—W. R. INGE, *Paddock Lectures*, p. 28.
"The two points which I wish to emphasise about the doctrine of the Trinity are, first, that popular theology, when it thinks of the Three Persons in one God, is usually much more tritheistic than the orthodox faith. This error has come about through the unfortunate use of the word ' Person,' with its misleading associations. The other is that the analogy between the ' Persons ' of the Trinity and our own complex nature is not an accidental or fanciful resemblance but rests on the belief that *man is really a microcosm, reproducing in little the Creator in whose image he was made.*"— *Ibid.*, p. 30.

See ABRAHAM, ABSOLUTE, ATMAN, BUDDHI, CHRIST, COSMOS, DEMIURGE, FATHER, FIRST-BORN, GOD, GODHEAD, HERMES TRISMEGISTUS, HOLY GHOST, IMAGE, INCARNATION, ISVARA, MACROcosm, Monad, Pyramid, Self, Son of god, Spirit, Triad, Trident, Tsurah, Witnesses (three), Zerana.

TRI-RATNA, THE THREE HOLIES :—

A symbol of the Soul in its three spiritual aspects,—Higher Self, lower Self, and individual Selves.

" This triad of personalities consisted of (1) the Buddha himself, that is to say, Gautama Buddha, or the Buddha of the present age of the world ; (2) his Dharma or Law, that is, the word and doctrine of the Buddha personified, or, so to speak, incarnated and manifested in a visible form after his Paranirvana ; and (3) his Sangha or Order of Monks, also in a manner personified—that is, embodied in a kind of ideal impersonation or collective unity of his true disciples, . . . the whole assemblage of monks, Arhats, Pratyeka-Buddhas, Bodhi-sattvas, perfected Buddhas, and not yet perfected saints of all classes, whether on the earth, or in any other division of the Universe."
—Mon. Williams, *Buddhism*, pp. 175, 6.

The Higher Self (Buddha) of the present manifestation, His Incarnation in the lower nature of the soul under the karmic law, and His multiple division into the myriad human souls now in all stages of progress towards ultimate unity in the One, constitute the Eternal Spirit.

See Arhats, Bodhisatvas, Buddha, Dharma, Monk, Paccekabuddhas, Saints.

TRISHTUBH METRE :—

A symbol of the buddhic plane in relation to the rate of vibration in the atoms of buddhic matter.

See Gatha (ahuna).

TROJANS :—

A symbol of the lower emotions.

" O gods ! surely a great sorrow comes upon the Grecian land. Verily, Priam would exult, and the sons of Priam, and the other Trojans would greatly rejoice in their souls, if they were to hear these things of you twain contending : you who in council and in fighting surpass the Greeks."—*Iliad*, Bk. I.

O Powers above ! certainly a great trial of endurance shall forthwith assail the mind (Greece). Assuredly the Causal Self (Priam), and its assemblage of higher faculties shall thereby be developed ; and the lower emotions (Trojans) will be greatly stimulated if the Desire-mind (Aga-

memnon) and the Personality (Achilles) be stirred up. For in the unwisdom of the lower self there consists greater wisdom than in the lower mental faculties. Emotion surpasses mind.

See Arabs, Countries, Greece, Hector, Helen, Ilium, Priam, Ships (Ilium), Troy, Warriors.

TROY :—

A symbol of the causal-body, the seat of the Self on the mental plane.

" The tale of Troy. Many of its incidents and characters are clearly symbolical ; and the entire story can now be treated only as a sacred legend, a drama of religious strife reflecting the supposed operations of nature. . . . Troy was a divine city, its capture a divine event."—R. W. Mackay, *Progress of the Intellect*, Vol. I. p. 168.

" Ye sons of Atreus, and ye other well-greaved Greeks, to you indeed may the gods, possessing the heavenly dwellings, grant to destroy the city of Priam, and to return home safely."—*Iliad*, Bk. I.

The appeal of the Spiritual mind (Chryses) is made to the Self through illusion (Atreus). ' From the higher planes (heavenly dwellings) may the Divine Power (gods) grant that the desires, in captivating the mind, become the means of apparently destroying the perfect causal-body, and so assist in furthering the evolution of the soul which is to return to its home above.'

See Atreus, Causal-body, Helen, Ilium, Priam, Ships (Ilium), Trojans.

TRUTH AND OBSCURITY :—

Symbolic of reality and illusion, or truth and error.

TSURAH :—

A symbol of the higher triad, atma-buddhi-manas.

" The Tsurah is the higher principle which remains above—the higher eternal principle of the continued life of the individual."—Myer, *Qabbalah*, p. 401.

See Atma, Buddhi, Manas, Pyramid, Triad. Trident, Trinity, Witnesses (three).

TUAT, OR DUAT, THE UNDER-WORLD :—

A symbol of the manvantara, or great cycle of life manifestation in nature (underworld). It is described as " night " because the Self (sun) is unapparent to the lower consciousness. The Sun-god Afu-Rā, the incarnate God, is the Hidden Deity

(Amen Rā) immured in his cabin on the Solar-boat (World-soul), which traverses the twelve divisions of the cycle in the twelve hours of the night. The Tuat embraces all nature below the plane of atma ; the first and last divisions being on the higher sub-planes of the buddhic plane, for the Soul (boat) commences in the first and finishes in the last ; it descends in the first six divisions, and ascends in the second six. The descent is the involutionary process of spirit entering matter, and the ascent is the evolutionary process of spirit rising from and ultimately discarding matter.

The Solar Boat on the river of Life (river Urnes), is a symbol of the World-Soul, or buddhic causal-body,—the vehicle of the Higher Self (Rā) and its powers (deities). The World-soul contains the complete collective experience of humanity. The higher mental causal-bodies are individualised in mankind, but there is only one buddhic causal-body for the human race, and in this all souls are one potentially.

See ABRAXAS, ADAMAS, ÆONS (twelve), AFU-RĀ, AMENT, APEP, ARIES, BOAT, CABIN, CAUSAL-BODY, COMPARTMENTS, EQUINOX, EVOLUTION, HADES, HOUR, INCARNATION, INVOLUTION, KHEPER, MANVANTARA, NET-RĀ, NIDANAS, NIGHT, OCEAN, RIVER OF LIFE, SAMSARA, SAU, SEVENTH, STRIDES, TATTU, TRIBES (twelve), TWELVE, UNDERWORLD, ZODIAC.

TUBA TREE :—

A symbol of the ray of the Divine Life.

See LOTE-TREE, PARADISE, TREE OF LIFE.

TUBAL CAIN, FORGER OF CUTTING INSTRUMENTS OF METAL :—

A symbol of the dawn of the intellect with its incisive powers of analysis and discrimination.

See BRASS, CUTTING, METALS, NAAMAH.

TUFARAPAINUU, TUFARAPAIRAI, AND ORO, BROTHERS :—

Symbols of aspects of the Higher Self,—namely, Wisdom, Action, and Will.

See NOAH'S SONS, ORO, TRIAD, TRINITY, VAIRAUMATI, VAPOUR (white).

TUMA-TAUENGA :—

A symbol of the mind, or mental plane of the soul.

"But Tuma-tauenga, or man, still stood erect and unshaken upon the breast of his mother Earth (Papa-tuanuku) and now at length the hearts of Heaven (Rangi), and of the god of storms (Tawhiri-matea) became tranquil, and their passions were assuaged."—G. GREY, *Polynesian Mythology*, p. 10.

The mind, which makes humanity what it is as the flower of creation, now became the balance and steadying element in the soul. The lower (earth) and the higher (heaven) natures had each their place assigned them by the mind ; and the passions and desires were placed under control of the mental factor.

See HAUMIA, RANGI, RONGO, TANEMAHUTA, TANGAROA, TAWHIRI, TRIBE-RULERS.

TUNA :—

See EEL-GOD.

TURQUOISE, OR BLUE HEAVEN :—

A symbol of the celestial regions of the buddhic plane, wherein the heaven-world consists.

See BLUE HEAVEN, KINGDOM OF HEAVEN.

TUSHITA HEAVEN :—

A symbol of the higher sub-planes of the buddhic plane, from which the germ-Soul descends to the lower planes as the two-fold monad, atma-buddhi.

See BODHISATVA, BUDDHA, ELEPHANT (white), HIRANYAGARBHA, MONAD.

TUSK :—

A symbol of spiritual power in overcoming ignorance and evil. In the mouth it expresses the force of that which is uttered on the higher planes, namely, Truth.

"A tusk in Scripture, and in ancient times, was called a horn, and a horn was the universal symbol of *power*. Just, therefore, as a horn on the head was the symbol of physical and worldly power, so a horn in the mouth was a symbol of spiritual or moral power, the power of the mouth, or of words and arguments."—J. GARNIER, *Worship of the Dead*, p. 262.

See BOAR (wild), DESERTS, ELEPHANT (white), FANG, HORN, TEETH PROTRUDING, TLALOC, TOOTH.

TUTE-WEHIWEHI, THE FATHER OF REPTILES :—

A symbol of the lower self which seeks gratification through the desires and sensations.

See IKATERE, PUNGA, RANGI, TANGAROA.

TWELVE, NUMBER :—

A complete number in relation to conditions of the manifest. The twelve divisions of the cycle of life (Zodiac, Tuat, etc.) correspond to soul-states (twelve tribes) and soul-qualities (twelve disciples). The sets of twelve are all interrelated.

"This number (of the twelve disciples) is typified by many things in the Old Testament; by the 12 sons of Jacob, by the 12 princes of the children of Israel; by the 12 running springs in Helim; by the 12 stones in Aaron's breastplate; by the 12 loaves of the shew-bread; by the 12 spies sent by Moses; by the 12 stones of which the altar was made; by the 12 stones taken out of Jordan; by the 12 oxen which bare the brazen sea. Also in the New Testament, by the 12 stars in the bride's crown, by the 12 foundations of Jersualem which John saw, and her 12 gates."—BP. RABANUS MANRUS (A.D. 857).

"The number *Twelve* divisiblest of all, which could be halved, quartered, parted into three, into six, the most remarkable number—this was enough to determine the *Signs of the Zodiac*, the number of Odin's *Sons*, and innumerable other Twelves. Any vague rumour of number had a tendency to settle itself into Twelve."—T. CARLYLE, *The Hero as Divinity*, Lect. I.

"And when Jesus was twelve years old, they went up (to Jerusalem) after the custom of the feast."—LUKE ii. 42.

The accomplishment of the age of twelve years signifies a full period of evolution when an initiation was undergone by the Chirst-soul. This took place in the inner mind (temple) and corresponded to an awakening of the logical and intuition sides of the soul. These are the father-mother principle, indicated by the presence of the parents.

"Twelve is symbolic of spiritual perfection and completion. It is 4 + 8, or the world and man renewed. It is also 4 × 3, or the world and man in intimate union with God, and it is 6 × 2, symbolic of Christ taking upon him the sin of man, and becoming subject to death for the sake of man's redemption."—J. GARNIER, *Worship of the Dead*, p. 221.

See ADAMAS, ADITYAS, ÆONS (twelve), BREASTPLATE, CROWN (twelve), DISCIPLES, HEROES, INITIATIONS, MEASURE, NIDANAS, SAVIOURS, SHEW-BREAD, TRIBES (twelve), TUAT, URDAR, YEAR, ZODIAC.

TWO, NUMBER :—

A symbol of the duality of manifestation, the One becoming Two,—Spirit and Matter. Also of the relative, the opposites, higher and lower, good and evil, etc.

"Two is symbolic of union, of Christ who was both God and man, and therefore of the union of God and man."—J. GARNIER, *Worship of the Dead*, p. 220.

See HEAVEN AND EARTH, INVOLUTION, LIVING THINGS, MALE-FEMALE, MARRIAGE.

TWO GREAT TRIPLE POWERS :—

Symbolic of Love and Wisdom, working on the three higher planes. These spiritual forces are the powers which control the working together of all things for good.

See ATMA, BUDDHI, MANAS.

TYPE AND ANTITYPE :—

The symbol and the truth symbolised. The figure in the lower illusion of what exists in the higher reality.

"For, as the typical is Divine truth on a lower stage, exhibited by means of outward relations and terrestrial interests, so when making the transition from this to the antitypical, we must expect the truth to appear on a loftier stage, and, if we may so speak, with a more heavenly aspect. What in the one bore immediate respect to the bodily life, must in the other be found to bear immediate respect to the spiritual life."—P. FAIRBAIRN, *Typology of Scripture*, Vol. I. p. 194.

See CREATION, IMAGE, PROTOTYPES.

TYPHON, OR SET :—

A symbol of the lower principle, or of the desire-mind.

"Typhon is the part of the soul that is subject to the passions. . . . And the name 'Seth,' by which they call Typhon proves this; for it signifies 'that which tyrannises and constrains by force.'"
"Typhon is called *Seth, Bebon*, and *Syn*; these names being meant to declare an impeding check, opposition, and turning upside down."
"The more learned among the priests call the sea 'Typhon.'"—PLUTARCH, *Isis and Osiris*, §§ 33, 49, 62.

The lower principle acts through the passions and desires, in opposition to the higher principle. Desire is Love inverted. "Sea" signifies the astral plane—the plane of the desires.

See AHRIMAN, DEVIL, MARA, RAVANA, SET, SUSANOWO, TAURT.

TYRANT, WICKED :—

A symbol of illusion which dominates the lower mind.

"The man that can strive against the wicked tyrant and smite him on the head."
—*Vendidad*, IV.

The "man" is the mind or ego that assimilates knowledge and thereby dispels illusion. The "smiting on the head" is the effort made to overcome illusion under its most subtle forms, such as pride.

See ASHEMOGHA, ATREUS, HIPPO-POTAMUS, ILLUSION.

TYRANTS UNDER ADAMAS :—

Symbolic of strong passions operating upon the lower planes,—such as lust of power, greed, war, cruelty,—all active under the "old Adam," the lord of the lower nature.

See ADAMAS.

TYRRHENIA :—

A symbol of the fourth sub-plane of the buddhic plane.

TYRUS OR TYRE, PRINCE OF :—

A symbol of the mind, intellect, or mental nature.

"Thus saith the Lord God : Because thine heart is lifted up, and thou hast said, I am a god, I sit in the seat of God, in the midst of the seas ; yet thou art man, and not God, though thou didst set thine heart as the heart of God. . . . Therefore, behold, I will bring strangers upon thee, the terrible of the nations ; and they shall draw their swords against the beauty of thy wisdom, and they shall defile thy brightness. They shall bring thee down to the pit ; and thou shalt die the deaths of them that are slain, in the heart of the seas."—EZEK. xxviii. 2–8.

The lower consciousness established in the incipient causal-body (seat of God) centralises the mind midway between the higher and lower natures (seas—waters above and below). The mind commences to act or observe as from itself, owning no superior rule or law. It gathers its knowledge intuitively from the higher planes, and rests unreflective and unprogressive in complete content with itself. But the Supreme requires the mind to be self-conscious and responsible, there-fore the lower qualities (strangers) are presented to it. They assail the "beauty of its wisdom" ; and the higher influences (brightness) are obscured and lost ; so the mind is brought down to the desires (pit) and subjected to the succession of deaths of the personalities on the lower planes. In the lives on earth, the lower mind must learn to serve the Spirit and to sacrifice itself.

"Thou wast the anointed cherub that covereth ; and I set thee, so that thou wast upon the holy mountain of God ; thou hast walked up and down in the midst of the stones of fire. Thou wast perfect in thy ways from the day that thou wast created, till unrighteousness was found in thee."—EZEK. xxviii. 14–16.

The mind originally observed the requirements and laws of the higher intelligence and Spirit to which through love it aspired. Its consciousness appertained to the higher planes (holy mountain) ; its development was brought about through the func-tionings of buddhi (stones of fire). The mind was perfect in its manifesta-tion from the first until it was deflected by the lower emotions and desires. The "anointed cherub that covereth" signifies the buddhic consciousness above the consciousness in the causal-body. On the descent of the mind, the buddhic becomes reflected on the astral plane (cast to the ground).

See ADAM (lower), ANOINTING, EDEN, FALL, GARDEN OF EDEN, INTELLECT, MOUNTAIN, PIT.

TZELEM, DIVINE OR HOLY :—

A symbol of the causal-body, or immortal soul.

"Come see ! That holy tzelem, in it man goes, and in it man grows up, and it is from that plastic likeness, and phan-tom of a tzelem—of him is made another tzelem, i.e. phantom image, and they are connected as one" (*Zohar*).—MYER, *Qabbalah*, p. 411.

This refers to the potential causal-body, and to man's actual causal-body which grows up into its likeness as man develops his qualities.

"The innermost fundamental spiritual principle or type of the individual, the Qabbalah asserts, remains as a something indestructible and as a *tzelem*, shadow of an image, or *d'mooth*, likeness or similitude of the previous upon earth living man. This is the body of the resurrection."—*Ibid.*, p. 392.

The inner vehicle of the individuality is the causal-body, which is immortal. It is in the similitude of the World-soul, and is built up by the transmuted qualities of the transient personalities. It is the body of the perfected individuality at the end of the cycle.

See CAUSAL-BODY, IMAGE, INDIVIDUALITY, KHABIT, RESURRECTION.

UATCHIT, OR UAZIT, GODDESS OF THE NORTH :—

A symbol of the higher or buddhic emotions which supplant the lower.

"And Horus took with him the goddesses Nekhebit and Uatchit in the form of two serpents, that they might consume with fire any rebels who still remained."—*Legend of the Winged Sun-disk.*

And in his ascent the Christ-soul takes with him the wisdom and love aspects of the Holy Spirit, which should overcome with good any evil yet remaining in the soul.

See BUDDHI, ENEMIES, FIRE, GODDESS, HORUS, NEKHEBIT, SERPENT (north).

UAUAT, REBELS OF :—

Symbolic of the various phases of intellectual pride, arrogance, vanity, and love of power.

See HIPPOPOTAMUS, NUBIA.

UDDER OF THE COW :—

A symbol of the means through which the higher qualities (milk) are derived for the soul's sustenance.

"Its body (the sky) is the cow, its udder the cow's udder (the cloud), its teat the cow's teat (lightning), its shower (of wealth) the shower of milk : from the cow it comes to the Sacrificer."—*Sata. Brâh.*, IX. 3, 3, 16.

From the buddhic plane (cow) by means of the buddhic functioning (udder), through the higher life activities (teat), comes the outpouring of wisdom, love, and truth to the spiritual mind (sacrificer).

See COW, FOOD, LIGHTNING, MILK, MILK (goat), RAIN, SACRIFICER, VACH, WEALTH (shower).

UDGÎTHA, OM :—

A symbol of Divine love, all embracing.

"The essence of the Sama Veda is the Udgîtha (which is Om). That Udgîtha (Om) is the best of all essences, the hi hest, deserving the highest place, the eighth."—*Khand. Upanishad*, I. 1, 2.

The first principle of the Divine nature is Love. Love of the Ideal transcends all states of soul ; it is the highest of endowments, surpassing all that is below (7) and entering upon a higher plane (8).

"The plane of the spirit is that of unity ; it is the plane of the flesh which is that of division, and love is the language of the spirit."—R. J. CAMPBELL, Serm., *Souls under the Altar.*

See EIGHT, LOVE OF GOD, OGDOAD, OM, SAMAS, VEDA.

UGLY FEMALES :—
See YOMI.

UKEMOCHI, THE FOOD GODDESS :—

A symbol of Buddhi under the aspect of transmuter of the qualities whereby the soul is fed with truth and love.

"The parentage of the Food-Goddess is variously given in different myths. One story makes her the daughter of Izanagi and Izanami, and another of Susa-no-wo (the Moon-God)."—W. G. ASTON, *Shinto,* p. 162.

The higher parentage is from the Divine Will and Wisdom ; the lower, from the Desire-nature (Susa-no-wo).

"Perhaps a trace of an identification of the food with the God is to be recognised in the myth which represents the Food-Goddess as producing from her mouth and other parts of her body viands for the entertainment of the Moon-God."—*Ibid.*, p. 161.

The food being wisdom and love can be identified with Buddhi, who transmutes the desires presented by the desire-nature (Moon-god).

See AMATERASU, FOOD AS GOD, IZANAGI, SUSA-NO-WO.

UMBRELLA :—

A symbol of the overshadowing from above of the higher nature.

"In Eastern countries the *Umbrella* symbol typifies supremacy. If a king is present no one else ought to carry an umbrella."—MON. WILLIAMS. *Buddhism,* p. 523.

See CANOPY, PROCESSION, TEE.

UNBELIEF, SIN OF :—

Man's unbelief in the higher nature springs from the fact of the operations from above being inversely reflected below in the astral vehicle of the desire-mind, and perceived thus by the brain consciousness.

" Thereupon Angra Mainyu created the sin of unbelief."—*Vendidad*, I.

The illusory principle of the lower mind, kama-manas, causes the lower nature to have the aspect of reality, and the higher nature to be unperceived or seem unreal and visionary.

See ANGRA-MAINYU, ASTRAL, ILLUSION.

UNCTION, EXTREME :—

A symbol of the bestowal, through higher qualities, of the Divine love (oil) on aspiring mental qualities whose lower nature is sick unto death, thus giving them the power of rising.

See ANOINTING, OIL (anointing).

UNDERWORLD OR HADES :—

A symbol of the lower nature. The four lower planes, usually reckoned as the lower mental, the astral, the etheric, and the physical. These are the planes that are under the heaven-world of atma, buddhi, and higher manas. " Darkness," i.e. ignorance, prevails in the underworld from which the light of the Higher Self (sun) is withdrawn. In the underworld, through much sorrow and suffering the struggling souls gain experience and attain perfection and ultimate liberation, when they rise to the heaven world above. Whether in incarnation or out of that state, the souls remain in the underworld throughout the cycle, the consciousness never rising above the lower mental levels.

See DUSAKH, HADES, HELL, MICTLAN, NIFLHEIM, PO, QUATERNARY (lower), RE-STAU, TARTARUS, TATTU, TUAT.

UNEN-EM-HETEP :—

A symbol of a state of consciousness in the higher mind or devachan.

" O Unen-em-hetep, I have entered into thee and my soul followeth after me, and my divine food is upon both my hands, O Lady of the lands, who stablishest my word whereby I remember and forget."—BUDGE, *Book of the Dead*, Ch. CX.

The Self having conquered the lower planes of existence, and being now safe above the possibility of being touched or harmed by the conditions thereupon, the Supreme nature becomes known to the ego, and so the soul is raised to a sense of Divine realisation. The directive effort, or will, becomes capable of being used effectively, and the Wisdom-emotion nature is the means whereby the Self declares Itself, for out of the fullness of the *Heart* the mouth speaketh.

" The Heart contemplates God as manifested in love, for love is the universal category of affectional cognition. To love God with the heart is to love him as manifested in love ; it is to love Love, not for its convenience, but for itself, because it is absolutely beautiful and lovely to the heart."—THEODORE PARKER, *Ten Sermons*, p. 4.

See BLISS, DEVACHAN, FOOD, HEART, LADY, NIRVANA.

UNGUENTS :—

A symbol of Divine love and harmony.

" Then they brought him (Buddha) as presents from the houses of his friends costly unguents of sandal wood, and strings of gems exactly like wreaths of plants."—*Buddha-Karita*, Bk. II. 21.

The " giving of gifts " is comparable to the joy which is brought to the Self from the preliminary experiences which precede its development. The " houses of his friends " signify the conditions which are established on the mental sub-planes between the centres of the mental mechanism. The whole statement denotes the organising of the mental functioning by the Devas (friends)—the builders of forms. The " unguents of sandal wood " are the rewards of righteous acts :— love, the " oil of gladness," is its own reward, i.e. it brings increased power and opportunity for well doing. " Strings of gems " signify the functionings upon the buddhic emotional plane. The allusion to " wreaths of plants " is made because there is the suggestion of the " budding " of the feelings which will afterwards yield " flowers and fruit," that is, virtues and higher emotions.

" I (Lakshmi) reside in one who associates with such as anoint their limbs with fragrant unguents, in one who is scented with perfumes himself, and in one adorned with bracelets and ear-rings."
—*Institutes of Vishnu*, XCIX. 19.

The principle of Wisdom (Lakshmi) is contained in those qualities which are associated with Divine love, faith, and the buddhic emotions.

" Among the objects presented to the deceased in these ceremonies (of purification) scents and perfumed unguents play a prominent part. To certain kinds of oil, magical properties have been attached from time immemorial in the East, and the important place which they occupied in the ceremonies and rituals of many nations proves that remarkable effects were expected to follow their use."— BUDGE, *Egyptian Magic*, p. 203.

See CEREMONIES, DEFUNCT, EMBALMMENT, FRIENDS, GEMS (strings), HOUSES (friends), JEWELS, LAKSHMI, MAGIC, MAISHAN, OIL, OINTMENT, PERFUMES, RITES, RITUAL, SCENTS.

UNION IN THE GARDEN OF REEDS:—

A symbol of the acquirement of Individuality germinal on the higher mental plane, and implying union between higher and lower, as the Self rises above the manifestation of the astral life.

See GARDEN OF REEDS, INDIVIDUALITY, REED-PLAIN, SEKHET-AARU, SELF.

UNION WITH GOD :—

A symbol of the soul's one-ness with the higher nature, implying complete freedom from any tie or attraction to the lower nature.

" By grace man regains the complete union with God, which he had originally. The soul, like all things, pre-existed in God. Then I was in God, not as this individual man, but as God, free and unconditioned like him. Then there were no real differences in God. Immanent in the divine essence, I created the world and myself. By my emanation from him into individual existence I gave God his divine nature (his Godship), and do give it him constantly, for I give him that possibility of communicating himself which constitutes his essence. God can only understand himself through the human soul ; in so far as I am immanent in the essence of the Deity, he works all his works through me, and whatever is an object of the divine understanding, that am I. . . . This breaking through and out from the limitations of creatureship is the end of all existence and of all change. God became man that I might become God. . . . But the soul is nevertheless not annihilated in God. There remains a little point in which the soul continues to show itself a creature " (Eckhart).—UEBERWEG, *Hist. of Philos.*, Vol. I. pp. 480–1.

" That unspeakable joy of life and intensity of individuality which God possesses in never knowing what self is, in possessing of choice, His being in the being of the spiritual universe. It is to *that* that we look forward ; not to a heaven of selfish rewards ; but to the loss of all consciousness of our lower being, in union with the being of God ; and to the gain of our true individuality in the feeling that we are at one with the individuality of all."—STOPFORD A. BROOKE, Serm., *Individuality*.

" All positive religions expressed for him (Bruno) one and the same truth, some more, some less adequately,—that the supreme end of human activity is the union of the soul with God, whereby it becomes one with God and is raised above the sphere of sense and reason, above nature, out of the ordinary cycle of human life and human death."—J. L. McINTYRE, *Giordano Bruno*, p. 305.

" What may be called the highest mystery is at the same time the highest truth, whether in Christianity or in Neo-Platonism, namely, the perfect union with God. Thus Macarius (c. 330) says in his Homilies (14, 3) : ' If a man surrenders his hidden being, that is, his spirit and his thoughts, to God, occupied with nothing else, and moved by nothing else, but restraining himself, then the Lord holds him worthy of the mysteries in much holiness and purity, nay, He offers Himself to him as divine bread and spiritual drink.' "—MAX MÜLLER, *Theosophy, etc.*, p. 482.

" The soul passing out of itself by dying to itself necessarily passes into its divine object. This is the law of its transition. When it passes out of self, which is limited, and therefore is not God, and consequently is *evil*, it necessarily passes into the unlimited and universal, which is God, and therefore is the true good " (*Mde Guyon*).—VAUGHAN, *Hours with the Mystics*, Vol. II. p. 228.

" So long as man cherishes the desire of being himself something, God comes not to him, for no man can become God. But as soon as he renounces himself sincerely, wholly and radically, then God alone remains ; and is all in all. Man can create no God for himself ; but he can renounce himself as the true negation, —and then he is wholly absorbed in God. This self-renunciation is the entrance into the Higher Life which is wholly opposed to the lower life—the latter taking its distinctive character from the existence of a self."—J. G. FICHTE, *Way towards the Blessed Life.* p. 159.

" Every existence tends towards the Higher, the first Unity, to obtain perfection. . . . The whole universe is one complex, the lower emanates from the higher, and is its image, but the Divine potentiality is active in each. Love and yearning for the original source of being, and the desire of Divine perfection, are the principles of motion common to all the created " (*Geberol*).—MYER, *Qabbalah*, p. 155

See ADOPTION, ÆON, ARC. MAN, ASCENSION, ASCETICISM, ATMAN, AUSTERITIES, BLISS, BRAHMA, BROTHER OF JESUS, CONSUMMATION, GARDEN OF REEDS, GOD, GRACE, IMAGE, INDIVIDUALITY, LIBERATION, MARRIAGE, PEACE, RESURRECTION, SEASONS, SHEEP (lost), SIMORG, WILL.

UNKULUNKULU :—

A symbol of the Higher Self or God manifest.

See REED-PLAIN.

UNLEAVENED BREAD :—

A symbol of purification through goodness and truth,—" leaven " in this case standing for desire and lower emotion.

" Purge out the old leaven, that ye may be a new lump, even as ye are unleavened. For our passover also hath been sacrificed, even Christ : wherefore let us keep the feast, not with old leaven, neither with the leaven of malice and wickedness, but with the unleavened bread of sincerity and truth."—1 COR. v. 7, 8.

Christ the passover that " hath been sacrificed," refers to the Divine sacrifice in involution, and the passing over to the present state of evolution in which the Divine love arises from within in measure as it is called forth by the most advanced qualities or virtues in the soul. These qualities, then, are exhorted to continue their purification no longer by means of the discipline of authority and moral coercion ; or of the strife of passion and desire, but by the gentle means of unblemished goodness and sincere love of Truth, thereby purging the mind of its lower qualities (old leaven).

See BREAD, CRUCIFIXION OF CHRIST, FOOD, LEAVEN, MAN (natural), MANNA, PASSOVER, SACRAMENTAL CAKES, SACRIFICER, SHEW-BREAD.

UNRIGHTEOUS, OR WICKED MAN :—

A symbol of the unpurified mind, i.e. the mentality which has not cast off its lower nature, which binds it to the process of incarnation with its recurring births and deaths in the lower life.

" Know ye not that the unrighteous shall not inherit the kingdom of God ? " 1 COR. vi. 9.

The unpurified qualities, being of the lower nature, cannot possibly have any part in the higher nature. Only through the transmutation of its lower qualities can the soul become an inheritor of heaven, when the lower consciousness, being raised, merges itself in the higher.

" When he (the wicked man) is judged, let him come forth guilty ; and let his prayer become sin. Let his days be few ; and let another take his office. Let his children be fatherless, and his wife a widow. . . . Let there be none to extend mercy unto him ; neither let there be any to have pity on his fatherless children."—Ps. cix. 7-12.

The imprecatory Psalms refer not to people but to qualities. The bad qualities are anathematised as enemies of goodness, and requiring to be killed or starved out of the soul, and not fed and nourished by the personality.

See CHILDREN OF MEN, ENEMIES, GATHA (kam.), HARLOT, INCARNATION OF SOULS, MAN (bad), SLAUGHTER, WAY OF THE LORD, WICKEDNESS.

UNVINTAGED SEA :—

A symbol of the unfructified lower emotion-nature on the astral plane. The lower emotions which have not yet borne fruit on the higher planes.

See ASTRAL PLANE, SEA.

UPABHRIT SPOON :—

A symbol of the mental-body on the lower mental plane, which is the seat of the personality.

See DHRUVA, GUHU, SRUK, SRUVA.

UPANISHAD :—

A symbol of the Word of God, that is, the expression of the Truth from within the soul, in Divinely inspired symbolism.

" The word *upanishad* has come to signify ' secret meaning, secret instruction, a secret.' For *upanishad*, derived as a substantive from the root *sad*, to sit, can only denote a ' sitting ' ; and as the preposition *upa* (near by) indicates in contrast to *parishad, samsad* (assembly) a ' confidential secret sitting.' "—DEUSSEN, *Phil. of Upanishads*, p. 13.

" The New Testament and the Upanishads, these two noblest products of the religious consciousness of mankind, are found when we sound their deeper meaning to be nowhere in irreconcilable contradiction, but in a manner the most attractive serve to elucidate and complete one another."—*Ibid.*, p. 49.

The late Professor Max Müller, while appreciating highly some thoughts to be discerned in the Indian scriptures, wrote despairingly of the "real difficulties in the Upanishads," which he said,—

" Consist in the extraordinary number of passages which seem to us utterly meaningless and irrational. Some of the sacrificial technicalities may perhaps in time assume a clear meaning, . . . but there will always remain in the Upanishads a vast amount of what we can only call meaningless jargon, and for the presence of which in these ancient mines of thought I, for my part, feel quite unable to account."—*Sacred Books of the East*, Vol XV. p. xx.

The "meaningless jargon" is, of course, the very obvious *sacred language* in which the Upanishads are written, the "secret meaning" of which is not revealed through the superficial researches of literalism.

See AMBAYAVIS, GOSPEL, INSPIRATION, KORAN, PEN, RAMAYANA, REVELATION, SACRED TEXT, SASTRA, SCRIPTURES, SIGN, VEDA, WORD OF GOD.

UPLIFTING OF RĀ IN THE SOLAR BOAT AT THE END OF THE NIGHT :—

The picture in the sarcophagus of Seti I is emblematical of the process of the unfoldment of the soul and its powers ; and the actual as well as potential facts of the case are symbolically given.

The "boat," or causal-body, is upheld, supported, or evolved through the powers of the universe (Nū), and these yield up, as it were, that which is accomplished through their agency. The symbols represent the ending of the path to Liberation and Union,— the glorified Soul rising from the underworld, or Way of the Tuat, into peace eternal.

The astral plane (water) is depicted below the Boat to indicate the process of the soul's achievement in overcoming desire for the lower life. The globe upheld by Khepera (beetle) is the Soul in its buddhic robe, and above this is the plane of Atma.

The symbols of the buddhic and physical planes, namely, Isis and Nephthys, relinquish their powers (crowns) and their functions, for they are no longer needed,—they both disappear as māyā.

The Soul is received into the higher space (Nūt) above the Tuat, that is, it is received into the highest heaven (atma) where even the buddhic robe is discarded.

The symbol of encirclement at the top signifies Realisation, that state which is perfect and complete, and represents the consummation of endeavour. It is described as " Osiris who encloses the Tuat," meaning that the Christ-soul has gained the experience of the lower planes, which enrichment is now enclosed within it. The position of the surrounding figure of Osiris is noteworthy, and is so depicted in that it represents the functions through which perfection is attained ; the parts of the human body being correspondentially related with the higher centres on planes above the physical, and it is through these centres that the soul-nature develops.

See AFU-RĀ, BOAT (sektet), ISIS, KHEPER, NEPHTHYS, OSIRIS, RĀ.

URAEI, SERPENT EMBLEMS :—

Symbols signifying the triumph of wisdom and buddhic emotion reflected upon the lower mental plane.

See CADUCEUS, CROWN (atef), SERPENT.

URANUS AND GAEA :—

Symbols of Spirit and Matter, the prime factors in the process of Involution.

" Now Heaven (Uranus) used to hide his children from the light in the hollows of earth (Gaea) which both she and they resented. The children conspired against their father, and their mother assisted them by producing iron, with which she bade them avenge their wrongs. But fear fell upon them all except Cronus, who determined to deliver his mother from Heaven's embraces. So when Heaven approached his wife, Cronus, armed with a sickle of iron, mutilated him. Thus Heaven and Earth were divorced ; but Oceanus clung to his father."—JOHN RHYS, *Hibbert Lectures*, p. 111.

Upon referring to Hesiod's *Theogony* (166–192), it will be seen that this story is a variation of the worldwide symbolism of the separation of Spirit and Matter at the commencement of the process of evolution. Matter, it is to be understood, has, through the preceding process of involution, been thoroughly impregnated with the seeds of all qualities and forms which are afterwards to be evolved. The symbol of emasculation is therefore used to denote the cessation of involution when its time is fulfilled.

Spirit (Heaven) is said to hide in Matter (Earth) his progeny of the essential conditions of manifestation, which, as it were, resent their state of latency, and are eager to see the light of life. Upon the dawn of mind (iron), brought forth of Matter, the means for separation of Spirit and Matter appear, for the mental plane is midway between the higher and lower natures. Then it is that cyclic Time (Cronus) is said to effect the termination of the process of involution. Mind becoming active in the multiplicity of ideas presented to it (jagged iron sickle), begins, through desire, to reverse the life currents outwardly, and so stop their course inwardly. Thus Spirit and Matter were separated in order that beings should be formed between them, and natural phenomena should appear. But the Spirit of Truth (Oceanus) was obscured, for evolution commences in ignorance and error.

See CRONUS, EARTH (primordial), EVOLUTION, FOAM, GE, HEAVEN AND EARTH, IRON, INVOLUTION, MATTER, OCEANUS, POSEIDON, PRAGÂPATI RELAXED, PROTOTYPES, RANGI, RHEA, SEPARATION OF HEAVEN AND EARTH, SEX PRINCIPLE, SICKLE, SPARK, SPIRIT, TITANS, VENUS, ZAGREUS, ZEUS.

URDAR FOUNTAIN :—

A symbol of the fountain of Truth expressed in the outpouring of the activities in the Cycle of Life.

" The third root of the great Tree of Life runs under the region of the Asar, or gods. Beneath it is the Urdar or primeval fountain. Twelve swans swim in this fountain, and are the parents of the race of swans. There, too, by the Urder fountain, dwell the three chief Nornor, or Fates."—HOWITT, *Literature of the North*, Vol. I. p. 45.

Behind the Unity which precedes the Duality of Time and Space is the Absolute Source of all. From It proceeds the Cycle of Life in twelve stages of progress, or states of the Self producing all other states. These are subject to natural laws.

See ABSOLUTE, ADITYAS, ASAR, CIRCLE OF EXISTENCE, FATE-SPHERE, FOUNTAIN, MOIRAE, NORNOR, OCEAN, SWAN, TREE OF LIFE, TUAT, TWELVE, WATER, YGGDRASIL, ZODIAC.

UR-HEKAU—THE MIGHTY :—

A symbol of the sacred scriptures as coming forth from Divine Wisdom.

" The papyrus sceptre Ur-hekau, ' Great one of words of power,' surmounted by a piece of flesh."—BUDGE, *Egypt. Heaven and Hell*, p. 52.

In Egypt, as in India and elsewhere, the sacred writings are the expression of Deity, and indistinguishable from It. The " piece of flesh " signifies the lower nature to which the Divine Word is addressed.

" The other (*Sem* priest) holds in his right hand the instrument Ur Heka in the form of a ram-headed serpent, the head of which is surmounted by a uraeus, and in his left hand an instrument in the shape of an adze. With the former he is about to touch the mouth and eyes of the mummy, and with the latter the mouth " (*Description of Vignette, Papy. of Ani.*)—BUDGE, *Book of the Dead*, p. 39.

The spiritual mind (priest), by means of veneration of the sacred symbols, stirs the religious consciousness so that it perceives (eye) and expresses (mouth) love (ram) and wisdom (serpent) within the soul. The higher intellect (adze) also is exercised to discern the truth.

See CUTTING, EYE, FLESH, IRON, MOUTH (opening), MUMMY, PAPYRUS, PLACE OF PEACE, PRIEST, SASTRA, SCRIPTURES, SERPENT, TUBAL, VEDA, WORDS OF POWER.

URIM AND THUMMIN :—

Symbols of Wisdom and Love.

" And thou shalt put in the breastplate of judgment the Urim and the Thummin ; and they shall be upon Aaron's heart, when he goeth in before the Lord : and Aaron shall bear the judgment of the children of Israel upon his heart before the Lord continually.—EXOD. xxviii. 30.

In the inner nature of the twelve disciplined qualities of the soul,—the virtues,—will be found the principles of Love and Wisdom, and these will rest in the affections of the spiritual mind (Aaron), when the soul passes inwards between each incarnation, to the judgment of the Lord, or karmic decision on results. The spiritual mind when it enters the causal-body (holy place) will bear with it the fruition of the twelve virtues (children of Israel), and that fruition will endure.

See AARON, BREASTPLATE, CAUSAL-BODY, HEART, INCARNATION OF SOULS, ISRAELITES, KARMA, STONE, TRIBES, TWELVE.

URNĀ OF BUDDHA :—

A symbol of spiritual Truth.

"The tuft of hair, Urnā, growing between the eyebrows of the Buddha, and which must be white as snow or silver."—*Lotus of the Good Law.*

Spiritual truth centralised by the intellect and intuition is of perfect purity.

See BALDER, BODHISATVAS, BUDDHA (marks), CIRCLE, HAIR, WHITE.

URNI-TENTEN (HORUS) :—

A symbol of the Self unified with atma-buddhi.

"After these exploits Rā ordered that Horus should be called Urni-Tenten, and that the enemies of himself and Horus,—Set and his confederates,—should be handed over to Isis and Horus for them to do with them what they pleased."—*Legend of the Winged Sun-disk.*

And afterwards the Logos directed that the Christ incarnate should be unified with the wisdom-love aspect, and that he should have conscious access thereunto. And that consequently he should now no longer work from the mental and causal plane, but should function through buddhi in order to gain complete mastery over the relative or manifest existence. This refers to evolution on another and higher globe of the planetary chain.

See ATMA, BUDDHI, CHRIST, ENEMIES, HORUS, INCARNATION, ISIS, PLANETARY CHAIN, RĀ, SET.

URNS, THE TWELVE :—

Symbols of the twelve virtues, or highest qualities of the evolving soul.

Epiphanius gives a theory of salvation by Manes as follows :—

"When the Son came into the world to effect the redemption of mankind, he contrived a machine containing twelve urns (cadi), which being made to revolve by the motion of the spheres attracts into itself the souls of the dying, These the Great Luminary (the sun) takes and purifies by his rays, and then transfers to the moon; and this is the method

whereby the *disk*, as we call it, of the moon is replenished."

When the Son of Righteousness, or Higher Self, manifests himself in the lower nature, he comes forth to the sons of God—the spiritual monads—to effect their redemption in the life process they voluntarily undergo. To this end the cycle of life (motion of the spheres) is ordained, containing vehicles (urns) in which the Self can operate from within; for the Christ cannot manifest excepting through vehicles. The twelve vehicles are the twelve most advanced soul-qualities, and in these the Christ germinally dwells and expands.

The "souls of the dying" are those personalities who are translated from the physical or solar state in which experience is gained for purification, to the *post-mortem* state on the astral plane, whose correspondency is the lunar symbol. The process of the revolution of the soul in and out of incarnation, therefore shows the transference of the soul from the physical to the emotional plane, and represents the condition into which the soul enters at the passing over from the physical life. The moon's changes (disk) are symbolic of the waxing and waning of the desire-nature. The "replenishing" of the desires is preparatory and prior to each incarnation.

See DANCE (circle), DEAD, DISCIPLES, GATHA (kam., ush.), GILGOOLEM, INCARNATION OF SOULS, MONAD OF LIFE, MOON (lower), MOON (waxing), NIGHTS (three), PERSONALITY, REDEMPTION, REINCARNATION, SAVIOURS (twelve), SEED, SONS OF GOD, SUN, TUAT, TWELVE, VESSELS, WHEEL OF LIFE, ZODIAC.

UR-UATCHTI CROWN :—

A symbol of the conqueror of the lower principle.

"And Horus said, 'Henceforward let the double snake diadem of Heru-Behutet be called Ur-uatchti,' and it was so."—*Legend of the Winged Sun-disk.*

And now the Higher Self commanded that the symbol "crown of the Kingship" should be known as the sign of him who has overcome and done valiantly.

See CONQUEROR, CROWN (double serpent), HORUS, NEKHEBIT, VICTORY.

URVA, LAND OF THE RICH PASTURES :—

A symbol of aspiration and fruitfulness on the astral plane, through buddhic transmutations.

See PASTURES.

URVAKHSHAYA, A JUDGE :—

A symbol of the gnosis, or the path of wisdom chosen by the soul.

See GNOSIS OF LIFE.

URVATAD-NARO :—

A symbol of the kama-manasic principle.

See ZOROASTER.

USERT GODDESS, OR POOL :—

A symbol of an aspect of wisdom.

"O Usert, I have come into thee at the head of the house wherein divine food is brought for me."—BUDGE, *Book of the Dead*, Ch. CX.

The lesser Self has come into the sanctuary of the greater Self as Wisdom, and all its needs are satisfied.

See AMBROSIA, FOOD OF GODS, POOL OF PEACE.

USHABTI FIGURES :—

See SHABTI.

USHNISHA :—

See URNA.

USHTAVAITI GATHA :—

See GATHA USHTAVAITI.

UTCHATS,—THE TWO EYES OF HORUS :—

Symbols of the Individuality and the Personality.

"The rubric of a late chapter (i.e. CXL) of the Book of the Dead directs that the amulet should be made either of lapis-lazuli or of *mak* stone. The Utchat is of two kinds, one facing to the left and the other to the right, and together they represent the two eyes of Horus, one of which, according to the ancient text, was white and the other black ; from another point of view one Utchat represents the Sun and the other the Moon, or Râ and Osiris respectively."—BUDGE, *Egyptian Magic*, pp. 55, 56.

The right, white, sun, and Râ utchat is the symbol of the Individuality, and the left, black, moon, and Osiris utchat is the symbol of the Personality. Both spiritual centres of consciousness being on the mental plane, the blue stone corresponds in colour. The tongue under each eye signifies expression and activity.

"O thou (Good Daimon), whose tireless eyes are sun and moon,—eyes, that shine in the pupils of the eyes of men !" (From a Papyrus).—MEAD, *T. G. Hermes*, Vol. I. p. 84.

See EYES (Horus), LIPS, MOON, OSIRIS, RÂ, SUN.

UZUMÉ, GODDESS :—

A symbol of the emotion-nature evolving from lower to higher states.

"Then this young Goddess (Ame-no-Uzumé) commenced to tread with measure upon the circular hollow box and cause it to resound ; sang a six syllable song or charm of numbers ; and gradually quickening her dance, such a spirit descended on the Goddess that she loosened her dress, revealing more and more of her loveliness, and at last, to the intense amusement of the Gods, discarded her dress altogether. With the laughter of the Gods the heavens shook."—*The Nihongi*.

Then were the re-incarnating cycles of earth lives full of the play and conflict of the emotions which sent up vibrations to the buddhic plane. These caused advance upon the six-fold path through harmony of qualities, and thus evolution proceeded. Then the soul realising its needs, consciously hastened its own progress ; the now exalted Emotion-nature cast away the bonds of opinion and convention, and revealed the beauty of the Truth within until finally all ideals were realised ; and the lower nature being purified, all its restrictions were discarded. Then with the animation of the Ideals the higher planes of atma-buddhi vibrated.

See AMA-TERASU, BUDDHI, CIRCULAR, CLOTHING, DANCE, EVOLUTION, FACES OF MEN, GILGOOLEM, GODS, HIDING PLACE, LAUGHTER, MUSIC, MUSICIAN, NAKEDNESS (higher), PATH, REINCARNATION, SIX, SONG, TAMAGUSHI.

VÂCH, DIVINE SPEECH :—

A symbol of the principle of Buddhi, Wisdom, the primal manifestation of life.

"Vâch, the melodious Cow who milked forth sustenance and water."—*Rig-Veda*.

The Holy Spirit, Wisdom (Cow), the source of Divine inspiration, who bestows higher emotion (milk) and truth (water).

" There is also with the Maruts, Vâk (the voice of thunder) like unto a courtly, eloquent woman."—*Rig-Veda*, I. 167, 3.

There is allied with the spiritual egos the buddhic principle (vâk), which expresses the higher emotions in peace and harmony within the soul. The " voice of thunder " signifies the manifestation of the higher life through wisdom, truth, and love.

" The Great Voice, ' the voice out of the midst of the darkness.' It is interior, imperceptible, without cessation or interruption. It is the house of the Eternal Wisdom and is female, as a house always is."—A. E. WAITE, *Secret Doctrine in Israel*, p. 50.

See BUDDHI, COW, FOOD FOR SOUL, MARUTS, MELODY, MILK, MUSIC, SPEECH, UDDER, VOICE, WISDOM, WOMAN.

VAÊKERETA LAND :—

A symbol of the etheric-physical plane.

VÂGAPEYA SACRIFICE :—

A symbol of the spiritual nature, atma-buddhi, which descends into the limitations of matter, in order that the individuality should be endowed with it.

" To the king (râgan) doubtless belongs the Râgasûya (sacrifice) ; for by offering the Râgasûya he becomes king ; and unsuited for kingship is the Brâhmana. And, moreover, the Râgasûya is the lower, and the Vâgapeya the higher sacrifice."—*Sata. Brâh.*, V. 1. 1. 12.

To the personality (king) there is added the mental nature (râgasûya), for it is through the mind that the personality rules the lower nature. The individuality (Brâhmana) is unmanifest to the lower nature, and therefore cannot rule it directly. Moreover, the mental is the lower, and the spiritual the higher, limitation and endowment.

" Vâga-peya doubtless means the same as anna-peya (food and drink)."—*Ibid.*, V. 1, 3, 3.

The spiritual nature is the " bread " of goodness, and the " water " of truth, for the nourishment of the soul.

See BRAHMANA, BREAD, FOOD, INDIVIDUALITY, PERSONALITY, RAGANYA, SACRIFICE, WATER.

VAHISTO-ISTI GATHA :—

Symbolic of the buddhic functioning of wisdom.

" That progress which is in the Vahisto-isti Gatha the supreme Zaratust should carry on."—*Shayast La-Shayast*, XIII. 14.

That development of the soul which is brought about by the functioning of the buddhic nature in transmuting the lower into the higher emotions, is due to the activity of the Higher Self in disciplining and purifying the lower nature.

" For the Lord giveth wisdom ; out of his mouth cometh knowledge and understanding. . . . For wisdom shall enter into thine heart, and knowledge shall be pleasant unto thy soul."—PROV. ii. 6, 10.

See BARSOM, BUDDHI, HEART, MOUTH, TRANSMUTATION, WISDOM, ZOROASTER.

VAHRÂM THE STRONG :—

A symbol of Divine energy and activity on the higher planes.

VÃI THE GOOD :—

A symbol of Wisdom, the principle of buddhi.

VAIMANIKA DEITIES :—

Symbolic of the spiritual egos or individualities. These are said to be " spirits moving in mid-air on their vimânas or chariots," that is, they are the human egos active on the higher mental plane (mid-air) seated in their causal vehicles.

See AIR, CAUSAL-BODY, CHARIOT, INDIVIDUALITY, MARUTS, MONAD (life), PHAEACIANS, SONS OF GOD.

VAIRAUMATÎ, DAUGHTER OF MAN :—

A symbol of faith, or sense of dependence upon the Higher.

" The two brothers of Oro searched through the whole of the islands from Tahiti to Borabora but saw no one that they supposed fit to become the wife of Oro, till they came to Borabora, here, residing near the foot of the red-ridged mountain, they saw Vairaumati. When they beheld her, they said one to the other,—' This is the excellent maiden for our brother.' "—ELLIS, *Polynesian Researches*, Vol. I. p. 231.

The manifesting Self in its aspects of Will and Wisdom is said to go forth from Itself to the lower planes whereon to seek for its evolving counterpart ; and at length among the lower emotions. It finds Faith, which is a perception of the spiritual nature which is coming in course of evolution. " Now faith is the assurance of things hoped

for, the proving of things not seen "
(HEB. xi. 1). This intuition of Truth is
to be the means by which aspiration is
to raise the lower self. The "red-ridged
mountain " symbolises the aspirations
which rise from the struggling lower
nature. When Wisdom, Will, and
Action are united to Faith, then is
perceived the application and need
of Faith in the soul to the end of the
life cycle.

See FAITH, HEAVENLY REGIONS,
HOA, MOUNTAIN, ORO, TAATA,
TAHITIAN, TUFARA, VAPOUR.

VAIRUPA AND VAIRÂGA (SÂMAN VERSES) :—

Symbolic of a state of utter
indifference both to form and
attachment to the life of form ; a
state in which there is not a vestige
of selfishness or attraction towards
the things that are less than the Self
of all.

See ASCETIC, AUSTERITIES, SAMAN,
UNION.

VAISVÂNARA :—

A symbol of the Divine Mind, or
the Higher Self on the mental plane.

Thus Adyta, the sun, rises, as Vaisvânara (belonging to all men) assuming all
forms, as spirit, as fire. . . . the golden,
who knows all things, who ascends highest,
alone in his splendour, and warms us ;
the thousand rayed, who abides in a
hundred places, the spirit of all creatures,
the Sun, rises."—Prasna Upanishad, I. 7, 8.

This refers to the Higher Self manifesting (rising) on the mental plane,
and producing and energising the ideal
forms of all things which actualise on
the astral and physical planes. The
Self is atma-buddhi (golden), and is
the informing Spirit within all
creatures ; knowing all things, and
ascending through evolution, to the
highest from which he had descended.
He gives life to all (warms up), and is
always and everywhere present within
his creatures.

See ADITYA, DAWN, EAST, HIRAN-
YAGARBHA, POTSHERD, SLEEPING
(waking), SUN, SUN-RISING, SURYA.

VAISYA, OR THE AGRICUL-TURAL CASTE :—

A symbol of the astral self or
desire-nature in the astral-body of
the human being.

" The Vaisya are commanded to tend
cattle, to bestow gifts, to offer sacrifices,
to study the Veda, to trade, to lend
money, and to cultivate land."—Laws of
Manu, I. 89.

The desire-nature is to nurture the
better emotions ; to help the lower
nature to develop ; to give up the
lower for the higher condition ; to
submit to the spiritual law (Veda) of
evolution ; to exchange a worse state
for a better ; to assist towards the
transmutation of qualities ; and to
discipline and make fruitful the lower
nature (land).

See ANDREW, ASTRAL, AUSTERITIES,
CASTES, CATTLE, CLASSES, CULTIVA-
TION, EVOLUTION, MERCHANDISE,
MONEY, RAGANYA, SACRIFICE, VEDA.

VAIVASVATA MANU :—

A symbol of the personality or
the lower mind.

" Manu of the present period, called
Vaivasvata, is represented as conciliating the favour of the Supreme Being
by his austerities in an age of universal depravity " (Deluge Story).—MON.
WILLIAMS, Indian Wisdom, p. 394.

" Manu " represents the Individuality on the higher mental plane, and
" Vaivasvata " the personality through
which it works on the lower mental
plane, therefore " Manu " here signifies
the lower mind which has been under
restraint of its out-going activities.
The lower nature is now required to
be disciplined by the mind, owing to
the vehemence of the lower desires.

See AUSTERITIES, CORRUPTION,
DEATH (Yama), DELUGE, DEPRAVITY,
LAKE, MANU, PERSONALITY, SHIP OF
MANU.

VĀJASRAVASA :—

A symbol of the Supreme Manifesting Spirit, or the Higher Self.

" Vājasravasa, with the desire of
recompense, offered sacrifice, and gave
all that he possessed to the priests. He
had a son named Nachiketas."—Katha.
Upanishad, I.

The Higher Self, desiring the results
of experience, limits Himself in the
manifestation of his nature, and
bestows all his powers and qualities
upon the spiritual egos or minds.
The son of the Highest is the Soul or
incarnate Self.

See EXPERIENCE, NACHIKETAS,
POVERTY, PRIEST, SACRIFICER, SELF.

VALE, LOKE'S SON :—

A symbol of force or energy in astral growth.

See LOKE, NARE.

VALHALLA :—

A symbol of the buddhic plane of the soul, to which the consciousness rises when the strife or struggle of life is over, and perfection has been attained.

"Odhin's hall, where Norse warriors who had fallen in battle renewed their martial life and feasted with the god. The hall was built round the trunk of a tree, Laeradhr, on the leaves of which browsed the stag Eikthyrmir and the goat Heidhrun, from whose udders flowed the inexhaustible stream of mead drunk by the heroes of Valhalla. . . . Every day the champions (Einherjar) ride forth to combat with each other on Odhin's field, and each night return to feast on boar and mead. When fresh heroes are expected, Odhin sends to meet them at Asgardh's gate with goblets of mead."—*Non-classical Mythology*, p. 179.

The qualities are transmuted, or the egos are raised, to the buddhic plane, where they experience bliss. The buddhic vehicle (hall) is permeated by the Divine Life (tree) which gives sustenance of truths of being (leaves), to the Individuality (stag) and the Personality (goat), through whose functioning the qualities and souls are developed. Every incarnation (day) the qualities go forth to strive in the arena of life ; and at each indrawing they acquire the results of effort. The Higher Self (Odin) bestows spiritual life (mead) on those in devachan (Asgard) who have overcome evil in the lower life.

See ASGARD, BUDDHIC PLANE, DEATH OF BALDER, EAST, HEROES, INCARNATION OF SOULS, INDIVIDUALITY, MISTLETOE, ODIN, PERSONALITY, TREE OF LIFE.

VALKYRIOR :—

A symbol of the host of heaven, or higher nature forces of the buddhic plane, and the higher emotions.

See BUILDERS, DEVAS (higher).

VALLEY :—

A symbol of the kama-manas, or lower mind ; the mountains on each side signifying the higher emotions.

"The Lord is God of the hills, but he is not God of the valleys."—1 KINGS xx. 28.

The Higher Self is the co-ordinator of the higher emotions, but not of the lower mental faculties (desire-mental).

"Man's whole nature longs for fuller satisfaction than it can find in the dark valley of material existence."—R. J. CAMPBELL, Serm., *The Function of Faith*.

"The angels of the lowest heaven dwell in valleys between the hills and the mountains."—SWEDENBORG, *Apoc. Rev.*, n. 896.

"Blessed the man whose strength is in Thee, in whose heart are the ways ! Who passing through the valley of weeping make it a place of fountains, Yea, the early rain covers it with blessings."—Ps. lxxxiv. 5, 6.

Exalted is the mind (man) in which the Self manifests, in whose centre of being is the realisation of the path of Truth that leads to liberation and eternal life. The mental qualities thus raised by love and wisdom during the soul's passage through the lower life of suffering replenish the mind with truth (fountains). The mind seeking the Ideal is responded to from above in an outpouring of truth (rain) which dissipates error and illusion.

"If a man has ' the ways ' in his heart, he will pass through ' the valley of weeping,' and turn it into a ' place of fountains.' His very tears will fill the wells. Sorrow borne as a help to pilgrimage changes into joy and refreshment. The remembrance of past grief nourishes the soul which is aspiring to God. ' The early rain covers it with blessings.' Heaven-descended gifts will not be wanting, nor the smiling harvests which they quicken and mature."—A. MACLAREN, *Expositor's Bible, Psalms*.

"It is a meeting of water from below and water from above. The wells fill themselves out of the ground, and the rain comes from the sky into the pools ; yet both from the same original source. Never so much as in suffering does the divinity which God gave to man come out and show itself to meet the new divinity which he sends down to it out of Heaven."—PHILLIPS BROOKS, Serm., *Valley of Baca*.

See BRIDGE OF GJALL, FOUNTAIN, HILL COUNTRY, KAMA, MOUNTAIN, PASSAGES, RAIN, WELL.

VALMIKI, THE POET :—

A symbol of the Divine Self, the inspirer of truth in the soul.

"The voice of Valmiki uttered its poetry which the great seer Kyavana could not compose ; and that medicine which Atri never invented, the wise son of Atri proclaimed after him."—*Buddha-Karita*, Bk. I. 48.

The efforts of the Divine Self to communicate itself to the Soul failed in the immature forerunners of the Soul. The means whereby the Divine nature was to deliver, heal, or redeem the Soul, the Eternal is said "not to have invented" and applied; since deliverance is to be achieved through the Son of the Eternal, that is, the Soul itself is to be its own deliverer.

" For the purpose of realising the nature of the Self, we have had to come out from our eternal home in God that we might strive and suffer amid the illusions of time and sense. We have to overcome before we can enter into the eternal truth that lies beyond all seeming. In that overcoming we have to master the flesh and magnify the spirit, despise the world to save it, lose the life to find it." R. J. CAMPBELL, Serm., *Winning the Divine Name*.

See ALCHEMY, ATRI, IMHOTEP, KYAVANA, MEDICINE, PHYSICIAN, PITRIS (lunar), SERPENT ÆSCULAPIUS.

VANANT PLANET :—
See MERCURY.

VANAR PEOPLE :—

A symbol of the mental qualities. *See* KISHKINDHA, VIBHISHANA.

VAPOUR AND SMOKE :—

Symbolic of illusion and ignorance which obscure the truth.

" And Ahriman passed even into fire, the visible symbol of Ormazd, defiling it with smoke and vapour."—*System of Zoroaster.—*J. F. CLARKE, *Ten Religions*.

The lower principle of relativity and separation " passing into fire " is a symbol of energising the matter of the lower planes ; whereupon ignorance and illusion accompany the process.

See AHRIMAN, AHURA-MAZDA, FIRE, FIRE OF AHRIMAN, ILLUSION, SMOKE.

VAPOUR, WHITE :—

A symbol of a homogeneous buddhic condition.

" When Oro emerged from the vapour which, like a cloud, had encircled the rainbow, he discovered the dwelling of Vairaumati, the fair mistress of the cottage, who became his wife " (The Tahitian " Legend of Oro ").—ELLIS, *Polynesian Researches*, Vol. I. p. 231.

And when the Self had come forth from the homogeneous condition which

represents the state on the upper planes, and had occupied the " bridge " of manas (rainbow) which led to the plane of the desires, the heterogeneous was descried, and therefrom was distinguished the Soul within which Faith abode, and to Faith the Self became attached.

See BABEL, CONFUSION, HOA, ORO, RAINBOW, TUFARA, VAIRAUMATI.

VARA,—AN ENCLOSURE, FOUR SQUARE :—

A symbol of the lower quaternary, —the arena of life.

" Then make that vara the length of a riding-ground on each of the four sides ; and bring thither the seeds of cattle, oxen, men, dogs, birds, and red blazing fires."—*Vendidad*, II.

The Supreme now directs that the lower quaternary be prepared in order that the six centres of the qualities for the manifestation of the Divine life may be introduced. The centres comprise two buddhic (cattle, oxen), two mental (men, dogs), two astral (birds, red fires). The "length of a riding-ground " signifies that the forms must be of sufficient effective capacity for the exercise of the qualities.

See ARENA, BRIDGES (nine), COURSE, DOOR OF VARA, FIELD, KARSHIPTA, KNOWER, QUATERNARY, SEEDS OF SIX, SETTLEMENTS.

VARENA, FOUR-CORNERED LAND :—

A symbol of the quaternary. *See* THRAETONA, VARA.

VARUNA, THE INVESTING SKY :—

A symbol of Truth-reality manifesting as the Divine Will in the cycle of life.

" Wise and mighty are the works of him (Varuna) who stemmed asunder the wide firmaments (heaven and earth). He lifted on high the bright and glorious heaven ; he stretched out apart the starry sky and the earth " (A prayer of Vasishtha to Varuna).—*Rig-Veda*, VII. 86.

The lower nature (Vasishtha) aspires towards the eternal Truth, in veneration for that which transcends the ignorance and illusion on the lower planes. The Divine Will differentiates between the spiritual and material natures, and elevates the higher planes above the lower in the consciousness of the soul.

See ADITYAS, ASURA, DEVAYANA, NOOSE, OCEANUS, POSEIDON, TANGA-ROA, TLALOC, VASISHTHA.

VASE :—

A symbol of a soul-sheath,—causal, mental, or astral.

In the Egyptian picture of the weighing of the heart, the vase with the heart stands for the causal-body, the vehicle of the Higher Self.

See CRATER, CUP, JUDGMENT HALL.

VASISHTHA :—

A symbol of the highest aspect of the lower nature, or the subtler forces on the lower planes of the soul.

" Yea, the son of Sarasvati proclaimed that lost Veda which they had never seen in former ages,—Vyasa rehearsed that in many forms which Vasishtha helpless could not compile."—*Buddha-Karita*, Bk. I. 47.

Verily, the Son of the Eternal (Atma-buddhi) declared that the Divine Word (Veda), or law of the direct action of Spirit in the Soul, which had been lost and unknown to the lower consciousness, was to be recovered in Himself. On the higher planes the law of the Spirit was known and interpreted, but the lower planes were incapable of directly responding to the vibrations from above.

See ASITA, COW OF PLENTY, GOLDEN AGE, LAW OF BUDDHA, SARASVATI, SON OF GOD, SPIRIT, VARUNA, VEDA, VYASA.

VASUDEVA :—

A symbol of the Divine Spirit operative within the soul.

See BIRTH OF KRISHNA.

VAULT OF HEAVEN :—

A symbol of the higher planes.

See HEAVEN, KINGDOM, SKY.

VAYU, THE WIND, OUT-BREATHING :—

A symbol of the Divine Spirit energising from within outwardly in the process of evolution ; or the spiritual principle active in evolution upon the higher mind.

See BHIMA, BREATH (divine) DEVA-YANA, EVOLUTION, SHU, WIND.

VEDA, OR SÂSTRA :—

A symbol of the " Word of God," which is the direct utterance of the Supreme within the soul. It is the Divine law of true life on the higher planes, as revealed in the sacred scriptures of all nations, symbolically interpreted.

" Of him who gives natural birth and him who gives the knowledge of the Veda, the giver of the Veda is the more venerable father ; for the birth for the sake of the Veda ensures eternal rewards both in this life and after death."—*Laws of Manu*, II. 146. S. B. of E.

Of the mind which gives birth to the ego in the natural order, and the Spirit which gives knowledge of the true life of the soul, the Spirit is the most to be extolled ; for the birth of the ego to the life of the Spirit ensures immortality and the spiritual fruits of experience and effort.

" Studying the Veda, practising austerities, the acquisition of true knowledge, the subjugation of the organs, abstention from doing injury, and serving the Guru are the best means for attaining supreme bliss."—*Ibid.*, XII. 83.

Striving to conform to the Divine law, restraining the outgoing activities, seeking truth, subduing the desires and passions, refraining from direct and indirect injury to others, and serving the Divine self, are the true means for attaining blissful heights.

" If you ask whether among all these virtuous actions, performed here below, there be one which has been declared more efficacious than the rest for securing supreme happiness for man ; the answer is that the knowledge of the Soul (the Self) is stated to be the most excellent among all of them ; for that is the first of all sciences, because immortality is gained through that."—*Ibid.*, 84, 85.

See AMBAYAVIS, AUSTERITIES, BIRTH (second), BOAR (avatar), GOSPEL, GURU, INSPIRATION, KORAN, PAPYRUS, PEN, REGENERATION, REVELATION, SACRED TEXT, SASTRA, SCRIPTURES, SELF, SIGN, SOMA, SOUL, UDGITHA, UPANISHAD, UR-HEKAN, VAISYA, VASISHTHA, VISCERA, VITAL AIRS, WORD OF GOD.

VEHICLES OF CONSCIOUS-NESS :—

The organised bodies on the different planes, in which the soul abides and expresses itself. The five vehicles are,—the Buddhic, the Causal, the Mental, the Astral, and the Physical. Sometimes a sixth is mentioned, namely, the Etheric, which is only to a small extent a vehicle.

See CASTES, CHILDREN OF HORUS, CLASSES, MARRIAGE (castes), VESTURES.

VEIL OF ISIS :—

A symbol of the higher mind inaccessible to the lower consciousness.

" The shrine of Minerva at Sais (whom they consider the same with Isis) bears this inscription,—' I am all that hath been, and is, and shall be ; and my veil no mortal has hitherto raised.''—PLUTARCH, *Isis and Osiris*, § 3.

It is through Buddhi (Isis), the Holy Spirit, Wisdom, that the Self works ; as is said,—

" I was set up from everlasting, from the beginning, or ever the earth was.''—PROV. viii. 23.

The veil of the higher mind which separates the lower self from Buddhi can never be raised by mortality. Only when the mortal has put on immortality will the " beautiful maiden '' be revealed to the risen soul on the " bridge '' of the higher mind.

" Horapollo says that Horus is the Sun, and that Isis is represented as saying, ' No mortal has raised my veil ; the fruit which I have brought forth is the Sun,' that is, the incarnation of Osiris.'—GARNIER, *Worship of the Dead*, p. 372.

This variation of the Isis statement has almost the same symbolism as the story of the nativity of Jesus. "No mortal man, etc." means, no mental quality united with emotion is capable of producing the spiritual factor in the soul. Isis (Buddhi) must be a pure virgin in order to bear Horus (Jesus) ; she must be fructified, not by mind, but by the Divine Self (Holy Ghost), in order that she may conceive and bring forth Horus the incarnate Christ (Osiris). Isis is the heavenly virgin, the Madonna of the Catholic Church, who holds her Divine Son in her arms.

See BIRTH OF JESUS, BRIDGE OF HEAVEN, BUDDHI, EVE, HOLY GHOST, HORUS, INCARNATION, ISIS, JESUS, MAIDEN (heavenly), MIRROR, OSIRIS, SUN, VIRGIN, VIRGIN MARY.

VENUS, GODDESS, OR THE PLANET :—

A symbol of astral love which being related to the buddhic function urges the Life to pour itself forth into the forms which await its

reception, and so this lower love of form life is an important factor in evolution.

See ADONIS, APHRODITE, CUPID, FOAM, FORMS, MESCH, NINGIS-ZIDA, PLANETS, POURUSHASPA, URANUS.

VESSEL, OR RECEPTACLE :—

Symbolic of a higher or lower form of thought, or fixed set of opinions.

" Moab hath been at ease from his youth, and he hath settled on his lees, and hath not been emptied from vessel to vessel, neither hath he gone into captivity : therefore his taste remained in him, and his scent is not changed.''—JER. xlviii. 11.

The lower nature (Moab) at first is at ease in the soul ; there is little effort towards improvement, and habits of thought bind down to things below. The lower nature hath not passed from form to form of better thought, neither has it become ruled by the higher will. Therefore its inertia remaineth, and its intelligence is still directed only to the senses and desires.

See BEASTS (wild), CUP, GEUSH, HYLAS, MAGICAL FORMULÆ, LEES, PITCHER, TAMAS.

VESTURES OF THE SOUL :—

A symbol of the vehicles of consciousness or bodies in which the spiritual ego functions on the several planes of the soul.

" Self is true ; the evermoving world is false ; and the migrating souls that seem to be, and do, and suffer, are nothing else than that one and only Self, clothed in the five successive vestures or *involucra*, the beatific, the cognitional, the sensorial, the vesture of the vital airs, and the nutrimentitious vesture or visible body in the world of sense.''—A. E. GOUGH, *Phil. of Upanishad*, p. 57.

Within the arena of changing phenomena the observant consciousness alone persists ; and the reincarnating souls achieve their experience by means of the mechanisms provided on each of the lower planes. These five vestures are :—

Beatific	= Buddhic,
Cognitional	= Causal,
Sensorial	= Mental,
Vital airs	= Astral,
Nutrimentitious	= Physical.

The Beatific vesture is the " robe of glory '' which will be assumed by the soul when the consciousness rises to the buddhic plane.

" Of this blissful vesture tenderness is the head, joy is the right wing, bliss the trunk, and Brahman is the tail, the prop."—*Brihad. Upanishad.*

" Bird " is a symbol of aspiration, and the Higher Self is the propeller or energiser of the soul.

The Cognitional vesture is the Causal-body on the higher mind plane, through which Truth is known.

" Of this cognitional body faith is the head, justice the right wing, truth the left wing, ecstasy the trunk, the intellect the tail, the prop."—*Ibid.*

The Sensorial vesture is the Mental body which receives the impressions made on the senses, and makes them known to the consciousness.

" Of this sensorial body the Yajush is the head, the Rik is the right wing, the Sāman the left wing, the Brâhmanas the trunk, and the Atharvāngirasa the tail, the prop."—*Ibid.*

This sensorial body is the organ of the lower mind, and its aspiration is energised from within by the spiritual qualities signified.

" Of the body of the vital airs the breath is the head, the pervading air is the right wing, the descending air is the left wing, ether is the trunk, and earth is the tail, the prop. Therefore there is this memorial verse : It is breath that gods breathe, and men and cattle, for the breath is the life of living things. Therefore it is called the life of all. They that meditate upon breath as Brahman live the full life of man."—*Ibid.*

The Astral body is the body of the "lower vital airs," namely, the instincts, desires, and passions. Desire and Love are the life-energies (breaths) of the soul. Desire is Love inverted. The higher qualities (gods) are energised by Love-divine, and the lower qualities (animals) by desire. All living things have the breath of life, either higher or lower. Only those who exchange the lower for the higher attain to immortality.

" The nutrimentitious body is the outermost vesture of the soul. Man in his visible and earthly body is made up of the materials of food."—GOUGH, p. 76.

The body of flesh is the passive instrument of the soul, and has no life of its own.

" In the Vedanta, the individuated soul, when separated off from the supreme Soul, is regarded as enclosed in a succession of cases (kosa) which envelop it and, as it were, fold one over the other. The first or innermost sheath is called the *Vijnāna-maya-kosa* or ' sheath composed of mere intellection ' associated with the organs of perception. This gives the personal soul its first conception of individuality. The second case is called the *Mano-maya* or ' sheath composed of mind,' associated with the organs of action. This gives the individual soul its powers of thought and judgment. The third envelope is called the *Prāna-maya* or ' breathing sheath,' i.e. the sheath composed of breath and the other vital airs associated with the organs of action. The fourth case is called the *Anna-maya.* or ' covering supported by food,' i.e. the corporeal form or gross body ; the three preceding sheaths, when combined together, constituting the subtle body. A fifth case, called *Ananda-maya* or ' that composed of supreme bliss,' is also named, although not admitted by all. It must be regarded as the innermost of all, and ought therefore, when five are enumerated, to be placed before the *Vijnāna-maya.*"—MON. WILLIAMS, *Indian Wisdom*, pp. 123, 4.

The spiritual ego (migrating soul), or spark from the Eternal Fire of Life, when manifesting upon the planes below atma, is enclosed during incarnation in five vehicles of consciousness, which are five human bodies, each composed of the matter of the plane upon which it exists and functions. These bodies do not fold over one another, but usually occupy the same space as the physical body, without interfering with each other. The five bodies are,—

Ananda-maya	=	Buddhic ;
Vijnāna-maya	=	Causal ;
Mano-maya	=	Mental ;
Prana-maya	=	Astral ;
Anna-maya	=	Physical.

The highest or innermost body, that on the buddhic plane, is at present latent in humanity. The first body to manifest is the Causal-body on the plane of the higher mind or higher intellect. The second body is the Mental, on the plane of the lower mind, the plane of action and conflict, knowledge, reason, judgment, and the strife of opposites. The third body is the Astral, on the astral plane, the plane of the desires, passions, and life of the lower nature which produces action on the lower planes. The fourth body is the Physical, on the physical plane : this is the servant (Sudra) of all the other bodies during the periods of incarnation.

"The natives of West Africa are the possessors of no fewer than four spirits each; the Sioux have three souls; some Dakota tribes rejoice in the sacred number four; and the Navajos, according to Dr. Matthews, think of one of their souls as a sort of 'astral body.' Other tribes of savages are proud of, or troubled with, no fewer than six or seven. Tâoism in China provides each individual with three souls; one remains with the corpse, one with the spirit's tablet, and one is carried off to purgatory. And lest the civilised sceptic scoff at this, he may be asked to remember, not only the threefold designation of the Hebrews, of the animal (*nephesh*), the human (*ruach*) and the divine (*neshamah*) soul, but also Plato's *thumos, epithumia,* and *nous*; or the various conscious, subconscious or 'subliminal,' and dual, triple, or quadruple selves of some modern psychologists."—G. T. LADD, *Phil. of Religion,* Vol. II. p. 488.

See ANDREW, ASTRAL, BIRD, BREATH, CASTLES, CAUSAL-BODY, CHILDREN OF HORUS, CLASSES, ELEMENTS, HEAD, HOUSE (clan), GODS, INCARNATION OF SOULS, JOB, KARANA, MAASEH, MARRIAGE (castes), NEPHESH, NESHAMAH, QUATERNARY, REINCARNATION, ROBE, RUAH, RULERS (world), SAHU, SAMKHARA, SELF, SHEATHS, SKANDHAS, STEM, STHULA, VEDA, VEHICLES, VITAL AIRS, WING.

VIBHISHANA, A BROTHER OF RAVANA :—

A symbol of the scientific mind which is related to the desire-mind.

"Vibhishana had fled through the air from Lanka, in dread of the consequences of the offence he had given his King (Ravana) by counselling conciliating proceedings towards Rama. Vibhishana, on account of his local knowledge and great wisdom, was of much service to the Vanar host."—OMAN, *The Great Indian Epics,* p. 64.

The scientific mind comes over to the higher nature from serving the lower nature, and thereby offends the desire-mind (Ravana). The mind of science being replete with facts and trained to accuracy, is of great use to the mental faculties (Vanar host) which work for the Self (Rama). "Travelling through the air" is symbolic of change of mind (air) by progress towards higher exercise of mental faculty.

See AIR, HANUMAN, INTELLECT, KISHKINDHA, LANKA, RAMA, RAMAYANA, RAVANA, VANAR PEOPLE.

VIBHU, HALL OF BRAHMAN :—

Symbolic of the condition previous to the soul's final liberation from the lower nature.

"He approaches the hall Vibhu, and the glory of Brahman reaches him."—*Kaush. Upanishad,* I. 2.

The ego enters the condition of final liberation on the higher buddhic level; and then it is that the glory of the Supreme is manifest to him,—for it can never be beheld so long as the thraldom of manifestation is imposed upon the Self from which the ego is indistinguishable in essence.

See BLISS, BRAHMA, GLORIFYING, ILYA, LIBERATION, ODOUR, SALAGYA, TASTE, UNION.

VICTORY, OR TRIUMPH :—

A symbol of complete subdual of the lower nature with its passions, desires and affections, and consequent liberation of the soul from the cycle of births and deaths.

"When this corruptible shall have put on incorruption, and this mortal shall have put on immortality, then shall come to pass the saying that is written, Death is swallowed up in Victory."—1 COR. xv. 54.

At the end of the cycle, when the purification of the souls has been accomplished, the mortal lower nature shall fall away, and the perfected individualities will enter as victors into the joy of their Lord the Christ.

"Of Victory there; of Glory there. . . I conquer by this my most mighty word which is within my body, for is not this my throne?"—*Book of the Dead,* Ch. CX.

The Higher Self subdues the planes of nature by means of the Life within the forms, and it does this from its "throne," the causal-body.

"It is our destiny to find our place in a glorious perfect Divine Humanity the complete expression of the Christ idea of which Jesus is the norm and centre, the express image of the Father, and towards the realisation of which every soul that has ever lived will in the end contribute his quota of spiritual experience. In this work past, present, and future are one; none can be omitted, none can be spared. Every victory over evil gained by an individual soul is gained for all humanity. Christ is the source and goal of the whole mighty process."—R. J. CAMPBELL, Serm., *Our Earthly Race.*

See ASCENSION, BRAHMAN, BATTLE, CONFLICT, CONQUEROR, COURSE, CRUCI-

FIXION (Jesus), DEATH, HIGH-PRIEST-
SHIP, INDIVIDUALITY, KILLING OUT,
LIBERATION, PILLAR (temple), RE-
DEMPTION, REMISSION, RESURRECTION,
SAINTS, SALVATION, SLAUGHTER,
SPENDYAD, STRIFE, THRONE, VOHU-
MAN, WAR.

VIGARÂ, THE AGELESS RIVER :—

**A symbol of infinity,—the river of
life eternal.**

"He comes to the river Vigarâ, and
crosses it by the mind alone, and then
shakes off his good and evil deeds."—
Kaush: Upanishad, I. 2.

The perfected soul arrives at the
border of Eternity, and crosses it by
pure buddhi, the "raft of wisdom,"
and so shakes off all relativity,—the
pairs of opposites.

See ARA, LIBERATION, OPPOSITES,
RAFT OF WISDOM.

VIKAKSHANÂ,—INTELLIGENCE:—

**A symbol of perfect self-govern-
ment.**

"He approaches the throne Vikak-
shanâ."—*Kaush. Upanishad.* I. 2.

The soul now approaches the
"throne," which is a symbol of
mastery over self,—the sign of absolute
poise and sovereignty.

See BRIHAT, ILYA, SALAGYA.

VILLAGE :—

**A symbol of the assembling of a
few qualities.**

See ASS (colt), CITY.

VILLAGE-RULER :—

**A symbol of the desire-nature
operating from an astral centre.**

See ASTRAL, HOUSE (clan), RULERS.

VINE, AS THE TREE OF LIFE :—

**A symbol of the Divine Ray from
the Supreme, projected through all
planes and beings, and returning to
Itself in spiritual fruition.**

"I am the true vine, and my Father
is the husbandman. Every branch in
me that beareth not fruit, he taketh it
away : and every branch that beareth
fruit, he cleanseth it, that it may bear
more fruit."—JOHN xv. 12.

Christ, the Higher Self, is the central
stem of the manifesting Divine Life
which proceeds from its unmanifest
root (the Father). The principal
branches on the line of return are the
"disciples," who typify the most

advanced qualities in the soul. Those
qualities of the lower nature which bear
no fruit, i.e. the desires—illusory and
transitory,—"wither away" when
their use is ended. Every quality
which bears fruit, i.e. every high
emotion for goodness and truth, is
purified more and more by the laws
of the Supreme.

"In one hymn to Marduk he is regarded
as the possessor of the 'plant of life.' In
another hymn he is himself called 'plant
of life.'"—A. JEREMIAS, *The Old Test.,*
etc., Vol. I. p. 76.

"The vine is tree of life, the ideogram
being 'wood of life' as wine is 'drink of
life.'"—*Ibid.,* p. 209.

"Man has his own part to play. Let
him choose Life ; let him daily nourish
his soul ; let him for ever starve the
old life ; let him abide continuously as a
living branch in the Vine, and the True-
Vine Life will flow into his soul, assimilating, renewing, conforming to Type, till
Christ, pledged by His own law, be
formed in him."—H. DRUMMOND, *Natural
Law, etc.,* p. 312.

"In *W. A. Inscriptions* 'the divine
Lady of Eden' is called 'the goddess of
the tree of life' in the Accadian of north
Babylonia ; 'the goddess of the vine' in
the Sumerian of south Babylonia. It is
clear from this that the sacred tree was
also conceived of as a vine."—SAYCE,
Rel. of Anc. Babyl., p. 240.

"Jesus called Himself the vine, and
His disciples the branches, and His Father
the husbandman. He said, 'Abide in
me, and I in you.' They are not in
Him in the same kind of way that He
is in them. And yet both always tend
to their advantage, and not to His. For
the relation of the branches to the vine is
such that they contribute nothing to
the vine, but from it derive their own
means of life ; while that of the vine to
the branches is such that it supplies their
vital nourishment, and receives nothing
from them. And so their having Christ
abiding in them, and abiding themselves
in Christ, are in both respects advantageous, not to Christ, but to the disciples.
For when the branch is cut off, another
may spring up from the living root ;
but that which is cut off cannot live
apart from the root."—AUGUSTINE,
Gospel of John, Vol. II. p. 302.

"The figure of an organism is the
truest and most instructive that we can
frame to express the relation of the
Divine Logos to His creatures. It is the
figure which Christ Himself chose, and
which is freely used in other parts of
the New Testament. Christ proclaimed
Himself the true Vine (not, be it observed,
the root or stem of the tree, but the Vine
itself), of which we are the branches. The
whole is not the resultant of the parts, but
their living unity. The members depend

for their existence on the life of the whole. If it dies, they die ; if they are severed, they die and are no more."—W. R. INGE, *Paddock Lectures*, p. 98.

See DIONYSUS, DISCIPLES, FATHER, FRUIT, GRAPES, HANGING, HOMA-TREE, HUSBANDMAN, QUALITIES, SACRAMENT, SKY, SOMA, TREE OF LIFE, WINE.

VINEGAR TO DRINK :—

A symbol of the experience of suffering and sorrow.

" And straightway one of them ran, and took a sponge, and filled it with vinegar, and put it on a reed, and gave him to drink."—MAT. xxvii. 48.

Through the action of a quality there was given to the Christ-soul the cup of sorrow which was to be drunk to the dregs ; this was willingly (reed) accepted under the rule of Divine law.

" And the vinegar which was handed to Him seems to me to have been a symbolical thing. . . . the reed signified the royal sceptre and the divine law."— DIONYSIUS, BP. OF ALEXANDRIA, *An Interpretation of Luke*.

See COW'S URINE, CRUCIFIXION OF JESUS, GALL, GETHSEMANE, PASSION, REED, SORROW, SUFFERING.

VINE-POLES :—

A symbol of channels for the expression of wisdom or buddhic emotion.

" And Mary said to Jesus,—I found thee in the vineyard ; Joseph was putting up the vine-poles."—The Story of the Infancy in the *Pistis Sophia*.

The purified lower nature perceives the Christ-soul in the place of spiritual wisdom, and observes the reason exercised in directing channels through which that wisdom shall find expression in the soul.

See BROTHER OF JESUS, CHANNELS, JOSEPH (Mary), TREES AND RIVERS, VIRGIN MARY.

VINEYARD :—

A symbol of the region of spiritual wisdom. It also signifies the larger aspect of the whole of nature as a means to a spiritual end.

" The kingdom of heaven is like unto a man that is a householder, which went out early in the morning to hire labourers into his vineyard. And when he had agreed with the labourers for a penny a day, he sent them into his vineyard."— MAT. xx. 1, 2.

The state of bliss on the higher planes as the result of victory over the lower is fore-ordained by the First Logos, who, as one who goes forth under many aspects, calls all the forms of His own life within His universe to discharge their appointed tasks. And when upon each plane of nature the law of cause and effect had been set in operation, the soul-qualities (labourers) are sent to undertake their business of development in the chains of worlds.

" The vineyard implies the culture of a pure spirit in man."—E. MAITLAND, *The Bible's own Account of Itself*, p. 64.

" A vineyard signifies the church, where the divine truth of the Word is, and where the Lord is known thereby ; because wine signifies interior truth."—SWEDENBORG, *Apoc. Rev.*, n. 649.

See BLISS, BUDDHIC PLANE, DAWN, DAY, EMPEROR, HOUSEHOLDER (higher), JUSTICE, KARMA, LABOURERS, MONEY, MORNING, PARABLE, PLANETARY CHAIN, STEWARD, VICTORY, WAGES, WINE, WORK.

VIRAJ :—

A symbol of the principle or plane of buddhi.

" Viraj, as a kind of secondary creator, is sometimes regarded as male, sometimes as female. *Manu* (I. 11) says that Purusha, ' the first male ' was called Brahmā and was produced from the supreme self-existent Spirit. In I. 32, he says that Brahmā having divided his own substance, became half male, and half female, and from that female was produced Viraj, and that from Viraj was born Manu—the secondary progenitor and producer of all beings."—MON. WILLIAMS, *Indian Wisdom*, p. 24.

" Viraj " as male is atma-buddhi. Purusha, or Brahmā, is God manifest, produced from the Absolute. The division of substance is into Spirit and Matter, and it is from the Matter aspect that the buddhic plane (Viraj) is formed. Then from buddhi (Viraj) is produced the mental plane on which the Divine Mind (Manu) creates the ideas of all forms for the reception of the lives.

See ABSOLUTE, BRAHMA, BUDDHI, HEAVEN AND EARTH, MANU, MATTER, PURUSHA, SPIRIT.

VIRGIN ; VIRGINITY :—

Symbols of the purified emotions, or purified lower nature, no longer fructified by the desire-mind (man).

"For the congress of men for the pro-creation of children makes virgins women. But when God begins to associate with the soul, He brings it to pass that she who was formerly woman becomes virgin again. For, banishing the foreign and degenerate and non-virile desires by which it was made womanish, He substitutes for them native and noble and pure virtues."

"For it is fitting God should converse with an undefiled, an untouched and pure nature, with her who is in very truth *the* Virgin."—PHILO JUDÆUS, *De Cherub.*, § 14, 15.

"What is the virginity of the mind? Entire faith, firm hope, sincere charity."—AUGUSTINE, *Gospel of John*, Vol. I. p. 191.

"Exceeding wonderful and glorious is virginity. . . . This most noble and fair practice is the flower and first fruits of incorruption. We must understand that virginity, while walking upon the earth, reaches the heavens. . . . The state of virginity, *which is the goal of the incarnation*, though all may not yet reach it" (Bishop Methodius).—HARNACK, *History of Dogma*, Vol. III. pp. 110, 111.

Here, "virginity on earth reaches the heavens," can be explained by the purified lower nature (earth) becoming raised and united with the higher nature (heavens), which union is the goal of the incarnation of the souls, or the goal of Christ the Higher Self primordially involved in matter.

"The idea of a special tie between the virgin soul and Christ, comes to the front (in the works of Ambrose)."—*Ibid.*, Vol. III. p. 130.

"Thou Virgin Mother, daughter of thy Son,
Humble and high beyond all other creatures."
—DANTE, *Divina Commedia*, last canto.

"The virgin and daughter of Zion is mentioned in many places; by whom is not meant any virgin or daughter there, but the church as to the affection of good and truth, the same as by the Lamb's bride. Mount Zion signifies heaven and the church as to love."—SWEDENBORG, *Apoc. Rev.*, n. 612.

"The character of virgins is principally given to those that adhere steadfastly to Christ, and abhor everything that has any show of violating their fidelity to him. The apostle says, 'I have espoused you to one Husband, that I may present you as a chaste virgin to Christ' (2 COR. xi. 2)."—*Cruden's Explanations*. p. 356.

See BIRTH OF BUDDHA, OF JESUS, CHURCH, HETHRA, INCARNATION, MAN, RACES, VEIL OF ISIS, WALKING, WOMB OF MĀYĀ.

VIRGIN BRINGING FORTH A SON :—

Symbolic of the purified emotion-nature giving birth to the Christ-soul.

"For this mystery the Naassene says is the Gate of Heaven, and this is the House of God where the Good God dwells alone ; into which House no impure man can come—no psychic, no fleshly man—but it is kept under watch for the spiritual alone ; where when they come, they must cast away their garments, and all become bridegrooms, obtaining their true manhood through the Virginal Spirit.

For this (he says) is the Virgin big with child, conceiving and bearing a Son —not psychic, not fleshly, but a blessed Æon of Æons" (Doctrines of the Naassenes).—HIPPOLYTUS, *Philosophumena*, Bk. V.

This mystery is the Celestial Abode, —the Causal-body or World-soul where dwelleth Unity, the Higher Self,—Atma-buddhi,—the Father-Mother of all. Into this entrance of higher-manas no lower mind, no kama-manas, can come. Only those souls who have put away the "old Adam," and have purified themselves of their lusts and limitations, and who have transcended the littleness of their lower selves can enter in. Those who have cast off the lower self, or nether garments, are to be clothed upon of the Spirit, and the love element is to be turned to the highest use in the sacrifice of such forms of thought as would retard progress along higher lines. For this purified lower nature is the holy Virgin, the immaculate one, who consecrates herself to the purpose of bearing and bringing forth the Christ within the soul, spiritual and exalted, who will heal, save, and uplift humanity throughout the cycle.

"With one voice Eckhart and Tauler, Ruysbroek and Suso exclaim—'Arise, O man ! realise the end of thy being ; make room for God within thy soul, that He may bring forth His Son within thee.'"—VAUGHAN, *Hours, etc.*, Vol. I. p. 300.

"Mary is blessed, not because she bore Christ bodily, but because she bore him spiritually, and in this everyone can become like her" (Eckhart).—UEBERWEG, *Hist. of Philos.*, Vol. I. p. 482.

"The inward mind is the Virgin that conceives the Son of God, and bears and brings him forth."—JOHN WARD, *Zion's Works*, Vol. VIII. p. 210.

"Christ, if He be 'formed within,' is made of the woman in us, that is, the human will, growing thence, and of the womb of human affections ; not by man, but by the Holy Ghost, who begets that new life, to be in due time born amidst beasts out of a pure virgin affection, like Mary, in us ; which is itself the fruit of numberless other affections, some grievously defiled, as Rahab and Thamar which have gone before."—A. JUKES, *Types of Genesis*, p. 66.

" The mystery of man ! He who does not believe in that cannot enter into the full glory of the Incarnation, cannot really believe in Christ. Where the mysterious reach of manhood touches the divine, there Christ appears. . . . To him who knows the hither edges of that mystery in his own life, the story of how at its depths it should be able to receive and to contain divinity cannot seem incredible ; may I not say, cannot seem strange ? . . . . Once feel the mystery of man, and is it strange ? Once think it possible that God should fill a humanity with Himself, once see humanity capable of being filled with God, and can you conceive of His not doing it ? Must there not be an Incarnation ? So only, when it seems inevitable and natural, does the Christhood become our pattern. Then only does it shine on the mountain-top toward which we can feel the low lines of our low life aspiring. The Son of God is also the Son of Man."—PHILLIPS BROOKS, *Light of the World*, p. 14.

See ADAM (lower), ÆON, BIRTH OF JESUS, CAUSAL-BODY, CONCEPTION (immaculate), FLESH, GARMENT OF SHAME, GATE (higher), HOLY GHOST, HOUSE OF GOD, INCARNATION, MAN, MULTITUDES, SON OF MAN, SPIRIT, WOMAN.

VIRGIN MARY BEARING THE CHILD JESUS :—

A symbol of the purified lower emotion-nature conceiving the Christ-soul through the brooding of the Spirit from above.

" And blessed is she that believed ; for there shall be an accomplishment of those things which are spoken unto her from the Lord " (LUKE i. 35). " Thus St. Ambrose says on this passage,— ' And ye also are blessed who have heard and believed ; for whatsoever soul hath believed, both conceiveth and bringeth forth the Word of God, and acknowledgeth His works. In each let there be the soul of Mary, that it may magnify the Lord ; in each let there be the spirit of Mary, that it may rejoice in God. If according to the flesh the Mother of Christ is but one ; yet, according to faith, the fruit which all bear is Christ.' " —I. WILLIAMS, *Our Lord's Nativity*, p. 49.

" Let God be active in thee, and then in thy love of God art thou certain of thy bliss which can never again be destroyed by the evils of the age. Ever and ever therein goes on the incarnation of God as in Christ, for the Father did not bear the Son only in eternity, but ever and ever does He give birth to Him in the soul of him who offers himself to Him,

and what the Son has taught us in Christ is merely this, that we are the self-same sons of God " (Eckhart).—PFLEIDERER, *Develop. of Christianity*, p. 153.

" Eckhart, to quote his *ipsissima verba*, represents the Father as speaking his Word into the soul, and when the Son is born, every soul becomes Maria [i.e. " Virgin Mary "]."—MAX MÜLLER, *Theosophy, etc.*, p. 520.

" The love principle in the soul is the Virgin Mary, who conceives the Divine and Spiritual Life. This love principle or spirit is called a virgin, because it would not be defiled with the world's love, but naturally loved righteousness and hated iniquity, therefore it conceived and brought forth the Divine Life, which was the babe Jesus."—JOHN WARD, *Zion's Works*, Vol. III. p. 278.

" Only when she (the soul) has regained her ' virginity ' (purity) and become ' immaculate,' can the Christ—man's Saviour—be born of her."—*The Perfect Way*, p. 187.

" I must become Queen Mary, and birth to God must give ;
If I in blessedness for now and ever-more would live."—SCHEFFLER.

" ' I believe in Jesus Christ, who was conceived by the Holy Ghost, born of the Virgin Mary . . . and the third day he rose again from the dead, ascended into heaven and sitteth on the right hand of God.' The Modernist does not ask for an alteration in the phraseology of these clauses. He acquiesces in the plain statements of fact being taught as the church's message, but he would plead that in the sphere of the scientific or critical intellect they should not be pressed in their literal meaning. They are in his view, symbolic statements : that is, statements which have certain spiritual values. . . . I agree that symbolism must be admitted to apply to the language of religion in general and of the Christian religion in particular—meaning by symbolism the use of material images, couched in the language of human experience, which are not to be understood literally by the trained intelligence, but only as the best available expression of transcendent spiritual realities."—C. GORE, Bp. of Oxford, art. " Symbolism in Religion," *Constructive Quarterly*, March 1914.

" The history of the Virgin Mary and her functions in regard to her Son, as presented alike in the Gospels and in Catholic tradition and ritual, are in every particular those of the soul to whom it is given to be ' Mother of God ' in man. Her acts and graces, as well as his life and passion belong to the experience of every redeemed man. As the Christ in him delivers him from the curse of Adam, so the Virgin Mary in him delivers him from the curse of Eve, and secures the fulfilment of the promise of the conquest over the serpent of Matter. And, whereas, as sinner, he has seen enacted in his own interior experience the drama of the Fall ; so as saint, he enacts the mysteries represented in the Rosary of the Virgin, his soul passing in turn through every stage of her joys, her sorrows, and her glories. Wherefore the part assigned to Mary in the Christian Evangel is the part borne by the soul in all mystical experience. That which first beguiles and leads astray the soul is the attraction of the illusory world of mere phenomena, which is aptly represented under the figure of the Serpent with glittering coils, insinuating mien, and eyes full of fascination. Yielding to this attraction, through directing her gaze outwards and downwards instead of inwards and upwards, the soul—as Eve—has abandoned celestial realities for mundane shadows, and entangled in her fall the mind, or Adam. Thus mind and soul fall together and lose the power of desiring and apprehending the divine things which alone make for life, and so become cast out of divine conditions, and concious only of material environments. and liable to material limitations. This substitution of the illusory for the real, of the material for the spiritual, of the phenomenal for the substantial, constitutes the whole sin and loss of the Fall. Redemption consists in the recovery of the power once more to apprehend, to love, and to grasp the Real."—ANNA KINGSFORD, *The Perfect Way*, p. 241.

" It is well to insist upon the true importance and value of favouring conditions in the production of moral character. Without these—which correspond, as it were, to a mould or matrix wherein the spiritual life is conceived and brought forth—it is certain no result whatever can be assured."—R. DIMSDALE STOCKER, *The God which is Man*, p. 130.

" Nature and man can only form and transform. Hence when a new animal is made, no new clay is made. Life merely enters into already existing matter, assimilates more of the same sort and rebuilds it. The spiritual Artist (Christ) works in the same way. He must have a peculiar kind of protoplasm, a basis of life, and that must be already existing. Now He finds this in the materials of character with which the natural man is previously provided. Mind and character, the will and the affections, the moral nature—these form the bases of spiritual life. To look in this direction for the protoplasm of the spiritual life is consistent with all analogy. . . . The mineral supplies material for the vegetable, the vegetable for the animal, the animal for the mental, and lastly, the mental for the spiritual. . . . In this womb the new creature is to be born, fashioned out of the mental and moral parts, substance, or essence of the natural man. The only thing to be insisted upon is that in the natural man this mental and moral substance or basis is spiritually lifeless. However active the intellectual or moral

life may be, from the point of view of this other Life it is dead. . . . The protoplasm in man has a something in addition to its instincts or its habits. It has a capacity for God. In this capacity for God lies its receptivity ; it is the very protoplasm that was necessary. The chamber is not only ready to receive the new Life, but the Guest is expected, and, till He comes, is missed."—H. DRUMMOND, *Natural Law, etc.* pp. 297–300.

" A Divine element, a spiritual quickening, is required for the evolution of anything God-like in our mundane sphere ; it is a Virgin Birth. Lower acting upon lower can never produce a higher. It is the downpouring and incoming of the higher to the lower which produces through the lower the Divine manhood which leaves the brute behind. This is the sense in which it is true that Jesus was of Divine as well as human parentage."—R. J. CAMPBELL, *The New Theology*, p. 106.

See ADAM (lower), ASSUMPTION, BETHLEHEM, BIRTH OF JESUS, CAVE, CONCEPTION, CROWN (stars), DEMIURGE, EVE, EVOLUTION, FALL, GOLD (frank.), HEBDOMAD, HEEL, HEROD, HILL COUNTRY, HUITZILOPOCHTLI, INCARNATION, MARJATTA, REDEMPTION, REGENERATION, SERPENT (subtil), SIMEON, VEIL OF ISIS, WOMAN.

VIRGINS OF THE PARABLE :—

Symbolic of ten faculties of perception. The five wise virgins signify five inner means of contacting higher planes. The five foolish virgins signify the five senses.

" Then shall the kingdom of heaven be likened unto ten virgins, which took their lamps, and went forth to meet the bridegroom. And five of them were foolish and five were wise. For the foolish, when they took their lamps, took no oil with them ; but the wise took oil in their vessels with their lamps."—MAT. xxv. 1–4.

The state of consciousness on higher planes is foreshadowed in the process of achieving that state. The " bridegroom " is the Christ, and the marriage is the union of Wisdom and Love, the bride being the condition which is implied in the soul's arriving at the higher state. The five senses have not the substance of love and Truth wherewith the Spirit feeds the flame of life in the causal-vehicle (lamp). The five higher faculties are possessed of it. When the period of union arrives, the higher faculties, being spiritual, take their part in it, but the senses remain outside and are of no avail ; they are referred to the means that science provides for the gathering of facts and approaching the Truth.

" The virgins are divided into two equal numbers of five, inasmuch as the one class preserved the five senses, which most people consider the gates of wisdom, pure and undefiled by sins ; but the others, on the contrary, corrupted them by multitudes of sins. . . . Now the oil represents wisdom and righteousness ; for while the soul rains down unsparingly, and pours forth these things upon the body, the light of virtue is kindled unquenchably."—METHODIUS, *Banquet of the Ten Virgins*, Ch. III.

The virgins all slumbered because they were unconscious of the highest happenings. " But at midnight there is a cry, behold the Bridegroom ! Come ye forth to meet him." Here, " midnight " signifies the period of attainment of the required conditions when the union of Higher and Lower can take place. It is then that Christ appears to the wondering and adoring soul. The thrill of His mighty presence calls on all the faculties of the vehicles of the ego to bestir themselves. They rouse from their sleep and look around.

See CHRIST, DOOR (shut), FIVE (number), FIELD, FIRE, KINGDOM OF HEAVEN, LAMP, MARRIAGE, NIGHT, OIL, PARABLE.

VIRGO, THE ZODIACAL SIGN :—

A symbol of the sixth period of the cycle of life. It signifies the completion of the process of involution resulting in the one perfect matrix of Matter fully permeated and informed by Spirit, and ready to bring forth the qualities and the Christ in the many souls during the subsequent six periods of evolution.

" Methodius holds that Christ is not only arch-shepherd and arch-prophet, but also archetypal virgin."—HARNACK, *Hist. of Dogma*, Vol. III. p. 112.

Christ, the Archetypal Man, who is perfected and dies in involution, is also the archetypal Virgo who brings forth, as Mother Matter, all things during evolution : " for in him were all things created, in the heavens and upon the earth, things visible and things invisible " (COL. i. 16).

See ADAMAS, ARC. MAN, CRUCIFIXION OF CHRIST, EVOLUTION, INVOLUTION, RACES, SIX, WOMB, ZODIAC.

VISCERA, OR VITALS :—

A symbol of the lower qualities of the personality enclosed, as it were, in the skin (physical body).

" These (four children of Horus) had charge of the viscera of the dead, and were bound to appear at the judgment, because according to Egyptian belief, it was not the divine Ego of a man which sinned, but only his internal organs."—WIEDEMANN, *Rel. of Anc. Egyptians*, p. 248.

The four vehicles of the divine Ego are the causal, mental, astral, and physical bodies to which the lower qualities are attached. The four bodies are said to appear at the judgment because it is through their being perfected that the divine Ego is liberated from the lower nature. The divine Ego, being the pure Spirit within, cannot sin, but in so far as it identifies itself with its manifesting personalities, it experiences evil states through the lower qualities.

" In Indian physiology the functions of the viscera are said to depend on the activities of the vital airs."—GOUGH, *Phil. of Upanishads*, p. 133.

See APPENDAGES, CHILDREN OF HORUS, HEART, JUDGMENT DAY, LIVER, PRANAS, PROMETHEUS, QEBHSENNUF, ROASTED FLESH, STOMACH, VITAL AIRS.

VISHNU :—

A symbol of the manifesting Logos or Higher Self,—the Divine Sacrifice and God-incarnate.

" It is as Vishnu that the Supreme Being, according to the Hindus, exhibited his sympathy with human trials, his love for the human race, his respect for all forms of life, and his condescension towards even the inferior animals as integral parts of his creation. Portions of his essence, they assert, became incarnate in the lower animals, as well as in man, to rescue the world in great emergencies. Nine principal occasions have already occurred in which the God has thus interposed for the salvation of his creatures. A tenth has still to take place."—MON. WILLIAMS, *Indian Wisdom*, p. 329.

The Higher Self sacrificed, or limited, himself in the process of involution, in order that he might become the Saviour of the many souls in evolution. In all forms of life he is involved, and he is the cause of development in all beings. In successive periods of the cycle of

Life, he is said to incarnate in the lower nature (symbolised by various animals and men) for the purpose of bringing about the development of soul appropriate to each period. Kalki, the tenth avatar, symbolises the final triumph of the Self at the end of the cycle.

" Hail to thee, mighty Lord, all-potent Vishnu ! Soul of the universe, unchangeable, holy, eternal, always one in nature, whether revealed as Brahmā, Hari, Siva—Creator or Preserver or Destroyer—thou art the cause of final liberation ; whose form is one, yet manifold ; whose essence is one yet diverse ; tenuous, yet vast ; discernible, yet undiscernible ; root of the world, yet of the world composed ; prop of the universe, yet more minute than earth's minutest particles ; abiding in every creature, yet without defilement ; im-perishable, one with perfect wisdom " (*Prayer of Parāsara*).—MON. WILLIAMS, *Indian Wisdom*, p. 498.

The manifesting Self is described as the inmost Spirit, and the Divine Life of the universe and of the human souls of which he is the liberator and Saviour. He is eternal Truth and perfection, everlasting Love and Wisdom.

See BOAR, CHURNING, EYE OF VISHNU, INCARNATION, KALKI, KRISHNA, LIBERATION, MAHAVIRA-POT, NARAYANA, RAMA, SERPENT (ananta), STRIDES, TORTOISE.

VISTASP, KING :—

A symbol of the Higher Self as organiser of the Soul in the process of involution on the buddhic plane.

" That (branch and period) of gold is when I (Auharmazd) and thou (Zaratust) converse, and king Vistasp shall accept the religion, and shall demolish the figures of the demons, but they them-selves remain for concealed proceedings." —*Bahman Yasht*, I. 4.

This refers to the first period of spiritual activity in the development of the soul. It is the " golden age " of involution on the buddhic (gold) plane, and in it the Divine Will and the World-soul " converse," that is, are in complete harmony in the activities of life. The Higher Self establishes the science of the spiritual life in the Divine scheme, and without strife overcomes ideally the imagined or arranged lower qualities which sub-sequently are to become active in the period of evolution on the lower planes.

See AHURA-MAZDA, BUDDHIC PLANE, CIVILISING, DEMONS, GOLDEN AGE, INVOLUTION, OANNES, RELIGION, ZOROASTER.

VISVAKARMAN :—

A symbol of the Higher Self as the Divine sacrifice and the Incarnate Self.

" The Seer and a Priest, who offering all the worlds as a sacrifice, came down as our Father, he, appearing first, entered among mortals, desiring wealth with blessing " (*Rig-Veda*).—MAX MÜLLER, *Science of Religion*, p. 162.

The all-seeing and all-knowing Self limits himself in manifesting the universe, and in descending into matter to be our progenitor, he becomes first the Archetypal Man in order to manifest in us the higher qualities, and attain through effort to supernal bliss.

" Sacrifice is the necessary condition for the revealing of the highest kind of life either in man or God."—R. J. CAMPBELL, Serm., *Jesus and the Life-Force.*

" The last in order of time, broadly speaking, so far as the world-process is concerned, is the highest in order of being."—*Ibid.*, Serm., *The Source of God.*

See ARC. MAN, BLESSING, FATHER, LAMB OF GOD, MELCHIZEDEK, PILGRIM, PRIEST, SACRIFICER, WEALTH, WORLDS.

VITAL AIRS, UPPER AND LOWER :—

A symbol of the life energies which are higher, buddhic, and lower, astral. These become active in the mind (air).

" From the upper vital airs Pragâpati created the gods, and from the lower vital airs the mortal creatures."—*Sata. Brâh.*, VI. 1, 2.

" Pragâpati fashioned animals from his vital airs, a man from his soul (mind). . . Animals are vital airs. The soul is the first of the vital airs ; man is the first and strongest of animals. The soul is all the vital airs, for in the soul all the vital airs are established. . . . Man is all animals."—*Ibid.*, VII. 5, 2, 6.

From the higher outgoing energies or soul-qualities (atma-buddhic) the Supreme created the ideals (gods), and from the lower outgoing energies (astral), the instincts, desires, and passions.

The Supreme produced the desires from his outbreathing life on the lower planes ; an ego from his spiritual effluence. The desires are energies on the astral plane. The spiritual effluence is the the highest, and is on the plane of atma. The ego is the greatest and most powerful of emotion-energies in his inmost being. The spiritual effluence comprises all the outgoing energies and qualities, for in the ego all the life forces and qualities inhere potentially, whether of the higher or the lower planes. The spiritual ego is a microcosm.

"Cast off the fetters of the senses, the 'remora of desire'; and making your interests identical with those of the All, rise to freedom, to that spontaneous, creative, artistic life which, inherent in every individual self, is our share of the life of the Universe. You are yourself *vital*—a free centre of energy —did you but know it. You can move to higher levels, to greater reality, truer self-fulfilment, if you will. Though you be, as Plato said, like an oyster in your shell, you can open that shell to the living waters without, draw from the 'Immortal Vitality.' Thus only—by contact with the real—shall you *know* reality."—E.UNDERHILL, *Mysticism*, p. 37.

See ANIMALS, ASTRAL, BEASTS, BREATH (divine), CHARIOT, CREATURES, FETTERS, GODS, HIGHER AND LOWER NATURES, LINGAM, LIVER, PRAGÂPATI, PRANAS, PROMETHEUS, QUALITIES, SENSE ORGANS, VESTURES, VISCERA.

VÎVANHÂO, OR VIVANGHAT, FATHER OF YIMA :—

A symbol of the Absolute, or the First Logos, the emanator of the Higher Self (Yima,—Jamshed).

"Then spake Zarathustra : Reverence to Homa ! Who was the first who prepared thee for the material world ? Homa answered : Vîvanhâo was the first man who prepared me for the material world."—*Homa Yasht.*

Then the soul inquires,—Who is it first prepared the Divine Life for the material existence ? The reply is that the Absolute or First Logos under its threefold aspect of Intelligence, Will, and Action, first prepared the Divine for the material or manifested world.

See ABSOLUTE, CREATION, FATHER, GODHEAD, HOMA, TRIAD, TRINITY, YIMA, ZOROASTER.

VOHU-KHSHATHRA GATHA :—

A symbol of the causal-body with its higher mental faculties and emotions.

See CAUSAL-BODY.

VOHUMAN, OR VOHUMANO, THE GOOD MIND :—

A symbol of Glorious Achievement in that the Higher Self attains his purpose, and vanquishes ignorance and evil in his creation.

"The first of Ormazd's creatures of the world was the sky, and Vohuman by good procedure produced the light of the world, along with which was the good religion of the Mazdayasnians, this was because the (future) renovation which happens to the creatures was known to him."—*Bundahis*, I. 25.

The first plane of the manifest universe and soul is the buddhic (sky), the first production from Atma. But Vohuman (good thought) had previously appeared in the ideal scheme of the Supreme, as signifying the principle of glorious achievement which should bring about the development of the manifest. Then was produced consciousness (light) in the union of spirit and matter, and the working of the spiritual life (religion) which should eventually entirely renovate the world and the soul.

See AKEM-MANO, AMSHASPANDS, ARCHANGELS, BAHMAN, HIGH-PRIEST-SHIP, INVOLUTION, LIGHT, MIND (good), RELIGION, RENOVATION, SKY, VICTORY.

VOICE OF GOD :—

Symbolic of the higher nature calling from within to the lower mind. The expression of the conscience in the personality.

"Behold I stand at the door and knock : if any man hear my voice and open the door, I will come in to him, and will sup with him, and he with me. He that overcometh, I will give to him to sit down with me in my throne, as I also overcame, and sat down with my Father in his throne."—REV. iii. 20, 21.

The Christ speaks from the higher mind. He stands in the higher mind and knocks at the door of the lower mind. If the lower mind hears and heeds the voice of the Saviour, and purifies itself, then it will open the door and in union with the Christ will partake of the heavenly feast. The victor over the desires and passions of the lower nature, i.e. the individuality, will become one with the Christ in the Causal-body, as the Christ victorious in his involution and evolution is one with the Unmanifest in potentiality.

"Voice here denotes the divine truth of the Lord from his Word."—SWEDEN-BORG, *Apoc. Rev.*, n. 37.

"The 'Voice of God' is, in Rabbinic literature, a companion idea to the Shechinah. Like the latter, it is immanent in man and the world."—J. ABELSON, *Immanence of God*, p. 83.

"The outermost is the animal, within are varying degrees of soul which are continually changing as the Spirit tries to utter itself. Your soul is the individualised *you*, the compound of thoughts, feelings and desires by which you give your spirit utterance."—R. J. CAMPBELL, Serm., *God in Man*.

"In the call of duty we must learn to hear the voice of God."—*Ibid.*, Serm., *Jacob's Wrestling*.

"Amidst the animal and selfish desires of our nature, there is a Voice which clearly speaks of Duty : Right : Perfection. This is the Spirit of Deity in Man—it is the life of God in the soul. This is the evidence of our divine parentage."—F. W. ROBERTSON, *Sermons, 1st Series*, p. 213.

"The soul, by its sense of right, or its perception of moral distinctions, is clothed with sovereignty over itself, and through this alone it understands and recognises the Sovereign of the Universe. Men, as by a natural inspiration, have agreed to speak of conscience as the voice of God, as the Divinity within us. This principle, reverently obeyed, makes us more and more partakers of the moral perfection of the Supreme being."—W. E. CHANNING, *Likeness to God*.

"The Kaffir view of conscience clearly shows the unconscious action of memory images. The qualms of conscience 'usually seem to him to come as unreasoned checks almost *ab extra*. It is as if he suffered from some alternation of personality, or as if some faculties of his soul had suddenly arisen out of the strange hidden depths of his own personality and made themselves felt' (D. Kidd). Frequently he hears a voice."—A. E. CRAWLEY, *The Idea of the Soul*, p. 282.

"Man will sooner doubt the solid earth he treads on than the Voice that speaks to him through the changes and chances of this mortal life. That Voice has not only or even chiefly to do with passionate intuitions and subconscious perceptions, for it seems to sound as clearly and more often in deliberate and reasoned conviction that this or that is right or wrong, and must at every hazard be done or left undone."—H. M. GWATKIN, *The Knowledge of God*, Vol. I. p. 115.

See CAUSAL-BODY, CHRIST, CONQUEROR, CONSCIENCE, DOOR (higher), EAR, EVOLUTION, EXILE, FATHER, FEAST, HECATOMB, HIDING, INDIVIDUALITY, INVOLUTION, JOB, MAN, NOISE, REDEEMER, SON OF MAN, SOUND, SUPPER, THRONE, THUNDER, UNION, VICTORY.

VOURU-KASHA OCEAN :—

A symbol of celestial Truth, the immanent Divine Reality.

"Tishtrya's most significant epithet is 'water-faced,' because he brings the waters from the celestial ocean, Vouru-kasha, down on the earth to fertilise the soil."—*Tir Yasht*.

"Tishtrya" is a symbol of the Ego or Mind seated in the causal-body. "Water-faced" signifies having a Truth-aspect, because whilst the mind is the great creator of illusion, it is also a means of discerning the true. The higher mind (the Ego) functions through buddhi and so derives its knowledge from above (Vouru-kasha). This can only be done insofar as the wisdom above is interpreted to the mind in the experiences which have been collected through the functioning of the Ego upon the lower planes (the earth).

See ANDUISUR, BUDDHI, EXPERIENCES, HARVISPTOKHM, HORSE (red), ILLUSION, IRIS, IRRIGATION, OCEAN, PUITIKA SEA, RAIN, TISTRYA, WATER (higher).

VOW :—

A symbol of the germ of conscience, or a partial conception of cosmic law in the soul's evolution.

See CONSCIENCE, HECATOMB, OATH.

VOWS, RELIGIOUS :—

A symbol of aspirations which yield results in the mind, capable of directing the evolution of the indwelling Self.

See LAW OF BUDDHA.

VRITRA DEMON :—

A symbol of the lower principle.

"In the *Rig-Veda* (see VI. 20, 2) the demon of cloud and darkness, called Vritra, is either identified or associated with the serpent Ahi ; and the god Soma is described as delivering over all evil speakers and slanderers into the power of this serpent."—MON. WILLIAMS, *Religious Thought in India*, p. 13.

The Divine Life (Soma) requires those qualities of the lower mind which express falsity and perversion to be re-embodied and thereby placed in the power of the lower principle, in order to gain experience and development.

See ARROWS (divine), DARKNESS, RAVANA, SERPENT, SOMA.

VULTURE, THE BIRD OF ISIS :—

A symbol of the transmuting power of Buddhi (Isis), whereby the lower nature (flesh), or the personality (corpse), is consumed.

" Isis cometh and hovereth over the city, and she goeth about seeking the secret habitations of Horus as he emergeth from his papyrus swamps, and she raiseth up his shoulder which is in evil case. He is made one of the company in the divine boat, and the sovereignty of the whole world is decreed for him."—BUDGE, *Egyptian Magic*, p. 48.

The 117th chapter of the *Book of the Dead* is associated with the amulet of the vulture which was placed on the neck of the mummy to be a protection. The amulet was made of gold in the form of a vulture hovering in the air with outstretched wings and holding in each talon the symbol of life.

Buddhi (Isis) " hovereth over," or descends, as it were, to the astromental centre (city) and establishes relations with the hitherto latent higher qualities which contain the germ of the incarnate Self (Horus) now emerging into actuality on the astromental plane (swamps). Buddhi is able, by raising the qualities, to set free the directive ability (shoulder) of the indwelling Self, for the soul in which the Divine nature is submerged is in an evil case. The incarnate Self now enters into activity amid the higher qualities in the causal body (boat), and the rule of the whole evolving nature of humanity is assigned him.

The " golden amulet in the form of a vulture placed on the neck of the mummy " signifies the alliance of the buddhic function with the purified emotions (neck) in the purified personality (mummy), so that the ego may be raised to the life immortal.

The symbology of the vulture explains the reason why the Parsis deliver their dead over to the vultures. The personality (corpse) must be transmuted and consumed by Buddhi (vulture) in order to liberate the ego from the lower nature and raise the consciousness to the higher planes. The Parsis devoutly regard their Divinely inspired scriptures, but they mistake the symbol for the reality, and believe they are bound by the letter of the Word.

" Sorrow comes, and weariness, and broken hopes. Sorer and heavier lies the burden of life upon the shoulder, for so only can some of us be freed from that devotion to the world, that nightmare of self that sits upon the breast of aspiration;—so only can we learn the hard, hard lesson that the invisible is the real, and the visible the unreal world. For in the darkness it is still God's pertinacity that is labouring for us, it is still His love which says, I will not leave you, till I have done that which I have spoken to you of. What I do thou knowest not now, but thou shalt know hereafter."—STOPFORD A. BROOKE, Serm., *Jacob's Life.*

See BIRTH OF HORUS, BOAT (sektet), BUDDHI, BUTO, CITY, COMPANY OF GODS, CORPSE, CORPSE DEVOURED, DEFUNCT, EAGLE, EMBALMMENT, FLESH, HOUSES (corpse), INCARNATION, ISIS, MARSH, MUMMY, NECK, PERSONALITY, PROMETHEUS, REED-PLAIN, SHOULDER, TRANSMUTATION.

VULTURE AS A BIRD OF PREY :—

A symbol of the Self emerging within the soul in a terrific guise ; which means that the Divine law of the Self is hard and obnoxious to the lower self, which is threatened with extinction.

See ANGER OF GOD, WRATH.

VYĀSA, THE DISPOSER IN REGULAR SEQUENCE :—

A symbol of the Divine Spirit Atma,—buddhi—manas, as the Author and Progenitor of the scheme of things, and of the process of the soul's development during the cycle of manifestation of the Divine Life.

See TRIAD, TRINITY, VASISHTHA.

WAGES :—

A symbol of payment in specific spiritual acquirements, for accomplished result or successful work of the lower self in developing the soul.

" God has sown something in you which is to bear its fruitage, and in the reaping thereof, here and now, if you are faithful to the vision He gives, you have your wages—namely, the sweet assurance that you have won something worth the winning, for earth and heaven. . . . And your wages in the service of God are that you are found worthy, made capable, of doing God's work just where you stand."—R. J. Campbell, Serm., *Reaping for Eternal Life.*

See Householder, Justice, Labourers, Money, Reaping the harvest, Vineyard, Work.

WALK :—

A symbol of progress or advance in development.

See Feet, Foot, Strides of soul.

WALKING DAY BY DAY :—

Symbolic of stages of the soul's activities upon the lower planes.

" I (Jesus) must walk to-day and to-morrow, and the day following : for it cannot be that a prophet perish out of Jerusalem."—Luke xii. 33.

This refers to the strenuous nature of the process of perfectionment which is arrived at through the activities upon the lower planes whereon the perfecting of the Christ-soul is fore-shadowed, and from which it, as it were, proceeds. Then having proceeded to the state signified by "Jerusalem," the soul cannot perish but must have everlasting life.

" Jesus saith unto him, Arise, take up thy bed and walk."—John v; 8.

Christ exercised his spiritual power within the soul and released it from impediments to progress.

" We bear our neighbour, and walk towards God ; but Him, to whom we are walking, we do not yet see : for that reason also, that man did not yet know Jesus. It is difficult in a crowd to see Christ : a certain solitude is necessary for our mind ; it is by a certain solitude of contemplation that God is seen. A crowd has noise ; this seeing requires secrecy. ' Take up thy bed '—being thyself born, bear thy neighbour ; ' and walk,' that thou mayest come to the goal. Do not seek Christ in a crowd ; He excels all crowd. . . . Even now as yet thou knowest not Jesus, nor yet seest Jesus : what follow thereafter ? Since that man desisted not from taking up his bed and walking, ' Jesus seeth him afterwards in the temple.' The Lord Jesus, indeed, saw him both in the crowd and in the temple ; but the impotent man does not know Jesus in the crowd, but he knows Him in the temple. The

man came then to the Lord : saw him in a consecrated, a holy, place. And what does the Lord say to him ? ' Behold, thou art made whole ; sin no more, lest some worse thing befall thee.' "—Augustine, *Gospel of John,* Vol. I. p. 245.

See Feet, Foot, Hiding, Jerusalem, Morrow, Three (number).

WALKING UPON THE WATER :—

A symbol of making progress against a tide of astral desires and passions.

"And in the fourth watch of the night he (Jesus) came unto them, walking upon the sea."—Mat. xiv. 25.

This happens only after the Christ has *realised* that He is able to save to the uttermost the striving qualities ; and therefore his preceding prayer upon the mountain is alluded to. After the Christ-soul has sought strength from above, he stems the tide of the astral plane, and comes to the aid of the toilers of the night who are fighting desperately hard—he being a great way off. So it is with many that at times of stress, the Christ within, who seems far away, is in reality only gathering power from above, which shall be used to aid the lower nature in its efforts to unite itself with the higher. The "fourth watch" signifies the fourth sub-plane of the astral plane.

See Astral, Mountain, Sea, Ship on sea, Water (lower).

WALKING WITH GOD :—

A symbol of the potential life of the unmanifest.

"And all the days of Enoch were three hundred, sixty and five years. And Enoch walked with God : and he was not, for God took him."—Gen. v. 23, 24.

" Enoch walked with God " is a symbol of the latent individuality on the higher mental plane, which is able to survive the attached person-alities with their terrestrial incarna-tions and their first (physical) and second (astral) deaths. The 365 " days of Enoch " indicate the length of the solar year, or Zodiac, a symbol of the great cycle of life, during which the individuality (Enoch) is permanent in the soul. " He was not " means that the individuality was not yet in manifestation. " God took him," or " he abode in God," signifies that individuality was potential—or yet in the bosom of the Absolute. "Jared," his father, is a symbol of the Divine source of Light and Life.

See ENOCH, INCARNATION OF SOULS, INDIVIDUALITY, NOAH, PERSONALITY, YEAR, ZODIAC.

WALKS, SIX :—

Symbolic of strides of progress on the lower planes, between six initiations on plane after plane.

"On this first walk I ask from thee, O Homa ! who expellest death, the best life (paradise) of the righteous, the splendid, the all-radiant with its own brilliancy."—*Homa Yasht.*

The " first walk " is the first initiation. The aspiration of the ego is for life which shall endure and contribute to the permanent advancement of the soul-state. This initiation occurs upon the astral plane, and is due to the attainment of perfect adjustment of the functioning upon the plane immediately above, i.e. the mental, which admits of the vibrations being steadied so that they transmit themselves downward again to the lower vehicle.

"On this second walk I ask from thee, O Homa ! who expellest death, the health of this body."

The second initiation corresponds to complete mastery by the ego of the astral vehicle with its instincts, desires and passions, so that the soul is no longer disordered by strife.

"On this third walk I ask from thee, O Homa ! who expellest death, the long life of the soul."

The third initiation is that which is to contribute understanding of the true function of the mental body. The "long life of the soul" is the prolongation of the life on the mental plane. It is the extension of the devachanic period—the period between two incarnations.

"On this fourth walk I ask from thee, O Homa ! who expellest death, that I may stand forth at will, powerful and successful upon the earth, putting down troubles and annihilating the destructive powers."

The fourth initiation is a comprehension of the mysteries attending the perfect controlling of the activities of the physical plane, which implies intellectual command of the will from the causal sheath downwards. This initiation is possible only after great advancement, as the acquirement of conscious power over the physical plane is incapable of being wielded by any but a highly evolved adept with complete knowledge of the relation of subjective thought to the form-life of physical nature.

"On this fifth walk I ask from thee, O Homa ! who expelled death, that I may stand forth as victor and conqueror in battle upon the earth, putting down troubles and annihilating the destructive powers."

The fifth initiation is that increase of faculty which comes from the buddhic awakenment, and this gives victory over lower conditions through the exercise of wisdom. The critical intellect is exchanged for the higher buddhic faculty.

"On the sixth walk I ask from thee, O Homa ! who expellest death, that we may first become aware of a thief, murmurderer, or wolf ; may no one else become aware of him sooner ! may we become aware of everything first."

The sixth initiation corresponds to the introspective character begotten of right contemplation, which detects every lurking desire, or lower quality, in its first attachment to the soul, so that no future personality be needed to draw it forth. This initiation is a sign of true self-government, in that the Self triumphs as it realises the true source of its power, and learns to fulfil itself. This initiation is from the atmic plane.

See ADEPT, ANAGAMIN, ARHAT, ASEKA, ASTRAL PLANE, ATMA, ATTACHMENT, BUDDHIC PLANE, CAUSAL-BODY, CONJUNCTION, CONQUEROR, DEATH, DEVACHAN, EARTH, FORTUNATE, HOMA, INCARNATION OF SOULS, INITIATIONS, INTELLECT, MAN (righteous), MURDERER, PERSONALITY, PLANES, REINCARNATION, STRIDES OF SOUL, VESTURES, VICTORY, WOLF.

WANDERERS, OR WAYFARERS :—

Symbolic of egos in their periodical descents into incarnation, in order to gain experience in the lower life.

"If the Kind One look with kindness, then is the True Guru obtained. The soul hath wandered through many births, and now the True Guru hath communicated the Word. There is no benefactor so great as the True Guru."—MACAULIFFE, *The Sikh Religion,* Vol. I. p. 223.

The Christ (True Guru) bestows the Spirit (Word) when the soul has gained its experiences, and entered into the joy of its Lord.

"My God will cast them away, because they did not hearken unto him : and they shall be wanderers among the nations."—Hos. ix. 17.

As long as the chosen qualities (Israel) do not unite with the higher but follow the lower, they are condemned to incarnate among other groups of qualities less advanced than themselves.

See CAIN, EXPERIENCE, FUGITIVE, GURU, INCARNATION OF SOULS, ISRAELITES, NATIONS, PILGRIM, SHEEP (lost), SOSHYANTS, WAYFARING MEN, Yt.

WAR, FIGHTING :—

Symbolic of conflicts between the higher mental qualities and the lower emotions and desires. Also of the activities of the Higher Self in subduing the lower nature, for "the Lord is a man of war."

"Blessed be the Lord my strength which teacheth my hands to war, and my fingers to fight."—Ps. cxliv. 1.

The soul acknowledges that all power to subdue the lower nature comes from the Higher Self, and that it is through the disciplining of the qualities by the Christ that a successful struggle can be carried on, and the Divine ends be accomplished.

"By wars in the Word are signified spiritual wars, which are wars of truth against falsity, and of falsity against truth ; wherefore by weapons of war, such things are signified as are made use of in spiritual conflict."—SWEDENBORG, *Apoc. Rev.*, n. 52.

"Only when we see sin as God sees it, only then can we be sure of using no weapons that are not divine, for its removal. Only when pity for it joins with horror at it in our hearts, as they join in the heart of God, each keeping the other strong and pure, only then can we go out to meet it with a perfect determination, bound never to lay down our arms so long as there is any sin left in the world, and, at the same time, with an absolute conviction that no impatience to rid the world of sin must tempt us for a moment to use any means for its destruction which are not pure and just : an absolute conviction that it is better that sin should be left master of the field, than that it should be fought with sin. . . . Never try to set a wrong right by another wrong. You are only putting off the day when the true right shall be established. Never fight God's battle with any weapon of

the devil. . . . The time comes when, without a hesitation or misgiving, the soldier of God sees that he may strike, and may call every good power to witness that he does right in striking. Then it is evident that his plunging of his sword in the eternal righteousness has not merely made it powerless for evil, but has made it fiery for good."—PHILLIPS BROOKS, Serm., *The Sword Bathed in Heaven*.

See BATTLE, BLACKSMITHS, CONFLICT, CONQUEROR, FINGERS, GOATS, HANDS, MAB, MENIS, PILLAR (temple), SLAUGHTER, SOLDIERS, STRIFE, SWORD, VICTORY, WEAPONS.

WARM AND COLD :—

Symbolic of love and hate.

See COLD AND HEAT, HEAT AND COLD, OPPOSITES.

WARP AND WOOF OF THE UNIVERSE :—

Symbolic of the organisation of spirit-matter on the buddhic plane as the pattern for the external universe.

See FABRIC, LINEN, LOOM, MANCO CAPAC.

WARRIORS, TWIN :—

A symbol of intellect and emotion in conflict.

"Yea, He gives rest to the twin warriors, who are their wardens, because He mourns on account of their wars ; yea, he crushes out the things that hinder the little ones, He places a limit to the hurtful power of the shining forms (Khus)."—*Book of the Dead*, Ch. CX.

The Self is the means of affording peace for the "twin warriors," inasmuch as intellect and emotion can never agree excepting as they take refuge in the Self—the mind then being sublimated and the emotions purified. The Self is the means of dispelling the illusions which are due to the imperfect conceptions of the immature individualities or unawakened minds. The Self by limiting its own manifestation is also the means of preventing the attraction to the form-side of life from alluring the personality to destruction.

See ARMY, GREEKS, KHUS (lower), LITTLE CHILDREN, SOLDIERS, TROJANS.

WASHED THE FEET :—

A symbol of purification of the progressive soul by truth (water).

"Jesus saith to him, He that is bathed needeth not save to wash his feet, but is clean every whit."—JOHN xiii. 10.

We stand upon the feet—the progressive lower activities of every-day life—and these correspond to the foundation of our being; when that is purified, the "washing" is complete.

"To wash the feet is to purify the natural man; and when this is purified, the whole man is also purified. The natural or external man is purified when he shuns the evils which the spiritual or internal man sees to be evils."—SWEDENBORG, Apoc. Rev., n. 49.

"Our human feelings themselves, which are inseparable from our mortal life on earth, are like feet wherewith we are brought into sensible contact with human affairs; and are so in such a way, that if we say we have no sin, we deceive ourselves, and the truth is not in us. And every day, therefore, is He who intercedeth for us, washing our feet: and that we, too, have daily need to be washing our feet, that is, ordering aright the path of our spiritual footsteps."—AUGUSTINE, Gospel of John, Vol. II. p. 198.

See BAPTISM, FEET, FOOT, FOOTSTEPS, MAN (natural), WALK, WALKING DAY BY DAY, WATER.

WASHED IN THE BLOOD OF THE LAMB :—

A symbol of the soul purified through the involved Divine Life which rises up from within, restoring and healing the soul.

Christ, the Divine Sacrifice, the incarnate Son of God, is latent or potential in the lower nature (flesh) of every soul, and becomes the Saviour as he is brought into actual being by the aspirations and efforts of the personalities. Those egos who have eventually transcended their lower selves are "washed," that is, cleansed, from imperfection and become spiritual, so that they inherit eternal life as a result of the previous sacrifice of Christ or involution of Spirit in Matter.

"'The blood of Christ' (that is, the given life, the sacrificial spirit of Christ), 'who through the Eternal Spirit offered Himself without blemish unto God, shall cleanse your conscience from dead works to serve the living God' (HEB. ix. 14). You notice that the effect of the sacrifice of Christ is an effect in the conscience, in the inner nature of man. Christ must live within us as a great cleansing, sanctifying presence, and as a power of consecration to the service of God. What are the merits of Jesus? His truth, His faith,

His tenderness, His mercy, His love. These must be in us, they are no use anywhere else; they are healing streams from the fountains of Eternal Purity, to carry life and health to our souls."—T. RHONDDA WILLIAMS, Serm., Redemption.

"Even in Greece itself, though the doctrine (of the 'blood of God') was utterly perverted, it was not entirely lost. As Servius tells us that the grand purpose of the Bacchic orgies 'was the purification of souls,' and as in these orgies there was regularly the tearing asunder and shedding the blood of an animal, in memory of the shedding of the life's blood of the great divinity commemorated in them, could this symbolical shedding of the blood of that divinity have no bearing on the 'purification' from sin, these mystic rites were intended to effect? We have seen that the sufferings of the Babylonian Zoroaster and Belus were expressly represented as voluntary, and as submitted to for the benefit of the world, and that in connection with the crushing of the great serpent's head. If the Grecian Bacchus was just another form of the Babylonian divinity, then his sufferings and blood-shedding must have been represented as having been undergone for the same purpose—viz. for the purification of souls."—A. HISLOP, The Two Babylons, p. 71.

See ATONEMENT, BLOOD, BLOOD OF LAMB, CRUCIFIXION OF CHRIST, DIONYSUS, INCARNATION, LAMB OF GOD, MEDIATOR, PASSOVER, PERSONALITY, SACRAMENT, SACRIFICER, SOMA-JUICE, TAUROBOLIUM, TRANSUBSTANTIATION.

WASTING DISEASES AND PUTREFACTIONS :—

Symbolic of the lowest aspects of the soul's lower desires, passing into dissolution and dissipation.

WATER (HIGHER ASPECT) :—

The great symbol of Truth or the eternal Reality and source of all manifestation. Water suggests unity, absence of parts, comprehensiveness, purity, motion; also disappearance in evaporation below, and outpouring from above in rain to fertilise the earth.

"Now that truth (of Agni's mouth) is the same as the waters, for the waters are the truth. Hence they say, 'Whereby the waters flow, that is a form of the truth.' It is the waters indeed that were made first of this universe. Hence when the waters flow, then everything whatsoever exists is produced here."—Sata. Brâh., VII. 4, 1, 6.

"In the beginning this (world) was water. Water produced the true, and the

true is Brahman."—*Brihad. Upanishad,*
V. 5, 1.

"I am the great God who created
himself, that is to say, I am Water,
that is to say, Nu the father of the gods,
or as others say, Rā the creator of the
names of his members which turned into
the gods."—*Papyrus of Hunefer,* XVII.

"And (the more learned among the
priests) think that Homer, like Thales,
had learnt from the Egyptians to lay
down that Water was the beginning and
origin of all things, for that his Ocean is
Osiris, and his Tethys Isis, as nursing
and helping to breed up all things."—
PLUTARCH, *Isis and Osiris,* § 34.

"Water and earth—these were the two
elements out of which the old inhabitants
of Eridu believed the world to have been
formed. It was the theory of Thales in
its primitive shape."—SAYCE, *Rel. of Anc.
Babyl.,* p. 139.

"Water is the first element in the
mundane system of the Chinese."—KIDD,
China, p. 161.

"The emanation which produced the
creation of the universe is like water
gushing out from its source and spreading
over everything near" (*The Geberol*).—
MYER, *Qabbalah,* p. 195.

"Plotinus compares the Cause of all
things to an overflowing spring which by
its excess gives rise to that which comes
after it (*Enn.* V. 2, 1). This similarity produces the next, and so forth, till at length
in matter pure indetermination is reached."
—T. WHITTAKER, *Neo-Platonists,* p. 56.

"The oldest element with the Indians
is water. In *Rig-V.,* X. 121, 9. Pragàpati
begets 'the great sparkling waters.'
These again appear in *Rig-V.,* X. 82, 1, as
the primeval slime in which in the beginning heaven and earth were plunged ;
and in *Rig-V.,* X, 72, 4-6, as the 'wave
surge' that is identical with *Aditi,* etc.
In the Upanishads also the conception of
the primeval waters still survives. 'The
waters are the body of that prâna !
(*Brihad. Upanishad,* I. 5, 13). 'This earth,
the air, the heavens, the mountains, gods
and men, domestic animals and birds,
vegetables and trees, wild creatures down
to worms, flies and ants, are nothing but
the water under solid conditions' (*Chând,*
VII. 10, 1)."—DEUSSEN, *Phil. of Upanishads,* p. 190.

"Sarasvati evolved from a river-
goddess into a goddess of wisdom. In
Celtic myth we find knowledge and
inspiration associated with running
water."—*Non-classical Mythology,* p. 151.

"The text (REV. xxii. 17) speaks not
of earthly water. No doubt the words
'Water of Life' have a spiritual and
mystic meaning. They had a spiritual
and mystic meaning already among the
heathens of the East—Greeks and barbarians alike. . . . And water—with its
life-giving and refreshing powers—what
better symbol could be found for that
which would keep off death ?"—CH.
KINGSLEY, *Water of Life,* p. 3.

"Compounding the water from five
springs in unyielding brass, cleanse the
hands."—*Empedocles,* FAIRBANKS, 442.

This refers to the truth (water)
which may proceed from either one
or more of five avenues of sense, and
must be sifted and defined by mind
(brass) ere it may be acted upon
(hands) to advantage.

"The prophet exclaims, 'Praise the
Lord, ye heaven of heavens, and the
water that is above the heavens' (Ps.
cxlviii. 4). Nor is this the only thing
that proves the dignity of the water.
But then is that which is more honourable
than all—the fact that Christ, the Maker
of all, came down as the rain (HOS. vi. 3),
and was known as a spring (JOHN iv. 14),
and diffused Himself as a river (JOHN vii.
38), and was baptized in the Jordan."—
HIPPOLYTUS, *Holy Theophany,* § 2.

"Zi-Kum, 'the spirit of the sky,'
ended by becoming a symbol of that
primordial deep from which Ea had
derived his wisdom, and whose waters
were above the visible firmament as well
as below it."—SAYCE, *Rel. of Egypt. and
Babyl.,* p. 307.

"'He bindeth up the waters in his
thick clouds, that they should not burst
forth alike beneath' (JOB xxvi. 8). For
what does he call 'the waters' in this
place but knowledge ; what 'clouds'
but the Preachers ? For that in Holy
Writ 'water' may sometimes be a term
used for knowledge, we have been taught
by Solomon bearing witness to it, who
says, 'The words of a man's mouth are
as deep waters, and the well-spring of
wisdom as a flowing brook" (PROV. xviii.
4). That by 'water' knowledge is denoted,
the Prophet David bears witness, saying,
'Dark water in clouds of the sky' (Ps.
xviii. 11), i.e. secret knowledge in the
Prophets. . . . But by the name of
'clouds,' what else is denoted in this
passage (of Job) but the holy Preachers,
i.e. the Apostles, who being despatched
in every direction through the regions of
the world, both knew how to shower in
words, and to flash forth in miracles ?"—
GREGORY THE GREAT, *Morals on the Book
of Job,* Vol. II. p. 301.

"The Spirit of God is still in the Waters
surrounding the Earth ; and when Spirit
and Water cease to be closely united,
the Divine Spirit will rise out of the Water,
and the end of the world will come."—
Doctrine of the Slovaki.

"The living water in the Egyptian
theology would appear to have signified
the same thing (as in JOHN iv. 13, 14);
it was in their doctrine the symbolical
support of eternal life to all who received
it, along with the fruit of the Tree of Life
which grew in the paradise of Osiris."—
BARLOW, *Essays on Symbolism,* p. 62.

"Waters denote truths, and in the
opposite sense falsities."—SWEDENBORG,
Arc. Cel., n. 10, 227.

"That waters signify truths, and specifically natural truths which are knowledges from the Word, is evident from many passages in the Word."—SWEDENBORG, *Apoc. Rev.*, n. 50.

"Thus the Spirit of God, which is Original Life, is always moving upon the face of the waters, or heavenly deep, which is original Substance."—*The Perfect Way*, p. 178.

See ANDUISUR, BAPTISM, BOAR (avatar), CHILDREN OF HORUS, DARKNESS (higher), DELUGE, EA, EGINA, FLOOD, GARHAPATYA, HOUSE OF BONDAGE, IRRIGATION, JORDAN, LAW OF BUDDHA, MOIST ESSENCE, NARAYANA, NILE, NU, OCEAN, RAIN, SERPENT (ananta), SUN (moon), THIRST, VOURU-KASHA, WASHED (feet), WELL, YIMA.

WATER (LOWER ASPECT) :—

A symbol of the astral plane in which are errors and illusions,—the inverted or distorted reflections of truths.

"And God said, Let the waters under the heaven be gathered together unto one place, and let the dry land appear: and it was so."—GEN. i. 9.

And the Supreme now directs that the "waters" under the higher nature, namely, the astral matter (green sea), shall be organised, so that preparation shall be made for the "dry land,' namely, physical matter, to appear; and so it came about.

"Loke frequently changed himself by day into the likeness of a salmon, and then concealed himself in the waters of the Frananger Force."—*Prose Edda.*

The lower self or desire-mind (Loke) varied its aspects on the astral plane. The "day" is a symbol of a period of kama-manasic activity, and the "night" signifies the submergence of the experiences with which the soul identifies itself.

"Sir, thou hast nothing to draw with, and the well is deep" (JOHN iv. 11). "Tropologically, St. Augustine · 'The water in the well,' he says, 'is the pleasure of the world in a dark abyss, which men draw with the pitcher of desire. For this makes men always to thirst, because cupidity is insatiable.' "—C. À LAPIDE, *Great Comm. St. John* iv. p. 138.

See ASHES, DOVE, FLOOD, HEALING (epileptic), NAVIGATION, RU, SEA, THIRST, WALKING UPON WATER.

WATER TURNED TO WINE :—

A symbol of the substitution of the divine life or love element for the duty element in the conduct of life. It is a transmutation of the lower mental into the higher spiritual condition of soul.

"The 'beginning of miracles' (JOHN i. 11) for the Man Regenerate is always the transmutation of the 'water' of his own Soul into the 'Wine' of the Divine Spirit."—*The Perfect Way*, p. 229.

"But by the Divine power the water is changed into wine when perfect love casts out fear."—ST. BERNARD, *Serm. I, in Dom. I, post. Oct. Ep.*

"By these nuptials and by wine, He signified the union, and as it were, the marriage of our soul, through grace and charity, with God."—C. À LAPIDE, *Great Comm. St. John*, p. 90.

"The miracle apart, there lies something mysterious and sacramental in the very fact. Let us knock, that He may open to us, and fill us with the invisible wine : for we were water, and he made us wine, made us wise ; for He gave us the wisdom of His faith, whilst before we were foolish."—AUGUSTINE, *Gospel of John*, Vol. I, p. 115.

"When the author of this (fourth) gospel asked himself what Jesus had done for them, he conceives of His work as the transmutation of the common ordinary life into a thing of spiritual value and religious reality, that is, He made water into wine. If this be the meaning of the story of the miracle at Cana, it is much more valuable than if we took it in a literal sense. To believe that Jesus on one particular occasion turned literal water into wine would not be a religious belief at all, nor of any value for religion now. But to believe that He, by the spiritual quality of His mind, showed the deeper meaning, and brought out the divineness, of the common ordinary life, is to recognise a truth of daily importance for ourselves."—T. RHONDDA WILLIAMS, Serm., *Miracle of Cana.*

See CANA, DISPENSATIONS, SACRAMENT, TRANSMUTATION, WINE.

WATERPOTS OF STONE, SIX :—

Symbolic of six vehicles of consciousness.

"Now, there were six waterpots of stone set there after the Jews' manner of purifying, containing two or three firkins apiece."—JOHN ii. 6.

The six vehicles of the consciousness or spirit (stone) are the physical etheric, astral, mental, causal, and buddhic ; which are formed for the growth and purification of the qualities (Jews), that they may attain perfection (three) through strife of the opposites (two).

"It was by waking the Soul that Jesus would change the world for men, turn the common into the heavenly, the water into wine. Everything is different to the man who realises the soul. All values are changed ; all things are put in a new scale, fall into a new perspective, appear in a different light. Fill the vessels at the command of Christ, and then draw, and you will find that the water has become wine. . . . Nothing can be ordinary after this ; life is transfigured, the water is turned to wine, the marriage feast of the soul is consummated in perfect union with God."—T. RHONDDA WILLIAMS, *ibid.*

See CANA, JEWS, MARRIAGE, STONE, UNION, VEHICLES.

WATER FROM HEAVEN IN TWO STREAMS :—

Symbolic of the outpouring of Truth and Purity from the higher planes.

"As soon as Buddha was born, the thousand-eyed Indra, well pleased, took him gently, bright like a golden pillar ; and two pure streams of water fell down from heaven upon his head, with piles of Man-dara flowers."—*Buddha-Karita*, Bk. I. 27.

Directly the Self or Soul was brought forth in the period of involution, the Infinite Spirit bore the Soul toward the planes whereon its development is to be accomplished. It appeared, as it were, radiant and pillar-like—erect and forming a link between the higher nature and the lower. Forth from atma-buddhi issued two clear streams, symbols of Truth and Purity, which were to clarify the Soul through the mind (head). The "flowers" signify the virtues with which the Soul is potentially endowed.

See BIRTH OF BUDDHA, BUDDHA, FLOWERS, GOLD, INDRA, INVOLUTION, MAN CRAWLED, PILLAR.

WAVES OF THE SEA :—

A symbol of the surgings of the lower emotion - nature, with its passions and desires on the astral plane (sea).

"The mind of man is the sea, and the thoughts of his mind, as it were, a wave of the sea ; which sometime swell in anger, are made calm by grace, and from hatred run out in bitterness ; but when man dieth, ' the waters of the sea fail ' (JOB xiv. 11), in that according to the words of the Psalmist, ' in that very' day his thoughts perish " (Ps. cxlvi, 4). —ST. GREGORY, *Morals on the Book of Job*, Vol. II. p. 51.

See SAILS (black ship), SEA, SHIP ON SEA, STORM OF WIND WHALES.

WAY OF DEATH :—

A symbol of the personality engaged in following after the transitory attractions of the lower life.

"Behold, I set before you the way of life, and the way of death."—JER. xxi. 8.
"For the Lord knoweth the way of the righteous : but the way of the ungodly shall perish."—Ps. i. 6.

The perfected soul (righteous man) is described as immortal, under the figure of an everlasting fruitful tree by the waters (truth) ; while the desires (the ungodly) "are like the chaff which the wind driveth away," that is, the husks from the heavenly harvest are dissipated by the spirit.

See ATTACHMENT, CHAFF, HARVEST, MAN (bad), MAN (righteous), PERSONALITY, TREE OF LIFE.

WAY OF DELIVERANCE :—

A symbol of the Self whose manifestation in the soul brings about its liberation from the lower nature.

"Jesus saith unto him, I am the way, and the truth and the life : no one cometh unto the Father but by me."— JOHN xiv. 6.

The indwelling and partially manifest Self explains that its further manifestation in the soul is the path to the unmanifest Self (the Father), and that it is only through the manifest that the unmanifest can be approached by the evolving souls of humanity.

See ABSOLUTE, DEVAYANA FATHER, HIGHER AND LOWER SELVES, INCARNATION, LOST (forest), PATH (twofold), SELF, SOUL (middle), WORKS (path).

WAY OF THE LORD :—

A symbol of the realisation of the path which leads the minds and mental qualities unto life eternal, —namely, Truth.

"Wait on the Lord and keep his way, and he shall exalt thee to inherit the land ; when the wicked are cut off, thou shalt see it."—Ps. xxxvii. 34.

The disciplined mental qualities are exhorted to be steadfast in well-doing, so that the Higher Self may exalt them to their inheritance above. When the lower desires are cut off from them, then they shall become conscious on higher planes. The desires (wicked) pass away and are dissipated, but the higher mental nature, buddhi-manas (the perfect man), enters into peace. (*See* verses 35-7).

See CONSCIOUSNESS, LAND, LOST (forest), MAN (bad), MAN (righteous), PATH (birds), QUALITIES, TRANSMUTATION, UNRIGHTEOUS MAN, WICKEDNESS.

WAY OF THE MIDST :—

A symbol of the astral plane.
See MIDST (way).

WAYFARING MEN :—

A symbol of the egos or souls which descend into incarnation for transitory lives in the lower nature.

"The way of holiness; the unclean shall not pass over it; but it shall be for those, the wayfaring men, though fools shall not err therein."—ISA. xxxv. 8.

The path of truth and righteousness is the higher mind to which only the purified souls can rise. It is for the spiritual egos who gain experience through many lives; but the personalities (fools) cannot traverse it because of their infirmities.

"For he is called a 'wayfarer,' who minds that the present life is to him a *way* and not a native land; who thinks it beneath him to fix his heart on the love of this passing state of being, who longs not to continue in a transitory scene of things, but to reach the eternal world."— ST. GREGORY, *Morals on the Book of Job*, Vol. II. p. 218.

See EXPERIENCE, FUGITIVE, INCARNATION OF SOULS, PERSONALITY, PILGRIM, SHEEP (lost), SOSHYANTS, WANDERERS.

WEALTH OF THE TREASURY :—

A symbol of the complete potential equipment of the powers of the soul as it descends into the lower nature.

"And of the wealth of our treasury, They (the Parents) had tied up for me a load."—*Hymn of the Soul*, GNOSTIC.

This is the atma-buddhic (Parents) spiritual endowment from above which is latent or germinative in the young soul.

"I walk in the way of righteousness, in the midst of the paths of judgment; that I may cause those that love me to inherit substance, and that I may fill their treasuries.—PROV. viii. 20.

The Self through the principle of Wisdom identifies itself with virtue and goodness in the plane of under-standing, so that the Soul and Wisdom are united to the Self and may come into their inheritance (treasuries) which has been laid up for them from the beginning.

"God's name is the pure wealth : God giveth it through the Guru" (*Nanak*).—MACAULIFFE, *The Sikh Religion*, Vol. I. p. 275.

That which distinguishes the Higher Self is his endowment of spiritual potencies, and this will be conferred on the soul through its indwelling Lord.

"The inner wealth of the soul, the spoil of its struggle in this world of sense, will be life's great survival after its last grim fight with death."—J. BRIERLEY, *Studies of the Soul*, p. 224.

See HEIR, HUSBAND (good), KUVERA, MAN (rich), MERCHANDISE, NALA, POVERTY, RICHES, SINGERS, TISTRYA, VISVAKARMAN.

WEALTH SHOWER :—

A symbol of the higher qualities forthpoured by buddhi upon the soul.

"Now, as to this same shower of wealth, the body from which it flows is the sky, the udder the cloud, the teat the lightning, and the shower of ghee is the rain-shower."—*Sata. Brâh.*, IX. 3, 3, 15.

The qualities of wisdom, love, and truth (shower of wealth) proceed from the buddhic plane (sky), and are dispensed through the buddhic functioning (cloud), and the activities of the Divine life (lightning). Love (ghee) and truth (rain) are the nutriment of the soul and of its ideals (gods).

See CLOUDS (rain), COW, FOOD, GHEE, GODS, MILK (cow), RAIN, SKY, UDDER.

WEAPONS OF OFFENCE AND DEFENCE :—

Symbolic of the outgoing energies of the soul directed against the incoming forces of the lower emotional environment,—the desires, passions, and sense attractions.

"For the weapons of our warfare are not of the flesh, but mighty before God to the casting down of strongholds."— 2 COR. x. 4.

"My last exhortation to ye is this : Let faith, prayer, and patience be your weapons."—*Savonarola's Last Advice to Friends*.

"Be you equipped with the armour of righteousness, and wear for all your

protection the white robes of God's priests
Be you armed with the weapons of
righteousness, and use, for your assaults
on evil, mainly a holy life. There is none
other in all the armoury like it. The
true power of the Christian soldier lies
in character, character, character ! "—
A. MACLAREN, *Sermons, 2nd Series*, p. 274.

See ARMS, ARROWS, BLACKSMITHS,
CONFLICT, PONIARD, QUALITIES,
SHIELD, SPEAR, SWORD, WAR,
WORKERS.

WEAVING OR WEB :—

See FABRIC, LINEN, LOOM, WARP.

WEDDING :—

A symbol of the union of the
Higher Self and the lower Self at
the end of the cycle ; or of the
union of Wisdom and Love.

See MARRIAGE.

WEDDING GARMENT :—

A symbol denoting that the nature
within and the nature without have
become one in the soul.

See MARRIAGE, PARABLE, WHITE.

WEEK :—

A symbol of the six periods of
Divine activity in the cycle of involution, together with the pralaya of
rest, passivity, or balance, which
precedes the opening of the present
cycle of evolution. Otherwise, a
week signifies a period of completion.

"A week in Daniel and elsewhere,
signifies an entire period, from beginning
to end, and is predicated of the church.
The same is signified by seven."—
SWEDENBORG, *Apoc. Rev.*, n. 10.

See DAYS, EVOLUTION, INVOLUTION,
SABBATH, SEVEN, SIX, SUNDAY.

WEEPING OF THE GODS FOR BALDER :—

Symbolic of the alliance of consciousness with matter, wherein the
Life becomes identified with the
forms.

"When at length they had somewhat
recovered themselves, they burst forth in
the first place into such loud weeping that
they were not able to express their grief
to one another."—*The Story of Balder,
Edda.*

When equilibrium of conditions is
established, the first act of sacrifice—
or identification of the Life with the
forms becomes possible. And in this
alliance—the One becoming the many
in diversity—the separation of the

Divine functions takes place, and
the spiritual energy is limited by
matter.

See ASAR, BALDER, CONSCIOUSNESS,
DEATH OF BALDER.

WEEPING OF ISIS FOR OSIRIS :—

A symbol of the flowing out of
Divine compassion towards the
monads or centres of consciousness
suffering on the lower planes.

"When at length Isis was alone, she
opened the chest, laid her face to that of
the dead Osiris and kissed him and wept."
—PLUTARCH, *Isis and Osiris*, § 17.

When at length the Wisdom principle
reaches the plane of action whereon it
is supreme, the time arrives when the
lower experiences are reviewed through
introspection, and then arises the
spirit of infinite compassion for the
sufferings of the lower nature.

See CHEST, DEATH OF OSIRIS,
EXPERIENCES, FACE, ISIS, MONAD,
OSIRIS, WISDOM.

WELL OF WATER :—

A symbol of the Divine fount of
Truth (water).

"Everyone who is saved becomes a
son of that Spring which gushes forth
out of the depths—the Wisdom of God.
And it is nowise marvellous that the
saint should be a son of wells. . . . ' O
the depth of the riches both of the wisdom
and the knowledge of God ' ! he can be
a son of wells, to whom the word of the
Lord comes."—ORIGEN, *Comm. on John*,
Bk. II. § 1.

"Under the root of the Rimthursar
(or Giants of Frost), lies the well of Mimer,
in which wisdom and understanding are
concealed ; a fact still in full consistency
with all that we are taught of the giants,
that they were mighty in knowledge,
and in the power of runes. Odin himself
desiring a draught of the well Mimer, was
obliged to leave one of his eyes in pawn
for it."—HOWITT, *Literature of the North*,
Vol. I. p. 45.

Underneath the manifest life (root
of tree) with its powers and qualities
(Rimthursar) may be found the
eternal Truth (well) by the souls who
seek for the wisdom and understanding which are concealed in human
experience and progress. It is by
means of the qualities and faculties,
and their transmutations, that Truth
will be attained. The Higher Self
(Odin), desiring the results of experi-

ence, was obliged to incarnate and confine his lower consciousness (left eye) in matter, in order that Truth might be attained by him in the struggle upward of the Spirit from matter.

"But whosoever drinketh of the water that I shall give him shall never thirst ; but the water that I shall give him shall become in him a well of water springing up unto eternal life."—JOHN iv. 14.

It is the Christ who bestows soul-satisfying Truth which dissipates ignorance and illusion ; and Truth shall be evolved in the soul until perfection is reached, and immortality attained.

"Truth lies at the bottom of a well." —HERACLITUS.

"A moment's halt — a momentary taste
Of Being from the Well amid the waste,
And Lo ! the caravan has reached
    The Nothing it set out from,
Oh ! make haste."—OMAR KHAYYÁM.

"Waste" has the same signification as "wilderness," namely, the arena of life. "Being" here means Truth (water). The "caravan" stands for the soul and its qualities. The "Nothing" is *Ain Soph*, the Absolute.

See AIN SOPH, EXPERIENCE, FOUNTAIN, MIMER, ODIN, RIMTHURSAR, SUN (moon), THIRST, WATER (higher), YGGDRASIL.

WEST QUARTER :—

A symbol of the buddhic plane whereon commences the great cycle of life. It stands also for the sun-setting, signifying the obscuration of the Self (sun) in the night of the underworld.

See ARIES, HORIZONS, QUARTERS, SAND, SUN-SETTING, TUAT, UNDERWORLD.

WETNESS :—

A symbol, in its higher aspect, of truth, and, in its lower, of error and illusion.
See MOIST ESSENCE, WATER.

WHALE OF JONAH :—

A symbol of the evolutionary process and cycle through which the soul passes.
See CIRCLE OF EXISTENCE, EVOLUTION, HINE, JONAH, KHWAN, LEVIATHAN, SIGN, SERPENT (ananta).

WHALES, OR GREAT SEA-MONSTERS :—

A symbol of the more primitive and gross passions of the lower nature of the soul.

"Am I a sea or a whale, that thou settest a watch over me ? "—JOB vii. 12.

The incarnate Self, or Soul, in passing through the sufferings and illusions of the lower life, identifies itself with the desires and passions, and is tormented by the prickings of conscience.

"Now I have gained release, and this world's bonds
Are cut asunder by the knife of knowledge.
Thus I have crossed the ocean of the world,
Filled with the shark-like monsters of desire,
And agitated by the waves of passion—
Borne onward by the boat of stern resolve."
(*From Buddha's outburst of joy at having achieved emancipation*). — MON. WILLIAMS, *Indian Wisdom*, p. 60.

"And God created great whales, and every living creature that moveth, which the waters brought forth abundantly, after their kind, and every winged fowl after his kind : and God saw that it was good."—GEN. i. 21.

And now the primitive and more turbulent passions are realised in the process of involution, and all the numerous instinctual motives to action, and all the varying phases of astral (waters) activity, shown in the lower emotions and desires. And the higher desires being raised (winged) yield then more complex emotions. And all is pronounced perfect and fully prepared for the evolution that is to follow.

"Which whales in the sea are types of the devils in the world."—J. BUNYAN, *Exp. of Genesis.*

See CREATURES, EARTH (specialised), JOB, MONSTERS, PRISONERS, WATER (lower), WAVES.

WHEAT :—

A symbol of that spiritual seed which is sown in the lower nature (earth) and its fruit reaped in the higher, and so becomes the nourishment of the causal-body, and the food of the ideals (gods). The Divine germ (wheat), operating in the lower emotions, causes eventually their transmutation into higher emotions.

"Except a corn of wheat fall into the ground and die, it abideth alone : but if it die, it bringeth forth much fruit. He that loveth his life shall lose it ; and he that hateth his life in this world shall keep it unto life eternal."—JOHN xii. 24, 25.

Except the Divine Spirit—the fructifying Germ—descend into the lower nature (ground) and "die," that is, become latent, it would abide alone on high ; but if it become latent in the evolving qualities of the soul, it will be the means of their transmutation to higher planes, there to constitute the treasure laid up in heaven for the many souls who have struggled upward to the light of love and truth. A soul that remains attached to the out-going desire-life, loses that life ; while a soul that detaches itself from the life of the lower planes is thereby possessed of the immortal life of the higher.

"Christ puts not bread into our hands, but seed corn ; and although we carry away the full sack whenever we go to our Brother and ask Him to feed our hungriness, it is germinal principles that He gives us rather than loaves, and we have got to cultivate them and watch them, and patiently, too, in the belief that He will bless the springing thereof, and after many days we shall find seed for new sowing, as well as bread for the eater ! " —A. MACLAREN, Sermons, 3rd Series, p. 76.

See AGRICULTURE, BARLEY, CHAFF, CORN, CULTIVATION, EARTH, FAN, FOOD FOR MAN, FRUIT, GERMS, HARVEST, MEAL, MONAD OF LIFE, PLOUGHING, REAPING, SEED, SOWER, SOWING, TRANSMUTATION, TREASURE.

WHEAT AND BARLEY :—

A symbol of wisdom and love.

" O white grain (wheat) and red grain (barley) of the Land of God ! I have come into Thee ; I have striven, and I have borne my burden, following first the purity of the Company of the Gods, and the mooring-post is fixed for me in the Pool of the Zenith."—Book of the Dead, Ch. CX., BLACKDEN.

Wisdom and Love are of the higher planes—the abode of the Self—to which the consciousness has now risen. The Self within has striven to take the responsibilities of the life cycles, following first the path of purification in seeking the ideals or Divine attributes. And the goal of righteousness is set before it in the highest as its aim.

" Fields of wheat and barley (in Sekhet-Aaru), the former being between seven and eight feet, and the latter between nine and ten feet high. The spirits who reaped this grain are said to have been nine cubits, i.e. over thirteen feet in height."—BUDGE, Egypt. Heaven and Hell Vol. II. p. 42.

The lower planes (Sekhet-aaru) are the fields of the soul, which are sown and tended, but the fruit is gathered on the higher planes of buddhi and atma ; hence the symbol of the heights. The spirits are the egos or individualities who have conquered the lower planes (nine).

See BARLEY, COMPANY OF GODS, FOOD FOR SOUL, GODS, KINGDOM OF GOD, MOORING POST, NINE (number), POOL OF ZENITH, REAPING AFTER SOWING, SEKHET-AARU, SOWING, ZENITH.

WHEEL OF LIFE :—

A symbol of the great cycle of Life,—the progress of the Spirit or Self through the lower nature. In it the Spirit descends, as it were, in involution on the one side, and rises in evolution on the other, thus completing the circle.

" The progression and the return (of things) form a circular activity. . . . In the great circle to and from the Principle of all, all things are involved" (Proclus). —T. WHITTAKER, The Neo-Platonists, p. 167.

" We meditate upon that deity, the Demiurgus (Isvara), as the wheel with one felly and three tires, with sixteen peripheries, with fifty spokes and twenty wedges to fix the spokes, a wheel that is multiform, with one cord, with three diverse paths, and with one illusion proceeding from two causes."—Svetas. Upanishad, I.

The one " felly " signifies the whole cycle of life ; the " three tires " are the three gunas that bind the qualities to the cycle ; the "sixteen peripheries " are sixteen powers and qualities exercised by the soul ; the " fifty spokes and twenty wedges " are the many conditions of the manifesting life on the different planes. The " one cord " is the one Divine Life ; the " three paths " are of duty, truth, and love ; and the " two causes " are the sense of separateness and ignorance which make the unreal appear to be the real.

" The originating principle is the glory of the deity that keeps the wheel of Brahman, the cosmic cycle, still revolving. It is the all-knowing author of time, all perfect, by whom this world is eternally pervaded."—Svetas. Upanishad, VI.

" He is the reality of reality ; from him spring forth, as sparks from the fire, all the vital spirits, all worlds, all gods, all living creatures ; in him they are all fixed, like spokes in the nave of a wheel."—DEUSSEN, *Phil. of Upanishads*, p. 232.

" Universe after Universe is like an interminable succession of wheels for ever coming into view, for ever rolling onwards, disappearing and reappearing ; for ever passing from being to non-being, and again from non-being to being. . . . In short, the constant revolving of the wheel of life in one eternal circle, according to fixed and immutable laws, is perhaps after all the sum and substance of the philosophy of Buddhism. And this eternal wheel or circle has, so to speak, six spokes representing six forms of existence."—MON. WILLIAMS, *Buddhism*, pp. 119, 122.

See CIRCLE OF EXISTENCE, DEMIURGE, EVOLUTION, INVOLUTION, ISVARA, SPARKS, SWASTIKA, TIME, VITAL AIRS, ZODIAC.

WHEELS OF BIRTH AND DEATH :—

A symbol of the periodic descents of the personalities into incarnation, and the ascents therefrom. The symbol may also signify the descent of the spiritual egos from the plane of atma to occupy forms on the lower planes, from which they rise on their return to their home above.

" Brahman pervades all created beings in the five forms, and constantly makes them, by means of birth, growth, and decay, revolve like the wheels of a chariot." (" The five forms are the five great elements, which produce all bodies.")— *Laws of Manu*, XII. 124.

Spirit (Brahman) is the essential underlying element of all beings produced in the manifested universe of five planes. The spiritual monads acquire experience by means of life-cycles of birth, growth, and death, which succeed one another until perfection is attained.

" God, our dwelling place before time began, brought forth the material universe to be a school of discipline for us, a necessary means to the reliasation of certain qualities of our nature."—R. J. CAMPBELL, Serm., *Our Solidarity, etc.*

See BOAT OF EARTH, CHARIOT, DEATH, ELEMENTS, FORMS, GILGOOLEM, GIRDLE (star), HOME, INCARNATION OF SOULS, MAASEH, MONAD OF LIFE, PERSONALITY, REINCARNATION, SONS OF GOD, SWASTIKA.

WHEELS, HOLY :—

A symbol of the Rounds of the Lunar cycle, in which the astral nature is developed.

" When the child of man is born, there is given to him a *Nephesth*, i.e. animated life from the animals, the clean side, from the side of those which are called *Auphaneh ha-Qad-dosh*, the Holy Wheels " (*Zohar*).—I. MYER, *Qabbalah*, p. 398.

When the spiritual ego descends to the mental plane, and so becomes the son of mind (manasaputra), there is provided for him a desire-nature (Nephesh) in an astral body, developed through animal forms to the highest extent ; and this desire-nature has been evolved for humanity during the Rounds of the Lunar chain of worlds. The " animated life from the animals " is the astral nature which is the basis of the human personality when the mental nature is superadded to the desire-nature and man appears on the earth.

See ANIMALS, ASTRAL, CHILDREN OF GOD, EVOLUTION, HIRUKO, LUNAR CHAIN AND CYCLE, MAN (born), MANA-SAPUTRA, METEMPSYCHOSIS, MONAD OF FORM, MOON-WAXING, NEPHESH, PITRIS (lunar), PITRIYANA, RACES, ROOTRACES, ROUND, SKINS OF ANIMALS, SOUL (middle and lower).

WHIRL OR EDDY OF THINGS :—

Symbolic of a system of vortices in matter, by which vibrations are set up.

See EDDY.

WHITE, OR WHITENESS.

A symbol of perfect purity,—the external nature as spotless as the internal.

"And his head and his hair were white as white wool, white as snow."—REV. i. 14.

And the mental and higher aspects of the Self were of immaculate purity.

" Since by the head is understood love and also wisdom in their first principles, it follows that by hair is to be understood love and wisdom in their ultimates."— SWEDENBORG, *Apoc. Rev.*, n. 47.

See HAIR, HEAD, HORSE (white), RAIMENT, SHINING, TRANSFIGURATION, WEDDING GARMENT.

WHITE-ARMED HERA :—

A symbol of Wisdom on the buddhic plane, pure and free from the lower nature.

" Then Hephaistos the famed craftsman began to make harangue among them, to do kindness to his dear mother, white-armed Hera."—*Iliad*, Bk. I.

Then the Creative Mind, or Christ triumphant, commenced to co-ordinate the higher qualities and so induced them to focus their activities upon Wisdom seated above.

See ARMS OF BODY, HEPHAISTOS, HERA, MUSE.

WHITE FLOWERS :—

Symbolic of purity in the aspects of qualities of the higher nature.

See FLOWERS (white).

WHITE FOUNTAIN, AS OF MILK :—

A symbol of an outpouring of spiritual energy from buddhi.

See FOUNTAIN, MILK, WEALTH SHOWER.

WHOREDOM :—

Symbolic of the soul seeking satisfaction from without instead of from within—whence cometh all good ; or of the soul's attachment to the lower emotions in preference to the higher.

" By whoredoms are signified adulterations of good and falsifications of truth in the Word."—SWEDENBORG, *Apoc. Rev.*, n. 134.

" Rebellion, and judgment, and imprisonment, and execution and war, are constantly used as the symbols of spiritual things : so are adultery, fornication, divorce, and I may say, every form of faithlessness. Natural life is altogether, by the Holy Spirit, made to be but one allegory of spiritual things : all the substantial attributes, or constant laws of life, are, to use a vulgar but very expressive similitude, the fount of types with which the book of inspiration is printed, in order to be made legible and intelligible to the whole human family."—ED. IRVING, *Works*, Vol. I. p. 71.

See ADULTERY, COURTEZAN, DEVILS, DIVORCING, FOLLY, HARLOT, MARRIAGE (lower).

WICKED MAN :—

A symbol of the mind or soul which is unperfected and full of the lower emotions and desires.

WICKEDNESS OF MAN :—

Symbolic of evil mental conditions in a phase of growth of the soul, which must be swept away.

"And the Lord saw that the wickedness of man was great in the earth, and that every imagination of the thoughts of his heart was only evil continually."—GEN. vi. 5.

And the Self beholds the necessity for its further descent into the manifest. And it sees that there is increased necessity and opportunity for its operations amid the discordant conditions which have been set up by the mental activities upon the lower planes.

See CORRUPTION, DEPRAVITY, GATHA (kam.),MAN (bad), UNRIGHTEOUS,WAY, WAY OF THE LORD.

WIDE-FORMED OCEAN :—

A symbol of manifestation in space, or expanse of manifestation of the Divine Life and Truth on the five planes of the solar universe.

See ADITI, OCEAN, WORLDS (five).

WIFE :—

A symbol of the emotion-nature (woman) in alliance with the mind (man).

" Therefore shall a man leave his father and his mother, and shall cleave unto his wife : and they shall be one flesh."—GEN. ii. 24.

The mind, recognising a superior duality within itself, shall quit sense and desire, its lower parentage, and go in search of the ideal higher emotions (buddhic, feminine). The twain are *one* when the mind and higher emotion-nature are harmonious and at peace together.

" The Sacrificer addresses his wife, ' Come, wife, ascend we the sky ' (by the ladder). . . . She, the wife, in sooth is one half of his own self ; hence as long as he does not obtain her, so long he is not regenerated, for so long he is incomplete. But as soon as he obtains her, he is regenerated, for then he is complete. ' Complete I want to go to that supreme goal,' thus he thinks."—*Sata. Brâh.*, V. 2, 1, 10.

The " sacrificer " is the ego manifesting as mind allied with the emotion-nature. He seeks the ideal on the buddhic plane (sky) ; for the emotion-nature is the complement of the mental-nature in the regenerate soul. When complete union is accomplished between manas and buddhi, then the supreme goal is attained.

" Wives be in subjection unto your own husbands, as unto the Lord. For the husband is the head of the wife."—EPH. v. 22, 23.

The emotions must always be ruled by the intellect, until the Spirit (Lord) rules both. For the intellect is the regulating, rationalising, and balancing factor. (The best emotions exercised without intelligence are productive of much evil). As the soul in its religious aspect is subject to Christ, so let the emotions also be subject to the intelligence in everything. The intelligence must love the higher emotions, as Christ also loved the spiritual soul.

"To keep our emotional nature well under control of reason and will is our duty."—A. MACLAREN, *Sermons*, 1st Series, p. 143.

See ADULTERY, CONCEPTION, DIVORCE, EPIMETHEUS, EVE, FATHER (lower), HEAD, HUSBAND, LADDER, MALE-FEMALE, MAN AND WIFE, MAN WITHOUT WOMAN, MARRIAGE, PANDORA, PARENTS, PERSEPHONE, REGENERATION, RIB, SKY, WOMAN.

WILDERNESS, OR DESERT :—

A symbol of the field or arena of the lower life, empty in itself of true life—the life of the Spirit.

"Then was Jesus led up of the Spirit into the wilderness to be tempted of the devil. And when he had fasted forty days and forty nights, he afterward hungered."—MAT. iv. 1, 2.

The Christ-soul emerged from the latent condition within, whereupon the Higher Self, foreseeing its needs, put it to the test of its potency, by driving it into the arena of conflict where it was placed in relation with the not-Self or lower principle. And when the Christ-soul had undergone abstinence from intuitive knowledge during the transitory conditions attending the soul's pilgrimage for a term of the re-incarnating cycle, he became dissatisfied with the things of sense and longed for spiritual sustenance.

"By wilderness is signified the church in which there is no longer any truth."—SWEDENBORG, *Apoc. Rev.*, n. 722.

"Every individual soul has its own particular rightful place in the totality of the life of God, and must come to it when all its labours are consummated, and its wanderings in the wilderness of illusion are over."—R. J. CAMPBELL, Serm., *Divine Restitution*.

"Numbers—giving the history of Israel in the wilderness, their services, their trials, and their failures there—brings out, I cannot doubt, repeated types of the

Christian's experience and pilgrimage in the world as a wilderness."—A. JUKES, *Law of the Offerings*, p. 26.

See DAYS, DEVIL, FIELD, FORTY DAYS, HOUSE OF BONDAGE, HUNGER, REINCARNATION, SERPENT (brazen), TEMPTATION.

WILDERNESS OF JUDEA :—

A symbol of a condition of solitude in which the soul is freed from illusions and the lower attractions.

"This Wilderness is the quiet desert of the Godhead, into which He leads all who are to receive this inspiration of God, now or in Eternity."—TAULER, *The Inner Way*, p. 323.

See DESERT, FOREST, JOHN BAPTIST.

WILL OF MAN :—

The spiritual centre of relative existence in the lower mind. From this centre the higher determinations of choice emanate, and these derive their power and also direction from the mind. That which may be called the lower, illusive, or inverted will is merely the blind self-assertion of the desire-principle which for a time dominates the mind and prevents the expression of the true will.

"Each of us is this eternally free âtman (which is exempt from the constraint of causality). We do not first become the âtman, but we are it already, though unconscious of the fact. Accordingly we are already free in reality, in spite of the absolute necessity of our acts, but we do not know it. . . . The constraint of the will, absolute as it is, yet belongs entirely to the great illusion of the empirical reality, and vanishes with it. The phenomenal form is under constraint, but that which makes its appearance in it, the âtman, is free. The real consistency of the two points of view is expressed in the words : ' It is he who causes the man whom he will lead on high out of these worlds to do good works, and it is he who causes the man whom he will lead downwards to do evil works ' (Kaush, III. 8). The eternally free âtman, who determines our doing and abstaining is not another, contrasted with us, but our own self."—DEUSSEN, *Phil. of Upanishads*, p. 210.

"The voluntary attitude of man as a self-determining will, to the Absolute Divine Will is the most fundamental element of religion. . . . No wisdom goes beyond that of the poet : ' Our wills are ours to make them Thine.' For it is, in fact, the choice of the Object of religion in a spirit of faith and self-surrender, which carries with it all else that is most essential to its supreme realisation as an experience."—G. T. LADD, *Phil. of Religion*, p. 342.

"Matter causes nothing at all; force causes nothing but motion, and cannot determine its own direction. Therefore whatever problem of originating and directing power arises from the present arrangement of things arises equally from their arrangement in the furthest past we can discern. One true original directing cause, and only one, is known to us in will. Our own will we know by direct experience, and other wills we infer from outward actions. . . . Deliberate choice as opposed to unreasoning impulse implies a pause for deliberation; and we know as certainly as we know any scientific fact that in the deliberation, we contribute from ourselves an irreducible element which prevents the issue from being anything like a mechanical result of those motives (which stir the will). . . . Though we are conscious of power to do anything whatever within certain limits, a man in his right mind has some principle or general aim, good or bad, to which he endeavours to subject that power, so that a choice of motives in particular cases resolves itself into a choice of means for carrying out such principle or general aim."—H. M. GWATKIN, *The Knowledge of God*, Vol. I. pp. 64, 65.

"The only transcendental thing in the world is Will, and this we know directly in ourselves. We are on the inside of things because we *will*, and we know everything to be part of the one evolution of life or will. There is no explanation of will; it itself is not known by the mere intellect although its different assertions may be. . . . As soon, then, as a man has grasped the notion of volition as the keynote of the self, he ceases to explain himself by things outside of himself. He has also at the same time done with *external* explanations of the world, and he is prepared to find the reality of the world in the one Will that is manifesting itself in himself and in all things. I must take to myself all the guilt of my finite existence, and admit that I too have willed to live, have willed the world. . . . It is literally true that liberty is a mystery. As finite will I am enslaved, but as infinite will I am free. The finite will must be made to die unto itself, and to affirm the eternal Ideas of the eternal Will. Whatever else religion is, it is first and foremost a perception of the radical evil that is in the finite will."—W. CALDWELL, *Schopenhauer's System*, pp. 393, 396-7.

"Nothing can make any change in you but the change of your will. For everything, be it what it will, *is a birth of that will* which worketh in you. You have nothing, therefore, to inquire after, nor anything that you can judge of yourself by, but the state of your will and desire. . . . where these are, there are you; and what these are, that are you: there you live, and to that you belong; and there you must have all the good and evil that can be called yours. . . . If your will is with God, you work with God; God is then the life of your soul, and you will have your life with God to all eternity."—WM. LAW, *The Way to Divine Knowledge*, p. 137.

"Now let us remember that 'our wills are ours, we know not how,' but they are ours: it is equally true that they are ours to make them God's. But when they are made God's, made to accord with His, they are no less ours; indeed, they will be ours more than ever when we have made them His; we shall never be our full and true selves until we have found ourselves in God. . . . The self that is lost is the little self; not the ego, but the egotism; the self that dreams it is separate, and seeks advantages as a separate entity."—T. RHONDDA WILLIAMS, Serm., *Dying in the Lord*.

"All the events that meet a man in his Outward Life are nothing else than the necessary and unalterable Outward manifestation of the Divine Work fulfilling itself in him, and he cannot wish that anything in these events should be otherwise than what it is, without wishing that the Inward Life which can only thus manifest itself should be otherwise; and without thereby separating his will from the Will of God, and setting it in opposition thereto. He cannot any longer reserve to himself a choice in these things, for he must accept everything just as it happens; for everything that comes to pass is the Will of God with him, and therefore the best that can possibly come to pass. To those who love God, all things *must* work together for good, absolutely and immediately. . . . To those who do *not* love God, all things must work together immediately for pain and torment, until by means of this torment, they are at last led to salvation."—J. G. FICHTE, *The Way Towards the Blessed Life*, pp. 164, 5.

See AEGAEON, APES, BRIAREUS, DOG, DOG-STAR, GEORGE AND DRAGON, GUARDIAN SPIRITS, JERUSALEM, MAISHAN, SERVANT OF GOD, SHEEP (lost) SWORD OF SPIRIT, UNION.

WIND, WORD, SPIRIT, MARUT, BREATH :—

Symbols of emanation, to which the forthpouring from the Absolute is comparable. Otherwise, "Wind" is a symbol of Spirit energising on the mental plane.

"It is not the wind, but the Divine energy, that is regarded as vitalising the germs which the Divine Word is about to call forth."—T. K. CHEYNE, *Origin of the Psalter*, p. 322.

"And God made a wind to pass over the earth, and waters assuaged."—GEN. viii. 1.

And the Divine power energises the mental vehicle of the soul, so that the lower vehicles are again to be prepared for the accommodation of the re-energised soul.

"In the Holy Scripture, by the rapidity and subtlety of the winds, souls are used to be denoted, as it is spoken by the Psalmist of God, 'Who walketh above the wings of the winds' (Ps. civ. 3), i.e. 'Who passes above the virtues of souls.' "—St. Gregory, *Morals on the Book of Job*, Vol. II. p. 399.

"The powerful operations and motions of God's Spirit, quickening or reviving the heart toward God, are compared to the blowing of the wind, John iii. 8."—*Cruden's Explanations*, p. 369.

See Absolute, Angels, Breath, Fan, Holy ghost, Maruts, Moon (higher), Shinatsu, Vayu.

WIND, ADVERSE :—

A symbol of surgings of sorrow and suffering.

See Ship on sea, Storm, Waves.

WIND,—HOT AND COLD :—

Symbolic of the activities of good and evil on the mental plane.

See Cold and heat.

WIND, STRONG, OF MAZDA :—

A symbol of the Self energising on the buddhic plane (Mazda-Sapandâr = Atma-buddhi).

"Invoke thou the strong wind created by Mazda Sapandâr, the pure daughter of Hormazd."—*Vendidad*, XIX.

Put thy trust in the Divine Breath —the Holy Spirit—which is the functioning of the Absolute upon the buddhic plane.

See Breath (divine), Gale (Apollo), Sapandâr.

WIND, SWEET, FROM THE SOUTH :—

A symbol of a pure and deep sense of truth flowing in from the buddhic plane, corresponding to the deeper aspect of the understanding.

See Maiden (heavenly), Perfume, Scent (sweet).

WIND FROM THE SOUTH :—

A symbol of vibrations of love proceeding from the buddhic plane.

See South wind.

WINDS, VARIOUS :—

Symbolic of diverse doctrines of the lower mind which proceed from error and illusion.

"That we may be no longer children, tossed to and fro and carried about with every wind of doctrine, by the sleight of men."—Eph. iv. 14.

See Crops, Egypt (higher), Gales, Phœdrus, Sharp air, Storm, Tawhiri.

WINDS, FOUR :—

A symbol of the quaternary,—the four lower planes of manifestation.

"And I saw the chambers of the winds, and I saw how He had furnished with them the whole creation and the firm foundations of the earth. And I saw the corner-stone of the earth ; I saw the four winds which bear the earth and the firmament of the heaven. And I saw how the winds stretch out the vaults of heaven and have their station between heaven and earth : these are the pillars of the heaven."—R. H. Charles, *The Book of Enoch*, Ch. XVIII. 1, 2, 3.

"Therefore give Thou unto me bliss and Thy peace : that the grasping of the four winds may knit together my parts."—*Book of the Dead*, Ch. CX.

For this reason (of self-knowledge) bliss shall be committed to me, inasmuch as it alone is of the true nature of the Self which in essence is pure bliss. The full control of the four planes—buddhic, mental, astral, and physical, which are the means of evolution, serves to knit together the nature which is to be expressed under manifold aspects.

"Four entrances into heaven. That of the north wind belongeth to Osiris, that of the south wind to Rā ; that of the west wind to Isis ; and that of the east wind to Nephthys."—Budge, *Book of the Dead*, Ch. CLXI.

The quaternary offers four means of developing the soul for the higher planes.

"Come unto me, O thou of the Four Winds, Almighty One, who breathest spirit into men to give them life. . . . O thou whose tireless eyes are Sun and Moon—that shine in the pupils of the sons of men" (*Invocation to the Good Mind*).—C. Lumans, *Papy. Gr.*

The soul seeks union with the Self incarnate within the lower nature (four planes), who emanates the spirit, or Life, into the minds of humanity to give them immortality. For the centres of consciousness and perception are higher and lower, namely, the individuality (sun) and the personality (moon) ; and these bring truth to the spiritual egos.

See Adam (lower), Bliss, Goddess, Going in, Mind (good), Moon, Quarters, Quaternary, Sun, Swastika, Tlaloc, Worlds (five).

WINDOW OF ARK OF NOAH :—

A symbol of the means whereby spiritual perception is established in the soul, so that the light of Truth may shine in.

"A window shalt thou make to the ark, and in a cubit shalt thou finish it above; and the door of the ark shalt thou set in the side thereof; with lower, second, and third stories shalt thou make it."—GEN. vi. 16.

The "window" is a symbol of the aperture towards the Divine or receptive attitude of the mind towards Truth. The direction "in a cubit, etc.," signifies the complete finishing to the pattern upon which the causal vehicle is to be constructed. It is to be finished "above," that is, it is to be capable of transmitting vibrations from higher planes. The "door" is the entrance to the mind for the vibrations from below —those proceeding from the desires, senses, etc. The "lower, second, and third stories" signify the three higher sub-planes of the mental plane.

"Some have supposed this 'window' (zohar, a word only occurring here, GEN. vi. 16), was an inward lamp or light connecting the word with 'oil,' and that again with the word mentioned 'the anointing' (1 JOHN ii. 27), which makes the light or instruction of this world unnecessary."—A. JUKES, Types of Genesis, p. 110.

As "oil" is a symbol of Divine love or life, the "anointing on the crown of the head" signifies the bestowal of spiritual perception on the mind.

"The three stories in the Ark illustrated the three degrees of mind on the three heavens, natural, spiritual, and celestial. The window taught that in temptation all light came from the Lord alone."— J. DEANS, Story of the Flood, 1909.

"The conscience stands between man's power of knowledge and the spiritual world, just as the eye stands between man's power of knowledge and the world of visible nature. It is the opened or unopened window through which flows the glorious knowledge of God and heaven." —P. BROOKS, Serm., Eye of the Soul.

See ANOINTING, ARK OF NOAH, BRAHMARANDHRAM, CAUSAL - BODY, CONSCIENCE, DOOR OF ARK, DOOR OF VARA, HEAD, LAMP, LIGHT, OIL, SUN AS DOOR.

WINDOW OR SKYLIGHT :—

A symbol of an opening in the soul towards the spiritual realm, whereby the light of Truth may enter in and illuminate the receptive mind.

"And furnish a door to the vara, and let a self-shining window be left."— Vendidad, II.

The "door to the vara" is the same as the "window in the ark of Noah," —it is the aperture to the buddhi-manas in the receptive lower quaternary, and is on the level where the lower Self becomes united to the Higher Self. It has the same meaning as the "bridge" of manas. "A self-shining window" remains, that the soul may receive a glimmer of the rays of the Self. The interesting fact is this,—that the higher Light of truth is seen and realised only as the reflection of the Divine radiance below in the lower self enables Truth to be perceived by the personality. It is through the experience of the lesser life that the Wisdom and Love of the Larger Life become known.

"Christ is our window, and self-consciousness the eye of the soul."— R. J. CAMPBELL, Serm., Man and Moral Freedom.

"If your soul gives way under affliction, it is because you have been identifying God and the eternal good with the partial and fleeting expression of both. When God withdraws anything, it is to give you something higher and better; when he withholds anything it is because you are not yet ready for the boon. I wonder why it so seldom occurs to us that the form under which we crave to possess it at any one time is of much less moment than the deepening of our capacity for possessing it."—R. J. CAMPBELL, Serm., Broken Souls.

"Man is conscious of a universal soul within or behind his individual life, wherein, as in a firmament, the natures of Justice, Truth, Love, Freedom, arise and shine. This universal soul he calls Reason: it is not mine or thine, or his, but we are its. . . . That which, intellectually considered, we call Reason, considered in relation to nature, we call Spirit. Spirit is the Creator. Spirit hath life in itself."—EMERSON, Essay on Nature, Ch. IV.

See BRIDGE OF HEAVEN, BUDDHIC FUNCTION, DOOR OF VARA, EXPERIENCE, EYE, HIGHER AND LOWER SELVES, LIGHT, PERSONALITY, QUATERNARY, SELF, SPIRIT, SUTRATMA.

WINDOWS OF HEAVEN OPENED :—

Symbolic of spiritual vibrations from the higher planes entering into the soul.

"Bring ye the whole tithe into the storehouse, that there may be meat in mine house, and prove me now herewith, saith the Lord of hosts, if I will not open you the windows of heaven, and pour you out a blessing, that there shall not be room enough to receive it."—MAT. iii. 10.

The mind is exhorted to acquire knowledge (meat), and offer up the lower to the higher, that the soul (house) may develop. Then the bestowal of spiritual gifts will be to the mind's utmost capacity.

See BLESSING, GIFTS OF GOD, HOUSE IN HEAVEN, MEAT, MELCHIZEDEK, OFFERING, TITHES.

WINDOWS OF HEAVEN STOPPED :—

Symbolic of the vibrations from buddhi-manas obscured in the soul.

"The fountains also of the deep and the windows of heaven were stopped, and the rain from heaven was restrained."—GEN. viii. 2.

The "fountains of the deep" are here those sources of error which produce illusion in the lower self—these were restrained. The "windows of heaven stopped" are the spiritual perceptions diminished. The "rain from heaven being restrained" signifies the withdrawal of the unmanifest Self from the manifesting Self, and the cessation of the buddhic outpouring of truth (rain).

See DEEP, FLOOD, FOUNTAINS OF DEEP, RAIN, SELF.

WINE :—

A symbol of wisdom, or spiritual life and truth, which when partaken of by the soul, intoxicates or paralyses the lower nature, but brings joy and satisfaction to the higher.

"And wine that maketh glad the heart of man, and oil to make his face to shine, and bread which strengtheneth man's heart."—Ps. civ. 15.

The Self bestows upon the receptive soul spiritual life and truth which bring joy and satisfaction to the causal-body ; and love (oil) to cause the mental aspect to radiate knowledge ; and truth-goodness which gives sustenance to the soul.

"Philo speaks of the 'wine of the divine love of God.' "—E. A. A., *Enc. Biblica, Gospels*, 54.

" 'Wine' is the mysterious vitality and spiritual energy of created things."—MYER, *Qabbalah*, p. 358.

" 'Wine' signifies holy truth, or truth from the good of love. In an opposite sense it signifies truth falsified and profaned."—SWEDENBORG, *Apoc. Rev.*, n. 316.

See CANA, CUP, DIONYSUS, GRAPES, INTOXICATION, SACRAMENT, SATYRS, SILENUS, STOMACH, TRANSUBSTANTIATION, VINE, WATER TO WINE.

WINGS ; PINIONS :—

A symbol of aspiration : indicative of rising in the mind (air).

"When perfect and fully winged, the Soul soars upward, and is the ruler of the universe ; while the imperfect soul loses her feathers, and drooping in her flight, at last settles on the solid ground—there, finding a home, she receives an earthly frame which appears to be self-moved, but is really moved by her power ; and this composition of soul and body is called a living and mortal creature. . . . And now let us ask the reason why the soul loses her feathers.

"The wing is that corporeal element which is most akin to the divine, and is intended to soar aloft and carry that which gravitates downwards into the upper region where dwell the gods. Now the divine is beauty, wisdom, goodness and the like ; and by these the wing of the soul is nourished, and grows apace ; but when fed upon evil and foulness, and the like, wastes and falls away" (PLATO, *Phœdus*).—JOWETT, *Dialogues, etc.*, Vol. II. p. 123.

Plato describes the World - soul (Archetypal Man) in its primordial state, as the Divine Ruler (Higher Self). The "imperfect soul" is the separated soul—the Divine Spark or Monad which descends to the lower nature (ground) and occupies a body prepared for it, that is subject to a transient life and death. The imperfect soul seeks to rise from that condition which tends downward (desire, etc.), and attain perfection so as to consort with the ideals (gods) on the upper planes—the ideals being beauty, wisdom, goodness, etc., which are the "fruits of the Spirit," to nourish the soul. Through the ideals aspiration (wing) is augmented, but if the personality becomes immersed in desire and sensation, aspiration declines.

"All the powers of God are winged, being always eager and striving for the higher path which leads to the Father."—PHILO, *Works*, Yonge, Vol. IV. p. 252.

"A few have left caterpillar and chrysalis behind even in this world ; they have found the wings of a larger spiritual consciousness and are in communion with a glorious world of more abundant life."—R. J. CAMPBELL, Serm., *The Son of Man Ascending.*

See BIRDS, FRUCTIFYING, HORSE (winged), MAASEH, SUN OF RIGHTEOUSNESS.

WINTER :—

A symbol of a period of latency and unfruitfulness ; of globe obscuration and extinction of the lower personality and lower planes ; of pralaya—absence of life.

"The five months of winter are cold as to water, cold as to earth, cold as to trees. There is the heart of winter ; there all around falls deep snow. There is the worst of evils."—*Vendidad*, I.

These "winter months" represent periods during which no manifestation occurs. There is no outpouring of life and truth (water), no lower nature (earth), and no growth of qualities. The "deep snow" signifies the latent condition of the lower planes before the awakenment of the Life takes place.

See ANGRA, DEARTH, DEVASTATION, FROST, PRALAYA, SABBATHS, SNOW, SUMMER.

WINTER FIEND :—

A symbol of the desire-nature, barren of itself, and unproductive of good apart from the higher influences.

WISDOM (FEMININE) :—

A symbol of the principle of buddhi, or the intuitive and transmuting activities of the buddhic plane, operating through the higher mind and upon the lower nature.

"She (wisdom) standeth in the top of high places, by the way in the places of the paths. She crieth at the gates, at the entry of the city, at the coming in at the doors. Unto you, O men, I call ; and my voice is to the sons of man."—PROV. viii. 2–4.

Buddhi occupies the heights of the soul, for the buddhic plane is the highest plane of the quaternary. The buddhic functioning is on the paths to perfection through Truth, Love, and Action. Buddhi appeals to the soul at the entrance from above to the higher mind's centre (city) which receives the vibrations from below. ' Unto you, O mental qualities, I call ; for the spiritual intuitions from me, are to raise the egos—the sons of mind.'

"The idea of ' wisdom ' appears to be parallel to the Old Testament idea of ' spirit '—a life common to God and man, breathed into man by God. . . . ' I, Wisdom, possess (Heb. *dwell in*) intelligence, I have knowledge and insight ' (PROV. viii. 12). The statement of the Hebrew is not that Wisdom dwells in friendly alliance *with intelligence*, but that she dwells *in intelligence*, an unexampled form of expression."—C. H. TOY, *Book of Proverbs*, pp. xvii. 167.

"Sujâta (of happy birth) is, of course, Dharma or Prajnâ, divine wisdom personified as a woman."—A. LILLIE, *Popular Life of Buddha*, p. 81.

"In reason no love can be found—there is much love in wisdom ; and all that is highest in wisdom entwines around all that is purest in love. Love is the form most divine of the infinite, and also, because most divine, the form most profoundly human. . . . Reason and love battle fiercely at first in the soul that begins to expand ; but wisdom is born of the peace that at last comes to pass between reason and love ; and the peace becomes the profounder as reason yields up still more of her rights to love."—MAETERLINCK, *Wisdom and Destiny*, §§ 29, 30.

"Love, which fills my mind continually with new and most exalted ideas of this Lady (Beatrice—Wisdom). . . . Philosophy is born when the Soul and Wisdom have become friends, so that the one is loved by the other. . . . God sees, then, this Lady the most noble of all absolutely, inasmuch as most perfectly He sees her in Himself."—DANTE ALIGHIERI, *The Banquet*, III. Ch. 12.

"Wisdom implies, whether in God or in man, both power and knowledge ; but it implies something more ; for wisdom is a moral attribute. This attribute, therefore, embodies the conceptions of knowledge and power employed in the interests of what is morally good. Goodwill is necessary to wisdom. And if the wisdom is to be perfect, not only must the power and the knowledge be perfect, but the good which is chosen and pursued by all the means that the perfect knowledge and wisdom provide, must be the highest and supremely valuable Good. This good, the human mind is obliged to conceive of as uniting the three recognised forms of good—the good of happiness, the good of beauty, and the good of morality —in one Ideal of all that has worth."— G. T. LADD, *Phil. of Religion*, Vol. II. p. 212.

"There is Wisdom guiding me, of whose existence I am certainly aware, but whose ways I cannot comprehend. But it shall not be always so. Now I am known perfectly, but I know in part, in the very least and weakest and dimmest way. But the time shall come

when I shall know as I am known."—
PHILLIPS BROOKS, Serm., *The Knowledge
of God.*

See AMATERASU, ARMAITI, ASHA-
VANUHI, ATHENA, BOAT OF WISDOM,
BUDDHI, COW, DHARMA, EARTH (great),
ESTHER, FIRE, FRIGG, GODDESS, GOLD,
GOLDEN FLEECE, GOLDEN HAIR,
HATHOR, HEAVEN, HELEN, HERA,
HIKOBOSHI, ISIS, ISTAR, KYPRIS, LADY,
LATONA, MOTHER, MUT, PRAGNA,
QEBSENNUF, SAPANDAR, SERPENT,
SERPENT (sparks), SOPHIA, TRANSMU-
TATION, UZUMÉ, VACH.

WISDOM (MASCULINE) :—

A symbol of the Higher Self—
atma-buddhi, the manifesting Spirit
on the higher planes.

" Christ the power of God, and the
wisdom of God."—1 COR. i. 24.

" The *Zohar* calls Wisdom the Divine
Word which announced and finished
creation, and says, that it is the foundation
of all spiritual and physical life. It calls
Wisdom the Upper Paradise or *Eden
illa-ah.* This superior Eden, the Wisdom
or the Ancient, is in the *Zohar* ' a Form
comprising all forms.' "—I. MYER, *Qabbalah*, p. 205.

" Ibn Geberol says in his *Kether Maḷk-
huth :* ' Wisdom is the fountain of life.'
The *Zohar* says : ' The seventh palace, the
fountain of life, is the first in order from
above, etc.' "—*Ibid.*, p. 199.

The higher " Eden " is the plane of
atma-buddhi ; the lower " Eden " is
a lower sub-plane of the buddhic plane.
The Monad (atma-buddhi) contains
all forms and qualities, and is the
source of the prototypes or patterns
of all things on the buddhic plane.

" Then I (Wisdom) was by him, as a
master workman : and I was daily his
delight, rejoicing always before him ;
rejoicing in his habitable earth ; and my
delight was with the sons of men."—
PROV. viii. 30, 31.

Then the Higher Self was present
on the upper planes guiding and
supervising. Wisdom or Intelligence
was the sole inscrutable wonder of
manifestation in which the Self realises
itself. Through evolution the Self
accomplishes its task upon the lower
planes, and thereon perfects its nature.
Through the spiritual egos — the
spiritual product of mind (men)—
the Wisdom principle is realised.

" This delight of the Wisdom of God
in men existed before there were any
men, or any earth for them to dwell in.
What can this mean but that from ever-

lasting that intelligent consciousness,
that principle of life and mind, which
now shows itself in us and constitutes us
human, is present in its fullness in the
eternal Son of God, whence we all derive ?
It is the light that lighteth every man
that cometh into the world, and, therefore, in a sense it is perfectly true that
God rejoiced over us before the world was.
To him time is not the succession of
experiences that it is to us. It is the
eternal Now—a state utterly inconceivable
to our present limited faculties. We
cannot even speak of it without an
intellectual contradiction. To say that
all that *is* was present to God in Christ
before time began is to assume the
reality of time in the very act of denying
it."—R. J. CAMPBELL, Serm., *The Timeless
Affinity.*

See CIRCLE, EDEN, GARDEN OF
EDEN, HOKHMAH, HOLY GHOST, MONAD,
PARADISE, PROTOTYPES, RONGO,
SEPHIROTH, SERPENT ÆSCULAPIUS,
SERPENT (solar), TIME, WORD.

WISE MEN :—

A symbol of intelligence or
intellect.

See ESTHER, GOLD (frank.), HEROD,
MAGI, STAR IN THE EAST.

WITNESSES, FALSE :—

Symbolic of states of mind which
misinterpret, or misunderstand, the
truths which are veiled in the
Divine utterances of which the outer
expression only has been seized.

" Now the chief priests and the whole
council sought false witness against Jesus,
that they might put him to death."—
MAT. xxvi. 59.

The intolerant creed of convention
appeals to the letter in order to kill
out the Christ from the soul. It cannot
succeed, but the false has first to be
seen, ere the true appears in its own
good time.

See CAIAPHAS, IDOL PRIEST, PHARI-
SEES, PRIESTS AND ELDERS, TRADITION,
TRIAL OF JESUS.

WITNESSES, TWO :—

Symbols of Love and Wisdom,—
atma-buddhi,—which witness the
process of the soul's development in
the lower nature. They appear to
be killed out of the soul by desire
(the beast) in its early stages of
growth, but afterwards they revive
and live through the power of the
Spirit of Christ.

" The Spirit's witness *comes from God,*
therefore it is veracious, Divine, omnipo-

tent; but the Spirit's witness from God *is in man*, therefore it may be wrongly read, it may be checked, it may for a time be kept down, and prevented from showing itself to be what it is."—A. MACLAREN, *Sermons, 1st Series*, p. 66.

"And after the three days and a half the breath of life from God entered into them, and they stood upon their feet; and great fear fell upon them which beheld them."—REV. xi. 11.

After a complete period of obscuration during which Love and Wisdom had lain, as it were, dead in the soul, while the lower qualities were full of activity, the time arrived when they should arise from latency to actuality, and confront and subdue the instincts, desires and passions of the astral plane. Through the evolution of the higher nature which has its life direct from God the lower nature is overcome and obliterated.

"The great city is no other than the world's materialistic system in Church, State, and Society, wherein perpetually the Lord, as the Christ in man or Divinity in humanity, is crucified. And God's two witnesses, who have so long lain dead in this city, are no other than the Intellect and Intuition, which represent, respectively, man's mind and soul."—EDWARD MAITLAND, *Bible's Own Account*, p. 69.

"These two articles—the acknowledgement of the Lord, and a life according to the commandments of the decalogue—are the two essentials of the New Church, and are meant by the two witnesses."—SWEDENBORG, *Apoc. Rev.*, n. 491.

See BEAST, BOOK STUDIES, BREATH, CANDLESTICKS, CRUCIFIXION (in Revelation), FEET, RETURN, THREE, WORLD.

WITNESSES, THREE, IN HEAVEN :—

Symbolic of the Trinity, or Divine Triad :—the Absolute (Father), the Manifest God (Word), and the Buddhic principle (Holy Ghost); and these three are One to us; for the lower mind cannot differentiate between them, or comprehend them. —*See* 1 JOHN v. 7.

See ABSOLUTE, FATHER, GOD, GODHEAD, HOLY GHOST, INCARNATION, TRIAD, TRINITY.

WITNESSES, THREE, ON EARTH :—

Symbolic of the Divine action in the lower nature (earth). Love (spirit), Truth (water), and Life (blood); and these three agree in one uplifting of the human soul. Love of the Higher is the force that attracts upward; Truth dissipates ignorance and illusion; and the Divine Life is the direct energy from God.

"The Divine Substance is, in its original condition, homogeneous. Every monad of it, therefore, possesses the potentialities of the whole. Of such a monad in its original condition, every individual soul consists. And of the same substance, projected into lower conditions, the material universe consists. It undergoes, however, no radical change of nature through such projection; but its manifestation—on whatever plane occurring—is always as a Trinity in Unity, since that whereby substance becomes manifest is the evolution of its Trinity. Thus—to reckon from without inwards, and below upwards—on the plane physical it is Force, universal Ether, and their offspring the material World. On the plane intellectual it is Life, Substance, and Formulation. On the plane spiritual—its original point of radiation—it is Will, Wisdom, and the Word. And on all planes whatsoever, it is, in some mode, Father, Mother, and Child. For 'there are Three which bear record in *heaven*,' or the invisible, 'and these Three are One. And there are three which bear record on *earth*,' or the visible, 'and these three agree in one,' being Spirit, Soul, and Body."—*The Perfect Way*, p. 17.

See CROSS, MONAD OF LIFE, PYRAMID, RELIGION, TRIAD, TRINITY, TSURAH.

WIZARDS :—

Symbols either of non-human intelligences directing lower plane activities, or of base minds attracted towards unpractical notions and false ideas.

See BLACK MAGICIANS, SORCERERS.

WOLF :—

A symbol of the lower mind attached to desire, fierce and cunning.

See BERSERKS, MURDERER, WALKS.

WOLVES WITH FOUR LEGS :—

A symbol of the desire-nature which functions through the fourfold aspect of the lower self.

See QUADRUPED, QUATERNARY.

WOLVES' LAIR :—

A symbol of the bad aspects of the sense-nature, which support and serve the lower desires.

WOMAN :—

A symbol of the emotion-nature of the soul, which is to be transmuted from the astral to the buddhic state.

"And the Lord God caused a deep sleep to fall upon the man, and he slept ; and he took one of his ribs, and closed up the flesh instead thereof ; and the rib, which the Lord God had taken from the man, made he a woman, and brought her unto the man. And the man said, this is now bone of my bones, and flesh of my flesh : she shall be called Woman, because she was taken out of Man."— GEN. ii. 21–3.

And the Love-Wisdom within the soul caused a state of latency to overtake the mind (man), so that it was for a time unable to carry on its activities. And on the mind plane, one of the higher sub-planes (rib) was specifically selected in accordance with the Divine scheme, as the abode of the higher soul related to buddhi, and thereon was the emotion-nature (woman) evolved ; and this new factor was brought into relation with the lower mind. And the mind acknowledges the better half of itself to be now of its own substance, and recognises in mind-emotion that which is apparently dual within the mind itself.

"Auharmazd spoke to Mashya (man) and Mashyoi (woman) : ' You are man, you are the ancestry of the world, and you are created perfect in devotion by me ; perform devotedly the duty of the law, think good thoughts, speak good words, do good deeds, and worship no demons.' Both of them first thought this, that one of them should please the other, as he is a man for him ; and the first deed done by them was this, when they went out they washed themselves thoroughly."—Bundahis, Ch. XV. 6, 7.

The Supreme uttered its commands to the evolving Soul through the mind (man) and emotion (woman) nature. ' Keep true to the ideals within you : fulfil the law of your own evolution : recognise the three-fold nature, spiritual, ethical, and expressive, underlying your activities : and bow down before no unworthy object.' Originally, mind and emotion were not in conflict, for desire had not entered in. The first process which was undergone within them was the instinctive, automatic, fulfilling of their own true natures lawfully and rightfully. They acknowledged unconsciously the Supreme source of their being. They acted truthfully (washed) in accordance with the Divine Law of growth at this stage of involution on the buddhi-manasic plane, prior to the *fall*.

" The woman was the first to sacrifice to the daêvas "—*Zoroastrian System*.

The emotion-element in the soul is the first to be implicated through desire (daêvas) ; just as signified in the *Genesis* story.

" Let a woman learn in quietness with all subjection. But I permit not a woman to teach, nor to have dominion over a man, but to be in quietness. For Adam was first formed, then Eve ; and Adam was not beguiled, but the woman being beguiled hath fallen into transgression ; but she shall be saved through the child-bearing, if they continue in faith and love and sanctification with sobriety."—1 TIM. ii. 11–15.

This symbolical Divine utterance has no erroneous reference to persons of different sexes. It teaches indisputable truth, as does all sacred scripture. The emotion-nature (woman) must be subject to the dictates of the reasoning mind (man), or truth, justice, equity, peace, mercy, are suppressed in the soul. The emotion-nature must assert itself in an orderly manner, but it is not its function to teach and lead. The mind (Adam) has first place, and functionally is not affected by motives either from above or from below. On the other hand the emotions (Eve) are functionally affected by the Spirit above and by desire below. The salvation of the emotion-nature is effected by its turning to the Holy Spirit, and through purification (virginity) bringing forth the Christ in the mind, whereby both mind and emotion are freed from desire, and the consciousness rises to higher planes.

See ADAM (lower), ANDROMEDA, BONES, BREASTS, CHURCH, CHILD, CONCEPTION (child), DIVORCE, EPIMETHEUS, EVE, FALL, FLESH, HEEL, HUSBAND, LAW OF ZOROASTER, MALE-FEMALE, MAN, MAN AND WIFE, MAN WITHOUT WOMAN, MARRIAGE, PANDORA, PERSEPHONE, PRODIGAL, QUALITIES, RIB, SERPENT (subtil), VACH, VIRGIN MARY, WASHED, WATER (higher), WIFE.

WOMAN AS GODDESS :—

A symbol of the Wisdom principle, Buddhi, from which the higher emotions proceed.

" I (Lakshmi) reside in milk, butter, fresh grass, honey and sour milk ; in the body of a married woman, in the frame of an unmarried damsel. . . . I reside in women who wear proper ornaments always, who are devoted to their husbands, whose speeches are kind."—*Institutes of Vishnu*, XCIX. 14, 21.

The "Goddess Lakshmi," being a symbol of the buddhic principle, the remaining symbols are found to signify the higher emotions in which buddhi resides. (The ancient writer gives a long and correct list of symbols of the buddhic emotions, only a few of which symbols are given above.)

See AMATERASU, ARMAITI, ATHENA, DEMETER, FRIGG, HATHOR, HERA, ISIS, ISTAR, LATONA, SITA, THETIS.

WOMAN AS MATTER :—

A symbol of the veil of matter in which manifestation takes place. Matter is the feminine, receptive principle in which Spirit, masculine, active, becomes involved.

"But when the fulness of the time was come, God sent forth his Son, made of woman, made under the law."—GAL. iv. 4.

For when the Absolute out-breathed, the Logos was emanated as the Divine sacrifice limited by matter (woman) and involved therein with all its qualities, according to the supreme law.

See BIRTH OF CHRIST, HETHRA, MATTER, MĀYĀ, MOTHER, MUT, TEFNUT.

WOMAN EMBODYING LOKE :—

A symbol of the physical nature, which is feminine, as used by the astral nature which urges it to action.

See LOKE, MISTLETOE, NEPHTHYS, THOCK.

WOMAN TAKEN IN ADULTERY :—

Symbolical of the emotion-nature in its lower aspect allied to the sense-activities.

"And the scribes and the Pharisees bring a woman taken in adultery; and having set her in the midst, they say unto him, Master, this woman hath been taken in adultery, in the very act. Now in the law Moses commanded us to stone such : what then sayest thou of her ? "—JOHN viii. 3-5.

The literalists and conventionalists endeavour to oppose the methods of the inspired inner teacher. "Moses," or the moral law, is appealed to. Now, the measure of the law conventionally interpreted, is a hard and fast one. Conduct and morals become a question of custom, line and rule,

engendering a habit of trusting to the formal crust solidifying without, instead of to the living source within. It is the Christ then comes to revivify, to re-animate, to raise. The "adultery" is a temporary falling away of the emotion-nature from the true and first love—the Christ. No external coercive method could cure this condition. "Jesus stooped down and wrote on the ground," because the Christ had to come down, so to speak, to limit and define in words for the soul's benefit those principles of wisdom and love which are above all definition. Christ, as the story shows, maintains a responsive attitude towards the soul. Condemnation is not of the Christ who wins by love, and is full of compassion. The going out of the accusers means the dispersal of the operations of the lower personality until the mind becomes tranquil, and love can do its work.

See ADULTERY, BAPTISM, CHRIST, DISPENSATIONS, MOSAIC, MOSES.

WOMEN'S LIFE IN DARKNESS :—

A symbol of the astral emotions devoid of the light of Truth.

"Verily, the life of women is always darkness, yet when it encountered her (Mâyâ), it shone brilliantly ; thus the night does not retain its gloom, when it meets with the radiant crescent of the moon."—*Buddha-Karita* I. 17.

Truly, the life of the unenlightened emotions is dark and blind. But as the light of Truth (queen Mâyâ) from above stirs the emotions, they are raised from their condition of ignorance, and become united with the Higher Self. Thus the "night" of negation does not remain without knowledge (dark) ; for at the coming of the Love-nature from above, this emotional state is informed and irradiated by the Higher Self. Christ, the light of Truth, illumines the personality (moon) through its emotion-nature (woman) within the mind (man).

See DARKNESS, LIGHT, MĀYĀ (higher), MOON, NIGHT, PERSONALITY.

WOMB OF MÂYÂ :—

A symbol of primordial matter—mental, astral and physical—in which the World-soul is conceived in the period of involution, and from which it is brought forth into the manifest existence of the involutionary cycle.

"Mâyâ also, holding him (Buddha) in her womb, like a line of clouds holding the lightning flash, relieved the people around her from the sufferings of poverty, by raining showers of gifts."—*Buddha-Karita*, I. 22.

The lower planes of matter being ready to be delivered of the Soul while Truth potential (Mâyâ) holds the Divine Life, so the lower nature becomes fructified of the Spirit within it, which is the means of developing the soul - qualities (people). The "clouds" stand for truth-potential, and the "lightning" for life. The generous donations symbolise the fructifying of the lower nature hitherto deficient in truth, wisdom, and love, which are the gifts of the Spirit and the wealth which puts an end to poverty or lack of the spiritual.

"First the Glory descends from the presence of Ahura-Mazda, where it abides in the Eternal Light ; it passes through heaven down to earth, and it enters the house where Zoroaster's mother is to be born. Uniting itself with her presence it abides in her until she brings forth her first-born child Zaratusht."—*Dinkard*, VII. 2, 3.

The Divine Ray, or Spark, of Truth and Life, goes forth from the Absolute, at a particular stage of involution ; passes through the upper planes, and descends to the astro-physical level (earth). The Divine Spark thereby enters the Womb of Matter (potential), and coming thus into relationship with the lower nature, indwells therein, until matter (mother mental, astral, and physical (earth), reaches the condition and period of delivery, when the Soul (Zoroaster) is born into the cycle of involution and into the buddhic causal-body, thus manifesting the World-soul.

See BIRTH OF BUDDHA, OF CHRIST, OF ZOROASTER, BODHISATVA, CLOUDS, DESTROYING EVILS, GLORY, HETHRA, INVOLUTION, LIGHTNING, KHEPER, MATTER, MÂYÂ, MOTHER, PEOPLE, POVERTY, PRAKRITI, SOUL, SPARK, VIRGIN MARY, ZOROASTER.

WOMB-COSMIC :—

A symbol of the Self, potential, prepared to manifest on the higher planes ; container of the scheme of existence, or the ideal germs of all qualities and forms which have to appear The upper matrix is buddhi-manasic, which is repeated as lower matrix on the astro-mental plane for the astro-physical universe. Creation for both the higher and the lower planes has its inception on the higher mental plane. This inception is symbolised by Ushas, the Dawn, and the god Shu, the Divine Will—the separator of Space (Nut) and Time (Seb).

See BULL (primeval), DEMIURGE.

WOOD :—

A symbol of the astral plane, or the desire- and astral-nature. The astral plane is the plane of the growth of the lower qualities, symbolised by "plants."

"The third (human being) from the east, is superintendent of Wood." (*Chinese Legend*).—KIDD, *China*, p. 167.

The third vehicle of the World-soul is the astral principle on the astral plane of manifestation.

"Aristotle was the first to use the word Matter (in Greek *Hyle*, wood ; in Latin *Materia*, building stuff), as a term of the schools, to denote the impalpable, invisible substratum of things, in contradistinction from the invisible Form."—C. BIGG, *Neo-Platonism*, p. 195.

"Chinese writers, on the theory of the earth, maintain that there are five original elements, whose names and order are : Water, Fire, Wood, Metal, Earth—of which the last occupies the centre of a circle described by the other four. The first two take precedence of the rest, both on account of superior importance and of priority of existence."—KIDD, *China*, p. 160.

The "five original elements" are the five planes of manifestation. The first two elements, "Water" and "Fire," signify the planes of Atma and Buddhi, which are the highest and most real planes, manifesting prior to the three lower planes. The element "Earth" signifies the Physical plane, which is the limit or foundation plane of the manifest existence. The elements "Metal" and "Wood," signify the Mental and Astral planes.

See AMERDAD, ASTRAL PLANE, ELEMENTS, SHELTER, SIMILITUDES, WORLDS (five), YANG.

WOOD, HOLY :—

A symbol of the astral plane in its aspect of growth, in which the Self begins to manifest.

"The first place where the earth feels

most joy is when the faithful one steps forward with the holy wood, the sacred twigs (barsom), the holy meat, the holy mortar in his hand, fulfilling the law with love."—*Vendidad*, III.

The awakenment of the Self must in the first place proceed from the physical plane; and the manner in which the Self is first aroused is through sensation and feeling, on the astral plane (wood). The "sacred twigs" signify the buddhic responses and growths which occur as the ego functions. The "holy meat" is a symbol of intellectual food—knowledge. The "holy mortar" is a symbol of the critical intellect—that which pounds up opinions. "Fulfilling the law with love" signifies the evolution of the higher intellect which supersedes the lesser mentality, and intuitively perceives the Divine truth, love, and wisdom of the higher nature of the soul.

See BARHIS, BARSOM, FULFILLING, KUSTI, MAISHAN, MEAT (holy), MORTAR AND PESTLE.

WOODEN PALACE OR HOUSE :—

A symbol of the astral body as an abode for the soul.

"The Gods also planted hemp and kodzu, and with their fibre and bark respectively wove clothing for the Sun-Goddess. They also cut down timber and built a palace."—*Japanese Legend of the Concealment of the Sun-Goddess.*

There was also formed an astral mechanism for the desire and sensation functionings, which should enwrap the germ of the higher emotions. And this was enclosed in an astral body formed from the matter of the astral plane.

See AMATERASU, CLOTHING, HOUSE, LOOM, SHELTER.

WOOL, WHITE : A SYMBOL OF WISDOM.

See CRANIUM.

WORD, DIVINE — UNUTTERED AND UTTERED :—

A symbol of the Higher Self potential, and of the Divine Life actual in the cycle.

"In Eckhart's system, the Godhead is the 'unnatured Nature,' i.e. the unoriginated Reality, the Ground of all revelation; God is the 'natured Nature,' i.e. the Divine expressed in Personal Form. The

Godhead is the *Worldless One ;* God is the *uttered Word*."—R. M. JONES, *Mystical Religion*, p. 227.

"I-am is the Hidden One of the mouth; it is the silence of his mouth whose uttered word is mystery, even the mouth of the Ruler of the Æon which grasps the eternity of ' Being in Peace.' "—*Book of the Dead*, Ch. CX., BLACKDEN.

The Divine Self is the Unspoken Word—the inherent power of the Logos—which is to be heard only within souls who have transcended the planes of form. The "Uttered Word" is the emanation of the Divine Life which is manifested through the period of the manvantara. The "Word of the Ruler of the cycle" is the power within the soul which makes for righteousness—interpreted in the natural, moral, and intellectual orders of the lower life, and which is realised when we perceive that all things work together for good; since such a perception is an intuition or direct sense of the eternal Love of God.

" ' The Word of God will come down and suffer and be crucified, and he will wet the crown of Adam's head with his blood '—said a voice from Adam's body."—*Book of the Conflicts of Adam.*

This utterance indicates the previsive power of the spiritualised lower mind, which is enabled to foresee the vision of the Eternal as it will manifest ultimately in the soul. The "wetting of Adam's head" with the "blood of the Lamb" is a symbol of the sacrificial part which the lower self must also take in order to benefit through the sacrifice of the Logos at the "foundation of the world" or lower nature.

"The eternal Word, when fully spoken, will be a song of many harmonies, a mosaic of many stones, a picture of many forms and hues. But we shall all be wanted therein. If you do not rise to the full measure of your spiritual capacities, I shall be the poorer, and shall have to wait for my complete felicity until you do. If I am a defaulter, you will suffer loss ; and all the race waits for us both and cannot fully find itself till we have arrived at what we *are*, which is what God means us to be. Nor in the nature of things can we possibly know what we really are till we get there."—R. J. CAMPBELL, Serm., *God's Life in Man.*

See ADAM (lower), ÆON, BIRDS (two), BLOOD OF LAMB, CRUCIFIXION OF CHRIST, HAWK, HETEP, I AM, MOUTH (speech), Peace, Sword of spirit, Themis.

WORD, LIVING AND MIGHTY :—

A symbol of the expression of the Divine life on each plane of nature.

"I conquer by this most mighty Word which is within my body, for is not this my throne ? And ' I am ' brings to my remembrance in Him what I had forgotten."—*Book of the Dead*, Ch. CX.

The Higher Self subdues the adverse forces of the lower planes of nature by means of the Life within the human forms ; and it does this from its seat in the causal-body (throne). The Individuality (I am), the true Self, is the container and source of all memory and self-consciousness. The Personality is enabled to recover the record of experiences which are collected by means of the Self.

"May Thoth, who is filled and furnished with words of power, come and loose the bandages, even the bandages of Set which fetter my mouth " (*Book of the Dead*).— Budge, *Egyptian Magic*, p. 126.

May the higher mind (Thoth), through which the Divine Life energises the soul-bodies, be the means of freeing me from captivity to the desires (bandages of Set) which prevent the expression (mouth) of my true nature on higher planes.

"My child, remember him that speaketh the Word of God to thee by day and by night. Thou shalt honour him as the Lord. For in whatsoever quarter the Lordship is spoken, there is the Lord."— *The Didache*, IV. 1,

"Within you and through you a word of God is being spoken, a divine idea is struggling to fruition through sorrow and pain and hard-won victory over all that is the denial of itself."—R. J. Campbell, Serm., *God's Use of Time*.

"We are individually fragments of a wondrous whole in various stages of unfoldment, and all that we are going through on earth is part of a process which will culminate in the production of a glorious humanity revealing the eternal perfections of God. What there will be after that only God knows—perhaps a new beginning, the utterance of some new Word of his infinitude."—R. J. Campbell, Serm., *The Eternal Self*.

"The written word of the letter is not *the Word itself*, that cleanseth and sanctifieth the man, or which procreateth the life. But it is a shadow or figuring out of the holy and true word, a serviceable instrument whereby we are made well-affected inwardly in our souls to the true word of vivification, to the end that through belief

and love we might in the spirit of our minds be made of like-being with the nature and being of the Good Life ; even as the words of Scripture witness "— (H. Nicholas).—R. M. Jones, *Mystical Religion*, p. 437.

"This is a primary position of all William Dell's teaching, that an inward change must occur, and that this inward change is wrought by the Divine Word, Light, Life or Spirit. He says : ' The living and eternal Word dwells in our hearts, and this Word dwelling in us by faith changes us into its own likeness. . . . This is not a word without us, as the word of the law is, but the Word within us. If thou live under the Word many years, and it come not into thy heart, it will never change thee.' In a fine sentence he says : ' The heart cannot be forced by outward power, but by the inward efficacy of truth.' "—R. M. Jones, *Ibid.*, p. 491.

See Experiences, Fetters, I am, Individuality, Kalchas, Magic, Mouth, Personality, Reminiscence, Speech, Thoth, Vestures.

WORD OF GOD :—

A symbol of the expression of Divine Truth in the various scriptures of the world.

"The spiritual sense of the Word is not that which shines forth from the literal sense. While one is searching and explaining the Word to confirm some dogma of the Church, this sense may be called the literal sense of the Word. But the spiritual sense does not appear in the literal sense ; it is interiorly within it, as the soul is in the body, as the thought of the understanding is in the eyes, and as the affection of love is in the countenance, which act together as cause and effect. It is this sense chiefly which renders the Word spiritual, not only for men, but also for angels ; therefore the Word by this sense communicates with the heavens."—Swedenborg, *T.C.R.*, n. 194.

"Propose me anything out of this Book (the Bible), and require whether I believe it or not, and seem it never so incomprehensible to human reason, I will subscribe it with hand and heart, as knowing no demonstration can be stronger than this ; *God hath said so, therefore it is true*. . . . I am fully assured that God does not, and therefore that men ought not, to require any more of any man than this : to believe the Scripture to be God's word, *to endeavour to find the true sense of it*, and to live according to it."— Chillingworth, *Works*, p. 354.

When the mind is fully convinced from evidence and reason that the Scriptures are the Word of God and of transcendental origin, in no way vitiated by human inventions and imaginings, then it consistently holds of the inspired Word—"God hath said so, therefore *it is true*." This is logical and straightforward, free from the ruinous contradictions of modern theology, but there remains the all-important question of the correct interpretation of the Word of Truth. Now, as the literal sense of the Scriptures is in most cases absurd and false, the logical mind is forced to imagine symbolical meanings. Preachers cannot do without them, and sometimes admit, as did Robertson of Brighton, that "Scripture language is symbolical."

See AMBAYAVIS, GOSPEL, INSPIRATION, KORAN, MYTHOLOGY, PAPYRUS, PEN, REVELATION, SACRED TEXT, SASTRA, SCRIPTURES, UPANISHAD, UR-HEKAU, VEDA.

WORDS OF POWER :—

A symbol of the higher qualities which are mighty to subdue and transmute the lower qualities. They are the expression of the Divine nature within the soul.

"The earliest name for the formulæ found upon amulets is *hekau*, and it was so necessary for the deceased to be provided with these *hekau*, or 'words of power,' that in the 16th century B.C., and probably more than a thousand years earlier, a special section was inserted in the Book of the Dead with the object of causing them to come to him (the defunct) from whatever place they were in, 'swifter than greyhounds and quicker than light.' "—BUDGE, *Egyptian Magic*, p. 27.

"Homage to you, O ye lords of eternity, ye possessors of everlastingness, take ye not this heart of Osiris (the deceased) into your grasp, and cause ye not words of evil to spring up against it ; for it is the heart of Osiris, and it belongeth unto him of many names, the mighty one whose words are his limbs, and who sendeth forth his heart to dwell in his body" (*Book of the Dead*, Ch. XXVII).—*Ibid.*, p. 32.

In the above text, appeal is made to the lords of Karma that the purified soul should not be required to again reincarnate and be subjected to the strife of the lower qualities (words of evil) in the underworld of the phenomenal life. For the causal-body (heart) is the seat of the Self on the higher mental plane ; and the manifest Self is the individuality whose expression is the higher qualities (limbs), and whose causal-body is made new

before the ideals, and proceeds forth as the immortal vehicle of the ego.

The power of the higher qualities is exceeding great in raising and transforming the soul. In the pursuit of ideals the lower qualities are deprived of all strength by the higher and swifter impulses from the Divine nature within.

"Spiritual freedom is the attribute of a mind, in which reason and conscience has begun to act, it is moral energy or force of holy purpose put forth against the senses, against the passions, against the world, and thus liberating the intellect, conscience, and will, so that they may act with strength and unfold themselves for ever. The essence of spiritual freedom is power."—W. E. CHANNING, *Works*, Vol. I. p. 105.

See ALCHEMY, AMULETS, CAUSAL-BODY, DEFUNCT, HEART, INCARNATION, INDIVIDUALITY, KARMA, LIMBS, MAGIC, MOUTH, OSIRIS, SCARLET, UR-HEKAU.

WORK :—

A symbol of the endeavour of the soul to attain perfection ; or the business of development during the incarnation of the ego in the lower worlds.

"I assure you that life as you and I are living it now matters only in relation to the eternal, and every thought we think and every deed we do, can only be rightly estimated by their spiritual effect."—R. J. CAMPBELL, Serm., *Judgment Deferred*.

See JUSTICE, LABOURERS, MONEY, SACRIFICE, VINEYARD, WAGES.

WORKERS OF METAL :—

Symbolic of qualities upon the mental plane, attached to high ideals which will endure and consolidate and overcome the lower desires.

"But Horbehudti was behind the enemies in the bark of Rā, a lance of iron and a chain were in his hand. With him was his following equipped with weapons and chains" (*Legend of the Winged Sundisk*).—WIEDEMANN, *Rel. of Anc. Egypt*.

But the Lord of heaven was behind his vehicles in the causal-body, and capable of wielding his instruments of high mental ideals so that he could gain entire mastery of the vehicles and their lower inclinations. With him were the raised soul-qualities who were working together with him.

See ARMS, BLACKSMITHS, CUTTING, INITIATIONS, IRON, METALS, QUALITIES, TUBALCAIN, WALKS, WEAPONS.

WORKS AND WISDOM PATH :—

Symbolic of the way of the soul to liberation and bliss, by means of effort and learning.

So far is it from being true that works cease when sanctification is attained, that it is not until after one's sanctification that right activity, love to all creatures, and most of all to one's enemies, and peace with all, begin. Ecstasies are soon over, but union with God becomes an abiding possession of the soul, even when, in the midst of the soul's outward activity, that union seems to be withdrawn" (Eckhart). —UEBERWEG, *Hist of Philos.*, Vol. I. p. 480.

See HYMNS, LIBERATION, PATH (two-fold), WAY.

WORLD :—

A symbol of the soul in its lower aspect ; the arena of the mental life ; the planes of form and illusion ; or the lower quaternary perceived in the mind.

" I am a king. To this end was I born, and for this cause came I into the world, that I should bear witness unto the truth. Every one that is of the truth heareth my voice."—JOHN xviii. 37.

The Christ is the great king of the inner realm ; he is the end and aim of all evolution. He enters the soul (world) in order to rule it through love, and his witness is the love of goodness and truth. Every quality that partakes of this love co-ordinates itself with him.

"'The world,' the name by which we describe the connected elements of experience in general, is regarded not merely as connected causally or otherwise from end to end; it is regarded as a whole. And these two—'Truth' (the aim of intellectual effort), and 'the world,' the unity of experience which lies beyond the causal connection of its facts—confront one another, and demand some further whole which shall include them both. These two wholes must become one in God."—W. RICHMOND, *Personality.* p. 109.

When the mental nature (world) perfectly conforms itself to Truth, Wisdom and Love, then the two Selves—the higher consciousness and the lower—become One.

" That the world is a phenomenon of mind is the fundamental thought of modern philosophy from Kant downwards; and that philosophy is accordingly in its essence idealism. . . . Mind is invisible nature, Nature is mind made visible ; mind is the inner side of all that is outward, the real working principle in all that is actual, as all that is outward is

but its representation of itself, all that is actual, the form and means of its self-realisation."—PFLEIDERER, *Phil. of Religion*, Vol. II. pp. 1, 2.

" Thus from that ether he (Brahman, the Highest Self) wakes all this world, which consists of thought only, and by him alone is all this meditated on, and in him it is dissolved."—*Mait. Upanishad*, VI. 20.

" You are not in this world, nor are you experiencing anything in connection with it, however dark and drear, because an almighty being sent you here without consulting you and without your having anything to do with the matter. That is not the way things are ordered. You are here by the operation of a law which is the law of your own nature. Being what you are, you could not choose but come, any more than a plant can help growing."—R. J. CAMPBELL, Serm., *The Eternal Self.*

"A child was born yesterday. How he lies to-day in his serene, superb unconsciousness ! And all the forces and resources of the earth are gathered about his cradle offering themselves to him. Each of his new-born senses is besieged. Each eager voice cries out to him, ' Here I am. I have waited for you. Here I am.' He takes what they all bring as if it were his right. Not merely on his senses, but even on his mind and most unconscious soul, the world into which he has come is pressing itself. Its conventionalities and creeds, its standards beaten out of the experience of uncounted generations, its traditions of hope and danger, its prejudices and limitations and precedents, all its discoveries and hopes and fears— they are the scenery in which this new life stands, they are the mountains in whose shadow and the skies in whose light he is to unfold his long career. They are here before him, and he comes into them. You cannot separate him and them from each other. He and his world make one system, one rich, complex unit of life, as he lies this Sunday morning in his cradle, sleeping his unsuspecting sleep."—PHILLIPS BROOKS, *Light of the World*, p. 42.

See AMENI, ARENA, EVOLUTION, FIELD, ILLUSION, KING (great), QUATERNARY, SETTLEMENTS, SOUL (lower), WITNESSES (two).

WORLD, THIRSTY :—

A symbol of the mental arena of the phenomenal and illusory activities of the soul. In this state, aspiration towards the real (thirst) is the means whereby the nature of the Self is realised, and Truth (water) gained.

See ARENA, FIELD, LAW OF BUDDHA, STREAM, THIRST.

WORLDS, FIVE :—

A symbol of the five planes of manifestation in the universe and the soul.

"I will adduce Plato, who says the World is one, but if there be other worlds around this, and this be not the only one, they are five in number, and no more. . . . Earth, Water, Fire, Air, Æther."—PLUTARCH, *On the E at Delphi*, § XI.

"The 'Five Worlds' of the Sufis. These five worlds are not five different localities, but five different planes of existence which loses in true Being as it descends ; they are consequently often spoken of as the 'Five Planes' (Hazrat-i-Khamsa). . . . Above and beyond the universe, yet compassing all things, and the Source of all things, is the 'World of Godhead,' of This nothing can be predicated, and It is not reckoned among the Five. The first of these is called the 'Plane of the Absolutely Invisible,' or the 'Plane of the Nebulosity,' and its world is the 'World of the Fixed Prototypes,' that is to say, the existences that people it are the Fixed Prototypes. The Second Plane is that of the 'Relatively Invisible,' and its world is the 'World of the Intelligences and the Souls'; (that is, of the Celestial or Spheral Intelligences and Souls), these are sometimes called the 'Spirits of Might,' and so this sphere of being is known also as the 'World of Might' (Alem-i Jebirut). (NOTE.—The terms *Jeberut* and *Jeberutiye* convey the idea of 'constraining,' as though the beings of this World exercised some constraining power over those below them.)

"The next plane is called the 'World of Similitudes,' or the 'Angel World.' . . . The Fourth Plane is the 'Visible World,' which is often called the 'World of the Kingdom,' i.e. the Physical World ; it is the world in which we move, and is the antithesis of the 'Absolutely Invisible.' (NOTE.—It is also called the 'Sensible World,' the 'World of Form,' the 'World of Generation and Corruption,' and so on.)

"The Fifth Plane is the 'World of Man,' which sums up and comprises all the others ; for Man, as we shall see, is the Microcosm epitomising in himself the whole universe."—E. J. W. GIBB, *Hist. of Ottoman Poetry*, Vol. I. pp. 54–6.

Above, beyond, or deep within the planes of the manifest, there is affirmed to be the Godhead, the Absolute, the unmanifest Source of all beings. The First Plane of manifestation is that of Atma (Absolutely Invisible), in which are the Monads of life and form (Fixed Prototypes). The Second Plane is the Buddhic Plane (Relatively Invisible), in which is the higher causal-body of all souls, also the

ideals and highest qualities of being (Spirits of Might), which constrain and bring about the transmutation of the lower qualities. The Third Plane is the Mental plane (Man) which focalises the other planes because on it the human consciousness resides. The Fourth Plane is the Astral plane (Similitudes) containing the forms of growth which take up physical matter in the next plane, and also the forces of desire. The Fifth Plane is the Physical plane (Sensible) which is perceived by the senses.

The Mental plane is apparently displaced in the Sufi system, probably to emphasise its peculiar significance in relation to humanity and the Soul.

The Sufi exposition of the Five Planes of Manifestation, is, perhaps, the fullest that has been derived through inspiration in the past from the One Source of all Truth. Every country, from America and Iceland eastward to Japan, and including New Zealand and Polynesia, has received the same information, but in a less explicit form.

Sometimes only four worlds, planes, or elements are indicated, in which case the Divine Being is implied as presiding above all as the highest state of manifestation, thus counting as a fifth plane or "world of Godhead." The four worlds or four planes below atma constitute the quaternary, the arena of life, underworld, samsâra, tuat, tartarus, etc.

See ABSOLUTE, ÆTHER, ARENA, ASTRAL PLANE, ATMA, BUDDHIC PLANE, CAUSAL-BODY, COSMOS, CREATION, DAYS (five), ELEMENTS (five), FIVE, GATHA DAYS (five), GODHEAD, GOLDEN AGE, HIGHER AND LOWER WORLDS, IMAGE, MACROCOSM, MICROCOSM, MONADS, PLANES (five), PRAGÂPATI, PROTOTYPES, QUATERNARY, REINGA, RULERS (five), SAMSÂRA, SEASONS (five), SIMILITUDES, TARTARUS, THIEVES (five), TUAT, UNDERWORLD, WORDS OF POWER.

WORSHIP OF THE WOOD OF ISIS :—

Symbolic of the veneration with which knowledge of words, forms, and rites in which wisdom is hidden,

is regarded by the lower mind at a certain stage in the growth of the soul.

"Thus it was that Isis made the 'wood of Isis' worshipped by the people of Byblos down to a late date."—PLUTARCH, *Isis and Osiris*, § 16.

Veneration for ceremonial knowledge may lead the lower mind towards aspiration and devotion.

"Symbolism remained, while the abstract thought, to which that symbolism should have been a stepping stone, failed to penetrate into the Egyptian religion. The Egyptian continued to be content with the symbol, as his father had been before him. But in the priestly colleges and among the higher circles of culture it became less materialistic; while the mass of the people still saw nothing but the symbol itself, the priests and scribes looked, as it were, beyond it, and saw in the symbol the picture of some divine truth, the outward garment in which the deity had clothed himself. —A. H. SAYCE, *Rel. of Anc. Egyptians*, p. 35.

See BYBLOS, CEREMONIES, ISIS, MYTHOLOGY, PAPYRUS BOAT, PEOPLE, RELIGIONS, RITES, SCRIPTURES, SIGN.

WRATH (MENIS) OF ACHILLES :—

A symbol of the violent out-going energy of the lower nature of instinct, passion and desire, in the nascent personality. This energy produces strife and suffering in the lower consciousness on the mental plane. The personality (Achilles) is immersed in the conflict of the mental qualities and emotions with which it identifies itself.

See ACHILLES, MENIS.

WRATH OF APOLLO :—

A symbol of the out-going energy of the Higher Self in the exercise of the striving functions for the overcoming of the lower desires and instincts.

"O Achilles! dear to Jove, thou biddest me (Calchas) to declare the wrath of Apollo, the far-darting king. Therefore will I declare it; but do thou on thy part covenant and sware to me, that thou wilt promptly assist me in word and hand."—*Iliad*, Bk. I.

'O personality, young soul! dear in the eyes of the Self; thou urgest that the laws of the Supreme are harsh and unequal, and cause suffering and sorrow, therefore will I (memory) so interpret them. But do thou for thy part vow that thou wilt render

me assistance voluntarily and actively, even though it cause distress to the lower mind.'

See ACHILLES, APOLLO, ARGIVES, FUNERAL, KALCHAS, PESTILENCE.

WRATH OF GOD :—

A symbol of the Divine aspect towards evil. In so far as the lower consciousness identifies itself with evil, the God within wears a forbidding aspect indicative of opposition to misdeeds. But the wrath exists only in the lower self, for the nature of God towards the evolving soul is always that of love and compassion.

"For the wrath of God is revealed from heaven against all ungodliness and unrighteousness of men, who hold down the truth in unrighteousness; because that which may be known of God is manifest in them; for God manifested it unto them."—ROM. i. 18, 19.

The conscience is the inner monitor which is manifest in the mind as a revelation from heaven, and this holds up the truth to the soul.

"Wrath is predicated of evil; and anger of falsity, because they who are in evil are the subjects of wrath, and they who are in falsity are the subjects of anger; and both in the Word are attributed to Jehovah, that is, to the Lord; but it is meant that they take place in man against the Lord."—SWEDENBORG, *Apoc. Rev.*, n. 635.

"If the Soul be in the Love of God, then beholdeth it God accordingly, and feeleth him as he is—Love. But if it hath captivated itself in the Wrath of God, then it cannot behold God otherwise than in the Wrathful Nature, nor perceive him otherwise than as an incensed and vindictive Spirit."—J. BEHMEN, *Supersensual Life*, Dial. 3.

"I saw no wrath, but on man's part, and that forgiveth He in us. It is the most impossible thought that may be that God should be wrath."—JULIANA OF NORWICH.

See ANGER OF GOD, CLEANSING, CONSCIENCE, JEALOUS GOD, JEHOVAH, MOSES, SIVA, SLAUGHTER, TEMPLE, VOICE, VULTURE (prey).

WREATHS OF PLANTS :—

Symbolical of the budding of the feelings which will afterwards yield the fruit of high emotions.

See GARLANDS, GEMS (strings), PLANTS, UNGUENTS.

WRITING :—

See PEN, SEAL, THOTH.

YAGNÂ-YAGNÎYA AND BHADRA, —SÂMAN VERSES :—

Symbols of Wisdom and Will in their interior aspects of mani- festation.

See SAMAN.

YAGUS, THE CROSS-SHEETS :—

These are a symbol of compassion, which is of the Spirit of Love.

See OM, UDGITHA.

YAJNOPAVITA,—THE SACRED CORD, OR SACRIFICIAL THREAD :—

A symbol of the Higher Triad or Divine Ray—Atma-buddhi-manas.

" This cord, which is a coil of three threads, is worn over the left shoulder and allowed to hang down diagonally across the body to the right hip, and the wearing of it by the three twice-born classes was the mark of their second birth."—MON. WILLIAMS, *Indian Wisdom*, p. 246.

The wearing of the triple cord signifies the acceptance by the ego of the means of progress in the spiritual life.

See BARKIS, BARSOM, BIRTH (second), BUCKLE, CASTES, EPHOD, KUSTI, SANNYASIN, SUTRATMA, TAMA- GUSHI, TRIAD, TRIDENT.

YAMA, KING :—

A symbol of the Causal Self or perfected personality ; an aspect of the Individuality or the Higher Self.

" Verily in him that exists, these deities reside, to wit, Indra, King Yama, Nada, the Naishadha king, Anasnat Sungamana, and Asat Pâmsava. Now Indra, in truth, is the same as the Ahavanîya (fire) ; and King Yama is the same as the Gârhapatya (house- holder's fire)."—*Sata. Brâh.*, II. 3, 2, 1–2.

Truly in the ego, or soul, that manifests on the lower planes, there indwells the Higher Self (Indra), the Causal Self (King Yama), the Per- sonality (King Nada), the mental faculties, and the desire-nature. Now atma-buddhi (Indra) pours forth spiritual activity on the buddhic plane, and the Causal Self is a centre of activity on the higher mental plane.

See AHAVANÎYA, BUDDHIC PLANE, CAUSAL-SELF, DEATH (king), GÂRHA- PATYA, INDRA, NACHIKETAS, PERSON- ALITY, SOMA-JUICE.

YANG AND YIN :—

Symbols of Spirit and Matter, or of Life and Form.

" The alternate action and inaction of *Li*, in the sphere of *K'i*, produced the positive and negative forms, *Yang* and *Yin*, variously represented as Light and Darkness, Heaven and Earth, Male and Female, etc., whose vicissitudes consti- tute the *Tao* or course of Nature, as reflected in the four seasons, the alter- nations of day and night, etc. The *Yang* and *Yin* contain the ' Five ele- ments ' in embryo, viz. metal, wood, water, fire, and earth, of which water and fire are regarded as the simplest forms. Each element possesses a *Yang* and a *Yin* quality, and all are pervaded by *Li* " (Chucius).—W. G. WALSHE, *Cosmogony (Chinese), Ency. Rel. and Ethics.*

The rhythm of the Great Breath produced the duality of Spirit and Matter, the active and receptive states of being. This primal duality is variously named in the sacred scrip- tures. Spirit and Matter unite in forming the five planes (elements) of the Cosmos, viz. Atma (water), Buddhi (fire), Mind (metal), Astral (wood), and Physical (earth). On each of the planes there is a Life (yang) and Form (yin) element, or active and passive aspects ; and the Divine Life (Li) pervades all things.

" Heaven represents the male (Yang) principle and earth the corresponding (Yin) female principle, on which two principles the whole of existence depends." —ALLEN, *Chinese Poetry*, Pref. 27.

" *Yang* and *Yin* signify ' light and darkness, perfection and imperfection, manifestation and obscurity, good and evil, the source of existence and the cause of decay.' . . . The superior of these powers, by whatever name it is distinguished, rules in heaven and con- trols celestial objects, while the inferior which is female, governs on earth and directs terrestrial things."—KIDD, *China*, pp. 137–8.

" The Master said :—' The trigrams Khien and Khwän may be regarded as the gate of the Yî.' Khien represents what is of the *yang* nature (bright and active) ; Khwän what is of the *yin* nature (shaded and inactive). These two unite according to their qualities." —*Yî King*, Appendix III. § 2, 6, 45.

" Man is yang, woman is yin, Heaven is yang, earth is yin, The south is yang, the north is yin, The sun is yang, the moon is yin."—J. EDKINS, *Religion in China*, p. 92.

Spirit (Khien—heaven) is masculine, active, indwelling, enlightening, per- fect, the Higher Self (sun). Matter

(Khwan—earth) is feminine, receptive, exterior, ignorant, imperfect, the lower self (moon). These two unite and produce forms and qualities. They are the prime dual principles of manifestation of the Divine Life.

"So far as observation can extend at present, life is a mysterious force or substance, or both in one, which seeks manifestation through matter without ever fully finding it. Life is free, matter is determined, and the whole history of the cosmos is the struggle of life to overcome the determinism of matter and use it as a medium for its own self-expression. Always it is more or less baffled in this endeavour, because of the resistance offered by matter to any attempt to turn it aside from its pre-ordained path or make it do anything new. And yet, but for that struggle and that resistance, we should have no such thing as creation at all. Life, or whatever the reality is which reveals itself as life, would be utterly helpless without matter as its instrument; and yet that instrument can never be a perfect one, nor can the results it obtains be a full, final, and complete expression of the potentialities of the life that makes use of it. . . . At first the forms with which life clothed itself were gross and clumsy, and comparatively simple in structure. But as ages went by it replaced these by other and more complex forms until at last it has produced the human body and brain. But apparently it has always been the same life, always fundamentally one, manifold as its expressions have been and are."—R. J. CAMPBELL, Serm., *God's Gift of Life.*

See EARTH (primordial), ELEMENTS, HEAVEN AND EARTH, IMPERIAL, KHIEN AND KHWAN, MALE-FEMALE, METAL AND TAO, WATER (higher), WOOD, YI, RANGI.

YÂO, CELESTIAL EMPEROR :—

A symbol of the Higher Self manifesting upon the buddhic plane, during the cycle of involution.

"Yaou was very young when he began to reign, but his heart was penetrated by a benevolence as extensive as heaven. His mother observed a red dragon, and was delivered of him after fourteen months' pregnancy. Fire was the element chosen to illustrate the virtues by which he reigned. Yaou was frugal in his food, and almost mean in his dress; to study the happiness of his people was his sole business. Unwearied in his researches, he made annual tours throughout the empire; his arrival was anxiously looked for; his presence was as refreshing as that of the rain upon the parched soil. 'Strive,' he said, 'for wisdom, and render virtue conspicuous, show obedience to your superiors; be kind.' Without effort he promoted virtue, his sole example being sufficient to render the whole nation virtuous. . . . Yaou's presence displayed the splendour of the sun; his deportment the majesty of the clouds."—C. GUTZLAFF, *Chinese History.*

The Self or Soul was born first upon the buddhic plane as Love wide-reaching throughout the manifest. Truth-matter (mother), becoming relative and conditioned, brought forth the Self after a full period of latency and complete preparation. Divine Love on the buddhic plane (fire) was the element characterising the higher qualities through which the Self ruled the activities of the plane. The Self was undergoing but little experience, and external manifestation was almost absent. The involution of the higher qualities was the great purpose of the Self. The manifestation of the Self is symbolised by the illuminating radiation of the sun, and his functioning by the outpouring of rain (truth) on the buddhic plane (clouds).

The "red dragon" has the same meaning as the "great red dragon" of REV. xii, which seems to threaten the "woman" before she brings forth the "man-child." It stands for the relative in the manifest which always must include in some degree the opposites of goodness, love and truth.

The period indicated is the golden age of involution wherein the qualities are involved in matter and the World-soul in peacefulness and to the utmost perfection, so that when the One Soul becomes the many souls, each soul will contain within it as a microcosm the perfections of the One, the Macrocosm. Each soul is perfect potentially, and awaits the evolution of all that is within it, so that it may be perfect actually.

See ARC. MAN, BIRTH OF MAN-CHILD, BUDDHIC PLANE, CIVILISING, CLOUDS, CRIPPLES, DRAGON (red), DYNASTY, ELEMENTS, EVOLUTION, FIRE, FOOD, GOLDEN AGE, INVOLUTION, LIMBS, MACROCOSM, MANCO, MAYA (higher), MEMBERS, OANNES, OHONAMOCHI, RESPECTFUL MANNERS, ROBE, SUN, VISTASP, YEAR.

YASODHARA, WIFE OF BUDDHA :—

A symbol of the form-side of the manifest soul in involution.

" Then King Suddhodana sought for his son Buddha, from a family of un-blemished moral excellence, a bride possessed of beauty, modesty, and gentle bearing, of widespread glory, Yasodhara by name, having a name well worthy of her, a very goddess of good fortune."— *Buddha-Karita*, Bk. II.

This statement signifies the linking the Divine Self in the mind with the sense objects which are pure and natural after their own order. And for the purpose of furthering the mind's involution, the most seductive and alluring environment is sought. The " widespread glory " and the " name " signify the pleasure of the Self in realising itself through the kama-manasic nature. (The last sentence is merely a comparison indicating success.)

See BUDDHA, NAME, RAHULA, SUDDHODANA.

YATIS PEOPLE :—

A symbol of atma-buddhic qualities without external activity.

" Yatis ' ascetics ' are a people living on Mount Meru."—*Laws of Manu, S.B.E.*, p. 495.

See ASCETIC, MOUNTAIN.

YATUS OF EVIL WITCHCRAFT :—

A symbol of a mental quality of " black magic," an art which leads to death of such unbalanced states of soul.

See ARA, BLACK MAGICIANS.

YEAR OF TWELVE MONTHS :—

A symbol of the Cycle of manifestation which comprises the twelve stages through which growth is accomplished.

" The (visible) form of time is the year, consisting of twelve months, made up of Nimeshas (twinklings) and other measures."—*Mait. Brâh. Upanishad*, VI. 16, 14.

" For the thunderbolt is the year: the day is Agni, the night Soma, and what is between the two, that is Vishnu. Thus he makes the revolving year. . . . By that year, as a thunderbolt, the gods clove the strongholds and conquered these worlds.—*Sata. Brâh.*, III. 4, 4, 15-16.

The spiritual energy manifesting on the higher mental plane is the Life cycle itself. One period in the cycle is for the outgoing life (Agni), and another for the indrawing (night), when the lower self (Soma-moon) is active. The period between is purely spiritual (Vishnu). Thus the Supreme establishes the Cycle and its Life-waves. By that Cycle, as a means for the liberation of Divine energy, the higher qualities (gods) manifest their nature by destroying the strongholds of ignorance and evil, and overcoming the desire for the illusions of the lower planes.

See ABRAXAS, ÆONS (twelve), AGNI, ALPHA, DAY AND NIGHT, GODS, MAN-VANTARA, NIGHT (primor.), PRAGÂPATI, PRALAYA, RÂ, SEASONS (five), SOMA (moon), STRIDES, THUNDERBOLT, TIME, VISHNU, WORLDS, ZODIAC.

YEARS OF PATRIARCHAL LIFE :—

Symbolic of the limited continuance of specific mental states, or stages of development of the soul.

" God does not measure by time, but by the end to be accomplished in any given instance."—R. J. CAMPBELL, Serm., *God's Use of Time*.

See PATRIARCHS, STRIDES OF SOUL.

YEDUD :—

A symbol of spiritual perfection attained by the soul by means of its progress through the states of the lower nature.

" And in it (the *Neshamah* Soul) is perfected Yedud (Y H V H)."—MYER, *Qabbalah*, p. 398.

When the consciousness has risen to atma-buddhic levels, then humanity is perfected.

" The chief symbolism is drawn from the Sacred Name, being *Yod, He, Vau, He* = Jehovah. *Yod* is the Father, *He* is the Mother, and *Vau* the begotten Son."—A. E. WAITE, *Secret Doctrine*, p. 41.

See JEHOVAH, NESHAMAH, TETRA-GRAMMATON, TRIAD, TRINITY.

YE'HEEDAH :—

A symbol of the personality, the lower mind, or lower consciousness.

" Ye'heedah, the only one, is the *personality* of man."

" The *Rua'h* forms with the *Nephesh*, the actual personality of the man, which is called if he deserves Ye'heedah."— I. MYER, *Qabbalah*, pp. 391, 397.

The lower mind (Rua'h) with the desire-nature (Nephesh) form, with the ego, the personality (Ye'heedah).

See GOSHURUN, NEPHESH, PER-
SONALITY, RUAH.

YELLOW COLOUR :—

A symbol of kingship—supremacy
over the lower nature.

" Yellow is a good example of the fact
the student in colour symbolism must
by no means overlook, that a colour may
be employed either in a good or a bad
sense. . . . It is the colour of jealousy
and treason, and Judas is often represented in old glass painting in a yellow
robe. Where, however, it is represented
by gold, or is a substitute for it, it signifies love, constancy, dignity, wisdom."
—F. E. HULME, *Symbolism, etc.,* p. 20.

See COLOURS, GOLD, POISON
(yellow).

YELLOW EARS OF HORSE :—

Symbolic of the aspiring intelligence coming into play.
See HORSE (red).

YELLOW DRESS :—

A symbol of the buddhic vesture
of the soul—the " robe of fire "
assumed by the ego when liberated
from the lower nature.

" He who has cleansed himself from
sin is well grounded in all virtues, and
regards also temperance and truth, he
is indeed worthy of the yellow dress."—
Dhammapada, I. 10.

See ASRAMAS, ORDERS.

YESHTIHA MOMENTS :—

A symbol of eternal duration out
of time.

" He comes to the moments called
Yeshtiha, and they flee from him."—
Kaush. Upanishad, I. 2.

The soul passes beyond the eternal,
that is, withdrawn above the possibility
of manvantaric manifestation. Time
now retreats, as it were, and the soul
becomes merged in the Absolute.

See APARAGITA, DEVAYANA, ILYA,
SALAGYA, TIME.

YETZEERATIC WORLD, THE WORLD OF FORMATION :—

A symbol of the astral plane containing the type-forms of life which
appear as growths on the physical
plane directed by intelligence.

" It is testified that Scripture makes
use of the three expressions, ' to create,
to form, and to make,' in allusion to the
three worlds which are below the world
of emanation. It follows that the four
worlds are those of Emanation, Creation,

Formation and manifestation, Action,
the material universe, or, as it is called
by Rosenroth, *Mundus Factionis.* The
Hebrew equivalents are *Atziluth, Briah,
Yetzirah,* and *Assiah.* The union of
God and His Shekinah takes place in
Atziluth, the world of Emanation, where
there is no separateness."—A. E. WAITE,
Secret Doctrine in Israel, p. 30.

Creation is on the mental plane,
formation on the astral, and materia-
lisation on the physical. The four
worlds are the buddhic, mental, astral,
and physical planes, in the order of
the symbols given. It is on the
buddhic plane that the union of
Love and Wisdom takes place in the
soul (Yetzirah *equals* Yetzeeratic).

See ASEEYATIC WORLD, ASTRAL
PLANE, ATZEELOOTH, BREEATIC
WORLD, BUDDHIC PLANE, QUATERN-
ARY, SIMILITUDES, SHEKINAH,
WORLDS (five),

YGGDRASIL, GREAT ASH TREE :—

A symbol of the Divine Life extending through all planes of manifestation.

" In the centre of Midgard stands the
great ash Yggdrasil. All life is cherished
by it, even that of serpents which devour
its roots and seek to destroy it. It has
three grand roots. One strikes down to
Niflheim, and into the fountain Hvergelmer, where Nidhogg, with all its
reptile brood, gnaw at its roots. A
second root penetrates to the regions of
the Rimthursar. The third root runs
into the region of the Asar or Gods.
Beneath it is the Urdar, or primeval
fountain. . . . On the topmost bough of
Yggdrasil sits an eagle, and between the
eagle's eyes a hawk. A squirrel runs
up and down the stem, and four stags
leap about beneath it, and feed on its
buds " (*Prose Edda*).—HOWITT, *Literature
of North. Europe,* Vol. I. p. 45.

The Ray from the Supreme, or the
Tree of Life, centres, as it were, on
the mental plane (Midgard). From
it proceeds the life of all things,
even of the desires which antagonise
it. It has three great currents of
energy. One current passes downwards to the lower nature (Niflheim),
and to the fount of illusion—the
astral plane of the desires (serpents).
A second current flows to the plane
of the primal mental qualities (Rimthursar). The third current outpours
on the atma-buddhic planes, whereon
is the fountain of Truth. The height
of attainment for the soul is atma-

buddhi (hawk-eagle). The consciousness passes, as it were, up and down
the Divine Ray ; and the four soul-
bodies are active on their respective
planes, and subsist on the life forces
which evolve as experiences.

"The three Norns have a certain
analogy to the three mythic Persian
destinies seated by the fountain of perennial life ; and the tree (Yggdrasil) itself
is evidently a symbol of that inscrutable
Power which is the life of all things.—
H. E. BARLOW, *Essays on Symbolism*, p. 87.

"Ling supposes Yggdrasil to be the
symbol both of universal and human
life, and its three roots to signify the
physical, the intellectual, and the moral
principles. Other writers cited by Finn
Magnusen take these roots to have been
meant for matter, organisation, and
spirit, and the Ash itself for the symbol
of universal, primordial vitality."—
MALLET, *North. Antiq.*, p. 493.

See ASAR, ASTRAL, FIG-TREE, GODS,
HVERGELMER, MIDGARD, NIDHOGG,
NIFLHEIM, NORNOR, OAK, RIMTHUR-
SAR, SERPENT, SYCAMORE, TREE OF
LIFE, URDAR.

Yî SYSTEM :—

A symbol of the Cycle of Life in
which the Soul, or causal-body, is
formed for the experience and individualisation of the monads of life,
or spiritual egos (sages).

"In the system of the Yî there is the
Grand Terminus, which produced the two
elementary Forms. Those two Forms
produced the Four emblematic Symbols,
which again produced the eight trigrams.
The eight trigrams served to determine
the good and evil issues of events, and
from this determination was produced
the successful prosecution of the great
business of life."—*Yî King*, App. III.
1, 11, 70–71.

At the commencement of the Cycle
of Life, the Absolute emanated the
dual principles, Spirit and Matter.
These two principles produced the
Four planes of manifestation below
Atma, which introduce the duality of
opposites, higher and lower. The
eight opposite conditions are for the
recognition of the mind in determining
the good and evil issues of actions, for
it is through choice exercised that the
growth of the souls is accomplished as
they progress through the cycle.

"The Yî was made on a principle of
accordance with heaven and earth, and
shows us therefore, without rent or
confusion, the course of things in heaven
and earth. The Sage, in accordance
with the Yî, looking up, contemplates
the brilliant phenomena of the heavens,
and looking down, examines the definite
arrangements of the earth ; thus he
knows the causes of darkness or what
is obscure, and light or what is bright.
He traces things to their beginning, and
follows them to their end ; thus he
knows what can be said about death
and life. He perceives how the union
of essence and breath forms things, and
the disappearance or wandering away
of the soul produces the change of their
constitution ; thus he knows the characteristics of the anima and animus."—
Yi King, App. III Ch. IV. § 1, 20, 21.

This refers to the archetypal universe on the higher planes, and its
reflection on the lower. The former
is perfect ; the latter imperfect
because not fully evolved.

The Life Cycle was established in
relation with both the higher nature
and the lower, and therefore becomes
the orderer and interpreter of the
operations and course of events in
the upper world (heaven) and the
underworld (earth). The Self (Sage)
seated in the higher mind, and
regarding the planes above, observes
the perfection of the archetypal order
of things, and looking below perceives
the partial and distorted reproduction
on the lower planes. Thus he is
aware of the causes of ignorance and
illusion, and their relation to knowledge and truth. He traces the phenomena of nature to their beginning,
and follows them out to their ending ;
thus he comprehends the meaning of
death and of life. He perceives how
the union of spiritual quality and
mentality produce forms of life, and
the disappearance from manifestation,
and the wandering again to re-incarnation of the soul, produce development of constitution of the souls of
humanity. Thus he knows the essential qualities of the phenomenal life,
and the spirit or soul within that life.

See CAUSAL-BODY, CIRCLE (existence),
COSMOS, CREATION, EXPERIENCE,
KHIEN, KHWAN, OCEAN, OPPOSITES,
PILGRIM, PROTOTYPES, QUATERNARY,
WANDERER, YANG.

YIMA-KHSHAÊTA (JAMSHED) :—

A symbol of the Higher Self or
Divine Ego.

"A son was born to Vivanhâo, Yima-
khshaêta, who had abundance of flocks,

the most glorious of those born; the most sun-like of men; that he made during his reign over the earth; men and cattle free from death; water and trees free from drought, and they were eating inexhaustible food."—*Homa Yasht.*

There proceeded from the Absolute, the Self who was formed from the interplay of those forces or Divine attributes which were inherent in the Monad of Life. The "abundance of flocks" signifies the qualities of the soul—those celestial qualities which enable the ego to aspire. The "sun-like of men" is symbolical of self-command, dignity and power, which subdue and conquer the lower nature (earth). The symbol "men and cattle free from death" implies that the soul-qualities persist through time and are preludes to the eternity of the existence of the soul. "Water" signifies truth, and "trees" are here the symbol of Divine intelligence. The "freedom from drought" is a symbol of the nourishing of the mind through pure truth. The "inexhaustible food" is the sustenance of wisdom and love which comes from the higher planes. This "happy reign of Yima" refers to the Golden Age of Involution, during which the "opposites" did not exist as activities.

See CATTLE (cows), DROUGHT, FOOD, GOLDEN AGE, JOB, MONAD, PONIARD, SHEEP, SUN-LIKE, VIVANHÂO, WATER.

YMER, THE GIANT :—

A symbol of the Archetypal Man, the consummation of the process of involution.

"From the twelve rivers of Niflheim which flow from the fountain Hvergelmer, and are called Elivogar, meantime were dropping the poison-drops into the abyss of Ginunga, which froze into rime-frost, blown by the winds and rain from the north, and then melted by the heat from Muspelheim in the south, and shaped itself into the giant Ymer. While he slept there grew under his right hand a man and woman, and from his feet a giant with six heads. From these singular developments proceed not mankind, but the Rimthursar, or Giants of the Frost" (*Prose Edda*).—HOWITT, *Literature of North. Europe*, Vol. I. p. 40.

From the twelve stages of the cycle of manifesting life on the lower planes (Niflheim), which proceed from relativity or illusion (Hvergelmer), the inverted reflection of the higher,

there came the astro-physical functionings (poison-drops), which being perfected in involution disappear, as it were, below (abyss), to appear above on the mental plane, and be transmuted to the buddhic (Muspelheim), and so complete externally the Archetypal Man (Ymer) in potentiality. Then in preparation for evolution there were formed the renewed planes of higher-manas (man) and buddhi (woman), and beneath these, the lower-mental, astral, and physical planes, each dual in manifestation (six-headed giant). The "heads" refer to the mental plane, the plane of origin and of the lower consciousness. After the planes are formed, then the primal powers and qualities (Rimthursar) begin to operate upon their own plane.

"Odin and his brothers Vili and Ve, having commenced their reign, killed the giant Ymer, and made the world of him. Of his flesh they made the land, of his blood the sea, trees of his hair, the heaven of his skull; of his eyebrows made they Midgard for the sons of men, and of his brains the clouds."—*Ibid.*

The Divine Will, Wisdom and Action in the new cycle, now evolve from the potential (Ymer) the actual. And so the lower nature (flesh—land) of the soul (world) is formed, with its life of desire (blood—sea), its aspirations (trees—hair), its higher nature (heaven—skull), its mental-nature (eyebrows—Midgard) for the egos, and its buddhic nature (brains—clouds).

See ABRAXAS, ARC. MAN, ASKR, AUDUMBLA, BRAINS, BUR, CLOUDS, CRANIUM, DEATH OF OSIRIS, DIONYSUS, DISMEMBERMENT, DWARFS, FROST, GINUNGA, MEMBERS, MIDGARD, MUSPELLHEIM, NIFLHEIM, NORTH, ODIN, POISON, PRAGÂPATI (relaxed), PURUSHA, RIMTHURSAR, SOUTH, ZAGREUS, ZODIAC.

YOKE OF JESUS :—

A symbol of the cheerful bearing of the troubles of life, through love of goodness and truth.

"Come unto me all ye that labour and are heavy laden, and I will give you rest. Take my yoke upon you, and learn of me; for I am meek and lowly in heart: and ye shall find rest for your souls. For my yoke is easy, and my burden is light."—MAT. xi. 28–30.

The invitation of the Spirit is to those who are oppressed with the cares of life, and full of worldly aims. The Christ points out the advantage of resting the mind upon the ideal which is above the lower ambitions and affections. The " taking of the yoke, etc.," signifies the joyful acceptance of the ideals of righteousness and truth—*burdens*, as the lower nature would regard them —which has the moral effect of transforming life with its environment into a joyous playground rather than a penitentiary.

" For this is the love of God, that we keep his commandments : and his commandments are not grievous."— 1 JOHN v. 3.

" ' To Buddha will I look in faith : he, the Exalted, is the holy, supreme Buddha, the knowing, the instructed, the blessed, who knows the worlds, the Supreme One, who yoketh men like an ox, the Teacher of gods and men, the Exalted Buddha.' "—H. OLDENBERG, *Buddha*, p. 339.

The Self within (Buddha) draws the mental qualities (men) and the ideals (gods) to himself by the bonds of love (yoke).

" For what heavy yoke does He put upon our mind's neck, who bids us shun every desire that causes disquietude ? What heavy burden does He lay upon His followers, who warns us to decline the wearisome ways of the world ? "

" The Lord beheld this heavy yoke of slavery set hard on the necks of worldly men—a weight of heavy bondage to be subject to temporal concerns, to court the things of earth, to retain things which are gliding away, to wish to stand in things which stand not, to seek after passing objects, but yet be unwilling to pass away with what is passing. . . . But the bands of each one are loosed, when by Divine help the inward bonds of carnal desire are burst asunder."—ST. GREGORY THE GREAT, *Morals on the Book of Job*, Vol. I. p. 132 ; Vol. III. p. 399.

" ' This restful labouring,' said Walter Hilton, ' is full far from fleshly idleness and from blind security. It is full of spiritual working, but it is called rest, for that grace looseth the heavy yoke of fleshly love from the soul and maketh it mighty and free through the gift of spiritual love to work gladly, softly, and delectably.' "—E. UNDERHILL, *Mysticism*, p. 60.

See HEART, JESUS, LABOURERS, LAW OF ZOROASTER, POOR IN SPIRIT, RICH MAN, RICHES (lower), SERMON, WORK.

YOMI (DARKNESS), LAND OF, OR BOTTOM COUNTRY :—

A symbol of the lower quaternary, or underworld.

" Yomi is spoken of as the abode of Susa-no-wo, who, according to one myth, was appointed to rule this region. We also hear of the deities of Yomi, the armies of Yomi, the ugly females of Yomi, and the Road-wardens of Yomi." —W. G. ASTON, *Shinto*, p. 54.

The lower planes constitute the realm over which the desire-nature (Susa-no-wo) presides. The " deities and armies of Yomi " are the desires, the " ugly females " are the lower emotions or passions, and the " Road-wardens " are aspirations on the upward path, or moral regulations in the lower mind to " make straight the way of the Lord."

See COMB, CUPID, DARKNESS (lower), PEACHES, QUATERNARY, SUSA-NO-WO, TARTARUS, WOMEN'S LIFE.

YOUNG MAN :—

A symbol of an immature mind, a state of prejudice or mental inaction.

See ADAH, BOY, DWARF, MAN (natural).

YUDHI-SHTHIRA, SON OF DHARMA (*MASC.*) AND PRITHA (*FEM.*) :—

A symbol of the spiritual mind produced by virtuous efforts (dharma) and the purified emotion-nature (pritha).

" Yudhi-shthira was born first, and at the moment of his birth a heavenly voice was heard to utter these words : ' This is the most virtuous of men.' "—MON. WILLIAMS, *Indian Wisdom*, p. 380.

The spiritual mind—atma-buddhi-manas—was first to manifest on the higher mental plane as creative energy of the Logos proceeding on a scheme of truth and righteousness.

See ARJUNA, CHRYSE, OSIRIS, PANDAVAS, PRIEST, POURUSHASPA, PRITHA.

ZACCHEUS, A CHIEF PUBLICAN :—

A symbol of the soul exercised about the things of this world, but actuated by better motives in regard thereunto than is ordinary.

" And he (Zaccheus) sought to see Jesus who he was ; and he could not for the crowd, because he was little of stature. And he ran on before, and climbed up into a sycamore tree to see him."—LUKE xix. 3, 4.

The well-intentioned mind desired to raise an ideal, and, as it were, to catch a glimpse of the " King in his beauty " (the Self), but is too much entangled with the cares of this world and the deceitfulness of desires to be able to do so, except by adopting the expedient of " climbing up a tree," that is of getting a view in advance of the means whereby progress could be accomplished. This " bird's-eye " view corresponds with an intuition of a condition beyond the state actually arrived at. It therefore answers to an aspiration of the subjective mind upon the deva-chanic plane, which had not yet been realised in the world of effects. " Zaccheus " is one " little of stature," that is to say, a soul not up till now raised beyond a certain point or degree of development : yet one who shall surely rise eventually and claim his inheritance. The " crowd " signi-fies the lower mental qualities which obscure the view of that which is higher.

" Zaccheus being small of stature, ascended a sycamore, and saw the Lord, because they who humbly choose the foolishness of the world, do themselves minutely contemplate the wisdom of God. For the crowd hinders smallness of stature from beholding the Lord, because the tumult of worldly cares keeps the infirmity of the human mind from looking at the light of truth."—ST. GREGORY, Morals on the Book of Job, Vol. III. p. 259.

See CROWD, DEVACHAN, NICODEMUS, RICHES (lower), SYCAMORE, TREASURE.

ZACHARIAS, THE PRIEST :—

A symbol of the subjective spiritual mind of a period of the soul's evolution.

" But the angel said unto him, Fear not, Zacharias : because thy supplication is heard, and thy wife Elisabeth shall bear thee a son, and thou shalt call his name John. And thou shalt have joy and gladness ; and many shall rejoice at his birth. For he shall be great in the sight of the Lord."—LUKE i. 13–15.

Then the messenger of the Spirit within reassured the spiritual mind in response to its aspirations, and so it had an intuitive perception of the new truth which was to spring from the two parents. For the spiritual

mind and the higher emotion-nature are now to give rise to the moral nature (John). And this will cause the spiritual nature to be re-inforced and raised, and many qualities shall be made better at its advent. For the moral nature shall be a great influence in the soul for goodness and truth.

See CHRIST INCREASES, CONCEPTION, HILL COUNTRY, JOHN BAPTIST.

ZAGREUS, THE MYSTIC DIONYSUS :—

A symbol of the involved Higher Self, or Archetypal Man.

" The myth which took a central position in the Orphics' creed is known as the legend of Dionysus Zagreus. As the son of Zeus and Persephone, Dionysus was still a child when his heavenly father entrusted him with the empire of the world. He was persecuted by the Titans, who had formerly been worsted in their struggle with Uranus. The divine boy escaped from their wily attacks in divers shapes and forms, till he was finally caught by them in the form of a bull, whom they tore to pieces and devoured. His heart alone was rescued by Athene, and Zeus presently swallowed it in order to create from it ' the new Dionysus.' To punish the Titans for their crime, Zeus struck them with his thunderbolt. Out of their ashes rose the race of mankind whose nature contained both elements—the Titanic and the Dionysic springing from the blood of Zagreus. The Titans are the embodiment of the principle of evil, Dionysus of the principle of good, and in their fusion were contained the seeds of that conflict between the godlike and the ungodlike which occurs but too frequently in the human breast."— T. GOMPERZ, Greek Thinkers, Vol. I. p. 128.

The buddhic emotion-nature (Perse-phone) fructified by the Supreme Spirit (Zeus) brought forth the Soul or Self on the buddhic plane to be the ruler of the lower nature. The Self being subjected to the primal laws and conditions of manifestation (the Titans) which ruled and limited him on every side, passed through the various stages of involution until he was perfected as the matrix of all forms and qualities (the bull). The primal laws then brought about his death and dismemberment of qualities, in preparation for the new cycle, that of evolution. Then intervened between the two cycles a period of rest and withdrawal of life, when the primal conditions were unapparent (Titans destroyed). " Zeus swallowing the heart " signifies that the inner life of the Spirit on the buddhic plane (Athene) was preserved within the Soul to manifest subsequently as the incarnate Self (the new Dionysus) in the souls of humanity. Through the potential conditions of nature (ashes of Titans) were then gradually evolved the astral, physical, and mental bodies of the races of mankind. The human being is made up of both natural and spiritual elements ; the spiritual springing from the life (blood) of the incarnate Self within. The natural or lower qualities (Titans) attract outwardly and so become the antagonists of the spiritual which attract inwardly.

" The stainless, indivisible Self is in that last bright sheath, the heart : it is the pure light of lights that they that know the Self know."—*Mundaka Upanishad*, II. 2.

See ARC. MAN, BULL (pri.), DEATH OF OSIRIS, DIONYSUS, DISMEMBERMENT, HEART, LIMBS, MEMBERS, PERSEPHONE, PRAGÂPATI (relaxed), PURUSHA, RHEA, TITANS, URANUS, YMER, ZEUS.

ZAIRIMYANGURA (TORTOISE) :—

A symbol of the lower desire will.

" The daêva Zairimyangura is an evil creature that destroys from midnight to dawn thousands of creatures of the good Spirit."—*Vendidad*, XIII.

This signifies the opposite of the true will, that is, the negative will which has no discrimination, and allows the higher impulses to pass unrecognised.

See CREATURES (small), DAEVAS, TORTOISE.

ZAMA, ZAMA, OZZA, RACHAMA, OZAI—FIVE WORDS ON THE VESTURE OF JESUS :—

Symbolic of the perfectly expressed personality in which is found— Faith, Peace, Love, Wisdom, Power.

" The interpretation. The mystery which is beyond the world, that whereby all things exist. It is all evolution and all involution."—*Pistis Sophia*.

The perfect expression of the highest qualities is the object of existence and the outcome of involution and evolution.

ZAREMAYA OIL :—

A symbol of love and gladness— the food of the Spirit which satisfies the mind that is growing in grace, i.e. learning to depend on the higher nature.

See AMBROSIA, FOOD, OIL.

ZENITH OF THE SKY :—

A symbol of the buddhic consciousness in which the evolving Self attains the summit of its powers.

See AUSHEDAR, COME, POOL (zenith), SKY, SUN-MOTIONLESS, WHEAT AND BARLEY.

ZERÂNA-AKERANA :—

A symbol of the Absolute, the Eternal unmanifest Being, the Emanator of the Universe.

" In the beginning, the Eternal or Absolute Being, Zerâna-Akerana, produced two beings : Ahura-Mazda (King of Light) and Ahriman (King of Darkness). The two became antagonists." —*Zoroastrian System*.

The Absolute at the emanation of the Universe creates the dual aspects under which manifestation proceeds. These are Spirit and Matter, God and Devil ; that which gives form and quality, and that which receives form and quality ; that which energises, or is positive, and that which is acted upon and used, or is negative. Truth (light) and Ignorance (darkness) become antagonists.

See ABSOLUTE, AHRIMAN, AHURA, AIN SOPH, DARKNESS, DEVIL, FATHER, FRAVASHI, GODHEAD, MATTER, SPIRIT.

ZETES AND CALAIS, THE WINGED SONS OF BOREAS :—

Symbols of the will and mind, begotten of the higher mind. They are said to fly through the " air," a symbol of the mental plane.

" The table was spread for Phineus : the Harpies instantly descended on and seized the victuals. Zetes and Calais, the winged sons of Boreas, drew their swords and pursued them through the air."—*Argonautic Expedition*.

When the higher qualities (Argonauts) have undertaken to deliver the ego's mental discrimination (Phineus) from the astral ensnarements of desire and sense (Harpies), opportunities are offered for the soul's exercise, and the sense-nature (Harpies) rushes forth to accomplish its purpose and so appropriate knowledge (food) to itself for its own ends. Then it is that the will (Zetes) and the mind (Calais) are brought into play on behalf of the ego ; the result being that they are said to pursue the senses on the plane of manas (air)—the great creator of illusion—wherein the senses are dangerous and deceitful.

See ARGONAUTS, BOREAS, HARPIES, NICOTHEA, OCYPETE, PHINEUS.

ZEUS, SON OF CRONUS :—

A symbol of the Higher Self ; begotten of Time (Cronus) and Space (Rhea).

" Zeus is called the father of gods and men, the most high and powerful among the immortals, whom all others obey."—*Smith's Class. Dict.*

" Hesiod calls Zeus the son of Cronos and Rhea, and the brother of Hestia, Demeter, Hera, Hades, and Poseidon. Cronos swallowed his children immediately after their birth, but when Rhea was pregnant with Zeus, she applied to Uranus and Ge to save the life of the child. Uranus and Ge therefore sent Rhea to Lyctos in Crete, requesting her to bring up her child there. Rhea accordingly concealed Zeus in a cave of Mount Ægaeon, and gave to Cronos a stone wrapped up in cloth, which he swallowed. . . . Zeus grew up in Crete. In the meantime Cronos, by a cunning device of Ge or Metis, was made to bring up the children he had swallowed, and first of all the stone, which was afterwards set up by Zeus at Delphi."—*Smith's Class. Dict.*

This strange story which has puzzled scholars for 2,000 years is simply a concise symbolic sketch of part of the world-process and the birth of the Soul. The six children of Time (Cronos) and Space (Rhea) are fundamental principles—planes of manifestation, i.e. physical (Hestia), astral (Hades), buddhic functioning below (Demeter), buddhic above (Hera), atma (Zeus), and Truth-reality (Poseidon) the manifesting principle. On their emanation, these principles are utilised or conditioned by Time in the world-process of *involution* of qualities, and are afterwards given forth (disgorged) to become active in the subsequent process of *evolution*. The atman (Zeus) principle being above the lower manifestation, cannot be conditioned by Time (swallowed by Cronos), so there is, as it were, substituted the implanting of the latent atman, the Spirit (stone) in vestures of the planes (wrapped in swathes) ; this is the Soul conditioned by Time and to be developed by the involutionary process. It is the first to appear in the evolutionary process as the perfect pattern (Archetypal Man) of the many souls. The " setting up at Delphi " signifies the establishment of the causal-body in the sanctuary of the higher mind. Spirit and Matter (Uranus and Ge) bring about the true birth of the Self (Zeus) on the higher buddhic plane in a state of perfect peace (Crete) apart from Time. The Self is brought up in the innermost soul (cave), being conditioned by the higher nature (mountain).

" The stone swallowed by Cronus is none other than the ' Philosopher's stone,' the ' Concealed Stone of many colours ' (*Golden Treatise*), ' the mystic seed ' of transcendental life which should invade, tinge, and wholly transmute the imperfect self into spiritual gold."—E. UNDERHILL, *Mysticism*, p. 170.

The " concealed stone of many colours " signifies the indwelling Spirit of many qualities.

" We are, so to speak, a portion of the Eternal Divine Substance, detached from its source (or feeling itself to be such), wrapped up in matter and put to sleep, rendered unconscious of its glorious origin, limited in a thousand ways, and then bidden to evolve towards that from which it came."—R. J. CAMPBELL, Serm., *Our Eternal Glory.*

" The Highest Truth, the Truth of God's being and action revealed to the finite thought of man, is necessarily mysterious. It comes to us as we can bear it, shrouded beneath symbols and encased in formulæ. These are the swaddling-clothes of the Everlasting."—H. P. LIDDON, *University Sermons*, p. 202.

See ARC. MAN, ATMAN, CAVE, COLOURS, CRETE, CRONUS, CURETES, DIONYSUS, EVOLUTION, GE, HEAVEN AND EARTH, HEPHAISTOS, INVOLUTION, KRONOS, LIGHTNING, METIS, NAVEL, PALACE, RHEA, STONE, THUNDER, TIME, TITANS, TLALOC, URANUS, VESTURES, ZAGREUS.

ZILLAH, WIFE OF LAMECH :—

A symbol of wisdom or practice, associated with reflection (Lamech).

See ADAH, LAMECH.

ZION OF THE HOLY ONE OF ISRAEL :—

A symbol of the causal-body, the seat of the Higher Self, the leader of the chosen qualities (Israel).

" And the ransomed of the Lord shall return, and come with singing unto Zion ; and everlasting joy shall be upon their heads : they shall obtain gladness and joy, and sorrow and sighing shall flee away."—ISA. xxxv. 10.

The qualities which have traversed the " way of holiness " are transmuted (ransomed) and perfected, and thereby raised to the higher mind plane on which is the " holy city," the causal-body wherein is everlasting joy to crown the qualities which are now above all sorrow and suffering.

" Zion is the living soul, ' where the Lord visiteth.' "—JOHN WARD, Zion's Works, Vol. VII. p. 158.

See CAUSAL-BODY, ISRAELITES, JERU-SALEM, JESHURUN, PRAISE OF GOD, RANSOM, STONE (corner).

ZODIAC OF TWELVE SIGNS :—

A symbol of the Cycle of Life through which the Soul's development is accomplished. The Soul, or indwelling Self (sun), proceeds in a spiral course, whose cyclic progression is in twelve stages corresponding to the twelve signs. These stages are related to human life inasmuch as they each answer to certain parts of the Archetypal Man, and each part has its stage of development in relation to the whole, and every department of human experience is expressed in them.

" In the Soul is the spiritual circle or Zodiac, wherein is fulfilled what the twelve signs represent in the natural Zodiacal system of the Universe or Macrocosm." — JOHN WARD, Zion's Works, Vol. II. p. 238.

" When he prepared the heavens I was there : when he set a circle upon the face of the depth."—PROV. viii. 27.

The Higher Self came forth on the upper buddhic plane (Aries), and the Cycle of Life was described in the mentality of the lower nature.

" Thou, Pragâpati, dividest thy person in twelve parts, and thou becomest the Twelve Adityas."—Vana Parva, v. 189.

The Archetypal Man as the " year " or Zodiac is dismembered in twelve parts, related to the twelve stages of the Cycle of Life.

" Zoroaster, Plato says, having been placed on the funeral pyre, rose again to life in twelve days. He alludes perchance to the resurrection, or perchance to the fact that the path for souls to ascension lies through the twelve signs of the zodiac ; and he himself says that the descending pathway to birth is the same, . . . after which the soul obtains release from this entire world."—CLEMENT OF ALEX., Miscellanies, Bk. V.

The Soul (Zoroaster) descends to the lower planes for experience and purification (funeral pyre), afterwards it ascends in the resurrection, and is liberated from the lower nature.

" Theologians admitted therefore two gates (between heaven and earth), Cancer and Capricorn, and Plato also meant these by what he calls the two mouths. Of these they affirm that Cancer is the gate through which souls descend, but Capricorn that through which they ascend [and exchange a material for a divine condition of being] " (Porphyrius).—MAX MÜLLER, Theosophy, etc., p. 144.

Cancer corresponds to the lower mind plane on the side of involution, that is, where the Soul descends into the lower nature ; while on the side of evolution, Capricorn corresponds to the higher mind plane, that is, where the souls of humanity ascend from the lower nature and put on immortality.

" The Indian Capricorn is an elephant emerging from a makara, or leviathan." —A. LILLIE, Budd. in Christendom, p. 7.

This signifies wisdom (the soul) emerging from the cycle of the lower nature (leviathan).

" Owing to the complex and manifold nature of existence, every sphere or plane of man's being requires for itself a redemptive process ; and, for each, this process consists of three degrees. Of these the first three relate to the Body, the second three to the Mind, the third three to the Heart, and the fourth three to the Spirit. There are thus, in all, twelve Degrees or ' Houses ' of the Perfect Man or Microcosm, as there are twelve Zodiacal Signs or Mansions of the Sun in his course through the heavens of the Macrocosm. And the Gospels set forth mainly the six of the Heart and Spirit. The crown both of the twelve degrees and of the six acts— that which constitutes alike the ' Sabbath ' of the Hebrews, the ' Nirvana ' of the Buddhists, and the ' Transmutation ' of the Alchemists—is the ' Divine Marriage.' "—The Perfect Way, p. 245.

The " Body " must be taken to mean the astral body of desire ; the " Mind," the mental-body ; and the " Heart " the causal-body, the " shrine of the Spirit of the man " *(ibid.,* p. 246). The "Perfect Man" is the Archetypal Man.

See ABRAXAS, ADAMAS, ADITYAS (twelve), ÆONS (twelve), APOSTLES, ARC. MAN, ARIES, CANCER, CAPRICORN, CELESTIAL STEMS, COMPARTMENTS, DECANS, ELEPHANT, EQUINOX, EVOLUTION, HORSE SACRIFICE, HOUR, IABRAOTH, INVOLUTION, LEVIATHAN, MACROCOSM, MANVANTARA, NIDĀNAS, PISCES, PRAGÂPATI, RĀ, SAMSARA, SEVENTH, SUN, TAURUS, TIME, TRIBES, TUAT, TWELVE, VIRGO, WHEEL OF LIFE, YEAR, YMER.

ZOROASTER, ZARATHUSTRA, OR ZARTUST :—

A symbol of the Soul or the Son of the Supreme ;—the Higher Self descending to incarnation on the lower planes in the period of involution, and ascending in human souls in the present period of evolution.

"Zoroaster's fitness for the prophetic mission which he is to undertake is divinely recognised, and Ahura Mazda selects him as his own messenger to the world" (*Avesta*).—A. V. W. JACKSON, *Zoroaster*, p. 27.

The Higher Self, in becoming involved in the lower nature, discerns the destiny which awaits him as victor over the lower principle, under the sub-cycles of evolution and re-birth. The Logos emanates or appoints His only begotten Son as His special interpreter of Himself to the lower self or consciousness.

"The archangel Asha replied to Ahura Mazda that there was only one man who had heard the orders issued by the council, viz. Zoroaster, he therefore was to be endowed with eloquence to bring their messages to the world" (*Yasna*, xxix).—M. HAUG, *Essays, etc.*, p. 148.

The messenger (Asha) of the Most High, which is a flash of intuition arrived at in the awakening mind, asserts that there is only One Intelligence who knows the Divine Law and Scheme, and he is the Son of the Supreme Himself. He it is who must be endowed with the means of expression on the planes ; that is, have the actual graces and virtues whereby that which has hitherto been potential shall manifest and fulfil itself below.

"Creator of the settlements supplied with creatures ; Who is their heavenly lord and earthly master ?—Then said Ahuru Mazda : Urvatad-narô, and thou who art Zarathustra."—*Vendidad*, II. end.

The question is now asked of Divine Wisdom,—Who is the creator of the lower nature and its activities ? The answer is given, that it is the desire-mental principle (Urvatad-narô), and also the Soul (Zoroaster) itself which collects through the interactions of mind and desire, all the experiences which are woven into the nature of the evolving Self. The advent of the Soul into the lower nature is a signal and an effective means for an entire reconstitution of the planes upon which its evolution is to be carried on and consummated.

"Plato (*Alcibiades*, I. 37) says the same as Agathias, calling Zoroaster a son of Ormazdes, i.e. Ahuramazda, Hormazd."—HAUG, *Essays*, p. 11.

Zoroaster is described as supernatural, the Son of God, the same as Jesus the Christ-soul.

Eckhart observes that—

"Between the Soul and the only-begotten Son there is no distinction ; for what the Son reveals to us is just this, that we are the same Son."—PFLEIDERER, *Phil. of Religion*, p. 4.

"When he (the Soul) shall have crossed over as the image to its Archetype, then he will have reached his journey's end."—PLOTINUS, *Enneads*, VI. 11.

"In the Vendidad and the Yashts Zoroaster is represented to us not as an historical, but as a dogmatical personality, stripped of nearly everything that is peculiar to human nature, and vested with a supernatural and wholly divine power, standing next to God himself and being even elevated above the archangels. The temptations of the devil, whose whole empire was threatened by the great Prophet, form a favourite subject of the traditional reports and legends. He was the concentration of all wisdom and truth, and the master and head of the whole living creation."—M. HAUG, *Essays, etc.*, p. 295.

The contention that Zoroaster was a man who trod the earth at some ancient date, is utterly inconsistent with what is said of him in the sacred books ; while the symbolic interpretation of the "prophet" harmonises completely with the inspired utterances.

See AHURA, ARC. MAN, ASHAVAHIST, AURVAITI, BIRTH OF ZOROASTER, CREATURES, EVOLUTION, EXPERIENCES, FORENOON, FRAVASHI, HOMA-TREE, HYMNS, INVOLUTION, MAGIC PRACTICES, OX, POURUSHASPA, REBIRTH, SETTLEMENTS, SON OF GOD, SOUL, URVATAD, VAHISTO, VISTASP, WALKING WITH GOD.

THE LIFE-CYCLE OF TWELVE STAGES

CELESTIAL-PLANE.

Involution.   Evolution.

ARIES   Wisdom and Love.   **PISCES**

Eden.   SPIRITUAL-PLANE.   Heaven.

TAURUS   Higher Emotions.   **AQUARIUS**

Individuality.

GEMINI   Higher Consciousness.   **CAPRICORN**

The Fall.   MENTAL-PLANE.   The Rise.

CANCER   Lower Consciousness.   **SAGITTARIUS**

Personality.

LEO   Lower Emotions.   **SCORPIO**

Hades.   ASTRAL-PLANE.   (Present stage of human evolution.)

VIRGO   Passions and Instincts.   **LIBRA**

Descent   PHYSICAL-PLANE   Ascent
into Matter.   from Matter.

SIX STAGES OF INVOLUTION.   SIX STAGES OF EVOLUTION.

The cyclic Path of the Higher Self (Sun).

THE ZODIAC OR GREAT CYCLE OF LIFE.

APPENDIX

PSYCHO-ANALYSIS AND THE SCRIPTURES

MYTHS and Scriptures bear a close resemblance to dreams, as comparison between them will show.

"Some dreams are very short; others are peculiarly rich in content, enact entire romances and seem to last a very long time. There are dreams as distinct as actual experiences, so distinct that for some time after waking we do not realise that they were dreams at all; others, which are ineffably faint, shadowy and blurred: in one and the same dream, even, there may be some parts of extraordinary vividness alternating with others so indistinct as to be almost wholly elusive. Again, dreams may be quite consistent or at any rate coherent, or even witty or fantastically beautiful; others again are confused, apparently imbecile, absurd or mad."

S. Freud, *Lectures on Psycho-analysis*, p. 73.

"Some Scriptures are very short, others are peculiarly rich in content, enact entire romances (*Esther*) and seem to last a very long time (*Pentateuch*). There are Scriptures as distinct as actual experiences, and therefore are mistaken for history (*Gospels*); others which are faint, shadowy and blurred (*Psalms*). In one and the same Scripture there may be some parts of extraordinary vividness alternating with others so indistinct as to be almost wholly elusive (*Isaiah*). Again, Scriptures may be quite consistent or at any rate coherent (*Kings*), or even witty or fantastically beautiful (*Job*); others again are confused, apparently imbecile, absurd or mad (*Daniel, Revelation*)."

Compared by present writer with Freud's statement.

"The dream as a whole is the distorted substitute for something else, something unconscious, and the task of dream interpretation is to discover these unconscious thoughts."—*Ibid.* 95.

Similarly, the Scripture as a whole is the distorted substitute for an underlying meaning, and the task of Scripture interpretation is to discover these sub-conscious thoughts which are expressed in symbolism.

Freud formulates three rules of interpretation, the first of which reads:—

"We are not to trouble about the surface-meaning of the dream, whether it be reasonable or absurd, clear or confused; in no case does it constitute the unconscious thoughts we are seeking."—*Ibid.*

Similarly, the surface-meaning of a Scripture is negligible whether reasonable or absurd, clear or confused; in no case does it constitute the undermeaning we are seeking.

With regard to a degree of ambiguity in the appreciation of meanings in the Sacred Language, this cannot be held to negative the language itself, but only to imply difficulty of comprehension until mastery is attained by close study of the Scriptures of all nations.

Freud points out : " In ancient systems of expression, for instance in the scripts of the oldest languages, indefiniteness of various kinds is found with a frequency which we should not tolerate in our writings to-day. Thus in many Semitic writings only the consonants of the words appear : the omitted vowels have to be supplied by the reader from his knowledge and from the context. Hieroglyphic writing follows a similar principle, although not exactly the same. The most confusing feature in hieroglyphic script is that there is no spacing between the words. . . . Chinese is so full of uncertainties as positively to terrify one. As is well known, it consists of a number of syllabic sounds which are pronounced singly or doubled in combination. For purposes of our comparison, a still more interesting fact is that this language is practically without grammar. We are assured that in spite of these uncertainties the Chinese language is a quite exceptionally good medium of expression."—*Ibid*, pp. 195-6.

These facts respecting the indefiniteness of some languages, which nevertheless are good means of expression, show clearly how unwise it would be to reject, merely for reasons of obscurity, a suggestion of the existence of an esoteric language whose terms are to be found in the ideas expressed in the various Scriptures of the world.

NOTES

NOTES

NOTES

NOTES

NOTES

NOTES